ROMAN MILITARY RECORDS ON PAPYRUS

PHILOLOGICAL MONOGRAPHS
OF THE
AMERICAN PHILOLOGICAL ASSOCIATION

NUMBER 26

Legati Hahniani ope
hic liber prodit

Accepted for publication by the Committee on the Publication of Monographs
of the American Philological Association

Edited by John Arthur Hanson, Princeton University

ROMAN MILITARY RECORDS ON PAPYRUS

By

ROBERT O. FINK

The State University of New York at Albany

PUBLISHED FOR

THE AMERICAN PHILOLOGICAL ASSOCIATION

BY THE PRESS OF

CASE WESTERN RESERVE UNIVERSITY

1971

Library of Congress Catalog Number: 69–11125
SBN: 8295–0174–6

Composed by William Clowes and Sons, Ltd
London, Beccles and Colchester, England

Photolithographed by Cushing-Malloy, Inc.
Ann Arbor, Michigan, U.S.A.

Preface

It is now thirty-five years since Michael Ivanovich Rostovtzeff proposed to me as the subject of my doctoral dissertation a collection and study of the Roman military papyri published up to that time. From that dissertation, accepted by the Graduate School of Yale University in 1934, the present corpus has grown.

The interval, however, has still not made it a work of which one may properly wish *plus uno maneat perenne saeclo*. It remains a collection of texts of whose imperfect state no one could be more conscious than the present editor, and is rightly destined to be superseded as rapidly as new insights and new readings produce improvements. In fact, its power to spur and assist in its own replacement might be a fair test of its worth. But however that may be, I take pleasure now in acknowledging with gratitude the aid and encouragement of all those who have contributed to the completion of this work.

Until I left Yale in 1941, Rostovtzeff gave generously of his interest and counsel; and only those who knew him can understand how much that counted for. During his absence in 1934, Prof. Ainsworth O'Brien-Moore supervised my dissertation and offered many suggestions which are incorporated into the present work. Those years were also the beginning of my collaboration with C. Bradford Welles and J. F. Gilliam, who were the first to publish many of the texts in the present volume and to whose sharp eyes, sound sense, and helpful criticism much of what is good here must be attributed. Their names will be found passim throughout the book.

I am also deeply grateful to the Government of the United States of America for a Fulbright Grant for research in Italy in 1956–57, to the Trustees and Administration of Kenyon College for leave of absence during that year, and to the Istituto Papyrologico "G. Vitelli" of the Università degli Studi di Firenze for its hospitality extended by its Director, Nicola Terzaghi, and especially by Prof. Vittorio Bartoletti, who not only did everything possible to facilitate my work there, but with his wife, Anna Maria Colombo, also entertained us in their home. The presence of Drs. Manfredo Manfredi and Eugenio Grassi added to the pleasure of my work in the Istituto and to its effectiveness.

Elsewhere in Europe I enjoyed the invaluable assistance of Dr. Herbert Hunger and Mr. Anton Fackelmann of the Oesterreichische Nationalbibliothek in Vienna and Mr. T. C. Skeat of the British Museum, and was welcomed and given every facility at the John Rylands Library in Manchester, the Bodleian Library, the Bibliothèque Nationale in Paris, and the Bibliothèque Publique et Universitaire in Geneva.

The Eli Lilly Foundation by a grant administered through Kenyon College assisted the continuation of these studies on a half-time basis in the fall semester of 1959–60; and very special gratitude for making possible the completion of the work is owing to the American Council of Learned Societies for a Research Fellowship which in turn enabled me to accept a full year's sabbatical leave from Kenyon College for 1963–64 and to visit both the University of Michigan and Yale more than once during that time in order to see papyri first-hand and to use their excellent papyrological and general libraries. It is a pleasure to record here the generous hospitality, both professional and personal, of Prof. and Mrs. H. C. Youtie at Michigan, and of Profs. C. Bradford Welles, Alan E. Samuel, and John F. Oates at Yale, and in particular to acknowledge my great debt to my colleague, Prof. William E. McCulloh, who made a notable contribution by taking over the entire burden of the Department of Classics at Kenyon during my sabbatical leave.

Photographs of various papyri have been obtained through the courtesy of the authorities of the Ashmolean Museum and the Bodleian Library, the John Rylands Library, and the University Library, King's College, Aberdeen. Prof. Leiv Amundsen has most obligingly supplied a photograph of *POslo* 122 accompanied by a detailed description and an expert copy of damaged lines which are somewhat obscure in the photograph. Particular thanks are due to Prof. Hermann Tiemann, Director of the Staats- und Universitäts-Bibliothek, Hamburg, for permission to publish the full text of *PHamb.* 39, and to Drs. Hellmut Braun and Herwig Maehler for a set of excellent photographs accompanied by Dr. Maehler's transcriptions of lines where the photographs seemed likely to be insufficient or misleading. Prof. Eric G. Turner helped to obtain a photograph of *PHawara* 19; and photographs of papyri in the University of Michigan were secured many years ago through the kindness of Prof. Henry A. Sanders. Prof. John F. Oates while at Yale supplied my requests for photographs of a number of Dura papyri. Similarly, my friend and former student, Dr. Fred C. Mench, now of the University of Texas, while a graduate student cheerfully checked or copied on many occasions material which was otherwise inaccessible to me.

I am also indebted for information about certain papyri to Profs. Marcel Hombert and Friederich Zucker, and to Dr. P. J. Sijpesteijn regarding two Latin papyri in the collection of the University of Wisconsin which he is publishing. All who work with Latin papyri are debtors to Robert Marichal for his publications in the magnificent *Chartae Latinae Minores*; and I, too, have profited, even when I have felt it necessary to disagree with him, from the acumen and the broad scholarship which his work displays, and no less from a pleasant personal correspondence.

Thanks are also due to the Yale University Press for permission to use some of Gilliam's and Welles' texts from *Excavations at Dura-Europos*, Final Report v; and to the Committee of the Egypt Exploration Society for permission to reproduce the texts of thirty-nine ostraca from Tait and Préaux, *Greek Ostraca in the Bodleian Library at Oxford*, vol. 2.

Any assistance not mentioned here has, I trust, been acknowledged in the appropriate place in the body of the work; but if anyone has been overlooked, I hope that he will understand and believe that my gratitude is not diminished by the inadvertence.

Remains now to thank the officers of the American Philological Association for including this book in their monograph series, and my editor, Prof. J. Arthur Hanson, for saving me from a host of inconsistencies, infelicities, and errors. Whatever shortcomings remain—and they will be found—are my own fault.

Finally, my wife has typed the entire manuscript of the book—some parts of it many times. No one else would have done it—or could have—at any price.

Robert O. Fink

State University of New York at Albany
June 21, 1968

Table of Contents

Bibliographical Abbreviations xv

Introduction 1

Chapter I: Military Records in the Period of the Republic 6

Chapter II: Records of Individual Personnel 9

Complete Rosters

1: *PDur.* 100, A.D. 219 18
2: *PDur.* 101, A.D. 222 52
3: *PDur.* 104, A.D. 238–247 82
4: *PDur.* 105, A.D. 250–256 83

Partial Rosters

5: *PVindob.* L 100 recto, A.D. 217? 87
6: *PDur.* 98, A.D. 218–219 90
7: *PDur.* 99, ca. A.D. 218 96
8: *PDur.* 102, A.D. 222–ca. 228 96

Special Lists

9: *PGenLat.* 1 verso, part v, A.D. 90–96 106
10: *PGenLat.* 1 recto, part II, probably A.D. 88 115
11: *PVindob.* L 112 recto, early II p. 120
11 bis: *PVindob.* L 4, end of III p. 122
12: *PDur.* 113, A.D. 230–240? 125
13: *PDur.* 106, A.D. 235–240 126
14: *PDur.* 108, A.D. 235–240 127
15: *PDur.* 107, ca. A.D. 240 128
16: *PDur.* 112, A.D. 241–250 132
17: *PDur.* 110, A.D. 242 to 250 or 256 133
18: *PDur.* 111, A.D. 242–256 135
19: *PDur.* 109, A.D. 242–256 136
20: *PMich.* III 164, A.D. 243–244 137
21: Princeton Garrett Deposit 7532 recto, A.D. 235–242 141
22: *PDur.* 93, ca. A.D. 230–240 143
23: *PDur.* 116, A.D. 236 144
24: *POsl.* III 122, A.D. 238–242 146
25: *PDur.* 96, ca. A.D. 245–255 148
26: *PDur.* 103, A.D. 205–224 149

27: *PDur.* 115, A.D. 232 150
28: *PRyl.* 79, A.D. 144–151 152
29: *PDur.* 121, probably A.D. 241 153
30: *PMich.* VII 454, II–III p. 155
31: *PDur.* 120, A.D. 222? 156
32: *PDur.* 122, ca. A.D. 241–242 158
33: *PDur.* 117, A.D. 236 159
34: *PVindob.* L 2 recto and verso, A.D. 115–117? 160
35: *PDur.* 123, after A.D. 238 164

Unclassifiable Lists
36: *BGU* 1083, time of Augustus, I a. 165
37: *PGenLat.* 1 recto, part III, A.D. 90 167
38: *PVindob.* L 99 recto, I/II p. 168
39: *PMich.* III 162, A.D. 193–197 169
40: *PMich.* III 163, A.D. 222–239 171
41: *PDur.* 114, ca. A.D. 215–230 173
42: *PDur.* 119, A.D. 230–240? 174
43: *PDur.* 124, A.D. 220–230 174
44: *PDur.* 118, A.D. 248–256 175
45: *PAberd.* 132, II p. 176
46: *PAnt.* 41 recto, A.D. 212–230 177

Chapter III: Records of Military Units 179

Morning Reports
47: *PDur.* 82, A.D. 223–235 183
48: *PDur.* 83, A.D. 233 189
49: *PDur.* 88, A.D. 218–222? 238–244? 191
50: *PDur.* 89, A.D. 239 192
51: *PSI* XIII 1307, early I p. 197
52: *PMich.* VII 450 and 455 recto, first quarter of III p. 201
53: *PMich.* VII 450 and 455 verso, ca. A.D. 225–250 204
54: *PDur.* 85, ca. A.D. 230 207
55: *PDur.* 87, ca. A.D. 230? 208
56: *PDur.* 84, ca. A.D. 233 209
57: *PDur.* 86, ca. A.D. 240 209

Monthly Summaries
58: *PGenLat.* 1 verso, part IV, ca. A.D. 90 210
59: *PSI* XIII 1308, A.D. 152–164 212
60: *PDur.* 90, ca. A.D. 225–235 214
61: *PDur.* 91, ca. A.D. 225–235 215
62: *PDur.* 92, ca. A.D. 225–235 216

Pridiana
63: *Briiish Museum Papyrus* 2851, A.D. 100–105 217

64: *BGU* 696, A.D. 156 228
65: *PDur.* 94, ca. A.D. 240 233

Unclassified Records
66: *PDur.* 95, A.D. 250–251 234
67: Bodleian Library Ms. Lat. Class. e 37 R, middle of III p. 239

Chapter IV: Accounts, Receipts, and Records of Matériel 241

Pay Records
68: *PGenLat.* 1 recto, part I, A.D. 81 243
69: *PGenLat.* 4, ca. A.D. 84 250
70: *PBerol.* 6866 and *PAberd.* 133, A.D. 192 254
71: *PVindob.* L 72 and 82, recto, late II p. 266
72: *PRyl.* 273a recto, II p. 267
73: *PFay.* 105, ca. A.D. 120–150 269

Receipts
74: *PSI* 1063, A.D. 117 277
75: *PYale* 249, A.D. 139 281
76: *PHamb.* 39, A.D. 179 283
77: *PMich.* VII 435 and 440, early II p. 306
78: *Sammelb.* III 6955–6976; *Ostr.Bodl.* 2003–2041; *Wilcken Ostr.* II 1128–1146, 1265; A.D. 157 to 187 or 217 310
79: *PClermont-Ganneau* 4a, second half of II p. 332
80: *PLond.* 482, A.D. 130 333
81: *POxy.* IV 735, and V app. I, p. 325, A.D. 205 335

Records of Matériel
82: *PRyl.* 223, II p. 338
83: *PDur.* 97, A.D. 251 340
84: *PVindob.* L 111, II p. 345
85: *PGissBibl.* Inv. 282, first half of III p. 346
86: *PGrenf.* II 110, A.D. 293 347

Chapter V: Official Correspondence 348

Letters Concerning Personnel
87: *POxy.* VII 1022, A.D. 103 352
88: *PDur.* 63, A.D. 211 355
89: *PDur.* 66, A.D. 216 356
90: *PDur.* 55, ca. A.D. 218–220 380
91: *PDur.* 64, A.D. 221 383
92: *PDur.* 67, A.D. 222–225 387
93: *PDur.* 76, ca. A.D. 210–225 393
94: *PDur.* 68, ca. A.D. 232–238 394
95: *PDur.* 69, ca. A.D. 235–238 395
96: *PDur.* 81, A.D. 243–244? 396
97: *PDur.* 74, A.D. 223–252 398

Letters About Finances and Matériel
98: *PDur.* 60, ca. A.D. 208 399
99: *PDur.* 56, A.D. 208 403
100: *PDur.* 58, ca. A.D. 240–250 406
101: *PDur.* 61, ca. A.D. 216 407
102: *POxy.* XII 1511, first half of III p. 409

Unclassifiable Fragments of Letters
103: *PDr.* 57, perhaps ca. A.D. 208 411
104: *PDur.* 70, A.D. 213 411
105: *PDur.* 71, ca. A.D. 219 412
106: *PDur.* 73, ca. A.D. 210–220 412
107: *PDur.* 75, ca. A.D. 210–220 413
108: *PDur.* 62, ca. A.D. 216–220 413
109: *PDur.* 65, A.D. 221 414
110: *PDur.* 72, A.D. 211–222 414
111: *PDur.* 78, ca. A.D. 210–230 415
112: *PDur.* 79, ca. A.D. 210–230 415
113: *PDur.* 77, ca. A.D. 220–230 416
114: *PDur.* 59, probably A.D. 241 417
115: *PDur.* 80, ca. A.D. 235–245 418

Tituli
116: *PDur.* 130, ca. A.D. 215–245 419

Chapter VI: Commentarii, Acta, Regulations, and Reference Materials . . 420
117: *PDur.* 54 (Feriale Duranum), ca. A.D. 223–227 422

Chapter VII: Unclassifiable Fragments 430
118: *PDur.* 134, A.D. 220–222? 431
119: *PDur.* 135, A.D. 210–230 431
120: *PDur.* 142, A.D. 220–230 432
121: *PDur.* 143, A.D. 221–242 432
122: *PDur.* 136, ca. A.D. 230 433
123: *PDur.* 133, A.D. 213–217 or 235–238 433
124: *PDur.* 145, A.D. 208–256 435
125: *PDur.* 137, III p. 435
126: *PDur.* 138, III p. 436
127: *PDur.* 139, III p. 436
128: *PDur.* 146, III p.? 437

Addenda 438
129: Bodleian Library Ms. Lat. Class. g 3 P, II p. 438
130: Bodleian Library Ms. Lat. Class. g 4 (P.), end of II p. 439
131: *PHawara* 19, II p.? 440
132: *PAberd.* Inv. 2h, II/III p. 441

133: *PAberd.* 150, early II p. 442
134: *BASP* 3 (1965) p. 28, III p. 443

Indices 445
1: Persons 445
2: Emperors and the Imperial Family 501
3: Notable Persons, Including Consuls 503
4: Military Affairs 507
5: Religion: Gods, Divi, Temples, Festivals 517
6: Calendar 519
7: Geography and Ethnics 521
8: Greek Words 524
9: Latin Words 532
10: Abbreviations and Conventional Symbols 556
11: Inscriptions, Ostraca, and Papyri 560
12: Classical Authors Cited 562
Concordance of Papyri and Ostraca 563

Bibliographical Abbreviations

AJA = *American Journal of Archaeology*

AJP = *American Journal of Philology*

Annone = Denis van Berchem, "L'Annone militaire dans l'Empire romain au IIIe Siècle," *Mémoires de la Societé Nationale des Antiquaires de France*, eighth series, vol. 10 (1937)

Archiv = *Archiv für Papyrusforschung*

ArM = J. Nicole and Ch. Morel, *Archives militaires du Ier siècle*, Geneva 1900

BASP = *Bulletin of the American Society of Papyrologists*

ChLA = Albert Bruckner and Robert Marichal, *Chartae Latinae Antiquiores*, Olten and Lausanne, 1954–

CP = *Classical Philology*

CPL = Robert Cavenaile, *Corpus Papyrorum Latinarum*, Wiesbaden 1958 (cited by number of text)

CRAI = Académie des Inscriptions et Belles-lettres, *Comptes-rendus des séances*

Daris = Sergio Daris, *Documenti per la Storia dell'Esercito Romano in Egitto*, Pubblicazione dell'Università Cattolica del Sacro Cuore, Contributi, Serie Terza, Scienze Storiche 9, Milan 1964

Degrassi, *Fasti* = A. Degrassi, *I Fasti Consolari dell'Impero Romano*, Rome 1952

Domaszewski, *Rang.* = A. von Domaszewski, "Die Rangordnung des römischen Heeres," *Bonner Jahrbücher* 117 (1908) 1–275

Dornseiff-Hansen = F. Dornseiff and B. Hansen, *Rückläufiges Wörterbuch der griechischen Eigennamen*, Berlin 1957

Dussaud, *Topog.* = R. Dussaud, *Topographie historique de la Syrie antique et médiévale* (Haut-Commissariat de la République française en Syrie et au Liban, Service des Antiquités et des Beaux-Arts, *Bibliothèque archéologique et historique* IV) Paris 1927

EL = J. Mallon, R. Marichal, Ch. Perrat, *L'Écriture latine de la capitale romaine à la minuscule*, Paris 1939

Final Rep. v = C. Bradford Welles, Robert O. Fink, and J. Frank Gilliam, *The Excavations at Dura-Europos, Final Report* v, part I: *The Parchments and Papyri*, New Haven 1959

HTR = *Harvard Theological Review*

Johnson, *Roman Egypt* = Tenney Frank, *An Economic Survey of Ancient Rome*, vol. 2: Allan Chester Johnson, *Roman Egypt to the Reign of Diocletian*, Baltimore 1936

JJP = *Journal of Juristic Papyrology*

JRS = *Journal of Roman Studies*

Lesquier = J. Lesquier, *L'Armée romaine d'Égypte d'Auguste à Dioclétien*, Mémoirs publiés par les membres de l'Institut français d'archéologie orientale du Caire, no. 41, Cairo 1918

Mallon, *Pal.* = J. Mallon, *Paléographie romaine* (*Scripturae Monumenta et Studia* III) Consejo superior de investigaciones cientificas, Instituto Antonio de Nebrija de filologia, Madrid 1952

Marichal, *Occ.* = R. Marichal, *L'Occupation romaine de la Basse Égypte*, Paris 1945

Marichal, "Solde" = R. Marichal, "La Solde des armées romaines d'Auguste à Septime-Sévère d'après les P. Gen. lat. 1 et 4 et le P. Berlin 6.866," *Annuaire de l'Institut de Philologie et d'Histoire Orientales et Slaves* 13 (1953) = *Mélanges Isidore Lévy*, 399–421

PIR = E. Klebs, H. Dessau, P. von Rohden, E. Groag, A. Stein, *Prosopographia Imperii Romani*, Berlin 1897–98; 2nd ed. Berlin 1933–

Preisigke, *Namenbuch* = Fr. Preisigke, *Namenbuch enthaltend alle griechischen . . . Menschenamen, soweit sie in griechischen Urkunden . . . Aegyptens sich vorfinden*, Heidelberg 1922

Prelim. Report = M. Rostovtzeff, A. R. Bellinger, C. B. Welles et al., *The Excavations at Dura-Europos, Preliminary Report of the First* (*Second*, etc.) *Season of Work*, New Haven 1928–

RE = Pauly-Wissowa-Kroll, *Realencyclopädie der klassischen Altertumswissenschaft*, Stuttgart 1894–

SB = Fr. Preisigke, F. Bilabel, E. Kiessling, *Sammelbuch griechischer Urkunden aus Ägypten*, Strassburg, Heidelberg, Wiesbaden, 1913–

Sel. Pap. = A. S. Hunt and C. C. Edgar, *Select Papyri* II, Loeb Library, Cambridge, Mass., and London 1934

Stein, *Präf.* = A. Stein, *Die Präfekten von Ägypten in der römischen Kaiserzeit*, Bern 1950

Synteleia = *Synteleia Vincenzo Arangio-Ruiz*, Naples 1964

TAPA = *Transactions and Proceedings of the American Philological Association*

TLL = *Thesaurus Linguae Latinae*

Wessely, *Schriftt.* = C. Wessely, *Schrifttafeln zur älteren lateinischen Palaeographie*, Leipzig 1898

Wessely, *Studien* = idem, *Studien zur Palaeographie und Papyruskunde*, Leipzig 1901–

Wilcken, *Chrest.* = L. Mitteis and U. Wilcken, *Grundzüge und Chrestomathie der Papyruskunde*, vol. I, ii, Leipzig-Berlin 1912

Wilcken, *Grundzüge* = ibid., vol. I, i

Wuthnow = H. Wuthnow, *Die semitischen Menschennamen in griechischen Inschriften und Papyri des vorderen Orients*, Leipzig 1930

YCS = *Yale Classical Studies*

Conventional Signs

In editing the texts, the Leyden system of conventional signs has been used, that is:

] or [ ] or [denote breaks or gaps in the papyrus;

[. . . .] or [*ca.* 12] denote gaps in which the approximate number of lost letters can be estimated;

a[*bc*]*d* denotes that the letters enclosed by the brackets are restored;

dots denote remains of illegible letters and show their approximate number;

dots below letters, e.g. *aḅc̣d*, denote that the letters (here *b* and *c*) are damaged to such an extent that without the context they could be read in more than one way;

kal(*endas*) denotes the expansion of an abbreviation;

abc{*bc*}*d* denotes that the letters enclosed are in the papyrus but should be deleted;

a⟨*bc*⟩*d* denotes that the letters *bc* were mistakenly omitted by the scribe;

a`*bc*'*d* denotes that the letters *bc* were added above the line by the scribe;

a⟦*cd*⟧*b* denotes that the letters *cd* were erased or canceled by the scribe.

Introduction

Even before the discovery of the archives of the cohors xx Palmyrenorum at Dura-Europos in 1931–1932, the steady accumulation of single texts deriving from the files of the Roman army would have warranted collecting them and undertaking a comprehensive discussion of the system of records employed by the Romans for military purposes. Now, with the publication not only of the Dura find but many others, those in the University of Michigan being but one example,[1] there is a real need to make this scattered material available in an orderly form and to offer some account of its significance. The present volume attempts to fill that need.

Scope and Limits. Since Roman provincial government was actually government by an army of occupation, since the soldiers upon leaving the army became civilians, and since even soldiers on active service engaged in many transactions of a private or semi-private nature, the dividing line between military and civil documents is not always a sharp one. A receipt, for example, given to a civilian in exchange for supplies delivered to the army is certainly both; so are letters concerning military matters addressed by officers to civilians; and so are discharge papers and the like. For the purposes of this book, however, in order to avoid endless proliferation into related aspects of life in the Roman world, military records are defined in a narrow sense as records and correspondence concerned solely with the internal administration of the army. This excludes correspondence with civilians, requisitions upon and receipts in favor of civilians, petitions addressed to, or judicial proceedings heard by, a centurion or tribune, and of course private contracts to which soldiers are parties, such as the well known purchase of the slave boy Abbas by C. Fabullius Macer from Q. Iulius Priscus, both of the trireme Tigris.[2] It also excludes epikrisis lists, certificates of exemption from service, such as *POxy*. 39, and the military diplomata. With the exception of a few special instances, all such texts have been omitted. Omitted likewise are all inscriptions such as e.g. *CIL* VI 1056–1059 (Dessau 2156 and 2157) and 220 (Dessau 2163), partly because they have been thoroughly edited and commented upon and are readily accessible, partly because repeating them here would add bulk to the present corpus out of all proportion to the value of additional data which the inscriptions might contribute.

The period covered here is the first three centuries of the Roman monarchy. The reign of Augustus is the starting point simply for lack of any texts of an earlier period, though Chapter 1 contains a discussion of what may be inferred regarding army records in the Roman republic. On the other hand, the reign of Diocletian constitutes an obvious stopping

[1] See the Concordance of Papyri at the end of this volume.

[2] British Museum, no. 229 = *Paleographical Society* ii (1894) no. 190; *ChLA* III 200. See also the references in *ChLA* and *CPL* 120.

point because of the great changes in military as well as civil administration which took place at the end of the third century and the beginning of the fourth. With Diocletian and after, we are in a new world whose military records would have to be treated separately even if they were included in this volume.[3] They have accordingly been omitted.

In general the body of the text deals only with the form, nature, and purpose of the documents collected here. No attempt has been made to exploit systematically at length their evidence on Roman military organization or historical events. On the contrary, it is the purpose of the book to make these materials available to historians. In the individual apparatuses to the various texts will be found numerous corrections of former readings and of interpretation; but for general discussions the reader should in every case turn to the separate publications of individual papyri.

Sources. As already indicated, this volume consists primarily of a corpus of Roman military papyri; but it also draws upon inscriptions and the historians and other literary sources. Even late technical authors like Vegetius are used whenever it seems possible to extract from them anything pertinent.

Terminology for Various Types of Records. It seems improbable that the Romans of the first three centuries of the Christian era employed a very extensive or exact technical vocabulary to designate particular categories of military records. One genuine technical term, it is true, known only from the papyri, is *pridianum*, which designates an annual inventory of the personnel of a legion or auxiliary unit. In Egypt there were pridiana for December 31 and August 31; but elsewhere in the empire there was probably only one a year, for December 31.[4]

Appian speaks of a *biblion ephemeron* which from his description must have corresponded to **47–57**, to which Rostovtzeff gave the name *acta diurna*.[5] But Vegetius uses the term *acta* in a context which makes it an extremely general term, about the equivalent of "records";[6] and other designations, such as *matrix*, *matricula*, *breuis*, *breuiculus*, and their Greek equivalents, though apparently distinguishable in the literary sources, cannot be attached with confidence to any of the existing papyri.

The nature of a matricula can be guessed from four passages in Vegetius:

> 2.2: legio . . . cum grauem armaturam . . . item leuem armaturam . . . proprios et sibi insitos equites legionarios isdem matriculis teneat . . .
>
> 2.5: . . . uicturis in cute punctis milites scripti, cum matriculis inseruntur, iurare solent.
>
> 2.7: . . . principalium militum et . . . principiorum nomina secundum praesentes matriculas indicabo. tribunus maior . . .
>
> 1.26: producendi . . . tirones sunt semper ad campum et secundum matriculae ordinem in aciem dirigendi.

[3] Dr. Gerald M. Browne will publish two military rosters (one in Greek) of ca. A.D. 312 as nos. 16 and 17 in his dissertation, *Documentary Papyri from the Michigan Collection = American Studies in Papyrology* 6 (1970).

[4] See chapter 3 below, pp. 180–82, and **63–65**.

[5] Appian, *Bell. Civ.* 5.46 (Lucius Antony's surrender at Perugia): *καὶ ὁ Λεύκιος ἔπεμπε τοὺς χιλιάρχους τὸ σύνθημα τῷ στρατῷ ληψομένους παρὰ τοῦ Καίσαρος. οἱ δὲ ἔφερον αὐτῷ τὸν ἀριθμὸν τοῦ στρατοῦ καθ' ἃ καὶ νῦν ἔθος ἐστὶ τὸν αἰτοῦντα τὸ σύνθημα χιλίαρχον ἐπιδίδοναι τῷ βασιλεῖ βιβλίον ἐφήμερον τοῦ ἀριθμοῦ τοῦ παρόντος.*

[6] Vegetius 2.19: totius enim legionis ratio, siue obsequiorum siue militarium numerum siue pecuniae, cotidie adscribitur actis maiore prope diligentia quam res annonaria uel ciuilis polyptychis adnotatur.

These citations show that for Vegetius the matricula was a complete roster of an entire unit (in this case a legion) in which the new soldier's name was entered when he took his oath, that is, in order of seniority. It also contained the names and titles of all the officers and principales, from the tribune down. In 1.26, however, *secundum matriculae ordinem* must mean "according to the order of the centuries and turmae in the matricula," since there would be no point to using the order of seniority in bringing out the tirones for the drills which Vegetius is recommending.

The evidence for breves is as follows:

> Vegetius 2.19: cotidianas etiam in pace uigilias, item excubitum siue agrarias . . . uicissim milites faciunt. ut ne quis contra iustitiam praegrauetur aut alicui praestetur immunitas, nomina eorum qui uices suas fecerunt breuibus inseruntur quando quis commeatum acceperit uel quot dierum adnotatur in breuibus.
>
> SHA, *Alex.* 21: . . . haberet breues et numerum et tempora militantum continentes semperque . . . et rationes eorum et numerum et dignitates et stipendia recenseret . . .
>
> Rufinus, *Adv. Hieron.* 2. 36: . . . si quis accepto breuiculo in quo militum nomina continentur nitatur inspicere quanti ex militibus supersint, quanti in bello ceciderint . . .
>
> Isidore, *Origines* 1.24.1: in breuiculis quoque quibus militum nomina continebantur propria nota erat . . . qua inspiceretur quanti ex militibus superessent quantique in bello cecidissent. . . . in stipendiorum quoque largitione propriae erant notae.

Since Rufinus and Isidore obviously derive from the same source, these citations can be reduced to three; and except for the passage from the *Vita Alexandri* they indicate that breves were temporary check-lists used for a wide variety of special purposes. What the *Vita Alexandri* means by *breues et numerum et tempora militantum continentes* is, however, not clear; and the further mention of rationes, dignitates, and stipendia may even refer to other kinds of records.

But any attempt to draw a sharp distinction between matriculae and breves may be futile. The words themselves in the sense of a list or catalogue first appear rather late. *Matricula* or *matrix* is first attested in an inscription of A.D. 199,[7] *breuis* in Diocletian's *Edictum de pretiis rerum uenalium*;[8] and in any event a brevis dealing with stipendia or with casualties and survivors after a battle would have to contain the names of all the personnel in the unit, while losses of any severity would entail drawing up a new matricula. In that case, the losses could be noted in the old matricula as readily as in a separate list. Conversely, the use of *breuis* to designate such different things as casualty lists, duty rosters, and records of leave shows that it was a generic term, not a specific or technical one.

The papyri seem to bear out the conclusion that there was no clear-cut differentiation into matriculae and breves, but that each list was drawn up for a specific purpose that determined its form and content. **1** and **2** may be matriculae in the sense that they are complete rosters of the entire cohors XX Palmyrenorum; but every name in both is accompanied by a notation which would be more appropriate to a brevis as described above, whereas **6**,

[7] *CIL* VI 1585: *domine permitta[s rogo aedificium me extrue]re et in matri[culam referri]*; but this is a civil property-list. (G. R. Watson, "Theta Nigrum," *JRS* 42 [1952] 60, note 28, would restore either *matri[cem* or *matri[ces* instead of *matriculam*; but the difference is not important for the present discussion.) W. Ensslin (*RE* 14.2252–53, s. v. "matricula") believed that the term was applied to military lists as early as the third century. There is nothing inherently improbable in his date, but also no evidence for it.

[8] *Edictum* ii 10: *pretia quae subditi breuis scriptura designat.*

although a select list, has no notations at all beside the names, and if one accepts Vegetius' description of a brevis, then **6**, **8**, **9**, **10**, the guard rosters, and all the other special lists will have to be lumped together in one category in spite of their obvious differences in form and purpose.[9] It is worth observing, too, that aside from the pridiana these texts do not have identifying headings. Within a given officium the men who prepared the lists and accounts and kept the journals were also the men who used them; and so they had no more need for headings and titles than for a special terminology.

The Dating of the Texts. The evidence of the consuls' names sometimes makes it possible to fix the date of a text within quite narrow limits; but even a single date in a military text defines a period of approximately 25 years within which the text must have been written, for legionaries served (in theory at least) first 16 years, then, beginning in Tiberius' reign, 20, and finally 25, while auxiliaries from the start served 25 years and classiarii 26 (later raised to 28). In practice, to be sure, these limits were frequently exceeded; but even if the soldier actually remained in service for 30 years, and few would live so long, calculation on the basis of a twenty-five-year term would miss the true terminus ante quem by only five years.

The Identification of Individual Soldiers. It may be laid down as a rule that the date on which he entered the service became an essential part of every Roman soldier's permanent identification, regardless of his rank. In addition the higher officers and the centurions and decurions were identified by the name of the legion, ala, or auxiliary cohort in which they were currently serving, while principales below the rank of centurion and all privates were further identified by their century or turma. These companies were known by the commander's cognomen in the genitive: a century or turma commanded by C. Iulius Gallus was the *centuria Galli* or *turma Galli*. In the not uncommon situation, however, when a century or turma was without a regular commander, the cognomen of the last incumbent was used in an adjectival form. If Gallus were removed by death, transfer, or other cause before a successor took charge, during the interim the company would be called the *centuria Galliana* or *turma Galliana*.[10] In the navy each ship's crew constituted a century for organizational and administrative purposes; and members of the crew are identified in inscriptions and papyri by the type and name of their ship—"of the trireme Fides," "of the liburna Mercury," and so on—but in the diplomata only by name, rank, filiation, and origo.

The nomenclature of soldiers with Roman citizenship in the papyri varies with the date and with their rank. The earliest text, **36**, probably of the time of Augustus, gave the praenomen and certainly the nomen, filiation, tribe, and origo. Apparently none of the men had a cognomen. **9**, **10**, **36**, and **68**, of the reign of Domitian, all use the praenomen, nomen, cognomen, and most of them the origo. **87**, A.D. 103, also uses praenomen, nomen, and cognomen. Shortly thereafter the praenomen began to disappear. **74**, A.D. 117, and **75**, A.D. 139, have names with and without the praenomen; and as late as A.D. 156, a text written in very full detail, **64**, shows praenomen, nomen, filiation, tribe, cognomen, and

[9] See further the introduction to Chapter 2, pp. 9–11.

[10] R. O. Fink, "*Centura Rufi*, *Centuria Rufiana* and the Ranking of Centuries," *TAPA* 84 (1953) 210–15; Eric Birley, *Roman Britain and the Roman Army* (Kendal 1953) 128–29.

origo for the prefect; praenomen, nomen, and cognomen for a new centurion, a decurion, and a group of tirones; but nomen and cognomen both with and without the praenomen for men received by transfer. **59**, however, A.D. 152–170, and **76**, A.D. 179, and **39**, A.D. 193–197, have nomen and cognomen only; in **70**, A.D. 192, nomen and cognomen are accompanied by the origo. Thereafter, in the third-century papyri, praenomina are not found as such, though they are commonly misused as nomina and cognomina.

At all periods non-citizens were identified by the time-honored system of personal name and filiation.

The combination of two names only, century or turma, and date of enlistment served surprisingly well to distinguish one man from another. Even in the great rosters from Dura, **1** and **2**, it was not often necessary to add *prior* or *posterior* or *alter* to a name to avoid ambiguity.

The foregoing comments apply to practices which are common to nearly all the military papyri. The forms and usages of particular types are taken up in the introductions to Chapters 2–6 and in the comments on individual texts.

I

Military Records in the Period of the Republic

Although it has already been said that no actual remains of Roman military records survive from the period before Augustus, their nature and extent are not beyond all conjecture. It is obvious on the one hand that records in the usual sense could not be kept before the Romans were made literate by the Etruscans, and on the other hand that purely military records in the sense understood in this book would be few until the growth of an empire beyond the bounds of Italy led to the creation of armies which were in fact standing armies, no matter what they might be in law or theory.

The very beginning, then, may well be placed in Servius Tullius' reign when he instituted the census,[1] for among the early Greeks and Romans the census was intended almost exclusively for military purposes. It served to give the responsible authorities needed information on the number of men available for military service and the amount of each man's property, which determined whether he could serve in the cavalry, the heavy infantry, the light infantry, or not at all. Livy is explicit about the first census at Rome (1.44.2): "milia octoginta eo lustro ciuium censa dicuntur; adiecit scriptorum antiquissimus Fabius Pictor eorum qui arma ferre possent eum numerum fuisse." But because the Roman army before Augustus was, in theory at least, simply the *populus Romanus in armis*, and conversely the *populus Romanus* in the comitia centuriata was the army *in toga*, and because the army was for generations, except during the siege of Veii, regularly mobilized in March and disbanded in October, the census lists were at most no more than half-military records in spite of their basic purpose.

The entries in the census could not have differed much from the formula prescribed in the lex Iulia municipalis (*CIL* I 206; Dessau 6085), lines 146–47: "nomina, praenomina, patres aut patronos, tribus, cognomina, et quot annos quisque eorum habet, et rationem pecuniae." How much of this was in Servius Tullius' census is of course impossible to say; but these are the essentials for identifying the person and deciding what service he should be assigned to in the time when every man served at his own expense; and the parallel with

[1] There is no need to discuss the historicity of the man, the correctness of his name, or the exact date of the first census. Somebody introduced the practice into Rome; and since the Romans credited Servius Tullius with the innovation, it is convenient to use his name. And the approximate date is reasonable enough.

the earlier of the extant military texts (see Introduction, p. 4) is unmistakable. They usually omit the man's age (but see **87**); and the *ratio pecuniae* was without military importance after Marius' reorganization of the army. On the other hand, the military texts often add the soldier's origo, which would not need to be stated for each person in the census rolls of a single municipium. Another item which may have been carried in the census lists in the time of the free republic was the number of stipendia each man had served, since a cavalryman was liable for 10 stipendia before he reached the age of 46 and a footsoldier for 16, which might be extended to 20 in emergencies.[2] Since these stipendia were not necessarily served consecutively, a record would have to be kept; and the census lists seem a logical place for it.

Down to the time of Marius the census was the basis for enrolling troops (Polybius 6.19–20); and the procedure in cities and tribes allied with Rome must have been much the same, for Polybius (2.23.9) reports that during the Gallic invasion of 225 B.C. the Romans *καθόλου . . . τοῖς ὑποτεταγμένοις ἀναφέρειν ἐπέταξαν ἀπογραφὰς τῶν ἐν ταῖς ἡλικίαις, σπουδάζοντες εἰδέναι τὸ σύμπαν πλῆθος τῆς ὑπαρχούσας αὐτοῖς δυνάμεως*, and in 204 B.C., according to Livy (29.15 and 29.37.7) twelve Latin colonies which were delinquent in their obligations were required to take their census by the Roman formula and forward the results under oath to Rome.[3] Once the troops were enrolled, rosters must have been set up for each legion, and men and supplies accounted for, in very much the same way as in the extant papyri. Probably the rosters were somewhat more complex because of the division of the soldiers into the four classes of velites, hastati, principes, and triarii; and Polybius' description in 6.34.7–36.9 of the manner in which the daily watchword was given out and the sentries checked implies that tesserae with distinctive marks were used, which would require a daily record of the men to whom each tessera was issued and the men who collected them from the sentries. In the period of annual armies all records would be closed when the army was demobilized in October.

In the earliest times there would have been no military financial records except the commander's accounts of public moneys received and expended and of booty and indemnities. Livy's mention (2.12.6–7) of a stipendium given to the soldiers in the regal period must be an anachronism, unless he assumed that it was abolished with the kingship, for he says quite explicitly (4.59.11) that in 406 B.C. the Senate voted "ut stipendium miles de publico acciperet cum ante id tempus de suo quisque functus eo munere esset," and in 403 (Livy 5.7.12–13) "ut tribuni militares . . . equitibus peditibusque gratias agerent . . . placere autem omnibus his uoluntariam extra ordinem professis militiam aera procedere; et equiti certus numerus aeris est adsignatus. tum primum equis suis merere equites coeperunt." These payments were at first intended only as subsidies in an emergency to enable men to perform military service whose private means were not adequate; but as Rome's wars continued and her territory grew, they proved indispensable. Polybius (6.21.4–5) reports that in his day the allied cities, when notified by the consuls of the number of soldiers they were to supply, conducted the levy, administered the oath, and sent the men under a commander

[2] Polybius 6.19. Cf. the lex Iulia municipalis, lines 90–94 and 100–104, establishing three stipendia in the legionary cavalry or six in the infantry as a prerequisite for holding public office.

[3] See also Polybius 6.21.4 and 5, and Mommsen, *Römische Forschungen* 2, p. 399; *Staatsrecht*, 3rd ed., vol. 2, p. 363, where he shows that at any rate Capua and its dependencies, whose citizens possessed Roman civitas sine suffragio, were already sending the results of their census to Rome at least as early as 225 B.C.

(ἄρχων) and paymaster (μισθοδότης). A little later, after stating the daily allowances in money and grain for both Romans and allies in the infantry and cavalry, he adds (6.39.12–14): δίδοται δὲ τοῖς μὲν συμμάχοις τοῦτ' ἐν δωρεᾷ, τοῖς δὲ Ῥωμαίοις τοῦ τε σίτου καὶ τῆς ἐσθῆτος, κἄν τινος ὅπλου προσδεηθῶσι, πάντων τούτων ὁ ταμίας τὴν τεταγμένην τιμὴν ἐκ τῶν ὀψωνίων ὑπολογίζεται.[4] Such deductions are precisely what one sees in **68** and **73** below; and the records in the earlier time must have been similar. With Marius the stipendium became an outright salary that would meet all of a soldier's expenses and perhaps leave something over; so that the accounts thereafter must have been even more like those of the standing army of Augustus' time and later.

Standing armies existed de facto, of course, in the First Punic War and almost continuously thereafter, when the necessities of the situation forced the Romans to keep armies in being and to retain the same soldiers under arms for a number of years consecutively; but this need not, and probably did not, modify the system of records, though it did mean that the records affecting a given man or unit would have to be preserved longer. Caesar throws no light on military record-keeping in general, except in so far as his works illustrate the range and content of a pro-consul's commentarii. (See the introduction to Chapter 6.) Perhaps the most interesting item in Caesar regarding military records is the information at the end of the Helvetian war (*Bell. Gall.* 1.29.1) that the Helvetians, too, had detailed census lists which at least included data on the number of men fit for military service.[5]

[4] "To the allies these things are given free; but for the Romans the quaestor deducts from their stipendium the official price of food, of clothing, of any equipment they need, of all these things."

[5] C. Wachsmuth, *Klio* 3 (1903) 281–88, argues that Caesar's figures for the total population of the Helvetii and other tribes are calculated from the number of fighting men in the ratio of four to one usually assumed in ancient authors; but I see no reason to reject Caesar's explicit statement that the lists enumerated women, children, and old men separately.

II

Records of Individual Personnel

The object of all military record-keeping is of course to provide accurate and up-to-date information on the availability of personnel and equipment; and since soldiers are even more essential than matériel, and more mobile, it is not surprising that the largest number of the texts in the present corpus belong to the category covered in this chapter.

They range from mere jottings, which were probably some clerk's memoranda for a task, to complete rosters of a whole unit, the coh. xx Palmyrenorum; but the existing texts still leave unanswered one question which can be discussed briefly here—that is, whether or not the Roman army's records included simple lists which merely registered the soldiers of each legion or auxiliary unit, with full name, filiation, tribe if a citizen, origo, date of enlistment, century or turma, and any other identification. At first thought it is natural for us to assume the existence of such a record; but all of the actual rosters about which anything definite can be said are what I have named "working" rosters because they carry beside each name a notation, altered from time to time as necessary, of the soldier's current status or assignment. (Some of the lists were entirely in capitals—**11**, **28**, **37**, **45**, and **46**; but the reason for the formal script eludes me, for in other respects these lists do not differ from the ones in cursive.) Further reflection shows that the records could scarcely be kept otherwise. A mere register would soon be hopelessly out of date because of transfers, promotions, deaths, and the like; only a card-index system could keep up with such changes. But the working roster could do so for a certain length of time until the alterations became too numerous for easy reference, while at the same time it automatically supplied the soldier's name in a form full enough for most needs, the year of his enlistment, and the century or turma in which he was serving. If more were needed, such as the month and day of his enlistment, he could be looked up in the appropriate year of the unit's journal, in the files of correspondence, in the payroll records, or in special lists.

For present purposes the papyri belonging to this chapter have been classified in four groups: complete rosters (**1–4**), partial rosters (**5–8**), special lists (**9–35**), and ten unclassifiable (**36–46**). Of the latter, **45** and **46** are doubtfully military but have been kept. On the other hand, *PMich.* 447 (*CPL* 121, Daris 26) is not a military list (see now R. O. Fink, "P. Mich. vii 447," *AJA* 68 [1964], 297–99); and *PMich.* 448 (*CPL* 131) is not a list at all but to all appearances a mythological or historical text. *BGU* 610 (*CPL* 115) is a list of veterans (*ex signifer*, *ex cornicularius*, etc.), not of soldiers.

All the rosters have in common listing of the men by centuries or turmae, and within the respective companies by year of enlistment in descending order of seniority. The complete rosters, however, aside from their length, are distinguished by having each century or turma identified by the commander's name in the genitive with his date of enlistment, followed in the next line by his title, *ord*(*inatus*) or *dec*(*urio*), and his name in full in the nominative. Then follow in order of rank rather than seniority his lieutenants' names, each preceded by the year of his enlistment. Thereafter the privates and all the other principales, even the cornicularius, follow in order of seniority. All of the names in these rosters are accompanied by notations indicating either rank, duty (e.g. *officio*, *ad equum probandum*), status (e.g. *non reuersus*, *translatus*), or the names of places where the soldier was on detached service. The variety of hands in these notations, and even more, the variety of abbreviations used for the same word even when no difference can be detected in the hand, is proof that they were not all inserted at the time when the list of names was prepared but were added or altered from time to time according to the situation. In **1** the names of the decurions and their lieutenants and all the men who do not have specific assignments, as well as the cornicularius and some others, are accompanied by one to four puncta, which shows that the roster was also used as a check-list for some purpose. There is also a numerical total after the last name in each century or turma. These two features are lacking in **2**; but the puncta are found in **3**.

The partial rosters differ from the complete ones in omitting the names of the centurions' or decurions' lieutenants and often the repetition of the commander's name in the nominative. Of the four texts in this class, only **6** repeats the name. The notations in these rosters are either few and repetitious, as in **5** and **8**, or altogether lacking, as in **6**, for the reason that these rosters are made up in the first place on some selective principle for a particular use.

Some of the special lists also divide the men by centuries and consulships, as do **23**, **29**, and **31**; but even in such lists the number of men for each year is seldom more than two or three at most and usually only one; and chronological order is frequently disregarded, while there are generally additional features which are not present in the rosters. Most of the special lists, however, differ completely from the rosters and from each other in their form. My introduction to each text states the characteristic features which led to its classification. Of particular interest are the unique duty roster (**9**), the individual records of detached service (**10**), the cluster of guard rosters from Dura (**12**–**19**, especially **15**), the record of the dates of promotion of decurions and centurions (**20**), and the casualty list (**34**).

In the nature of the case very little can be said about the miscellaneous group; but **36** is of some interest as a list of legionaries which is perhaps to be dated within twenty years after Actium and is certainly the oldest text in this corpus. It may or may not be part of a complete roster; there is no way of knowing. **39** is all in capitals and may be a special list of some sort. **44** could be part of a roster, and **40** of a roster or special list. The others are mere scraps.

Other sorts of texts also contained lists of soldiers' names, particularly letters, of which **87** and **92** are prime examples. Financial records were kept under individual names; and a strip from the left edge of **73**, cols. i, ii, or iii, would look like any check-list. Monthly summaries of unit strength also included names and assignments, as in **58**; and the daily journals of units (**47** and **50**) frequently had to list individual soldiers. It may well be, therefore, that some of the fragmentary lists included here, particularly **36–46**, are actually parts of a different kind of record.

133, in "Addenda and Corrigenda," was published in *ChLA* as part of a list of discharged soldiers. It appears to me more probably a legal document.

The Notations in the Lists of Individual Personnel. In the following pages, I discuss the meaning of all conventional signs or abbreviations which occur four or more times as notations in the lists of individual personnel. The frequency of some of them in **1** and **2** particularly both recommends this approach and makes it possible. For occurrences of these symbols and abbreviations in other texts of the present corpus, the reader may consult Index 10. Those which occur three times or fewer are discussed in the apparatus.

Bars and Angles. By far the commonest is the horizontal bar which appears before names with no other notation (but see under *magdala* below) and therefore obviously denotes that the soldier in question is present at headquarters but has no particular assignment. This bar occurs 299 times in the extant parts of **1** and 345 times in **2**, although the latter as a whole contains fewer names. It is also found in **3**, **4**, **5**, **8**, **9**, and **23**.

A variation on the bar is found with the designations of military rank, *ord*(*inatus*), *dec*(*urio*), *sig*(*nifer*), and so on. These, too, precede the name and are sometimes accompanied by other notations as well; but when they are not, they are regularly enclosed in an angle consisting of a horizontal bar above the title of rank and a stroke beginning at the right end of the bar, so that the apex of the angle points toward the name, and slanting downward toward the left. (Five examples appear in Plate XLIV of *Final Rep.* V; and see the plates in *ChLA*.) In a few instances at the end of **2** the apex of the angle touches the left side of the title, which is entirely outside the angle (**2** xxxvi 16; xxxviii 25, 26, 28; xli 4, 6, 8; xliv 12). Testimony that this angle is the equivalent of the horizontal bar is provided by the fact that in **1** and **2** no title which stands alone lacks the angle, while of the seventeen titles which are accompanied by a word or phrase denoting some assignment—e.g. *singul*(*aris*) *dupl*(*icarius*), *ad hordeum dec*(*urio*), *ad frum*(*entum*) *ord*(*inatus*)—only four have the angle, and in two of these cases the designation of the assignment is certainly a later addition (**1** xxxix 16 and xli 2), while it may have been added in the other two as well (**1** xxxvi 2 and **2** xl 19). The angles, that is, observe the same limitations as the bars; and the puncta (see below) likewise behave the same with both. This angular symbol also occurs in **4**, and in the same circumstances, with the exception of **4** b i 6. There a word has been erased before *sesq* and a horizontal bar substituted.

The titles which are regularly enclosed in the angle are *actua*(*rius*), **1** xvii 3, **2** xxii 13; *buc*(*inator*), **2** xiii 1; *cor*(*nicularius*) **1** xxxii 29, **2** xxxiii 10; *dec*(*urio*), e.g. **1** xxxi 22 and see the index; *dupl*(*icarius*), e.g. **1** xi 6 and see the index; *ord*(*inatus*), e.g. **1** xi 2; *sesq*(*uiplicarius*), e.g. **1** xxxiii 30; *sig*(*nifer*), e.g. **1** xxvii 7; and *uex*(*illarius*), e.g. **1** xxiii 12. (Duplicarius and sesquiplicarius are of course pay grades rather than names of military ranks: *Final Rep.* V, pp. 32–33.) In **2** viii 24 and xxxiii 9 is a title which I have not been able to read but which belongs in this series because it is enclosed in the angle. In **1** xxviii 21 [*im*]*ag*(*inifer*) seems possible. In printing the texts in this volume, the angular symbol has been represented conventionally as follows: ———→, with no attempt to enclose the letters below within the angle, as occurs on the papyrus.

Symbols for Century and Turma. The symbol Ꮍ is well known in inscriptions with the two values of *centurio* and *centuria.* The Dura texts use it for *centurio* only as an appositive preceded by the name (**13**, 18 note; **15** i 22; **50** i 7); and this is the usual practice in the other papyri (e.g. **10** 14), though in **63** the totals at the ends of the various sections run *in is* Ꮍ *vi, dec iiii*, and so on (ii 1, 15, 39, 42). By the third century the word *centurio* seems to have been replaced by *ordinatus.*

Ŧ is the common symbol for *turma*; but in two Dura texts it is replaced by Tu: **15** i 6, 11; ii 1, 2, 4, 12; and **23** ii 2, 5, 9.

Puncta. A heavy dot or black disk (the size varies), a punctum, served the Romans as a check-mark. It is found in four of the papyri in this chapter (**1**, **3**, **8**, and **38**) and also in **73**. **1** and **8** illustrate particularly well the numerous possibilities in the employment of this symbol.

In **1** it appears in two sizes and always at the left of the bar or angle, seldom before notations in words. For a discussion of such exceptional cases, see below, on *magdala.* Five dromedarii, including one sesquiplicarius, seem to have no punctum before the bar (xliii 20, 21, 23, 25, and 31). I have no explanation but the possibility that the puncta here may have been lost through scaling of the surface of the papyrus. The larger puncta are used singly or in combinations up to four (for the cornicularius, xxxii 29); the small puncta, except for two doubtful cases (ix 27 and xi 4) are always combined with a large one. Two decurions and one duplicarius have two large and two small puncta (xxxi 22, 24; xxxviii 12); and two large puncta are either present or can be restored with confidence in the case of three decurions, three duplicarii, two sesquiplicarii (xxxiii 30, and xli 8), the actuarius (xvii 3), two signiferi (xxxii 16 and xl 19), five vexillarii, the imaginifer, if that is his rank (xxviii 21), a soldier whose title is *ad hostias* (xxxvi 22), two others whose rank cannot be ascertained (xxv 11 and xli 6) and one soldier (xxxvi 23) who seems not to hold any rank. A combination of one small and one large punctum occurs 23 times before a bar and 12 times before notations in words. A single large punctum is used before the bar 178 times, four times with the angle (vii 11: *s*[*ig*(*nifer*) *?*]; xxxix 13: *uex*(*illarius*); two unidentifiable: viii 17 and xxxiii 34), and 36 times before notations in words. Five doubtful cases in which either the existence or the number of the puncta or the nature of the notation which they precede has not been determined are xiii 30, xxii 15, xxviii 28, and xli 14 and 15.

What the puncta in **1** implied is difficult to say. They clearly had something to do with rank, for the cornicularius has four puncta and the decurions, duplicarii, and sesquiplicarii, as well as other principales, all have at least two large puncta. (Evidence is lacking, as it happens, for the centurions.) On the other hand, the puncta seem not to have had any direct connection with the payroll, because the numerical totals at the end of the roll of each century and turma must include all the enlisted men and principales, whether their names are accompanied by puncta or by notations in words.

Theta and thetati. *Θ* as a special notation indicating death, perhaps death in combat, is also known from literary sources. See G. R. Watson, "Theta Nigrum," *JRS* 42 (1952) 56–62, and R. O. Fink, "Hunt's Pridianum," *JRS* 48 (1958) 113, on col. ii, 3–12. The only military list in which the symbol occurs is **8** (vi 13, 22; vii 6; and x 22); but it is also found in **73**, and the word *thetatus*, as a notation abbreviated *te*, in **34** recto i 12, 13, and 17; written out in **34** recto ii 8; verso ii 14; and **63** ii 11. It is doubtful, however, whether it occurs in *PMich.* 435 (see **77** below).

Notations in 8. The notations in **8** seem to follow basically the same practice as in **1**, but with considerably less variety among them and more accumulation of notations before some of the names. At the outset each name seems to have been preceded by a bar except for the man in iii 4, who apparently died or was killed (see on *ϑ* above) before the list actually came into use. During the use of the list, some names received additional notations, of which the commonest is a punctum above the middle of the bar. At the left end of the bar *app(adana)* was added in 10 instances, *n s* (not certainly explained, but see below) in 6 and perhaps 11, *disposit(us)* once (v 16) and *remans(it)* once (viii 4). At least six of the notations with *app* have a punctum added on the left, and at least two of those with *n s*, to one of which in turn a bar was added on the left of the punctum. Finally, one of the doubtful cases of the notation *n s* which had both a punctum and a bar on the left of the punctum had a *ϑ* added over the middle of the original bar next to the name (x 22). It seems evident that this variety of notations reflects changes in the status of the men on the list, and that each notation as it was added canceled the one on its right.

In **38** and **73** the puncta stand immediately before the names, without the horizontal bar.

Intercolumnar Notes in 1. A unique feature of **1** is a set of 41 notations scattered at intervals in the spaces between the columns. All consist of the abbreviation *p* followed by a name, sometimes clearly in the ablative, but often abbreviated and without a case-ending, and sometimes in forms certainly not ablative. The variety is well illustrated by the series *p natali* (xxxv 3), *p natales* (xxxvi 23), and *p˙ natal˙* (xxxvii 6). Nonetheless, the most acceptable explanation is to read *p(ro)* and understand the entries as indicating that the man beside whose name each is found substituted in some capacity for the person named in the notation. Most of the men in the intercolumnar notes cannot be identified; but there can be no doubt that *p heliodor sig* at the left of **1** xxviii 14–15 is the signifer Aelius Heliodorus of **1** xxvii 7 and **2** i 12.

Notations in Words. The notations in words follow, in alphabetical order of the first word in each phrase. Since all the texts are more or less damaged, the number of appearances for each notation is a minimum; but the ratio of one to another is perhaps the same as when the texts were complete.

ad dom(inum) n(ostrum); *ad domin(um)* (**1** xxix 6).
This notation occurs only in **1** and must refer to an escort provided for Elagabal on his way from Syria to Rome in the autumn of 218. It is worth noting that only three of the 55 men so designated are equites.

ad leones; ad leon(es) (**2** xiii 6 and xv 19). 7 occurrences in **1**, 4 in **2**. Very possibly a place name (see *TLL* s.v. "ad," cols. 527–28); but there was an amphitheater at Dura, and the Dura graffiti depicting lions and lion hunts may not be entirely conventional. See *Prelim. Rep.* IX, pp. 46–49; *Final Rep.* V, p. 41 and note 17. See also under *magdala* below.

ad m̊ ambul, ad man′ amb, m′ ambul, m˙ amb˙ (20 times, all in **1**);]*ṃ˙ amaụl.* (**1** xli 19); *ambul* (**2** xli 25, 29; xlii 18; xliii 4); see also under *ad mamm.* The middle element in this phrase is obscure; but the last evidently is a form of *ambulare* or *ambulatio*, referring to cross-country marches as a training exercise. Cf. Vegetius 1.27. Note that this phrase and the next are applied only to equites. But the noun *ambulatio* is also a possibility, denoting a colonnade or bazaar at Dura at which a detail was stationed. Cf. *porta* and *templo* in the guard rosters, p. 128 below. In that case *man* is probably a proper name in the genitive, e.g. *Mannaei.* See also under *magdala* below.

ad mamm. Found 18 times, including one sesquiplicarius (**2** xxxii 6), in **2** only. This notation bears a tantalizing resemblance to the preceding one; and the total of these entries in **2**, along with the occurrences of *ambul*, is 21 as compared with the 20 instances of *ad man ambul* in **1**. But *mamm* is not necessarily the same as *man*; and no form of *ambul* is associated with *mamm.* Since the text belongs to 222, the first year of Alexander's reign, perhaps *ad mamm(aeam)*, comparing *ad dominum nostrum* in **1**.

ad op(inionem) stip(endii), ad opin, ad opinio, ad opinion, ad op stipen. 10 times in **1**, including one centurion (xxi 2); 19 in **2**. Obviously this has reference to the payment of the soldiers' stipendium, though the precise meaning is not clear. Gilliam (*Final Rep.* V, p. 291) in discussing **66** conjectures that *opinio* means either a preliminary examination and approval of the payroll and supporting documents by the governor or the procurator or, alternatively, an audit after the soldiers were paid. R. W. Davies, *Historia* 16 (1967) 115–18, prefers the former. Note the phrase *ad opinionem peten(dam ?)* in **66** ii 1, and the possibility of *ad opinionem quaerendam* in **65** 6.

ad praetori(um), ad praetor. Twice in **1**, including a sesquiplicarius, and twice in **2**; possibly once, a duplicarius, in **4** a i 9. "Serving at the headquarters of the governor." See **47** ii 7 and 8. The *a* of *praetora*, **2** xl 11, is unexplained.

ad sacrahim, ad sacrahimag. Only in **1**, six times, including one duplicarius (i 4). Perhaps a place-name (cf. on *ad leones*), perhaps a duty. Morton Smith, *CW* 53 (1960) 264, proposes *ad sacra {h}imaginis* or *{h}imaginum*; R. W. Davies, *BASP* 5 (1968) 31–32, suggests *ad sacra(s) {h}imag(ines).* These expansions are not impossible; but *sacra(s)* seems unlikely, and the *h* is a difficulty. Since they were nearly all recruited from Semitic-speaking communities, the clerks of the XX Palmyrenorum were quite familiar with the sound represented by *h.* They might omit it occasionally (perhaps under the influence of Greek spelling), but there is no certain instance in the Dura papyri where it was prefixed incorrectly to a word with an initial vowel. Cf. the apparatus on **47** ii 18. Since the *h* seems to appear regularly in this notation, I doubt if the word *imago* is involved. On the other hand, *sacrahim*, in spite of the ending, apparently cannot be a Semitic plural noun. If it at least represents a separate word, *ag* can be expanded as *ag(ens)*, and the first element will designate a place.

If, however, Smith and Davies are right, the *imagines* are of course representations of the emperor and his family; and the service may be a parallel, as Davies observes, to the *excubatio ad signa* in the morning reports, **47–57**. One could even suppose that the imagines had replaced the signa; but there is no proof.

See also under *magdala* below.

appadana, app, appa, appad, appada, appadan. 63 times in **1**, including one duplicarius (xxxi 26); 50 in **2**; once in **3**; 11 times in **8**; once in **23**. This is of course the town at the junction of the Chabur and the Euphrates north of Dura. It also appears at the end of **98** with three other places which were evidently dependent on Dura.

barbal(issus). Occurs only in **2**, six times altogether. It is on the Euphrates about 170 miles north of Dura, just where the direct route to Antioch left the river. The presence of soldiers of the xx Palmyrenorum may imply difficulties with communications.

becchuf(rayn), *becuf*, *becch*, *bechuf*, *bechch*, *becchufr*. 93 times in **1** including one centurion, one duplicarius, and one sesquiplicarius; 37 times in **2**, including one duplicarius. Perhaps two more in **1** xxiv 18 and **2** vii 16. The full name of this place appears in a soldier's private letter, *PDur*. 46, line 3; but its location is unknown. The number of soldiers on duty there shows its importance.

birtha; twice *bartha* (**1** xv 9 and xxiv 12). Eight men, all infantry, have this notation in both **1** and **2**. Dussaud, *Topog*. 455–57, wishes to identify its site with that of Zenobia on the Euphrates about 70 miles north of Dura. This seems more likely to be the one meant here than the Birtha, also called Apamea, near Zeugma. See also under *magdala* below.

castell(um) arab(um), *castel ar*, *castelo ar*, *castelo ara*. 7 occurrences in **1**, 3 in **2**. The site is unknown; the place may be the same as Kastello in **65**. The number of men is roughly the same as for Birtha and Chafer Avira.

chafer auira, *chaf˙ auira*, *chafer a*, *chafer auir*, *chaferị;* twice *caper auir* (**2** xix 16; xxxiii 31). 7 times in **1**, including a vexillarius; 4 in **2**. The first word means "village"; the meaning of the second is uncertain. Welles cites Aramaic ᶜWYR "blind" in *Final Rep*. v, p. 40. "Village of blind men"? The location is not known. See also under *magdala*.

disposit(us), *dispos*, *disposi*. 14 times in **1**, 15 in **2**, once in **8**. "Relay rider." All are cavalrymen. See also under *magdala*.

exploraṭọṛ, *explorato*, *explorat*, *explora*, *explor*. 15 times in **1**, 8 in **2**. "Scout."

magdala, *magdal*. 11 times in both **1** and **2**. 5 more instances are possible in **2** (ix 23, 24; x 30; xxi 8; xxv 14). A place-name, "tower"; its location is unknown. This notation also illustrates a problem which involves a good many of the preceding notations in **1**, particularly *ad man ambul* and *dispositus*, but also *ad leones*, *ad sacrahim*, *birtha*, *castell arabum*, and *chafer auira*. In the discussion of the puncta it was said that puncta did not as a rule appear before notations in words; but seven of the eleven entries for *magdala* have puncta; and two of the remaining four are damaged in such a way that one cannot say whether or not puncta were once present. In **1** ix 28, however, and xx 1, there was no punctum. In all cases but one (**1** xiv 1), on the other hand, there is also a horizontal bar which in some cases seems to cancel the word *magdala*, in others to underline it. Actually, the situation seems to be that where there is a punctum the word was written first and canceled by the line, while in the two instances where there is no punctum the line came first and the word was written over it. Some support for this explanation is furnished by **1** xli 2, where the notation *ad hor(deum)* is written above the horizontal bar in a different hand, clearly an addition later than the two puncta on the left. The same is true of *chafer auir* in **1** xxxix 16; but the case is muddled by the fact that none of the four (or five) notations *ad leones* which are accompanied by a punctum (**1** xxii 7; xxvi 5, perhaps 6; xxxiv 30; and xxxvi 9) shows a bar at all. The notation *ad man ambul* seems to be written above a bar when a punctum is present in every instance but **1** xxxvi 12; *dispos(itus)* similarly except for **1** xxxii 23. The only occurrence of *ad sacrahim* with a punctum (**1** ii 12) has been canceled; but neither of the two similar instances of *birtha* (**1** xii 6; xviii 10) has a bar, nor the two of *castellum arabum* (**1** vii 6 and xxx 14); but one *chafer auira* has a punctum with no bar (**1** xliii 1), one is canceled but has no punctum (**1** xl 8), one with the symbol *z* beside it is canceled (**1** xxxv 17), and three with the punctum seem to be underlined by the bar.

I find no clear pattern in this welter; but no doubt when the roster was in use the difference in ink between original notations and those substituted later was more apparent, and doubtless, too, the clerks who made the alterations and used the roster read it in the light of their own knowledge of the situation which they carried in mind.

n s. Found only in **8**, 5 times certainly, possibly in 5 more cases. The meaning is unknown; but perhaps *n(on) s(anus)*, ill or wounded, since at least four men in the list have died and two of the dromedarii are without their camels.

officio, offici, offic, off, of. 30 times in **1**; 18 in **2**; twice, perhaps three times, in **4**; once in **8**. Both the instances in **4** are *off(icio) proc(uratoris)*. In Antioch? In **92** v 16 and ix 14 are the notations *ex off* and *ex of*. These men were all serving as clerks.

parthia. Occurs only in **1**, five times. On the analogy of the other notations, this must be a topographical term rather than geographical or national. Dussaud, *Topog*. 471–72, mentions a "Parthen ou Parthes" which bequeathed its name to Parsa Dagh, southeast of Cyrrhus.

singul(aris), sing, singl, singul(aris) co(n)s(ularis). 22 times in **1**, including three duplicarii; 58 times in **2**, including one duplicarius; once in **4**, a decurion; 7 times in **8**, including one duplicarius; once in **23**. The singulares were orderlies. The *singulares consularis* (4 each in **1** and **2**) served on the staff of the governor, presumably in Antioch.

tra(n)sl(atus). Indicates transfers. This notation occurs only in **1**. Twice it refers to men leaving the xx Palmyrenorum for another cohort (**1** viii 30 and xxxi 9), twice to men received from other cohorts (**1** xii 28 and xiii 9). The notation *legio*] *iiii scy(thica)* in **1** xxvi 21 was undoubtedly of the same sort.

Numerical Totals. Nos. **1**, **6**, and **8** have a number at the end of the roster of each century and turma which obviously is a total of some sort; and **38** ii 11 has a similar number just after the name of the centurion or decurion. In **6** and **8** the totals are without question a unit count of the men listed. This is particularly clear in the century of Marianus in **8**, where in vii 25 the number originally read 64 and was later reduced to 62 by cancellation of the last two *i*'s in the numeral. 64 names can still be counted for this century in cols. v–vii; but in vi 13 and 22, two names are marked with a theta and canceled. Other totals in this text cannot be checked; but in **6** ii 21, where the century of Danymus has a total of 55, there are still 48 names although the beginning of the roll is missing; and in **6** iv 15, the total of 52 compares with 43 names extant and some lost at the foot of both col. ii and col. iii.

In **1**, however, the situation is more complex; and I have really no better explanation of it than the one in *Final Rep*. v, pp. 32–33, unsatisfactory as that is. In this text two totals are given, first the overall, then the number of "duplicarii," by which pay-grades are certainly meant. For the pedites we have 140, including 3 duplicarii, for the century of Marcus in **1** x 28, where 127 names can be counted and an estimated 12 lines are lost. The three duplicarii cannot be identified with confidence because the opening section of the century's record is lost, so that we do not know how many lieutenants Marcus had, but one duplicarius, one sesquiplicarius, and the signifer in vii 11 would be a reasonable conjecture. The general total for the century of Antonius is lost; but the number of duplicarii is either three or four (xvi 4). Actually, three is probably the correct number—the two duplicarii in xi 4 and 6, and the man, whatever his rank, in xii 22. For the century of Marianus only the general total survives, 146 men, where 114 names can be counted and an unknown number, but perhaps 25, are lost. The centuria Malchiana provides the clearest evidence, with a total of 140–149, including five duplicarii. The papyrus is in better condition here; and 139 names can be counted, including one canceled, and five can be estimated as missing. The five duplicarii are the two in xxvi 14 and 16, the man in xxvi 24, the signifer in xxvii 7, and the imaginifer, if that is his rank, in xxviii 21.

It is reasonably sure, then, that the totals in **1** for the pedites are a simple unit count as in **6** and **8**, though this leaves out the dromedarii, for whom no totals are given, and who are listed and counted with the pedites in **8**.

The totals for the equites present a much more difficult problem. The turma of Zebidas has an overall total (xxxiii 20) of 140–49, including 5 duplicarii, but only 60 names can be counted, even though the papyrus here is well preserved. Similarly the turma of Tiberinus has an overall total of 130–39 (xxxv 33) with an actual count of 66; the turma of Demetrius 122–31 (xxxviii 9) against a count of 68; the turma of Octavius 120–39 (xl 25) with a count of 71; and the turma of Antoninus 134 (xliii 16) with a count of 61, perhaps 4 names lost, and two canceled. For the turmae of Tiberinus and Antonius, the overall total is or could be exactly twice the number of the names; but what is one to say of the turma of Octavius (and probably Demetrius), where the total is considerably less than the number of actual names, or of the turma of Zebidas, where the total given is twenty or more higher than twice the number of names?

The duplicarii present no such problem. The five in the turma of Zebidas are clearly the two in xxxi 24 and 26, the signifer in xxxii 16, the vexillarius in xxxii 21, and the cornicularius in xxxii 29. This count is good evidence that the number of puncta with a name does not concern pay directly, for all of these men are lumped together as "duplicarii," though the cornicularius has four large puncta, and the duplicarius in xxxi 24 two large and two small, while the duplicarius in xxxi 26, at Appadana, has none. The puncta may, however, have something to do with the discrepancy between the actual count of men and the stated overall total for this turma, though that still leaves unexplained the discrepancy in the opposite direction in the turmae of Octavius and Demetrius.

The three duplicarii in the turma of Demetrius must be the duplicarius in xxxvi 4, the sesquiplicarius in xxxvi 6, and the vexillarius in xxxvi 18. If so, the *ad hostias* in xxxvi 22 and 26 is proved not to be a rank, in spite of the angle associated with the notation.

In the turma of Octavius the six duplicarii are the duplicarius in xxxviii 13; the four vexillarii in xxxviii 23, and xxxix 9, 13, and 16; and the signifer in xl 19. Conversely, the presence of the two duplicarii and the sesquiplicarius in xli 4, 6, and 8, without any indication of other ranks, justifies the restoration of ị[*ii*] as the number of duplicarii in xliii 16, unless we allow ị[*iii*] to account for Zebidas []ạlac[, who appears as a vexillarius in this turma in **2** xliii 3. But this is unnecessary because the rank of vexillarius seems not to have been permanent. Zebidas Egla and Zabathes Malchi, for example, are vexillarii in **1** xxxix 9 and 16; but in **2** xxxix 13 and 19, the former is stationed at Chafer Auira, and the latter is *ad mamm.*

Complete Rosters

1

Complete Working Roster of the Coh. XX Palmyrenorum

PDur. 100 (inv. D. P. 12 recto) A.D. 219

Transcription: *Final Rep.* v, no. 100; *edidi.*
Facsimile of cols. xxx–xxxii: ibid., plate 44.

Commentary:

1. Ibid., pp. 36–46.
2. R. O. Fink, "*Centuria Rufi, Centuria Rufiana*, and the Ranking of Centuries," *TAPA* 84 (1953) 210–15.
3. J. F. Gilliam, "Dura Rosters and the *Constitutio Antoniniana*," *Historia* 14 (1965) 74–92.

The following are incomplete, inaccurate, and obsolete:

1. Transcription of col. xxxix in *Rep.* v, pp. 301–2 = *CPL* 335.
2. Transcription of col. xxxviii in R. O. Fink, "The *Cohors XX Palmyrenorum, a Cohors Equitata Miliaria*," *TAPA* 78 (1947) 159–70.

This is the earliest of the complete rosters described above, p. 10. It lists the personnel of six centuries and five turmae, each headed by the name of the centurion or decurion and his lieutenants, followed by the other members of the company in order of seniority. At the end of the roster are the dromedarii who were attached to the various centuries, with the centuries in the same order as before. Each name is accompanied by a notation of some sort (see above, pp. 11–16), mostly in the same cursive hand as the names. The whole roster was evidently prepared by one clerk; but it must have continued in use for a certain time, for a number of the notations were changed or added by several hands, notably in cols. xxxiv–xxxix.

The date A.D. 192 in xxi 7, xxxviii 14, and xli 9 would in theory have led to the honesta missio in 217; and the names of three of the four men under 192 have in fact been canceled. But xxxi 14–15 and xliv 17–18 have the date of 219. This must accordingly be the actual date of the text.

The verso of this papyrus contains another complete roster, **2**.

Col. i

7 ḍạṇ[y]ṃi	[mu]ç̣iano et fạbiaṇo cos	A.D. 201
bẹ[c]ç̣huf ord aurel	septimius ḍaṇỵṃus	
	messaḷa [et] ṣabino c[os	214
ad sacrahim dupl aurel	cocceius	
	ṭert[u]llo cos	195
ạppada aurel	abẹdlahạṣ bụç̣çạẹi	
becchuf aurel	maṃmaeus ạụ[i]da	
–]——— aurel	aelịụṣ mạṛịnus	
	ḍ[ext]ro iị ç̣os	196

–]…———→ aurel f[lauiu]ṣ ṇịc̣omachus
–]——— aurel ạ[e]ḷiụṣ bassus
offic aurel anṭonius max[i]mus
lạ[te]rano cọṣ A.D. 197
]. . cịlariụṃ aurel ụlpị[us s]ịluaṇụs
ạnulḷịṇ[o] ii c̣[o]ṣ 199
o]ffic ạ[ur]el fausṭụs
]. . . [ ]ạgṛ[i]ppas [th]ẹṃạṛṣạ
]ṃu[ci]ano c[o]ṣ 201
]ḷa . [. us] tḥeṃạ[rs]ạ[
]ị[a]ḍ[ib]ẹḷụṣ ẓ[ebida

Cf. **2** vi 18–30, vii 1–2; **6** i 1–6.

1. The date is that of the centurion's enlistment. For all abbreviations and conventional symbols not found in the apparatus, see above, pp. 11–16.

10. *ṣiġ(nifer)*? Cf. **2** vi 23.

14. The notation has not been satisfactorily read.

19. The vertical alignment suggests that *la-* is the beginning of the man's name.

Col. ii

]aurẹ[l] . [A.D. 201–205?
]auṛẹḷ iuḷiụ[s
● [
One line lost
]aurel ṭḥẹ[
ad dom n a[u]rel[
a]d ḍọṃ ṇ ạ[u]rel ḅassus[
of]fic ạ[u]rẹl moṇ[im-
]offịc̣[a]ụṛẹl ạ . ẹạ[
aur]ẹ[l
Consulate? 202–206?
]●⟦[a]ḍ ṣ[ac]ṛạhiṃ[ ]⟧
]d[

8. *moṇ[imus*: D.

13. Possibly *ad] d[om n*

Cols. iii, iv, v

Frags. a–b–c **Frag. d**

(a) A.D. 214

appa]ḍa[
ad] dom n[
bec]chuf ạ[urel
]ḅecchuf ạ[urel
]ạp̣padan[
]ạp̣p̣ạḍ[an]. [. . . .]. ẓẹḅ[
a]p̣p̣ạḍ[an au]rel th[eme]s zẹḅ[
au]rel iad[ib]ẹḷus
au]rel aeli[u]s bolan[-
]ba[ ]. [
(b) **(c)**

]ụị . [
aurel]ḍị[u]ṣ g̣[
aur]ẹḷ g̣ẹṛṃạ[nus
aurel]theṃ[
aurel]ma . [
]. [

Frag. e

].[
au]ṛel[
au]ṛẹl[]ọ[
] aurel [
]ạur[el

Frag. f

].[
]. . . ran [
barba]essaṃ[en
].ẹṇụṣ[
]an[t]ọninus
]. heḷiọḍ[or-
]ẹḍ.[. .].[

Frag. g

].[
–]———ạ[u]ṛ[el
Consulate
ap]p̣ạda auṛ[el
bec]c̣h ạ[urel

Frag. h

]ạ[
] ad[
] ạḍ ḍom n ạ[urel
]ad dom ṇ a[urel
a]d dọ[m] ṇ [aur]el[

Frag. i

].ạ.[
a]ụrel ma.[
au]rel ṃarin[-
a]ụrel theọ[
a]ụrel lon[
].oḷ.[

Frag. j

]eṃ[
]ṃạ.[
]ueṣ[
a]p̣ro [cos? A.D. 207?

Frags. a–b–c belong to col. iii. Frag. d contains a series of names which recurs in **2** ix 28–31, well down in the roster of the century of Danymus. It probably belongs at the foot of col. iv. Frag. e may belong in col. iv on the level of frag. a; and frag. f at the corresponding point in col. v. Frag. h could come from either col. iii or col. v at the level of frag. d. Frag. i may align vertically with b–c at a level above a; and j could be at the foot of any of the three columns, since the reading *apro* is little more than a guess. Frag. g has no convincing assignment.

Frag. d, 1 and 5. The alignment of *ụị-* and *ma-* with *dius*, *germanus*, and *them-* shows that these are the beginnings of names.

Frag. e, 3. Since the lacuna after *aurel* is very small, *o* is probably the first letter of the name.

Frag. f, 2.]*ḥạẹran*?

Frag. i, 3. *marin*[*us*: D.

Frag. i, 5–6. Could be *longinus* and *apollinarius*. Cf. **6** ii 11 and 15; **2** x 15 and 24–25. These men enlisted in 216.

Col. vi

About two lines lost. Century of Marcus
]ḅịda
]o cos
]sọṇ
About eight lines lost
]ịṃ[
].ṃb[
]ịmạ.[
]d.[
].[.]. .ṣ[
⟦ au]ṛẹ[l] marr. .[⟧
au]ṛẹl occḥạ[
aur]ẹḷ niṣaṃṣụs ạḍḍ[aei
a]ụrel barchalb[as
]. [aur]ẹḷ ịẹṛḥaeus zeḅịḍa[
———]– ạụ[r]ẹ[l] themarsa barn.[
becchu]f aurẹl a[e]lius germaṇ[-
]. aụ[re]ḷ bạ[r]naeus zabdil.[
●[aur]ẹḷ iulius ṣạḷṃan [

]-[———] ạ[ure]ḷ heliodorus zebiḍạ[
] seuero iii cos [A.D. 202
-]——— aụ[r]ẹḷ iụḷiụṣ dometius [
——]—— aureḷ iẹṛaḅole themarsa [
geta sẹṇ[ior]e ii cos [203
]n aurel seleucụṣ ḅarbaeṣsaṃ[en

Cf. **2** xii 6–12; **6** iii 4–12; **8** iii 7–8.
3. Probably *zebida.*
25. *germaṇ[us*: D.

Col. vii

● ——— ạụ[rel ma]ṛiṇ[us barathe
●[m]ạṛ[is ier]ḥạẹị
.[ ]ạ[......]mṣi
● ——[——]ṛ[.....].[.].[
●[ ]ḷẹ.[.....].us
p haeranạ.ḷ ● [ca]ṣteḷ [ ] se.[.....].ẹḷḍṣ.ạ[
ad do[m n]ḥe[
[cilone ii cos] A.D. 204
appad[bernician]us sị[luan-
sing[ul iulius so]emus[
●——s[——]maxim[
●-[———]- ạ[urel barzas] marẹ[a
]ṇ ạ[urel priscus] abdoṇ[a
bec]c̣ḥụf ạ[urel mauel]as abeḍ[adadi
app]ạdan ạ[urel]ṛas afṛọ[
offic]ịo ạ[urel sel]eucus ṃ[
sal]ṃạ[nes signa-

About four lines lost

]ṇ[
bar]ṇaeụṣ[
m]ạṛị[nus
anton]ịno ị[i cos 205
zabdes mal]c̣hi
-lus mal]c̣hi
]..[
-hes malc]ḥ[i
-rus serapio]n
apro et maxi]ṃo cos 207

Cf. **2** xii 20–31, xiii 2–12; **6** iii 13–21; **8** iii 10–17.
3.]*a*[: D; *mṣi* was on a tab of papyrus now lost.
6. The letters at the right end of the line are a notation which may be in a different hand, at any rate by a different pen. For the intercolumnar notation see p. 13.
9. *siluani*: D.
11. *s[ig(nifer)*? Not *s[ing(ularis)* because the angle which encloses the title indicates a permanent rank, not merely an assignment. *maxim[us*: D.
28. Perhaps *zabdibolus hammae-*; cf. **2** xiii 7.
29.]*h*[: D.
30.]*n*: D; but cf. 2 xiii 9.

Col. viii

—]——— aurel zenọdọ[rus artemidori A.D. 207
]officio aurel ḅaṣṣ[-

]——— aurel p̣[ri]scus . [
] p̣omp[eiano cos 209
] appaḍạ aurel a[b]ḍaṣ [z]ẹḅị[da
f̣[a]us[ti]ṇo c[os 210
—]——— aurel [quin]ṭus ị[u]ḷ[ianus
———]— aurel [iuliu]ṣ menaṇ[drus
appa]ḍa aurel ṃ[a]lchus bel[
] aurel ạṇtonius clẹ[men-
] ḍ[u]obus aspr[is cos 212
] aureḷ c̣ḷạudius t[i]bẹṛiṇ[us
]ạ aurẹ[l ier]ab[oles u]ḍatḥ[i
]s au[rel ulpiu]s aṇtoniṇ[us
aurel anto]ninus hiạ[
a]ṃạẹụṣ ẓẹbịdạ[
●-[———
One line lost: messala cos? 214?
.[
app̣[ada
ạp[pada
ạ[
ḅ[
ḅ[
ad op̣ [stip
becc̣[huf
One line lost: messala cos? 214?
appạ[da
app[ada
ṭṛasl in cọ[h
ap̣[pada
b[

Cf. **2** xiii 13–28; **6** iii 24–32.
2. Perhaps *bassus diomedi*; cf. **2** xiii 13–16.
3. Perhaps *priscus abbosa*; ibid.

Col. ix

bẹ[cchuf aurel a]ụidạs A.D. 214
ad ḍ[om n bol]ịadaẹụs iẹrhaei
ad [dom n]ạẓịzus aaṭhibeli
ad [dom n i]erhaeus zebida
ad doḿ [n aurel gai]us
ạ[ ]s marini
ạḍ ḍ[om n] ạ[u]ṛ[el anti]gonus
———]- auṛ[el]ịus ualens
.[aurel] z.[ ]
.[ ] [ ]ụs
au]rel .[ ]
.[ ]a[u]rel d[ ]

●[———]-   a[u]rẹḷ ualẹ[......]ṣ
].[ ] baṛ[
aur]ẹḷ[ ].e.[
]aụ[r]eḷ   abbạ[
]ạuṛẹ[l]   baṛ[
ad] do[m n] aurel iulius   .[
ad] ḍoṃ [n] aurel   ze[
a]d dom ṇ aurel   ḍ..[
ạd [dom] ṇ ạurel   gaị..[
ạp̣p[ada]ṇ aurel malchụṣ[
ṣ[ing]uḷ ạụrel domẹ[ti-
appa]dan auṛẹḷ amṛ[
bec]chuf aurel ualeriụṣ[
be]c̣c̣ḥuf aurel bas..[
●[ ]● [—]—— aurel cal[
⟦mạ[gd]ạla⟧ aurel   ..[
b[ecchu]f aurel   .[
● [———]- aurel   m[
Cụ[......]. aurel mạ [
———]- ạurẹ[l]   .[
——]-[——

Cf. **2** xiv 12–18; **8** iv 4–8.

9. The alignment shows that the *z* is the initial of a name.

23. *dome[tius*: D.

24. *amṛ[us*: D.

27. *calpurnius gaulianus*? Cf. **6** iv 2.

28. The cancellation of *magdala* is not certain. The word may have been written over an existing line. See pp. 15–16.

31. The *c* is written large in the papyrus. Probably *cụ[m*, the first word in nine other notations in **1** and **2**. This notation could not have contained more than about nine letters.

33. A line should not ordinarily appear under the column of names. Therefore it probably indicates that the name which stood here was canceled.

Col. x

laeto] ịị coṣ[A.D. 215
]ṣ ạ[urel]ṣ ọc̣c̣[...]ṃsa
sa]ḅino ịị [co]ṣ 216
———]— ạ[urel do]ṃeṭius ṇ[icola]us
bec]chuf a[u]ṛẹ[l] quint[ ][
be]cchuf aụṛ[el] bassus[ ][
]..s auṛ[el] demeṭ[rius][
].[..].io ạ[urel] ṃaximus[
becch]uf ạ[urel] philọṇ[
———]— [au]ṛel dometius [
]ạụrel seleục̣[u]s [
]aurel ṛọmaṇụ[s
]ạurel[
]aurel .[
———]— aurel p̣[ri]ṣcian[-
———]— aurel barlaḥạ[s
———]— a[u]ṛẹḷ[ ]b[

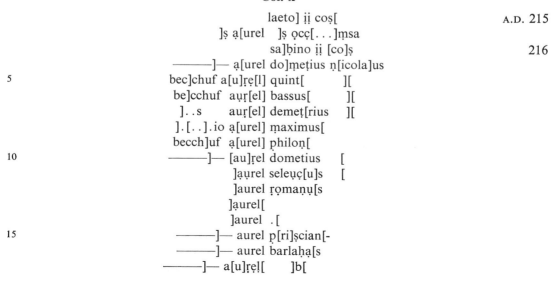

becchu]f auṛ[el].
becchu]f aurẹ[l
———]— aurel[ ].[
———]— ạ[urel].rus
]ạ[urel an]ṭoṇị[
]. ạ[urel].us[
———]— a[urel fl]auiuṣ[
]aụṛ[el]ṣ
]ạurel[ ]nus
a]urẹ[l]..[.....]ṣ
cx̣ḷ˙ ị[n] dụpḷ iii
Remainder of column blank

Cf. **2** xv 12–14; **6** iv 5–14.
4. Cf. **6** iv 6.
7. The notation before the name is in a different hand and different ink.
8. *o*[*f*][*fi*]*ç io*?
15. *p*[*ri*]*ṣcian*[*us*: D.
28. For the totals at the end of the roll of each century and turma see pp. 16–17.

Col. xi

ϒ aṇ[tonini uictorino] cos A.D. 200
] [ ] o[rd aurel dometius] ạṇ[toninu]ṣ
apro et m]ạxị[mo cos] 207
● singul du[pl]..[.......].
]ịnọ [cos] ?
●●——— ḍ[u]p̣l ạ[urel].es salṃ[ ]
er]ụcio clarọ [cos] 193
●——— ạ[urel malchu]ṣ anaṇ[i
tertu]llo [cos] 195
●——— ạ[urel iulius ba]ṛhạ[dadus]
bec]chuf auṛẹ[l]ị[e]ṛaẹi
dextro ii] cos 196
]..[.]n aurel[ ].ces
].s.f aurẹ[l]aior
b]ecchuf aurẹ[l malchus d]iogeni
—]—[— a]ụreḷ[zabdaath]ẹs mocimi
anulli]no ii cos 199
].us zabḍ[i]b[o]lị
demet]ṛịus baṛ[n]ạẹi
iulius apo]llonius [
]ṇo cos[
].ua[.....]ẹi
].[
]ṇ[.....]ṣ
mammaeu]ṣ bela[ca]b[i 201
mambogeu]s za[o]ṛ[a]
habibas n]ebudaei
hanina-]bellaei

]s
]bia.[
One or two lines lost
]us

Cf. **2** xxvii 2–16; **6** iv 16–32.

4. The dot before *singul* may be accidental. If not, it is the only example of an isolated punctum of this size. The absence of the angular symbol around *dupl* is to be noted. See above, p. 11.

5. The date might be any of nine years from 198 to 216.

13. Probably *app*]*ạḍ*[*a*]*n*

14. The cognomen may be *maior*. Cf. Marcus Maior, below, xxxiv 21 and **2** xxxiv 19. The notation has not been explained.

19. In **6** iv 26 the patronymic appears as *bannaei*. Perhaps the same should be read here.

21. *mucia*]*ṇo*: D; but **2** xxvii 8–13 and **6** iv 27–31 suggest restoring *uictorino* here and *muciano* in line 23 or 24.

28. Probably *haninas*.

Col. xii

] –[–]——[–] ạ[ur]el ni[A.D. 201–203
ạ[d sacr]ạḥiṃ ạ[ur]el [
p̣ h[.]aruạl.[.].●aḍ ṃ[.].. ṃạ. aurel [
ad doḿ ń aurel .[
ad doḿ ń aụre[l]..[
ci[lone ii co]ṣ 204
●———— ạ[ure]ḷ iuliụṣ[
●[—]——— a[u]ṛel geṛ[
bec]c̣huf aurel add[ ]ṇdṛ[
●———— ạ[ur]el auidiṇ.[ ].[
ad] ḍọḿ ń [au]ṛel aṇṭ[o]ṇiuṣ [
becc]huf[ ] aeḷị[u]ṣ b[
].[aur]ẹḷ ṃagnuṣ[
.[aur]ẹḷ m.[..]iṃ[
].[ ].[ ].s
About five lines lost
●———— ạ[urel]ẹị
●———— ạ[urel
●[●—]-̣——› ạ[urel
[co]s 205–207
c̣ọ[ ].ḷiọṇe ạ[urel
cuṃ[ ].[
ọ..[
tr]ạ[s]ḷ ex coh ị..[
].[.]a.[.]
●[●

3. The notation *aḍ ṃ*[.]..*ṃạ*. was apparently written above an existing line. The ink of these letters is somewhat paler than on the remainder of the page. This may be a form of *ad man ambul*. The intercolumnar note is not certainly read.

9. *add*[*as alexa*]*ṇdṛ*[*i*: D.

25. The notation has not been satisfactorily read.

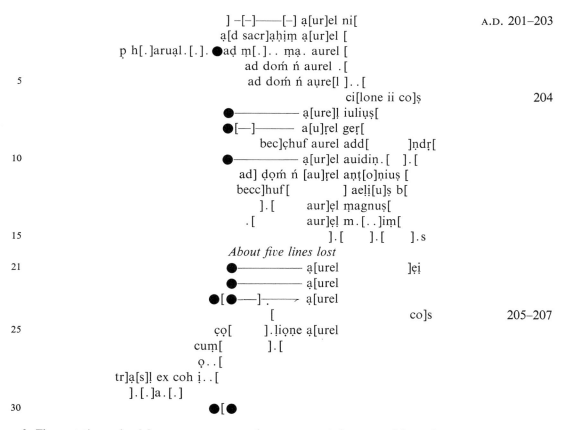

Col. xiii

ạ[ppa]ḍaṇ ạurel ạ[bed]ḷạhạ[s — A.D. 207
ḅ[i]ṛtḥ[a] ạ[u]ṛel .[..]..[
ad dom̄ ń aurel ọgạṣ .[
[ ].[ ] aurel c̣laudius ạ[ntoninus
diụ[o] aṇ[t]ọṇ[ino iii cos — 208
p.[....]..●[bir]ṭha aurel hẹlịọḍor[us apolloni
aḍ ṣac̣ṛ[a]ḥịṃ ag˙ aurel [ ]ạntiọc̣ḥ[ianus
cum ṃ..eạeliḅes[...] aurel [ ]flauius flạ[uianus
traṣḷ ẹx coh ˙i˙ ascol˙ siṇ[gul a]urel ịụlius maṛ[c]ị[anus
[po]mpeiạno cos — 209
ex[plor a]urel ạ[g]ṛippaṣ ṭhem[
●—[——— a]ụrel [ ]ụs [r]omanus [
.[a]ụre[l]ḥẹraclidạ[s
faus]ṭino cos — 210
be[cchuf aurel] .ḍ[.]s ḥẹlio[dor-
●..[
Consulate? — 212 ?
●———[—
ap̣p̣a[d
becc[huf
offị[cio
ad dom̄ [ń au]rel .[
appạ[d au]ṛel .[
●———[—— a]urel [
●[—]-[—— a]ureḷ [
•[●—]—[——] au[rel
● ——[——
● ——[——
●[—]—[——
]p̣[—]—[——

Cf. **2** xxviii 20–28; **8** x 15–17.

8. I cannot explain the notation.

9. The name of the cohort is almost certainly to be read *ascal(onitanorum)* though the *o* is clear in the papyrus.

12. *iulius romanus*? Cf. **8** x 16–17.

15. *helio[dorus*: D.

Col. xiv

]ṃagdạ[la au]rel ḅaricạ[s] ịeṛ[haei — A.D. 214
●———[—] aurẹ[l]za[b]dibo[lus
ạ[p]pada[n] aurel ierhaẹ[us] ẓẹḅị[da-
●———[— aur]ẹ[l] ạbedsalṃ[as] ịerḥạ[ei
●———[—] ạurel moc̣[i]ṃus
●———[— a]urel maṛ[in]us
ạp̣p̣[a]da ạ[u]ṛel abḍ[u]ṣ
●——— ạ[urel] zabda[s aua]ḍa
●——— ạ[urel] nisṛ[aeu]ṣ

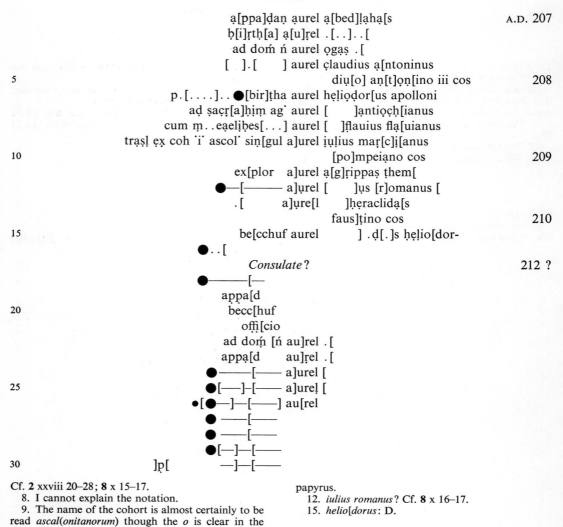

ap]pada ạ[urel] gerṃ[a]ṇus
ad] doḿ ń ạ[urel] ạbed.[..]ṃṛa
ad do]ḿ ń[ ]a e[
].[ ]ạṇus
About two lines lost
ad] doḿ ń .[
a]ḍ doṃ́ ń ạ[urel
a]ḍ doḿ ń ạ[urel
a]ḍ ḍoḿ ń ạ[urel
ad] ḍoḿ ń a[urel]..[
ad do]ṃ́ ń a[urel]ma[
becc]huf a[urel z]ebida[
]. .[ ] p[
⟦]iuṇ[⟧

Cf. **2** xxix 23–29.
1. The notation is either a later entry, written over a line, or has been canceled.

Col. xv

bẹ[c]c̣huf ạụrel ạ[eliu]ṣ hẹḷ[io]ḍorus
la[eto] ii cos A.D. 215
app]adan aụṛ[e]ḷ ḍ[o]mettị[u]s
ṣạ[bino ii co]ṣ 216
bec]c̣huf aurẹ[l] ṇ[eo]ṇ
becc]huf a[u]rel[ ].eus
bec]c̣huf aurel ạ[poll]ọnius
].[bec]chuf aurel [ ]ṣ
]el[ ]ḅạrtha aurel a[*ca.* 9].
].c̣.[.].ụṇ ⟦appạdạ auṛẹḷ a[*ca.* 9].⟧
●————[– aurel] c[yrillus]
offic̣ aụṛ[el] g[ordius]
becchuf aurẹ[l].[*ca.* 9].
explora aụ[r]ẹ[l
●⟦magdaḷ⟧
becc̣h[uf
].[
iṇ[aur]el ị[u]ḷiuṣ[
aur]el ma[
aur]ẹl mo[
aure]ḷ ma.[
]...[ ] baṛṛil.[
]bars.[
aurel]ḷongiṇ[us
]ạ[

Cf. **2** xxx 11–27; **6** v 19–21.
9 and 10. The intercolumnar notation has not been satisfactorily read.
15. The notation seems to be in another hand, written over an existing line. See above, p. 15.
24.]*ḷongiṇ*[: D.

Col. xvi

extr[i]c̣aṭ[o ii co]s A.D. 217
]a aụ[rel ab]g̣aṛụṣ ṭḥemạ[rs]ạ
———]— a[urel g]ạdde ḅ[ore
]dupl iii[
Three lines blank
Y] caṣ[trici] antoṇino ii c̣ọ[s 205
or]ḍ ạ[urel . .]ịus castriciụṣ [
]p̣ antoṇị[
]c̣ilone ii cos 204
ad ḍ[ ]mocimus thẹṃaṛ[sa
]diụọ ṣẹ[u]ẹ[ro c]ọs 194
]aurel marrịụṣ .[. .]ṃaṇ[
tertullo c̣[o]ṣ 195
]●[———]- aurel zaidibolus m[alacheli
]●[———]- aurel iulius[
———]— aurel zaiḍ[ibolus sad. . .i]
——]—— aurel [
c]ọs[196–201
——]—— aurẹ[l a]ḷẹx̣anḍ[r-
——]—— ạ[urel]ṃalc̣hi[
]f̣[ ]ṭheṃarsa[
]ọ cos 197–202
]l. ạ[urel *ca.* 9 di]ọmedi
]a aụ[rel *ca.* 10 z]ebida
].n au[rel *ca.* 12]ḷe
]ṣ a[urel th]ẹṃạrsa
]. a[urel].
———]— a[urel

Cf. **2** xxxi 14–16; **6** x 27–30.

2. *themarsa* corrected from *themes*. The same correction in this name is found in **2** xxxi 15; and cf. **92** iii 18.

4. For these totals see pp. 16–17.

9. *ạ[lexand]ṛus*: D, without sufficient basis. *aurel* seems much more likely, in view of the prevalence of *aurel* elsewhere in this text, though this leaves space for only about three letters in the lacuna. Possibly *d]ius*, *iul]ius*, *ael]ius*, or even *ạ[urel]ius* written out in full.

10. For the marginal notation see p. 13. Presumably the name of a duplicarius who enlisted in the same year as Castricius stood in this line and the notation applied to him.

12. This man was either a duplicarius or a sesquiplicarius.

16 and 18. **6** x 28 has *zabdibolus*.

27. *ma]ḷe*: D; but *ierabole* and other names are possible.

Col. xvii

moci]m[us] thẹṃe[A.D. 203
●[ ]s .[.].[. . .]ṣ
●● a[——⌐ ul]p̣iụ[s seueru]s
.[ ]ịụlius [salman]
]ciloṇ[e ii cos] 204
]——[——]halạ[s
ad dom ṇ[ ]ịụḷiuṣ [marin]ụs

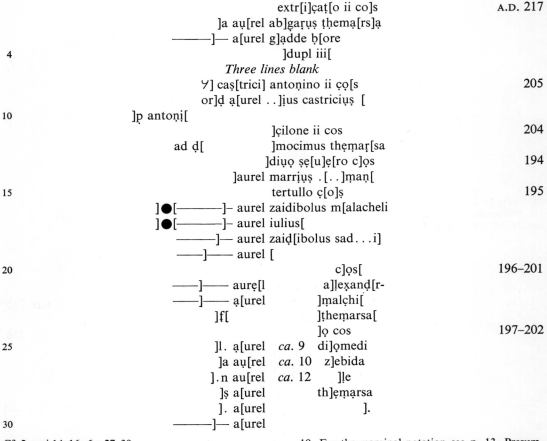

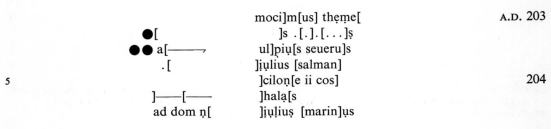

appa[dan]ḍ[.]a[nus]g̣ại
officịọ a]be[dmalchu]s marọṣa
]———[— maximus]ḥotaraei
●———[— iulius] ḥelịọdọṛus
ạd doṃ n[t]ḥeṃes malchi
]——[—— ul]pius puplianus
becchuf[aurel] domnus
] priscus annona[
] baricbelus basṣ[i
] didas sal[man
] iadaeus [themarsa
aure]ḷ .ạ[
] diụṣ[
]ị[
] .[
] s.aụ[
aurel] mu[
] iuliụ[s
] iuliụṣ[
]ạb[
].[

Cf. **2** xxii 12–27; **6** xi 1–9; **8** viii 1.
3. *a*[*ctuar*(*ius*): cf. **2** xxii 13.
4. The notation began with *b*, *d*, or *o*.
8. Perhaps *hadrianus*; cf. **2** xxii 18.

Col. xviii

].[.]ṇụs
]nọ [co]s A.D. 205–209
ạ[d] ḍọṃ ṇ[ ].[
fausti]no c̣[os 210
●—[—]——[ierh]aeus z[ebida
[becc]huf ạ[urel]eus[
as]priṣ [cos 212
[appa]da au[rel art]eṃ[idorus
ạ[pp]ạda a[urel the]ṃes [zebida
p˙.[ ]● [bir]tha aurel[themarsa nisa]ṃṣi
o]f̣f̣ị[c] aurel[ ].haei
]aurel[macrin]ịus maximi
———]- aurel[mocim[us antonini
ṃ[essal]ạ c̣ọs 214
aur]ẹ[l ierab]ọle obean
[aurel g]aius
moci]ṃus antoni[
[aurel]ḍalạṭhụ[s
]gṇ[
.[ ].a.[
] ●——[——].[

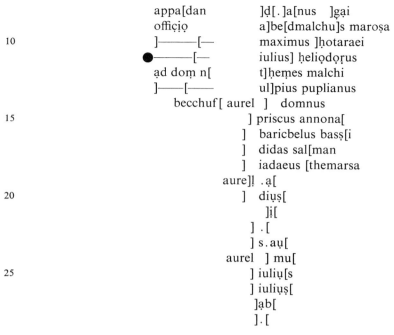

].ẓ[
] ●——[—— aurel bars]imsus[
ierhae]us niṣ[
]eṣam[
].al[

Cf. **2** xxiii 18–28; **6** xi 20–33; **8** viii 13–21.

2. Probably *pompeiano cos.*

16. In **6** xi 28 the second name appears as a patronymic: *aurel gai.*

18. Either *abdalathus*, *auidalathus*, or *sadalathus* is possible.

24. *niṣ[raei*: D; but see on **6** xi 33. The man there seems to be the same person as here; but *iarhaeus th-* in **8** viii 24 is different, since his name does not follow *aurel barsimsus* directly, as here.

Col. xix

ọfficiọ ạu[r]ẹ[l
becchụ[f
p̣arthia aureḷ[
].ṇauem họṛ[d a]urel .[
ad doḿ ń [a]urel [*ca.* 9].
ạd doḿ [ń a]urel ze.[
a]ḍ doḿ ṇ́ [au]ṛel iuliụ[s
ad] doḿ ń [au]ṛel ẓ[
ad] doḿ ń [a]ụrel .ar.[
ad] ḍoḿ ṇ́ aurẹ[l] ma[
ad] ḍoḿ [ń aur]ẹḷ zaḅ[
aur]ẹḷ iulius p̣[rior?
]ạurel iụ[l]ius p̣[o]s(terior)?
].[ ]...[
]bedṣus
].
]s
i]ẹrhaei
]..[

About two lines lost

● [
● [——]—[—
b]ecch[uf].[
Cuṃ[n]aueṃ[ ].us
ṣin[gul]s
]a

4 and 25. For the notations cf. **1** xxix 24. In 4 read *hor[d(eariam)*, "barley ship"?

Col. xx

⟦ṃag[d]ạl⟧ aurel i.[..].[
si]ng[ul] aurel m[
sạ[bi]ṇo ịị [cos A.D. 216
●⟦ṃạg̣ḍạ[l]⟧ a]urel d[e]ṃeṭṛi[us

[becc]huf aurel pr[isc]us ab[bosa
[becch]ụf aurel ṣ[um]marẹs
●–[———]– aurel .[. . . .]ụs
a]urel aṇ[toni]nus
aur]ẹl hẹ[lio]ḍorus
aur]ẹl [bass]us
aur]ẹl ṣ[il]ụanus
•●—[——— aur]el [ ].[.].[.].ius
aurel bas]ṣụs
aurel silu]ạṇus
About two lines lost
b]ẹcc[huf
–]———[—
bẹçch[uf
ad ḷeonẹ[s
explọṛ[
–]———[– au]rel [
becchụ[f a]ụrel [
ḅẹ[c]ḉh[uf a]ụrel [
]ạurẹ[l

Cf. **2** xxv 13–22; **8** ix 13–17.
6. *summareus*?

Col xxi

Ɣ mạ[ri]ani dịụo aṇ[to]niṇo ii [cos A.D. 205
ạd [o]p̣iṇ[i]on orḍ ạurel iulius [ma]ṛ[ianus
].[.]..[ ] geta ṣ[eniore ii cos 203
ṣingul ḍ[u]p̣ḷ ạurel iulius [ap]olị[narius
cilon[e i]i cos 204
becchuf ṣ[esq] ạurel lucius [t]hemạ[rsa-
comoḍ[o vi]i cos 192
ad p̣raẹṭọṛ[a]urel abḍ[as t]ḥẹmarsa
erucị[o clar]ọ cos 193
●———[—]ịạdaẹ[u]ṣ [ier]haei
ad sacṛ[ahim].th[. . . .] ṃalchi
te]ṛtụ[llo] cos 195
beç[chuf i]ẹṛḥ[aeu]ṣ barnaei
]ṣạt[urnino cos 198
●—[——— agripp]ạs ṃạle
[anullino] ii cos 199
●[
]ạ[urel
———]— a[urel
Consulate 200 or 201
].in auṛ[el
———]— auṛ[el

———]— auṛ[el i]er.[
———]— auṛ[el].siur.[
———]— auṛ[el] ṃalc[h-
]zeb[
]b[

Cf. **2** xvi 16–22.
8. *abd* corrected from *aba*. This is the only man of this year still active. The others (xxxviii 15 and xli 10–11) have been discharged.

Col. xxii

a]ḍ doṁ [ń] ạurel bạṛlạ[has iarh-
seuero [iii cos A.D. 202
p̣[art]ḥia aurel buccaeụ[s
geta ṣ[eni]orẹ [ii cos 203
bẹ[cchu]f̣ṛ ạ[urel] ulpius .[..]ịnus
●———[— a]urel aelius [h]ẹracl.[
● ad lẹ[ones a]urel them[es] ṃalchi
ẹmans˙ ex erạ.[au]ṛẹḷ iuliuṣ[ ].anus
cil[one ii c]os 204
●———[—]ṃaṛ[cus ui]ctor
].[ab]edla[ha]ṣ maxiṃi
●——[—— iul]ius [ab]ẹdsẹṃia
casṭ[el arab].a[.......]ẹi
[uareus ba]ṛ[si]ṃṣi
p′ helió max ●[maximu]ṣ ẓaoṛ[a
●[
]. ạ[urel
]ọffi[c] a[urel
—]——[—] aụṛ[el
app]ạdạ aur[el
Consulate 205–207
].n aurẹ[l i]er.[
becchu]f aure[l z]ebida[
]. aurẹ[l]hab[
a]ụṛ[el]abb[
]ḍ[

Cf. **2** xvii 9–21; **8** v 10–15.
1. *iarhaei*: D.
8 and 13. The notations may be in a different hand. *emans(it)* means "was absent without leave". What follows should name the post from which he was absent, the time at which the absence began, or the reason for it; but no satisfactory interpretation of *era.* occurs to me.
15. *p(ro) helio(doro) max(imi)*? The notation is in a different hand, the same as *-nans*, xxiii 15.

Col. xxiii

● [———]— ạụrel ie[r]ạbọḷ[es bu]ccaeị
● [—]——— ạụrel iulius ạ[...]ṇi.[
———]— ạ[u]ṛẹḷ b..ḍs.[....]ae.[
diuo anṭ[oni]ṇọ ị[ii cos A.D. 208

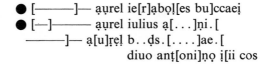

be[.]f̣ ạ[urel]ụalerius [m]ụcịạ[n-
bec̣[au]rel ulpius ṃ[ari]nus[
of[fic a]urel iulius m[a]ximụṣ[
singụḷ [a]urel mạ[rinu]ṣ
●———[— aurel] ruṃ[as
pom]p̣eịạ[no co]s A.D. 209
appạ[d a]elius[. . .]ụs
●●-[——— uẹ[x]ius ṃ[a]ṛinus
fa]us[tin]ọ c̣ọṣ 210
]ạḍ[daeus m]ạ[c]caei
]nans •● ap̣[pad]ḍa.ṇus
●——[—— iulius th]emarsa
One line lost
———]— ạ]urel
e]x̣plor a[urel
——]—— a[urel
Consulate 212–214
] aurẹ[l
ap]p̣ạd aurẹ[l]ṇao.[
———]— aurẹ[l] ṃoci[m-
———]— aurẹ[l] iuliuṣ[
].[ ]ha[
]..[

Cf. **2** xviii 9–23; **8** vi 1–3.
2. Probably *antoninus*.
5. *m]ụcịạ[nus*: D.
5 and 6. The notations may be in a different hand. It does not seem possible to read *becuf* in 5 for lack of space before the *f*; and this renders the restoration in 6 doubtful.
12. *ṃ[ ]inus*: D; in app., *m[ar]inus?*
14.]..[*m]ạ[c]caei*: D.
15. See on **1** xxii 8. Read *e]mans*? or *re]mans(it)*? Cf. **8** viii 4.
19. The notation is in a different hand.
24. *ṃoci[mus*: D.

Col. xxiv

ạppadạ aurel iulị[us] ṃạṛ[inus A.D. 214
[becc]hụf aurel ma.[. . .]ụs .[
ạp̣[p]adạ aurel baṣṣụ[s n]ạṣ[sibeli
●———[ ]thẹ[m]ẹs ḥ[eliodor-
●———[—] ạurel baḅụiuṣ
app̣[ada]ạurel mục̣ian[u]s
●———[— a]ụreḷ aelạ[mis] belsur
appạ[da aurel] m[ann]us
●———[—]iuliụṣ[he]ṛacla[
ạḍ ḍ[aurel]ni.[..]eus
becc̣ḥ[uf aurel]mạṛinus
barthạ[ ]clạ[u]ḍ[ius] ṣoteric̣us
castẹ[l arab]s zebida[
b[ ]s mar[..]us
One line lost

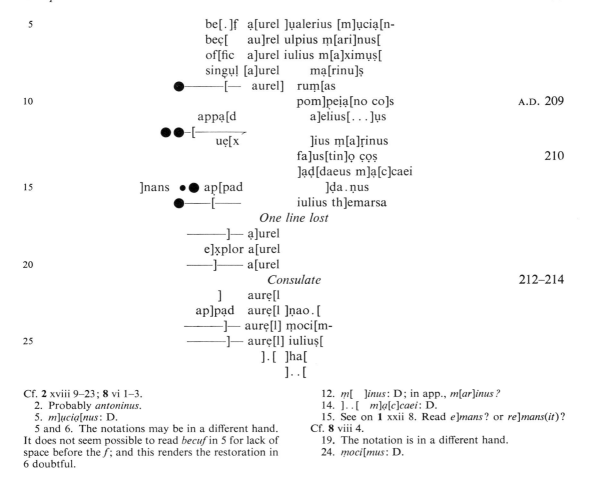

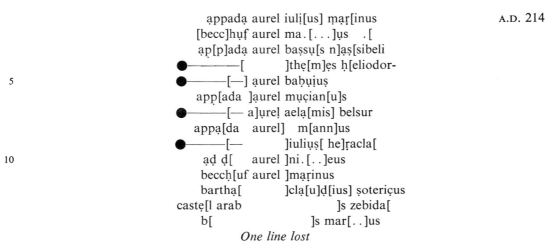

●[———]— auṛ[el
]di.ḅ.[castel a]ṛab auṛ[el
]be.[ ].n aureḷ[
———]— ạurel[
———]— aurel[
]. aurel[ ] m[
]aurel[ ] [
a]ureḷ[ ] [
]...[

Cf. **2** xix 7–16; **8** vi 15–19. Throughout the column a rough joint in the papyrus causes a wide space between *aurel* and the name which follows. Lines 22–23 are blank for this reason below *m* in line 21.

4. *ḥ[eliodori:* D.

5. *bu* corrected from *ba* in *babuius.*

9. The papyrus is broken after *heracla*; but the last *a* has the final form.

10. Probably *ad dom ń*; and perhaps *nisraeus.* Cf. **2** xxix 29.

17–18. The intercolumnar note has not been satisfactorily read.

Col. xxv

ad doṃ ń aurel ṣab.[
●——— aurel claụdius[
offị[cio] aurel iuliuṣ ṃ[arc-
caṣṭ[el] ạ[rab] aurel ṃar.[
●——— aurel rụfus[
——— aurel ạẓizus
•●——— aurel [bassu]s
●——— ạurel t[hema]rsas sạ[lma]ṇ[
ad[aur]el [...]us
●mag̣[dala aur]el m[axi]mus ṣ[a]ḷṃ[an
●●[——— au]ṛel p̣riscus
au]ṛeḷ[ ]ḅ[..]s
●[ ]ṃạḷc̣hus
la]ẹṭo ii cos[A.D. 215
One line lost
ma]gḍala[
becchuf[
becchuf[
]biṛtha.[
——]——[
]ṣinguḷ[a]urel[
b]ecc̣hụf ạurel[
sin]g̣ụ[l] c̣os aurel[
]auṛ[el

Cf. **2** xx 2–8.

6. No punctum at beginning of line, but a faint mark as if a stroke had been begun and then erased.

7. D in app.: [*bassu*]*s?* Cf. **2** xx 4.

10. *m*[ ]*mus:* D; in app., *m*[*axi*]*mus?*

11. Cf. **2** xx 8.

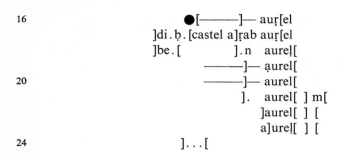

Col. xxvi

]p̣ aụ[r]eli ●——— aurel aḅbosaṣ[A.D. 216
ḅ[ec]c̣ḥuf̣ aurel siluaṇ[us
●———[– a]urel lic[in]ṇi[us
bec̣[ch]ụ[f aur]el g̣ẹ[r]ṃanụ[s
p p̣a[ ]● ad leọ[ne]s aurel ieraboleṣ[
p.[ ]ad lẹọṇ[e]ṣ aurel d[o]ṃetius
becc[huf] ạụ[r]el c̣[....]ụs
bịrṭ[ha aur]ẹl .[....].us
c]xlvi [i]ṇ dupl[ ]i[
Three lines blank
Ɣ malc̣hiaṇ[a] diuo seue[ro] ii coṣ[194
si]ṇg[ul] ḍ[u]p̣l aurẹ[l]ḍ[...].[
Consulate
●[●]——— dupl aur[el
Consulate 193–197
explora ạ[ur]el[
—]——— ạ[urel
Consulate 194–198
]iiii scy ạ[urel
—]——— ạ[u]ṛel[
Consulate 195–199
——]—— aurel[
——]—— aurel[
Consulate 196–200

Cf. **2** xxi 4–9; **8** vii 12–14.
9. For these totals see pp. 16–17.
21. The name may have been canceled. In that case, the notation must have run *translatus in legionem iiii scy*(*thicam*). The *y* has a cross-bar through it.

Col. xxvii

●——— auṛel coddạẹus A.D. 197–201
—]——— a[u]ṛẹḷ abgarụ[s] tḥ[em]e
●——— a[urel] ocbane ạ[..].ạẹị
—]——— a[u]ṛẹl seleus mạ[l]chi
—]——— [a]ụrel acibas ginn[aei
seuerọ ịịị coṣ 202
–]——— sig [aur]ẹḷ aelius[helio]dorus
]——— ạ[urel ẓabdi[bolus] theoboḷi
gẹṭa seni[ore ii c]os 203
●——— aur[el] ịụḷius aṛ[is]ṭon
becchuf aụ[rel] momḅogeus
•●——— auṛ[el] iaqubus tḥẹṃarsa
●——— auṛ[el] zebidas saḷṃan
aḍ ọpinio au[rel] abednạbus them[ars]a

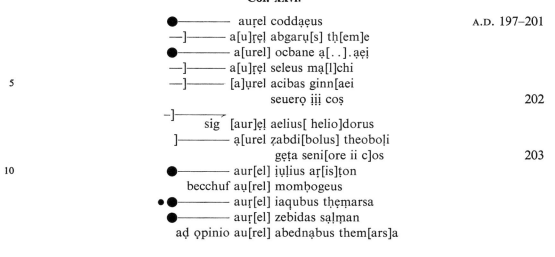

●——— aurẹ[l] addas maḷc̣ḥ[
]. aurẹ[l] themarsa ma[
]n aurel adda[s] ẓ[
———]— aurel ạẹḷius ṃarcia[n-
———]— aurel[ ]ẹus ni.[
becc]ḥuf aurel[
——]—— aurel ạ[
———]— aurel ạntị[ochus
a]urel malc[h-
] cilone [ii cos 204
aurel] cassiạ[nus ni...ṛ]
].ạ[
]ṣign.ị[

One line lost

]●[

Cf. **2** i 7–15 and ii–iv, frag. a 3–5; **6** ix 4–14; **27** a ii 3; **92** ix 8–9.

3. *ocbaneṣ*[ ].*ạẹị*[*:* D. The second name appears garbled. In **6** ix 6 it is clearly *ocbanes abidlaha*, and **2** i 8 does not contradict this reading; but the traces in the present text fit no such name.

7. *sig* is in a different hand.

15. *maḷc̣ḥ*[*i:* D.

18. *ṃarcia*[*nus:* D.

23. *malc*[*hus:* D. Cf. **6** ix 15 and app.

27. Possibly]*ṣignịf*[

Col. xxviii

cuṃ e...ṇ aurel marin[u]s maxiṃị
●——— aurel cassius sacoṇ[a
aḍ ḍ[o]ḿ ń ạ[u]rel iulius i[.]ṇu[...]ṣ
officio [au]rel marinuṣ lu[ci
birtha aurel maxiṃ[us]ạḷ[..]i
●⟦magdala⟧ aurel iulius maxị[mu]s
diuo ạ[ntoni]no ii cos A.D. 205
●——— aurel ualeṛ[ius f]ịrmus
●———[- aur]el iulius [al]ẹxandrus
beç[c]ḥ[u]f̣ ạuṛ[el] iulius [za]bde
castell arab[aur]ẹl mar[ ] ṣalman
●———ạ[ure]ḷ hammaeus ogel[i]
albino et emeliaṇo cos 206
p̣ [he]l[i]odor. ●——— ạurel iulius [m]ạṛinụs·
sig ●———[a]ụṛel titius ṭịberius
ad [o]pin ạurel abedmalc̣ḥus
ad opinio ạụrel iulius h[....].[
apro et ṃax[imo cos 207
●——— aurel abedạḷạ[th-
●——— aurel aẹḷius th[
●●———
]ạg ạ[urel m]azabạ[nas
●——— ạ[urel m]oçịṃ[
●——— ạ[urel].ạ.[

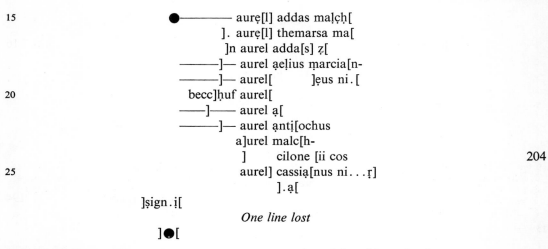

ṣ[in]gul aụ[r]el [ ]b.[
pọ[mpeiano cos A.D. 209
appa]ḍa aurel .[
]aurel[
p paç..m ●[
Two lines lost
●[
Two lines lost
●[

Cf. **6** ix 19–23; **92** ix 10–11.
1. The notation has not been satisfactorily read.
3. *ianuarius*?
5. *maximus malchi*?
17 and 21. The notations are in a different hand.
19. *abedalath-*, rather than *abedạlạ[has*: D. The latter name regularly appears as *abedlahas*; but cf. *'Αβδάλλαθος*, *PDur.* 17 A 3, and *'Αβδελάθ*, *PDur.* 26, 17 and 18.
21. *im]ag(inifer)*? Cf. **2** xxii 16.

Col. xxix

offiçio aur[e]ḷ mociṃ[us] ẓabd[
becchuf aurel clạ[u]dius antoni.[
ạ[d] ọpinio aurel ṣ.[..]ṃius leonid.[
ḅecchuf aurel iaḍ[..]ẹus aithibẹḷị
m]ẹssalạ [c]os A.D. 214
ad domin aurel ị[u]ḷius baṣsus
appadan a[ur]ẹ[l] bargạ[
●⟦.[ ]...⟧ a[ure]ḷ euxeṃon
ap]p̣adan a[urel] iulius flaụ[i]ụs
b]ẹçchuf a[urel] addas ẓ[e]bida
ḅ[e]çchuf aurel maṛ[inu]ṣ
[o]ffịcio au[r]ẹl malçh[us z]ẹbidạ
ạ[p]padan auṛ[el] ṭrạ..[.]us
ạ[p]p̣adan aurel malçhus
ạ[p]p̣adan aurel ạ[nto]ṇiuṣ [b]assus
●——— aurel ạ[........].manus
●——— aụṛẹḷ [ ].as thẹṃarsa
●——— aurel [ ]ẹṃ[ ]
●——— aur[el].us[
●——— ạụ[rel
ạ[ ] ạ[urel
bẹcchụ[f] ạ[urel
●———[—
]çum nauẹṃ[
—]——[—].ius
]ṣ
]ị
ha]ẹṛan
]s
]ṣ

]hus h[ae]ṛan
d]ẹmetṛịụs
].[..]ṣ

3. The letter after *d* of *leonid* is certainly not *a*; it resembles *u*. The notation is in a different hand.
6 and 8. The notations are in another hand.

13. *traianus*?
24. For the notation cf. **1** xix 4 and 25.

Col. xxx

ad dom̃ ñ aurel erenṇ[A.D. 214
ad dom̃ ñ auṛẹḷ malchus ṭ[hemar]ṣạ
ad dom̃ ṇ̃ aụ[rel] malchụ[s
ad dom̃ ñ auṛ[el] siluanus
ad dom̃ ñ ạurel erennius marịnụṣ
ad dom̃ ṇ̃ aụṛel andronicus
ad dom̃ [ñ] ạurel siluanus
ad dom̃ ṇ̃ aurel silụ[a]nus alṭẹṛ
pạrthi[a] aurel thẹṃarsa
becc[huf] aurel ieraboles
appad[an] aurel aṇ[to]ninus
–]——— aurel ier[ha]ẹ[u]s abgari
●——— aurel ḥadriạṇus
p baṣṣo • ● cạ[st]ell arab aurel ierhạẹus theoboli
appadan aurel demetrius
l]aeṭ[o ii] cos 215
parthia aur[el apollo]ṇius mẹsenus
ịn proseq hoṛḍ auṛ[el bas]ṣus
sabi]ṇọ ii çọṣ 216
●——— aụṛ[el].ạs
beç[c]ḥuf aurel .[.....]..[...]..
ḅẹ[cc]ḥuf auṛẹl [ ]..[.]sci
ḅẹcchụf auṛẹl [
●⟦magdala⟧ aurel .[
●——— ạurel [
be[cchuf au]rel [
be[cchuf aur]el [
–]—[——]– auṛ[el ale]x̣ạndrụs
]ạ ạụṛ[el]ḅelus
au]ṛ[el]es
aurel basi]ḷẹụs
aurel helio]dor[u]ṣ
]ḷ[.]cus
]ụṣṇ[.]ṣ
]ọle[
]..[.]ḷ[..]...

Cf. **6** x 5–17.
1. *erenṇ[ius:* D; but *erenṇ[ianus* is equally possible.
18. *in proseq(utione) hord(iatorum)*. See **47** ii 5; and cf. also **1** xxxvi 10 and **2** xxxiv 24.

29. *iadi]belus:* D.
31.].*ẹụs:* D.
32. *helio]dor[u]ṣ:* D.

Col. xxxi

becchuf aurel ḅ[a]rsiṃ[
●——— aurel liuian[us
ad leones auṛẹḷ addaeus[
]——— ạuṛ[el] marinuṣ[
becchuf auṛ[el] barhaḍạḍ[
becchuf ạ[u]rel dometius marcị[a]ṇus
● ⟦magdala⟧ aurel zebinnus
ad op ṣṭịp aurel baṛnaeus
trasl in coh .[..] ⟦aurel alexandṛuṣ⟧
offị[cio] aurel marinus
● magdal[a] aurel barsemia
cato
⟦d⟧extri⟦o⟧ ii cos — A.D. 217
●——— aurel ẓabde
imp aṇṭonino aug ii
et sacerdote ii cos — 219
●——— aurel seleucus
●——— aurel gạius germanus
]c̣[ ]ḷ[ ]iṇ dụpl v
Two lines blank
Ƭ zebida aṇuḷ[lin]o [ii cos — 199
● ●●●——— dec aurel zeḅ[id]ạṣ ierḥ[ae]i
.[....... co]s — ?
● ●●●——— dupl ạ[ur]ẹḷ ṃ[......].ma[
dị[uo seuer]ọ iii c̣[os — 202
appada dupl aurel aḍ[.....]gṇ..[..]i
e[rucio] c̣ḷ(aro) c̣[os — 193
●——— aurel ..[*ca.* 11].n
]..[*Consulate* — 194–195
●——— ạ[urel]ḍaduṣ ṃombogei
–]——— ạ[urel].us thẹmarsa
]——— a[urel]ạs hala
s[in]guḷ ạ[urel]ạṇṭoninus
dextro i]i cos — 196
....esur]us [a]ẹḷạṃi
anullin]o [ii] cos — 199
barhada]dus heraṇ[
ieraboles t]hemarsa
ulpius m]ẹṇạndr[u]ṣ
]ḥ[

Cf. **2** xxxii 5–11; **6** x 19–25.
7 and 11. The notations are in a second hand.
12. *dextro* corrected to *extricato*. The *i* of *extricato* is drawn through the *o* of *dextro*.
13. **6** x 25 and **92** ix 4 have *zabdas*.
18. For these totals see pp. 16–17.
26. Note the absence of the angular symbol from *dupl*.
30. *ạ*[ ].*adụs:* D. Possibilities are *abeda-*, *baada-*, and *barha-*, all attested for Dura.
40. Possibly *belaacabus hala*; cf. **2** xxxii 12–13.

Col. xxxii

becchuf aurẹ[l] boreṣ [nisa]ṃṣi
uictori[no cos] A.D. 200
explorato aurel naheṣ[tabus the]ṃạṛsa
mucia[no cos] 201
becchuf ạụrel haguṣ [mal]c̣hi
●——— aurel abianes ṃ[acc]ḥana
●——— aurel themarsa [ha]ẹran
●——— aurel aẹlius b[o]ḷạ[n]ụs
p marinuṣ •● ⟦dis[po]ṣ⟧ aurel themarṣạ [ab]gari
beç[ch]uf aurel ierạbole addḍ[a]ẹi
●——— aurel iuliuṣ themarsa
ad sacṛ[ahi]mag· aurel bassus tiberini
becchuf aurel i[u]ḷius marinus
●——— aurel iulịus mạṛinus alter
●——— aurel male maçchana
●●——— sig aurel flauius euclides
●——— aurel iẹ[r]haeuṣ themarsa
dịụo seuẹṛo iii cos 202
●——— ạ[urel h]ẹḷịọdorụs seleuci
●——— aurẹ[l mal]chus momḅ[o]gei
●●——— uex aure[l ba]ṛạth[es . . . .]. . i
●——— aurẹḷ [ ]ạḷ. [.]ḅịụṣ [silu]ạni
● disposit aurel[ ]ius marinus
g̣[et]ạ ṣẹṇ[ior]ẹ [ii] c̣[o]s 203
●——— ạure[l] uạ[l]ẹṛius ṃ[o]ṇ[i]ṃus
●——— aurel ị[uliu]ṣ saṭ[urnilu]s
becchuf aurẹḷ iẹ[rha]ẹụṣ bẹḷạạ[cab]i
offic̣ịọ aur[el] ị[ulius] ṃạ[xi]ṃus
●●●●——— cor aurẹ[l alexa]ṇḍ[ru]ṣ antonini
●——— ạ[ure]ḷ [ ].a. . .[i]amlichi
●——— aụrẹḷ [aeliu]ṣ heliọḍọṛus
●——— ạụṛ[el bar]ḅ[a]ẹṣsamen mal[e
[cilone ii]cos 204
●——— ạ[ur]ẹ[l fronton] ṃare[a
–]—[—— aelius al]ẹxạṇḍṛ[us
–]—[—— iulius cassi]ạnuṣ[
–]—[—— abe]ḍḷạḥ[in
exploratọṛ[

Cf. **2** xxxii 12–26; xxxiii 1–17.
6. *ṃ[att]hana:* D; but see Index 1, s.v. "Matthana."
10 and 23. The notations are in a different hand.
12 and 16. The notations are in another hand.
15. *maṭthana:* D; see on line 6.
27. *bẹḷạc̣[abi]?*
38. *exploratụṃ?*

Col. xxxiii

diu[o antonin]ọ ịị coṣ — A.D. 205
● <u>ad ṁ ambul</u> aurel ualeṛ[ius firmu]ṣ
ex[plo]ra aurel iuliuṣ [bassus]
●——— aurel uabalạ[th. . .]ẓ[. .]i
●——— aurel zabdiḅọḷ[us sal]ṃan
appaḍ[ ] aurel mocimus z[e]ḅida
●——— aurel ierhaeus ṃ[a]rea
●——— aurel zebidaṣ ịẹṛḥaei
●——— aurel gabrioṇ [o]bean
p baroṭaro •●——— aurel azizus antonini
sin[gu]l cos aurel mocimus mocimi
ạpṛo et maximo cos — 207
beccḥuf aurel dometius antoninus
•●——— aurel iulius iulianus
pompeiano cos — 209
●——— aurel f̣ḷauius demetrius
●——— ạụrel ạeḷius ḷicinnius
dụob[u]s aspris cos — 212
● <u>ad man ambul</u> ạụ[rel] iul[i]us ạḷexạ[n]drus
cxḷ[ ]ị[n d]upl v
Two lines blank
Ƭ tiberinị apṛọ eṭ ṃaxim[o co]ṣ — 207
●●——— dec aurel ṭhemarṣ[a] ṭ[i]ḅerini
geṭa ṣẹ[niore] ii cos — 203
ad hordeum dupl aurel iulius ạnṭọninus
ạpro eṭ maximo cos — 207
becchuf dụpḷ ạ[urel a]ẹḷ[i]ụṣ ḅarnaeus
aḷḅiṇ[o co]s — 206
●●——— sesq ạ[urel] f̣ḷaui[u]s demetri[
ẹṛụ[c]ḷio cl(aro) cos — 193
●——— a[urel]ẹ. thema[rsa
● [ ].ḷ.st[
● [———]euṣ .[
tertu]ḷḷo coṣ[— 195
●-[———].t.[
]-[———]de.[
] ●———[-

Cf. **2** xxxiii 18–31; xxxiv 1–6.

2 and 19. The notations are in a different hand.

4. *uabalathus azizi*?

10. The notation is in another hand, possibly the same as that of the similar notes in the next column.

20. For these totals see pp. 16–17.

24. The lacuna between the second and third names is too small to restore [*as*].

26. *ad hordeum* is in another hand: "Detailed to the barley supply."

26 and 28. Note the absence of the angular symbol from *dupl*.

Col. xxxiv

●———— aụrel [iadi]ḅẹḷụṣ malcḥi
●———— auṛel ụ[. . . . . mo]ṃbogeus
●———— auṛel .[. . . . . .] ṃaccaei
•● ạḍ ṃań amb aurel ḍ[i]ụs iẹrhaei
●——— a[u]ṛel barṇ[a]eus zebida
●———— aụṛel antoṇ[inu]s marinus
ḅẹçchuf a[u]ṛel tḥ[e]ṃ[ar]ṣa addaei
dẹxt[ro] ịi cos A.D. 196
● diṣpos ạ[u]rel sim[a]ọnes auidalatḥi
● ad mań amb aurẹl maronas gadde
appadan aurel ualeras quirini
saturnino ⟦ii⟧ cos 198
●——— au[r]ẹl barathes zebida
aṇullino ii cos 199
●———— aurel maesomas aciba
ụictorino cos 200
appada au[rel] gạianus themarsa
●———— ạụ[rel] bọlaeus mocimi
p fṛa. . . •●———— ạ[urel] ieṛhaeụ[s] themarsa
mụçia[no] ços 201
●———[–] ma[r]çus ṃaior
●——— aụ[rel] malçḥ[us] themarsa
p raịbelo ● dispós[ ].[ ] ụlpiuṣ dẹṃetrius
•● ad ṃan ạ[mb] ạuṛ[el] bela[acab]us abgari
⟦appadaṇ⟧ auṛ[el i]uḷius [sc]ạurianus
p rạibelọ ● chafer auiṛ aurel̩ flaụ[ius] ṃonimus
[diuo seuer]ọ iii cos 202
bec[c]ḥ[uf do]ṃetius barnaei
●———[–]mus marini
p̣ sing ● ad leoneṣ[ ]bạrbaẹ[ssamen
cum pẹ. . .[ ].[.]s the[
g]ẹ[ta se]niorẹ [ii cos 203
● [ ].[. . .]ṣ th[
[ ].sa .[
[ ]bus[
]diṣ[po]ṣ[
–]———[–

Cf. **2** xxxiv 7–29.

2. *ụ[lpius:* D.

4, 9, 10, 23, 26, and 36. The notations may all be in one hand, different from that of the names.

17. The notation is in another hand.

19, 23, 26, and 30. The marginal notations seem to be in the same hand as the one in xxxiii 10.

25. The notation is in another hand.

29. **2** xxxiv 27 has *mo]ç[i]mus barnaei* between *d]omittius barnaei* and *barbaesamen.* Should one assume an error and read *mocimus marini* here and in **2**; or is this *-mus marini* a different person?

31. For the notation cf. **2** vii 19 and xiv 20, and the note on the latter, though the meaning of all is unclear.

31 and 33. The restoration of *theme* in these two lines in D is without any sure basis.

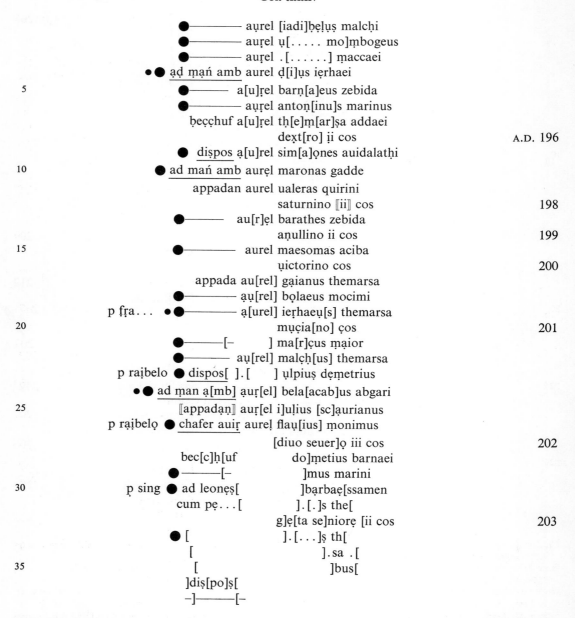

Col. xxxv

ạp̣p̣ạḍan au[rel] ịsidọṛ[u]ṣ . . sidon
becuf aụ[rel za]bḍịbo[lu]s themarsa
p natali˙ [ ] ad ṃan ambul aụ[rel gem]ẹḷlus thẹṃarsa
–]——— a[urel ḅạṛatḥes hạgus
cilone ii coṣ A.D. 204
o]ffịcio aurel ụ[l]pius ḅarsiṃṣus
●——— aurel ṃ[a]ḷchus bodẹ
●——— aurel[ ]bọlianus
●——— ịulịus[ ] aristus
appadan aurel [ul]pius maṛcẹḷḷus
●——— aurel ạntọṇinuṣ
diuo aṇtọṇịṇo ii cos 205
officio aurel ierhaẹụṣ bora
p˙ addaạ˙ị˙ ● ⟦disposit⟧ aurel iaquḅụṣ ẓebida
becchuf aurẹl iul maximus
●——— aurel mocimus siṃon
z ⟦chafer a[u]ịṛ⟧ aurel germạnus
●——— aurẹl fḷauịụṣ ṃarinus
●——[— a]urel mocimus ṭheme
apṛ[o] et maximo cos 207
explor[a]ure[l] sạ[m]ṃas gai
appadan [a]urẹ[l] ạgṛ[ipp]as male
p[ompei]ạno cos 209
ẹx̣[plo]ṛ[a]urel ạ[zizu]ṣ zaora
du[obu]ṣ aspris cos 212
●——— ạ[ur]el m[a]x̣imus seleuci
●——[— aur]ẹl [ier]ḥaeus malchi
● ⟦disp[o]sịt[ ]⟧ the]marsa buzi
. [ ]ius mocimus
●——[—— ua]balathus hanina
mes]sala coṣ[214
● ⟦dispọ[os]⟧ th]ẹṃarsa[mocimi
c̣x̣x̣[in dupl]

Remainder of column blank

Cf. **2** xxxv 4–30; xxxvi 1–6.
3. The intercolumnar notation is in a different hand from previous ones and from *p natales* in xxxvi 23.
3, 14, 17, 28, and 32. The notations are in a different hand, apparently the same as in 4, 9, etc. of xxxiv.
6. *barsumius* in **2** xxxv 10.
9. The whole line is inserted, in small letters, between 8 and 10. Note the absence of *aurel.*
10. The notation is probably in the same hand as in xxxiv 17.
15. *iul* was inserted by a different hand.
16. *simaoni* in **2** xxxv 17.
17. The symbol *z* appears to be in the same hand as the names. Gilliam on *PDur.* 82 ii 8 proposes ζ(ήτει), probably rightly. Cf. **8** i 12, **47** ii 8, and **65** 4.
33. For these totals see pp. 16–17.

Col. xxxvi

Ŧ [d]emetṛị [uic]ṭorino cos A.D. 200
●●——— ṃ ạṃ[bul d]ẹc̣ aurel ulpịus demetrius
eruc̣io cl(aro) cos 193

●● [dup]ḷ ạụrel claụḍius mombogeus
cilọne ii cos 204
[ ] sesq aurel prisc̣[u]s gai
ad praẹṭor erucio cl(aro) cos 193
●——— aurel salm[e] marini
p.[ ] ● ạḍ leọ[nes] aurel luciạnus themaṛ[sa
]hoṛḍ[ ] aurel muciạnus ẓạbdị[bo]l[u]ṣ[
•●——— aurel abdasṭhor mocimi
•● ḿ ambul˙ aurel aelius fronton
seuero ii cos 194
●——— aurel lucius aurelius
p sorẹcho •●——— aurel luciuṣ salme
tert[u]llo cos 195
offic aurel malc̣ḥus theme
●● u[e]x̣ aurel barathẹs abgari
ạḍ doṃ́ ń aurel acrabaṇes simon
ạ[pp]adana aurel salmaneṣ naamaei
●——— a[ur]eḷ heranes ạịthibeli
●● [ad h]ostị[as] a[urel] ulpius marea
p nataleṣ ●●——— au[rel] hagus salme
[offi]cio ạ[ure]ḷ aelius gaius
saturnino cos 198
a]ḍ [ho]ṣtias˙ ạ[ur]el iadibelus ierhaei
anullino ị[i] cos 199
•● ⟦dis[po]sit⟧ [au]rel salmanes ṃaccaei
•● ⟦di[sposit]⟧ a]ụrel nisamsụs ẓabdiboli
[ ] ạurel uictor heṛan
uictorino cos 200
p antiọc̣ḥi •[● a]ụrel mạ[cc]ạẹus ṭhemạ[r]ṣa
ṃ[uciano co]ṣ 201
● [au]rel .[z]ẹbida
]. ạ[u]ṛel [ab]gaṛị
]ạurẹ[l
]aureḷ[ ]ṭẹ.[
a]uṛẹ[l ze]ḅida[
a]bgari

Cf. **2** xxxvi 15–29; **26** b 1–2.

6. Note the absence of the angular symbol from *sesq*.

7. The notation *ad praetor* belongs with *sesq* in line 6.

8. The lacuna hardly affords room for the *e* of *salme*; so it is not possible to restore *salmes*.

10. For the notation cf. *ad hord*, **1** xxxiii 26 and xli 2, and **2** xxxvi 18 (a duplicarius and a decurion); *in proseq hord*, **1** xxx 18 and **2** xxxiv 24; and *]nauem hord*, **1** xix 4.

15, 23, and 32. The intercolumnar notes are perhaps in the same hand, differing from that of the names and of similar notations in preceding columns.

20. The notation is in a different hand.

22 and 26. "In charge of sacrificial victims"? The angular symbol implies that this is a rank; but the notation, canceled, appears without the angle in xlii 23. See also under *ad sacrahim*, p. 14, and on the duplicarii of this turma, p. 17 above. In 26, D omits the angular symbol which there is written *under* the notation *ad hostias*.

28–29. The notations are in another hand, the same as that of similar notations in xxxiv and xxxv.

Col. xxxvii

appạ[ ]aurel mocimus ierhaei
●——— aụṛel marimelus ṛeibeḷị
[b]ẹ[c]ḥ offịç ạurel ulpius marinus
explora aurel didas çoççei
●——— aurel goreṃis iadaei
p˙ ṇ[a]ṭal˙ ●——— aurel ierhaeụ[s t]ḥemarsa
]. . r. [ ] •● ⟦ḍịsposịṭ⟧ ạ[u]ṛel zabbae[us ba]rchalba
sẹụero iịi ç[o]ṣ A.D. 202
ạ[pp]ạ[d]ạn aure[l] iulius germanụṣ
geta seniore ii cos 203
●——— ạụṛel iuliụṣ gorippus
●——— a[u]rel zabbaeus malchi
p˙ nisạṃṣo ● ⟦dispọṣịṭ⟧ aurel barathes buccaei
singul˙ ạ[ur]ẹl longinus nume[i]
p˙ hammẹo ● ⟦disposit⟧ ạụṛel iamlichus mocịṃi
•●——— aurel iulius germanus
cilone ii cos 204
•●——— aurel marinus hoṭaraei
•●——— aurel malchus muc[iani
ẹ[xp]ḷora aurel mar⟨a⟩s themarsa
appadan aurel signas matrhaeị
●——— aureḷ iulius maximus
●——— aureḷ ierhaeus ḅarnaei
● [m] ambul aurel [z]ebidas maççạei
●——— aurel [u]ạlerius maxịmụs
a]d dom̄ n̄ aureḷ amrus milens
] ——— aurel ụlpius marinus
diuo antoninọ ịi coṣ 205
]m̄ ambul aure[l] çlauḍ[iu]ṣ ṇạṭalius
m] ambul[au]ṛ[el] ịeraḅọḷe ḷụçi
]offic[ ]demetrius z. [. . .]ṇ. [
sin[gul cl]ạudius siḷụạṇ[u]ṣ
–]—[—— iul]ius ạṇṭọ[ni]ṇ[-
]m ạ[mbul
]ịul[ius . .]. . [
]qụ. [. . .]ụs ua[
] iulius lọ[. .]. . [
]ạeliuṣ [a]ṇto[ninus

Cf. **2** xxxvii 1–29; xxxviii 1–8; **26** b 3–8.

6. *p natal* is in the same hand as in xxxv 3.

7, 13, 15. The notations are in a different hand, the same as in xxxiv–xxxvi.

13 and 15. The intercolumnar notes may be in the same hand as in xxxvi 15, 23, and 32.

20. The name is corrected from **2** xxxvii 21.

24, 29, 30, 34. The notations are in a different hand, perhaps the same as in 4, 9, etc. of xxxiv; 3, 14, etc. of xxxv; and 28–29 of xxxvi.

35. Quite possibly *iulius marinus*; cf. **2** xxxviii 5–7.

Col. xxxviii

]ḍispos aurel addạeus ierhaei
albiṇo et emeliano c[os — A.D. 206
].. singul cos aurel aelius mạrcẹllus
ḅẹc̣c̣ḥụf ạurel bar[n]aẹus themarsa
aprọ et maximo cos — 207
●●——— auṛẹ[l] ịulius beḷac̣ạbus
duobus ạsp̣ṛịs cos — 212
singul ạ[urel] abeḍṇamạ[r]eṣ maronạ[
cxx[.]ị iṇ dupl iii
One line blank
Ŧ octaui muciano cos — 201
● ●●●——— dec aurel luciị[u]s octaụịus
●●——— dupl aurel sal[m]ạnes zebida
com[o]do vii cos — 192
ṃ ẹ ⟦sesq aurel roṃanus allaei⟧
eruc̣ịo cl(aro) cos — 193
●——— aurel amạeus iadibeli
ad equm prob aurel saedus magdaei
● c̣ḥạf· auịra aurel mạ[lc]ḥus nisamsi
diuọ [s]ẹuero ii cos — 194
ḅẹcchuf aurel iuliị[us] iuliạnus
teṛṭụḷlo cos — 195
●●——— uex auṛẹḷ bassụṣ salṃ[a]ṇ
●——— aurel ị[u]ḷ[i]us romanus
●——— aurel ie..[..].ene.nis
● m [a]ṃbul aurel malc[hu]s abg̣ari
p· ..[.].o ●● m ạṃbul aurel hia.[..]..[..]ṇ
]..p.. ●● m ạṃbul aurel si.ba.[..]ụs uabalathi
dextro [ii co]s — 196
●——— ạ[u]ṛel fl[aui]uṣ [m]ạ[r]ịnus
●[●———]- a[urel] ber[o]sạ[s] ụa[l]ens
anụ[ll]ịn[o i]i cos — 199
]. aurel iul[ius] ạṇ[t]ọṇ[i]nus
]..ị.tio[———]-[aur]ẹḷ m]ariṇus
].nisa[
———]-[au]ṛẹl[ ]amaḷ[
——]——— au[r]el [ulpius ba]rṇ[eb-
———]—— auṛẹḷ ụ[l]pius ap]ọ[llona-
———]—— ạ[ur]ẹl[

Cf. **2** xxxviii 9–31; xxxix 1–6; **26** c 1.

1, 18, 19, 26, 27, 28. The notations are in a different hand, the same as in xxxiv–xxxvii.

3. The name in **2** xxxviii 11 is *marcellinus*.

8. *singul* is in another hand.

9. For these totals see pp. 16–17.

15. *m*(*issus*) *e*(*meritus*); cf. xli 10–11. All three men enlisted in 193.

18. *ad equ*(*u*)*m prob*(*andum*): "to inspect a horse." Cf. **83**.

28. The marginal note is in a very small hand.

34. The inter-columnar note has not been satisfactorily read.

37. *ba*]*rn*[*ebus:* D.

38. *ap*]*o*[*llonas:* D.

Col. xxxix

becchuf aurel alexạ[ndrus] antonini
●● ⟦m ambụḷ⟧ aurel mocị[mus b]arlaḥa
uicto[rino c]ọṣ A.D. 200
●——— aurel iulius ạ[nton]ịnus
ọffic aurẹl iulius ạ[nt]ọṇị[nu]ṣ al[te]ṛ
mucian[o] c[o]ṣ 201
–]——— ạurẹl malchus ṃạc[c]aei
app̣[ad]ạ aụṛel marcell[u]ṣ
–]———]uex aurel zebida egla
●——— aurel abedsalmas themạ[rsa
p̣[ ].nt˙ ●● m ambul aurel malchus heṛan
expḷ aurel iulius saḷman
●——— uex aurel themaṛṣạ ụ.[
p .[..].uani ●●——— aurel themarṣạ [c]ḥaseti
appạḍ aurel malchu[s] ierhạẹ[i
●● c̣ḥạfer aụ[i]ṛ˙ uex aurel zabatheṣ [ma]lcḥi
●——— aurel bolanus bolani
●——— aurel themes salṃạn
●——— aurẹl gaius abif[u]ṛ
●——— aurel seleucus ier[h]aei
appad aurel mazabanas ḅẹlacabi
●——— aurel zebidas iạdaei
–]——— ạurel barhadad[us] ạbifuṛ
⟦appadana⟧ aurel iulius marịṇ[u]ṣ
explora ạ[u]ṛẹ[l] zebidas ier[h]ạei
becc̣ḥụf a[ure]ḷ iulius barlạ[h]a
●——— aurel ierhaeus zab[.]ua
aḍ op [stip] ạ[u]reḷ mannas thẹ[m]arsa
● [chaf]ẹṛ auị[r]ạ ạ[u]ṛe[l] iulius[ ]s
aḍ doṁ [ń] ạ[ur]ẹ[l] bar.[.......]. ierhaei
●–[——— aur]el zeb[.......]ại
s[euero iii cos] 202
au]ṛel ṃ[...mus iar].[
au]ṛel ị[ulius anto]ṇ[i-
aur]e[l alexandrus t]ḥẹo[fil-
geta seniore ii] cos[203

Cf. **2** xxxix 7–28; xl 1–8; **26** c 2.

2, 11, 16, 29. The notations are in a different hand, the same as in xxxiv–xxxviii.

5. The notation is in another hand.

9. **2** xxxix 14 has *zebidas.*

14. **2** xxxix 17 has *themarsas.*

15 and 21. The notations may be in the same hand as in line 5.

16. The name in **2** xxxix 19 is *zabdaathes.* Cf. also **13** 19.

18. **2** xxxix 21 has *themarsas.*

22. There is an erasure between *i* and *a* of *iadaei.*

24. The notation is in another hand, different from that in 15 and 21.

35. *t]ḥẹo[fili:* D.

Col. xl

paṛ[thia a]ụrel ulpius siluanụs
bẹ[cchuf a]urel ṭhemarsa ierḥaei
●—[——— aur]ẹḷ [o]g̣ẹḷụṣ ụạbalạ[t]hi
●———[— aur]ẹḷ [ ].[za]bḍịboli
●——— ạ[ur]ẹḷ .[
c̣[ilone ii cos] A.D. 204
singụl ạ[ur]ẹḷ ṣ[iluanus moci]ṃi
⟦chaferị⟧ ạ[urel maron]ạṣ [di]ṇaei
•●——— a[urel gorip]pụs uạḷẹṇti
becchuf auṛ[el rabbul]ạṣ bạ[ssi
singul aurẹ[l].ḅịdạ[ ]
officị[o] auṛ[el do]ṃẹṭịus p̣[r]ọclus
●——— aurel ạ[b]ẹḍmalcḥ[us] authaei
[di]ụo antoninọ ii cos 205
p̣ fra.. •●———[— aur]ẹḷ [flauiu]ṣ sil[ua]nus
●——— ạ[ur]ẹḷ a[eliu]ṣ f⟦.⟧ọ[r]ṭunatus
becchuf a[ur]el iụ[li]us maṛ[i]ṇus
ạ[p]ṛ[o et] maximo cos 207
●●——— sig aurẹl ḷụ[c]ịus ualeṛịanus
duọ[bu]ṣ aspris c̣ọs 212
●——— ạ[u]ṛel og[a]ṣ haninạ
ṃ[ess]ạḷạ cos 214
●——— ạ[u]ṛel [.].[..]ṣ gaiạ[n]us
officio a[u]ṛel u[al]ẹns
cxx[ ] in dụ[p]ḷ ṿi
Remainder of column blank

Cf. **2** xl 9–31; **26** c 4.
2. **2** xl 10 has *themarsas.*
8. The notation is in a different hand.
9. In **2** xl 16 the name is *ualentini.*
11. The *bi*, if correctly read, is in an unusual ligature. The name at this point in **2** is *bassus bibi.*
25. For these totals see pp. 16–17.

Col. xli

Ŧ antonini aḷ[bino et] ẹṃẹḷịanọ cos A.D. 206
●● ad hor / dec aurel uḷ[pius an]toninus
[co]ṣ ?
●[●]ḍ[upl] ạ[ur]ẹ[l alexand]ṛụṣ[
].[*Consulate*?
●[●]...[
diuo seue]ṛọ [iii cos 202
●[●]ṣ[e]ṣ[q] ạụṛ[el iulianu]ṣ ṭheṃ[arsa
como]do vii cos 192
[ ] ḿ é ⟦a[urel] ṣalmanes za[ ]⟧

[ ] ṃ́ é ⟦auṛ[el s]adalaṭhụ[s . . . . . .].i⟧
erục̣io c̣[laro cos A.D. 193
]——— aurel aem.[ ].i
p˙ ụ[. .]ṇina[ ]——— aurẹl amaeus zạ[bdibo]li
p ạ[. .]b.b[—]——— aurel boliạ[d]ạẹụṣ ẓ[a]ọṛa
tertu[llo cos 195
]ad mạ[n a]ṃb aurel zebị[da]ṣ ṣalman
becc̣ḥuf aurel bassuṣ malchi
]ṃ amaụl. aurel hadadsabuṣ⟦.[. .].aei⟧ (barsimsi)
offịc̣io aurel asadus themạ[rs]a
dexṭṛọ ii cos 196
singul [c]os aurel ualerius uạ[l]ẹntiṇuṣ
—]——— aurel ieraḅ[us] ebuc̣[a]ẹi
saturnino cos 198
ạd opiniọ aurel themarsạṣ zeb[id]a
anullino iị [cos] 199
●——— aurel barhotarus ạụidalathi
p mal˙ siluaṇ[.] •●——— aurel guris nisamsi
●——— aurel bassuṣ ṃọṇṭa[n-
uic̣[tor]ịno c̣ọṣ 200
ḅ[ec]c̣[h]ụf aurel tḥ[emars]ạ dinaei
● [ ]m[ ] aurel ḍ[emetr]ius macc[ae]i
ṃucị[ano cos] 201
———]— auṛ[el o]ge[lus] . .[. .]ḅoli
———]-[ael-]ṣạ. .sius
theodo]ṛụs z[ebi]dạ[

Cf. **2** xli 1–24.

2. *ad hor* is in a different hand. The proper expansion is uncertain: *ad hor*(*deum*), as in xxxiii 26, or *ad hor*(*reum*)? "In charge (?) of the barley supply."

6. This man was either a duplicarius or a sesquiplicarius.

10–11. *m*(*issus*) *e*(*meritus*). Cf. xxxviii 15. *s*]*adalaṭh* .[. . . . . . .].*i*: D.

19. The name .[. .].*aei* has been corrected to *barsimsi*. The notation seems to be correctly read; but unless it is a mistake for *m ambul*, its meaning is unknown.

28. The intercolumnar note is in the same hand as in xxxvi 15, 23, and 32. For the name see also **115** c 1, app.

31. In **2** xli 19 the name is *themes*.

32. Possibly *m a*]*m*[*bul*.

34. The first letter of the last name is *c*, *g*, or *t*; the second is *a*, *r*, or *m*. Possibly *gaddiboli*. Cf. Wuthnow, *Γαδδειβωλιοι*.

35.]*ṣạ. .sius:* D; but cf. **2** xli 23.

Col. xlii

p .aṣṣẹṛ ●[●———]˙- aurel belacabus z.[
•[●———]- aurel salmes zebid[a
p iar.[ ]aurel bassus anṭ[onin-
]ṣẹḷe[uc]us ạ[ntonini ?
About one line lost
]ạ[urel
———]-[
am]bul[ ]ṃ[ocimus

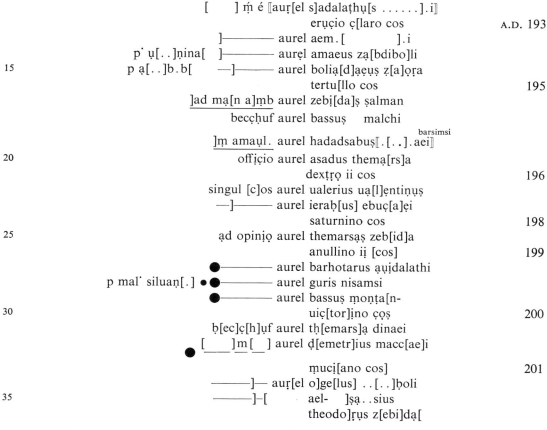

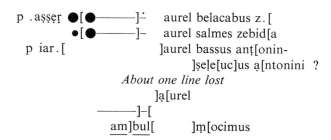

ạ[p]p̣ad[ ]ạ[b]ḅas [zebida
●-[———]iul[i]ụs ṃ[agn-
[ ]iulịụs m[arinus
●-[——— aur]ẹl ab[d]aeus ḅạṛaei
●——— ạụrel antonius bassus
seuero iii cos A.D. 202
ạppạ[d] a[u]ṛẹl sẹ[l]eucus barathe
sịngul aurel tiṃon marini
ge[t]a sẹ[ni]ọ[r]ẹ [i]i cos 203
non reuer aurel hẹṛaneṣ ị[e]rabole
●——— aurel h[a]gus ierhaei
ạ[p]p̣ad aurel barṇaeus ierhaei
o]ffic ạ[u]ṛel iuli[u]ṣ salman
•●——— auṛẹl afạ[r]nes bassi
● ⟦ad hosṭịaṣ˙⟧ ạuṛẹl aeli[u]s longinus
●——— ạ[u]rel baṛạṭḥes abgari
● m˙ ambul aurel zebidạs malchi
ç̣ịlone ii cos 204
•●——— ạu[r]el neb[u]daes themạrsa
●——— aurel zabdịḅolus gora
●——— [a]urel themarsa nisạṃṣ[i]
b.[aur]ẹl gạrmelụṣ be[l]iabị
]aurẹl ḷuçius caṣ[sianus
a]ụrẹ[l]..[
au]ṛẹ[l

Cf. **2** xli 25–29; xlii 1–22.
3. *anṭ[onini:* D.
4. Cf. **2** xlii 28.
8.]*ṃ*[*:* D.
10. *ṃ*[*agnus:* D.
18. *non reuer*(*sus*)*:* "failed to return." Cf. **2** xii 18 and **47** ii 6–8.
23. For the notation see above on xxxvi 22 and 26.

Col. xliii

● chaf[er]boliadaeus zebida[
●———[–]mocimus zaora
● [a]ç̣hilleus malch[
diuo antoni]ṇo ị[ii cos? A.D. 208?
About three lines lost
]..[
abgarus] ịeṛ[haei
iulius] gẹṛṃ[anus
● [clau]ḍiuṣ dạ[dona
ẹx̣[p]loṛ[lici]nnius ap[o]llọṇ[inus
●———[– s]almes malcḥị
[duo]bus aspris cos 212
●——— auṛ[el nis]ạmsus heliodori
]ç̣xxxiiii in dupl ị[ii]
One line blank

ḍ[ro]madaṛi[i
Y dan̩[y]ṃị teṛṭullo c̣ọs — A.D. 195
——— auṛẹḷ ḥeraneṣ ṃalchi
p̣ . . [. .]. ——— ạ[u]ṛẹ[l] ṭhemarsas themuạṃi
Y marci dẹxtro ii c[o]ṣ — 196
⟶
sesq aurel dometị[u]ṣ barbaessamen
eruciọ cḷ(aro) cos — 193
——— aurel dicaẹus themarsa
ter[t]ụḷlo cos — 195
●——— aurel aziẓ[u]s salạmalathi
ṃụciano c[o]ṣ — 201
ạd opinion aurel aelius anṭ[o]ṇinus
Y anṭọṇini tertụ[l]ḷo cos — 195
] ——— a[urel m]ạḷẹ mannạ[e]ị
a]ṇu[lli]ṇo ii [co]s — 199
i]ụḷịus bạṣs[u]s

Cf. **2** xlii 25–26: xliii 7–11.

3. *malch[i:* D.

16. For these totals see pp. 16–17.

20, 21, 23, 25. Note the absence of puncta before the bar. The one in line 27 has been partly destroyed by surface scaling; but it is not certain that the same thing happened in these four lines.

21. *themuạṃạ:* D.

23. This man must be the same as *dometius barsemia* in **2** xliv 12.

29. The notation is in a different hand.

Col. xliv

Y castrici .[ ]c̣os — A.D. ?
Cum episul auṛẹ[l]ḥeliodorus
●———[–]ḍạṣ runnaei
About six lines lost
Y] ṃạḷ[chiana dextro ii] c̣[os — 196
–]——— ạ[urel themarsas] ḅuc̣c̣ạei[
–]——— a[urel ? dalathu]ṣ theoboḷị[
]m˙ amb˙ auṛ[el ierabol]ẹ zebida
–]——— auṛẹ[l g]abrion
[cilon]ẹ ii cos — 204
●——— au[r]ẹḷ[m]oṇiṃi
imp a]ṇ[tonino aug] ịị
e]ṭ sạ[cerdote ii c]ọṣ — 219
●——— g[. . . .]eụ.[ ].[
Remainder of column blank

Cf. **2** xliii 15–21.

2. Read *cum epis⟨t⟩ul(is).*

12. Either *abedalathus, auidalathus* or *sadalathus* is possible, though the spacing in **2** xliii 17 favors the last.

13. *auṛ[el bol]ẹ:* D. The name must be *iarhaboles* because other compounds of Bol, e.g. *theobolus,* are *o*-stems.

16. A nomen seems to have been lost here; but there is no room for one in **2** xliii 21, though the patronymic there is anomalous with *aurel.*

19. The absence of *aurel* is noteworthy.

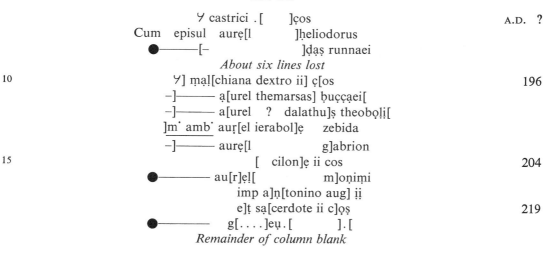

2

Complete Working Roster of the Coh. XX Palmyrenorum

PDur. 101 (inv. D. P. 12 verso) A.D. 222, after March 13

Transcription: *Final Rep.* v, no. 101; *edidi.*

Facsimile of cols. xxx–xxxiii: ibid., plate 45.

Commentary: the same as for **1**.

This is a complete roster, like **1** in all respects except that the name Aurel(ius) is not applied to everyone, there are no intercolumnar notations, and no totals for each century and turma. See pp. 13 and 16–17 above for a general discussion of both. The body of the text through col. xli 16 is in one hand, from xli 17 to the end in another. The notations beside the names, as in **1**, are mostly in the same hand as the names but also exhibit a certain variety.

The earliest date in the roster is 195 (xlv 3) and the latest 222 (xvi 5; xxvi 10; and xxxi 20). The theoretical term of 25 years would have led to discharge in 220 for men who enlisted in 195 and in 221 for those of 196 (e.g. vi 22 and xxxviii 5), but in the nine entries under the latter date none of the 18 extant names has been canceled. On the other hand, there are only three entries, with a total of 10–15 men, for 222, in all of which Alexander is *d(ominus) n(oster) Augustus* and sole consul. The date is therefore certainly later than the fall of Elagabal on March 13, 222, news of which may not have reached Dura until the middle of April, while in col. xxvi at least it is certain that there was no entry later than 222. Most probably, then, this text was written in the middle of 222, and at the latest before any recruits of 223 had been admitted. But if **31** is correctly dated in 222 and if there was then only one centurion Antoninus, the present text must be later than September 29, 222, the latest date in **31**.

The recto of this text is no. **1**.

Col. i

Century of Malchus

ad] ọp̣ ṣṭịp̣[A.D. 196–199

Consulate 197–200

]——— a.[

Consulate 198–201

——]—— ...[

—]——— ạ[ ]..[

——]—— aḅg̣[arus]ṭḥeṃ[e]ṣ

ọfficịọ ọc̣ḅạṇ[es abid]laḥ[a

——— selẹụṣ [m]ạḷc̣[hi

——— ac̣ịḅạṣ [g]ịṇṇẹị

se]ụẹṛ[o] ị[ii] c̣ọṣ A.D. 202
s[i]gnif aeḷịụ[s he]l[i]ọḍọṛ[us
ḅirtha ẓaḅḍị[bolus] theoḅọ[li
geta se]niore ị[i cos 203
ḅịṛṭḥa iuliụ[s ari]ṣṭọn

Cf. **1** xxvii 1–10; **6** ix 4–7. The name of the centurion here is taken from xliii 15, the beginning of the roster of dromedarii. In **1** (219) and **6** (218) this century is *malchiana*, that is, formerly commanded by Malchus but at the time without a centurion. (For this use of the adjectival form of a former centurion's name see p. 4.) In view of the great frequency of the name Malchus, the present centurion is probably a different person from the other Malchus; but since we do not know the full name of either, it is also possible that the original Malchus has returned.

7. **1** xxvii 2 has *tḥ[em]e*.

Cols. ii, iii, iv

Frag. a, col. ii

]. . [
]. . [. .]. [
aurel a]ṇṭioc̣[hus
cil]one iị cos[A.D. 204
aurel cas]sianus[
]nus[
]. . [
]. . [

Frag. d

—[———
—[———

Frag. f

].f̣l[. .] .[
s]ẹlẹục̣ụ[s
ia]qubus .[
].ṇus
]. . [. .].ṇes
]ịaḍib[el-
]. . . . [

Frag. g

].[
].ẹa
]ba.na
]haṣ[

Frag. h

] . . [. .]. . [
]. . zebida
]ạuiḍ[a]ḷathi
]. zaḅḍ.[
]. . [

For the placing of the fragments, see in general on **1** iii, iv, v. The verso of frags. b, c, e, i, and j is blank; but the date on a proves that it belongs in col. ii. In **1** xxvii 9–24 there are 14 names under *geta seniore cos.* Here in col. i and on frag. a traces of four remain; so that the first line on a could not have been lower than line 12 of the complete col. ii. Since the papyrus was rotated on a horizontal axis in order to use the verso, if frag. d was correctly placed at the foot of col. iv of the recto, it will be at the top of col. iii here; and frag. f in the same way will be at the foot of col. iv.

Cf. **1** xxvii 22–25; **6** ix 14–16.

a 5. The position of *cas*]*sianus* implies that *aurel* preceded; but this must be the same man as in **92** ix 9 where *cassianus* is the nomen. The use of three names is anomalous in this roster; but *cl*(*audius*) *iulius marinus* and *cl*(*audius*) *iulius secundus* occur in xxxi 21 and 22.

Col. v

].ṃẹṣ
One line lost
extric]ạto ị[i c]ọṣ ? A.D. 217?
]e.[
About four lines lost

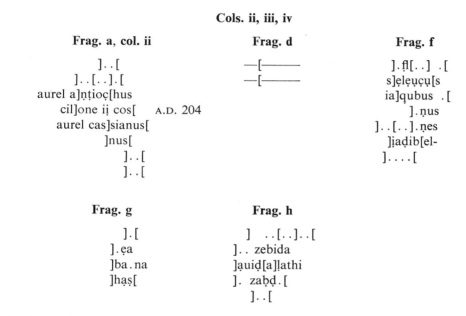

]. . . [
]aurẹ[l
]aụ[rel
]aureḷ[
]ạụ[r]ẹl[
]ạ[u]ṛẹ[l
]. . [.]. [

Col. vi

offiçio . [
——— ạ[
barḅ[al
Consulate A.D. 219?
——[—
sin[gul
Consulate 221?
of[ficio
——[—
Consulate? 222?
—[——
About six lines lost, some of them blank
[Ɣ danymi muciano et fabia]ṇo ç[os 201
[ord septimius dany]ṃụṣ[
]ṃẹṣạ[la co]ṣ[214
dupl aure]ḷ coçç[eius
]ḍẹxtro iị [cos 196
sịgn fḷ[auius] nicoṃ[achus
—]——— ạẹḷị[u]s basṣ[us
ḷạ[te]ṛạṇ[o cos 197
——— ulpịụṣ [siluanus
aṇul[lino ii cos 199
. . [.]. . . aurẹ[l faustus
aḍ [.]. . . a[grippas themarsa
ṃụ[c]ịano cos 201

Cf. **1** i 1–18; **6** i 2–5.

Col. vii

]ḷ[a.]. us tḥẹṃạrṣạ
]ịadibelụs zeḅida
]ṭheọbọlus gadḍẹ
]ṃeheridates barginnaia
——]—[–] babuiụ[s m]ọçịṃ[
———]–[– ze]biḍ[as] zebida
a]ppạ[d]. iụ. [.]. gaani

seuero] iii cos A.D. 202
]—[———].rini
]ṣiṇ[gul]llus ṭḥẹọḍ[o]ṛ[i]
g]ẹṭạ [se]ṇiore ii cos 203
].[. . .]. .[
]. .[.] ṃạlchi
]b[. .].ạṣ themaṛṣạ
]ạ[nto]ṇinus
ḅẹ[ ]ẓạḅḍib[o]ḷi
——[——]ṣạḷṃ[e]s
—[———].ṇụs
]mpe.[ma]ṛinus
–]——[—]us
–]——[—]ḷụṣ
cilone ii] ç̣ọṣ 204
be]ç̣ç̣ḥ[uf
About two lines lost
]. . .[
———]— bassṣ[us
]. .[
]ạ[
]s . . .
]. ma[
]b[

Cf. **1** i 19–20; **6** i 6–10.
1. See on **1** i 19.
10. *gemellus*?

19. Possibly *cu]m pe*.[; but not enough remains of the notation to yield sense. Cf. however **1** xxxiv 31 and **2** xiv 20, with the note on the latter.

Col. viii

antoni]ṇo iị [cos A.D. 205
].ebụ[
]ṇus
ma]xi[m-
]r.[
About two lines lost 205–207
].[.]ạnus
Consulate? 206–208
]ṇs
a]ṇtoṇiṇ[
ṣ[i]ṇg[u]ḷ[ ]llạẹ[u]ṣ
singụl fl.[ ].sus
pompei]ano co[s 209
].[ ]. m.[ ]ẹi
——— a.[ ]ṇus
duobus? co]ṣ 212?

———[-   ]..[ ]
———[-   ]..[ ]ṣ
—]—[—   ]..b..[
—[—]-[—   ].[ ]ṣaḷṃ[
—[—]-[—   ]ụạbaḷ[ath-
[   ].ḅ.[
——[— p̣aṛ[   ]ṣ..[
].[
messal]a ç[os?   214?

4. *ma]xi[mus:* D.
11. *a]ṇtoṇiṇ[us:* D.
12. Both *allaeus* and *bellaeus* are found in these rosters; and other possibilities exist.
24. For the notation cf. **2** xxxiii 9.

Col. ix

A.D. 214

-]—[——
-]—[——
.[
——[——
apṗ[ad
ạḍ.ṛ.[
———[—
apṗạ[d
appaḍ[
appa[d
app[ad
———[—
beçç[huf
becçḥụ[f
exp[lor
ad op ṣ[tip
——[——
-]—[——
a]ppạ[d
a]ṗpạ[d   ]ạ[.]ụṣ
beç[ch au]ṛel [ ]nioṇ
——[—— i]ạrhẹ[us] ṭhẹmarsạ
ṃ[ ]ṃocịṃ[us] baṛṇẹ[ ]
ṃ[a]urel ḅarathe
]ḷ ạurel ḍemetrịụ[s
appa]ḍa aurel ḅassus
——]—— aurel [so]ṣsiaṇ[us
———]— dius [ ]g.[.].us
ma]gdal aurel g[er]ṃaṇ[us
becc]ḥụf aurel ṭh[e]ṃ.[
ẹxploṛ aurel ma..[

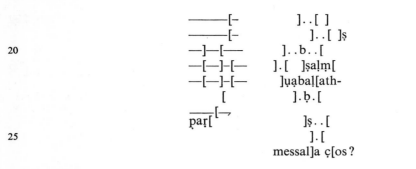

———— aurel ba[
—]——— aurel sopạ[
ba]ṛbạḷ aurel filo . . s

Cf. **1** iii–v frag. *d*; **8** ii 9–13.

5. The notation may have been canceled.

6. The notation is in smaller letters. It may have been substituted for *appad* in 5; or it may belong with the line in 7. Perhaps *ad frum*.

21. Perhaps *cronion*.

24. This is the only certain instance in **2** of *aurel(ius)* followed by a patronymic; so it is probably a clerk's error.

29. The entire line has been inserted between 28 and 30. It is in small letters and paler ink, possibly in a different hand.

33. Perhaps *sopatros*.

34. *filotas*?

Col. x

th]ẹ[marsas] ịarhẹi[
———]— zabḍ[ibolus] ṭhẹme
———]— ṃục[ianus] zabbei
—]-[—— aurel apolḷọnius
a]p̣p̣ạ[d] . . [. .] . iuṣ marinus
m]ạgdạḷ ṭhẹ[m]ạṛsas barnebus
—]-[——]zabdibolus
—]-[——]antoninus
] ḷ[ae]ṭo ii c̣ọs A.D. 215
—]-[——] . [ ]orinus
—]-[—— aurel] ḍẹṃẹtrius
ap̣p[ad] . s ạṇṭiochus
sin[gul]ṇdon
sabi]ṇo ii c̣[os 216
———— a[urel ma]ḷcḥ[u]s
———— ạ[u]rel[ ]nus
becch ạ[ur]ẹ[l
]posụs . [
] . diaṭ[
—]——— ạụrẹḷ . [
]ndra ạ[u]ṛẹḷ . . [
ḅẹ[c]c̣h aurel m . . . . ṣ[
ap[pa]ḍ ạurel . [
——[—— a]urel ḷọ[
——[—— a]urel[apo]ḷḷ[inarius
[ ] bass[us g]ọṛạ[
] . [ ] ạure[l]ụ[
]ḅ[aur]ẹl[b]ạṣsụṣ
]b[au]ṛel[ ]ṃuci[anu]ṣ
]mạ[au]ṛẹḷ[ ] . [.] . . [

Cf. **1** iii–v frag. *i*; **6** ii 1–20; **8** ii 15–29.

16 and 24. One of these names may be *aurel longinus*. Cf. **6** ii 10–11, where *longinus* follows immediately after *aurel malchus*, and **1** iii–v frag. *i* 5–6, where *aurel lon*[comes just before a name which could be restored as *apollinarius*.

18.]*posus* seems to have been corrected from]*poss*; but *poses* could be read. In any case, the meaning is uncertain. Perhaps *dis*]*pos*⟨*it*⟩*us*?

19. Possibly *ad iatr*, with reference to the hospital? R. W. Davies, *BASP* 5 (1968) 32: [*ho*]*ṛdiat*(*or*). Cf. **47** ii 5.

21. The notation is in a different hand over a partial erasure. Perhaps *ad mandra*, "detailed to the stable"?

22. If 16 is *longinus*, this could be *aurel magnus*, who follows *longinus* in **6** ii 13.

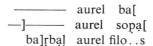

Col. xi

].
].
About four lines lost
].s
..ṃ[ ]dṣus
About five lines blank
[ᛉ marci muciano et fabian]o cos A.D. 201
[ord iulius marcu]ṣ
[dupl]
[ ]. cos
]ḍụ[p]ḷ ị[ar]ḥe[us].i
ḍ[extro ii co]ṣ 196
——— ạbbạ[s l..– –
ṣ[aturnin]ọ cos 198
——— acib[a-]ṇi
[anullino] ịị ç[o]s 199
——— h[ ].[..]ẓạ[
——— m.[ ]addei
——— .[ ]ḷifa
[uictori]no ç[os 200
ad op sṭị[p ma]xịṃ[
[muciano] ços 201
———[—]nuṣ[
ad ọp ṣtip ..[..]ẓ[ ].[

Cf. **6** ii 22–30.

Col. xii

]—[———
]——[——
biṛ[tha
——[——
beç[chuf
——[—— ịu]ḷị[u]ṣ [salman
birthạ[h]ẹḷiodọ[rus zebida
ṣẹụ[ero iii cos A.D. 202
———[— iuliu]ṣ dọṃ[ittius
ad op stip̣[iar]ḥaboḷ[- themarsa
g]ẹ[ta seniore ii cos 203
———[—
barḅạ[l
——[——
——[——
——[——
—[———]ụạ[
non re]ụersụ[s].ṇụs

———[— ual]ẹṛ [malc]hi
cilo]ṇẹ [i]i c[o]ṣ A.D. 204
app[ad iuli]us [cri]spinụs
singul[ ]us ị[u]ḷịanus
———[— b]ẹṛniciaṇus siluạ[n-
o]ffịcịo ịụlius sọ[e]ṃus
ḅẹc̣[c]ḥ barzas [ma]ṛea
ap]p̣ad priscus abḍọṇa
——— gerelius asc̣ḷ[epiades
mis· .[.]dquere cuṃ[.]e.upe.[ṃauelạṣ abiḍ[adadi
app[a se]leục̣us ṃ[
ap]pa salmạnẹṣ signạ[

Cf. **1** vi 27–32; vii 9–17; **6** iii 7–19; **8** iii 14–17.

5. The notation is in a different hand.

10. *iar]ḥabol[es:* D. In **1** vi 31 the name appears as *ierabole*, in **6** iii 11 as *iaraboles*.

18. The notation is in another hand. "Failed to return." Cf. **1** xlii 18 and **47** ii 6–8.

19. The space permits only *ualer*, as in **6** iii 16, instead of *ualerius*.

23. *silvạ[ni:* D.

27. **92** v 13 has *g̣ạleris*; but *gerelius* is also found in **8** iii 16.

28–29. The notation is in very small letters and seemingly applies only to Mauelas Abidadadi. There is no gap in the list of names. The first line may be read *mis(sus) ad qu(a)ere(ndum)* (cf. **2** xxxv 17 and xli 17): "to search", or "to lodge a complaint"? See also under *ad opinionem*, p. 14. Nothing intelligible has been made of the second line.

Col. xiii

——]—[–].[
b]ecc̣ḥ[uf]ḅạrnẹ[us
ṣịṇ[gul]ṃaṛịnus
diu]ọ ạnṭonị[no ii cos A.D. 205
—]——— zaḅ[d]ẹṣ malc̣[hi
ad lẹ[o]n [..]ụ[...]ḷus malc̣ḥ[i
—]——— ẓ[a]bdibolus haṃṃ[ae-
–]——[—]hes malchi
———[—].rus serap[ion
a]lbino cos 206
ṣịngul auṛ[el] priscus
] ạpro cos 207
b]ẹc̣[ch z]ẹ[nodo]rus artem[i]ḍ[ori
——[——]diọṃedi
——[——]ṣ ạḅboṣa
pomp[e]iạ[no cos 209
ap̣p̣ạḍ aḅ[da]ṣ zẹbi[da
faust]ịno [cos 210
——— quị[ntus] ịuḷịạṇ[us
–]——[— iulius] ṃenand[rus
singul [co]ṣ aṇt[oniu]ṣ clemẹ[n-
singul aurel ịuḷius
duobus aspṛi[s cos 212
——— clauḍị[us] ṭiberiṇ[us
——— iarhaḅ[ol]eṣ [u]ḍạṭhi

aḍ[ ]ụlp̣[ius] ạnṭ[on]ịnus
———— moṇ[im]us [ ]. . a
]ḷ amạ[eus] ẓeḅ[i]da
]g̣ iulị[u]ṣ ạṇtọṇịṇ[u]ṣ
mesạ[la co]ṣ 214
buc̣[ ]. aụ[r]ẹl pṛị[scus

Cf. **1** vii 23–31; viii 1–16; **6** iii 20–32; **92** viii 11–15.
6. *malc̣ḥ[us:* D.
9. *serap[:* D.
14. Perhaps *bassus diomedi*; cf. **1** viii 1–3.
15. Perhaps *priscus abbosa*; cf. **1** viii 1–3.
31. *buc(inator);* cf. **50** i 2 and 9.

Col. xiv

A.D. 214

]ẓẹṇ[
]ṣạ[
]ḷ[.]e.[. .].[
]ss. .[.].[
].ṣas d.[
]. bạṛs.[
]b[
].[
]baṛ[
belaca]bus [i]ạṛḥ[ei
] saḷmaṇ[
aurel] auidaṣ[
bol]ị[a]ḍeus iarḥaei
].i [azizus] aethibeḷi
———[— iarheu]ṣ zebida
ạd leoṇ[aurel]g̣aius
]———[—]ṃarini
———— ạ[urel a]ṇtigọnus
———— .[ ]es ẓe[
Cum p[ ].c.[
offi[cio]ma.[. . .]ṣ
—[———] de.[
-]—[——] ba.[
—[———]g̣[ ].[
—[———]bạ[ssu]s
[ ]zẹṇobi
]. .[ ]hạ[e]ṛan

Cf. **1** ix 1–7; **8** iv 2–8.
20. For the notation cf. **1** xxxiv 31 and **2** vii 19. I cannot explain any of the three; but there may be a connection with *ad pen(um) comp(arandum)*, **2** xxxiii 15 and xxxv 19.
24.]*ḍ*[: D.
26. Cf. **8** iv 12: *zen]ọbius.*

Col. xv

].[ ]bạṛbaḷ[
———— ạ[

Consulate A.D. 215 or 216
bec]c̣h b[
sing]ụḷ ạ[
About six lines lost
aurel phi]ḷọ[n 216
aurel] ṣẹleu[cus
bec]c̣ḥ[aure]ḷ romạ[nus
——]—— ạ[ure]ḷ diodo[rus
——]—— c̣[ha]ẹremon se.[ ].
be]c̣ch a[ur]ẹl de.[
—]——— aụ[re]ḷ m[
ad leon a[ur]ẹl ba[
becch a[u]ṛel [
——— a[u]ṛel [
becch aurel [
a[p]p̣ada auṛel[
——— ạụṛẹḷ[

Cf. **1** x 9–12; **92** v 16.

Col. xvi

].[
]maẓ[
]doṃẹ[tti]ụs zeṇ[
⟦p̣˙[*ca.* 12]os liciṇ[niu]ṣ gaị[⟧
ḍ [n al]exạ[ndro aug cos A.D. 222
sin]gul aurẹ[l
si]ṇgul ma.[
si]ngụḷ ịul[ius
Space of about seven lines,
at least four of them blank
𐅃 ṃ[ariani d]ịuo an[to]ṇino ii cọs 205
ad frum ọṛd [iulius] mariạ[nu]ṣ
]g̣eta sẹ[nio]ṛe ii cos 203
siṇgụḷ ḍ[u]p̣[l i]ulius apolḷ[i]ṇarius
saturṇ[i]ṇo c̣ọs 198
——— agṛippas ṃạḷe
anulịṇọ ịị [cos 199
——— apọ[l]]ḷọni[us] ḅạ[

Cf. **1** xxi 1–4 and 14–16.
2. Perhaps *comazonte cos*, A.D. 220.
4.]*os* is probably *disp*]*os*(*itus*); but cf.]*posus*, **2** x 18.
17. *ad frum*(*entum*): "in charge (?) of the wheat supply." Cf. *ad hordeum*, **1** xxxiii 26 and xli 2.

Col. xvii

].[
]ḅ[
—[———

b.[t]ḥẹmarṣ[a
app̣[ad]ṃarini
—[———]es iarhẹ[
[ ]nisams[
[ ]es theṃ[
[barla]has [i]arḥ[-
[di]ụo sẹụer[o iii cos A.D. 202
———[— aurel buccaeus]
[geta seniore ii cos] 203
becch ul[pius ... inus]
———— aelius ḥ[eracl-
———— tḥeme[s] ṃaḷ[chi
ci]ḷon[e ii cos 204
——]—— marc̣us uị[ctor
———]— abidlahaṣ [maximi
–[——]— iulius ạ[bidsemi]ạs
–]-[——]— uareus b[arsi]msi
—[——]— maximus [zao]ra
—[——]— alexaṇ[d]ṛuṣ [ ].ụṣ
—[———]- mari[n]us .[.].ṛon
—[———]- iuli[us] ṃ[..]nus
—[———]- .[..].anus[..]mni
———— [aci]bas ḅ[or]a

Cf. **1** xxii 1–15; **8** v 9–18; **92** iii 6.
9. [*i*]*arḥ*[*ei*: D.
24. Possibly *magnus*.
25. *siluanus domni*?

Col. xviii

]..[
].ụs[
] gạ[
a]pro co[s A.D. 207
]baṇ.[
About two lines lost
].[
d]ịuo [antonino iii cos 208
ualeri]us mu[cian-
ulpius] ṃariṇ[us
iulius] maxim[us
aurel] marinus
———— ạ[urel]rumas
siṇguḷ[ ]marinus
singul[p]hịlotas
pomp]ẹ[i]ạṇọ c̣ọṣ 209
ạppad[ ]ṣ
——— ——→
uẹ[x -ius] m[arinu]ṣ
fa]uṣ[tino cos 210

magḍ[al addaeus] ṃ[accaei
———[—]ṣ .[. . . . .]s
—[——— iuli]us th[emars]ạs
—[——— malc]ḥus [uabala]thi
[———— siluan]ụs ṣ[adala]ṭhi
f]iṛṃus

Cf. **1** xxiii 5–16; **8** vi 1–5; **92** v 20.
5. Either *bannae-* or *ocbane-* is possible.
10. *mu[cianus:* D; *m]ụciạ[nus: PDur.* 100 xxiii 5.
18. **1** xxiii 11 has *a]elius* [. . .]*ụs*
19.]*m*[ ]*ṣ:* D.
21.]*ṃ[accaei:* D.
23. **1** xxiii 16 and **8** vi 3 have *themarsa.*

Col. xix

-]—[——
Consulate A.D. 212
ap]p̣adaṇ[
ad] ọp sti[p
-]—[——
About five lines lost
].[214
b]ạssus ṇạssị[beli
t]ḥẹṃes he[liodor-
—]—[— aure]ḷ babụ[ius
a]p̣paḍ[an] ạurel mucị[anus
c]ạperạ[ ]ạelamis beḷ[sur
] appaḍ[a]ụrel .[
off[ic au]ṛel ṃ[
———[— c]laudius ṣ[otericus
castel aṛ ḅarnẹ[
appạ[d]iuliuṣ[
appạ[d] ạnṭ[
app[ad] .[
———[—] .[
———[—] ḷ[

Cf. **1** xxiv 3–12; **8** vi 16–18.
3. The notation is in a different hand.
13. *he[liodori:* D.

Col. xx

]ạ.[
]iụliuṣ ṃarc.[
]. aureḷ mar.[
]. aurel bas[sus
——]—— thẹ[marsas salman]
——]—— aurel[. . . us]
——]—— ṃaẋ[imus salman]
——]—— ạuṛ[el
].[

About three lines lost

sing̣[ul]ṛa.[
—[———].ur.[
sabi]no ii [co]ṣ ? A.D. 216?
singul[ ]ṇeote[riu]ṣ
magḍạ[l]ṣ the[mars]a
becc̣ḥ[aur]ẹl iarhe[us
barḅạl [aur]el romaṇ[us
———— ạ[urel]abidlahas
sị[ng]ul ạ[ure]ḷ baṣṣ[u]ṣ
ex .[.].. [au]ṛel luc̣[ius
ṣingul ṃ[a]ṛinụs heli[od]ọṛị

Cf. **1** xxv 1–4 and 8–11; **8** vii 4–6; **92** v 21.
5. *thẹ*[*:* D.
6. *aurel*[*:* D.
7. *ṃa.*[*:* D.
8. Probably *aurel priscus*; cf. **1** xxv 11.
22. *explor*(*ator*)?
23. .[.]*ạsṃuṣ heli*[*od*]*ọṛ*[*u*]*ṣ:* D; and in app.: *ẹ*[*r*]*ạsṃuṣ?*

Col. xxi

]ṣị[ngul
]siṇg̣[ul
]. cuṣṭọḍ[ ].[...]ṣ[
bec̣[ch aurel ab]bosas
——[—— aurel s]ịluanus
aurel] lịcinni[us
].[aurel] geṛmaṇ[us
]ṃ[aurel] ịarḥabọ[les
ṃạg[dal aurel] ḍoṃit[tius
ọffịc̣ịọ[ ]..[
Consulate A.D. 217 or 219
singul auṛẹ[l
siṇgul aurẹḷ[
grạ[to cos 221
singul iulius th[
sị[n]guḷ aureḷ[
Remainder of column blank

Cf. **1** xxvi 1–6; **8** vii 12–14.
3. *in custodia; cum custodib*(*us*)? Cf. **63** ii 36–37.

Col. xxii

Century of Antoninus prior
———]— .[
Consulate A.D. 197–201
——]—— .[*ca.* 8 diom]ẹḍị
——]—— ạ[*ca.* 9 zeb]ida
ḅịrṭhạ[d]ọmitti
h]ạẹran

–]—[——]ẓabbei
si]ng̣[ul].nṇọsa
diuo s]euẹ[r]ọ iiị [cos A.D. 202
cast]ẹlọ ạra ạ[u]ṛ[el]ẹi
[geta seniore ii cos] 203
cas]ṭelo ar mọciṃ[us theme
—]——— ..tua. ulpius [seuerus
—]——— iulius s[a]ḷṃ[an
cilọne ii cos 204
] .ạg. halas [
iu]ḷị[u]ṣ mari[nus
]anus gạ[i
be]ççḥ[abi]ḍmalchus ṃ[arosa
——]—[– ma]x̣imus hoṭ[arei
]o.[iuli]us hẹḷị[odor]ụs
becç[h ulpiu]s pupḷ[ianus
bec[ch aure]ḷ do[m]ṇu[s
——]—[– pri]scus [an]nọṇa
——]—[– bari]cbẹ[l]ụs bạ[s]ṣ[i]
bi]ṛth[a] didas salm[a]ṇ
of]f̣i[c] ịadeuṣ [t]ḥem[ars]a

Cf. **1** xvii 1–18; **6** xi 1–9; **8** viii 1. In **1** this is the century of Castricius; in **6** it is the centuria Seleuciana.
3. .[*ca.* 12].*ḍị:* D; but cf. **1** xvi 25.
4. *ạ*[ ]*ida:* D; but cf. **1** xvi 26.
13. The notation is in a different hand. Read *actuar*(*ius*), comparing **1** xvii 3.
16. Possibly *imagi*(*nifer*)? Cf. **1** xxviii 21.
18. Perhaps *hadrianus*; cf. **1** xvii 8.

Col. xxiii

].[A.D. 205
]a[
].[
ab]bọ[sa-
———]— bass[us barsimsi
[albino et emiliano c]os 206
———]— sep[timius heliodor-
[apro et maximo co]s 207
].ṇ[ ]ạ
].[ ]ei
sin]g̣ul[ ]nus
———]— iulị[us]ụs
d[iuo antonino iii cos] 208
si]ṇgul iulius f̣[
] pomp[eiano cos] 209
———]–– iulius romaṇ[us
sin]gul aurel anto[n-
] f̣ạ[ustino cos] 210
za]bd[i]bolus mal[
iar]ḥeus zebida

bec]c̣ḥ[ ].s haerạ[n-
sin]gul[ ]thus m[
[du]ọbus cos[212
appạḍ[aure]l̥ artẹ[mid]ọ[ru]ṣ
appạ[d th]ẹmes z[e]ḅida[
bi]ṛṭhạ[the]ṃarsạ [n]ịsạṃsi
——]—[-].n.s[.].ạaṭh[
m[esa]l̥a cos
——]—[-] flaui[us]erni[a]ṇus

Cf. **1** xviii 5–10; **6** xi 13–26; **8** viii 6–16.
7. *heliodorus:* D.
19. *mal[chi:* D.
27.].*n*.*s* [.]*paṭh*[*:* D.
29. Possibly *maternianus* or *paternianus.*

Col. xxiv

]ḅạ[
]ṃạṛ.[
]ọn.[
]conọṇ[
a]eliụ[s].n
[laeto ii cos] A.D. 215
].[
].[ ]
———]— .[ ]li
———]— i[u]l̥[ius]us
———]— ạụrẹl[ ]as
ap]p̣ad aurel[
—]——— aurel qu.[
mag]ḍal aurel ẓo.[
]l iulius basṣ[u]ṣ
——— auṛel longi[n-
——— ạ[ur]ẹl̥ baṛ...[
alexạ[ṃ.[ ]zabbeus
———]— ạ[ ]mannus
———]— ṛ[ ]malchus
]al ạ[ ] ṣabinus[ ]ṣ
——]—— ạ[ ] ṃalch[
——]—— aụ[rel]zabaẹ[u]ṣ
———]— a[ ]ẹs siuṣ[
———]— aẓ[i]ẓụs z[e]b[i]ḍa
]ael̥[i]us g̣er[ma]ṇus

14. *l̥o*.[is also possible.
15. *magdal*? Cf. 14.
16. *longi[nus:* D.
18. The notations are in small letters opposite the name *zabbeus* only. There is no gap in the list of names. The place is probably Alexandria ad Issum.
19–22. All these men may well be Aurelii.
21. *magdal*? The trace to the right of *sabinus* may be only a chance stroke.
22.]*ṃalch[us:* D.

Col. xxv

]·[
]ạ· ·[
]ab·[
———]— ạ[
]· iarḥ[
]· auṛ[el
One line lost
]ul[*ca.* 12]s
]ṃạ[
]ạuṛeḷ ·[
]a[u]ṛel [
———]— aurel p̣[u]p̣ḷ[
sabin[o ii cos A.D. 216
m[ ]aurel demeṭ[rius
b[ ]· priṣcus abbosa [
—[———] ạuṛẹ[l] summaṛẹṣ[
b[aurel]antoninus[
c̣ụṃ[aurel]ḥeliodorus[
]ạuṛ[el]ḅạssus
]ạuṛ[el sil]uanus
]auṛ[el b]ạssus
bec]c̣h auṛ[el si]luanus
]ḷ au[rel a]bidmạ[lch]ụs
———]— auṛ[e]ḷ ṃaṛiṇ[u]s
]auṛel ḍẹṃ[et]ṛiụṣ
]ạụ[r]ẹ[l] ha·[. . .]s

Cf. **1** xx 3–14; **8** ix 13–21.

17 and 18. D omits *aurel.*

Col. xxvi

]·[
Consulate? A.D. 217–220?
]· ·[
au]ṛẹ[l
au]ṛeḷ[
gṛạ[to cos 221
]flauius [
]aurel tḥeọ[
siṇ[gul]iulius gaiụ[s
] d́ ń alexaṇḍṛọ [aug cos 222
si[ngul]aurel dionusius
sị[ngul]f̣ḷạ[ui]us numeṛi[
Remainder of column blank

Col. xxvii

Century of Antoninus posterior
becc]h du[pl
[dextro ii cos] A.D. 196
a]p̣paḍ[ ].[
malchus dio]g̣eni
zabdaat]ḥes moc̣imi
anul]ḷ[i]no ii c̣os 199
]s zabḍ[i]b[oli
—[——— iulius] ạpolo[nius
]ụict[o]riṇ[o cos 200
——[——]c̣ius anṭ[o]nin[
birthạ [. . . ụṃ . .]ṣ [o]g̣a
mucia]ṇo cos 201
——— mạ[mm]ẹụs [b]el[a]ạc̣aḅ[i
——— maṃ[bogeus z]ạorạ
——— habibạ[s ne]ḅudai
appad haṇi[na- b]ẹḷẹị
diụo s[euero iii] cos 202
——— malchụṣ[
——— bareus[ ]c̣hi
]a iulius[ ]entianụs
]. aurel ṣabinus
g[eta] ṣeniore ii [co]s 203
——]—— ael[i]us ḥ[e]ṛennianus
——]—— bu[.]ṛaṇ[.].us maccei
expl[o]ṛat aụdas zebida

Cf. **1** xi 15–28; **6** iv 22–32.
10.]*ṭius* is also possible. *anṭ[o]nin[us:* D.
11.]*ṣ*[*o*]*ḷa:* D.
19.]*ṭhi* is also possible.
20. *terentianus*?

Col. xxviii

-]—[——
-]—[——
of̣[fic
-]—[——]ṇus
].ṇini
]ụaḷẹns
di]uo antoṇino [ii cos A.D. 205
—[———] abgar[u]ṣ
-[———]. uabala[th-
barba]esamen.[
—[— —].[ ] maxiṃ[u]ṣ
al]bino co[s] 206

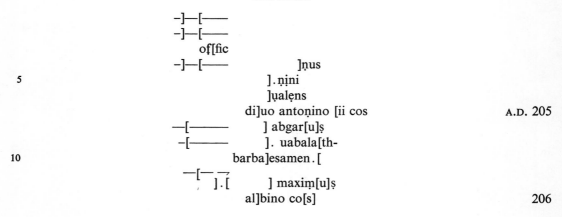

offi[c].[a]riṣton
barbal a[urel] maṛ[i]ṇus
singul a[u]ṛel baṣ[su]s
apṛọ ç[o]ṣ A.D. 207
———— macceus h[ae]ṛaṇ
becch mocimus ṃ[
appa malchus uaḅal[a]ṭhi
———— claudius [anto]ṇinus
diụ[o an]ṭọnino ị[ii cos 208
singul] cos aurel ạṇtoninus
].a heliọḍọṛus apolloni
] aurel ạṇṭ[i]ọçhianus
]p fla[u]ịus f̣ḷạui{u}anus
sing]ụl cos iul[iu]s ṃarcianus
singul ḷụçịlius luci
p[o]ṃpeiạṇọ ç[o]ṣ 209

Cf. **1** xiii 4–10; **8** x 14–15. 10. *]esamen.[:* D.

Col. xxix

].[
]si[ngul
Consulate A.D. 210?
——[——
]ạḷ[
]ḷ[ ].[
———[—]dem.[
duobus coṣ 212
———— g̣[..]sces maxiṃ[
ạp̣p̣[a].esuṛ.ṃiuṣ he[
———— ḅachareụ[
———— ịulius .[.......]ụs[
meṣ[a]ḷ[a co]s 214
ạp[pa]ạurel ịaquḅ[u]s
———— ṣeleuc[u]ṣ theṃẹ[
———— ạṇtoniụṣ zabbei
magḍạl [i]arhe[us] themạrsa
———— aurel romanus
———— zebi[da]s salman[
———— seleục̣us cassi
magdal zabd[i]ḅ[o]ḷ[us] ṃaẓḍ.[
———— iạ[r]h[eus] bạrnei
ṃagdal bari[cas i]arhei
ad op stip auṛẹ[l]ẓabdiboḷ[us
———— aụṛẹ[l]mocimus

explor aurẹ[l]marinus
ạppad aurẹḷ ạbdus
——— ẓabḍ[as]auada
——— ạurẹḷ nisreus
——— ạḅgelḷụs bassi
——— ạurẹḷ anṭọṇ[i]ṇụs

Cf. **1** xiv 1–9.

9. The first letter could be *b* or *d* as well as *g*. *maxiṃ[us:* D.

10. There is probably only one letter missing before *e*; and *n* is possible instead of *m*. The letter after *r* is probably *c*, but perhaps *p* or *t*. Cf. **15** ii 11: *ualeṛ[.]eṣ-surṃius*.

16. There is an erasure, with the remains of an *l*, to the left of *antonius*.

Col. xxx

—[———
—[———
—[———
—[———
—[———].[
ọf̣f̣ị[c] pa[
. [n]isreus uaḅ
ạp̣p̣[ad] ạurel maṛ[
siṇ[gul] aurel[ ]a[..].io
appad habiḅạ[s].m.[
bec̣c̣ḥ aelius[hel]iodor[us
laeṭọ ii c̣oṣ A.D. 215
siṇ[gul] ṛạạṃmas ḅaṛ[.]..[
——— aurel demeṭṛ[iu]ṣ
siṇ[g]ụl aurel domitti[u]ṣ
——— aureḷ munnis
sabino ii cos 216
——— aur[e]ḷ neoṇ[
becḥch aur[el]ạpolḷonius
——— au[rel]romạ[nu]s
singul[ ]. gerṃ[a]ṇus
singul iụ[lius] mari[nu]ṣ
——— ạụrel curiḷḷ[u]s
ad op stip aụrel gordius
——— ulp̣ius mariṇ[
becc̣ḥ aụṛ[el] romaṇ[u]s
——— aụṛẹḷ iulius
bẹc̣[c]ḥ antonius bạrlaḥạ
bẹc̣[c]ḥ aụṛel siḷụạṇus

Cf. **1** xv 1–12; **6** v 19–21.

7. Lack of any notation before the name is probably caused by scaling of the surface.

8 and 10. The notations may have been erased.

13. The name was inserted in small letters between 12 and 14.

28. *ha* is in an unusual ligature resembling *hd*.

Col. xxxi

]ugṇ[
a]ụṛẹḷ[ ]ṃa[
]l aurel[
ṣ[i]ṇgul aurel[
———— aụṛel u[
ạḍ naues df au[rel] gr[
appada au[rel].nṣịo[
becc̣ḥ auṛ[e]ḷ ṃalc̣ḥ[u]ṣ
becch aurel ḷongiṇ[us
m]ạgdal aụṛel apoll[.]n.[
b]ẹcch a[ur]ẹl zenobiu[s
———— aurel malchus
———— a[u]ṛel castor
extric[a]ṭọ ii cos A.D. 217
———— ạḅgarus thẹm{e}arsa
———— [ga]ḍḍes bọre
sacẹ[r]ḍote ii cos 219
oḟ[fic a]urel heṛ[mo]genes
ọf̣f̣ị[c au]ṛel an[to]ṇinus
d n aḷ[exa]ndro aug c̣[os 222
singuḷ cl iul maṛinus
singuḷ cl iul secuṇdus
singuḷ flauius ṛọṃạṇ[u]ṣ
singul ạụṛel ṣe[l]ẹuc̣[us
s[i]ṇgul ạpollinarius g[ai]ani

Cf. **1** xv 24; xvi 1–4; **6** v 28–30; **92** iii 18.
3. *singul*, as in 4?
6. The letters *df* are unexplained. *d*(*iscens*) *f*(*abrum*)?
15. *themarsa* has been corrected from *theme*. Cf. **1** xvi 2 and **92** iii 18.

Col. xxxii

[Ŧ zebida anulli]nọ[ii cos A.D. 199
Two lines lost
].[
].[
ḅ.[.]..p̣.ị rom[ ]ni
.[*ca.* 9] cos
ạḍ mamm sesq[ ].[
deẋ[tro ii cos] 196
————..[.].esurus [aelam]ị
aṇ[ullino ii co]ṣ 199
———— baṛḥ[a]ḍạ[dus haeran
———— iarhabọlẹṣ [t]ḥemạṛṣạ
———— ulpius ṃ[enan]dṛ[u]ṣ
———— belaac̣[a]b[us h]ạḷa

becch boreṣ[nis]amsị
u̧[i]ctọrino c̣[o]s 200
——— nahestabuṣ themarsa
muciạno cọs 201
——— hagus mạlchi
——— abianes ṃ[a]c̣chana
ạd mamm tḥemarsaṣ ḥaeran
——— [ae]ḷius bolạnus
disposi ṭḥemarsa[s] aḅgarị
——— [i]aṛhaboles addei
——— ḅaṣ[s]ụs tiberini
disposi i[u]ḷiụ[s] ṃarinus
ad op stip [iu]ḷiụ[s] ṃarinus al[ter
——— iarh\`[eu]s´ ⟦aboles⟧ ṭ[hemarsa
seuẹ[ro] ịii coṣ 202

Cf. **1** xxxi 34–40; xxxii 1–18.

1–2. D has no readings.

4. This man is probably a duplicarius (note *sesq* in 6); but the notation has not been satisfactorily read.

10. *PDur.* 100:]*sus heraṇ*[; *PDur.* 101: *baṛ*.[.]..[, proposing *baṛṣ*[*i*]*ṃṣ*[*us heran.*

19. *ṃ*[*a*]*ṭṭhana:* D; but see Index 1, s.v. "Matthana".

23. *addei* has been corrected from *abb.a.*

27. *iarheus* has been corrected from *iarhaboles.*

Col. xxxiii

——[——
—[——— malchus m]ạmbọ[gei
—[——— -al..bius si]ḷụani
-ius ma]ṛinụs
geta s]ẹṇịor[e ii cos A.D. 203
——— u̧[alerius] ṃonimus
——— [i]ụl[ius] ṣatụrnilus
ad mamṃ [iarhe]ụs bẹ[l]ạacabi
paṣ Y[ ]ịụ[lius m]ạ[xi]mus
cor ạḷẹ[xan]ḍṛ[us a]ntonini
ad pretori· aeliụ[s] ḥeliọ[doru]ṣ
ad mamṃ b[ar]ḅ[ae]ṣạm[en] ṃạḷe
c̣[i]ḷ[one] ịị c̣oṣ 204
ad mamm froṇ[to]n ṃạ[r]ẹạ
ad pen comp aẹ[li]ụ[s] alex̣[andr]us
——— iụ[lius] caṣsiaṇụs
———[—]. ab[i]dlahin
dịuo antonino ii cos 205
——— ualerius firmus
——— iulius baṣsus
in perfunc ⟦zabdibolus salman⟧
——— mocimus zebida
chaf[e]r a iarheus marea
——— zebiḍạṣ iarḥei

———— gabṛịon ọ[b]ẹan
———— azizus antọ[n]ịni
sịṇ[gu]ḷ mocimus ṃ[o]c̣[i]mi
apro [cos] A.D. 207
———— [i]ulius iụ[lianu]ṣ
duọ[bus cos] 212
caper auir iuḷ[iu]ṣ al[exandr]ụs

Cf. **1** xxxii 20–37; xxxiii 1–19.

9. The notation has not been satisfactorily read. It might begin with either *p* or *a* (cf. *apro*, line 28) and could have *si* for the next two letters instead of *as*. Instead of the centuria-symbol, *li* is possible.

15. *ad pen(um) comp(arandum):* "to collect food". Also in **2** xxxv 19.

21. *in perfunc(tione)*. Since the name is canceled, probably "(dead) in line of duty".

Col. xxxiv

[Ŧ tiberini] ạpṛ[o et maxi]mo cọs A.D. 207
[dec] ṭḥ[e]ṃạ[rsas tiberi]ṇi
g[eta seniore ii c]ọs 203
. [dupl] ị[ul]ius [anto]ṇịnuṣ
ạ[pro et] ṃaximo coṣ 207
ḍụpḷ aelius [barn]eus
ḍẹ[xtro ii] cos 196
. [ ] . . [ ] ṣimaones auidalathi
] ṃaronas gadde
saturnino cos 198
———— b[ar]athes zebiḍa
anulino ii cos 199
———— ṃạesamas aciba
uictorino cos 200
ạppạ[d] gạ[ia]ṇus themarsa
———— bolae[u]s mocịmi
ad ọp stịpẹn iarheus themarsa
muciano cos 201
———— marcus maior
———— malchus tḥemarsa
———— males macchana
disposit belaacabus abgari
appaḍ [i]ụlius scaurianus
in proseq[ ] . [f]ḷauius ṃonimus
diuo ṣẹuero iii cos 202
———[— d]ọmittius bạrnei
——[—— mo]c̣[i]mus barnei
ad le[ones]barbaesamen
gẹta seniore ii cos 203

Cf. **1** xxxiii 23–28; xxxiv 8–32.

2. **1** xxxiii 24 apparently has *themarsa*; but I do not feel justified in restoring it here.

4. Since Aelius Barneus in line 6 is a duplicarius, Iulius Antoninus must have been of the same rank.

13. **1** xxxiv 15 has *maesomas*.

17. The notation is in a different hand.

21. *matthana:* D; but see Index 1, s.v. "Matthana."

24. Cf. on **1** xxx 18.

27. Cf. on *-mus marini*, **1** xxxiv 29.

Col. xxxv

ia]ṛhei
].[ ]me
———]— g̣[apo]ḷḷọ[
o]f̣f̣ị ị[sidorus ..s]ịḍọ[n
——— ẓ[abdibol]ụs theṃ[arsa
[di]sposi ge[mellus]ṭhemarsa
——— baṛ[athes]hag[u]ṣ
——— haguṣ iarhei
cilone ii cos A.D. 204
offi ulpius barsumius
——— ṃalchus bodẹ
app[a]ḍ ụlpius ṃarcellus
diuo antonino ii cọṣ 205
———[— i]arheus bora
[di]spos[..] ạd [i]aqubus zebida
ọ[f]fic [i]ụḷius maximus
]ạd queren mocimus ṣimaoni
——— aurel germanus
aḍ pen comp flauius marinus
——— mocimus theme
apṛo et maximo cos 207
explor sammas gai
——— agrippas male
ad op stiṗ. domittiụṣ antoninus
poṃpeiano cos 209
——— azizus zaora
fạustino cos 210
——— mocimụṣ salmaṇ
ḍụobus cos 212
——— iaṛheus malchi

Cf. **1** xxxv 1–27.
2. *the*]*me:* D.
10. *barsimsus* in **1** xxxv 6.
17. Cf. on **2** xii 28. *simon* in **1** xxxv 16.
19. Cf. on **2** xxxiii 15.

Col. xxxvi

the]ṃạ[rs]ạs buẓi
ạpp[a -ius m]ọci[mu]ṣ
ad op] sti[p uabalat]ḥụ[s hanina
di]ṣpoṣ[a]ṗọḷ[l-
mes]ạla cos A.D. 214
——— ṭ[hemars]ạṣ mocimi
s]abino cos 216
——— aurẹl demetrius
About six lines blank

Ŧ demetri uictorino cos — A.D. 200
———⌝ dẹç ulpius demetrius
pọmpeiano cos — 209
ạḍ hord dupl aelius licinnius
mesala cos — 214
———⌝ sesq aurel marinus
saturnino cos — 198
——— iadibelus iarhei
anulino ii cos — 199
——— salmanes maçç̣ẹ[i
ḍ[i]ṣposi nisạmsus zabdị[bo]ḷ[i]
ḅecch uicṭọr hae[r]ạn
uictoriṇọ cos — 200
——— ṃacceus themarsa
muciano cos — 201

Cf. **1** xxxv 28–32; xxxvi 1–2 and 25–33.
16. Note the unusual position of the angular symbol.
20. *sesq* is in a different hand.

Col. xxxvii

]ẹlus .[
.[ ].eus[. . .].[
———[—].e.[
[ ]uṣ[. . . .]. .[
———[— ulpius] mariṇụṣ[
e[xplor didas] coççei
ạd mamṃ [g]ọremis ịạḍei
ad mamm iarheus themạ[rsa
a]d mamṃ zaḅḅeus barchạḷḅạ[
diuo seuero iii cos — A.D. 202
appa iulius german[u]s
geta seniorẹ [ii cos — 203
——— iulius gorippus
——— zabaeeus malchi
——— barathes buccei
ad mamm iamḷichus mocimi
ad mamm iulius germanus
cilone ii cos — 204
——— ma[ri]n[u]s hotarei
——— malchus muciani
ad mạmṃ maras themarsa
——— signas matharei
——— iulịus maxịṃus
ad mamm i[a]rhẹus b[ar]ṇei
——— zebidas ṃ[a]çcei
——— uạlerius [m]ạximus

[di]sposit ụḷpius m[a]rinus
ḍiuo anton(ino) iị [c]os 205
————⌝ claudius nạtaliụs

Cf. **1** xxxvii 2–29; **26** b 3–7.
11. The notation is in a different hand.
29. Perhaps [*sig*(*nifer*)]; cf. **47** i 17.

Col. xxxviii

]s iarh[a]bọ[les luci
]. d[e]ṃẹṭṛị[us z. . . .n.
]. .[*ca.* 10]ṣ[
].[ ]. . .[
]. iuliụs ạṇṭ[oni]ṇ[-
]s iulius maṛ[in]ụ[s
———— iuliụṣ l[o. .]. [.
————⌝
uẹx ϒ aeliụs ạṇt[o]ṇị[nu]ṣ
dispọs addeus iarḥẹị
albino çọs A.D. 206
ẹs siṇgul aeliụs ṃạṛçẹḷlin[u]s
explor barneuṣ ṭḥẹṃarsa
apro ço[s] 207
magdala iulius beḷ[a]ạçạbus
duọ[bus c]os 212
singul abidnạmares marona
mesạḷa cos 214
dispos aureḷ aẓizus
About five lines blank
Ŧ octaui muciano cos 201
————⌝ dec luç[ius] octạụiuṣ
————⌝ dupl saḷ[ma]nes zebida
mesala et sabino cos 214
————⌝ sesq ụḷp[i]ụs gaiaṇ[us]
dextro ii [co]s 196
———— flauius mari[nu]s
a]d mamm berosas ualeṇṣ

Cf. **1** xxxvii 30–38; xxxviii 1–13 and 29–31; **26** b 8.
1. The name in **1** xxxvii 30 is written *ierabole* without final *s*.
5. *ạṇṭ[oni]ṇ[us:* D.
8. *uex*(*illarius*) (*centuriae*) although the man is a member of a *turma*.
11. The meaning of *es* is unknown. The name in **1** xxxviii 3 is *marcellus*.
14. The *a* after *c* is blotted and resembles *o*.
17. The date is inserted in small letters between lines 16 and 18.
25, 26, 28. Note the unusual position of the angular symbol.

Col. xxxix

———— a[ ].o.[
]nisạ[
]ụs aṃ[

diṣpos ụlp[ius] ḅạṛneb[
——— ulpịụ[s ap]oḷlonạ[
——— maḷ[ch]ụṣ ḥạeran
——— ạlexaṇ[d]rus antọnini
——— moc̣im[us] bạrlaha
u[i]ctoṛ[i]no cos — A.D. 200
ad mamṃ iụliụs ant[o]ṇịnus
officio i[u]ḷịus antoninus alṭer
muciano c̣ọs — 201
——— maḷ[c]huṣ maccei
chafer a zeḅ[i]ḍas egla
ad mamm ṃ[a]ḷc̣hus haeran
——— iulius salman
——— themarsas chaseti
appada malchus iarhei
ad mamm zaḅḍaathes malchi
——— boḷanus bolani
——— thẹmarsas salman
——— gạ[i]us ạbidfur
——— ṣẹ[le]ục̣[u]ṣ ịạṛḥei
app̣[ad]ạ mạẓabbanaṣ belaacạbi
——— zebidaṣ ịạḍẹi
——— bạrh[a]dạḍụṣ aḅịḍ[fur
——— zebidas iarhẹ[i
——— iulius barḷ[aha

Cf. **1** xxxviii 35–38; xxxix 1–26; **26** c 1–2.
3. *a*.[*:* D.
4. *ḅạṛneb*[*us:* D.
5. *ap*]*oḷlonạ*[*s:* D.
14. Cf. *zebida* in **1** xxxix 9.
17. Cf. *themarsa* in **1** xxxix 14.
19. In **1** xxxix 16 the name is *zabathes*. Cf. also **13** 19.
21. Cf. *themes* in **1** xxxix 18.

Col. xl

].s ẓ[
] loṇ[
]as ṃ[
]ḍịuo sẹ[uero iii cos — A.D. 202
appạdạ ṃ.[..]ṃụs iaṛ[
——— iụḷ[i]ụs ạntoṇị[
ṣịngul c̣ọṣ [a]ḷẹ[x]andrus theofiḷ[
geta seniore i[i] c̣os — 203
uex Y ụḷ[piu]ṣ siluanus
——— ṭ[h]emạrsas iarhẹ[i
p̣[r]ẹtora ọgelus uabalathi
——— ụlpius bassus
cilone ii cos — 204
——— ṣiluạṇus mocimi
——— ṃaronas ḍinei

———— gorippus ualentiṇi
ad mamm rabbulas bassi
singḷ bassus bibi
uexiḷ ḍomittius proç[ul]us
Çụṃ ạḷḅọṣ
———— abidmalchus aụṭḥei
diuo anton(ino) ii cos 205
———— f̣lauius siluanus
———— ạelius fortunatus
ḍ[i]spos ịụḷịụṣ ṃarinus
apṛo cos 207
ṣị[g] luc[i]us ualerianus
ḍuobus asp[ri]ṣ ç[os 212
aḍ mamm [o]gas haṇ[in]a
mesalạ [cos] 214
disposit aurel ualẹ[ns
———— abidsalmạ[them]arsa

Cf. **1** xxxix 32–36; xl 1–24; **26** c 4.

7. *theofịḷ[i:* D.

9. Perhaps *uex(illarius) c(enturiae)* as in xxxviii 8 (see ad loc.), or possibly *uexl*. There seems no room for *uexil* as in line 19 below.

9 and 19. The notations are in another hand.

10. Cf. *themarsa* in **1** xl 2.

11. See on *ad praetori(um)*, p. 14. The *a* which follows *pretor* is unexplained.

16. Cf. *ualenti* in **1** xl 9.

18. Cf. **1** xl 11: *aure[l . . . .].bida*, and note.

19. The letters below *uexil* are small and form part of the same notation. There is no break in the list of names. If the notation is correctly read, it must mean "with the name-lists," though *albos* is the wrong case and the wrong gender.

24 and 30. The notations are in another hand, different from that in 9 and 19.

Col. xli

]Ŧ[antonini] ạ[lbino et emiliano c]ọṣ A.D. 206
ad] ọp sṭị[p dec ulpiu]ṣ [antoninus
].[ ].[?
———— [dupl ale]xaṇḍrụṣ .[ ].a
pompeian[o co]ṣ 209
———— dupḷ[ ]em.[ ]ạb[.]..
dị[uo s]euẹṛ[o] ịịi ços 202
———— sesq iulịanus theṃ[a]rsa
d]ẹx̣tro ii c[os 196
singul uạḷeriụṣ ualeṇṭịnụs
———— iạṛhabụṣ ẹbuc[a]ẹi
sa]ṭụrnino cos 198
sig ṭhemạ[rs]as zeḅida
ạ[nu]lino ii cos 199
———— bạṛḥọ[ta]ṛus auiḍalạṭḥị
———— g[u]ris ṇisamṣị
ad querend b[as]ṣus [m]ọntaṇ[
[uictori]ṇo coṣ 200
bechuf ṭhem[e]ṣ dinaei
———— ḍ[e]metṛịụṣ maccei

m]uc̣ịano coṣ A.D. 201
——— ogeḷus [ ]ịbọḷị
——— ael[- sa . .]ṣiuṣ
——— th[eo]ḍ[orus ze]bida
ambul b[elaca]ḅus[z . -
——— ṣạ[lm]es zeḅ[ida
——— ḅ[assu]ṣ ạ[nt]oni[n-
appad[seleuc]us ạṇtoṇiṇ[.]n
ambul[iarh]ạboleṣ theme

Cf. **1** xli 1–8 and 21–36; xlii 1–4.

4, 6, 8. Note the unusual position of the angular symbol.

13. The notation is in a different hand.

17. This line and all the rest of the verso are in a hand different from that of the preceding columns. The notation is in still another hand. For the notation see on **2** xii 28.

19. Cf. *themarsa* in **1** xli 31.

22. Cf. **1** xli 34 and note.

23. *ael*[*ius:* D; but *ael*[*ami*]*s* is more likely on the basis of the spacing. Cf. **1** xli 35.

27. *ạ*[*nt*]*oni*[*ni:* D.

28. The *n* at the end of the line seems to be by the hand and pen of the upper half of the column. *ạṇtoṇiṇ*[*i*]*ṇ:* D.

Col. xlii

]ḷ[ ]ḷạṭḥ[
ba]ṛatḥ[es] . [ ] . . [
ḍị[spos] ṃocimus [ ] . [
appạḍạ ạbbas zeḅ[ida
——— [i]uḷius magṇ[
———[— iu]ḷịus marinụs
ọfficio ạ[bda]eus barhaei
dio seuero ịịi cos A.D. 202
——— sẹ[l]eucus barathe
ṣ[in]g̣ul tịmon maṛ[i]ni
geta seniorẹ [i]ị coṣ 203
app]ạda bạrneus iarhaẹị
] . . ṇṣ ạfarneṣ bassi
——— ạẹlius longinus
——— bạrathes abg̣[ari
] . . l zẹbidas malcḥ[i
cilone ii c[o]s 204
a]mbul ṇẹbudaes theṃ[a]ṛṣạ
———]— ẓạbdibolụ[s] g̣[o]ṛa
———]— ṭ[h]emarṣạ[ ]nisamṣi
———]— gạrmẹlus bẹ[l]ịhabi
. [luci]us cạ[ssi]anụṣ
—[———]s th[
—[———,] . [. . . . .]ḥus ḅ[.]ḷ[
——— bọliadeus zẹ[bid]ạ
——— mocimus zạ[ora

Cf. **1** xlii 8–31; xliii 1–2.

5. *magn*[*us:* D.

13. For the notation see on **1** xxii 8 and xxiii 15.

20. There is room for an *s* in the lacuna between the names; but there is no way to decide whether it was written.

Col. xliii

ach]ịllẹ[us malch-
diụ[o an]tọnịn[o ? cos — A.D. 205 or 208
———[—
uex̣ ze]b[i]ḍaṣ[ ]. . [.]ạlac[
aṃb[ul]iụlius maṛinus
——— habibis zẹbida
disposịi zebị[d]ạṣ ḥab[i]bi
appada abgaṛus ịaṛhaei
——— iuḷ[i]ụs geṛṃạṇ[u]s
——— cl dadọna
explọṛ liç[i]ṇnius apolloniṇ[u]ṣ
——— salmes malchi
About two lines blank
DROMadaṛịi
ϒ malchi dextṛo ii cos — 196
ad op ṣ[tip]ṭḥẹ[m]arsas buccei
———[—]dạlathus tẹọboli
ạ[d] op stiṗ[iarha]boles [z]ẹbiḍa
ad o]p ṣ[t]ịp[ ]. ẹs gabṛ[ion
cil]ọṇẹ ii ç[os — 204
——— auṛ[el] m[o]nim[i
]b[*Consulate*
——— tẹ[
One line lost
———]— ạ[. . . . .]. [.]. . [
ad[ ]. antonius romanụṣ
sabino ii cos — 216
——— ạurel paulus

Cf. **1** xliii 3–13; xliv 10–15.

1. *malchi:* D.

9. *cl(audius)*.

14. *drom* is in roughly formed rustic capitals with a serif at the foot of the hasta of *r*; the rest of the word is in large cursive letters.

17. The spacing on the papyrus suggests *sa*]*dalathus* or even *dalathus* rather than *aui*]*dalathus* or *abe*]*dalathus.*

18.]*boles:* D; but see on **1** xliv 13.

21. See on **1** xliv 16.

22. The consulate is either *al*]*b*[*ino*, 206, or *duo*]*b*[*us aspris*, 212.

Col. xliv

ϒ [danymi]. [
—]–[——]m[
] [ ]. . [*Consulate*
——— auṛel ḅaṛça. [
sabinọ ii çọ[s — A.D. 216
——— aurel cạlpurniụs
——— aurel roman[u]ṣ
——— aurel aạdeus
——— aurel sabin[u]ṣ

——— aurel roman[u]ṣ .

ϒ maṛci deẹ[x]tro ii c̣[o]ṣ A.D. 196

———→ sesq doṃeṭ[i]us barṣẹṃea

ṃ[uci]ạno c̣[o]s 201

ad .[ ] aeliụṣ antoṇ[i]ṇụṣ

ṃessala cọs 214

——— aurel ualens

——— aụ[r]ẹḷ[ma]rinus

[sa]bino ii cos 216

——— ḍ[ometius] ṇicolaus

ad ọ[p stip]aṣ[

]. co[s 217–222

—[———]..[

About three lines lost. Century of Marianus

ạḍ op [stip

m]ẹssala cos 214

———[—] heraclas

Cf. **1** xliii 22–23; 28–30; **8** iii 1–5; vii 21–22.

12. This man must be the same as Dometius Barbaessamen in **1** xliii 23. Note the unusual position of the angular symbol.

28. Probably *iulius heraclas*; cf. **1** xxiv 9.

Col. xlv

[ ]s *Consulate*

ạd ọp sti[p] auṛ[el]s

ϒ aṇtonini p̣ṛ [tert]ulḷ[o] c̣ọṣ A.D. 195

——— gaius baṛḥạ[d]aḍ[u]s

——— ṃalchus salman

duobụṣ asp(ris) cos 212

——— macrinus maximi

sabino ii cos 216

——— aurel siluạ[nus

ϒ antonini post ạn[to]ṇịno iị[cos 205?

——— iulius [ ]b[ ]ṣ

ṃẹ[ssala cos] 214

——— iulius ..[......]ius

ạḍ ọp stip abiḍsalṃaṣ [iarh]ei

Remainder of column blank

7. This is the Macrinius Maximi of **1** xviii 12, **6** xi 24, and **8** ix 27.

10. Or *ii[i*, A.D. 208.

3

Complete (?) Working Roster of the Coh. XX Palmyrenorum

PDur. 104 (inv. D. P. 30 recto) A.D. 238–247

Transcription and commentary: *Final Rep.* V, no. 104; *edidi.*

This papyrus has been somewhat hesitantly classified with the complete rosters because of its apparatus of notations beside the names (frags. b and c) and horizontal lines with puncta (frags. c and d). In these respects it resembles **1** in particular; but its extent is too small for one to be sure that it is not a partial roster like **8**, which also has the horizontal lines and puncta, though they are differently arranged, and a few notations.

The earliest consulate which can be read is in frag. a 6 (*crispino*, 224); but another preceded in line 2, and there are traces of a name in line 1 which must then belong to a man who enlisted not later than 222. His 25 years of service would have expired in 247, which therefore constitutes an approximate terminus ante quem. Crispinus, on the other hand, was the junior consul for 224, so his colleague must have incurred damnatio memoriae. But the name of his colleague, Ap. Claudius Julianus, is still used in **23** (A.D. 236) and with *diuo alexandro cos* in **24** (A.D. 238–242). Julianus, therefore, who had been proconsul of Africa and probably praefectus urbi under Severus Alexander, survived both Alexander and Maximinus but fell victim to damnatio memoriae under Gordian III or Philip. In view of the resemblances between Gordian's policies and Alexander's, Philip appears the more likely to have condemned Julianus. In that case, this text would date 244–247.

The spacing of the line and the date of the text as a whole would justify the restoration *d(iuo) alex(andro) cos*, 226, in frag. a 11; but the remaining traces do not favor the reading *ḍ(iuo)*.

The verso is **35**.

Frag. a

]. . [
Consulate A.D. 223 ?
]. el. [.]s[
]ạṃạẹụṣ[
]g̣erṃ[a]nu[s
criịspino cos 224
]abdeus [
] fusc̣[o] ị[i cos 225
]malchụṣ [
]ṛabbelus[
ụị[

a 3. Possibly *aelius.*

a 11. The traces align with the consulships in lines 6 and 8; but they are faint, as if erased, and they do not suit the name of any consul of appropriate date.

Frag. b

].[ ]ṃạ.[
]salmes mac̣[
]....ạṇụṣ ẓ.ḅ...[
].[....]. [al]ẹxạṇ[dr-
]. ẓạ[
].[.].[.]....[ ]ị
]ṭ[h]ẹṃẹṣ[ ]..[
].ṣi[.]..eḷius ..o..ṛ.[
]...ị bac̣[.]ḅ..ịụs malch.[
]ḥ[

b 8. The notation preceding the name has been canceled. The name was probably *aelius*.
b 9. The notation to the left of the first *b* is in the same ink as the notation in the preceding line.

Frag. c

]———[–
●———[–
Two or three lines lost
]——[——
One line lost
appad[
]————[–

Frag. d

●[
One line lost
●[
●[
—[–]∸[–

4

Complete Working Roster of the Coh. XX Palmyrenorum

PDur. 105 (inv. D. P. 34 verso); *vidi* A.D. 250–256

Transcription and commentary: *Final Rep.* v, no. 105; *edidit* Gilliam. Facsimile (frag. b): ibid., plate 63.

There is little to add to Gilliam's discussion of the reasons for and against regarding frag. a as part of the same text as frag. b and the smaller bits. Against the assumption of unity are the very different hand of frag. a and the seeming lack of consuls' names. The usual heading, however, including the decurion's name, is now evident in lines 7–13. In favor of accepting all the fragments as one text is the fact that the rectos of both frag. a and frag. b contain parts of a single text, and that the present lists both follow the pattern of **1** and **2**—names accompanied by notations of rank, status, or assignment. This is far from conclusive, and frag. a may well be a separate text; but it has been left with the other fragments for lack of proof that it belongs by itself.

The pattern of frags. a and b is also the reason for including these lists with the complete rosters. The partial rosters, **5**–**8**, differ in either omitting the commanding officer's full name at the head of each century or turma, or in having no annotations beside the names.

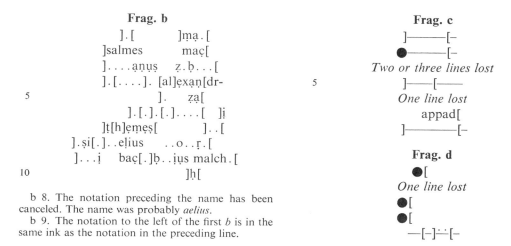

The date must be later than that of the recto, which is A.D. 250–51, and of course before the capture of Dura by Shapor in 256. Aurelius Castor (b i 4) seems to be the same person as in **2** xxxi 13. He enlisted in 216 and would have been eligible for discharge ca. 241; but here he is a duplicarius and may be serving longer than a normal enlistment. Dessau 2529 names a sesquiplicarius alae who served 36 years; and a centurion in Dessau 2653 (*CIL* VIII 2877) served 45.

The recto of this papyrus is **66**.

Frag. a (*First hand*)

Col. i | **Col. ii**

]ṃ.[
.[ ].ic.[
]————[ ]..sas
]—————[ ]aziz..[
—r ILLI....[...]s
One line blank
]ṣịngul deç˙ i romVLL[u]ṣ si[
. ..[——[—
ad pr]ạetor dup.. ç .[...].[
.[*Consulate*?
dupḷ
].[
]ṣẹṣ[q].ellus
].[ ].ṣ.s
].[

Quoted matter is from Gilliam's commentary in *Final Rep.* V.

i 1.]..[*:* D.

2.]..*c*.[*:* D. "[*M*]*ọcị*[*mus*] may be possible"; but the letter before *c* is pretty clearly *i*.

3.]...*as:* D.

4. "*Azizụ*[*s*], presumably; but *Azizị* is at least as good a reading."

5. *Ru*....[..]*s:* D. "Possibly *Rufin̈*[*ianu*]*s; Rufi-* at any rate is an attractive reading though the traces of ink would not suggest *n* as the next letter. If we have a single letter to the left, it appears to be an *r*. It is uncertain whether the same letter or symbol was used in the next few lines; in no instance does the ink that remains show much resemblance to what we have here. A ditto mark, to avoid repeating *Aurel* endlessly, would explain why there are no nomina, but I can cite no parallel. There seems to be a very short horizontal line in the margin."

7.]...*lde:* D. "The marginal notation might be read]*emulde* ...".

8. "The margin opposite this line seems to be blank." The letter in the column of notations could be *c* or *l*.

9.]...*rdụ*..[..]*.:* D. "One can read *ord*(*inatus*) in the notation: perhaps *et ord u*..[;]*etor dupl* can also be read. Possibly there are consulships in lines 7, 9, and 11." Read *duplic*?

13. "Possibly *ṣẹṣ*[*q*(*uiplicarius*) in the margin, enclosed in an angle."

ii 1: *sig*(*nifer*) or *singul*(*aris*).

Frag. b (*Second hand*)

Col. i

ɣ .[*ca.* 12]ọ[
——— ɣ ạụṛ[el ...]ụṣ[
ṣ[abino ii] cọṣ A.D. 216

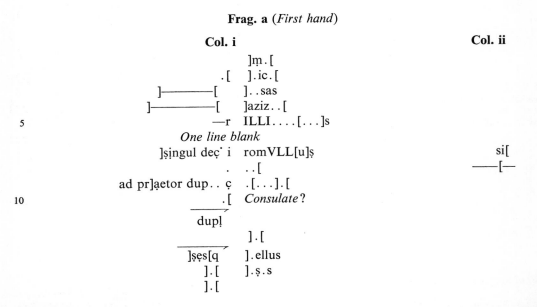

sing dupl au[r]ẹ[l] caṣṭor
[d a]lex iị [co]s A.D. 226
⟦[. . . . .]⟧ ——— sesq luc̣ị[us] ịụliaṇ[u]s
f̣[u]scọ iị cos 225
singul aurel doṃiṭianus
].nṣạpunc /] /]. . .ḷ epulis ——— iul apoliṇaṛius
d alex̣ [ii cos 226
——— ạurẹ[l] iaddạẹ[
——— ạụṛẹḷ ia. . [
——— ạurel d[
albiṇ[o cos 227
—]-[——] aụ[rel] . . .us
ṃ[o]ḍẹṣ cos 228
].[.]lo[.].[.]ḷus
]d alẹx iịị cos 229
]aurel antoṇ[i]nus
a]urel asclepiạdẹs
]ạurel ualẹns
]agricoḷa cos 230
—]——— aụṛẹḷ [b]ạḅuius
——— ạụṛẹ⟨l⟩ siḷ[ua]ṇus
]l .[. .]geṇ.ḷ.ụs

Quoted matter is from Gilliam's commentary in *Final Rep. V.*

b i 1. "The *o*. . . may be part of *cos*."

2.]. . .[. . . . . . .].[: D. "The centurion's nomen. . . quite possibly is *Ạụ*[*rel*(*ius*)]." At the beginning of the line is the tail of a long stroke sweeping downward from right to left, probably the remains of the symbol Ⴤ used instead of the abbreviation *ord* found in **1** and **2**. The horizontal bar before the centurion's name is exceptional; but cf. line 6.

3. .[. . . . . .] *cọṣ:* D.

6. This line too appears to be an exception to the rule that in the Dura rosters such designations of rank are accompanied by an angular symbol (above, pp. 11–12); but a word seems to have been erased, possibly *chaf au*, and the horizontal bar substituted. Even this is not regular. "One must assume that the last two letters of *Lucius* are rather crowded in the lacuna."

9. The notation is in a third hand. Gilliam read].*n*. .*uoc* and]. . . .*epulis*, suggesting also the possibility of].*nfṛọ* for the first line. Like him, I can make no sense of any of these readings. Can *epulis* be an error for *epistulis*? R. W. Davies, *BASP* 5 (1968) 33, compares **76** FF 4, where an epulum is commuted for money; but such matters would hardly be noted in a roster.

Apoliṇạris: D; but the *u* is represented by the hook on the left of the *s*.

11. *Iaddạ*[*eus*]*:* D.

12. "Possibly *Iaṛḥ*[*aboles*. The *h* is possible; but the *r* is hard to reconcile with the remains."

16. [*Modest*]*o iị*: D.

17.]. . .*o*[.]. .[.]*s:* D. "Possibly *Aure*]*l O*[*g*]*ẹl*[*u*]*s*."

23. *Aur*[*el*]. .*ụ*.*s:* D.

25. *singu*]*l* .[. .].*e*. .*ḷ*.*s:* D. "Possibly *Ị*[*ul*(*ius*)]."

Col. ii

-]—[——
-]—[——
-]—[——
——[—]-
——[—]-
.[ ]. .[

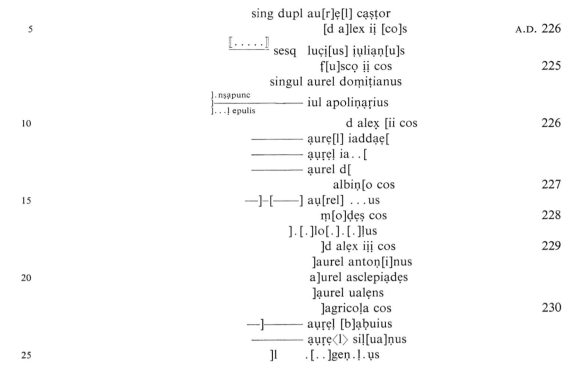

Consulate A.D. 231
si]ng[ul]. . [
. [si]ṇgul ạụ[rel
si]ngul au[rel
o]f̣f proc au[rel
ḷụp[o cos 232
——— aurel ṭḥeṃ[
siṇgul aurel baṛ. [
——— aurel zeṇ[
——— marinus m[
——— aure⟨l⟩ gerṃ[anus

b ii 12. "There may have been about two dates in the nine or so lines lost at the top of the column. If so the date in the present line should be *ca.* 234 . . . I cannot read the consuls of 233–235 in the faint traces left; *Ḷupọ* [*cos*] (232) might be possible, which would mean that seventeen men had enlisted in 230. Ardashir's invasion of Mesopotamia and preparations for Alexander's Persian campaign would offer an explanation. . ." Actually, the date seems fairly certain. The first letter of the consul's name is either *g* or *l*; and the preceding sequence of consuls calls for one not many years after 230. The addition of as many as seventeen or eighteen men in one year to the same century is paralleled in **1** ix, xiv, and xxix, all of A.D. 214, and xxi, A.D. 216. **2** xxiv shows a similar long run for 215.

13. *Ie*. [*:* D.

Fragments c, e, and g–i are blank on the verso

Frag. d

]. upp[.]. [
]a[u]ṛẹl . . . . aṣ. [

Frag. f

—]—[——
–]———[–
offịç p̣ṛọ[c

Frag. j

]fpoc aurẹ[l
sin]gul aurẹ[l
One line blank: Consulate?
–]—— h[
]ç[
]ọp̣inio. . [

Frag. k

]. [
a]ụṛẹ[l] . . . . . o. [
]ạureḷ çṛị[s]p̣ị[nus
] africa[no cos
]. [.]ccei. . . . [

Frag. l

]. . [
aur]el long [
]. . ṭoṛ [
]. [.]. [. .]o[
]. [.]ṣ

Frag. m

———[ ]. . . [
]ụal. . [
——]-[——] . ụṛạeniạ[
—]——[—] ḥ[.]ḍṛẹ. [
]. eoṇ[ ] isịḍ. . [

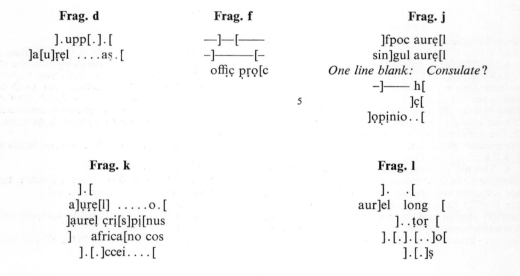

of]fici[ ].ạ...[
]ṣ[i]ng[ul]..a.a[
].[..].[

d 1. The letters are in large cursive, perhaps a heading, or conceivably *pupp(ieno) cos*, A.D. 234.
2.]..[..].[..]..[: D.
f 3.]*off proç*[: D.
j 1.]*fp.ç*: D. Read *of*]*f p⟨r⟩oc*?
4–6. No readings in D.
k 2. *A*]*ụṛ*[*el*]: D.
3. *A*]*urel C*.[..]..[: D. The *l* and *c* are fused in a sort of ligature.
4. *Afric*[*ano*: D; in app., "The date, in which Maximinus' name is suppressed, shows that this scrap probably came from the column following Frag. b ii."
5.].*cei*...[: D.
l 2. *Long*[*inus*: D; but there is a space between the *g* and the edge of the papyrus, and the name could be variously restored.
3.].*o*.[: D.
5.]..[.].[: D.
m 2.].*al*[: D.
3–4. No readings in D.
5.]*eo*. *I*....[: D. Possibly *ad leones*.
6. No readings in D.
7.].*g*[..]...[: D.

Partial Rosters

5

Annotated Partial Roster of a Unit in Egypt

PVindob. L 100 recto July, A.D. 217?
Papyrussammlung der Oesterreichische Nationalbibliothek

Transcription, facsimile, and commentary: R. O. Fink, "Two Fragments of Roman Military Rosters in Vienna," *La Parola del Passato* 55 (1957) 298–311.

Text: Daris, no. 19.

Commentary: R. O. Fink, "*Damnatio Memoriae* and the Dating of Papyri," *Synteleia* 232–36.

This text most resembles **8** among the Dura papyri. In both, the names are listed by centuries and within each century in order of seniority by consulships; and in both, the names are accompanied by notations, though in the present text fewer than half the names are treated so. Failure to repeat the centurion's name in full in the nominative at the beginning of his century (col. ii) shows that this list differs in form from the complete rosters like **1** and **2**. The date by day and month in ii 1 is a unique feature of this list.

The soldiers all appear to have Roman names; but since the date is after the constitutio Antoniniana the names do not provide a means for deciding whether this is a roster of the one legion in Egypt or an auxiliary cohort.

The date is not easy to fix. The earliest date of enlistment which can be read is 190 (ii 5), and this would lead to 215 as the first possible year for the soldier's discharge. One must also consider the possibility that even earlier dates of enlistment occurred elsewhere in the complete text. On the other hand, the names of the consuls in ii 5, 7, and 9 show that at this time Commodus was under damnatio memoriae and Falco was not, whereas in **1** (219) Commodus is found as consul for 192, and in both **1** and **6** (218) Erucius Clarus, Falco's junior colleague, is named alone for 193. Since Commodus had been deified by Septimius Severus in 197 at the latest, his omission here indicates a renewed damnatio, most probably in Macrinus' reign, for Commodus was back in favor in **1**, under Elagabal, and there is no known reason for Caracalla to rescind Commodus' original deification. The date in ii 1 then leads to July 217 as the date of the text, because Macrinus' short reign extended only from April 217 to June 218.

The verso is in Greek.

Col. i

].i.[.]ṇ. iị c̣ọṣ A.D. 205?
]. . . . . . .ịnuṣ
]. . . . . .ṇ
].[. .].ụạs
]. . . .ṣ.thus
albi]no et aemil cos 206
].ịc̣om. .
]plution
]ạnus
].pḥus
m]aximo cos 207
]. .nus
ant]ọni iii cos 208
arte]midorus
]mḷas
]. *Consulate*? 212?
]ṃaximus
]ṃ. .ọus

i 1. The consul's name, if that is what we have here, should be one of those for 205 or one or two years before; but I cannot fit any of them to the remains.

6. Expand *albino et aemil(iano)*.

11. Since the name of the junior consul is so far to the right, one should probably restore *apro et maximo*. I know of no evidence to support Degrassi's placing Maximus first (*Fasti Consolari*, p. 58).

13. Probably *divo antoni(no)*. Caracalla's colleague was Geta Caesar, who had incurred damnatio memoriae. Daris restores *Imp. Ant*]*oni*(*no*), depending on my former dating of the text ca. 215.

16. The names in lines 8, 14, and 17 show that little is missing from the cognomina in this column. The blank here consequently implies a consulship requiring very few letters, such as that of 212, which appears frequently in **2** as *duobus cos*.

18. The first extant letter is probably *m*, but perhaps *b* or *o*. The next two look like *t* but could be *a*, *r*, or *s*.

Col. ii

. .[. . .].i kal augustas
Ɣ aurel theopropi
duobus aspris cos A.D. 212
——iul—— maximus
sepṭim[i]ano cos 190

p̣ṛef —— iul maximus
pretinace cos A.D. 192
iul eupranor
falcone cos 193
iul serenus
diḅi seuero cos 194
[a]ụrel sempr⟨o⟩n⟨i⟩us
ael s.[.]ọn
castri ulpius ṃ......
———— longinus ru[....].[
ante aurel neṃas
aurel sp[
aṛṛ.[
[ ].ruṭịcia cl[
Consulate 195?
iuḷ[
iụ[

ii 1. The name of the month has been corrected from one which was two or three letters shorter, perhaps *maias*; and *kal* appears from the odd loop on the left of the hasta to have been corrected from *id*. The character preceding *i* can be read as the numeral *V* (cf. the *u* of *maximus*, i 17) or less probably as *e* (cf. *falcone*, ii 9).

3–4. The fact that the date is not in sequence with those which follow indicates that this man was a duplicarius or sesquiplicarius, not a private.

4. The bar is drawn through *iul*.

6. Previously I read *prep* for the notation; *pr.p*: Daris. If the present reading is right, it implies a form of *praefectus*; and it is tempting to read the notations in this column as a unit—*praef(ect-) castri ante* [.].*ruticia*, though the final word is unclear. *castri* may be an error for *castrorum* but is perhaps better understood as "fort," "castellum." If the notations belong together, all the soldiers in lines 6–19 have the same assignment.

7. Read *pertinace*.

11. Read *diuo*. The numeral *ii* has been omitted after *seuero*.

13. Previously *sḷ*.[.]*ạn*, also in Daris. Possibly *sỵ*[*ri*]*ọn*?

14. For the case of the notation, if it is correctly read, see above on *pref*, line 6.

16. *Ante(opoli)*: Daris; but see on *pref*, line 6.

19. See on *pref*, line 6.

22. *Iu*[*l*(*ius*): Daris; but other names are possible.

Col. iii

.[
—— d[
—— p.[
————.[
roma.[
a
ḳạ[.]. ..[
Consulate
ofici .[
p[

———— ṣ[
aụ[
———— iụ[
Consulate
[ ]ịu[
auṛ[
One line lost
....[
iu[
———— .[

iii 2 and 3. There is a light horizontal stroke before each of these lines which differs from the strokes used elsewhere in this text to indicate availability for any duty. The purpose of these two strokes is not apparent.

2. The indentation of this line may indicate a consulship, though it is not as great as for the consulships in col. ii. *d*[*extro ii cos*], A.D. 196, would be suitable.

5–6. The notations here may belong together; and seem to be in a second hand. It is tempting to read *romae a kal n*(*ouembribus*).

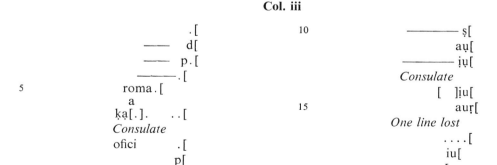

6

Partial Roster of the Coh. XX Palmyrenorum

PDur. 98 (inv. D. P. 11 recto) A.D. 218–219

Transcription and commentary: *Final Rep*. v, no. 98; *edidi*.

Facsimile of frag. a: ibid., plate 43.

The following are inaccurate and obsolete: (1.) Transcription of parts of frag. a ii, iii, and iv in *Rep*. v, p. 300 = *CPL* 333. (2.) Commentary in R. O. Fink, "The *Cohors XX Palmyrenorum*," *TAPA* 78 (1947) 164–65.

The classification of this text as a partial roster is assured by the absence of any notations except *ord* and the name of the centurion in the second line of the entry for each century, and by the small total number for each century, ranging from 52 to 58. This would give a total of 350 pedites at most for the six centuries, only about half the number which this cohort, a cohors equitata miliaria, should have had. On the other hand, the men in each century are divided by consulships, unlike the lists accompanying letters, where the names are in order of seniority but the dates of enlistment are not given.

It is certain that at least one column is missing before the present column i, because about ten names are lacking from the beginning of the century of Danymus. These, however, with the consulates, would fill only about half a column. What filled the upper half of the column and any which preceded it can only be guessed at. Possibly the equites preceded the pedites in this list, as on the verso (**27**). It is also clear that another column is missing at the end with about 20 names of the centuria Seleuciana and perhaps other material.

The purpose of the list is unknown.

The date is calculated on the basis of the fact that the earliest enlistments recorded here are for A.D. 193 (ii 24 and iv 18) while the latest are for 217 (v 28 and x 24). The latter are the terminus post quem, while the usual 25-year term starting in 193 would produce 218 as the date of discharge. Since, however, this is only a partial list, there may have been others in the cohort at the time who enlisted earlier or later than these dates. But **6** names men who are not found in **1** in spite of its much greater extent, and hence **6** should be the earlier of the two. It cannot be later than **1**, because in **1** the centuria Seleuciana has become the century of Castricius. Consequently 217–219 are the limits for the date of this text. It is probably very little earlier than **1**, for the centuria Malchiana is found in both, and it is unlikely that a century would be left without a centurion for a number of months.[1]

The verso, as said above, is **27**.

[1] It is worth noting that of the 19 consulates found here, 4 are represented by the junior consul: 193, C. Iulius Erucius Clarus in place of Q. Pompeius Sosius Falco; 200, C. Aufidius Victorinus instead of Ti. Claudius Severus Proculus; 201, M. Nonius Arrius Mucianus instead of L. Annius Fabianus; and 217, T. Messius Extricatus in place of C. Bruttius Praesens. All of the men omitted must have incurred damnatio memoriae, though the circumstances are not known. The case of Praesens is striking, for unless we assume that he was condemned by Caracalla, from whom he received the consulship, in the first three months of 217, his absence speaks for dating the text in the reign of Macrinus or early in Elagabal's. Similarly, the use of Erucius Clarus for 193 in this and all later Dura texts in contrast with Falco in **5** ii 9 seems to show that Falco was condemned by Elagabal and in any case puts **6** later than **5**.

(*Frag. a*)

Col. i

Century of Danymus
ạṇ[toniu]s maximus A.D. 196
anulino ii cos 199
aụṛẹl faustụs
ạgrippas themarsa
muciano cos 201
iadibelụṣ zebida
iul malchus
theobọlus gadde
zebidas zebida
geta seniore ii cos 203
mocimus bolani
iul antoninus
magnus uabalathi
cl zebida
cilone ii cos 204
monimus aufei
abidsemias pupli
maximus ermogeṇị
monimus monimi
abbedas nicaei
monimus salluma
charifas iuli
apro cos 207
zebidas barnaei
seuerus antonini
pompeiano cos 209
ael heliodorus
faustino cos 210
ael theodorus
b]ạṣṣus tiberini
].aeus ṃạlchi
messala cos 214
mocimus zebida
ịạdibelus ammaei
b]ạṛneus iaraḅ[ol-
aurel roṃ[
ṃocị[mus

Cf. **1** i 12–20; **2** vi 27–30; vii 1–15.
10. *s* of *cos* has been corrected from *r* or *a*.
36. *Roṃ[anus:* D.

Col. ii

ṭḥemarṣạṣ [iaraei
zabdibolụṣ [th]ẹ[me
aurel apọḷ[lon]ịus
laetọ ịị c̣os A.D. 215
iul bạṣsus
aurel marinus
aurel bargas
aurel demetrius
sabino ii cos 216
aurel malchus
aurel longinus
aurel calpurnius
aurel magnus
aurel malchụs
aurel apollinarius
aurel aprianus
bassus gora
aurel romanus
aurel bassus
aurel marinus
lv

7 marci muciano cọ[s 201
ord iul marcus
erucịọ c̣ḷ[aro co]ṣ 193
malc̣hus ẹ[
ṭerṭ[ullo cos 195
barṣemịạs bụḅ[
dextro i[i cos 196
abbas l..[
]ṣạṭụṛṇ[ino cos 198
]ḅas baraḅ[
]omo[

Cf. **2** x 1–28; xi 14–22; **8** ii 15–29.
27. *e* is possible instead of *u*, and *d* instead of the second *b*.
30.]..*ṣạṭụṛṇ[ino:* D; but the traces before the consul's name are the top of the *b* in the line below.

Col. iii

ḍomittiụṣ salman A.D. 201
abgarus iaraei
marinus seḷẹuci
nisamsus adḍẹị
ạụrel barchalbas
iaraeus zebida
iul salman
ħeliodorus zebidạ
seuero iii cos 202
iul domittius
iaraboles themaṛṣa
geta senịọṛe ii cos 203
marinus barathe
salmanes iamlichi
maris iarhaei
ualer malchi
cilone ii cos 204
iul soemus
mauelas abidadadi
antonino ii cos 205
zabdes malchi
zabdibolus hammạẹ[
apro et max[imo co]ṣ 207
zenodorus artẹṃịḍọṛị
faustino cọs 210
quintus iuliạṇ[u]s
ịul ṃenandrụṣ
duobus aspṛịṣ cos 212
cl tiberinus
iarhaboles ụdạṭḥ[i
⟦i⟧ulpius aṇṭọ[ninus
amạẹ[us zebida

Cf. **1** vi 21–32; vii 1–2 and 9–14; viii 1–16; **2** xii 6–28; xiii 4–28; **8** iii 7–10.

15. The *h* in *iarhaei* is unusual for this text. It seems possible that lines 15 through 20 are in a different hand.

Col. iv

aurel[
calpụ[rn]ịụṣ g̣aulianus
mamṃ[e]us bobe.[
aurel ma.h[..]s
sabino i[i] cos A.D. 216
domittius nicolaus
auṛel demetrius
aurel maximus
aurel domittius
aurel barlahas
aurel zabdas
aurel apollonius
aurel bassus
aurel flauius
lii

Y antonini uictorino cos 200
ord domittius antoninus
erucio c̣laro cos 193
malchus anani
tertuḷḷo cos 195
iul baṛ[h]ạḍadus
dextro ị[i] c̣ọs 196
malchus diog̣eṇị
zabdaathes ṃọcimi
anulino ii cos 199
demetrius bannaei
iulius ạpollonius
uictorino cos 200
....ụṃ.[ ]ṣ oga
muc̣ịạno cos 201
mamṃẹus b[e]ḷạcabi
mabog̣[e]uṣ[za]ọra
]s

Cf. **1** x 3–24; xi 1–26; **2** xxvii 2–14; **8** v 3.

2. Cf. *aurel cal*[in **1** ix 27.

3. *Marịṇus Bọbe*.[: D. The first vowel of the second name could be *a*.

16. The consul's name appears to have been written *uictorini*.

17. The last *n* has been corrected from *u*.

26. **1** xi 19 has *baṛ*[*n*]*ạẹi*; but see the apparatus there.

29. ...*u*...[: D.

Col. v

About five lines lost
bạ[
Consulate A.D. 202–215
aṇṭọ[
About three lines lost
.[
ạ[
iul ḅ[
aurẹl gerṃ[anus
cocceiụṣ s.[
iul haḍ.[
aurel hadṛịạ[nus
sabino i[i cos 216
aurel antọṇ[
aurel cyrillụṣ
aurel mạ[. . .]ị[
aurel .[.]ḷ[
aurel bạ[
aurel sạ[
ạ[ure]ḷ g̣[.].[
aurel g̣[
ẹxṭṛị[cato ii cos 217
abg̣aruṣ [themarsa
g̣ạḍḍẹ[s bore

Cf. **1** xv 11; xvi 1–3; **2** xxx 23; xxxi 14–16.
16. *Cocceian*[*u*]*s*.[*:* D.
19. *sabino i*[*i cos* is inserted in smaller letters between the lines.
20. *aurel* is corrected from *iul.*
26. Possibly *g̣ạ*[.

Frag. c

Col. vi

An unknown number of lines lost
Century of Marianus
m]ạḷc̣hụs[ ]..[
faụṣṭịṇ[o] c̣ọ[s A.D. 210
mo]cimus ṣ. . .[
duobu]ṣ ạspṛịṣ [co]ṣ 212
]ṣ ẓẹbịḍa
]ḍi
]us
]ọ.[.].[.]ṣ
]messạḷ[a] c̣ọs 214
]ạ[.]..ạ.n
].ṛ[.] s
]ṭḥẹ[m]ạṛsa
]ṣ

Col. vii

An unknown number of lines lost
]h[
[*Consulate?*]
ṭḥemarṣạ[s
[co]s
ạụṛ[el
[*Consulate*]
zaḅḍịḅ[olus
]ị[

6. *ḷ*.[*:* D; "Possibly *ḷạ*[*eto cos*: A.D. 215." But at least one other consulate intervenes (line 4 and possibly line 2) between this line and *messala cos*, A.D. 214, in vi 9. *g̣ṛ*[*ato cos*, 221, is too late. Actually the traces seem to be the top of the second *b* in line 7.
7. *zaḅ*..[*:* D.

Col. viii

One line lost
Frag. e
]ẹi
]..[
]..[..].
]i
]ḅẹi
]. cos
An unknown number of lines lost
Frag. d
]ạ
].
]x̣l.
Y m]ạlchiaṇạ [a]nulino ịị [cos A.D. 199

]ṛubaṭhus s . . [
tertullo c̣ọ[s 195
] . . . eus nisaṃs[-
sal]ṃanes tḥ[e]ṃe
dexṭṛọ ii cos 196
maṛị[nus] themarsa[
ṣạ[tu]ṛnino cos 198
thẹṃạ[rs]a . [ ] . . [

10. If this is a numeral, it cannot be the correct total, which was certainly 60 or more. The trace after the *l* may be a mark of punctuation, though there is none after other numerals in this text, but is probably an *i*.

12. Rubathus must have been acting commander of the century, for his date of enlistment (199) is not in sequence with the dates which follow.

Frag. b

Col. ix

One line lost
]c̣ọṣ A.D. 199–201
ṣạlmẹ[s] . . [
aụ[rel co]ḍdeus
ạbgạṛ[us t]ḥẹ[me]s
ọcbanẹṣ ạbiḍḷa[h]a
sẹ[l]eus ṃalc̣hi
]ạṣ
One line lost
geta seni]ọre ii [co]s 203
ma]lc̣ḥi
]nịṣạmsi
t]ḥẹmaṛṣa
aurel a]ntiochus
] . zebiḍa
cilo]ne ii cos 204
]narieus
] . us
marinu]ṣ maximi
cassiu]ṣ ṣạcona
marinu]ṣ luci
anton]ino ii cos 205
hammaeus o]gelị[
po]ṃpẹịano cos 209
b]ạraṭḥẹ
] . . [
] .

Cf. **1** xxvii 1–22; **2** i 7–9; ii–iv frag. a 3–4. The left ends of the first five lines in this column are on frag. c.

15. Probably *malchus zebida*. Cf. **1** xxvii 22–24.

Col. x

aurel marinụs A.D. 214
aurel flauius
cl hairạn
aurel monimus
iaraeus abgari
aurel marinus
iaraeus theoboli
laeto ii cos 215
aurel apolloniụs mesenus
aurel bassus
sabino ii cos 216
aurel muc̣ịạ[n]us
aurel paulụs
aurel alexa[nd]ṛus
aurel baṣịlẹus
aurel zinnẹ[..]ṣ
aurel heliọdorus
aurel antoninus
aurel liuianus
aurel addeụs
aurel marịnụs
alter marinụs
aurel barsemias
extric̣ạṭọ ịị c̣ọs 217
aurel zabdas
lviiii

tẹṛtụllo cos 195
ϒ seleucianạ ⟦ḍẹxṭr[o ii] c̣ọs⟧ 196
za]bdibolus malac̣heli
zabdi]bolus sạḍ[..].i
] .[ ].....s
]..[

Cf. **1** xxix 12–32; xxxi 2–13; xvi 15–18.
9. *aurel* is in the same hand as the rest of the text, *apollonius mesenus* in a different hand.
15. *baṛ.elus*?
25. Cf. *zabde* in **1** xxxi 13.
27. *dextro ii cos* is in the same line as *seleuciana*; *tertullo cos* has been crowded in close above in the same line.
28–29. Cf. *zaidibolus* and *zaiḍ*[in **1** xvi 16 and 18. In 29 possibly *sadachi*; cf. *Σαδάχ* in *PDur*. 49, line 5.

Col. xi

ulpịụṣ seuerus A.D. 203
i[ul]ịus [sa]lṃạn
c̣ịlone ii cos 204
abiḍmalchụs marosạ[
maxịṃụṣ [ho]ṭarei
iul hẹḷ[iodor]ụs
iul ạb[.....] s
bariçḅeḷus ḅạṣṣị
iade[u]s theṃ[a]ṛsa
dịụo antonino ii cos 205
iul bassus
ạurel mucianus
basṣụs barsimsi
albino cos 206
septimius heliodoṛ[
apro ẹṭ ṃaxiṃ[o cos 207
iul romanus
abbis marona
iaraeus barnaei
faustino cos 210
ịaraeus zebida
duobuṣ ạspriṣ [cos 212
themarsas nisamsi[
macriniụs maximi
mocimus ạṇtonini
messạḷạ c̣ọs 214
iaraboles ọbeạn
aurel gai
mocịmus anto[ni-
ạụṛẹḷ seleuc̣[
abdeus zabḅ[
aurel barsimṣ[us
iaraeus ṇịṣạṃṣ[-
fl deṃẹṭṛius[
aurel ḅ...[
aụṛẹ[l
ạ[

Cf. **1** xvii 3–18; xviii 4–24; **2** xxii 13–27; xxiii 5–26; **8** viii 1–26.
15. *Heliodoṛ[us:* D.
28. **1** xviii 16 seemingly has *aurel g]aius*.
30. *Seleuc̣[us:* D.
33. Apparently *ṇịṣạṃṣ*[corrected from *nisraei*; but there is a confusing stroke above the *m*. *Ṇịṣṛẹụ[s:* D.

7

Partial (?) Roster of the Coh. XX Palmyrenorum

PDur. 99 (inv. D. P. 55) ca. A.D. 218

Transcription and commentary: *Final Rep.* v, no. 99; *edidit* Gilliam.

Little can be said of this text except that it is part of a list of names which were divided by years of enlistment. Too little is preserved for certain classification as either a complete or a partial roster.

The hand resembles those of **6**, **47**, and **48**. That, and the possibility that it may be a fragment of **6**, are the basis of the dating.

The verso is blank.

Frag. a		**Frag. b**	**Frag. c**
]zebida .[		]. .s	].i
mẹsala co[s	A.D. 214	].aei	
]. . . . .[		]. .ẹs	
		]ṛịi[	

8

Annotated Partial Roster of the Coh. XX Palmyrenorum

PDur. 102 (inv. D. P. 16 recto) November 4, A.D. 222, to ca. 228

Transcription and commentary: *Final Rep.* v, no. 102; *edidi.*

Facsimile of cols. iv–vii: ibid., plate 46.

Mentioned in *CPL*, no. 338, but without a text.

The small number of men for each century, only a little more than in **6**, and the lack of the centurion's name, with his lieutenants' names, at the beginning of the roll for each century is evidence that this is a partial roster rather than a complete one. The inclusion of the dromedarii at the end of each century rather than at the end of the whole, as in **1** and **2**, suggests that this list did not comprise the equites and that what we have is, allowing for losses by damage, all there ever was.

It is further observable that the overwhelming majority of the names where it is possible to judge are accompanied by the horizontal bar. The only reasonably certain exceptions are iii 4, v 27, vii 4 and 10, viii 12, and ix 3 and 5. The list may accordingly have been one of pedites and dromedarii available for assignment to any task. It seems clear, too, that the puncta and other notations in words, such as *app*, were added from time to time and in effect canceled by a punctum or bar on their left when the soldier completed his assignment. The appearance of ϑ in iii 4, vi 13 and 22, and x 22 shows that the list also served for checking casualties, while the notation *sine dromon* in iii 5 and vii 22 and the cancellation of other names where the notations are missing (ii 8, iii 18 and perhaps 23, vi 29, and ix 20, with dates running from August to November) may imply a series of skirmishes.

Dating this text is difficult. The death of Aurelius Romanus (dromedarius, century of Danymus, enlistment A.D. 216) which is recorded in iii 4 seems to show that this list is later than **2**, A.D. 222, where in col. xliv 7 and 10 two Aurelii Romani, both of A.D. 216, appear as dromedarii of this century. On the other hand, in **2** xliv 19 Domitius Nicolaus is also a dromedarius, though not in **1** x 4, **6** iv 6, or the present text, col. v 3. His service as dromedarius may, however, have been temporary; and if **8** is in fact later than **2**, then the date in ix 20 fixes the terminus post quem of this text at November 4, 222. The terminus ante quem would ordinarily be provided by the verso, **92**, which is certainly earlier than December 225; but the Mambogeus whose name is canceled in **8** iii 18 must be the same as the Mombogeus Barnebus of **92** v 14, for in both lists the man belongs to the century of Marcus and is preceded by Gerelius Asclepiades and followed by Aurelius Antoninus and Domitius Nicolaus. If then the cancellation of Mambogeus' name means that he is dead, as in the case of the names canceled in iii 4 and vi 13 and 22, **8** must be later than **92**. The name in ii 8, however, seems to have been canceled without the notation ϑ for death; and the same may have been true of Mambogeus and two other canceled names (vi 29 and ix 20) where evidence concerning the theta is missing. But if Mambogeus was removed from this list for another reason than death, **8** may still be earlier than **92**. Calculation from the only other evidence available, the dates of enlistment, which begin with A.D. 203 in **8** (iii 7 and v 9), leads to A.D. 228 as a reasonable terminus ante quem.

The verso, as stated, is **92**.

Col. i

Century of Danymus

].e..[
]bbaei [
]......[
]..[
]..[.]ṣa [
].[

Col. ii

Century of Danymus

]..[ ].rius A.D. 214
]..[.].[ ]iṃ[.]us
]ṃe..[.]bị.[

au]ṛel ḅ[e]lạc̣ạ[b]ụs
——— a]ụrel ṛomạ[nu]s
].[ ] aure[l] f̣ḷ.[ ]
●...[———]- [a]ụṛẹḷ ḥẹ[
●———⟦[a]ụṛẹḷ[ ]⟧].[..]..[
[ ]ṃọc̣iṃus [barne-
.-[——— aur]ẹ[l] deṃ[e]ṭrius
].[a]ụṛẹḷ baṣ[sus]
●——— ạụṛẹḷ sos[si]ạṇ[u]ṣ ● z
[———]- ạurel gẹṛmạṇus
[———]- ḅ..ba.[..]d......[
[t]hẹṃạ[rs]ạs iar[hae]i
[ ]ṃuc̣ia[n]us[zabbae]i
aur]el[apolloniu]s
].[ ]. ṃaṛ[i]nus
them]arṣ[as barne]ḅ[us
]..[
ḷ[aeto ii cos 215
———]- ạụṛel ḍ[
c]laụḍị[us
a]ụṛ[el
].[
].[ ].[
]..[ ]ṇ[
sạ[bi]no [ii c]ọs 216
au]ṛẹl [m]ạ[l]c̣ḥụṣ
aur]ẹ[l
aur]ẹḷ[

Cf. **2** ix 23–29; x 1–15; **6** i 36–37; ii 1–10.

12. For the *z* after the name cf. on **1** xxxv 17.

Col. iii

]p̣ius
]ṣạbiṇọ iị [c]ọs A.D. 216
———]- ạ[urel] c̣ạlpurṇị[us
ϑ ⟦ạ[urel] romạ[nus]⟧] . kal sẹp̣ Aug. 14–31
——— ạ[urel] addaeus[sin]ẹ dromon
lxiii

ϒ ma]ṛc̣i gẹṭa seniore ii [c]os 203
———]- seleucus barbaeṣ[am]ẹn
———]●—— salmanes iamlịc̣[h]ị
]ṃạris iaṛḥaei
a]ụrel sentian[u]ṣ
]ụlp̣ịụṣ maṛịṇụ[s]

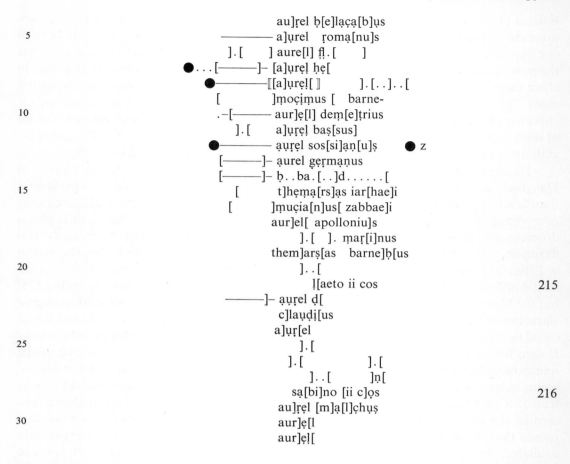

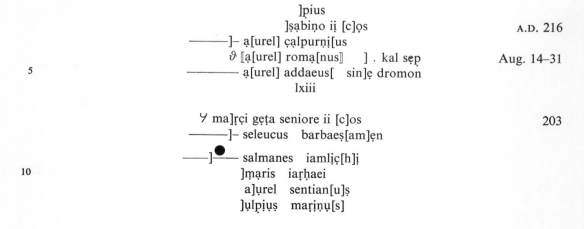

———]- ṇịsraeus ṃạḷẹ[
ciḷọ[n]ẹ ị[i cos   A.D. 204
——]—— ị[u]l[i]ụs c̣ṛ[i]ṣp[inus
——]—— gẹṛelius ạ[s]clep̣[iades
]ạpp ——— salmanes ṣị[gna
——]-[—⟦ mam]bogẹụ[s barnebus ⟧] ḳạl oc̣t   Sept. 14–Oct. 1
].[
About two lines lost
]..[
]. kal ọc̣ṭọbṛ[Sept. 14–30

Cf. **1** vi 32–33; vii 2 and 17; **2** xliv 5–8; xii 20–31; **6** iii 14–17; **92** v 12–14.

1. Probably *aurel ulpius*.

2. The date is repeated because the men who follow are *dromedarii*, not infantry.

4. ϑ indicates the death of the person named. The date is in another hand.

5. The notation *sine dromon(e)* also occurs in vii 22. This is the only known testimony to the use of this word in Latin in the sense of "dromedary", for which *dromas* was the usual term. For the meaning, cf. the *amisit equum* entries in **83** and Gilliam's commentary on *PDur*. 97.

16. **92** v 13 has *g̣ạleris*; but **2** xii 27 reads the same as this text.

17, 18, 23. The notation *app* and the dates are in the same hand as the date in line 4.

18. ⟦*[mam]bogẹụ[s]*⟧*:* D; but cf. **92** v 14. The date and the cancellation of the name imply the man's death. Cf. line 4 above.

23. See preceding note on 18.

Col. iv

].ṣ -[——— a]ụrel ạṇ[to]ṇịṇụs   A.D. 214
-[——— be]ḷ[a]cabụṣ ị[arha]ei
]ṣ[a]lṃ[a]n
-[——— aurel a]ụiḍạs
———[- bo]l[i]aḍạeus ịarhaei
].[azi]ẓụṣ[aa]ṭḥ[ibe]ḷị
[iarhaeus z]eḅiḍạ
[m]arini
-[———]si[..]ṣ
.[ ].[ ].
[ ].sụṣ[
zen]ọbiụṣ
]ḍemetriuṣ
-[——— he]l[i]ọdori
—[—— mo]cimus
—[——

Cf. **1** ix 1–6; **2** xiv 10–17 and 25–26; **92** v 15.

11. Probably *bassus*; cf. **2** xiv 25.

12. Cf. **2** xiv 26: *]zenobi*, where the loss of the letters *us* after the *i* is possible.

Col. v

-]—[——].[A.D. 216
—]—— ạ[ ]..ḥ[.].[
—— ṇs ——— doṃ[i]ṭtius nị[colaus
ḍṛom mẹ[ssala cos   214

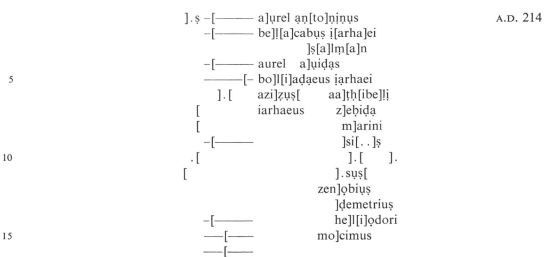

——●—— aurel maṛ[inus
sabiṇ[o ii cos 216
———— aur[el] zabḍịḅ[ol-
[ ] [ ]l.[
Ꮍ mariani gẹta sẹṇị[ore ii cos 203
——●—— aelius hẹṛa[cl-
——●—— tḥemeṣ ṃal[chi
cilọ[n]e [ii cos 204
——●—— abiḍlạ[ha]ṣ ma[ximi
——●—— iulius abiḍ[semias
——●—— ṃ[a]ximụ[s z]aọ[ra
]ḍ[ispo]sit —.e..— alex̣[andrus ....us]
——●—— mariṇ[us ...ron]
—]●—— acibạ[s bora
ḍ[iuo antonino ii cos 205
—]●—— iulius bạssus
——]—— anto[ ]siṇ[
aḷ[bino cos 206
——]—— nisaṃ[sus
——]—— anṭ[
—]●—— ...[
——]—— aụṛ[el
]..[ ].[ ]ḷ[
——]—— ụ[
—]●—— i.[
—]●—[——].[

Cf. **1** x 4; xxii 4–15; **2** xvii 14–26; **6** iv 6; **92** v 18; iii 6.
3. The notation is in another hand.
8.]*l*.[is a numeral, part of the total for the century.
14. *Abiḍ[semia:* D.
16. The notations are in another hand. *Alex̣[andrus:* D.
17. *Mariṇ[us:* D.

Col. vi

f̣[austin]o coṣ A.D. 210
—]-[—— ạdḍạẹus [maccaei]
——●—— iuliu[s] tḥẹ[m]ạṛsa
———— mạ[lc]ḥus uạḅạlathi
——●—— siḷ[ua]nus sadalathi
duobus aspriṣ c̣[os 212
]ạpp̣ —[—]— iar[h]ạeus salman

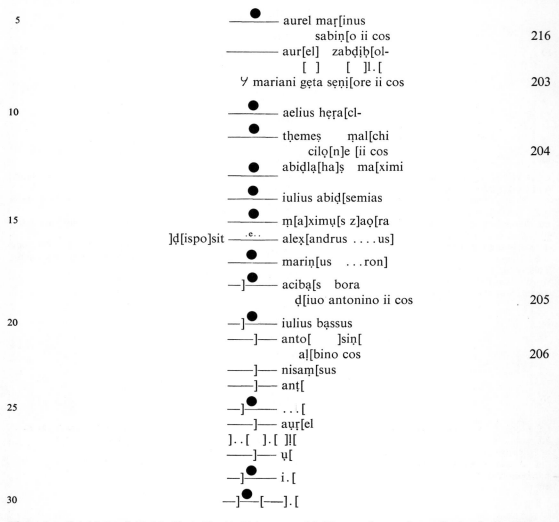

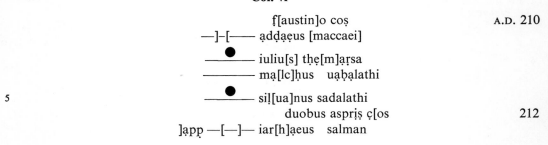

—[—]— zebidas ị[a]ṛhaei
—●— habbis ọg̣ẹli
messala cos A.D. 214
—●— claudius milens
—●— ạ[ur]el mannạeus
—ϑ— ⟦ạ[u]ṛel domittị[us]⟧
—●— aelius aurelị[u]s[
● app —[—]— iulius maṛ[in]ụs
● ạpp —[—]— bạssụ[s] ṇạṣṣ[i]ḅẹḷi
[———]- [t]ḥẹmes helịọḍọr[
[———]- ạilạ[m]is ḅ[e]lasur
● ạpp [———]- [aure]ḷ mạnnuṣ
● ạp[p ———]- iuḷiuṣ gaịanus
]ạnṭoniuṣ[ ]ụs
——]—ϑ—⟦ aurel ṃ[. .].suṣ⟧
——]— ịulius ṣ[a]binụ[s
——]— mazạb[anas
——]— ạurel[
——]— ṭḥẹ[
One line lost
]aurẹ[l
——]·—⟦ aur[el]⟧
——]— uạ[

Cf. **1** xxiii 16; xxiv 1–7; **2** xviii 23–25; xix 12–16; **92** v 20.

2. *Aḍḍạẹus*[*:* D.

4. A punctum written over the line in the notations has been erased.

7, 15–16, 19–20. All the notations are in another hand, the same one as in preceding columns.

12. *Aurel Man.deus:* D.

22. The initial could be *n. ṇ*[*isa*]*ṃsuṣ*?

Col. vii

]ṣ[
]ọ[
● nṣ —[——]n[u]ṣ
[aur]ẹl romanus A.D. 216
— .[.]ḍ.[.]ạn iṇ . .erapu[—— aur]ẹl abịdlah[a]s
—●[—— aur]el l[u]cịụs
]nṣ —[——] a[u]rel ṃọcimus
—[——] aurel ọḥrasus
[—]—— aurel ṃaximus

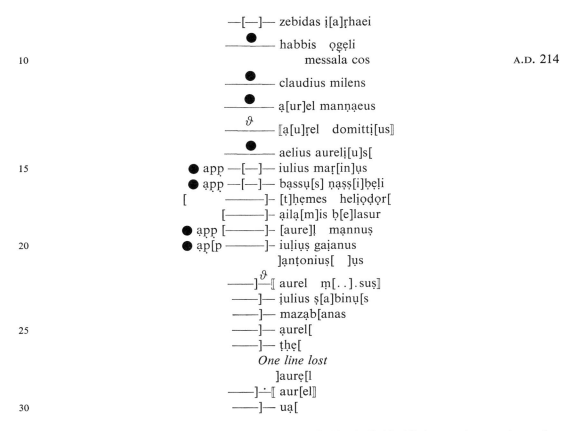

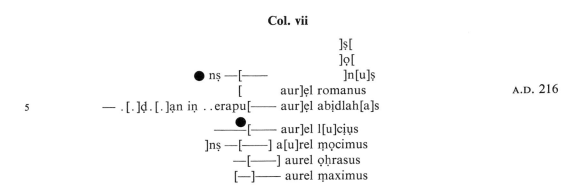

]ḍ . . [ ]s . [.] . [.] . ḍza . ro ạụrel barbaesomen
———●——— ạ[ure]l mariṇ[u]s
———●——— ạ[ur]ẹḷ silu[anu]ṣ
———●——— aurel iarhaboles
———●——— auṛẹl [d]omiṭtius
[ ] ii cọs
———●——— ạ[ur]ẹl m]aṛọṇ[a
ḍ[ro]ṃ fauṣtịṇo cos 210
———●——— auṛẹ[l] ṣ[i]luạṇụ[s]
[du]ọḅus aspris cos 212
———●——— ḥ . . . [ ]ṣ . [ ]ṣ[ ]
mes]ṣa[la] cos 214
——— . [h]eraclas sine ḍṛomo
[laeto] ịị cos ? 215?
———●[— g]aiaṇus
lxii⟦ii⟧

Century of Antoninus prior

Ɣ [ ] . [
] . . [—]●[—] [
]aro . . [
] . r[

Cf. **2** xx 19–22; xxi 5–9; xliv 27–28; **92** v 21.

5 and 10. The notations are in another hand. Neither has been satisfactorily read.

7. *ns* is in a different hand from the text and the other notations.

15.]*ii cọs:* D. The space admits only a very short name. *fusco*, A.D. 225, would serve, but is later by five years than any other date in the text.

22. For the notation see above on **8** iii 5.

26. The century of Antoninus prior is the same as the centuria Seleuciana, **6** ii–iii, and the century of Castricius, **1** xvi–xx.

Col. viii

——[— iadaeus them]ạṛṣạ[
ḍ[iuo anto]nino ii cos A.D. 205
———●——— ịulius [bassu]ṣ
remaṇṣ[. .]. . .——— ạurel[muci]anus
[i]ulius[ ] . ṇ[.]eus
———●——— ḅassụ[s ba]rṣịmsi

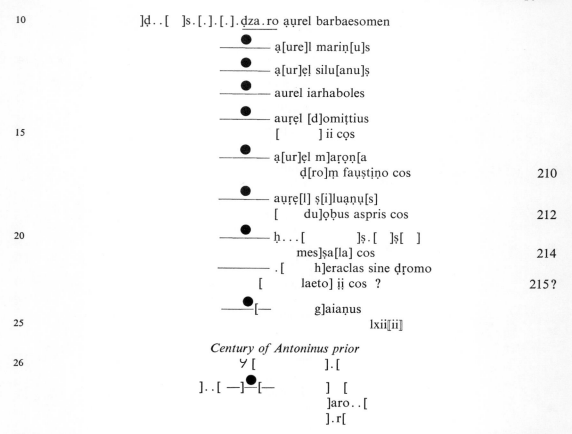

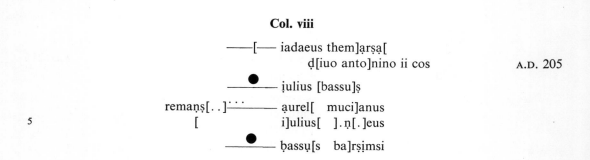

ạp[ro] ç̣os A.D. 207
●——— ịụ[liu]s ṛomanụṣ
[——]— ḥabḅiṣ ṃaronạ
.. [——]— iarhaeus ḅ[arn]a[e]i
p̣[o]mp̣[e]ị[an]ọ cos 209
[ ]. iulius romanus
ḍuobus asp̣ṛị[s c]ọṣ 212
app [———]- ṭḥẹṃes zẹbiḍạ
●——— tḥemarsạ[s] ṇisạṃsi
messạḷa ç̣os 214
●——— ạ[u]rel ṃạgṇụṣ
———]- themarṣas ṭḥ[e]ṃẹ
———]- aurel ṃuciạ[nus
———]- ạbdạeus ẓabḍ[
—.[–]——— ạurel bạṛs[imsus
● ạp̣[p –]——— mocimụs ma.[
● ạpp̣ [–]——— iu[liu]s ma..[
[——]— ịạ[r]ḥae[u]s tḥ[
[——]— ḟḷauius[
—]—— aureḷ ḅ[
———]- aụṛẹ[l
———]- aụṛ[el
——]— ạụṛẹḷ[
———]- ạ[u]ṛẹ[l
]ạụ[rel
]..[

Cf. **1** xvii 18; xviii 7–10; **2** xxiii 5, 15–16, and 23–26; **6** xi 9–36; **92** iii 13–14; vi 4.

4. *remans(it)*: "remained behind" for good reasons. Cf. **66** b ii 6: *aeger remansit.*

4, 14, 22–23. The notations are in the second hand.

9. **6** xi 18 has *abbis*; but the traces here show more than *a* before the first *b*. Cf. *habbis ogeli* in vi 9.

20 *abdaeus* is in a different hand. **6** xi 31 seems to have *zabḅ*[.

23. Either *marinus* or *maximus* is possible.

25. *flauius demetrius*? Cf. **6** xi 34.

Col. ix

au]ṛẹl ....[
——]— ạụ[re]ḷ[ ].ạẹ.heus
].[ ]ạ[ ]us c.[ ]●
a]el[iu]s ge.[...]s ●
]..[i]ụḷius ua[b]ạḷạ[t]ḥụṣ
]....[.]eus ṭ[he]ṃạṛsạ[

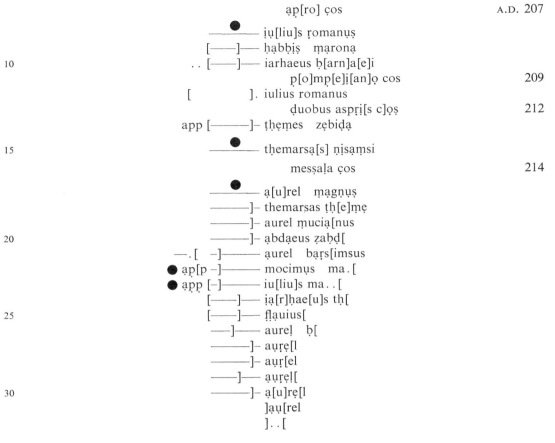

laẹṭ[o ii] cos A.D. 215
———— ạụreḷ marịnus
a]ụṛẹ[l].eus
]ạureḷ m.l[.]abiṃị
● app ———— aụṛ[el].[
●[ ].———[– ro]manus ḅarsimsi
sabino ii cos[216
.[ ].[———]– ạ[u]ṛẹḷ deṃetri[u]ṣ[
⟦. . .⟧———— ạụrẹ[l]ṣ[u]ṃṃạṛ[es
⟦. .⟧——●—— ạurel heliọḍ[o]ṛus
——●[— aur]ẹḷ basṣ[u]s
–[———] aurẹl demẹṭ[rius
[ ] ạụrẹḷ romanụṣ
[ ]⟦aụṛel barçha[⟧ pri]die n nouembr Nov. 4
——]˙— aurel marinus
] ẹxtṛicato ịị [co]s 217
——]— auṛẹl l[u]ciụṣ
c]omazọṇ[t]ẹ [ii co]s 220
a]urel iulius
dṛọṃ ḍụ[o]ḅ[us aspris cos 212
ma]criṇ[ius] ṃạx[imi
] ṣạḅiṇ[o i]ị [cos 216
].[

Cf. **1** xx 3–6; **2** xxv 13–24; xlv 6–8.
6. Possibly *iarhaeus*.
11 and 20. The notations are in the second hand.
20. *barchalba*? On the date see above on **8** iii 4 and 18.

Col. x

Century of Antoninus posterior

ϒ [
–[———
–[———
[ ].[
———— ạ[
[ ].[
———— ịạ[
—● ṇs ———— .[
[———]– [
●[———]– ḅ[
]ẹger. .[–]–[–]p̣— .[

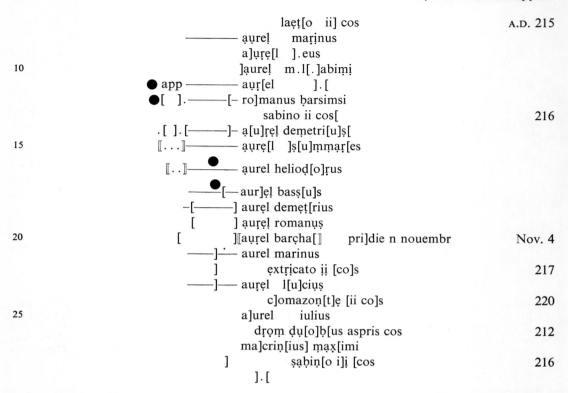

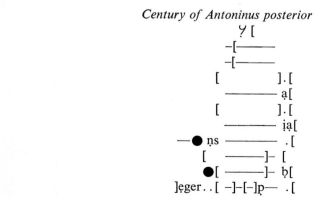

–[–]nṣ ——— .[

—●.[———]– .[

Consulate? A.D. 208?

–[–]ṇṣ ——— h[

—●— flạ[u-

Consulate? 209?

—●— ag[

—[———]– iulị[

Consulate? 210?

—]●— mạ[

—]●— ba.[

—●— ṃ[

Consulate? duobus aspris? 212?

—●[—]—ϑ— .[

Cf. perhaps **1** xiii 6–11; **2** xxvii 23–26; **92** vi 11. See on 15–16.

11. The notation is in the second hand. Its meaning is not known. R. W. Davies, *BASP* 5 (1968) 32, suggests *a*]*eger* for the beginning of the notation.

13–14. The spacing suggests a consulate between these lines. A.D. 208?

15–16. Consulate between these lines? A.D. 209? *fla*[*u*- in 15 may be *flauius flauianus*: **1** xiii 8; **2** xxviii 25. *h*[in 14 would then be *heliodorus apolloni*: **1** xiii 6; **2** xxviii 23. Both enlisted in A.D. 208. *ag*[*rippas them*- (**1** xiii 11) and *iuli*[*us romanus* (**1** xiii 12) belong to the year 209.

17–18. Consulate between these lines? A.D. 210?

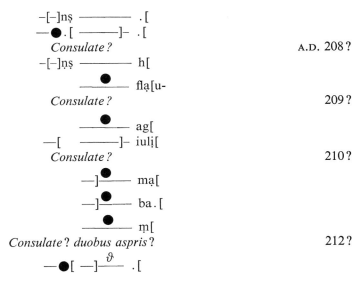

Special Lists

9

Duty Roster of the Legio III Cyrenaica

PGenLat. 1 verso, part v — A.D. 90–96
P. lat. 1, Bibliothèque publique et universitaire, Genève

Transcription, facsimile, and commentary:

1. J. Nicole and Ch. Morel, *Archives militaires du Ier siècle* (Genève 1900); cited as **ArM**.
2. *ChLA* I, no. 7, a and b, pp. 12–18.

Commentary (selected list):

1. H. Blümner, "Aus den Akten eines römisches Militärarchives in Ägypten," *Neue Jahrbücher für das klassische Altertum* 5 (1900) 432–43.
2. R. Cagnat, "J. Nicole et Ch. Morel. Archives militaires du 1er siècle," *Journal des Savants*, 1900, pp. 375–82.
3. E. Espérandieu, "Observations sur le papyrus latin de Genève no. 1," *CRAI*, 1900, ii, pp. 442–58.
4. Lesquier, 138–42, 228–32, 244, and 248–49.
5. Marichal, *Solde* 403–12.
6. Th. Mommsen, "Ägyptische Legionäre," *Hermes* 35 (1900) 442–52 (= *Gesammelte Schriften* 6.118–27).
7. A. von Premerstein, "Die Buchführung einer ägyptischen Legionsabteilung," *Klio* 3 (1903) 1–46.
8. Wilcken, *Grundzüge*, pp. 369, 393, 396–98.

Text: *CPL*, no. 106, v, pp. 212–14, and Daris, no. 10 (6), reproduce the text of *ChLA* except that both make two lines of some entries, such as *d decri* ꓘ (line 8), which are a single line in the original. Daris sometimes omits dots which indicate traces of letters.

The nature of this text is self-evident. It is what is known in the American armed forces as a "duty roster"; and its purpose is adequately described by Vegetius (2.19):

> cotidianas etiam in pace uigilias item excubitum siue agrarias de omnibus centuriis et contuberniis uicissim milites faciunt. ut ne quis contra iustitiam praegrauetur aut alicui praestetur immunitas, nomina eorum qui uices suas fecerunt breuibus inseruntur. quando quis commeatum acceperit uel quot dierum adnotatur in breuibus.

The commentaries cited agree that this table is the complement of **58**, in which col. ii concludes with 31 men available for any assignment. These are the first 31 of col. a in the present text, whose names are all in capitals. The last five names were added in a mixture of capitals and cursive at some time after the blank table was drawn up. At least three hands wrote the dates in cursive at the top; and the notations on successive days following each man's name are all in cursive and in several hands.

58 i 1 shows that these men belonged to the leg. III Cyrenaica.

The use of the name *domitianus* for October is evidence that this table was in use during the latter half of Domitian's reign; but fortunately it is not necessary to become involved in the question of the exact year when the new name was adopted. This is the verso of the papyrus; and it is obvious that the two pieces (Marichal's a and b) which form the present sheet were put together without regard for the texts which they bore on the recto in order to provide material for part IV and the present V. The latest date in part II is September 19, 87; and Marichal would therefore date part V to October 1–10, 87 (*ChLA*, p. 18, on V 1–10; *Solde* 405–9), on the ground that II and V belong together as parts of the same set of records, II accounting for men on detached service away from the camp and V recording the assignments of the munifices. This is attractive; but see **10** for a discussion of part II, and note that in **10** 25 the month is still called "October" on September 19, 87. In any case, there is a later date on the recto of this papyrus: part III is clearly dated A.D. 90; and however we interpret it (see **37**), it must indicate that the recto of that piece was scrapped in that year. And the fact remains that the two rectos were treated as waste paper in gluing them together in order to use the verso. A.D. 90 seems therefore to be a reasonable terminus post quem; and since Domitian was not killed until September 18, 96, it is possible, though unlikely, that the news of his death had not reached Alexandria by October 10 and that the table was being used in that year.

The recto of this papyrus is occupied by **10**, **37**, and **68**.

	a	b	c	d	e
1.		k domitia[	vi nonas[domitianas[	v nonạs[domitia[	iv no dọm[
2.	C ḌỌMỊṬỊVS CE[LE]R[ ]. .	ṛ[ ]	[		]
3.	C AẸṂILIVS VALẸṆṢ[ ]. .	[ ]g[.]e	ornatus	heli	———
4.	C IV[LI]VS VẠLẸṆS	harena	phal	ad cuṇic	ụḷ cal
5.	L IVLIVṢ OC.ỴIANỴṢ .	———	[		]
6.	P CLODIVS ṢẸCVNḌ[VS]	pro	quṇị	ta	ṇe
7.	M ARRIVS ṆIGẸṚ			in Ƴ	
8.	L SEXTILIV[S] G[E]RṂẠNỴ[S]	sta por	spẹcḷat	ballio	phal
9.	C IVLIVS ḶO[. .].[ ]		phal	specula	
10.	Q CASSIVS ḌỌ[R]VS . .	insula			
11.	C IVLIVS LONGỴṢ SIDO	pro	quin	ta	ṇe
12.	C IVLIVS LONGVS ẠṂISO	———		exit cu	m asin
13.	T FLAVIVS PRISCVṢ			ṛ[.]. .	
14.	T FLAVIVS NIGẸṚ	de.se.se	triḅ	———	———
15.	M ANTỌṆỊ[V]Ṣ CṚỊ[SP]V[S]	ballio	fercla	ụịḷ. .ṛ.	paganọ cultus
16.	Ṃ NỴM[. .].VỊVṢ. .[	]	. . .cs ạndriṇi	[ ]	
17.	Ṃ PEṬṚ[[ṆỊVṢ .[	]	pr. .ụṣ ạṃ.ọc̣ụḷa	ḍḅ. Ƴ	ballio
18.	. DỊR. .[. .]ẠṂVṢ.[	].ṛe	—[—		—]—

f	g	h	k	m	n	
iii no dmi[	pr no do[	nonis dom[i]ti[	ỵiii idụṣ[domitian[	vii idus doṃ[	vi idus dọṃ[	(1)
s[..]ṛ	[ ]	[ ]		b pref com	C	(2)
———	[ ]	go..[.]s	ạrma ṃẹṇṭạ	baḷlio	peç.[	(3)
arma ṃeṇtar	arma menaṛ	baḷliọ	gạḷẹari ato	in Ꮍ	ba[llio	(4)
in Ꮍ	baḷlio	sta prin cịpis	uia nico	in Ꮍ	pạ.[	(5)
ṣio	[ ]	sta por	calceṃ	cal heḷ[i]	—[—	(6)
strig[i]s	strigis	strigis	strigis	strigiṣ	ṣṭ[	(7)
d d[ecr]ị Ꮍ	d˙ decri Ꮍ	d decri Ꮍ	d decri Ꮍ	d deçṛi [Ꮍ]	d deç[ri Ꮍ	(8)
ṣeṛen Ꮍ	seren Ꮍ	sereni Ꮍ	sereni Ꮍ	sereni Ꮍ	ser[eni Ꮍ	(9)
					çạ[	(10)
sio	in Ꮍ heli	———	———		in[	(11)
ṃịṣṣ.[ ].	ịṇ..				[	(12)
stati[o]ṇ ad .eṛẹnu					[	(13)
———	———	———	———	———	[	(14)
in Ꮍ	.[.]..	ṣṣçụṃ ọṣ	ṭṛ	———	[	(15)
in Ꮍ	in Ꮍ		uia nico	in Ꮍ	[	(16)
ballio	pro	quin	ta n	ẹṣị[o		(17)
[–]—[—]	———	———	——— [	].[		(18)

	a	b	c	d	e
19.	Ç AEMILIVS[ ]. [	]	ạrạ. . . –[–	– –]–	———
20.	C V.Ḷ.Ṛ.Ẋ[. .]. . .Ṣ.Ṣ	cum pilọ[	]ḷụṇ	[ ]. [ ]. .	[ ]
21.	. FLAVIỤṢ[ ]. [	]	[	]	b[.]. . [ ] a[.]. [
22.	Q FABIVṢ ÇAPṬ[ ]	ḅaḷḷio	stạ por[	]	bạḷ[io]
23.	A MẠṚ[I]ỴṢ ÇḶẸMEN[S]	ẹx̣it in	ḍịṃ. . .us	aẹg	
24.	Ḷ VALERIVS FELIX	ç.çḥ	———	[ ].	[—]–[—
25.	C CERFICIVS FVSCVS[	]	[	]. . [ ]	[ ]ịạ.
26.	Ç FV.Ģ. . . . . .ṚÇ. .		[	].niụ. . [	]
27.	L CAL. . [ ].ỴS	[	]. [ ]	.peçụạ	
28.	Q ANṆỊỴ[S]. [ ]	scopari	us	[ ]	
29.	Ṗ VX̣Ị.NỴ[S].O	sç[o]pạ in Ꮍ		[	]ẹṣ
30.	M LONGINV[S]sus			ṣ. [.]a	[
31.	M DOMITIVs[ ]. . ạṭo		. . .	. . exit	ạd f̣ṛụṃ
32.	M LONGInuṣ ap[. . .]. [ ]		ṃ	ḥ . .	
33.	M iuLius FeLịx	çọme	ss ——	———	———
34.	t fLauius uale. . .				
35.	c sossius celer [			]	
36.	L uịNçLẹịus serenus	[	]		
37.	M iVLIVs LOnGVs				

f	g	h	k	m	n	
–[———]	p̣ṛọ	quin	tanẹ	sị[o		(19)
ḍ ḍ[ecri] Y	d ḍecrị Y	d decri Y	d ḍeç[ri Y	]ṣ[.].[		(20)
ba[l]ḷi[o]]..	ballio	ṣ[t]a pọṛ eṭọṛ	...[..a[			(21)
baḷ[io]	ḅạ[ll]iọ	baḷli[o]	ḅạḷli[o]	ḅ[allio		(22)
				[		(23)
]———	———	———	———[–			(24)
stạ [p]ọṛ			.[.]..ạ[			(25)
iḍ.[..].	in Y	arṃa ṃẹṇṭạ	–[——]–[–	—]—[—		(26)
[	]	sta pr[i] c[ipis]	uia [n]ịc[o]	ạ[		(27)
[	]	[				(28)
[	]	ṣṭạ... [				(29)
	]	.[.].[	]	[		(30)
[e]ṇtụm	ṇeap	ạ ...	.ṛo	[		(31)
	ụicạḷ stercus..	———	———	[		(32)
———	sta por	———	———	[		(33)
		...		[		(34)
				[		(35)
				[		(36)
				[		(37)

For lack of time I was unable to study this text in the original at Geneva. The present revision was made from a new photograph. In order to avoid confusion with the Roman numerals of the five parts of this papyrus, I have assigned Arabic numerals to the lines, and lower-case letters to the columns, omitting the letters *i*, *j*, and *l* because of their resemblance to numerals.

1 **b.** First hand. *k(alendis) domitia[nis]*. **c.** First hand. *nonas:* ArM; *nonis*: ChLA; *domitiani*: ArM and ChLA. **d.** Second hand. *domitia(nas)*. **e.** Third hand. *no(nas) dom(itianas)*. **f.** Third hand. *no(nas) d⟨o⟩mi-(tianas)*. **g.** Fourth hand. *pr(idie) no(nas) dom(itianas)*. **h.** Fourth hand. *domit*[: ChLA. **k.** Fourth hand? *domitiani*: ArM and ChLA. **m.** Fifth hand? **n.** Fifth hand? *dọ*[: ChLA.

2 **a.** *ÇE[LẸR]:* ChLA. The first name looks like *DOMCIIVS*; but cf. 31 a. **a**, **b**, and **f**. The photograph shows traces of letters here; but not enough to read. Possibly *a* or *r* in col. b. The traces may be remains of an earlier text. Previous editors offer no readings. **f.** Edd.: no reading. **m**, **n.** *b(eneficiarius) pref(ecti) com-(meatu):* ArM; *b(eneficio)*, *com(meatus)*, *C(ommeatus):* Premerstein. "On leave by the kindness of the prefect"—presumably the praefectus castrorum; hardly the Prefect of Egypt. On the praefectus castrorum see now J. F. Gilliam, "The Veterans and *Praefectus Castrorum* of the *II Traiana* in A.D. 157," *AJP* 77 (1956) 359–75.

3 **a.** *VALẸ[NṢ]:* ChLA. **b.** Edd.: no reading. **c–d.** "Working on Helius' parade (?) uniform." Cf. 6 m. Premerstein argues, p. 21, that Helius was senior centurion of a maniple of which the present century was the second half. Helius' rank as centurion is explicit in 11 g. The bars in **e** and **f** may indicate the continuation of the same assignment, but more probably denote exemption from duties. Cf. line 14. Repetitions and continuations seem to be shown as in lines 6 and 7. Blank squares probably mean that the man was available but was not assigned any special duties or, line 10, that he was not in the camp. **h.** *gọṣṣ:* ArM; *gon.i:* Premerstein; *gosṣ*[..]..: ChLA. Marichal hazards a guess: "perhaps *Gossipion*, Pliny *Hist. Nat.* XIX, 2, 6, 'cotton' from Egypt, survey of the cotton's harvest?" The reading, and hence the meaning, remains a mystery. At the beginning *gon*, *gosi*, or *goss* are all possible, though the *s* is very doubtful; and at the end the top of the *s* runs over into col. k. There is also a good possibility that the whole entry is a continuation of a word or phrase begun in col. g. Cf. 12 d, 28 b and 33 b. **k.** *armamenta:* ArM; *arma/metor:* ChLA, "to be read *armame(n)tor(ium)*, variant of *armamentarium*?" "Working on gear" or "in the armory." **m** (and elsewhere). Premerstein first explained *ballio* as *balneo*—"on bath duty." Cf. **47** ii 9: *missus lig(nator) balnei mil(es) i.* **n.** *ḥeḷ:* ArM; *in* Y: ChLA, comparing 16 m. The reading is quite uncertain; but perhaps cf. *pecua* in 27 d.

4 **a.** *VAL[EN]S:* ArM; *IVḶỊVS VAL[E]ṆS:* ChLA. **b.** *harena:* ArM; *harena* Y*:* ChLA. The stroke which is interpreted as the centuria-symbol appears actually to be the lower right-hand stroke of the *a*, as in *ta*, 6 d. "Digging sand" or "working in the arena"? **c.** ArM Morel: *phal(aricis)* or *phal(is)*, less probably *phal(aris)*. This entry recurs in 8 e and 9 c; but there is no clue to a really convincing explanation. **d**, **e.** In d, *cunic(ulos):* ArM Morel; *clinici:* Nicole; *cunic* Y*:* Premerstein. In e, *cal(cem):* Morel; *cal(ceamenta):* Lesquier, p. 232 n. Actually *ad cunicul(os) cal(carios)* or *cal(cis):* "at the limestone quarries" or "at the lime-kilns." For the shape of the first *l* cf. *ballio* in 3 m, *cal heli* in 6 m, and *ballio* in 17 f and 22 g. **f**, **g.** *armamenta:* ArM; *armamentạ*, *armamentar;* ChLA, "the ending *r* is certain" in col. g but not in f. In both, however, the *r* runs into the following column; and in g the *t* is missing. **h.** *ba[l]lio:* edd. **k.** *galeariatu:* ArM; *galeariato:* ChLA; Marichal: "interpreted by Premerstein, p. 39, and Lesquier, p. 232, as 'ordinance', *to* [instead of *tu*] seems to me certain, it should be, therefore, the ablative of *galeariatus* or *galeariatum* in the sense of wagon-train, Vegetius, II, 11, cf. Morel, p. 28." The letters between *g* and *r* are extremely doubtful. The *a* looks more like *h*; the *l* is a mere dab; and the *ea* resembles a theta. Vegetius 2.11 contains no reference to *galearii* or to this word; and Morel's guess seems strained. Premerstein (p. 39) compares *caculatus* from *cacula* and the *TLL* proceeds in the same way, though the editors there take the reading of ArM: "*cum officium unius diei significat, fortasse substantivum ad exemplum vocis* tribunatus *et sim.*, *i. q.* galeariatus, ūs, *officium* galearii." Vegetius equates galearius with *lixa* (1.10) or *calo* (3.6). Lesquier (p. 232, n. 18) says, "Il s'agit sans doute de l'entretien des casques et armures," but the form of entries like *ornatus Heli* (3 c–d), *armamenta* (3 k), and *fercla* (15 c), none of which is ablative, makes his idea unlikely. The present entry is rather to be compared with *strigis* (7 f–m) and *ballio* (3 m et alibi). **m.** *in (centuria)*; but the meaning is doubtful. Marichal quotes Lesquier p. 239 as noting that this entry recurs four times in col. f, lines 5, 15, 16, and 26, and points out that four is the regular number of sentries contributed by a century. But the reading of 26 f is highly uncertain; and in col. d, *in* Y occurs only once, though there are, to be sure, damaged squares where it might have stood. There is also the question of how *in* Y *Heli*, 11 g, relates to this entry. In view of *scopa(rius) in* Y, 29 b, and entries like *via nico*, 5 k and elsewhere, this entry may denote guard duty within the area occupied by the soldier's own century. *d decri* Y, *sereni* Y, and *in* Y *heli* would then indicate the same duty in the grounds of other centuries.

5 **a.** *OC[TA]VIA[NVS]:* ArM; *OCṬ[ẠṾ]IA[ṆṾṢ]:* ChLA. The *S* of *IVLIUS* is abnormal. The scribe seems to have written the first stroke of a *V* and then to have added other strokes in an attempt at correction. The resulting figure most resembles an *X*. Between *C* and *V* of the cognomen there is not room for both *T* and *A*; either would fill the space. Close after the *C* there is a vertical stroke. **b.** For the meaning of the bar see on 3 e–f. **h.** Premerstein: *sta(tio)* or *sta(tione) principi⟨i⟩s:* "guard duty at headquarters." Morel would read *Principis* as the genitive of a proper name. **k.** *via nico(politana):* edd. The camp of the legions was in Nicopolis, a suburb of Alexandria. Two other men were detailed to the same duty on this day: lines 16

and 27. Guard duty or road repairs? **n.** *pr*[*:* ArM; *pr. . . :* ChLA. Both reading and meaning are obscure.

6 **a.** [*S*]*ECVN*[*DVS*]*:* ArM; [*Ṣ*]*ẸCVNḌṾ*[*S*]*:* ChLA. **b–f.** Premerstein seems to be right in explaining (p. 39 and note 4) these entries as work setting up training equipment. Cf. the meaning of medieval "quintain" and Vegetius' description (1.11 and 14–15) of recruits exercising *ad palos*. The entry is also found in 10 b–f and 17 and 19 g–n. **c.** The *n* is clear; a lapsus pennae. **f.** *c̣ḷọ:* ArM; the reading in the text is Premerstein's. **h.** Premerstein: *sta*(*tione*) *por*(*tae*) or *por*(*tus*); but *por*(*torii*) seems equally possible. Cf. Ramsay MacMullen's comments on the *stationarii* in *Soldier and Civilian in the Later Roman Empire* (Cambridge, Mass., 1963) esp. 56–59, and the sources which he cites. **k.** *calcem:* ArM and ChLA, ("limestone" or "lime"?); but Premerstein's *cal*(*ceamenta*) *cen*(*turionis*), "working on foot-gear of the centurion," is attractive in view of the entry for the next day, which is certainly *cal*(*ceamenta*) *Heli*. **n.** ChLA offers no reading.

7 **f–m.** The *strigae* were the secondary streets of the camp. Guard duty? Military police? Cleaning up grounds? The same duty may have continued in n.

8 **a.** *SEXTILIV*[*S*] *G*[*E*]*RM*[*A*]*N*[*VS*]*:* ArM; *SEXTILIVṢ G*[*E*]*R*[*MẠ*]*N*[*VṢ*]*:* ChLA. It appears very possible that the final *S* of *SEXTILIVS* was omitted altogether. There is scarcely room for it before the *G*. **c.** *signis:* ArM and ChLA; but cf. 9 d. Read *specula*(*tor*). Literally, "scout," but really body-guards, aides, and particularly executioners. **f.** *d*[*ecri*]*:* edd. **n.** *de*[*cri:* edd.

9 **a.** *F*[*:* ArM; *F̣. . . . :* ChLA. The first letter of the cognomen might be any of those which have a vertical stroke on the left; but because of its height *F*, *H*, *I*, or *L* seems the most probable. The *O* is fairly convincing. **c.** Cf. 4 c and 8 e. **d.** Cf. 8 c. **f** and **g.** *sereni:* ArM and ChLA. **n.** *se*[*reni:* edd.

10 **a.** *RV*[*F*]*VS:* edd. The first remains hardly suit an *R*; but they are exactly on the lines of the *D* of *CLODIVS*, line 6. Similarly, the second letter is much more like *O* than *V*. There are also traces of ink at the right side of this column. **b.** The island was of course Pharos; and the next eight squares are blank because the soldier was not in camp and available for duties there. Note the blanks in lines 12 and 23 after the entries with *exit*. **n.** *cal:* edd.

11 **a.** *LONG*[*V*]*S SIPO:* ArM; *LONGṾS SIDO:* ChLA, i.e. *sido*(*ne*), the soldier's origo. The origo is added to distinguish this C. Julius Longus from the one in 12. **f.** *ṣc̣ọ:* ArM; *sio:* Premerstein.

12 **a.** *MISO:* ArM; *AṾSO:* ChLA, for *auso*(*nius*)—"from Ausonia." But *ausonius* is a poetic word; there is a stroke too many for *AV*; and the *A* could conceivably be read as *R*. The most natural reading would be *MISO*, if it made sense. I have guessed in the text that *AMISO*, "from Amisus," was intended. **d–g.** *asin. . . . . :* ArM; *asin ạḍ c̣ạ* [*l*]*:* ChLA, "*exit cum Asin*(*io ad cal*(*cem*)?" Another possibility is *asinạṛi*⟨*i*⟩*s*. One might compare **10** 32: *exit cum frum*[*entariis ?*]; but until the entries in f and g have been read with certainty, the interpretation must remain doubtful.

13 **a.** *PRISCV*[*S*]*:* ArM. **d.** Edd.: no reading. **f.** *stati*[*o*] *ad Serenu*(*m*)*:* ArM; *stati*[*o*] *ad terenu:* ChLA, "*terenu* for *terrenum*, to complete *aggerem ?*" The first letter of the last word looks in fact more like *c*, *l*, or *p*; and the *r* is highly uncertain. *leaenu* would suit very well if it were intelligible. Note that the squares from g through m are blank.

14 **a.** *NIGE*[*R*]*:* ArM; *NIG*[*ẸṚ*]*:* ChLA. **b–c.** *de . . . . e:* ArM; *de.e.e:* ChLA, "We could read *dessesse*, from *deses* 'idle'? Cf. a form *desses*, Thesaurus, but it is a barbarism and how to connect it with *trib*?" From the point of view of sense, Premerstein's reading *de nene*, which he explained as a miswriting for *de bene*(*ficio*) *trib*(*uni*) is attractive; but the *n*'s are not convincing paleographically, and there is no need for *de*. Cf. 2 m. The man seems at any rate to have had an exemption from duties through col. m.

15 **a.** *ANTO*[*N*]*I*[*V*]*S CRI*[*SP*]*V*[*S*]*:* ArM; *ANTOṆỊVṢ CṚI*[*SPVS*]*:* ChLA. **c.** "litters," "stretchers." **d.** *in* Ɣ*:* ArM and ChLA; but this may well be a continuation of the entry in c. The true reading is very doubtful; even *ḅaḷḷi*[*o*] looks possible. **e.** *pagane cultus:* ArM; *pagano cultu:* ChLA. The *o* is open at the right, like a *c*; so that *pagạṇic* would be a more satisfactory reading. The final *s*, if it is one, has no downstroke; and the syntax of the phrase is not clear. "In plain-clothes." Morel cites Pliny, *Epist*. 7.25.5: "Sunt enim ut in castris sic etiam in litteris nostris plures cultu pagano quos cinctos et armatos et quidem ardentissimo ingenio diligenter scrutatus inuenies"; Premerstein adds Tacitus, *Hist*. 1.85, and Epictetus, *Diss*. 4.13.5. **g–k.** Edd.: no reading in g; *com* in h; in k, *tr:* ArM; *ẹstr:* ChLA. Premerstein reads *com*(*es*) *tr*(*ibuni*). There are traces of writing in g, with a tall letter which crosses into h and another tall letter in h before the *c*, which itself might be read as *e*. The remaining letters are badly distorted except for *r*. The *t* is corrected from something else; the *o* is almost triangular; and the *s* could be *e* or an *s* with a small *t* below it.

16 **a.** *.NṾṂ. . . S. . . . V:* ArM; *.NVM. . . . . . . :* ChLA. The letter before the second *V* looks like *A* or *V*. **c.** *. . . . . /. . . mprinci:* ArM; *ṣṭạ/pṛịncip:* ChLA. The letters before *cs* might be *ri*; the last *n* may be *m*. It does not seem possible to read *alecsandrini*. **d.** ChLA reports traces of three letters.

17 **a.** *Q PETR*[*ONI. . .*]*V*[*S*]*:* ArM; *Q̣ PEṬR*[*ON*]*ỊVṢ:* ChLA. The first letter of the cognomen is rounded: *O* or *Q*. **c.** *pr. . . us/amenta:* ArM; *. . . . . . ./ ạṛṃ. . . . :* ChLA. The final *a* of the entry is in col. d on the line between 17 and 18. No one has offered any guesses about the meaning. **d.** No reading in ArM; ChLA reports traces of three letters. **k–m.** *n*[*esio*]*:* ArM; *nẹṣ*[*io*]*:* ChLA.

18 **a.** *.CAR. . . . . MO. . . :* ArM; *.CAR. . . . . Ṣ:* ChLA. **b–c.** *c̣ọṃẹṣ:* ArM; ChLA reports traces of three letters in b, one in c. **e.** *ḅạḷḷịọ:* ArM; traces of three letters in ChLA. **f–m.** Edd.: no readings.

19 **a.** ArM and ChLA report traces of eight letters after the nomen. **b.** ArM: no reading; ChLA: traces of three letters. **c.** *. . .ones:* ArM; *c̣ọṃesser:* ChLA, "*comes Ser*(*eni*)," with reference to 9 f–n. **d.** ArM: no reading; ChLA: traces of three letters. **e–f.** Edd.: no readings. **m.** *sc:* ArM; *sio:* Premerstein; *s*[*ịọ*]*:* ChLA

20 **a.** *VALER[I]V[S].....SVS:* ArM; *VALERỊVṢ ....:* ChLA. The second letter of the nomen begins with a vertical stroke. It most resembles an *I* followed by and combined with the left stroke of *V*. **b.** Edd: *com(es) pili.* Marichal, "orderly of the primipilus," citing Premerstein, Lesquier, and Morel; but the entry may have run one or two columns farther. **c.** ...*cus:* edd. **d.** Edd: no reading. **f.** ArM: no reading; ChLA: traces of three letters—"Perhaps the same text" as g–k. Cf. 8 f–n. **g.** *[d]ec[r]i* Ƴ*:* ArM; *ḍecr[i* Ƴ*]:* ChLA. **k.** *[d]ec[ri* Ƴ*]:* edd. **m.** Edd.: no reading. Perhaps after all *ḍ [d]ẹ[cri* Ƴ*].*

21 **a.** *T FLAVIVS......:* edd. **e.** *b[al]l[io]:* ArM; *b[allio]:* ChLA. **f.** *ba[l]lio:* ArM; *ba[l]li[o]:* ChLA. **h.** *papili:* ArM; *s[t]a por:* ChLA. **k.** Edd.: traces of 9 letters.

22 **a.** Cognomen, *[F]ABE[R]:* ArM; *ḌABEṚ:* ChLA. But there is a clear trace of the upper right quarter of a curved letter crossing the upper tip of the right-hand stroke of *A*; and an *F* should have left more traces above. The third letter is too low for *B*; and the fourth, if *E*, should show the middle horizontal stroke. **b.** *[b]a[l]lio:* edd. **e.** *b[al]li[o]:* edd. **f.** *ba[l]lio:* edd. **k.** *[bal]li[o]:* edd.

23 **a.** *M MA[R]Ç[IVS]:* edd.; *CL[E]MEN[S]:* ArM. There is not sufficient space for *M MARCIVS*. **b–d.** *exit uino cum ......rel...:* ArM; *exit ạḍ horṃ ....ạeḷ:* ChLA. There is no doubt about *exit in*; the *d* could be *o*, but the next letter can scarcely be *r*; the final *g* might be the centuria-symbol.

24 **a.** *C VALERIVS:* edd. **b.** *gel:* ArM; *çaeç:* ChLA, "*Caec(ilii) (centuria)?*" The third letter seems to have been corrected from *s*. **c–k.** It appears that each of the days was marked with a horizontal stroke. If so, perhaps the entry in b should be read *com(meatus)*.

25 **d.** Edd: no readings. **e.** Traces of four letters reported in ArM; *[sta] p[o]r:* ChLA. **f.** *sta [p]o[r]:* ArM. **g.** *ḅ....:* edd. **k.** ...*ir:* ArM; *[i]ṇ* Ƴ*:* ChLA.

26 **a.** *Ṭ FV[RI]V[S......]RVS[...:* ArM; *Ṭ FVṚ[I]ỊVS..........:* ChLA. For *C* rather than *T* as the initial of the praenomen cf. the *T* in line 13 and both *C*'s in line 25. The *G* in the nomen seems certain. **d.** ...*niç:* edd. **f.** *i[n* Ƴ*]?:* ArM; *ị...:* ChLA. **h.** *arma/ [m]ẹṇ[ta]:* ArM; *arm[a]/[ṃ]ẹntạ:* ChLA. **k.** Edd: Traces of eight or nine letters.

27 **a.** *GALL.........:* edd. **d.** *pha[l]:* edd. The entry could end with *r* instead of *a*. But possibly *pecua(rius)*? **h.** Edd.: Traces of three letters. **k.** *[ni]co:* edd.

28 **a.** *Q ANN[IVS]:* ArM; *Q ANNỊV[Ṣ]:* ChLA. The initial of the praenomen could equally well be *C*. **b–c.** "Sweeper."

29 **a.** *VẠ[....]V[.....]CO:* ArM; *V........... ÇO:* ChLA. **b.** *st[a] prin:* edd.; but there is another long vertical stroke after *n*. "Sweeper in the company area." **e.** Edd.: no readings. **g.** *ArM*: Traces of eight letters. **h.** *sta p[or]:* ArM; *st[a po]ṛ:* ChLA.

30 **a.** *LONGINV[S RVF]VS:* ArM (*ṚỴḌVS*, Nicole); *LONGINV[S].....:* ChLA. The letters at the end are in cursive. *Longinus* appears five times as a nomen of legionaries in Egypt in *CIL* III 6627 (=Dessau 2483) and once in *CIL* III 6607 (=Dessau 2247), both of the early first century A.D. **d.** Edd.: no readings. **h.** Edd.: no readings.

31 **a.** For the cognomen, ...*ISO:* ArM; .....*Ọ:* ChLA. The final *s* of the nomen and the letters at the end are in cursive. **c.** Edd.: no readings; but there appears to have been an entry at the top of this space which ran over into d, above the *e* of *exit*. **e.** *ad [fru:* ArM; *[ạḍ fru:* ChLA. **f.** *men]tu:* ArM; *me]ṇtụ:* ChLA. **h.** *oli:* edd. **k.** Edd.: no readings. Cf. **10** 2, 5, 8, 23, and 27; and **51** ii 23.

32 **a.** For the cognomen, *au.....:* ArM; *A......:* ChLA. The name begins with capitals and trails off into cursive. **c–d.** ArM: no reading; ChLA: ..*r* in d. The remains in d look like *h*, or perhaps *ei* at the top of the square with another letter or two below on the level of *ṃ* in c. **g.** *in/stercuss:* ArM; *ad/stercus* Ƴ*:* ChLA. Possibly *uic(o) al(exandrino)*? *stercus* implies "cleaning stables" or "latrine orderly." There seem to be two strokes after the final *s*, and another letter in h.

34–37. Marichal calls attention to the fact that these men were assigned no duties during the first days of the month, as far as the papyrus is preserved. One may carry farther his argument (*Solde* 407–8) that Julius Felix (line 33) was added to the list at the last minute to replace Marius Clemens (line 23) who *exit* on October 1. Four other men became unavailable in the first days of the month: Cassius Dorus (line 10), *insula* on October 1; Julius Longus (line 12), *exit* October 3; Flavius Niger (line 14), *commeatus* October 1; and Domitius (line 31), *exit* October 3. Without attempting to say who replaced whom, it seems reasonable that Julius Felix and those who follow were added to take the places of the five just named. It must be admitted, however, that this does not account for Flavius Priscus (line 13), who went on a *statio ad*? on October 5 and does not reappear in the next four days.

34 **a.** *VALENS:* edd.; but the final letter cannot be *S*. After the *e* the remains look most like a *t* followed by *a* with another *a* in ligature dropping below it. Perhaps read *ualeṛia(nus)*?

36 **a.** *vi....leius:* ArM; *VI.....EIVS:* ChLA.

37 **a.** *i[uli]us:* ArM.

10

Record *viritim* of Detached Service Between February 80 and September 87

PGenLat. 1 recto, part II; *vidi* — Probably A.D. 88
P. lat. 1, Bibliothèque publique et universitaire, Genève

For bibliography see above, **9**.

Transcription, facsimile, and commentary: *ChLA* I, pp. 12–13 and 15.

Text: *CPL* no. 106, ii; Daris, no. 10 (3).

Translation: *Roman Egypt*, no. 407, p. 675, translates the text in *ArM*.

This text lists the departures and returns of individual soldiers detached for various duties outside the camp. Presumably the men belonged to the same legion and perhaps the same century as those named in the other four parts of this papyrus; but proof is wanting. What we have here is clearly based on the material in duty rosters, such as the *exit* entries in **9**, and in morning reports, like the *reuersus* items in **47**. Cf. also the records of replacements on detached service in **11 bis**.

The precise object of such a list as this, however, and the reason for beginning and ending with the dates found in it, are not evident; nor is it certain whether it was compiled all at one time or kept as a running record. Marichal was at first of the opinion that sections B, C, and D were in a hand different from that of A (*ChLA*, p. 13, on B 1–2), and calls attention especially to the *a*, *d*, and *m* in the different entries; but in "Solde" he states (p. 406) that the writing and the ink are homogeneous except for the last line of section C, which contains the date of September 19, 87. There can be no question that he is right about this line (numbered 25 in the text below), and that it constitutes a sort of terminus ante quem for the rest of part II. From the date in September and the fact that there is no notation for the soldier's return, he then goes on to deduce that part V (my **9**), which begins with October 1, followed part II immediately and was also composed in 87. He appears to me, however, to have been right in his original opinion that more than one hand wrote the other parts of the text. As he says, the *a*, *d*, and *m* are particularly distinctive; and so to some degree are the *n* and *r*. I feel, in fact, that as many as six hands can be distinguished in the cursive lines: the first in lines 2–6 and the second in lines 7–9; hand 3 in lines 12–15, 18–19, and 27–29; hand 4 in line 16; hand 5 in lines 20–24 and 30–33; and hand 6 in line 25. The samples are small and the hands are admittedly similar, so that judgments can easily differ regarding particular lines; but if it is true at all that more than one hand is represented in the entries under each soldier's name, then this text is not a summary produced at one time but a record kept open for new entries as needed. In favor of the latter interpretation is the form itself, with the names set wide apart but the entries made in a tiny, space-saving script so that two or three centimeters of blank papyrus still remain under each name. It will be observed, too, that lines 20–25 do not keep the same margin as lines 18–19, and that 30–33 begin a bit farther left than 27–29. And finally, line 16, as well as 25, records a soldier's departure which is not followed by a statement of his return. In short, this seems to be a check-list of soldiers absent from their century.

These considerations, in turn, have a bearing upon the date of this piece. If it was not all composed at one time between July 7, 86, and September 19, 87, when the latest extant entry was added (Marichal, "Solde" 406), it is not necessary to assume that 87 is the latest possible date. Only four soldiers are named here; but there must have been a similar record for every man on detached service. Even of these four, Celer has no missions later than 83, so that if his record alone survived we should be inclined to date the papyrus four or five years earlier than we do. It is consequently very possible that dates later than 87 would be found if the entire text were extant. Conversely, lines 3, 18, and 29 must be dated in Titus' third year; and it is probable that 27 belongs to his second year, while if we had the whole papyrus we might find even earlier dates elsewhere. This record, then, probably started no later than 79; and one may reasonably assume that it ran for 10 years. If so, it would have been closed in 88. It may be observed that part I of this papyrus (**68** below) is dated 81 and had become scrap paper by 90, when part III (**37** below) was written.

Certainly part II had been discarded before it was glued to part I so that the verso could be used for parts IV and V, for the right edge of I once covered the left ends of a number of lines of II. This is explicitly stated by Nicole (*ArM*, p. 7) who adds in note 1 on the same page, "Nous avons réussi à dégager entièrement la plus grande parti du texte ainsi oblitéré en enlevant le bord droit de la feuille A," that is, the sheet containing part I. The notation at the left of lines 15–16 seems to contradict my view, for Prof. Victor Martin, who kindly re-examined the papyrus at my request, reports, ". . . it seems clear to me that [the two pieces of papyrus] were glued together before the note was written and that it goes across the junction." From the photograph in *ArM*, however, it appears that the right edge of I originally covered the whole *M* in line 1 of this text and, extending vertically downward, covered the first *r* of *febrar* in the notation and half of the *m* in *domiti* (line 16). In that case, the writing at the left of the joint belongs to the text of part I; and in fact line 23 of col. ii of **68** extends to a point under *e* of *febrar* and *d* of *domiti*, while the stroke to the left of *febrar* resembles the foot of the *f* in *fit*, col. ii, line 12 of **68**. However that may be, it should also be noted that in line 25 of the present text (the latest entry) the month of October is still called by that name on September 19, 87,[1] whereas on the verso, **9** above, the month is called Domitianus. The order for the change of name may have reached Egypt in 87 during the eleven days between September 19 and October 1 (not even the year of the change is certainly known), thus permitting **9** to follow **10** directly, as Marichal wishes; but probability favors the supposition that a year or more separates the two texts, and that the sequence of September 19 and October 1 is coincidental.

[1] Charlesworth in *CAH* 11.24, note 3, evidently misled by the name of the emperor, erroneously cites this same line as the earliest certain instance of the use of *Domitianus* for October.

It follows that there is little likelihood of any direct connection in the system of records between this text and **9**. The latter, on the verso of **68**, cannot be earlier than 90 and may be considerably later, and there is no proof that the *t flauius uale.*[in line 17 is the same person as the *t flauius uale*. . . of **9** 34. At any rate, none of the other three men here is found in **9**; and the name Flavius and those based on *ual-* are too common to be conclusive.

This text, short as it is, shows that there was nothing mechanically regular about the assignment of detached service. The period of absence varied from a minimum of four months or less (lines 20–21 and cf. 31–32) to a minimum of seven months (lines 6–8), with a possible maximum of ten and a half months (lines 5–6). At the date of the papyrus Celer had had no missions outside the camp for four or five years; and *uale.*[had only two between January 17, 82, and September 19, 87. Most of the detached service for all four was concentrated in the years 80–82; and there is none that can be ascribed with certainty to 84. This last item of course adds confirmation that the text once included the records of many more soldiers than the four represented.

The verso, as stated, contains **9** and **58**.

Sect. A

M PAPIRIVS RVFVS C.[
exị̣ṭ ad frumentum neapoli ex epịṣṭ[ula t suedi]
clementis praef· castrorum anno· iii ịṃ[p titi 2–8] A.D. 80
octoḅres r anno eodem xii k februariaṣ[81
exit ad frumentum mercuri anno ·i· imp· dọmitiano .[5–10]
r anno eodem ·iii· idus iulias exịṭ cụs [10–15] 82
.[..]..na anno iv ḍomitiani xi k maia[s r anno v domitiani 2–8] 85
ḍẹ[c]ẹmbṛes exit ad frumentum mercuri ạṇṇ[o vi (?) domitiani 86?
[...].[..]... r anno eodem nonis iulis

Space of about 2.2 cm.

Sect. B

ṾṆP̣Ṿ...ẠỊṂNṾFẠ.[
T FLAVIVS SATVR[
ẹxịṭ ad hormos confodiendo[s anno ? imp ?
xix k febrarias r anṇ[o *ca.* 27]
exịṭ cum timinịo ⅄ ạṇ[no *ca.* 25 r]
anno eodem iv k decẹm[bres
].[.]februa].[.]ọ domiti — exit cum maximo libert[o *ca.* 25]

Space of about 3.2 cm.

Sect. C

T FLAVIVS VAḶẸ[
exit ad chartam comfịcị[endam anno iii imp titi] 81
xiix k febrarias r anṇ[o *ca.* 25]
exit ad moneta annọ [i] i[m]p [domitiani *ca.* 10 r anno] 81/82
eodem xvi k februariaṣ [exit *ca.* 18 anno ?] 82–85
imp· domitiano idibus a[7–8 r anno *ca.* 13]
exit ad frumentum mercuṛ[i anno .. domitiani *ca.* 8]
r anno eodem pr· idus iuliaṣ [exit *ca.* 20] 83–87
. chora anno vii domitiani xiii k octoḅ[res 87

Space of about 3.3 cm.

Sect. D T FLAVIVS CELẸR[
exit ad frumentum neạ[pol]ị[*ca.* 10 anno ii imp titi]
iii idus februarias r anno e[odem 80
exit cum potamofulacide· ạ[nno iii imp titi *ca.* 10] 80/81
r anno eodem ix k iunia[s exit *ca.* 22]
anno ·i· imp domitiano ·v· n[onas octobres r anno eodem] 81
x k martias exit cum fruṃ[entariis anno ii domitiani] 83
xiii k iulias r anno iii doṃị[tiani 83/84

TRANSLATION

Marcus Papirius Rufus, *castrensis* (?).

Left for the granary at Neapolis in accordance with written orders of Titus Suedius Clemens, prefect of the camp, [*Sept. 14–Oct. 14*], 80. Returned the same year, January 21, [*81*]. Left for the granary in the Mercurium quarter [*month, day*], 81/82. Returned July 13, 82. Left for [*guard duty?*] April 21, 85. Returned [*Nov. 14–Dec. 12*], 85. Left for the granary in the Mercurium quarter [*month, day, 86? 87?*). Returned the same year, July 7.

Titus Flavius Satur[

Left to dredge harbors, January 14, [*81 or later*]. Returned [*the same (?) year, month, day*]. Left with the centurion Timinius [*month, day, year*]. Returned the same year, November 28. Left with Maximus the freedman [*of the emperor? month, day, year*]. *In the margin:* February, Domitian.

Titus Flavius Vale[

Left to make papyrus, January 15, 81. Returned [*month, day, year*]. Left for the mint, [*month, day*], 81. Returned January 17, 82. Left April 13 [*or August 13*], 82–86. Returned [*month, day, year*]. Left for the granary in the Mercurium quarter [*month, day, year*]. Returned July 14, 83–87. Left to --- from the countryside, September 19, 87.

Titus Flavius Celer

Left for the granary at Neapolis, February 11, 80. Returned the same year, [*month, day*]. Left with the river patrol [*month, day, 81?*]. Returned the same year, May 24. Left [*destination lost*] October 3, 81. Returned February 20, 82. Left with the grain-convoy (?) June 19, 83. Returned [*between August 29, 83, and August 28, 84*].

The original length of full lines in the cursive entries is fixed by 3, 7, and 31, where not much restoration is needed and where the content of the restoration is certain within very narrow limits. Lines 3 and 7 can vary only in the choice of a numeral and *k*, *nonas*, or *idus*, while in 31 the month is certain because *v nonas* is a possible date in only four months, of which October alone falls in the interval between the beginning of Domitian's first Egyptian year, September 13, 81, and the end of the mission on February 20, 82 (line 32). Similarly *anno eodem* is required because Domitian's second year would not begin until August 29, 82. These restorations would produce lines with a minimum of 39 letters and a maximum of 52. There are 41 letters in line 31; so about 45 letters may be considered normal for lines in these entries.

The photograph seems to show slight and illegible traces of three or four lines of writing above *M PA* and the *R* of *RVFVS* in line 1.

1. *C*[*:* ArM, ChLA, and Daris. ChLA "C must indicate the *origo*: CASTR(IS)?"

2. *exeptor:* ArM and Daris, for *exceptor*, "secretary"; *exepṭ*[*or:* ChLA; *ep*[*istulis:* Mommsen.

3. [*Imp. Tito . . . . . .*]*:* ChLA and Daris. The clerks, however, were impartial in their use of cases with the emperor's name. Among the certain instances, *domi-*

tiano occurs three times and *domitiani* twice. Gilliam, reviewing Daris, *AJP* 88 (1967) 100, suggests restoring *divo* or *divi* instead of *imp*; but cf. **63** i 21.

4. *februaria*[*s:* ArM and ChLA; *Februari*[*as:* Daris. The barred *r* could be expanded *r(edit)* to parallel *exit*, or as *r(euersus)* as in **47** and **50**. This line seems complete as it stands. It proves that the Egyptian calendar is being followed, for February belongs to the same year as the preceding October.

5. *Domitiano*[*:* edd.

6. *Maias:* Daris, a slip; *cu*[*m:* ArM; *cụṃ*[*:* ChLA. If *cus*[is correct, perhaps *cus*[*tos* or (*in*) *cus*[*todiam*?

7. . . .]*a anno:* ArM; . . . . . *anno:* ChLA; [. . . . .] *anno:* Daris; *maias*[*:* edd.; [*R anno eodem* . . . . . . *:* ChLA and Daris. At the end of the line *anno v* must be restored if one reads *decembres* in line 8, because a new year began August 29.

8. . . .]*ma*[*rti*]*as*, *neapoli* [*anno:* ArM; *ṇọṇạṣ m*[*ạ*]*ias*, *Neapoli ạṇ*[*no* . . . *Domit* . . . *:* ChLA; *nonas M*[*a*]*ias*, *Neapoli*, *ạṇ*[*no:* Daris. The year is probably 86, possibly 87; and the numeral to be restored could be either *v*, *vi*, or *vii*, depending on both the year and the month.

9. Edd.: traces of three letters before *r*.

10. . . . [.].*ÇA.MV*[.]. . . [*:* ArM; . . . . . . *N.ANIV. ṬI*[*:* ChLA and Daris. Marichal: "Seeing the exceptional presence of two names and the *exit*, line 3, we think the first was cancelled." The readings offered in the text are intended merely to give some notion of what the remains look like. It would be equally possible, and just as unintelligible, to read *ṚẠÇV* . . . *ṂIẠNOFỊ*. [There may be a horizontal bar over the *O* (or *V*); but I see no signs of cancellation. The line may have been a heading for a section of the text.

11. Edd: *SATVR*[*NINVS;* but Saturnianus, Saturnilus, and other restorations are possible.

12. *confodiendos*[*:* ArM. The *f* and *o* of *confodiendos* are superimposed, producing a character like a Greek phi. Domitian's name should perhaps be restored here to make a line long enough to account for carrying *xix k* over into line 13.

13. *xiịx*, *ann*[*o eodem:* ChLA and Daris.

14. *pr*[*:* ArM. The reading in the text is Marichal's.

15. *dece*[*mbres:* ArM. The line seems to be complete as it is.

16. *Liber*[*ali:* edd. The photograph makes it clear that there is a *t* after the *r*. One should perhaps read *libert*[*o aug(usti*). In the margin: [*f*]*ebrua*[*rias*], *Domiti:* ChLA, "We don't know, to what the date *februarias* and the name *Domiti*, on the margin, refer: correction or addition to be inserted in the last part of the text?" Marichal is obviously right in this conjecture. The entry in the margin may in fact be the date of this man's return from the mission noted in line 16; but in that case one would expect it to have been added to the text. More likely it is an addition to or correction of the date in the lost part of line 16. Nicole may be right in his conjecture (ArM, p. 8) that this is the date of the third *exit* for *Satur*[, and that line 16 may therefore have contained in its lost portion the entry for his return; but this depends on the assumption that the *exit* items were not entered until the absent soldier had returned, which line 25 seems to disprove.

17. *VA*[*LEN* . . . . *:* ArM; *VAḶE*[*NS:* ChLA and Daris. Cf. **9** 34; but note that the identification is by no means sure. The name could be Valerianus, Valentinus, or others.

18. *confici*[*endam:* Daris. Since this line is indented about three letters, the name of Titus makes a long enough line; and it must be used if the reading of line 20 is right.

20. *anno*[*:* edd.

22. The month is either April or August.

23. The tail of a letter in the line above runs through the *u* of *mercuri*.

25. *III k(alendas):* Daris. There is a mark before *chora* which resembles a small *c* with a vertical stroke through it. A *c* canceled, a punctum, or the preposition *e*? The case of *chora* is probably ablative and implies *in*, *e*, or some similar preposition at the end of 24.

26. Celer may be the whole cognomen; but Celerianus and Celerinus are possible.

27. *nea*[*pol*]*ị:* ArM; *Nea*[*poli:* ChLA and Daris. The year must be in Titus' reign because the first year of Domitian is not mentioned until line 31. Titus' second year has been restored here because the first *exit* in lines 27–28 took place on February 11 and the second return in lines 29–30 on May 24. This would entail crowding both missions and the intervening stay in camp into a period of three and a half months if the four lines are assumed to belong to the same year; and though not wholly impossible, such an occurrence seems extremely improbable in the light of the other entries. The same reasoning leads to the restoration of *anno iii* in line 29.

29. ChLA: ". . . deals perhaps with the escort of the convoy of grains: the employ of legionaries in this case is attested, cf. J. Schwartz, 'Le Nil et le revitaillement de Rome,' *Bull. de l'Inst. français d'Arch. orientale* 47 (1948) p. 45; O. Guéraud, 'Un vase ayant contenu un échantillon de blé,' *Jour. Juristic Papyrology* 4 (1950), p. 107." For the year see on line 27.

30. *iunias*[*:* ArM.

31. *domitiano vii*[*:* ArM; *n*[*onas r anno:* ChLA and Daris.

32. ChLA: "*frumentarii* . . . form only in Hadrian's reign a special corps, cf. M. Rostovtzev, *Storia economica e sociale dell'Impero Romano* (Firenze, 1946) p. 416, n. 10. The text proves, that the abovementioned four legionaries are not *frumentarii*." The year must be Domitian's second, because the next line has *r anno iii* instead of *anno eodem*. The year of the *exit* was therefore different from the year of the return.

33. *do*[*mitiani:* ArM; *Dom*[*itiani:* ChLA and Daris.

11

Detached Service Record

PVindob. L 112 recto; *vidi* Early II p.
Papyrussammlung der Oesterreichische Nationalbibliothek

Transcription and facsimile:
1. Wessely, *Schriftt.* no. 9; *Studien* 14, p. 3 and plate 8; cited as **W**.
2. L. Schiaparelli, *La Scrittura latina nell' età romana* (Como 1921) p. 115 and plate 4.
3. *EL*, no. 20.

Text: *CPL*, no. 116, reproduces Wessely's text; Daris, no. 17, follows the dating of *EL*.

In content this scrap is to be compared with **10**. It appears to record the departures of soldiers detailed to various services outside the camp. It differs, however, in several respects. First, the entire text is in capitals, which implies a rather formal document, though we have no way of guessing why capitals were used. Then each soldier is identified by the consular date of his enlistment; and finally, it seems that all three men are away from the camp and only the occasion of their absence is recorded, with no mention of anyone's return.

The consular dates are a hopeless crux. The most promising series of years is perhaps 126, M. Annius Verus III and C. Eggius Ambibulus; 128, L. Nonius Calpurnius Asprenas Torquatus II and M. Annius Libo; and 129, P. Iuventius Celsus, etc., II and L. Neratius Marcellus II. But the cognomen of Verus' colleague does not begin with *D* (nor is any other Verus known whose colleague is suitably named); Torquatus' colleague is similarly ineligible; and in 129 Marcellus was the junior consul and regularly named second, not first. Marcellus is named first, to be sure, in *CIL* XV 1435; but one hesitates to assume that liberty here. Degrassi wishes to make the Torquatus of the present text the consul of 143, C. Bellicius Flaccus (?) Torquatus, whose colleague was L. Vibullius Hipparchus Ti. Claudius Atticus Herodes; but there is doubt whether he was really *cos II*, and the date will not fit into a reasonable sequence with those of any Verus or Marcellus.

Since none of the soldiers named is otherwise known, there is no means of fixing the date more exactly.

The verso is blank.

Col. i

]C̣Ọ S
]. IS
]
]
]
]COS
]
]
]C̣OS

Col. ii

VER̤Ọ III˙ ET D.[
DIONYSIVS LVC̣Ạ[
RAN HERACLIAN Ỵ [
TORQVATO II ET A[
C ANTONIVS PRI[
BER̤ẸNIC[
MARCELLO II . . . [
C IVLIVS F̣RONT[
CVM EPISTṚẠ[TEGO

i 1.]. : W; no reading in EL. These ends of lines in this column show that the columns of the text were no broader than the consuls' names.

2.]*IS:* EL.

ii 1. *et* .[*:* W; *ET DỌ*[*:* EL; *D*[*:* Daris. The numeral after *VERO* seems to have been corrected from an *E* or a ligature of *E* and *T*. EL's statement that the only "Verus III" is A.D. 126 is of course mistaken. The emperor Verus was *cos III* in 167, though this does not solve the problem of the dates in this text.

2. *luc*.[*:* W and Daris; *LVCẠ*[*:* EL. The *N* of *DIONYSIVS* is corrected from a *D*. This man has neither a praenomen nor a nomen and is therefore not a Roman citizen. Consequently, if all the men listed here belonged to the same unit, it must be an auxiliary cohort or an ala.

3. Probably [*AD*. . . *CHOR*]*AN*. Cf. **10** 25, and *BGU* 372, col. ii, 5–8 (A.D. 154): *Τοῖς κρατίστοις ἐπιστρατήγοις καὶ τοῖς στρατηγοῖς καὶ τοῖς πεμφθέσι ʽυπ' ἐμοῦ* [Sempronius Liberalis, Prefect of Egypt] *προς τῆς χώρας ἀσφάλειαν καὶ ἀμεριμνίαν στρατιώταις*. *Heracliano*[*:* W and EL; but the last character has a tail which extends down to the line below. In either reading *Heraclian* is not easy to explain. Possibly *Heraclian*(*a*) or *Heraclian*(*i*) (*centuriae*); but one is also reminded of the entries in *PMich*. 447 which contain adjectives formed from the names of prefects of Egypt and without case-endings—"Syriacian," "Proclian," "Munatian," and others. (On this papyrus see above, p. 9). Stein, *Präf.* 161–62, mentions a T. Fl(avius) Frontinus Heraclius (*PIR* s.v. "Flāvius," no. 274a) who *may* have been a prefect of Egypt—he was a *uir perfectissimus*—and whom Stein considers probably different from the prefect Heracleus of *POxy*. x 1313.

4. *a*[*ttico:* W and CPL (A.D. 143); *A*[*NNIO:* EL and Daris (A.D. 128).

5. *Pri*[*mus:* W and EL; but Priscus and other names are possible.

6. *berinic*[*es:* W; *BERINI C*[*:* EL, with W's query (*Schriftt.*) "Tiberini?" "Stationed at Berenice" or "in the century of Tiberinus"?

7. *et*[*:* W and CPL; *EṬ* [*CELSO II:* EL and Daris (A.D. 129). On this inverted order of the consuls' names, cf. the introduction above.

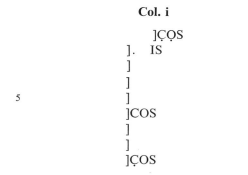

11 bis

Replacements of Men on Detached Service

PVindob. L 4 End of III p.
Papyrussammlung der Oesterreichische Nationalbibliothek

Transcription and facsimile:
1. Wessely, *Schriftt.* no. 23.
2. Idem, *Studien* 14, p. 3 and plate 9; cited as **W**.

Text: *CPL*, no 322, has parts as noted, using Wessely's readings. Daris, no. 25.

The general pattern of the entries in these fragments can be reconstructed with some confidence. Each begins with a date in capitals (frag. a, line 1; frag. b, i, lines 1 and 15; frag. c, line 1) followed in the next line by a place-name and the number of soldiers concerned—frag. b, i, line 16: *a]frodito eq i.* The next line contains the identification of a turma (a 17; b i 17); and the next a soldier's name in the nominative (a 4; b i 18). Then comes the word *loco* in a line by itself (a 13 and 20), and in the line after, a soldier's name in the genitive (a 21; cf. a 14).

From the foregoing it is clear that this text was at least in part a record of men sent on detached service as replacements for others. There is no indication, however, whether these were routine exchanges, replacing men who had completed their tours of detached service and were returning to headquarters, or were substitutions occasioned by some incapacity of men stationed at the various posts. The intercolumnar notes in **1**, discussed on p. 13 above, may be compared; but they almost certainly indicate substitutions of the latter sort.

The blank lines in frag. b, i 19–20 and 22, and ii 7–8 and after line 16, may mean that *loco* and the name in the genitive did not appear in these parts of the respective entries, that is, that the man sent out was not a replacement for another; but the papyrus is too damaged to permit a decision.

The correct order of the fragments cannot be determined because the *IDVS* in a 1 and in c 1 may not belong to the same month, and neither need belong to the month of August which is named in b i 1 and 15. Nevertheless, since some order is necessary, I have arbitrarily assumed that *ịV* in b ii 25 is from the date *IV Idus Augustas* and have placed the other fragments accordingly as belonging to the records of the same month.

Wessely dated the text (*Studien* 1 [Leipzig 1901] pp. i–ii) at the end of the third century but before the Diocletianic inflation on the basis of the Greek in frag. c, 6–7, which he read as 110 (drachmas or denarii?), 4 obols, and 17 and 1 obol. Whether the Greek had anything at all to do with the Latin text is doubtful; but if not, it must have been written after the Latin was discarded and so in any case it constitutes a terminus ante quem.

The verso is not mentioned and may be presumed blank.

Frag. a (*CPL* Frag. II; Daris Frag. B)

Ṿ[I]Ị ỊḌVṢ[
.[ ].ṃ Ƴ cḥ[
....ạgr.[.]e
aelius [.].[...].t..r[
.l[.]..
ạlẹ.ẹ[..]dr..[
it[e]ṃ ..ị[.].[
ṃe... .gụ.[
..[
...[
...[
..laitin[.].[
loçọ[
]ḅ. didumi ẹ[
]..
]item˙ cercesḍite eq i .[
Ŧ sereni [ ]..[
...[ ].. .[..].....[
]....ll .[ ]....[..]oạtṃịctḍ[
loco
aụrelị iu.[
]..[

a 1. *AVG]VṢ[T:* W.
2–3. ....*q*....[*:* Daris, 2; no readings in W.
4. *aelius:* W.
5. *ale:* W; Daris' line 6.
5–6. Possibly *l[o]çọ ạḷẹx̣ạ[n]drị*?
6. No reading in W.
7–12. No readings in W.
7. (*turma*)[*:* Daris.
8. *Aelius* [*:* Daris.
9–11. Blank in Daris.
11. (*turma*)..........[*:* Daris 12(?).
12. ....*:* Daris 13 (?).
13. *loc:* W; *loc.*[*:* Daris 15.
14. *didym. le*[*:* W; *Didym.le*[*:* Daris 16.
16. *ea*: W; *eq:* Daris 17 and Fink, independently. The name of the place could also be read *cercesaite* or *cercesthe*. Possibly another variant of Cercasorus? See **70** a iii 8 app.
18. No readings in W and Daris.
19. *ll:* W; no readings in Daris. The letters at the end of the line are a notation in a different hand.
20. *loc:* W.
21. *aureli i:* W; *Aureli* (*centuria*)*:* Daris.

Frag. b

Col. i (*CPL* Frag. III; Daris Frag. A I)

A]ṾG[V]ṢṬ
].nṣ.e.ḍex
].
].i..[..]s
]
]e.
].[..].[..].
].ạnụes
About six lines blank

15]. AVGVST
a]f̣rodito eq i
]ni
].eịnus
Two lines lost?
21].[.]ḅ...o.ỵs
One line lost?
]..ani
]odis..ṣ[

Col. ii (Daris Frag. A II; not in *CPL*)

. . [
ua . . . . [
Ŧ . [
ị . . [
Ŧ[
ạ[u]relịụ[s
Two lines blank
item˙ ẹ . . . . [
[
iul [
[
[
item′ bạḅỵ[lone
Ŧ . [
auṛeḷ[
About eight lines blank
ỊV [

b i 1–8. W has no readings.
1. *Au]gust(as):* Daris.
2.] . . . *XXX*: Daris.
3. Daris 3–4: no readings.
4. *]l:* Daris 5 (?).
8.] . . . *us:* Daris 9.
16. *[Item a]frodito eai:* W; *eq(ues) I:* Daris and Fink, independently.
18. *se]ṛenus:* W.
21. No readings in W;] . . . *onis:* Daris 24 (?).
23. *]ani:* W.
24. *]odis:* W.
b ii 1–4. No readings in W.
1. No readings in Daris.
2. *ḅḅ*[*:* Daris.
6. *a[u]reli[us:* W; *Aureli[us:* Daris.
7–8. (blank). Daris has *Iu*[as line 9.
9. *Item* and nothing more: W and Daris 10.
14. *Item b*[*:* W and Daris 15.
15. Ŧ: W and Daris 16.
16. *aure[lius:* W and Daris 17.
25. . *V:* W; *ỊV*[*:* Fink and Daris 28, independently.

Frag. c (*CPL* Frag. I; Daris Frag. C)

P̣RID IḌ[VS
μεγιστε[
δεδομεν̣ —[
]ογου ζ̣ . β̣ . . σ^{υ}——
] . κρατου . . . μο̣ν̣ λδ^{e}——
] . [.] . . . [κ]ανωπου ρχε–
] . . . ιζ—

c 2–3. μεγιστε[αυτοκρατορ επι]δεδομεν: W; δεδομ[: Daris. If it made sense, μετιστε would be a more acceptable reading. Even in reading μεγιστε, the vocative arouses suspicion.
4. λόγου ζ οβ [*3*]*:* W; λ]όγου ζ οβ: Daris.
5. αρ]ποκρατου ερμου λδ: W.
6.] κανωπου ριε–: W; ρις[: Daris.

12

Guard Roster?

PDur. 113 (inv. D. P. 31 verso) A.D. 230–240?

Transcription and commentary, frag. e only: *Final Rep.* v, no. 113; *edidi.*

Under this inventory number are five scraps of papyrus, one of which, frag. e, is blank on the recto and so cannot be proved to belong with the others. But it joins another scrap found among the fragments of **15** and so at least is a part of this group of papyri which have morning reports on the recto (**48**, **50**, **54**, and **56**) and guard rosters on the verso (**12**–**15**). All that can be read on any of these five fragments is names; but their arrangement in a continuous text rather than in columns is sufficient grounds for classifying the text as a guard roster.

The date is based partly on the hand, partly on the mention of the centurion Naso in a-b-c line 10, and partly on the possible presence in frag. e 4 of a centurion Themarsas, not otherwise attested. His tenure, if he was a centurion, cannot be dated; but the greatest number of openings for it lies in the years between 225 and 240. A date nearer 240 seems most likely because Naso is otherwise attested only in **15** and **16**, both of 240 or later.

The recto of these fragments is **54**.

Frags. a–b–c

]. . [
].[
].ọ.ụṣ[
].[ ]ḅassụ[s] .[
]ḥ.[ ]abseus ḅ[.].ḅ[
]. . . .[ ].[ ]. . . . .[
]ṣ[ ].aụ.[ ]ụs zaḅdiḅ[ol-
]. .ṃi[ ]ẓ[.].ḅạ[ ]ṣ malcḥ[
]. .[ ].rị. . . .[.]s th. .[
].[ ] ϒ naṣọṇ[i]ṣ mo. . . .[
]. .iọạụ[ ].lqụ[
]. .[ ]. . .[ ]ẓebiḍ[
].[ ]. .sam.[ ]e.ạ[
]. au.[
].i. . .[
].ad[
].[
]io[
].[
]aụṃ[

a–b–c 9. The letter after *th* is not *e* but may be *i*.
10. There is a remnant of a letter or symbol, like a flattened *a* or *r*, above and to the left of the first *n* of *nasonis*, to the right of the centuria-symbol. I do not know what it means.

Frag. d

]. . .[
]ṣ a[. .].[
]b.elba[.]. .[
].e.ụṃ.[
].e.[ ].[
]ọ[

Frag. e

].[.].l[
mom]bogeus m[a]lc̣ḥ[
]. fl· demeṭr[ius
] ϒ thẹmaṛsạ[
].[

e 2. Since the names are not in columns, *mombogeus* and *malch* may be parts of the names of two persons.
4. The traces read as the centuria-symbol may be *ẹi* instead.

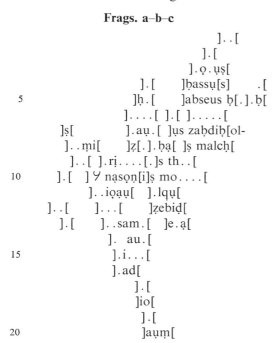

13

Guard Roster

PDur. 106 (inv. D. P. 17 verso) A.D. 235–240

Transcription and commentary: *Final Rep.* v, no. 106; *edidi.*

Facsimile: ibid., plate 58, 1.

The mention of three gates (lines 6, 12, and 13) and of a horreum frumenti (17), as well as the arrangement of the names in a continuous text rather than in columns, are sufficient evidence that this is a guard roster. For a complete description of such rosters see on **15**. This text differs slightly in form from **15** in that *porta pretoriana* (6) and *porta f. . sia* (12) are followed directly by names instead of the designation of a century or turma.

The names of the centurions Heliodorus (8), *Al.*[(16), and Germanus (18) show that this roster is later than no. **27** (Nov. 30, 232), which accounts for five of the six centurions of the cohort without naming any of these. Germanus first appears in 236 (**23**) and is still in service in 250–251 (**66**). Heliodorus is otherwise attested only in **15** and **29**, ca. 240 and 241. By about 240 (**15**) all of the centurions of the period 216–235 had been replaced; and *Al.*[is not among the six named in **15**. From then until the fall of Dura there are only five texts where he could have appeared: **30**, **32**, and **16**, all of 241–242; **66**, of 250–251; and **19**, of 242–256. Probability therefore favors dating the present text earlier than **15** and later than **23**.

The first fourteen lines and *iulius* in line 15 are in a large, rough hand like that of **15**. The remainder is in a different and smaller script.

The recto of this papyrus is **48**.

]. . [
]. . [. .]. . . [.]ṣ ba. [
]ṛị. . ạụṛẹḷ [. . .]ḥ. . . . . . . [
]. . . [. .]ṇas. . . sti[
ı]ạṛhạḅ[o]l[.]. as. p̣ạọ. [
]p̣[o]ṛıạ [p]ṛetoriạṇa alexaṇ[dr]ụṣ . [
]. [. .]. . . oụp̣ẹị ạurẹl bargạs . [
] ϒ ḥ[e]l[io]ḍorị ạụṛẹḷ cọ[
]arṣi. . grạ. . . . . qụọạḍ. [. .]. . . . [
]. [. .]ạṛẹạ. . . . [. . . .]. . . ṣạṛạ ạel. . . l. aẹ. s zebiḍa . . . [
]. ọgeneṣ ḅạ[. . .]ẹ. . . a aụṛ[e]l [ ]. . . . . ṣ. p̣. . p̣ạẹṣ. [
]ạḅẹḍ[. .]. c̣ṛẹ[. . .]. . malchi p̣orṭạ f̣. . sia aurel cḷạụdius[
]. el˙ ḅạṣṣụṣ [. . .]. . aḍ ḅạḷịṣṭạs [.]lạ. ṭịọ. ạc̣us porta q[

]ạg̣ṣ[.]sg̣ạs sias˙ aurel bargas[
]iulius (*vacat?*) . . . ị . . . ṣ Ƴ . [
] . . . [.]a . . . . . ạ.c̣ụs Ƴ al.[
].rụṃṭii oṛeo frumenṭ[i
]eị Ƴ germani ụ.[. . .].[
]ạthes [m]ạlc̣[h
] . . . [

Few of the new readings in the text are of any help in understanding it; but it is hoped that they represent a closer approach to deciphering what was actually written.

2.]. . [. . .]*r*. . [.]*ṣba*.[*:* D.
3.]*ṛị*[. .] . . . . . [. . .] . . [. .] . . . . [*:* D.
4.]*ṇas*. . *uṣ ṛạ*[*:* D.
5.]*ḥ*[. .]*ḷ*[. .]*as.ọṇ*.[*:* D. The second letter after *s* may be *p*.
7. *Ạurẹl Basṣụs*[*:* D.
8. D shows only six doubtful letters.
9.]*ạṛịi*. . *rạ* . . . . . *; quẹ* . . . [*:* D. The remains at the beginning may be the end of *themarsas*. For *quọạḍ*.[cf. **15** ii 13.
10.]*aṛẹạ* . . . [. . . . .]*ṃ; Ạel* . . . *l*. . *ẹ.s:* D.
11. *ṣ* . . . [.]*pṛịṣ*.[*:* D.
12. *Ạbẹḍ*[. . .].*ạ*.[*:* D.
13. *aḍbạl* . . . . *s; ḷaṛṭiọ.aç̣us; porta aq*[*uaria:* D.
14.]. . *ṣgas siạṣ:* D.
15. . . *ụ* . . . *ṣ:* D.
16.] . . . *a*. . [.]*ịạg̣ụs:* D.
17.].*ḍ.ịṇtii:* D. The two *i*'s may be a numeral.
18. *Ẓ*[*:* D. The character after *germani* looks very much like the top of the centuria-symbol; but it is hard to imagine a reason for the use of the symbol at this point. Possibly *germani* (*centurionis*) *p*[*rinc*]*i*[*pis*, comparing **50** 1 and 8?

14

Guard Roster

PDur. 108 (inv. D. P. 67 verso); *vidi* A.D. 235–240

Transcription and commentary: *Final Rep*. v, no. 108; *edidit* Gilliam.

Facsimile: ibid., plate 58, 2.

As Gilliam notes, this piece may be from the same roll as **13**. The hand seems the same as that in lines 1–14 of **13**; and on the recto the hand is like that of **48**. The date follows from these considerations.

The recto of this piece is **56**.

Ƴ ge]ṛṃạni aurel ẓ[a]ḅḍ[
]ẹ aurel [a]lẹx̣ạṇ[drus
] . . . . oreo f̣ṛ[u]m[enti
au]ṛẹ[l] hel[

1. *Aurel* . . . [*:* D.
4. *Hel*[*iodorus:* D. *aurel* seems probable; but one might read *ạ* Ƴ *hel*[*iodori*.

15

Guard Roster

PDur. 107 (inv. D. P. 9 verso) ca. A.D. 240

Transcription and commentary: *Final Rep.* v, no. 107; *edidi.*

Facsimile of col. i and left edge of col. ii: ibid., plate 59.

This is the largest of the guard rosters and provides material for a general outline of their form. The essentials are:

1. a date by day and month: col. ii 7, *viiii kal iun.*
2. a designation of the places to which soliders were assigned: col. i 9, *hospitio*; i 14, *hospitio* (?) *dec(urionis) apoloni*; i 17, *porta*; i 18 and ii 11, *porta praetoriana*; i 22, *hospitio (centurionis) praepos(iti)*; col. ii 8, *porta*; ii 9, *groma*; ii 10, *porta aquaria*; ii 15, *porta f.ri*; ii 16, *hospitio*]*ạọị ạḍ preposi*[; and ii 22, *templo*. The mysterious *sfetules* of col. i 5 and 19, ii 12 and 14, and frag. c 3 (cf. **17** 3: *sfetl*) probably belongs here, though an explanation of it is still to seek. So likewise *quo arabu*[*m*, ii 13, and some of the other unexplained readings. **13** and **14** add a *horreum frumenti*; **13** perhaps *ad ballistas*; and **17** *ad signa.*
3. the names of the soldiers assigned to each post, with their identification by century or turma.

A sprinkling of numerals is also found; but the principle of their distribution is not clear.

The breadth of the column is considerable; col. ii 11 and 12 both number over 100 letters (ca. 108 and 102). The number of men is also great. All the lines in col. i are full to the end, as well as the first five lines of ii; and ii 6 is nearly full. Each day's entry must then have occupied about thirty lines; so that a conservative estimate of six men's names to the line leads to a minimum of about 180 men detailed for this duty daily.

The date is derived partly from the fact that the recto is dated in the second half of May, 239, partly from the names of the centurions. Bargas and the two Marini, centurions in **66** (A.D. 250 or 251) along with Achaeus and Germanus, are not yet present; but Heliodorus, who seems to have had only a brief career with the xx Palmyrenorum, is here; and he is attested for either 239 or 241 by **29**. Cf. also the discussion of the date of **17**.

The recto of this papyrus is **50**.

Col. i

[*ca.* 65–75].ịṃ[*ca.* 12 Ɣ p]ṛisc[i] auṛ[el] iarhaeus
[*ca.* 40–45]...[– – –]ịạḍ.[.]..[– – – i]arhaeus ṇiṣṃosa
[*ca.* 40–45]. flau[ius ...]...[.].[*ca.* 7].ṛoṃ..[..].....[– – –].us aurel clauḍ[i]ụs
[*ca.* 40–45].[s]almeṣ auṛ[e]l ṃe..ḍ[– – –]ẹl ḍ[...]. [.] .[...] .[.]..l[– – –]ṣ..ṣọ.
ṃọbiaeus addẹị
[*ca.* 40–45]ma f[l]ạuius ṇẹ..[..].ṣ[...].ina[– – –]ẹ̣ị.[– – –]..ọ.[– – –] ṣ[i]ḷuanus
ṣf̣ẹṭuleṣ ị
[*ca.* 40–45]ṃe T^{u} ṛomulḷị ḅạ[*ca.* 10].s[*ca.* 10]e..ṃ..[– – –]...ṇa Ɣ achaei

[*ca.* 35–40 iar]ḥạḅọles .a.[.]c̣iạ.i ạ.[*ca.* 7] aurel ạḷ..[*ca.* 7]l.ḅ.sḅạ..[– – –] e....ụs absaẹṛịa
[*ca.* 40–45]ẹ.ọ[....]elạ...ọṃ[*ca.* 6]ạs ϒ f̣eḷi[cis *ca.* 6].[.]...[– – –]Ṭᵘ antiochi aurel
[*ca.* 45–50]ọgelus ṃạ[lc]ḥ[i o]ṣpiṭịo auṛẹḷ[.].[– – –]germa[n – – –]antiochus ϒ heliodori
[*ca.* 40–45]ṣịọ[*ca.* 15]ṃḅriussuṛi..us ϒ ạc̣ḥ[aei ..]...[..]...ill[.] ito..o ϒ germani
[*ca.* 60]ntụs ạụṛel ṃ[o]c̣imụṣ[aurel]ṇebumarius Tᵘ ⟦ϒ naṣọṇis⟧ (above: coc̣ẹi[a]ṇa)
[*ca.* 59]..ḍ..[.].. ḍemẹtṛiụṣ ....[– – –]..s aurel barṇạeus ạụṛẹḷ
[*ca.* 62].ṃụṣ ạụṛel ..[– – –].ṣ..[a]ụṛel iạṛ.[.].ṣo
[*ca.* 55 os]piṭịọ dec̣ apọlọṇi.[......]. [.]su [– – –] ϒ [a]chaei aurel ọg[as] iarạḅoleṣ
[*ca.* 62]f̣lauius marị..[.]..[– – –]s. ṇ[i]samṣi ϒ nasonis aurel
[*ca.* 53 aure]l ḅạṛ[s]ẹṃeas zaḅ...ṣ.....[.].ẹ..[.....].[au]rel siluanus prior
[*ca.* 56]ṃonim[u]s prior [...].[..]ḅ[.....]pọṛṭ[a ......]a ϒ prisc̣i bassus maccei
[*ca.* 56].ri auṛẹl ṃarinuṣ u . .[.]l. aụṛẹḷ[...].ṛ pọṛṭạ pṛẹtorriana
[*ca.* 56]ṣf̣eṭụles i ϒ feliḉiṣ aurel bassụs .ị ii aurẹḷ uictoriṇus iii iulius
[*ca.* 56]ṭo ḷẹg ϒ ạchaẹi zebịṇṇuṣ haṣc̣ia ii aurel [t]heọdọrus iii aurelius
[*ca.* 56] ϒ ..[.].[.]....[.]ṭẹṣia ϒ nasonis occ̣ḅạnas .[....] aurel antoninus pọs
[*ca.* 56]... theṃarṣạs malchi ospitio ϒ pṛepọs ... ϒ nasonis aurel bạṛṇisianụṣ
[*ca.* 56] aḅbalmaei ϒ achaei ogelus thẹṃarsas ϒ pṛ⟨i⟩sc̣i flau[i]ụṣ demeṭṛius

i 1.]..[;]*risc̣[:* D.
2.].*a*.[; *ṇismoṣi:* D.
4.]*l*[; *ṃẹ*[.]*c̣ọ*[; no reading for *l* in the middle of the line;]...*s*..: D. The last name could be simply *biaeus addaei;* but the letters before the *b* remain an enigma.
5. No reading for *ṣ* after *ṇẹ* or for *o* after *c̣ị*; *ṣẹẹṭules:* D.
6. After *romulli,* .*ạ*[*ca.* 14].[: D.
7. *iar*]*ḥạḅọle* ..*ạ*.[.]*c̣iạ* ϒ ..[;].*ḅ*..[;]*e*...*ẹs absaẹṇa:* D. For the last name cf. col. ii 13 app.
8.]..[....] *ịụ*..*ọṃ*[;]...*i*[*ca.* 6]. *ạntiochi:* D.
9. *ọgeluṣ* .[..].[;].*ṛsịto*.*au*...[: D.
10.]..[;].*ẹṃ*.*uscuṛi*.*ṇṣ*; *ạc̣*[*haei:* D. The letters *ito*.*o* are written large.
11.].*c̣hụs;* ⟦..*ṃ*...[.]*i*⟧: D.
12.]..*od*..[;]..*ḍem*.*ṣ*[..]...[; *barṇạeus ạuṛ*[*el:* D.
13.].*ṣ*...[.].*us iạṛ*....*o:* D.
14.]...*ọc̣ṣṭạ*.*olg*. ϒ[;]*ṣụ*[*s*] ϒ *ạchaei; ịg*[..]; *iarạḅole:* D. In *apoloni* the *p* is corrected from *e* or *s*; and there is a correction in *on*. At the end of the line *iaraboles* is written over an erasure, where traces of an *l* remain.
15.]*ṣ*..[.]*sam*..*i:* D.
16.]*lọ*..[..]*ẹmeas; a*]*ụrel:* D.
17. The *a* before *prisci* is written large. Very possibly *port*[*a aquari*]*a;* cf. **17** a 6.
18. *ụ*[ ] ...*l*....: D. The *u* after *marinus* is probably a numeral. On either side of the doubtful character which follows there is about half a centimeter of blank papyrus.
19.]*ṣẹẹṭụles:* D. The *i* after *bassus* is probably a numeral.
20. *ẹr*.*ṣcia:* D. The letters *to leg* are written large.
21.]*ẹ*...[; *gẹsia:* D. At the end, *pos*(*terior*). Cf. *prior* in i 16 and 17.
22. *prepọṣọ*..; *ḅaṛ*[.]*ṇnianạṣ:* D. One might possibly read *prepoṣiṭị ạ*; but how account for the last letter?

Col. ii

.ạụ.r.[...].ạnaṭị.ị auṛẹl [....]..[.....].[*ca.* 5].us helioḍori Ṭᵘ c̣oc̣[eia]ṇa ạụrel z.[.]..[.]sṆẠOCi.[
bassus sịạ...ṇ. Tᵘ anṭịọchi aurel th[*ca.* 8].as Tᵘ coceiana aurel ṃạlchus .... [.]..[
[.]ṣ.[...].ṛẹịp..iṇạṣiạṇus g̣[er]ṃạ[nus *ca.* 7]pṛo ϒ ..... au[rel a]bianẹ[s] ạụṛẹḷ ḥẹlioḍọṛụ[s
ịạṭo.. [Tᵘ] ṛọṃulli auṛẹl pạ[..]ṃ....[.].[*ca.* 6]..ṣ.[.]...ṃuṭị[...]....ạṣ ṃạlchi aurel ṣạlṃ[
iul helioḍọṛụs aurẹḷ .[..].[*ca.* 9]ṣ[.....].ḅ..ụalạh.ị[..]ụl..ẹḥ..[..].. ϒ nasọṇị[s
ϒ heliodọṛị [....]ṃ.[*ca.* 14].[..]..[..].ị.uḷ. ϒ g̣ẹṛṃ[ani a]u[r]ẹl am..[...]ịụṣ (*vacat*)

viiii kal iuṇ[. . . . . . .].eṛ[u]nṭ aḍ. .g.[*ca.* 5]. .ẹiḅ ạ[u]ṛel .[.].[. . .] prior Y n[a]ṣ[o]ṇ[i]ṣ
.[. . .]. .ḥu.[
asclẹpiad[es Y p]ṛisci bạṣṣụṣ [. . . .].ịṃi Y [a]c̣ḥạẹi herṃ[o]geṇeṣ maç̣c̣io.[.]s poṛṭ-
[a *ca.* 22]ru[
moc̣iṃ[u]s ṭ[he]ṃạrsas ạụṛel [. . .].eịaḅụs groṃa Y ṇasonis a[ure]l [. .]. .eṛ.[*ca.* 22
]. .a.[*ca.* 15]erṃ[
aurel . . . . .[. . . . . au]ṛel antọ[*ca.* 7].[.].s ii portạ ạquaṛị[a] Y germạṇi aurel
. .[*ca.* 17].aṛus aụ[rel *ca.* 3].ṛo ṃarịṇus
ṃ[a]lc̣ḥi aurel malç[hu]ṣ auṛẹl .[*ca.* 12]. .abbu[.].[. . .].isọ. ualeṛ[.] eṣsuṛṃius. .
[. . . .].[.].[. . . . .] porta pṛetoriaṇ[a *ca.* 6]ṣ menander
[b]arsịnes mannọsịn Tu anti[ochi *ca.* 7]th[. . .].[. . . . .] Tu [coceian]a aurel ṃalchus
sf[e]ṭuleṣ Y heliọdọri m[o]c̣iṃụṣ ṣalme Tu pauḷini
aurel abdas Y heliodọri ṃarinus . .[*ca.* 27]ḍṛus deṃ[et]ṛị[us] a.ṛe.[.]ạṣ tereṇṭịạṇụṣ
qụọ arabu[m Y] heliodori auṛẹḷ
absas malchus salme cci Y feliçịṣ [*ca.* 18]us ṃilen[s] ạụṛel .[.].imus ạụṛẹl simạoṇẹs
ṣfeṭuḷẹ[s *ca.* 9].ạs. .[.].[
aurel barhadadus porta f̣.ṛi[*ca.* 21] Y nasoniṣ ạụṛẹl ḅelahaḅẹaṛus Y ḥeliọdori auṛ[el
. . .].[. . . . . . .].[
Y germani aurel zeṇodorus . .ọ.[*ca.* 20].[.] ṭḥ[ema]ṛṣ[a]s oṣpitiọ[.]ạọịạḍ pṛeposị
[. . . . .] ulpiụ[s . . .]. . .[
Y ṇạsọṇịs ḷicinnius alexaṇ[d *ca.* 15 a]ntoṇịṇụṣ [Tu] anṭị[oc]ḥi aurel ab.[*ca.* 11
]elp.[. . .].[.].[.]ṣ[. . .]ạụṃ.[.]i[
aḅḅạlṃaei Y achei aurel tibeṛ[*ca.* 15] aurel diomed[e]s ạ[ure]l . .[. .]. . [*ca.* 17 a]-
ụṛẹl ḥeliodọṛus .[
Y pr⟨i⟩sci aurel coceius aurel [*ca.* 20]ạs aurel nebụṃaṛị[u]ṣ auṛẹ[l . .].[*ca.* 23
]ḍ[. .].ei[
addei cassius malç[h]ụ[s] .[.]ẹ[. . ant]ịọchuṣ [*ca.* 7 Y] felicis aurel salmạ[n . . . . .].[
ịạṭọẹṣso Y ac̣ḥẹị aurel ḅ[. . . . .].eias ogeluṣ [themar]ṣ[a]s aurel barsummạṛẹ[s
aụṛel ạṛṭemịdorus iu[li]us ịuḷịanus templ[o Tu] ạpoloṇi ulp geṛṃaṇ[us

ii 1.]. . .*ạṭị; z. . . .*[.]*s. .oci.*[*:* D. The letters *naoc* may be in small capitals.

2. *ḅassuṣ. . . .ṇ.:* D.

3.]. . . . . . .*ịnṭịạrus;*]*ṭṛo; aḅ*[. .]*bianu*[*s*]*; ḥeliọdoṛị*[*:* D. Germanus' first name may be Asianus; but that name is not otherwise attested at Dura.

4.]. . . .*auti*[*:* D.

5.]*ị. .ụạḷụhç.*[;]*ọl:* D.

6.]*ạ. .*[;]. . .*uḷ.; ami.*[*:* D.

7. *iuṇ*[*ias;*]*c̣io* before *aurel;*].*aḥu.*[*:* D. After the date one would like to read *excub*]*ụer*[*u*]*nṭ aḍ ṣigṇ*[*a;* but the letter before *e* is either *e, f,* or *s*; and *s* is possible in place of *t*. Perhaps *man*]*ṣeṛ*[*u*]*nṭ*.

8.]*s pụ. .*[*:* D.

10.]*ṃarus a.*[;]. .*a.:* D.

11. *aurel ṇ.ị. . .ṣ;*].*a abdạ*[.].[.].*sḅi;*]*eḅsuṛṃius* . .[*:* D. Possibly *ualeṇ*[*s* instead of *ualeṛ*[.]. For the next name cf. .*esur.mius* in **2** xxix 10.

11–12. The designation of a century or turma should follow *pretoriana*; but that would leave a series of three names. Cf. however **13** 6, where *alexandrus* comes immediately after *pretoriana*.

12. [.]*arṛịṃes ṃaṇṇọṣịn; aurel au.*[.]*chus ṣẹ*[*e*]*ṭules:* D.

13. There is a correction in the name after *demetrius*, perhaps *aụre.*[to *aḅṣe.*[.

14.]. . .*ṃil. .*[*; si. . . .ṣẹs ṣeeṭuḷẹ*[*s:* D. The letters *cci* are written large. A numeral?

15. *portaṣ. .*[*; nasonis* [.].[. .]*ẹl.:* D. The traces at the end are on frag. a. *porta* is in large letters. *porta fori*?

16. *zenodorus. . .*[;]. .[. . . . .]. .s;]*ạc̣ịạ:* D. At the end *ulpiu*[*s* and other traces are on frag. a. The next two letters after *ospitio* are written large.

17. The traces following *elp*. are on frag. a.

18. The last two names are on frag. a.

19. The traces at the end are on frag. a.

21. *f̣aṭọṭro:* D. The second name of Ogelus Themarsas is restored from i 23.

22. *ạr.emụṣdorus:* D. The first two names are written over an erasure. There are remains of an *h* under *ur* of *aurel*; there is something under the *t*; and *mi* has an extra stroke. The restoration [Tu] *apoloni*, thought doubtful in D, is now confirmed by the reading in i 14.

Frag. a

Frag. a is now incorporated into the text, as noted in the apparatus to col. ii 15–19.

Frag. b

Not previously published. The papyrus is quite dark and the surface is much abraded. The hand is small and very different from that of the main body of this text and the other fragments. It is certainly from a different column, if not from a different text, though the recto (**50**) is clearly a morning report, as with the other parts of **15**, and the arrangement of the names implies a guard roster. The first line is also the top of the column.

].[ ].b...[
]ḷVỊỊỊ. 𐆛 .[.].[
]..[a]ụṛelius .[
].qu...a[.]g̣.....ạs *Illegible traces*
]...ạṛịẹs ṇaṛ.[..]ḥ.[
].[.].[.]n[ ]niụs [.] *Illegible traces*
].oụ[
One line lost?
].ạ[.]...[
Illegible traces].ḍ.[
]..[ ]f̣elici m[
].. auṛẹḷ[i]us zẹṇọbius[
].. ṃ..ḷ[ ]ṛ ụ[

Frag. c

].[
]ḍ..[ ]..[
]..m.. sf̣ẹṭuḷẹ[s
]ḥi 𐆛 germani f̣ḷ[
]. 𐆛 heḷiodori aụ[rel
]...ṃ. aurel ..[

Frag. d

]..[
].. 𐆛 f̣[e]ḷ[i]cis .[
]xx̣.. themarṣ[a
].s
].

Frag. e

].ḅ[..].[
]. ạụṛel ḍ[
].ṃaṛị.[
]ḅus.

Frag. f

].bel[
]. aḅṣṣ.ạ.ịeị.[
]ṛus

Frag. g

] 𐆛 naṣọṇ[is

Frag. h

]...ṃus[
].ṭọ..[

Frag. i

]...[
]...i[
].u.[.].i.[
au]ṛel .....[
]....[

Frag. b 2: The numeral (if it is one) may be in small capitals.
4. Perhaps *porta*] *ạquạṛịa*.
7. The letters may be small capitals.
10. The last letter visible of the name is *i*; but it is hard to believe that a dative was used here. More probably this is an error for [𐆛] *felicis*.
c 4.].*i*: D.
e 2.].*ạṣ*.*el*.[: D. The letter after *l* may be either *d* or *b*.
f 1.]. *bel*[: D.
h 1.].*uṃus*[: D.
2.]....[: D.
i 3.].*u*...[: D.
4.]*ṛel*.....[: D.

16

Guard Roster

PDur. 112 (inv. D. Pg. 17) A.D. 241–250

Transcription and commentary: *Final Rep.* V, no. 112; *edidi.*

Facsimile of recto only: ibid., plate 61, 2.

Only the arrangement of the names and designations of centuries leads to classifying the recto (hair side) of this parchment as a guard roster. The nature of the verso is even less clear. Presumably the numerals are the total of the men in some category in each century, with a grand total of 417 for the entire cohort.

On the date, see the detailed discussion under **17**. Since the names of Achaeus and Naso are on the flesh side, Naso must have been active after Bargas and Mocimus became centurions. This text, like **17**, must be later than **29**, A.D. 241, and probably earlier than **66,** A.D. 250.

Recto

]l . . [
a]ụṛẹḷ siluanus . . ϒ barga aurel . . . . l[
]ṣ marcus ulp siluanus ϒ mocimi[

Verso

ϒ ạc̣haei ḷvii
ϒ ṇạṣọ[nis] ḷxiịị c̣cccxvii

Recto 2. *siluanus pṛ(ior); aurel ọạ. . . l*[*:* D. Instead of *o* one could read *b*, *d*, or *u*.

17

Guard Roster

PDur. 110 (inv. D. Pg. 19); *vidi* — A.D. 242 to 250 or 256

Transcription and commentary: *Final Rep.* v, no. 110; *edidit* Gilliam.

Facsimile: ibid., plate 61, 1.

The arrangement of the names in a continuous text and the mention of the *porta aquaria* (line 6) and *porta praetoriana* (7) are sufficient to assure that this text is a guard roster.

The date is based on the hand, very similar to that of **15**, though more expert, and on the names of the centurions Bargas, Germanus, and Marinus. Gilliam tentatively suggested A.D. 241, *Gordiano II et Pompeiano*, on the basis of his reading of frag. b, 1; but it seems impossible to reconcile the traces at the beginning of the line with the name of Gordian. The centurions named are all found in **66** of A.D. 250–251; but in **66** there are two Marini, prior and posterior, whereas here there is only one. The present text is therefore either earlier or later than **66** and certainly later than **15**, for **66** shows that, in addition to the three centurions named here, Achaeus was active until 250, so that only two places remain in this text for the other four centurions of **15**—Felix, Heliodorus, Naso, and Priscus. **16** proves that Naso was still present after Bargas and Mocimus joined the cohort; so, since Germanus is also present in **66** and must therefore be assumed in **16**, there is room there for only one of Felix, Heliodorus, and Priscus. Like Bargas in **16**, Felix is associated with Mocimus in **32**; it is therefore likely that in both **16** and **32** the complete roll of centurions was Germanus, Mocimus, Achaeus, Felix, Naso, and Bargas. But since Heliodorus is present in **29**, A.D. 241, it follows that **16** and **32** are later, and that the present text is still later because the introduction of Marinus requires the omission of either Felix, Mocimus, or Naso. One at least of the other two was eliminated in **66**, when the second Marinus was added; but there appears to be no way of deciding the order of **17** and **66**. General probability perhaps favors placing **17** earlier, merely on the ground of the somewhat greater interval of time from 241 to 250 than from 250 to 256, and the obvious fact that more papyri have survived from the period before 250 than after.

It is to be noted that this text is on parchment, not papyrus. As Gilliam points out, this may be evidence of a shortage of papyrus at Dura.

The verso, that is, the flesh side, is blank.

Frag. a

]. ϒ marini ạp̣ọḷḷ[
iarha]ḅoḷẹṣ ϒ bargạ[ ]. . . .i[
]. ius sfetl ϒ bạṛg̣[a]ṛẹịọqu. .ariṣ[
].c̣hi ϒ barga[ ]l[ ].[ ]e. .ṛiasa.[
].am ϒ [g]ẹ[r]ṃ[a]ṇi aḅ. .[ ]l[ ].sfe. .ẹss.[
]. .ṛịus pọ[rta a]quaria ϒ bạṛg̣ạ[ ]ṛiḷlus
]pọṛṭa pṛaẹṭorianạ [ϒ] g̣ermani iul. . .[. . .].[
]. . . .ḥariod.[ ]ϒ g̣ẹrmani aurel ạṛi.[. . . .]. . . . . .[
]. .ị.c[.].es ϒ [ba]rga a[u]rel abeḍṃạḷc̣ḥ[. . . . .]. . .[
]. .o.uṣ . .ṣi. .ac̣hi mạṛinus ṃ[.]l[
]uṭ. .ṛuṣ.s ạ[*Illegible traces*
]. . .us ḥalas aṭ signa ord ạuṛẹl[
].[ ]h. .[ ].[

Frag. b

]ḅẹ.ẹdiọ.m[
]ṭ[ ]. . . .[
]ṇdri.[

a 1. *Mạriṇi* . .[*:* D.

2.]*ọlhi:* D;]. .*ọ* . . .[at the right end.

3.].*us ṣ.ẹ.ḷ:* D. The reading *sfetl* appears to be an abbreviated form of *sfetules*, found in **15** i 5 and 19; ii 12 and 14, and frag. c 3. No one, to my knowledge, has proposed an explanation of it. Right end,]. . . . *quiṇṭis:* D.

4.].*lhi:* D;]. .*ianạ*[at the right end.

5.].*m*.[. .].[.]. . .*ị*. . .[*:* D;]. .*ḟ*. .*ṣ*. .[at the right end. Possibly *sfetules*? Cf. line 3. After *germani* perhaps *aḍ* instead of *ab*.

6.]. .*nus:* D;].*lus*[at the right end. Perhaps *cy*]*rillus*? **15** i 17 may also mention the *porta aquaria*.

7. *p*]*ọṛṭạ; Iul*. . .[*:* D.

8.]. . .*ṛiod:* D. Gilliam: "*prae*]*ṭọṛịo duḳ*[*cis* and *Aurel Ạc̣i*[*bas* are possible, though a parallel would make the first more plausible."

9.]. . .*es; Abeḍṃạḷc̣ḥ*[*us:* D.

10.]. . . . . . .[. .]*ạc̣hi;* .[*:* D. Gilliam: "The name preceding *Marinus* may end -*athi*." At the end, *a* is possible instead of *m*.

11.]. . .[.]*rg*[*:* D.

12.]. .*ṣ*. .*ḷạṣ*. .*sigṇa:* D. Gilliam: "*ad signa* does not seem possible"; but *at* is an extremely common spelling of *ad*.

13. No reading in D.

b 1.]. . .*et pom*[*:* D. The *b* seems clear; but *boga* or *bro* could be read. I am not sure that the hand of this fragment is the same as that of frag. a.

2–3. No readings in D.

18

Guard Roster?

PDur. 111 (inv. D. Pg. 15) A.D. 242–256

Transcription and commentary: *Final Rep.* v, no. 111; *edidit* Gilliam.

The classification of this scrap is highly uncertain; but the projection of the date into the margin recalls **15** ii 7; and the names and centuries seem intermixed as in the guard rosters.

The date depends upon the similarity of this piece to **17**.

Gilliam's text is reproduced here.

After illegible traces of three lines:

sil[uanus?
iii iduṣ[
7 [. .] . [
7 [

19

Guard Roster

PDur. 109 (inv. D. Pg. 14) A.D. 242–256

Transcription and commentary: *Final Rep.* v, no. 109; *edidi.*

Facsimile: ibid., plate 60, 3.

The word *groma* in line 6 assures that this is a guard roster, even if the arrangement of names did not.

The dating rests upon the presence of the centurion Bargas. See the detailed discussion under **17**.

The verso (flesh side) is blank.

]·[
]··[
] ϒ . . . [ ] . . . . [
]. a ạụrel gaian[us .]c̣. . [
] . . . aụṛẹl ṣimọạṛus[ ]ϒ̣ baṛ[ga
]. ṛus groṃa ϒ [g]ẹṛṃạṇi ịẹạṣtel[
]. ẹ aurel ḅaṛsuthẹ[ ]b[
]ṣ aụṛẹḷ . oraṛẹẹṛạḷị[
]·[·]. . . [

1 and 2. No readings in D.

3. The first letter of the centurion's name begins with a stroke slanting down from right to left: *a*, *m*, or *r* is most likely.

4. ϒ *bar*]*ga*? Cf. **66** b ii 21–22.

5.]. . . *ạ*. . . *l*. *ṭiṃ*. *i*. *a*: D, line 3. The first letter of the second name is probably not *t*; but could just possibly be *a* or *r*. The letters *ọạṛ* could also be read *pṛ* or *ọṃ*.

6.]. *ius*: D; *c̣ạṣṭel*[*lo* cannot be read because a personal name is needed.

7.]. ; *ḍạrṇac̣hẹụ*[*s*: D, with a comment that *ụar-ṣuṭheu*[*s* is possible and that the initial cannot be *b*. In the apparatus (Welles?) "The unidentified name can be read *ḄAṚA*. *ṬH*, and the last two letters may be *OR*, with some difficulty. It would be easier to explain Barasthor (Introd. p. 63) but the letter in the middle resembles an overly large *U*, not an *S*."

8. *ạụṛẹ*[*l*] . *orạṛf*. *ṛi*. [: D.

20

List of Decurions and Centurions with Dates of their Promotions

PMich. III 164 (inv. 1804); *vidi* April 243 to April 244

Transcription, commentary, and facsimile:

1. Henry A. Sanders, in *Classical Studies in Honor of John C. Rolfe* (Philadelphia 1931) 265–83. See also Wilcken, *Archiv* 10 (1932) 278–79.
2. J. F. Gilliam, "The Appointment of Auxiliary Centurions (P. Mich. 164)," *TAPA* 88 (1957) 155–68; cited as **G**.

Transcription with notes: Sanders, *PMich.* III 164. Cited as **S**.

Text: *CPL*, no. 143, reproduces Sanders' readings in *PMich.* III. These are now obsolete. Daris, no. 27, reproduces Gilliam's.

Commentary: J. Frank Gilliam, "The *Ordinarii* and *Ordinati* of the Roman Army," *TAPA* 71 (1940) 127–48.
Idem, "Egyptian 'Duces' under Gordian," *Chronique d'Égypte* 36 (1961) 386–92.

The nature of this text is sufficiently indicated by the pattern of the entries. With the exception of the heading in lines 16–17, each entry begins with a name in capitals, followed in cursive by (1) the date of the soldier's enlistment, (2) *factus dec(urio)* or *factus ord(inatus)*, (3) a statement of the rank from which the man was promoted, and in a second line (4) the name of the person who promoted him, and (5) the date of the promotion. Since the promotions were not all made in the same year (cf. line 3 and 20), this is not a list of men who were being promoted, but of centurions and decurions in the order of their seniority within their unit and rank. Gilliam observes in *Chron. d'Égypte* 36.387, note 5, that this text must come from a bureau above the level of a single military unit.

How much of the text is lost is difficult to say, but in all probability not very much on the left and right. The names in capitals were probably not preceded by a praenomen; and the lines immediately after the names could hardly have begun with more than a date by day and month. Line 6 suggests that at most 15 letters are missing from the left ends of the cursive lines, while in line 9 only 6 letters are needed. On the right side the necessary restorations in lines 9, 15, and 20 prove that about 12–15 letters are lacking.

The date of the text is fixed within narrow limits. Line 15, if the restoration there is correct, shows that it is later than April 6–12, 243, while line 12 guarantees that it can be no earlier than November–December 242. In line 11, on the other hand, the title *gordiana* proves that the list was compiled before Gordian's assassination in March 244 was known in Egypt. The most probable limits for the date are therefore April 243 to April 244.

Gilliam ("Ordinarii" 141–42) has already observed that the unit in lines 1–15 was either an ala or a cohors equitata miliaria; and in fact the former choice is the likelier. The present text shows at least five decurions entering the unit in one year. This would mean that the entire staff of decurions was replaced if this was a cohors miliaria organized like the coh. xx Palmyrenorum. An ala quingenaria, however, according to Hyginus (*De mun. castr.* 16) had 16 decurions, and an ala miliaria 24; so that a turnover of five men in a year, though large, would not be impossible. There is no way of being sure whether this text is to be dated before or after the battle of Resaina in 243; but the losses which would occur in any case during a campaign in difficult country help to account for the high proportion of decurions appointed in 242–243.

The verso is blank except for the ends of six lines in Greek along one edge. All that remain appear to be numerals: *C′*, *H′*, *Δ′*, *IC′*, and two unidentifiable strokes.

2–3]F̣IDIVS VICTORINVS
[7–13 p]ṛaesente et ẹxṭricạ[to] c̣[o]ṣ factus dec′ ex eq˙ leg ị[i traiana fortis — A.D. 217
[a(b) 6–12].[.].ụ′ p̣′ tụnc dụce iiị noṇaṣ apriles attico et pṛaeṭ[extato cos — April 3, 242
2?]ḌỊMVS PEṬỌSIRIS
[12–18]g̣ṛaṭ[o] ẹṭ seleucọ c̣[o]ṣ [f]ạctus dec′ ex sesq˙ alae .[— 221
[9–15]bṛẹṣ aṭṭico et praeṭẹx̣ṭaṭo c̣ọs a basileo p̣[raef aeg — Aug.–Oct. 242
A]NTONIVS ẠMMONIANVS
[7–13]. ṃạximo et urban[o] c̣[o]s factus dec′ ex sesq˙ alaẹ[— 234
[3–12 a basil]eọ u′ p′ praef [ae]g viiii˙ kal˙ nouembr attico et pr[aetextato cos — Oct. 24, 242
AV]RẸḶIVṢ HIERAX
[17–23 cos factu]ṣ ḍ[e]c′ ex dupḷ alae gall gorḍ[ianae
[26–32]. . . ḍec aṭṭic̣ọ ẹṭ praeṭẹxta[to cos — Nov. 14–Dec. 13, 242
]ORIGEṆ[E]S
[9–15 diuo] ạ[l]ẹx̣ạṇḍṛo ẹ[t dion]e cos f̣[actu]ṣ [de]c̣′ ẹx eq .[— 229
[9–15].ọ[.]. coḥ vi p[r]′ . .[. .]ạ.[. .].ọ[i]ḍuṣ a[pr]iles a[rriano et papo cos — April 6–12, 243

] COH III ITVRẠẸ[O]ṚỴṂ[
] ORDD [
PET]ẸṆEFOTES HIERAX [
[9–15 ag]ṛic̣ọla eṭ c̣lementino cos factus dec′ ex̣[— 230
[a ianuari]o tunc praef aeg iii kal sẹpṭ agricola et c̣[lementino cos — Aug. 30, 230
A]ỴṚẸLIVS Ạ[R]POCRA[T]ỊOṆ[
[6–12]ṣ ạg̣ṛic̣ọla eṭ c̣lementino c̣[os] f̣ạctus ord [e]x̣ eq[— 230
[21–27].an[5–8 pr]aef̣ aeg n[onis

TRANSLATION

]fidius Victorinus: [enlisted] 217; promoted to decurion from cavalryman of the legio ɪ[ɪ Traiana fortis] [by . . .] vir perfectissimus, at that time dux, April 3, 242.

]dimus Petosiris: [enlisted] 221; promoted to decurion from sesquiplicarius of the ala [. . .] [August–October] 242 by Basileus prefect of Egypt.

Antonius Ammonianus: [enlisted] 234; promoted to decurion from sesquiplicarius of the ala [. . .] by Basileus, vir perfectissimus, prefect of Egypt, October 24, 242.

Aurelius Hierax: [enlisted . . .]; promoted to decurion from duplicarius of the ala Gallica Gordiana [by . . . November–December], 242.

]Origines: [enlisted] 229; promoted to decurion from cavalryman [. . .] [. . .] cohors VI praetoria, April [6–12], 243.

Cohors III Ituraeorum

Centurions

Petenefotes Hierax [enlisted] 230; promoted to decurion from [. . .] by Ianuarius, at that time prefect of Egypt, August 30, 230.

Aurelius Harpocration [enlisted] 230; promoted to centurion from cavalryman [. . .] [by . . .] prefect of Egypt, on the [5–7] of [*month, year*].

1. *AU*]*FIDIUS:* S and G. There is no trace of the top bar of the *F*; but no other letter is possible. On the left, above the cross-bar are remains which are hard to reconcile with *A*, *M*, or *V*. Perhaps *DE*]*ḶFIDIVS*, assuming that phi was rendered as *F*. Other possibilities besides Aufidius are Fufidius, Amfidius, Nymfidius, and Xifidius. See Dornseiff-Hansen, *Rückläufiges Wörterbuch der griechischen Eigennamen* (Berlin 1957). Gilliam *ad loc.* is probably right that no *praenomina* were used.

2. [*E*]*xtrica*[*to*]*:* G; *ex q*(*uaestionario*)*:* S; *ex eq*: Fink and G, independently. Expand *dec*(*urio*) *ex eq*(*uite*) *leg*(*ionis*) *ị*[*i traianae fortis*. Gilliam points out that line 11 makes it probable that the legion was named, and that only the *II Traiana* was in Egypt at this time; but these units may not have been in Egypt (see on line 15), so that some uncertainty remains. Line 15 shows that it is possible to have as many as fifteen letters beyond the present right edge of the papyrus; and this agrees well with the indications of line 6 regarding the left margin. That is, the names in capitals were approximately centered over the lines in cursive, which began about 8–10 letters to the left of the names and ran about 15 letters farther on the right.

3. [*a Bas*]*ị*[*l*]*ẹọ praẹf Aeg II Nonạs:* S;].[.]. . . . . *ṇc*. . .*IỊII':* G; and in his textual notes Gilliam suggests *tụnc ḍuç*(*e*) as a possibility, citing Pearl as reading]. .*ụ'p' tụnc duc*( ). The *u* of *tunc* looks like an *o*; but Youtie agrees that there can be no doubt of *tunc*, or of *duce*, with the *ce* in ligature. There is no trace of the upper half of the loop of *p*; but *praef* in line 20 shows that the top of the letter was sometimes left open. The remains before *u'p'* are those of two letters which drop below the line. The one on the right is the tail of *F* in line 1; the other could be *f*, *h*, *p*, *q*, *r*, *s*, or *t*.

The title vir perfectissimus in this context suggests that the holder, at the time when the text was composed, had become Prefect of Egypt, just as Domitius Philippus had advanced from dux to Prefect between 240 and 242 (Gilliam, *Chron. d'Égypte* 36.386–92). But this is not possible because Aurelius Basileus is attested as Prefect from August 18, 242, to April–May 245, whereas this text was written between April 243 and April 244. Perhaps we should suppose that the former dux had been promoted to another post, such as praefectus annonae, which also carried the title perfectissimus.

The date is *iii nonas*, not *iiii*. The seeming fourth stroke is the tail of the first *t* of *extricato* in line 2.

4. *C*]*ORDIUS:* S;]. . . . *ỤS:* G. Wilcken, *Archiv* 10, suggested *mus* as the last syllable. The letter before *M* most resembles *T*; but the cross-bar does not extend to the right. The first letter preserved is almost certainly *D* because of the curl inside the top of the curve; *O* is formed otherwise. Didymus is an obvious guess; but Nedimus, Hadymus, and others are found in Dornseiff-Hansen.

5. *Graṭ*[*o e*]*t;* [*f*]*ạctus:* S; *Gr*]*ạṭọ* [*e*]*ṭ:* G. The *g* and *r* are obscured by the top stroke of an *e* coming from the line below. The top of the *e* of *et* is visible above the hole. Expand *dec*(*urio*) *ex sesq*(*uiplicario*).

6. *et praep*[*osit cọḥọr et praefẹç*[*tus*] *arçis:* S; the names of the consuls restored by Fink and G, independently;]*ḅṛ; Praeṭẹ*[*x*]*ṭato:* G. Since the first four entries, lines 1–12, all record promotions made in 242, and lines 3, 9, and 12 show the dates *iii nonas apriles*, *viiii kal novembr*(*es*), and]. . . *dec*(*embres*), it is almost certain that the date in this line lies between August 14, *xviiii kal septembres*, and October 24, *viiii kal novembres*. This in turn establishes that a maximum of 15 letters is lost from the beginning of the line and thus sets the approximate position of the left margin for all the other lines in cursive. If allowance is made for the fact that the *i*'s in *xviiii*, *viiii*, and the like take up only half the space of other letters, the true maximum is probably 13 letters. In line 9, moreover, only 6 letters are certainly to be restored; so it is probable that in most lines 8–10 letters are missing at the left end.

8. Gilliam is right in saying that the letter before *maximo* may well be *s* and if so is probably the end of a month-name.

9. *ba*]*ṣiḷẹọ; prae*[*f*]*; xvi kal':* S; *prae*[*f*] *IIII' Kal':* G. The *v* of the numeral is faint but perfectly visible; it connects with the preceding *g* and the following *i*. The four *i*'s could easily be read as *iul*.

10.]*ḶIUS CHIERAX:* S;]. . .*LIỤṢ:* G. The *C* in Sanders' reading was recognized by Hunt as part of the cross-bar of *H*. The middle of the *R* and *E* of *AVRELIVS* are clearly visible on a strip of papyrus which hangs vertically below the *L* on the photograph. It should be rotated 90° clockwise to bring it into its original position.

11. *f*[*ac*]*ṭ*[*u*]*ṣ:* S. Expand: *dec*(*urio*) *ex dupl*(*icario*) *alae gall*(*icae*) *gor*[*dianae*.

12.]. *Oct:* S.
13.]*ỤṢ ORIGEṆ*[*E*]*S:* S.
14. *F*[*u*]*ṣco Ị*[*I et dextr*]*e; f*[*actus*] *d*[*ec*]*' ex sesq*[*:* S;]. . .[.]. . . . . .*ọ*.[. . . . . .]*ẹ; f*[*actus dec*]*' ẹx eq* [*leg:* G. In his apparatus Gilliam suggests the possibility of *Ç̣om*[*azont*]*ẹ cos*. The reading *alexandro* seems reasonably sure from the loop of the first *a*, the stroke from upper right to lower left of the *x*, the top of the *d*, and the *o*, as well as the spacing. The *c* of *dec* and the *e* of *ex* are very uncertain. The spot of ink after *q* is certainly not part of *u*; but any restoration of the end of this line must be highly conjectural because of the uncertainties occasioned by the reading in the first part of line 15. See the comments below.

15. *ab Honoratia*]*ṇo p ṿ praẹf Ạ*[*eg* . . . . . *N*]*ovẹ*[*mbr Se*]*veṛ*[*o et Quintiano cos*]*:* S;].*ọ*.*ṛiṣ*. . .[. . .]. [. . . . .].*ụ*.*ạ*[. . .].*ḷe*.*ạ*[*:* G. The top of the *p* in *pr* is open, like that of *u'p'* in line 3. There is no doubt about *apriles*; the loop of the *a* is visible above the *A* of *ITURAEORUM* (line 16) and *les* at the end is certain. The apparent hook at the top of the *s* is actually the tail of the *q* of *eq* in line 14. Following the series of month-names in lines 3, 6, 9, and 12, the last of which is December 242, this reading leads to the year 243 and justifies the restoration of *a*[*rriano et papo cos*] at the end of the present line.

The reading *coḥ vi p*[*r*]*'* and the unread traces which follow are much more troublesome. The usual pattern of all the entries which precede and follow calls for the identification of Origenes' former unit to follow *eq* in line 14, with the name and title of the person who promoted him at the beginning of line 15. There is always the possibility that some sort of error has confused the order of the wording in lines 14–15, just as in line 6 above; but if the regular pattern is being followed here, line 15 should begin with something like [*a* (nomen) *trib*(*uno*)] *coh*(*ortis*) *vi p*[*r*(*aetoriae*) and line 14 might end with *ex eq*(*uite*) [*coh*(*ortis*) *vi pr*(*aetoriae*)]. But this will not really do. It would be quite as normal for a praetorian *eques* to be promoted to the decurionate as for an *eques legionis* (above, line 2; and cf. *CIL* VI 2977 [Dessau 2173]: *d.m. M. Aur. Augustiano . . . . lectus in praetoria, eques sive tabularius ann. V, factus centurio in Syria*); but there is no evidence known to me that a tribune of a praetorian cohort could appoint decurions or centurions. One must rather suppose that the tribune was the person who recommended the promotion, like the legate in *CIL* VIII 21567 (. . . *et pro salute M. Aemili Macri leg. Aug. pr. pr.* . . . *propter cuius suffragium a sacratissimo imperatore ordinibus adscriptus sum*) and restore *nominante* N. *tribuno* (cf. **24** below), *suffragio* N. *tribuni*, or the like. And since praetorian tribunes were also commanders of the *equites singulares imperatoris* (*Rangord.* 106 and 137) it is quite possible that line 14 ended *ex eq*(*uite*) [*singulari*], as Gilliam suggests, p. 159, note 12, and cf. especially *CIL* VI 31151: *decurio factus ex n*(*umero*) *equitum singularium Augusti.*

On this reasoning the name of the person who actually made the promotion must have followed *coh vi pr* in line 15; but the remains are too few and scattered to support any restoration. Even the number of missing letters is uncertain, though *a ḅạ*[*sil*]*ẹọ* [*praef aeg*] might be crowded in before the date. *ab imp gordiano aug* contains the same number of letters but is harder to reconcile with the traces.

Before *coh* the photographs show parts of two letters between lines 14 and 15. Actually they are on a bit of papyrus attached to the main piece by a single fibre which, if straightened, would bring the letters into line 15, two or three spaces to the left of *coh*. Presumably they are part of the name or rank of the tribune; but they are puzzling to identify. The one on the left looks like the top of the two left-hand strokes of *n*; and the one next to it resembles an elliptical *o* with the long axis slanting downward from left to right.

Origenes' transfer from either the praetorians or the equites singulares to the present Egyptian unit is readily explicable on the supposition that all were together in Syria and Mesopotamia during Gordian's campaign against Shapor in 242–244. Compare the praetorian Aurelius Augustianus (above) *factus* (*centurio*) *in Syria* and the equites singulares in *CIL* VI 228 (Dessau 2187, A.D. 205) who were *factus decurio in Syria Foinicia* and *factus decurio in provincia Dalmatia.*

16. *ITURAE*[*O*]*RỤ*[*M*]*:* S and G. Gilliam: "Apparently the name of the cohort was not followed by *Gordiana*, unless the line was very badly centered."

17. *OR DD:* S, expanded *or*(*do*) *d*(*ecurionum*); but certainly to be read as *ord*(*inati*). See Wilcken and Gilliam *ad loc.*, and Gilliam, *TAPA* 71.127–48.

18. *Ç̣*[*AL*]*EFOFES:* S;]. .*EFOṬES:* G. Of the other names which end with the same letters, Senephotes is two letters too short and Pachompetenephotes is much too long.

19. *ag*]*ṛic*[*o*]*la:* S. In view of the heading *ORDD* and the appearance of *ord* in line 22, Gilliam is undoubtedly right in supposing that *dec* in this line is a clerical error for *ord*. Since the years of enlistment and appointment are the same, read *ex* [*pagano*, comparing **64** i 20–24?

20. [. . . . .]*oṛino praef; et Ṃ*[*aximo II:* S;]*ọ ṭụnc praef; et Ç̣*[*lementino:* G; "the beginning of the line is probably to be restored [*a Ianuari*]*o*."

21. *A*]*Ẹ*[*MI*]*ḶIVS* [. .]*ẸOCRAṬẸṢ:* S;]. . .*LIUS:* G. The reading *Arpocration* is credited by Gilliam to Pearl.

22. *f*]*ạctus orḍ* [*de*]*c' ex*[*:* S; *orḍ* [*e*]*x eq:* Fink and G, independently. For possible restorations after *eq*(*uite*) cf. above, lines 2 and 14.

23. . . . . .]*ạ et Ạeṣ:* S;]. . .[ ].*ẹ*. . .*ẹ*. .[*:* G. The prefect must be one of those who held office between 230 and 244. Of those known, only the names of Ianuarius, Honoratianus, and Annianus are possible. The remains here would permit one to read [*honora*]*ṭiaṇ*[*o*, and his long term, from December–January 232 at least until November 20, 236 (Stein, *Präf.* 131–32), makes such a reading likely; but since the prefects from 236 to 240 are not certainly known (Stein 134, and cf. Gilliam on line 15), other possibilities remain open.

21

List of Legionary Principales

Princeton Garrett Deposit 7532 recto — A.D. 235–242

Transcription, commentary, and facsimile: R. O. Fink, "A Fragment of a Roman Military Papyrus at Princeton," *TAPA* 76 (1945) 271–78.

Text: *CPL* no. 138, and Daris, no. 21, reproduce the readings in the foregoing article, except as noted.

The identification in terms of cohort as well as century of the soldiers listed here shows that they are members of a legion (cf. particularly *CIL* III 6592 = Dessau 2345: *Aurel Alexandrus quandam* (sic) *signifer leg. II Traianae for. Ger. cohor. II hastati pr.*; and Dessau 2653–55), while the fact that in at least three instances two or three of the men belonged to the same century (lines 1, 5, and 10; and 8, 14, and 15) proves that they are not centurions. The heading in line 17 may therefore indicate that the men in lines 18–21 are cornicularii; but if a numeral follows, as seems likely, the genitive *corniculariorum* needs a noun to modify. One might understand *officium* on the basis of *CIL* III 3543 (Dessau 2391): *adiutori offici corniculariorum cos.* (Cf. also Dessau 2390 and 3035). On that assumption the men in 18–21 are probably adiutores. Whatever their exact title, the men in lines 1–16 must have ranked immediately above or below them.

The only legion in Egypt at this period was the II Traiana; but it is possible that the papyrus originated in some other province.

The only means of dating the text is the consuls' names in lines 13–16 and 18–21. Since 219, in which Elagabal was consul, is represented only by his colleague Sacerdos, the list must belong to a time after Elagabal's overthrow in 222. On the other hand, the men in lines 19–21, all of whom enlisted in 216, would have been discharged about 242 even if they served twenty-six years.[1] On the consulate of Praesens, line 18, see below, pp. 146–147.

Neither the few surviving dates of enlistment nor the order of the cohorts and centuries are in regular series. Hence Gilliam's suggestion is probably right (*CP* 48 [1953] 97 and note 8) that the men are listed in order of seniority within their rank, that is, by the dates of their appointment or promotion.

The verso contains accounts in Greek.

[1] On the length of the period for which legionaries served, see G. Forni, *Il Reclutamento delle Legioni da Augusto a Diocleziano* (Milan and Rome 1953) 37–38 and 142–44; and Abdullatif Ahmed Aly, "A Latin Inscription from Nicopolis," *Annals of the Faculty of Arts, Ain Shams University* 3 (1955) 113–46. Twenty-five or twenty-six years became the commonest term of service for legionaries as well as auxiliary troops, regardless of Augustus' initial regulations.

]l[.
Y ss ualerius hispạnu[s
Y ii pil pos iunius martiaḷ[is
Y iiii pṛ pr aụrelius caeciliạ[nus
Y vi pr pos aụrelius eracḷịḍ[
⟦ Y v pr pos hẹḷụịus p̣[e]ṛ[tin]ạx . . [⟧
Y viiii p̣ịl p̣ọs flauius ulpiạ[nus
Y ii pṛ p̣ṛ uibius c̣ṛẹṣcenṣ[
Y ii pr pos fụṭṭianiụs demẹ[trius?
Y vi pr pos iulius alẹxandẹr . [
Y v pr pos neṛatius firminuṣ [
Y viiii h pos aureliuṣ maximụs . [
Y x pr pos aspriuṣ maximụs saceṛ[dote cos A.D. 219
Y ii pr pr aurelius ḍemosteṇes graṭ[o cos 221
Y ss aurelius theocles g̣ṛạto cos[221
Y i pr p̣ṛ aurelius titus c̣ọs ss[221
CORNIC̣VLARIOṚVM .X. [
Y x h pr uibius faustinus presente c̣ọ[s 217
]ds Y i h pr flauius seuerianus sab(ino) cos[216
Y ii h pr aurẹḷius aplunaris sab(ino) cos[216
Y iii pr pr ulpịus quiriṇus sabino c̣[o]ṣ [216

1. No reading in TAPA.
2. *ịṣ.ṣ.ịạṇu[s:* TAPA.
2 and 15. (*centuriae*) *s*(*upra*) *s*(*criptae*). The use of the symbol Y here when the numeral is omitted shows that the symbol is being used throughout the text in its normal signification, not as *c*(*ohors*).
3. (*centuriae*) (*secundi*) *p*(*ili*) *pos*(*terioris*).
4. (*quarti*) *pr*(*incipis*) *pr*(*ioris*).
5. (*sexti*) *pr*(*incipis*) *pos*(*terioris*). *ṃạllịọ*[*:* TAPA; *Ṃallịọl*[*:* Daris.
6. *p*[*ertin*]*ạx:* TAPA. The name is very doubtful. The traces could be read as *ṣạṃ..ṇạ* or *ṣạṇ..ṃị*.
9. *fuṣc̣ianius demọ*[*:* TAPA.
10. The consul's name probably began with *c*, *p*, or *t*.
11. *me.aṣius:* TAPA. The present reading is doubtful because there is no other example in this text of an *n* ligatured with the next letter, and because the *r* is not certain.
12. (*octaui*) *h*(*astati*) *pos*(*terioris*).
13. *aṣṣorius:* TAPA; but for the *p* cf. *aplunaris* in line 20. The name Asprius is attested in e.g. *CIL* x 7845 (Dessau 6107).
14. *Gratọ:* Daris.
15. *g̣*[*r*]*ạto:* TAPA.
16. [*c*]*oṣ:* TAPA. Expand *co*(*n*)*s*(*ule*) *s*(*upra*)*s*(*cripto*). It is just possible that this is the same person as the decurion Titus in **24** 5 and 18, or the Aurelius Titus, Y *deputatus*, in Dessau 4932 (*CIL* VI 32415).
17. *M*[*:* TAPA. Before the *x* are very slight traces of a vertical stroke along a fold in the papyrus. Accidental, or remains of an *l*? After the *x*, either *x* or *v*, but not *i*.
18. (*decimi*) *h*(*astati*) *pr*(*ioris*).
19. *Sabino:* Daris. *d*(*e*)*s*(*ideratus*)? *d*(*e*)*s*(*eruit*)? *d*(*iscens*) *s*(*igniferum*)? On the last see Domaszewski, *Rang*. 45, and on signiferi legionis, pp. 41 and 43.
20. *Sabino:* Daris; *apollịṇạris:* TAPA.
21. *cos:* Daris.

22

List of Principales

PDur. 93 (inv. D. P. 41 recto) ca. A.D. 230–240

Transcription and commentary:
Final Rep. v, no. 93; *edidi.*
R. O. Fink, "A Fragment of a Roman Military Papyrus at Princeton," *TAPA* 76 (1945) 277–78.

Facsimile: *Final Rep.* v, plate 33, 7.

Text: *CPL*, no. 341, reproduces the readings in *TAPA.*

This text resembles **21** and **24** in being a list of names in cursive divided by headings in capitals which designate various ranks. In the present text were duplicarii and men of the next higher or lower rank. The Princeton and Oslo papyri, however, list the names individually, with each man's century or turma and date of enlistment, while here the names seem to be grouped by dates as in the rosters. Whether their century was individually noted cannot now be determined.

The consulate in line 4 is most probably 223, 234, or 236; but 227, 232, 253, and even 256 seem possible. The dating consequently rests on paleographical grounds.

The verso is *PDur.* 141, four lines of Greek which yield no connected sense.

].[ ]ẓ. . . . [
]iulius prọculus[
a]urel thẹṃarṣạ[
] maxiṃ[
a]urel quinṭ[
]DVP̣LICIẠ[R
]. . . [

3. *Th*[*e*]*ṃạṛṣạ*[*s:* D.
6.]*DVPLICIA*[*R*(*IORVM*)*:* D; but the restoration on the analogy of **21** 17 is not very probable because it is not clear what noun could be supplied here for *dupliciariorum* to modify.

23

List of Principales?

PDur. 116 (inv. D. P. 76 recto) A.D. 236

Transcription and commentary: *Final Rep.* v, no. 116; *edidi.*

Facsimile: ibid., plate 53.

Although the general form of this text, and especially the notations beside the names in cols. i–iii, produces a resemblance to the partial rosters, it has none the less been classified, with some misgivings, as a list of principales. The reasons are (1) the small number, never more than two, from each century or turma, though the dates of enlistment cover a period of fifteen years; (2) the fact that Aelius Licinnius (ii 10) is known to have been a duplicarius as early as 222 (**2** xxxvi 18) and Apollonius Mesenus no later than 232 (**27** b i 7); and (3) the notation *singul*(*aris*) in col. i 5 and 7.

If we may assume that both Licinnius and Mesenus stayed in the same turma, this list shows that the decurion Romullus succeeded Demetrius and Antiochus replaced Antoninus; but the considerable transferring which took place within the cohort (*Final Rep.* v, p. 35) makes this uncertain.

The date rests upon Gilliam's brilliant explanation (*Final Rep.* v, p. 388) of the entry *cos stip xv* in i 8 and ii 7 as a way of designating a year for which damnatio memoriae had made it impossible to name either consul. He writes, "It would be equivalent more or less to '—— and —— consuls (fifteen years' service).' The two consuls would appear to be those of 222, Elagabalus and Alexander." A soldier who enlisted in 222 would be in his fifteenth year in 236; and the date is further confirmed by the fact that the verso (**33**) is occupied by a text which is certainly dated 236.

If Gilliam is right, as he appears to be, this papyrus shows that the formula *III et I cos*, *III et II cos*, etc., for years in which neither consul could be named had not yet been devised.

The verso is **33**.

Col. i

]. . .[
].mụ.[
. . .[ ]ụ.[ ]. .c̣i. . .[.].[
ϒ anton p̣ṛiọṛ [ ]iuḷi[a]no ii eṭ crispino cos A.D. 224
sịngụl aurel aṛṭeṃidorus
ϒ nigriṇi iuliano ii et cṛịṣpiṇ[o] cos 224
singul aurel mocimus
ϒ gẹṛmani cos˙ stip˙ xv 222

Col. ii

—— . . . ṣ . [
Ṭ[^{u}] . . . [
. [ ] .
] . . c̣ụ . . [.]ụl . . [.] . ẹṣọp̣[ ]aureliụ[s] . ạ . . [ ] .
] . T^u ạṇṭiocḥi[l]ạẹṭọ ịị et cerealẹ [c]os A.D. 215
appạ[d]ạn apolloniu[s] meṣṣeṇus
cos˙ [st]ịp˙ xv 222
aṃḅ[u]l . . marcus uic̣ṭor
T^u romulli [p]ọmpeiano et au[ito] cos 209
—[——]– aeliuṣ [lici]ṇṇius

Col. iii

–]–[——] . l[ ]ẓ[e]ṇoḍọṛuṣ
. [ ] . cu[.]l trib eq[u]ị[
ịuliano ii et crispịno cos 224
——— aurelius ụạḷerius
Remainder of column blank

Col. iv

] . . . . [ ] . . [. c]os
aurelius zeḅ[. . .]ṃ . . [
ṣ[ac]erḍote iị cos 219
aurẹḷ[iu]ṣ ạlexander
aurẹḷ[ius] ḍiodorus
[iuli]ạ[no ii] et c̣ṛịṣp̣ịṇ[o (?) co]s 224?
auṛẹl[iu]ṣ r . . . ụṣ [
ϒ rufiaṇ[l]ạeto ii ẹṭ c̣ẹṛẹ[ale cos 215
aụr[eliu]ṣ . [.] . eṃ . [ ] . [

i 2. Perhaps read *maximo ii et aeliano cos*, A.D. 223.
3. D offers no reading for *u*.
4. *Antoṇ . . . :* D. The name of the centurion is difficult; but the second stroke after the second *n*, slanting down from left to right, probably belongs to an *l* in the line above. Cf. **27** i 7 and **33** ii 1 for the abbreviated name.
ii 2.] . . [. . . *co*]*s:* D.
4. . . *c̣ụ* . *l*[;]*ẹ* . *o aurel* . . . [.] . . . . [*:* D. The meaning of the notation is not known.
9. *pompeiano:* D.
10. [*lic*]*ịṇnius:* D.

iii 1. *he*]*l*[*i*]*oḍọṛụṣ:* D. The position of the first *l* in the line suggests that the nomen was *aelius*. The *z* is doubtful because the only other example of the letter (iv 2) is quite different; but *heliodorus* is also doubtful because the space between the *l* and *o* is much too great for an *i*.
2.] . *cu*[.]*l* . . . . *ẹq* . [*:* D.
iv 7. *auṛẹ*[*l*]*ius ṛ* . . . . . *:* D.
8. The century could be either *rufiani* or *rufiana*. See above, p. 4. An Aurelius Rufus appears in **1** xxv 5 (enlisted 214) and **47** i 4.

24

List of Principales

POsl. III 122 A.D. 238–242

Transcription and commentary: Leiv Amundsen, "A Latin Papyrus in the Oslo Collection," *Symbolae Osloenses* 10 (1931) 16–30.

Transcription and facsimile: *Papyri Osloenses* III, no. 122 and plate 10.

Commentary: R. O. Fink, "A Fragment of a Roman Military Papyrus at Princeton," *TAPA* 76 (1945) 276.

Text: *CPL*, no. 139, reproduces the text of *POsl.*, citing two of Fink's readings in the apparatus; Daris, no. 24.

This text most nearly resembles **21** and **22** in that all three are characterized by headings in capitals which indicate that they are lists by rank of various categories of principales. **21**, however, deals with legionary personnel, whereas the present text, like **22**, is a list of auxiliaries, as shown by the name in line 21. Since only turmae are mentioned, it may come from the files of an ala; but only seven different decurions are named, or eight if we assume that the illegible name in line 9 is another person, so that the possibility of a cohors equitata miliaria cannot be excluded until we are sure that the limitation to five turmae seen in the coh. xx Palmyrenorum was general at this time.

The Oslo text differs from the others in the fact that the names in lines 4, 6, and 8 are preceded by the single letter *s* and followed by the notation which Amundsen read as *cdot* and I as *pnt*, both of us with some hesitation. The *s* might be expanded *s*(*esquiplicarius*), in view of line 11, *s*(*ingularis*), or even *s*(*ignifer*); but there is no real evidence for its significance, and the same is true of the notations after the names. The men in lines 1–10 were presumably duplicarii; and the lack of a heading for this section implies that at least one other column preceded the present text. The variation in the order of the turmae (5, *titi*; 7, *flamini*; 14, *flamini*; 18, *titi*) and the failure of the consulships to follow chronological sequence make it necessary to assume that the men are listed in order of the dates of their promotion to the rank they hold (Gilliam, *CP* 48 [1953] 97–98 and note 8); but there is no clue to the purpose of the list.

The date, fixed by Amundsen, is derived from the consulships. Since Alexander (line 18) is *diuus*, the time must be after Maximinus' death in 238, while the men who enlisted in 217 (lines 12 and 20) would have completed their twenty-five years of service in 242, though of course they may have remained longer. The dating of lines 12 and 20 by Praesens is of some interest because all of the Dura papyri from 218 to perhaps 235 (**1**, **2**, **6**, **8**, and **31**) use the name of Extricatus alone for this year. During that time Praesens was evidently under damnatio memoriae, but must later have been rehabilitated. I have found nothing to explain either action; but it is worth noting that a Bruttius Praesens was consul in 246, who may have been the son of the consul of 217. The names of both Praesens and Extricatus are used in the dates of *CIL* VI 2009 (Dessau 466) and 1984 (Dessau 5025); but it seems doubtful if any conclusions can be drawn from this. The former shows many erasures, but only of emperors' names; the latter seemingly had no erasures.

The verso of this papyrus is blank.

]Ŧ nicolae iuliano ii cos[A.D. 224
] aurel cronion[
] Ŧ quintiani uaḷ comaẓ[o]ṇṭẹ c̣[os 220
] s aurel hermaiscus pnt [
] Ŧ titi modesto cos [228
]ṣ[ ]ḷius horigẹnes p̣nt [
Ŧ]fḷamini ạgric[o]ḷa cos [230
]ṣ[a]ụṛẹḷ h[.].[....]s pnt [
Ŧ].ṇị[.]..[a]g̣ṛicola cos[230
aur]ẹḷ ...ṛṃ[
SES]QVI⟨P⟩ḶỊC̣ỊẠR′ X [
]Ŧ ammoniani post p̣raesente cos[217
] aelius sarapion [
]Ŧ flamini iuliano ii cos [224
] aurel ammonianus [
]Ŧ sarapionis grato cos [221
] iulius sarapion [
]Ŧ titi diuo alex˙ cos [222
] auṛẹ[l] heras [
Ŧ amm]ọniani pr p̣raẹṣẹṇṭ˙ c̣ọṣ[217
]theon serẹ[

I have not been able to visit Oslo to see this papyrus; but I owe warm thanks to Prof. Amundsen, who has furnished me with a new photograph accompanied by an expert tracing of lines 12 and 20 and a letter with further descriptions and explanations.

1. *Nicolai:* POsl.

3. *Va˙*; "read *Val(erio)*"*:* POsl. *c̣[o]ṣ:* POsl. The traces after the *z* are too small to identify as particular letters.

4, 6, and 8. *c(ivitate) do(natus) t(estatur)* or *t(estatus)*: POsl.; *p(romotus) n(ominante) t(ribuno):* Fink; CPL and Daris follow POsl. Amundsen did not publish the *s* at the beginning of these lines, but notes its presence in his letter. Its meaning is doubtful.

5 and 18. Titus is attested as a cognomen in numerous inscriptions, e.g. Dessau 2210, 2891, and 4932, and in Aurelius Titus, **21** 16, who may be the same person as here.

5. This was Modestus' second consulship; but the papyrus omits the numeral.

6. *Iu]lius:* POsl.; but *ae]lius* is also possible.

7 and 14. The name of the decurion is troublesome. Either he had no cognomen, which seems impossible at this date, or this is an abbreviated form of Flaminus, or the name was Flaminus, which is not attested elsewhere.

9. *T(VRMAE)* .....[.*:* POsl.; *t(urma)*.....[.*:* Daris; but the plate in POsl. shows that the symbol for "turma" was lost and should be bracketed. Just possibly [Ŧ *f]ḷạṃịṇị*, but very uncertain.

10. *[A]ṛṭẹṃ[idorus cdot:* POsl.

11. *SES]QVI⟨P⟩LICIAṚ(II):* POsl.; *]Q̣VỊḶI-C̣ỊẠ.Ṃ[:* Daris. **21** 16 suggests that the expansion should be in the genitive case; but cf. **22** 6 app.

12. *Ammoniani Cosa(ni):* POsl.; but Amundsen's tracings of this line and 20 make *post(erioris)* almost certain here. Cf. the Antonini, *prior* and *posterior* in **2**, **27**, and **92**, and the Marini in **66**.

18. *Alexandro:* Daris.

19. *Aur[e]l:* POsl.

20. *Am]ṃọniani Praesent˙:* POsl.; but there are more letters than these, and *pr(ioris)* appears certain in view of the reading of line 12. For the form of the *r* cf. *aurel* in 4 and 15. Amundsen says in his letter, ". . . the spot of ink following the *t* can hardly be meant as an *e*—abbreviation mark or accidental?"

21. *Serẹ[ni f(ilius):* POsl.; *Serẹ[n:* Daris.

25

List of Ranks with Names

PDur. 96 (inv. D. P. 36 recto) ca. A.D. 245–255

Transcription and commentary: *Final Rep.* v, no. 96; *edidit* Gilliam.

The ranks named on frag. a make it probable that this was a list of personnel in descending order. There is no way of knowing how inclusive it was originally.

The date is based on the hand.

The verso is unpublished. The hands are different on the two fragments; and only a few letters are legible on either.

Frag. a

]ord[
].ịḅ[
]ụex a[
]mens[
]disc .[

Frag. b

].[. .].[. .]ṛ. .dị[
]iul hel[
]iarab[ol]ẹṣ[
]ṃ[

a 2.].*i*.[: D. In place of *b*, perhaps *d*. The letter before *i* is *n* or *s*. Gilliam suggests *ṣịg̣*(*nifer*) with a question.

3. *uex*(*illarius*) and presumably the first letter of a name.

4. *mens*(*or*).

5. *disc*(*ens*). The next letter could belong to a name or to a rank, such as *discens librarium*.

b 1.]*ṛ*. . .[: D.

2. *heliodorus:* D.

3. *iarab*[*o*]*lẹṣ:* D.

4.]. .[: D. The letter could be either *m* or *n*.

26

List of Cavalrymen

PDur. 103 (inv. D. P. 38 recto) A.D. 205–224

Transcription and commentary: *Final Rep.* v, no. 103; *edidi.*

Frags. b and c are proved by the names to list cavalrymen of the turmae of Demetrius and Octavius. Frag. a has only a few letters on the recto; but its connection with the others is reasonably well assured by the verso.

The date derives from the fact that Nisamsus Zabdiboli (b 1) and Ulpius Apollona- (c 1) both enlisted in 199, so that their 25-year enlistment would have expired in 224, while Iarhaboles Luci (b 8) did not enlist until 205.

The verso is **60**.

Frag. a

ạụṛẹ[l

Frag. b

Turma of Demetrius

nisamsus] ẓạbdibo[li
maccaeus t]ḥeṃ[a]ṛsa
ulpius ma]ṛiṇus ..[
didas c]ọccei
goremis]ịạḍei
iulius germ]anus
ierhaeus b]ạrnaei
ieraboles] ḷuc̣i
].[.]s
]a

Frag. c

Turma of Octavius

ulpiu]ṣ apoll[ona-
ma]ḷchus mac̣[caei
]us mocị[
ogel]us uaḅ[alathi
]..[
] felix̣[
Remainder of column blank

Cf. **1** xxxvi 29–32; xxxvii 3–5, 9, 23, and 30; xxxviii 38; xxxix 7; xl 3; **2** xxxvi 25–28; xxxvii 5–8, 11, 24; xxxviii 1; xxxix 5, 13; xl 11.

c 1. *Apoll[onas:* D.

27

List of Names by Turmae and Centuries

PDur. 115 (inv. D. P. 11 verso) November 30, A.D. 232

Transcription and commentary: *Final Rep.* v, no. 115; *edidi.*

Facsimile of frag. a: ibid., plate 49, 2.

Text: *CPL* 334 reproduces frag. b i 1–6 from *Prelim. Rep.* v.

This text exhibits a number of puzzling features. It may be complete along the left edge of frag. b; but the size of the numbers there removes them from any probable connection with the few soldiers listed. The equites, too, are quite exceptionally put first and the pedites last, with those of the century of Marcus on frag. c at the bottom of the space between frags. a and b and in a column to the right of b ii. The answers to these problems probably lie in the notations at the top of frag. b ii and frag. a i. One may conjecture that frag. b i names men who were already members of the cohort and that the first lines of b ii refer to the incorporation of men transferred from another unit or new recruits, also cavalry, *accepti ex epistulis* (cf. **29**, **30**, and **64** ii 13–15) of the legate of Syria, though the different hand of *accep epistul* tells against this idea unless the words were added later to correct an omission. The rest of b ii and the space above frag. c may have been occupied by the names of these new men. Frag. a i seems to mean that the men who follow have been made equites (cf. **65** 7 and **64** ii 32) from infantry. None of them can be identified elsewhere with certainty, so this idea cannot be tested; but it would make the whole text refer in one way or another to cavalry.

The repeated dates at the foot of a ii probably accompanied some sort of attestation of the document; but the middle one seems to have been struck out.

The recto is **6**.

Frag. b

i m̄ [i]id[ ]
ii m̄ iidx̣iiii
m̄ iixxviiị

Col. i

Ŧ tiberini
dupl lucilius ar̩t̩or̩ius
⟦males themar̩[s]a̩⟧
aurel mocimus
aurel isidorus

Ŧ antonini
dupl a polonius mesenus

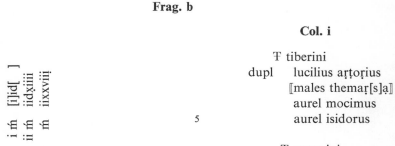

i xxxv
ii [[xl]] lxxiiii
iii [[liii]]
ḿ iid xxvii

]eṭem
]ḅ[.]i[.]beḷeṣ

Ŧ cocei
cl maximus
fl heliọdorus
themarsas addaei
a[u]ṛel monimus

Ŧ nifṛạọṭes
[a]ẹl antoninus
]l antoninus

[Ŧ] paulịṇi
[o]geḷus .[

Col. ii

X̣Ṿ● [*ca.* 7].ṛṣ[....].[
ḍẹ[..]..[.]os
].ạ.c̣...ṭ[
ạ[c]c̣ep X̣Ṿ[ ]kạ[l]. ọc̣ṭọbṛeṣ
epịsṭul[

Frag. c

]dorus
].
].[..]s
aur]eḷ maximus
].[.].ṛ
]ni.aḷoṛ IṾ[

Frag. b, numerals: *ḿ(ilia)*. Line 3, *]ịṭem*? *d]ẹc̣em*? Line 4. *]ḍ[..].[.]de.ẹ:* D. The first letter could be *i* or *d* as well as *b*.

b i 7. There is a hole in the papyrus between *a* and *p*; but there is no way of saying whether anything was ever written there.

13. *nahạṛoṭis:* D. The reading remains uncertain; *nihạṛọṣes* also seems possible. The third letter may have been corrected from *l*.

14. *]fl* is also possible.

17. Perhaps *o]geḷus ṃ[alchi*. Cf. **47** i 17: *option ii ogelus malchi*.

b ii 2. *ḅẹ[:* D.

4. *ḳạ[l]...ṃ..ọbṛẹṣ:* D. The letter after *kal* has a vertical hasta. Perhaps *kạ[le]ṇ*; but such an abbreviation would be quite unusual.

c. 6. *]ṇi.ạ.oṛ:* D.

Frag. a

Col. i

].ẹm X̣X...[.].[.] equos acceper
[[Ŧ]]
ϒ ṃạṛianị
ṭhemạṛsa gora
nịṣạmsus malchi
ụạbalathen ballaei
ạṇtonius alexandri

ϒ anton(ini) prioris
salmạṇes zabdiboli
aurel bernicianus
zebidas iarhaei
mocimus themarsa
zabdibolus malchi

ϒ ant[on p]ọsṭ[
maḷc̣hus themarsa
zab[dibol]us g̣ọra[

Col. ii

ϒ puḍ[e]ṇṭiṣ[
theoteç̣nus aciba
aurel mombogeus
aurel bolaeus
⟦aurel alexander⟧

ϒ gaiani
theacabus themarsa
obeanes themarsa
auṛẹl maximus
⟦iarḥạẹus themarsa⟧
ạụ[r]ẹl achileus
iụ[l] mammes
pr kal decembres
ḷupo cos
]. . [ ]⟦lụpo ẹṭ ṃạx̣ịṃo ç̣ọ[s]⟧
]. . [ ]lupọ eṭ ṃạximo cos
]en[.]s[

a i 1.]*ṇ.ṛix̣* ⟦Ϯ:⟧ .[.].[.]*ẹqụos:* D. The letter after the *m* could be a large *X*.
7. *anton*[*ini*] in D is a misprint.
ii 11–12. There is a space between *l* and *e* of *achileus* and the two *m*'s in *mammes* to avoid an imperfection in the papyrus.
12. *i*.[. .] *mammus:* D.

28

List of Classiarii

PRyl. 79; *vidi* — A.D. 144–151

Transcription and facsimile: *PRyl.* II (1915) no. 79 and plate 23.

Transcription, commentary, and facsimile: *ChLA* IV, no. 241, cited as **M.**

Commentary: J. F. Gilliam, "A Roman Naval Roster: P. Rylands 79," *CP* 48 (1953) 97–99. This article renders obsolete Fink's comments in *TAPA* 76 (1945) 276–77.

Text: *CPL*, no. 125, reproduces the text of the editio princeps, citing Fink's and Gilliam's readings in the apparatus. Daris, no. 28, adopts Gilliam's *lib*(*urna*).

Gilliam is undoubtedly right in expanding the abbreviation in line 10 as *lib*(*urna*)—or in the genitive—and hence in interpreting the text as a list of classiarii from two different ships. The small number of men under each date shows that this is not a complete roster but a special list of some sort. It is impossible to say why capitals were used throughout; but they suggest a formal document.

The date is based on the consulships. The latest (line 7) makes A.D. 144 the terminus post quem, while the earliest (line 11) implies 151 as the approximate year of discharge for the soldier in question, since classiarii served 26 years at this period (*CIL* XVI, dipl. 79, 92, and 100).

The verso is blank.

COMMODO] EṬ PỌṂ[PEIANO COS A.D. 136
].ỊṾS Ḥ[
STLOG]Ạ ET SEVERỌ [COS 141
]VS POLY.[
RUFIN]Ó ET QVADRẠ[T]Ọ [COS 142
]VS SEṚẸṆ[
AVITO] ET MAXIMÓ [COS 144
DO]ṂITIVS Ṿ[.].[
]ỌNIVṢ .[
]LIB MERCVṚ[
ASIA]ṬICÓ II ET AQṾ[ILINO COS 125
]ṬERIVṢ .[
GALLI]C̣ANO ẸṬ ṬỊT[IANO COS 127
]NA IV[
].[

2. *]CIVS T[:* Ryl.; [. . . .]. . .*S T*[*:* M.
4. *POLYB*[*:* M.
5, 7, and 11. Note the apices over the final *O*.
6. *SEREN*[*VS:* Ryl.; but the name could have been in the genitive.
8. . . .[: Ryl.; [. .*DO*]*MITIUS* .[. .]. .[*:* M.
10. *LIB(ERTVS?):* Ryl.; *LIB(RARIORVM) MERCVR*[*I:* Fink; [. . . . .] *LIB(URNA) MERCURI*[*:* M. Read *LIB(VRNA* or *-AE) MERCVR(IO* or *-II)* with Gilliam.
12. *VA*]*LERIVS* .[*:* Ryl.; [. . *VA*]*LERIUS* . .[.]. .[*:* M. But]*C̣ERIVS* is also possible.
15. [. . . . .]*NA* [.]. . . *I*.[*:* M.

29

Record of Accessions by Transfer

PDur. 121 (inv. D. P. 26 recto) May or June, probably A.D. 241

Transcription and commentary: *Final Rep.* v, no. 121; *edidi.*

Facsimile: ibid., plate 55, 2.

The phrasing of this list is paralleled by **87** 4–9: *tirones sex . . . in coh cui praees in numeros referre iube ex xi kalendas martias;* **50** i 15: *in n(umeros) in coh(ortem) xx palm gordianam;* and **64**, e.g. ii 19–21: *in (centuriam) candidi, torquato et iuliano cos, horatius herennianus ex iv idus nouembres.* In the last, as in the present text, the consulship is the year of the soldier's original enlistment, the day and month is the date of enrollment in the particular unit. **66** shows much the same arrangement. Since line 12 shows that Aurelius Macrinus enlisted in 225, he is not a tiro and so must be entering the xx Palmyrenorum by transfer. There is no evidence whether or not the same is true of the other men in the list.

The date results from the consulship of Gordian and the name of Attius Rufinus. Gilliam points out in his introduction to *PDur*. 59 (**114**) that only 239 and 241 come into consideration, and that **50** i 14 named a different legate of Syria at the end of May 239. Unless one assumes that the present text is to be dated in June rather than May, and that Rufinus took over the governorship in that month of 239, it is practically certain that the year is 241.

The purport of lines 4 and 11 is obscure, though the latter may perhaps be compared with **94** b ii 2.

The verso is **45**.

g]ọṛḍị[ano cos
ṛ[e]l in nu ẹx [epistula
ạṭṭị ṛufinị [u c cos n
].is eraṭ[
Ɣ ge[r]ṃanị[
iul aṇṭ[
iiii kal iu[— May 29 or June 28
gordia[no cos — A.D. 239 or 241
ṛel in ṇ[u ex epistula
atti rufini u c cos ń[
erạṇt denum m[
Ɣ heliodori fusc[o] ịị [cos — 225
aurel maçṛ[i]nus
vii[
gordịa[no cos — 239 or 241
]....[

2 and 9. Probably *rel(atus) in nu(meros)*, though the abbreviation *nu* is unusual.

3 and 10. *u(iri) c(larissimi) co(n)s(ularis) n(ostri)*.
4. Possibly *[i]ṇ is*.

30

List of Accessions by Transfer?

PMich. 454 (inv. 509); *vidi* II–III p.

Transcription, commentary, and facsimile: Henry A. Sanders, *PMich.* VII: *Latin Papyri*, no. 454 and plate 13a. Cited below as **S.**

Commentary: Jean Bingen, *Latomus* 8 (1949) 71–72; J. F. Gilliam, *AJP* 71 (1950) 436–37; Sergio Daris, "Note per la storia dell' esercito Romano in Egitto," *Aegyptus* 36 (1956) 235–46, esp. 242–44.

Text: *CPL*, no. 146, reproduces Sanders' text, noting the readings in Gilliam's review for col. ii, lines 8 and 9. Daris, no. 20.

Too little remains of this text for any certainty regarding its nature and purpose; but a few facts emerge.

The unit concerned must be a cohors equitạta. It cannot be a legion, for it included a non-citizen (line 12), nor an ala, because it had a centurion (line 9); but it was made up in part of turmae (lines 1, 4, 6, 11, 14).

Four of the seven men named in col. ii are being transferred from other units; and perhaps all were transfers. It seem at any rate that all are in process of being incorporated into the present unit. Cf. **29**, **31**, and **64**.

The date is on the basis of the script.

The verso is blank.

Col. i

]us

]ḍọcẹs

]ẹni. . g̣us

Col. ii

Ŧ eạ[.]. . c̣[

One line lost or left blank

iulị[us

iteṃ ẹọṛ· iṃṃ[u]ṇẹ[s] . . [.]. . 1. [

Ŧ saturnini

One line blank because of defect in papyrus

aurelius isidorianus[

Ŧ maximi [

One liṇe blank

aurelius serenus [

item sagiṭ[.] ex n emẹṣenoṛ [
aelius marinus hordinaṭus[
sempronius ḍ[e]ṃetrius ṣc̣ṛ[
Ŧ rufi
suaemus ṭaeṣii
[i]ṭem ex n′ or⟨i⟩ẹntalium
Ŧ rufi
iulius ualens
Remainder of column blank

i 2.].*ocṛus:* S. Perhaps *cappa]doces*?
3.]*ṿarius:* S. The letters in the center look like two overlapping *a*'s. The *e* and *g* might both be read as *c*. Dornseiff–Hansen cite a name *Diadumeniacus* which is possible here.
ii 1. *Ṭ(urma) c̣ṛ[:* S. Nothing is certain in this line except the symbol for turma.
3. *item foṛti[ ]cas:* S. Nothing is certain here but *item*. For the *r* of *eor(um)* compare the *r* in *isidorianus*, 5.
8. *Item Ṣac̣ọt[.]ix Ṇemọṣenoi:* S. The reading in the text was proposed by Bingen and Gilliam independently. There was probably nothing in the lacuna before *ex*. Expand *sagit(tarii) ex n(umero) emesenor(um)*.
9. . .]*relius; hordinacus:* S. The readings adopted are Gilliam's.
10. *Ṃ[.]ternus scr[:* S, restoring *scr[iba]*. Gilliam suggests *ses[q(uiplicarius)*, which is not impossible, though the upper part of the *e* is hard to find. The remains look most like *sce* or *spe*.
12. *Murenus Taeni:* S. The first letter can hardly be anything but *s*; the second, either *u* or *y*. The name seems probably a variant of *Sohaemus*. The second name is more difficult; the *t* and the *s* are both uncertain, and both Sanders' reading and mine are unexampled names, though the feminine Taesis or Thaesis is common enough.
13. *Ịtem; Ọrọntalium:* S. The letter before *n*, however, is in ligature with it, and perhaps with the preceding *r*, and is open on the right so that it most resembles a *c*. The papyrus is badly wrinkled at this point; but the letter can best be read as a damaged *e*. It is possible, too, for an *i* ligatured with the *r* to have been lost here. Daris (*Aegyptus* 36.243–44) points out that col. v of *PFlor.* II 278 begins ἀρι]θμοῦ ἀνατολικῶν, hitherto ignored or treated with scepticism. The two texts appear to be contemporary, whether the Florentine papyrus is placed in the reign of Marcus Aurelius or Septimius Severus, for it also mentions sagittarii in col. v. The two texts thus confirm each other. Bingen makes the same connection.

31

Names by Centuries, with Dates by Day and Month

PDur. 120 (inv. D. P. 29 recto) A.D. 222?

Transcription and commentary: *Final Rep.* v, no. 120; *edidi.*

Facsimile: ibid., plate 55, 1.

This text has been placed among the accessions by transfer with some hesitation because of its partial resemblance to **29**; but it should be noted that the dates by day and month could refer to any important event, such as a promotion, in the career of the men named. **66** a i–ii and b i is very similar; so perhaps this text should be classed with it in Chapter 3.

As *PDur.* 120 the papyrus was dated 233–235 on the ground that the centurion

Antoninus in line 4 is not distinguished as *prior* or *posterior*, as he would have been between 222 (**2**) and 232 (**27**). But an *Antoninus prior* is also found in **33** ii 1 in 236, under Maximinus. Hence, if the omission of these designations in the present text is significant, the list must be dated in 222, but earlier than **2**, where the second Antoninus, distinguished as *prior*, first appears. If this reasoning is correct, it follows that the present Antoninus is Domitius Antoninus, *posterior*.

The verso is **96**.

Col. i

]. . [
]. . [ ]. . [.]. . [
].n. . . [ ]. . ụ[
Y antoniṇị laetọ ii cọṣ — A.D. 215
aụṛel antọṇinus
aurel siluanus
aurel ṣịluaṇụ[s] ạḷṭẹṛ
]g̣ạ iiii kal ṇọu(embres)
]ṣ ex̣tricato ii cos — Oct. 29, 217
]ṣ aurel domitiụṣ[
x̣. . kal auguṣṭạṣ — July 17–26, 222?
d n alexanḍ[ro] ạụg [cos

Col. ii

].[
aụṛẹl g̣ṛạṭụṣ
iii kal ọ[ct — Sept. 29, 222?
ḍ n alexanḍ[ro aug cos
]. .[ ]. . . .
One line lost
]. . . [
].[

i 8.].*ạ*: D.

i 12 and ii 4. *d*(*omino*) *n*(*ostro*).

32

Soldiers of the Same Year, by Centuries

PDur. 122 (inv. D. P. 46) ca. A.D. 241–242?

Transcription and commentary: *Final Rep.* v, no. 122; *edidi.*

The soldiers in this list may be tirones, though more probably men who have served out their enlistment and are ready for the honesta missio; but all that is certain is that all enlisted in the same year.

The date depends upon the names of the centurions, Felix and Mocimus in particular. The introduction to *PDur.* 122 incorrectly states that Felix was still present in 250 or 251 (**66**). Actually his only known date other than the present text is about 240 (**15**); and Mocimus is attested only in this text and **16**, the date of which is highly uncertain but later than that of **15**. See also the discussions of the dates of **15** and **17**.

The verso is blank.

𐆛 g]ẹṛmaṇ[i eod]ẹṃ [cos
] auṛẹl ḅerniçịaṇ[us
] ṃarin[u]s ạḅboṣ[a
𐆛 mo]ciṃi eoḍem ç[os
]ạuṛel hẹlla[ni]çụ[s
]aurel anṭoninụ[s
]aurel abgạrus
] 𐆛̣ ạçheị eodem cos
aure]ḷ maxiṃ[us
ạụ[re]l marin[us
[a]ụṛẹl [za]ḅdib[o]ḷ[us
]. 𐆛̣ f̣elicis eodem cos
] aurel salmanes .[ ].....[
aur]ẹ[l] p̣ạụ...ạ[

3. The *m* begins with a strongly curved stroke, unlike any other initial *m* in the text; but *çḥarin*[*u*]*s* seems improbable because of the form of the *h* in *achei*, line 8.

4. The traces of the centurion's name could be read]*ciạṭi*; but a centurion Mocimus is attested in **16**.

13. The traces after *salmanes* seem to be a notation, not part of the name.

14. The traces could be read as the name Pautina, attested in Dessau 7226.

33

Names by Centuries, with Notation *pdcc*

PDur. 117 (inv. D. P. 76 verso) A.D. 236

Transcription and commentary: *Final Rep.* v, no. 117; *edidi.*

Facsimile: ibid., plate 54.

The nature of this list could probably be understood if the notation *dcc* or *pdcc*, which apparently preceded every name, could be explained. As it is, one can not even be sure whether *dcc* is a numeral or the initial letters of a phrase. Thus far I know of no proposals for the elucidation of this puzzle.

To the description of the papyrus formerly published should be added the observation that there are traces of ink in six lines above the present heading in col. i. These, however, are so faint and uncertain that one must assume either that they were erased before the present text was written, or that they are offset from another layer of the papyrus. The one possible exception is the line just above the capitals, where with sufficient good will one might read *v ḳ[a]ḷ* above *IMI* of *MAXIMINO*.

The year at least is certain, since Maximinus held only one consulship.

The recto is **23**.

Col. i

IMP̣ Ḍ Ṇ [M]AXỊM[I]NO [A]VG
[et afric]ạṇọ c̣os
]. [ ]ṇ[
]. [

i 2. The name may have been in small capitals, but *cos* is in cursive.

Col. ii

Ỵ aṇtoṇ	p̣ṛiọ[r
] ḍc̣c̣	iạṛhae[us] zebida
] dc̣c	malchụ̣[s z]eḅiḍa
]ḍcc	iul . . . [. .]ục̣.ṣ
]p̣dc̣c̣	ạụṛẹl lọ[. .]oṇụṣ
]ḍc̣c̣	ạ[. .].ẹ.[.]. . . .i
	]ḷṃ. . ạs.
	].[. .].g̣.[

ii 7. Possibly *n* instead of *m*.

Col. iii

]ḍcc	seleucu[s m]ạlchi
]p ḍc̣c̣	aurel ṃ.[..].ịus
]dcc	aurel h[..]ofuṛ
]dcc̣	abgarus ịạṛḥaẹi
]ḍcc	ṃal[c]ḥus ṃombogei
..[..]ṇ.. AG̣G̣	aurẹ[l] bạṛḅesomeniuṣ
]..[	].us s[..]g̣ill[
	]..ẹ.[

iii 3. For the final element of the name cf. *abidfur*, Index 1, Personal Names.
6. The reading of the notation is very uncertain; but part at least seems to be in small capitals.
7. *s[i]gill[*: D.

Col. iv

dc̣c̣	ạụrel sịṭoṛṛ[
pḍ[cc]	ḍụṃanus na.[
dc]c̣	aurel sa.a.[
dc]c̣	auṛel bassạ..[
pḍ[c]c̣	aurel .earc̣ḥẹs
dc]c	iul ..[.]sus
	aụṛeḷ ḅaḅạ
	]..[ ]..[ ]ḍ.[

iv 1. *sạc̣ọṇạ[*: D; but the second letter is surely not *a*.
2. The *du* has been corrected, probably from *au*. Perhaps *ma[* in place of *na[*.
5. *..ạṛc̣ḥẹs*: D.
7. The name *aurel baba* is in the margin.

Col. v

pdcc	ịạ[rha]eus theṃạṛṣạ
pdcc	aụ[rel] g̣eṛṃanus
p̣dc̣c̣	.[...]ḥ[...]ẹleạ..[
dc̣c̣	ạ[ur]ẹl apolloṇius
dcc	ạ[ur]ẹl ṭhẹodoṭus
p̣ḍc̣c̣	ạ[ur]el zeṇ.[.]o.ṛ
ḍ[cc	au]ṛẹl[ ]..[

Col. vi

pḍ[c]c.[
One line lost
..[
...[
Two lines lost
pḍ[cc

34

Casualty (?) List of Legionaries and Summary

PVindob. L 2, recto and verso; *vidi* — A.D. 115–117?

Transcription and facsimile of the recto:

1. Wessely, *Schriftt.*, no. 8.
2. Idem, *Studien* 14 (Leipzig 1914) plate 8; cited as **W**.
3. *EL*, plate 12, no. 17.

Text: *CPL*, no. 110, and Daris, no. 13, reproduce Wessely's text.

The rough, unskillful hand, vacillating between capitals and cursive, the crude phonetic spelling, the lack of any systematic form, the insertions and corrections, and the admixture of Greek letters and terminations combine to prove that this list was drawn up by someone not at all accustomed to writing. No attempt has been made here to reproduce all the vagaries of the script.

The date must be earlier than A.D. 127, when the leg. III Cyrenaica is attested for Arabia (Ritterling, *RE* 12.1510, s.v. "Legio"). Its latest certain date in Egypt is August 4, 119 (Lesquier 63); while the names Cocceius (recto i 5) and Ulpius (recto i 20, and recto ii 23 and 24) point to a time long enough after Nerva's and Trajan's accessions for men with their nomina to be enrolled in the legions. The high proportion of deaths recorded here, seemingly 9 out of 28 men, therefore makes it reasonable to conjecture that this may be a casualty list dating from the Jewish revolt of 115–117. Cf. the introduction to **74**, pp. 277–78. Note also that two or probably three of the nine centuries named are without centurions, whereas in the great inscription of the leg. II Traiana of A.D. 157 (Abdullatif Ahmed Aly, "A Latin Inscription from Nicopolis," *Annals of the Faculty of Arts, Ain Shams University*, 3 [1955] 113–46) among 51 centuries only 3 are without centurions.

The text of the verso, hitherto unpublished, seems in part to be the same sort of text as the recto but to conclude with a numerical summary of the data; but it is too badly preserved and too small for any certainty.

Recto

Col. i

LEG I[II] CYṚ
ↃNẸRO
ϒ nini rufi
cereli rufi
cocceus clemes
o. ⟦iulius maximus⟧
cladius antoninus
pr ⟦iulius cutratus⟧
fanius ṛulius
ϒ subureana
cladius zenon
tẹ cladius feanus
te flaus gerfeanus
tr anto nius maximus
]. gra.[ ]ius . . .ẹanus
]ṣ salius capiton
te bius longon
flaus clemes
LEG XXII ↄnro
ϒ upian(a)

Col. ii

barẹton
ϒ aufri aç̣ụḷị
iulius ruticus
petucaeus otaus
LEG III cyr
ϒ antoni longini
antonius satụnịḷ[us
domitius germạ[n-
balini ecatẹus[
ϒ capitoeana
licin loce
ϒ aufri aculi minọṛ(is)
cladius agaϑo
LEG˙ III
ϒ antoni longo
paconi egnati
iulius niger
One line blank
tetates
ϒ pompei epane
cladius clemes
cladius apulinar
antonius uales
upis satunilus
upis alexa

Recto. The left edge of the recto is cut clean; so that the text is probably complete on that side. It may also be complete at the top; but the verso, for which the papyrus was rotated on a vertical axis, shows that it is probably not complete on the right of the recto. It is very likely incomplete at the bottom as well, for no name follows the designation of the century in line 20 of col. i.

i 1. *ỊỊỊ:* EL; *[III] Cyr(enaica):* CPL; also in ii 5.

2. *onero:* W and EL. The first character cannot be *o*, for both here and in line 19 it is clearly open on the left side, which is true of no certain *o* in the papyrus. A reversed *c* is a well-known symbol in inscriptions; but none of its usual meanings—e.g. centuria, conductor, sextarius—are of any help here. Presumably *ɔnero* here and in line 19 are headings which apply to the personnel of each legion who are listed below.

3. *Noni:* W and EL. The first name of the centurion might be read as *uini*; but the first and third letters appear identical on the papyrus. Read *ninni*; and for the single *n* cf. *fanius* in i 9.

4. The genitive does not call for the addition of the centuria-symbol. It is a mistake induced by the genitive in the preceding line or a vocative. Cf. ii 15–16, and also *CIL* VI 1057, where many gentilicia are given a pseudo-genitive form by lopping off the final *us* to abbreviate them. For the first name cf. *Λουκίῳ Κερελ[*, *POxy*. 965 (3rd cent.); but it may be *celerius* with metathesis, or even *caerellius*.

5. Read *cocceius clemens*.

6. *ϑ:* W; *O:* EL. There are traces of a tall letter after the *o*; but it cannot be *b* (for *obiit*) in the same hand as the body of the text. The annotation might, however, still be read as *ob(iit)* on the supposition that it was added by a second hand; and *of(ficio)* is also possible.

7. Read *claudius*. W's *antonius* in *Studien* must be a typographical error, since *Schriftt.* has *antoninus*.

8. *tr:* W; *tr(anslatus):* EL; but the *p* is clear. *pa* is possible; but probably one should read *(ad) pr(aetorium)* or *(in) pr(aetorio)*. Cf. **1** xxxi 8 and xxxvi 7, and **2** xxxiii 11 and xl 11: *ad praetori(um)*; and **63** ii 70: *ad praetorium cum librariis*. Or *pr(omotus)*? Read *iulius quadratus*.

9. This name is an addition crowded into the space between lines 8 and 10. Read *fannius rullus*? Daris has transferred *(centuria)* to this line from line 10.

10. *subur fanii:* W; EL has the same, but in the apparatus "lire Suburani"; *Subur(ani) Fanii:* Daris. EL is right in regarding this as one word; but the sixth letter must be *e*, not *f*. The *r* has been corrected from *e*. The last letter is not clearly *i* or *a*; but it consists of two strokes, so that *a* is more probable. Read *Subureana* accordingly. The name of the centurion may derive from that of Sex. Attius L. f. Volt. Suburanus Aemilianus who was adiutor of Iulius Ursus, Prefect of Egypt in 84 and later consul in 101 and 104 (Stein, *Präf.* 42 and note 135).

The adjectival form of the centurion's name shows that this century as well as the Capitoniana (ii 10) and the Ulpiana (if i 20 is correctly read), were temporarily without centurions. On this point see R. O. Fink, *TAPA* 84 (1953) 213, and Eric Birley, *Roman Britain and the Roman Army* (Kendal 1953) 128–29.

11. Read *claudius*.

12, 13, and 17. *te:* W; *te(tates):* EL; *te(tatus):* Daris. The *e* is faint and damaged but the letter can hardly be *r*. Since the recto ii 19 reads *tetates*, and **63** ii 11 has *ϑetati*, it is difficult to guess what form the scribe had in mind here for the singular. On the meaning of *thetatus* see above, p. 13.

For the name in 12 read *claudius theanus*? Cf. on 13.

13. *gerfennus:* W and EL; but cf. *Γερθιᾶνις* (genitive), *POxy*. 1446, introd., p. 126. Read *flauius gerthianus*.

14. The annotation could be *tr* corrected from *te*, or vice versa. There is a gap of 0.3 cm. between *o* and *n* because of a rough joint in the papyrus. *tr(anslatus)* or *te(tatus)*.

15. *gra[t]ius . . . eanus:* W and EL. Either *gra[tt]ius* or *gra[n]ius* could be restored. The second name could be Alfeanus.

17. *Bius* is not elsewhere a nomen; but the reading is certain.

18. Read *flauius clemens*.

19. *onro:* W and EL; but see on line 2 above.

20. *upi[s] pei:* W; *Upi Pei:* EL; but cf. *an* of *antonius* (ii 7) and the *n*'s of *capiton* (i 16) and *bariton* (ii 1). Read *ulpian(a)* or less probably *ulpian(i)*. The papyrus is damaged after the *i*; but apparently no letters are lost. There is no trace of ink. The space here may have been caused by the joint in the papyrus as in lines 14–15. If the reading offered here is correct, this century, too, like the Suburiana (i 10) and the Capitoniana (ii 10), lacked a centurion.

ii 1. *bariton:* W, in app., "*Βαρίδων?*"; *Bariton:* EL; but cf. the verso, ii 13, where the fourth letter is clearly *e*. This entry, consisting of a single word, cannot be a name but must be a heading like *ɔnero* in col. i. My colleague at Kenyon College, Prof. R. A. Henshaw, once informed me that there is a late Hebrew word *brit*, meaning "outside, outside the group, foreign," which with the nunnation *-on* would produce a noun *bariton*. Is it possible that the peculiarities of this list result from its being the work of a Jewish rebel, not a Roman army clerk?

2. *ac̣ụl:* W; *Acụl(i):* EL. W proposes to read *Auferi Accolei*; Lesquier, *Aufelli Acculei*. It seems more probable that the name was *Afrius Aquilus*. The substitution of *au* for *a* in the first name is the result of the same confusion which produced *cladius*, but working in the opposite direction. For the spelling *aculi* cf. Greek *'Ακύλιος* and *"Ακυλας*.

3. Read *rusticus*.

4. W proposes *peducaeus octavus*, rightly. L. Peducaeus Colonus was Prefect of Egypt in 70 (Stein, *Präf.* 39, and *POxy*. 2349); and the soldier's name probably derives from his.

7. *Saturn[ilus:* Daris.

8. W and EL restore *Germạ[nus*; but *Germa[nicus* is equally possible.

9. W suggests *Beleni* for the first name; Lesquier, *Varini*. *ecat[.]?:* W; *Ecat.us:* EL; *ecat:* Daris. Read *hecataeus*.

10. *Capito Fana:* W and EL. W would disregard the centuria-sign on the ground that it is followed here by a nominative. But read *capitoniana* and see above on i 10 and 20.

11. The nomen is of course *licinnius*. W suggests *Locceius* for the second name, but cites no examples. See, however, *SB* I 1319, line 6, and 4595, line 6; and *BGU* IV 1046 and III 8. A cognomen is wanted; and one might also think of one of those based on *luc-*, e.g. Lucius (Dessau 2200; and **2** xx 22; **8** vii 6; ix 23), Lucianus, Lucillus, and the like.

12. This line is an addition made after line 13 was written. The name is the same as in line 2. On *minor* cf. the use of *prior* and *posterior* to distinguish centurions of the same name in **1**, **2**, **24**, and **66**.

13. The theta in this name, like many of the spellings, shows that the scribe was more accustomed to Greek than to Latin. On the other hand, he has omitted final *n* here and in *longo* (ii 15), retained it in *zenon* (i 11), *capiton* (i 16), and *longon* (i 17).

14. *LEG:* W. The lower dot seems possible but not certain. The repetition of *LEG III* here is an error, for it is not needed and the title is not completed with *Cyr*; but no attempt has been made to correct it.

15. Is this the same centurion as in line 6? Lesquier, p. 520, questions the name *Longo*; but cf. *Longon* in i 17, and *Λώγγων* in *BGU* 67, 5.

16. *Paconi(us) Egnati(us):* Daris. See above on i 4 for the genitive here. Read *paconi(us) egnati(anus)*?

19. See above on i 12 and 13.

20. W proposes *Eppani* without citing parallels. I have no suggestion.

21. The *m* has been corrected from another letter. Read *claudius clemens*.

22. Read *claudius apollinarius*.

23. Read *ualens*.

24. *Saturnilus:* Daris. Read *ulpius saturnilus*.

25. *alexa* is complete in itself; but in view of the abbreviations elsewhere, it might represent *alexa(nder)*.

Verso

Col. i

] ϒ ḍomịti cạẹlị
]cornelus
]. uales
] .ạụṣ ḍoṃitius

Col. ii

].s[
].[ ]XXIII
.[ ].
..[ ]X̣X̣Ịỵ
.[
.....u[....].
ṣ[ ]ṛ...
ọṇ...
LEG [ ]ḷ[
XII
ḶEG̣ X[XI]I XVII
].ạbḷị II IV
bareton Ị[
ṣ tetatị
. X
ṛ[..]utor
ị. item ii

Verso. The surface of the verso is spongy with decay and badly abraded. The hand is perhaps the same as that of the recto. It appears slightly taller and thinner, though in fact it is not. The capitals on the recto measure 0.3 to 0.5 cm.; those on the verso 0.4 to 0.5. The cursive of the recto varies from 0.2 to 0.4 cm.; on the verso from 0.2 to 0.3 cm.

i 1. Read *caeli(ani)*? A cognomen is needed.

2. Read *cornelius*? But a cognomen is needed; and *cornelus* would serve, though unexampled.

4. This line is slightly separated from the other three and seems to be in a different hand. The scribble which is read as *.ạụṣ* is highly uncertain, but cannot be part of the name.

ii 1–10. These lines appear to contain summaries of data for two legions, with one total, 23 or more, in line 2, and the name of the second legion and the numeral 12 in lines 9–10, followed by *LEG XXII* in line 11. The remains in line 8 can be read as *dn* or as *on*, which recalls the *onero* formerly read in col. i, recto, 2 and 19.

12. It is tempting to read *tran]ṣ ạb LẸ[G] II*, that is, the II Traiana.

13. The *t* has a peculiar form, with one horizontal stroke about 0.1 cm. above the other and the vertical hasta connecting them, as if the scribe had begun the letter too high and had then written it again immediately below without erasing the upper stroke.

14. Read *s(umma)*?

16. *a[di]utor?*

17. It is not certain whether the first two traces are the remains of letters or numerals, or whether anything is lost between them and *item*. The latter might even be the end of *[mil]item*.

35

List of Absentees?

PDur. 123 (inv. D. P. 30 verso); *vidi* After A.D. 238

Transcription and commentary: *Final Rep.* v, no. 123; *edidit* Welles.

Facsimile: ibid., plate 31, 1.

The interpretation of this text as a list of absentees rests upon the possibility that the repeated ἀφοσητάων in lines 2, 4, and 8 may be a phonetic spelling of *absentium*. The use of the Greek alphabet is puzzling, especially in view of Welles' observation that the scribe seemed to be more familiar with Latin.

The date must be later than **3**, which occupies the recto and which must be dated 238–247.

. . φιων . . σ̣αν
ιτεμ αφοσσηταω[
ιουλι[
ιτεμ αφοσσ[η]ταω[
]πρριω κελε̣[
. . . . [
μαρρινος γλαυκι[
[ι]τεμ α[. .]σ̣τ̣[α]ω[
. . . [
. . . . [ ] . . . [ ] . [
αβιδγινει
αυ⟨ρ⟩ηλιος θεμαρσ[
. . . . . . [ ] . . [

1. . . φιων . . . αν: D.
5. κέλε̣[ρος: D.
7. γλαυκί[ου: D.
12. θεμαρσ[ᾶς: D.

Unclassifiable Lists

36

List of Legionaries

BGU 1083 (inv. 13319) Time of Augustus; I a.

Transcription: P. Viereck, *BGU* 1083.

Transcription with facsimile:
1. *EL*, no. 21.
2. Mallon, *Pal.*, plate II, no. 1.

Text: *CPL*, no. 109, reproduces Viereck's text. Daris, no. 14.

There is no direct evidence that this is a military text; but the Roman alphabet, the Roman citizenship of all the persons listed, and the formal completeness of the names, with filiation, tribe, and origo, establishes a strong probability that such a list, especially at so early a date, is a roster of soldiers. The fact that they are all citizens points to their being legionaries; and the nature of the nomina, with perhaps one Iulius (line 6) and no Claudii or Flavii, coupled with the absence of cognomina, indicates an early date. Comparison with the very similar early inscription which lists men of the III Cyrenaica and XXII Deiotariana, *CIL* III 6627 (Dessau 2483), however, reveals a decisive difference. There too the soldiers are without cognomina; but 26 of the 36 men named belong to the tribe Pollia, two are castrenses, and seven others have cities in Egypt as their domus. Sanders is surely right in dating the inscription "a full generation or more after Actium" on the ground that the preponderance of the tribe Pollia shows that these men are in fact illegitimate sons of soldiers whose origo reflects their mothers' nationality.[1] Nineteen of the soldiers in the inscription are from Galatia, Pontus, Paphlagonia, and Bithynia; but six are from Alexandria, one from Paraetonium, and two are castrenses. By contrast, none of the 15 men in this papyrus is in the tribe Pollia, and none is from Egypt.[2] Two are from the transpadane region (Cremona and Altinum), two from Africa (Hadrumetum and Utica), and the rest from Galatia, Phrygia, Lycaonia, and Bithynia, unless the Apamea of line 8 and the Laodicea of 12–13 are the Syrian cities of that name. (Philomedia, 10, is a puzzle unless Philomelium in Phrygia is meant. Ruge, *RE* 19.2521, s.v. "Philomelion," states that Procopius [*Anecd.* 18.42 Haury] calls the city Philomede.) All of this points to a date not more than a generation after Actium and makes this much the oldest of extant Roman military records.

1 "The Origin of the Third Cyrenaic Legion," *AJP* 62 (1941) 84–87.

2 It is interesting to note that the veterans of the leg. II Traiana who were discharged in A.D. 157 were likewise all drawn from outside Egypt and that none were castrenses. 65% came from Africa, the rest from Italy, Syria, and Asia Minor. See Abdullatif Ahmed Aly, "A Latin Inscription from Nicopolis," *Annals of the Faculty of Arts, Ain Shams University*, 3 (1955) esp. pp. 126–30.

The names Granius and Trebius in col. i of *CIL* III 6627 may also occur in lines 7 and 8 of the papyrus, but in the inscription Trebius belongs to the tribe Pupinia, while]*bius* in line 8 of the papyrus belongs to Romilia or just possibly Pomptina. This precludes any direct relationship. Nevertheless, if the papyrus is military at all, it is the earliest evidence for the presence in Egypt of either the III Cyrenaica or the XXII Deiotariana, antedating *Ann. Epigr.* 1910, no. 207, by ten years or more.

The purpose of the list is unknown.

]enucius˙	c˙ f˙	aẹm(ilia)	pesinuntem
c]anidius	c˙ f˙	poṃ(ptina)	ancyra˙
]ḅaebius	q˙ f˙	[po]ṃ *or* [ro]ṃ	ancyra˙
]cornelius	sex f	pọṃ	ancyra
⟦]sulpịcius	l f	aem	pesinuntem⟧
].lius	m'˙ f˙	c̣la(udia)	cremona˙
].ranịus	q f˙	ṛom(ilia)[	..]a[...].ịạ
]bius	. f˙	ṛoṃ	apạṃ[e]ạ
o]ctauius	a˙ f˙	ṛoṃ	adrymeto˙
]ius˙	c˙ f˙	...	philomedia˙
sal]lustius˙	c˙ f	ṣạḅ(atina)	utica˙
]untịus˙	ḷ f˙	cor(nelia)	laudicia
a]ṇtonius	l˙ f˙	cor	laudicia
]ṭọrius	[.] f˙	fab(ia)	altino˙
].[		] ..[.	chr]ỵṣọpoli pạ[.].ṃ[

1.].*nucius:* CPL and Daris. Tribe, ...*a*˙: BGU. Restore the name as Genucius?

3. Tribe, [...]: BGU.

4. Tribe, [...]: BGU.

5. Tribe, *Lem(onia)*: BGU.

6. Perhaps *I[u]lius*: BGU. Filiation, *M˙ f˙*: BGU and EL; but there is a vertical stroke above the *m* to the right and a dot of abbreviation as well, lower and farther right. Tribe, [*L*]*eṃ*: BGU; [*C*]*la*˙: EL.

7. *Tur*]*ranius:* Daris. Filiation, *Ḷ˙ f˙*: BGU; *.f˙*: EL. Origo, [..].[...]..: BGU; .....*a:* EL. Perhaps [*l*]*a*[*udic*]*ia*. Restore the name as]*granius*?

8.]*dius:* BGU and EL. Filiation, *Q f˙*: BGU and EL. Origo, *Ap*..[.].: BGU;]*Ap*[*amea*]: Daris, independently. Restore the name as Trebius? Vibius? Baebius?

10.].*us:* BGU;]...*us*˙: EL.

11. Tribe, *Çor*˙: BGU; ..*s*: EL.

12.]*nutius:* BGU. Filiation, .*f*˙: EL. Origo, *Laudicea*: BGU and EL. Restore the name as Arruntius?

13. *an*]*tonius:* BGU and EL.

15. Origo, *Ch*]*ryṣọpoli*.......[: BGU; *Ch*]*rysopoli*˙ *b*.....: EL. The initial of the word after *chrysopoli* could be *d* or possibly even *r*, but hardly *b*.

37

List of Legionaries

PGenLat. 1 recto, part III; *vidi* A.D. 90

For the bibliography see no. **9**. *ChLA* I, p. 12.

Text: *CPL*, no. 106, III, p. 210, and Daris, no. 10 (4), both reproduce the text of *ChLA*.

This small text has given rise to discussion out of all proportion to its extent. The use of capitals throughout gives it a formal air; but it is ten years later than the accounts which occupy the rest of the sheet (**68**) and upside down to them. Héron de Villefosse (*CRAI*, 1900, i, 270–75) restored the first line to make this a list of veterans discharged in A.D. 90. Espérandieu (*CRAI*, 1900, ii, 442–58) thought the text a list of soldiers ready for discharge but not yet released. Premerstein (p. 22) conjectured that it was the beginning of a complete roll of a century; Morel (*ArM* 16), that it was "une sorte d'étiquette" which gave the date when the accounts on the sheet were assumed to be obsolete. But these five lines come up against the last line of the accounts, leaving twice as much blank space above as they themselves occupy; and there seems to be no reason why a list of any importance should be written in a chance space of an obsolete record. Marichal is therefore probably right in saying (*ChLA* 13), "We could imagine a quill-test or a sample for a *matricula*." Similar exercises in penmanship cover the walls of the clerks' rooms in the temple of Artemis Azzanathkona at Dura (*Report* VI [1936] 482–95, with references to and corrections of *Report* V).

The date is in the first line of the text.

The verso contains **9** and **58**.

IMP DOMITIANO XV COS M.[..].[
C AEMILIVS C F POL PROCVLVṢ ..[
Q IVLIVS Q F COL PONṬICVṢ ÇAṢ[
C VALERIVS C F POL BASSVS CAṢ˙ a[
M ANTONIVṢ M F POL ALPỊNV[S] ḍṛ[

1. *COS A*[*VG:* ArM; *M*(*issi*) *H*(*onesta*) *M*(*issione*): Villefosse; *Ṃ*...[*:* ChLA, and in the apparatus *M*[*ATRICVLA*...? The strokes after *COS* could be *M*, *AM* or *AV*; but nothing more is certain. Possibly even *M* [*COCCEIO NERVA II*, Domitian's colleague in this year; but the position of *COS* between the two names would be anomalous.

2. *PROCVLVS:* ArM, with no indication of letters following; *PROCVLVS* ...[*:* ChLA, and in the apparatus, "The indication of the tribus *Pol*(*lia*), which is ordinarily that of the *ex castris*, should incite to read, at the end, CAS, also palaeographically seductive."

3. *PONTICVS*...*:* ArM; *CẠỊ*[*:* Premerstein, suggesting either *GA*[*D*(*ARA*) or, because of the tribe *Col*(*lina*), *CAE*[*S*(*AREA*). The latter is reasonable; but *CAS*(*TRIS*) seems a likelier reading despite the tribe. Collina appears to have been the tribe of *spurii*: cf. Dessau 6276, 7570, and 8292.

4. *BASSVS* ...[*:* ArM; *CAṢṬṚ*[*:* ChLA. But the last extant letter is certainly a cursive form.

5. .*F; ALBINVS* .[*:* ArM; *M F; ALB*[*V*]*S CẠṢ*[*:* Premerstein; *ALBỊṆV*[*S*] *Ç*.[*:* ChLA. A *B* seems impossible for the third letter of the cognomen because the *B* in line 4 rises high above the line. The last two extant letters are cursive. Presumably they are the beginning of the soldier's *origo*, like *CAS*(*TRIS*) in line 4.

38

Check-list of Soldiers

PVindob. L 99 recto I/II p.
Papyrussammlung der Oesterreichische Nationalbibliothek

Transcription, facsimile, and commentary: R. O. Fink, "Two Fragments of Roman Military Rosters in Vienna," *La Parola del Passato* 55 (1957) 298–311.

Text: Daris, no. 15.

The puncta and other notations with the names give this list some resemblance to the rosters, as does the name in the genitive, presumably that of a centurion or decurion, in i 11. But the names are not divided by consulships as in the rosters, nor do the names or notations supply any indication of the principle on which the text was composed; so it has been classified with the miscellaneous lists. Col. i 3 also seems to be something foreign to the usual content of a roster. The puncta show that at any rate it was a check-list of some sort.

The mixture of Roman, Greek, Egyptian, and Semitic names shows that the unit to which these men belonged was an auxiliary. If i 10 ends with *dec*(*urio*), which is quite uncertain, they were members of an ala or a cohors equitata.

Since none of the persons here is otherwise known, the date is based upon the hand. If *fl*(*auius*) is correctly read in ii 13, the time is at least as late as Vespasian's principate.

The verso is in Greek.

Col. i

] ụị
One line blank
]ạ[p]ync̣ḥ[is]ẹchnutas
].n˙ ss (*vacat*)
]nepherọ[s] ịudi
]horion isidori
]tosthnes armais
]zenon ẓẹ(non)
]ḍionyṣius heraclei
]didymus ḥọrigenes
]maximus atrei exruḥụḍec
Two lines blank
].RLIANI xlvii
]● serapion demetri
] achles pibechas
] ammonius mṛci
] uettienus ṃạtinus dupl
]...[..]..ṇ..[..]..ạṇ[u]s

Col. ii

]et [
One line blank
● ps[e]ṇạm[.].[
● papọntos ṣ.[
● papontos s[
● ofilius c̣ạ[
paasec̣hus ṃ[
[.]. ṛcius ṛu[
● ạ[...].[.]s ạṭ[
ạ.l[ ]..ui[
[ ].ạṇera[
● ạrrius us[
gaius coṃ[
fḷ cronṇ[
iọṣepus i.[
● marius m[
● artemon .[
[.].ạetẹnuṣ[
....[.].[

i 1. The two characters may be a numeral; cf. the *vi* in the numeral of i 11. But conceivably they may be a variant of the T with a cross-bar which is used as a symbol for *turma*.

2. The second name may be *pechnutas*, though Preisigke, *Namenbuch*, cites only the form *Pachnoutis*. Note that the present text has *Serapion* for *Sarapion* in i 12. The name may end in *-is*. Cf. on i 13 below.

3. Read *a*]*ṇn*(*o*) *s*(*upra*)*s*(*cripto*)?

6. No other name except that of the officer in line 11 projects into the margin; hence one must apparently read *Tosthenes* here, perhaps a mis-writing of *Sosthenes*.

7. The cipher following Zenon's name is in the same position as the cognomina and patronymics of the other names and presumably serves the same purpose. The resolution of the cipher presented here was proposed by Dr. Manfredo Manfredi of the Istituto Papirologico "G. Vitelli" of the University of Florence. Cf. the name of Fortius Fortius in **39** 12. One might also expand the cipher as *ze*(*nonis*).

9. *horigenes* is corrected from *heraclei*, repeated by mistake from the preceding line. The first *e* was changed to *o* and *igenes* written above the line.

10. The name is an addition by a second hand; and the notation is by a different pen in darker ink, perhaps a third hand. The notation remains a puzzle. I previously supposed that it might represent something like *ex a*(*la*) (*quinta*) *h*( ) *u*( ), *dec*(*urio*); but I now read the third letter as certainly an *r*. On the analogy of the entries in **10** one might think of *ex*(*it*); *r*(*ediit*) (*quintum*) . . *dec*(*embres*); but once again the characters read as *hu* stand in the way.

11. Restore *centuria* or *turma* [ ]*.rliani*. The name is a problem because the combination *rl* requires a vowel before it and the remains of the letter before *r* do not suit any of the vowels. On the assumption that a vowel may have been omitted between *r* and *l* (note the omissions in i 6, 13, and 14), *Egrilianus* is a possibility, since a Cornelius Egrilianus is attested as a centurion of the leg. III Cyrenaica in an inscription from Bostra (*CIL* III 103 = *IGRR* III 1328), though probably later than the time of this papyrus.

13. Read *achilles*. Preisigke, *Namenbuch*, offers only the spelling *Pibechis*; so perhaps the ending here should be *-is*. Cf. on 2 above; but note that *armais* in 6 has an *i*-longa before the *s* and that *i* is not found elsewhere in this text in ligature with the letter which follows.

14. Read *marci*.

15. Vetienus is a good Roman gentilicium, though not in the *Namenbuch*; but Matinus is cited there only from *PGiess.* 54, 16, of the IV/V century. Read *martinus*? The notation *dupl*(*icarius*) may be in the same hand as the notation in line 10.

ii 5. The gentilicium is a variant spelling of Ofellius, moderately common in Egypt.

7. Perhaps [*m*]*ạṛcius*; but the remains could also be read as [.]*ṛạcius*.

9. The position of *ạ*.*l*[shows that it is a marginal notation, not part of the name. Its meaning is unknown to me.

39

List of Principales?

PMich. III 162 (inv. 3240 recto); *vidi* A.D. 193–197

Transcription, commentary, and facsimile: Henry A. Sanders, *Memoirs of the American Academy in Rome* 9 (1931) 81–85 and plate 3; cited as **S.**

Commentary: Wilcken, *Archiv* 10 (1932) 277–78; H. I. Bell, *JEA* 17 (1931) 268–69; and R. O. Fink, "*Damnatio Memoriae* and the Dating of Papyri," *Synteleia* 232–36.

Text: *CPL*, no. 129, and Daris, no. 16, reproduce the text of *PMich.* III 162.

The nature and purpose of this list are uncertain; but the fact that it is in capitals, that each soldier's origo is formally stated, and especially that only one or two men are named under each year, whereas in complete rosters the numbers show a considerable increase from the earlier years under each century to the more recent ones, all point to the probability that this is a selective list of some sort, perhaps a list of principales. Cf. **10**, **13**, and **37**. The patronymics in lines 2, 9, 22, 23, and 25 show that these men were not citizens and therefore must belong to an auxiliary corps.

The date could not be much after 198 at latest, since the consuls for 173 appear in line 1; but it is fixed more closely by the omission of Commodus' name as consul in lines 8 and 15. This restricts the possibilities to the time when Commodus was under damnatio memoriae, perhaps 193–195 and certainly no later than 197.

The verso contains only an address in Greek: ἀπόδο̣[ς . . .]π̣ετε. . χ̣ω ἀπὸ ἀπλωναρίου ἀδελφ[οῦ].[1] This has occasioned some discussion; but Sanders appears to be right in believing that the address and the Latin text belong together. Wilcken's idea that the Latin was a palimpsest is not confirmed by an examination of the papyrus, which shows no trace whatever of any previous writing; and it is in itself improbable that the Roman army at this period and in Egypt should be using second-hand papyrus for a formal list in capitals. Bell's explanation that a Greek letter once occupied the verso above the address likewise has no evidence to support it and assumes an arrangement of letter and address which would be unique. It is true that this piece was cut, for whatever reason, from a longer list, for the present left edge cuts through the *S* of *SARAPION* in line 25 and the right edge cuts letters in lines 7, 16, 18, 19, 22, and 23. But the papyrus was then folded once on a line from *T* of *ET* in line 1 to the second *I* of *ISIDORI* in line 25; and the address was written parallel with the fold just below the middle of that half of the verso. It might be helpful to us to know the name of the addressee; but it is not necessary to understand ἀδελφός literally, as in a private letter. Cf. the use of *frater* to mean "brother-officer" in **87–89** below.

[1] Read by Youtie. Sanders read ἀπόδος [. .]α[. .]ποτ-[. .] × [.]; but there is a question whether the character in the middle of the line is a tie-mark or a chi.

SẸṾ[E]ṚỌ E[T] POMPEIANO COS[A.D. 173
LVCOFṚỌṆ H[. .]Ṿ[.]LIṚI LVCOP[
GALLO EṬ F̣ḶẠ[CC]Ọ C̣OS [174
IVLIVS AMMỌNỊANVS CASTR˙[
EPONVCHVS AP̣OLLINARIVS CAST[R
PISOṆE ET IṾLIANỌ COS [175
CLAVDIVS APOLLINARIVS LVCOP[
QVIN[TI]LLO COS [177
CASSIVS S. . .MI SOENI[
AVREḶIVS VICTOR LỴC̣OP˙[
ORFITO ET RVFO COS [178
FORTỊVS FOṚTIVS PR[O]SOP[
P̣RAEṢENTẸ ỊỊ COS [180
PL[V]TIỌN P̣LVTI[. .]CIS LVCOP[
VICTORINO II COS [183
CASSỊVS HERONIANVS CAST[R
MARVḶLO ET AELIANO COS [184
AELỊVS HIERONVMVS CAST[R
CRISP̣INO ET AELIANO COS [187
IVLIVS PANISCVS COPTIṬ[

FVSCIANO II COS [A.D. 188
RVFVS CASSIANI CAST[R
POMPEIVS SARAPIONIS CAST[R
SILANIS DVOBVS COS 189
SARAPION ISIDORI ANTI·[

1. *Sẹṿ[er]o:* S.
2. *H[. . . .]liri:* S. The letter read as *Ṿ* might be *A*, *M*, or *N*. The *R* in the second name is doubtful because the tail of this letter does not curl up as here. Perhaps *D* might be read (cf. *CLAVDIVS* 7 and *ISIDORI* 25) or *C* as in *CASTR* 5, *CLAVDIVS* 7, or *CASSIVS* 16. For the *I* before *R* cf. *CLAVDIVS* 7 and *SILVANIS* 24. Expand *Lucop(olites)*.
3. *e[t] Fḷ[acc]ọ:* S.
6. *I[u]liano:* S.
9. A large number of names fit the pattern *S. . . MOS*; but the traces of letters in the middle are hard to reconcile with any of them, particularly the letter in the center, which shows a stroke slanting downward from right to left like part of an *X*. Possibly *Sozymus*? Expand *Soeni(tes)*.
12. Second name, *Fo[r]tius:* S. Daris omits the origo. Expand *Prosop(ites)*.
13. The *R* of *Praesente* has been corrected from *L*. The consul whose name is omitted was Sex. Quintilius Condianus, executed with the other members of his family by Commodus. Since his name is still used in the consular date of *PBerol.* 6866 ii 30 (**70** below) of A.D. 192, the execution must have taken place later that year and not in 182 as conjectured in *PIR*, s.v. "Quintilius" no. 20. See Fink, "Damnatio."
14. *Pl[u]tiḷu[s] Pluti[l]us:* S. There is almost no doubt that both names begin *PLVTI-*; but the second certainly ends with *-CIS*. In the lacuna there is space for two letters at most, perhaps only one.
16. The first *N* of *Heronianus* resembles the ligature N̄T. A Iulius Heronianus, decurion of the ala veterana Gallica, appears in Dessau 2543 (= *CIL* III 14; III S 6581) and an Aurelius Heronia[nus in Wilcken *Ostraka* 1487; but *SB* I 2067, a list of persons, has in line 11 a *Ἡρῶντις Ψεναμο(ύνιος) Ἀβῶτ(ος)*, so perhaps *Herontianus* should be read here.
17. *Maru[l]lo:* S.
20. Expand *Coptit(es)*.
21. The other consul was M. Seruilius Silanus. This text proves that it was he and not Q. Seruilius Silanus, consul in 189 (cf. line 24), who was executed by Commodus. *PIR*, s.v. "Servilius" no. 48, is undecided.
25. Expand *Anti(noites)*: Wilcken, *Archiv* 10.277.

40

List of Soldiers, with Annotations

PMich. III 163 (inv. 1003); *vidi* A.D. 222–239

Transcription, commentary, and facsimile: Henry A. Sanders, *Memoirs of the American Academy in Rome* 9 (1931) 87–88 and plate 4 b; cited as **S**.

Transcription with notes: Sanders, *PMich.* III 163.

Commentary: J. F. Gilliam, "*P. Mich.* 163," *CP* 51 (1956) 96–98.

Text: *CPL*, no. 130, reproduces Sanders' text, noting Gilliam's dating and his readings of lines 6 and 16. Daris, no. 22, adopts Gilliam's readings in his text. The alignment of names is distorted in both; and neither makes clear that the text consists of parts of two columns.

This is another annotated list of soldiers, but too small, as Gilliam points out, to permit a determination whether it is from a complete or partial roster. It is not even completely certain that the men are not legionaries, though the flavor of the names strongly suggests an auxiliary ala or cohort.

The date has also been fixed by Gilliam. The starting-point is *praesentei cos* in 6 and *aduento cos* in 16. The latter must be the consul of 218; and this leads back to a date no later than 215 in line 2 and a terminus ante quem for the papyrus of 240, since recruits of 215 would have been discharged about that year. Actually, however, the remains of a name in line 1 imply enlistment not later than 214 and hence a lower limit of 239. On the other hand, the use of Adventus' name alone shows that his colleague Elagabal had already been killed and sets the terminus post quem as March 13, 222.

The verso is blank.

Col. i		Col. ii
].ṛịu[	A.D. 214?	
laeto ii ?]cos	215?	
]donatụṣ		
sab]ino ii cos	216	
] antoninụs		
]praesentei cos	217	.l[
]ṇụs clemens		
]nus syrion		
]. besarion		
]. isidorus		
] monimus		
]. apollinaṛi[u]ṣ		
]. ạṇṣịrapọ..		
] eudaemoṇ		a.[
]. marcellinụ[s]		
] ạḍụento cos	218	
]ṣ hiçṃạ		f eq in coḥ[
]corneliaṇ[		casṭ[
		i.[
		it[
		[
		[
		çạ[

i 1.]ḷịtọ[: S.

2. Given the consulship in 6, the spacing permits this restoration, while earlier consuls, such as *Messala*, 214, or *Antonino IIII*, 213, are too long. But certainty is not possible.

4. [*Commodo IIII et Victor*]*ino II cos:* S; *Sab*]*ino II:* Gilliam.

6.]*cẹṛetentẹị çọṣ:* S; the reading adopted is Hunt's.

7.]*ns:* S. The ligature of *n* and *u* is peculiar. *ns* corrected to *nus* or to *ans*?

9. *Caesarion:* S.

13. *..deramuṣ:* S. The reading in the text is gibberish, of course. It is intended merely to give some notion of how the traces look to me.

16. [*Condiano et P*]*raesente cos:* S; *ạḍụento:* Gilliam.

17. *Hi caṣ*[*:* S; *Hicaṣ*[*:* Gilliam, as a proper name. The reading adopted is still unsatisfactory.

18. *Corneliụ*[*s:* S.

ii 6. *iu*[*:* S. The first letter could be *a*, *e*, *f*, *i*, *r*, or *s*.

14. *rẹ*[*:* S.

17. *sẹsq:* S. But there are only two letters before the *q*; so that one should probably read *f*(*actus*) *eq*(*ues*) *in coh*(*orte*). Cf. **64** ii 32 and **65** 7. This does not help to identify the unit, for the man could have been made an eques either in his own cohort or another.

18. *iteṃ*[*:* S. It might be possible to read either *caes*[or *cass*[. Cf. *castri* in **5** ii 14.

19. *it*[*em:* S, perhaps rightly.

20. *it*[*em:* S, perhaps rightly.

23. Sanders offers no reading. *sa*[is also possible. See also on 18 above.

41

Names

PDur. 114 (inv. D. P. 63 recto) ca. A.D. 215–230

Transcription and commentary: *Final Rep.* v, no. 114; *edidi.*

Facsimile: ibid., plate 48, 2.

The drastic abbreviation of some names and the seeming brevity of the list mark it as a mere jotting for some temporary purpose.

The date is based on the names of Barnaeus Zebida, **1** xxxiv 5, turma of Tiberinus, 195; and Theobolus Gadde, **2** vii 3 and **6** i 8, century of Danymus, 201. If the men of the same name in the present text are the same persons, the former would have been eligible for discharge in 220 and the latter in 226. In addition, three Aurelii Zabdiboli are known who enlisted in 214 and 216. But since none of the men in this list can be identified with any certainty, the date remains a guess.

The verso is **100**.

aur]ẹl zabdib
deme]ṭrius ẓạabal
aure]l mocimus
za]ḅdibol malchi
aur]ẹl marinus
aure]ḷ barneus zebi
] theobol gadde
] iul ualentinus
] g̣ạiaṇụṣ
]us zebida
] ạuiḍas
] geṛṃanus
] iulianus

3 and 6.]*l:* D.

42

Names

PDur. 119 (inv. D. Pg. 16) A.D. 230–240?

Transcription and commentary: *Final Rep.* v, no. 119; *edidi.*

The most that can be said of this text is that it was a list of names. The dating is on the basis of the hand. The verso (flesh side) is blank.

]. . ạnu[
]a. . . ṇ[
]. ạḍ. ṃ[ ]. [ ]. [
]ctụ[. . . .]n ẓ. [
i]ulius g̣. . [
]. ạẹtagụs p̣. [
]antonius ṃ[
]ḅẹạṣṭ[. .]s ạ[

43

Names

PDur. 124 (inv. D. P. 39 verso) A.D. 220–230

Transcription and commentary: *Final Rep.* v, no. 124; *edidit* Gilliam.

A list of names, dated only by the hand. The recto is **120**.

]. [
]. . [
]. . . [ ] ẓebida
]. . ianus
]. . [. . . .]. . . .
]. . . . themarsa

44

Names

PDur. 118 (inv. D. P. 26 verso) A.D. 248–256

Transcription and commentary: *Final Rep*. v, no. 118; *edidi*.

Facsimile: ibid., plate 66, 2.

The names are the usual ones at Dura; and the purpose of the list is not apparent.

The date depends upon the reasonably certain reading in line 9. Thereafter two more consulships follow, in lines 11 and 14; and both require the numeral *ii*. The earliest possibility, then, is the consulship of the two Philips in 248. The proposal in the former publication that *Gallieno ii cos* might be read in line 14 is rendered impossible if the detached strip of papyrus on the left of the plate is brought up to the edge of the large fragment, as it can be in lines 8–9, 11, and 15. Line 10, however, stands in the way of doing so; and in line 12 the traces on the detached strip might be read, doubtfully, as *uolu*]*si*[*ano* but cannot be reconciled with *iii et*. In line 14 similarly the traces on the strip might be *g*[*a*]*ḷ*; but Gallus' name followed by *ii* and nothing else would mean that his son's name was omitted, while the use of these letters as part of Gallienus' name would require too large a gap between the strip and the larger fragment. The date therefore cannot be made precise.

The recto is **29**.

]. . [
]ụṣ ạc̣ịḅạs
]. . anus
]. sus
]ịus
ant]ị[o]chus
]ạṃes
]. ṭhemarsa
arriano]eṭ p̣ạpo cos ? A.D. 243?
]llus
]eus
iii et]ii cos ? 248?
] messianus
]. . ii cos 255?
]ạḍallathụs
iar]ḥaboles
]. germanus
iaq]ubus
]. ia. . us
]. e. [
]. o[

No readings are offered for the detached strip of papyrus on the left of the plate because of the uncertainty regarding its position.

15. *s*]*ạḍallathụs* or *u*]*ạḅallathụs*.

45

List of Names

PAberd. 132 (inv. 2e) ii p.

Transcription:

1. E. B. Windstedt, *CQ* 1 (1907) 267.
2. E. G. Turner, *Catalogue of Greek and Latin Papyri and Ostraca in the Possession of the University of Aberdeen* (1939), no. 132.

Transcription, commentary, and facsimile: *ChLA* iv, no. 227.

Text: *CPL*, no. 68.

Though Cavenaile places this text among the miscellaneous papyri, its form gives it a claim to be a military list in capitals like **28**, **39**, and **46**. The indentation of line 2 certainly suggests a consular date; and the right-hand one of the strokes in the margin to the left of line 3 may be the remains of the symbol for century/centurion. Marichal reads it so and attaches it to the name in line 4. This may be right (see app.); otherwise the lack of a praenomen for Serenus shows that he was not a Roman citizen and hence that the list, if military, belonged to an auxiliary corps.

Turner dates the list tentatively in the third century; but both the hand and the use of praenomina incline me rather to the second, perhaps A.D. 125–150. Marichal dates the text 131–160; see on lines 2 and 4.

The verso is blank.

]. .   L· GAE.[
]   PO.[
]. . .   C PỌN[
].   SEREN[
]   C ṾỊṾ[

1. Turner does not mention the traces in the left margin. *GAE*[*:* Aberd.

2. *Ḷo:* Aberd.; *POṆ*[*tiano et* . . . . . . *cos:* ChLA. Too little remains, however, for certainty about the date; nothing is left of the third letter but a dot level with the top of the *O* and near it. Hence *pollione*, *pompeiano*, and *pontiano* are possible. If a date in the second quarter of the second century is right, then *Pontiano et Rufino*, A.D. 131, or *Pontiano et Atiliano*, A.D. 135, have a good claim. Marichal prefers them. But *Pollione II et Apro II*, A.D. 176, should probably be considered as well.

The nearly vertical strokes in the left margin seem to be an extension of strokes begun in line 1. Marichal assigns them to line 3.

3.]*ssi:* ChLA; in app.: "Should we understand *iu*]*ssi* as in ChLA, iii, 218 (P. Lond. 2723, ii, line 3, and infra no. 261)? This seems most likely, but in view of the state of the text I have preferred not to admit it as a conjecture." See also **46** 2 app.

4. *SEREN*.[*:* Aberd.;](*centuria*) *SEREN*[*I:* ChLA. Marichal may be right; but the stroke which he interprets as ⅄ appears to start in line 3 and would be an improbably large and sweeping character.

5. Three dots: Aberd.; *C. UIT*[*:* ChLA.

46

List of Names

PAnt. 41 recto — A.D. 212–230, perhaps 219–21
Ashmolean Museum, Oxford

Transcription and commentary: C. H. Roberts, *The Antinoopolis Papyri*, Part I (London 1950) no. 41 and page 107.

Transcription, commentary, and facsimile: *ChLA* IV, no. 261.

Text: *CPL*, no. 135, and Daris, no. 24, both reproduce Roberts' text.

This small text has little of interest aside from being in capitals throughout except for two notations in the margin. Too little remains to show whether it should be placed among the partial rosters or special lists. It is not even certainly a military text; but the listing of the names by consulships and the marginal notations at least indicate that it is a roster or name-list of some sort rather than a pridianum, as the editor suggests.

The date derives partly from the consulships, partly from the names. The men in the first three lines must have enlisted no later than 205; and so the usual 25 years' service would produce 230 as an approximate terminus ante quem. But since all the men are Aurelii, the text must be subsequent to the constitutio Antoniniana in 212. The peculiarity that at least three men (lines 3, 5, and 7; perhaps also 6) have a gentilicium in addition to Aurelius suggests that it belongs to the time of Elagabal like **1**, which exhibits the same practice. (See in detail *Final Rep.* V, p. 38.) The present text goes even further and includes the praenomen. Because of the date, the nomenclature gives no clue to the sort of unit in which, if this is a military roster, the men served, whether a legion or an auxiliary corps.

The verso is in Greek, "part of a document, perhaps a letter from a high official."

	]F̣.Ṿ..[.].ON[	
].ṣi	M˙ AVRELIVS[	
	M˙ AVR˙ LOLḶỊṾṢ[	
	ẠḶḄỊṆỌ ẸṬ ẠẸṂ[ILIANO COS	A.D. 206
]ṣi	M˙ AVR˙ ỊVLIVS F̣[	
	] M˙ AVR˙ ṾẠḶERỊ.[	
	] M˙ AVR˙ IVL˙ HI..[	
	] APRO ET MAX[IMO COS	207
	].M˙ AVR˙ ANTIN[OVS	

1. *AU*[*R*(*ELIUS*)*:* Ant. and ChLA; *Aur*(*elius*)*:* Daris; but a photograph obtained through the courtesy of the Ashmolean Museum shows a distinct horizontal stroke, as of a *T*, after the *V*. *ḶON*[*GUS:* edd. Other possibilities exist, however, such as *longinus*; and reading *aur long* leaves a space of about two letters unaccounted for between them.

2. *AUR*(*ELIUS*) *ELIUS:* ChLA, i. e. *aelius*. This is possible and ingenious; but even if there is an abbreviation stroke after *AVR* (my photograph seems to show some damage to the papyrus there, but appears to have the remains of a stroke), the space of a wide letter between *M* and *A*, unlike any of the entries below, leads me to believe that *aurelius* is the man's real gentilicium and hence written out in full. In marg.,]*iri*( )*:* Ant.; [*Iu*]*ṣsi:* ChLA, in app.: "one could read *Iusi*", comparing *PMich*. 447 + *PLond*. 2723 = *ChLA* 218 (see also R. O. Fink, "P. Mich. VII 447," *AJA* 68 [1964] 297–99 and **45** app. 3). In the present text *iussi* may be possible but is far from certain.

3. *LOḶḶỊỤ*[*S:* Ant.

4. *ẠḶḄ*[*I*]*ṆỌ ET* [*AEMILIANO:* Ant.; *ẠḶḄỊṆỌ ẸṬ ẠẸ*[*MILIANO:* ChLA.

5.]*.i*( )*:* Ant.; [*Ius*]*si:* ChLA; *IULIUS* .[*:* edd.

6. [*Ius*]*ṣị:* ChLA. My photograph shows no trace. *AỤF̣ELḶỊ*[*US:* Ant., in app.: "*Apuleius* is a possible reading." *ỤALERỊỤ*[*S:* ChLA, with credit to Barns for assistance. The initial *V*, however, seems to have a stroke below on the left (*A*, *M*, or *X*?) and the *AL* could be *N*.

7. In marg., [*Iuss*]*ị:* ChLA. *HILA*[*RI:* Ant.; *HILA*[*RIUS:* ChLA. In the last name, the third letter is identical in form with the second. The fourth letter is *T* (less likely, *E*) with an additional short stroke on the left slanting downward from right to left. This may represent the left-hand stroke of an *A* inserted as a correction; but I cannot find any sign of the right-hand stroke, of which the top should certainly be visible.

9. In marg., [*Iuss*]*ị:* ChLA. *ANTIN*(*OUS*)*:* Ant., in app.: "Less likely *Antin*(*oites*)."

III

Records of Military Units

The records of individual persons covered in the preceding chapter were of course the basis of all the other records of the Roman army, since the only reason for the existence of military organization is to insure the presence of suitable persons in certain places at given times. Official correspondence, furthermore, as Chapter 5 will show, proves a surprisingly detailed awareness of individuals even when they were remote from provincial headquarters; but the organization exists so that the commanding general will not have to deal entirely with single persons. In order to secure this result, the records of persons must be digested into records of legions, cohorts, and alae which will enable the responsible authorities to manipulate large numbers of men as units. **47–66** provide a notion of how this was done by the Romans. They are classified in four categories—morning reports, monthly summaries, pridiana, and a puzzling one which Gilliam has dubbed a "strength report," **66**.

Morning Reports. The type of record in which unit and personnel records meet most intimately is the unit journal, called *βιβλίον ἐφήμερον* by Appian,[1] and *acta diurna* or *cottidiana* by Rostovtzeff, and very similar to the so-called "morning report" of the present-day American army. In the passage of Appian just cited, the emphasis rests upon the daily report of the number of men present; but comparison of **47** and **50** shows that they have features in common, which may therefore be regarded as the essential elements of these journals. In **47** the items in each day's entries run as follows. (All except the fourth are in single long lines. The fourth item consists of a varying number of short lines, each devoted to one set of men.)

1. The date by day and month and the grand total of the men on hand, with separate statements of the number of centurions and their lieutenants, the number of dromadarii with their minor officers, and finally the number of equites with the number of decurions and their lieutenants.
2. In a separate line the full official name of the cohort, in the genitive case.
3. The name of the tribune in command, followed by the daily password and sometimes other material.

[1] *Bell. Civ.* 5.46: καὶ νῦν ἔθος ἐστὶ τὸν αἰτοῦντα τὸ σύνθημα χιλίαρχον ἐπιδίδοναι τῷ βασιλεῖ βιβλίον ἐφήμερον τοῦ ἀριθμοῦ τοῦ παρόντος.

4. Departures and returns and other particulars of special interest.
5. The announcement of the orders of the day and other items, and the oath of obedience.
6. The names and ranks of the guard of honor who performed the excubatio ad signa on that day.

The same components appear with only slight variations in **50**; but there the cycle for each day begins with the orders of the day (the fifth item in **47**) and closes with the password, the third item in **47**. The fourth item, movements of individual personnel, does not occur in **50**. See the commentary on that text. **48** and **49** reveal some of the same elements.

The variations noted in the order of the different sections of data are probably not significant. Without the modern device of printed blank forms, the clerks of each officium were necessarily left somewhat to their own discretion in setting up the pattern of various records. What is significant is that all of these acta diurna had the same content.

Of the texts already discussed, it is obvious that **10** and **11** were probably summaries drawn from the acta diurna.

Monthly Summaries. The next group, **58–62**, may likewise have been taken from the *acta diurna*; but they may also have been independent texts from the start. It is fairly certain, too, that they are not all of exactly the same sort; but in spite of their extremely fragmentary condition it is possible to say that they are all summaries, probably monthly, of one kind or another, and that they are not quite so much concerned with individuals as the morning reports. **62** is certainly dated by the kalends of October, and **60** may be dated by the kalends of January; and this implies a kind of monthly inventory. **61** may have been another of the same type; and **58** was without question an analysis of the personnel of a legionary century who were not available at the beginning of the month for the sort of duties recorded in **9**, of which **58** is the complement. **62** at least resembles **58** in analysing the praesentes into various categories; and it may probably be assumed that **60** and **61** did the same, while **58** (and possibly **59**) no doubt was like the others in beginning with a division into *absentes* and *praesentes*. But **60–62**, instead of being limited to one century, differ from **58** in taking in the entire coh. xx Palmyrenorum, as the high numbers, ranging from at least 300 to 766, clearly show.

62, on the other hand, diverges from the rest because it contains no names, in this respect resembling **63** and **65**. **58** is inconsistent. In col. ii the armorum custos is not named, whereas the conductor, the carrarius, the librarius, and the rest are named, some with one name, some with two. And in col. i it is doubtful whether there are enough lines to contain the names and titles of all the members of the century not included in the 40 who begin col. ii.

58 and **59** contain titles of various ranks along with the names; and **59** approaches the rosters in that it gives the men's dates of enlistment as well.

All of these differences, especially in view of the very small amount of text in any one of this group, render impossible any convincing guess as to their use or uses, except in the case of **58** which has already been described as the companion-piece of **9**.

Pridiana. **63** and **64** are less of a problem. **64** in particular has an obvious form and purpose in the extant part, and together with **63** gives a reasonably clear idea of a pridianum, the one sort of military record known to have a specific technical name. **64** begins with a detailed heading—its title, pridianum, the name and titles of the unit, the date by day, month, and year, the location of the unit's headquarters, the date of its arrival there, the name, filiation, tribe, and origo of the commander, the date of his enlistment, and the name of his predecessor. **63** contains, in i 23–25, the same data, but in the briefest possible form. Both documents then report the situation of the unit's personnel at the date of the preceding pridianum, first the total enrollment, then the number of centurions, decurions, equites, and pedites. **64** has dromedarii as well; and **63** adds the number of duplicarii and sesquiplicarii in both cavalry and infantry. The remainder of each text is concerned with changes in personnel since the last report. In the extant part of **64** there are only accessions and promotions—a centurion and decurion are appointed, nine recruits are received and distributed among the centuries and turmae on six different dates, five soldiers are transferred from other units, and at least two are promoted to equites. All these items are treated in detail, with name and identification of each soldier and the date by day and month of his incorporation into the cohort. In **63**, by contrast, 50 accessions are disposed of in five lines, and no soldiers are mentioned by name except men who have been discharged. The rest of **64** after the promotions to eques has been lost; but **63** continues with categories of permanent losses, *absentes intra* and *extra provinciam*, and *praesentes*. The last extant item is for *aegri* among the *praesentes*; but it is possible that the record continued in much the same way as **58**.

What, then, is a pridianum? On the ground that both of the known examples begin with the first of January and proceed at once to the situation of September 1, I proposed in my former publication of **64** (see bibliography there) that a pridianum was ordinarily an annual report on January 1 covering all changes in personnel between the previous January 1 and December 31 and detailing the current disposition of the unit's soldiers. In Egypt alone, where the administrative year ended August 28, a second pridianum was submitted; but because the army operated with the Roman calendar as well as the Latin language, the date of the report was moved to the pridie Kalendas Septembres so as to take in the whole month of August.

This is still my view, though Gilliam (see bibliography under **63**, "The Moesian 'Pridianum'," 752–54) questions it, arguing that the pridiana make no mention of the Egyptian year, that the periods covered do not coincide with it exactly, that if accessions were entered in only one pridianum there would be no complete annual report in Egypt for either the Egyptian or the Roman year, and that the pridiana of December 31 and August 31 would cover periods of different length. He suggests rather that a number of pridiana—the number not specified—were submitted at intervals during the year, each carrying forward items of continuing importance such as accessions and losses, until all were summed up in the pridianum of December 31. Such a procedure is certainly possible; and if Gilliam is right, the preceding category of monthly summaries (**58–62**) may be illusory, these texts being really interim pridiana. None is complete, so that certainty is impossible, but they seem to me not to contain sufficient data to qualify as pridiana; and if they are not, then there is no evidence for interim pridiana except the two pridiana mensis Augusti. On the other hand, I see no objection to supposing that these were interim reports intended only for the internal use of the Egyptian administration while the pridianum mensis Decembris would be *the* pridianum for Egypt as for other provinces, accumulating all the items of importance for the entire year, as Gilliam envisages, and conceivably intended, not for the governor of the province, but for the emperor and his general staff in Rome.

66 is unique and unclassifiable except for the obvious facts that it is concerned in large part with the strength of the coh. xx Palmyrenorum, that most of the absences and returns whose occasion can be read are concerned with preparations for payment of the stipendium, and that in the course of the year 250 not less than eleven soldiers, all but two of whom had ten years or more of service, were affected, singly or in small groups, by important changes.

96, too, may belong in this section as a fragment of a morning report, a monthly summary, or a pridianum.

Morning Reports

47

Morning Report of the Coh. XX Palmyrenorum

PDur. 82 (inv. D. P. 3 recto); *vidi* A.D. 223–235

Transcription and commentary:

1. J. F. Gilliam, "Some Latin Military Papyri from Dura," *YCS* 11 (1950) 209–46; now superseded by the following.
2. *Final Rep.* v, no. 82; *edidit* Gilliam.

Facsimiles:

1. Frag. c. only: *Illustrated London News*, August 13, 1932, p. 240.
2. *Final Rep.* v, plates 50–51.

The following are incomplete and no longer of any value:

1. M. I. Rostovtzeff, *CRAI*, 1933, pp. 313–14.
2. Idem, *Münchener Beiträge* 19 (1934) 367–70.
3. E. T. Silk and C. B. Welles in *Prelim. Report* v (1934) 296–97.

Text: *CPL*, no. 326, reproduces Gilliam's text from *YCS*.

The characteristics of this and similar unit journals have been described above, pp. 179–80. This text was dated ca. 233 by Gilliam on the ground that it is later than **27** (November 30, 233) and close in date to **48**; but the evidence is not conclusive. It is certainly later than **92** (223–225), which has the same centurions as **2** except for Pudens, who has replaced Malchus; but **27** actually names only Marianus, Antoninus prior, Antoninus posterior, Pudens, and Gaianus. It is probable that Gaianus had replaced Danymus, while Marcus, who enlisted in the same year as Danymus, 201, may have been replaced by Nigrinus, though this is not provable. The present text, on the other hand, names Marianus, Antoninus prior, Pudens, Gaianus, and Nigrinus, and in i 12 an Antoninus who is not distinguished as *prior* or *posterior*. But *prior* is used in i 15 and implies a *posterior*, so that this text may be contemporary with or earlier than **27**.

All that can be said with certainty is that **47** is later than **92** and, as shown by the honorific epithets "Severiana Alexandriana," prior to Alexander's death early in 235. An exact terminus ante quem is supplied by Gilliam's demonstration that by April 20, 235, Laronius Secundianus had taken Iulius Rufianus' place as tribune (*YCS* 11.219–20 and note 18; *PDur.* 125 and 126); but nothing requires **47** to be dated much after 223.

The verso is **83**.

Col. i

ṿi ḳal apṛ[iles n p mil ca]l dcc̣c̣cxx̣ị[i]i in his [o]ṛḍ viiii d{i}upl viii ṣ[esq] ị drom xxxiiii in his sesq i eq ccxxiii in his dec v dupl vii sesq iiii

coh xx̣[palmyrenor s]ẹuerianae alexa[nd]ṛianae *vacat*

[iu]liụ[s] rụ[f]iaṇ[us t]ṛ[ibun]ụs signum mẹ[r]c̣uri ṣ ex sepṭezoṇ[i]s ṃ[isit] *vacat*

[m]ịṣsi .[*ca.* 5].[*ca.* 7] mịl ṿ ịn h drom .[. . eq i] ϒ ṃaṛ[i]ạṇi auṛẹl licinnius ϒ puḍẹṇṭis aurel demetrius ϒ nigrini aurel romanus aurel rufus Ŧ anton iarhaboles odeati

ṛẹụersi q[d]p cum .[. . . .] appạ[d]ạn[. . .].Ŧ tiberini . .[*ca.* 16] *vacat*

Space of one and a half lines

ṭ[i]ṃ[i]ṇius p[aulinus decurio ad]ṃissa pṛọṇụnṭịauiṭ[quod imperatum fuerit faciemus] et ad omnem tesseram parati eirimus excubant ad signa d n alexandri aug

dẹc̣ ṭ[iminius pauli]ṇ[u]s ạ[edit a]urel si[luanu]ṣ [*ca.* 30]ṣ uabalathi curator aurel rubathus ci iarhaeus malchi curator ii cl agrippas eq

[. . .]. . .[*ca.* 15]. . .[.]ṣ. . .ị. . .[.].[*ca.* 30] *vacat*

Space of three lines

[v kal ap]riḷẹṣ n p ṃ[il] cal dc̣c̣c̣cxx[in his ord . . . . dup]l ṿiii ṣẹṣq i drom xxxiii in his sesq i eq ccxx̣ịịị in his dec v dupl vii sesq iiii

[co]h x̣x̣ p̣[alm] seụẹṛ[i]anae alexạṇḍ[rianae] *vacat*

[iulius rufi]a[nus tribunu]ṣ [signum . . .].ẹ.ịṣ ẹx̣ ṣepṭẹzoṇịs ṃ[isi]ṭ *vacat*

[*ca.* 30]. . ạṇṭoninus ϒ anṭọn aurel mariṇ[us] ⟦aurel hẹliodorus⟧ ϒ gaiani iarhaboles iarhaei ϒ nig(rini) aurel apolinarius

[missi ad fr]ụṃenṭ[um compara]nḍụṃ ṃi[l . .].[*ca.* 11]ẹ . . .ịạnes iarhabole *vacat*

[*ca.* 8 be]cchufṛ .[. .]ị[n] ụex[i]l ṃil i ϒ g̣aian[i] . .[. .].[*ca.* 10] *vacat*

[*ca.* 8].ig.[. . .].[*ca.* 6] ϒ anton prior ạ[ure]ḷ[ ] *vacat*

[*ca.* 8]ṭ[iminiu]ṣ pạ[u]liṇus dec adṃissa proṇ[u]ṇt[iauit *ca.* 23] iiii kal april expungẹṇṭur suplicatio immolatio et ad omnem tesseram parati erimus

ẹxc̣ubạ[nt] ạḍ signa d n ạlexandri aug dẹc̣ [timinius pau]l[inus] ṣẹṣq ạụṛẹḷ ạḅṣas aedit aurel siluanus sig cl natalius lib aurel capiton ci anton ual opt[io]n ii ogelus malchi eq

[*ca.* 18]ṃalchus zebịḍa eq ael heliod[orus . . .].[.]. . . .l ạẹl mẹnanḍer . .ḥ[.]. . .ẹi

i 1. *DCÇÇXIIII:* D; but plate 50 shows a gap between the fourth *c* and the remains of the *x*. An *l* might be restored; but the size of the lacuna suggests that an *x* is preferable. There is not room for *lx*.

Read with Gilliam *n*(*umerus*) *p*(*urus*) *mil*(*itum*) *cal*(*igatorum*), comparing **63** ii 14 for *purus*. Or perhaps *n*(*umero*) *p*(*uro*) *mil*(*ites*) *cal*(*igati*), understanding a verb like *sunt*, as in **50** i 5 and 11. The *caligati*, as this line proves, comprised all enlisted men up to and including centurions and decurions. See also J. F. Gilliam, "*Milites Caligati*," *TAPA* 77 (1946) 183–91.

Since all the evidence shows that the cohort had only six centuries at this time, three of the nine centurions on the rolls must be supernumeraries.

Two letters are lost at the right edge of plate 50 in all lines which continue on plate 51.

3. *signum* . .[. .]. *ṛis ex Sep*[*t*]*ezo*[*ni*]*ṣ:* D, omitting *misit*, and in the apparatus, "*Sep*[*t*]*ezo*[*ni*]*ọ*, with a looped *o* at the end, may not be entirely impossible, but a final *s* is a much easier reading. *Ṃẹṛ*[*c*]*ụri s*(*ancti*) probably follows *signum* if a planetary deity is to be supplied . . . it is uncertain whether we should understand a verb (*misit* in [*PDur.*] 89 [= **50**])." But the plate shows clear traces of ink which can be read as *m*, *r*, or *a* after the final *s* of *septezonis*; and this may justify the restoration in the text. The letter before *ex* curves to the right too much for a good *s*, but not enough for a *c*.

4. [*Mis*]*si; drom* . . [—6—] ϒ *Ṃạṛịạṇị:* D. The number and identity of the dromedarii is uncertain; but there are two named Aurelius Romanus in **2** xliv 7 and 10, at that time the century of Danymus. One of these is thetatus in **8** iii 4. The single entry Ŧ *anton*(*ini*) at the end of the line makes the restoration *eq*(*ues*) *i* certain.

5. [*R*]*eṿersi; cum* . [—6—]. . . . .[. . .]. Ŧ*:* D.

Expand *q*(*uondam*) *d*(*e*)*p*(*utati*)? Not wholly satisfactory because in inscriptions *qd* alone represents *q*(*uon*)*d*(*am*) and the contexts in which *deputare* is found are not suitable to the situation here. *d*(*is*)*p*(*ositus*) is even less acceptable because in the rosters it clearly means "relay rider." The abbreviation *qdp* occurs in these papyri only with forms of *reversus*, which in turn contrasts with *missus*, perhaps *emanserunt* (see on ii 17), *non comparet*, *mutatus*, and *remansit* (**66** b ii 6). The meaning, then, must be "formerly detailed."

6. *Ṭị[mi]ṇius; ạḍṃịssa:* D. Gilliam: "The first part of the oath is restored from [**48** and **50**]; cf. however below, i, 16. I earlier read *excubare*, and that is at least as easy a reading here. However, in [**49** and **50**] *excubant* is much to be preferred, or certain, and in [**51**] one finds *excubuerunt ad aquilam et signa*."

7. The readings *timinius* through *siluanus* are taken from Gilliam's text in *Final Rep.* v. The *aedituus* must have had charge of the *aedicula* where the signa were kept. Cf. the *sacerdos* in **50** i 2 and 9, and frag. b 2. Gilliam: "The abbreviated title of Iarhaeus Malchi is *ci* or *pi*; perhaps *ci(rcitor)* which is found written out in [**49**] in a similar list." The two curatores may have had oversight of the stables: Domaszewski, *Rang.* 51.

8. The readings are Gilliam's.

9. *D[C]CÇCXI[III; drom(adarii) XXXIIII; eq CCXXIII:* D. The last numeral in the grand total might be read as *v*, though it seems too broad and upright for this hand. Since the number of reversi in line 5 is unknown and the grand totals in line 1 and here are both doubtful, it is impossible to say absolutely whether or not the missi-reversi items affect the totals, though the totals for the dromedarii here and in line 1 indicate that they did. In the figure here for the dromedarii there are four strokes following the three *x*'s; but one is not a proper *i*. It appears rather to be the start of a fourth *x*, not finished but not erased. In the total for the equites in this line the second *x* is peculiar and the numerals which follow it are blurred.

10. *P̣[a]ḷ[m]; Sevẹṛianae:* D.

11. Conceivably [*signum ue*]*ṇẹṛịṣ*? D omits *misit*. The *m* and *t* are mere shadows on the papyrus; but cf. on line 3 above.

12. *Marinus:* D; ϒ *Gaianin:* D, a misprint.

13. [10]. . . [10]. . . . . . . [. . . .]. . [15].[. .]. . . *Ç̣ạianụs Iarhabole:* D. A Haeranes Iarhabole appears in **1** xlii 18; but he enlisted in 203 and is noted as *non reuersus*, hence is unlikely to be the person named here.

14.].*ex*[. . *m*]*il:* D.

15.] ϒ *Anton(ini)*. . . . . . [. . .]*ḷ*[*:* D.

16. *Ṭ[imin]ịụṣ* [*Pau*]*linus; proṇụṇ*[*tiavit:* D. Gilliam: "This line, after the long lacuna, remains puzzling. . . .*IIII Kal Apriles* was of course the next day. No unusal event was recorded on it. . . . Nor did any of the occasions contained in the Feriale Duranum [**117**] fall on March 29. . . . *Expungere* can mean 'discharge' in military language (*P.Oxy.* 1204 and *Schol. Pers.*, 2, 13, cited in *TLL* v, cols. 1813 f.), and possibly we should understand it in that sense here. If so, a formula such as one of those in the Feriale may have been used: [*quod emeriti m(issi) h(onesta) missione*] *IIII Kal Apriles expungentur, supplicatio immolatio.* [Cf. **117** ii 22, and *YCS* 7 (1940) 193–202.] Even if this should represent substantially the content of the lacuna, the exact wording would of course be quite uncertain. . . . In any event, it should be stressed that the nature of the occasion being celebrated here is uncertain."

Col. ii 18 may confirm that discharges are meant (see below for my interpretation); but as an alternative it may be worth noticing that *expungere* also commonly means "to check off" items on a list, and that the occasion here might be a liberalitas of the emperor or something similar. Cf. Tertullian, *De corona mil.* 1.1: "Proxime facta liberalitate praestantissimorum imperatorum expungebatur in castris. Milites laureati adibant."

Gilliam: "Whatever the content of the middle of the line may have been, the abrupt transition to *ad omnem tesseram*, with the change of subject and the omission of the first part of the oath, is strange. I can think of nothing better than . . . that the clerk omitted the first clause by error. If there was another *quod* clause earlier in the line, the lapse might be somewhat easier to understand."

17. [*Paulinus*], ... *Aurel* . . . .*s; .i Anton(ius) Val(entinus* ?)*:* D. Gilliam: "For. . . the title of *Anton(ius) Val(entinus)*, see above under line 7. Other expansions are possible for both parts of his name. . . . In 7 one finds *curator* . . .*curator II*, but no optio seems to be listed earlier in this line. The title of the second man appears to be something else, to judge from the few traces left. *Hogelus* [instead of *II Ogelus*] would remove the difficulty, but the reading is not attractive. Ogelus Malchi may be the man with this name in [**27**] *b* i, 17." The reading *sesq* may perhaps solve the problem, since the rosters show duplicarii and sesquiplicarii as lieutenants of the centurions and decurions and hence with the status if not the title of optiones. Note that in **20** 5 and 8, two sesquiplicarii are promoted to decurion. The cognomen *absas* seems reasonably certain.

18.]. . . . *Ç̣ḷ(audius) Iul(ius) Menander* .[.]. . . . .*i:* D. The *c* of *cl* could be almost anything; and the word is probably a title of rank. For *ael* in place of *iul*, cf. the *ael* earlier in the line.

Col. ii

iiii kal april n p mil cal ḍçcç[c-
coh xx palm seueriạ[na]e a[l]e[xandrianae
iulius rufianus tribunus . . ụẹṣṣụṣ . . [
missi ad hordeum comparandum ṃ[il . .] in h eq . . [
missi in prosec hordiator mil [.]i ϒ mariani .[
reuersi q d p adatha mil ii ϒ nigrini iul zabdibolus[
reuersi q d p ad praet praẹṣidis cum epistul[i]ṣ .[
z reuersus ex q d p cum eis ad praet praes ex coh ii eq[

missus lig balnei mil i Y nigrini zebidas barnei . [
⟦reuersus⟧
timinius paulinus decurio admịṣṣạ pronuntịa[uit
dec tẹịnnius paulinus aed aurel siluạṇụs ṣị[g
iii aurel bassus, iiii aurel heliodorus [
Space of two and a half lines
iii kal apriles ṇ p mil cal dccccxịịii[
coh xx palmyreṇ[o]ṛụm seueriạnae alẹx[andrianae
iulius rufianus tṛ[i]ḅ[u]ṇus pṛiṃo . [
vacat ẹx ṃị[l] in ḥ d[upl
h e mansẹṛunt mil iiii Y . [
mariani moṃḅọg[eus] themarsa Y [
non çọmparet [ ] eq i [
mụtatị tul ex q d p ạ[d . . . . .] ḟrum eṭ ịnḍ[
m[u]ṭatus . tul ex [*ca.* 9]. [

ii 1. *ḌÇÇÇ[CXIIII:* D.

2. *Ale[xandrianae:* D.

3. *tribunus* [. .]. *ụẹṛ*. . . [.]. . [: D. In i 3 and 11 the tribune gave out the password at this point; but here and in line 16 below the word *signum* does not follow *tribunus*. Conceivably the difference in the present line may be an action pursuant to the entry in i 16. Gilliam: "After *tribunus*, [*r*]*ẹụẹṛṣụṣ* is quite possible and then, a much more dubious reading, *ẹx*." *reuersus* is very possible; and in that case, either *ab* or *ad* at the end of the line.

4–5. On the collection of barley see Gilliam, *YCS* 11.243–44, and Index 9 of this corpus, s.v. "hordeum." Gilliam ad loc. in *Final Rep.* v seems to be right in supposing that the men in line 4 were those who actually bought or requisitioned the barley while those in line 5 acted as their escort, citing Pliny, *Epist.* 10.27. He prefers, however, to suppose that the men in 5 arranged the transportation of the grain which the others collected; but in that case there seems no reason why they should be sent out together on the same day. He notes, too, that this is the first appearance of the word *hordiator*.

6. *ad Atha:* D. Gilliam: "Atha does not seem to be otherwise known, at least in this spelling. There was an Attas or Athis a few miles below Barbalissus; see Dussaud, *Topographie Historique*, p. 453. If one assumes that *ad* is not the preposition but part of the name, another possibility is Adatha in the Palmyrene (Dussaud, p. 270–71), though it was in a different province."

7. Expand *praet(orium)*. *ṃ[ilites:* D; but the next word may have been the name of the writer or the addressee.

8. For the marginal note see above on **1** xxxv 17. Gilliam: "The cohort, the *II Eq(uestris?)*, may be that named in an inscription from the Dolicheneum, having been transferred to Dura by 251–253; *Preliminary Rep.* IX, 3, pp. 112–114, no. 972."

9. *lig(nator)*. Without *balnei*, one would prefer *lig(natum)*. Cf. **63** ii 18, *uestitum*, and 20, *equatum*.

12. *Timinius; Silvaṇụṣ* .[: D. Gilliam in *YCS*: "*Timinius* was written carelessly . . . and here may actually have been spelled *Teiminius*"; but the fourth letter is like the fifth.

13. Gilliam is of course right in supposing that the numerals show that two other men with the same title were named in the preceding line.

17. . . . . [.]*ịn*. . [: D. Gilliam: "The line is deeply indented and may be a heading for lines 18–22. At the end *in h(is)*.[is possible." Rather than a heading, I should consider this line a continuation of 16, probably added after 18 was begun. Note that 19 is also crowded in between 18 and 20. In 16–17 the tribune did something *primo*, then something else which involved certain soldiers.

18. Gilliam: "*Hemanserunt* = *emanserunt*. These men were absent without leave but were not yet considered deserters; *Digest*, xlix, 16, 3–4 and 14." It may be significant, however, that the first *e* as well as the *h* is written larger than usual; and in view of the entry in i 16, perhaps announcing discharges on the following day, I should propose here, on the second day after, *h(oneste) e(meriti) manserunt mil(ites) iiii*, that is, that these men re-enlisted at once after their discharge and remained in the cohort, perhaps as *evocati*.

19. *Mariani* . . . . . . [. . .] *Themarsa* Y [: D. This line, as already stated, is an addition crowded in between lines 18 and 20.

20. Gilliam notes that probably nothing is lost in the lacuna.

21. *Mutati* . . . *ex qdp* [. . . . .]*e*. . *merin*.[: D. Gilliam: "*Mutatio militiae* is a punishment; *Digest*, xlix, 16, 3–6. But possibly *mutatus* is equivalent here to *translatus*, meaning simply 'transferred.' The three letters before *ex* seem to be the same in both lines. One possible reading is *tul*"; and in *YCS*, "The middle letter might even be *d*, which would suggest *adl(ecti)*. The meaning of these lines is quite obscure, but one would expect them to list men in a certain status, as do lines 18 and 20." One might also read *m[u]ltati*, *m[ul]ṭạtus*; but the key to these lines lies, of course, in the syllable *tul*, before which there is another letter or blot in line 22.

TRANSLATION

Col. i

March 27. Milites caligati, net, 923, among these 9 centurions, 8 duplicarii, 1 sesquiplicarius; camel riders, 34, among these 1 sesquiplicarius; cavalry, 223, among these 5 decurions, 7 duplicarii, 4 sesquiplicarii

of the cohors xx Palmyrenorum Severiana Alexandriana.

Iulius Rufianus, tribune, sent the password (chosen) from the seven planets, "Mercury s(anctus?)."

Sent [ ] 5 soldiers, among them [ ] camel-riders, 1 cavalryman: century of Marianus, Aurelius Licinnius; century of Pudens, Aurelius Demetrius; century of Nigrinus, Aurelius Romanus and Aurelius Rufus; turma of Antoninus, Iarhaboles son of Odeatus.

Returned, previously detailed with [ ] Appadana (?) [ ] turma of Tiberinus [ ]

Timinius Paulinus, decurion, announced the orders of the day. Whatever may be ordered, we will do; and at every command we will be ready. There are standing watch at the standards of our Lord Alexander Augustus:

decurion, Timinius Paulinus; shrine-keeper, Aurelius Silvanus; [*title, name*] son of Vabalathus; care-taker, Aurelius Rubathus; inspector of sentries, Iarhaeus son of Malchus; care-taker 2, Claudius Agrippa; cavalryman,

[*nothing legible, but continues the preceding list.*]

March 28. Milites caligati, net, 92[-?, among these ? centurions], 8 duplicarii, 1 sesquiplicarius; 33 camel-riders, among them 1 sesquiplicarius; 223(?) cavalry, among them 5 decurions, 7 duplicarii, 4 sesquiplicarii

of the cohors xx Palmyrenorum Severiana Alexandriana.

Iulius Rufianus, tribune, sent the password (chosen) from the seven planets [ ]

[ ] Antoninus; century of Antoninus, Aurelius Marinus, Aurelius Heliodorus (*canceled*); century of Gaianus, Iarhaboles son of Iarhaeus; century of Nigrinus, Aurelius Apollinarius.

[Sent] to get wheat, [?] soldiers [ ]e...ianes son of Iarhaboles.

[ ] Becchufrayn [ ] 1 soldier, century of Gaianus [ ]

[ ] century of Antoninus prior, Aurelius [ ]

Timinius Paulinus, decurion, announced the orders of the day. [*because*] on March 29 (soldiers) will be checked off, a supplicatio and immolatio and at every order we will be ready.

There are standing watch at the standards of our Lord Alexander Augustus: decurion, Timinius Paulinus; sesquiplicarius, Aurelius Absas; shrine-keeper, Aurelius Silvanus; signifer, Claudius Natalius; clerk, Aurelius Capito; inspector of sentries, Anton( ) Val( ), lieutenant 2, Ogelus son of Malchus; cavalryman [ ]

[ ] Malchus son of Zebidas; cavalryman, Aelius Heliodorus; [ ] Aelius Menander [ ]

Col. ii

March 29, milites caligati, net, 9[ ]

of the cohors xx Palmyrenorum Severiana Alexandriana [ ]

Iulius Rufianus, tribune, having returned (?)[ ]

Sent to get barley, [?] soldiers, among them [?] cavalrymen [ ]

Sent to convoy the barley-collectors, [?] soldiers; century of Marianus [ ]

Returned, previously detailed to Adatha, 2 soldiers: century of Nigrinus, Iulius Zabdibolus [ ]

Returned, previously detailed to the headquarters of the governor with letters [ ]

Check! Returned, from among those previously detailed with the men at the governor's headquarters, from the cohors II Eq[ ]

Sent as wood-gatherer for the bath, 1 soldier, century of Nigrinus, Zebidas son of Barneus [ ]

Returned (*canceled*)

Timinius Paulinus, decurion, announced the orders of the day [ ]

decurion, Timinius Paulinus; shrine-keeper, Aurelius Silvanus; signifer [ ]

[ ] 3, Aurelius Bassus; 4, Aurelius Heliodorus [ ]

March 30. Milites caligati, net, 914 [ ]

of the cohors XX Palmyrenorum Severiana Alexandriana [ ]

Iulius Rufianus, tribune, first [ ]

from soldiers, among these [?] d[uplicarii]

Honorably discharged, there remained (*in the cohort*) 4 soldiers: century of [ ]

century of Marianus, Mombogeus son of Themarsa; century of [ ]

Missing, 1 cavalryman [ ]

Exchanged [ ] from those previously detailed [ ] wheat (?) and ? [ ]

Exchanged [?] from [ ]

48

Morning Report of the Coh. XX Palmyrenorum

PDur. 83 (inv. D. P. 17 recto); *vidi* ca. Sept. 4, 233

Transcription and commentary: J. F. Gilliam, "Some Latin Military Papyri from Dura," *YCS* 11 (1950) 215, 220–21, 223–26, and 246–48.

Transcription, commentary, and facsimile: *Final Rep.* v, no 83 and plate 52, 1; *edidit* Gilliam.

Text: *CPL*, no. 339, reproduces the text of *YCS*.

The formula *quod imperatum fuerit faciemus* in line 7 and the phrase *signum Iouis* in 12 are enough to show that this is a fragment of a morning report. Gilliam is undoubtedly right in supposing that a new entry began with line 7 so that this text follows the pattern of **50** rather than **47**. The whole can now be reconstructed in outline in terms of the six component items named above, pp. 179–80:

Line 7 contained item 5, the admissa and oath of obedience.
8–10: item 6, the excubatio ad signa.
11–12: item 1, a new date and the numbers of men on hand.
13: item 2, the full name of the cohort.
14: item 3, the commanding officer's name and the password.
1–6: item 4, departures and returns and other matters of special interest.

In this section lines 4–6 are a copy or at least a summary of a letter, unless the first person of the verb *praecepi* is misread. **51** i 15 offers a parallel. The name of the cohort in 4 is then part of the address: [*name*, *title*, to *name*, *tribuno cohortis*] *XX*, etc.

The amount lost at the beginnings of the lines is considerable but cannot be calculated exactly. In 7 a name and title corresponding to *Timinius Paulinus decurio* (**47** i 6 and 16; and ii 11) and the words *admissa pronuntiauit* are certainly missing, perhaps 45 to 50 letters; but the letters]. ạs before *quod* show that there was something else as well. Similarly in 11 a date such as *VI Idus Septembres* with the formula for the numbers through the dromedarii amounts to about 65 or 70 letters; and in 14 we must suppose that the name and title of the tribune was followed, as in **47** ii 16, by other remarks before the mention of the watchword. In this, too, the present text resembles **50** (cf. i 7 and 13) rather than **47**.

The date of this text cannot be far from that in line 6, though **50** i 11 and 14 show that it may differ by two or three weeks. Consequently, even if **47** belongs to the same year, which is doubtful in view of the different arrangement of the items, it must be separated from the present text by an interval of at least 5 months.

The verso is **13**.

].[
]ẹli Ƴ pudentis ptolaemeus ṃ[
] *vacat*
coh]x̣x̣ p̣almỵrẹnorum seuerianae al[e]x̣[andrianae
]rẹs mạx̣iṃ[o] ẹṭ p̣a[tern]o cos et proficisci ad castra praeçẹp̣i offị.[
].[....].[ ]ṃa pṛidie n[o]nạṣ ṣeptembrẹs maxiṃo et pạṭerno cos [
] *Space of two lines*
].ạs quod imperạṭụm fuerit f̣ạçiẹṃu[s] ẹṭ ad ọṃnem tẹ[sseram
]ḍeṃẹṭ[r]ius ṃag çạmpi bellaeus oga ṣig ṃạḷçhus zebida [
]..ṃp.[.]l ad bonoṣẹ[.].[..] aurel g̣ọṛa aurel ạḅiḍṇ[
] *vacat*
].[ ]. eq cxx iṇ ḥiṣ dẹç[
] *vacat*
] *vacat*
]. sigṇ[u]m iouis [
Remainder of column blank

1. Gilliam, *YCS*, p. 247: "The single letter that survives . . . may be *l*."

2.] . .*ị:* D. Gilliam: "The line may begin]*ẹḷị*, e.g., *Og*]*ẹḷị*. The name Ptolemaeus is so unusual except in Egypt . . . as to suggest that the soldier came from that province. . . ."

4. *Palm*[*y*]*renorum; Al*[*exandrianae:* D.

5.]. *Ṃạx̣iṃọ; prae.ẹ..da*..[*:* D. Gilliam: "The consular date may be preceded by *Au*]*g*." At the end of the line, "*Praeçẹp̣ị* is perhaps worth considering." Before *maximo* the most likely possibility is *septemb*]*res*; cf. the next line. But *octob*]*res*, etc., are not excluded.

6.].*a; Septembr*[*e*]*s; Pa*[*t*]*erno:* D.

7. *f̣ạciẹ*[*m*]*uṣ;* [*o*]*mnem:* D.

8. *Bellaeus Ọ.a..g̣:* D. Gilliam: "For the office *mag*(*ister*) *campi* see Domaszewski, *Rangordnung*, pp. 48 f.; R. Cagnat, *L'Armée Romaine d'Afrique* I (1912), p. 188. After Bellaeus there may be first a three-letter name in the genitive, ending in *a* (*Oga* ?); then the title of Malchus Zebida. It is carelessly written, but *sig*(*nifer*) is not an attractive reading." The *a* preceding the title has the final form, so that *oga* is almost obligatory; and this leaves little choice but *sig* for the title, even though *si* is in an unusual ligature.

9.] . . . . . . *l aḍ bonos* .[. . . . .] *Aurel* . . .*a Aurel* . . .*oṭ*. .[*:* D. Gilliam: "With *ad bonos* cf. *ad bonis* in [**50** i 4 and 10]. The next letter may be *c*, *p*, or *t*. Following the lacuna *Aurel Ç̣ọṛa* is just possible, but each of the two middle letters can be read in several ways." The letter after *abid* might be *m* as well as *n*.

11. At the beginning of the line Gilliam suggests, "Possibly *ses*]*q*(*uplicarius*) *Ị*"; but the traces nearest *eq* look like the remains of an *m*. Noting that the number of cavalry is only about half that in **47** and **50**, Gilliam says, "This fact may reflect losses, but possibly some cavalrymen were on detached duty and were not included in this summary." Cf. also **49** 4, and esp. **50** i 11 and note.

14. Gilliam: "This is the watchword. . . . An epithet of some kind quite possibly followed *Iovis*."

49

Morning Report of the Coh. XX Palmyrenorum

PDur. 88 (inv. D. P. 22); *vidi* — A.D. 218–222? 238–244?
On loan to the museum of West Point

Transcription and commentary: J. F. Gilliam, "Some Latin Military Papyri from Dura," *YCS* 11 (1950) 218–19, 221, and 252.

Transcription, commentary, and facsimile: *Final Rep.* v, no. 88 and plate 67, 3; *edidit* Gilliam.

Text: *CPL*, no. 340, reproduces the text of *YCS*.

The formula for the excubatio ad signa in line 1 is the evidence for including this text among the morning reports and also shows, since it is preceded in the same line by the formula for the admissa, that this fragment comes from the extreme right edge of the column. Since the first line is at the top of the column (the papyrus is complete along the upper margin), this text, too, may have begun each day's entries with item 5, the admissa and the oath of obedience; but the space between lines 3 and 4 implies rather that the entries began as in **47** with the date and the summary of the cohort's strength. The space between lines 4 and 5 is rather wide and may have contained the cohort's official name. In that case, 5 would have contained the tribune's name and the daily watchword.

The later date suggested in the heading above depends upon the possibility of reading Gordian's name at the end of line 1. In my opinion, that reading is very dubious, though I have nothing certain to put in the place of it. I suspect, however, that the order in which the items in each day's entry are presented indicates a time earlier than **48** and about the same as **47**.

The verso is blank, and so gives no help with the dating.

eri]ṃụs excubanṭ ad signa domini n iụ.ḷ. . . . .[
]c[ir]citoṛes aurel ạch.[ ]. . .es g̣aius sal[
h]ẹl[i]ọdorus ṭ.c˙ ag̣. . .s. .ṃịạ. . ual. . . . . ịịị . .[. . .].[
Space of two and a half lines
]drom x̣xxii iṇ ḥis sesq̣ ị ẹ[q c]xxxx̣[
]ṣ *vacat*

1. *n Iṃp*[. .]. . . . .*ị*. .[: D. Gilliam: "At the end of the line a possible reading is *domini n(ostri) Iṃp(eratoris)* [*M*] *Ạnṭọnị G̣ọ*[*rdiani*." But the letter read as *m* in *imp* is convex above and must be either *r* (cf. *heliodorus*, line 3) or the right half of a *u* (cf. *heliodorus* and *ualentini*, also line 3). Too little remains, however, for any convincing guesses about the identity of the emperor, though the range of possible choices is narrow. Perhaps *ạụṛẹlị ạṇṭọṇịṇị ạ*[*ug* is least difficult, i.e. Elagabal.

2. I have taken the reading *circitores* from Gilliam, who cites *TLL* s. v., and adds, "Here they are probably discharging a temporary function, going the rounds and checking sentries, not holding an office; cf. Vegetius 3.8. Circitor was a regular rank in the late empire." But in e.g. **47** i 17 the circitor is listed between a librarius and an optio; so the term may designate a rank in these papyri.

3.]*Heliodorus* . .*a*. . . . . .*s*. . .*ual*. . . . . *III*.[: D. Gilliam: "At the end of the line, possibly *Ɣ Ɣ III*."

4. *X̣X̣XỊ in ḥis sesq IỊ eqq*[: D. As I read the line, there is room for only one *c* in the number of the equites. See on **50** i 11, and cf. **48** 11.

50

Morning Report of the Coh. XX Palmyrenorum

PDur. 89 (inv. D. P. 9 recto); *vidi* May 27–28, A.D. 239

Transcription and commentary: J. F. Gilliam, "Some Latin Military Papyri from Dura," *YCS* 11 (1950) 215–18, 220, 222–37, and 248–52. Now superseded by the following.

Transcription, commentary, and facsimile: *Final Rep.* v, no. 89; and, col. i only, plates 56 and 57; *edidit* Gilliam.

Text: *CPL*, no. 331, reproduces the text of *YCS*.

The general nature of this text as a morning report is self-evident; but differences between it and **47** have already been noted above, pp. 179–80. Aside from the changed order of the component items, the chief difference is the absence of item 4, the missi and reversi. This is accounted for, I believe, in lines 6 and 12 by the statement *omnes permanserunt*, that is, that no one left or returned. Cf. **66** ii 9–15, where after a grand total on XV Kal. Octobres the next six days report simply *n*(*umerus*) *p*(*urus*) *mansit* until the abbreviation *q d p* reappears. The relative numbers in the two reports are discussed below on i 11. Whether or not the number of excubitores remained constant is not possible to determine accurately; but they are still principales and immunes. Instead of the aedituus we now have a sacerdos, whose office as a military rank is well treated by Gilliam, *Final Rep.* v, p. 282. In the present text the list of excubitores is followed in lines 4 and 9 by a formula which is not found in **47** and has not been satisfactorily read; and in i 15 is the beginning of either the full text or a summary of an official letter which has been copied into the journal. Other details are covered in the apparatus to the text.

The date is restricted by Gordian's consulship, i 14, to the years 239 and 241; and all considerations speak for the former. In i 14 the date is not *II cos*, though this is a highly official document dating two soldiers' entry into active service; and Gilliam points out that in 241 the governor of Syria was probably Attius Rufinus, not the]*nio* of i 14 in this text. The extremely full form of Gordian's name and titles in i 2 and 8, in contrast with the simple *d n Alexandri Aug* of **47** i 6 and 17, also implies a date early in Gordian's reign if one may assume that the nomenclature in the papyri showed the same tendency as that of the coins to be full and explicit when an emperor was new and relatively unknown, becoming progressively simpler in the course of his reign as familiarity with it grew.

The verso is **15**.

Col. i

(*First hand*)

1 [aurel g]ermanus ord principis adṃịssa proṇ[un]ṭịạ[u]ịṭ [e]ṭ quod imp fueṛit fac̣ẹṃụṣ ẹṭ ạd ọmnịam tesserạ[m] paṛaṭị ẹremus exc̣ubant ạḍ [sig]ṇạ ḍ ṇ ị[mp

2]ṃạṛc̣i ạṇṭọṇị g̣ọrdiani pii f̣ẹlicis inuicti a[u]g̣[u]ṣ[ti o]ṛd aurel germạ[nu]ṣ p̣rinps singnif uḷpius mariạ[n]ụs buc aurel priṣc̣uṣ [sacer]ḍos ṭhemes mocimi˙ .[

3]tess auṛel mocimus m̈ ulpiụs siluạṇus ṣịgnif ii˙ flauius demeṭrius alt signif iii˙ aurel maḷ[chus] disc mens[orem] ạurel iarhaboles ạc̣[

4]ẹt ad bọnis ṇ us eq˙q˙ iiii paṛaṭị ṣunt *vacat*

5 [vi kal iun sun]ṭ in hibeṛ[ni]ṣ coh xx paḷm g̣ọṛ[dian]ạe n p ṃ[il caliga]t[o]ṛ dc̣clxxxi in his ordd vi dupl v[i]ii sesq i drom xxxvi[in his eq i]n his decc iiii dupl vi sesq ịị .[

6 coh x]x̣ palm g[or]ḍịanae sumṃ[a omnes p]ẹrmạ[nserun]t *vacat*

7 auitus] Ƴ leg praẹp̣ . . . . u[. .]l[.].u. .[. .].ec̣[.]. . . . .ṇịụit signum ṣẹc̣uṛịṭatis misit *vacat*

Space of five lines

(*Second hand*)

8 ạ[urel german]ụṣ ọṛḍ pṛịnc̣ẹp̣ṣ [ad]ṃịṣ[s]ạ pṛ[onun]ṭịạụ[it] e[t qu]od imp fu[e]ṛit faceṃụṣ et ad ọṃ[n]em tes[se]ṛạ[m] p[arati eri]ṃụṣ excubaṇṭ [ad sig]ṇạ d n imp m antoni gordi[a]ṇị pị[i] f[e]l ịnuic̣ṭ[i aug

9 ọṛ[d aurel germ]ạṇus sig ụlpịụṣ [m]ạṛ[ianu]ṣ ḅ[uc aurel] pri[scus sace]ṛ thẹmes moc̣imi [te]ṣs aurẹḷ [mo]cịmụṣ [. . . . . ulpius] siluaṇụs s[ig] ịị fḷ[de]ṃ[e]ṭṛị[u]ṣ ṣị[gni]f ị[ii] auṛẹl malchus disc m[e]ṇs ḅạṛ.[

10 ạụṛel ị[*ca.* 12]. .c̣ et ad [bo]ṇis.[. . . . .]. . . p̣ạṛ[ati sun]t. *Illegible traces, ca. 20 letters. Erased?*

11 ṿ k[a]l iun [s]unt [in hiberni]ṣ coh xx palṃ[gordian]ạẹ ṇ p d[c]c̣ḷx̣[xxi] ị[n hi]s ordd vi dupl viii ṣẹ[sq] i drom xxx̣[vi] ị[n] h[is eq c]lxxxṿiii ị[n] ḥị[s] ḍ[e]c̣c̣ ịị[ii] d[u]p̣l vi sesq ịị *vacat*

12 coh[xx palm gordia]ṇae ṣ[umma om]nes peṛṃạṇṣerunt *vacat*

13 i ạẹḷ ạ[uitus Ƴ le]g praep ḥịbeṛṇ[is coh x]x̣ p̣[alm . . . . . .]nic̣ịt signum iouis doḷịc̣heni s misit *vacat*

14]tiroṇẹṣ p[r]oḅati ạb[*ca.* 10]nio u c cos n′ n′ ii˙[*ca.* 10] abb.[.]sarị Ƴ˙ aurel germanus ex vi idus maias d n˙ gorḍ[ian]o aug cos *vacat*

15]ẹ [*ca.* 9].[. . tirones] ḍụọs quorum noṃi[na et iconismo]s item staturas subịci pṛạecepi˙ ar. . . . .s agita. . . . .e.ṭọṣ pṛọḅaṭos [i]ṇ n′ in c̣[o]h xx palm g̣ọṛḍịạṇạm [.].ạ *vacat*

i 1. *proṇ[u]ṇṭ[iav]ịṭ* [.].; *fac̣⟨i⟩ẹmus; erimus:* [*Im-p(eratoris)*]: D. Gilliam: "The *ord princeps* was the senior centurion of the cohort. . . . Before *quod* I formerly read]*ṇ*, but this now seems impossible. For the unexplained letters between *pronuntiavit* and *quod* cf. line 8. The second scribe also wrote *facemus* but did not repeat the more remarkable *omniam*."

The broken letter before *quod* most resembles *r*; but in line 8 there is an unmistakable *e* at this point, and there is room for three letters at most between *pro-nuntiauit* and *quod*. With these limitations, an *et* correlating with *et* after *faciemus* seems unavoidable. Cf. the form of the *t* in *inuicti*, line 2; and see Gilliam on line 8 below. The letters in the middle of *faciemus* are blotted, as if some correction had been attempted; and the *et* which follows is also blotted.

2. *A̩[u]g(usti) ord(inatus); Germ*[*anus*] . . .*n*. .: D. Of the word after *Germanus* Gilliam says, "Neither . . . *princip(is)* nor *sinnif(er)* is attractive." In favor of the reading in the text are the reasonably sure *n* (cf. the first *n* in *singnif*), *p*, and final *s*; and for the ligature of *ri* one may compare *fuerit* in line 1. Read, of course, *prin⟨ce⟩ps*. Expand *buc(inator)*.

3. . .*ị Ulpiụs; Mạ*[*lchus; mens*(*orem*) [. . .] *A̩ụrel*(*ius*) *Iarhaboles* . .: D. Gilliam: "Whether the office of Ulpius Silvanus is represented by a symbol or by ordinary letters, I can make nothing of it. There are two points directly over it, which may indicate that

two words are abbreviated.... Presumably Flavius Demetrius was the second man with this name in his century [*and with the same year of enlistment*]. *Mensorem* may have been written out, but cf. Col. i, 9." If the characters before *ulpius* are letters, the last is certainly *i* and either of the other two could be *c*, *p*, or *r*, and the second could be *t*.

Expand *tess(erarius); alt(er)*.

4. *ẹṭ ạḍ..nis s s u s e d˙ d˙ IIII:* D. Gilliam: "cf. Col. i, 10 and Frag. *b* (possibly also [**47**] i, 8).... From *us* the readings seem certain; the *ss* that precedes might be read as *h* or *n*.... At the beginning of the line... I can find nothing more plausible than *et ad bonis*. The clerk was quite capable of making errors, and there would be no objection to the corrections *ad bonos* or *ad bona* if a suitable meaning was thus obtained... it does not seem helpful to recall that soldiers might be called *boni* or that bona castrensia might be deposited ad signa. No expansion of the abbreviations that has occurred to me seems at all plausible. To encourage others to do better I will record two: *s(upra) s(cripti) v(otis) s(usceptis) e(xcubare) d(ies) (quattuor) parati sunt* and *s(upra) s(criptis) v(erbis) s(acramenti) ed(ictis) d(ictis) (quater) parati sunt*. Expansions which would be obvious in another context seem out of place here, e.g., *s(umptu) s(uo) v(otum) s(olverunt)*."

I share Gilliam's bafflement; but "to encourage others" I offer a different, though not necessarily better, reading and expansion. First, *eqq* instead of *edd*. Cf. the *q* of *sesq*, line 5. The only other *q* in this hand (*quod* in line 1) is made differently; but it is not the final letter, and final *d*'s, as in *ord*, line 1, are also different. Then, if **48** 9 is the same expression, as it seems to be, the variation between *bono* and *boni* points to a compound word such as *Boniportus*, *boniuolentia*, *bonouiratus* (see *TLL* s. vv.), and the *-us* to a *u*-stem accusative plural. One could then read *ad bonis[e]ssus* (or *bonosessus*) *eq(uites) (quattuor)*. I have no suggestions for interpretation, however, except to point out that *sessor* can mean "rider of a horse," as in Suet. *Iul.* 61; so that Bonisessus could possibly denote minor deities of cavalrymen, patrons of a firm seat. The convincing explanation consequently still remains to be found.

5. *hibẹ[rn]ịs:* D. Gilliam: "Possibly *ṃ[ilit]ụṃ* follows *n p*, though the most one can say for the initial letter is that it does not exclude the reading.... There may have been as many as thirty-nine dromedarii." For the number of equites see below on line 11.

6. *Gọ[rd]ianae ṣụṃ[ma:* D.

7. *praep........[.]l..u..ẹç[..]..nivit:* D; but cf. line 13.

8. *Ạụr[el(ius) Germanu]ṣ [o]rḍ; pṛ[onu]ṇṭịạ[vit..]ẹ[. qu]od; fuẹṛit; omṇem; pa]r[ati er]ịṃus; Pi[i Fe]l(icis):* D. Gilliam: "The upper part of a tall *e* seems certain before *qu]od*, which suggests perhaps *it]e[m* or *e[t*. In line 1, above, the same *[e]t* might be restored, formed as in *Demetrius* (line 3)."

9. *Mạṛị[anu]s; Deme]ṭṛị[u]s; mens(orem) ....:* D. Gilliam: "I print *Aurel(ius) [M]ocimus* because the name is certain in i, 3. Actually *]cianus* is much easier to read here. Perhaps the clerk wrote *[Mu]cianus*, rightly or wrongly. At the end of the line *III* is possible." *[mar]cianus* is another possibility. A name should follow *disc mens*; but it cannot be *aurel* as in line 3. The first letter is a tall one, perhaps *b* or *h*, though not a convincing example of either, or *i*. Just possibly *ịạṛạḅ[oles* or *ḅạṛṇ[aeus iarabol-* (**6** i 35) and so after all the same person as in i 3.

10. *Ạụṛẹḷ(ius) Ị[arhaboles]..; ad [..]ṇịṣ.[:* D. Gilliam: "The unexplained letters after *Iarhaboles* may be the same as in line 3. The second, or last, could be *c* in both."

11. *Kal; DCÇLX̣[XXI in hi]s; eq(uites) c]ḷçxxxịịị (?):* D. Gilliam: "One has to choose between 133 and 233 as the number of *equites in hibernis* at this time. The first figure seems too low, the second too high. In [**47**]... the 223 equites included 5 decurions, 7 duplicarii, 4 sesquiplicarii. The last three figures here are 4, 6, 2." He also notes that the grand total drops from 914 to 781, but the number of dromedarii rises from 34 to 36–39, and that in **48** the total number of equites (line 11) is 120.

The choice, however, may be wider than supposed. The letter before the first *x* is represented at the top by a mere dot; but below the *x* there is a curved stroke which must be the tail of an *l*. Then between the third *x* and the first *i* is a trace of another letter which does not descend as far as the *i* and is slightly curved, hence *u*. This permits restoration of a *c* in the lacuna for a total of 188 equites, a sum which accords well with the other figures. The grand total is about 83 per cent of that in **47**; and the same proportion of the 223 equites in **47** yields 185, while the four decurions are 80 per cent of the usual five. Gilliam reminds us that the difference in numbers between **47** and **50** may result simply from having fewer men *in hibernis*; but the alternative possibility that it reflects real losses seems more likely. The Persians had raided Dura not more than a month before, the tribune Julius Terentius had fallen in combat, and the cohort is currently under a legionary centurion as praepositus. (Cf. lines 7 and 13.) On the Persian raid, April 30, 239, see *Prelim. Rep.* IV [1933] 112–14, no. 233. On Terentius' death and epitaph, see C. B. Welles, "The Epitaph of Julius Terentius," *HTR* 34 [1941] 79–102.

12. *Gordiana]e:* D.

13. *...[...Avitus]; pṛạep.....[...]m[-12-] nivit:* D. Cf. line 7. The verb before *signum* ends with *-nicit*, *-niuit*, or *-nigit* in both. Gilliam's suggestion of Aelius for the centurion's name is attractive. There is just room for *ael a[uitus* ⅄ *le]g*. Gilliam questions whether *s* after *dolicheni* is a mistake or an abbreviation, *s(ancti)*; but it may be a regular element in the formula of the password whenever the name of a deity was used. Cf. **47** i 3.

14. *pṛoḅati ab [......]nio; II [-12-] abb.ṣ.. ui; Gọṛḍị[an]o:* D. Gilliam: "*Tirones* probably begins the line.... Following the second lacuna we have all or part of the name of a recruit, e.g., *Abbas ..[.]vi...* There is a dot of ink after these letters (or the centurial sign) which may be meant as punctuation, and also a blank space of several letters. I prefer to see in Aurel(ius) Germanus the second of two recruits, followed by the date of their probatio, rather than the ord. princeps [of the same name]."

The name which begins with *abb* seems to be in the genitive and should therefore be preceded by another name, such as Heliodorus. Wuthnow cites both *Αβδεσαρος* and the genitive *Αβδισαρου*; so I am tempted to hazard *abbḍ[i]sari* here, even though the double *b* is anomalous if the *d* is retained. The symbol which follows is surely the sign for centuria/centurio; and so it appears that this man was appointed centurion. Six centurions are present; but one may have been retiring or being transferred. For tirones appointed directly to the rank of centurion, cf. **64** i 20–24, and **20** 19; and see Gilliam, "*Paganus* in *B.G.U.* 696," *AJP* 63 (1952) 75–78, and "The Appointment of Auxiliary Centurions," *TAPA* 88 (1958), esp. pp. 164–68.

I agree that the Aurelius Germanus is the second recruit; but the date, whether or not that of the probatio, is probably entered here in the cohort's journal as the effective date of the new men's enrollment in the cohort. Cf. **87**, lines 4–7 and 24: *in coh(orte) cui praees in numeros referri iube ex xi kalendas martias* and *accepta vi k martias*, which show that the letter was received five days after the date on which the tirones were to be incorporated into their unit.

The governor's name poses difficulties. His identity has not been discussed by Gilliam in either *Final Rep.* v or "The Governors of Syria Coele from Severus to Diocletian" (*AJP* 79 [1958] 225–42); but the size of the lacuna after *ab* shows that the remains are probably part of his second name, while the *i* before *o* implies a gentilicium. Perhaps a man with two gentilicia? At the beginning, *ab* may imply a name with an initial vowel, or could be divided *a B*[. One might consider L. Iulius Apronius Maenius Pius Salamallianus, consul about 226 after governing Galatia and Numidia, or [C]aese(nnius?) Vinius, governor of Moesia Inferior under Gordian (Degrassi, *Fasti*, pp. 63 and 67). Expand *u(iro) c(larissimo) co(n)s(ulari) n(ostro) n(umero) ii* and *d(omino) n(ostro)*.

15.]*e*[–8– *tirones*]*; noṃi*[*na* –15–]. ; *pr*[*a*]*ecepi˙ar*. . . *sagitare*. . *ẹ*.*ṭo*[.]. ; . . . *in c̣*[*o*]*h Gor*[*d*]*ịạṇam* [.]. . *:* D. Gilliam: "The line . . . may begin [*e*(*xemplum*)] *e*(*pistulae*), with the governor's name and title in the lacuna that follows." He suggests on the model of **87** 7–9 restoring *nomi*[*na et iconismo*]*s* here, and continues, "The words between *praecepi* and *probatos* may be a phrase giving additional information about the recruits. My tentative suggestion is *Arabes agitare expertos*, 'experienced Arab (camel?) drivers.' *Arabas* of course is the much more common form, and the infinitive is awkward. Palaeographically, the only difficulty is the *x* in *expertos*, more of which would be expected to show above the lacuna." This is ingenious; but the infinitive, the meaning attached to *expertos*, and the abrupt and rather pointless introduction of this phrase combine to restrain whole-hearted acceptance. The difficulties are compounded by a blot—or erasure or correction—between *ar* and *s* and a correction or extra stroke where Gilliam reads the *e* of the infinitive. If it made sense, *agitatae* would be an easier reading; and the *to* could very well be *ad*, while many of the other traces can be read in several ways. The phrasing of **87** 4–5 (see above on line 14) suggests [*i*]*n n*(*umeros*) after *probatos* and recommends Gilliam's *c*(*ui*) *p*(*raees*) at the end of the line, though the last letter, as he says, is not much like *p* elsewhere in the text. The shape may be modified because it is the last letter in the line.

Col. ii

(*First hand*) ạ[urel germanus ord princeps *etc.*
Two lines lost
]l. .l[
iiii kal iunias ṣụnt in [hibernis co]h xx̣ p̣ạlm[
[coh x]x̣ palmyrenorum gọṛḍ[ianae
]ṣ auitus Ɣ prepos coh i. [

ii 4. Gilliam: "The most attractive reading . . . is *Aure*]*l*(*ius*) [*M*]*al*[*chus*]. If this is correct, these lines differed in length or content from i, 1–4." Perhaps no more need be assumed than a different order of the names of the excubitores.

5. This line is the basis for the dates restored in col. i.

7. *coh ḳ*[*:* D.

Frag. a

(*First hand*) ạ[u]rel german[us ord princeps
ọṛ[d] ạurel [g]erṃ[anus
ạ[. .]. .e.[

Frag. b

]. . . . [
(*Second hand*) buc aurel p]ṛiscus sacer thẹṃ[es mocimi
pa]ṛạṭi sụṇt
]. . [.].pp̣.[.]. . ṭe. . *Illegible traces*
].i.s *Illegible traces*
].[.]. . . . ssụ.[
About seven lines blank
(*First hand*)].s quod iṃ[p fuerit
]bdạṣ aureḷ[
]. . [.].a. .asus .[

Frag. b 3. *par*]*ati:* D.
4–6. No readings in D. *ssri*[is also possible.
7.]ṣ*:* D.
8.]. . *Aurel*(*ius*)[*:* D.
9.].*sssus*[*:* D. Cf. i 4 and 10.

Frag. c has traces of four, and **frag. e** of three, illegible lines. **Frags. d, h**, and **i** have two more or less doubtful letters each. **Frag. g** is blank.

Frag. f

]ṭiron. . . . . . .[

Frag. f.]. .*on*. . . . . . .[*:* D. This fragment may very well belong in the gap at the beginning of i 15; but neither side of the papyrus confirms or refutes this possibility.

TRANSLATION

Col. i

Aurelius Germanus, first centurion, announced the orders of the day. We will both do whatever may be ordered and be ready at every command. There are standing watch at the standards of our Lord the Emperor

Marcus Antonius Gordianus Pius Felix Invictus Augustus: first centurion, Aurelius Germanus; signifer, Ulpius Marianus; bucinator, Aurelius Priscus; priest, Themes son of Mocimus;

tesserarius, Aurelius Mocimus; (?) Ulpius Silvanus; signifer 2, Flavius Demetrius, the second; signifer 3, Aurelius Malchus; apprentice surveyor, Aurelius Iarhaboles; . . [ ]

and for (?) four cavalrymen are ready.

May 27. There are at the base of the coh. xx Palmyrenorum Gordiana, net (sum of soldiers?), 781, among these 6 centurions, 8 duplicarii, 1 sesquiplicarius; 36 (?) camel-riders, [among them?; cavalry ?] among them 4 decurions, 6 duplicarii, 2 sesquiplicarii.

Total of the coh. xx Palmyrenorum Gordiana. No change in strength.

[? Avitus], legionary centurion, acting commander at the base of the coh. xx Palmyrenorum [*verb*], sent the password "Security."

Aurelius Germanus, first centurion, announced the orders of the day. We will both do whatever may be ordered and be ready at every command. There are standing watch at the standards of our Lord the Emperor Marcus Antonius Gordianus Pius Felix Invictus Augustus:

centurion, Aurelius Germanus; signifer, Ulpius Marianus; bucinator, Aurelius Priscus; priest, Themes son of Mocimus; tesserarius, Aurelius Mocimus; [?] Ulpius Silvanus; signifer 2, Flavius Demetrius; signifer 3, Aurelius Malchus; apprentice surveyor, (?) [ ]

Aurelius [ ] and for [ ] are ready.

May 28. There are at the base of the coh. xx Palmyrenorum Gordiana, net, 781, among these 6 centurions, 8 duplicarii, 1 sesquiplicarius; 36 (?) camel-riders, among these [?; cavalry; ? 1]85, among these 4 decurions, 6 duplicarii, 2 sesquiplicarii.

Total of the coh. xx Palmyrenorum Gordiana. No change in strength.

Aelius (?) [Avitus], legionary centurion, acting commander at the base of the coh. xx Palmyrenorum [*verb*], sent the password "Jupiter Dolichenus Sanctus."

[ ] recruits approved by [ ]nius, vir clarissimus, our governor, two in number: [*name*] son of Abdisarus (?), centurion, and Aurelius Germanus, from May 10, 239.

[ ] two [recruits] whose names and marks of identification, also heights, I have ordered appended. [?] (men) approved into the ranks of the coh. xx Palmyrenorum Gordiana.

51

Morning Report? of Legionaries

PSI XIII 1307; *vidi* Early I p.
Biblioteca Medicea Laurenziana, Florence

Transcription, commentary, and facsimile: Medea Norsa in Norsa and Bartoletti, *PSI* 13 (1939) pp. 103–7 and plate 7.

Transcription and facsimile: Mallon, *Pal.*, plate XI.

Commentary:

1. J. F. Gilliam, "Notes on *PSI* 1307 and 1308," *CP* 47 (1952) 29–31. Cited as **G**.
2. Sergio Daris, "Osservazioni ad alcuni papyri di carattere militare," *Aegyptus* 38 (1948) 151–58.
3. Sergio Daris, "Note di lessico e di onomastico militare," *Aegyptus* 44 (1964) 49–50.

Text: *CPL*, no. 108, reproduces Norsa's text with an apparatus based on readings proposed in Gilliam's article. Daris, no. 11, takes Gilliam's revisions into his text except for i 14 and independently reads *aqui[lam* in ii 11.

The kinship of this text with the morning reports is evident in ii 17: *excubuerunt ad aquilam et sig[na*, and the next three lines which record the ranks and names of the excubitores, and probably in ii 6, which can reasonably be restored *adm[issa pronuntiauit*. Col. ii 23 may be an entry, [*reuersus*] *a frumento neapol*[*i*, comparable to **42** ii 6–8. On the other hand, the *uigiliae* mentioned in ii 11–16 and 21–22 recall the guard rosters, **12**–**19**, though they obviously do not name all the sentries individually. Gilliam calls attention to the lack of dates and totals of the various categories of soldiers on hand.

It may be, then, that this is a different kind of text and not a morning report at all, or it may be that the pattern of such journals change between the date of **51** and those of **42**–**50**; but it seems most likely that the differences result from this unit's having more to record each day, because of its location and responsibilities, than the XX Palmyrenorum. Of the five headings, where lines project into the margin, only two are similar, ii 11 and 21. Both of these begin with *uigilias* and contain the name Varius ϒ, but the words between are different. One must consequently infer that the extant text is only a part, perhaps a small part, of the entry for one day in this unit's journal.

Gilliam (p. 30) cautiously mentions the possibility that this papyrus may be a record of the leg. XXII Deiotariana; and the possibility certainly exists. But the evidence is tenuous and ambiguous;[1] and in any case it is not certain that the report is for a whole legion. Only ten centurions at most are named, without reference to their cohorts; and of these Bovi[(i 1) and Bassus (ii 16) may not be centurions, while Baebius' title of hastatus primus (ii 5) and Minicius' of princeps (ii 6) imply that they belong to the primi ordines and are on a different footing from the other centurions here. This leaves only six men who are certainly ordinary centurions; so that the text may be the journal of one cohort only. How the excubatio ad aquilam was assigned is unknown and so offers no help in answering this question.

The date is on the basis of the hand, and is supported by the rarity of cognomina among the names. If either the Gaius Sossius C.f. Pol., a gregalis in the century of Aquila in *CIL* III 6627 (Dessau 2483) or the Gaius Sossius, optio in the century of Celsus in the same legion (*CIL* III 6591), is the same as the centurion Sossius in col. i 14, or if all three are

[1] Aside from the papyrus, the evidence consists of three inscriptions: *CIL* III 6627 (Dessau 2483), 6591, and 6600. All are undated; but the first is certainly no later than the reign of Tiberius and may well belong to that of Augustus. The second is of approximately the same period; the date of the third is quite uncertain. The first, from Coptos, provides the basis for the whole discussion by listing in two parallel columns personnel from two legions which are presumed to be the III Cyrenaica and the XXII Deiotariana since those are well attested in Egypt and the identity of the third legion mentioned by Strabo is unknown. (In any event its stay in Egypt was brief. See H. A. Sanders, "The Origin of the Third Cyrenaic Legion," *AJP* 62 [1941] 85.) The left-hand column of this inscription has been ascribed to the III Cyrenaica because it names in line 12 a C. Sossius C. f. and *CIL* III 6591 has a C. Sossius who is an optio in the III Cyrenaica. (Lesquier, p. 57; Ritterling, *RE* 12.1506–7, s. v. "Legio.") But it is far from certain that they are the same man; the name Sossius/Sosius is not especially uncommon, and the man in 6627 is a private in the century of Aquila while the one in 6591 is an optio in the century of Celsus. Alternatively, if the two men are the same, one must take account of the possibility that with his promotion Sossius was also transferred, so that his belonging to the III Cyrenaica in 6591 may equally be evidence that he was in the XXII Deiotariana in 6627. The latter inscription itself provides evidence for such transfers, for in col. i the second century of the fifth cohort is the century of Gauisidius (lines 15–16) while in col. ii the sixth century of the fifth cohort is the centuria Gauisidiana. Evidently Gauisidius had been promoted and transferred so recently that a new centurion had not yet taken command of his former century. Similarly, the present papyrus has a centurion Sossius (i 14) who may be the same person as the optio; but this does not prove that the papyrus is a record of the III Cyrenaica. 6600, cited for a centuria Neri (as in the papyrus, ii 18), really provides no evidence at all, for the obvious restoration of lines 1–2: *L. FLA*[*VIVS* . *F*(*ilius*) / *HOR*(*atia tribu*) *SEV*⟨*E*⟩*RV*[*S* points to a date after the middle of the first century. This in turn makes it likely that the centurion's cognomen rather than his nomen was used to identify his century, while the spacing of lines 3–4 in the published inscription indicate that *NERI*, which stands at the broken edge of the stone, probably continued as e.g. *NERI*[*ani*] or *NERI*[*tani*].

identical, the papyrus must be later than either of the inscriptions, hence perhaps in the time of Tiberius.

The verso contains one line in Greek, another with a few Greek letters, then *I*]*VLI*, and two more lines repeating *AENEAS DAPDANIAE*.

Col. i

]. Ɣ bọui[ ]
]
].tḷe.us.[ ]
]s bucina[ ]
]m Ɣ lepidiạṇ[i]
]ịus
]ṣọngbeiuii.f̣
]ciṣ.s ịuṣtus
]
]
]...ṇacis
].[.].[.].u.
]ṣ.u..ẹperei
]iam Ɣ sossi
].
].p̣˙ laịsọ
]
]
]
]ṇaris
].ụammillus
]rentes
]ad dec̣ụmạ
]maemịl.us
]
].p̣o..[

i 1.]*pibuṣ*[...]: PSI. The letters after the centuria-sign may be the name of the centurion; but they could be another word. Cf. ii 11 and 16. They can also be read *bẹui*[.

3.]...*ẹ.us*[...]: PSI.

4. PSI: "Cf. Premerstein, o.c., p. 125 (bucinatores)"; but the plural is too long and probably not wanted. Cf. **50** i 2 and 9.

5.]*ṃị Lepidian..*: PSI; "forse]*m i*(*n*) *Lepidian*[*a*," citing a *cohors Lepidiana*.]*ṃ* Ɣ *Lepidianị*: G, comparing ii 3.

6.].*us:* PSI.

7.]*con..ḅe tutius:* PSI "Lettura incerta." Most of the letters seem reasonably clear; but they offer nothing intelligible. The first might be *c*, *l*, or *p*; and instead of *g* one might read *c* or *p*. The last *i* has a final form and so implies the end of a word. After it is a short horizontal stroke high in the line which resembles no letter in this hand and may be a mark of abbreviation. For *f* possibly *s*.

8.]*lị ṣịṭ tu*[*t*]*ius:* PSI. But *minicius iustus*, as in ii 6, cannot be read.

11.].*ịnacis:* PSI.

12.]....*us..*: PSI.

13.].*u. referes:* PSI. Lesquier, p. 528, cites a centurion Crepereius from *IGRR* 1333 (A.D. 84) and 1337 (A.D. 85); but his dates are too late for this text.

14.]*iam i*(*n*) *possi:* PSI, in app., *possi*[*denda;*]*iam* Ɣ: G. For Sossius see the introductory comments.

16.]*t˙ la..s.:* PSI. The final *o* could be read as *t*.

17–19. PSI estimates the blank at only two lines.

20.].*aris:* PSI. Perhaps *apollinaris*.

21. *q*]*ua anụlus:* PSI, "sigillo?"

23. *PSI:* "*ad decuma*[*nam portam*? o sim."

24.]*ma.a...us:* PSI. *M. Aemilius*?

26.].*d..*: PSI. Perhaps *s* in place of *p*.

Col. ii

]..[ ].....[
loṇgiṇo adl.[.]q...... ualesceṇ.[
et tirọnes spectatum dụxit lepid[ianus (Ɣ ?)
legị[o]nis duaṣ
ḅ[ae]bius iu[..]us haṣ[t]atu[s p]ṛimus inṭ[
minic̣ius iu[s]ṭus princeps adm[issa pronuntiauit ?
quam et hodie habụiṣṭis rec̣og[nitam res- ?]
pọndẹrunt ex eis qui ad cunioṣ.[
in caṣtris non sunt non eniṃ[
si et [..]n totum saẹpius recogn[
uigiliaṣ ḍeduxit uaṛius Ɣ ạḍ ạquiḷa[m et signa

duaṣ ịṇ uallo ex cọh singụ[l]a.[
ad pọndera macelli duos ad ca.[
unam quibus ṣignum suụ[m dedit ?]
uigiles a[d] noṃem rẹcognitos in[
bassus Ɣ n[u]mero ḷxx̣viịi ẹx[eis ?
excubuerunt ad aqu[i]ḷam et sig̣[na
18 Ɣ nerị antistius Ɣ seruili seṇ[
18a ....
Ɣ uari turranius et tesser[arius
dom[i]tius ˋsignifˊ ad ualetudinari[um
ụigilias g[.] c̣ụm uex ịṇ eịṣ uarius Ɣ [
ẹ Ɣ f̣ịrmi lucreṭịuṣ *vacat*
]...an[..] a frumentọ neapol[

No translation is offered because the text makes so little connected sense. If the length of the lines in **47** and **50** is more or less standard for these journals, then the present text, with about 30 letters to the line, has only about one-fourth of the original content of the long lines.

ii 1. [..].[.......]*qu*[.....]....[: PSI. The *q* is possible, since the traces resemble the triangular head of the letter in *quam*, line 7. But elsewhere the tail does not extend farther than the third line below, whereas here it touches the *u* of *hastatus* in line 5. The *q* therefore probably stood in line 2.

2. *ad li*[.]... [*con*]*ualesceṇ*[: PSI, "*ad li*[*tora con*]*ualescen*[*tes* ovvero --[*ti*, o sim." The letter after *l* is either *i* or *a*; and the traces following the *q* are probably the top of the *m* in *spectatum*, line 3.

3. *Lepid*[: PSI; *Lepid*[*us*: Daris. G compares i 5 and ii 3.

4. *dua*[.]: PSI. Cf. lines 12 and 13 below.

5. *Ḅ*[*a*]*ẹbius Ṭu*[*sc*]*us haḅeatuṛ primus inṭ*[*er*: PSI; *Ḅ*[*ae*]*bius Ṭu*[*sc*]*us; i*..[: Daris; but the initial of the second name is *i*, not *t*. Perhaps *iustus*. *hastatus primus*: G. Perhaps *in p*[*rincipiis*? *p* is certainly possible instead of *t*.

6. *ad m*[: PSI; but cf. **47** i 6 and 16; ii 11; **50** i 1 and 8.

7–10. 7, *recog*[*nitam;* 8, *ponderunt:* PSI. The second person of the verb, *habuistis*, if correctly read, implies the text of a letter, as in **50** i 15, or if *res*]*ponderunt* is right, the report of a colloquy between some official and others, perhaps *ei qui ad cuni*..[. It is impossible to say who spoke the next two lines.

8. *cunioṣ*[: PSI.

10. [*i*]*n:* PSI, who notes that *si* could be the last syllable of a word in the preceding line.

11. *Ua*[*r*]*ius ịṃạ qui*..[: PSI; *Varius* Ɣ: G; Daris omits Ɣ ; *ạquiḷạ*[*m:* Fink, and *aqui*[*lam:* Daris, independently.

12. *excịịt; singula*.[: PSI. The adjective *duas* must agree with *uigilias*—"two squads of sentries," while *duos* in line 13 means "two soldiers." Read *singu*[*l*]*aṛ*[*is*] as a title (cf. lines 19 and 20); or is this a mistake for *coh*(*ortibus*) *singulis*?

13. *ca*[: PSI. On *ad pondera macelli* as supervision of weights used in the market, see Gilliam, p. 30. At the end of the line, possibly *ad car*[*cerem*]; cf. **52** b 15.

14. Gilliam, p. 30, doubts *suu*[*m* and adds "*Signum* may mean 'watchword' here, in which case it would be followed by a word in the genitive," as of course in **47**, **48**, and **50**. But there may have been a special reason for giving this party of sentries a separate recognition-sign.

15. *aḍnomera recognitos:* PSI, with a question whether the clerk meant to write *adnomerare cognitos* or *ad nomen* (written *nomem*) *recognitos*. The latter is surely right. Gilliam, p. 30, suggests an inspection and roll-call, comparing Livy 28.29.12: ... *stipendium ad nomen singulis persolutum est*.

16. *Bassus i*(*n*)*; XX̣XVIII* .[: PSI; *Bassus* Ɣ: G; *Bassus* (*centuria*) *Numeri:* Daris, mistakenly ascribing *Numeri* as well as Ɣ to Gilliam. Since the symbol can be expanded (*centuriae*), it is not certain that Bassus was a centurion.

17. *ad aq*[*u*]*ḷam et si q*[*uis:* PSI; but in "Addenda and Corrigenda," p. xiii: "*ad aqu*[*i*]*ḷam et sig*[*na* (*legionis*) (a noi communicato verbalmente dal prof. A. Vogliano)." Gilliam proposed the same reading independently. *aquilam et sign*[*a:* Daris.

18. *iners i*(*n*)*; seṛ*[: PSI; Ɣ *Neṛ*[*i*]; Ɣ: G; *Sem*[: Daris.

18a. There is an addition in small letters above *ur* of *turranius*, just as *signif* was added above 20. I have not been able to read it; but it begins with a tall letter, possibly *bene*(*ficiarius*).

19. *iuari:* PSI; Ɣ *Vari:* G.

20. *Domitius:* PSI. *signif* is an addition in small letters like 18a. It must apply to Domitius, for a signifer assigned to hospital service is impossible to understand.

21. *uigilias* .[..].*mu*..*nt*.. *Uarius i*(*n*)[: PSI, "*mutantes?*"; *Varius* Ɣ : G. Read]*c̣um uex*(*illatione*) *ịṇ eịṣ*?

22. *x iuratu:* PSI; Ɣ *Ḟirmị:* G, without mention of Norsa's *x*.

23. [...].[.]*a; Neapoḷ*[*is:* PSI. For *a frumento neapol*[, cf. **9** 31 e–f and **10** 2 and 27.

52

Morning Report? Unit Unknown

PMich. vii 450 (inv. 2761) and 455 (inv. 2758) recto — First quarter of iii p.
Now in Cairo

Transcription, commentary, and facsimiles: Henry A. Sanders, *PMich.* vii: *Latin Papyri*, nos. 450 and 455, and plates 11 and 14 (no. 455, frag. a only); cited as **S**.

Commentary:

1. Jean Bingen, *Latomus* 8 (1949) 71–72.
2. J. F. Gilliam, *AJP* 71 (1950) 436–37; cited as **G**.

Text: *CPL*, nos. 132 and 133, reproduces Sanders' text with notes from Gilliam's review. Daris, no. 12.

There can be no doubt that these two texts are part of the same original, as Gilliam (p. 436) was the first to observe, noting that the hand of the recto is the same in both and that Aprius (or Arrius) Ammonianus appears in both, while on the verso the date in *PMich.* 450, col. ii, is *v idus aug*[, and in *PMich.* 455 the date is *iiii idus aug.* He could have added that both were rotated on a vertical axis, not the usual procedure, to use the verso; and it even seems possible that the top of the largest fragment of 455 verso fits onto the bottom of col ii verso of 450. The hand of col. i of 450 verso is the same as that of 455 verso; but the first four lines of 450 col. ii are different. This combination of the two texts also explains the otherwise puzzling rustic capitals on the recto of the small piece of 450 which I have labeled frag. f. They must come from a heading such as that of 455, 7–10, or the fragment which I have renumbered frag. c.

The precise nature of the text is harder to define. In frag. b 2 and 14, *admittenda pronuntiauit*, and in frag. b 3, *excubare* of course point directly to such morning reports as **47** and **50**. Likewise *signum* in frag. a 6 may be part of the formula for giving out the password for the day, and *uigili-* in a 10 recalls **51** ii 11, 15, and 21. But *reliqui praesentes* in b 7 and c 2 suggests a summary like **58**–**62** or even a pridianum. Cf. **63** ii 41. The summaries and the pridiana, however, do not contain the admissa and the excubatio; so this text was probably a morning report. The entries with *reliqui praesentes* are in capitals and hence a heading. One may conjecture, then, that these lines began each day's entry and reconstruct them in outline as follows: date by day and month; total strength of the unit; *in his* ϒ (number), *dupl* (number), *sesq* (number); *drom* (number) *in his* (title, number); *equites* (number); *absentes* (number and perhaps *in expeditione*, *cum praefecto*, or the like); *reliqui* *praesentes* (number): *ex his* (men assigned to various duties named, perhaps including *custodiarum bal.*); *reliqui ad signa* (that is, available for any duty); *in his* ⅄ (number), *dec* (number).

The nominative case of *cohors I nomidarum* in frag. c 6 may mean that the text is a journal of that cohort; but unfortunately the history of the I Numidarum is almost unknown. It may be the same as the coh. I Numidarum which was stationed in Syria in 88 (*CIL* XVI, Dipl. 35); and an inscription from Samos (Dessau 8865) includes the prefecture of a coh. I Numidarum in the career of the person honored. The coh. I Flavia Numidarum, however, which was in Lycia Pamphylia in 178 (Dipl. 128) was probably different because its commander was a tribune, which implies a cohors miliaria. **63** shows that the unit need not have been stationed in Egypt for some of its papers to find their way there. The unit of our present text was at any rate a cohors equitata and included dromedarii, like the XX Palmyrenorum and the I Augusta Praetoria Lusitanorum (**64**). The small number of centurions probably indicates a cohors quingenaria; but this is not certain because the number of *absentes* is unknown and could be very large. In **61** it reaches the startling sum of 766.

The date is uncertain, too. None of the personnel named here is otherwise known; and the mention of the ala veterana Gallica on the verso (**53** b 25) at most establishes a tentative terminus post quem of about A.D. 130, when the ala is first known in Egypt. On the evidence of the hand I should date it in the first quarter of the third century.

The verso is **53**.

Frag. a (*PMich.* 450 recto; Daris A recto)

]   ọ ciuitatis p̣. . [. . .]a[.]ụ[.]ṃ[
]   *One line blank*
]c̣ịụịṭạtibus qu. . ṇt˙ . . . [
]. . sarapion . . . . . . ṛọni[.].[.].[
]. . ṭọ p̣raẹf̣. . . . . ṭ   .[
]primo mạ. . . . ṃ[i]l i
ap̣riụṣ ạmmonianụṣ ⅄ signụm . . [
ạ. . [.].[.]. . ị . . . . [   ]. . .
]. . . . . [
].[   ].ssit   fạusṭiụs uib.[
One line blank
]uịgili.ṣ. . . . . . [
].ạ[ ]ḷ. . [ ]ṣ ịn ḥị[s

After publication these papyri were returned to Egypt. My text is consequently based only on the study of photographs, some of which were kindly supplied by Prof. Sanders.

a 1. *Fa*[. . .]*ṇ*[.]*ụ*[.]*ṃ*[*:* S; *Fa*[. . . . .]*m:* Daris. There is papyrus to the left of the *o*, but the writing has disappeared.

2.]*c̣*[*i*]*ṿịtatibus quarụṃ* .[*:* S. The mention of civitates here and in line 1 evidently belongs to a letter or similar material as in **50** i 15; **51** ii 7–10; and **53** ii 8–29.

3.]*i Sarapioni Orạpo*[*ll*]*oni*[*:* S.

4.]*ṭo praesen*[*:* S, also possible; *praesen*[*te:* Daris.

5.] *primorụm fru*[. . . . .]*bụs*[*:* S.

6.]*arriçam monian*[. .]*c̣*[.] *signum ṣṭ*[*:* S;]*Arriọ Ammonianọ*[*:* Bingen; *Arri. Aṃmonian*[*:* Gilliam. The nomen as written here could be *arrius*; but b 15 shows that it was probably *aprius*. The *signum* is probably the daily password given by the centurion. Cf. especially **50** i 7 and 13, but also **47** i 3 and **48** 14.

7.]*ḷ*[. .]*ḷ*[.]*ṃạṣ:* S;]. . .*l*[. .]*l*.*mas*[*:* Daris.

8. No reading in S.

9.] *opsit frustinuibụ*[*s:* S.

10.]*ṿigili t*[. .]*ṣịṣtum*[*:* S. Cf. **51** ii 11 and 21.

11.]*ạ*[. . . .]*nẹ*[*:* S.

Frag. b (*PMich.* 455a recto; Daris B recto)

]ḷ..ḷ[
]admittenda pronuṇṭ[iauit
pa]ṛati excubaṛ[e
]... ạṃmoniani hoṛ[
] *One line blank*
]g̣elorum sc̣enopọ[
]. ịṣidori ḍẹḍ[.]c̣c̣tuṣ[
] *Two lines blank*
]Ṿ RELIQVI PRA[ESENTES
]ḌES CVSTODIAR[VM BAL
] DROM I RELIQ[VI AD SIGNA
]ỊN HIS Ƴ IV DEC˙ Ị[
] *Two and a half lines blank*
]. mil˙ numero x [
a]ụrelio ammoniano Ƴ [
]diosḍọrus didumacḥi [
] *One line blank*
ad]ṃittenda pronuntiauiṭ[
]. ḳạrc˙ aprius aṃmonianus[
] ịṇ ... eqụẹs i aṃṃ.[.]..[
] *One line blank*
] ex...ụ..ẹṛroe..[

Frag. c (*PMich.* 455b recto; Daris C recto)

]..[ ]....NṬ .[
RELI]QVI PRAESENTES[
CVSTO]DIARVM BAL II[
]RELIQVI AD SIGN[A
]IN HIS Ƴ III DE[C
]c̣[o]hors i nom[idarum
s]euerianus [

Frag. d (*PMich.* 455c recto; Daris D recto)

]ạ...[..].[
]. s.c̣ạro[
]..ṣ c̣ọh˙ [

Frag. e (*PMich.* 455d recto; Daris E recto)

]ạ.oạ[
]ḷ [

Frag. f

(*PMich.* VII, p. 84. Not in *CPL* or Daris.)

]BE[
]. C̣Ạ[

b 1. The reading is Sanders'. This line is cut off in the photograph. Daris omits it.

2. *pronunṭ*[: S; in app.: *pronunt*[*iavit*.

3.]*VII excubarẹ*[: S. **47** and **50** have *excubant* and **51** *excubuerunt*; but the letter after *a* cannot be *n*.

4.]*Amoniani Hos*[: S; Gilliam: "perhaps *hoṛ*-[*dinat*-." Sanders may be right in supposing that the centuria-symbol preceded *ammoniani*; and *t*(*urma*) is also possible. In that case *hor*[would be the beginning of a soldier's name. In this text there is no certain instance of *ord*(*inatus*) for *centurio*.

5.]*ṃelorum ṣtenoco*[: S, suggesting tentatively *ca*]*melorum stenoco*[*riasis*. The first word could be an ethnic. The second word, if correctly read, seems to be a compound recalling such Egyptian place-names as Scenae Veteranorum and Scenae Mandrae; but *p* is possible for *c*, and the *e* has been corrected from something else. Possibly, however, some case of *scenopoios*.

6. *demissu*[: S. Over the first *i* of *isidori* is a curled stroke from the top of a preceding letter—*c*, *e*, *s*, or *t*. The *s* here has an abnormal looped form resembling the *d* of *admittenda* in line 1.

7. *praẹ*[: S; in app., *prae*[*sentes*.

8.]*ṭes:* S; in app., [*pedi*]*tes* or [*equi*]*tes custodiar*[*um*]. The first letter cannot be *T* but may be a somewhat angular *D*. There is also a thin stroke from the top of it which slants down to the right through the *E* and *S*. *custo*]*ḍes custodiarum* seems too good to be true. *bal* is probably *bal*(*nei*) because of the single *l*; but *bal*(*listarum*) may be possible. **13** 13 has a guard *ad balistas*.

9. *reliq*[: S; in app., *reliq*[*ui; reliq*[*uus:* Daris.

10. *I*[*I:* Daris.

11. ...... *ṇuṃẹro:* S.

12.]*erelịo:* S, restoring *C*]*erelio*, perhaps rightly.

13.]*ḍioso Rossi Dumanti*[*s:* S; "Perhaps *Ḍioscorus Didumaṇṭị* . . .": G; *Didumant*[: Daris.

15.]*Ç̣yṃe Aṛrius Aṃonianu*[: S. The beginning of the line is difficult; but cf. Domaszewski, *Rang.* 39, citing *CIL* III 3412 for a *beneficiarius legati legionis, agens c*(*uram*) *c*(*arceris*). The spot of ink before the *k* may be an oblique stroke of abbreviation. The second and third letters of the cognomen have one stroke too many for *apro*-, one too few for *amm*-, but frag. a 6 shows that *amm*- is right. The different nomina prove that this is another person than the centurion in line 12.

16.]*ṃenti Amm*[: S. After *in*, if that is right, one expects *his*; but it cannot be read. The letters look most like *mi* or *pri*.

17. *ex tyṛ* [..]*e*[: S; "Only the first two letters are read with certainty."

c 1. ...... *mil'*[: S; *mil.*[: Daris.

2.]*ṣ qui:* S.

3. *custo*]*diarum bal*(*listarii*)*:* S in app.; but see on frag. b 8.

6. *c̣*[*o*]*hors I Noṃ*[*idarum:* S; ". . . probably gives the name of the cohort whose daily record was to follow. A First Cohort of Numidians is reported from Pamphylia, but not from Egypt."

Frag. d. *ẹgo*[and *coh*[: S.

Frag. e.]*anṭ* and]*q*[: S.

Frag. f. *OP* and *CA:* S.

53

Morning Report? Unit Unknown

PMich. vii 450 (inv. 2761) and 455 (inv. 2758) verso — ca. 225–250
Now in Cairo

Transcription, commentary, and facsimiles: see **52**.

The reasons for uniting these two papyri have been stated above in the introduction to **52**. This is a singularly frustrating text, which is classified here because of the indications of the pronuntiatio and the daily oath in frag. b, 29–30. It is plain, too, that the document is a journal; but nothing can be made of frag. a, col. i, and very little of the rest except that most of the extant part of frag. b is occupied with a narrative in a letter, or a report of some sort of hearing which involved soldiers of at least a legion and the ala Veterana Gallica. In all likelihood about seven-eights of the text is missing.

The date is likewise indeterminate, a guess on the basis of the hand.

The recto is **52**.

Frag. a (*PMich.* 450 verso; Daris A verso)

Col. i

(*First hand*)].ui
]araḅs
]ebrusạdus
]ṃissị . . . . .ḍior
]p̣ṛeṣs iv
].[.]. .ạṛius epị[.].c̣. .
]f̣. .ṛus. .[
].ụ.ṛatuṣ p̣ṛ[.].us
]iul ạlex̣ạṇdṛụṣ .
]ụs *vacat*
]ạ. . . . . .ạ. . . . .[
].[ ].[
]n[

Col. ii

(*Second hand*) v˙idus aug̣[
ag leg˙ ṛ[
perfo.[
perfe.[
[
[
vacat .[
vacat .[
.[
—]——[—

a i 1.]*sui:* S.
2.]*ṇib*(*u*)*s:* S.
3.]*sẹnsus:* S.
4.]*ṣumm*[. .]*errim:* S.
5.]*p*[.]*uṛes:* S.
6.]*perste*[. . .]*rriṃ:* S.
7.]*firves:* S.
8.]*ạṇteriị*[. . .]*s:* S. At the end, perhaps *p̣ṛ*[*i*]*ṃus*?
9.]*iuṣti erroṇẹus:* S.
10.]*eius:* S.
11.]*eos t*[.]*a*[.]*ui*[. .]*sus:* S.

a ii 1. There is an abbreviation dot on each side of the right-hand stroke of the numeral.

2. *ab leg I*[*I:* S. Not *ab*; but I do not know what to do with *ag* unless perhaps *uices*] *ag*(*ens*) *leg*(*ati*) *ạ*[*ug*(*usti*). It is not certain that this text originated in Egypt. See under **52**.

3. *perfor*[*tes:* S.

4. *perfec̣*[*ti:* S.

5–8. No readings in S.

Frag. b (*PMich.* 455a verso; Daris B verso)

(*First hand*) et .. eq[
]i ị[dus a]ug˙ ad ṿ ịd[us easdem ?
]iiii idus aug ịṃ[
singul˙ cọ[s
p̣arc̣i p̣ṛẹḅ[
emansioṇ[
singul e.[
acti e e *vacat* [
illa die domi ạ[
uel feriatae.[
]ṣaluṭauit˙ in ci[u]itatem[
⟦ṃilitẹ[⟧
iṇṭerfuit iṭeṛụ[m
in aḍỵṭi theṛạpẹ[
in aedem aqụ[ilae
c̣ẹ˙ pụtateṣạ[
fuit uel imfiṭị[
hora illa noṇ[a
rumpantes si q[u-
ṣaluṭaụit acṭuituṃ[
hora viiii principia .[
crpf˙ ṣṣạ usque si.[
c̣[o]ṇṭemsit˙ reuersus tes.[
eaṃ... ḷegionariorum di\r/ọta p̣ọṣṣ.[
teṛịgụṣ prosedit˙ ille pṛạ[e-
Ɣ ṃ[i]l x̣˙ transseuntes˙ in.[
ala u gall et ille praef̣.[
teṣṣ ịurauerunt actuituṃ in.[
eas ḥ qụạli usque et proṇunṭi[
imp̣[ ]eratum fuerit faciemus[

Frag. c (*PMich.* 455b verso; Daris C verso)

]ṇtuc̣ọ [
]nibus xli
]ṣtui lxxxxi
].. ii
]ṣẹḍ.ubus eius vii
]....
]ụs

Frag. d (*PMich.* 455c verso; Daris D verso)

]. Ɣ ius.[

Frag. e (*PMich.* 455d verso; Daris E verso)

iḷ[
a[
uị[
.[

Frag. f

(*PMich.* VII, p. 84. Not in *CPL* or Daris)

]ṃf̣[
One line blank
]. ṣ[
].me.[
].ỵio.[
].ụ.[

b 1. The reading is Sanders'. The line is cut off in the photograph.

2. *.ṿi; ad c*[*:* S; Daris has nothing before VI. This appears to be a notation of the period covered in a large preceding section of the journal. For the shape of the *v* after *ad*, cf. the numeral in a ii 1.

3. S does not report the two tall, thin strokes after *aug*. They seem to be letters in a chancery hand, as in lines 8 and 22, and may be the start of a consular date with the title and name of the emperor. A horizontal stroke divides this line from the preceding one.

4. *p*[*:* S.

5. *Ɨ Narsi tre*[*:* S, assuming that the symbol represents *turma*. I first read it as a form of the centuria-sign, *Ɣ Marci*; but I now think it is accidentally formed from the tails of the *s* and *n* in the preceding line. The last four letters cannot be read as *trib* because the third cannot be *i*; but the whole line can be read in several ways.

6. If correctly read, this means overstaying one's allotted time.

7. *ex*[*:* S. Perhaps *eṃ*[*ansit*. A horizontal stroke divides this line from the section which follows.

8. *acti˙ s˙ s˙:* S; G suggests *e*(*xemplum*) *e*(*pistulae*). The two *e*'s are in a chancery hand like *PDur.* 59 (*Final Rep.* V, plate 40, 2). Cf. the similar notations in lines 3 and 22.

9. *Iḷladi Eumaṛ*[*:* S. Gilliam, *AJP* 88 (1967) 100, agrees on *illa die*.

10. S: "... probably describes cohorts or *alae* [or legions?] as idle or unemployed." The letters could also be divided *feriat ae*.[.

11. *iṇṣeruit in chortem*[*:* S. The first *t* of *salutauit* is bad; but cf. line 20. The only other possibility I can see,]*s adnauit*, is a less attractive alternative. The word is in the margin.

12. *ạṛiṭị:* S. The word was inserted in small letters between lines 11 and 13 and then canceled.

13. *et c̣ṛẹ[:* S, perhaps rightly.

14. *inṭẹrsit detrịṃ[:* S.

15. S notes that this probably means the shrine of the military standards. Cf. **51** ii 11 and 17.

16. *CE¯ putat ẹsṭ[:* S; "*C(ilicum) E(quitatae)*... the First Flavian cohort of Cilicians." Possible (cf. line 22) but suspect. The first two characters are written with a coarser pen, and the supposed *e* has a peculiar form like a reversed numeral 3, while the first letter, if Latin, could equally well be *p*. There is a horizontal dash level with the top of the *e*, and a dot of abbreviation as well. The notation may mark the entrance of another person into the narrative or debate; but I do not actually know what to make of it. The rest of the line could be divided variously: *puta te ṣạ[*, *putat e ṣạ[*, or *putate ṣạ[*.

17. *inụṣti[:* S. The last word may be a form of *infitiari* or *infitiae* with *m* for *n* through a false assimilation.

18. *hora˙ II vanoṛ[:* S. For *non[a* cf. line 21.

19. *nuntiantes sibị[:* S; *nuntiante:* Daris. Except for the first letter, *nuntiantes* would be acceptable.

20. *peṛlusịṿit actuituṃ[:* S; "*actuitum* occurs here and in l. 28. It must be a variant spelling of the adverb *actutum* or an unknown name." The first word seems to have been written with an initial *t* and corrected by writing an *s* through the *t*.

21. *`si´ .ịṭịrạsem ṃinịṣịṛia[:* S. Cf. *hora illa noṇ[a* in line 18.

22. *CRS* |·|.; *si[:* S; "*C R S* is probably for *c(ivium) R(omanorum) s(cutata)*." This seems basically right; but the reading seems rather to be *c(iuium r(omanorum) p(ia) f(idelis)*, with the rest of the cohort's (or ala's) name at the end of the preceding line. If correctly read, these titles limit the choice of units to four: the ala III Asturum (*CIL* XVI, Dipl. 73), the ala I Flavia singularium (Dipl. 23, 36, 55, 94, 117–118, 121), the coh. II Brittonum miliaria (Dipl. 46 and 110), and the coh. III Delmatarum equitata (*CIL* III 8010). None of these was ever in Egypt; but it may be a matter of the transfer of a centurion or other personnel. I am not sure whether the letters are written with the same pen as *cẹ* in line 16. There appear to be three strokes of the chancery hand, as in lines 3 and 8, after the four letters; but the third is very faint. Read *s(upra) s(cript)a*?

23. [..]*pemfis; tesṭ[:* S. *tesṭ[atus*, *tesṣ[eram*, and *tesṣ[erarius* are all possible.

24. *ịṇ legionariorum defection[:* S. *eam* projects into the margin; and only the feet of the next three letters remain. Sanders' reading makes sense and mine does not; but *defection[* is impossible and any connection with *deiotariana* seems out of the question because of the date. A large cursive *r* is written over the next three letters after *d. diota*, if correct, may be a vessel taken from the *adytum* (line 14) or the *aedes aquilae* (line 15). In that case perhaps *r(eddita)*.

25. *ad [e]ọṣ:* S; *prae[:* Daris. Again, the reading offered here is absurd; but the line certainly begins with *te*. The *u* is especially doubtful. Perhaps the end of *Sotericus* or a similar name.

26. *ϯ Attae; in ị[:* S; "The sign for *turmae* seems clear; and *Atta* is a known cognomen." The symbol cannot be a form of T, but must be ϒ. The letter after the symbol may be *a*, and I cannot find the *i* of *mil*; but *l* is certain and *ae* at the end is very difficult.

27. Gilliam, *AJP* 88 (1967) 100, believes that *alae* is also possible. *praefẹ[:* S. Expand *ala u(eterana) gall(ica)*.

28. *tes voverent actuitum* [ ]*in:* S; "*tes* is perhaps the end of *equites* or *cohortes*, the subject of *voverent*." It might equally well be the end of a participle; or if the two *s*'s are right, an abbreviation of *tessera* or *tesserarius*. There is no gap between *actuitum* and *in*.

29. *dus Ịṇịutliusque et pro*[ ]*uetẹ[:* S. The letters between *eas* and *ali* could also be read *ẹṣuid*. Perhaps understand something like [*eadem mente se*] *eas h(abere) quali usque. eas* could refer to legions (cf. line 24), alae (line 27), cohorts, or even civitates (line 11). At the end of the line *pronunti[auit* seems reasonable and is supported by the next line. There is no gap after *pro*.

30. [..]*im*[.]*eratur fient ẹṭ ṣi*[ ]*emve:* S. Gilliam proposed the reading adopted here. There is a gap between *imp* and *eratum* where the clerk skipped over a defect in the papyrus, but no gap after *faci*.

c 1.]*ạṭuṭị:* S.

3.]*ẹq˙:* S.

4.]*ạg˙:* S.

5.]*s*[.]*ṇibus; ϛ I:* S.

6. No reading in S.

7.]*s:* S; omitted by Daris.

Frag. d. ϒ *Ius[:* S; *(turmae):* Daris, mistakenly.

e 1.]*me[:* S.

2 and 3. No reading in S.

4. *a[:* S. The traces could also be read *q*[or ϒ [.

5. ϒ [*:* S; (*turma*): Daris.

f 1.]*reis:* S.

2.]..*l:* S.

3.]..*e:* S.

4.]*mis:* S.

5.]*esion:* S.

6. No reading in S.

54

Morning Report? of the Coh. XX Palmyrenorum

PDur. 85 (inv. D.P. 31 recto); *vidi* ca. A.D. 230

Transcription and commentary: *Final Rep.* v, no. 85; *edidit* Gilliam.

This text is placed among the morning reports because of the mention of the tribune and the principia in frags. a–c.

Dating is on paleographical grounds.

The verso is **12**.

Frags. a–b–c

]·[
]·ạ[
Two lines blank
]··[ ]·····[ ]·i cal Ỵ [
]·[········]····[··]···l····[
]·[··]·s tṛ[i]ḅụnus in princ̣[ipiis
]ṣ tribụ[ ]bres ·[··]ạ·[

Frag. d

]ṣalu··[
]exẹṃ[

Frag. f

]sep·[
]i *vacat*
]·[·]ṣ[·]us

Frag. e is blank on the recto.

a–c 3. *c̣ạl* ·[*:* D; "*m*]*ịl*(*itum*) *c̣ạl*(*igatorum*)*?* The next letter is not a good *d*, though one would expect a number beginning with *D* to follow *mil cal.*" The centuria-symbol does not follow naturally either.

5.]·*us:* D.

6.]*ḅr*·*s* ·[··]··[*:* D; "Probably]*ḅṛẹs* or]*ḅṛịs*. *O*]*b res* is less attractive than *Octo-* or *Novem*]*bres*, which the arrangement of the fragments excludes." To be precise, there is room for *v k octo-* if we read *tribu*[*s*, or, on the basis of f 1, [*septem*]*bres*. But there are other possibilities as well, such as [*salu*]*bres* (cf. d 1) or [*cele*]*bres*.

d 1.]··*lụ*·[*:* D. Perhaps *signum*] *ṣalụtị*[*s misit* (cf. **50** i 7 and 13; **48** 14), but perhaps the greeting from a letter.

2.]*exeṃ*[*pl:* D. This could be either *exem*[*plum epistulae*] or a form of *eximere*.

Frag. f is not labeled in the mounting. D offers no readings.

55

Morning Report? of the Coh. XX Palmyrenorum

PDur. 87 (inv. D. P. 65 recto) ca. A.D. 230?

Transcription and commentary: *Final Rep.* v, no. 87; *edidit* Gilliam.

These scraps are included here because of the readings in a 4: *in prin[cipiis*; c 1–2: *nomin[a* and *]erunt*; and i 1: *e]q cc[*, which recall entries in **54** a–c 5; **50** i 15; and the totals of over two hundred equites in **47**. But Gilliam properly emphasizes that the nature of the text is very uncertain.

The date is necessarily on paleographical grounds.

The verso is **125**.

Frag a

].[
].[
]...[
]in priṇ[cipiis ?
]..brịt [
].[ ]..[

Frag. b

].[
pri]ṇc̣eps ..[
an]ṭọninus ..[
]ṇri gaṛ..[
]ỵ [.].ụḥ ..[
vacat

Frag. c

]nomin[a] [
].[.]erunṭ [
].m c̣ạri.i *vacat*
vacat

Frag. d

].[...]..um[
]..[..].pṛ....[
].[...]abed[

Frag. e

]![......]...ịị.[
]eq lx[

Frag. f

]dec[

Frag. g

].[.] Ŧ ..[
].[....]iii ẹ[
]..i[

Frag. h

]..h.[
]......[
]...[
]mo[...]........[

a 5.]*ḅạt*.[: D.

b 2. ....*ṣ*[.]..[: D.

3. ....*us*.[: D.

4.]..*ṛị gạịạ*[*n:* D.

5. Gilliam: "The line may begin with the centurial sign. Otherwise, a possible reading is]*ṾỊ* [*M*]*ạlchus*[".

c 1.]*nomin*[: D.

2.]*erunt:* D.

3.]*um p̣ṛịṣc̣ị:* D. An accusative followed by a genitive is hard to understand if this is a morning report.

d 2. Gilliam: "Possibly *praep* or *praef*, but the next letter is not *c*, i.e., *c*[*oh*."

g 1. Gilliam: "The name of the decurio, following the turma sign, may begin with *a* or *r*."

2. Gilliam: "Possibly the third consulship of Elagabalus (220) or Alexander (229)." But it need not be a consulship at all.

i 2. Gilliam: "*s*]*ẹsq*(*uiplicari-*)?"

56

Morning Report? of the Coh. XX Palmyrenorum

PDur. 84 (inv. D. P. 67 recto) ca. A.D. 233

Transcription and commentary: *Final Rep.* v, no. 84; *edidit* Gilliam.

Facsimile: ibid., plate 52, 2.

This text is ascribed to the morning reports on the grounds of the resemblance of its script to **48** on the recto and of both script and content to **13** on the verso. This association is also the basis of the dating.

The verso is **14**.

]. . [. .]. . . [
]. [.]. . lḅạ[. . .]ḷus[
]s ạụrel h[.]. . . [.]g̣[

1.]. . [: D.
2.]. . . *ḷ*. [. . . .]. [.]*ṣ*[: D. The reading suggests the name *ba*]*ṛ*[*c*]*ḥạlḅạ*[*s*; but the traces are too slight to confirm or disprove the possibility.
3. *Au*]*rel H*[: D.

57

Morning Report? of the Coh XX Palmyrenorum

PDur. 86 (inv. D. P. 54) ca. A.D. 240

Transcription and commentary: *Final Rep.* v, no. 86; *edidit* Gilliam.

The numeral followed by a name recalls the lists of excubitores in the morning reports, e.g. **47** ii 13, and **50** i 9, and is the reason for placing this scrap in the present category.

The date rests on the similarity of the hand to the first hand of **50**.

The verso is blank.

]. [
]iiii ulpius[

58

Monthly Summary of a Century of the Leg. III Cyrenaica

PGenLat. 1 verso, part IV; *vidi* — ca. A.D. 90
P. lat. 1, Bibliothèque publique et universitaire

Bibliography under **9**; but *ChLA* I, pp. 16–17.

Text: *CPL*, no. 106, IV, reproduces the text of *ChLA* with a few readings from *ArM* and Premerstein in the apparatus. Daris, no. 10 (3), does the same except for lines 9–11 of col.. ii.

This text and **9**, which occupies the rest of the verso, are mutually complementary. The present text accounts rather summarily for all the immunes of the century, leaving a balance of 31 men who are available for any sort of day-to-day task. **9** covered in detail the routine assignments for October of these 31 and 5 others added after the list was made up.

The date is certainly subsequent to September 19, 87, the latest date in **10**; and may be later than A.D. 90 (**37** above); but Marichal's surmise that **58** and **9** followed immediately after **10** in chronological sequence, though attractive, involves difficulties which prevent its acceptance. See the introduction to **10**. The terminus ante quem is of course the date of Domitian's death, September 18, 96; but the possibility remains open that **58** and **9** were written in 88–90 and that **37** was written on *their* verso, not on the recto of **10** and **68**.

Col. i

leg iii]c̣yṛ
]ụii . . .   ỵ . . .
]iii
].ụị. i
]
]i
]
]x
]iiị
]
]i
]iṿ
]ị
]ii
]
]i
]
]xii
]i
]ii
]
]ii
]
]. . .
]ụạ
] x̣ḷ[.]x
] .
]·
]ụṣ
]ẹq
]ạg̣.aṭ.
]imus
]x̣xṿ ỵ
].
]ẹṛ. ỵ ỵ
]equites ii
]c̣ina celsus
]crispus

Col. ii

reliqui x̣xx̣x
ex eis
opera uaçantes
armorụṃ custos i
cọnductọṛ porçịus i
çạrrarius plọṭịnus i
ṣẹçutor ṭri [i]uḷịus ⟦ọạ⟧ seuerus i
custọs domị ploti tr[i]ḅuni fḷauụṣ i
]ḷibrarii et cịẹạpi ii
cuṛ. . ịtịụṣ çạpra
aurẹḷ[iu]ṣ . . [. .]ḷ. r . ị
supranumẹṛạṛ. [.] i
dọ. ọ. . ṣ[ ]
ṣṭationem a[g]ẹṇṣ i
ị domitius f̣. . [. .].
ṣ ịx̣
reliqui x̣xxi

Previous estimates of 45–50 lines in col. i are too high. The entire written space is only ca. 34.0 cm. high; and lines 2–4, 18–20, and 32–38 show a consistent average of about 0·9 cm. for each line, including one interlinear space. There is room then for only 38 lines.

i 1. No reading in ArM and ChLA. The *y*, however, is clear in the new photograph; and the first stroke and top of the *r* are preserved. Since the columns are narrow, as shown by col. ii, and since the numerals at the ends of the lines in col. i are sufficient, with those in col. ii, to account for the total strength of a century, this line is probably a heading rather than an entry dealing with a transfer or some other transaction with the legion. If it is a heading, it proves that the whole of the verso of this papyrus belonged to the archives of the III Cyrenaica.

2.]. . . : ArM and ChLA;]*ni* ⅄*:* Prem. If the preceding line has been correctly interpreted, this one may have contained the identification of the century, something like (*centuria*) [*name in genitive*] (*septimi*) *h*(*astati*) *pr*(*ioris*)*:* (*centurio*) [*name in nominative*], as in **21**. This cannot actually be read. There is a bar over the *uii*, indicating a numeral or an abbreviation, but what follows is quite uncertain. It looks most like *h* or *l* followed by a horizontal bar passing through two *x*'s. There may be more than three letters to the right of the doubtful centuria-symbol.

3.]. . . : ArM and ChLA;]*iii:* Prem.

4. No reading in ArM;]. . .*i:* ChLA;]*uic i:* Prem.

8.]⟍ : Prem.

11.]*x:* ArM;]*i:* Prem.

12. Edd., no reading.

16. No reading in ArM;]*ii:* Prem.

18.]*xi:* ArM;]*iṇ:* ChLA; ⫞ *i:* Prem.

19.]*s:* Prem.

20.]8 *i:* Prem.

22. Edd., no reading.

24–27. Edd., no reading.

29. Edd., no reading.

30.]. . . : ArM; no reading in ChLA.

31.]. . : ArM;] . . . . : ChLA;]*M:* Prem.

32.].*mus:* ChLA;]*mus:* Prem.

33.]*ix:* ArM and Prem.;]*ix* .⅄: ChLA.

34. No reading in ArM and Prem.;]. . . . . : ChLA.

35.]*VII:* ArM;]. . . . . ⅄ *i:* ChLA;]. . ⅄ *i:* Prem., and in app., "etwa [*bucinator*] (*centuriae*) (*unus*)."

37.]*c̣ọrnelius:* ArM;]*Çornelius:* ChLA; *c*]*ornelius:* Prem. Perhaps *in armorum offi*]*cina*, or the like. Note the carrarius in ii 6.

ii 6. *ṣịuinius:* ArM. Prem. first read *Plotinus.*

7. *tri*[.].*tius:* ChLA; *tri*.*nutius:* Prem. Read *secutor tri*(*buni*), a member of the tribune's bodyguard. Gilliam has the same in his review of Daris, *AJP* 88 (1967) 100. Specifically on this entry, Domaszewski, *Rang.*, p. 41, no. 37. [.]*ṇius* could be read for [*i*]*uḷius*.

8. *domi*. . .*iti*. . .*staius:* ArM; *Cọṭi*.*r* . . . . .*Staur:* ChLA; *domi iti sallusti staius:* Prem. For the *n* ligatured with *i* in *tribuni*, cf. *nu* in *supranumerar*, line 12. The *us* of *flauus* is doubtful; but the letters are crowded against a patch on the papyrus. *st* would be possible instead of *fl*; or perhaps read *flauịạ*(*nus*).

9. *et ḍịṣçẹṇṣ:* ArM; *et ce*[*r*]*ại*[*u*]*s:* ChLA; *et ce*[*r*]*aiu*[*s*]*:* Prem.; *cẹ*[*r*]*ạri*[*u*]*s:* Daris. The final *i* of *librarii* is a correction over a *c*. I am baffled by the last word. *cerarius* would be an excellent reading; but I cannot find any form of it in the remains, which could be read *clerici* if that made good sense.

10. *curiati*[*us* . . . . .]*s:* ArM and Prem.; *Curịạti* . . . .*:* ChLA; *Curiatius*. . . .*:* Daris.

11. *aureli*[*us:* ArM; *Aurel*. . . . .*:* ChLA; *Aureli*[*us* . . . . .]*s:* Prem.; *Aurelius* . . .*:* Daris.

12. *supranumer* . . . .*:* ArM; *supranumẹṛạṛ*[*ius*]*:* ChLA; *supranumerari*[*us*]*:* Prem.

13. *do*[*mitius*]*:* ArM; *Do*[*mitius*]*:* ChLA; *Do*[*mitius* . . . . .*:* Prem.
14. *a* . . . . .*:* ArM; *a*[*ge*]*ns:* Prem. and ChLA.
15. .*domitius:* ArM; *Domitius* . . . .*:* ChLA. The character to the left of *domitius* is blotted, perhaps to cancel it. Possibly *l*(*ucius*)?

15–16. ChLA has a series of seven dots, beginning under *s* of *stationem*, line 14, between lines 15 and 16.
16. *F* . . .*:* ArM and Prem.; *F*. . . . . .*:* ChLA, and in app., "*f*(*iunt*) *ix*, total of the preceding lines." Very possible. With *s*, as in the text, read *s*(*umma*).

59

Monthly Summary of a Naval Century

PSI XIII 1308 A.D. 152–164

This papyrus was destroyed during World War II. My readings are based on the plate in *PSI*.

Transcription, commentary, and facsimile: Medea Norsa in *PSI* 13 (1939), pp. 108–9 and plate 5.

Commentary:

1. J. F. Gilliam, "Notes on *PSI* 1307 and 1308," *CP* 47 (1952) 30–31.
2. Sergio Daris, "Osservazioni ad alcuni papyri di carattere militare," *Aegyptus* 38 (1958) 151–58.

Text: *CPL*, no. 144, reproduces Norsa's text and dates, with notes from Gilliam in the apparatus. Daris, no. 29, adopts Gilliam's dates in lines 2, 4, and 6, but retains Norsa's readings in lines 15 and 18.

The nature of this text is quite uncertain. It might be regarded as a list of *immunes* and *caligati* similar to the lists of *principales* in **21–25**; but it has been placed here because of its resemblance to the list of *immunes* in **58** ii 3–15. There is an important difference, however, because the present text gives dates of enlistment as well as names. The fact that the dates are not in chronological sequence shows that the names are in order of rank; and the titles *gubernator*, *faber*, and *ascita* prove that these are classiarii.

Gilliam has already shown that the approximate date of the text is fixed by the consulships in lines 3, 5, and 7. Greater exactness might be possible if the name of the consul in line 15 could be read. See also the apparatus on i 13, 15, and 18.

Col. i		Col. ii
]. . . [		
].ṭẹar.[		
]. claro it˙ cos′	A.D. 146	
]. .ius apolinaris[		
]s gub˙ auito cos′	144	.[
].l[.]ẹsa[. . .]. firmịc̣ụs		
]. .rie. . hom˙ cos′	152	.[
]ualeriụs rufus		
] fab˙ aug˙ n˙		
]. iulius maximus		
]sia.iu. .[.].us aponịaṇus		h[
] ascita		
]uolusius seneca		.[
] caligati		
]. ạ. . .c̣t˙ cos		
]. . .s. nephyạs		—— l[
]ṇ pachny. . .		+ ạ[
]anton [i]ị c̣[o]s′	139	
]h.s˙ neoh. .[. .]ḍus		
]ṃịṣ. .ḍ[. .] a		ς [
]. . . . . . .[ ].		
] [		
] [		
]. . .ụs		.[
]		
]		
]. . . [. .].[		
]. .[		

i 1. No reading in PSI.
2.].*teṛṛ*.[*:* PSI.
4.].*ius:* PSI.
5.]*gub˙:* PSI; *gub(ernator):* Gilliam.
6.]. . *Firmus:* PSI.
7.]*l*. .*e*.*:* PSI. Read *hom(ullo) cos.* In the letters which precede, perhaps *gl*]*ạḅri*(*one*) *eṭ*, since Homullus was the junior consul for this year and we do not know that Glabrio ever incurred damnatio memoriae.
9.].*:* PSI. Read *fab(er) aug(usti) n(ostri)* or *n(aualis)*. Domaszewski, Rang., does not index *faber* as a rank, but does have a *doctor fabrum legionis*, an *optio fabricae*, and *fabriciesis legionis*—all p. 46. Cf. however the references in Gilliam, p. 31, note 16: Dessau, *ILS* III, part 1, p. 506; C. G. Starr, *The Roman Imperial Navy* (Ithaca 1941) 42, 51, 56, 60, 61, 65, n. 46. For *aug(usti)* cf. *CIL* XI 630: *mil. coh. III pr(aetoriae) architectus Augusti* (*Rang.*, p. 25). The *n* has a stroke above it which combines to resemble the ligature of *NT*, but the stroke may be only a mark of abbreviation.
10.]*Iulius:* PSI.
11.]. . . . . . *Apontinus:* PSI.
12. The meaning of *ascita* can perhaps be derived from *ascia*—axe or adze—as a formation with the Greek agent-suffix -της, which becomes -*ta* in Latin, as in *poeta*. *ascita* would stand in the same relation to *ascia* as ὁπλίτης to ὅπλα and would mean "one who wields an ascia," an adzeman or broad-axe man, a hewer of timbers. Daris, *Aegyptus* 38 (1958) 158, equates the word with ἀσκητής in the sense of Latin *curator*. If Volusius owes his name to L. Volusius Maecianus, Prefect of Egypt in 160–161 (Stein, *Präf.* 88–90), the date of the papyrus is narrowed accordingly.
14. Soldiers of the rank of centurion or lower. See on **47** i 1.
15.]*Aspero˙ cos:* PSI. Here the remains seem most nearly to resemble *ạpaṛc̣ṭọ* or *ạṃạẹṭọ*; but neither suggests the name of any consul known in this period unless one hazards *ḷạẹṇạt*(*e*), A.D. 131, who may be too early (cf. on line 13) or *ḷụpẹṛc̣ọ*, A.D. 135. Perhaps a consul suffectus?

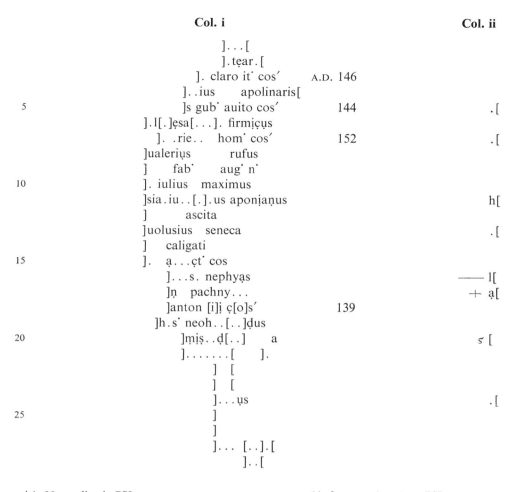

16.].*us Nechutus:* PSI.
17.]. *Pachẹ. . :* PSI.
18.]*Anton*[*in*]*o* [*co*]*s*˙*:* PSI. If my reading is right, the date in line 15 should fall between 127 and 139 because all the men in lines 16–19 are in the same category of caligati and hence in order of seniority.
19.]. . . *Nechu*[*tus:* PSI. Instead of]*ḍus*,]*bis* is possible.
20.].*mullu*.[*:* PSI. The transcription in PSI ends here.

ii. The apparent *h* in line 11, which could be read as *l*, and the marks in lines 16 and 17 are heavier strokes than in the body of the text and are presumably marginal annotations of some sort. Note the "digamma" below in line 20. The letter after the sign in line 17 could be either *a* or *m*.

60

Monthly Summary? of the Coh. XX Palmyrenorum

PDur. 90 (inv. D. P. 38 verso) ca. A.D. 225–235

Transcription and commentary: *Final Rep.* v, no. 90; *edidit* Gilliam.

The numerals on all three fragments, *kạl ịạṇụ*[in frag. b 3, and a general likeness to **61** and **62** are the reasons for placing these scraps of text in this category. What little can be made of the form of the document indicates that it is less likely to be a morning report (**47–57**) or a pridianum (**63–65**).

The date is based on paleography.

The recto is **26**.

Frag. a

].[
]ccc.[
One line blank
]c̣cc̣[
Two lines blank
].[

Frag. b

].[.]. . . .n
].ṇṃḥ
One line blank
] kạl ịạṇụ[
]. [ ]ccc.[
]cccḷx̣v
One line blank
]ẹṣ[ ]sṣ[.].

Frag. c

].ḍcx̣.

61

Monthly Summary of the Coh. XX Palmyrenorum

PDur. 91 (inv. D. P. 19 recto) ca. A.D. 225–235

Transcription, commentary, and facsimile; *Final Rep.* V, no. 91 and plate 48, 1; *edidit* Gilliam.

The item *abs*(*entes*), implying also a category of *praesentes*, in line 8, suggests a kinship with both **51** and **62** and is the basis for classifying this text as a monthly report. It might, however, be a letter accompanied by a list of names like **92**.

Gilliam notes that the traces of writing at the left edge of the papyrus (col. i here) need not belong to the same text and are almost certainly not part of the same column as the main body (here col. ii).

The date rests on paleographical considerations.

The verso is *PDur.* 140, the language of which has been identified as Greek, but of which Welles reports that he is unable to read anything consecutive.

Col. i	Col. ii
	]. ẹụ[
	]. . . . ụs. . . [
].	sa[l]mes them[
]. . . .	iulius ṃạṛị[
	ṃạ. . [
	ṃ. [ ]ḥ. . [
].[	*One line lost?*
	i. . . c̣c̣x̣x̣ṿi abs mil dcclxvi
	ḍṛọm xxvii
]. . . . ạ	]. . . . tesdẹḍ. [
	]. . . . [
	].[
	]. [.]l . ẹṇṭạ[
]. . c̣iṇus	]. . ẹn aḅẹḍ. ẹ. [
]us. . . . . [	]ṇiṃị[ ]. ṛiṃ[
	]. . ṭụẹ. . . . [
	]. ṇo. [.]. . . [

ii 7. This line may have contained a date; but the fibres have been stripped from the surface, leaving a bare trace of ink at the left side.

8. *abs*(*entes*) *mil*(*ites*).

10. Very possibly]*ẹqụites*, since in the totals of **47** and **50** the caligati, dromedarii, and equites appear in that order. Otherwise perhaps *pra*]*ẹṣẹṇtes*.

62

Monthly Summary of the Coh. XX Palmyrenorum

PDur. 92 (inv. D. P. 27) ca. A.D. 225–235

Transcription, commentary, and facsimile: *Final Rep*. v, no. 92 and plate 49, 1; *edidit* Gilliam.

The date by the Kalends followed by a grand total and the number of *absentes* and *praesentes*, the latter being further divided into successive categories, makes this text seem the beginning of a text like **58**, col. ii of which appears to be the end of such a list. And just as **58** was a report of the status of one century only, it is possible that the present text was limited to the equites of the xx Palmyrenorum.

The date is on paleographical grounds.

The verso is blank.

kal ọc̣toḅ[r]ẹṣ n ẹq ccclxxxviiii
ex eis
abs n xxxi
reliq praẹṣ[c]c̣clỵiii ịn ḥịṣ[
ẹx̣ arṣ iiii
p̣ṛinc˙ i
ḍẹc̣ur xxx̣ị
].[
]...[
].[
]....[ ]viiiị[
]ḷx[in]ḥịṣ.[

Minute traces of five or six more lines

1. *Octoḅ*..[..]..*q:* D; Gilliam, "It is possible to read... *n*(*umerus*) *eq*(*uitum*).... The reading is supported by Welles."

3. Expand *abs*(*entes*); *n*(*umero*).

4. [*CC*]*CL*[*V*]*III:* D. Expand *reliq*(*ui*) *praes*(*entes*).

5. *ẹ*....: D; Gilliam, "Possibly *ẹ.arc*". I am at a loss to explain the sense of either reading.

6. ...*n:* D; Gilliam, "Possibly *princ*; if so, perhaps *princ*(*ipiis*) rather than *princ*(*eps*) or *princ*(*ipalis*)."

7. .*ẹc̣*.. *XXX:* D; Gilliam, "Possibly *decur*; if so, *decur*(*sores*)? The number makes *decur*(*iones*) impossible."

11.]...[..]..[: D.

Pridiana

63

Pridianum? of the Coh. I Hispanorum Veterana

British Museum Papyrus 2851; *vidi* ca. Sept. 17, 100? 101? 104? 105?

Transcription, commentary, and facsimile:

1. A. S. Hunt, "Register of a Cohort in Moesia," *Raccolta di Scritti in Onore di Giacomo Lumbroso* (Milan 1925) 265–72; cited as **H**.
2. R. O. Fink, "Hunt's *Pridianum*: British Museum Papyrus 2851," *JRS* 48 (1958) 102–16; cited as **F**.
3. *ChLA* III, no. 219.

Transcription and facsimile: *New Palaeographical Society*, series 2, vol. 2, plate 186; cited as **NPS**.

Commentary:

1. U. Wilcken, *Archiv* 8 (1927) 94–95.
2. G. Cantacuzène, *Aegyptus* 9 (1928) 63–96, and *Revue historique du Sud-Est européen* 5 (1928) 38–74. The two papers are identical.
3. R. Syme, "The Lower Danube under Trajan," *JRS* 49 (1959) 26–33; cited as **S**.
4. J. F. Gilliam, "The Moesian 'Pridianum'," *Hommages à Albert Grenier*, Collection Latomus 58 (1962) 747–56; cited as **G**.
5. R. W. Davies, "Optatus and the Roman Army: P. Lond. 2851, 1–22," *BASP* 5 (1968) 121–28.

Text: *CPL*, no. 112, reproduces mostly the readings of NPS with notes in the apparatus from Hunt and Wilcken.

In spite of all the contributions of the scholars named above and in the apparatus below, many questions about this text remain unresolved, including the basic one of its classification. Gilliam (pp. 753–54) argues that there may have been more pridiana yearly than the one (or in Egypt two) which I envisage and asks whether such reports could not have been requested by governors at other than the usual times. Marichal (*ChLA*, p. 127) picks up the latter suggestion and draws the conclusion that this is not a pridianum at all but "a special 'statement of strength' called for by the general staff during the Dacian campaign, at the time when operations were about to be interrupted by the approach of winter and the spring offensive prepared." Since **64** is the only certain pridianum known, and it is incomplete, there is no sure means of settling the matter; but i 24 suggests that the part of the text which follows bears at least some resemblance to a pridianum, and comparison with **64** supports this belief. Consequently, I have grouped this text with **64** in spite of the differences between the two; but because of the lack of particulars, such as the names of the men newly added to the cohort, I believe that it is a summary rather than a full pridianum, while the date in i 23 persuades me that it summarizes the pridianum of August 31. (See above, p. 2.) **58** should be compared as an example of the way in which the present text may have continued after ii 44.

A more difficult problem is the relationship of i 1–22, and especially 11–20, to the rest of the text. Gilliam (755) and Marichal (*ChLA* 127) refer these lines also to the coh. I Hispanorum. In the present state of the papyrus, certainty seems impossible; but the full identification of the cohort in i 24–25 appears to me to indicate that it had not been mentioned before, just as the blank line between 22 and 23, with the capitals in 23, implies the opening of a new section. Moreover, lines 11–20 pretty certainly list men who have left the service (line 20: *recesserunt*), while lines 23–28 open a new section with a formal heading and a statement of the strength on December 31, followed in lines 29–36 and ii 1–2 by accessions and a new total, after which losses are detailed in ii 3–13. If i 1–22 are in fact concerned with the I Hispanorum, at the very least they must constitute a different record from the one which begins in i 23. Otherwise the separation of the two sets of decreases is hard to understand. But there is no necessity for both i 1–22 and the text from i 23 on to be records of the same unit. If the "pridianum" section is a digest (implied, too, in Marichal's proposal of *secundum* or a similar preposition before *pridianum* in i 24), the upper part of col. i is probably also a digest; and both may well have been prepared at a central office from the pridiana or other reports of various units. This would also explain the absence of a year-date in i 23–25. The year would be the same for all the reports and would appear at the head of the entire document.

What can be said of these first lines is that 1–10 seem to end, most of them, in numerals, whether in reference to personnel, money, or supplies, and that 11–20, by using capitals and naming the men individually in separate lines, single out for special mention five (or six) men who had left the service. Line 11 stated the fact of the discharge (and perhaps the reason for it) and the number of men; lines 12, 15, and 17, the dates of enlistment of the soldiers; and lines 13, 14, 16, 18, and 19, the full name of each with his origo. Line 20 contains, as Marichal saw, a date by day and month, and a notation in a second hand, *qua die recesser(unt)*. This last must refer to something which happened on the day mentioned, presumably the award of military decorations or the praemia militiae. The occasion of the discharge need not have been the same for all. *Recesserunt*, if it was chosen to contrast with *accesserunt* (i 29 and 35) and *decedunt/decesserunt* (ii 3 and 12), may denote resignations, while diploma 10 (A.D. 70) is for *causari . . . qui bello inutiles facti ante emerita stipendia exauctorati sunt et dimissi honesta missione*, and diploma 17 (A.D. 71) includes not only classiarii who have served their full enlistment but also those *qui ante emerita stipendia eo quod se in expeditione belli fortiter industrieque gesserant exauctorati sunt*. The presence of men of three different years at any rate makes it certain that some of them and perhaps all had either served longer than the twenty-five-year norm or were being discharged early. For that reason the consulships offer only an approximate clue to the date of the text; but they should not be ignored. See the discussion below.

The fact that four of the men here are natives of Stobi and a fifth of Nicopolis has a bearing also on the not yet conclusively settled question of the cohort's identity. Because the papyrus was found in Egypt, Hunt assumed that this cohort was the coh. I Hispanorum equitata known from Egypt in 83 and 98/99. If Hunt was right, it is not easy to understand how so many men from Stobi got into an Egyptian unit twenty or thirty years before the date of the papyrus; and so this identification becomes an argument against accepting i 1–22 as part of the same text as the remainder. On the other hand, if the men in i 11–22 had been members of the I Hispanorum veterana, perhaps it should be identified with the coh. I Hispanorum attested for Pannonia in A.D. 60 (Dipl. 4), because it is more likely to have received recruits from Stobi and Nicopolis. Conceivably, however, all three cohorts are the same. Dessau 2720 does not, as Syme supposes, show that the Pannonian cohort was still in that province in A.D. 97; so it could have been transferred to Egypt about A.D. 80, brought to Moesia for one or both Dacian wars, sent back to Egypt, perhaps to help quell the Jewish uprising of 116, and then brought to Dacia to form part of the permanent garrison. But that is speculative. For details see the apparatus on i 24.

Lines 21–22 are both easier and more difficult. At least there is a firm date, A.D. 79, as Marichal has shown. It is clear, too, that Optatus' circumstances are different from those of the men in 11–20 because he is being made the subject of a special entry. Marichal regards these lines as recording a normal discharge from an ala or cohors Gallorum; Syme and Gilliam do not discuss them. Marichal rejects my idea that Optatus was buying his discharge before the expiration of the full term of twenty-five years on the grounds of (a) the date of the document, (b) his reading of].*GAL ˙T˙* in place of]*ẸMIT*, (c) the use of *IIS* instead of *HS* for sestertii, and (d) the order *M IIS* instead of *HS M*. Of these, the most serious obstacle to my interpretation would be the date, if 105 is right; and taken together they are enough to cause me to retract my restoration but not my readings. See the apparatus on i 21. Another solution is offered in the suggestion (by letter) of R. W. Davies of Leeds, who proposes for line 21 [*DEPOSITA AD*]*EMIT*, noting that a thousand sesterces is precisely the maximum set by Domitian in A.D. 89 for the savings of individual soldiers.[1]

As for the date of the text, it is clear that my former proposal of A.D. 99 must be revised. Syme has argued convincingly for A.D. 105–108, "either just before the outbreak of the Second War or soon after the annexation of Dacia" (pp. 28, 32, and 33); Gilliam prefers September, 105, with 106 as the only alternative (749–50); Marichal says 16 September 105. The date in i 23, as Gilliam remarks (753), may be that of the document's "dispatch or receipt, or the effective date of its figures, assignments, and so on", or, one may add, the date of its composition. Its chief importance is that it eliminates consideration of any time before the outbreak of the Second War if the year is 105. Since Trajan got the news of Decebalus' attack in time to leave Rome on June 4 (S, p. 28), the war had already been going on for five months or so by the middle of September, and the first summer's campaign was drawing to a close. Cf. Marichal (*ChLA* 127), who had arrived at the date 105 independently. Syme, however, has presented the case for 105 most completely (26–28). It rests on a combination of Faustinus (i 30), Herennius Saturninus (ii 7), and Fabius Iustus, whom Syme discovered in ii 25. (Faustinus and Iustus also appear now in ii 4 and 5, but were not in my earlier text.) Faustinus is known as a governor of Moesia Inferior from a diploma of May 13, 105 (*CIL* XVI 50) and Saturninus as governor of Moesia Superior from a diploma which may be dated between November 19, 102, and August 11, 106 (*CIL* XVI 54, cf. 160

[1] Suet. *Domit.* 7: "geminari legionum castra prohibuit nec plus quam mille nummos a quoquam ad signa deponi." But *adimere*, as proposed by Davies, does not appear to be a suitable verb to express the withdrawal of a man's own *deposita*, because of its regular connotations of forceful or undeserved deprivation.

and S, p. 27). Syme now makes Iustus the successor of Faustinus as governor of Moesia Inferior in 105 (though his reason for wanting the change to take place before May 105 is not clear to me), and ousts Q. Sosius Senecio, placing him instead in Moesia Superior about 100–103 (S, pp. 28–29).

But consistent and logical though these arguments are, they fall somewhat short of proof. Saturninus was certainly governor of Moesia Superior before August 11, 106; but he was consul suffectus in May 100, and nothing proves that he was not governor by 101. Nor is it certain that he was governor at the time of this text, for the papyrus breaks off immediately after his name and we do not know what title he had. Faustinus and Iustus, too, have only the title *legatus* without further definition; but if Faustinus had been replaced by the date of the papyrus, one would expect him to be entitled *tunc legatus*;[2] and this is not the case. As for Iustus, the only evidence that he was governor of Moesia Inferior is the title *legatus* in this papyrus and the fact that he has singulares, whose service is described as *intra prouinciam*, supplied by the I Hispanorum. In an earlier paper Syme envisaged for Iustus "a post on Trajan's staff in the first campaign against the Dacians, or . . . the command of a corps in the field";[3] and in either of these positions he would still have the title *legatus* and there would be singulares on his staff. The same would apply to Faustinus and Saturninus.

Another possible objection to the date of 105 lies in its disregard of i 15. A second examination of the papyrus in 1965 convinces me that the numeral in line 15 is correctly read. Hence only *IIII* or [*V*]*IIII* are possible, for of course none of Domitian's consulates were named because he was under damnatio memoriae. The names of the consuls must also fill the line completely, a space of about 30 letters, as measurements in lines 21–27 show. The only consulate within a reasonable time range which satisfies both these conditions is that for A.D. 75: *Imp. Vespasiano VI et Tito Caesare IIII*; but if the man under this date was not discharged until 105, he had served for thirty years, and the men in i 12–14 a year or more longer if they are listed in order of seniority. This is not impossible but it is unlikely in view of the wholesale discharges which took place in this region in 99 and 100 in preparation for Trajan's first Dacian war.[4] The consulate in i 17, to be sure, which requires about a dozen letters, is best filled by *Imp. Tito VIII*, A.D. 80; but that entry could easily be a causaria missio. All of this seems to point to the year 101, since 99 and 100 should perhaps be eliminated because of Faustinus' and Saturninus' consulships.

But there is reason for supposing that 101 is too late. The time is mid-September, and the fighting in 101 was severe; but so far as can be judged, the cohort had suffered few casualties. There were 119 cavalry on the preceding December 31 (i 27); and if the fifty accessions who came in thereafter were distributed proportionately between infantry and cavalry, the number of the latter may have totaled 130 before deductions. (It is of course possible that all or none of the new men were assigned to the cavalry.) In ii 15, however, after all deductions, the number of cavalry is 110 or more, a reduction of nine to twenty men at most, for all causes. Of these no fewer than 2 and no more than 8 were removed

[2] Cf. **20** 3: *tunc duce;* 20: *tunc praef aeg;* **83** lines 2, 5, 10, 19: *tunc praeff;* lines 4, 8, 14: *tunc cos;* lines 21, 23, 24: *tunc duc.*

[3] R. Syme, "The Friend of Tacitus," *JRS* 47 (1957) 131–35, particularly 132 and 134.

[4] *CIL* XVI 44, 45, 46; Carl Patsch, *Der Kampf um den Donauraum unter Domitian und Trajan* (Beiträge zur Volkerkunde von Südosteuropa, vol. 2, Wien und Leipzig 1937 = Sitzungsber. Akad. Wiss. Wien, philol.-hist. Klasse 217, 1, pp. 3–252) pp. 60–61.

from the cohort by transfer (ii 5 and 6) and one was killed by bandits (ii 10). If there were any losses in combat, they were among the *thetati* in ii 11; but this line contains no notation *in is eq* like ii 5 and 6. It appears a reasonable conclusion that the cavalry at least had had few if any combat losses during the period from January 1 to September 17. This and the various activities detailed elsewhere in the document have the air of preliminaries to a campaign rather than active war; and if that is true, 101 should be eliminated in favor of 100, unless we assume that the cohort spent this entire season in a rear-echelon assignment. The same reasoning would equally rule out 102, 105, and 106; while 104 is less likely because the outbreak of the second Dacian war seems to have caught the Romans by surprise. On the other hand, the fact that the cohort began the year over strength by forty men and added another fifty before the middle of September does not accord well with a date in 103, after the first war was over, or in 107 or later, when Dacia had been annexed.

Nor need the consulships necessarily stand in the way of a date in 100. Even a consulship would require a man's presence in Rome for only a short while if at all.[5] But if the true date proves to be either 101 or 105, with the emperor himself in the field, all three of the men named in this text, Faustinus, Saturninus, and Iustus, could have been Trajan's legati (he would need many such) without holding the governorship of a province.

The date of the text, then, appears to me not finally determined and not likely to be until further evidence becomes available. A.D. 105 is reasonable and attractive but nevertheless based in part on conjectures. I now prefer 100 because of the entries in i 15 and 21–22; but it is clear that their testimony is not conclusive either.

The verso is blank.

[5] Cf. R. Syme, "Consulates in Absence," *JRS* 48 (1958) 1–9.

Col. i

[*ca.* 32]. . [. .]. ḍḷxỵ
] . . . .
]. . . . x . .
]. . . ịọ
]. ḷx[.].
]. [. .]. [.]c̣ị.
]. .
]. . . .
]. cḷx̣[x]x̣[.]iii
]. [.]ṣṣạ

One line blank ?

[*ca.* 32] V.
] C̣OṢ
] SṬOBIṢ
] NICỌP̣OL(i)
[*ca.* 30]I[I]II C̣ỌṢ
]Ṣ STOBIS
[*ca.* 24]. COS
[*ca.* 20] [ ] SṬỌBIS
[*ca.* 19].S [ ] STỌBỊ[S]

[*ca.* 16]Ị̣ḌỊḄỴS [SEPTEMB]Ṛ[I]ḄỴS qua die rẹçẹsser(unt)
One line blank
[ ]ẸMIT M· IIS $\overline{\text{QMC}}$· IMP· VESPAṢ[I]ANO $\overline{\text{VIIII}}$ CỌS
[ ].ẠẸVS OPTATVS anṇo ạẹt
One line blank
[ ] XVI K OCTOBRES *Sept. 16*
[pr]id[i]anum coh ị ḥịṣp ụeter d ṣtobịṣ
[ ].ụṣ arrụn[t]iạnus praef
[summa militum] p· k· ianuarias dxxxxvi
[in is 𐆛 vi dec ii]ịị ẹq [i]ṇ ịs dup [. . .] sesq iii cxix
[ ]ḍ[u]p ped ị sesq ị[.]
[ACCESS]Ẹ[R P]OSṬ K ỊANVẠRIAS
[*ca.* 14] f̣ạustino lẹg ịị
[*ca.* 16]. .ịg [ ] [ ] x̣xx̣[
[*ca.* 20]. .[.].ṃ[.]p̣[. .].nịsus. .lẹg[. . .]ex.[
[*ca.* 13].rạ. .[.]ṣ[.]. . .[. .]ẹ. . . . . .
[*ca.* 12 no]n ṣecutiṣ[. .] [.]i
[summa ac]çẹṣserunt ị[n i]ṣ . . . . . ị
] dḷxxx[x]vi

ChLA has the following readings for lines 1–14 of col. i.

1.]. . . .[. .]. .*ḌLX:* "traces of two large characters (XI?) at the extreme right, apparently not part of the original text."

2.]. . . . . .*Ç*. . .

4.]. . . . .*o.*

5.].*K*. . . . . [*X̣*]. .

6–8. Traces only.

9.]. . . . . . .*ÇḶ*.[.]. . *ỊII*

10.]. . .[. .]*ṣṣ*. . . .

11.]. . . .*VI*[. .]*;* but the number cannot be more than six because only that many names at most follow in lines 13–19. The reading *VI* is possible, though the trace of the *I* is infinitesimal and could be an accidental fleck. In the apparatus Marichal argues that the entries which follow do not represent discharges because all these men "must have entered the service in the same year"; but such is not the case. Discharge was not automatic upon completion of the theoretical term (cf. Tacitus' account in *Annales* I, esp. 17.3–4 and 8, 26.2, 35.2, and 36.4, of the mutinies in Pannonia and Germany); and in the military diplomata the formulae *qui quina et vicena stipendia aut plura* or *quinis et vicenis pluribusve stipendiis emeritis* persisted at least until after the middle of the second century (*CIL* XVI, pp. 157–58). It was also common practice to discharge simultaneously the soldiers of two successive years. See e.g. Dessau 2097 (*CIL* VI 209) and Abdullatif Ahmed Aly, "A Latin Inscription from Nicopolis," *Annals of the Faculty of Arts, Ain Shams University* 3 (1955) 113–146, section a, lines 9–11. Marichal moreover recognizes the possibility that some of these men may be receiving a missio causaria. See also below on line 15, and above, p. 218.

12.]. . . . . . . *CoṢ*

13.]. . . *S*[*t*]*ob*[*ịịs*]

14.] *NIC*[*Ọ*]*ṔOL*(*i*). Nicopolis must be the city in Epirus, for Nicopolis ad Haemum (ad Istrum) and Nicopolis ad Nestum were founded by Trajan and could not have contributed men who were being discharged at this date.

15.]*cos:* NPS;].*ỊỊ* . . .[*ÇoṢ*]*:* ChLA. Marichal, convinced that lines 11–20 cannot refer to discharges, here interprets lines 12–19 as a list of soldiers transferred from another unit (presumably to the coh. I Hispanorum? See also on line 21). This is not impossible; but because of the spacing line 20 is more naturally taken with lines 11–19 than, as Marichal wishes, with 21–22. See below on line 20. For the names of the consuls see p. 220 above.

16.]. . . .*Stoḅịṣ:* ChLA.

17. The blank space before *COS* shows that the consul's name was centered in the column like the headings in ii. It must therefore have contained only about a dozen letters. *IMP. TITO VIII*, A.D. 80, contains eleven and would be suitable. *DIVO* instead of *IMP* would make twelve. Titus' colleague, Domitian, would of course not be mentioned. The fleck of ink remaining at the edge of the papyrus shows that the name did not end with *O*.

19. ChLA makes separate lines of].*S*[and *STOBI*[*S*] (read there as *St*[*ọḅịṣ*]); but lines 20 and 21 show that the papyrus is warped. In line 21 the letters *QMC* rise above *VIIII* by the same amount as *S* in line 19 rises above *STOBIS*. The space between *STOBIS* in this line and line 18 is, however, a bit greater than usual, so that another line is possible; but it could be a consular date as easily as the name and origo of a soldier. In the latter case, read *VI* in line 11. Conversely, if *VI* were sure in that line, the presence and content of ChLA's line 19 would be confirmed. As it is, both remain somewhat less than certain.

20.]. .*post;*]*i̤s qua:* NPS;].*L*.*U̧S*;]*o̤s qua:* F; [*I*]*D*[*I̧B*]*US;*]. .*U̧S:* ChLA. *qua . . . recesser* is ascribed to a reviser. Marichal in the apparatus to this line wishes to make it apply to lines 21–22 because of the date here and the belief that lines 11–19 cannot refer to discharges. But a blank line separates 20 from 21; and the verb *recesser*(*unt*) is plural, whereas there is only one name in 21–22. The first part of the line may have read *donis milit. donati*, *praemiis donati*, or *ciuitate donati*.

21.]*e̤mit*. .*i̤is;* *c*(*oeperunt?*); *Vespasiano* *V̧III:* NPS; [*sacramentum red*]*e̤mit; VIII:* F;].*G̨AL* ·*T*· *MIL*(*ites*) *I*(*nfra*) *S*(*cripti*)*; C*(*oeperunt*)*; VIIII:* ChLA, in app., *d*(*imissi*) *h*(*onesta*) *m*(*issione*) *alae I Fl*(*auiae*) *Gal*(*lorum*) *T*(*auriana*) *mil*(*ites*)—or *mil*(*es*)—*i*(*nfra*) *s*(*cripti*)—or *s*(*criptus*)—and the alternative suggestion that some cohors Gallorum may have been given the surname *T*(*raiana*). Since Marichal has already argued in the apparatus on lines 1–23 that those lines refer to the same unit as the rest of the text, it is not clear how this apparition of an ala or cohors Gallorum is to be reconciled with the presence of the I Hispanorum veterana in line 24. Moreover, ChLA's two supposed *L*'s in *GAL* and *MIL* appear indistinguishable from the *I*'s in the same capital hand and so are probably not *L*'s at all, while *infra scripti* or *scriptus* seems pointless when the only name concerned appears in the very next line. At the beginning of the line,].*G̨A* is no more certain than]*E̤MI*; and the dots on either side of the *T* do not exist. All in all, then, while acknowledging the force of Marichal's arguments against interpreting *M IIS* as *mille sestertiis*, and accepting the reading *VIIII*, I prefer to retain my readings at the beginning of the line as being closer to what was actually written. Expand *c*(*oepit*).

It is somewhat surprising that Vespasian is given the title Imperator instead of Divus.

22.]*o̤rius* or]*e̤rius:* NPS;]. .*e̤us:* F;]. .*LIUS:* ChLA, with *anno s*(*upra*) *s̤*(*cripto*) in a separate line below; in app.: "IULIUS should probably be read." The gentilicium appears to me to be one formed like *Peducaeus* or *Poppaeus*. On *anno* . .*t*, Hunt notes "*antio* might be read for *anno*." ChLA's second *s* instead of *t* is believable, but not the first *s*. As for the spacing of the lines, *anno* is the same distance below *VIIII* as *TVS* of *OPTATVS* is below *QMC* and so belongs in the same line as *OPTATVS*. In the apparatus Marichal states that *anno* refers to what follows; but the cursive hand of *anno* and the blank space of a line between 22 and 23 make this an unattractive proposal. Could *anno* have been added by the same hand as *qua die recesser* in line 20?

23. *a.d.*] *xvi:* NPS; *xv:* F;]*XVI; OCTOBRE*[*S*]: ChLA. In favor of *XVI* is the fact, to which Gilliam calls my attention, that the date *xv kal octobr* begins a section in **66** b ii 9. On the other hand, W. F. Snyder reminds me that *xv kal octobres* was the eve of Trajan's birthday. It is uncertain whether anything preceded *XVI* in the line, but probably nothing.

24. *coh* [*I*]*:* NPS; *Ad p̣ṛ*]*id*[*i*]*anum;* [*His̤*]*p;* [*S̤*]*tobiis:* ChLA; *d*(*egentis*)*:* G. Of the numeral and the next two letters almost nothing remains; but the *p* is certain and the title *ueterana*, as Hunt saw, limits the choice, at least among known cohorts, to the I Hispanorum veterana known from Dipl. 44 to have been in Moesia Inferior in 99 and in Dacia Inferior in 129 and 140 (Dipl. 75 and Boris Gerov, "Zwei neugefundene Militärdiplome aus Nordbulgarien," *Klio* 37 [1959] 196–216). It is possibly the same as the I Hispanorum which was in Pannonia in 60 (Dipl. 4); but Hunt identified it with the coh. I Hispanorum known from Egypt in 83 (Dipl. 29) and in 98 or 99 (*CIL* III 14147[2] = Dessau 8907). The date of the inscription does not preclude the identification, as Lesquier and Cichorius thought; and it seems not to have been noticed that the inscription, though it names the prefects of the I Hispanorum and the II Ituraeorum equitata, states explicitly that P. Claudius Iustus, the prefect of the I Thebaeorum equitata, is the curator of the other two cohorts. This I take to mean that the other two prefects and the bulk of their soldiers are absent from Egypt, leaving Iustus as locum tenens to handle the routine affairs of the token formations which remained at headquarters. Syme's discussion of possible equations of the I Hispanorum veterana with other cohortes I Hispanorum (S, 29–30) reaches no firm conclusions and illustrates very well the difficulties of the question; but the fact that the papyrus comes from Egypt favors the identification with the Egyptian cohort.

Gilliam does not inquire into the identity of the cohort but questions the interpretation of *d* in this line as *quingenariae* (750–51). He prefers to understand *d*(*egentis*) *Stobis*; but this seems open to the objection that *degere* is always used of persons, never of military units, for which *tendere* was the usual verb.

Before *pridianum* there is room for only about seven or eight letters. A consulate might follow the date in line 23, now that there is no consulate in line 30; but the year might have been given at the top of this column, or in a preceding column, so that there is really no basis here for any restoration. I do not understand ChLA's *ad*. The suggestion of *secundum* (ChLA, app.) seems better.

25.]. . .*arro̤n*. .*anus:* NPS;].*s̤s̤a arro̤ afṛ*[*i*]*c̣anus:* F. Marichal reads *Arrun*[*t*]*ianus* independently. Arruntianus' nomen filled some of the lacuna at the beginning of the line; but not necessarily all of it. He is not otherwise known.

26.]*I̧ K*(*al*)*:* H; *summa ad pri*]*d̤*(*ie*)*:* NPS. Expand *p*(*ridie*) *k*(*alendas*).

27. *dup* [*ii*]*:* NPS; *e̤*[*q*(*uites*)*; dup*(*licarii*) [*II*]: ChLA. Expand (*centuriones*), *dec*(*uriones*), *sesq*(*uiplicarii*).

28. *d̤u̧p; sesq v̤*[*i*]*:* NPS; [.*d̤*]*u*[*p*(*licarius*) *p*]*ed*(*es*) *I ses*[*q*(*uiplicar*. .)*:* ChLA. Marichal keeps my former restoration of the number of pedites; but I now believe that the spacing forbids it. Cf. ii 1–2 and 15–16.

29. *ACCEDUN*]*T̨:* G, and see below on lines 35 and 36; *et decesserun*]*ṭ:* NPS; *CEDUN*]*T̨:* F; but the traces before [*P*]*OST* are too angular at the foot for *T*, and **64** i 19 has the perfect tense.

30.]. . .*s̤ta̧no* . . . . .*:* NPS; *barbaro e*]*t* [*f*]*a̧ustino c*[*o*]*s:* F; *tirones probati a Caecili*]*o̤* [*F*]*a̧ustino l̤e̤g:* G; Marichal reads *leg* independently and adds [*p*(*ro pr*(*aetore*)]. There is not room enough, however, for

both *caecilio* and *tirones probati*. A. Stein's suggestion of *uipstano* (*Die Legaten von Moesien* [Budapest 1940] 112–13) is eliminated by the new reading, but was impossible anyway because Vipstanus is a gentilicium. Marichal doubts the existence of the numerals; but the remains of two vertical strokes are plain directly below the first two *x*'s of the numeral in line 26.

31.]*ụṣ:* NPS. G, p. 749, note 1, suggests considering *l*]*ẹg*, with the observation that the line might be shorter than 30 because Fabius Iustus was named instead of Faustinus. ChLA restores accordingly. This reading is possible, as likewise]*ạụg* or]*ṣịg*; the remains are too slight for a choice. But as before, there is not room for *tirones probati* and both names. In the column of numerals there were no previous readings.

32.]. . .[.]*t* . . . . .*c̣*[*o*]*s*. . .*:* NPS; *dat ?*]*i ạ* [*F̣au*]*ṣtịno s*(*upra*) [*ṣ*(*cripto*)] *l*[*e*]*g*(*ato*) *ỊX̣:* ChLA. Not impossible; but the *o* of *Faustino* would be open at the top, unlike any other *o* in the text; and the point of *supra scripto* is not obvious.

33.].*ṭ*. . . . . .[.]. . . . . .*:* NPS; ChLA reports only traces.

34.]. *secutis:* NPS; *cum tyo*]*n secutis*[. .]*:* F; [*accepti ?ex no*]*n:* ChLA. Hunt saw a connection with ii 13; but the circumstances are unclear. Marichal's explanation of *non secuti* as stragglers from other units temporarily added to the strength of the cohort (app. on ii 13) is persuasive; but *accepti ex* scarcely fills the line.

35. *ac*]*c̣ẹṣserunt; l:* G; *summa ? de*]*cesserunt ị*[*n*] *ịṣ eq* . .[. . . . . .]*ị* [*x*]*:* NPS; *summa*]*c̣ẹṣserunt* .[. .]. . . [.]. . *x:* F. Gilliam's detection, confirmed by Skeat, of the correct numeral in line 36 shows that the entries in lines 30–34 are all concerned with accessions, and justifies the altered restorations in lines 29 and 35.

36. The reading is by Gilliam and Skeat; [*reliqui*]*; dx̣xxvi:* NPS and F. Marichal restores [*summa mil*(*itum*) *perfecta*].

Col. ii

in] ị[s ⅄ v]i dec iiii eq̣ in [is d]up̣ ii ṣẹ[s]q̣ iii[
          dup̣ p̣[ed   ]. .[. .]. .[
               EX̣ EIS DECEDVNṬ[
[d]ạṭụṣ ịṇ [c]lasṣẹṃ f̣ḷ moesicam ạdmin[. . .] iusṣu fạustị[ni leg   i
     ]. .[. . . .].ḅ.[. . . . .].ṃ iussu iust[i] leg in is eq i[
. .ọ.[. .]ṇṭ[. . . i]ṇ is eq   i[
remissus ad [he]reṇṇịum saturninụṃ[i
translatus in exeṛc[i]ṭum p̣ạnnọ[n]ị[-   i
perit in aqua   .[i
˙occisus˙ a latroṇ[i]bus   eq ị[
ϑetati   [
  summa decesserunt in is[
restitutus ex non secutis   [i
˙reliqui˙ numero puro . . . . .   [
in is ⅄ vi dec iiii eq in is dup ii sesq iii cx[
          dup peḍ ị ṣesq vi   [
          EX EIS APSENTES   [
in gallia uestịṭụṃ   [
item fumiṇṭat[u]m   [
traṇṣ ẹr.ṛ[e]m equatum in is eq   [.]i   [
ḳạsrae ịṇ praeṣidio in is eq ii   [
ịṇ dardanịa aḍ metella   .[
summa ạpsenṭes extra prouinciam in is eq   . . . .[
          INTRA PROṾINCIAM
sịngụlares fabị˙ ịụṣti legạṭ ịṇ is carus deç ẹ[
officii latiniaṇị p̣roc ạụg   [
piṛob[o]ridauae in p̣ṛaesidio   [
buridạuae in uexịḷḷaṭione   .[
traṇs danuuium in ex̣p̣ẹḍitionem in iṣ ṣẹṣq[
                    eq xx̣iii ṣesq ped ii [

iṭem tras ad annonạ[m] ḍẹf̣ẹṇdendam [
iṭ[e]m exploraṭum [c]ụṃ ạ..uino Ƴ eq˙ [
iṇ.ạ.ạrio ad ṇaues frụmenṭạrịạṣ in is dec i[
aḍ p̣ṛaetorium c[um] librarịịṣs . [
ad ḥaemum ad arṃeṇta addụ[cenda] [
in custodia iu[mentorum i]n ị[s s]esq[*ca.* 7]. ṿ[
iṭem in custodịa .[.]..[ ]. e[
summa uṭraque ạpṣẹṇṭ[es
in is Ƴ i deç ịịị ẹq in iṣ[
ṣ[es]q ped ii [
reliqui p̣ṛạẹsentes [
in is Ƴ v dec i eq in is d[up
dup ped i seṣ[q
ex eis aegri in iṣ[

ii 1. *ị[s] Ƴ [v]ị; ịṇ ịṣ dup:* NPS; *[in is (centuriones) V]I; [ḍ]up; [CX..]:* ChLA.

2. *dup [ped .. s]ẹṣq [...:* NPS; *p[ed(es) I sesq(uiplicarii) VI] ....:* ChLA.

3. The entries which follow show that *decedere* means permanent removal from the rolls of the cohort.

4. [.]....*caṇẹ*.[...]*ạḍẹ..ạṃ..ụiṇ*[.].*us uerecun-[dus:* NPS; *moesicam ạḅ miṣẹ*[...] *iussu k.ecut*.[: F; *Da]ṭụṣ; aḍmiss[us]:* ChLA, and independently *Fausti[ni*, noting that the name is written over the name *Iusti*. I believe that what the clerk first wrote was *ad ministerium fabi iusti*, and that the stroke rising out of the present *f* is the remains of the *b*. I do not understand *admissus*, for *iussu faustini* certainly must be taken with *datus*. For *ministerium* cf. **89** *4* i 3–6 app., and Pliny, *Epist.* 10.27. Expand *fl(auiam)*.

5. [.......]..[....]....*ṣṣ*......*ụṣ:* NPS; *iussu ḷẹgati [a]ug:* F;]..[.......]. *iussu; ḷẹg(ati) V.. in:* ChLA, and *Iusti* independently. I do not see where *V..* comes from. These letters are surely *leg*, with a space after *iust[i*. Cf. i 30.

6. ...[...]...[... *i]n.:* NPS; .*ṛọ*.....*ṣu*.[: F;]...[.].......[... *iṇ*]; *eq(uites) ỊI:* ChLA.

7. *ad*[..]*ṛẹç...um:* NPS. The term *remissus* seems to mean that the man had been attached to the I Hispanorum without being incorporated into it and was now being sent back to his own unit. L. Herennius Saturninus was proconsul of Achaea in A.D. 98/99, consul suffect in 100, and governor of Moesia Superior at some time in the years 102–106 (S 27, and above, pp. 219–20).

8. *exercitum ḍaçịcụṃ:* NPS; *exerc[iṭ]um; P̣anno-[ṇicum:* ChLA. Either *panno[n]i[cum*, implying an undivided province; or *panno[n]i[ae*, to be followed by *inf(erioris)* or *sup(erioris)*.

9. ChLA does not report the traces at the right edge of the papyrus. Possibly *ẹ[q*.

10. ChLA places *eq* in line 11. Marichal noted the dot before *occisus*.

11. *ϑetati [in] ịṣ eq* .[: NPS; ...*[iṇ ịṣ eq( )[:* ChLA; but the *is* is extremely doubtful, and *eq* belongs to line 10.

12. *in is [eq] ị* [: NPS; *is* ...[: ChLA.

13. *ex Tyon:* NPS and F; Hunt: "Tyon is apparently a personal name; but the form is strange." *non:* ChLA, confirmed by Skeat. For *secuti* see on i 34.

14. ChLA records the dot before *reliqui* and the traces which follow *puro*, noting as well that this line is by a second hand.

15. *cx*[is the number of equites; cf. i 29. The net difference between the figure in col. i and in this line is therefore something between a loss of nine and an increase of thirty.

16. *ped* [ ]*ị:* NPS; *peḍ .ị:* F.

18. *Ģṛẹçia vest....:* NPS; *uest[i]ṭ[ụ]ṃ:* ChLA. Hunt: "*Gallia* might well be read but is hardly credible in this context." The *s* is corrected from a *t*.

19. *frụmẹṇtat[u]m:* NPS; *fumị..ṭatum:* F; *fur-ṃẹṇtat[ụ]m:* ChLA. Hunt: "*frumentat[u]m* is very doubtful and in some ways *alimentatum* would be a more satisfactory reading." The word must be an error for *frumentatum*; but the letter after *m* has a serif at the foot and so cannot be *e*. *Item* of course refers to *in gallia*, line 18.

20. *M.r[.]m:* H, "presumably the name of a river"; *mar[u]m:* NPS; *eraṛ[.].n:* F; .[.]*r[ụ]m:* ChLA. The first letter might be *f*; the one between the *r*'s most probably *t*. Before the *m* there is room only for *e*, not *u* or *a*.

21. *ṭyrae:* NPS; *K..rae:* ChLA. For the omission of *t* from *castra*, cf. Arabic *Kasr*, *Qasr*; also *cum epis⟨t⟩ul(is)*, **1** xliv 2, and *e quaes⟨t⟩ur(a)*, **83** 16. The place meant may be the Castra in Dalmatia on the road from Salonae to Servitium, the one in Macedonia on the via Egnatia west of Heracleia Lyncestis, the Castra Augustoflavianensia in Moesia Superior, or Ulcisia Castra in Pannonia Inferior. At all events, it is outside Moesia Inferior: line 23.

castra as a feminine singular is found as early as Accius, *trag.* 16: *castra haec uestra est*; and in *CIL* III 6627 (Dessau 2483, time of Augustus), VI 3289, IX 795, and VIII 9725 = 21531 (A.D. 339).

22. *daṛdaṇịṣ:* NPS; ChLA does not report any traces on the right edge.

23. *eq iii*[: NPS; *eq iii*.[: F; *eq III* [: ChLA. After *eq* one expects numerals; but the characters here are not

easily read so. The first could be *b*, *d*, or *l*, the second is *c*, and the third looks like *i* with a short diagonal stroke through it sloping down from right to left. On the edge of the papyrus is a blur which may be another character. Just possibly *CI*.[corrected to *L*.[?

25. *ịụṣti:* Syme, confirmed by Barns, Turner, and Skeat; *ex. . . . . i leg(ione ?) . . . . tarus dẹçẹ*[*:* NPS; *fabị ụṣẹti lẹgạ*.[. .]. .*ṣạlarus deṃ*[*:* F; *leg(ati) ỊỊỊỊ* [*ị*]*ṇ; dec(urio) I*[*:* ChLA. Gilliam (749, note 2) suggests the possibility that the line ended [*i*]*n is carus deç* .[, "Carus being a decurion included among the *singulares*." Between *leg* and *in* there is space for two letters at most; and I believe that faint traces are visible in the photograph which suit *at*. I do not understand ChLA's *IIII*. The number of singulares would have been entered as in col. i at the right edge, now lost, of the present column. At the end of the line perhaps *ẹ*[*q(uites)*. Aside from the praefectus, the only other person mentioned by name is a centurion in ii 32, though the *sesq* in line 36 may also have been named. But there is no room for a name after *dec* in line 33.

26. *Aug(usti) I:* ChLA. Expand *proc(uratoris) aug(usti)*. Hunt: "possibly the Cornelius Latinianus to whom Hadrian addressed a rescript according to Ulpian ap. *Dig*. XLVIII 5, 28, 6."

27. *piroboridavae:* NPS; [*p*]*raesidio I:* ChLA.

28. *boridavae; vexillatione:* NPS *uexịḷla*[*t*]*ione:* F; *Boridauae; uẹxịḷḷationẹ:* ChLA.

29. *iṣ* ? *i ḍẹ*[*c:* NPS, F, and ChLA; but this is impossible because there are six centurions in line 15 and five in line 42, with *A. . uinus* absent in line 32.

30. *eq x˙iii:* H; *xiii:* NPS; *XVII:* ChLA.

31. *r. . . . endam:* NPS.

32. [*cu*]*m . . ụịno:* NPS; [*c*]*ụṃ pạụlịạno:* F; [*cu*]*ṃ P*[*ạ*]*ụḷḷino:* ChLA.

33. *i.a.ạrio:* H; *. . a.ạrio:* NPS; *iṇ aụario:* F; *in aḷario:* ChLA. NPS: "The line may begin with *in*, but nothing satisfactory then suggests itself for *a.ario*. *c*, *l*, or *t* would be suitable for the letter after the first *a*. Perhaps it is a place-name." F: "one might consider '*in* ⟨*n*⟩*auario*,' understanding '*navarium*' as the equivalent of 'navalia'. No such word is in the lexica; but in view of the scribe's other neologisms it may not be impossible." ChLA: "*Alarius*, 'of the wing', *alarii*, 'auxiliary cavalry' is classical; *alarium* then could designate in camp parlance 'the quarters of the wing' for example."

34. *ẹụ*[*m*] *librariis:* NPS; [*p*]*ṛaetorium; c*[*um l*]*ịbrariiss:* ChLA. The doubling of the final *s* of *librariis* remains unexplained.

36. *ịu*[. . . . .]. .[. . .].*ọ*[*:* NPS; ChLA does not report anything to the right of *sesq*. The restoration *iumentorum* is Rostovtzeff's. To fit the space, it would have to be abbreviated to *iument*.

37. *custodia ạ*[– – 15 – –]*ẹ*[*:* NPS; *custodia. . . .* [. . . . .].[*:* ChLA.

38. *utraque:* Skeat and ChLA; *apsen*[*ṭẹṣ:* ChLA; *vera que apṣẹṇ*[*s erat:* NPS; *uera que ạpṣẹṇṣ*[*:* F.

40. [*ṣẹṣq(uiplicarii)*]*:* ChLA.

TRANSLATION

i 20 . . . . on the day on which they retired from service.

21–22 . . EUS OPTATUS, WHO ENLISTED IN A.D. 79, 1000 SESTERCES. . . . YEAR . .

SEPTEMBER 16,

pridianum of the cohors I Hispanorum Veterana quingenaria at Stobi,

25].us Arruntianus, prefect.

Total of soldiers December 31, 546

among them 6 centurions, 4 decurions; cavalry 119,

among them [ ] duplicarii, 3 sesquiplicarii;

1 infantry duplicarius, [ ] sesquiplicarii.

ACCESSIONS AFTER JANUARY 1

30]Faustinus the legatus 2

31 [ ] 30

34 [. . .] the stragglers

35 [Total] accessions 50

[Grand total] 596

ii 1 among them 6 centurions, 4 decurions; cavalry [ ]

among them 2 duplicarii, 3 (?) sesquiplicarii,

[ ] infantry duplicarii,

FROM THESE THERE ARE LOST

given to the Classis Flavia Moesica, for [?] by order of Faustinus the legatus

5] by order of Iustus the legatus, among them 1 cavalryman

. . . among them 1 cavalryman

sent back to Herennius Saturninus [1

transferred to the army of Pannonia [1
drowned [1
10 killed by bandits, 1 cavalryman [1
11 killed (in combat?) [
Total lost, among them [
restored from the stragglers [1
Balance, net,
15 among them 6 centurions 4 decurions; cavalry, 110 (or more)
among them 2 duplicarii, 3 sesquiplicarii;
16 infantry duplicarii [ ], sesquiplicarii 6

FROM THESE, ABSENT,

in Gaul to get clothing
likewise to get [grain?]
20 across the Erar? (river?) to get horses, among them [ ] cavalrymen
at Castra in garrison, among them 2 cavalrymen
in Dardania at the mines
Total absent outside the province, among them [ ] cavalrymen

INSIDE THE PROVINCE

25 orderlies of Fabius Iustus, the legate, among them Carus, decurion[
in the office of Latinianus, procurator of the Emperor
at Piroboridava in garrison
at Buridava in the detachment
across the Danube on an expedition, among them [ ] sesquiplicarii
30 23 cavalrymen, 2 infantry sesquiplicarii
likewise across to defend the crops
likewise scouting with the centurion A..uinus, [ ] cavalrymen
in ? at the grain-ships, among them 1 (?) decurion
at headquarters with the clerks
35 to the Haemus (mountains) to bring cattle
on guard over draft animals, among them [ ] sesquiplicarii
likewise on guard over ?
Total absent of both categories
among them 1 centurion, 3 decurions; cavalry, among them [ ]
40 2 infantry sesquiplicarii
Balance present
among them 5 centurions, 1 decurion; cavalry, among them [ ] duplicarii,
1 infantry duplicarius, [ ] sesquiplicarii
from these, sick, among them [

64

Pridianum of the Coh. I Augusta Praetoria Lusitanorum Equitata

BGU 696 (inv. 6870) — August 31, A.D. 156

Transcription, commentary, and facsimile: Th. Mommsen, *Ephemeris Epigraphica* 7 (1892) 456–67 and plate 3; cited as **M**.

Facsimile with transcription:

1. *Palaeographical Society Facsimiles of Manuscripts and Inscriptions*, ser. 2, vol. 2 (London 1889–94) no. 165.
2. Wessely, *Schriftt.*, no. 6.
3. H. Delitsch, *Geschichte der abendländischen Schreibschriftsformen* (Leipzig 1928) plate 1; contains only col. i 1–21.
4. *EL*, plate 16, no. 24; stops at col. i, line 38; col. ii, line 35.

Transcription and commentary:

1. Th. Mommsen, *Gesammelte Schriften* 8.553–66; repeated from *Ephemeris Epigraphica* 7.
2. R. O. Fink, "Mommsen's *Pridianum*: *B.G.U.* 696," *AJP* 63 (1942) 61–71; cited as **F**.

Commentary:

1. J. F. Gilliam, "Paganus in *B.G.U.* 696," *AJP* 73 (1952) 75–78.
2. Idem, "An Antonine Consul Suffect," *CP* 55 (1960) 177–78.

Text and translation: *Sel. Pap.*, no. 401; Mommsen's text. Only i 1–33 and ii 13–28 are used.

Text: *CPL*, no. 118; Daris, no. 9.

This text contains none of the perplexities of the preceding one. It carries its title in full in lines 1–2 and an exact date in the combination of lines 2 and 11.

Mommsen's numbering of the lines is retained here to facilitate comparison. Actually, col. i contains only 40 lines.

Col. i

PRIDIANVM COH Ị AVG PR LVS EQ
MENSIS AVGVS`TI′ SILVANO ET AVGVRINO COS A.D. 156
QVAE HIBERNATVR CONTRAPOLLO
NOSPOLI MAIORE THEBAIDIS EX VIII

IDVS IVLIAS PONTIANO ET RVFỊṆ[O] COS July 8, 131
P̣ṚẠẸFẸCTVS M ỊVLỊVS M F TRIBV
QVIR SIḶVANVS ḌỌMO THVBVRSI
CA MILITARE COEPIT EX IX KAL MA
IAS COMMODO ET LATERANO COS April 23, 154
LOCO ALLI PVDENTILLI
Two lines blank
PRỊDIE KAL ṢEPTEMBRES
SVMMA Ṃ. . . . .Ẹ KAL DV
IANVARIAṢ ỊN IS ɣ VI DEC IỊI
ẸQ CXIV DṚOṂ XVIIII
PEDITES CCCLXIII
One line blank
ET POST KAL IANVARIAS ACCESSER
FACTVS EX P̣ẠG̣ẠNO A SEMPRO ɣ I
NIO LIBERALE PRAEF AEGVPT
siluano et augurino cos
sextus sempronius caṇdidụṣ ex v kal April 27, 156
maias
REIECTVS AB ALAE I THRAC DEC I
MAVRETANIAE AD VIRCAM CHOR
TIS
uibio uaro cos
a flauius uẹspasianụs ex vi nonas March 2, 134
ṃartias
TIRONES PROBẠTI VOLVN VIIII
TARỊ A ṢEṂP̣RONIO LIBERALAE
PRAEF AEG IN IS EQ I DROM I
in ɣ herculani siluano et augurino cos
philon isiognis ẹx̣ [. .] ṇonas maias May 2–6, 156
a[p]ọllos hẹrminuṣ ẹx̣ idibuṣ ssis May 15
in ɣ marci eodem cos
anubas amṃ[on e]x̣ [i]ịi nonas May 5
ṣṣạṣ
in ɣ gaiani [eodem] cos
c sigillius ual[e]ns
in ɣ semproniani eodem [cos
ammonius[

i 1. Expand *coh(ortis) I Aug(ustae) Pr(aetoriae) Lus(itanorum) Eq(uitata)*.

5. *RUFIṆỌ:* EL; *iudus:* Daris, a misprint.

7. The last *V* of *SILVANVS* has been corrected from *O*.

10. *AELI:* M and EL; but the reading is clear. This may very likely be the Q. Allius Q. f. Col. Pudentillus, *augur curiae xxiiii* and *minister Larum Aug.* of *CIL* x 7953 (Dessau 6766). See now P. Clermont-Ganneau 1 b, *JJP* 4 (1950) 327–37, and J. F. Gilliam, *CP* 55.177 and note 5. Daris cites *SB* vi 9228, 23.

14. *SUMMA AD [PR]*x*:* M; *SUMMA AḌ PR.:* EL; *SUMMA MỊḶ(ITUM) [PE]ṚF̣(ECTA):* F. Gilliam, *PDur.* 82, note 6, rejects Fink's restoration and proposes *SUMMA ṂỊ[L(itum)] P̣Ṛ[I]ḌỊE.* This is attractive, but perhaps too long for the space. All that is certain is that the next letter after *SUMMA* is either *A* or *M*, and that the last letter before *KAL* is *F* or *E*.

15. *Ianuaria[s i]n:* Daris.

17. *CCCLXII[I]:* EL, surely a misprint.

20. The centurio-symbol between *SEMPRO* and the numeral was regarded by Mommsen and in EL as simply a mark of division. On *pagano* see Gilliam,

AJP 73.75–78, who demonstrates that in such a context as this the word means merely "civilian."

25. *ALA EI:* M and EL. Mommsen corrects to *Ala II*, stationed in Mauretania; but Cichorius is probably right in reading *Alae I*, which was then in Egypt, since all the other units named here were also in Egypt. See further Fink, *AJP* 63.66. *Reiectus* here means "sent back"; and *uircam* (read *uirgam*) is the *uitis*, the centurion's and decurion's staff of authority.

28. Vibius Varus is named alone as consul because his colleague, L. Iulius Ursus Servianus, was executed by Hadrian in A.D. 136. See Groag, *RE* 10.888–90, s.v. "Iulius."

28–29. This is the date of Vespasianus' original enlistment, not of his transfer.

32. Daris reports *ex [n]onas* incorrectly as the reading of F.

35. *[ap]olloni[u]s ..is ex ..nonas:* M; *Ạpolloṇịụs ....is ex̣ ..nonas;* EL; *e]x nonas:* Daris. H. I. Bell suggests in a letter than Philon's second name may have been "Isiogenes on the analogy of Origenes, incorrectly written." Cf. also "Diogenes," "Hermogenes," and possibly "Theognis."

36. *a[po]llo ....min ....idibus ....:* M; *A[p]ollos Iu..min..ẹx̣ idibus ....ịs:* EL and Daris; *a[p]ọllos .. ia.minuṣ:* F. Expand *s(upra)s(cript)is* here and *s(upra)s(cript)as* in line 39. These are at present the oldest known examples of abbreviation by contraction in a secular document, antedating by thirty-five or forty years the *IIo* for *(secund)o* of *PBerol.* 6866 (**70**), on which see Marichal, *Occ.* 77–79. The Chester Beatty papyri are even earlier; but Bell points out in his letter that one cannot argue from these purely Christian texts that similar practices were already followed in pagan secular documents.

37. *Masịci:* EL and Daris.

38. *Am... i nonas:* EL; *Ammṃ[on.. e]x nonas:* Daris; *amṃ[on e]x .i nonas:* F. There is room only for *ammon* as the second name. The date follows from the fact that both *ii nonas* and *vii nonas* are impossible and *iiii nonas* highly improbable for reasons of space.

39. This line and the rest of the column are not reproduced in EL. M offers no reading; but see above on line 36.

41. *Valens.[:* Daris.

Col. ii

in ϒ gaṇ[seuero et sabiniano cos] 155
c iulius [ex kal] December 14–31
ian[uarias]
siluano et a[ugurino cos]
heraclammon q[ex ..] March or May 2–6, 156
nonas m[
in turma artemidọṛ[i eodem cos]
eq hermacis apync̣[his ex] March 16–April 12
apriles
in turma saluiani ẹọdẹ[m cos]
dro cṛọnius barbasatis ex xvi[April 14–16
kal maias
ACCEPTI EX LEG II TR FORṬ[I]
DATI AB EODEM PRAEFECṬ[O]
AEGVPTI
ịn ϒ lappi condiano et maximo cos
ualerius tertius ex viii kaḷ March 25, 151
apriles;
in ϒ c̣andidi torquato et iuliano cos
horatius herennianus ex iv idus Nov. 10, 148
noụembres
TRANSḶATVS EX COH I FL CIL
in ϒ candidi comṃ[odo] et pompeianọ cọṣ 136
mae`ui´us margellus [ex]
ITEM TRANSLAṬ[I EX

in 7 lappi seuero [et stloga? *or* sabiniano? cos] — Feb. 6–12, 141 or 155

c longinus apollọ[ex]
idus feb[ruarias]
in 7 semproniạ[ni ex]
commodo et[pompeiano? *or* laterano? cos] — 136 or 154
eros ẹ[
ITEM FACTI ẸQ̣[VITES
in turma arte[midori ex]
seuero et[stloga? *or* sabiniano? cos] — 141 or 155
ision petsireoṣ .[
in turma s[
glabr[ione et homullo cos] — 152

ii 1. *gai[ani:* M; *Ga[iani]:* EL and Daris; *ga⟨ia⟩ṇ[i:* F; but this cannot be the same man as the centurion of i 40. When more than one man was assigned to a century, they were listed together, like Philon and Apollos in the century of Herculanus (i 34–36) or Iulius and Heraclammon here (ii 1–6). Therefore if these men had been assigned to the century of Gaianus they would have been listed in col. i where Gaianus first appears. There were already six centurions on January 1, before the addition of Sempronius Candidus; and it appears that for at least a time there were seven centurions in the cohort, since all are named—Herculanus (i 34), Marcus (i 37), Gaianus (i 40), Sempronianus (i 42), Gan- (ii 1), Lappus (ii 16), and Candidus (ii 19)—this in spite of Hyginus' statement (*De mun. castr.* 27) that a cohors equitata quingenaria had six centuries. Perhaps Herculanus or one of the others was later discharged or transferred; but there is no indication in the extant part of the papyrus that this had happened by August 31.

The seeming lack of order in the month-and-day dates of enlistment of the nine tirones is to be explained by the fact that the order adopted is that of the centuries (see R. O. Fink, "*Centuria Rufi, Centuria Rufiana*, and the Ranking of Centuries," *TAPA* 84 [1953] 210–15).

The restoration of the names of the consuls follows from *ian*[in line 3 and *siluano et a*[*ugurino* instead of *eodem cos* in line 4. These show that Iulius' enlistment was effective as of December 155, but came too late in the year to appear in the previous pridianum. Cf. the situation in **87**, where the letter announcing six recruits was received five days after the effective date of their incorporation into the cohort.

2. [*ex kal.*]*:* Daris.

5. *Heraclammon Us*[*:* M and EL.

8. *..i hermacisapyni:* M; *i*J *hermacisapyni:* Pal. Soc.; *in* (*centuria*) *hermacisapyni:* EL; *eq*(*ues*) *hermacisapyn*.[*:* F. But for the second name see Preisigke, *Namenbuch*, s.v. Ἀπύγχις; from this the division and hence the first name follow.

11. *..ccinius barbaiatis ex xv*[*:* M; *nuocrịnis barbaiatis ex*[*:* EL; *....i Cronius Barbasatis:* Daris. The *d* of *dro*(*madarius*) is to the left of the *i* of *in* in the preceding line so that *dro* appears to have been added after the name was written. This may account for the unusual abbreviation.

16–17. From this point to the end of the papyrus the dates are those of the soldiers' first enlistment, not the date of their assignment to the coh. I Lusitanorum.

23. *Commodo:* Daris; *co*[*s:* EL.

25. *TRANSLAT*[*US:* EL; but the plural is necessary because the names of two men follow.

26. Mommsen, followed by EL, restored Stloga as the name of the second consul, but there is no basis for a choice between him and Sabinianus.

29–31. The appearance of the consuls' names in the line following the indication of the century shows that the dating formula has changed from consulship-name-day-month, as in all preceding entries, to day-month-consulship-name. The latter order continues to the end of the papyrus. If the difference is significant, I do not see the reason, since lines 26–28, in the same division of the text, retain the original order. The spacing out of the consuls' names in lines 30 and 34 shows that they occupied the whole line by themselves; and the same is true of the soldier's name in line 31.

30. As in line 26, there is no way to choose between Pompeianus and Lateranus. M and EL print [*Laterano? cos.*

31. *Eros e*[*x:* EL; but the letter at the edge of the papyrus must be the beginning of Eros' second name. The form of the letter is abnormal for an *e* in this hand; but no better reading is apparent.

32. [*equites:* Daris. The restoration *ẸQ̣*[*VITES*, first proposed by Cumont (see *PDur.* 94 and Cumont, *Fouilles de Doura-Europos* [Paris 1926] 314–17), is confirmed by the fact that the next two men are assigned to turmae instead of centuries.

35. *..spon Petsireo*.[*:* M and EL; *Petsireo*.[*:* F; *Petsireo:* Daris. But the second name is in the genitive, as often. The last *s* has a peculiar form because it was ligatured with the following letter.

36. *S*[*alviani:* Daris.

36–37. These two lines are not reproduced in EL.

TRANSLATION

PRIDIANUM OF THE MONTH OF AUGUST, A.D. 156, OF THE COH. I AUGUSTA PRAETORIA LUSITANORUM EQUITATA, WHICH HAS HAD ITS HEADQUARTERS AT CONTRAPOLLONOSPOLIS MAIOR OF THE THEBAID SINCE JULY 8, 131. THE COMMANDER, MARCUS IULIUS SILVANUS, SON OF MARCUS, TRIBE QUIRINA, HOME THUBURSICA, ENTERED THE SERVICE APRIL 23, 154, IN THE PLACE OF ALLIUS PUDENTILLUS.

13 AUGUST 31.
TOTAL OF SOLDIERS JANUARY 1: 505
AMONG THESE 6 CENTURIONS, 3 DECURIONS, 145 CAVALRY, 18 CAMEL-RIDERS, AND 363 INFANTRY.

AND AFTER JANUARY 1 WERE ADDED:
20 COMMISSIONED FROM A CIVILIAN BY SEMPRONIUS LIBERALIS, PREFECT OF EGYPT: 1 CENTURION
Sextus Sempronius Candidus, April 27, 156.
25 SENT BACK FROM THE ALA I THRACUM MAURETANA TO A COMMISSION IN THE COHORT: 1 DECURION
30 Aulus Flavius Vespasianus, enlisted March 2, 134.
RECRUITS, VOLUNTEERS, APPROVED BY SEMPRONIUS LIBERALIS, PREFECT OF EGYPT, AMONG THEM ONE CAVALRYMAN AND ONE CAMEL-RIDER: 9
in the century of Herculanus, 156,
35 Philon Isiognis, May [2–6];
Apollos Herminus, May 15;
in the century of Marcus, same year,
Anubas Ammon, May 5;
40 in the century of Gaianus, same year,
Gaius Sigillius Valens, [*month and day*];
in the century of Sempronianus, same year,
Ammonius [*surname, month and day*];
ii 1 in the century of Gan[-, 155]
Gaius Iulius [*name*], January [1–13];
156,
5 Heraclammon Q[*name, March or May 2–6*];
in the squadron of Artemidorus, same year,
cavalryman Hermacis Apynchis [*March 16–April 12*];
10 in the squadron of Salvianus, same year,
camel-rider Cronius Barbasatis, April [*14–16*];
RECEIVED FROM THE LEG. II TRAIANA FORTIS, SUPPLIED BY THE SAME PREFECT OF EGYPT:
in the century of Lappus,
Valerius Tertius, enlisted March 25, 151;
in the century of Candidus,
20 Horatius Herennianus, enlisted November 10, 148.
TRANSFERRED FROM THE COH. I FLAVIA CILICUM:
in the century of Candidus
Maevius Margellus, enlisted [*month and day*], 136.

ALSO TRANSFERRED FROM [
in the century of Lappus
Gaius Longinus Apollo [ ], enlisted February [*6–12, 141 or 155*].
in the century of Sempronianus [*enlisted month and day, 136 or 154*]
Eros E[*name*].
ALSO PROMOTED TO CAVALRYMEN
in the squadron of Arte[midorus, *enlisted month and day, 141 or 155*]
Ision son of Petsiris;
in the squadron of S[*name, enlisted month and day*] 152.

65

Summary of the Dispositions of Soldiers at Dura

PDur. 94 (inv. D. Pg. 6 recto) ca. A.D. 240
Now in the Bibliothèque Nationale, Paris, numbered Suppl. Gr. 1354, 3

Transcription, commentary, and facsimile:

1. F. Cumont, *Monuments Piot* 26 (1923) 40–46 and plate 7.
2. Idem, *Fouilles de Doura-Europos (1922–1923)* (Paris 1926) no. 6, pp. 314–17 and plate 107; cited as **C**.
3. *Final Rep.* v, no. 94 and plate 60, 2; *edidi.*

Text: *CPL*, no. 345, reproduces Cumont's text.

This bit of parchment is too small for an unquestionable classification of the text. It bears some resemblance to both the monthly summaries and to **66**; but the monthly summaries seem to be concerned entirely with *absentes* and *praesentes*, not with *facti equites* (line 7), who might be in either category, and *missi honeste emeriti* (8), who are neither. Similarly, **66** has several entries with forms of *opinio*, but no entries like *chafer aura* (2) or *kastello* (3). Consequently, this text has been placed here as having some resemblance to the pridiana, though I cannot affirm that it is one. The unit concerned may be the XX Palmyrenorum; but since the parchment did not come from the archives of the cohort in the temple of Azzanathkona, it could equally well belong to any of the detachments stationed at Dura.

The date is based partly on paleographical considerations, partly on the fact that the material used is parchment, since all of the military texts from Dura on parchment seem to be relatively late.

The verso is *PDur.* 48, a list of women's names. The alphabet is Greek; but the women clearly belong to Arabic or Palmyrene families. On the recto, too, the numerals in lines 4–6 have been scribbled over with another text in Greek which is upside down to the Latin.

	].[	].	iii[
	c̣ḥafer aụra	ṃ[i]l	ii[
	kastello	mil	i [
z	ad[...]mọpiṇị	drom	ii [
	ad[op]inion	mil	iv[
	item ad opin[	]ạṛẹṇḍ[	
	facti equites	mil [	
	missi h emer	mil	ii[
		toti	m[
	ṛel numerare		✳[
		]f̣ạc̣ṭ [.]..[	

2. ..*tferara:* C; *ạ.ra:* D; but cf. *chafer auira* in **1** and **2**.
3. Cf. the *castellum arabum* in **1** and **2**.
4. *a....mopimadac̣:* C. Probably *ad* [...]*m opini*(*on*-). For the notation *z*, see on **1** xxxv 17. *drom* has been corrected from *mil.*
5. *ad...imium* and *ịịị*[*:* C; *ii*[*:* D.
6. *ad opim....:* C. It does not seem possible to read *p*]*ẹṭẹṇḍ*[*am*, as in **66** b ii 1; but the traces might be the remains of *quaerendam*. Cf. **2** xii 28, xxxv 17, and xli 17.
9. The use of *toti* instead of *summa* or *omnes* is remarkable at this date.
10. *el numerare:* C. The construction of the infinitive is not evident. The traces at the end of the line are probably the symbol for denarii.
11. *ẹṇḍ:* C.

Unclassified

66

Strength Report of the Coh. XX Palmyrenorum

PDur. 95 (inv. D. P. 34 recto) — Between October 250 and July 251

Transcription, commentary, and facsimile (frag. b only): *Final Rep.* v, no. 95 and, frag. b only, plate 62; *edidit* Gilliam.

Commentary: R. W. Davies, "Ratio and Opinio in Roman Military Documents," *Historia* 16 (1967) 115–18.

Gilliam in his publication of this enigmatic text has described its difficulties very lucidly. It is not all of a piece; nor do we know the relationship of one section of it to the others, or how much of the whole is represented by the existing fragments.

The one element common to all is that they are somehow concerned with the strength of the cohort. Frag. a i 6 and 8, and a ii 4 certainly designated categories of soldiers who were then named individually; and the same is true of frag. b i 6 and 24. Frag. b i 29–33, and ii 1–8 and 27–29, are occupied with returns, or failure to return, of soldiers *q d p* on various assignments; and b ii 9–15 state the total strength of the cohort on September 17 and repeat on consecutive days through September 23 (or even September 24 in line 16) that the strength has remained unchanged. This series of no changes is broken by either line 16 or line 17; in line 18 a *q d p* reappears; and in lines 21–26 the entries are like those of frag. a i 9–13 and ii 5–18.

Entries of the last sort all begin with the usual identification by century and year of enlistment in one line, with the soldier's name in the next, then a date by day, month, and year, either immediately after the name or after a series of several names, as in a ii 5–12. The date of enlistment proves to be 240 in five of the nine places where it can be read; the others are 238, 244, 246, and a doubtful 233. The year of the day-and-month dates is 249 twice and 250 four times. Eleven men in all are affected by the circumstances, not necessarily the same for everyone, which produced these entries.

Gilliam rightly notes (*Final Rep.* v, p. 290) that the entries follow a chronological order of the months and days, clearly shown in b i 9–10, 20–21, 26–27, and ii 9–10. Dates by day and month also occur in **29**, which seems to record accessions by transfer, **31**, and **64**. The last, of course, is a pridianum; but **31** has not been securely classified and may be part of just such a text as the present one.

Most of the *q d p* items are concerned with preparation for payment of the stipendium. In this preparation Gilliam distinguishes two steps, the ratio and the opinio. Whether the opinio preceded or followed the ratio is uncertain: but Davies argues persuasively that the opinio was an estimate and came first, followed by the ratio as an audit after the pay had actually been given out to the soldiers.

The date of the text can be fixed within fairly narrow limits. The latest year mentioned is Decius' second consulship, 250; and in b ii 25 the clerk may at first have written *octobribus*, perhaps the Kalends or the Nones, but in any event later than *ṿịị[ii kal o]c̣ṭ* in line 15. On the other hand, Decius is called *dominus noster* throughout, so that the text must antedate the arrival in Dura of the news of his death, which occurred no later than the middle of June, 251. The text can therefore hardly be later than the end of June or the beginning of July of that year.

The verso is **4**.

Frag. a

Col. i

k[a]l aụ[g
]ạd praeṭọṛi[ ]ṣ
] a.[..]....[
]Ṭ^{u} romul[l]ị ...[.].ọ.[
]........eṛị[
.[.].. mil iị...[.]ẹ ṃịḷ .[
].........soni.
.e.˙ praesidis mil i
Ƴ] ṃ[arin]i pos sabino ii cos A.D. 240
]ḍionyṣius iịị id
ạug[u]ṣṭạ[s d n]
[d]ẹc̣ị[o] ạụg ii ẹṭ g[rato cos 250
]...s.ị.cị.......[

Quoted matter in the following commentary is from Gilliam's apparatus in *PDur*.

a i 1. Elsewhere in the text, e.g. line 10 of this fragment, such dates by day and month follow the name of a soldier.

2.].*ḍ*.*rạẹ*. . . [*:* D. "In all other cases where the day is given, the year is 249 or 250, but I cannot read the names of the consuls of either year . . . in line 2. Perhaps line 1 ended with *cos s*(*upra*)*s*(*criptis*) or the like. A possible reading in line 2 is]*ạḍ prạẹṭọṛ*[*ium*." Probably *praeṭọṛi*[*um praesidi*]*ṣ*.

4.]. *Roman*[*u*]*ṣ* . . [. .]. [*:* D. Possibly *romul˙*.

5.]. . . . . . *ẹ*. [*:* D.

6.]. *mil II*[.].*ẹ*. . . [*:* D. This line perhaps introduces a category of soldiers of which the assignment in line 8 is a subdivision.

8. "*ad pr*]*ạẹṭ*(*orium*) *praesidis* may be possible." There are no traces of ink to the left of .*e*.; so perhaps *ọff˙ praesidis*, though the second *f* is not satisfactory.

9. [𐆛 *Marin*]*i:* D.

10. It is odd that this man has but one name.

11. No reading in D.

12. [*d n D*]*ẹc̣ị*[*o*]*:* D.

13.]. . . *c*. . . . . . [*:* D.

Col. ii

ad .[.]. m[i]l . . . .[. .]. .[
aç̣[.]ṣ[.]ul. .e tuṇç̣ p̣ṛ[
. .[.]ẹṣex. . .si iteṃ[
pḷ.ụ.tụ. . .ṭ mil x[
𐆛] geṛ[m]ạṇ[i] .[. . .]. .[
]i.[ ].[.]. .[
]aụrel max̣im. .[
𐆛 mạṛini pr sạbinọ [ii cos 240
aụrel malchus
𐆛 ṃariṇị p̣ọṣ sabin[o ii cos] 240
aurel antoninus kal i[
aẹmilliạṇo ịị ẹṭ ạq[uilino cos] 249
𐆛 achei sạbino ii cos 240
aụṛẹl . . . .[.]anus iị[i]ị kạ[l]
aug aemiḷliano ii et [aquilino cos] 249
𐆛 germani praesenṭe eṭ ạḷḅ[i]ṇ[o cos] 246
[. . . .]idaṣ c̣ḷ.ḅ. . . .[
]xii kal feḅ[

a ii 1–18. "Presumably lines 1–4, which may have continued the end of Col. i, state some circumstance or event which affected the men in lines 5–18."

1. *ad*. . . . .[. . .]. *:* D.

2. No reading in D.

3. . .[.]. .*ẹxạụinite*.[*:* D; "At the end of line 3 *item* is possible."

4. *p̣*. . . . . *:* D.

5. 𐆛 *Ç̣ẹṛṃạṇi:* D.

6. No reading in D.

7. "It is impossible to decide between *Max̣iṃụṣ* and *Max̣iṃịṇ*[*us*"; but there is no instance of the latter name at Dura.

11–12. Gilliam suggests that this date may apply also to the names in lines 7 and 9.

14. *Ị*[*II*] *Ḳ*[*a*]*ḷ:* D.

16. *Ạlb*[*ino:* D.

17. [. . . .].*ḍạocl*. . . . .[*:* D; "Though the traces . . . would permit one to read [*Aure*]*l Ḍạoclẹ*[*i*]*ḍẹṣ*, they offer no particular support for the last few letters, and *Dao-* for *Dio-* raises doubts." Perhaps [*zeb*]*idas* or [*au*]*idas*.

Frag. b

Col. i

m]ai ḍ[n] ḍecio
aug ii et grato co]ṣ A.D. 250
]id˙ aug
]

atilio] c̣ọṣṃino u c

]ṃịl i

d n]decio

aug ii et grato co]ṣ A.D. 250

]x̣iiii kal

].

Three lines lost

]ạug ẹṭ[

]ṭṭịṇị . . . [

]

Ƴ m]ạrini pr ṣạḅịṇo ii c̣ọs 240

]aurel antoṇịnuṣ

].iẹra poṇ[t]ịano c̣ọṣ 238

]aurel maximus x̣ṿ[ka]l

sep d n decio aug iị

eṭ grato cos 250

].. eṭ ịn [i]ṣ q d p ad hor..ṣ

]pr mil i

]... pẹṛegrino cọṣ 244

si]luanus iii n°

sept ḍ n dẹc̣io aug ii

e[t g]rato cos 250

].[.]. ẹx̣ q d p ad opini

ọṇeṃ stip kal maiar˙

ṃịḷ[..] in ḥịṣ [o]ṛ[d] i[

]..[.]..ẹl ii

]. e[.].ṣis ex iṣ q d p[

b i 5–10. "One might reconstruct . . . these lines as: [*Probatus ab Atilio*] *Cosmino u*(*iro*) *c*(*larissimo*) [*co*(*n*)*s*(*ulari*) *n*(*ostro*)] *mil i* [his century, *d*(*omino*) *n*(*ostro*)] *Decio* [*Aug ii et Grato co*]*s* [the soldier's name] *XVIII Kal* [*Sept cos s s* or the consuls repeated in full]. Atilius Cosminus is named as governor (*consularis*) in January and March, 251, in [**83**]."

9.]*X̣ṾỊII:* D.

14. *A*]*ug:* D; "*A*]*ug* is part of a consular date, i.e. *Decio Aug*, . . . if the chronological sequence proposed . . . is correct." If *et* is right, as it appears to be, *ii* was omitted. Is this then Decius' first, suffect, consulship, held perhaps under Philip?

15.]..*ịnị*[..].[*:* D. A soldier's name?

19. "The centurion's (or decurion's) name . . . may end]*aieura* or]*aioura*." With him, if a centurion, we should have the full complement—Germanus, Bargas, Marinus prior, Marinus posterior, Achaeus, and].*iera*. Gilliam also notes that the senior consul of this year, Fulvius Pius, is omitted, implying damnatio memoriae.

23.]..*e*..*n* [.]*.:* D; "Possibly *ad hor*(*deum*)." The last three characters in the line might be *cos*, or the last could be the centuria-sign. Cf. also *corcosio* in ii 28.

24. "Perhaps (*centuria*) *Marini*] *Pr*(*ioris*) should be restored." But this is doubtful because of the position of *pr* in the line.

25.].[.. *P*]*ẹregrino:* D.

26. Expand *no*(*nas*). The *o* is written above the *n*.

29.]. . . . . *q d p:* D; "*Reversi*, *r*(*eversi*) *ex is*, or the like, presumably began this line."

30. [*on*]*em:* D.

31. *in* [..].[.].[*:* D; "The first lacuna . . . contained a number, followed possibly by *in* [*is e*]*q*(*ues*) *Ị* and another such sub-total in the next line."

32.]. . . *II:* D.

33.].*e*[..]. . . *ex:* D.

Col. ii

ad opinionem peten ṃịḷ ịịị[

ṇọn secuti opinioṇe mil iii [

ịr is q d p ad rat′ stip kal sept mil iiii [

r ex is q d p ad raṭ st[ip] . . . . ẹ . ṭ mil ii[
in ịṣ[ ]i eq i
aeger reṃansiṭ [ex i]ṣ q d p ad rat
ṣṭiṗ . [ ] . . [ ] . . mil i
rr ex is q d p ante ạḍ . . [ ]ḷ[ ]ḷ ii
One line blank
xv ḳạḷ octobr ṅ ṗ dçç[. . . .]xv
xi[i]ịị kal oct ṅ p man[si]ṭ
[x]ị[i]i ḳạl oct n p ṃạṇ[si]ṭ
x̣[ii ka]l ọçṭ n p man[si]ṭ
[xi kal o]çṭ ṅ ṗ mans[i]ṭ
[x kal o]çṭ ṇ p manṣ[it
ṿịị[ii kal o]çṭ ṇ p ṃạnṣ[it
] . . [ ] . [.] . . [
. . . [ ]ṃ iii[
ṣ[ ]ẹ q ḍ p̣[
baṛ[ ]b . [
. [.] . [
ꟹ barg[a]ọ[
aụṛẹḷ [g]aiạṇus
ꟹ mariṇị pr pạṭẹ[r]ṇ[o ? cos 233
ẓạbdas barathẹ[
octobr d n deç[io
aug ii et grato co[s 250
rr ex ịṣ q d p off proc mil iii[
rr ex [i]ṣ q d p corcọsio ṃ[il
r[r] ẹx̣ ị[s] . . . . [.] . . [
]p̣ . [
] . . [
]ḅ[

b ii 2. . . . *secuti:* D; "An uncertain *non* can be read at the beginning of the line. If this is correct, *non secuti* may be equivalent to *non reversi cum eis* (the preceding group). *Opinione* is perhaps to be translated 'from the audit'." An accusative, rather, with final *m* omitted? For *non secuti* cf. **63** i 34 and ii 13.

3. *R(eversi)* ⟨*ex* ?⟩ *is:* D; "The initial *r*'s are large, as also in lines 8, 27, 28, and Frag. *d*. All are marked as abbreviations by a stroke which runs through the letter. The obvious expansion is *reversi*. . . . The letter is doubled . . . to indicate the plural in all but one of the other occurrences . . . . At the beginning of line 3, above and to the left of *r*, there is a stroke which seems to be accidental . . . I assume that *ex* is omitted carelessly, but *R is* and *Rr is* are found in Frag. *d*. Presumably there was some difference in the wording of lines 3 and 4 (aside from *ex*) or the men would not be listed separately." Perhaps read *i(n) r(euers)is*?

4.] . . . . *mil:* D; "It is possible that *Kal* was written after *stip* and then corrected, with an *o* replacing *l*. . . . *Sept* might be read before *mil*, with no certainty at all. After the superimposed *o* there is a tall letter which may be *h*, suggesting [*c*]*oh*." The tall stroke, however, has a sort of serif at its foot extending toward the right; and this seems to rule out an *h*. A large *r* like the one at the beginning of the line has been scribbled over the *o* and extends down into line 5.

5. In the lacuna Gilliam suggests *ord* or *dec* or a similar title. This line is an addition, squeezed in between 4 and 6.

7. *ṣṭip(endii)* [*Kal* . . . .]. *mil(es) I:* D.

8. *ạnṭe* . . . . [. . . .] . [. *mi*]*l(ites) I*[*:* D. Possibly *ad ra*[*t;* cf. the *r*'s in *aeger remansit*, line 6.

9. "The space appears to admit restorations ranging from *DCC*[*LXXX*]*XV* to *DCC*[*CCLX*]*XV*."

10. Expand *n(umerus) p(urus) mansit*, that is, the net total remained unchanged. Cf. **50** i 6, and ii 12: *omnes permanserunt*.

11. No numeral; *K*]*al; m*[*a*]*n*[*si*]*t:* D.

12. No numeral in D.

13. No date; *man*[*sit*]*:* D.

14. No date; *man*[*sit*]*:* D.

15. No date in D.

16. "*One line lost*"*:* D.

17. . . [–*ca. 10*–]. *III*[*:* D.
18.] *q d p* [*:* D.
19. *b*. . [*:* D.
21. *Barg*[*a* . . .]. [*:* D.
22. *A*[*ure*]*l* [*G*]*aiạ*[*n*]*us:* D.
23. *P*. . . [.]. [*:* D. "There is difficulty in identifying the consul. His name seems to begin *Pa*-. There are objections to *Praesente*, *Peregrino*, *Papo*, and *Pontiano*." The reading in the text is far from certain, and is not even possible except on the assumption that Paternus' colleague, L. Valerius Maximus, had incurred damnatio memoriae like the senior colleague of Peregrinus (above, b i 25). But **44** 9 seems to show that Papus' colleague was still in good standing in 255; and a name must be found which begins with *pa*.

25. Gilliam: "*D n* is written over something else which I have not read. The date in these lines (24–26) may serve as that of the whole entry back to line 16 or 17." In the traces under *d n*, I am inclined to see the last four letters of *octobribus*.

28. *cor*. . *ịọ*. [*:* D; "*Cor*(*niculario* or -*ariis*) *ç*ọ(*n*)*ṣ*(*u-laris*) is a rather dubious possibility. Or one can have recourse to a placename: *Corçọṣịọ ṃ*[*il* (*Circesio* cannot be read.)" Dussaud, *Topog.* 87, mentions a Corcois in the region of Tripoli, due west of Palmyra. Cf. also i 23 above, where one may read *ad horcos*.

32.]. [*:* D.

Frag. c

]. [
]. . . ạ. .

Frag. d

]ṛr is q d p ọf̣f̣[
]r is q d p̣[

Frag. e

]ç̣ọṣ

Frag. f

]q ḍ [p] . . . [
l]eg iiii ṣçy[th
]. n. . ssum[
]. . . [

Frag. g

]. . . [
]p̣. [
]. an. [

Frag. h

]em. [
]. . . [

67

Morning Report?

Bodleian Library Ms. Lat. Class. e 37 R — Middle of III p.

Transcription, commentary, and facsimile: *ChLA* IV, no. 270.

Marichal, to whom we owe the rediscovery of this papyrus, classifies it with the morning reports, comparing **47**–**51**. He is probably right. It is perhaps most like **51**, though the mention of *ciuitas* may link it with **52**. Had I known of it earlier, it could have followed **55**; but in view of the obscurities and small extent of the text, no harm is done by placing it here. And if *sal*]*utem* in line 1 is right, it may be a letter.

My transcription is from a photograph obtained through the courtesy of the Bodleian Library.

The hand and the name *aurelius an*[in line 11 are the grounds for the date.

The verso is blank.

sal]utẹṃ[
]ṣtatioṇem [. . .]. . .c̣iuita[t-
]ẹ.res xx et ṣịg cuṃ[
]us xxx et princ̣ ạ. . . .e[
].ṣoṛ˙ ị ad custodias xxiii[
]. . . . . ạḍ ḷẹgatum ñ faciet˙ antoṇ[
]ṃau. .ị. . . . ϒ adboṇas c̣ạ[.]usc̣. .ṭṭus iii pṛ[
One line blank
sp]ḥaeṛọmachiam agọnas filaḍẹlpḥ[i-
]ụịt.[. . .]. . . .ịịs eṭ uigiliạm ii circumiu.[
]ubic ualerius serenuṣ[
].[ ]. .[ ]iulius cornelianus ϒ auṛẹl aṇ[
].us ϒ cornẹ[lii] iuliani [

1.]*ṇtia*.[*:* ChLA. The word *salutem* could be either the greeting in a letter, or perhaps more likely the daily password, like *signum securitatis* in **50** i 7.

2. [*ịṇ*] *ciuita*[*te:* ChLA.

3.].*res; sịg*(*nifer*)*:* ChLA; in app. Marichal suggests *fossores*; but there is the end of a horizontal stroke at the left of the *r* which precludes *o*.

4. *Ṃạṛc̣ẹ*[*llus:* ChLA. This may be possible; but the *c* is very doubtful and the only certain letter is *e*. The initial, for example, could be *a*. *princ* is Marichal's reading. The abbreviation could be expanded as a form of either *princeps* or *principia*.

5. *p*]*roxi*(*me*)*; XXXIII*[*:* ChLA; in app., "*roxi* is sure. The following stroke seems to me only explicable as an abbreviation mark." The *r* is possible; but in my photograph the letter after *o* does not appear to be *x*. It could be *a* except that everywhere else in this hand the right-hand stroke of *a* rises high above the line, unless it is in ligature with the preceding letter, e.g. *agonas*, line 8, and *ualerius*, line 10. The only other possibility is *r*; cf. the *r* of *cornelii*, line 12. In any case the letter is followed by a raised dot as a mark of abbreviation. The *i* is then a numeral; and the next stroke, I believe, is the first stroke of an *a* which the clerk saw was too close to the *i* and so repeated a little to the right. The numeral in ChLA is a misprint.

6. *ịṃpẹratum n*(*ostrum*)*; Anton*[*ius:* ChLA. The expansion *n*(*ostrum*) is probable; but I do not see its construction with *imperatum*, which seems impossible because the feet of four letters, not three, remain between the supposed *m* and *at*. If one assumes an error in the case of *legatum*, *ab* could be read instead of *ad*. The name might easily be Antoninus or Antoninianus.

7.]*ṃal*. . . . . *ad bo*[*ṇọ*]*s Caṣ*[*i*]*us Co*[*ṭ*]*tius; pa*[*ratus:* ChLA. Marichal is right in comparing **48** 9, *ad bonos*, and **50** i 4 and 10, *ad bonis*; but these shed little light. See the apparatus on **50** i 4. Here the space between *n* and *s* is too wide for *i* or *o* but *a* seems possible. Just as in **50** 4, I can make no real sense of what follows; but I do not believe that it consists of personal names. Instead of *ṭṭ*, two *c*'s or *ct* are possible. At the end of the line *pṛ*[seems preferable to *pa*[*ratus* because the second letter does not rise above the others like *a* in this hand.

8. . . . *ad ? ṣpḥ*]*aeromachiam agonis:* ChLA. The construction of *agonas* is not clear; but the accusative rather than genitive is certain. The vertical stroke hooks to the left at the foot, whereas all *i*'s in this text hook to the right; and there is a plain line connecting *n* and *s* which forms the nearly horizontal right-hand stroke of the *a*. Cf. the *a* of *ualerius*, line 10.

9.]*uit* . . . .*s; circumiue*[*runt:* ChLA. Marichal's proposed expansion of *ii* as (*secundam*) seems all but certain.

10.]*ubit;* ChLA; but the crossbar of the last letter does not extend to the left of the hasta. Otherwise Marichal's suggestion in the apparatus of *eunt excubit*(*um*) is very attractive.

11. *An*[*tonini:* ChLA. The name Cornelianus recurs in **40** i 18, from Egypt, about A.D. 218.

12. *Corneḷ*(*ii*)*:* ChLA. The parentheses are surely a misprint for brackets.

IV

Accounts, Receipts, and Records of Matériel

Besides keeping track of individual soldiers and whole units, a system of military records should also furnish current information regarding foodstuffs, arms, tools, raw materials and all such supplies, so that the appropriate officers of all ranks up to the commanding general may know what is available to the troops in a given area, foresee and provide what is needed, and give a proper accounting for what has been expended. According to Vegetius, the praefectus legionis was responsible for arms, horses, clothing, and food, the praefectus castrorum for tents, baggage, the sick and their expenses, vehicles, pack-animals, tools, wood, bedding, and artillery.[1] How extensive and complex the inventories of equipment and supplies were likely to be can be guessed from Vegetius' account of specialists and activities under the charge of the praefectus fabrum[2] and his list of a legion's equipment: 55 *carroballistae*, 10 *onagri* (with of course wagons and oxen), dugout boats with very long ropes or sometimes with iron chains; *harpagones ferrei*; *falces ferreae* mounted on long poles; *bidentes*, *ligones*, *palae*, *rutra*, *alvei* and *cofini* for excavating; and *dolabrae*, *secures*, *asciae*, and saws for cutting and working timber.[3]

Among the texts in this chapter, all such inventories of equipment and supplies are represented only by **82** and **83**. Whenever supplies were issued or money changed hands, a receipt was of course required; and of these a fair number survive, **74**–**81**, though they are scattered over a century of time and concern only a narrow range of items, mostly grain and wine. Pay and deposits, a matter of utmost interest to the individual soldier, are covered in **68**–**73**.

It is obvious that the texts in this chapter contain data of great value both on Roman military record-keeping and on pay and prices in the army; but the facts are extremely difficult to interpret, as the comments on the individual texts make clear. None of the explanations thus far advanced for the odd sums entered as pay in **68**–**70** is wholly satisfactory; and many of the other papyri are too poorly preserved to be of much use.

One or two facts do, however, emerge. It is certain from nos. **68**–**72** that the system of three pay-periods a year was standard; and *POxy*. 1047, with its λόγος . . . στιπενδίου

[1] Vegetius 2.9 and 10.

[2] 2.11: "Habet praeterea legio fabros tignarios structores carpentarios ferrarios pictores reliquosque artifices ad hibernorum aedificia fabricanda, ad machinas turres ligneas. . . . Habebant etiam fabricas scutarias loricarias arcuarias in quibus sagittae missibilia cassides omniaque armorum genera formabantur."

[3] 2.25. Cf. also 3.2, 3, 7, and 4.6–9, 11, and especially the discussion of ship-building in 4.34.

καλανδῶν σεπτεμβρίων, shows that the same practice continued into at least the fourth century.

Second, the receipts, which are almost all in Greek, show that the Romanization of the soldiers did not extend, in Egypt at any rate, to the language which they normally used among themselves.

Finally, these records enable us to make a rough calculation of the rate of loss among military papyri. A minimum figure of 25 legions of 5000 men each, with an equal number of auxiliaries, with three pay-records annually for each man, would have produced, in the 300 years from Augustus to Diocletian, at the very least 225,000,000 individual pay-records. Of these all that survive in intelligible form are **68** and **70**.

Four additional fragmentary accounts, **129–132**, not all of them certainly military, will be found in "Addenda and Corrigenda."

The following texts are omitted from this chapter:

1. *POxy.* XII 1511 is not an account but a book of copies or summaries of letters. See **102**.
2. Manteuffel's ostraca from Tell Edfou (B. Bruyère, J. Manteuffel, K. Michalowski, and J. Sainte Fare Garnot, *Fouilles Franco-Polonaises, Rapports I: Tell Edfou, 1937* [Cairo 1937] pp. 173–76, and cf. J. Manteuffel, "Mittheilungen über die Ausgrabungen in Tell Edfu," *Actes du Ve Congrès International de Papyrologie* [Brussels 1938] 257–58, and *CPL*, nos. 238–98) have been shown by Youtie not to be military but bath-records. See H. C. Youtie, "Records of a Roman Bath in Upper Egypt," *AJA* 53 (1949) 268–70.
3. Préaux's ostracon from Mons Claudianus (see below, p. 311, note 1) has been shown by Gilliam to be a civilian text.
4. M. Norsa, "Un papiro Greco-Latino del Museo del Cairo," *Raccolta di Scritti in Onore di Giacomo Lumbroso* (Milan 1925) 319–24, reprinted in *Sammelbuch*, no. 7181, and *CPL*, no. 137, is a receipt given by an *apolusimos geometrês* to T. Flavius Valerianus, eutheniarch of Oxyrhynchus. It concerns supplies for the comitatus of the Prefect of Egypt, which of course included soldiers; but neither of the parties in the receipt is a soldier, and so the text cannot be classed as military.
5. *POxy.* I, 43 recto, records deliveries of chaff to representatives of various military units; but in col. iii 1–23 three *bouleutai apodektai achyrou* give a receipt for chaff to the *epimeletai achyrou* of Oxyrhynchus. This text, then, like the list of city watchmen on the verso, must come from the civil records of Oxyrhynchus. On the whole matter of the rôle of the *bouleutai* and *epimeletai*, see Denis van Berchem, "L'Annone militaire dans l'Empire romain au IIIe Siècle" (*Mémoires de la Societé Nationale des Antiquaires de France*, ser. 8, vol. 10, 1937, pp. 117–202), especially pp. 158–64 and 196–97. This papyrus belongs with *POxy.* 1115, 1194, and similar ones cited by van Berchem.
6. *PDur.* 129 is a receipt given by a decurion and a cavalryman; but it is for public money, possibly of the city of Dura, and the transaction takes place in the presence of *μεσῖται*. The date, moreover, is by the Seleucid era. I conclude, therefore, that this is a half-civilian matter. Even if the barley which is to be bought is destined for military use (nothing is said of the object of the purchase), it seems certain that the money was not being supplied through normal military procedures.
7. *PMich.* III, 161 (*CPL*, no. 128) is not a receipt for the stipendium of a classiarius, but a promissory note. Line 7 reads *chirographo*; and this text should be added to those in Arangio-Ruiz' "Chirografi di Soldati," *Studi in Onore di Siro Solazzi* (Naples 1948) 257–59.

Accounts

68

Pay Record of Legionaries

PGenLat. 1 recto, part I; *vidi* — Jan.–Sept. 81
P. lat. 1, Bibliothèque publique et universitaire. Geneva

Transcription, commentary, and facsimile:

1. J. Nicole and Ch. Morel, *Archives militaires du Ier siècle. Texte inédit du Papyrus latin de Genève No. 1* (Geneva 1900); cited as **ArM**.
2. *ChLA* I, no. 7, pp. 12–13.

Commentaries:

1. A. von Premerstein, "Die Buchführung einer ägyptischen Legionsabteilung," *Klio* 3 (1903) 1–46; cited as **P.**
2. *Roman Egypt*, pp. 670–76; cited as **Johnson**.
3. P. A. Brunt, "Pay and Superannuation in the Roman Army," *Papers of the British School at Rome* 18 (London 1950) 50–71; cited as **Brunt**.
4. Marichal, *Solde*.
5. G. R. Watson, "The Pay of the Roman Army: Suetonius, Dio, and the *quartum stipendium*," *Historia* 5 (1956) 332–40; cited as **Watson**, "**Stip.**"
6. G. R. Watson, "The Pay of the Roman Army: the Auxiliary Forces," *Historia* 8 (1959) 372–78; cited as **Watson**: "**Aux.**"

Text: *CPL*, no. 106, I, and Daris, no. 30, reproduce the text of *ChLA* except that they simply bracket letters which Marichal dots as well as bracketing. Neither indicates that the traces along the left edge are the remains of a separate column.

Translation: Johnson, no. 407 (pp. 673–75) is a translation of the text in *ArM*.

This text is also used in Lesquier, *Armée*, and Marichal, *Occ.* (see **70**). Consult the indices of these works and also the bibliographies in *ChLA* and Watson, "Aux." 372, note 2.

No interpretation of this text thus far proposed has yet won universal acceptance. Even its status as a pay record is denied by Watson ("Stip." 338), who calls it a "record kept by those in charge of the deposita . . . intended to show the amounts standing to the men's credits." Those who regard it as a pay record are in turn divided over the explanation of the amount of each stipendium. (The new reading of 247½ drachmas instead of 248 does not, so far as I can see, lessen the difficulties.)

Since legionaries at this time were paid 75 denarii, worth four drachmas each, in each stipendium, the expected figure here would be 300 drachmas. To account for the discrepancy, Mommsen supposed that the Roman government worked a sleight-of-hand upon the soldiers in Egypt by means of the exchange. The 75 denarii due in each pay period were regarded as the equivalent of 300 drachmas, but drachmas of billon, not silver, and hence worth only 1800 obols. Then the 1800 obols were converted into silver drachmas of $7\frac{1}{4}$ obols, giving 248 drachmas. This reasoning has been accepted by Lesquier, Premerstein, and most recently Brunt and Marichal; but it is open to serious objections:

1. The arithmetic is not exact. 1800 obols in silver amount to 248 drachmas, 2 obols. The difference seems negligible; but **70** shows that in A.D. 192 the army was taking account of even $\frac{1}{4}$ obol. And the new reading in the present text makes a difference of an additiona half a drachma.
2. If the government was determined to pay the troops in terms of billon coinage, converting the number of billon drachmas into the equivalent value of silver was altogether pointless. What purpose could it possibly serve except to call attention to the fact that the soldiers were not getting 300 silver drachmas?
3. As a corollary to the foregoing, the fact that the account shows the soldiers receiving none of their pay in cash makes the medium of exchange a matter of indifference until such time as the soldier died or was discharged, when his deposita would have to be paid to him or his heirs. What is more to the point is that the amounts withheld from the stipendium are in the same denomination. If the payment was in billon drachmas, so were the deductions; so that if the government was cheating the soldiers in their pay, it was allowing itself to be cheated in the matter of clothing, food, and similar items. Watson, moreover, is almost certainly right in doubting whether the amounts deducted were anything but conventional. In the Dura papyri relating to horses, of 10 animals in **83**, A.D. 251, whose valuation is certain, 9 are rated at 125 denarii. (The exception is **83** 15–16, a special case of some sort.) The same rate of 125 denarii holds for two others in **99** A and C (A.D. 208); and at least two are rated at something over a hundred in **99** B, while another is also rated at one hundred and something in a receipt of A.D. 139 (**75**). Such uniformity in valuation over a period of at least forty and perhaps a hundred years, and without regard to the age or sex of the horse, can hardly be imagined to be the result of strict equality in actual worth.
4. The effect on morale of such manipulation of the exchange would be grave, as Watson ("Stip." 336–38) has shown. In addition to his already cogent arguments it should be pointed out (a) that the very soldiers who made these calculations and kept these accounts would themselves have been victims of the system; (b) that units from Egypt served outside that province, as the III Cyrenaica did in the Jewish war of 68–70, and that detachments of the Alexandrian fleet regularly did so, all of whom would soon have discovered that soldiers in identical branches of the service were being better paid in other provinces; and (c) that soldiers were commonly transferred into and out of Egyptian units from and to legions and auxiliaries in other provinces. How could this have been managed without serious discontent if centurions, for example, being transferred to Egypt from a legion elsewhere knew that they were taking a cut in pay?

Allan Chester Johnson, followed by Passerini and Forni, found a different explanation of the stipend of 248 drachmas.[1] Noting that it is approximately five-sixths of the 300 drach-

[1] Johnson, pp. 670 and 673; A. Passerini, *Le coorti pretorie* (Rome 1939) 101, note 2; and G. Forni, *Il Reclutamento delle Legioni da Augusto a Diocleziano* (Milan and Rome 1953) 31–34.

mas which the stipendium of a legionary ought to comprise, and convinced that Domaszewski was wrong in assuming that the pay of auxiliary troops was only one-third that of legionaries, they propose to see in the present text a pay-record of auxiliaries, probably equites, in spite of the tria nomina of both soldiers. But here again the arithmetic is not exact; five-sixths of the legionary stipendium are 250 drachmas, not 247½ or 248; and Marichal (*Solde* 403–12) has effectively proved that these men are not Roman citizens serving in an auxiliary unit. Brunt and Watson also believe them to be legionaries.

Watson, as already stated, does not consider this a pay-record at all. For him the 247½ drachmas of each instalment are merely a portion of the stipendium retained to cover the amount each soldier owed, the balance of the 300 drachmas being paid to him in cash for pocket money to do as he pleased with. This avoids imputing to the government chicanery in manipulation of the exchange; it allows the two soldiers, who are certainly citizens, to remain legionaries; and it explains why they appear to draw no money for any purchases outside the camp. On the whole, it may be the most acceptable of the proposals offered thus far.

And yet certain facts occasion some uneasiness. Watson's theory does not explain how the figure of 247½ drachmas was arrived at, nor why it appears to be invariable for every stipendium-period and for all soldiers. The text, too, says only *accepit stip(endium)*, not *de stipendio* or *ex stipendio*; and as for pocket money, **70** regularly designates withdrawals in cash by *reliquos tulit*, whereas here we have only *reliquas deposuit*.

It seems very possible, in fact, that we think too much in modern terms when we worry about Roman soldiers having pocket money. It is certain that most of them managed to have some and to carry on all kinds of activities outside their military duties;[2] but it is doubtful that the Roman government felt much responsibility for providing its troops with entertainment. For the official attitude the moralizing tone of Vegetius 2.20 rings true, combined as it is with considerations of the bluntest practicality. He speaks only of donatives, because in his day the soldiers were supported by the annona; but his remarks would be just as applicable to the stipendia of earlier times:

> . . . pars sequestraretur apud signa et ibidem ipsis militibus seruaretur ne per luxum aut inanium rerum comparationem ab contubernalibus possit absumi. Plerique enim homines et praecipue pauperes tantum erogant quantum habere potuerint . . . . Miles deinde qui sumptus suos scit apud signa depositos de deserendo nihil cogitat, magis diligit signa, pro illis in acie fortius dimicat, more humani ingenii ut pro illis habeat maximam curam in quibus suam uidet positam esse substantiam.

Finally, it may be well to bear in mind that the present text represents only two accounts out of 5000, more or less, which were kept for this year for one legion alone, and that they may well belong to men who had been in service only a year or two. Consequently they may not be wholly typical, even for their own time and unit. Perhaps the most that can be said of them with assurance is that they are pay-records of legionaries. The evidence now available does not seem to warrant any more detailed interpretation.

[2] One need only point to the fact that so many maintained "wives" and children. Note also the active trade in all sorts of goods revealed in the letters of Claudius Terentianus published by H. C. Youtie and J. G. Winter in *PMich.* VIII, nos. 467–71; and cf. others, such as 464, 476, and 481.

The date of the text is supplied by the consulship in the heading—A.D. 81. The first stipendium was paid early in January (see **71**), the second in May, the third in September. Strictly speaking, only the first two fell within Titus' third Egyptian year; but the date which mattered from the Roman official point of view was the consulship. The three different hands are evidence that the accounts were posted at intervals during the year.

The verso contains **9** and **58**.

Col. i		**Col. ii**		
]		L AṢINIO COS		A.D. 81
] . .		Q ỊṾLIVS PROCVLVS ḌAM		
	(*First hand*)	[accepit] stip i an iii do dr ccxlvii s		
		ex eis		
		f̣ạẹṇạria	ḍṛ x	
		ịṇ ụ[ic]ṭum	dṛ lxxx	
		caḷ[i]gas fascias	dr xii	
]x̣ s		ṣaṭuṛṇạlicium k	dr xx	
]ịi s		. . . . r . . torium	dr lx	
		ex[p]ẹṇsas dr clxxxii		
		reḷiqụạs deposuit dr lxv s		
		et habụiṭ ex prio d[r] cxxxvi		
		fiṭ ṣuṃm	dr cci s	
	(*Second hand*)	accepit stip ii anni eiusd ḍṛ c̣cxḷvii s		
		ẹx̣ eis		
		f̣aenaria	dr x	
] . lvi s		iṇ ụictum	dr lxxx	
		caligas fascias	dr xii	
		aḍ ṣigna	dr iv	
		exp̣ensas dr cvi		
		reliquas deposuit	dr cxli s	
		et habuit ex p̣ṛor[ ]	dr cci s	
] . s		fịt [su]mma omnis	dr cccxli[ii]	
	(*Third hand*)	ac̣c̣ẹ[pit sti]p̣ iii a[nn ei]ụṣ[dr] c̣c̣xlvị[i] ṣ		
		[e]x̣ e[i]ṣ		
		faenạṛịa	[dr x]	
		[in uictu]ṃ	ḍṛ [lx]x̣x̣	
		[calig]ạṣ [f]ạṣc̣ias	ḍṛ [xii]	
		ịṇ uẹstim[e]ṇṭ[i]ṣ	dṛ c̣[xl]v s	
		expensaṣ	[dr c]cx̣ḷvii s	
		ḥabet in deposito	dr cccx̣ḷịiii	
	(*Fourth hand*)	rennius innocens		

i 3.] . . ; ChLA; but this reading was apparently meant for line 2, since the apparatus on 2 reads, "On the margin traces of 'capitals,' perhaps OC, corresponding with a name."

8. No reading in ChLA.

9.]*iii:* ChLA, and in the app., "On the margin *iii* (and not *ii s*, cf. I a, 3 [col. ii 3 in the present text]), preceding account." But see below on ii 3.

17–18. ChLA: "On the margin *ob*(*olos*) *vii* belongs to a precedent account, the number 7 confirms, that the drachm is worth, in this text, 7 oboli ¼, cf. Marichal, *Occup.*, p. 36." *o*]*b vi s* would be a possible reading and would prove that the drachma contained at least 7 obols; but the reading is unsure, and I prefer the one in the text. For the *l*, cf. ii 3, 9, and 24. Otherwise *ha]ḅuit* or *de]ḅuit* are possible.

23. No reading in ChLA.

ii 1. . .*L:* ChLA; but a new photograph shows no traces of ink to the left of the *L*. Degrassi, *Fasti*, questions the praenomen of Asinius, apparently because Morel read *et* in place of *L*. But the reading here is perfectly clear; and the combination with the third (Egyptian) year of the emperor leaves no doubt that the year is 81. Marichal, ChLA, apparatus on line 3, is entirely right as to the date. I had already come to the same conclusion in my dissertation (see the Preface above) in 1934.

2. *OMT* (?) or *CAN:* ArM; *DAM:* P. The last two letters could equally well be *MA*. Expand *Dam(asco)*. The abbreviation could be expanded as in ChLA, *Dam(ascenus)*, for which see Marichal, *Occ.* 28–29, who follows the analogy of *coptit(es)* in **39** 20. But cf. **36** 9, *adrumeto*; 14, *altino*; and 15, *chrysopoli*; and **63** i 13, 16, and 19–20, *stobis*.

3. *Do(mitiani):* ArM and Daris; *do(mini):* P, pointing out that Domitian's third regnal year did not begin until August 29, 83. Titus died September 13, 81. *ccxlviii:* edd.; but the last two letters are exactly like those of *eis* in all three hands and quite distinct from the two *i*'s in the *xii* entered for *caligas fascias*, or in ii 10 and 20, iii 9 and 29. See further on ii 31. Read *stip(endium) (primum) an(ni) (tertii) do(mini), dr(achmas) ccxlvii s(emis)*.

5. The purport of this charge is uncertain. The hay has been variously explained as bedding, as each man's share of the maintenance of a pack-animal for the use of a contubernium, and as fodder for an eques' horse. See also on **76**, below.

8. For *saturnalicium* cf. iii 7. Since this reading is secure, it is hardly possible to reject *k(astrense)*, in spite of Blumner's objections (*Neue Jahrbücher für das klassische Altertum* 5 [1900] 434) accepted by Hoey, *Feriale Duranum* 161, note 737. On the occasion see **117** iv 7–8, and *Feriale Duranum* 160–62 and 168–72.

9. *ịṇ ụẹṣṭịtorium:* ChLA. The word *in* is possible though not certain; but the fifth letter is a clear *r*, and so *uestitorium* is impossible.

10. *Expẹṇsas:* ChLA.

11. *lxvi:* ChLA.

12. *priore:* ArM; *dṛ:* ChLA.

13. *sụṃṃạ; ccii:* ChLA.

14. Read *stip(endium) (secundum) anni eiusd(em)*. *[dr cc]xlvii:* ChLA.

15. *[E]x:* ChLA; *[Ex]:* Daris.

19. *[ad]:* ChLA. This might be a contribution to the legion's burial fund (Vegetius 2.20) or for the cult of the *signa*. See Marichal, *Occ.* 40, and *Feriale Duranum* 116–18.

21. *cxlii:* ChLA.

22. *prịọr[e]; ccii:* ChLA. Read, of course, *ex priore*.

23. *summa; ccxl[iv]:* ChLA.

24. *A[c]cepịṭ; anni eius[d] ḍṛ c̣c̣xlviii:* ChLA; in app., "*eius[d]*, the *d* is uncertain, cf. I b, 13" (iii 13 in the present text).

25. *ẹịṣ:* ChLA.

27. *[uictum]; [dr lxxx]:* ChLA.

28. *[dr] x̣ịị:* ChLA.

29. *ụẹṣṭịmẹṇṭịṣ; c̣[x]ḷvị:* ChLA.

30. *[d]ṛ c̣cxlviii:* ChLA.

31. *ccxlịṿ:* ChLA. It is necessary for Marichal to read *ccxliv* here because he reads *cxlii* and *ccii* in lines 21 and 22 and the amount here is the same as the sum in line 23. But the last letter in this line is pretty certainly not a *v*, as comparison with the forms in iii 23–29 will show. The reading *s(emis)* in various lines of this column thus gains support.

32. *T. ENNIUS:* ArM; *RENNIUS:* P. The name, however, is not in capitals but large letters of cursive form. Its connection with the rest of the text is uncertain; but ArM may be right in supposing that it is the signature of a signifer or auditor who has checked the accounts. It need not, however, be anything more than an idle bit of practice, as **37** probably was.

Col. iii

C VALERIVS GERMANVS TYR
(*First hand*) accepit stip i an iii do dr ccxlvii s
ex ẹis
faenaria dr x
in u[i]ctum ḍr lxxx
caligas fascias dr xii
satụrnaḷịc̣ịụṃ k dr xx
in uestimeṇ[t]ịṣ dr c
expensaṣ dr ccxx̣ii
reliquas depọ dr xxṿ s
et habuit dr xx̣[i]
fit summạ omṇịṣ dr x̣lvi s
(*Second hand*) accepit stip ii anni eius dṛ ccx̣lvii s

ex eis
faenaria [d]r x
in uictum ḍr ḷx̣x̣x
caligas fascias dr xii
ad signa dṛ ịv
expẹnsas dr cvị
rẹ[li]qụas deposuit dr cxli s
eṭ ḥabuit ex pṛiore dr xlvị ṣ
f[it s]umma omn⟨i⟩s dr [c]ḷx̣x̣x̣vị[ii]
(*Third hand*) aç̣cepịt stip iii anṇ[i] ẹ[i]ụ[s] ḍṛ ccxlvịị s
ex eịs
fạe[n]ạria ḍṛ x
ịṇ ụictum ḍṛ lx̣x̣x̣
ç̣al[i]g̣as fascias dr x̣ii
ịṇ ụestimentis dr cxlv s
habet [i]n deposito dr clxxxviii

iii 1. *CYR:* ArM; *TYR(O):* P; *TYR(IVS):* ChLA.
2. *Do(mitiani):* ArM and Daris; see on ii 3 above. ChLA: "The copyist has written *stip III an IIII*, with correction." *ccxlviii:* ChLA.
8. *uestimeṇ[tu]ṃ:* ArM and ChLA; but cf. line 28 below.
10. *deposuit:* ArM; *xxvi:* ChLA.
11. *x̣x̣:* ChLA.
12. [*x*]*lvi:* ChLA.
13. *eiusd:* ArM; *ccxlviii:* ChLA.
20. *rẹḷiqụas; cxḷịị:* ChLA.
21. *et* omitted by ArM; *xlvi:* ChLA.
22. *fịt summa omnis; ç̣ḷx̣x̣x̣vịịị:* ChLA.
23. *annị* [*eiusd*] *ḍr ccxlvịii:* ChLA.
25. *fạeṇaria:* ChLA.
26. [*d*]*r:* ChLA.
27. *ç̣ạḷịgas:* ChLA.
28. *cxlvi:* ChLA.
29. *in:* ChLA. In this entry the total of expenses for the pay-period (cf. ii 30), which should have followed *in uestimentis* in line 28, has been omitted, and also the line *et habuit ex priore*. The omissions may be the result of an oversight; but they may have been deliberate because the expenses exactly equaled the amount of the stipendium. In ii 29–31, where the situation is the same, *expensas* appears, but not *et habuit ex priore*.

TRANSLATION

Col. ii

A.D. 81
Q. Iulius Proculus, born at Damascus,
received the first pay of the third year of the Emperor, 247 ½ drachmas
out of which
hay money (?) 10 drachmas
for food 80 drachmas
boots, socks 12 drachmas
camp Saturnalia 20 drachmas
. . . . r . . torium 60 drachmas
spent 182 drachmas
deposited the balance 65 ½ drachmas
and had from before 136 drachmas
total 201 ½ drachmas
received the second pay of the same year, 247 ½ drachmas
out of which
hay money (?) 10 drachmas
for food 80 drachmas

boots, socks 12 drachmas
to the standards 4 drachmas
spent 106 drachmas
deposited the balance 141 $\frac{1}{2}$ drachmas
and had from before 201 $\frac{1}{2}$ drachmas
entire total 343 drachmas
received the third pay of the same year, 247 $\frac{1}{2}$ drachmas
out of which
hay money (?) 10 drachmas
for food 80 drachmas
boots, socks 12 drachmas
for clothing 145 $\frac{1}{2}$ drachmas
spent 247 $\frac{1}{2}$ drachmas
has on deposit 343 drachmas

Rennius Innocens

Col. iii

C. Valerius Germanus, born at Tyre,
received the first pay of the third year of the Emperor, 247 $\frac{1}{2}$ drachmas
out of which
hay money (?) 10 drachmas
for food 80 drachmas
boots, socks 12 drachmas
camp Saturnalia 20 drachmas
for clothing 100 drachmas
spent 222 drachmas
deposited the balance 25 $\frac{1}{2}$ drachmas
and had 21 drachmas
entire total 46 $\frac{1}{2}$ drachmas
received the second pay of the same year, 247 $\frac{1}{2}$ drachmas
out of which
hay money (?) 10 drachmas
for food 80 drachmas
boots, socks 12 drachmas
to the standards 4 drachmas
spent 106 drachmas
deposited the balance 141 $\frac{1}{2}$ drachmas
and had from before 46 $\frac{1}{2}$ drachmas
entire total 188 drachmas
received the third pay of the same year, 247 $\frac{1}{2}$ drachmas
out of which
hay money (?) 10 drachmas
for food 80 drachmas
boots, socks 12 drachmas
for clothing 145 $\frac{1}{2}$ drachmas
has on deposit 188 drachmas

69

Pay Record of Legionaries

PGenLat. 4 — ca. A.D. 84

P. lat. 4, Bibliothèque publique et universitaire, Geneva

Transcription, commentary, and facsimile:

ChLA, part 1, no. 9, pp. 22 and 24–25.

Transcription and commentary:

1. J. Nicole, "Compte d'un soldat romain", *Archiv* 2 (1903) 63–69; cited as **N.** Superseded.
2. Marichal, *Solde*.
3. G. R. Watson, "The Pay of the Roman Army: Suetonius, Dio, and the *quartum stipendium*," *Historia* 5 (1956) 332–40; cited as **Watson, "Stip."**
4. Robert Marichal, "Le Papyrus latin 4 de Genève," *Studi in Onore di Aristide Calderini e Roberto Paribeni*, vol. 2 (Milan 1957) 225–41; cited as **M 4.**

Commentary: Lesquier, 506–509, and Johnson, *Roman Egypt*, 671 and 676–77, are obsolete.

Text: *CPL*, no. 107, reproduces Marichal's text in *ChLA* and the reconstruction offered there. Daris, no. 31, was able to use M 4 as well.

It has always been obvious that this must be a pay record similar to **68**; but the task of reading the scanty text and reconstructing the account has been formidable, and was rendered worse by the clerks' many errors and corrections. This being the case, every scholar must be grateful to Marichal for his meticulous re-examination of the papyrus and his patient study and elucidation of the resultant text. The text printed here retains his numbering of the lines in M 4, and differs from his only where there is an explicit statement to that effect. That there should be differences is inevitable; the data do not permit a final and incontrovertible disposition of every item. But the differences are matters of detail; in the main Marichal's reconstruction is sound and convincing even though difficulties will always remain.

As in **68**, a different hand made the entries for each of the first three pay periods; and Marichal distinguishes a fourth hand in that of the corrector, a fifth in line 18. Line 27 he refers to the third hand. These differences in the hands, however, and the corrections in lines 17, 17a, and 25a (cf. M 4, p. 240) surely refute the idea (M 4, p. 233) that the second and third accounts were mere rough drafts, since it is plain that they were added at intervals of four months, just as in **68**. It is evident that lines 3, 11, 19, and 27 each recorded a stipendium of 297 drachmas, that lines 10 and 18 state the balances left after the deductions itemized in lines 4–8 and 12–16, and that both the amount of the stipendium and the amounts of the deductions are higher than in **68**. At this point, however, general agreement stops.

The four stipendia, whether one inclines to Marichal's or Watson's view (see on line 27), at any rate point to a date after Domitian's increase in soldiers' pay, while the hand shows a close kinship with that of **68**. Marichal's date of January to September 84 can therefore be accepted as close to the truth.

The verso is reported by Nicole to contain only the left ends of a dozen lines of Greek.

1 QV]ADRATV[S ....
1a [lvii]
2 (*First hand*)].uṃịạ Y ḍṛ ⟦[lx]x̣x̣x̣..⟧
3 [accepit stip i an] dr ccxcvii
3a [ex eis]
4 [faenaria] dr xiii
5 [in uictum ?] dr cxxiix
6 [caligas fascias d]r xvi
6a] lvii a ii s
7 [in uestimentis ?]dr ⟦lxxxxiii a ii s⟧
8 es]ṭ s ss ccxiṿ a ii s
8a] ii
9 d]ẹp dr lxxx⟦xṿị⟧ a iii s
10]..um dr lxxxii a[
10a]
11 (*Second hand*) [accepit stip ii an] dr ccxcv[ii
11a [ex eis]
12 [faenaria] dr xiii
13 [in uictum] dr c
14 [caligas fascia]ṣ dr xvi
15]ḷ dr xx
16]. cx
17]ẹst s ṣs dr cxḷ[viiii
17a]
18] dr xxxxv[
19 (*Third hand*) [accepit stip iii an]ị. dr cc[xcvii
20 [ex ei]ṣ
21 ?]. dr x[ii]ịị a[iii
22 [in uictum] dr c
23 [caligas fascia]ṣ dr xvi
24 dr xx]x̣ịii a ii
25 [summa ss d]ṛ clxiii a v
25a] xlvi a ii[i] s
26]cxx a ii s
27] c̣cxc̣[v]ịi
28]. .[

No translation is offered because of the many conjectural restorations in the text and the other uncertainties which remain.

1. When Nicole published the text, the final *s* had not been broken off; and he apparently saw traces of four additional letters.

1a. On the bit of papyrus now lost Nicole read *lvii* here, a correction of the number canceled in line 2. Marichal prints line 1a in his transcription of the papyrus in ChLA but not in his reconstructed text.

2.]*uita* ϒ*d*. .⟦*LXXXX*. .⟧*:* N;].*v*. .*a* ϒ⟦*ḶX̣X̣X̣X̣ỊỊ* ⟧*:* M 4. All but the lowest tips of the numerals were lost with the fragment which carried away the ends of lines 1 and 1a. Marichal (M 4, pp. 234–35) proposes to read [*deb*(*et*) *in vestitori*]*um* (*arcae*) (*centuriae*) *dr LXXXXII*[*I a II s*] corrected to *LVII* [*a II s*], the amount and the correction being repeated in lines 7 and 6a. The order of line 7 among the items in the column leads him, through comparison with the order of the items in **68** ii 3–9, to assign the charge in line 7 to *uestitorium* and to explain its presence here in line 2 by assuming a debit carried over from the last accounting of the previous year. This may be right, even though the word *uestitorium* will not do (see on **68** ii 9) and though the repetition of the identical amount in line 7 implies that Quadratus had had no expenses in this category since the previous stipendium.

Marichal's *arcae centuriae* is much more dubious, as he himself says. It seems to me preferable to see here the end of a centurion's name and his title and to explain the money as a deposit to Quadratus' account, like the transactions in **74**. Even if the amounts in 1a and 2 were the same as in 6a and 7, which is not certain, they need not be entered in the two places for the same reason.

3. Marichal simply states that 297 drachmas equal 75 denarii without explaining why there are not 300. Watson ("Stip." 338) suggests that 3 drachmas were deducted as a "commission on the exchange."

3a. Restored by Marichal on the analogy of the entries in **68**.

4. *faenaria* is likewise restored in accordance with **68**. See on **68** ii 5.

5. *CXXXIX:* N. Marichal believes that this amount is greater than those in lines 13 and 22 because it included the saturnalicium. For the last, cf. **68** ii 9 and iii 7.

6. Restored by comparison with **68**. .*r:* N.

6a. *LII a II s:* N. This line was inserted as a correction for line 7. In the photograph, the second letter after *v* looks more like *g* than *i*. Read (*obolos*) *ii s*(*emis*). Marichal rightly explains that the letter *a*, properly *a*(*sses*), is used archaistically in this text as a symbol for obols.

7. .*r LXXXXIII a* .. *I* (or *S*)*:* N.

8.]*ụs C̣CCXIV*. .*I*.*IS:* N;]*ụs 314* [*4*] ½*:* Lesquier; [*es*]*t s*(*umma*) *s*(*upra*)*s*(*criptarum*)*:* M 4. Marichal reports that the numeral is written over an erasure. This explains Nicole's three *c*'s, and perhaps also explains why the *v* in the photograph looks like a Greek psi.

8a. These two numerals were inserted between the lines in correcting *xxxxvi* in line 9 to *lxxxii*.

9.]*o dr XXXXVII a IIII* (or *S*)*:* N. Expand *d*]*ep*(*osuit*)? The *p* looks more like a *d*.

Marichal in ChLA explains that the total of expenditures before the correction of line 7 was 250 drachmas, 2½ obols, leaving a balance of 46 drachmas, 3½ obols, which was entered in line 9. Then when line 7 was reduced to 57 drachmas, 2½ obols, the amount in line 9 was correspondingly increased by prefixing an *l*, canceling *xvi*, and writing *ii* above the canceled numbers. Then the corrector struck out the whole, noting that the right amount was given in line 10. Much the same explanation appears in M 4, pp. 231–33.

It is not certain, however, that the entire number for the drachmas was canceled (that for the obols was not); nor is it clear why the corrector should have found the right amount already entered in line 10 (see below). The few letters remaining at the beginning of lines 9 and 10 seem rather to show that the two amounts are of different character. The fact that both amount to 82 drachmas may be coincidental; and the number of obols in line 10 is unknown.

10].*rum dr LXXXX a* . . . *:* N; [*et habuit ex priore ad aera*]*rium:* M 4. Marichal's restoration is based on the equation of this line with those reading *et habuit ex priore* which follow the entries *reliquas deposuit* in **68**, and on the assumption that line 10a was a short one stating the total of Quadratus' deposits. But he also explains (M 4, pp. 233–34) the identity which he assumes of the amount here with that in line 9 as the product of an odd expedient of the clerk's. Finding this figure in his notes and not knowing what to do with it because he had already calculated and entered in line 9 the balance after expenditures resulting from the original charge in line 7, the clerk simply put down the 82 drachmas in line 10 as a balance brought forward from the preceding stipendium-period.

This explanation will hold, if at all, only if the number in line 9 is canceled. Otherwise we must assume that the corrector let both stand as corrected. The remains at the beginning of the line are not helpful, because they can also be read as]*ṃum*,]*ạum*, or perhaps even]*ṇum*. I have no proposal for the identification of this line. It might be the total of Quadratus' deposits, if he is a recent recruit, in which case my idea of line 2 must be given up.

10a. Marichal restores [*fit summa dr CCXXIX a I*]. This may be right; but see on line 10.

11. *CCXCV*. .*:* N.

14. ChLA indicates traces of a letter before *dr* (Nicole does not); but no use is made of them in the restoration.

15. [*ad signa* ?]*:* ChLA; and Marichal argues for this attribution in M 4, pp. 237–38. But the letter at the edge of the papyrus before *dr* cannot possibly be *a* and seems probably to be *l*. At any rate, it has a vertical stroke from the foot of which a horizontal stroke extends to the right. Nicole shows nothing before *dr*. The amount is five times the charge *ad signa* in **68**. I can think of nothing to propose.

16. *ḍr CX:* N; [*in vestitorium*] *dr cx:* ChLA. Observing that the numeral is not aligned in column with the other amounts deducted, Marichal questions (M 4, pp. 236–37) whether this sum is to be included in the

total of expenses. He decides in the affirmative on the ground of corrections which he believes were made in lines 17 and 17a. But there are uncertainties. The corrections are not obvious; and the letter before *cx* is troublesome. It is not the same as any other *r* in the text; and if read as *d* it leaves no room for an *r*. It might be a doubtful *b*; but that suggests only *ha*]*b*(*et*) or *de*]*b*(*et*), neither of which is appropriate here.

17, 17a, and 18.]*ṣ ṣum dr CX. . . . :* N;]*est s*(*umma*) *s*(*upra*)*s*(*criptarum*) *dr CÇḶ*[*IX:* ChLA 17; *C:* 17a; [*reliquas deposuit*] *dr XXXXV*[*:* 18, corrected by Marichal to *XXXVIII*. I cannot find on my photograph the additional *c* in line 17 and the *c* in line 17a which Marichal reads; but something of the sort must be accepted to account for the balance of 45 to 49 drachmas clearly read in line 18. Nonetheless, this reasoning is only as strong as the assumption that line 17 is the total of deductions for this pay period and that line 18 contains the balance left after all deductions. Even so, lines 17 and 18 in Marichal's text do not agree. Either 17 should read *ccxlviiii* or 18 should read *xxxviii*; and so Marichal supposes (M 4, pp. 236–37) that one clerk wrote line 17, that he or another corrected the number in 17, adding 17a, and that still another clerk then misread 17, made the subtraction, and entered the incorrect balance in 18. This may well be the case; but it seems better to leave the question open.

19. *dr CÇ. . . . . . . :* N;]*dr:* ChLA, with no mention of the traces on the edge of the papyrus. The first is a nearly vertical stroke; the second resembles the peculiar second *i* of *lvii* in line 6a. Perhaps read, as in **68** iii 13, *ei*]*ụṣ*(*dem*)?

20. ChLA notes a stroke, described as very uncertain and without meaning, under the second *c* in line 19. N shows a series of 9 dots. Do these represent actual traces of letters?

21. *XIII:* N; [*faenaria*] *dr X*[*I*]*II* (*obolos*) [*III:* ChLA. The number of obols is restored by calculation from lines 27, 27a, and 28. M 4 (p. 239) asserts that the additional three obols do not render the ascription to faenaria doubtful; but the size of the lacuna makes other readings probable for the number of drachmas: *x*[*ii*]*ii*, *x*[*v*]*ii*, or *x*[*l*]*ii*. Only the position of the item in the list speaks in favor of *faenaria*.

23. Nicole shows nothing before *dr*.

24. . . . . *III a v* (?)*:* N; [*in vestitorium dr XX*]*X*[*I*]*II* (*obolos*) *II:* ChLA. The gap after *x* does not seem large enough to restore another *i*; but the sum of lines 21–24 is still correct because of the reading *x*[*ii*]*ii* in line 21. The numeral here is displaced far to the left.

25. . . . .*ṛ CLXIII a II S* (?)*:* N.

25a. . . . . *XLVI a II S:* N; [*recessit?*] *XLVI* (*obolos*) *III s*(*emis*)*:* ChLA. Three obols are needed here; but it seems better not to use the stroke at the foot of the right-hand stroke of *a*, because nearly every *a* in the text has such a stroke. (Cf. M 4, pp. 229–30 on the *a* and the number of obols in line 9.) The item must be an expense of some sort, since it figures in the total in line 27; so Marichal may be right in equating it with the *recessa* of **73**.

26. . . . . *CCX a III* (or *s*)*:* N. Marichal points out that this is the sum of the amounts in lines 25 and 25a, and also that the unexpended balance of Quadratus' stipendium, 86 drachmas, 3½ obols, is not entered in this account as in lines 9 and 18.

27. . . . . *CCXÇ . II:* N;]*CCXCVII:* ChLA. Watson ("Stip." 334–36) takes this line as proof that Domitian left the stipendium at 75 denarii but paid four stipendia annually after 83–84, when he raised the soldiers' pay, and dates the papyrus within a "fairly short interval" after that date. Marichal (M 4, pp. 240–41), accepting late 83 as the time when the quartum stipendium was added, dates the entry in September 84 and explains that the payment was in the form of a congiarium, on the ground that when the increase in pay was granted it was too late to include the appropriate amount in the first stipendium and that this separate payment was made in addition to the last stipendium of the year rather than dividing the money equally between the second and the last. He quotes in support *Inscriptiones Italiae* 13 (1947) p. 193: [*Imp. Domitianus congiarium diuisit*] (*denarios*) *LXXV*, dated A.D. 84. The congiarium would be classed among the seposita, and this accounts for the lack of a final balance for the third stipendium: the congiarium was still to be added.

Watson may nevertheless be right that there were four pay-periods a year thereafter, at least while Domitian lived; but it is certain that if there ever were four, the practice soon reverted to three. See **71** and **72**.

70

Pay Account of Auxiliaries

PBerol. 6866 and *PAberd.* 133 (inv. 2g) May, A.D. 192
I have worked from photographs given to me by Rostovtzeff.

Transcription and facsimile: *EL*, plate XIX, no. 27, contains all of frag. a, but not others. Superseded by the following.

Transcription, commentary, and facsimile: R. Marichal, *Occ.*; cited in apparatus as **M**.

Transcription and commentary: Eric G. Turner, *Catalogue of Greek and Latin Papyri and Ostraca in the Possession of the University of Aberdeen* (Aberdeen 1939) no. 133. This fragment consists of three lines only.

Commentary:

1. A. Passerini, "Il papiro berlinese e il soldo militare al tempo di Commodo," *Acme* 1 (1946) 366.
2. Idem, "Gli aumenti del soldo militare da Commodo a Massimiano," *Athenaeum* 24 (1946) 145–59.
3. P. A. Brunt, "Pay and Superannuation in the Roman Army," *Papers of the British School at Rome* 18 (1950) 50–71; cited as **Brunt**.
4. Marichal, *Solde*.
5. G. R. Watson, "The Pay of the Roman Army: The Auxiliary Forces," *Historia* 8 (1959) 372–78.
6. R. O. Fink, "*Damnatio Memoriae* and the Dating of Papyri," *Synteleia Vincenzo Arangio-Ruiz* (Naples 1964) 232–36.
7. Eric G. Turner, "P. Aberdeen 133 and P. Berlin 6866," *JEA* 33 (1947) 92.

Lesquier, *Armée*, and Johnson, *Roman Egypt*, also made use of *PBerol.* 6866; but since they necessarily had only an imperfect text to work with, their results require modification.

Text: *CPL*, no. 122, reproduces the text of *Occ.* with some apparatus from Lesquier and *EL* and a summary of Marichal's findings; Daris, no. 35. *CPL*, no. 123, is *PAberd.* 133, omitted by Daris.

Except for the certainty that the soldiers here are auxiliaries, this text has been interpreted in as many different ways as **68**, by the same scholars, and with the same arguments. Marichal and Brunt consider that the amount of the stipendium is the result of manipulation of the exchange, operating with a basic sum of 100 denarii, while Watson believes that these are records primarily concerned with the soldiers' deposits and that the pay installment of 84 denarii $15\frac{3}{4}$ obols (i.e. $84\frac{9}{16}$ denarii) is only a fraction of the whole stipendium retained to cover any deductions which might have to be made.

An important difference, however, is Marichal's conviction, in which he follows Lesquier, that the payments recorded here are for a whole year instead of a period of four months. Watson seems tacitly to have adopted the same view; but Brunt (64–66) argues that the payments here are for the same period as in **68**, chiefly because (1) "stipendium" ought to mean the same thing in both texts and whenever used of pay, and (2) a rate of less than 85 actual denarii (to be exact, 345 drachmas, 7 obols) per annum would have been impossibly low for a man to live on. See also on **78**, p. 313 below.

Much of the discussion, however, has been beclouded by inexactness regarding the date of the text. Marichal came closest when he concluded (*Solde* 416–17) that the text should be dated between August 29, 192, and August 28, 193, and probably after Septimius Severus was proclaimed emperor on April 9, 193. This is reasonable in itself; but frag. b ii 7–8 fix the year as 192 without any question. In those lines Commodus as consul has the title *Imp*; and his colleague is Pertinax. But the title could have been used only during Commodus' life, for after his assassination on December 31, 192, his memory was immediately damned and he would not have been named at all, while after his deification by Severus he would have had the title *diuus*.[1] With this dating all question of pay increases, frumentum menstruum, donatives, or other benefactions by Severus disappears. If such there were, they were granted by Commodus.

The arguments in favor of believing that these are annual accounts seem insufficient in any case. The principal one is the conviction that the pay of auxiliaries at this time was one-third that of legionaries. Even if this were certain, it would prove little because we have no adequate evidence for the pay of legionaries at this time; and it needs to be emphasized strongly that a hundred and eleven years intervene between **68** and the present **70**. Any conclusions reached by combining the two are sure to be insecure unless otherwise supported. On the other hand, **66** b i 30 and ii 3, by their mention of the *stip. kal. maiar*(*um*) and *stip. kal. sept*(*embrium*), are proof that the coh. XX Palmyrenorum was being paid three times a year in A.D. 250–251; and **71** (cf. **72**) shows that some troops were being paid in May during the second century. It is not known whether these were legionaries or auxiliaries; but on general grounds it would seem that paying some soldiers thrice yearly and others only once would be sure to create friction. Finally, all the *debet* accounts of the present text contain an item for *collatio* (*secund*)*o stip*(*endio*) (e.g. frag. a i 29; b i 10) which parallels the charge *ex eo* (i.e. *stipendi* in the line which precedes) *collatio* in the other accounts. Marichal takes this mention of the *secundum stipendium* as evidence that the account is for a whole year (*Solde* 412); but it appears to prove the opposite. In itself, *secundum* implies a *primum* and a *tertium*; and the payment of the collatio falls upon all the soldiers alike, aside from the quite exceptional case of a i 1–3. The natural time for withholding a payment is on the payday when it becomes due; and so if this is the *collatio secundo stipendio*, then we must believe that it is the second stipendium which the soldiers are being paid. But the second stipendium was due about the Kalends of May; and so the exact date of the text is early May 192.

A consequence of this dating by the consulate in b ii 7–8 is that one of the smaller fragments with traces of consulates may be used to complete b ii 8, but all the others must

[1] See in detail R. O. Fink, "*Damnatio Memoriae* and the Dating of Papyri," *Synteleia* 233.

either be placed higher in the same column, or somewhere to the left of either frag. b or even frag. a. Since I see no way of identifying the consuls in any of these fragments, I have put them all between frag. a and frag. b as the location with the greatest degree of probability. The designations "c", "d", "e", and so on are not intended to suggest that the fragments originally followed in that order.

A word may now be said about the form *stipendi*, not discussed in *Occ*. Except for the mention of the secundum stipendium, this might be read as *stipend i* for *stipend*(*ium*) (*primum*); and there is still the question whether it is to be taken as *stipendi*(*um*), the object of *accepit*, or as *stipendi*, a partitive gentive. If the latter, then Watson's contention that the odd amounts of the pay in **68** and **70** represent only a part of the total due finds support; but I see no way of deciding the matter.

On the other hand, the suggestion in *Occ*. (55) that the amounts owed in the *debet* entries may be an accumulation of installments of the collatio is not borne out by the figures in a i 26–32 or b i 7–13, in neither of which are the debita a multiple of 4 denarii, 22½ obols. Moreover, a ii 18–21, and probably b ii 14, show that the soldiers were subject to other charges than the collatio, and it is quite possible that the total of such charges at times exceeded the stipendium. But Marichal is right in emphasizing that none of these soldiers with debita is said to have received any pay, and is probably right in supposing that they were absent from headquarters at the time when the record was made up.

To return now to the text as a whole. It must be a pay record because of the formula *accepit stipendi* and the withholding of the collatio. But the form is quite different from that of **68**; and reasons may be suggested. In **68** it is evident that when the first stipendium of the year was paid, a skeleton account was made up for the entire century with each man's name at the top of a column, followed by the accounts for the first stipendium, and room for the second and third. The roll would then be laid away until May, when the second stipendium was entered with the appropriate deductions and balances and the roll put away until September. But this was clumsy in itself and would need endless revisions because of deaths, transfers, promotions, and the like during each interval of four months. Moreover, Domitian had forbidden soldiers to accumulate more than 250 denarii of savings in their accounts (Suet. *Dom*. 7.3); and it is obvious in the present text that involuntary savings are limited to the 100 denarii *in deposito* and the 75 *in uiatico*. Under these circumstances elaborate accounts were not needed; and so by the time of this text a new roll was being made up for each stipendium in which all the accounts followed continuously. This also made it unnecessary to name each stipendium in each man's account as first, second, or third, as was done in **68**, because the roll would have a statement at its head telling which stipendium was being recorded.

Frag. a

Col. i

]O COS
]. . CASTR
]ạr ⚹ c̣cxliii ob x s

One line blank

ORFITO ET M]ẠX̣ỊṂO COS A.D. 172
]PVS˙ CASTR
[loric- in dep ✳]ịn uiatico ✳ lxxv
[accepit stipendi ✳]ḷxxxiv ob xv s e
[ex eo collatio ✳]ịịịị ọb xxii s
[reliquos tulit ✳ lx]x̣ịx ob x̣x̣i e
[habet in dep ✳ in uiatic]ọ ✳ lxxṿ[
One line blank: Consulate? 174?
]ṂẸ[
About eight lines lost
loric- in dep]✳̣ ç[in u]ịạ[tico ✳ lxxv
accepit stipe]ṇdi ✳ lxxxiv ob x[v s e
ex eo col]latio ✳ iiii ob xxi[i s
reliquos tu]lit ✳ lxxix ob xxi e
habet in dep] ✳̣ c in uiatico ✳ lx[xv
P]ỌḶLIONE II CỌṢ 176
].ṬHEHVS˙ CASTR
loric- in dep ✳]ç in uiatico ✳ lxxv
accepit stipendi] ✳ lxxxiv ob xv s e
ex eo collati]ọ ✳ iiii ob xxii s
reliquos tulit] ✳̣ lxxix ob xxi e
habet in dep ✳ C in]uiatico ✳ lxxv
[IMP LVCCIO COMMODO ET]
QVINṬỊḶ[LO CO]Ṣ 177
MA]X̣IMVṢ N[. . . . .]IANVS˙ ÇASTR
loric]titis in dep ✳ c [i]n ụiaticọ ✳̣ lx̣xv
deb]et ex priore ratiọṇ ✳ x̣[v]ị[ii] ob xxiv s
ite]ṃ collatio íío stiṗ ✳ iiii ob xxii s
]f′ quos debet ✳ xxiii ob xix
habe]ṭ in dep ✳ c in uiatiçọ ✳ lxxv
debet ✳ xxii[i] ob xix

Frag. a i 1–3. This entry is unique in consisting only of a date, the soldier's name, and one other line, followed by either a line too short to reach the edge of the papyrus or a blank line. Possibly the man had died or been transferred or discharged.

3.].ṛ: M.]ṭr is a less likely possibility. Expand: *(denarios) ccxliii ob(olos) x s(emis)*.

4. *MA]X̣ỊṂO:* M.

6. *[lorictitis]:* M; but in a iii 22 and b ii 10, the word *loricem* is used. A. Piganiol, in his review of *Occ.* (*REL* 25 [1947] 435) explains *lorictitis* as a "déformation de *loricatis*" to be understood as "dans les coffres-forts." This makes good sense, but is phonetically unsatisfying; and he does not discuss *loricem*. Gilliam, *AJP* 88 (1967) 101, suggests that the word may be connected with "cuirassed statues of emperors standing before a strong-room in the *principia*," and cites the *procurator a loricata*.

7.]*(ḍẹṇạṛịọṣ):* M. Expand: *xv (dodrantem)*, and see *Occ.* 72–76 for the symbol.

9. *LXX]ỊX:* M. Expand: *xxi (quadrantem)*, and see *Occ.* 72–76.

11.]*M[:* M; and in the apparatus Marichal proposes *SEVERO ET PO]M[PEIANO II COS*. The *M*, however, falls under the *O* of *MAXIMO* in line 4; so the numeral must have been expressed with Severus' name, if this line is a consular date. But the line need not contain a consulship at all. I am inclined to believe that this is the soldier's name or origo, and that the consulship was in the preceding line, here blank. *gallo et flacco cos*, 174, would do very well.

17. M restores *Apro ii et P]ollione*; but that inverts the customary order of this pair of names; and *POLLIONE* is far enough left to cause some doubt whether there was another name in the line. The *E* is under the *O* of *MAXIMO*, line 4, and the *M* in line 11.

In line 4 there are thirteen letters before this point; in line 11, twelve letters, of which seven spaces are needed for *POLLION*, leaving only five or six for the eight letters of *APRO II ET*. It seems quite possible that Aper had incurred damnatio memoriae.

18.]. .*Ṭ̣HOHUS:* M; but for the possible *E* cf. the second *E* of *PRESENTE*, col. ii 30. Perhaps Dositheus, Pitheeus, Pitheous, or Pseutheous. The second *H* probably represents a Greek eta; cf. *TINHIVS* in b ii 9.

19. Daris does not bracket *denarios*.

24–25. M prints the names of both consuls as one line; but *quintillo cos* is too far left to permit it. Cf. b ii 7–8, which has the arrangement adopted here.

26. Surprisingly few names suit the requirements of the cognomen here. Dessau and Dornseiff-Hansen offer only Nemaesianus, Neptunianus, Nigrinianus, and Numisianus.

28. *X̣Ṿ[III]:* M. Expand: *ration(e)*.

29. *collatio (secundo) stip(endio):* M, which Marichal explains as an ablative of time. See *Occ.* 39 and 77–79. This is not, however, the oldest example of abbreviation by suspension. See **64** i 36 and 39.

30. *f(iunt)*.

Col. ii

LVCCIVS AGILLIVS· CASTR
lorictitis in dep ⚹ c in uiatico ⚹ lxxv
accepit stipendi ⚹ lxxxiv ob xv s e
ex eo coḷ[la]tiọ ⚹ iiii ob xxiị s
reliquos ṭ[u]ḷit ⚹ lxxix ob xxị ẹ
habet in dep ⚹̣ c in uiatico ⚹ lxxv
ORḞỊTO ET RVFO COS A.D. 178
P̣OLION[ ]Ḍ̣IOSCORI CASTR
ḷorictitiṣ ị[n] dep ⚹ c in uiatico ⚹ lxxv
accepit s[ti]pendi ⚹ lxxxiv ob xv s e
ex eo c[ol]ḷatio ⚹ iiii ob xxii s
r]ẹḷiquos [t]ụḷ[i]t ⚹ lxxix ob xxi e
ha]bet in [dep ⚹] ç in ụ[i]aṭico ⚹ lxxv
].Ṣ.[. . .] PANTARCHVS CASTR
lorictiti]ṣ in dep ⚹ clxxxxv ob viii s in uiạ[tico
accepit] stipendi ⚹ lx̣xx̣[iv o]ḅ xv s e
ex eo] ç[o]ḷḷatio ⚹ iiịi ọḅ [xxii] s
q]ụẹsturam pro contụctione[
].meịlocụṣoụbilateris ⚹ lị[iii
]x̣ ṛ. . .ṭa ⚹ lviii ob xxii s
reliqu]ọṣ tulit ⚹ xxv ob xxi e
habet in]ḍep ⚹ clxxxxv ob viii s in uiatico ⚹ lxxv
]S MAXIMVS· CASTR
loricti]tis in dep ⚹ c in uiatico ⚹ lxxv
d]ẹbet ex̣ priore ration ⚹ xviii ob xxiv s
item collaṭio íío stip ⚹ iiii ob xxii s
f· quos debet ⚹ xxiii ob xix
habet in dep ⚹ c in uiatico ⚹ lxxv
debet ⚹ xxiii ob xix
PRESENTE $\overline{II}$ ET CONTIANO Ií COS 180
rinoc PATHERMVTHIS PTOLEMEI· HELIOPOL
loricititis in dep ⚹ c in uiatico ⚹ lxxv
accepit stipendi ⚹ lxxxiv ob xv s e

ex eo colḷatio ✳ iiii ob xxii s
reliquos tulit ✳ lxxix ob xxi e
h[a]bet in dep ✳ c in uiatico ✳ lxxv
ostraci Ḥ. . . Ṇ[.]NVS PHLEI˙ ANTEOPOL˙
lorictitis in dep ✳ ccvi in uiatico ✳ lxxv
accepit stipendi ✳ lxxxiv ob xv s e
ex eo colḷatio ✳ iiii ob xxii s
reliquos tulit ✳ lxxix ob xxi e
habet in dep ✳ ccvi in uiatico ✳ lxxv

ii 5. [*tuli*]*t:* M.

6. [(*denarios*)] *C:* M; but my photograph, which is much older, shows a small fleck of the symbol for denarii.

7. Rufus seems to have survived Commodus in spite of the statement in SHA, *Comm.* 4.10. See Fink, p. 235.

9. [*i*]*ṇ:* M.

12. [*tuli*]*t:* M.

14. Between *S.*[and *P* three letters is the maximum possible; but there may have been fewer. The first name may have ended].*SV*[*S* or].*SI*[*VS*.

15. *uiaṭ*[*ico:* Daris.

16. *LX̣XX*[*IV ob*(*olos*)]*:* M.

18. *in qua*]*ẹsturam:* M, with credit to Lesquier. *contuctione* is interpreted, probably rightly, as a variant of *conductione*, making Pantarchus a conductor of some sort. But the vowel after *t* differs very little from the final *e*, so that it is just possible that one should read *contectione*, "a roofing over." Without more of the context, one can hardly decide. See also on line 19.

19.]. .*ẹellocuo ubi laterit:* M, comparing *debet*, i 31, and *habet*, ii 42, for a final *t* rather than *s*, and commenting, p. 59, note 1, "Quant à la forme *laterit*, elle n'étonnera aucun romaniste." But the final letter here stands free, whereas the *t* of *debet* and *habet* is in ligature with the preceding *e*; and neither *lateris* nor *laterit* seems an acceptable form of the verb *latere* in 192, even in Egypt. The line appears to me a hopeless crux; but to assist in its solution, which is essential to the understanding of line 18 as well, I add these notes. Only the top stroke of the first letter is extant, at first horizontal and then curling upward as it moves to the right. It is not precisely like anything else on the papyrus, but might be *m* or *c* (cf. the first two letters of i 29), *g*, or, less likely, *f* or *t*. The next letter, read *ẹ* in *Occ.*, is almost certainly *m*; *e* is sure; the next could be *l*, but could as easily be *i*. The character after *c* has a hook at the top of the left-hand stroke which may indicate *us* as in *helius*, iii 13 (*locus* is at least a word); but it could also be *u* or *e*. Next is probably an *o*, small and filled in; and the remaining letters are certain. Very tentatively I suggest that at the end *bilateris* might be read as an adjective derived from *later*, *lateris*, or *latus*, *lateris*. No such word is found in *TLL*; but in Greek both δίπλινθος and δίπλευρος do occur. The choice of meanings, if either is to be accepted, depends on making sense of the first part of the line.

20.]*f*(*iunt*) *ṛẹliçta:* M. The word *relicta* can be accepted, though all but the *ta* are no more than dots in my photograph; but the first letter on the papyrus is almost certainly *x*, not *f*. The number at the end of the line is clearly the sum of the amounts in lines 17 and 19. Marichal's explanation seems certain: Pantarchus ceded this amount from his pay and received the balance shown in line 21. The amounts in line 22 show no change from line 16; therefore his entire stipendium is accounted for in lines 17–21.

25. *de*]*bet:* M.

26. See on i 28.

30. The second consul is Sex. Quintilius Condianus, executed by Commodus later in 192. See Fink, p. 234. The *t* for *d* supports the reading *contuctione* for *conductione* in line 18.

31. *rinoc*(*orurae*) is a later notation by a second hand. Cf. a ii 37; iii 1, 8, and 13; and b ii 9. See *Occ.* 66–69 on the place-names. *Heliopol*(*itanus*), like *castr*(*is*) in the preceding entries, is the soldier's origo.

37. *P̣*.[.].*UNUS:* M. As in line 31, *ostraci*(*nae*) is a later notation in cursive, by the same hand as *rinoc*. The date of enlistment is omitted because it is the same as in line 30 above.

Col. iii

heracIus IV[
loṛ[ic-
a[ccepit
[
[

haḅ[et
[*Consulate* A.D. 181–186
ce]rkas˙ go ANṾ[
] gendụṃ loṛị[c-
a[ccepit
About fourteen lines lost: see apparatus
h[abet
.[ ].[ ].[182–187
helius MELAS˙ L[
lorictitis iṇ[dep
debet ex[priore
item [collatio ííо stip
f[quos debet
habet ị[n dep
[debet
One line lost: consulate 183–188
ANTO[
loricẹṃ[in dep
accep̣[it
[ex eo collatio
.. ṛ[eliquos tulit
ḥ[abet
.[*Consulate* 184–189
Ṿ[

iii 1. *heraclus* is another notation in cursive in the second hand like those in ii 31 and 37. It signifies, of course, Heracleous(polis) Parva, in the Delta. See *Occ.* 66–69.

6. *ha[bet:* M.

7. This line, and 12, 20, and 27 below, contained consular dates which must fall between 180 (ii 30) and 190 (b i 6–7). The date in this line is therefore limited to 181–186, or if frag. c is regarded as still belonging to a column between frags. a and b (see the apparatus on frag. c), then to 181–185.

8.]....˙ *go AN*.[: M. The name of the place is variously given as Cercasora, Cercasorum, or Cercasorus. It occupied a strategic site at the apex of the Delta, about ten miles north of Babylon.

9. *g.ub.m:* M. Perhaps one should combine this line with the preceding: *gogendum*, i.e. *cogendum*? But the meaning is not clear.

10a. The fourteen lines which measurements on the plate show to be missing are exactly enough to complete the entry which begins in line 8 and the one which ends in line 11, with a complete one between, now entirely lost. None of the three could have been of the *debet* type, which creates entries of seven lines instead of six; and there could have been no mention of a consulship.

12. The limitations described under line 7 restrict this consulship to 182–187 or 182–186; but the traces are too slight and uncertain to encourage any attempt at greater precision.

13. As Marichal saw, *helius* must be Heliopolis, north and a little east of Babylon.

14. *i[n:* M.

16. *iteṃ [ex eo collatio:* M.

20. For the dates, see on line 7.

22. Marichal refers to b ii 10 for the form *loricem* found in these two places instead of *lorictitis*. Since both words are known only from this text, the difference between them is not clear. See also on a i 6.

25. *ṛ[eliquos:* M; but my photograph shows traces of at least two letters before the *r*.

26–28. No readings in M. The tip of a stroke visible in 28 cannot be the *l* of *lorictitis* and so must be the first letter of either a soldier's or a consul's name. If a consul's, it is the second line of a consular date such as b ii 7–8; and 186, *commodo v et glabrione ii*, would be a suitable date. But the stroke in line 28 cannot be part of Glabrio's name and so must belong to the soldier. The consul's names remain in doubt.

Frag. c (Marichal: 6.866 B, frag. C; *Occ.* p. 16)

HE.[
loric̣[-
accc̣[epit
[ex eo
ṛ[eliquos tulit
habẹ[t
[*Consulate*
]ṭḥaub Ṃ[
l[oric-

Frag. c. On the left edge of the papyrus there are traces of ink level with line 3 and a reasonably certain *e* (for *quadrantem*) in the next line. In the middle are traces in line 5 which might be *i* and *e*; but they may be accidental.

7. *t]ḥạub(asti) M*[--- *COS*]: M. Marichal in the apparatus proves that this fragment cannot be attached to the right side of frag. a in the gap of 14 lines between the lines presently numbered 10 and 11. But marginal notations like *thaub* elsewhere are placed beside the soldiers' names; and so this line cannot contain a consulship as Marichal supposed. Instead, the consulship was in the preceding line, now lost except for the blank space between lines 6 and 7. With the consulate, all hope of dating or placing the fragment vanishes. It could come from the left side of frag. a or frags. b, d, or e, or be part of a column not otherwise represented.

8. *Ḷ*[: M.

Frag. d (Marichal: 6.866 B, frag. D; *Occ.* pp. 20–21)

collatio ✳ iiii ob xxii]s
tulit lxxix ob xxi]ẹ
uiatico ✳]lxxv
Consulate]
]IT
in uiatico ✳ lx]x̣v ogḍo[
stipendi ✳ lxxxiv ob xv s] e ṣ[
collatio ✳ iiii ob xx]ịi s
tulit ✳ lxxix o]b xxi e
in uiatico ✳]l[x]xv
CA]ṢTR
in uiati]c̣o ✳ lxxv
ob]xv s e
ob]x̣xii s
ob x]x̣i e
in uiatico ✳ lx]x̣ṿ
]. .
in u]ịatico ✳ lxxv of[
]ṣ ẹ
]ṣ
]ẹ
] ✳̣ lxxv
]. .

Frag. d 1–3. These are the last three lines of a regular entry, from *ex eo collatio* in 1 through *reliquos tulit* (2) to *uiatico* ⚹ *lxxv* in 3.

5.]*IT(ES)*: M, surely right. Cf. frag. b i 7: *THINIT(ES)*.

6–7. *Ogbo*[: M. The remains in *ogḍo*[and *s*[are parts of a marginal notation such as those in frag. a ii 31 and 37; iii 1, 8, 13 and b ii 9. It belonged with a name in the adjoining column on the right, and *ogḍo*[should designate a place; but I have not identified it. The alternative reading *ogḅo*[does not help; for a miswriting of "Ombos" seems unlikely on the score of both pronunciation and geography, and the choice of *d* over *b* is supported by comparison of *gendum* (a iii 9) with *bab* (b ii 9). Can it refer to the obscure 'Ογδοηκοντάρουρος (*Corp. Pap. Raineri* 28, 14) placed "probably at Theogenous or Mendes" in *PTeb.* II, p. 392?

14. Daris has no bracket after *ob(olos)*.

16. *LXX*]*V*: M.

17. This line must have contained a soldier's name and origo, and should be in capitals; but the vestiges remaining look like a cursive *es* or *et*.

18. *Os*[*traci*(*nae*)?: M, with a suggestion in the apparatus that *of* should perhaps be read in place of *os*. This is another marginal notation like *ogḍo*[in 6 but may perhaps be *of*[*ficio* rather than a place-name. The entries for depositum and viaticum are displaced far to the right; so the line must have begun with something more than the usual *lorictitis*.

23. These traces reported by M are not visible in my photograph.

Frag. e (Marichal: 6.866 D, frag. E; *Occ.* p. 21)

]NVS OXYR [
loric- in dep]⚹ clxxxvii s in u[iatico
accepit stipe]ṇdi ⚹ lxx̣xiv ob x̣[v s e
ex eo]c̣ollatio ⚹ iiii ob x̣[xii s
reliquo]ṣ tulit ⚹ lxxix ob x̣[xi e
habet in dep] ⚹̣ clxxxỵii s in uiaticọ[
]COS
]NIVS .[

Frag. e 7. *CO*]*S*: M.

Frag. f (Marichal: 6.866 B, frag. F; *Occ.* pp. 21–22)

]i ob xxị[
f quos debet ⚹ o]b xii
]⚹ lxxṿ[

Frag. f. I have taken these readings from M because my photograph does not include this piece. Marichal seems to be right in restoring these lines as a *debet* account like b i 7–13.

Frag. g (Marichal: 6.866 B, frag. G; *Occ.* p. 22)

.[
[*Consulate*?
IṾ[
]. ẹrro lọ[ric-
a[ccepit
[ex eo
[reliquos
hạ[bet
THE[
loric[-
a[ccepit

Frag. g. There seems on the plate in *Occ.* to be an ink-stroke not recorded in Marichal's text. The short line which precedes the soldier's name could be either the last line of a *debet* entry (cf. a i 32) or a consular date.

I have taken the marginal notation from *Occ.*, though on the plate the *e* looks more like *a* and though I do not understand the double *r* if the place meant is Heroonpolis (*Occ.* 68). *ḥẹro* does not look possible.

PAberd. 133

]COS
].S· HELIOPOL
i]ṇ uiatiç̣ọ ⚹ ḷx̣x̣[v

Frag. b (Marichal: 6.866 B, frag. A; *Occ.* pp. 17–19)

Col. i

[loric- in dep ⚹ c in uiati]ç̣ọ ⚹̣[lxxv
[accepit] ṣtị[p]ẹndi [⚹ lx]x̣xiv ob xv[s e
e]x̣ eo c̣ọḷḷat[io ⚹]iiii ob xxii s
reliqu]ọs tulit ⚹ lxxix ob xxi e
habet in d]ẹp ⚹ ç̣ in uiạtico ⚹ lxxv
SE]PTIMIANỌ ỊÍ COS A.D. 190
]TIBERIS· THINIT
[lorictiti]ṣ in dep ⚹ c iṇ uiatico ⚹ lxxv
[debet]ex p̣riore rati[on] ⚹ vi ob xxii s
[item collatio íío stip ⚹ i]ịii ob xxiị s
[f quos debet ⚹]x̣i ob xvii
[habet in dep ⚹ c in uiat]ico ⚹ lxxv
[debet ⚹ xi ob]xvii
]S· C· R·
[loric- in dep ⚹ c in uiati]ç̣ọ ⚹ lxxv
[accepit stipendi ⚹ lxxxiv]ob xv s e
[ex eo collatio ⚹ iiii]ob xxii s
[reliquos tulit ⚹ lxxix ob] x̣x̣i e
[habet in dep ⚹ c in uiatico]⚹ lxxv
]Ṣ . . . .
[loric- in dep ⚹ c in uiatic]ọ ⚹ lxxv
[debet ex priore ration ⚹].ix ob xvii s
[item collatio íío stip ⚹]iiii ob xxii s
[f quos debet ⚹ o]ḅ xii
[habet in dep ⚹ c in uiatico ⚹] ḷxxv

Frag. b i 1. *uiati]ç̣ọ* [*(denarios)*: M. Only a soldier's name is certainly missing above this line.

6. *IMP LUCCIO COMMODO VI ET SE]PTIMIANO*: M. The position of *SEPTIMIANO* in the line, however, shows that at most there is room for only nine or ten letters before it; and of these at least three must be allowed for the usual indentation of the consular date. Cf. this fragment, ii 7–8. It is hard to believe that the clerk overlooked the emperor's name; but he seems to have done so, for *VI ET* alone would take up nearly all the available space.

14. Expand *c*(*iuis*) *r*(*omanus*).

20.]· *CASTR*(*IS*): M.

Col. ii

At least six lines lost

.[.].[.].[
..[..].ixṭ.[
trạṇ.[.].[
[ ]ḥe magni.[

4a pọscu.[*Second hand*
5 ex eis in dẹp̣[
5a ex yscription.[
6 habet in dep[
IMP· LVCC̣Ị[O COMMODO VII ET
PERṬ[INACE II COS A.D. 192
bab TINHIVS VAL[
10 loricem in dep ✳̣[
debet ex prioṛẹ[
item collati[o
13 accepit sụṃ[
13a mis ad praesi bab[
14 cincturas c.[
15 f· quos ḍ[ebet
habet in dep ✳ x̣[
debet ✳ .[
IVḶ[I]ỴS[
lor[ic-
20 acç[epit
[ex eo collatio?
pin. [
poss [

Frag. b ii 1. .[: M.

2. . . . [*co*]*ḷḷạṭị*[*o*: M, who says that the *a* is made to look like an *x* by a stroke from above; but that stroke is not continuous with the one which makes the *x*.

3. *ṭṛạ*. . [: M. The letter after *n* is not *s*, but could be *a*.

4. *iṭem an*. . [: M. The surface of the papyrus is scaled before *h*; but the tops of letters should be visible. Expand *h*(*oneste*) *e*(*merit-*)?

4a. This line is inserted with a coarser pen and in a different hand.

5. Marichal says that this line has been canceled; but I do not see any signs of cancellation in the photograph.

5a. This line is also inserted by the same hand and pen as 4a. Read *inscriptione*[.

6. This line appears to have been added by the same hand and pen as 4a and 5a.

9. *UAṚ*[: M. The marginal notation, *bab*(*ylone*), is a later addition, like those in frag. a. It is certainly in a different hand from the additions in lines 4a, 5a, and 6. The soldier's name probably derives from that of Tineius Demetrius, Prefect of Egypt in 189–190. The use of eta for *e* is noteworthy; but cf. a i 18 above, *CPL* 310: *COH I APAMHNORVM*; and the verso of **51** (*CPL* 61): *AENEAS DAPDANIAE*. For Roman *h* as a Greek rough breathing see on **76** xvi 1.

10. The difference between *lorictitis* and *loricem* is not known. Cf. frag. a i 6 and iii 22.

13. *suṣ*.[: M; in "Solde" 416, note 3, he reads *stip*; but the second letter cannot be *t*. The last three letters of *accepit* and the rest of the line seem to have been written by the hand which wrote lines 4a, 5a, 6, and 13a.

13a. . . . . . *praesi*(*di*.) *Bab*[*yloniae*: M. This line is inserted by the same hand as 4a, 5a, and 6, but with a better pen. Expand *mis*(*sus*) *ad praesi*(*dem*) *bab*(*ylone*) or more probably *ad praesi*(*dium*) and perhaps *bab*(*ylonis*).

14. *cḷ*[: M.

16. (*denarios*) [: M.

17. (*denarios*)[: M.

22. M prints these letters as capitals, but the *n* is a cursive rather than capital form. Lines 18–23 are part of an abnormal account somewhat like that of Pantarchus, a ii 14–22.

Frag. h (Marichal: 6.866 B, frag. B; *Occ.* p. 22)

]lx̣[xv
]lxxv
]✳ lxxv
]✳ ḷx̣x̣ṿ

]lxxv
]lxxv
]✱̣ lxxv
]✱ lxxv
]✱̣ [l]x̣x̣[v]

Frag. h. Marichal seems right in supposing that this fragment comes from a summary at the end of the text (*Occ.* 23) and in comparing it with **73**, col. iii (*Occ.* 62–63).

8. Daris brackets (*denarios*).

TRANSLATION

Since the text is so repetitious, I translate only a sample of the two commonest types of entries. Frag. a i 1–3; ii 18–19; and b ii, entire, would be more interesting but are either too fragmentary to make sense or have not been satisfactorily read.

Frag. a ii 7–13: Consulate of Orfitus and Rufus
Polion son of Dioscorus: camp-born.
in the strong-box; on deposit, 100 denarii; as viaticum, 75 denarii.
  received of his pay 84 denarii, 15 $\frac{3}{4}$ obols
    from that, contribution, 4 denarii, 22 $\frac{1}{2}$ obols
  took the rest, 79 denarii, 21 $\frac{1}{4}$ obols
has on deposit 100 denarii; as viaticum, 75 denarii.

Frag. a ii 30–36: Second consulate of Praesens and second of Condianus
at Rhinocorura. Pathermuthis son of Ptolemeus: Heliopolitan.
in the strong-box: on deposit, 100 denarii; as viaticum, 75 denarii
  received of his pay 84 denarii, 15 $\frac{3}{4}$ obols
    from that, contribution, 4 denarii, 22 $\frac{1}{2}$ obols
  took the rest, 79 denarii, 21 $\frac{1}{4}$ obols
has on deposit 100 denarii; as viaticum, 75 denarii.

Frag. a i 24–32: Consulate of the Emperor Lucius Commodus and Quintillus
Maximus N[. . . . .]ianus: camp-born.
in the strong-box: on deposit, 100 denarii; as viaticum, 75 denarii
  owes from the previous accounting, 18 denarii, 24 $\frac{1}{2}$ obols
  also contribution, second pay, 4 denarii, 22 $\frac{1}{2}$ obols
    sum which he owes, 23 denarii, 19 obols
has on deposit 100 denarii; as viaticum, 75 denarii
    owes 23 denarii, 19 obols.

Frag. b i 6–13:]second consulate of Septimianus
    ]son of Tiber: native of This.
in the strong-box: on deposit, 100 denarii; as viaticum, 75 denarii
  owes from the previous accounting 6 denarii, 22 $\frac{1}{2}$ obols
  also contribution, second pay, 4 denarii, 22 $\frac{1}{2}$ obols
    sum which he owes, 11 denarii, 17 obols
has on deposit 100 denarii; as viaticum, 75 denarii
    owes 11 denarii, 17 obols.

71

Pay Records

PVindob. L 72 and 82, recto; *vidi* — Late II p.
Papyrussammlung der Oesterreichische Nationalbibliothek

Unpublished.

Both the hand and the content confirm that these two pieces belong to the same text; and the little that can be read shows that they are pay accounts of much the same sort as **70**. The main difference is that the stipendium is described as the stipendium of May 1 and that they seem to contain more details of charges; but there are only three accounts here, so the impression of more detail may be misleading.

The phrase *stip(endium) kal(endarum) maiar(um)* here, and the similar formulae in **66** b i 30 and ii 3, and **72**, give ground for supposing that the stipendium was paid or due on January 1, May 1, and September 1, as Gilliam argues.[1] The Feriale Duranum, however, has been restored so that the first stipendium comes on *vii idus ianuarias.* (See **117** i 7–9.) But the two opinions do not necessarily exclude each other. A stipendium which was due on January 1 would not necessarily be paid on that date, for the precise number and status of the men to be paid could not be known until the records for December 31 were in. Or even if the day fixed for payment were *vii idus*, the stipendium might still be referred to as the stipendium of the Kalends for convenience' sake instead of the exact but awkward *stipendium diei septimi ante idus.*

No fractions of the denarius happen to appear in these pieces; and so it is impossible to say how many obols it contained.

The dating is on the basis of the hand, which seems approximately contemporary with that of **70**.

The verso is in Greek.

[1] J. F. Gilliam, "The Roman Military Feriale," *HTR* 47 (1954) 191; *Final Rep.* v, p. 291.

Frag. a (=L 72)

accep stip]ḳạḷ ṃ[aiar
]𐆖 iii suṃ[
]. . . refec ạṛ[m
]. 𐆖 xxxvii[
]𐆖 lxii dḟ. ạṣa[
]𐆖 xxxi [
c]oṣ
].˙ AẸLVRI[
d]ẹp̣ọsiti 𐆖 xc̣viii [
ac]c̣ep st⟨i⟩p kal maiar[
]ṭịo ad 𐆖 iii sumifṣṇọ[
]. . ẹṭẹị refec arm 𐆖 x̣[
]ẹ 𐆖 xxx. ii c̣o. . . . [

Frag. b (=L 82)

]. [.]. [
One line blank: consulate?
]ẠẸ hoR[
]. 𐆖 xv[
accep]ṣṭip kal maịạṛ ẹ. . . [
]ạḍ 𐆖 iii suṃ[
]. ṛẹf s. . . 𐆖 c̣x̣[
]. iṣ˙ 𐆖 xx̣. [
]. 𐆖 lii iṇ. . [
]pe 𐆖 xlvii [
One line blank: consulate?
]ỊẠḤỌ. EṚỊ. . [

Frag. a (L 72) is a piece incomplete on all sides, with a maximum width of 4·6 cm. and a maximum height of 8·0 cm. At the top at least two lines are missing. Frag. b (L 82) is likewise incomplete all around, with a width of 3·7 cm. and a height of 8·5 cm. The height of the letters varies from 0·2 to 0·3 cm.; the symbol for denarius is 0·4 cm. high. The interlinear space varies from zero to 0·4 cm. The width of the columns is of course unknown.

a 2. This line corresponds to line 11, of which I can read neither the beginning nor the end. Could the charge here—if it is a charge— be the *collatio* of **70**? The amount is different; and I do not know what to make of *ad* before the symbol for denarius.

3. This line corresponds to line 12. I cannot decipher the beginning of either; but the charge seems clearly to be for *refec*(*tio*) *arm*(*orum*).

4. The letter on the left edge could be *c*, *s*, or *t*.

5. After *d*, *f* seems more likely; but *e* might be possible. I can make nothing of the letters here.

8. *F* is possible instead of *E*. Dessau 2636 (*CIL* VIII 2494) names a C. Iulius Aelurio who was a centurion of the leg. III Augusta in the time of Caracalla.

9. Does the genitive perhaps imply *tulit d*]*epositi*, "he withdrew a part of his deposit"?

11. See on 2.

b 5. Cf. a 1 and 10. Possibly *eṭ ṣẹp*[*t*(*embrium*)?

6. Cf. a 2 and 11.

7. Except for *ref* and the denarius symbol, the whole line is very uncertain.

8. One could also read].*ịịọ*

9. On the left edge of the papyrus *c* or *s* may be possible. The remaining stroke is nearly horizontal and at the top of the denarius symbol.

12. Aside from *E*, none of the letters is at all certain.

72

Pay Record of Auxiliaries

PRyl. 273a, recto; *vidi* II p.

Description: *PRyl.* II, no. 273 a, p. 399, lines 5 and 7 only.

Transcription, commentary, and facsimile: *ChLA* IV, no 243; cited as **M**.

Text: *CPL*, no. 126, and Daris, no. 32, reproduce the readings in *PRyl.* See the apparatus on lines 5 and 7.

Only enough can be read here to prove that this is a pay record very like **70** and even more like **71**. The nomenclature in line 5 is not Roman; so the men must have belonged to an auxiliary unit.

The dating must rest on paleographical grounds because the reading of line 10 is too uncertain to date by, if it is in fact a consulate.

The verso is in the Roman alphabet and may have been military. There appear to be remains of two columns with at least 13 lines in the second, in groups of 7, 3, and 3. The second line may read Ꮍ *ạ*. . [or *uiạ* or *vi ạ*. . [; the third may be *ẹọdẹṃ* or *ẹọṛụṃ*; the sixth, *ẹx̣ ạgṛ*; the seventh,]*ụḷit*; and the tenth,]. . . *ḷiụịus* followed by traces of more letters. None of this suffices to prove the nature of the text.

]. ⋇ c̣[
ka]ḷ [i]ạṇuạ[ri-
].a.   ṭṛ.[
ṭuḷ ẹtọ   ⋇[
One and a half lines blank
ṂẠṚIN˙ CRISP.[
...⋇̣ c̣c̣lx̣xi ṛsp rat˙ .[
ac̣c̣ẹp˙ sṭip˙ kal ianuarị[
].x.o.ạiaṣ.   [
.[ ]....[ ]ṭul[i]ṭ ịgạ..[
About three lines blank
ṂẠẸG̣ ..[
IṬVS   .[
ḥạḅ⋇ ...   [
ac̣c̣ẹp ṣtip kạḷ .[..]..[
i[   ].[   ].ṛ .ar [
]l.ṛ. ⋇ cclxx[
].[

1.].*US*[*:* M. Perhaps *ḥạḅ(et)*; cf. lines 6–7 and 12–13.

2. [*accep(it) stip(endii) Kal I*]*ạṇụạ*[*ri....:* M. Cf. line 7.

3. [*debet ex priore rat*]*ịoṇẹ* (*ḍẹṇạṛịọṣ*) *X*[*:* M.

4. *reli*[*q*(*uos*) *tu*]*lit*. .(*denarios*)[*:* M. Perhaps one should read *tul(it)* here and in line 9 on the analogy of *reliquos tulit* in **70**; but no such reading can be combined with Marichal's restoration of *debet* in lines 3 and 8. Cf. e.g. **70** a ii 8–13 with ii 23–29.

5. *Ṃ. ỊỤN. CRISPU*[*S:* Ryl, *CPL*, Daris; *Ạ.....N˙ CRISPU*[*S:* M. *Crispị*[*nus* is also possible.

6. ....*a.r.l.co rsprat˙* .[*:* M. Perhaps *ḥạḅ(et)* ⋇ etc.; cf. line 12. Marichal is right in seeing *ṛ s p* as a series of abbreviations; but if *hab(et)* in line 12 is right, then the sense of this line (and of 1 and 12) should be something like *habet denarios* (tot) *ex priore ratione* followed in the next line by the report of the receipt of the current stipendium. But I can think of nothing more appropriate as an expansion than *r(elictos) s(ecundum) p(riorem) rat(ionem)*; and this is not very convincing.

7. *a*[*c*]*cep(it) stip(endia) kal(endis) Ianuari*[*is:* Ryl, CPL, Daris. On *kal ianuar* see under **71**.

8. [*debet*] *ex pr*[*i*]*ore ra*[*tione:* M. I cannot find these words.

9. *reliq(uos) tul*[*i*]*t* .....[*:* M. The remains before *tulit* are only the feet of letters; but I do not find *l* or *q* among them.

10. [*APOLLINARI ET M*]*AMERT*[*INO COS:* M. But this restoration would extend far beyond the left-hand margin of the column, established by line 5; and in any case Apollinaris and Mamertinus were suffecti, not consules ordinarii. Nor is it certain that this line contained a consular date. With this reading the ground for Marichal's date of A.D. 150–170 also disappears.

What actually stood here is difficult to say. It may well have been a personal name, as in line 5; but even the letters are uncertain. The *E* seems sound; but at the beginning *AM* and *MA* are equally possible. After the *E*, Marichal's *R* is not convincing; the other traces are mere flecks.

11.]*ICUS:* M; but the second letter has a right angle at the foot. There is space for an *I* in the break between the *T* and *V*, or *IDVS* might be possible. The sense remains unclear.

12. .... (*denarios*) ...*:* M. Expand *hab(et)*.

13. *acc*[*ep(it)*]*; Ia*[*nuari:* M.

14. Only dots in M.

15. ...... (*denarios*) *CCL ex*[*:* M.

ChLA publishes an accompanying scrap as a second fragment, reading (1)]*ME*.[, (2)]...[The letters look more like Greek to me, possibly (1)]λλεḷ[They are on the recto.

73

Summary of Withdrawals, Amounts Owing, and Sums on Deposit

PFay. 105; *vidi* ca. 120–150
British Museum, no. 1196

Transcription and commentary, frag. a only:
1. Bernard P. Grenfell, Arthur S. Hunt, and David G. Hogarth, *Fayûm Towns and their Papyri* (London 1900) no. 105; cited as **Fay.**
2. Marichal, *Occ.*, pp. 41–53, 56–57, 62–66, and 72–76.

Transcription, facsimile, and commentary: *ChLA* III, no. 208; cited as **M.**

Text: *CPL*, no. 124, reproduces the text of *Occ.* except in a iii 22; Daris, no. 34, was able to use *ChLA* but retains several readings from *Occ.* and ignores most of the dots under letters.

The heading of frag. a ii and the summary at the end of a iii show that this text is basically an accounting, perhaps at the end of a four-month pay period, of the moneys held in or owed to various funds by the soldiers of a turma in the auxiliary forces. Since a iii 27–29 state the totals of deposita, seposita, and viatica, while a ii is devoted to withdrawals from the deposita, we should probably assume that there were also columns recording additions to these three accounts. Frag. b, in fact, which repeats the names found in a ii 12–15, must either be a part of such a column or belong to the records of a different accounting period. Marichal is no doubt right in supposing that seposita were accessible to the soldier only upon his discharge (*Occ.* 50 and 53); but there is no reason why viatica should not be subject to withdrawals; and in fact a i 14 ought perhaps to be restored as [*recessa*] *uiaticorum* (cf. a ii 1). It is to be noted that only two names follow—too few for a list of the men with viatica to their credit, or of those making additions to their viatica. Line 17 in the same column should begin like ii 3, with [*item de*]*bitores*; and the eight names which follow must be those of men who are indebted to this fund.

Since frag. a, col. iii, is on a separate piece of papyrus, the question arises whether it is part of the records of the same turma as cols. i–ii. *ChLA*, p. 90, argues that it is not because only two names, and those common ones, appear in both i–ii and iii. But the same men would of course not have deposita and at the same time be *debitores* (*depositorum*); and the total of the two categories in ii 14–18 and iii 2–26 is not too large for a single turma. The name in capitals at the top of iii must, to be sure, be a heading of some sort and consequently shows that iii was not a direct continuation of i–ii, even though there is no way of knowing whether Longinus is the commander of the whole unit, a decurion, a signifer, or something else. But since i and ii seem to deal only with recessa, the totals for seposita and viatica at the end of iii must come from other columns no longer extant, and the possibility remains that the whole set of accounts was for one and the same turma.

This possibility is strengthened by the fact that in frag. b 2–5 the same four names recur in the same order as in frag. a ii 12–15, with a good chance that the name in b 6 is the *fabianus* of a ii 16. Marichal in *ChLA*, p. 90, supposes that the name Pasion is found twice in frag. a i (15 and 23) and Serenus twice in frag. a ii (11 and 13) because "the book-keeper simply copied out in order the more detailed and dated entries in a Day Book." Pasion may, it is true, be one person because this name occurs in three different accounts, the third time in a ii 6. But it is hardly credible that the five men in frag. b should turn up by chance in the day-book in the same order as in frag. a ii. Rather, the clerks were observing the customary order of seniority within the turma which sufficed to distinguish Serenus 1 (ii 11) from Serenus 2 (ii 13) and they could manage with only one name apiece for these men because they did not have to keep them separate from Sereni, Apollinarii, and Gemelli in other turmae. Cf. **80**.

The sums held on deposit by the individual soldiers named in col. iii, and the totals in iii 27–29, are important evidence on the adequacy of soldiers' pay. The non-Roman names of the men in this text show that they were auxiliaries, and the symbol ₮ in a ii 19 is proof that they were equites. There is of course no evidence on the length of service of the men, but it is worth noting that average of the deposits for the last twelve, from Neferos (line 15) to Turbon, is 387 denarii, even though Saturninus (line 24) had only 38, while the average for all 25 members of the turma is 445 denarii. Dionysius (ii 1 and 18) makes a withdrawal of 1458 denarii and receives 103 for arms; and there is reason to believe that Argotius (iii 14 and app.) had a deposit of 2000 or more. The mere fact, too, that as many as 25 members of the turma had money on deposit is significant in this connection.

Marichal, *Occ.* 49, states that **70** and **73** are complementary to each other; and this is certainly true up to a point. The list of depositors in **73** a iii is paralleled by **70**, frag. h, which certainly listed soldiers with the amount of their viatica, perhaps, though not certainly, preceded in each line by the amount of the depositum. Conversely, frag. h of the present text mentions a stipendium and frag. e may contain references to hay and boots which recall the deductions in **68**. All this suggests the possibility that a summing up like the present text formed the concluding section of every such pay account as **68** and **70**. But the data now available do not enable us to determine the exact relationship between the two sorts of records.

It has been said that the personnel in this text are auxiliary equites; but it is still an open question whether they belonged to an ala or a cohors equitata. *ChLA* in effect withdraws the proposal in *Occ.* to identify the unit as the ala veterana Gallica; and the possibility of the identification breaks down completely if the new dating of **73** is right.

The original editors dated the text about A.D. 180, chiefly on the ground that the addressee named on the verso was a strategos of the Heraclide meros of the Arsinoite nome in either A.D. 176–179 or 186. Marichal, *Occ.*, publishing in 1945 when the papyrus was inaccessible, contented himself with the observation that this date could only be a terminus ante quem but advanced the date of the text only five years, to about 175, a date retained in *ChLA*. The hands, however, appear to have much more in common with those of **68** (A.D. 81), **10** (A.D. 87), and **63** (A.D. 100–105) than with **70** (A.D. 192), though the editors' dating would make it roughly contemporary with the last; and the hand of frag. a, i–ii, appears earlier than that of col. iii. In this connection it may be significant that in a iii 27–28 and 30 the bars over the figures for thousands drop down at both ends, a usage described by Cagnat (*Cours d'Épigraphie*[4] 32) as characteristic of the time of Hadrian. At any rate, a date of 120–140 does not seem unreasonable.

The verso contains only an address in Greek: *'Απολλω[ ] 'Αρσι(νοίτου) 'Ηρακλ(είδου) μερίδος*. Both the editors and Marichal doubt that it has anything to do with the accounts on the recto; but the example of **39**, though Marichal rejects it, nevertheless keeps the possibility open that the text was being sent to *apollo-*, whoever he was. His official status is not actually known, though it has been restored as *στρ(ατηγῷ)*; and in any case we have too little information about the relationships of civil officials and the army to be sure that this sort of data would never be sent to a civilian. But if this address is to be taken as evidence that the papyrus had been discarded and used to wrap a package (*Occ.* 47), it is also an argument for dating the text of the recto much earlier than the decade 176–186.

Frag. a

Col. i

(*First hand*)]x̣xviiii b xxv s
About three lines lost
]b s
]s
Two (?) lines lost
] .[ ].[ ].[.].iiii s f̣
]● ba..[.].[ ].[ ]
]● apollịnar[....]ṿ b xiiii s
]● longinus ✳ xxv
]● dioscorus ✳ xxv
One line blank
]uiaticorum ✳ xx[vi]i b xii s
]. pasion ✳ ii b xii s
] crispus ✳ xxv
One line blank
de]bitores ✳ ccccxvi b x̣vi s f
]● uictor ✳ lvi b v s f
● diọnụṣius ✳ vii b ii
● ḥịerax̣ ✳ xviiị b s
● psois ✳ xviii b s
● hermofịḷ ✳ xxv b iii
● pasion ✳ xxiii b x̣vi
● maximus ✳ clxx̣vị b xṿii
...artes ✳ lxxxx[i]i
One line blank
Ŧ ..[re]c̣ẹṣṣạ ✳ mlxxiiii b xiii f

The letters *i* and *l* have not been used for identifying fragments because they are too easily mistaken for numerals. Frag. n is nearly blank, showing only two or three slight traces.

No translation is offered because the text consists so much of names and numerals.

a i 1.]*XVIIII:* Fay. and Daris;]*XVIII:* CPL, a typographical error. Text, Fink and M independently. Read (*denarii*)]x̣xviiii (*oboli*) *xxv s*(*emis*).

2–4. The amount of space between lines 1 and 5 suggests that there may have been a blank line at some point between, like those after lines 13 and 16.

5. (*oboli*) *v s*(*emis*)*:* Fay. and Daris; (*obolus*) *s*(*emis*)*:* Fink and M, independently.

6. No reading in Fay. and M.

9.]*IIII s:* Fay.; ● . . . [;]. (*oboli*) *IIII s*(*emis*)*:* M. Expand (*oboli*) *iiii* (*dodrans*), i e. $\frac{1}{2} + \frac{1}{4}$. For the *f*, see on line 17. The trace at the beginning of the line looks like a stroke rather than a punctum. It may indicate a word started in the margin as a heading, like *uiaticorum*, line 14, and *debitores*, line 17.

10. *Ba*.[*:* Fay. Fay. has omitted all the puncta, in this line and elsewhere, but mentions them in the commentary.

11. *Apoḷ*[*l*]*inar*(*ius*) [*denarii*. .]*V:* Fay. and Daris; *Apoḷ*[*li*]*nar*(*ius*) [(ḍẹṇạṛịị). .]*Ṿ:* M.

14. The amount in this line, as Marichal observes, is the sum of the amounts in lines 15–16.

15. Before the name there is the top of a stroke slanting upward from left to right. No punctum is visible beside this name in the photograph; but it may have been carried away by a small tab of papyrus which curls down into the next line.

16. The photograph shows no punctum with this name; but the tab of papyrus just mentioned may conceal one.

17. (*oboli*) *XVI s*(*emis*) (*quarta ?*)*:* Fay.; *XVI* (*quadrans*)*:* Occ., an oversight for (*dodrans*); *XVI* (*bes*)*:* M. But I believe that Marichal was right in the first place in interpreting the final symbol as *quadrans.* His analysis in *Occ.* 72–76 shows how the three-stroke symbol $\equiv$— for *quadrans* evolved in *PBerol.* 6866 (**70**) into a sign similar to an *e*. But in ligature, as often happened with a preceding *s* for *semis*, this could be read as *s* plus ꞅ, the form which it takes here in col. i where the *s* does not form a ligature with it. In col. iii, however, the three bars of the original form are clearly visible in line 23. Cf. frag. f 4, which appears to contain the symbol = for *sextans*.

The sum in this line is the total of the individual entries in lines 18–25.

18. *V s*(*emis*) (*quarta* ?)*:* Fay.; *V* (*quadrans*)*:* Occ.; *V* (*bes*)*:* M. See on the preceding line and expand *v* (*dodrans*).

19. *Dioṇụ*[*s*]*ius; VII:* Fay.; *Di*[*onus*]*ius:* Daris; *VIIỊ:* M. But the sum in line 17 shows that the figure here must be *vii*.

20. .*neran*(*us*)*:* Fay.; *Ịperan*. . *:* M. The last *i* of *xviii* appears to be corrected from *s* and the number of obols to be corrected from (*quadrans*) to *s*(*emis*).

21. *Ṣịsois; XVIII:* Fay.; *XVII:* M, who agrees with my reading of the name.

22. *Hermofi*(*lus*)*:* Fay.; *Hermof*(*ilus*)*:* M.

25. . . [.]*ertes:* Fay.; *Ạḅẹrtes:* M, preceded by a punctum. *LXXXXII:* Daris.

26. *T su*[*nt re*]*cessa:* Fay.; the bit of papyrus with *T˙ su* is not on my photograph, and has evidently become detached since the original publication. Marichal is of course right in expanding (*turmae*).

XIII (*quarta* ?)*:* Fay.; *XIII* (*dodrans*)*:* Occ.; (*sextans*)*:* M. See on line 17 and expand here *xiii* (*quadrans*).

Col. ii

recessa depositorum			
● ● dionusius	✳ mcccclviii		
One line blank			
item ḍẹbiṭọres	✳ dclx.i	b . . .	
● capiton	✳ [.]. . [.]	b	xxvii s[
● apollos	✳ [ ]xxi	b	xii[
● pasion	✳ c̣vii	b	xii[
● amṃọnius	✳ lxxi	b	xxvi . [
● protas	[✳] l[x]vịi	b	xviị . [
● hermaiṣg[us	✳] iiii	b	xxvii s
● muntanus	✳̣ lxv	b	xiii s
● serenus	✳̣ iiii	b	xxvii s
● gemellus	✳ iiii	b	xxvii s
● serenus	✳ lxxii	b	xx s
● nefotian	✳ iiii	b	xxvii s

● eponuchoṣ ⚹ iiii b xxvii s
● fabianus ⚹ lvi b xxvii s
● apollinar ⚹ clxxii b xxvii s
(*Second hand*) item armorum dionysi ⚹ ciii
One line blank
(*Third hand?*) Ƭ˙ sunt recessa ⚹ iiccxxvịị[i

ii 2. Fay. does not report the traces to the left of the punctum. There is only the top of a stroke, tilted a little to the left, which most resembles *d* but might be *b*.

3. *DCLXVI:* Fay., with no reading for the obols but a report that the figure has been erased; *DCLXVII* (*oboli*) [*XV:* M. The sum in this line is the total for the entries in lines 4–17; but since the number of denarii in Capiton's debt (line 4) can be restored as any amount needed to suit one's calculations for the entries in 5–17, it seems best to leave this total in doubt. The upper left stroke of the numeral after the certain *x* seems too horizontal for a *v*, and there is too little room for *vi* between the *x* and the other *i*. But if the damaged letter was an *x*, the lower left stroke should appear next to the first *x*. At any rate, the symbol for obols is certain; and the total of the obols in lines 4–17, no matter how the individual sums are read and restored, comes to 11 denarii and a fraction. Consequently numerals must have followed the *b*; and their loss is due to abrasion of the surface.

4. (*denarii*) [*LXXX*]*:* M. See on line 3. One might equally well read [*i*]*ịị*[*i*], comparing lines 9, 11, 12, 14, and 15. (*oboli*) *XXV*[*I*]*I:* Fay. and Daris. There are a number of strokes at the extreme right edge of the papyrus at the level of this line. They appear to be offset from the numerals in the column of obols.

5. The spacing does not require another letter to be restored in the lacuna here.

6. (*denarii*) [.]*VII:* Fay.; [*X*]*VII:* M; but *v* is ligatured to the preceding letter which must accordingly be *c*, since *x* in this hand does not ligature.

7. (*oboli*) *XXVII:* Fay.; *XXVIỊ* [*s*(*emis*)*:* M. The last stroke, however, appears to be almost horizontal and hence cannot be an *i*.

8. (*denarii*) *L*[*XX*]*ṾỊI:* Fay.; *Ḷ*[*XX*]*ṾỊI; XVII ṣ*(*emis*)*:* M; but there is not enough space for two *x*'s in the figure for denarii.

9. *Hermaisc*[*us:* Fay. and M; but cf. the *g* of *gemellus*, line 12.

16. (*denarii*) *LXI:* Fay. and M.

18. M explains this reasonably as a sum added to Dionysius' deposit by the armory in payment for arms surrendered on his discharge.

19. *IICCXXṾII*[*II* (*oboli*) *XV:* M. This is the sum of the denarii in lines 2, 3, and 18; but it provides no evidence on the question of the obols in line 3.

Col. iii

(*Third hand*) M LONG̣[I]NVS .[
● camaṛịusis .[
● baibulas ị[
● posidonius [
● helius [
● ualerius .[
● horus [
● paninutas .[
. . ḍ. . . . . . ● chares [
C̣Ạ ● publius ḥ[
[ ]p̣ammoneṣ .[
● gaḷaṭes .[
● [an]tonius h ḍ[
● argoteṣ h [d]. —[
● neferos [h d]⚹ d.ṿ[
● alexaṇdrus [h] d ⚹ d [ ]. .
● collutes [h] d ⚹ ccccIxxxx b ii . . . g[
● claudius ḥ d ⚹ ccxxviii————[
● ptolemeus [h] d ⚹ d ————[
● antonius [h] d ⚹ ccccxvii ————[
● rufinus [h] d ⚹ d ————[

	● longinus	[h]	d	⚹	ccccliị f̣
	● saluius	ḥ	d	⚹	cclxxxv b xxvi f
	● saturninus	ḥ	d	⚹	xxxviii
tran‹s›lati in ala apriana	longinus	[h]	d	⚹	cclxv
	ϑ turbon	ḥ	d	⚹	cccclxx b v[i]i[. .]. [
	summa depoṣitọrum			⚹	x̅i̅cxxviiii ọb i ṣ
	sepositọr[u]ṃ			⚹	i̅i̅i̅dcxxv[i ob v]ii s
	uiatiçọṛum			⚹	mccccxvi ọb xx[v] f
	fit summa numo(rum)			⚹	x̅v̅i̅clxxii [o]b vi f
					. . . . ạ .
					. . . . . . m . . . [ ] . . . . . .
					ṃạṭị
					d
				⚹	c . . . ṿ[

iii 2. Fay. and M do not report the stroke on the edge of the papyrus.

3. The *l* is faint but appears certain, though Fay. and M do not report it.

5. After *helius* there is a single stroke, slanting downward from right to left at an angle of forty-five degrees, under *us* of *posidonius*. No report in Fay. and M.

8. The remains at the edge consist of two strokes originating together and slanting downward from left to right, one at about twenty degrees from the horizontal, the other at about forty-five degrees. Fay., no report.

9. I cannot decipher the notation, which Fay. and M do not report. Cf. lines 10 and 25.

10. For *h* see on line 13. *CA*, if correctly read, may be a continuation of the marginal notation in line 9. *ç(ustos) ạ(rmorum)*? *ç(ohors) ạ(pamenorum)*? *ç(iuis) ạ(lexandrinus)*? Possibly even *ç(iuis) ṛ(omanus)*. Fay. and M mention neither note.

11. *Ammoniụs:* Fay.; *Ạṃmonius:* M.

12. *Gaḷa[t]es* [*:* M.

13. *h(abet)* [*d(epositos):* Fay. and M. The expansion of the letters *h d* is confirmed by line 27. Cf. *habet in deposito*, **68** ii 31, and **70** passim.

14. *Argotịus:* Fay. and M, with nothing in the column of numbers. The strokes visible in that column resemble the right end of the overlining of the numerals for "thousands" in lines 27–28 and 30. If that is the case, this man had a deposit of 2000 denarii or more.

15. *DÇX̣Ṿ*[*:* Fay. and M. The character after *d* can hardly be *c*; the part which remains looks most like the top half of an *e* with the middle stroke twice the length of the curved upper one. The next two strokes may form a *v* like that in line 25; but even this is not certain.

16. No report in Fay. and M of traces at the right end.

17. *ḥ(abet); CCCCLXXXXVII (obolos) II s(emis):* Fay. and M. The supposed *v* is impossible; the character consists of a small loop with a tall, perfectly vertical hasta and must be either *b* or *d* though it is unlike any other example of those letters in this text. The letters on the right edge appear to be *g* preceded by *oh* or *bh*. I can make nothing of them.

22. *(obolos) XXIII:* Fay. and Daris; *XXIII s(emis):* CPL; *XXIỊỊỊ:* M. The numeral is not clear, but is more than 23. I have ventured to read *xxiii (quadrantem)*. Cf. the symbol at the end of line 23 and see on i 17.

23. *(obolos) XXVI s(emis):* Fay. and M.

25. *alam prima:* Fay. The notation is possibly in the first hand. Since it is all opposite Longinus' name, the reason for the plural is not clear, unless it implies that the denarii have been transferred along with their owner. M agrees independently with my reading.

26. *(obolos) V[I]I:* Fay.; *Ṿ[I]I:* M; *V[I]I*[*:* Daris. I see no way of determining the number with certainty.

27. *ob(oli) X s(emis):* Fay.; *(oboli) X̣ ṣ(emis):* M. See also on line 30.

28. *ṣepositor[u]m; IIDCXXV[I o]b(oli) [X]II:* Fay.; *IIIDCXXVI[I o](oli)*, a misprint for *o*]*b(oli)* ?; [*I*]*II:* Daris; *sepositor[um]; IIIDCXXVỊ* [*(oboli) I*]*II:* M. See also on line 30.

29. *ob(oli) XX*[*I:* Fay. and Daris; *(ọḅọḷị) X̣XỊ:* M. See also on line 30.

30. *numo(rum):* Fay. and Daris; *numo[rum]:* M; *(oboli) VI s(emis):* Fay. and M. The last character in the line is clearly not *s* but the symbol for quadrans; and this in turn requires a re-examination of the number of obols in lines 27–29. In 27, *x* is impossible; the first *i* is certain, so that only *ii*, *i s*, or *i f* can be read. In 28 the first *i* drops far below the line, implying a ligature of *v* and *i* as in the numbers for obols in line 23 and for denarii in line 29. In 29 the number for the obols is the worst damaged of all; but all three parts of the quadrans-symbol remain.

31–35. Fay. reports vestiges of four obliterated lines. It is possible that 31 and 33 were in capitals. The *d* in 34 and the denarius-sign in 35 are clear. These lines may have been purposely erased; but abrasion of the surface is apparent in line 30, so that the loss here may be accidental. M reads (31) . . . . . .; (32) . . . . . . *X̣X̣X̣X̣Ṿ*. . . . .; (33) *.X. .*; (34) nothing; (35) *(denarii) C. . X.* [. . .]. . [

Frag. b (*ChLA* 2)

(*First hand*)].[
ge]mellus
ser]enus .[
ne]fotiaṇụs ⚹̣[
epo]nuchos ⚹̣[
].ạnus ⚹̣[
..]c̣raṭṣ[.]us ⚹[
apol]ḷịnarịus ⚹[
]r...r[
].an.. sesq˙ .[
].to.[...].s a.[

Frag. b 1–5. These names occur in this order in frag. a ii 12–15, in the list of debitores under *recessa depositorum*.
1. *s*]*ẹṛ*[*enus:* M.
2. *C:* M.
6. This may be *fab*]*ịạnus*, the name in a ii 16; *Faḅi*]*anus:* M.
7.]*c̣rat*..[*ụ*]*s:* M;]*c̣ra*..[*u*]*s* [(*denarii*)*:* Daris. The *r* is formed as in *crispus*, a i 16. In a ii 17 the name following *eponuchos* and *fabianus* is *apollinar*(*ius*); but nothing of the sort is possible here. Instead of *ts*, perhaps *hi*; but both are unsatisfactory.
8. The reading is M's.
10.]...[*a*]*rm*[*o*]*r*[*um:* M.
11.].*to*.. .*ụs ṣ*. [*:* M.

Frag. c (*ChLA* 3)

(*First hand*)]..[.].[
]⚹ iiii [
]⚹ iiị ḅ[
]⚹ c̣c̣clx[
]⚹ xxxxi[
]⚹ clxxi b[
]rṛ...[
]enum ṣ.[
].anẹhip.[
]. f̣enum[
].um h.[
].calị.[
]...[

Frag. c 1. Not reported in M.
2.]..*III*[*:* M; but for the denarius sign in lines 2–6 cf. the ligature of ⚹ with the following numeral in i 14, 15, 19; ii 12, 14, 17, and 19.
3.]*C̣III*..[*:* M.
4.]*C̣C̣CLX* [*:* M. 5.]*C̣XXXXỊ*[*:* M.
6.].*CLXX̣II* (*oboli*)[*:* M. The number could be *clxxii*; a fold in the papyrus makes it impossible to say whether or not a second *i* was present.
7. (*one line blank*): M.
8.]*b num s*[*:* M. Read *f*]*enum*? Cf. line 10.
9.].*anthip*.[*:* M. The letters are clear except for the *e*, which is connected to the *n* with a thin line at the top. If we restore]*x̣anṭhipp*[*us*, more of the *x* ought to show on the edge of the papyrus. It is hard to believe that this is a transliteration of ἄνιππος; but nothing else comes to mind. Cf. d 3.
10.]..*c̣unus*.[*:* M. The *f* is unusual and could be read as the turma-symbol.
12. Perhaps *calịg*[*ae* or *calịg*[*atus*; but the *i* could be a damaged *s*.

Frag. d (*ChLA* 10)

(*First hand?*)]⚹ x[
]ẹṛ.. .[
]ịpposcor..[
]ṛemitṛ..[
]eụ... [
].xx.
]iịcccc.[
]ṭc̣..... [
].[

Frag. d 1. The letters are on a small, nearly detached bit which M reports in the app. on his line 141, which is line d 4 in this text.
2.]...[*:* M.
3.]*ippostoc̣ọ:* M. Cf. e 6 and 7.
4.].*en*..*tr*.[*:* M. Perhaps]*ḍemeṭrịuṣ*[?
5.]. *VIII* [*:* M. Perhaps ⚹̣ *viii*
6.].*XXV*[*:* M.
7.]*IC̣C̣LỊIII*[*:* M. 8.].*C̣*...[*:* M

Frag. e (*ChLA* 7)

(*Hand ?*)]...[
].s [
]is [
One line blank
].[..]is [
]. ⚹ cxxi[
].orḍi ⚹ .[
].oscor ⚹ .[
]...ṛ ⚹̣[

Frag. e 5.](*ọḅọlị*)...*I s*[*:* M, who also reports traces of five letters in a line above this one and below the blank line. I do not find them in my photograph.
5. *CXXII*[*:* M.
7.]. *ordi*(*narii*) .[*:* Daris. M agrees independently with the reading in the text.
8. Perhaps *D*]*ịoscor*(*us*) as in M; but note also d 3 and e 6.

Frag. f (*ChLA* 1)

(*Hand ?*)]ṃṃạ
].ẹṣ
]xs
]𐆖 iiii ob xviii = [
About two and a half lines blank
] ọ ..
] ọb xv [
].[.] iii f̣ [

Frag. f 1.]*m* . [: M. Read [*su*]*ṃṃạ*?
2.]. [: M.
3.].*CX*.[: M. Expand *s*(*emis*).
4.]*XIIII* . *ob*(*oli*) *XVIII* (*sextans*): M. Since the symbol at the end of the line apparently consists of only two strokes, *sextans* is probably right. Cf. on i 17.
5. No reading in M.
7.]...[: M.

Frag. g (*ChLA* 8)

(*Hand ?*)]ụm[
–]—[–
]g̣.ọ.[
–]——[–
]...[–]—x.[
]. 𐆖 iiị[
]...ọ[
].[ ]————[
].[..].ṣc....[
]ọo ṭi iii[
]..[

Frag. g 1.].*m*[: M.
2.]...[: M.
3. No reading in M.
4. No reading in M.
5.]..[..].*XI*[: M.
7.]....[: M.
8.]....[: M.
9.].[..] (*ḍẹṇạrịị*) *CX̣*[.]*II*[: M.
10.]*XI CḶIII*[: M.

Frag. h (*ChLA* 11)

(*First hand*)] 𐆖̣ ...[
]x˙ stip kaḷ ị[an-
]profers.[

Frag. h. Cf. **70**, **71**, and **72**.
1.]...[: M.
2.]*II*° *stip*(*endio*): M. The statement in the app. on line 147 that "the second *stipendium* must be the one payable on January 1" is refuted by **68** ii 1 and 3, where the combination of consulate and regnal year shows that *stip. i* must have fallen in January, A.D. 81. Similarly in Gilliam's review of Daris, *AJA* 68 (1967) 101.
3.]*oroferṇ*[: M.

Frag. j (*ChLA* 4)

(*Hand ?*)]so .[
]te .[
].[..]p [
p]ṭoḷemạ[eus

Frag. j 1.].*o*[: M.
2.]..[: M.
3.]. [: M. Just possibly]*ṣ*[*ti*]*p*
4.]*ç̣oh*..[: M.

Frag. k (*ChLA* 9)

(*Hand ?*)]..[
One line blank
]l[.]f̣i.ụṣ[
]ere debe.[

Frag. k 1.].[: M.
3.].*ṭip*.[: M; in app., *s*]*tip*(*endio*) or *S*]*TIPẸṆ*-[*D*...
4.]*re debit*[*ores*: M. The last letter is rounded at the bottom: *b*, *o*, or *t* are possible. Read *h*]*erede be*.[(cf. **77**), or make]*ere* an infinitive depending on *debe*.[?

Frag. m (*ChLA* 5)

(*Hand ?*)]..s
].
]ḅ
]ṣ

Frag. m 1.]*II s*[: M.
3.].[: M.
4. No reading in M.

74

Receipts for the Deposits of Tirones, Coh. I Lusitanorum

PSI 1063 September 3, A.D. 117

Transcription and commentary: G. Vitelli in *PSI* IX, no. 1063; cited as **V.**

The first and second receipts are reprinted without change by Arangio-Ruiz in Riccobono, Baviera, Ferrini, Furlani, and Arangio-Ruiz, *Fontes Iuris Romani Antejustiniani*, III: *Negotia* (Firenze 1943) pp. 398–99.

Text and translation, first two receipts: *Sel. Pap.*, no. 368.

Translation: *Roman Egypt*, no. 410, pp. 677–78.

Text: Daris, no. 33.

Commentary: J. F. Gilliam, "An Egyptian Cohort in A.D. 117," *Antiquitas*, Reihe 4: *Beiträge zur Historia–Augusta–Forschung*, Band 3 (Bonn 1966) pp. 91–97.

This text is part of a book of receipts of which **76** is a complete example. As usual elsewhere, each receipt is an autograph of the person who gave it. The content cannot be better expressed than in Vitelli's summary: six signiferi of the six centuries of which the coh. I Lusitanorum was composed give receipts to Longinus Tituleius, centurio princeps, for money credited on deposit to a varying number of *tirones Asiani* who have been assigned to each century. Johnson (p. 677) explains, "On enlistment the recruit received a lump sum from the state which was partly for expenses of equipment and partly for defraying the expenses of transportation to his assignment. . . . On arriving at his destination the recruit deposited the balance of his credit in the military treasury." From the receipts themselves, however, it would seem rather that the money was entrusted to and deposited by the centurio princeps on behalf of the recruits; but Johnson is probably right in seeing the deposits as the unexpended balances of viatica. Marichal (*Occ.* 53, 56, and 64) unaccountably speaks as if these receipts attested withdrawals by the soldiers from their deposits. The amounts are not large; they average just over 14 denarii for each tiro overall, with a range from 8.3 denarii for each tiro in the sixth century to 22.6 denarii each in the third century. The average for the first century is 21 denarii; for the second, 13.6; for the fourth, 9.13; and for the fifth, 13.

The very large number of tirones deserves notice. In **64** only 9 tirones were added to this cohort between January 1 and August 31 of A.D. 156, while in the present text the smallest number added to a single century is 17 in the second. The first and third have 20 each; the fourth, 22; the sixth, 23; and the fifth, 24. Since the theoretical strength of a century in a cohors quingenaria equitata such as this was only 60 men (cf. the totals in **64** i 15–17), these replacements amount to a minimum of 28 per cent and a maximum of 40 per cent of the personnel of each century. The date seems to provide the explanation—

the cohort had had severe losses in the Jewish rebellion of 115–116 (cf. **34**) and its ranks were being replenished with recruits brought from outside Egypt.[1]

Since these are documents of the internal military administration, Vitelli is justified in commenting that we should have expected them to be in Latin. But in fact, the great majority of such military receipts are in Greek; and that fact, as well as the quality of the Greek, gives us a glimpse of the actual speech of Roman army camps in Egypt.

The date is certain even though Trajan did not even complete his twentieth year. Vitelli cites *POxy.* 489, 1 and *Sammelbuch* 4117 as additional evidence that the news of Trajan's death had not reached this part of Egypt at this time.

The verso is blank.

The text offered here is Vitelli's.

[1] Cf. now Gilliam's commentary, "Egyptian Coh.," pp. 94–96.

(*First hand*)

Col. i

λονγεινος λονγ[ος] σημεαφορ[ο]ς [σπ]ειρης α̅
λουσιτανων ⳨ τιτουληιου λ[ο]νγεινωι
τιτουληιω ϊατ̣[ρω] ⳨ χαιρειν ελ[αβ]ον παρα σου
[δη]ναρια τετρακοσια εικοσιτ[ρι]α οβολους κ̣
υ̣περ δηποσιτο̣υ̣ τ̣ι̣[ρωνων] ασ[ιανω]ν δ̣ι̣σ̣-
τριβουτων εν τη κεντυρια ανδρων
εικοσι ετους εικοστου και εν ⟦. .⟧ τραια[νου]
αριστου καισαρος του κυριου θω[θ] ϛ̅ — Sept. 3, 117

(*Second hand*)

ουαλεριος ρουφος σημεαφορος σπειρ̅ α̅ λουσιτανων ⳨
κρησκεντος λο̣ν̣γε̣ι̣ν̣ω̣ τιτουληιω ⳨ χαιρειν
ελαβον παρα σου δηναρια αργυρα διακοσια τρια-
κοντα⟦τρια⟧ ^(δυο οβολους τεσσαρες) τα χωρηγεντα εις δη[πο]σιτον τειρω-
νων ^(ασιανων) αριθμω δ̣εκ[α]ε̣π̣τα ετους εικοστου πρωτου
τραιανου αριστου και[σαρο]ς του κυρ[ιο]υ θωθ ϛ̅

i 2. V cites *BGU* 568 (a second-century registry roll) line 9, for another occurrence of the name Longinus Tituleius. It provides no information about him.

3. The title ἰατ̣[ρῷ], if rightly read and restored, is of considerable interest. It appears only in this receipt; but this one was made out by the signifer of Tituleius' own century and should be correct in its terminology; as for the reading, the iota is certain, the alpha is probable, and the tau is possible. The combination of ἰατρός with the symbol for centurio, however, inevitably suggests *medicus centurio* or *medicus ordinarius*. In general, *ordinarius* or *ordinatus* as an equivalent for *centurio* is familiar enough, and by the third century, as in the Dura papyri, had completely displaced the earlier term (see J. F. Gilliam, "The *Ordinarii* and *Ordinati* of the Roman Army," *TAPA* 71 [1940] 127–48). However, *medicus ordinarius* has regularly been interpreted as "medicus qui in ordine meret," that is, a medicus who was actually an enlisted man, not a civilian attached to the army without being a member of it. Only Sanders was of the opinion that the medicus ordinarius "may even have had centurion rank." (For evidence and opinion on the whole question see Gilliam, *TAPA* 71.147 and notes 83–85. In "Egyptian Cohort," p. 92 note 5, he dissents from the present reading and proposes ἰδί[ῳ].) The present set of receipts supports Sanders' view, for Tituleius is given the title of centurion in all six. The fact that ἰατρός is found only once may help explain why *medicus centurio* seemingly never appears in inscriptions, and *medicus ordinarius* only rarely; *centurio* was a more honorific title and sufficed.

7. V suggests that the signifer may have written εναυ for ἕν or ἑνὸς αὐ(τοκράτορος) and then canceled αυ.

12. V: *lege* χορηγηθέντα for χωρηγεντα.

(*Third hand*) **Col. ii**

[. . . .]ιος μαξιμος σ̣η̣μ̣[ε]αφορ[ος σ]π̣ε̣ι̣ρ̣ης ᾱ
λο[υ]σι[τ]ανων ☧ κ[ελε ?]ρος λογ̣[γι]ν̣ω τιτουληιω
☧ [σ]πειρης της αυτης χαιρειν ελ̣[αβ]ον̣ παρα σου
[δ]ηναρια τετρακ̣[οσ]ι̣α̣ πεν[τηκοντ]αδυ̣ω οβο-
[λ]ους δυω υπερ δηποσιτ[ου τιρ]ωνων [α]σι[α]νων
διστριβουτων εν τη κ[εν]τυρι[α] α̣ν̣δρων εικοσι ∟ κᾱ τραια[νο]υ α[ρι]στου καισαρ[ο]ς του
κυριου θωθ εκτη

(*Fourth hand*)

γ δομιτιος ρουφος σημεαφορος σπειρης ᾱ λουσιτανων ☧ τα. . . .
λονγεινω [τ]ιτουληιω ☧ χαιρειν ελαβον παρα σου δηναρια
διακοσ[ι]α̣ δεκαεν οβολους εικοσιεξ υπερ δηποσιτου [τ]ιρω-
ν̣ων ασιανων διστριβουτων εν τη κεντυρια αριθμω
εικοσιδυω ετους κᾱ τραιαν[ου] α̣ρ̣ι̣[σ]του καισαρος του
κυριου θω[θ] εκτη

ii 9. V notes that it is unusual for the praenomen to be mentioned.

(*Fifth hand*) **Col. iii**

[ca. 12]ρ̣ιανος σημεαφορο[ς σπειρης ᾱ]
[λουσιτανων] ☧ αργιου λονγειν[ω τιτουληιω ☧]
[σπειρης της α]υτης χαι[ρ]ειν ελαβ[ον παρα σου]
δη[ναρια]ιακοσια δεκαεξ οβολ[ου]ς τ̣[ρεις υπερ]
δηπο[σιτ]ου [τι]ρωνων α[σ]ιανων διστρι[βου]των
εν [τ]η κε[ντ]υρ[ι]α ανδρων εικ[ο]σιτε[σσ]αρων
∟ κᾱ [τ]ραι[ανο]υ αριστου καισαρος του κυρι[ου] θωθ εκτη

(*Sixth hand*)

κο̣υιντος ερεννιος σημιαφορος σπερης ᾱ
λουσιτανων ☧ λωνγειανου̣ λωνγεινω
τειτωλ̣ηιω ☧ σπειρης της αουτης χαειρεν
ελαβον παρα σου δηναρια εκατων
ενενηκονταδυο οβο(λους) εικοσ̣ε υπερ δη-
πωσ̣ετων τερωνω⟨ν⟩ εικοσιτρειων ασσε-
υ
ανων διστριβοτε εν τ[η] κε[ν]τ̣ο̣υ̣ρ̣ι̣α ⟦ετος⟧ ∟ κᾱ
αουτ[ο]κρατωρο[ς] καισαρος [ν]ερουα ⟨τρα⟩ιανου αροστου
και[σ]αρος τ⟨ου⟩ κυριου θωθ εκτην

iii 4. V prefers τρ]ιακόσια to δ]ιακόσια.

7. V reports a sort of coronis at the end, "unusual in documents like this."

8. Cagnat, *Cours d'Épigraphie*[4], p. 38, note 4, states that the practice of writing a praenomen in full followed by the nomen or cognomen is quite rare and begins only in the second century.

12. εἰκοσιτρειῶν: Daris, an oversight.

13. V reports that the writer first wrote an iota and then changed it to epsilon in δηπωσέτων.

TRANSLATION

i 1–8: Longinus Longus, signifer of the coh. I Lusitanorum, century of Tituleius, to Longinus Tituleius, medicus (?) centurio. I have received from you denarii four hundred twenty-three, obols twenty, for deposit for the Asian recruits assigned to the century, twenty men. Twenty-first year of Trajan Optimus Caesar our Lord, Thoth 6 (Sept. 3, A.D. 117).

i 9–14: Valerius Rufus, signifer of the coh. I Lusitanorum, century of Crescens, to Longinus Tituleius, centurio. I have received from you silver denarii two hundred thirty-two, obols four, supplied for deposit for the recruits from Asia, in number seventeen. Twenty-first year of Trajan Optimus Caesar our Lord, Thoth 6.

ii 1–8: [. . . .]ius Maximus, signifer of the coh. I Lusitanorum, century of Celer, to Longinus Tituleius, centurio of the same cohort. I have received from you denarii four hundred fifty-two, obols two, for deposit for the Asian recruits assigned to the century, twenty men. Twenty-first year of Trajan Optimus Caesar our Lord, Thoth 6.

ii 9–14: C. Domitius Rufus, signifer of the coh. I Lusitanorum, century of Ta. . . ., to Longinus Tituleius, centurio. I have received from you denarii two hundred eleven, obols twenty-six, for deposit for the Asian recruits assigned to the century, in number twenty-two. Twenty-first year of Trajan Optimus Caesar our Lord, Thoth 6.

iii 1–7: [*ca.* 12]rianus, signifer of the coh. I Lusitanorum, century of Argius, to Longinus Tituleius, centurio of the same cohort. I have received from you denarii three (?) hundred sixteen, obols three, for deposit for the Asian recruits assigned to the century, twenty-four men. Twenty-first year of Trajan Optimus Caesar our Lord, Thoth 6.

iii 8–16: Quintus Herennius, signifer of the coh. I Lusitanorum, century of Longianus, to Longinus Tituleius, centurio of the same cohort. I have received from you denarii one hundred ninety-two, obols twenty, for deposit for twenty-three Asian recruits assigned to the century. Twenty-first year of Imperator Caesar Nerva Trajan Optimus Caesar our Lord, Thoth 6.

75

Auxiliaries' Receipts for Money

P Yale 249 May?–June, A.D. 139

This papyrus is unpublished. It appears here by permission of Professor C. Bradford Welles, who supplied most of the transcription of the two Greek receipts.

This text consists of three receipts from a book like **76**. One is in Latin, the others in Greek; and all are in different hands. It appears, too, that the lines, just as in **76**, were not of the same length for all, making restoration very uncertain. The only evidence on the nature of the payments concerned is *pretium equi* in line 3; but this is enough to indicate what a pity it is that more of this papyrus has not survived.

The date is fixed by lines 16–17, supported by lines 4, 8, and 22–23.

The verso is blank.

s. . tius martius . g̣ . [
herenio diogenị[salutem acce-]
pi a te pretium ẹqu[i probati ab]
auidio heliodoro prạ[ef aegypti
ḍenarịọs c̣ẹnṭụm[
apollọṣ didimi e[ques (?) turmae]
longiṇị p̣ọụḷịlfuṣo d[
[p]ṛ[i]ḍ[i]e i[d]us ṃ[.]iḅ[.]e [
scripṣ[i]. . ṃ . [.] . . [
imp antoniṇ[

One line blank

(*Second hand*)

ιου̣λ̣ιος ουαλεριανος ηλ[.].[
σατορνιλο̣υ̣ ερεννιω δ̣[ιογενει
χαιριν ελαβον παρ[α σου
το. . σα . χρ̣τησ . [
τουρμα λογγινι δ[
ε̣τ̣[ου]ς̣ δ̣ε̣υ̣τ̣[ε]ρ̣ου αιλ̣ι̣ο̣υ̣[
σεβαστου̣ παυνι κ̅δ̅[

(*Third hand*)

γαιος απωνιος ουλπ̣[
ερεννιω διογενη .[
ελαβα παρα σου την[
τι. δηνα̣ρια εβδομ[ηκοντα
ετους δευτερου αιλ̣[ιου αδριανου
αντωνεινου σεβασ[του

1. Although the writer of the third receipt uses his praenomen (line 18), the first letter here must be part of the nomen—Sattius, Sextius, Sittius, or the like. The name should be followed by the man's identification by rank, unit, and company, as in **76**; but I can make nothing of the three letters at the end of the line. The first might be *b*, *k*, *p*, or even *il*; the second is probably *g*; and the last *a* or *m*.

2. All three of these receipts are addressed to Herennius Diogenes; but his rank is unknown unless one restores ϛ[ουμμω κουρατορι] in line 19 on the analogy of **76**.

3. *equi* was probably followed by a description of the horse. Cf. **83** and **99**.

5. In **83** and **99** the standard valuation for horses is 125 denarii. It is a great pity that the number here is not preserved complete for comparison with the third-century rates.

6. Comparison with **76** suggests that Apollos signs here as the actual writer of this receipt. The restoration *e[ques* assumes that his name was followed by an identification, as in **76**, while *turmae* is supplied from line 15. The unit was therefore either an ala or a cohors equitata, since the filiation *didimi* shows that Apollos was not a citizen and hence could not belong to a legion.

7. The name of the decurion is clear; but I am unable to make sense of the remainder of the line. The readings reported for the doubtful letters are intended merely to give some idea of the appearance of the remains. Instead of *s*, an *f* is possible.

8. If this line really contains a date (there is a large ink-blot at this point), the name of the month makes difficulties. *m[a]i* is the most likely reading because the next receipt is dated in June (line 17); but I do not know what to make of the *b* which follows.

9. The second *s* is extremely doubtful.

10. Cf. lines 16–17 and 22–23.

11. At the end of the line ηλ should be the first letters of Valerianus' rank, like ἱππεύς in **76**; but I can think of nothing suitable.

12. The case of the first name is not certain; and Welles once read it as nominative. But it seems most likely to be a part of Valerianus' identification, the name of his centurion or decurion. At the end of the line only Diogenes' title is needed.

14. Welles notes that lambda is possible instead of chi, and adds that χορτης is just possible, though there is hardly room for it. The line should be either part of the description of the payment received by Valerianus or part of the name and identification of the person who wrote for him. The identification continues in line 15.

15. This is presumably the turma of the writer. Restore δ[ηναρια?

16. Cf. line 22. The emperor's name gives a clue to the length of the lines in this receipt, for the minimum restoration possible is αντωνινου while the maximum is αδριανου αντωνινου του κυριου. Since, however, only Diogenes' title seems to be lacking in line 12, it seems likely that αδριανου was omitted.

17. The date, June 18, A.D. 139, is written somewhat larger than the letters elsewhere in the receipt.

18. The last name is presumably Ulpianus.

19. The letter at the margin could be epsilon, omicron, sigma, or omega. It is probably the initial of Diogenes' title; but too little remains to be helpful. *Exceptor*, *optio*, or *summus curator* (see **76**) are obvious possibilities; and others may exist. The length of the lines (see on lines 22–23) suggests that οπτιωνι is the most probable of these three.

20. Supply τιμην to parallel *pretium*, line 3?

21. The third letter could be omicron, sigma, or omega. This must be the end of a word or phrase stating what Aponius was getting money for.

22–23. The only possible restoration here is αδριανου. The lines in this receipt were therefore only 25–30 letters long.

76

Receipts of Alares for Hay Money

PHamb. 39 January 9–April 10, 179

Staats- und Universitäts-Bibliothek Hamburg, inv. no. 184

Commentary, transcriptions, and facsimiles: Paul M. Meyer, *Griechische Papyrusurkunden der Hamburger Staatsbibliothek* III, no. 39, pp. 158–80 and plates 11–13; cited in the apparatus as **M**. Meyer published the full text of only eleven of the receipts: iii 20–26; vii 16–22; xi 12–21; xii 1–10; xv 2–9 and 10–17; and BB, FF, GG, and HH. The content of the others he summarized in a table which gives the name of the soldier, his rank, his turma, the post to which he was going, the name and rank of the writer, the hand, and the date by day and month. Plate 11 shows col. xvi, receipts 45–47; plate 12, col. xvii, receipts 48–50; and plate 13, the single sheet GG, receipts 65–66. (The serial, arabic, numbers attached to the receipts are those of Meyer's publication.)

Text and translation, receipt 33 only: *Sel. Pap.*, no. 369.

Text: Daris, no. 40, prints four receipts: iii 20–26, xi 12–21, xii 1–10, and BB. There are some misprints.

The text is here published entire for the first time by permission of Professor Hermann Tiemann, Director of the library. Dr. Hellmut Braun, Keeper of Manuscripts, assisted in obtaining photographs; and Dr. H. Maehler supplied a meticulous transcription of the lines where the photographs were less clear. Even where I have not agreed with him I have found his readings extremely useful.

For a complete discussion of the content the reader should turn to Meyer's indispensable commentary. Briefly, the text is a book of receipts given by soldiers of the ala Veterana Gallica for their hay allowance for the year. Meyer (p. 159) says that this year coincided with the Egyptian regnal year; but the fact that the earliest receipt in the book is dated January 9, and that two-thirds of all the receipts were given in that month, speaks rather for the use of the Roman calendar in keeping these accounts, for if the accounting year had begun on Thoth 1 (or September 1) these men should already have drawn one-third of their allowance for hay before January. The amount of the allowance on an annual basis is approximately three times that in **68** and **69**.

All these receipts are addressed to the summus curator of the ala, Iulius Serenus.[1] Besides these, the four separate sheets which were attached to the roll contain five receipts and

[1] Meyer is probably mistaken in stating that his praenomen is given in receipt 24 (col. viii, line 14). See the apparatus ad loc. But he is no doubt the same person, as Meyer says (p. 162), as the veteran ἀπὸ δεκαδάρχων who appears in *PHamb.* 40–53.

a letter, all likewise addressed to the summus curator. Three of the receipts are for the hay allowance, one of them for a period of two years (GG 1–8); one is for money for *epulum* (FF), and one is for money for an item which has not been read (BB). The letter (HH ii 1–8) requests Serenus to pay the writer's hay allowance to another soldier.

As for the form of the book, except for the four separate sheets, it is a continuous roll in which the individual receipts were written in succession, not a *tomos synkolesimos*. Meyer correctly saw that the numbering of the columns, which survives at the top of cols. vii–xv, shows that we have all of the book except for the lost parts of cols. i and ii. The blank spaces in cols. xxi–xxiv and the fact that the receipts in cols. xxi and xxiv are not in chronological order after those in cols. i–xx, show that this end of the roll was being used for receipts of stragglers who for some reason did not sign at the time when they received, or should have received, their money.

Meyer does not comment on the numerals which appear in the margin at the left of all the receipts except nos. 58–62. It is obvious, however, that they were added by a clerk to facilitate calculation of the amounts involved, and that they indicate the number of persons, from one to three, who are named in each as recipients of money. Some of the ostraca under **78** similarly have the number of denarii and obols added at the bottom in a second hand.

Four names (xiii 1, xix 12, xx 1, and xxii 1) are also preceded by a small oval punctum which Meyer ignored in the first two instances and misinterpreted in the last two. (See the apparatus ad locc.) There is no indication of the reason for checking these names only.

Meyer notes that the language of these receipts is Greek instead of the Latin usual in military texts, but does not comment further. Greek, in fact, seems commoner than Latin in receipts; **74**, **75**, **78**, **80**, and **81**, as well as the present one, are either entirely or almost entirely in Greek, though I believe that col. xvi 1–9 of this text shows a tendency to lapse into the Roman alphabet. The linguistic interest of the pronunciations reflected in the various spellings (Meyer argues too, p. 161, that many of the receipts were written at dictation) is sufficient reason for publishing the text in full.

A detailed commentary on the language is not in place here; but the confusion of *m* and *n* in xii 19–25 and xiii 1–8, the sixteen different ways of spelling the accusative singular of *κράστις* (or *γράστις*), and the uncertainty regarding cases and case-endings illustrated by the genitives *σερηνου μελανατος* (i 10), *σερηνου μελανι* (vii 9), *σερηνου μελανος* (x 3), *σερηνου μελας* (xii 19), *σερηνου μελανις* (xx 8), and *σερηνι μελανι* (xx 20) may be mentioned as examples of the kind of evidence which can be found here. The whole papyrus illuminates clearly the many gradations of dialectal background, education, and intelligence to be found in a Roman army unit at this period.

A little more can now be said about the nomenclature in these texts and about the decurions. Meyer's observation (p. 174) that the names of the gregales consist usually of gentilicium and cognomen, once of praenomen and cognomen (vii 2 and 13), and once of praenomen and filiation (viii 14 and 23) is only partly right because it is based on the concept of the tria nomina as the norm for Roman citizens, while he says nothing explicitly about the nomenclature of non-citizens but tacitly emends all such names to the pattern of name and filiation. This is theoretically sound; but in actual fact, both patterns of nomenclature were breaking down and usage was quite fluid. The indices of Dessau as well as the texts in this collection show names like Gaius and Lucius being used as gentilicia and cognomina; and other praenomina are employed in the same way. The same sort of evidence shows that the names of non-citizens are often both in the nominative. Aside from the papyri, it is enough to cite Dessau 2543, A.D. 199, where two decurions of the ala Veterana Gallica are recorded as Secundinus Verus and Marcus Fuscus, and one of the ala I Thracum Mauretana as Annellus Quodratus. Moreover, Meyer does not take note of such cases as "Nepheros, otherwise Nephos" (xix 18), without filiation; Cenes (xxi 1), with only a single name; and Marcus in the present text who signs himself *Τιτος* in viii 14 and *Τιτου* in viii 23. Obviously, to normalize the name-patterns under these circumstances is to distort the text.

Among the names of the decurions, Meyer accepts *Melanatos* (genitive) as the form in i 10 but has *Melanos* (gen.) elsewhere for the same man. In iii 20 he reads *ογτατιανι* and emends to *'Οκταουιανοῦ* but *οπτατιανι* is as good paleographically and certainly preferable. The decurion Serenus in BB 2 (January 17) and xvii 9 (February 9) he identifies with Aelius Serenus (p. 176); but this seems the least likely choice among the three decurions named Serenus. Receipts mentioning Serenus Melas run from January 9–13 (i 10) to April 10 (xx 20), and those with Pactumeius Serenus from January 16 (iv 21) to January 21 (xiv 11), while Aelius Serenus first appears in a receipt of January 26 (xv 11). Serenus and Pactumeius Serenus seem to be distinguished in BB 2 and 5, leaving Serenus Melas as the one most likely to be the decurion called merely Serenus. *Melas* may in fact not be an actual name but a distinguishing epithet.

It seems probable, to return to Aelius Serenus, that he came to the ala as a replacement at the end of January. Meyer correctly notes (p. 176) that after making all the identifications possible we are still left with the names of 18 decurions when it is known that such an ala had only 16, and concludes that two of the nomina used of decurions must designate the same person as two of the cognomina. Petronius, however, can be eliminated; for he left the ala between January 23 and February 8, as is proved by the change in terminology from *τουρμης πετρονιου* (xv 2–3) to *τουρμης πετρωνιανα* (xvii 2). But Aelius Serenus did not replace Petronius, for he is present while Petronius' former turma is being called Petroniana.[2] He must therefore have taken the place of one of the decurions who are named only once and early—Optatianus (iii 20, January 15), Subatianus (ix 13, January 17), or Clarus (xii 17, January 18), or possibly Gemellus or Ammonianus, who do not appear after January 19 (xiii 9 and xiv 3).

The date is of course provided by the receipts themselves.

The verso is blank.

In view of the kind of Greek which these soldiers wrote, there would seem to be no more reason to supply breathings, accents, and subscript vowels than to normalize the spelling. To do so would, moreover, obscure the fact that a few of the men were careful to provide iota and upsilon with a mark of dieresis (ix 13–19, x 15–24, and xi 1–10, all by hand 20) or sometimes to write iota adscript in the dative singular (iv 21, xii 20, xiii 3, xiv 3, and xx 10). In the transcription which follows I have therefore tried to present each text exactly as it was written; but for evident reasons I have not given separate, explicit affirmation to every abnormal spelling.

2 See R. O. Fink, "*Centuri Rufi, Centuria Rufiana*, and the Ranking of Centuries," *TAPA* 84 (1953) 213–15.

Col. i (A, col i)

1. (*Hand 1*) January 9, 179

ιπ]πευ̣ς̣ ιλης ουε̣τ̣ρ̣ανης
[γαλλικης τουρμης *ca.* 12 ι]ουλιω σερηνω σ̣[ο]υ̣μμο κου-
[ρατορι χαιρειν ελαβον παρα σου τη]ν γρασσημ μου ε̣ν̣ προχρια
[υπερ του εννεακαιδεκατου ετο]υ̣ς̣ ε̣ξερχομενος ι[ς] αφροδιτω
[δηναρια εικοσι πεντ]ε̣ ∟ [ιθ]α̣υ̣ρ[η]λ̣ι̣ω̣ν αντωνινου κ̣α̣ι κομοδο[υ]
[των κυριων σεβαστων τ]υβι $\overline{\iota\delta}$
τουρ]μης ηροδιανω εγραψα υπερ αυτου
δια το μη ειδεν]ε̣ αυ̣τ̣ο̣ν γραμματα

2. (*Hand 2*)

ιππ]ε̣υ̣ς ειλης γαλλικης τουρμης η̣ρωδιανου
[και τουρμ]ης σερηνου μελανατος και αγηνορ
[ ]. . . σερηνω σουμμω κουρατορι
[χαιρειν ελαβαμεν παρα σου τη]ν̣ γρα̣σ̣τιν ημων εν προχρεια
[εξερχομενοι εις *ca.* 10] δηναρια εικοσι πεντε πλη-
[ρες ∟ ιθ αυρηλιων αντωνινο]υ και κομμοδου καισαρων των̣
[κυριων τυβι . . *ca.* 9 ο πρ]ο̣γ̣ε̣γραμμενος [εγ]ραψα υπερ
[*ca.* 18 δια το μ]η ειδεναι αυτους γραμ[μ]ατα̣

3. (*Hand 3*)

τουρμης]α̣μμωνιαν̣[ο]υ
[σερηνω σουμμω κουρατορι χαιρειν ελαβον παρα σου τη]ν γρα̣σ̣τιν
[μου εν προχρεια εξερχομενος εις *ca.* 10 δηναρι]α̣ εικ[ο]σι
[πεντε υπερ του ∟ ιθ αυρηλιων αντωνινου και κομμοδο]υ̣ καισα-
[ρων των κυριων τυβι . .

4. (*Hand 4*)

]ου σερη-
[νω σουμμω κουρατορι χαιρειν ελαβον παρα σου την γρασ]τ̣ιν μ[ο]υ
[υπερ του εννεακαιδεκατου ετους δηναρια εικοσι πεντε π]ληρε̣[ς
[∟ ιθ αυρηλιων αντωνινου και κομμοδου καισαρων των κ]υριων̣
[τυβι . . τουρμης τ]ης
[αυτης εγραψα υπερ αυτου δια το μη ειδεναι αυτον γραμμ]α̣τα

The letters A, B, C, etc., in parentheses are Meyer's designations for the parts into which the papyrus was divided for mounting. Meyer is cited in this apparatus as **M**.

i 7. M points out (p. 176 and note 5) that Herodianus may be identical with Iulius Heronianus, second in the list of decurions of this ala in Dessau 2543 of A.D. 199.

Col. ii (A, col. ii)

5. (*Hand 5*)

]ε̣ιλης ουατρανα γαλιγα τουρμα
ι]ερακις ιππευς ειλης της αυου-
[της τουρμης της αυου]της ι̣ουλιο σερηνο σουμμο κου-
[ρατορι χαιρει]ν̣ ε̣λαβ̣α̣μεν παρα σου την γρασσιν
[ημων εν π]ροχρια υπερ του εννεακαιδεκατου ετους
[εξερχομε]ν̣ο̣ι̣⟦ς⟧ εις̣ ταπο̣σιριν εκ δηναριων εικοσι πεντε
[∟ ιθ αυρηλ]ι̣ων αντονινου και κομοδου τον κυριον σεβαστον
[τυβι . . ερμ]ι̣ας ερμι[ο]υ ι̣π̣πευς οπτιον καμπι ειλης της
[αυτης του]ρ̣μ̣ης̣ ιουλ[ι]ο̣υ εγραψα υπερ αυουτον ερωτηθις
[δια το μη ει]δ̣ε̣ν̣η̣ α̣υο̣[υ]τους γρ̣α̣μματα

6. (*Hand 6*) January 13

[*ca.* 10]. .[. . . . . . .]ειλης ουετρανης γαλλικης
[τουρμης . . . .]υ̣[*ca.* 8]ιουλιω σερηνω σο[υ]μμο
[κουρατορι χαιρειν ε]λ̣αβον παρα σου την γρα̣[σσ]ιν
[μου εν προχρεια υπ]ε̣ρ̣ του ε̣ννεακαιδεκα[το]υ̣ ετους
[εξερχομενος εις τα βουκο]λ̣ι̣α̣ δηναρια εικοσ̣[ι] π̣εντε
[πληρες ∟ ιθ αυρηλιων αντ]ω̣νινου και κομοδου̣ [τ]ω̣ν
[κυριων σεβαστων τυ]β̣[ι ι̅]η̅

7. (*Hand 7*)

ουετ]ρ̣α̣νης
]ο̣υ κα̣ι
α]υτης
]υ̣μ̣. .

ii 6. The writer first wrote εξερχομενος, then struck out the sigma and inserted an iota before it.
15. Dr. H. Maehler of the Staats- und Universitäts-Bibliothek Hamburg, reads α]ν̣α δηναρια, which is equally possible.
18–21. Too little remains here for any attempt at restoration; but one can say that the lines are about the same length as in the two preceding receipts, or perhaps a letter or two longer. Line 19 must have begun with γαλλικης; and και at the end shows that this was a multiple receipt. Line 20 probably ended [ειλης] or [τουρμης της α]υτης.

Col. iii (A, col. iii)

8. (*Hand 8*) January 14

διονυσις α̣ρ̣τ̣[εμιδωρος] ι̣π̣[π]ευς ειλης γαλλικης τουρ̣μ̣[ης]
ηρωδιανου κα̣[ι . . . . .]ς διο̣ν̣υσι[ο]υ ιππευς ειλης της αυτης
β {αυτης} τουρ[μης της α]υτης̣ σ̣ερηνω σουμμω κουρατορι
χαιρειν ελ̣λ̣α̣[βαμεν] π̣α̣ρα σου εν προχρεια την γραστιν ημων
εξερχομενο[ι εις] μαρε̣ωτην ανα δηναρια εικοσι πεντε πληρης υπερ τ[ο]υ ενν̣εακαιδεκατου ετους αντωνεινου
και κομμο̣δου τω̣ν κυριων σεβαστων τυβι ι̅θ̅
αχιλλες α̣χιλλεω̣[ς] ιππευς ειλης της αυτης αυτης τουρμης
ηρωδιαν[ου εγραψα] υ̣περ αυτων ερωτηθεις δια το μη ειδενε̣
αυτους γρ̣[αμματ]α̣

9. (*Hand 8*) January 14

ηλιοδω̣ρ̣[ος . . . . . .]ι̣ο̣ς ιππευς ειλης γαλλικης τουρμης
αγριππ̣[α σερηνω σο]υμ̣μ̣ω κουρατορι χαιρειν ελα̣βον παρα
α σου την̣ [γραστιν μου το]υ εννεακαιδεκατου ετους αυρηλιων
α̣ν̣[τωνινου και κομ]μ̣οδου καισαρων των [κυ]ρ̣ιων εν προ-
[χρεια εξερχομενος εις] σ̣κηνας μανδρας δηναρια εικοσι
[πεντε ∟ ιθ αυρηλ]ειων αντωνεινου και κομμοδου
[και]σ̣α̣[ρ]ω̣ν̣ τ̣ων κ̣[υ]ρ̣ι̣[ων] τ̣υβι ι̅θ̅ αχιλλευς ιππευς τουρμης
[ηρ]ω̣διανου εγραψα υπερ αυτου ερωτηθεις δια το μη ειδεναι αυτον
[γ]ραμματα

10. (*Hand 9*) January 15

αιλ̣ις καιπιτον ιππευ ειλης γαλικης τουρμης οπ̣τατιανι
ειολιων σερηνω σουμω κουρατο̣ρι χαιρι ελαβον πα[ρ]α̣ σου την
γ̣ρασι μου του ενηακαιδεκατους ετος αυρηλιω̣[ν α]ν̣τω̣νι-
νου και κομωδου των κυριων αυτοκρατωρο ε̣ν ποχριας
εξ̣ε̣ρχομενος εισκηνας μογαλος δηναρια {δηναρια}
[εικ]οσι πντε φ̣λ̣ηρ̣ε̣ς ∟ ιθ αυρηλιων αντωνινου
[και κ]ομοδου καισαρων των κυριων τυβιν κ̅

iii 1. For the name cf. the separate leaf BB, line 1.

5. In the place-name it is impossible to say whether alpha has been corrected to epsilon or vice versa.

11. The second name could also end -*νος*.

15. M reports *κηνας* as the reading of the papyrus.

17. The first half of the line I owe to Dr. Maehler.

20. M reads the name of the decurion as *ογτατιανι* and emends to Ὀκταουιανοῦ.

24. Μ̣ε̣κάλος: M; but there is no trace of the cross-bar for epsilon. The gamma is corrected from alpha.

25. The first epsilon of *πεντε* is omitted. The phi appears to be superimposed on a pi; and the lambda has a cross-bar from the middle of the left side to the foot of the right.

Col. iv (B, col. i)

11. (*Hand 10*) January 15

[ανουβ]ι̣ον αρποκρ̣α̣τ̣ι̣[ω]ν̣[κο]υ̣[ρα]τ̣[ωρ ιλης γαλλι]κ̣[ης
β [τυρμη]ς̣ αγριππας και πεχυσις πε̣[.]υρ.ι̣ς τυρμη̣ς̣
[ηρωδι]ανου ιουλιω σερηνω συμμου κουρατωρι
χ̣[αιρει]ν̣ ελαβαμεν παρα σου την γρασιν ημων
του ιθ ʃ′ εν προχριας εξερχομενοι εισκηνας δηναρια ικοσι πεντε
∟ ιθ αυρηλιω αντωνεινω και κομμοδω των κυριων
αυτοκρατορων τυβι κ̅
ανουβιων ο προγεγραμενος εγραψα υπερ πεχυσις
δια το με ιδενε αυτο γραμματα

12. (*Hand 10*) January 15

[.]. . .[.] κ̣ο̣λλουθι ιππευς ιλης καλλικης τυρμης ιουλιου
α [*ca.* 7 σ]ε̣ρηνω συμμου κουρατωρι χαιρειν ελαβον
[παρα σου τ]η̣ν γρασιν μου του ι̅θ̅ ʃ′ δηναρια ικοσι
[πεντε] ε̣ν προχριας εξερχο[μ]ενος ισκηνας
[∟ ιθ αυρηλ]ιων αντωνινω και κομμοδω των κ̣[υριων]
[αυτ]ο̣κρατορων τυβι κ̅
α̣[ν]ο̣[υ]β̣ιων κουρατωρ ιλης της αυτης εγραψα [υπερ]
αυτου̣ δια το μη ιδενε αυτον γραμματα

13. (*Hand 11*) January 16

ιουλις σερηνος ιππευς ειλης γαλι^κ τυ̣ρμης ηρωδιανο̣υ κ[α]ι ι̣[ο]υ̣λις
νεπωτιανος τυρμης της αυτης και παθερμο̣[υ]θις ο̣ρσενου̣φις
γ τυρμης πακτουμηνιου σερηνου ιουλιω σερην̣ω̣ σουμμωι
κουρατωρι χαιρειν ελαβαμεν πα̣[ρ]α̣ σου την̣ γρασσιν ημων
υπερ του ι̅θ̅ ∫′ ⟦δηνα⟧ εκαστος ημ[ων] δηναρια εικοσι πεντε
⌊ ιθ́ αυρηλιων αντωνινου και κομοδου των̣ κυριων σεβαστων
τυβι κά σοσσις ευδαιμων σημεαφορος τυρμ[ης] ηρωδιανου
εγραψα υπερ αυτων ερωτηθεις δια το μη ειδε̣[να]ι̣ αυτους
γραμματα

iv 1. αρποκρατι[ων] in pap.: M.
2. π[.].[.]υρ[..].ς: M.
5. κηνας in pap.: M.
14. κηνας in pap.: M.
20. The first theta of παθερμουθις has been corrected from another letter, perhaps epsilon.
24. σεβαστων was added in smaller letters by the same hand over a flourish extending from the nu of κυριων.

Col. v (B, col. ii)

14. (*Hand 8*) January 16

θεων στιλβο̣υν̣ο̣ς̣ ι̣[ππευς ειλης γαλλ]ικης [το]υρμης̣ πακτου̣μ̣ηι[ου]
σερηνου και ϊσιδωρος απολλωνι τουρμης απ[ολλιν]αριου αρεσ-
χις νεχθερωτις ιππευς ειλης της αυτ̣η̣[ς του]ρ̣μ̣η̣ς̣ ϊουλιο̣υ
σερηνω συμμω κουρατορι χαιρειν ελαβα̣[μεν π]αρα σου εν
προχρεια την γραστιν ημων του ιθ ∫ αυρη̣λ̣ι[ω]ν̣ αντονεινου
γ̄ και κομμοδου καισα̣ρ̣ων των κυριων ανα δηναρια εικοσι
πεντε εξερχομενοι ⌊ ι̅θ̅ αντωνε[ι]νου και κομμοδου
των κυριων σεβαστων τυβι κ̅α̅ αχιλ̣[λ]ες αχιλλεως
ιππευς τουρμης ηρωδιανου εγραψα υ̣[π]ε̣ρ αυ̣τ̣ων ερωτηθεις δια το μη ειδεναι αυτους γραμμ[ατ]α

15. (*Hand 8*) January 16

πετεμινις ψενο̣σιρις ιππευς ειλης γαλ̣[λικη]ς̣ το[υρ]μ̣ης πετρωνιου σερηνω σουμμω̣ κουρατορι χαιρ̣ι̣ν̣ [ελαβον παρα σου τη]ν̣
α γραστιν μου εξερχομενος εις σκην[ας *ca.* 7 του ιθ ∫]
αυρηλιων αντωνεινου και κομμοδ[ου των κυριων]
σεβαστων εν προχρεια δηναρια̣ [ε]ι̣κ̣[οσι πεντε]
⌊ ι̅θ̅ αντωνεινου και κομμοδου τω̣ν̣ κυρ̣ι̣[ων σεβ]αστ[ων]
τυβι κ̅α̅ αχιλλευς ιππευς τουρμης ηρωδι[α]νου ε[γ]ραψα υ̣περ
αυτου ερωτηθεις δ[ι]α το μη ειδενα̣ι̣ αυτον γραμματα

v 2. M reports απολιναριου in the papyrus. Evidently a scrap has broken off since his publication.

Col. vi (C, col. i)

16. (*Hand 12*) January 16

..[..]....[..].[...].πι̣φ.[.]. του[ρ]μης φ[ο]υρι.[
α ιο̣υλιω σερ̣η̣νω σο̣υμμω κο̣υρατ̣ορι χ̣[αι]ρειν ελ̣αβων̣
πα̣ρα σου την γρατιν μου υπερ το̣[υ ι]θ ε̣[το]υ̣ς εν

προχρ̣ιες εκξερχομηνος εις̣ [τα β]ουκ̣ο̣λ̣ια δηναρια εικοσι πεντε ∟ ιθ αυρηλιων̣ α̣ν̣τ̣ωνινου̣ και
κομοδου των κυριων σεβαστων τυ̣βι̣ κ̅α̅ μεμνων
σημιαφωρος τυρμης πετρωνιου ε̣γραψα̣ υ̣περ αυτου
δια το μη ειδηνε αυτων γραματ̣α

17. (*Hand 13*) January 16

ουαλερις σεραπιον ιππευς ειλης γαλλι[κ]η̣ς τυρμης πακτου-
α μηιου σερηνου ιουλιο σερηνω σουμ[ω] κουρατορι χαιρειν
ειλαβον παρα σου την γρασιν μου υ[πε]ρ̣ του ιθ ετους
εν προχρεια εξερχομονος εισκη̣[ν]α̣ς̣ μα̣[νδ]ρ̣ας̣ δηναρια
εικοσι πεντε ∟ ιθ αυρηλιω̣ν [αντο]ν̣ιν̣[ου και κομμοδ]ο̣υ
των κυρι[ων σ]ε̣βαστων τυβει [κα ιουλιος σερηνος κου]ρατωρ
τυρμης λ̣[υ]κ̣αριονος εγραψα [υπερ αυτου δια το μη ι]δ̣ενε α̣υ̣τον
γραματα

18. (*Hand 13*) January 16

μενκης ανουβας τυρμ̣η̣ς̣ [η]ρ̣ω̣δ̣[ι]ανου σ̣[ερ]η̣ν[ω] σ̣ου̣[μ]μω
α ειλης γαλλικης χαιρειν αιλ̣α̣βον̣ παρα σου την γρασιν μου
του ι̅θ̅ ετ[ο]υς εξερχομεν̣ος εις τα βουκ[ο]λ̣ια δηναρια
εικοσι πεν̣τε ∟ ιθ αυρηλιων αντωνινου και κομοδου των κυριων
σεβαστω̣ν̣ τ̣υβει [κ̅]α̅ σερηνος κ̣ο̣υρ̣ατωρ τυρμης λυκαριονος εγραψα
υπερ αυτο̣υ̣ δια̣ [το μ]η̣ ειδενε αυτ̣[ο]ν γραματα

vi 1–8. The entire receipt has been canceled by cross-hatching.

1. Since there is no room for ειλης γαλλικης,].πιφ.[is probably a title, as in x 9, where the name of the ala is omitted; but it may be part of the soldier's name. Cf. vi 17. The name of the decurion is probably Furianus. He may be identical with the decurion Messius Furianus in Dessau 2543. See Meyer, p. 176, note 5.

17. For the omission of κουρατορι cf. x 10.

19. The ξ of εξερχομενος is written over a character which is either a Roman *x* or a chi.

Col. vii (C, col. ii)

ζ

19. (*Hand 14*) January 16

γαιος σερηνος ιππευς ιλης γαλλ[ικης] του̣ρ̣μ̣ης γεμελλου̣
α ιυλιω σερηνω σουμμου κουρατ̣[ορι] χ̣αι[ρει]ν ελαβον
παρα σου την γρασσιν μου υπε̣[ρ τ]ο̣υ ∟ ιθ δηναρια
ικουσι πεντε ∟ ιθ αυρηλιων αντο̣νινου και κομμοδου
των κυριων σεβαστων τυβι κ̅α̅ εξερχομενος ις αφρ-
λ̣ινωι̣

20. (*Hand 14*) January 16

παθερμουθις παλαμο̣τ̣ης ιπ̣πευς ιλης γαλλικης
τουρμης σερηνου μελανι ι̣[ο]υλιω σερηνω σουμμου
α κουρατορι χαιριν ελαβον π̣α̣ρα σου την γρασσιν μου
υπερ του ∟̣ ιθ αυρηλιων αντ̣[ω]νινου κα̣[ι] κομμοδου των

κυριων σεβαστων δενα[ρια ει]κ̣ουσ̣[ι π]ε̣ν̣[τ]ε τυβι κ̅α̅
γαιος σ̣ερ̣ηνος ιππευ̣ς̣ ι̣[λης τη]ς̣ [αυτης] τουρμης
γεμελ̣[λου] εγραψα υπερ α̣υ̣[του ερωτηθεις δια] των μη
ιδενε α̣υ̣τον γραμματα

21. (*Hand 15*) January 17

λογγινος αριανος ιππευς [ει]λ̣η[ς] γαλλικη̣[ς τουρμη]ς̣ λουκιλλιου
βασσου σερηνω σουμμω [κου]ρατορι χαιρει[ν ελ]α̣β̣[ον] π̣α̣ρα σου την
α γρασσιν μου υπερ του ιθ / δ[η]ν̣αρ[ι]α εικοσι π̣εντε ε̣ν προχρεια
εξερχομενος εις σκηνας μανδρα̣ς̣ ∟ ιθ α̣υρηλιων αντωνινου
και κομμ[ο]δου των κυριων σεβαστων τυ[β]ι κ̅β̅ ερεννις μελας
σησκουπ̣λικαρις ειλης της αυτης εγραψα υπερ αυτου ερωτηθεις
δια το μ[η] ε̣ιδενα[ι] α̣υτον γραμματα

vii 1. The zeta at the top is the number of the column in the roll. This shows that the present col. i was the beginning of the roll, which therefore opened with the month of January.

6–7. M reports the place as Ἀφρ̣ο̣τινῳι̣, but the photograph shows only αφρ in line 6 and λινωι in line 7, with no sign of the omicron, and the final iota is very doubtful. M's suggestion of Aphrodito is nevertheless probably right.

8. παλαματης: M; but the letter after mu is quite different from any alpha in this receipt.

10. The tau of την is corrected from another letter, perhaps pi.

16. Since *longinus* is well attested as a nomen (see Index), there is no reason to emend αριανος to the genitive case.

19. Μανδρ[α]ς: M.

22. [α]υτον: M.

Col. viii (D, col. i)

η
22. (*Hand 16*) January 17

ιουλεις σερηνος ιππ[ευς] ε̣ι̣λης̣ ου̣ε̣τρανης γαλικης τουρμης λυκαριωνος
α ιουλιω σερηνω σουμμ[ω κο]υ̣ρατορ̣ι χαιρειν ελαβον παρα σου την γρασιν
υπερ του ι̅θ̅ δηναρεια [ει]κοσι πεντε εν πρ`ο´χρια εξερχομενος εις σκη-
νας μικρας ∟ ι̅θ̅ αυρηλιων̣ αντωνινου και κομοδου των κυριων σεβαστων
τυβι κ̅β̅·

23. (*Hand 16*) January 17

απωνις γερμνος ιππευς ειλης της αυτης τουρμης αμμωνιανου
ιουλιω σερηνω σουμ̅ω κουρατορι χαιρειν ελαβον παρα σου την
α γρασιν μου υ̅π̅ερ του ιθ δηναρεια εικοσι πεντε εν προχρεια εξερχομενος εις σκηνας μ̣ι̅κρας ∟ ιθ {αυ} αυρηλιων αντωνινου και κομοδου
των κυριων σεβασ̣τ̣ω̣̅ν τυβι κβ ειουλεις σερηνος ιππευς ειλης της
αυτης τουρμης λυκ̣[α]ρ̣ιωνος εγραψα υπερ αυτου δια το μη ειδαιναι
αυτον γραματα

24. (*Hand 17*) January 17

μαρκος τιτος ιππευ̣ς ε̣[ιλ]ης γαλλ̣[ικ]ης̣ τ̣ουρμης αγριππα λιουλιω σερηνω
σμουμω κουρατορ̣[ι χαι]ρ̣ειν ε̣[λαβον] π̣αρα σου την γρασιν μου υ̣[π]ερ του
α ∟ ιθ δηναρια εικ̣[οσι π]εντε ε[ν προχρι]α εξερχομενος εις τ[α βο]υ̣κολια
∟̣ ιθ αυρηλιων α[ν]τ̣ωνι̣[νου και κομ]μοδου των κυριων α̣υ̣τοκρατορων
τυβι κ̅β̅

25. (*Hand 17*) January 17

ορσενουφις ανναε.[..] ι̣π̣π̣[ευς ειλης γαλ]λ̣ικης τουρμης σωτηριχι λουλιω σερηνω σμουμω κο̣υρα̣τορι χαι[ρειν ελαβο]ν παρα σου την γρασιν μου εν προχρ[ει-
α υπερ του ∟ [ιθ ε]ξερχομενο̣[ς ε]ι̣σ̣κ[ην]ας μικρας δηναρια εικοσι πεντε
α ∟ ιθ αυρηλιων̣ αντωνινο[υ] και κομοδου των κυριων σεβαστων
τυβι κ̅β̅ μαρκος τ[ι]του εγρ̣α̣ψα υπερ αυτου ερωτηθεις δ[ια] το μη ειδαι
αυτον γραματα

26. (*Hand 18*) January 17

σαραπιων παθερμ̣ουτις ιππευς ε̣ιλης γαλλικης τουρμης ηρωδιαν̣[ο]υ̣ ιου[λι]ω σερηνω
σουμμω κουρατ̣ο̣ρι χαιρειν ελαβον παρα σ̣ου την γραστιν μο̣υ ε̣ν̣ [π]ρ̣[ο]χρια υπερ
[ε]ξερχ̣ο̣μενος ⟦εις μαρεωτην⟧
α τ[ου ι̅]θ̅ ∟ ∟ ιθ α̣υ̣ιρηλιων αντωνινου και κομμοδου των κυρ̣[ιων] α̣υ̣τοκρατορων
τ̣υ̣βι κ̅β̅ διον̣υ̣σιος σαραπι^ω σημιαφορος ⳨ α̣π̣ολιναριου εγραψα υπερ αυτου μη ει[δοτο]ς̣
γραμα̣∫

viii 7. *Γερμανός*: M.

14. Meyer, p. 158, note 2, implies that one should divide and read λ(ουκιω) ιουλιω; but the iota after the lambda is blurred as if from an attempt at erasure, and in viii 19, by the same hand, the name is written λουλιω. The lambda seems therefore to be simply another effort to render the sound of an initial Roman consonantal *i*. If the lambda is intended for a praenomen, it is the only instance of one in the whole papyrus.

19. *'Ανναρίου*: M.

21. κηνας in pap.: M.

22. The first sigma of σεβαστων has been corrected from another letter.

23. The alpha of μαρκος has been corrected from another letter, perhaps epsilon.

Col. ix (D, col. ii)

θ

27. (*Hand 19*) January 17

ι̣ο̣υλιος χαιρημονιανος ιππευς ιλης γαλλικης τ̣ορμης
αγριππα και σαραπιων ισιδωρου τορμης λυκαριωνος
γ και αμμωνιος σερηνος τορμης σ̣ε̣ντιου ιουλιω σερηνων
σουμω κουρατορι χαιριν ελαβαμεν παρα σου την
γραστιν ημων εν προχρια ε̣ξερχομενοι ις τα βοκολια ∟ ι̅θ̅ αυρηλιων αντωνινω κα̣[ι] κομοδω̣ των κυριων
σεβαστων εκαστες ημων δηνα̣ρια ικοσι π̣εντε
∟ ιθ αυρηλιω αντωνινων και κομοδου των κυριω̣ σε̣-
βαστ̣ων̣ τυβι κ̅β̅ ιουλιος χαιρ̣η̣μ̣ονια̣νος ο προγε-
γρα[μμεν]ο̣ς εγραψα υπε[ρ α]υτ[ω]ν̣ [ε]ρ̣ω̣τηθις δια
τ[ο μη ειδε]ν̣αι αυτους γραμ̣ατα

28. (*Hand 20*) January 17

κο.[.....]ς θηων ϊππευς ϊλης γαλλ̣ι̣κ̣[η]ς̣ τ̣ο̣υρμ̣[ης] σουπατιανου
ϊουλ̣[ι]ω̣ σ̣ε̣ρηνω σουμμω κουρατορε̣ι̣ χ̣αιρειν̣ ελ̣εβον παρα σ̣ο̣υ την γραστιν μου εν προχρ̣ι̣α εξερχομενος
α εισκηνας μεγαλας ετου̣ς ι̅θ̅ αυρ̣ηλιων αντωνινου
και κομοδου των κυρ[ιω]ν̣ σεβ̣α̣στ̣[ω]ν̣ τυβι κ̅β̅
ηρων ϊσιδωρος ϊππευς ϊλη̣ς̣ τ̣[η]ς αυτ̣[η]ς̣ τ̣ο̣υρμης λουκιλλιου
εγραψα ϋπερ αυτου ερωθ̣η̣θεις

ix 16. κηνας in pap.: M.

Col. x (E, col. i)

ι

29. (*Hand 21*) January 17

ιουλιος απολιναριος ιππευς ιλης γαλλικης τουρμης
σερηνου μελανος ιουλιω σερηνω σουμμω κουρα-
α τορι χαιριν ελαβον παρα σου εν προχρεια την γρασσιν
μου υπερ του ∟ ι̅θ̅ αντωνεινου και κομοδου
των κυριων εξερχομενος εις σκηνας μεικρας
δηṿ[αρια] ε̣ι̣κοσι πεντε ∟ ι̅θ̅ αυρηλιων αντωνινου
και κομο̣δ̣ο̣υ των κυρι̣ω̣ν σεβαστων τυβι κ̅β̅

30. (*Hand 13*) January 17

ιουλιος σερηνος κωρατορ τυρμης λυκαριονος σερηνω
σουμω ειλης της αυτης χαιρειν ειλαβον παρα σου
α τη̣ṿ [γρασ]ιν μου υπερ τ̣ου ι̅θ̅ και δεκατου ετου δηναρια
ει[κοσι] πεντε εξερχομενος ε[ι]ς̣ α̣ρ̣σ̣ι̣[νο]ειτην
∟ ιθ αυρηλιων αντονινου κα̣ι̣ κομ[οδο]ṿ των κυριων σεβαστων
τυβει δευτερα κ̣[αι] ε̣ι̣κ̣ο̣σ̣τ̣[η]

31. (*Hand 20*) January 18

ηλιοδωρος̣ [π]α̣τροκ̣λ̣ος ϊππευς ϊλης γαλλικης τουρμη̣ς̣ α̣γριπα ϊουλιω σερηνω σουμμω κουρατο̣ρει χαιρειν ελαβον παρα σ̣ο̣υ
α την γρασιν μου εν προχρεια εξερχομενος
ε̣[ι]σκηṿας μα̣ρδας ϋπερ του ∟ ι̅θ̅ δηṿαρι̣α
εικ̣[ο]σι και πεντε ετους ι̅θ̅ αυρηλιων [αντ]ωνινου
και κ[ο]μοδου των κυριων σεβαστων τυβι κ̅γ̅
ηρων ϊσιδωρος ϊππευς ϊλης της αυτης τουρμης
λουκιλλιου εγραψα ϋπερ αυτου δια το μη ειδεναι
αυτον γραμματα

x 1. The iota is the number of the column.
5. The upsilon of υπερ has been corrected from another letter.
11. The reading of the whole line is perfectly clear except for the first two words. The wording at the end seems to be the result of telescoping into each other two different expressions, ∟ θ και δεκατου and ιθ ετους.
19. κηνας in pap.: M.

Col. xi (E, col. ii)

ια

32. (*Hand 20*) January 18

κασις απιτος ϊππευς ϊλης γαλ[λι]κ̣η[ς] τ̣ουρ-
μης λουκιλλιου ϊουλιω σερηνω σουμ̣μ̣ω
α κουρατορει χαιρειν ελαβον παρα σου την γραστιν μου εν προχρεια εξερχομενος εις-
κ̣ηνας μεγαλας ϋπερ του ∟ ι̅θ̅ δηναρεια
εικοσει πεντε ετους ι̅θ̅ αυρηλιων αντωνινου

και κομοδου των κυριων σεβαστων τυβι κ̅γ̅
ηρων ϊσιδωρος ϊππευς ϊλης της αυτης τουρμης της
αυτης εγραψα ϋπερ αυτου ερωθηθεις
κασις απιτος ελαβον (*Casis' own hand*)

33. (*Hand 8*) January 18

ηλιοδωρος σερηνου ιππευς ειλης γαλλικης τουρμης αμμονιανου
β και ιουλις σερην̣[ος] ιππευς ειλης της αυτης τ̣ουρμης της αυτης
σερηνῳ σ̣[ουμμω] κουρατορι χαιρειν ελαβ̣α̣μεν παρα σου την
γραστιν [ημων] εν προχρεια εξερχομενοι εις τα βοκολια
ανα δ[ην]αρια εικοσι πεντε υπερ του ιθ ∫ αυρηλιων
αντων̣[ε]ι̣νου και κομμοδου καισαρων των κυριων
τυβι κ̅γ̅ αχιλλες αχιλλεως ιππευς ειλης τ̣ης αυτης
τουρμης ηρωδιανου εγραψα υπερ̣ αυτων ερωτηθεις
δια το βραδεως ηλιοδωρου γρ̣α̣φοντος ⟦και⟧
ηλιοδορος ελαβα ως προγιται (*Heliodorus' own hand*)

xi 1. The letters are the number of the column.
2 and 11. The name may well be Cassius Habitus; but I see no way of being sure. Ἄπιδος: M, without explanation.
6. The kappa of κηνας is in the margin.

11. This line is of course Kasis' (Cassius?) signature.
12. Ἀμμωνιανοῦ: M.
21. This line is Heliodoros' signature.

Col. xii (F, col. i)

34. (*Hand 22*) January 18

ο̣υ̣α̣λ̣[ε]ρ̣ι̣ο̣ς̣ σαραπαμμων ιππε̣υ̣ς̣ ειλης ουατρανης
καλλ̣ι̣κης τουρμης ιουλιου πρωταρχου ιουλιω
α σ̣ε̣ρ̣η̣[ν]ω σουμμῳ κυρατορι χαιρειν ⟦ομολογο⟧
ελ̣α̣β̣[ον] π̣α̣ρ̣α̣ σο̣υ την κρασι μου προχρεια⟦α⟧ς εξερ-
χομ̣ε̣ν̣ο̣ς ⟦λ̣α̣υ⟧ εις αφροδιτω δηναρια εικοσι πεντε
∟ ιθ α̣υ̣ρηλιων αντονινου και κομμοδου των κυριων
σεβ̣αστων τυβι κ̅γ̅ ζωιλος σημιαφορος
εγ[ρα(ψα)] το σομα αυτου υπογ(ρα)φ(οντος) το ο̣νομα αυτου
ουα[λ]ε̣ρις σεραπαμων ο προγεγραμμενος ως προ-
κιτ̣[α]ι (*Sarapammon's own hand in lines 9–10*)

35. (*Hand 23*) January 18

ιουλ̣ι̣ο̣ς̣ καστορ ιππευς ειλης ουετρανης γαλληκης
τουρ[μ]ης πακτουμηις σερηνου ιουλιο σερηνω σουμμο κου-
α [ρα]τορ χ̣ε̣ρ̣ι̣ν ελαβον παρα σου την γρασημ μου ε̣ν̣ π̣ρ̣οχριας
[εξερ]χ̣ο̣μ̣ε̣νος ισκηνας μαντρας δηναρια εικ[ο.]σι πεν^τε^
[∟ ιθ α]υ̣ρη̣λ̣ι̣ω̣ν αντονινου κε γομοτου των κυρ̣ω̣ν σεβαστω^ν^
[τ]υβι κ̅γ̅ α̣ντηνορ αχιλλι ιππευς ιλης ουετρα̣νης γαλλη-
κ̣ης τ̣[ου]ρ̣μ̣ης κλαρου εγραψα υπερ αυτου δια το μη ι-
δενε α̣[υ]τ[ο]ν̣ γραμματα

36. (*Hand 24*) January 18

βησαρ̣[ι]ων ισι̣δ̣ωρου ιππευς ειλης γαλλικης τουρνης σερηνου μελας
και αρμειυσει αρνει[. .]ο̣υ̣ τουρνης φρουριανου ιουλιωι σερημωι
σουμω̣ι̣ κουρατορι χαιρε̣[ι]ν ελαβα̣μεν παραι σου την γρασιν
β ημω̣ν ε̣ν̣ προ̣χειρωι εξερ[χο]μενομεν βησαρ εις τα βουκολια
αρμε̣ι̣υ̣[σ]ε̣ι̣ εισκαινας μ̣α̣ν̣τ̣ρας αικαστος τηναρια εικοσει πενται
∟ $\overline{\iota\theta}$ αυ̣[ρη]λ̣ι̣ω̣ν αντωνινου και κομοδου των κυριων σεβαστων
τυβι̣ κ̣γ

xii 1. Ο̣ὐ̣α̣λ̣έ̣ρ̣ι̣ς̣ : M.
3. Σ̣ε̣ρ̣ή̣ν̣ῳ; κουράτορι; ⟦ὁμολογῶ⟧: M.
4. προχρεία⟦α⟧ς: M. The writer appears to have written προχρειαες first, then to have corrected the second epsilon to sigma without erasing the final sigma.
8. ὑ̣π̣ο̣γρά(φοντος): M.; but there is not room for ρα. The phi is unlike those above—probably not a letter at all but a flourish of abbreviation.
9–10. These lines are Sarapammon's signature.
13. Either [ρα]τορ̣ or [ρα]τρι̣ because space is lacking for [ρα]τορι. I owe χεριν to Dr. Maehler. The first letter of γρασημ has two horizontals like a digamma.
14. κηνας: M.
15. Omega of κυρων is like no other omega in this receipt; but it is impossible to read as ιω.
20. Ἀρνείτου: M; but two letters are needed to fill the lacuna. The decurion is Furianus; see Meyer, p. 176, note 5.
23. καινας: M.

Col. xiii (F, col. ii)

ι̣γ

37. (*Hand 24*) January 18

● θεω̣δωρος ανμ̣ιοχου [ιππ]ευς ειλης γαλλικης τουρνης
ηρωδιαμου σερημ̣ωι σ̣[ο]υ̣μω̣ι καιρατορρι χαιρειν
α ελαβον παρα σου τη̣ν̣ γρα̣σ̣[ι]ν̣ μ̣ο̣υ εν προχριας εξερχαμενος
εισκηνα^s ν^α αρτρας τηναρ̣[ι]α̣ ε̣ικοσι πενται ∟ $\overline{\iota\theta}$ αυρηλιων
αντωνινου και κομοδ[ου] τ̣[ων κυρι]ω̣ν σεβαστων τυβι $\overline{\kappa\gamma}$
βησαριων ισιδωρου το̣υ̣ρ̣[μ]η̣ς̣ σ̣ερημου μελανει εγραψον υπερ
αυτου ερωτηθις τια το μ̣η̣ [ειδ]ε̣ν̣αι αυτον κρανατα

38. (*Hand 25*) January 19

καμης ορσει ιππευς ιλη̣ς̣ [γ]α̣λ̣λικης τουρμη̣ς̣ γεμελι
ιουλιω σερηνω σουμω κ[ου]ρ̣α̣τορ χαιριν ελαβον παρε σου
α την γρασαν μου εν πρ̣[ο]χρια̣ς̣ υπερ του ενναικαιδει-
κατου ετους αντω̣ν̣ι̣νω και κωμωτου των κριων
σεβαστων δηναρια εκωσι πεντα̣ι ετους $\overline{\iota\theta}$
αυρηλιων αντωνινω κ̣αι κωμωτου των κυριων
σεβαστων τυβι $\overline{\kappa\delta}$

39. (*Hand 25*) January 19

πασιον διοσκωρου ιππ̣ε̣υς ιλης γαλλικης τουρμα γαιμελι
α σερηνω σουμο κουρατωρ χαιριν ελαβον παρα σου την
γρασαν μου εν πρωχιας υπερ του εννεκαιταικα-
του αντωνινου και κωμ̣ωτου τω κυριων σεβαστων
δηναρια εικοσι πεντη ετους $\overline{\iota\theta}$ αυρηλιου αντωνινου

και κωμωτου των κυρ̣ιων σεβαστων τυβι κδ
——— καιμης ορσε ιπ̣π̣ε̣υς ιλης της αυτης τουρμα της αυ-
της εγραψα υπερ αυτ̣ο̣υ ερωτηθις δ̣[ι]α̣ τω μη ιδαιναι
αυτον γραμαται

xiii 2. *αννιοχου*: M, interpreted as *'Αντιόχου*, probably rightly. He does not report the punctum preceding the name.

5. *κηνας ναaρτρας*: M, interpreted as *Μανδρας*. The final sigma of *εισκηνας* and the first alpha of *νααρτρας* are inserted by the same hand above the line.

7. *τουρνης*: M.

9. Eta of *τουρμη̣ς̣* is corrected; sigma appears unfinished.

11. The letter following alpha of *προχρια* resembles a Roman cursive *s* or a narrow Greek pi in this hand.

Col. xiv (G, col. i)

ι̣δ

40. (*Hand 26*) January 19

ιουλις αγαθ[ο]ς δαιμων ιππευς [*στατωρ*] *ιλης γαλλικης*
τουρμης αμμωνιανου ιουλιω σερηνω σουμμωι
κουρατωρ χαιρειν ελαβον παρα σου την γρασσιν
α *μου εν προχρεια εξερχομενος ις αρσινοιτην*
υπερ του ιθ αυρηλιων αντωνινου και
κομοδου των κυριων σεβαστων δηνα-
ρια κε ∟ *ιθ αυρηλιων αντωνινου και*
κομοδου των κυριων σεβαστων τυβι κδ

41. (*Hand 27*) January 21

τιθοης πλουτιωνος ιππευς ειλης ουετρανης γαλλικης
τυρμης πακτουμηιου σερηνου ιουλιω σερηνω σουμ-
μω κουρατορι ειλης της αυτης χαιρ̣ε̣ιν ελαβον παρα σου
την γραστιν μου εν προχρεια εξηρχομεν[ο]ς ις σκηνας
α *μεικρας υπερ του ιθ* ∟ *των κυριων σεβαστων* ∟ *ιθ*
αντωνεινου και κομοδου των κυριων σεβαστ̣ω̣ν τυβι κς
μαιμινς ποτιολανος δουπλικαρις ειλης της αυτης τυρ-
μης αγριππα εγραψα υπερ αυτου ηρωτηθεις δια το μη ει-
δηναι αυτον γραμματα

xiv 2. M reports *ιππευς* but not *στατωρ*..

Col. xv (G, col. ii)

ι̣ε̣

42. (*Hand 23*) January 23

αμμονις κασις ιππευς ιλης ο̣υετρανης γαλλικης τουρμ̣[ης] π̣ε̣τρο-
νιου και λυκαριον πασαυς τουρμης απολιναριου και ορος πιατ[.]. .
τουρμης ιουλιου ιουλιο σερηνω σουμμο κουρατορ χεριν
ελαβαμεν παρα σου την γρασσιν υμων εν προχριας υπερ του ε̣ν̣νεα-
γ *κεδεκατου ετους εξερχομενοι ις τα βουκολλια εκαστος υμω̣ν̣*

δηναρια εικοσσι πεντε ∟ $\overline{ιθ}$ αυληριον αντονινου και κομοδου τω̣ν
κυριον σεβαστων τυβι $\overline{κη}$ αντηνορ αχιλλι αρμορου εγραψα υπερ αυτων
δια το μη ιδενε αυτους γραμματα

43. (Hand 28) January 26

χαιρημων μαξιμου ειππευς ειλης ουαδρανης ⟦γαλλικης τουρμης ελιοσε. .⟧
γαλλικης τουρμης ελιο εερηνω και παησις δχηουτος ειππους ειλης της αυτης
τουρμης λουκιλιω βασ ειολιω σερηνω σουμμω κορατωρι χαιριν
β ελαβαμεν παρεσο την γρασν ημων εν προχρια εκξερχωμενοι
υπερ του εννεκαιτεκατου ετους αντωνινω και κωμωδου των κυριων
σεβαστων εκαστες ημων δηναρια εικιει πεντε
∟ $\overline{ιθ}$ αυρηλιων αντωνινω και κομω̣δω των κυριων σεβαστων μεκιρ $\bar{α}$
χαιρημων μαξιμου εγραψα

44. (Hand 29) February 4

αντωνιος ρωμανος ιππευς ιλης ουαε̣τρανης γαλλικης τουρμης
ηρωδιανου ιλιω σερηνω σουμω κουρατωρι χαιρειν αιλαβον
παρα σου την γρατιν μου εν προχρια εξερχομενον εις
α λαυραν υπερ του ∟ $\overline{ιθ}$ αντωνινου κα̣[ι] κομοδου των κυριων
σεβ̣[α]στων δηναρια εικοσι πεντε μεχειρ ι´

xv 10. ⟦Σερη⟧: M.
11. Σερήνῳ: M; but the cross-bar is plain in both epsilons in the name. Δχηοῦτος = Διηοῦτος: M; but Dornseiff-Hansen lists a name Δχηους of which this could be the genitive in a variant spelling or pronunciation.
13. γρασην μων: M.
14. Ἀντονίνῳ: M.

Col. xvi (H, col. i)

45. (Hand 30) February 5

hερμιας ḥεβερι ιππευ[ς ειλης ου̣ε̣τ̣ραν̣η̣ς γ̣α̣λλ[ικ]ης
τουρμης λουκιλλιου βασσου ιουλιω σ̣ερηνω σομμω κουρατωρι μου χαιρειν ελαβα⟦β⟧ν παρα σου την γρασιν μου
εν προχρειας εκξερχομενος εις τα βουκολια υπερ του ⟦∟ $\overline{ι.}$⟧
α ∟ $\overline{ιθ}$ αυρηλιων αντωνεινου και κομμοδω των κυριων
αυτοκρατορων δηναρια εικοσι πεντε χμεχει̣ρ̣ $\overline{ια}$
αντονις μαρκιανος ιππευς σιμιαφορος ειλης της αυτης
τουρμης λουκιλλιου εγραψα υπερ αυτου δια το μη ηδεναι
αυτον γραμματα

46. (Hand 31) February 7

οππιος λειτωρεινος ιππεους ειλης ουετρανης
γαλλικης τουρμης σεντιου ιουλιω σερηνω
σουμμω κουρατορι μου χαιρειν ελαβον
παρα σου την γρασσιν μου εν προχρειας
α εξερχομενος ις τα βουκολια υπερ του
∟ $\overline{ιθ}$ αουρηλιων αντωνεινου και λουκιου
αουρηλιου κομμοδου των κυριων
αυτοκρατορων δεναρια εικοσι πεντε
μεχειρ $\overline{ιγ}$

47. (*Hand 18*) February 7

διονυσιος σαραπιων̣ο̣ς σημιαφορος ειλης γαλλικης τουρμης
α απολιναριου ιουλιω σερηνω σουμμω̣ κουρατορι χαιρειν
ελαβον παρα σου εν προχρια την γρασσιν μου του ι̅θ̅ ʃ
αυρηλιων αντωνινου και κομμοδου των κυριων σεβαστων
εξερχομεν̣ο̣ς εις αφροδιτω δηναρια εικοσι πεντε πληρης
με̣χειρ ι̅γ̅

xvi 1. *Ηγρω*[.]*ιας .εβερι*: M; *Π̣εβερι* in app. In the second letter, the horizontal is too low for gamma; and mu is possible instead of omega for the fourth letter because mu begins in this hand with an exaggerated curl. Cf. *κομμοδω* in line 5. Dornseiff-Hansen lists no *Πεβερος* but does offer *Ἑβερος*. Consequently I believe that the initial in both names is a Roman *h*. Note the possible Roman *r* at the end of *μεχειρ̣*, line 6, and the correction of *x* to *ξ* in col. vi 19. For the use of Greek letters in Latin words in these papyri, see on **70** b ii 9.

6. The chi at the beginning of the month-name may be a cancellation of another stroke. The name itself can be read *μεχερ̣.* or *μεχει̣ρ̣*: the next-to-last letter is more like rho than iota; and the last is most like a Roman *r* whose bow touches the hasta only at the top. The alpha of the numeral is an elaborate figure like a three-petaled flower.

Col. xvii (H, col. ii)

48. (*Hand 12*) February 8

μαρ̣[κ]ο̣[ς] ουα[λ]ε̣ρι̣ς̣ ιππευς στατορ[ει]λ̣η̣ς̣ [ουε]τ̣ερανης γα[λ]λικης
τ̣ουρμης πετρωνιανα ιουλιω [σε]ρηνω σουμμω κουρατορι
χαιρειν ελαβων παρα σου εν̣ προχρειας την γρ̣ατι μου
υπερ του [ι̅]θ̅ ʃ αυρηλιων αντονινου και κομοδου των κυ-
α ριων σεβαστων εξερχομενος εις αρσινωιτου δηναρια
εικοσι πεντα̣ι πλ̣η̣ρις μεχειρ ι̅δ̅ μεμνων ψενπρης σημιαφωρος εγρ̣α̣ψα̣ υπερ αυτου δια το μη ειδε̣ι̣ναι αυτον γραματα

49. (*Hand 32*) February 9

φλαυεις σερηνος κουρατωρ ειλης γαλλι^κ
τουρμι̣ς σερηνου και σαραπιων ταυριν
τουρμης της αυτης̣ ιο̣υ̣λ̣ιω σερηνω σουμμω κουρατ̣ω̣ρι χαιρει̣ν̣ ελαβαμεν παρα
σου την γραττειν εκ δηναριων̣ εικοσι
πεντε ∟ ι̅θ̅ αυρηλιω̣ν̣ αντωνινου και
β κομοδου των κυριων σεβαστων μεχειρ ι̅ε̅

50. (*Hand 33*) February 12

ναρωους μιλονος ειππεους ιουλις σηνος
σου̣μο κουρατορ χαιριν ελαβα παρα σου
α δην κρασιν μου ∟ ι̅θ̅ αυρηλιου αντονινου και
γομοτου των κυριων σεβαστων μεχιρ ι̅η̅

xvii 1. *ουαλερις*: M; *ουα*[*λ*]*ερις*: Dr. Maehler.

9. *Ταυρίνου*: M; but Dornseiff-Hansen lists *Ταυρις*, and a mixture of cases does not trouble the authors of these receipts.

15. *Ναρῶσις*: M; but cf. Dornseiff-Hansen, *Ναα-ραους*, *Ναρωους*. The letter after omega is not sigma.

16. The upsilon of *σουμο* may be corrected from tau.

Col. xviii (I, col. i)

51. (*Hand 34*) February 24

[θ]εοφιλος [αλ]εξανδρι ιππε̣[υς ειλης γαλ]λικης
τ̣ουρμης λ̣[υ]καριωνος ιουλ̣[ιω] σ̣ερη̣ν̣ω σουμω̣
κουρατορι [χ]αιρειν ελαβον π̣α̣ρα̣ σου̣ την γρασ̣-
α τιν μου εν̣ π̣ροχρεια εξερχομ̣ενος ις κλυσμ̣α
υπερ του εν̣νεακαιδεκατου̣ ετους αυρηλι[ω]ν
αντωνιν[ο]υ και κομοδου τω[ν] κυριων σεβα̣[σ]των
δηναρια εικοσι πεντε μεχε̣ι̣ρ λ̄ ουαλεριος
νεπωτιανος ιππευς ειλης της αυτης τουρμης της αυτης εγραψα υπερ αυτου ερωτηθεις δια το μη ειδεναι αυτον γραμματα

52. (*Hand 34*) February 24

αμεριμνος αμμωνι ιππευς ειλης ουετρανης
γαλλικης τουρμης λυκαριωνος και απολλως
σερηνος ιππευς ειλης της αυτης τουρμης
αιλιου σερηνου ιουλιω σερηνω σουμμω κουρατορι χαιρειν ελαβαμεν παρα σου την γραστιν
β ημων εν προχρεια εξερχομενοι ις κλυσμα
υπερ του εννεακαιδεκατου ετους αυρηλιων
αντωνινου και κομοδου των κυριων
σεβαστων δηναρια εικοσι πεντε μεχειρ λ̄
ουαλεριος νεπ̣ωτιανος ιππευς ειλης της
αυτης τουρμης λυκαριωνος εγραψα υπερ
αυτων ερωτηθεις δια το μη ειδεναι αυτους
γραμματα

53. (*Hand 35*) February 24

μηνοδορος μαρκι ιππευς ειλης ουετρανης
γαλλικης τυρμης σερηνου μελανος ιουλειω
σερηνω σουμμω κουρατορει χαιρειν ελαβον
α παρα σου την γρασσειν μου εν προχρεια
εξερχομενος εις αρσεινοειτην υπερ του ῑθ̄
αυρηλειων αντονεινων των κυρειων και κομοδου
σεβαστων δηναρια εικοσι πενται μεχερ λ̄
ιουλειος μαρκος σημειαφορος εγραψα υπερ
αυτου ερωτηθε̣ς̣ δια το μη ειδειναι αυτον γραμματα

xviii 13. Omicron of σερηνος may be corrected from eta.

29–30. The order of names and titles is confused; but και κομοδου does not appear to have been added after the rest was written.

Col. xix (I, col. ii)

54. (*Hand 5*) March 12

διο̣[νυσι]ο̣ς̣ π.[.]ο̣[.]..ε̣ς ι̣π̣πευς ει̣λης γαλληκ̣η[ς]
τουρμ̣ης λυκαρ[ι]ω̣νος και οννοφρις κ̣ολλου-
τι ιππ̣ε̣υς ειλης τ̣ης αυουτης τουρμης σεντιου

ιουλιω σερηνω σουμο κουρατορι χαιριν ελαβαμεν παρα σου την γρασσιν υμον εν προχρια
εξερχομενυ εις λαυο̣υρ̣αν εκ δηναριον εικοσι
β πεντε υπερ του ενεακαιδεκατου ετους
αυρηλιων αντονινου και κομοδου τον κυριον
σεβαστον φαμενοτ ις̅ ερμιας οπτιον καμπο̣υ
εγραψα υπερ αυουτον εροτηθις δια το μη ειδενε
αυτους γραμματα

55. (*Hand 36*) March 12

● ιουλις απολιναρις ιππευς ειλης γοτρανης
γαλλικης τυρμης απολιναρειου ειουλιω σερηνω
α σουμω κουρατορι χαιρειν ελαβον παρα σου
την γρασην μου εν προχρεια υπερ του ιθ ∟
αυρηλιων αντωνινου και κομοδου των κυριων
σεβαστων δηναρεια εικοσει πεντει φαμενωθ ις̅

56. (*Hand 37*) March 16

νεφερως ω και νεφως ιππευς ιλης γαλλικης
τορμης σωτηριχου ιουλιω σερηνω σουμμω
α κουρατορι χαιρειν ελαβον παρα σου
την γρασσιν μου εν προχρια εξερχομενος
εις λαυραν υπερ του ιθ̅ αυρηλιων αντωνινου και κομοδου των κυριων σεβαστων δηναρια εικοσι πεντε φαμενωθ κ̅

xix 1. *Διονύσιος Π.*[.].[.]ο̣ρ̣[.]υ̣ς: M; διο[νυ]σ̣[ι]ος πα̣[.]ε̣[.]ο̣ρ̣[.]ο̣ς: Dr. Maehler, "(very uncertain)."

12. M does not report the punctum before the name.

19. σωτηριχου corrected from σφτηριχου: M.

Col. xx (κ, col. i)

57. (*Hand 38*) March 16

● ιουλις σερηνος ιππευς ιλης γαλλ̣ι̣κ̣ης ⳨ ηρωδιανου
ιουλιω σερηνω σουμων κουρατου χαιρειν αιλαβον
α παρα σου την κρασις εν προκρια εξερχομενος ις σκηνες
μεκαλας υπερ του ιθ̅ ∟ αυρηλιων αντωνινου
και κομοδων των κυριων σεβαστων δηναριον
εικοσπεντε φαμενωθ κ

58. (*Hand 30*) March 17

αντωνις χαιρημονιανος ιππευς ειλης ουετρανης
γαλλιγης τουρμης σερηνω μελανις και αρρις αρριανος
ιππευς ειλης της αυτης τουρμης λουκιλλιου βασσου
ιουλιω σερηνωι σομμω κουρατωρι χαιρειν ελαβαμεν
παρα σου την γρασιν ημων εν προχρειας εξερχομενοι

ϵις λαυρα υπϵρ του ϵννϵακαιδϵκατου ϵτους αυρηλιου
αντωνϵινου και κομμοδου των κυριων αυτοκρατορων
ϵκαστος ημων δηναρια ϵικοσι πϵντϵ φαμϵνωτ κ̅α̅
αντωνις μαρκιανος ιππϵυς σημιαφορος ϵιλης της
αυτης τουρμης λουκιλλιου ϵγραψα υπϵρ αυτων ϵρωτηθϵις
δια το μη ϵιδϵναι αυτυς {ϵιναι} γραμματα

59. (*Hand 39*) May 10

πουονσις πανϵχατϵς ιππϵυς ϵιλης ουϵτρανης γαλλικης
τουρμης ιουλιω και λογγινος νϵριος ιππϵυς ϵιλης ουϵτρανης
γαλλικης τουρμης σϵρηνι μϵλανι ιουλιω σϵρηνω σουμμω
κουρατωρι χαιρϵιν ϵλαβαμϵν παρα σου την γρασσην ημων
υπϵρ του ι̅θ̅ ∟ αυληριου αντονϵινου και κομοδω των κυριων
αυτοκρατορων ϵκαστος ημων ανα δηναρια ϵικοσι πϵντϵ
παχων ι̅ϵ̅ παμινις πακοιβϵος κιτατορ καμπι τουρμης
αιλιου σϵρηνου ϵιλης της αυτης ϵγραψα υπϵρ αυτων ϵρω-
τηθϵντων δια το μη ϵιδϵναι αυτω̣ς γραμματα

xx 1. *Φούλουιος* (pap. *φουλις*): M, who has been misled by a stroke slanting down from right to left before the name. The same mark, really a narrow oval punctum, is also found before the names in xiii 1; xix 12; and xxii 1. The phi of *φαμϵνωθ*, line 6, is quite different.

20. *σϵραινι*: M; but cf. eta in *τουρμης*, line 19, and the alphas everywhere.

24. M reports the date incorrectly as April 10.

Col. xxi (κ, col. ii)

60. (*Hand 40*) May 5

κϵνϵς ιπ̣ϵυ̣[ς] ι̣[λη]ς γα̣λ̣[λ]ι̣κης τουρμης αιλϵιου σϵρηνου σϵρηνω
σουμμω̣ κουραϵτορϵι χαιρϵιν ϵλαβον παρα σου την γρασσιν μου
του ιθ ∟ αυρηλιων αντωνινου και κομμοδου των κυριων
αυτοκρατορων δηναρϵια ϵικ̣ο̣σ̣ϵ̣ι̣ πϵντϵ παχων ῑ
καλλ̣ι̣γονος κλϵονικου κουρατωρ ϊλης της αυτης τουρμης
της αυτης ϵγραψ̣α υπϵρ αυτου δια το μη ϵιδηναι αυτον γραμματα

Remainder of column blank
Cols. xxii and xxiii are entirely blank

xxi 2. I am not sure that any vowel followed the second mu of *σουμμ*; but an omega like that in *αυρηλιων*, line 3, is just possible.

4. M reports the date incorrectly as April 5.

5. The gamma of *καλλιγονος* is doubtful because of an apparent stroke extending upward above the horizontal bar. No letter in this hand resembles such a character; and so I have accepted M's reading.

Col. xxiv (L, col. iii)

61. Remains of eight or nine illegible lines, either lost through abrasion of the surface or washed off while this file was still active. Then a space of about five lines blank.

62. (*Hand 41*) March 6

● ιουλι̣[ο]ς̣ σερηνος ιππευς ιλης γα̣λ̣[λ]ικης [τουρμ]η̣ς̣ [
ιουλω [σ]ε̣ρηνω σουμ̣μ̣ω κουρατ̣[ορ]ι χ̣α̣ι̣ρ̣ε̣ι̣ν̣ [ε]λ̣α̣β̣[ον]
παρα σου την κρασ̣ι̣ν̣ μ̣ο̣υ υπερ̣ τ̣ο̣υ̣ ι̅θ̅ ∟ α̣υ̣[ρηλ]ι̣ω̣ν̣
αντωνε̣ινου̣ και κομμοδου των̣ [κ]υριω̣[ν σεβαστων εκ]
δηναριω̣ν εικοσι πε̣ν̣[τ]ε̣ι̣ φαμ[ε]ν̣[ω]θ ι̅

Remainder of column blank

xxiv 1. ε̣ιουλ[ει]ς: M; but the first epsilon is a punctum. See above, on xx 1.

5. M reports the date incorrectly as March 4.

The texts which follow are described by Meyer, p. 158, as written on four separate sheets of papyrus which were then laced to the papyrus of the roll at the points indicated by their letters—BB over col. iv, FF over col. xii, GG over col. xiv, and HH over col. xvi. I have kept Meyer's designations of these single sheets.

BB. (*Hand 18*) January 17

διονυσιος αρτιμιδωρος ιππε̣υς ε̣ιλης γαλλ̣ικης τ[ο]υ̣ρ̣μης ηρωδ̣[ια-]
νου και θεων στιλβωνος τουρμης σερηνου ιου[λιω σ]ερη[ν]ω̣ σουμ̣-
μω κουρατορι χαιρειν ελαβαμεν παρα σου αλλα τ̣.[. . .]μ̣ν̣.φ.α̣ ε̣ξ̣
καλανδων σεπτεμβριων ορφιτου και ρουφου υπατι̣[α]ς̣ [.]ε̣σπου̣α̣ι̣γευ- Sept. 1, 178
θημεν εν μαρεωτη μετα πακτουμηϊ σερηνο̣υ δεκαδαρχου
εκαστος ημων δηναρια εικοσι πεντε πληρης
∟ ιθ αυρηλιων αντωνινου και κομμοδου των κυρ̣[ι]ω̣ν αυτοκρατορων
τυβι κ̅β̅ διονυσιος σαραπιωνος σημιαφορος ει[λη]ς της αυτης
τουρμης απολιναριου εγραψα υπερ αυτων προ̣[σφ]ερομενων μη
ειδεναι γραμμ/

BB 1. Ἀρτε̣μίδωρος; Ἡρωδ̣ι̣[α]-: M.
2. Σ̣ερη̣[ν]ῳ̣: M.
3. τ[. . . .]α̣λ̣.[.].φ.λ̣ιου: M. Dr. Maehler writes, "τ seems certain, then a faint trace of the bottom end of a vertical stroke (α, ε, and the like, less likely ι); after the first gap ω seems certain (not α, as M read), then almost certainly λ (just possibly ν, not χ); after the second gap, φ or ψ, then faint traces of what could be ο̣ν̣ο̣υ (ν more likely than λ, but all rather doubtful)." What is wanted, of course, is a term denoting a particular item, like the κράστις, in addition to the other things, for which payment had been owing since the previous September 1.
4. [. .]α̣σπολ̣α̣ι̣γευ: M. Dr. Maehler writes, "]ασπ or]εσπ, then λαι almost certain (not λλι, λλα, νι, etc.)." There is probably space for only one letter, not two, in the lacuna. The verb expressed the reason for the men's absence in Mareotis. The date is September 1, 178.
5. Σερήν[ο]υ: M.
9. The spacing seems to require προ[σφ]- rather than προ[φ]-.
10. γράμμα(τα): M; γράμμα[τα]: Daris.

FF. (*Hand 20*) January 18

[ϊουλις σερηνος ϊπ]π̣ευς ϊλης̣ [γ]α̣λ̣[λικ]η̣[ς] τουρμ̣η̣ς̣ ηρωδιανι και ϊου-
[λι]ς̣ [νεπωτι]α̣ν̣[ος] τ̣ουρμης της αυτης και πατερμουθις̣ ορσενου-
φι̣ς̣ τ̣ο̣υ̣ρμης πακτουμηνιο̣υ σερηνου ϊουλιω σερηνω σουμμω κουρατορει χαιρειν ελαβαμεν το επουλον ημων
αυτοκρατορος κομοδου το β̅ και ουηρου το β̅ ϋπατειας
εκ δηναρειων δεκα οβολων οκτω ετους ι̅θ̅ αυρηλιων

αντωνεινου και κομοδου των κυριων σεβαστων
τυβι κ̅γ̅ ηρων ϊσιδωρος ϊππευς ϊλης της αυτης τουρμης
λουκιλλιου εγραψα ϋπερ αυτων ερωθηθεις δια το μη ειδεναι αυτους γραμματα

FF 1–2. The restorations of the names are M's. They seem highly probable but are not certain.

4. As M saw (p. 160), *επουλον* is a transliteration of Latin *epulum*, and the item is to be compared to (but not necessarily identical with) the *saturnalicium castrense* of **68** ii 8 and iii 7. The *collatio* which recurs regularly in the entries of **70** may also be similar.

5. This entire line is omitted from the transcription on p. 165 of Meyer. The date is A.D. 179.

9. *με̣ ϊ-*: M. There is a stroke too many for *μει*, but an eta cannot be read after the mu.

GG. (*Hand 42*) March 5

. . . .]φερω ιπ[π]ε̣υ̣ς̣ [ειλη]ς ο̣υ̣ετραν̣η̣[ς] γα̣λ̣λ̣ι̣κης
τυρμα φουρωνι ϊουλι̣ω̣ σ̣ερηνω σ̣ουμμω κουρατορι χαιριν
ελαβον παρα σου την γρ̣α̣στιν μου ϋπερ του οκτωκαιδε̣-
κατου ετους ομοιως και του εν̣νεακαιδεκατου ετους
αντωνινου και κομοδου των κ̣υνιων σεβαστων
φαμενωθ θ̅ ιουλις αμερυς ιππευ ειλης της αυτης
τουρμης της αυτης εγραψα υπερ αυτου δια το μη ϊδεναι
αυτον γραμματα

(*Hand 43*) March 1

σωπατρος διονυσιος ιππευς ειλης ουε̣τρανης γαλλικης ⳨ αιλιου σερηνου
ϊουλιω σερηνω σουμμω ⟦ε̣. .⟧ κουρατορι χαιρειν ελαβον παρα σου την γραστιν μου
υπερ του ι̅θ̅ ετους αντωνεινου και κομμοδου των κυριων σεβαστων
φαμενωθ ε̅ πο̣μπηϊος διογενης ιππευς ειλης της αυτης ⳨ ιουλιου
εγραψα ϋπερ αυτου ερωτηθεις παροντος αυτου δια το μη ειδεναι αυτο̣ν̣ γραμματα

GG 1. [. . . . . . . *Νε*]*φερῶ*: M. The restoration is possible; but several others are equally possible.

5. The tau of *των* is corrected from iota.

6. It is strange that this receipt should be dated four days later than the one which follows it. Probably the numeral theta here is an erroneous repetition of the last letter of the month-name. The iota of *ιππευ* is corrected from epsilon. M reports the date incorrectly as March 3.

9. *οὐο̣τρανῆς*: M.

10. ⟦*ειο̣*⟧: M.

12. The first omicron of *ιουλιου* is corrected from epsilon. M reports the date incorrectly as February 24.

HH. (*Hand 44*) April 5

Col. i

ισας σαραπιωνος ι̣π̣π̣) ϊλης ο̣[υε]τρανης γαλειγης
τουρμης αγριππα ιουλιω σερηνω σουμω κου-
ρατωρει χαιρειν ελαβον παρα σου την γραστιν
α ι̣μου του ι̅θ̅ ∫ δηναρεια εικοσι πεντε
Ḷ ιθ∫ αυρηλιων αντωνινου και κομμοδου
των κυριων σεβαστων φαρμουθι ϊ

Col. ii

ισας [σερ]ηṿω̣ τω τιμιωτα̣τω
χαιρειν
καλωṣ π̣[ο]ι̣η̣σις δουṣ διοσκωρω τω
αδελφω τ̣η̣ν γραστιν μου του ιθ∫
επι προ̣εχ̣ρησαμην παρ αυτου
εν αρσινο̣ειτου δηναρεια εικοσι
πεντε παρ ου και λημψη την απο-
χημ μου ερρωθ σε υχο^κ πρ̣οκοπʹ αει

HH i 1. *ι̣π̣ε̣υ̣ς*: M; but there is room for only three letters, and the final downstroke is much too long for a sigma. It is either iota or a mark of abbreviation. I have assumed the latter. The whole word, however, is so badly damaged that any reading is uncertain.

3. *ρατωρες*: M.

4. *μου*: M; but the mu is indented by one letter and there is a stroke before it in addition to the shaft of the year-symbol which rises from the line below.

5. The year-symbol has a peculiar shape, with a sharp angular hump slightly left of the center of the horizontal stroke and a short vertical stroke descending from the middle of the right half of the horizontal, producing a sort of tau.

ii 7. The published transcription omits *την*.

8. *'Ερρῶσ̣θ(αί) σε ὔχομ(αι) π.οκοπ* ‾...‾: M. He is right in his interpretation of the first word; but I can find no trace of a sigma. After *σε* read *⟨ε⟩υχο(μαι) κ(αι) προκοπ(εσθαι)*. The stroke over *αει* which puzzled Meyer seems actually to be a mark of abbreviation after *προκοπ*.

TRANSLATION

Because of the repetitiousness of the individual texts, I have translated only a few typical examples which illustrate most of the variations occurring in the phraseology. No attempt has been made to imitate errors in spelling or syntax.

Col. iii 20–26 (*10*): January 15, 179.

Aelius Capiton, cavalryman of the ala Gallica, turma of Optatianus, to Iulius Serenus, summus curator. I have received from you my hay allowance of the nineteenth year of the Aurelii Antoninus and Commodus, the Lords Emperors, in advance (*since I am*) leaving for Scenae Megalae, denarii 25, in full. Year 19 of the Aurelii Antoninus and Commodus, Caesars and Lords, Tybi 20.

Col. iv 19–27 (*13*): January 16, 179.

Iulius Serenus, cavalryman of the ala Gallica, turma of Herodianus, and Iulius Nepotianus, same turma, and Pathermouthis Orsenuphis, turma of Pactumeius Serenus, to Iulius Serenus, summus curator. We have received from you our hay allowance for the 19th year, each of us 25 denarii. Year 19 of the Aurelii Antoninus and Commodus the Lords Augusti, Tybi 21. I, Sossius Eudaemon, signifer of the turma of Herodianus, have written for them on request because of their not knowing how to write.

Col. ix 2–12 (*27*): January 17, 179.

Iulius Chaeremonianus, cavalryman of the ala Gallica, turma of Agrippa, and Sarapion, son of Isidorus, turma of Lycarion, and Ammonius Serenus, turma of Sentius, to Iulius Serenus, summus curator. We have received from you our hay allowance in advance (*since we are*) leaving for The Bucolia, the 19th year of the Aurelii Antoninus and Commodus the Lords Augusti, each of us 25 denarii. Year 19 of the Aurelii Antoninus and Commodus the Lords Augusti, Tybi 22. I, Iulius Chaeremonianus named above, have written for them on request because of their not knowing how to write.

Col. xi 12–21 (*33*): January 18, 179.

Heliodorus son of Serenus, cavalryman of the ala Gallica, turma of Ammonianus, and Iulius Serenus, cavalryman, same ala, same turma, to Serenus, summus curator. We have received from you our hay allowance in advance (*since we are*) leaving for The Bucolia, at the rate of 25 denarii for the 19th year of the Aurelii Antoninus and Commodus, Caesars and Lords, Tybi 23. I, Achilles son of Achilles, cavalryman of the same ala, turma of Herodianus, have written for them on request because of Heliodorus writing slowly. *Second hand:* I, Heliodorus, have received as stated.

Col. xii 1–10 (*34*): January 18, 179.

Valerius Sarapammon, cavalryman of the ala Veterana Gallica, turma of Iulius Protarchus, to Iulius Serenus, summus curator. ⟦I acknowledge⟧ I have received from you my hay allowance in advance (*since I am*) leaving for Aphrodito, 25 denarii. Year 19 of the Aurelii Antoninus and Commodus, the Lords Augusti, Tybi 23. I, Zoilus, signifer, have written the body, he himself subscribing his name. *Second hand:* I, Valerius Serapammon named above, as stated.

BB: January 17, 179.

Dionysius Artemidorus, cavalryman of the ala Gallica, turma of Herodianus, and Theon son of Stilbo, turma of Serenus, to Iulius Serenus, summus curator. We have received from you the other things [ ] from September 1, consulate of Orfitus and Rufus (178), [?] in Mareotis with Pactumeius Serenus, the decurion, each of us 25 denarii, in full. Year 19 of the Aurelii Antoninus and Commodus, the Lords Emperors, Tybi 22. I, Dionysius, son of Sarapion, signifer of the same ala, turma of Apollinarius, have written for them, they alleging that they do not know how to write.

FF: January 18, 179.

Iulius Serenus, cavalryman of the ala Gallica, turma of Herodianus, and Iulius Nepotianus, same turma, and Patermuthis Orsenuphis, turma of Pactumenius Serenus, to Iulius Serenus, summus curator. We have received our epulum, consulate of the Emperor Commodus for the second time and Verus for the second time (179), of 10 denarii, 8 obols. Year 19 of the Aurelii Antoninus and Commodus the Lords Augusti, Tybi 23. I, Heron Isidorus, cavalryman of the same ala, turma of Lucilius, have written for them on request because of their not knowing how to write.

GG: March 3, 179.

[?], son of [ ]pheros, cavalryman of the ala Veterana Gallica, turma of Furonius, to Iulius Serenus, summus curator. I have received from you my hay allowance for the eighteenth year and similarly for the nineteenth year of Antoninus and Commodus the Lords Augusti, Phamenoth 9. I, Iulius Amerys, cavalryman of the same ala, same turma, have written for him because of his not knowing how to write.

Sopatros Dionysius, cavalryman of the ala Veterana Gallica, turma of Aelius Serenus, to Iulius Serenus, summus curator. I have received from you my hay allowance for the 19th year of Antoninus and Commodus the Lords Augusti, Phamenoth 5. I, Pompeius Diogenes, cavalryman of the same ala, turma of Iulius, have written for him on request, he being present, because of his not knowing how to write.

HH, col. i: April 5, 179

Isas son of Sarapion, cavalryman of the ala Veterana Gallica, turma of Agrippa, to Iulius Serenus, summus curator. I have received from you my hay allowance of the 19th year, 25 denarii. Year 19 of the Aurelii Antoninus and Commodus the Lords Augusti, Pharmouthi 10.

HH, col. ii.

Isas to the most honored Serenus. Kindly give to Dioscorus my brother (-soldier?) my hay allowance of the 19th year, since I borrowed from him in the Arsinoite nome 25 denarii, from whom also you will get my receipt. With best wishes for your perpetual health and prosperity.

77

Soldiers' Receipts for Legacies

PMich. vii 435 (inv. 510) and *PMich.* 440 (inv. 511) Early II p.
vidi 435

Transcription, commentary, and facsimile: Henry A. Sanders, *Michigan Papyri* vii: *Latin Papyri*, nos. 435 and 440, plates v and viii b; cited as **S.**

Text and Commentary: R. O. Fink, "Soldiers' Receipts for Legacies," *BASP* 1 (1963–64) 39–46.

Commentary:

1. J. F. Gilliam, *AJP* 71 (1950) 433 and 435; cited as **G.**
2. Idem, "The Minimum Subject to the Vicesima Hereditatium," *AJP* 73 (1952) 397–405.

Text: *CPL*, nos. 219 and 190, reproduces the texts of *PMich.* with some notes from G; Daris, no. 37, uses G and combines the two texts of *PMich.*

Sanders' description of this text as a "camp record of inheritance," kept in a central office and covering the soldiers of all the units in the camp, was not contested by Gilliam in his review; but the variety of hands and spellings and the differing lengths of the lines in the present, more complete, text combine to show that it is more probably a book of receipts like **74** and **76**. The certain connection of nos. 440 and 435, first recognized by Gilliam, also eliminates Arangio–Ruiz' reconstruction of 440 as a soldier's promissory note, in his "Chirografi di Soldati," *Studi in Onore di Siro Solazzi* (Naples 1948) 257–59.

It seems possible also to be more precise than in Sanders' discussion about the nature of the inheritances in question. Youtie has called my attention to the fact that the sum of 95 drachmas which recurs in every receipt is the balance which would be left after deducting the vicesima hereditatium from a hundred drachmas (cf. line 3). This observation at once reminded me of the accounts in **70** where at least three-fourths of the soldiers have exactly 100 drachmas *in deposito*. I believe, then, that except for the receipt of L. Egnatius (i 7–12), which certainly includes more, these receipts involve only legacies of the hundred drachmas which the deceased held *in deposito*.

The dating is on the basis of the hands.

The verso is blank.

Frag. a (*PMich.* 435)

Because of variations in circumstances and hence in the phraseology, it is not possible to restore the text with certainty; but the readings in lines 2, 9, 14, and 16 make it appear that about 12–15 letters are lost between the two parts.

Col. i

(*First hand*)

]dṛo.ọṛṭịḍạṣ op[ ]ṇ *illegible traces*
ϒ]claudi romani ṣạ[lutem fateor me a]c̣c̣eṗ[i]s[se
]dṛạchmas centuṃ[ex quibus] *illegible traces*
].eṭi. dṛ ṇọnagen[ta quinque]....[....]..c
]ṃe. legato tres s.[
].[ ]ṣiti i ṃẹṣị ϒ [
One line blank

(*Second hand*)

coh [ ]cuṣ ● ● ḷ egṇaṭius opṭio ϒ iuli[*ca.* 17]..ị ϒ claudi romani
ṃ.ạṛ.ḅụç̣
saḷuṭem ḟate[o]r ṃ[e accepisse legati i]nstar ..ṛ ⟦...ire...⟧
ḍụ
a iulio maxịṃo ϒ ḍeḟ[uncto drachmas]c̣ ex quibus dec̣ụṇ-
tur ụiṭ[.]c̣ensim[a *ca.* 16].[.]cc eṭ drachmas
ṇọ[na]giṇta qụị[nque actum in castris] aug iv nonas
iulias
One line blank

(*Third hand*)

● ●̣ ●̣ ● aprilis petṛ[o]ṇ[ius ϒ *ca.* 12]..ịoni optioni
ϒ .a....[salutem fateor me] accepisse legaṭọ
]nto.
petroni blanḍ[*ca.* 11 iulii] maximi ϒ defụṇcti
drachumas c̣[.... ex quibus dedu]c̣untur
uicensima .[.].[ ]s quinque
reliquae drac[hmae nonaginta]quinque ẹṭẹ...
ḍ dr lxxxxv ḍan[tur]ạc̣ṭ[u]ṃ ị[n castris aug]
iiii nonas iul[ias
One line blank

coh ii th[ebaeorum

a i 1. . .*Diophaniụṣ Op*[*:* S. The name is highly uncertain; but *d* is probably not the first letter. What is wanted at this point is a succession of two names in the nominative, if *op*[is to be restored as *optio*, which seems likely. Cf. line 7.

2. .*Ç̣laudi, f*[*:* S; *ṣạ*[*lutem:* G; (*centuria*) *Çlaudi:* Daris. Sanders' *f* may be right. The letter is crossed by the tail of an *i* or similar stroke coming down from line 1, and is followed by traces that may be *a*. Read *fạ*[*teor*, assuming that *salutem* stood in line 1?

4. .*ucit:* S; (3) [*de-*] (4) *ducit*(*ur*)*:* Daris. These letters at the beginning, whatever they are, seem to reappear after *quinque* in line 18. Sanders notes that this is the earliest example of the spelling *nonagenta*.

5. . . .*ṛepleunt ressi*.[*:* S. The letter after *me* looks like a squarish *u*. Possibly *cu*]*ṃ eọ legato*?

6. . . .*oṣitọ IṾ Non*[*:* S. The tall *i* in the middle of the line may well be a numeral; but it is not followed by *u*. I am at a loss for the letters which follow. The stroke which I have taken as the upper part of *e* may be a mark of abbreviation over the next two letters.

7. *L II'*[*I*] *Cúr o L Egṛịlius Opṭuṣ Iuli*[ ]*II:* S; *iuli* [*maximi:* Fink in *BASP*. Perhaps one should restore ꝩ *iuli*[*ana*, since the centurion is dead; but such adjectives are usually formed from the cognomen. Gilliam may be right in proposing *optioni* (*centuriae*) for the lacuna; in that case *opti*]*ọṇị* should be read. This leaves a space of about ten letters after *iuli*[*ana* for the name of the optio. Sanders' *o* for *obitus* or *obiit* appears to be a punctum used as a check-mark (see p. 12 and no. **1** passim), and may be preceded by another. In the name of the unit I cannot find Sanders' *L* and regard *coh* as certain. The numeral is missing; and what follows can be read as either *cus* or *cur*. The latter is possible if the stroke which rises from the last letter is taken as the tail of the first letter in the last line of the preceding entry. The identity of the unit is a problem. Perhaps the most likely cohorts are the coh. I Corsorum civium Romanorum, which was in Mauretania Caesariensis in 107 (*CIL* XVI 56), a province which had military ties with Egypt, or the coh. Cyrenaica equitata in Arrian's *Contra Alanos* (Cichorius, *RE* 4.278, s.v. "cohors"). But the letters are so abraded and smudged that it would be possible to think of *coh.* [*II I*]*tur*(*aeorum*). There are also other cohortes Cyrenaicae, but all of them belong in Germany or the Danube region. In any event, if *coh* is correctly read here and in line 21, the chief basis for Sanders' dating in 116 disappears with the mention of the leg. III Cyrenaica and II Traiana.

8. *Saṭuṛeti Ṭatera*[*i*]*nstar ṂḌÇ ḍṛạc̣ḥṃạrum* with *dṛ P*[*t*]*ọl Ạụg* inserted above *drachmarum:* S; *salutem fate*[*o*]*r ṃ*[*e:* G. At the end of the line the original wording has been canceled and something written above which I am unable to read except that *m* is reasonably sure at the beginning. I cannot find support for Sanders' *dr Ptol Aug*. In the line itself perhaps *i*]*nstar ḥẹṛ*[*editatis*], since a hereditas differed legally from a legatum, and the sum here is apparently more than the hundred drachmas of the legata in the other receipts.

9. *ạ Pulịọ Mafịṇọ* ꝩ *Ter*[ ]*i ex quibus DC ḍẹḍucụ̄* with *dṛ* inserted above *DC:* S; *Maxịṃo; deduci* in place of *DC ḍẹḍucụ*(*n*)*:* G; *cc*]*ç:* Fink in *BASP*. For *ḍef*[*uncto* cf. line 15.

10. *uic*[.]*ensim*[*a*].*cẹṭ:* S. *BASP* omits the right half of the line. There is no doubt that the word is *uicesima* miswritten in some fashion.

11. *ṇoṇ*[*a*]*ginta:* S; *qui*[*nque act in castr*]*:* Fink in *BASP*.

13. *Co*]*h Ị C E Θ:* S; *Petro*[*nius:* S and Fink in *BASP; Petro*[*nianus:* G. Sanders may be right in reading *C*(*ilicum*) *e*(*quitata*) where I have indicated the remains of two puncta. On their left is the top of a tall letter which slopes a little to the left; but I can find nothing else in that area but unintelligible dots. Sanders' theta appears certainly a punctum. His *Petronius*, however, gets support from *petroni* in line 15; the two men may have been kinsmen. The order of nomen and cognomen is probably inverted. Cf. a ii 8. In the lacuna about 10 letters are available for the names of Aprilis' centurion and the optio.

14. ꝩ *Maximi:* S; [*salutem fateor me*]*:* G. The character read as the centuria-symbol is very doubtful; but "century" or "turma" is necessary for the identification of the optio at the end of line 13. Cf. lines 7 and 8.

14a. Inserted above the line,]*ạrio:* S; but compare *nt* in b, line 1, below—ꝩ *canti.*]*nto* ꝩ*:* Fink in *BASP*.

15. *maximi* and *defuncti* have been corrected from the ablative to the genitive. A maximum of 11 letters remains for the rest of Petronius' name and his rank.

16. *Ṿ*[*:* S; *ç*[*ex:* Fink in *BASP*. The numeral to be restored in the lacuna is unknown; it may have been *ç*[*entum* written out.

17. Very probably *ḥẹ*[*reditatium drachma*]*s*.

18.]*quinque mil-* (19) *lia:* S.

19. *d* in margin; *lia LXXXXV;*]*ịṭọ:* S. .*an*[*;*]. . .[*:* Fink in *BASP*.

I can make nothing of the *d* in the margin, if it is a letter intentionally written. In *dr lxxxxv*, I assume merely the repetition in numerals of the sum already stated in words. For *ẹṭẹ* cf. line 4.

21. *Ḷeg II Tr*[*:* S. See above on line 7. *thebaeorum* was probably abbreviated; but there is no way of knowing how.

Col. ii

It is not possible to ascertain how this fragment was related to the other two. The upper part seems not to have been spaced on the papyrus in the same way as the lower, but it is so badly smeared and blurred that nothing certain can be said about it. Sanders indicates only illegible traces, probably rightly.

traces ṣ[
One line blank? [
———→ ● C L. . . ụs[
●̣●̣ ạ. . . [
ẹ
ç̣
Two lines blank?
(*Fourth hand*) ḷụ.[.].ẹm.[
ḍr[ac]ḥ[m]ạ[
nigro ulp̣[i-
x n. . .u[
Remainder of column blank

ii 2. The traces after the angular symbol might also be read *GCḶ. . .ṛịs*[

4 and 5. Where these lines began and ended is doubtful.

6. *qụ*[.]*m*[*:* S.

7. *N. . .*[*:* S.

8. *Nigro* ϒ *Ṃ*[*:* S. The name may be *ulpius niger* inverted. Cf. a i 13.

9. *X n. . . II*[*:* S.

Frag. b (*PMich.* 440)

Like the preceding fragment, this one cannot be placed with certainty. It cannot be inserted between the two parts of 435, col. i; nor does it match with the readable lines of col. ii. But the similarity of the hands to those in col. i as well as the identity of content assures that it comes from the center of a column in the same roll.

(*Fifth hand*)]ṛo ϒ c̣anti pr.[
salute]ṃ ḍịc̣it fateọr me a[ccepisse
]ẹạ ḍ uicesima qụ[
].quas dṛ[
nona]g̣intu quiṇ[que
in castris]ạug iv non[as iulias
Two lines blank
(*Sixth hand*)]ṛ.aui antoniṇị ϒ u[
fa]teor me accepi[sse
]nị ϒ u.[
].ạṣqu.[

b 1.]*ịo* ϒ *O*[.]*ạnti prạ*[*:* S; ϒ *qụarti pri*[*ncipis:* G, as a possibility.]*ro* is the end of the name, in the nominative, of the soldier who was giving the receipt. For the name *canti* cf. *CIL* XIII 583 (=Dessau 3732) and 5677 (=Dessau 4609). The letters which follow may represent *prioris*.

2.]*ẹne*[. . .]*ịt fatior:* S; *s*]*aḷụ*[*te*]*m fatior:* G. The *e* of *fateor* is very like *i*; but cf. *uicesima*, line 3.

3.]*ṭro; qụ*[*:* S; *ḍṛ*[*:* G; *q*[*:* Fink in *BASP*. The spot which Sanders read as *o*, I have taken as a *d*; cf. *dr*, line 4. But it may be a small punctum. If *d*, can it represent *d(educuntur)*? At the end of the line Sanders' *q* looks probable, the *u* less so. *qu*[*inque* would be a very satisfactory reading.

4.]*q̣*[. .]*s quas Id*[*:* S. I can find no trace of Sanders' first *q*. It is tempting to restore *rel*]*iquas*; but the remains before *q* can hardly be made into an *i*.

5.]*ṃẹnṭọ c̣ṛị*[*:* S. The second extant letter may be *e* instead of *i*, and the fifth is either *u* or an open *o*; but the other receipts make it clear that *nonaginta* is meant. Dessau's indices (III ii, p. 827) provide examples of *o* in place of *a*.

6. *A*]*ug Iuṇio R*[*ustico II Plautio Aquilino cos:* S; the reading adopted is G's.

7.]*ạṛat si Antoniụṣ Iu*[*stinus:* S; . .*avi* (*Flavi*?) *Antoniṇị* .[*:* G. The second name might be *antoniani* if one reads an *i* in ligature with the preceding *n* instead of ϒ; but]*niani* cannot be read in line 9.

8.]*ṭ ẹrant et cc et o*[*:* S; *fa*]*tior:* G, otherwise the reading in the text.

9. *Anto*]*ni Iust*[*ini:* S. The letter after *u* could be *m* or *t*.

10.]*uis qu*[*:* S; no reading in *BASP*.

TRANSLATION

(Because the text is so fragmentary, only the most complete receipt, *PMich.* 435, i 7–12, is translated, even though it may not be wholly typical.)

coh. [ ]cus L. Egnatius, optio, century of Iulius Maximus, to [—]. . .i, century of Claudius Romanus. I acknowledge that I have received in the form of a legacy from Iulius Maximus, centurio, deceased, (?) hundred drachmas, from which are deducted the five per cent inheritance tax [- - - Remainder?] (?) hundred and ninety-five drachmas. Done in the Castra Augusta, the fourth day of July.

78

Receipts of Cohortales for Food and Wine or Money Equivalents

April 1, A.D. 157, to 187 or 217

These texts are ostraca, nearly all from Pselcis (modern Dakkeh), which have been published in three series as follows. The texts are taken from these editions (from *GOB* by permission of the Committee of the Egypt Exploration Society) with only the changes noted in the apparatus.

1. U. Wilcken, *Griechische Ostraka aus Aegypten und Nubien* 2 (Leipzig and Berlin 1899), and vol. 1, p. 20; nos. 1128–1146 and 1265; cited as **Ostr.**
2. Fr. Preisigke and Friedrich Bilabel, *Sammelbuch griechische Urkunden aus Ägypten* 3 (Berlin and Leipzig 1926), nos. 6955–6976; cited as **SB**. These ostraca are republished from H. G. E. White, "Graeco-Roman Ostraca from Dakka, Nubia," *CR* 33 (1919) 49–53.
3. John Gavin Tait and Claire Préaux, *Greek Ostraca in the Bodleian Library at Oxford* 2 (London 1955), nos. 2003–2041; cited as **GOB**.

Commentary, aside from the above: Claire Préaux, "Ostraca de Pselcis de la Bibliothèque Bodléenne," *Chronique d'Égypte* 26 (1951) 121–55. Cited as **Préaux**.

Text: Daris prints five of these receipts: 15 (his no. 44), 32 (41), 36 (43), 39 (42), and 40 (45).

Translation: Johnson, *Roman Egypt*, pp. 680–81, translates nos. 15, 30, 32, 33, 36, 37, 39, and 42.

Two related questions arise immediately about this group of receipts—first, whether they are truly military in the sense defined above (Introduction, p. 1), and second, if they *are* military, why ostraca are used rather than entering the receipts in a papyrus roll like **74–77**.

Not only does the use of ostraca awaken doubt of the military character of these receipts, but also the term *cibariator*. It is certainly not a regular military rank, and, with the possible exception of these receipts, is nowhere found in a military context.[1] None of the cibariatores named here is given any military title, but in no. 23 the optio M. Aurelius Asclepiades dispenses wine just as the cibariatores Petronius, Alexander, and the others do. Moreover, the personnel who give these receipts, so far as can be determined, are exclusively military; and the form and wording of the receipts parallel closely those in **76**. It seems therefore that *cibariator* may be simply a term for the man's current assignment, not the title of a permanent post or rank. One might compare the notation *ad hordeum* in the rosters. The receipts for the grain ration, nos. 1–14, present a clearer claim to be regarded as military, for in them the same Asclepiades is the dispenser and is called both *optio* simply and *optio paralemptes sitou*. Since Préaux observes (pp. 126–27 and 133) that these ostraca form two parallel series, one for the grain ration, which was a separate account, and the other for the *cibarium*, which included everything else, such as wine, salt, lentils, and vinegar (cf. nos. 15 and 18–71; nos 16 and 17 may belong to a third series), and that a number of the decurions and centurions are found in both series, the wine receipts should be military if those for grain are.

For all these reasons I have concluded that the receipts are probably military; but I cannot guess why they were not entered in a papyrus roll unless it was because of the small sums of money involved, usually only two or three denarii, eight and a fraction at the most (no. 37). These ostraca are probably best understood as temporary records which would be sorted out at intervals, daily or monthly, and entered on a roll which constituted the permanent account.

One cannot even be sure that all the soldiers represented in these receipts belonged to the same unit; but that is certainly the most probable assumption, and since both turmae and centuries are named, the unit must have been a cohors equitata. The possibilities, as Wilcken saw (*Ostr.*, p. 706), are the I Hispanorum, the I Thebaeorum, and the II Ituraeorum. Of these, the last is the most likely choice, because it may have had its headquarters at Pselcis (Cichorius, *RE* 4.306, s.v. "cohors").

Dating these texts is troublesome. Twenty-nine of the forty with readable year-dates fall in the 15th, 17th, 18th, 20th, and 22nd regnal years, thus limiting the possibilities, in view of the paleography, to the reigns of Antoninus Pius, Commodus, and Caracalla. Wilcken (*Ostr.* 1, p. 20) chose the last because the optio Asclepiades had the name Aurelius in nos. 3, 7, and 9; Wilcken took this as evidence of a date after the constitutio Antoniniana, because the praenomen Marcus is lacking. Préaux, however (p. 128), points out that in nos. 3 and 7 Aurelius is not to be read or restored, that in no. 9 the letter before αυρηλιω may well be a mu for μ(αρκω), and that Wilcken did not hesitate to date no. 69, in which an Aurelius without "Marcus" also appears, to the reign of Antoninus Pius because he read the regnal year as 27. For some reason neither Wilcken nor Préaux mentions the Marci Aurelii in nos. 1, 8, 11, and 39; but actually these names do not prove as much as they have been thought to. Préaux is right in saying (p. 127) that the Marci Aurelii could not be as

[1] It occurs in Préaux's ostracon from Mons Claudianus (*Chronique d'Égypt* 26 [1951] 354–63; but Gilliam has shown (*Chronique d'Égypt* 28 [1953] 144–46) that the parties named are probably civilians, and the cibariator perhaps even a slave.

early as Antoninus Pius and that Aurelii without "Marcus" are fairly common before the constitutio Antoniniana; but **2** and many other papyri in this corpus show that after 212, as well as before, there were large numbers of soldiers who did not use the name Aurelius.[2] Except for nos. 69 and 73, in short, all these ostraca could readily be dated to Caracalla's reign; and in no. 69 the year is somewhat doubtful, for Wilcken placed a dot under the kappa. The choice can only be between κζ and ιζ; and presumably enough remains of the letter to convince Wilcken that it was not iota. On the other hand, Préaux notes that the cibariator of no. 69, Petronius, is attested between the 15th and 20th years, thus creating a slight presumption in favor of emending Wilcken's reading to ιζ. But even this is inconclusive, because Petronius, though he appears as early as the 11th year (no. 18), not the 15th, may nevertheless still have been active in the 27th. He is not attested, to be sure, in the years 21–26; but neither is he attested for the years 12–14 and 19, and as it happens the years 19–26 are represented in the wine series by only three ostraca, the latest for the year 21, though there are six within the same period in the grain series, the latest for the year 23.

If Wilcken's κζ could be established as the correct reading in no. 69, it would, paradoxically, confirm Préaux's dating of these texts to the reign of Commodus, for Caracalla's regnal years do not extend beyond the 25th. But one must also bear in mind that no. 73, which was certainly written by a soldier and is unequivocally dated April 1, 157, is a warning that these ostraca are not an altogether homogeneous body of evidence—that there are gaps in the established series and stray pieces which do not fit into any series.

The nature of the transactions here also creates uncertainty about the date. If, as Préaux says (p. 133), the grain ration is not given a cash value because it was part of the soldiers' pay, then the date of the ostraca cannot be earlier than the reign of Septimius Severus, who is credited with being the first to give free grain to soldiers other than the praetorians.[3] But, as Marichal observes ("Solde" 417, note 2), the receipts may not mean that the soldiers are getting free grain. The receipt is only an acknowledgment that the soldier has been given his monthly ration of grain; and the deduction for it could still be taken from his next stipendium. The lack of any indication of the price of the grain can be explained on the ground that both the amount and the price were fixed, whereas in the issue of wine both the quantity and the price for a given amount varied and therefore had to be stated.

On the whole, I am somewhat inclined to favor Wilcken's dating because, in addition to the considerations discussed above, the soldiers in nos. 1 and 8 bear a second nomen, Iulius, as well as Aurelius, like many of those in **1**. This doubling of nomina seems more likely to have happened under the Severi than under Marcus Aurelius. But certainty is unattainable without further evidence.

Préaux is right in saying that the price of wine and its place in the soldiers' expenses cannot be assessed because the measures used are unknown,[4] and likewise the period for

[2] See in greater detail J. F. Gilliam, "Dura Rosters and the *Constitutio Antoniniana*," *Historia* 14 (1965) 74–92.

[3] Herodian 3.8.4: τοῖς τε στρατιώταις . . . πολλὰ συνεχώρησεν ἃ μὴ πρότερον εἶχον· καὶ γὰρ τὸ σιτηρέσιον πρῶτος ηὔξεν αὐτοῖς; D. van Berchem, "L'Annone militaire dans l'Empire romain au IIIe Siècle," *Mémoires de la Société nationale des Antiquaires de France*, ser. 8, vol. 10 (1937) 129.

[4] Wilcken shows (*Grundzüge u. Chrestomathie* I, i, p. lxxi) that κεράμιον is interchangeable with μετρητής, but that either may contain 5, 6, 7, 8, or 12 choes. Since a chous was slightly less than 3 quarts, a triceramon might vary from 45 to 72 quarts. To judge from the prices, a colophonion must have been about the same size as a triceramon.

which a given quantity of wine was expected to suffice. None the less, some comparisons can be made. Johnson (*Roman Egypt*, p. 311) cites texts showing that between A.D. 153 and 191 the price of an artaba of wheat varied from 2 to 5 denarii, with a state-fixed price in 155 of 2 denarii. In the same period the wages of watchmen, ox-drivers, masons, clerks, mechanics, and gardeners range from 4½ to 10 denarii a month; but nearly all get 6 or 7 denarii (Johnson, pp. 307–8). These men's wages would therefore have been used up by the purchase of one artaba of wheat and one colophonion of wine a month. (A colophonion could scarcely be expected to last more than a month, simply because the wine would not keep; and the fact that among this comparatively small number of ostraca two soldiers are represented by two receipts each in the wine series may be reason for believing that they claimed their wine-ration at fairly short intervals. The soldiers are Eponuchus son of Heracleides, nos. 20 and 53, and Antonius Hierax, nos. 48 and 49.) This in turn has a bearing on the question of the stipendium in **70**. Marichal's figure of 100 nominal and 84 actual denarii annually (Préaux's 60 denarii a year must be a slip of some sort) would amount to only 7 denarii a month, or just about the same as the ox-drivers, masons, and clerks cited by Johnson, and would certainly not cover clothing, arms, hay, and other such expenses, not to speak of any surplus such as the deposits in **73** reveal. This strengthens my belief that the stipendium in **70** is for the normal four-month period, or about 21 denarii a month.

Eight of these ostraca (nos. 24, 25, 45, 57, 65–67, and 70; and cf. no. 22) have at the end a notation in a different hand which repeats the number of denarii and obols in the body of the receipt. There is little doubt that these notations were added to facilitate the accounting processes in which these receipts were used, just as in **76** the number of soldiers named in each receipt is noted in the margin. The most interesting, and puzzling, feature of these notations is, however, the otherwise unknown symbol preceding the numeral for the denarii in all but no. 22. Préaux (pp. 136–37) describes it as two vertical strokes of unequal length crossed by a horizontal one; and her fig. 16 shows that the left-hand vertical is about twice as long as the other. White transcribed the symbol as a *θ* in nos. 57, 67, and 70, which led Bilabel in the *Sammelbuch* to regard it as a barred *o* and to expand it as *ὁ(μοῦ)*. Préaux transcribes it as *H* and interprets it as (δηναρια). Youtie agrees that it must be something of the kind, especially since the receipts in which it occurs are all for a single item each, making *ὁμοῦ* inappropriate.

Grain Series

1. Ostr. 1130 November 19, 179 or 211

μαρκ(ος) αυρηλις ιουλις ηρακλειανος στρα(τιωτης)
⳨ τιθοηρ̣ο̣υς ασκληπιαδη οπτιων[ι]
παραλεμπτου σιτου χαιρειν ελαβον
παρα σου τον σιτον μου υπερ μηνος
χυακ [α]ρταβη μιαν ιουλις (?) κλειδης
ιππευς εγραψα ∟ κ∫ αθυρ $\overline{κγ}$
πατερμουθι (*Hand 2*)

1 2. The symbol ⳨ represents *(ἑκατοντ)(αρ)χ(ία)* = *centuria* here and in most of these receipts.

2. Ostr. 1131 — November 20, 179 or 211

ιουλι̣ς̣ . . . λογ[
ασκληπι[αδ]η ο̣π̣τ̣[ιωνι]
χαιρειν ελαβον επι προ[χρεια]
πυρου αρτ(αβην) μιαν υπ(ερ) μηνος
χυακ αλεξανδρος συνστ(ρατιωτης)
εγραψα ∟ *κ αθυρ κδ̣*
διονυσιανο ⳨ [(*Hand 2*)
σεσ(η)μ(ειωμαι)

3. Ostr. 1140 — January–February, 179–189 or 211–217

τ̣ε̣ρ̣.χων (?) πετεψα[ιτος?]
ιππευ τυρμης ιμ[ουθου?
ασκληπιαδη π[αραλημπ-]
τη σ̣ι̣τ̣ο̣υ̣ χαιρειν ε[λαβον]
παρα σου σιτου [αρταβας]
δυο υπερ μη[νων τυβι και]
μεχιρ ∟ *κ̣[. . . . . .]*

4. Ostr. 1132 — November 21, 181 or 213

[. . . . .]υ ασκληπιαδ[η]
[οπτιωνι χαιρει]ν̣ ελαβον παρα σ[ου]
[τον σιτον μ]ου υ[π(ερ)] μηνος χο[ιακ]
[αρταβην μιαν ∟*] κβ // αθυρ κε*
[ερμι]νος τυρανος χ. . ρ˙α
[. . . .] εγραψα υπ(ερ)
[αυτου]
[. . . . .]θιν ερμειν[(*Hand 2*)
[. . . . .] σεσημ(ειωμαι)

5. Ostr. 1134 — November–December, 181 or 213

[. . . . .] ⳨ *απιανου ασκληπια(δη)*
[οπτιωνι παραλ]ημπτης σιτου χα(ιρειν)
[ελαβον π]αρα σ(ου) τον σιτον μου
[. . . . .]η ∟ *κβ // χυακ*
[. . . . . .] απογρ(αφομαι?) το ιδιον ονομ(α)

2 6. Ostr. prints *Παόν(ι)* for the month; but Préaux, p. 133, says that Gau's facsimile shows *Ἀθύρ*.

2 7. The symbol ⳨ here stands for *(ἑκατοντ)(αρ)χ(ης)* = *centurio.*

3 2. Préaux, pp. 143–44, and GOB on no. 27, lines 1–2, suggest reading *Γε[μέλλου* here instead of *Ιμ[ούθου*, read by Ostr.

3 2–3. *Αὐρη-] | λίῳ:* Ostr.; but Préaux, p. 128, says that line 3 begins with *ασκληπιαδη*, nothing preceding it.

3 6. *μη[νῶν Τῦβι]:* Ostr.

4 5. [. . . . . .]*νος Τύρανος:* Ostr.; but cf. no. 60. At the end of the line read *χ̣ο̣υ̣ρα-* and restore [*τωρ*] in line 6, comparing no. 60, lines 2–3, and no. 34, line 1?

4 8. *ερμειν[ου:* Ostr.

5 5. Surely *υπογρ(αφομαι)*?

6. Ostr. 1136 181/182 or 213/214

[.]αρ[. . . . .]
ωριον[. . . . .]
ασκληπιαδ[η . . .]ρως παραλημ-
πτου σιτου χαιρ[ε]ιν ελαβον π[α]ρα σ[ου]
σειτου μηνων [. . . . . . .]α . . μηνος
αθυρ και χοιαχ κ[αι] τυβ[ι] μεχειρ φαμενωθ φαρμουθι παχων γεινοντε
μηνων επτα ∟ κα πυρ(ου) αρτ(αβας) εξ μι[.]. . .
ρ.ν̣. . . .[.].ρ. εγραψα υπερ [αυτου]
∟ κβ // . . . . κϛ
διασ. . . . πρ̣α̣κ(τωρ) (*Hand 2*)
δια ωριωνος

7. Ostr. 1137 January 16–24, 183 or 215

βαλλησιανος στρατιωτ(ης) [. . . .
. . . . ασκληπιαδη ο[πτιωνι παραλη-]
μπτου σιτου χαιρειν [ελαβον πα-]
ρα σ(ου) τον σιτον μου [αρ]τ̣(αβην) [μιαν]
[υ]περ μηνος χ[οιακ]
∟ κ̣γ τυβε κ.

8. Ostr. 1144

μ(αρκος) αυρηλις ϊουλις [. . . . . .]
ιππευς τ(υρμης) κονου̣[ος ασκληπι-]
αδη οπτιων[ι παραλημπτη]
σιτου χαιρ[ειν ελαβον παρα σου]
τον σιτο[ν μου υπερ μηνος]
χυα[κ . . . .].

9. Ostr. 1139

[. . . . . . . αντω?]ν̣εινος α.α.
[. . . . .] μ(αρκω) αυρηλιω ασ-
[κληπιαδη οπτι]ωνι χαιρειν ελαβο[ν]
[παρα σου το]ν σιτον μου εν προχρ̣[εια]
[υπερ μη]νος φαμενωτ
[∟ . . //] μεχιρ κθ κλαυδιος
[. . . .]τιων εγραψα υπερ αυτου
μη ειδοτος [γρ]αμματα

6 2. The name should probably be restored in the genitive as that of a centurion or decurion.

6 11. Just possibly διὰ Σ. . . .

7 1–2. Ostr. proposes in the apparatus to restore [Αὐρ-] | ηλ̣ί̣ῳ; but Préaux, p. 128, points out that here we must have the name of a centurion or decurion.

8 2. Κονού̣[φιος: Ostr.; but Dornseiff–Hansen lists no such name. For κονου̣[ος cf. nos. 29, 63, and 66.

9 2. [. . . . .]. Αὐρηλί̣ῳ: Ostr. The reading adopted is from Préaux, p. 128.

9 7. [οπ]τιων or a second name?

10. Ostr. 1141

[. . . . . στ]ρατιωτης ☧
[. . . . . ασκλ]ηπιαδη παραλημ-
[πτη σιτου χαιρ]ειν ελαβον παρα
[σου σιτον μου υ]περ μη[ν]ος
[. . . . .]. . νσ. . . . .
[. . . . . . .]. ṿ. βησαρịον
[. . . . . . εγρα]ψα υπερ αυτου

11. Ostr. 1135 March 6, 182 or 214

μ(αρκος) αυρη(λιος) ισιδωρος οπτιων ασκληπ[ιαδη]
και παμβηκι παραλημπτα(ις) σιτ(ου) χα(ιρειν)
παραδεξον πετεησιω στρ(ατιωτη) υπ(ερ) εμου
+ ∸ αβ˙/ + ∸ μιαν διμυρον
αχρι λογου συναρσ̣εως ∟ κβ φαμε(νωθ) ι
βηκις νεωτ σειτου αντι κριθ(ης)
∸ ς
σεσημ(ειωμαι)

12. Ostr. 1143

[. . . . . .]. κ̣ω̣στ . ρ τεσσεραριος
[ασκληπ]ιαδης οπτιων χ(αιρειν)
[ελαβον] παρα σου σιτου αρταβη
[μιαν υπ]ερ μηνος αθυρ
[. . . .] β // . . . . . ονομ[. . .].

13. Ostr. 1145

ευ]δαιμων πατερμουθι . . . α
εν πρ]οχρια

14. Ostr. 1133 December 6, 181 or 213

]. ς αυρη(λ. . .) ιερ[
∟] κβ // χοιαχ ι
]ναι̣ (?) ☧ και απο. . . .[
] πετησιου παπ̣α ∸ β (*Hand 2*)

11 3. Ostr. app.: "Read παραδείξατε?" But the suggestion of *Παμ*]βηκις in line 6 seems needless.

11 4. Expand *(πυρου) (αρταβας)* (1 2/3).

11 6. *νεώτ(ερος)*: Ostr.; but this may be the name Neout, Neoterus, or Neoterius.

12 1. In commenting on no. 71, line 1, Préaux, p. 138, suggests reading αρμ]ο̣κο̣υ̣στωρ here. This, however, would leave a space of only three letters for the man's name and would conflict with the title "tesserarius." This is evidently a name such as Zoster, Gnoster, Castor, and Thestor; but one would need to see the original before making a definite proposal.

12 5. Cf. nos. 5, line 5, and 18, line 6. Restore ι̣δ̣ι̣ο̣ν or α̣υ̣τ̣ο̣ς̣ ονομ[α εγ]ρ(αψα)?

13. The phrase εν προχρια is the reason for placing this ostracon among the grain receipts. The second name may be either a patronymic or the name of an accountant in the dative, as in no. 1, line 7.

14. The note in the second hand, to be expanded (*αρταβας*) *β*, is the reason for including this ostracon in the grain series. The name πετησιου suggests a connection with no. 11.

14 3. Préaux, p. 127, note 1, suggests ☧ κασιανου. Cf. no. 69, line 2.

ADAERATIO OF LENTILS, SALT, AND VINEGAR

15. *SB* 6967 = Daris 44 December 29, 162 or 194

πρισκος π̣α̣υ̣λος ιππευς
⳨ ερμεινου απολλοτι κει-
βαριατορι χαιρειν ελαβον
παρα σου απο τιμης φακου
και αλος και οξεος δηναρι-
α τεσσερα οβολοι
οκτο ∟ γ // τυβι γ
γρα

BREAD?

16. *GOB* 2007 March 27–April 25, 175 or 207

. . . λεις χρη̣σ̣τ̣ο̣ρ̣α̣ν̣ . [
κειβαριατωρι χαι[ρειν ελαβον εκ του κλ- ?]
ειβανω υπερ κ . . [
∟ ιε̣ φαρμουτι[

17. *GOB* 2031

[ ] ελαβα παρα
[σου εκ του ?] κλειβανου δια
] . . . . . ηρευς
] . . . ις

WINE SERIES

18. *SB* 6970 July 25–August 23, 171 or 203

[. . .]δοντης στρατιωτης [⳩]
γλυκωνος πετρωνιω τω̣ κι-
βαριατωρι χαιρειν ελαβον
παρα σου εκ του κιβαριου οινου
κολοφωνιον εν δηναριων
τριων οβολ(ων) ζ αυτος [εγραψα]
∟ ια επειφ .
δι ερμ[ ]

19. *GOB* 2006 173/174 or 205/206

] ⳩ ε̣ν̣[
] . . κιβα[ριατορι]
[χαιρειν ε]λ̣αβον παρ[α σου]
[κολοφων]ιον εν δη[ναριων
∟ ι̣δ // . [

15 4. Daris omits ἀπό.

15 8. ⟨ε⟩γρα(ψα)? Omitted by Daris.

16 and *17*. εκ του κλειβανου, if rightly restored, should mean "from the oven." Did the soldiers get a ration of baked bread; or is this phrase somehow the equivalent of εκ του κιβαριου in e.g. nos. 18, 20, and 22?

16 1. Perhaps ι̣ο̣υ̣λεις.

18 1. The only name in Dornseiff-Hansen which ends thus is Μαρδόντης.

18 8. ερμ[εινου?]: SB.

20. GOB 2005 — January 26–February 24, 174 or 206

επωνυχος [ηρακλειδου
One line illegible
κιβαριατορι χ̣α̣ι̣ρ̣ε̣ι̣ν̣ [ελαβον παρα]
σ̣ο̣υ̣ εκ του κιβαριου [οινου . . . .]
δηναριων . . . [
∟ ιδ // μ̣ε̣χ̣[ιρ
One line illegible
. . δ̣ι̣α̣ . . . .

21. GOB 2008 — April 20, 175 or 207

[ ]νιλου στρατιωτης
[⳨ η]ρακλιανου πετρωνιω
κι]βαριατορι χαιρειν ελαβον
[εκ τ]ου κιβαριου οινου κολοφ(ωνιον)
ε]ν δηνα̣ρ̣ιων τριων οβολ(ων) [. .]
[∟] ιε // φαρμουτι κε
α

22. SB 6974 — May 29, 175 or 207

One line illegible?
[. . . .]ων̣ι̣ ερμεν[κιβαριατο-]
ρι χαιρειν ελαβον π[αρα σου]
εκ του κιβαριου . . . [
οινου ⳩ β ερμιων
υιος αυτου εγραψα υπερ αυτου
μη ειδ(οτος) γραμματα
∟ ιε παωνι δ
⳩ β
σεσημιο-
με

23. Ostr. 1129 — July 26, 175 or 207

κομαρος κομαρου στρατιω-
της ⳨ ηρακλιανου ασκληπιαδη
οπτιωνι χαιρειν ελαβον παρα σου
οινου ⟦π̣∫.⟧ κεραμον κοπτιτικον εν
αχρι του οψωνιου μαξιμος . . . υ̣ . . [. .]
συστρατιωτ(ης) ⳨ γλυκωνος εγραψα
υπερ αυτου γραμ[α]τα μη [ει-]
δοτος ∟ ιε // μεσορη β . . . . .

20. No. 53 is another receipt given by the same soldier.

21 1. *Νίλου*: GOB; but only two or three letters are lost before the nu, not enough for the man's own name. Here we probably have the remains of *πανιλου, οινιλου,* or *κονιλου.*

21 2. Cf. no. 23, line 2, for the name of the centurion.

21 7. The alpha perhaps gives the number of colophonia.

22 2.]ωνι is the name of the centurion or decurion; ερμεν[, of the cibariator.

23 4. The letters erased may be τρι of τρικεραμον.

24. *GOB* 2009 April 21, 176 or 208

σα]τουρνιλος
πε]τρωνιω κ[ιβ]αρ-
[ιατορι χαιρειν] ελαβον παρα σου
[οινου κο]λοφονιον εν δ̣η-
[να]ρια τριων οβολ(ων) η
[ ]ξ απολλωνιδης
εγραψα ∟ ις //
φαρμουθι
κ ϛ
Ⱶ γ ο̣β̣(ολοι) η (*Hand 2*)

25. *GOB* 2010 November 27–December 26, 176 or 208

– – – – –
πετρ[ωνιω κιβαριατορι χαιρειν ελαβον]
παρα σου οινου κο[λοφωνιον εν δηναριων]
τριων ∟ ιζ // χυακ[. . εγραψα ι-]
δια χιρι [
Ⱶ γ (*Hand 2*)

26. *GOB* 2011 December 27, 176 or 208, to January 25, 177 or 209

– – – – –
κολοφων]ι εν δηναρ[ιων
] ∟ ιζ // τ̣υ̣β[ι
]γ̣ρ̣αμμ. . εγρ̣α̣[ψα

27. *GOB* 2012 176/177 or 208/209

λογγεινος ερ[. . . . . . ιππευς Ŧ γε-]
μελλου πετρω̣[νιω κιβαριατορι χαιρειν]
ελαβον παρα σο[υ οινου κολοφωνια δυο]
δηναριων εξ[
∟ ιζ //

24 5–6. Préaux, p. 149, and GOB suggest [ἔ]ξ for line 6, and suggest that eta in line 5 was added later as a correction. Cf. line 10.

24 10. For the notation in the second hand see above, p. 313.

25 3–4. χυακ[| δια χιρι[στου: GOB; cf. no. 64. My restoration is based on no. 60, line 1.

25 5. For the notation in the second hand, see above, p. 313.

26 1. GOB notes that there is no sign of abbreviation after κολοφων]ι and compares modern Greek neuters with final iota. Cf. also nos. 28, line 3, and 40, line 6.

26 3. Préaux, p. 144, and GOB object to προγε]γραμμ[ενος and γραμμ[ατ(εως) as "insolites"; but Préaux says that a name *Παμμ*. . . is an even less attractive reading. Comparing no. 5, line 5, and **76** xi 11 and 21, and xii 9–10, one might restore [*name* ο προγε]γ̣ρ̣αμμεν(ος) followed by εγ̣ρ̣α̣[ψα or ελ̣α̣β[ον. Only a check of the original would decide whether the latter is possible.

27 1. The decurion Gemellus also appears in nos. 33, 34, and 66. See also on no. 3, line 2.

27 3. Instead of colophonia, tricerama could be restored. Cf. e.g. no. 31, line 3, and no. 36, line 4. Préaux, p. 140, says that the triceramon (or triceramion) is not mentioned elsewhere than in these receipts; but of course the simple ceramion is common as a unit of measure. Cf. also no. 23, line 4.

28. GOB 2015 — 176/177 or 208/209

– – – – –
χαι]ρειν [ελαβον παρα σου
εκ το]υ κιβαριου [οινου
κολοφ]ω̣νι εν δηναρ[ιων
∟ ιζ // φ[
δι απι . . (*Hand 2*)
]λας αν[

29. GOB 2013 — February 3, 177 or 209

ισιδωρο[ς Ŧ]
κον̣ο̣ν̣ος[. . . . . κιβαρι-]
ατορι χ̣α̣ι̣ρ̣ε̣ι̣ν̣ [ελαβον παρα]
σου οινου κολοφω[νι-
∟ ιζ // μεχειρ θ

30. SB 6960 — February 5, 177 or 209

– – – – –
δρασα . . . . ε̣
λεων βησαριων
ιππευς Ŧ αντωνι(ου)
πετρωνιω κιβαριατορι
χαιρειν ελαβον παρα σου εκ του
κιβαρειου οιν(ου) κολ(οφωνιν) εν Ӿ γ
∟ ιζ μεχειρ ια
πρισκος αμμω-
νιανος εγραψα

31. SB 6964 — March 7, 177 or 209

[ ]δ̣ιανος ⳨ σαβινου
[. . . κιβαριατ]ορι χαιρειν ελαβον
[παρα σου οινου τρι]κεραμιον εν αχρι συν-
[τιμηθη] ∟ ιζ φαμενωθ ια
[ ] . εινευς οπτιων εγραψα

32. SB 6957 = Daris 41 — August 27, 177 or 209

ιουλιος γερμανος στρατιω(της)
⳨ σαβεινος πετρωνιω κιβαρατορι
χαιρειν ελαβον παρα σ(ου) οινου
κολοφονια δυο δηναριων
τεσαρων οβ(ολων) ιε (γιγνεται) Ӿ δ οβ ιε
∟ ιζ επαγωμενω δ πασιον
. . . .

33. *SB* 6959 October 17, 177 or 209

[. . . .]ης ιππευς Ŧ γεμελλου
[κ]ιβαριατωρι χαιρειν
[ελαβον πα]ρα σου εκ του κιβαρ-
[ιου οινου] κολοφωνιν εν εως συ[ν-]
[τυμηθη] ∟ ιη φαωφι κ
[ ] ε̣γρ̣αψα

34. *GOB* 2016 December 20, 177 or 209

(*Hand 2*) δια ερμ̣ι̣ν̣ο̣υ̣ κ̣ο̣υ̣ρ̣α̣[τορος]
ι]σ̣ιδορος αθ̣μονις
[ι]ππευς Ŧ γεμελος αλεξ(ανδρω)
κιβαριατορι χαιρε ελα-
βον παρα σου εκ του κιβα-
[ριου] οιν̣ου κ̣ο̣λ̣ο̣φ̣ω̣ν̣ι̣ον ε̣ν̣
δηναριων δυο δραχμη[ς
∟ ιη χυακ κδ κασις
αρτεμιδορος ιππευς̣
εγραψα

35. *GOB* 2018 177/178 or 209/210

ερμα[στρατι-]
ωτη ☧ [
κειβαριτορ[ι χαιρειν ελαβον εκ του]
κειβαριου κο[λοφωνι-
∟ ιη // φα

36. *SB* 6963 = Daris 43 March 16, 178 or 210

νεφερως νεφερωτος
οπτιων αλεξανδρῳ κει-
βαριατορι χαιρειν ελαβον
παρα σου οινου τρικεραμον
εν ⳨ τριων οβολων εικοσι
∟ ιη φαμενωθ κ

33 1–2. The spacing in SB leaves room for only three letters as the name of the cibariator, and four for the rest of the cavalryman's name. These lines probably began farther left than lines 3–6; but cf. no. 31, line 2.

33 6. Perhaps [αυτος].

34 1. Préaux, p. 144, reports that the reading κουρα[is very uncertain; but Herminus Tyranus has the title curator in no. 60, line 3, and no. 4, lines 5–6. See ad locc.

34 6. The last name is probably that of a centurion or decurion. Herminus' cognomen is lost in the lacuna.

36 2. ὀκτίων: Daris, a misprint.

37. *SB* 6962 — June 8, 178 or 210

αμμωνις αμμωνις σημε-
αφορος αλεξανδρου κιβαρια-
τωρι χαιρειν ελαβον εκ του
κιβαριου οινου δηναρια
οκτω οβολ(ων) οκτω ⳨ η οβολ(ων) η
ερμειν[. . . . .] αντιοχου
. . εγραψα ∟ ιη παοινι ιδ

38. *GOB* 2019 = *SB* 6975 — 178/179 or 210/211

]πε̣λ̣[
αλεξανδρου κι[βαριατορι χαι-]
[ρειν ελα]βον παρα σου ο̣ιν[ου]
[τρικερα]μον εν ∟ ιθ //
[. . . . . .]ς̣ εως συντιμθν
[ ]. . .

39. *SB* 6961 = Daris 42 — August 5, 180 or 212

μ αυρηλις ασκληπιαδης ερμιν. .
⳩ αλεξανδρου πετρωνιου κειβαριατωρι
χαιρειν ελαβον παρα σου οινου κολοφονιν
εν δηναριων δυο δραχμας δυο μαρκ̣[ος?]
αυρηλιος ωριον σαραπιων αρμωρω
κουστωρ εγραψα υ(περ) αυτου μη ιδοτος
γραμματα ∟ κ // μεσορη ιβ

40. *GOB* 2020 = Daris 45 — April 10, 182 or 214

(*Hand 2*?) *ΓΛΥΚΩΝ*
ασκληπιαδης δεμονρους κορνιξ
⳩ ολυμπους ισιδωρους ιεραξ
κοιβαριατωρι χαιρειν
ελαβον παρα σου οινου
κολοφωνι εν και τρικερα-
μον εν εως ⟨σ⟩υντιμη-
θη ∟ κβ //
φαρμουθι ιε
ι]ουλις εγραψα

41. *GOB* 2034

ιουλιος ωριω̣ν̣ ο̣πτιων
αλ̣εξανδρω κιβ[αριατορι
χ̣α̣ι̣ρ̣ε̣ι̣ν̣ ελαβον παρα σ̣ο̣υ̣
οι[νου κολ]ο̣φ[ωνιον?
. . [

37 4. The number of colophonia appears to have been omitted. By the writer, or in White's copy?

40 2. GOB: κόρνιξ equals *cornicen.*

40 3. GOB: "Read Ὀλυμποῦτος Ἰσιδωροῦτι Ἱέρακι."

42. SB 6958

ιουλις νιλος ιππ[ευς]
Ϯ λονγινω αλε[ξανδρω]
κιβαριατορι χαι[ρειν ελαβον]
παρα σου οινου κ[ολοφωνιον εως]
συντιμιθη β.[...]
τεσσεραριο[ς εγραψα υπερ αυτου]

43. GOB 2039

]..[
αλε]ξανδ[ρω κιβαριατορι χαιρειν]
[ελαβον παρα σου οινου τρικε]ραμ[ον]
]αρ [
].. [
].. [

44. Ostr. 1142

ερασμιος χ̣ρησπ̣[......]
ερμας κιβαριατ[ορι χαι-]
ρειν ελαβον π̣[αρα σου]
οινου και[
δην[αρι- ....]
κ[..........]

45. GOB 2026

ασκληπιαδης ερ[ιππευς]
Ϯ λογγεινον ερμειν[κιβαριατορι]
χαιριν ελαβον παρα [σου τρικερα-]
μον εν δηναρι[ω]ν [τριων? οβολων?]
εν φιλαις (ετους?)[
Ḥ ( ) α ʃ′ (*Hand 2*)

46. GOB 2023

] κ̣ο̣πρητι κιβαριατορ[ι
[χαιρειν ελαβο]ν παρα σου οινου τρικερ[αμον εν]
[δηναριων τριω]ν οβολων τεσσαρων
] αυρηλις ισιδ̣ω̣ρ̣[(*Hand 2*)

44 3. π̣[αρὰ σοῦ ἀπὸ τιμῆς]: Ostr.; but the last phrase is not necessary, since the genitive οινου is used throughout with *colophonion* and *triceramon*.

44 4. και[νοῦ: Ostr. But cf. no. 15, line 5, and no. 49, line 4, and read οινου και [, e.g. αλος or οξεος. Or perhaps restore και[ραμον; cf. again no. 49, line 4.

45 6. Cf. above, p. 313, for the notation in the second hand. There is a difficulty about the amount. Préaux, p. 141, points out that δηναρι[ω]ν in line 4 seems to be plural, and that in any case one denarius, four obols, is too little for a triceramon, which elsewhere is rated at about three denarii.

46 4. ισιδωρ[ος: GOB; but cf. *isidorianus* in **30** ii 5.

47. *GOB* 2024

αιλις ερμ[
πετρωνι[ω κιβαριατορι χαιρειν]
ελαβο̣[ν παρα σου εκ του κιβαρι-]
[ο]υ̣ οινο[υ

48. *SB* 6966

αντωνιος ιεραξ δρομ[αδαριος]
Ŧ λονγεινου πετρων[ιω κιβαρια-]
[τορι] χαιρειν ελαβον παρα [σου εκ του]
κιβαριου οινου τρικερα[μα β ? δηνα-]
ριων πεντε οβο(λων) θ[
νιδης στρα(τιωτης) ⳨ γλυκ[ωνος εγραψα]

49. *SB* 6965

αντωνις ιεραξ δρομαδαρ(ιος) Ŧ [λονγεινου]
πετρονιω κιβαριατορι χαιρ[ειν ελαβον]
παρα σου εκ του κιβαριου[
και τρικαιραμον ε[ν δηναριων]
οκτω οβολ̣[ων
. .

50. *SB* 6955

[. . . .]ε̣π̣τ̣ι̣α[. . . στρα-]
[τιω]της ⳨ ποσ[πετρω-]
νιου κιβαρει[ατορι]
χαιρειν ωμολογ[ω ειλη-]
φηναι παρα σου ε[κ του]
[κιβ]αρειου οινου [. . .]
[   ]υν[. . .]

51. *GOB* 2029

[   ] ισιδ̣ορου
[στρατιωτης] ⳨ . . . . .
[πε]τρωνιω κιβα-
[ριατο]ρι χ̣α̣ι̣ρειν ελαβον π̣[α-]
[ρα σου] οινου τρικεραμον ε[ν]
[δηναριω]ν̣ τ̣ρ̣ι̣ω̣ν̣ ο̣β̣ο̣λ . .
[. . . . . .]δ̣ρ̣α̣ι̣ο̣υ̣ . . . ε̣ρ̣μ̣. . . . .

49 4. ἓ[ν *δηναρίων τριῶν*?]: SB; but the number of denarii is in line 5; and three denarii would be too little anyway for a triceramon and whatever was named at the end of line 3 before the *και* which begins this line.

50 2. *Ποσ[ίου?*: SB, as the name of the centurion; but there is no evidence to support this restoration in preference to another. No. 62, line 1, begins with the word *ποσιτος* which is probably a proper name.

51 7. Perhaps Ŧ *ερμ̣ι̣ν̣ο̣υ̣*? Cf. no. 15, line 2. But *π̣α̣θερμο̣υ̣θι̣ς̣* is equally possible.

52. GOB 2040

]. . . . .
]. . . . . πε-
[τρων]ιω κιβαριατορι
[χαιρε]ι̣ν̣ ελαβον
[παρα σ]ο̣υ̣ οινου
]. . . .
]. . . .

53. GOB 2027

επωνυχος ηρακλε̣ι̣δ(ου) στρατιω̣[της]
⳨ ε̣. . . ν̣ι π̣ε̣τ̣ρω̣[νιω κιβα-]
ρι̣α̣τορι χαι(ρειν) ελ[αβον παρα]
σου οινου τρικεραμ̣[ον]
[ε]ν δηναριων τ[ρι-]
ων οβολου ενος
. . . .
∟ . . // φαρμ(ουθι)
ι̣β̣
. . .

54. GOB 2035

ασκλας ασκλα[τος?
πετρωνιων κιβα̣ρ̣[ιατορι χ(αιρειν) ελαβον εκ του]
κιβ(αριου) οινου κολοφωνι[ον εν δηναριων]
τριων οβολ(ων) δεκα ∟ [
επειφ κζ αρειος δι. [
στρα(τιωτης) εγραψα

55. GOB 2032

[. . .]α̣ριων ⳨ γλυκων[ος]
[. . .]θι κειβαριατορι χ̣[αιρειν]
[ελα]β̣ον εκ του κειβαρι̣[ου]
[κολ] εν ✳ δ οβολ(ων) κϛ
]μαξιμος
]τεσεραρις
]α εν̣ ταγη̣?
].

53. No. 20 is in the same hand and from the same man. The centurion's name may be Herennius.

55 4. Expand: *κολ(οφωνιον)*. Préaux, p. 146: the numeral for the obols has been corrected from *κα*. Twenty-six obols as a fraction of a denarius is proof that the 28-obol denarius was being used.

55 7. *ἔγραψ]α?:* GOB. Préaux, pp. 146–47, says that ἐν ταγ̣ῃ is an insecure reading, and from the point of view of meaning, ἐγ̣ ταμι̣(?), referring to the treasury, might be preferable. It is not clear, however, what treasury she has in mind, whether the quaestura of the cohort or something else. Perhaps εν ταγη could be interpreted as "on command," "at dictation."

56. GOB 2030

] ☧ διδυμιανου
κιβαριατο]ρ̣ι̣ χαιρειν ε[λαβον]
[παρα σου κ]ο̣λοφωνιν εν δη[ναριων τριων?]
]. // φαρμουθι ιη
].αρις εγραψα
[υπερ αυτου μη ει]δοτος
[γραμματα].δ̣ρις.
]...

57. SB 6976

– – – – –
[κιβαριατο]ρι χ[αιρειν ελαβον παρα σου]
[οινου κο]λοφωνι εν δ[ηναριων
[∟ . .] επιφ κ ιουλιος[
[. . . . . συνε]υ̣δωκω κ[αι εγραψα]
[. . .]η ς̣ σ̣υ̣ν̣ε̣υ̣δ̣ω̣κ̣ω̣ κ[αι εγραψα]
[. .] ιεραξ κι-
κ κολ(οφωνια) β αυρηλις ερμ[
Ḥ δ̣

58. GOB 2038

– – – – –
κιβα]ριατορ[ι χαιρειν ελαβον παρα σου]
[ε]κ του κιβαρι[ου οινου κολοφωνιον εν]
δηναριου τ̣ρ̣[ιων
φαρμουτι κβ[
κουρατωρ [εγραψα
υ̣π̣ε̣ρ̣ α̣υ̣τ̣ο̣υ̣
.α̣ (*Hand 2?*)

59. GOB 2028

πε]τ̣εησις ιππευς
]ενβωμου δι εμου
]κολοφωνιν εν

56 2–3. The text is printed as in GOB; but the name of the cibariator must have begun line 2. In line 3, therefore, one should also restore *οινου, εκ του κιβαριου*, or both, to make the line long enough.

56 5. Perhaps *τεσσε]ραρις*; cf. no. 55, line 6.

57 3–4. SB restores *τεσ-*] | [*σαρων*, apparently on the ground of the total in line 9; but there are two items in the receipt—the wine (?) in line 3 and the cicus (?) in lines 7–8, and the total must include both. The amount in lines 3–4 must accordingly be less than 4 denarii.

57 7–8. SB proposes expanding *κικ(εως)*, probably rightly.

57 9. SB reads θ and expands *ὁ(μοῦ)*; but see above, p. 313.

58 2. Triceramon is possible instead of colophonion.

59 2. GOB has no proposal for]*ενβωμου*; but Préaux, p. 142, says that it must be either part of the name of the cavalryman's decurion or the phrase *ἐν Βωμῷ* as a place-name. Cf. no. 45, line 5: *ἐν Φίλαις*; but a decurion's name is more likely.

60. *SB* 6968

– – – – –

[εγραψα] ιδια χιρι
δι ερμινος τυραvος
κουρατ(   ) τρικ(εραμον) α
κουρατορσι τρικ(εραμον) α

61. *GOB* 2025

]μονις στ[ρατιωτης ☧ – – κιβαριατορι]
[χαιρε]ιν ελαβο̣[ν παρα σου εκ του κιβαριου]
οινο]υ̣ τρικερ̣[αμ-
]εου ⳨ τ̣[ριων
∟ . .] // μεχ[ιρ

62. *SB* 6972

ποσιτος κοινωδις
τοις ⌊ον τρικ(εραμον) α
δια πιοαν

63. *GOB* 2033

]ιππευς ⳨ κονονι
[κιβ]αριατωρι χαιριν
[ελαβον παρα σου εκ] του κιβαριον
] εως συν-
[τιμηθη

WINE? AND A VINEGAR CRUET

64. *GOB* 2041 = *SB* 6969

πετρωνις χιριστη-
ς κολ(οφωνιον) ᾱ οξιδιν
α

60 3. SB expands *κουρατ(ορσι)*; but this seems just as likely to be Herminus' title, to be expanded *κουρατ(ορος)*. For *κουρατορσι* in line 4, cf. no. 68, line 5: *τοις λιβραριοις*.

61. The lines are printed as in GOB, though it is clear that placing the names of both the centurion and the cibariator in line 1 makes it inordinately long—perhaps 50 letters, including two names for the soldier—against 33 in line 2. Other distributions of the wording could be found; but it would be futile to propose any without knowing the original shape of the ostracon.

62 2. SB: "Very possibly [αὐ]τοῖς ὀν(όμασι), in which case a lost text must have preceded."

64 3. GOB notes that the alpha may be only a flourish rather than a real letter.

Adaeratio of Wine

65. *GOB* 2004 — December 4, 169 or 201

[κε]ντουριας γλυκωνος
[κιβαρι]ατọρι χαιρειν
[ελαβον παρα σου] απο τιμης οινου
] L ι̣ // χυακ η
]ωρος ιππευς εγραψα
H α (*Hand 2*)
H α

66. *GOB* 2014 — February 10, 177 or 209

ιππ]ευς Ŧ κονωνος
κιβα]ριατορι χαιριν
[ελαβον παρα σου] απο τιμης οινου
]οβ(ολων) . L ιζ μεχιρ ις
].λιανος ιππευς Ŧ γẹμελλου
[εγραψα
H α ʃ' (*Hand 2*)
ʃ'

67. *GOB* 2017 = *SB* 6971 — January 5, 178 or 210

διδυμος παχωμ[
αλεξανδρω κιβαριạ[τορι χαιρειν ελαβον]
παρα σου απο τιμης οιν[ου δηναρια δ?]
L ιη τυβι ι εγρα[ψα ιδια χειρι?]
τοις λιβραριοις (*Hand 2*)
H δ (*Hand 3?: White*)

68. *SB* 6956 — 177/178 or 209/210

διοσκορος δ[
πετρωνιω [χαιρειν]
εσχον παρα σ[ου απο]
τιμης οινου δηναρι-
α δυο L ιη
[ ]ιβ
εσημιοσομην

65 5. [? Ἰσίδ]ωρος: GOB; but of course many other restorations are possible.

65 6–7. For the notations in the second hand see above, p. 313.

66 7–8. The notation is the same as in no. 45, but not certainly by the same hand. See also above, p. 313.

67 1. παχωμ[ιου ?: GOB.

67 3. SB brackets παρα; but Préaux, pp. 136–37, reports that it can be read.

67 5. Cf. κουρατορσι in no. 60, line 4.

67 6. For the notation see above, p. 313.

69. Ostr. 1265 August 27, 187?

αυρηλις ευδαιμων
στρατιωτης ⳨ κασιανου
πετρωνιω κιβαρατορι χαιρειν
ελαβον παρα σου απο τιμης οινου [κο-]
λοφωνιου δηναρια δυο οβολοι οκτω
∟ κ̣ζ // επαγομενων δ

70. GOB 2021 = *SB* 6973

ερμεινος η[. . . στρατιωτης]
⳨ τρουννιου [. . . κιβαρια-]
τωρι χαιρει[ν ελαβον παρα]
σου υπ(ερ) τιμ[ης οινου δηνα-]
ριων δυο ∟ [
διοσκορος παλ̣[
δια τρουν⟨ν⟩ιου
Η β (*Hand 2*)

71. GOB 2022

[ ]. εου αρμουκουστωρ
[αλ]εξανδρου κιβαρια-
[τορι χαιρειν ελα]βον παρα σου δι̣ ε-
[απο τ]ι̣μης οινου

Adaeratio?

72. Ostr. 1128 June 30, 173 or 205

ευδαιμων σαρ[απα]μ[μων-
στρατιωτης [⳨] ωρη⟨γε⟩νο̣υ̣ς
και . . . α . . . πι . . . . [. . ⳨]
τιθοης ασκληπιαδη [ο]πτιωνι
χαιρειν ελαβον παρα σου δι̣ . .
. . . . . ν δηναρια ε̣πτα κ̣α̣ι̣
οβολους ικοσι
∟ ιγ // επειφ ς̄
In the left margin:
πετ̣αλι̣
πολυδας

69 6. On the date see above, pp. 311–12.

70 5. ο̣β[ολούς: SB; but Préaux, p. 137, note 6, states that the symbol ∟ for ἔτους is beyond question.

70 8. On the symbol Θ in SB see above, p. 313.

72 1. Σαρ[απα]μ̣[μωνος]: Ostr.

72 5–6. The shaky syntax of these receipts leaves it a question whether Eudaemon and the other soldier are getting money or some commodity named in δι̣ . . . . ν which is worth 7 denarii, 20 obols. Cf. nos. 24 and 37, both of which have δηναρια instead of the genitive of value.

Money for Burial?

73. GOB 2003 April 1, 157

[.....].ς αλεξανδρος ⳨ λονγιε[νου
[... φ]λαουιου αντωνιν[ου ....]
[   ]α̣ρ̣ι νεκροτα̣[φ............]
[......]ητι χαιρειν̣ [ελαβον?]
[πα]ρ υμων εις λογον ι̣[....]
τ̣ανας (δραχμας) εικοσι ∟ κ αυτοκρα̣τ̣[ο]ρ̣[ος]
καισαρος τιτου αιλιου αδριανου
αντωνινου σεβαστου ευσεβους
φαρμουθι ς

Unclassifiable

74. GOB 2037

– – – – – π̣ε̣τ̣ρ̣ω̣[νιω
κ̣ιβαρια̣τ̣ο̣ρ̣ι χ̣α̣ι̣ρ̣ε̣ι̣ν̣
ε̣λ̣α̣β̣ο̣ν̣ π̣α̣ρ̣α̣ σ̣ο̣υ̣
Three lines made illegible by fading of the ink

75. Ostr. 1146

τεσσ]εραριος εγραψα

76. GOB 2036

ιουλ(ι-) ισιδ[ωρ-
⳨ ουιππι̣[
παυνι ε̣

77. Ostr. 1138 June 30, 161 or 193 or 217?

πασηνις πτολε[μαιου]
και οι συ(ν) αυ(τω) πρακ(τορες) ορ[....]
διοσκορους πανα[.....]
..του ανδρος πα̣ε̣ρ.[.....]
∟ α // επειφ ς
π̣αη[σις? (*Hand 2*)

73. This ostracon is included here only because of its mention in line 1 of a century of *Longie-*. Préaux, p. 151, equates the name with Longinus, which is not certain, and states that this centurion in not mentioned elsewhere in the texts from Pselcis. The probable reason is that this receipt dates from April 1, 157, and only seven of these ostraca can be earlier than 174/175.

75. The title *tesserarius* is the only evidence that this scrap belongs with these receipts.

76 1. Ἰούλ(ιος) Ἰσίδ[ωρος: GOB.

76 2. GOB restores Οὐιππί̣[ου; but the name may have been longer, perhaps Vibianus. It is not sure that this is a receipt.

77. This text may not be military at all. There is nothing to show that it is; but I have kept it because it is included in the series in Ostr.

Translation

Only a sampling is offered here, as with **76**, because of the repetitiousness of the texts.

No. 1. November 20, 179(?)

Marcus Aurelius Iulius Heraclianus, soldier, century of Tithoes, to Asclepiades, optio, receiver of grain. I have received from you my grain for the month Choiak, one artaba. I, Iulius Kleides, cavalryman, wrote. Year 20, Hathyr 23.

Second hand: For Patermouthis.

No. 2. November 21, 179(?)

Iulius . . . log [– –] to Asclepiades, optio. I have received in advance one artaba of grain for the month Choiak. I, Alexander, his fellow-soldier, wrote. Year 20, Hathyr 24.

Second hand: I, Dionysianus, centurion, have signed.

No. 6. 182(?)

[.]ar[– – – century? of] Horion [– –] to Asclepiades [– –] receiver of grain. I have received from you of grain for [seven ?] months—the month Hathyr and Choiak and Tybi Mechir Phamenoth Pharmouthi Pachon—make seven months, year 21, of wheat six artabas [– – –] I, [ ].r wrote for him.

Year 22, [*month*] 26.

No. 15. December 29, 162(?)

Priscus Paulus, cavalryman, turma of Herminus, to Apollos, cibariator. I have received from you from the value of lentils, salt, and vinegar 4 denarii, 8 obols. Year 3, Tybi 3. I wrote (?).

No. 18. July 25–August 23, 171 (?)

[. . .]dontes, soldier, century of Glycon, to Petronius, cibariator. I have received from you from stores (? *or* from my ration?) of wine one colophonion of 3 denarii, 7 obols. I wrote myself. Year 11, Epiph [*day*]. Through Herminus.

No. 23. July 26–August 23, 175(?)

Comarus son of Comarus, soldier, century of Heraclianus, to Asclepiades, optio. I have received from you of wine one Coptite ceramon toward my ration. I, Maximus [– – –], his fellow-soldier, century of Glycon, wrote for him being illiterate. Year 15, Mesore 2(?).

No. 36. March 16, 178(?)

Nepheros son of Nepheros, optio, to Alexander, cibariator. I have received from you of wine one triceramon of 3 denarii, 20 obols. Year 18, Phamenoth 20.

No. 40. April 10, 182(?)

GLYKON

Asclepiades Demonrous cornix(?), century of Olympus, to Isidorus Hierax, cibariator. I have received from you of wine one colophonion and one triceramon awaiting valuation. Year 22, Pharmouthi 15. I, Iulius, wrote.

No. 69. August 27, 187(?)

Aurelius Eudaemon, soldier, century of Cassianus, to Petronius, cibariator. I have received from you from the value of a colophonion of wine 2 denarii, 8 obols. Year 27, intercalary day 4.

79

Cavalryman's Receipt for Grain for Two Months

PClermont-Ganneau 4a — Second half of II p.

Transcription and commentary: A. Bataille, "P. Clermont-Ganneau 3–5," *JJP* 6 (1952) 186–88.

Text: *SB* VI 9248; *CPL*, no. 136; Daris, no. 47.

This text is like those under **78** in relating to the rations of one person; but it resembles **81** in that the transaction is with a civil official and in the use of the verb *μετρέω* (line 11). Finally, though Bataille apparently thought of it as a single receipt, the use of two languages points rather to a book of receipts like **75**. Too little remains of the Latin text to prove anything except that it too dealt with the grain ration and mentioned a *dispensator Caesaris*, a title rendered in Greek in line 10 as *οἰκονόμος Καίσαρος*.[1]

The dating is on paleographical grounds; but line 12 should be re-examined for the possibility that the two letters after *ἔτ(ους)* are a numeral for the regnal year.

The verso is not mentioned and may be presumed blank.

[1] D. van Berchem, "L'Annone militaire," 144, cites *CIL* III 333: *Caesaris Aug. seruos uerna dispensator ad frumentum*, *Καίσαρος δούλου οἰκονόμου ἐπὶ τοῦ σείτου*, noting that the dispensatores are not soldiers but slaves of the emperor attached to the military service.

sido.[
ẹṛ.....[...].a.[....].o..[
p...t scriba [..].ạṇ.[
dispensatore ca[e]saris
dari mihi frumẹṇṭ..
tẹ..ṛ....dị..l.........
ṣe.......sal...
]ε̣ι.ι̣τος σα̣ραπιων ιππευς
προγεγραμμενος τρε̣θονιω
οι]κονομω καισαρος χαιρειν
ε]μετρηθην παρα σου σιτο μ̣ο̣υ̣
τ]ου προτερ(ου) ετ(ους) αν(   ) υπερ μη-
ν]ων δυο γ(ινονται) αρταβα[ι] δυο
.]..ιμης τ̣α̣υρεινου μελα̣νο ι̣π̣(πευς)
ε]γραψα ϋπερ αυτυ

1. *sidoṇ[ius? [po]sidoṇ[ius?* Name? Ethnic?

4. Bataille's publication indicates no break in the papyrus after *caesaris*. If that is indeed the case, the lines of the Latin text were only about 20 letters long.

8–9. It appears from *ἱππεὺς προγεγραμμένος* that this is a different text, although it concerns the same person.

11. *σιτο(ν)*: Bataille.

12. It was suggested above that *αν( )* might conceal a numeral; but *ἔτ(ους) ἀν(ομένου)* is also possible—"of the end of the preceding year."

14. *Μέλανο(ς)*: Bataille. I have translated on the assumption that the beginning of the line is to be restored *τ]ọυṛμης*; but of course a name such as *Καιμης* or *Τειμης*, son of Taurinus Melas, is also possible. Since the two letters *ιπ* at the end of the line are doubtful, it is uncertain whether they should be expanded as *ιπ(πευς)*. The whole text might well be studied again in the light of the parallels mentioned above.

15. *αὐτοῦ*: Daris.

Translation

Lines 8–15:]ei.itus Sarapion, the cavalryman aforementioned, to Trethonius, imperial oeconomus. I have been measured out by you my grain of the preceding year, the [—th?] for two months. Total, two artabas. [I, – – –, turma (?)] of Taurinus Melas, cavalryman, have written for him.

80

Receipt for Hay for a Turma

PLond. 482; *vidi* — May? 130

Transcription and facsimile: *EL*, no. 18.

Transcription, facsimile, and commentary: *ChLA* III 203.

Transcription:

1. Lesquier, p. 503, published a text based on transcriptions by H. I. Bell and J. P. Gilson; cited as **L.**
2. Premerstein, *Klio* 3 (1903) p. 32, no. 4, is a less accurate transcription by Seymour de Ricci; cited as **P.**

Description: F. G. Kenyon, *Greek Papyri in the British Museum* 2 (London 1898) page XLII.

Commentary: A. von Premerstein, *Wiener Studien* 24 (1902) 378–79, is obsolete because based on an inaccurate text.

Text: *CPL*, no. 114, reproduces Lesquier's text; Daris, no. 38, follows *ChLA*.

Although Serenus has the unmilitary title of procurator, he is at the same time identified as a member of the turma of Donacianus, ala Veterana Gallica. Similarly, the conductores faenarii to whom he addresses the receipt may be civilian but can be military, as shown by

58 ii 5, probably **70** a ii 18, and Dessau 9103 (*CIL* III 14356, 3a).[1] Moreover, all thirty members of the turma are listed; and, unlike most such receipts, the text is in Latin. It therefore clearly belongs in this corpus.

As in **73**, the names are in the informal style without cognomina or patronymics.

The verso is presumably blank.

[1] The latest, but not wholly satisfactory, comment on such conductores is Ramsay McMullen, *Soldier and Civilian in the Later Roman Empire* (Cambridge, Mass. 1963) 9.

A.D. 130

alae uetrane galliga turma
ḍoṇaciani serenus procuratọr
conduc̣toribus fenaris ṣalute
accipi fenum contur[m]alibus
meis mensis iuni et naulum
sọḷḷui per me et tibi fiunt
eccutes triginti catulino
et afro cos
alafes
solas
iulius
platon
germanus
domittius
neruas
cocas
atestas
gaianus
paulus
nilas
bitecus
aululanus
dolens
domittius
ṣerenus
ẹcatus
bitsius
aululanus
felix ·
[. .]urinus
ḍ. . ṛspor
ṭ. b. ụs
teṛẹntius
. . . ules
ṃạximus
acillẹus
sarapịọṇ
androstenes

1. *ale:* P, of which Bell says "perhaps a misprint."
4. *accịpi:* L, "but *e* is not impossible."
5. *mexficium:* P; *mensis iuni:* L and Bell.
6. *ṣụ*[ ]*ṛui:* P; *ṣ.*[..]*.ui:* L; *ṣụ*[*stu*]*li:* EL; *s*[*ụstụ*]*li:* ChLA. But this is too long; and there can be no question about the *u* before the *i*. Between *s* and the second *l* there is room at most for two letters, part of which is taken up by a hole which may have come from a defect in the papyrus present when the text was written. For the gemination of the *l* in *sollui* cf. Dessau's indices, III, p. 803. The name of Catullinus in line 7 exhibits the opposite error of writing only one *l*.
8. Read *apro* for *afro*. Cf. *nefotianus* for *nepotianus*, **73** a ii 14 and b 4. ChLA makes *cos* a separate line.
9. *Aufis?:* Gilson; *alafes:* Bell.
17. *Atestus:* L; Bell adds, "... or *atecṭus*; the *u* is quite doubtful and *a* or perhaps *o* are also possible."
24. *Domiṭṭị*[*u*]*s:* L.
25. *Ģ...ụṣ:* L; "... or perhaps *gainus* (sic)": Bell; *Serenus:* EL and ChLA.
26. *.çạṭ..:* L; *Ẹcatụṣ:* EL and ChLA. Perhaps *hecatus*, though in Dornseiff-Hansen only as a deity.
27. *ḅiṭẹcus:* Bell; *Bitsius:* EL and ChLA.
28. *Aụlulạṇ*[*u*]*s:* L.
30. Perhaps [*ta*]*urinus*?
31. *Ḍ....or* or perhaps *...upor:* L; *d or* or *d upor?:* Bell; *D...por:* EL; *D...uspor:* ChLA.
32. *ṭụbạṣ:* Bell; *T.b.s:* EL; *Tibẹrịus:* ChLA. Possibly *tạrb.ụs*.
33. *n....tius:* Bell; *Te*[*ren*]*tius:* EL and ChLA.
34. *....ụlis:* EL; *...ulis:* ChLA.
36. *Acilḷ*[*i*]*us:* EL and ChLA.

Translation

Ala Veterana Gallica, turma of Donacianus, Serenus, procurator, to the hay contractors. I have received hay for fellow-members of my turma for the month of June and I have paid the freight myself and they total thirty cavalrymen for you. Consulate of Catullinus and Afer. *The thirty names follow.*

81

Receipt for Wheat for Cavalrymen and Infantry

POxy. IV 735 and *Oxyrhynchus Papyri* V, app. I, p. 315 — Sept. 4, A.D. 205
Present location unknown.[1]

Transcription, commentary, and facsimile:

1. Bernard P. Grenfell and Arthur S. Hunt, *The Oxyrhynchus Papyri* IV (London 1904) no. 735 and plate 5.
2. *ChLA* IV, no. 275.

Text: *CPL*, no. 134, reproduces the text of the original editors with an apparatus drawn from *Oxyrhynchus Papyri* V, p. 315. Daris, no. 39, also uses Gilliam, *Études de Papyrologie* 8 (1957) 51, note. 1. Neither prints col. i.

Unlike the conductores of **80**, who may be military personnel, the addressee of this receipt, a vicarius of the imperial oeconomus, must be a civilian. The piece is included here nevertheless because of its otherwise military character.

[1] This papyrus is supposed to have been sent to the Pierpont Morgan Library in New York; but the officials of that institution assure me that it was never received.

As the editors saw, the list of pedites was probably followed by another receipt like that in lines 5–11; and conversely, that receipt must have been preceded by fifty names of the equites for whom the wheat was intended. Probably all of the present col. i and the upper part of col. ii were taken up by this list, while that of the pedites began at col. ii 13, and continued in col. iii or farther, for the symbol in line 12 is not the numeral *vi*, as the editors read it, but the sign for "centuria." This eliminates the need to find six names in col. ii 13–17. Whether the papyrus is a single sheet like **80** or out of a book of receipts like **76** is not now determinable; but the former seems more likely.

On the date the editors say, "The receipt is dated in the 14th year of a joint reign, which on palaeographical grounds is probably that of Septimius Severus and Caracalla." The nomenclature, with the numerous Semitic names, reminding one of Dura, also speaks for a third-century date.

The editors do not mention the verso, which may therefore be presumed to be blank.

Col. i

]. l.
]. ụs
]n
]. us
]. ṣ
]as
]ṣ
]. a
]sus
]. s
].
]s
]
]ạ

Col. ii

. . g̣[.]l[
ṣạdus . . . [.]. [
marrius co. . ṇụṣ
[u]ạḷerius isidori
μαλωχως .[. .]μ̣ι̣[ο]υ οπτιων ουικτω-
ρι κωμαρινω καισαρων οικονομου
ουικαριου χα̣ι̣ρει̣ν εμετρηθησαν
οι προκιμεν̣ο̣ι ιππεις πραιτων αριθμω ν̄
υπερ μηνος θωθ πυρου αρταβας πεν-
τηκοντα ∟ ιδ // των κυριων σεβαστων
θωθ ζ
item pẹdites ⅄ belei
beleus zabdeus
ad cognlega claudius sabinus
ierraeus macchana
gaddẹs auidus
themes malichi

Col. iii

ịẹḍḍạel[
ṛịex barichius [
sadus [
themes [
salmes [
zebidas [
malichus sạ[
psenosirius [
roman ạ[
cumeṣṃẹṣ ⟦tru⟧ fon h[
[i]ulius . [
eponuchus . [
pacebis [

Col. i. The first remains are at the level of the space between lines 2 and 3 of col. ii. *POxy.* offers no readings but reports "a few Latin letters (apparently belonging to names)." *CPL* and Daris omit col. i altogether.

i 1. ChLA has]. on a level with ii 1, but no indication of any traces where I read].*l*.

2–3. ChLA puts these lines on a level with ii 3–4 and shows a blank line between my 3 and 4.

4.]*us:* ChLA.

5.]*s:* ChLA.

6.]*us:* ChLA.

8.]..*:* ChLA.

9.]*ius:* ChLA.

10.]*us:* ChLA.

11.]*s:* ChLA.

ii 1. *Ç*[.]*l*[*:* Oxy.; .... *Ç* [...]*l*[*:* ChLA.

2. *Ṣạdus* [*:* Oxy.; *Ṣạdus* ...[*:* ChLA.

3. *Coṃạṛ*[*:* Oxy. and ChLA. Possibly *cosanus* or *coranus*.

4. *Valerius;* Oxy.; [*Ụạḷ*]*erius:* ChLA.

5. *Ṃ*[..]*ν̣α̣ν̣*[ο]*υ:* Oxy. and ChLA.

6. *Κωμαρινου ... οἰκονόμῳ οὐικαρίῳ:* Oxy. in app. On *οἰκονόμος* see introd. to **79**, note 1.

7. Oxy. in app.: "First *ε* of *ἐμετρήθησαν* corr. from *ο* (?)."

8. *πραίτων ἀριθμῶν:* Oxy.; in app.: "lege *πρώτων*"; *ἀριθμῷ ν̄:* de Ricci. ChLA in app.: "The most probable explanation is ... a misreading of the abbreviation *πραιτωρ* for *πραιτωρ(ίοι)* ...," assuming that these equites are called praetorii because they were serving at the Prefect's headquarters; but misunderstanding of an abbreviation implies that this receipt was being copied from a written text, which seems unlikely. Lesquier's supposition (p. 97) that there were two units "de recrutement identique," a *numerus I equitum* and a *numerus I peditum*, is not really supported by *CIL* III 20996, which he cites, and must certainly be discarded. R. W. Davies, *JRS* 56 (1966) 243, proposes to interpret as "the above-mentioned cavalrymen of the afore-stated number"; but it is not clear how this is derived from *πραιτων*. That there is some miswriting here seems certain; a wholly satisfactory explanation is still to be found.

12. *vi Belei:* Oxy.; *v (centuria):* Daris. Gilliam arrived independently at the same reading as mine. We also agree on ii 13, 15, and 16, and iii 5 and 6.

13. *Zabdius:* Oxy.; and under 3–4, "*Beleus* and *Zabdius* certainly seem to be separate names." This is of course mistaken; Beleus Zabdius is the full name of the commander of the centuria Belei.

14. Oxy.: "The marginal notations here and in [iii 2] are obscure; *cognlega* is perhaps *collega*, but what is *riex*?" Wilcken *POxy.* v, p. 315) proposes *ad cogn(oscendum) lega(tur)*; de Ricci, *ad cogn(itionem) lega(ti)*, adopted in ChLA. But what legatus in Egypt? The governor was an equestrian prefect; and there were prefects, not senatorial legati, in command of the legions there (Wilcken, *Grundzüge*, p. 391). The obscurity remains.

15. *Serraeus:* de Ricci.

16. *Gradius:* Oxy.; *Gaddius:* de Ricci. *auidus* may be a variant of *auidas* or of *auitus*.

iii 1. *Ịẹḅạẹl:* Oxy. and ChLA. Instead of *ieddael* perhaps *iebbael*.

2. *Alex(andreae):* ChLA, credited in the introduction to de Ricci, but not mentioned in Oxy. v. The plate in Oxy. IV nevertheless shows no trace whatever of the horizontal stroke of the *l*. It might be possible to read *ae.x* or *nex*; but these do not help.

5. *Salmeus:* de Ricci.

6. *Zebidius:* Oxy.

10. *Çumeṣịụ*[*s*] *et Trufon:* Oxy.; *cum epistrat(ego):* de Ricci; *cum epist(ratego):* ChLA, which is certainly possible. But *cum ep(istulis) ṃịṣ(sus)* seems equally likely. The first three letters of *trufon*, but not the last three, appear to have been canceled.

11. *Iulius:* Oxy.

12. *Eṭiopịus Chu.*[*:* Oxy.; *Eponuchus:* de Ricci.

13. *Pacebius P*[*:* Oxy.; *P̣acebius* [*P:* ChLA. The plate shows no trace of the second *p*. It must have stood on a tab of papyrus lost before the photograph was taken.

TRANSLATION

ii 5–12: Malochos son of – – –, optio, to Victor Comarinus, vicarius of the dispensator Caesarum. The aforenamed cavalrymen, *praitôn* (?), 50 in number (?), have been measured out for the month Thoth of wheat fifty artabas. Year 14 of the Lords Augusti, Thoth 7.

Also infantry of the century of Beleus:

Beleus Zabdeus. *Other names follow.*

82

Naval Supplies Expended

PRyl. 223; *vidi* II p.

Transcription, commentary, and facsimile:

1. J. de M. Johnson, Victor Martin, and Arthur S. Hunt, *Catalogue of the Greek Papyri in the John Rylands Library, Manchester* II (Manchester 1915) no. 223, p. 370, and plate 23; cited as **Cat.**
2. *ChLA* IV, no. 242.

Transcription and facsimile: Mallon, *Pal.*, plate VIII, no. 2. Dates text in I p.

Text: *CPL*, no. 312.

The items composing this list—pitch, oil, grease, nails, wax, and iron sheets—clearly belong in the category of naval supplies and justify the editors' expansion of *lib* as *lib*(*urnam*) in line 3–4, 9–10, and 16. Whether these supplies were being acquired or expended is less obvious; but the small quantities point to the latter interpretation.

The dating is on paleographical grounds.

The verso is blank.

v idus maịạ[s
picis liq(uidae) in ịṣteg amp˙ i[
olei in lib˙ luci˙ emṇạ s[
sebi in lib˙ luci p ṣ[
].. teres ñ˙ ḷ.[
iv idus mạịaṣ
claui iṇ praetorium˙ fer˙ p˙ viiị[
cerae in ịṣtegis ueterib p xcv [
claui [i]n lib˙ luci˙ fer p i [
clauum in lib ṭimeti fer p iị [
claui in ịṣtegis ṇọụis fer p xi [
resinae [i]n ịṣteg˙ uasa ii [
lamnas ferream ii in lib
ueterem timeti fer p ix s[
iii idus maia]ṣ
].[ ]ḷịb[ ]..[

TRANSLATION

May 11.
liquid pitch for the decks, amphorae 1[?
oil for the liburna of Lucius, half-jar? ½

grease for the liburna of Lucius, pounds ½?
]. . *teres* number 50?

May 12.

nails for the praetorium iron, pounds 8[?
wax for the old decks pounds 95[
nails for the liburna of Lucius, iron, pounds 11
spike for the liburna of Timetus, iron, pounds 2?
nails for the new decks iron, pounds 11
resin for the decks pots 2
iron sheets, 2, for the old
liburna of Timetus iron, pounds 9½

May 13.

]lib[urna

2. *in Piteg(ium); amp(horae):* Cat., and in the apparatus, "*p* seems rather more suitable as the initial letter than *c* or *l*, but is not clearly formed; cf. however the *p* of *empti* (?) in l. 3. In any case the word is no doubt a proper name like *Luci* and *Timeti*." Marichal accepts the reading *Piteg(ium)* but rejects the idea of a personal name, explaining it as a place-name, "perhaps the equivalent of πιττουργεῖον, Strabo 218, the 'place where pitch is prepared', the name of a harbour or dock, for example." The word is a crux, without doubt, partly because the sample of the hand is so small that it offers little comparative material on possible ligatures and variations in the forms of single letters. In lines 8 and 11, however, the ending must surely be the ablative *-is* because of *ueterib* (8) and *nouis* (11). The first two letters of the word resemble each other very closely; and one of Marichal's arguments against reading the initial as *i*, that it has a hook to the right at the foot, applies equally to the second letter in lines 2 and 8. But the first *i* of *timeti* (14) has a hook to the right; and in *in* (10) the whole shaft of the letter is concave on the right. Marichal's other criterion, that the cap at the top of the first letter is suitable for *p* but not for *i*, is refuted by the *i*'s in *liq* (2), *lib* (3), and *in* (10 and 11). Moreover, the second letter is always ligatured with the *t* which follows, whereas *i*, if ligatured at all, is regularly joined with the preceding letter. Cf. *olei* (3), *luci* (4), *claui* (7, 9, 11), and *timeti* (14). For all these reasons I have proposed, in view of the naval context, to see here and in lines 8, 11, and 12 the word στέγη ("deck" or "roof") with a prothetic *i*. The *s* before the *t* is admittedly difficult because of the hook to the right at the foot of the letter in lines 2 and 8. But the hook is absent in lines 11 and 12 and is equally an argument against reading the letter as *i*, while the ligature with the *t* favors *s*.

3. *empti s(emis?):* Cat.; *emin(a) .s(emis)[:* ChLA. The amount, I believe, is right; but before the numeral a unit of measure is wanted, and here one of liquid measure. Perhaps the word began with *(h)emi-*, though Marichal's *(h)emina*, about half a pint, would be an extraordinarily small unit. A numeral could have preceded *s(emis)*. Expand *lib(urnam)*. The names *luci* in lines 3, 4, and 9, and *timeti* in lines 10 and 14 are those of the commanders. One might have expected the name of the liburna; but since each ship's company was regarded as a centuria, it is natural to identify them and the vessel by the name of the trierarch, just as centuries of infantry were identified by their centurions.

4. *p(ondo?) i[:* Cat. The expansion appears certain.

5. [.].*oteres n( ) b[:* Cat.; *Cl[aui u]eteres:* ChLA. Expand *n(umero)*. Against Marichal's reading is the fact that in lines 7 and 9–11 nails are measured by the pound. More probably we have here the plural of κωπητήρ or τροπωτήρ, a leather thong for attaching an oar to a thole-pin, or less likely, of λαμπτήρ, a ship's light. See the glossary in Lionel Casson, *Ancient Mariners* (New York 1959). The *l* is not very satisfactory because the upper stroke tilts to the left; but compare the *l* of *claui* in line 9. Other possible numerals are even less acceptable. ChLA offers no reading.

7. *fer(ri) p(ondo) vii[:* Cat.; *VII*.[*:* ChLA. The expansion *fer(rei)* is also possible.

8. *in Pịtegii veṭẹrib(us):* edd.

10. *clavom:* Cat.; but the spelling with *o* is unlikely at this date; in this hand *o* and *u* are not always distinguished. Cf. the two letters in *praetorium*, line 7. ChLA also reads *clauum*. For the amount, ChLA reads *II*.[; but *i s* is possible.

11. *in Pịtegii:* edd.; *ạctis:* Cat.; *nauis; X̣[:* ChLA. For the *n* of *nouis* cf. *lamnas*, line 13. *nouis* pairs naturally with *ueteribus* in line 8. I do not see how *nauis* would construe as either nominative or genitive.

12. *keramae in Pịtegii vạdạs:* Cat.; *una:* ChLA. I have adopted *resinae* from Marichal.

13. *kamạras:* Cat., and in the apparatus, "*s* of *kamaras* was written through an *m*, and the numeral *ii* has been added above the line. In making this alteration the scribe neglected to emend the termination of *ferream*." ChLA also reads *Lamna*⟦*m*⟧*s*.

14. *Etimeti:* ChLA; I do not understand the notes in the apparatus.

16. [. . . . . .]. *[in] lịb[:* Cat.;]. *ị[n] l[i]b(urnam)[:* ChLA.

83

List of Men and Their Horses, Coh. XX Palmyrenorum

PDur. 97 (inv. D. P. 3 verso) A.D. 251, after August 31

Transcription, commentary, and facsimile: *Final Rep.* v, no. 97 and plates 64–65; *edidit* Gilliam.

Transcription and commentary: J. F. Gilliam, "Some Latin Military Papyri from Dura," *YCS* 11 (1950) 189–209.

Commentary:

1. J. F. Gilliam, "The Prefects in Papyrus Dura Inventory 3 Verso," *CP* 47 (1952) 229–30.
2. J. F. Gilliam, "Trebonianus Gallus and the Decii: III et I Cos," *Studi in Onore de Aristide Calderini e Roberto Paribeni* 1 (Milan 1956) 305–11.

The brief comments in *CRAI* 1933, p. 314; *Münchener Beiträge* 19 (1934) 370–72; and *Prelim. Report* v, p. 297, are no longer of value.

Text: *CPL*, no. 325, reproduces Gilliam's text from *YCS.*

All that is certain about this text has been said by Gilliam in his able discussion in *Final Rep.* v. It is a list of cavalrymen, quite possibly of the same turma, in which all the names but one are accompanied by a description of the man's horse or a statement that he lost it on a given date. The one name, in line 20, stands alone; and this, in view of the failure to give valuations for the horses in lines 19–24, raises the suspicion (which cannot be tested) that the document may for some reason have been left incomplete.

The men are probably named in order of seniority as they appeared in the roster of the cohort; but they are not identified even by date of enlistment. The only information about them is their status in regard to mounts, while conversely, in Gilliam's phrase, "a listing by equites was the most practical way of presenting data about horses." Other peculiarities which he notes are the fact that the descriptions of the horses are clearly taken over unchanged from the letters, such as **99** and **100**, which accompanied their original assignment to a member of the xx Palmyrenorum; that the action of the official who approved the horse is variously expressed by *probatus*, *aestimatus*, and *signatus*; and that the valuations of the horses in lines 2, 4, 5, 9, 10, 11, 13, 14, 16, and 17 appear to have been added after the body of the text was written. At least, that is what line 13 seems to indicate, for there the clerk first added, then erased, a valuation which was out of place because the entry is one for the loss of a horse.

The best evidence that the descriptions are unchanged from the letters, even though the names of emperors who have undergone damnatio memoriae are duly suppressed, is line 5, where a horse acquired in A.D. 245 is still called *bimum* in 251.

With all this, many uncertainties remain. Gilliam points out that we do not know whether this is a routine report or a special one (it should be said that at any rate it is all in one hand and drawn up at one time), that the purport of the valuations is not evident, and that line 18 in its present state merely complicates the problem. If we restore *sal[ui* in its literal sense, then by implication the men in lines 1–17 are casualties in some sense; and in any case this heading divides the turma, if all these men are members of the same one, into two series.

Certain conclusions can none the less be drawn. Whatever the actual purpose of the text, it is obvious that it could have served three interrelated functions. First, it was an inventory of the horses in the possession of the equites of the cohort. Second, it was a summary of the cohort's situation in respect to cavalry—the number of men without mounts, the length of time since they lost their horses, the ages of the horses available, and so on. Finally, the list was a financial record. From it the lost horses could be debited to the appropriate accounts, whether of individual soldiers or some quaestura, and the current valuation of horses in service could be ascertained, along with the name of the soldier responsible for each.

The date of the text, Gilliam shows, is after August 31, 251 (line 22), but probably not a great deal later. Six of the nineteen horses mentioned have been lost, and nine of the rest range in age from seven to over thirteen years old. (Five are nine or older.) Moreover, five of the 19 horses were acquired in 251, between January 22 (line 14) and May 14 (line 17). If this is a representative sample, it shows a desperate state of affairs, with a fourth of the cohort's horses having to be replaced in a period of four months and a third of the personnel still lacking mounts, while one of the three newly acquired horses whose ages are known was already *aequatus*, i.e. seven or more years old (see Gilliam in *YCS*, p. 199). But the other two are only four years old; and the papyrus itself is evidence of strenuous effort by both the government and the army to cope with the situation.

The recto is **47**.

amịsit eq ex prịḍ[ie *ca.* 18 co]ṣ *vacat*
[o]g̣ẹḷus mạlchi ⟦eq quadrimum ṭe.[*ca.* 24]ụs albis ⟦ṇ f⟧ n′ f a′ d prob˙ a tunc preff xiii
kal nouembr pres et aḷbino cos 𐆖 cxxv⟧
[m]alchus goṛaṣ amiṣịṭ eq ị[*ca.* 27] *vacat*
[aur]ẹḷ alex[a]ṇḍ[rus] e[q a]equatuṃ .[*ca.* 25] prob˙ ab attilio cosmino tụṇc cos xvii kal
april iii et i cos 𐆖 cxxv
[*ca.* 22] . [*ca.* 25]. [. .]ẹạṭ bimum nigrum n f a d pṛọb˙ a tunc preff iiii kal ianuarias
tittiano cos 𐆖 cxxv
[. . .].[. . .].[. . . . . . .].[. .] ạṃịṣị[t eq *ca.* 25] *vacat*
ṃ[o]ç̣iṃụs aṇ[ton]ini amiṣịṭ [eq *ca.* 25] *vacat*
[.]ẹ.ị[. a]beḍṣạḷṃe eq cọṃṃa[genum(?) *ca.* 22]proṛẹṣạratum pedibus posṭẹrioribus albis
s n prob˙ ab atiliọ cosmino tun⟨c⟩ cos
xviị ḳ[a]ḷ april iii et i cos 𐆖 cxxv
[. . . .]ṛnab[u]ṣ [o]gạ eq e.[.]. . .[.]ạṛ.[.].[*ca.* 23] ṃuṛiṇum n′ f d′ et a′ s′ prob a tuṇç̣
pṛẹf̣f iiii kal ianuarias tittiano cos 𐆖 cxxv

[. . . . .]. . o. . . usa. eq ẹ.ẹ. . [. .]. . . . [*ca.* 23] p̣rob a tunc preff diẹ ẹṭ c̣ọṣ ṣṣ 𐆖 cxxv
. [.]. . us ụhạbalathi ẹq [. . .]. [*ca.* 23] probatum a tunc preff iiii idus septẹmbr ạemil ii et
aqul cos 𐆖 cxxv
a[u]ṛẹl bạrs[. . . .]ṣ aṃịsiṭ ẹq [e]x̣[*ca.* 21 co]ṣ ⟦𐆖 . . x̣⟧
. . . [. . . .]ḥ. lc̣uṣ ẹq qụạḍ[rimum *ca.* 22 pe]dibus posterioribus albis s n proḅ aḅ aṭịlio
c̣osmino tunc [c]ọs xị kạl f̣ebr ii[i] et i cos 𐆖 cxxv
ạ[. . . .] ạbuṃạṛius . . . . . . [*ca.* 25] russeobadium n a′ d′ aestimatuṃ a p̣ọṃp̣ọ[nio] letiano
u e proc aug̣g ṇṇ ị[d]ib april
iii et i cos 𐆖 xxxxv ẹṭ ẹ quaesur 𐆖 lv
ạ[ur]ẹl ṃaṃbogeus [eq] qụ[a]ḍriṃ[um *ca.* 10]. . . . [*ca.* 6 a] pomponio letiano u e proc
augg ṇ ṇ . . . . [pridi]ẹ [i]dus maias iii et i cos 𐆖 cxxv
iṭeṃ sal[*ca.* 13] *vacat*
barhạthes maesọm eq aeqụ[atam *ca.* 10]. . . ạlidam s n′ prob˙ a tunc preff xi kal octobr
aemil ii et [a]qul c̣os
a[u]ṛẹl ṭheodorus *vacat*
. . . [.]e. s ṣạḍạḷạthi ẹq qụạḍ[ri]ṃạṃ bạḍịo. . nam p̣ẹdib[u]s prioribus inalbis s n′ signata ạ
l[ic]iṇnio p̣acatiano tunc dục iiii iḍus aug tittiano cos
ịạṇ[5 amisi]ṭ eq[ ] p̣rịḍịe ḳạl ṣe[p]ṭẹmbr i[i]i et i cos
ba. ạ[*ca.* 12 e]q aequạtaṃ russeọṣọṛdịḍạm ṇ[. .] s[ ] signata a licinnio pacatiano tunc duc
iii iduṣ [au]g tittiano ⟨c⟩os
⟦b. . e⟧ e. [*ca.* 10]. . eq aeq[u]ạ[tu]m . c̣eriṇ[. .]m gla[6 n] f′ s′ probatum ab ulpio
tertio tunc duc xv ḳ[al m]ạias iii et ii cos

1. This line was written to take the place of the canceled part of line 2. Gilliam, in app., "The date . . . is quite possibly the same as that in line 22."

2. [. .]. *lus:* D; in app., [*Og*]*ẹlus; . ẹ.* [*;* in app., *c̣ẹr*[or *ṭẹr*[, perhaps *ceruinum* or *cerinum.* Expand: *eq*(*uum*)*; n*(*otatis*) *f*(*emore*) *a*(*rmo*) *d*(*extris*)*; prob*(*atum*)*; pr*(*a*)*ef*(*ectis*)*; pr*(*a*)*es*(*ente*). On the identity of the prefects see Gilliam's article listed above under "Commentary."

3. *C̣ọra:* D; Gilliam, in app., noting that *eq* seems to be followed by a date not preceded, as in line 1, by *ex*, "If there is any real difference . . . *ex* may indicate the effective date for the records as distinguished from the actual date," comparing **64** i 23, 29, 35, and elsewhere, **87**, and **99**.

4. *alex*[*a*]*ṇḍ*[*er*]*;* a]*equatu*[*m* . .]. [*:* D. Six letters are needed for the space between *alex* and *eq.* Expand *co*(*n*)*s*(*ularis*), i.e., governor of the province. Gilliam in app. notes Rostovtzeff's suggestion that this man is the Agilius Cosmianus of *Cod. Just.* 8.55.1 (A.D. 249), accepted in *PIR*[2] II, xi, no. 457a.

5.]. *bimum:* D; in app., "The letter before *bimum* is either *c* or *t.*" Similarly, *f* is possible instead of *e.* This line evidently began somewhat differently from the others, for in 2, 4, 17, 19, and elsewhere the abbreviation *eq* follows the soldier's name and in turn is followed immediately by the word indicating the horse's age, while here *bimum* is displaced far to the right. Line 8 may also have a different pattern; and lines 10–12 and 15 are doubtful. For the expansion of the abbreviations, see on line 2.

7. [.]. . *iṃ* [. .]*us:* D. The first *m* is highly uncertain; *ti* is possible in place of *ci*; and there is space for another letter between the second *m* and *u.*

8. [. . .]. [. *A*]*beḍṣạḷ*[*m*]*ẹ; cum* . . . [;]*proroṣtratum:* D. For *com* instead of *cum*, cf. the combination *co* in *cos*, lines 8, 17, and 21, and in *cosmino*, line 4. The reading *prorostratum* has the virtue of making sense, though the word is not otherwise attested and it is not clear how a horse's muzzle would protrude enough to be a distinguishing mark; but the letter after the second *r* can hardly be *o.* In *YCS* Gilliam, after *prorus*, reads "possibly *c̣ịṛạ*," and says "*c̣ịṛ*⟨*r*⟩*ạṭum* may be suggested in desperation." I have been unable to study the original and have nothing to propose. Expand *s*(*ine*) *n*(*ota*).

9. This is a line run over from the entry in line 8. The *x* of the numeral is under the last *s* of *posterioribus.*

10. [. . . . . .]*rnab*[.]. [.]. *.:* D. Gilliam in *YCS*: "]*ṛṇab*[suggests *Ba*]*rnab*[*i* or some other form of that name, but . . . space requires about four letters both before and after]*ṛṇab*[, and there should be two names." If *commagenum* in line 8 is right, the word here after *eq* may be a similar descriptive term. Expand: *n*(*otatis*) *f*(*emore*) *d*(*extro*) *et a*(*rmo*) *s*(*inistro*).

11. [. . . .]. *.o. . . usa eq* . [.]. . [. . .]. . . [*:* D; in app., "Apparently *-usa* is the end of a name in the genitive."

12. . [. . .]. *.us; eq* [. . . . . .]. [*:* D; in app., "The name of the Palmyrene prince is spelled *Vhabalathus* on his coins; H. Mattingly and E. A. Sydenham, *The Roman Imperial Coinage* v, 2 (1933), p. 585. Except for the present text, the spelling *Vabalathus* is regularly used in these papyri."

13. *ẹq* [.].[*:* D; in app., "*Bars[emia]s* is one of several possibilities. The denarius sign and numerals at the right edge of the column and the line connecting them with the entry to the left [which were added by mistake] were sponged out when the clerk discovered his error. He had completed at least three figures, presumably *cxx*."

14. [.......]...*ḷẹ*.. *eq q*[.......].[*:* D; in app., "*Eq q[uadrimu]ṃ* is an attractive restoration."

15. *Ạ* [.....].*bu*.[.]..*ius* ..[....]..[*:* D. The first name is probably *a[urel]*; *abumarius* is unexampled and hence doubtful. Expand: *n(otato) a(rmo) d(extro); u(iro) e(gregio) proc(uratore) aug(ustorum) n(ostrorum) (duorum)*. The emperors are Gallus and probably Volusian.

16. This line, like line 9, is run over from the preceding one. The first *i* of *iii* is under *c* of *proc* in line 15.

et .quaesur: D; in app., "*Et*... appears sound.... However, above the *t* there is a small, hooked stroke such as is found elsewhere only in the cap of *f* and, occasionally, *e*. There is also a slanting stroke across the lower part of the *e* of *et*... perhaps a correction was made at this point. If the two superfluous strokes are combined, they can be read as *f*, superimposed on the *et*. An *e*, combined with the *t*, is perhaps a more doubtful possibility...*f(it) quaes⟨t⟩or(ia)* or *e quaes⟨t⟩ur(a)* may be suggested.... Possibly *f(it) quae sor( )* or *sur( )* is more promising. At present it cannot be determined whether the two sums are to be added or whether the second includes the first." The reading adopted in the text assumes that in this one case the liability for the value of the horse was divided between the soldier and the treasury (of the cohort or garrison? [Cf. **98**, no. 2] or of the province?) and that the total was only 100 denarii. Note that in **75** 1–10 the soldier has been given the price of a horse, not less than 100 denarii. For the loss of the *t* of *quaestura* cf. **1** xliv 2: *cum epis⟨t⟩ul(is)*, and **63** ii 21: *kas⟨t⟩rae.*

17. *ṇṇ* ....[..].... [*I*]*dus:* D. The restoration [*pridi*]*ẹ* is of course only as secure as the reading of the final *e*.

18. The line is deeply indented, *i* of *item* coming under [*eq*] in line 17. It is evidently a heading or subdivision of some sort. Gilliam (*Prelim. Report* v, p. 297) suggests that *sal*[may be a place-name giving the post of the men whose names follow, or *sal*[*ui*, contrasting with an earlier category of casualties. He notes that the entries in lines 19–24 show examples of both of the types in 1–17 and follow the same pattern except that there is no money valuation at the end of the descriptive entries in lines 19, 21, 23, and 24.

19. *Ṃaesuṃṃ;*]..[..]. *ạlidam:* D; in app., "Perhaps ... *calidam*, though the *c* is not entirely satisfactory," quoting Isidorus, *Etym.* 12.1.52: [equi] *qui frontem albam* [habent], *calidi* [appellantur]. Paleographically, *pal⟨l⟩idam* might be more acceptable.

20. D in app., "This line may have been left incomplete, though a long entry could not have been added later since lines 19 and 21 tend to converge at the right. Otherwise, apparently one must conclude that Theodorus had never been assigned a horse. If so, it is almost certain that the men under the heading [in line 18] are not arranged according to their dates of enlistment."

21. ...[..].*s*.[.].*ṭhi; ba*.[.].[..]*nam; Ḷ[i]ẹiṇṇiọ:* D. App. in *YCS*: "The first letter in the line may be *r* or possibly *g*." The first three letters could also be read *pri* or *pae*. App. in *Rep.* v: "The word beginning *ba-* is probably a compound of *badius*, perhaps *baḍ[i]ọ[ca]nam*.... The *TLL* lists *inalbeo*, *inalbesco*, and *inalbo*, but not *inalbus*." The case of *signata*, if actually nominative, implies a new sentence, as also in line 23.

22. .*ạ*..[–7– *amisi*]*ṭ:* D; in app., *YCS*, "The line begins with *s* or *i*"; *Rep.* v, "There is room to restore *ex* before *priḍie*, to make the form of the entry correspond to that in line 1, but see the commentary on line 3."

23. *Ba*..[*; Tittiano cos:* D; in app., "*Russeosordidus*, if correct, is new. For the letters that follow I propose *n(ota)* [ ] *s(inistro)*." For *signata* see on line 21.

24. ...*ẹ*. [–14–].; .*eriṇ*[..]*m gla*[*ucum n.*] *f's'*; *XV*[......]*ias:* D; in app., "The word after *aeq*[*u*]*ạ*-[*tu*]*m* may be *ẹerin*[*u*]*m*, perhaps spelled with two *n*'s or -[*eu*]*m*, though the color elsewhere is used only of fruits and vegetables. *Glaucus* might describe either the horse's color or, if that was already given, his eyes." The plate seems to show a trace of ink after *m* of *aequatum* and before the *c*, which could also be *t*, of *cerin*. In place of *eri*, just possibly *elu*; and *gla* might be completed as *gla*[*br-* instead of *gla*[*uc-*, noting a hairless patch somewhere on the horse's skin.

In the date, only *kal* could follow a numeral as high as *xv*; but the first *a* of *maias* is very uncertain, so that *iun*]*ias* and *iul*]*ias* remain possible. Expand: [*n(otat-)*] *f(emore) s(inistro)*.

TRANSLATION

lost his horse effective [date]

Ogelus son of Malchus: *canceled:* horse, four years old, [– – feet] white, right thigh and shoulder branded, approved by the then Prefects October 20, 246: denarii 125.

Malchus Goras: lost his horse [*date.*]

Aurelius Alexander: horse seven or more years old [– – –] approved by Atilius Cosminus, then governor, March 16, 251: denarii 125.

[*Name* – – –] two years old, black, right thigh and shoulder branded, approved by the then Prefects December 29, 245: denarii 125.

[*Name*]*:* lost [his horse *date.*]

Mocimus son of Antoninus: lost [his horse *date.*]

[*Name*] son of Abedsalmes: horse, Commagenian (?) [– – –] (?), white hind feet, no brand, approved by Atilius Cosminus, then governor, March 16, 251: denarii 125.

[*Name*] son of Ogas(?): horse [– – –], mouse-colored, right thigh and left shoulder branded, approved by the then Prefects, December 29, 245: denarii 125.

[*Name*] horse [– – –] approved by the then Prefects, day and year above: denarii 125.

[*Name*] son of Vabalathus: horse [– – –] approved by the then Prefects, September 10, 249: denarii 125.

Aurelius Bars[emias(?)]: lost his horse effective [*date*]

[*Name*]: horse, four years old [– – –] white hind feet, no brand, approved by Atilius Cosminus, then governor, January 22, 251: denarii 125.

Aurelius(?) Abumarius(?): [horse – – –] red-bay, right shoulder branded, appraised by Pomponius Letianus, vir egregius, procurator of our two Augusti, April 13, 251: denarii 45 and from the treasury 55.

Aurelius Mambogeus: horse, four years old [– – – –] by Pomponius Letianus, vir egregius, procurator of our two Augusti, May 14, 251: denarii 125.

Also *sal*[

Barathes son of (?) Maesomas: mare, seven or more years old [– – –], no brand, approved by the then Prefects September 21, 249.

Aurelius Theodorus

[*Name*] son of Sadalathus(?): mare, four years old, frosty(?) bay, white front feet, no brand, sealed by Licinnius Pacatianus, then dux, August 10, 245.

Ian (?) [– – *name*: lost] his horse August 31, 251.

Ba[– – – *name*]: mare, seven or more years old, red-sooty, left [– –] branded, sealed by Licinnius Pacatianus, then dux, August 11, 245.

[*Name*]: horse, seven or more years old, wax-yellow(?) bald(?) [– –] left thigh [branded], approved by Ulpius Tertius, then dux, April(?) 17, 248.

84

Expense Account?

PVindob. L 111; *vidi* II p.

Transcription and facsimile:

1. C. Wessely, *Studien* 14: *Die ältesten lateinischen und griechischen Papyri Wiens* (Leipzig 1914) plate VIII. Cited as W.
2. Idem, *Schriftt.* no. 11. Superseded by 1.

Text: *CPL*, no. 313.

The only reasons for supposing that this may be a military text are the language and script and the fact that the account is in denarii. None of these is conclusive. The ablatives in lines 2 and 6–7 suggest a record of prices paid but may instead be valuations, as in an inventory of household goods or a list of items in a dowry. Since none of the things named has been identified, no decision is possible. The papyrus appears to be complete at the top, right, and bottom, and so may have been cut from a roll expressly for this list.

The dating is Wessely's, on the basis of the hand.

The verso is blank.

]ṃịṣem	𐆖 uginti quinque
].niṣem	𐆖 tribus
]ạṭer	𐆖 sexs
]..idem	𐆖 octo
]um	𐆖 quatuor
].m	𐆖̣ ụno
].ạḷem	𐆖 uno

1.]*icem:* W.
2.]*nicem:* W.
3.].*rem:* W. One could also read]*ṭạer*
4.].*dem:* W.
5.]*em:* W.
6.]*m:* W.
7.]*em:* W.

85

Record (?) of Delivery of Barley

PGissBibl. Inv. 282 First half of III p.

Transcription and commentary: Hans Georg Gundel, *Kleine Beiträge zum römischen Heerwesen* (Giessen 1940).

Text: *Sammelbuch* vi, ii, no. 9202.

Although the recipients of the barley in this text all have military rank, it is impossible to be sure whether this is a military text or half civilian. It may be an order to deliver the grain or a memorandum that a given person or village has delivered it. At least it is not a receipt; nor is it necessary to suppose that all the men named were members of the same unit. They may have been assigned to get barley for a number of alae and cohorts; and so much of the editor's discussion of the centurion's position and the distribution of the grain is left with no firm basis.

The dating is the editor's and is on paleographical grounds.

φρανιω σευηρω ☧ και φλαυιω δημητριω
δουπλικαριου και δημοσθενη επονυχω
σησκουβλιταριω και σεραπιωνι γερμα-
νω σιμιαφορω κριθ(ης) (αρταβας) σ̄

1. Read φρανιω, i.e. φλαυιω, in place of φρανιω? Or perhaps [α]φρανιω?

TRANSLATION

To Franius (Flavius?) Severus, centurion, and Flavius Demetrius, duplicarius, and Demosthenes Eponuchus, sesquiplicarius, and Serapion Germanus, signifer, of barley artabas 200.

86

Money for Equites Promoti?

PGrenf. II 110 A.D. 293

Transcription and facsimile:

1. Bernard P. Grenfell and Arthur S. Hunt, *Greek Papyri, Series II: New Classical Fragments and Other Greek and Latin Papyri* (Oxford 1897) no. 110 and plate 5.
2. *EL*, no 30 (plate 21).

Transcription, facsimile, and commentary: *ChLA* III, no. 205.

Text: *CPL*, no. 142, reproduces the text of Grenfell and Hunt.

Next to nothing can be made of this scrap. The mention in line 1 of equites promoti (if correctly restored) establishes the possibility of its being a military record; but if the beginning of line 4 ought to be read *data fide*, as seems likely, then the text may concern a loan, deposit, or some other fiduciary transaction, one party to which may be civilian. *PDura* 129, in which a decurion and a cavalryman get public money in the presence of witnesses for the purchase of barley, illustrates this sort of possibility nicely.

The month-date in line 3 is of course not directly connected with the consulate in line 6 and may refer to a wholly different year.

The verso is presumably blank.

No translation is offered because of the lack of any connected sense.

[*ca.* 15 equit]ịbụṣ promotis dd nn diocletiani et ma[x]ịṃịạṇ[i augg] ẹṭ
[constantii et maximiani] nobịlisṣimorum caẹsarum ạgẹsç. .a[. .] . . . . . .i.[
[*ca.* 20].enṭum uịginti ex ḍịe septimum k[al] ịạnuạṛịas
Hand 2 [*ca.* 20]. date fidẹị num HS o[ct]ogentum uig[inti] . . . . . .ti
[*ca.* 17] . . . .uus ịị ẹ. . .s eṭ qụạ[dring]enti decem ṭạ[. . .]m[. .]ṣui
[diocletiano aug v et] ṃaximiano aug iiii coss ạsserente marciano a[ct]ụario vi

1. [*equit*]*ịb*(*us*)*:* ChLA. Expand: *d*(*ominorum*) *n*(*ostrorum*)*; aug*(*ustorum*).
2. *ag*. . .[. .]. .[. . . . . .]. .*i:* Grenf.; *ag*. . . . .*:* EL;]. . . .*ḍi:* ChLA.
3. *ḍ*[*i*]*e:* edd.; *Ianuar*[*i*]*as:* Grenf. Perhaps restore [*octo*]*gentum*, as in line 4?
4. *uig*[*inti*] . .*ịṇ*. . .*ti:* ChLA. Read *dat*⟨*a*⟩*e*, *num*(*morum*) (*sestertium*).
5. *ỊỊ ẹqụas:* Grenf.; *uus ỊỊ ẹ*. . .*e:* EL; *uụs ḥ*. . . . . .*:* ChLA; *te*. . .*ṃ*. . .*ṣụi:* Grenf., EL; *tạ*[. . . . .]. .*sui:* ChLA.
6. *decerente:* Grenf., "lege *decernente*"; *ạsserente:* EL; . . . *VI*: Grenf.

V

Official Correspondence

A very large part of the public as well as the private business of the Roman world was conducted in the formal guise of letters. Governors of provinces and field commanders of armies reported to the Senate or the emperor, as the case might be, in the epistolary form; and their reports were called merely *litterae* or *epistulae*.[1] A special genus of such reports is formed by the *litterae laureatae*, or simply *laureatae*, announcing victories;[2] but the fact is that all sorts of communications, outside the army and within it, took the form of letters. In Cicero's correspondence we find reports and commands passing as letters between Pompey and other officers of the senatorial party;[3] the classic example of the exchange of reports and instructions between an emperor and a subordinate is of course Pliny's correspondence with Trajan; and examples of communications between generals or armies or even single legions are to be found passim in Tacitus' *Histories* in his account of the intrigues of the year 69. At a still lower level, the countless petitions, receipts, directives, and the like among the papyri furnish examples ad libitum of the epistolary form. It is cause for astonishment, then, as well as for regret, that so few examples of official military correspondence survive. For the entire period covered by this study, only two military letters have come to us complete or nearly so (**87** and **98**, no. 2) and only half a dozen more in sufficiently large pieces to make their content reasonably clear. The state of **89** is consequently all the more to be deplored, for its 57 letters of A.D. 216 would obviously have been of extraordinary interest.

89, however, at least supplies considerable information on the forms observed in military epistolography and the routines of handling it. The opening formula is the customary one in Roman letters—the name of the writer in the nominative, the person addressed in the dative, and *salutem*—except that in nos. 6–8 the recipient's name stands first, followed by those of the two writers. This may have been a mark of respect, since the letters are addressed to the tribune of the cohort and the writers are of lower rank. In **99** Marius Maximus, governor of Syria, addresses the prefect of the cohort as *ualentino suo*; and *suo* recurs in **87**, **88**, **100**, and **105**, in which the relationship, where known, is the same. In the

[1] E.g. Suet. *Iulius* 56.6: "Epistulae quoque eius ad senatum extant"; Tac. *Ann.* 15.8: "composuit [Paetus] ad Caesarem litteras quasi confecto bello, uerbis magnificis, rerum uacuas."

[2] Pliny, *Hist. Nat.* 15.133: "laurus Romanis praecipue laetitiae uictoriarumque nuntia additur litteris," and cf. e.g. Livy 45.1, Tac. *Agric.* 18.

[3] E.g. *Ad Atticum* 8.12 A–D.

body of the letter officers address each other as *domini* (pl.) or *domine*,[4] *domine frater*,[5] or *frater*,[6] *ἀδελφέ* in Greek.[7] The governor of Syria uses no closing formula in **99**, and possibly not in **100**. In **98**, no. 2, line 3, a circular letter, the formula is *opto bene ualeatis*; and in **87** 10, *uale, frater karissime*. In **89** the more elaborate *opto te, domine frater, felicissimum bene ualere* seems to have been used regularly in the Latin letters,[8] *ἔρρωσο* in the Greek.[9]

The address on the verso of the letters in **89** has the name and title of the addressee in capitals and the name and title of the sender in cursive, except in **89**, no. 18, where the dative case implies the recipient although the name is in cursive. (But see ad loc.) It is noteworthy that the titles are limited to *tribunus cohortis* and the like, without specifying the number and name of the unit. This may be an indication that the letters traveled in large packets which were addressed to the headquarters of the various units, so that the individual letters needed only the name and title as address. It seems likely that the cursive notation of the writer's name and title may have been added when the letter was received; but it is possible that it too was written by the clerk who addressed the letter. In any case, its presence undoubtedly facilitated the process of finding a particular letter in the roll.

It is certain at least that each letter was docketed upon receipt with the day, month, and year in full; and at some point, whether or not at once, single letters were glued together to make a roll for filing. The first label in **116** reads *epistulae equorum e*.[, and may be from a roll of letters like those in **99** and **100**. The crossing out of Geta's name in **99**, no. 1, of A.D. 208, which must be connected with his damnatio memoriae in 212, is interesting evidence not only for the vindictive thoroughness with which his memory was expunged but also for the fact that such files of letters were still regarded as "live" material four years after the letters were written.

Additional details are found in the literary sources. Under both the republic and the empire, the commander of an army included his army in the salutation of his letters to the Senate;[10] and Caracalla added the name of Julia Domna, as is natural in view of her title of "mater castrorum."[11] Caesar is credited by Suetonius with introducing an improvement in the form of these official epistolae, which Roberts believes consisted in the use of papyrus as a codex.[12] And finally we learn from Tacitus (*Hist.* 4.25) that at least occasionally, perhaps regularly, official correspondence was read to the soldiers: "Hordeonius exemplares omnium litterarum quibus per Gallias Britanniamque et Hispanias auxilia orabat exercitui recitauit, instituitque pessimum facinus, ut epistulae aquiliferis legionum traderentur, a quis ante militi quam ducibus legebantur." How long this procedure was followed is difficult to say. The verb *instituit* implies at least some continuance; and an alleged letter of Marcus

[4] **89**, no. 1, lines 2 and 9; no. 4, i, line 3; perhaps no. 12, i, line 7.

[5] **88**, no. 2, line 5; cf. *domine fili* in **91**, no. 1, i, line 5; no. 2, i, line 4.

[6] **89**, no. 43, line 7.

[7] **89**, no. 16, line 2.

[8] It is found in nos. 12, lines 7–9; 38, lines 7–10; 39, lines 9–10; no. 46; and 48, lines 6–9. In **89**, no. 1, lines 9–12, it is extended further: *opto uos, domini, felicissimos multis annis bene ualere*. Cf. no. 5, lines 11–12.

[9] **89**, no. 9, line 7. In nos. 17 and 29, the formula becomes *πολλοῖς χρόνοις εὔχομαι ὑγιαίνειν* and *ἔρρωσθαί σε εὔχομαι, ἀδελφέ, πολλοῖς χρόνοις*.

[10] Cicero, *Ad. fam.* 5.2, 7, 10a; 15.1 and 2. Cf. Dio 69.14.3: *ὁ Ἁδριανὸς γράφων πρὸς τὴν βουλὴν οὐκ ἐχρήσατο τῷ προοιμίῳ τῷ συνήθει τοῖς αὐτοκράτορσιν ὅτι "εἰ αὐτοί τε καὶ οἱ παῖδες ὑμῶν ὑγιαίνετε, εὖ ἂν ἔχοι· ἐγὼ καὶ τὰ στρατεύματα ὑγιαίνομεν."*

[11] Dio 77.18.2: *τὸ ὄνομα αὐτῆς ἐν ταῖς πρὸς τὴν βουλὴν ἐπιστολαῖς ὁμοίως τῷ τε ἰδίῳ καὶ τῷ τῶν στρατευμάτων, ὅτι σῴζεται.*

[12] Suet. *Iulius* 56.6; C. H. Roberts, *JRS* 23 (1933) 139–42.

Aurelius in SHA (*Niger* 4.1–2) runs: "Pescennium mihi laudas. . . . itaque misi litteras recitandas ad signa quibus eum . . . mille nostris praeesse iussi." The letter which was read *ad signa* was of course an officer's commission,[13] so that the parallel with Hordeonius' action is not exact; and there is little if any doubt that the letter of Marcus Aurelius is a forgery.[14] But a forgery to be convincing must be as like the real article as possible; and the alleged usage of reading commissions *ad signa* may indicate that Hordeonius' innovation lasted until the time when the biographies in the SHA were written. The idea is unlikely to be a complete invention of the author of the life of Niger, for it would have been quite as natural in giving commissions to notify the commanding generals and let them announce the appointments.

The letters in **89**, to return to the papyri, are typical of military correspondence in general in other respects. For example, the bulk of them are in Latin, the normal official language of the army; but there are a fair number in Greek—e.g. nos. 2, 9, 16, 17, 19, and 23—enough to prove that Greek as well as Latin was used on occasion by the army.[15] Six of the letters certainly, and others possibly, involve procuratores Augusti.[16] The *signifer* of no. 15, since signiferi were responsible for the rationes of their units, the *equum* of no. 42, and the *pecoribus* of no. 43 point to the possibility that some of the letters in the roll are concerned with financial affairs or the annona; but these are only hints which do not suffice even to establish a probability. Most of them, it is clear, are about personnel of the xx Palmyrenorum. (See further under **89**.)

It is to be noted that both no. 4 and no. 12 consist of letters to which are appended lists of names, and that the names in no. 4 are in a different hand from that of the letter.

Of the other letters, **87** is to be connected with **54** i 14–15, **64**, and **74**, as one step in the process of incorporating recruits into the army; **99** and **100** illustrate how horses were supplied, not merely to the cohort but to specific equites; **90** and **91**, and perhaps **88**, are concerned with the enforcement of regulations. **98** is a file of circular letters, all concerned with finances in one way or another; **101** mentions *frumentatio* but the actual subject may be discipline. **102**, wrongly published at first as a financial account, is a file of letters or copies of letters whose subject cannot be ascertained. **92** is the outstanding example of a letter accompanied by a list of names. The letter, unfortunately not restorable with any continuity, occupied two or more columns and dealt with three separate detachments of soldiers and at least one expeditio, while there were eight columns of names with somewhat over 200 men in all. The names are arranged by centuries and turmae in three lists according to the three detachments with a total at the beginning of each list. The soldiers' dates of enlistment are not used.

Since **92** is on the verso of a slightly older partial roster (**8**), it is very probably not an original letter but either a draft of a letter to be sent or a copy of one either sent or received.

94 and **95** are from the recto and verso of the same roll. The variety of hands in the

[13] Cf. Vegetius 2.7: "tribunus maior per epistolam sacram imperatoris iudicio destinatur. minor tribunus peruenit ex labore."

[14] David Magie, *The Scriptores Historiae Augustae*, Loeb ed., vol. 1, introd. xix–xxi.

[15] The Greek letters in **89** are probably from or to civil officials; but the receipts in Greek in **74**, **76**, and **78** are for transactions within the army.

[16] Nos. 4, 5, 6, 14, 15, and 18. The phrase *τοὺς δοθέντας μοι στρατιώτας* in nos. 2 and 41 could be a civil official speaking. Cf. Pliny's scruples about supplying escorts for a procurator (*Ep.* 10.27–28) and note that no. 4 in this roll contains two columns of soldiers' names. **88** and **98** also concern procurators.

surviving fragments is evidence that the recto probably consisted of a roll of letters. The verso is more of a problem because the arrangement of the names in frag. b by consulships, with notations besides the names, would be unusual in a letter, while the appearance of at least four hands on the verso makes it improbable that the text was a roster of any sort.

Most of the remaining texts in this category (**93**, **97**, **104**–7, **111**–**13**, and **115**) are probably bits of the letters and rolls already discussed; but thus far it has been impossible to place them in any connection with the larger fragments.

Letters Concerning Personnel

87

Certified Copy of a Letter About Recruits

POxy. VII 1022; *vidi* — ca. February 24, 103
British Museum inv. no. 2049

Transcription, commentary, and facsimile of lines 1–25: Bernard P. Grenfell and Arthur S. Hunt, *The Oxyrhynchus Papyri* VII, no. 1022 and plate 1.

Transcription, commentary, and complete facsimile: *ChLA* III, no. 215.

Transcription and commentary: Wilcken, *Chrestomathie*, no. 453. The text is that of Grenfell and Hunt.

Transcription and translation: *Sel. Pap.*, no. 421. Line 1 is omitted.

Transcription and facsimile: Mallon, *Pal.*, plate 13, no. 1. Lines 1–24 only; and a few letters are cropped from the right end of some lines.

Text and commentary: Daris, no. 4.

Commentary:

1. J. F. Gilliam, "Enrollment in the Roman Imperial Army," *Eos* 48, 2: *Symbolae Raphaeli Taubenschlag Dedicatae* (Warsaw 1957) 207–16.
2. Sergio Daris, "Osservazioni ad alcuni papiri di carattere militare," *Aegyptus* 38 (1958) 151–58.

I have not seen the next two, which I cite from Cavenaile.

3. A Calderini, "Reclute romane in Egitto," *Varietas* 15 (1918) 303.
4. R. Cagnat, *Bulletin de la Société nationale des Antiquaires de France*, 1918, pp. 122–24.

Text: *CPL*, no. 111, reproduces the text of the original editors.

The purport of this text is so obvious as to need little comment beyond reference to Gilliam's demonstration (see above) that *in numeros referri* (lines 5–6) means "to have one's name officially placed on the roster." What we have here is a copy of the original letter, including the docket which recorded the date of its receipt. The cornicularius of the cohort certifies the copy; but the purpose for which it was made is unknown.

February 24 is the date when the letter was received at the headquarters of the cohort. It was of course written not long before; but the date of this copy is unknown. It may have been made several years later.

The original editors distinguish a second hand in lines 24–31; and Wilcken supposed that line 1 was by a third hand. Since there are only two letters in line 1, certainty is not possible; but the sense makes it probable that the two letters are simply larger forms of the same hand as the body of the copy. Lines 24–26 also seem to be in the same hand, as comparison of *priscum* in lines 13 and 26, and *er* of *frater*, line 10, with the last letters of *per*, line 25, will show. Only the notation of Avidius Arrianus in lines 27–31 may be different; but the sample is too small for certainty. In the original letter Minicius Italus' subscription in line 10 must also have been in a different hand, his own.

The verso is blank.

ẹx̣(emplum)
c] miniciuṣ ịtalụ[s] c̣elsiano suo .[
sal[u]ṭem
tirones sex̣s probatos a mẹ iṇ
coh· cui praees· in nume-
ros referri iube ex x̅i̅ February 19
kalenḍas martias noṃi-
na eorum et icon[i]ṣmos
huic epistulae subiec̣ị
uale frater karissiṃ[e]
c· ueturium gemellụṃ
annor· xxi· sine i
c· longinum priscum
annor· xxii i supercil· sinistr
c· iulium maximum ann xxv
sine i
[.]iulium secundum
annor· xx· sine i
c iuḷium saturninum
annor xxiii i manụ sinistr
m antonium ualenteṃ
ann· xxii· i froṇṭịs
parte dextr
accepta vi· k· martias ann· v̅i̅· February 24, 103
imp· traiani n̄ per
priscum singul
(*Hand 2?*) auidius arrian cornicụlar
c̣ọh ii[i] iṭ[ura]eorum
scripsi· authenticam
epistulam· in ṭabụlario
cohortis esse

1. *c̣ẹ:* Oxy.; [*e*]*x̣e*[*mpl*]*u*[*ṃ*]*:* ChLA; *e*(*xemplum*) *e*(*pistulae*)*:* Daris, following Gilliam; *ex:* Mallon. Cf. **98** *2* 4.

2. [*C*]*elsiano:* Oxy. Above and to the right of *suo* there is an unexplained stroke, possibly the remains of an *s* which has been erased. Italus was Prefect of Egypt from A.D. 100 or 101 to the middle of 103; Celsianus was prefect of the cohort.

12. *annor*(*um*)*; sine i*(*conismo*).

13. *Longium:* Oxy. Cavenaile credits Wilcken with the reading *longinum*; but the *Chrestomathie* has *Longium.*

14. *i*(*conismus*) *supercil*(*io*) *sinistr*(*o*).

17. *Lucium:* Oxy.; but there is no trace of the top of a *c*, and cf. the *l*'s in *gemellum*, line 11. The *l* in *iulium*, line 19, may have been of the same form. ChLA also reads *Iulium.*

20. *sinistr*(*a*).

23. *dextr*(*a*).

24. *ann*(*o*) (*sexto*). Note that the letter was received five days after the effective date of the recruits' enrolment in the cohort.

25. *imp*(*eratoris*)*; n*(*ostri*).

26. *singul*(*arem*).

27. *Arrianus cornicular:* Oxy.; *Arrian*(*u*)*s:* ChLA. There is an extra stroke between *a* and *n* of *arrian*; and there is not room for *us*, especially since there is a space between words elsewhere in lines 27–31.

28. *III Ituraeorum:* Oxy. and Daris; *II*[*I*] *Iṭ*[*ụra*]-*eorum:* ChLA. The identity of the cohort is by no means certain; it could quite well be the II Ituraeorum.

TRANSLATION

Copy

Gaius Minicius Italus to his Celsianus.

Order the six recruits approved by me to be put on the roster in the cohort which you command effective February 19. I have appended their names and marks of identification to this letter. Good health, my very dear brother.

Gaius Veturius Gemellus, 21 years, no mark.

Gaius Longinus Priscus, 22 years, mark on left eyebrow.

Gaius Iulius Maximus, 25 years, no mark.

? Iulius Secundus, 20 years, no mark.

Gaius Iulius Saturninus, 23 years, mark on left hand.

Marcus Antonius Valens, 22 years, mark on right side of forehead.

Received February 24, sixth year of our Emperor Trajan, delivered by the dispatch-rider Priscus.

I, Avidius Arrianus, chief clerk of the coh. III (*or* II) Ituraeorum, certify that the original letter is in the files of the cohort.

88

Agathonius' Copies of Letters to Saturninus

PDur. 63 (inv. D. P. 10) July 1, 211

Transcription, commentary, and facsimile: *Final Rep.* v, no. 63 and plates 33, 3 and 35, 1; *edidit* Gilliam.

Text: *CPL*, no. 332, reproduces the text, now obsolete, of no. 2 from *Prelim. Rep.* v.

These are two letters, or rather, copies of letters, from a liber epistularum. The glued joint between them is plainly visible in plate 35.

The identities of all three of the persons named here are unknown; but Agathonius was probably tribune of the coh. xx Palmyrenorum and received copies of these letters because they concerned soldiers under his command.

Nothing is certain about the content of either letter except that no. 2 involved at least two men, Themarsas and Hiereus, who are not identified as soldiers, and that no. 1 mentioned a sale and *dupla bona.* In Gilliam's quite reasonable reconstruction Pomponianus is asking Saturninus in no. 1 to send him a soldier of the century of Seleucus who may be accused of using violence to force a sale. No. 2 may or may not have had a similar intent.

The date is that of the docket of no. 2.

1.

]agathonio
satur]ṇino ṣ[u]ọ
s]ạluteṃ
].as ad me
].[ ] ϒ̣ ṣeleuci
]ọstrum qui ui
]ṃ uendidisse ḥe[
].o proc̣˙ dupla bona
]...[..]ḍus ei.[

1 1. On the name Agathonius, not otherwise attested, see Gilliam ad loc.

2. [*Iul Pomponianus Satur*]*ṇino ṣụọ:* D; but there is no evidence that Pomponianus was the writer.

4. [*Peto, domine frater, mit*]*ṭas:* D, app.

5. D in app.: "The line probably contained only a name and ϒ] *Seleuci.*"

6. D in app.: "Possibly *n*]*ostrum* or even *v*]*ostrum*, agreeing with some title or designation of the soldier. Perhaps *vi-* rather than *vi.*"

7.]. *vendidisse .e*[..]*:* D.

9.]...[..].*usei.* [– *7* –]*:* D.

2. Recto:

agathon]io
.[ ].[.]ṣ[
iul pọṃp[o]nianus sạ[turn]ịno suo
(*Hand 2*) acc kal iul gentiano et baṣṣ[o co]ṣ ṣạḷụtem July 1, 211
peto domine frater themaṛ[sam zebi-(?)
da˙ et hierum abẹ[d-
de quibus tibi ṣ[c]ṛ[i]ḅ[-
meus dọṃinus .[
appada[na
[.]ẹ[

Verso:

AGATHONIO[
a iul p[o]ṃp̣ọṇ[iano

2 2. D does not mention these traces of letters. Those over *pom* could very possibly be [*e*]*x*(*emplum*). Cf. **87** 1.

4. This line is the docket with the date of receipt: *acc*(*epta*) *kal*(*endis*) *iul*(*iis*), etc., written in at the left of *salutem.*

5–6. D in app.: "Perhaps *Themar*[*sạ* (*or -sam*) *Zebi*]*da*, two very common names." This combination of names occurs in **1** xli 25 and **2** xli 13, an eques of the turma Antonini who enlisted in 198.

6. D in app.: "St. Augustine mentions a *Hierius*, a *homo Syrus*, in *Confess.* iv, 14, 21. Hiereus' father's name, beginning *Abed-*, probably took up the rest of the line."

7. *tibi* . . . [– *11* –]*:* D. Probably *ṣ*[*c*]*ṛ*[*i*]*ḅ*[*sit*.

8. D in app.: "*Meus* might be the end of a name, instead of the possessive. *Dominus* here is possibly 'owner'."

89

File of Letters of the Tribune Postumius Aurelianus

PDur. 66 (inv. D. P. 13) July–December, 216

Transcription and commentary: *Final Rep.* v, no. 66, and plates as noted with individual letters; *ediderunt litteras Graecas* Welles,˙*Latinas* Gilliam.

These letters are the remains of a liber epistularum regarding which I can do no better than to quote Gilliam, who has extracted more meaning from these discouraging scraps than anyone would have thought possible. "It seems reasonable to describe the roll as primarily one of incoming letters addressed to the tribune commanding the cohort, in which some copies of outgoing letters were inserted and to which a few letters written neither by nor to him were added, probably because their content was relevant." The letters in **88** illustrate this same practice of making copies of letters available to third parties who might have an interest in the matters concerned.

Continuing Gilliam's remarks: "It is clear that the letters . . . belong to the last half of 216 and were filed in order of receipt. . . . A considerable number of the letters refer to soldiers of the Palmyrene cohort, sometimes naming them; quite often they also mention procurators. The letters were written at a time when Caracalla was passing through Mesopotamia into Adiabene in the opening phase of what promised to be a major war. . . . It seems a reasonable assumption therefore that the present file was primarily concerned with members of the unit who had been assigned to procurators or were on detached duty elsewhere and who were now being recalled . . . in order that the cohort might be made a more effective combat force. . . . This hypothesis would explain the letters in Greek, most of which probably came from members of the civil administration, Imperial freedmen, and the like, to whom a few soldiers had been assigned. It is likely that the man to whom the tribune writes in Greek (no. *9*) is a civilian."

About the general content of the letters, this statement is unquestionably right; but the range of dates over a full six months, from July to December, would seem to fit a routine correspondence better than an effort to concentrate the cohort's personnel for possible combat.

I have undertaken a review of only a few of these exiguous fragments because it seemed that the results of gleaning after two such able and careful editors would not repay the expenditure of time and effort. Most of the texts which follow are taken over unchanged, with their permission, from Gilliam and Welles. Quotations in my commentary are from *Final Rep.* v, all from the apparatus there unless otherwise identified.

1. Outgoing. Same hand as nos. 10 and 11. Ca. July 3. Plates 33, 4, and 36, 1.

Recto:

1]. . [
1a a
2 p. [. .] domini . . . . . [*ca.* 16]. s [co]ḥ xx̣ [p]almy-
[re]norum antoṇ[i]ṇiaṇ[ae . . . .] ḍẹgeṇ[tes] quodaṃ siluae
[. .]b . . . [.] . . . . d. [*ca.* 13] ⟦.a⟧[. .].ạs. . ṇ. [.]. . misi
5 ạd uos p[e]ṛ aure[l *ca.* 14]. . . [.]ụm sta[tor]em
5a aurel mu[ci]anum ⟦Ч ṃ[a]ṛị[ani]⟧
6 coh eiusdẹṃ quem diṃ[*ca.* 10]quintuṃ [n]onas iul
sabiṇo ii ẹṭ anụḷḷịno cos[*ca.* 8]rla[.]ạm p. [. . .]es scribatis op[t]o uos doṃịni[
feḷicissimos mul-
10 ṭịṣ [ann]is bene
[ualere]

Verso:

]Ọ . . [. .]. . . ỊẠNO P̣F˙ ET AVRELIO REGVLO PP˙. [
ANTOṆỊṆIA[NAE

a
postumio auṛ[el]iano trib coh

"The letter may be concerned with two connected matters: soldiers of the Palmyrene cohort who perhaps were on detached service under the jurisdiction of the addressees, and earlier messages about these men which the addressees had ignored. The tribune may end by asking whether a previous letter was received" (p. 237).

1. "The partially preserved letter[s are] from the second line of the address."

1a. "The solitary *a* . . . is presumably a correction" of the word below.

2. *domini* .[.]*n*..[: D; but the letters after *domini* look most like *fra*...[or *kar*...[, though neither *fratres* nor *kari* seems possible. "The letter may have begun with a verb introducing a request; *pe*[*to*] is not possible. Nothing is lost to the left unless this line projects into the margin, as is possible. After *domini*, *ṣ*[*i*]*nẹ m*[*ora*] is worth considering, and at the end of the long lacuna *milit*]*ẹṣ* is an attractive restoration." In view of the tenor of the other letters in this roll, *remittatis* seems a good possibility for filling the rest of the lacuna.

3. "One might restore [*qui*] or [*quos*] *ḍẹge*[*ntes*. . . . Then followed perhaps *quo*⟨*n*⟩*dam silvae* (corrected ... from *silve*), the locative of a place-name? . . . see *CIL* III 3490: *Surus ex regione Dolica vico Arfuaris Silva*."

4. "The line may begin [*su*]*b*, followed by *ṛạ* or *ạr*. Toward the end, after *ạṣ* or *ṛṣ*, possibly *ọṣ* or *ọg̣ị*."

5.]*iṭẹm sta*[*tor*]*ẹm*: D. "After *Aure*[*l* his cognomen is lost, and perhaps also his title and *coh s s*. What I take to be the bottom of *t* in *iṭẹm* raises considerable doubts. The name of the stator (who carried a second letter or second copy?) was omitted in the first draft. It was added in the nominative, -*us* being later corrected to -*um*, with his century, which was then cancelled as superfluous. An Aurelius Mucianus belonged to this century, probably the same man [**1** xxiv 6; **2** xix 15]." The man in the rosters enlisted in 214. The reconstruction offered in D is reasonable but not certain. We do not really know why the corrector inserted Mucianus' name; and I prefer to understand the letters before *sta*[*tor*]*em* as the end of the stator's cognomen.

5a. This line is a correction, as noted, in another hand.

6. *diṃ*[*isi ad vos*]: D. Perhaps *diṃ*[*isistis*], though in fact there are many other possibilities.

7–8. "The letter may end [*Peto ob pe*]*rla*[*t*]*ạm*, *pạ*[*tr*]*ẹs*, *scribatis*, with *perlatam* agreeing with *epistolam*, the lost object of *misi* in line 4. *Patres*, which fits the space and traces of ink exactly, is rather unexpected. Cf. however *P. Gen.* 52 and the Latin letters in *P. Mich. VIII*." The meaning of *ob* is not altogether clear to me; *num* might be preferable.

Verso 1. "The first cognomen begins with either *N* or *A* and probably ends -*fiano*, -*riano*, or -*siano*. Possibilities include *Ṇ*[*u*]*ṃịṣiano* and *Ṇ*[*u*]*ṃẹriano*, though the *e* is not all one would desire. At the end of the line probably *ḷ*[*eg*, though *ṇ*[*umeri* is at least as good a reading. Possibly *ḷ*[*eg XVI F*(*laviae*) *F*(*irmae*)." "The positions of the two addressees are indicated only by the abbreviations following the names. . . . For the first I see no alternative to p(rae)f(ectus), though the abbreviation is quite rare. . . . The other might be *p*(*rae*)*p*(*ositus*), *p*(*rimi*)*p*(*ilus*), or *p*(*rimi*)*p*(*ilaris*). If both men were from the same unit, it would presumably have been a legion. . . . It seems strange . . . that the tribune should address his letter to two officers of the same unit, even if the second of these was primipilus iterum and so very close in rank to the prefect" (p. 237).

2. Incoming. Plate 15, 1. Since this letter is in Greek, it is probably from a procurator or other civil functionary and no doubt reported what the writer had done about sending back the soldiers who had been assigned to his use. Their names occupy the last four lines.

[. . .] . [
τριβ̣υ̣ν̣[ω] αυ-
[ρ]η̣λια[νω] . . . ν̣[
[. .]ιιτα̣ [χ]αιρειν
τους δο̣θεντ̣ας
μοι στρα̣[τ]ιωτας
και .[. . . .] . [
της .[. . . . . .]με
εις γε̣[. . . .]αν
αιτε[. . . . .]τρια
κα.[. . . . .]σιου
του.[. . . . .]ρου
τεσ̣[. . . .]ο̣στου

ιτε[. . .]τους
ε̣[ρρωσο
θ[εμαρσ]α̣[ς
[. . . . . .]κ̣αιος
[. . . . . . .]δαδος
[. . . . . . .].ο̣[.]. . [

2. [*Τ*]ριβύ̣ν̣[ω̣. .] *Αὐ*[ρη-]*:* D. "Except for the *ΑΥ*, nothing is certain, and the reading of the beginning of this line is only a possibility."

3. λ̣ια[νῷ̣ . .]. . .ν*:* D.

4. [.]ιιτα*:* D. "Probably we should read πλ]ῖστα."

9. "The word following εἰς may be a place name."

10. αιτα[*:* D.

14. ". . . the obvious ἔ]τους" (p. 238).

16. The restoration of the name is little more than exempli gratia. The name Themuamus would fit the space; and Themes followed by a patronymic would do.

18. The name could be Abedadadus, Barhadadus, or Baadadadus, all known from Dura.

19. [. . . . . . .].α[ιο]υ*:* D.

3. "The writer, addressee, and subject of this scrap are all unknown. It is from the right edge of a column" (p. 238). In line 5, however,]*misi* could refer to the sending or sending back of soldiers; and no. 4, line 6, suggests restoring *re*]*misi* here.

].[. . .]. . . .[
]ḷue.[. . .]. . . .[
]aḍ.[. . .] τιων[
].[. . . . .]e οπ[
]misi τ̣ι̣ω̣ν̣
]enọ[.]ạrum
Two lines blank
]. .ollioneco.[

"There are traces of Greek writing at the right of lines 2–5. . . . In spite of the wide space between lines 4 and 5, this may be taken as ὀπτίων" (p. 239).

"A possible reading in line 7 is *pollione coḥ*(*ortis*); cf. *pollio legionis*, *ILS* 2430 (*CIL* III 5949) and 9493, and Domaszewski, *Rangordnung*, p. 47" (p. 238). One might also think of *pollione coṣ*. Claudius Aelius Pollio was governor of Upper Germany in the first half of the third century, perhaps in 218/219, and so must have held the consulship earlier (see Degrassi, *Fasti Consolari*, p. 61), in which case he may have been suffectus in 216 and with Caracalla in Mesopotamia. But see also *PIR* , s.v. "Claudius" no. 770, where it appears that he may have been raised by Elagabal from the rank of centurion.

4. Incoming. July 8–15. Plate 37. This is the most complete of the letters in this roll and so in a sense provides the key to the meaning of all of them. "As the opening lines have been restored, the writer, who is presumably the governor, states that he is returning twenty-eight men belonging to the cohort who had been assigned to a procurator, Aurelius Theodorus . . . probably the provincial procurator if in fact as many as twenty-eight soldiers had been assigned to him" (p. 239).

Col. i

Recto (*hand 1*):

].[
].[ ]ṣạḷụṭ[em
[milit]ẹṣ ṇ ụigintị̣ octo d[omine coh]
[xx palm c]ụi pṛ[a]ẹ[e]ṣ tiḅ[i ex mini-

ṣ[terio a]ụrẹli tḥ[eo]ḍọri proc̣ ạ[ug cui]
q[uoru]m in loco a[l]ị[o]ṣ dedi remiṣ[i]
ex hị[s]
ṛ[. . . .]gri et i.m[. . .]. . .erunt ṃ[
quạ[e] summisi[. . . . . . .]. ex his quị[
ṇ[. . . .]exilḷ.[. . . . . . .].[. .]ṛunt[quo-
rụ[m no]mina .[*ca.* 10]c̣i p.[

Verso:

]TRIB(VNO) C[OH(ORTIS)]

TRANSLATION

Recto 3–6: I have sent back to you, dear sir, from the service of Aurelius Theodorus, procurator Augusti, to whom I have given others in their place, twenty-eight soldiers of the coh. xx Palmyrenorum which you command . . .

2. *ṣ[a]l̇ụṭ[em:* D.

3–6. "The restorations here may be excessive, especially since many of the dotted letters are mere traces. For *ex ministerio*, cf. Pliny, *Ep.*, X, 27."

4. *]c̣ui; minis-]:* D.

5. *[terio:* D.

6. *remisi:* D.

6a. These words are an addition between the lines in small letters by the same hand.

7. *ạ[. . .].ri et i. .[. . . .]. .erunt* .[–5–]*:* D. "The line may begin *r*[. The letter before the second lacuna is *m* or *n*; possibly *iṇ ṇ*[or *iṃṃ[unes.*" For the end of line 6 and the beginning of line 7, I suggest [*qui eo-*] *ṛ[um ae]gri*; the word after *et* would then be something similar in meaning to *immobiles*, though that word will not fit the remains before *erunt*, which in any event are probably part of the verb. At the end of the line perhaps *ṃ[anent.*

8. *qu.*[.]*:* D; "Probably *quạ* or *quị* with nothing lost in the lacuna." The neuter *quae*, however, as the object of *summisi*, seems a good possibility.

9. *ṇ*[. . . *v]ẹxillạ[tion* – 6 –]*:* D. "Possibly *qui [degu-] n[t in v]exilla[tione.*" But *u]exillạ[ri-* or even *]ex illị[s* is equally possible; and a word-division like *degu/nt* seems very unlikely.

10. .[*–12–* -]*c̣i:* D. "Quite possibly *nomina i[tem* and *subie]ci*. One would expect *subi]ci pr[aecepi*, but the partly preserved letter after *p* does not look like an *r*."

Col. ii

(*Hand 2*)].[
]ịus
.[. . . . . .]. barṣẹ[mias?
ulp̣ [sil]ụanus
cl zebidas
.[ ]auidas
.[ ]anus
.[ ]arreus
.[ ]ụabbaḷlathi
. .mun iụḷ[ ]ṇus i
ạ[urel s]eleucus
ạ[urel]alex̣[a]ndrus
. . . .[ ]aḅ. .ga
]annas
dem]etrius
Two lines lost
].s

Col. iii

]. . . .[
].ṃ.ogyṇ[
]ḷianus

[acc id]us iul
[sabino ii]ẹt anul-
[lino] c̣os

This list of names was prepared by a different clerk and attached to the covering letter.

ii 2.].*us*[*:* D.

8. *Ị*[*ul* . . . .]*asreus:* D, certainly a possible reading.

10. [. . . . .].*us I:* D; "[*Im*]*mun*(*is*) is the most obvious restoration." Cf. col. i, 7, and app. "The last two letters in *Iul* are very faint traces."

13.]*a*. . .*a:* D.

14. Probably *m*]*annas*.

iii 2.]*n*.*og*.*ị*[*:* D.

3. *Iu*]*lianus:* D; but a great many other cognomina end the same.

4. "In the docket *Idib*]*us* is . . . also possible."

5. Incoming? Plate 42,1. Nothing is certain about this letter; but it probably mentioned a procurator Augusti and a praepositus in line 3, who may be one person.

]. . [. . . . .]. . [
].[. . . . . .]p̣ṛ[.]. . . [
proc̣ ạ[ug] p̣raeposi[
aurẹ[liu]ṃ flauium ṃ.[
.[ ].ḍ.[ ]um . .[
ṇ[ ]meḷḷsạ[
sẹ[ ]aṭam h.ṣ.[
pa.[ ]ẹc̣ạesenṭ[
ṭụ.[ ]. . .as ut t.[
]ṃ portetur
(*Hand 2*) fra]ṭṛẹṣ fẹlicisṣ[imos
]. m[u]lṭis annis
(*Hand 1*)]ẹp̣ịṣṭụl
]ạṃi[.]ị ẹpis
].por
]Ṭ ẹạ

3. *proc̣ Ạ*[*ug* .]*rec̣ọsi*[*:* D. "One could read *pro p*[*r*]*ạ*[*eto*]*re*."

4. *Aure*[*l*] *Flavium* .[*:* D. There are traces of ink between the two names, though -*lium* is somewhat crowded in the space.

5. .[. . . .]. .[. .]*uṃ* . .[*:* D. The letter in the middle could also be *b*.

6.]*ṃeḷḷọṣ*[*:* D. Instead of the two *l*'s possibly *i*'s. I can find no trace of an *o* unless a dot over the second *l* is so read. It appears to be accidental, or perhaps a mark of abbreviation. R. W. Davies, *BASP* 5 (1968) 33–34, proposes [*ca*]*ṃeḷḷọṣ* on the basis of Gilliam's reading.

7.]*ạpaṃit*. . .[*:* D. "The *i* is tall and hooked at the top, presumably as an initial letter."

8.]*ec̣*. .*sent*[*:* D. Possibly]*e p̣resent*[.

9. *t*. .[. . . .]. .*asutt*.[*:* D. "The letters beyond the lacuna are probably to be divided]. .*as ut t*." Perhaps restore *ut ti*[*bi scripsi*] or [*praecepi*].

10.]*ạ:* D.

11.]. . . . *felicisṣ*[*:* D.

11–13. "The traces of letters in line 11 could be read as *do*]*ṃịnẹ* . . . and -*imu*]*ṃ* is possible in line 12. The two lines would then have the same left margin. But whatever stands in line 13, it is not any part of *bene valere*." If *fra*]*ṭṛẹṣ* is correctly read, this is an outgoing letter from Postumius Aurelianus.

13.]. . . .*ṣeḷ:* D.

14.].*ni*[.].*ẹpis:* D. Obviously *epis* | [*tul-*].

15. "Possibly *Moc*]*ọpor*." Most probably the first syllable of a form of *portare*, cf. line 10.

16.].*ci:* D.

6. Incoming. Same hand as nos. 7 and 8. July 16–August 1. "There is nothing to suggest the content of the letter, and the identity of the writers is unknown. The cognomen of the first, which ends -*genianus* (no. *7*, line 2), may be *Eugenianus*. However, the traces of the initial letter preserved in this text and in no. *8* do not suggest an *e* but rather *a*, *i*, *r*, *s*, or some other letter that curves slightly to the left at the bottom of the first stroke. *Ingenianus* is found in *CIL* VIII, 9786 but is not common, if it does in fact appear anywhere else" (pp. 240–41).

The fact that Postumius Aurelianus' name is first in all three of these letters may indicate that the two writers were beneath him in rank. What title they addressed him by is unknown.

pos]tumio [aureliano
[a]elius .[.ge]nianus [et] aureḷ[
saḷu[tem
[*ca.* 10]..[7].rum.[
[*ca.* 10]us[8].[..]ana[
[.].[..].[......]ep.[10] ⟦scr[.]..[⟧
[..]mutṇ[*ca.* 15].at[.]ịṇ[
[.....]da.[10 domine] frater dimiṣ[*ca.* 17].eci
(*Hand 2*) [acc]ḳal aug ..[*ca.* 17].oseo[
] *vacat* [ ]....[(*Hand 3?*)

10. The date is in hand 2. "The year is regularly given in these dockets, but the blank papyrus . . . below the line indicates that the consuls were omitted here. The two letters before the lacuna (ç or p̣ and perhaps ạ) are in the first hand. This is the last line of the letter proper; evidently it was indented *ca. 7* letters."

11. "These vague, wavering letters are probably from a signature."

7. Incoming. Same hand as nos. 6 and 8. The only clues to the content of this letter are the name in the accusative in line 4, perhaps *remisimus* in line 8 and *dimis*[in line 11, and the mention of a praefectus or procurator and of the xx Palmyrenorum in line 10. All of these are consistent with the interpretation of the roll in general as a file of letters regarding the return of soldiers who had been assigned to detached service, especially with procurators; but there is not enough to guarantee such interpretation of this letter.

See also above under no. 6.

Recto:

postu[mio aureliano
aeli[u]s [..]genia[nus et] a[urel
[salutem
].[*ca.* 20]ṃ et aureliu[m
]ẹb[.....]ṃ[.].ṭ.[
]..[10]ss[
].[.].[..].[10]..[
]emis[*ca.* 13].[....]i[
]liṛ.[*ca.* 15]um[
]a lupo pr[*ca.* 10 coh xx p]almur˙[
]..tine[*ca.* 15]. dimis[
]ṣorian[*ca.* 15]...

8. "*r*]*emis*[*imus*?"

10. "*a Lupo pṛ*[*aef*, *pṛ*[*aep*, or *pṛ*[*oc*."

Verso:

]..[
a
aurel[

"From the left edge of the address. Unless the order of the writers is reversed, Aelius -genianus' name may have followed *a* in line 2. There is enough blank space for about six letters before *Aurel*."

8. Incoming. Same hand as nos. 6 and 7. As in the preceding letter, the name in the accusative (line 4) and the mention of the xx Palmyrenorum and a procurator (lines 5 and 8) are in harmony with the general purport of the other letters in the roll.

post]umio [aureliano
ạelius .[.g]ẹnianus [et] aurel[
sal[utem]
[...... a]ur[el za]bḍ[i]ḅolụ[m
[.......].[... coh xx p]alm[
ḍ[e]ḍiṃ[u]ṣ[10].m[
[.]ṭtẹ[*ca.* 12]ṭo....[
(*Hand 2*) ac]ç [.]il.[*ca.*12 pr]ocuṛạ[tor-
augus[ti 11 e]x̣ littẹ[ris
me.[*ca.* 15]....[

8. "The single letter to the left of this line is in another hand, like those found in dockets recording receipt."

9. "One would restore *meị[s*, if there were not two writers named in the heading."

9. Outgoing. "The sense of the letter has not been recovered. We have no explanation of the identity of Themarsas, son of Verus. It is interesting that Postumius addressed him in Greek, and kept a copy of his letter which included the signature (ἔρρωσο) and the address . . . the length of the lacuna in the center is not certain" (p. 242).

Recto:

[.]..[ ]π̣[.]α̣[
μαρ.[ ]εως η[
θιαν[ ]α̣σα α[
μ.[ ]η[.]..[
οι.[α]ν̣τωνε̣ι̣[ν
.[ ]α̣ν[
(*Hand 2*) ερ̣[ρωσο

2. "If the round *kappa* was used, this could be Μάρκ̣[-; otherwise μαρα̣[At the end . . . *kappa* is possible unless the writer used the round form."

4. "The trace following *mu* could be the lower tip of a long *iota*."

Verso:

θε]μα̣ρ̣σα ουη[
α-
πο ποστ[ομιο]υ

"The *alpha* standing alone is a Latin *A*, under the influence of the Latin addresses; as an afterthought, the *ΠΟ* of the Greek ἀπό was added in the following line."

1. Οὐή[ρου: D. But other names are possible.
3. "The first *omicron* is so faint that it need not be read, except for the sense."

10. Outgoing. Same hand as nos. 1 and 11. Plate 33, 5. "Since there is an address on the verso, one would suppose that . . . [the letter] was originally prepared to be sent out, not to be kept as a file copy. I see nothing to suggest the subject of the letter" (p. 243).

Recto:

m[. . .]ụs ạḅ.[. . . .]ạbep.[*ca.* 12]. .
[. . .] anto[. . . . . .]i in[*ca.* 12].e
[. . . . . .]li. . .[. . . . .]. .s[*ca.* 12].
[. . . . .]i.u. .[. . . .].r[. .]. .[
[. . . . .].[*ca.* 12]. .[
qụ[. .].[
pe[
mị[*ca.* 15]. .[7].[
qu[*ca.* 15].en. .[. . . . .]ụs
hib[ern *ca.* 12]be[7].lo
coḥ[*ca.* 15]s[7].e
. .[*ca.* 23].o.[
].[

Verso:

[au]re[l *ca.* 10] *vacat* Y
a postumio aureliano ṭ[rib coh]
Across the fibers along lower right edge of sheet:
]![. . .]. . .[

1. *m[iss]ụs?*]*ạb epị[stul-?*

11. Outgoing? "This appears to be in the same hand as nos. 1 and 10 and, if so, is presumably a file copy. Its contents are entirely obscure" (p. 243).

]. . .[9]. . .[
]ḅ[.].[. . . . . .]s q[
]seraṭị[. . .] esse[
]analib.[.]s. .ṭ[
]iume.[. . .]. . .e.[
].[.]. . . .[. . . . . .]qu[
]. . o[*ca.* 10]. .[
Two lines lost
].l[
].dur[a?
].l.[
]x.[

4. "*libr*[or *liba*[" But perhaps *c*]*analibụ*[*s*?
5. Perhaps *iumeṇ*[*ta*, draft animals. Cf. no. 42, line 10, *cum pecoribus*.

12. Incoming? July 22? "A covering letter in col. i . . . was doubtless concerned with the men listed in col. ii. The centuries to which they belong show that they were already on the rolls of the Palmyrene cohort and were not, e.g., new recruits. The hand in col. ii is of a type found in lists of names rather than letters. Too little remains of the first column to determine whether the same hand was used in it" (p. 243).

Col. i

]ạ
].[
].u.[
]o
(*Hand 2*) d]ecimum
]
opto te d]omine
feliciss]ị[m]ụṃ
[bene ualer]ẹ

Col. ii

(*Hand 1 or 3*)
].ạ[
One line blank
Ɣ ṣelẹ[uci
aurel me[. . . . . the]marsa
One line blank
Ɣ marci
aurel iar[haeus zebi]da
ụ[lp] barsẹ[mias]
ạuṛẹ[l
One line blank
]a.[
Ca. three lines lost
.[
..[

i 5. "Perhaps *decimum* follows *data*. It is uncertain whether the interlinear interval permits the insertion of line 6 of the transcription. . . . However . . . if *decimum* is part of a date . . . space has to be provided for the rest of it." Since *decimum* is in a second hand, and in view of the dates in nos. 6 and 20, it appears simplest to take this as a docket and restore here [*acc d*]*ecimum* | [*kal augustas*].

ii 3 and 5. "For this type of name combined with *Aurel* see *Final Report* V, i, Introduction, p. 38."

8. "A possibility is [Ɣ] *aṇ*[*tonini*."

13. "Blank papyrus . . . except for three incomplete letters at the extreme right, each of which begins a line" (p. 244).

14. "Letter of Aurelius A- to Barchalbas. The identity of neither is known. . . . The hand resembles those in nos. 5 and 16. The content of the letter is entirely unclear" (p. 244).

Recto:

]ḷ.ạ.[
].[
]..g...[7]l[
co]ḥ xx pal[m...] cum
]o proc a[ug ...]...la
]ẹṭ[
].u.[
cọ[..]
dạ[..]..[
.[
i.[
ri.ụ[

3-5. "... could be restored: *mi*]*l* [*co*]*h XX Pal*[*m qui*] *cum* [*Lup*]*o proc A*[*ug*. For Lupus see [no. 7], line 10."

Verso:

]BARCHẠḶḄẠ[
]ạḅ a[u]ṛel a.........[

15. "Probably not addressed to the tribune, Postumius Aurelianus. A procurator is mentioned once more. The signifer is probably a soldier of the cohort" (p. 245).

Recto:

].a.[9].l..[
].[.].[.].[9].reç..[
].o.[....] aurel [.... pr]oc aug̣[
sig]nifer[.....].l..[
]...[..]..[7]..[
]..[
]..[
]ṭ.[.]..[
].ọ.[
]ṇ[

3. "It is uncertain whether the lacuna contains -*iano* or a short cognomen."

Verso:

AV]ṚẸL[
ab a ..[

"Since *Au*]*ṛẹl*[is toward the top of the sheet, it is probably a nomen (of Barchalbas? [see no. 14]) rather than part of *Aurelianus*. The writer's nomen may also be *Aurel*, with the *u* tipped over on its side."

16. Incoming? "This is a text of somewhat uncertain character. There is a free space of 2 cm. between the traces of line 1 and the main body of the text, and one of 3 cm. between this and the lower text. The latter might be expected to be a list of names, and line 8 may be so interpreted, but lines 9 and following seem to deal with other matters" (p. 245).

]κ.[
vacat
]τερ[αδ]ελφε[
]εν̣[ ].νοις .[
]ο̣ις γρ.[
]..[..]να̣[
]ρι[
]...ι[ ]ν̣[
vacat
(*Hand 2*) ζα]βειδ[
].ν κυρι[
γρα]μμασιν κ.[
]αρ..[..]..[
]ετως̣[...]η[

2. "Probably κύριε ἀδ]ελφέ."
4. "Probably γρά[μμασιν, as in line 10."
9. "Either τ]ο̣ν κύρι[ον or τ]ῶ̣ν κυρί[ων." But this could also be a personal name, such as αυρηλι]ο̣ν κυρι[λλον. A man of that name enlisted in 216: **1** xv ii; **2** xxx 23; **6** v 21.

17. Incoming? "The text consists of a number of fragments, in different hands, located by the skill and logic of Ibscher, but not yielding any connected text. I am inclined to believe that they do belong to one letter because of the shape and location of the fragments. . . . The health wish at the end is a translation of the Latin formula, and not an expression native to Greek epistolography" (p. 245).

]ν̣σ̣[
μ[ ]ον[
]σι[ ].
]α.[ ].
].
].
(*Hand 2*)]ν.ι̣μ[ ].
]ατ[
]φε[
(*Hand 3*)]θα[
αδε]λφε πο[στομιε πολλοις
χρο]νοις ευχ[ομαι υγιαινειν
(*Hand 4*)]sa[b]i[n]o ii
et annullino c]os

11–12. Welles, p. 245, notes that the same hand recurs in the signature of no. 29.

18. Incoming? or to Leo, tribune? "Since Leo is a tribune, one would assume that he commanded the Palmyrene cohort. But Postumius Aurelianus is found in several letters both before and after this in the roll. It is more likely that a completed outgoing letter was retained as a file copy than that one received by another tribune was inserted in this file. [But cf. p. 356 and nos. 14 and 15.] Another possibility, especially since the addressee's name is usually in larger letters, is that *Leoni* is ablative and not dative . . . the scrap has the characteristic content of many letters in this roll, referring to soldiers and a procurator" (p. 246).

Recto:

]mil˙[
]onini[
]. proc˙ a[ug
]e.[

"One could restore lines 1 and 2 as *mil*[*coh. XX Palm Ant*]*onini*[*anae* . . ." (p. 246).

Verso:

]. leoni trib[

19. Incoming. "No sense connection has been established between the five fragments which comprise this letter. . . . Their location is approximate. The Latin docket . . . shows that this was an incoming letter" (p. 246).

]ρο[   ]α̣[   ]. .[
]ων[   ]αντου[   ]σιεπ.[
]επ.[   ]ειαν[   ]νμ̣ο[
].[   ].τ̣ωπ.[   ].[
]σι[..]εν[   ]ν̣[
]..[
]μο[..]σ[
]σο.[.].[
]τ̣ο̣[

vacat

acc .[sabino ii et
anu]lli[no cos

20. Incoming. July 16–August 1.

[*ca.* 10] ṃị[l coh] x̣x̣ p̣ạ[lm]ụr′
[antoninia]ṇae [....].dp ṃ.[..]..[.].[
[*ca.* 15] iussi co.[
[*ca.* 15] sab[ino ii
[*ca.* 10].sso..[
[*ca.* 12]...
(*Hand 2*) [acc] kal aug̣ [sabino ii]
[et anu]ḷḷịṇo cos
].[

2. "Possibly *q(uondam) d(is)p(ositos)*? Cf. *Final Report* v, i, Introduction, p. 42."
4. "Part of a date, which took up much of lines 4–5."
9. "Possibly from the signature."

21. Incoming. July 16–August 12. (Cf. no. *23*) "One line from a short second column, followed by a docket. The first column ... is entirely lost" (p. 247).

]...[
acc   ]ạug[
sabino ii et anu]lli[no cos

22. "The first of these two lines is probably not from the heading of the letter. ... Either *Aeliu.*[or *Au*]*ṛeliu*.[can be read, and at the end either *ṣ* or *ṃ*" (p. 247).

].eliu.[
].u..[

23. Incoming. August 12. Plate 15, 2. "The letter consists of four fragments, the relative location of which was established by Ibscher and seems confirmed by the hand. ... There is no clue either to the subject of [the] letter or to [the writer's] identity" (p. 247). The use of Greek, however, implies that the letter was written by a civilian.

]α̣ρα[ ] (προ)[
].εξ̣[ ]αυτης
].α[δη]λ̣ουμ̣ε̣νοις κε[
]ν̣μα̣[ ]τεων δυ[
]..[ ]. αυτων[
]ξαντο αν[
].ο δε αυτοις[
]...ειν βαλλ[
]ει και συν[
].τω[
]πρωτ̣[
]π[.]ρον̣[ ]...[
].σ̣ο̣υ τα[ ]..[
].σα.[ ].[
]. τον[
].[
].σα[
vacat
(*Hand 2*) acc p]rịḍie iduṣ [aug
sabi]no ị[i] ẹ[t anul]ḷịn[o cos

1. "The sign interpreted as *πρό* is a clear *rho* written across what seems to be a *pi*. The same symbol occurs at Dura in the Palace of the Dux (*Rep. IX*, 3, p. 50, no. 956)."

24. Incoming? "The free space above the first line suggests that this was actually the first line of the letter. . . . There is . . . no clue to the subject or to the writer. . . . The fragment of an address on the verso . . . may be from the same pen but has not been read; it looks Latin rather than Greek" (p. 248).

πρ̣[
ευν[
.σα[
.[

25. Incoming. August 22. Plate 36, 2.

Recto:

]..[...].ṇ..[.].ṇ[
t]ri[b]cohor[t]ịṣ ṃi[l coh xx
palm]ureno[rum
]. duxiṭ[
]ọ dec̣[e]m.[.].[
]..[.].p̣..[
]anuḷḷịṇ[o cos
(*Hand 2*) acc]xi˙ kạ[l sep]teṃ[bres
sabi]no [ii] ẹ[t a]ṇụ[l-
li]ṇ[o cos

1. "Both dotted letters could be *m*."

2.]*ṛị*[. .] *cohor*[.]. . . .[*:* D; "*Cohor*[*t*]*is XX* is barely possible. What remains of the last two letters could be read more easily as *na*, though partially preserved *n*'s and *x*'s in this hand can hardly be distinguished." In the text adopted, one can imagine, e.g., some such construction as *ex epistulis* N.N. *tribuni cohortis milites coh. XX palmyrenorum . . . numero decem remisi.*

5. "Possibly]. *deç*[*e*]*m*". This seems certain; and the whole line might be restored *numer*]*ọ deç*[*e*]*m ṛẹṃ*[*isi.*

Verso:

[POSTV]ṂỊ[O A]ṾṚELỊAṆ[O] ṬRỊḄṾN[O COH
ab aurel . . . .[. .]. . . .[
(*Hand 3*)].p. . . .f. . . . . .[. . . .]. .[

2. "No letter is fully preserved after *Aurel.* The cognomen might begin *Abed-*."

3. "Possibly *Aure*]*ḷ* and a cognomen."

26. Incoming. August 23. "The letter is in six fragments, of which three are blank" (p. 249).

].να[
]ạπọλυσ[ ]τηṿ
]. απο τηṣ[ ].ϵ
]σα[ ]. . .[
]. .[
acc d]ecim[u]ṃ [kal sept
sabino] ii eṭ [anullino cos

2. "The reference may be to ἀπολύσιμοι, *missicii*, who were recalled to service, or to the discharge (ἀπολῦσαι) of the unfit in the field." In view of the references in other letters of this series, could it not rather be "I (have) released" soldiers assigned to me? Cf. nos. 2, lines 5–6, and 4, lines 4–5, and the occurrences of *dimittere* in nos. 1, line 6; 6, line 9; and 42, line 13.

5. "The writing does not occur on the papyrus fragment to the left, and this is, accordingly, probably the signature ἔρρωσο. No letter can be recognized."

27. Incoming?

].[. .].[
]. .υ.[
στρατ]ιωτη[

2. "The letter before *upsilon* may be *lambda* (or *alpha*), but it is not possible to read απ]ọλυσ̣[ιμ."

28. Incoming. September 6 or 7. Since no. 29 is docketed *septem idus*, this letter must have been received no later but might have been received *viii idus*.

Recto:

.[. . . . .]um[. .]. .u.[
[x]x̣˙ palmyṛ. . . .[
3 [. .]. .ra[.]ṭ.[
3a [.]ọ
[. .]. .[. .]um.[

.[...]. [....]n[
re.[..].[
ẹt[.].n.[
(*Hand 2*) acc [vi]i id[us septem-]
bres ṣạbịṇ[o ii et]
anullin[o cos

3a. Apparently an addition or correction of a few letters between the lines.

8. [*V*]*I:* D.

Verso:

[POSTVMIO A]ṾRẸḶIANO [TRIB COH
]n.[..]ị[

2. Possibly [*a leo*]*nẹ* [*tr*]*ị*[*b*? Cf. no. 18.

29. Incoming. September 7. "The letter is contained on seven fragments. . . . It is followed after about 1 cm. by three entries in different hands, probably names. The signature is in the same hand as that of no. 17, although the other hands are different" (p. 250).

].[
α]ṿρ̣ηλ̣ι̣.[
].ας [
.[δωσ]ειν εξουσιαν̣[
]ηνα[.]β[
].τ[..]μ.[
].ρ̣.ν̣[...].σσε[

vacat

(*Hand 2*)]..[..]....α.[ ]ε̣ς
(*Hand 3*)].δ̣.[ ]α̣.[
(*Hand 4*)].ιωσ̣[..]βερ̣[
(*Hand 5*)].[ ]ε̣ρρω̣[σθαι σε ευχομαι
α]δ̣ε̣λ̣φε̣ [πολλοις
χρον[οις
(*Hand 6*) acc sep]tem
idus sept sab]ịno [i]i
et anullino] c̣os

2. "This is probably part of the address, but it is hard to read the last letter as *alpha*, for *A*]ὐρηλια[νῷ."

30. "A scrap with a few strokes . . ." (p. 250).

]ẹ..[
].ṇt[

31. Incoming. September 6–9. "On seven fragments of papyrus. . . . The subject seems to have been the usual one, the disposition of soldiers in the hands of the writer and apparently wanted back by the cohort" (p. 251).

.[
τ[ους στρα]ṭιωτα[ς]. . . . [
α[ ]ηνων ω[ ]σι[. .]ς
κ̣[ ]προς με[
]ν[.]τηṿ[
]. .[
]εṣ[ ]αṿ[
vacat
(*Hand 2*) a]cc .[idus septem(bres)
s[a]ḅi[no ii et anullino
c̣ọṣ

3. "There may be room for παλμυρ- before]ηνῶν, or perhaps it may be possible to read π] | α[λμυρ]ηνῶν."

32. Incoming. September 9. "It is not certain whether these scraps belong together or whether, if so, they are from one letter" (p. 251).

]. . .ṣe.[
vacat
]ẹl[.]. . .[
].r[
(*Hand 2*)]εινου *vacat* [. . . .].[
[
[
(*Hand 3*) acc v idus [sept(embres)
sabiṇo ii et [anullino cos

33. Incoming. "Four fragments of mostly blank papyrus, with occasional traces of ink toward the edges at the bottom, as if from dockets otherwise lost" (p. 251).

μ̣αρ̣[
αυρ̣η[λι-
α.[
αντ[
]ν[
]ηλ[

34. Incoming. "The marginal note opposite lines 6 and 7 may have begun *data*. . . . The three letters at the beginning of line 8 come at the same interval as the other lines but are in a very small hand written with a blunt pen. There is something below the docket . . ." (p. 252).

[. . .]ex .[
vacat
aurel[
[.]r[.]m.[
[. . .]ḷ. .e.[
[. . . . . .]i.[
(*Hand 2*) sept]em sab- . .[. . . .]. . .[
[.]ḍ[
(*Hand 3*) [. .]mar[
]. . . .[
vacat
(*Hand 4*) aç̣c̣[
[
(*Hand 1?*) .[
.[
.[

6–7. The notation would have read in full: [*data* (?) -- *idus sept*]*em*(*bres*) *sab* | [*ino ii et anullino cos*].

35. "A scrap from the irregular left edge of a column. The small round hand is of a type not usually found in letters. The lines are crowded together" (p. 252).

i. .[. . .].[
. .[. .]. . .[
epulụ.[
p̣e. . .[
ạ. . . . .[
. .[
]. . . .ici.[
s .[
[
.[

3–4. R. W. Davies, *BASP* 5 (1968) 33, proposes *epulum* and *penus*.

36. Incoming.

Recto:

[. .].[
. . .[   ]aḅ[. .]ụ.[
⟦$\overset{c}{q}$⟧ui[   ]ụṇọ.[.]. .[
[.]ṃ.[   ]ṛ.[. .]ṭạ[
. . .[

Verso:

]. ẠV[RE]ḶỊẠṆỌ TRIB
..[
]..[

1. "A slanting stroke at the left edge can hardly be from *o*. Enough papyrus is preserved at the end to make it probable that *coh* was omitted."

37. Incoming.

]ιανω[
]χαιρε[ιν
]μαληθ.[
]ετ[..].[
]..[
]ṿα[
].[

1. "Probably to be restored as an incoming letter: *Ποστομίῳ Αὐρηλ*]*ιανῷ̣*."

3. "The letter following *eta* may equally well be read as *alpha*."

38. Incoming, because the signature is in a different hand from the signature of no. 1.

].[
].[..]..[
]et anul[l]ịṇọ [cos
]..[.....].al[
]..[*ca.* 12].ol
]e[*ca.* 15]m
(*Hand 2*)].[.]o cos opt[o]
te domine fra-
ter felicis[si]mum
bene uale[r]e

7. Probably [*sabino et anull*]*ị*[*n*]*o cos*; cf. nos. *1* 7; *20* 4; and *25* 7.

39. Incoming. Plate 42, 2.

]c̣ạ[
]m[
].ul[.].arạ[..]n[
].i..tum dim[.....]ig̣[
]ḷ[a]nia [a]nṭ[o]ṇiṇiana [.]nti[
]..[..].[. sa]b[ino ii] eṭ anulliṇ[o
].[ ].[ ].ṃiḅ..[
]ḅ..[....].mi.[.]...[
].ṛtin..[opt]o te domine fṛ[ater (*Hand 2*)
[f]ẹ[lici]ṣṣ[i]mum beṇẹ ụạḷẹṛ[e]

1.]..[*:* D. Possibly]*c̣ṛ*[or even]*pṛ*[.
3.].*ul*[..]..*rạ*[...]*n*[*:* D.
4. *dim*[......]...[*:* D. Probably *dim*[*isi*; cf. nos. *1* 6; *6* 9; and *42* 13; and see on *26* 2.
5. "An obvious restoration is *ala Thracum Hercu*]*l*[*a*]*nia*, but that unit seems to have been transferred to Egypt by 185." The objection is not insurmountable; the ala could have been brought to Syria for Caracalla's campaign, or individual soldiers or centurions could have been transferred in either direction.
6.]..[...].[... *sa*]*b*[*ino:* D. The date must fall between *v idus sept* (no. 32) and *iii* — *dec* (no. 42); but the few remains seem not to fit any of the possibilities.
7.].[– – –].....[*:* D. Perhaps *d* instead of *b*.
8.]...[.....].*mi*.[.]...[*:* D. Instead of *b*, a *d* is possible.
9.]... *tin* .*:* D.

40. Incoming. "The writing is a fine block capital, suitable to a bookhand" (p. 254).

]ω
χαιρ]ειν
].α̣
].ς

41. Incoming. "The beginning recalls that of no. 2. Presumably lines 12–13 contained names, and lines 14–16 the signature, but nothing has been recognized certainly" (p. 254).

]..[
του]ς̣ δοθε̣[ντας μοι στρατιωτας της σπειρης κʹ παλμυρηνων αντ]ω̣νειν̣[ιανης
]ου[
– – – – –
].δ[
]..[
[.]π̣ροει...εν[
[..]ε̣μμα[..]ν αλλα̣[
]..[.] επεμ̣[ψα
]εντετ...[
[..].ι̣θε̣[..]αβομ̣[
[.]δωνα.[...].ουα
.[...]υτ̣ευθηνα̣[
εχειν σοι δεομε.[
δ..η[..].[.]α̣ις̣[

2–3. "Restoration is based on no. *2*; cf. also no. *4*, col. i, etc."
5. "The arrangement of the fragments by Ibscher leaves room for one line here, which is entirely lost."
8. "It would be possible to read προείπομεν, but the traces do not establish this."
10. "Any other person and number of the aorist or imperfect of πέμπω would be equally acceptable."
11. Restore ἀριθμῷ π]έντε τ...[?
13. "The name might be restored as 'Α]δωναῖ[ος, but the formation is properly an adjective .... and I have found no instance of its use as a name ..." Easier restorations are [δα]δωνα .[(cf. Claudius Dadona in **1** xliii 11; **2** xliii 9) or [αβ]δωνα .[(cf. Priscus Abdona in **1** vii 13; **2** xii 26), both from Dura.
14. "This may be a verbal form in -ευθην or -ευθηνα[ι."
15. "We may think of a wish, καλῶς (for example) ἔχειν σοι, but the verb should be εὔχομαι rather than δέομαι."
16. "It would be possible to read δοχη. The next partially preserved letter has a long tail, so *iota* or *rho*."

42. Outgoing? Ca. November 29–December 11. "This column is written in a small, irregular scrawl and is perhaps a draft of an outgoing letter. The scratchings or corrections in lines 8 and 11 support this supposition" (p. 255).

]..[
]um[....].o[
]...ḅ[...]c̣ḥ[
]..   .[..]...[
sabị[n]o ii cos
]..[....].ọ....[....].u..a. [.]
]..[.....]..[.....]..[
].[*ca.* 10   ]⟦...[]⟧
]esidis
]..[....].....[......]ium
]... .ḷ......eq qui ḍẹsiderạ[-
]equum sibi probandum
]q̣uem dimisi ad ụọ[s] ii[i..].. [d]ec· sabiṇ[o ii cos

3. "Possibly *Ḅ[ar]c̣ḥ[alb*, but none of the dotted letters is a secure basis for further conjectures."
9. "Possibly *pra]esidis*."
11. *ḍẹsiderạ[t:* D. "The letters before *eq* are corrected and overwritten."

43. "The subject is uncertain, though line 10 may refer to soldiers acting as guards for herds, perhaps migrating flocks of sheep" (p. 255). More probably animals collected for the use of the army. Note the possibility of *iumenta* in no. 11, line 5.

]m[
]*vacat*   [*ca.* 10]...[
]ṇ item[*ca.* 10]..n.[
a]ntoṇ[*ca.* 12   ]..[
]..[.....]...[
]ṭi.[..]...[.]u...[
].tei[.. f]ṛaṭer .[
].[8   ]e...[.]..i.[
].....i....[.]u.ant.[
c̣um pecoribuṣ ẹsse[

9. "Possibly *m]uṭant* followed by the centurial sign."

44. Incoming? "A few letters . . . apparently from the right edge of a column. There is a gap of 3 cm. between lines 3 and 4" (p. 256).

].[...].ti
c]astra
]ane[..].
Three lines blank
(*Hand 2*)]...[.]

45. Incoming.

]kas
]us[
Two lines lost
]us
(*Hand 2*)].en...[
anu]ḷḷịṇo cọṣ

1. "*kas*[*tra*?"
4. "*De*]*c̣enḅr ṣạ*[*bino ii*?"

46. Incoming, because the subscription is not in Postumius Aurelianus' hand.

]felicis-
[simum be]ne uale-
[re]

47. Incoming. "The address on the verso shows that Aurelianus was still tribune of the cohort. The writer may be praepositus praetenturae" (p. 257); cf. **91** *1* ii verso 3 and *2* ii verso 3.

Recto:

[..].[
[.]..[
One line lost
...[
[.]ịuị[

Verso:

postumio ạụreliano trib [coh]
ạ [ ]p praet

2. "*prae*]*p praet*?"

48–50. "This and the two scraps that follow were placed in the same folder by Ibscher and may come from adjacent columns. All are in small, undistinguished hands" (p. 257).

48.

]..[
]. sabino ị[i e]t
[anulli]ṇọ c[o]s [.....]
].
]..[
(*Hand 2*)]opt[o te]
[domine fra]ter f̣[eli-
[ciss]ịṃ[u]ṃ [bene]
[ualere]

49.

]. . . [
]. . . . [.]. [
]ḷọṇgi[nu]ṣ . [

50.

]. [
]. el. [
]. aurẹ[l
]. [
]ịno[
]ḷ[.]. ci. [.]. . . [
]ṣ. ụṣ. [. . .]. ṛ. s[

5. Perhaps [*sab*]*ịno* [*ii et anullino cos*]; cf. nos. *1* 7; *20* 4; *25* 7; and *38* 7.
6–7. "The last two lines might be a docket or signature. The first could be read, with some effort, as *fe*]*ḷiciṣ*[*s*]*im-* but the next line does not yield any part of the formula" (p. 257).

51–57. "The following fragments are all in the same small, irregular hand and probably come from two or more columns of the same text. Despite their number and extent, their contents are not at all clear. The hand is very much like, and probably identical with, that in [**101**] and a connection with that text is suggested also by *fru*[*ment-* in no. 56. It is possible therefore that that text [**101**] should be combined with these fragments. However, it seems to be a directive of a kind quite out of place in the present roll. [Note, too, that *fru*[in no. 56, line 3, could be a part of the verb *frui.* ROF.] Another possibility is that these fragments do not belong here" (p. 258).

51. "Complete at the top."

]ẹo. . . . . [
]. .
]. . ec̣ta
]o. [. . . . .]
]ṣ

52. "Complete at the top and right. *Valere* is possible at the end of line 2."

]. ef. . ei. . . .
]. . . . ale. e
Two lines blank
]. of. . [
]. . . . [
]te. . . [
]. . . [
]. . [

53. "Complete at the top."

].[.]l..[
].a.[..]io′....[
i]unxi et c̣..[
].......[
]....[
]..[

54. "There is a blank space of 2.3 cm. between lines 1 and 2."

]ẹ.....e
vacat
]..[.]..um
]...ḅ.ạl[.].[
]..xx ṃil[..]..[
]quarum exeṃ[pl-
].... ḥọs si[
]..[.]......[
]..e[

5. A reference to letters or orders which the writer is citing.

55. "Complete at the top."

]....at sci.[
]. tabul[
]ṣṭur....[
].ulṭe..[
].[

3. *quae*]*stura-*?

56. "Incomplete on all sides."

].[.......].[
]..[.].re.[......]ent .. et[
t]ribuṇo coh[..].i.[.].re eos fru[
]...[.].[..].[..].....[.].ṭiṣ..[
].[...].[...]..ṛou..[
].[......]...[

3. *fru*[*ment:* D.

57. "Incomplete on all sides."

].[
pal]ṃuṛeno′[
]...[

"There are, also, numerous smaller and larger unplaced fragments, which yield no sense and have been omitted here" (p. 259).

90

Letters Demanding Restoration of Discipline

PDur. 55 (inv. D. P. 105) ca. 218–220

Transcription, commentary, and facsimile: *Final Rep.* v, no. 55 and plate 17; *ediderunt Latinas* Gilliam, *Graecas* Welles.

Although one is Latin and the other Greek, and although they are in different hands, both of these letters are on one sheet of papyrus. The best explanation seems to be the editors' suggestion (p. 214) that the Latin letter "included a copy of a Greek document . . . to which it . . . served to call official notice. The Greek text can have been a memorandum addressed by local magistrates to the governor or others, complaining of soldiers' misbehavior, and the Latin text may have been an order to their commanding officer to correct the situation. It may be noted that the Greek text shows a literary and discursive quality which removes it from the category of purely routine communications."

On this assumption, the author of the Greek letter would be a magistrate at Dura; the *Παρ' ἡμεῖν σπείρῃ* would be the xx Palmyrenorum; *δẹ́ọ[μ]αι* would be perfectly proper in frag. a, line 3; and the plural in *καθ[ο]ρῶμεν* (a 1), *ἡμεῖν* (a 4), and *ἡμῶν* (a 6) would be literal, not a pluralis maiestatis. Nevertheless, it remains true that "the relationship between the two texts is unknown" (p. 214); and Welles (p. 216) offers a different analysis of the Greek text. See below.

The date is at least within the reign of Elagabal; and the editors are probably right in arguing for a time shortly after Macrinus' defeat in June of 218 (p. 213), or at least before Comazon became consul in 220. As a matter of fact, it seems very likely that he is writing in the capacity of praetorian prefect; cf. Rudolf Hanslich, *RE* 7A, 2412–13, s.v. "Valerius."

The verso is blank.

1. "The two larger fragments (*a* and *b*) are evidently from the same text. . . . The first is from the upper part of a column, the second from the lower part, and, to judge by the amount of papyrus left blank, from the end of a text; there is no closing formula such as *opto te bene valere* . . . at least one column has been lost at the left. Presumably the small Latin fragments come from this, though only the content in Frag. *c* offers any confirmation" (*PDur.*, p. 214).

Frag. a

[7].em d n sanctissimo
[imp] ṃarco aurel˙ inụịc̣ṭọ
[7]. litteras ṣụas quas
.ụṇ..[.]ạṣi.[.]ṣ ạḍ[

uehementer n.[8].
miḷiṭeṣ coḥ x̣x̣ [palm]ỵrenorum
sublạṭ[i]s sạṇt....[.]ṣ derelictis
c̣astrị[s 7] ḍịṣc̣iplina
[....]..[8]a pạṛạ[po]ṭamiạ
[*ca.* 12].[...]..ṛ...[

Frag. b

[..].ụm ualeri c[o]ṃạzonṭị[s
[a]ụctoritate sacra de.[
ṭe sine mora˙ commilit[ones in castra]
sua inducere et de ceterọ [curare]
ut ex diṣc̣iplina ạg̣ạ[nt

Frag. c

lit]ṭerarum uaḷ[eri comazontis?
].. quoda.[
]ṭa.[.].. paḷmyrẹṇị ..[
]....[

Frag. d

].sci.[
].[

Frag. e

]ạrios ei[
].[.]ṃdeṣ.[

Frag. f

].ṣ˙ s˙ u.[
].exe..[

Frag. g

...[
rọge.[
....
[..].ma[

Frag. h

]...t.[
]..ṇt..[

Quoted matter in the following commentary is from the editors' apparatus in *PDur*.

1 a 1. "The first partially preserved letter . . . is most likely *s*; *De*]*c̣em* is possible but unattractive."

2. *inụ*[*icto* . . .]: D.

4. . . *ụṇ*. . [. .]*ṣc̣iṭ* [.]. . [–7–]: D. After the first lacuna,]*ạḍ* might be read instead of]*ạṣ*

7–8. *sublạṭ*[.]*s sa*. . . . . . . [. .]. *:* D; "Possibly *sublạṭ*[*i*]*s sạṇc̣ṭịṣ* [*s*]*ịg*[*ni*]*ṣ*, *ḍerelictis c̣astrị*[*s*, *soluta?*] *ḍịṣc̣iplina*."

10. I have taken this line from Gilliam.

b 1. [. . .]*ẹm:* D; "Possibly]*ụm*, not]*ẹm*, at the beginning of the line."

2. *dep*[*osc*. . . .]*:* D; "Presumably *dep*[*osco*], but the subject and form of the verb are uncertain." The letter after *de* has a flourish at the top which crosses both *d* and *e* and seems not to be repeated elsewhere. It may be *p*, but could be another letter, such as *a* or *r*.

3–5. The restorations are Gilliam's.

c 1. Perhaps, if these smaller fragments come from the column which preceded frags. a and b, one should restore *exemplum lit*]*ṭerarum* here and understand frags. a and b as part of the text of the copy.

2. Divide and restore *quod aḍ*[– – *pertinet*? Or *quodaṃ*[?

3. "Line 4 and the first three letters of line 3 are on a separate piece. Why it was attached here, and whether correctly, I do not know."

d. "Possibly *p*]*ọscịṭ*[or *p*]*ọscịṃ*[*us*. The trace of the letter in the second line seems to make it impossible to attach this to frag. *b*, 2–3."

f 2. "There appears to be an abbreviation mark or small *u* above the fourth letter."

2. "The Greek letter occupies the right part of frag. *a* and a number of smaller fragments. The hand seems clearly the same in all except frag. *q*, which, nevertheless, was found with the rest, and that hand is rather similar. The first line of the preserved text can be understood as having stood near the beginning of a letter. . . . The writer uses the *pluralis maiestatis*, and . . . [his] horizon is evidently wide. He mentions 'the cohort which is here with us' . . . and so was above the level of a unit commander. . . . A question attaches to the phrase ἐπὶ Συρείαν in line 5; if someone . . . was coming 'to Syria' he . . . was coming from outside. This would exclude taking the reference to apply to the Dura soldiery" (*PDur.*, p. 216).

Frag. a

καθ̣[ο]ρ̣ω̣μεν ο̣τ̣[ι
εις π[α]ντα υπεικ[ουσι
δε̣.[.]αι σου υ.[
ται γαρ της παρ ημ̣ε̣ιν σπε̣[ιρης
τερω̣ ως επι συρειαν και γενομ[εν-
ανων [. . .]ω ημω̣ν ως επι με[.]λ̣α̣[
[. . .]. .[. . . .]. . ηλθαν .[. . .]α̣.[

Frag. i

]σ̣τρα[τιω-
]προ̣[

Frag. j

]μας[
]φορου̣[

Frag. k

].[.]ι̣. .[
]. ουεξι̣[λλα-
]. . . . εις την πολ[ιν
στρατι]ωτων κα. . .[

Frag. l

]. .ιας .[
]εν[
]ειν.[

Frag. m

].π. .[
].[. . . .]ρ̣ω̣ς τ̣.ηλε[
]αμα κα[. .]χειν αρ[
]. .[

Frag. n

].α.[
]ρατ̣ος[
].επ[

Frag. o

]ρα[

Frag. p

]μ[

Frag. q

].ηπ.[
στρα]τιωτα[
vacat
].[. .]. . .[

2 a 1–2. "The sense may be restored . . .: καθ[ο]ρῶμεν ὅτ[ι οἱ στρατιῶται (or the like) οὐκ] | εἰς π[ά]ντα ὑπεί-κ[ουσι τοῖς ὑπὲρ αὐτοὺς τεταγμένοις]: 'We observe that the soldiers are not in all respects obedient to their commanders.' This is just the kind of understatement we should expect in an official notice sent about at the beginning of a new and perhaps still somewhat precarious reign. Probably conditions were actually chaotic." This, of course, is all on the assumption that the Greek letter emanated from the emperor or another very high source.

3. "The obvious and quite possible reading and restoration is δέ̣ο̣[μ]αι, but the writer uses the plural of himself elsewhere and this does not seem to be the place in the letter where he would make a request, even if we may suppose the writer of such a letter to request at all, and not give orders."

6. "If με[.]λ̣α̣[is part of a place name (I have not identified it), the line might have continued πρὸς ἡ]μᾶς."

k 2. οὐεξι̣[λλατιων-: D; but a form of *uexillarius* is equally possible.

m 3. "Perhaps κα[τέ]χειν, but something of the *epsilon* should be visible."

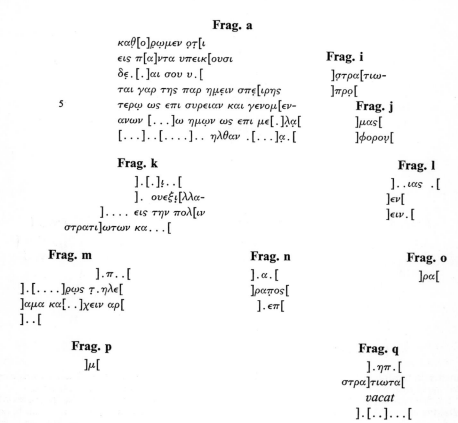

91

Requests for Enforcement by the Tribune of the XX Palmyrenorum

PDur. 64 (inv. D. P. 15) Between late June and December 31, 221

Transcription, commentary, and facsimile of no. 1 recto: *Final Rep.* v, no. 64 and plate 39; *edidit* Gilliam.

Transcription, commentary, and facsimiles of both nos. 1 and 2, recto and verso: J. F. Gilliam, "Two Latin Letters from Dura-Europos of A.D. 221," *Études de Papyrologie* 8 (1957) 49–58 and plates 1–4.

Commentary: R. W. Davies, "A Note on *P. Dura* 64," *Latomus* 26 (1967) 67–72.

CPL, no. 337, is a brief description without any text.

These two letters were both written by Aurelius Rufinus, a procurator Augustorum who is also praepositus praetenturae, that is, in charge of a sector of the frontier. They are addressed to Iustillus, tribune of the coh. xx Palmyrenorum; and both once included copies of letters from Antonius Seleucus, governor of Syria, as authority for the requested action.

In the first letter Rufinus asks Iustillus to force a libertus Augustorum to furnish barley from praedia fiscalia to cavalrymen and muleteers who are stationed at Appadana. The second requests the tribune to compel a librarius of the leg. xvi Flavia Firma to *satisfacere* a man who was apparently named but not otherwise identified. Nor is the nature of the desired action clear. The verb normally means to apologize or to make verbal amends; but it can also mean to give security or to pay a creditor. Which is meant here is impossible to determine.

In regard to the situations here Gilliam says (*PDur.*, p. 230): "The relations of the . . . men involved might be clearer if the procurator's title were read with more certainty and his position better understood. . . . He does not appear to write to the tribune as the latter's immediate superior in a chain of command. His request is based on a letter of the governor rather than on his own authority. Further, it is somewhat uncertain why the procurator should choose to obtain the action he desires through the tribune. While the librarius was quite possibly under the command of the tribune, one would not assume that the freedman was ordinarily subject to his orders."

Davies argues convincingly that Rufinus was a procurator concerned with the cursus publicus and that the soldiers at Appadana were at least in part assigned to that service. The procurator, however, did not have complete and exclusive authority over the soldiers and so was forced on occasion, as here, to appeal to the governor of Syria and the tribune of the xx Palmyrenorum to secure obedience.

1. Recto:

Col. i: *Rufinus' letter*

[aurel rufinus iustillo suo]
ac̣[c]..[s]ạlute]ṃ
(*Hand 2*) grat[o et se]leu[co co]s
(*Hand 1*) quid ṃiḥị scṛiber[e] ḍignạt[u]ṣ sịt
antonius seleucus u c˙ c[o]s noster
domine fili ut scires subieci
et peṭọ compellas ordinatum augg
n′n′ lib equiṭịbus siụ[e] mulionib[us q]ụ[i]
iṇ uexiḷḷ′ p̣padanenṣ[i] ḍeg horḍ[e]ụṃ
ex praedis f̣ịṣc̣alib[u]s dare ṣẹc̣un-
[dum . . .].[*ca.* 17]. . . . .
].[.].

Col. ii: *Copy of governor's letter*

(*Hand 3?*) ḥ[ord]euṃ[
ạ. . . . .[
dari prae. .[
mem
Remainder of column blank

Verso:

].[.]. .ỊO IVSTILLO Ṭ[RIB COH]
[aur]ẹl rufinus proc augg nn
praep p̣raeṭent

TRANSLATION (col. i)

[Aurelius Rufinus to Iustillus.]

Received [*day, month*], 221.

What Antonius Seleucus, vir clarissimus, our governor, has condescended to write to me I have subjoined, respected son, so that you may know; and I request that you compel Ordinatus, freedman of our Augusti, to give according to [ ] barley from the farms belonging to the fiscus to the cavalrymen or muleteers who are serving in the vexillation at Appadana. . . .

Quoted matter in the following commentary is from Gilliam's edition in *Final Rep.* v.

i 2. "*Acc(epta)* was followed by the day and month of receipt. Dockets in this position are found in [**99** and **88**]. In [**89**] dockets . . . are at the bottom of the sheet as also, e.g., in [**87**]." Both lines of the docket are in a smaller hand and occupy the space left blank in the line to the left of *salutem*.

3. *scṛiber[et] .ị. . . . .:* D. For the *d* of *dignatus* cf. *domine* in line 5; for the *g*, cf. *augg* in line 6. The *t* at the end is almost certain. Nothing in this reading conflicts with the description of the traces in *PDur.* ad loc.

4. Expand: *u(ir) c(larissimus) co(n)s(ularis)*. On the identity of Antonius Seleucus, see Gilliam ad loc. He may well be the Julius Antonius Seleucus known as governor of Moesia Inferior under Elagabal; but the present letters are the only evidence for him as governor of Syria.

5. "The procurator addresses the tribune as *domine fili* probably because of a difference in age rather than in rank. One finds, e.g., the prefect of Egypt addressing the commander of an auxiliary unit as *frater* [**87**, line 10], (A.D. 103)."

6. The Augusti meant are Elagabal and Severus Alexander, though the latter was actually only Caesar. See Gilliam ad loc. As he says, this limits the date of the letters to the time from late June, when Alexander became Caesar, to the end of 221.

"For *ordinare* as a technical term meaning to appoint to an office, see O. Hirschfeld, *Die kaiserlichen Verwaltungsbeamten bis auf Diocletian*[2] (1905), p. 313, n. 3; p. 443, n. 1; also Bang in Friedlaender, *Sittengeschichte* IV[9], p. 51. It is somewhat strange that the procurator does not give the freedman's name, but one would desire other examples before accepting Ordinatus as a personal name." But perfective participles are used as proper names, especially of slaves. Dessau's indices, for example, yield Acceptus, Ampliatus, Auctus, Doctus, Emeritus (see also **102** frag. a, 6), Inventus, Mandatus, and others in addition to aristocratic names like Torquatus. And *ordinatus* in the sense of "appointed to an office" without any mention of the office would be even stranger, especially in a military context where the word would naturally be understood as "centurion."

6–7. Expand: *aug*(*ustorum*) *n*(*ostrorum*) (*duorum*) *lib*(*ertum*).

8. *horḍẹ*[*u*]*m:* D. Expand: *uexill*(*atione*)*; deg*(*unt*). See especially **1** and **2** for men of the xx Palmyrenorum stationed at Appadana.

9–10. "Perhaps *secun* | [*dum morem . . .*"

ii 1. .[. . .]. .[: D. The copy appears to be in a slightly smaller hand than the procurator's own letter.

2. . . . . . .[: D; "A possible reading . . . is *Ạppạḍạ*[*n*-." This is very likely.

3. ". . . *praec̣ẹ*[*pi* cannot be read. *Praeḍị*[is possible."

Verso 1. "The first letter, of which very little is preserved, may be *a*; the last three, *c* or *tio*."

2–3. "The most obvious possibility for the nomen . . . is [*Aur*]*ẹl*, and the restoration is supported by no. *2*, col. i, 1, which can be read as *Ạụ*[*rel* . . . Apparently the procurator was *praep*(*ositus*) *praetent*(*urae*). Support for the reading is found in [**89**, no. *47* verso, line 2]. I know of no parallel for the office, though one does find a senatorial *leg*(*atus*) *Aug*(*usti*) *ad praetenturam* under Marcus Aurelius: *ILS* 8977; and cf. Ritterling, *RE* 12.1301, s.v. 'legio.' Cf. also the Mauretanian praetentura of the time of Septimius Severus: Fabricius, *RE* 13.668, s.v. 'Limes'. The combination *proc Augg praep* in itself is not a difficulty; see, e.g., *proc Aug limitis* in *ILS* 3251 [a close parallel, it would seem: ROF] and *proc Aug et praep vexillation* in *ILS* 1327."

The nominative case of Rufinus is most unusual. I have no explanation for it; but it recurs on the verso of no. 2.

2. Recto:

Col. i: *Rufinus' letter*

. . . [ ]p̣ạl
(*Hand 2*) acc̣[*ca.* 13]. . [ ]ṣạḷụṭ[e]ṃ
2a gṛạ[to et seleuco cos]
(*Hand 1*) qui[d] mihi scriṗ[s]ẹṛịṭ ạṇṭọṇius
se[l]eucuṣ [u] c cos ṇ [do]ṃiṇ[e f]ịḷi ụt
scires subieci et peṭ[o] c̣ọmpel[l]as
sozontem librari[u]ṃ leg x̣vi f̣ f̣ ạṇtọṇi-
ṇianae satisfacẹre hạ[ni]ṇạe antonius seleucụs u˙ c c̣ọs n .[. . . .]. . . .e
dịgṇạṭus ẹṣt (*Hand 3*) ọpṭọ tẹ ḍominẹ f̣ịḷị [felicissimum]
vacat mul[t]is annis ḅẹṇe ualeṛẹ
] *vacat*. . [*The governor's letter:*
]el˙ ṣ[*ca.* 11]. . [
]. ae q. [
]l[.]a ad ṃe[

Col. ii: *The governor's letter, continued*

(*Hand 4*)]. [
]. [
]. [. .]e. . [
. . . . [
coḷḷegam . . . [
sente eo ḥ[a]ṇ[ina
poterit de. . . [
aeṣtima cuṛạm
Remainder of column blank

Verso:

]IVSTILLO TR[IB COH
]ṛufinụs pṛọc̣ aụgg n
pṛaep pṛaet

TRANSLATION (col i 1–11)

[Rufinus to Iustillus, tribune of the coh. XX Palmyrenorum.]

Received [*day*, *month*], 221.

What Antonius Seleucus, vir clarissimus, our governor, has written to me, I have subjoined, respected son, so that you may know; and I beg that you compel Sozon, librarius of the legio XVI Flavia Firma Antoniniana, to give satisfaction to Hanina. Antonius Seleucus, vir clarissimus, our governor, has condescended to write. . . .

The copy of the governor's letter follows, but is too fragmentary to make sense. In Rufinus' own hand, lines 10–11:

I hope, respected son, that you most fortunately enjoy good health for many years.

i 1. *Ạụ[rel Rufinus Iustillo suo]:* D; "There is a trace of ink at the end of the line but not enough to identify the letter or letters: *s]ụ[o]*?" All the remains are very ambiguous; but the plate in *Études de Papyrologie* seems to show a clear *l* preceded by a possible *pa* at the end of the line. This, however, implies some such restoration as *ṛụf[inus iustillo trib coh xx] pạl[m,* given the spacing of the remains. But the omission of Rufinus' nomen and *suo* would be anomalous; Gilliam's reconstruction is the normal phrasing which one would expect. It is also possible that Rufinus' names and titles occupied a whole line, now lost, and that only Iustillus' names and title appeared in the present line 1.

2. As in no. 1, the two lines of the docket occupy the blank space at the left of *ṣạlụt[e]m*. I have taken over the latter from Gilliam; the plate reveals only the *m*.

On the docket: "Possibly]*ḅṛ* at the end of the line; i.e., *Novem]br(es)* or *Decem]br(es)*." This seems a very acceptable reading; but of course September and October must also be considered.

3. *scri[b]ẹṛẹṭ:* D; "*Scri[ps]ẹṛịṭ* is perhaps a better reading, but distrusting the faded ink I have followed the parallel in [*1* i 3]." The new reading in no. 1 now allows Gilliam's preferred reading here.

4. *[do]miṇ[e] fị[l]i:* D.

6. Expand: *leg(ionis); f(lauiae) f(irmae).* "A vexillation of the Legio XVI Flavia Firma was in Dura at this time, and presumably the librarius was a member of this. . . . It seems reasonable to conclude that the tribune is addressed as the senior officer in the Dura garrison, though it has been argued that a dux ripae was already established in Dura under Elagabal; see [*Final Rep.* v, p. 24]."

7. *ḥ.[. .]ṇạẹ:* D; "*Satisfacere* is probably followed by *ha*[or *hi*[, and the name *Ḥạ[ni]ṇạẹ* is a possible restoration. A Haninas Bellaei, a soldier of the Palmyrene cohort, was in a vexillation at Appadana at this time [**2** xxvii 16]. It is uncertain whether there was a financial obligation or whether the satisfaction to be given was of another kind." It is somewhat odd that Haninas is not further identified; but that matter was probably sufficiently covered in the governor's letter.

8. *ṇ(oster).[– 6 –]. . .e.e:* D; "A new sentence begins with *Antonius Seleucus.* At the end of line [8] a possible reading is *ere.*" See also under line 9.

9. *d. . .a. scit:* D; "In line [9], *d* may have been preceded by another letter. Possible readings after *a* include *r* or *tu* (written as in *ordinatum* in [no. *1* i 6]. . . *Opto te*, etc., is in a small, irregular hand, the procurator's own. There are traces of ink after *fili*, presumably from *felicissimum*, which I have restored, but they are not enough to permit any letters to be identified." At the end of line 8 perhaps restore *ṇ(oster) m[ihi] ḍịc̣ẹre*, though the last two letters look most like *me*, and *scribere*, which one would expect, seems impossible. At any rate, the blank line which follows, in part of which Rufinus wrote his subscription, shows that the copy of the governor's letter began in line 11.

10. *mụltịs:* D.

11. *vacat* [. .].[*:* D; "In [11] one might expect *exemplum*;" and in fact these traces, isolated in the middle of an otherwise blank line, are very probably the abbreviation *ex*, as at the top of **87** and in **98**, no. 2, line 4.

12.]*el* . [– *10* –]. . .[. . .]*:* D; "The letter following *el* . . . is not *r*; i.e., *Aur*]*el R*[*ufinus.*" A very possible restoration is *aur*]*el ṣ*[*ozon.*

ii 3. [.].[*:* D.

6. *sente eo* .[*:* D. Either *praesente* or *absente* could be restored, since we know nothing of the other circumstances.

7. Possibly *dec̣ẹṛ[nere.*

8. *aestima. .m* [*:* D; "perhaps *aestimarem* should be read; if so, *re* is very carelessly formed. Valuation of damages may be involved."

Verso 2. Here too, as in no. 1 verso, line 2, the name of the writer is in the nominative instead of the expected ablative with *a*(*b*).

92

Letter with Three Lists of Names by Centuries and Turmae

PDur. 67 (inv. D. P. 16 verso) Between March 13, 222, and December 225

Transcription, commentary, and facsimile of cols. iii–vi: *Final Rep.* v, no. 67 and plate 47; *edidi.*

This text is similar to **89**, nos. 4 and 12, in that it consists of a covering letter followed by a list of names of the personnel involved. It is much the longest text of the sort; the covering letter occupied at least two columns, and over one hundred names followed.

Almost nothing remains of col. i; but in col. ii, 9 and 13, two separate detachments of soldiers are mentioned, and in line 12, *ex]p[e]ḍitione* is fairly certain. There was a third detachment, for the names are divided into three lists, each headed by several lines ending in a total. The best-preserved heading is in col. v, 1–4; but enough remains in col. viii, 1–3, to show that it was similar. The heading of col. iii is almost entirely lost. This triple division into lists contained in cols. iii–iv, v–vii, and viii–ix is further supported by the blank space at the foot of col. vii, and by the recurrence in all three of the century of Pudens and the turma of Antoninus along with other centurions and decurions who appear in only two of the lists, always in the same order as in **8**, which occupies the recto. Within each list the soldiers are identified by century or turma, but not by date of enlistment.

The date of the letter can be fixed only approximately. It may or may not be later than **8**, the recto (see above, p. 97), which in turn is not earlier than November 4, 222. On the other hand, it is certainly later than **2** (after March 13, 222) because the centurion Malchus has been replaced by Pudens. By December 225 (*PDur.* 129), however, Aurelianus had replaced one of the four decurions named here who are also in **2**—Zebidas, Tiberinus, Octavius, and Antoninus. (Demetrius' name is lost from col. vii; but he appears in *PDur.* 129, so he was not the one replaced.) Consequently this text belongs in the three years between March 13, 222, and December 225.

The fact that it is written on the verso of a list of names needs explanation; and no obvious one comes to mind. There is a date in ii 16, which could be a docket; but there seems to be no subscription by the sender, and there may be a cancellation in line 10. Perhaps, then, this is the draft of an outgoing letter which was kept on file when the fair copy was sent off.

Col. i

]. . [. . .]. [
]. [.]a[
]ṣṣ
About four lines lost
]. [. .]. [.]ṃḅị. [
]. [

Col. ii

].[
].ẹ..[*ca.* 25].[..]ṇṭ.[
].[
].ṣ[
]ẹạ[.]l.[
]. Ɣ[
s]ụbḍạ[......]ḷ[.....]...[.......].p̣[..]..ṃiae.[
].[.].m[*ca.* 12]ẹndum ad.[.].[..]ṭiọnẹm mu[
].ṛ[*ca.* 11]ṃil lx ịṇ ḥịṣ eq i
]..ạḍ [*ca.* 14].ns....[.]..sit[.]ṣ[
]...[*ca.* 12]misaḍ.ịi.ṛi.tem
]e.[ex]p̣[e]ḍitione tẹ.ṭari
].ẹ...... lxxxxiii iṇ [hi]ṣ ṃi[
].[...]..ṛị[.] qu[or]ụm noṃ[ina a]ḍplị[ca]ṛi
].ad.[..].ni.[....]ṇoṭụṃ .[..]ẹio
].a[.....]ḳ[a]l m[
].[

7.]..*ṇiae* or]..*ụiae* is possible in place of]..*ṃiae*; not *par*]*ạp*[*o*]*ṭamiae* because the letter to the left of *p* is a tall one: *e*, *i*, or *n*. The *p*, too, is very uncertain.
10. *ns* and the next letter seem to have been erased.
12. *tẹṇṭari*? *tẹṣṭari*?
16. Possibly *a*[*cc*(*epta*)...] Either March or May, of course.

Col. iii

]ụṣ...
One line lost
]..[.].[
Ɣ mari] [
]. ḅannạẹi
acibas] b[o]ra
]
]us
Ɣ [anton p]ṛ
[ ]l[.]..[
iul .[.....]ius
]...[ ]ẓeḅ[id]a
iul romanus
aurel magnus
Ɣ anton post
ze]biḍạ iarḥaei
aurẹ[l ro]manus
abgarus themasa
Ɣ pudeṇ[t]ịs
aurel[....].ṛius
ạurel .[...]ṣ
a]ụrel baṛnaeus

4. [Ɣ *mari*(*ani*)]; cf. col. v, 19, and **1** xxi 1–2.
9. (*centuria*) *anton*(*ini*) *pr*(*ioris*).
15. (*centuria*) *anton*(*ini*) *post*(*erioris*).
20. *deme*]*ṭrius*?]*ṣṣius* is also possible.
22. *bạṇnaeus* is also possible.

Col. iv

About half a column lost

].
].m
ze]ḅiḍa
satu]ṛnịli
].[
.[ ]..[
.[
[ ]....[
[ ]ṃẹ...[.]ṣ
]..[....].l[
[Ŧ ant]ọn(ini)
]..nḍ[..].ṇ.[
]nus
i.[ ]apọḷ[

12.].*ṇṣ:* D. Perhaps the duplicarius *alexandrus* .[...].*a*, **1** xli 4; **2** xli 4.
14. The first letters in the line are a marginal annotation as in v 16 and vi 8. The name may be *ḷị*[*cinnius*]*apọḷ*[*loninus*; cf. **1** xliii 12; **2** xliii 10.

Col. v

⟦].es..[⟧
].[.].[
].....[
]ḷv in his[
]
Ɣ da]ṇụ[mi]
]ṇ.ṣ iarhaei
]. ṃạx̣imi
].balaç̣ḥi
aur]ẹḷ[ ]ue.ṣụṛus
au]ṛel [m]ạṇṇus
Ɣ ṃạrci
gạleris asclepiạ[d]ẹs
ṃọmbogeus barnebụṣ
ạụrẹl [a]ntoṇinus
ex off [a]ụrel diodorus
ạurel bassus
ḍomitiụs niç̣[ol]ạus
Ɣ ṃ[a]ri(ani)
ṃ[a]l[c]ḥus [u]abalathi
aurel ab[i]ḍlaḥạs

9. *uabalathi*? Or read].*balaẹi*?
11. ..*ṇṛus:* D.
13. **2** xii 27 and **8** iii 16 have *gerelius*.
14. Expand: *off*(*icio*).

Col. vi

].e.[
Century of Antoninus prior
]nṣ[
].[..]...[.]us
aurel] ḅ[a]ṛṣị[ms]us
]...[ ]..ei
]..[
]uṣ[..].[
[e]x̣ of[f].[ ].[
Century of Antoninus posterior
].[
]l...
heliodorus]ạpoloṇi
].[
].....ụs
]...ṣ
]ạb[..]..[.]i
]ṭhemasa
].n.[
a]ụṛẹl .aṣiliạ[
ϒ p̣[ud]ent[i]s
z.....[.].ạieṛ[
⟦.a[.]ṭoṇ⟧
ạẹṣon mo[.]ị[
ḅ.[ ]bḅi.[

8. [*e*]*x of*[*f* omitted in D.
18. *basilianus*?

21. *anton* seems to have been written and then canceled, evidently a mistake for *ạẹṣon*, which follows.

Col. vii

].[
]idạlạ[
].ṣaḅ[
].l..[
Turma of Demetrius
i]arhaei
]ṃax[i]ṃus
ṣ[ ]i
ạ[elius m]ạṛc̣ẹḷlus
Ŧ [o]c̣ṭaụi
[a]ẹl[i]us f̣[ort]ụṇaṭus
Ŧ ạnṭon(ini)
iul g̣ermanus
ṣalmeṣ ṃạlchi
ϒ mạṛc̣i
anṭonịus maxịṃus
Remainder of column blank

2. The name is probably *auidalathus*, and the man must have belonged to the turma of Tiberinus or perhaps Zebidas, but he is unlikely to be the Simaones Auidalathi of the turma of Tiberinus (**1** xxxiv 9; **2** xxxiv 8) who enlisted in 196, for he would be too old.

15–16. Since this is a century following the entries for equites, Antonius Maximus was probably a dromedarius. The same order of pedites, equites, and dromedarii is followed in **1** and **2**, although the dromedarii are attached to centuries. In **8** they are listed at the end of their respective centuries.

Col. viii

].[
].[..]ṛ.[
].[..]x̣ịị.[
[ϒ da]ṇuṃi[
m]ạgnus uaḅạ[lathi
cl] ẓeb[id]a
ḅassus[ ].bọl[.]a
aurel fronton
[...]ṣalṃus an[.].ọ[
aur]ẹl romanus
ϒ ṃạṛc̣ị
ạbḍạṣ zebida
]..[ ]...ạl....ụs
].[ ]ạṇtoninus
]l ạṇtọniṇ[u]ṣ
].l bassus
]ạ[
iul anṭọ[n]ị[u]s
ạ[u]ṛel baṣṣ[u]s
ạụṛẹl ḍọmiṭ[ius
a]ụṛẹḷ mo.[imu]s

3. Cf. v 4: *]lv in his*[.

21. Either Mocimus or Monimus.

Col. ix

].[
One line lost
ϒ ..[
.[....].[....].[.].[
aurẹ[l] iuliuṣ
aurẹ[l .]ṇti.[.].[
ϒ pudentis
abidṇạḅ[u]ṣ ṭḥ[emas]a
c̣assiạṇụṣ ni...ṛ
ṃạṛinuṣ [l]ục̣ị
iul ạlẹxạṇḍ[r]ụṣ
iul fla[uiu]ṣ
aurẹl ṃ[ ]ṣ
ex of aurẹl zạḅ[da]ṣ

Ŧ zẹ[b]ịda
ạbdoṇ ạbḅ[a]l[. .] . [
Ŧ tibẹ[ri]ṇị
ẓạḅdiḅọlus tḥẹmasa

6. *aurel antiochianus*? Cf. **1** xiii 7; **2** xxviii 24. If so, this is proved to be the century of Antoninus posterior, which is probable in itself, since the century of Pudens comes next, even though the traces after the centuria-sign do not look like *an*. An Aurelius Iulius also appears in this century in **1** xii 7.

16. Probably *abdon abbalmaei*; cf. **15** i 23; ii 18.

Col. x

]l[
Ŧ ọc̣ṭạuị
ḅạṛnaẹ[us . . . .]ḷ
Ŧ antoniṇị
ṇẹbudaeṣ [t]ḥema[s]a
Remainder of column blank

93

Four Fragments of a Letter

PDur. 76 (inv. D. P. 37) ca. 210–225

Transcription and commentary: *Final Rep.* v, no. 76; *edidit* Gilliam.

These fragments are classified with the letters dealing with personnel because of the phrase *mitte qui petat* in frag. b, 1; but there is not enough to indicate what the subject was.

The date is based on the hands.

The verso is blank.

Gilliam's text.

Frag. a

].cumque aḍ te[
]ṣc̣ribe..[
vacat

Frag. b

]mitte qui petat qu.[
].e eius ṃ[
Hand 2]...[
]...mu[
vacat

Frag. c

]...[.]..ạ...[
]..[..] coh s ṣ[
Hand 2].[..]. *vacat*
]....b.[.]. *vacat*

Frag. d

]..[
].et d[
].[

"One might expect the lines in the second hand on Frags. *b* and *c* to be either a docket . . . or . . . *opto te bene valere* or the like. I cannot read it as either" *PDur.*, p. 267.

a 2. *PDur.*, app.: "Probably *ṣc̣ribeṛẹ* or *ṣc̣ribeṃ*"; more likely, *scribe ṃị[hi*; cf. **98** *2* a 8.

c 2. *PDur.*, app.: *coh*(*ort*-) *s*(*upra*)*s*(*cript*-).

94

Fragments of Letters with Lists of Names

PDur. 68 (inv. D. P. 40 recto) ca. 232–238

Transcription and facsimile of frag. b only: *Final Rep.* v, no. 68 and plate 40, 1; *edidi.*

Under *PDur.* 68, I described these texts as consisting of eleven layers of a block of papyrus; but I can now account for only ten of them. All are incomplete on all sides, and none but frag. b yields any sense; but the variety of hands proves that this was a roll of letters which in some cases were accompanied by lists of personnel like **92** and **89**, no. 4.

Mention of the turma Paulini shows that these letters are later than **92** and contemporary with **27**, **47**, and **15**. On the other hand, they cannot be later than the list on frag. b, verso (**95**). The Gaulianus of frag. b ii 3 in the present text is probably the same person as in **6** iv 2, who probably enlisted in 214 (cf. **1** ix 27) and would then have been eligible for discharge in 239.

In lettering the fragments, *i* has been omitted to avoid confusion with the numeral.

The verso is **95**.

Frag. a

]c
]c̣ị ỵ

Frag. b (a small, neat hand)

Col. i

]ụl

Col. ii

]c̣tu
demnu.[
gaulian[
uibianị[
Ŧ paulịṇ[i
halas [
].[

Frag. c (medium large, sweeping cursive)

]l .c̣.[.].riạ...[
a]ụṛel gaianus ḥ[.]c̣[
]baṛḅ...[

Frag. d

Traces of letters in two lines

Frag. e

Traces of three letters in large cursive

Frag. f

Traces of four lines in a chancery hand

]ṇus..[

Frag. g (medium large cursive)

] ia.[
One line blank
] max[
].[

Frag. h

]. [
]. .[
One line blank
]. xuị ẹṭ[
].
]..ẹḷ.[
]ụṣ[

Frag. j

Illegible traces of four (?) lines in medium large cursive; then, with a heavier pen and in a vertical hand:
]ṣoṛ

Frag. k

]..[
]....ṃ[
].p̣.ạo[

a 2. Possibly *mar*]*c̣ị*, enlisted 201, but more probably *pris*]*c̣ị*, ca. 215–240, if this is the name of a centurion at all.

b ii 2. This should probably be a name; but cf. **29**, line 11.

95

Names, Perhaps from Letters

PDur. 69 (inv. D. P. 40 verso) ca. 235–238

Transcription and commentary, frag. b only: *Final Rep.* v, no. 69; *edidi.*

The notations at the left of the names in frag. b and the arrangement by consulates recall **1**, **2**, and **8**; but the brevity of this list, coming between two fragments, a and c, which are blank on the verso, forbids us to think of it as a regular roster. It may be a continuation of the list begun on the recto of the same fragment (**94** b). Frag. k may also contain names; and in any event is in a different hand.

The date is fixed by the entries in frag. b, 2: *aufidio mar*[*cello ii cos*, and 7: *cassio dion*[*e ii cos*. In both instances the other consul was Severus Alexander; and the omission of his name puts the list in the period between his death in 235 and his deification, which followed Maximinus' death in May–June, 238, and had taken place by the date of **24**, no later than 242 and perhaps even under Pupienus and Balbinus.

Frags. a, c, e, f, g, h, and j are blank on the verso. (The letter *i* has been omitted to avoid confusion with the numeral.) The recto is **94**.

Frag. b

]ạl.[
]ạụf̣idio ṃạṛ[cello ii cos A.D. 226
ze]bidas iarh[
]ṃ lọ.[.]us salmẹ[

]   albino et max̣[imo cos 227
]nd   themarsas .[
]..[.]..
]   cassio dioṇ[e ii cos 229
–]$\frac{}{p}$[–]——, f   f̣l demetri[us
]ạurel ṃ[

Frag. d

Remains of an address:

]ṚỊ   [
].   c̣ạ....[

Frag. k

Remains of four crowded lines in a small cursive:

]ṇot..[
]ḅẹọeṗ.ṇgri.[
]ạurel maal
]eṃṇ.rc̣.[

96

Copy of a Letter?

PDur. 81 (inv. D. P. 29 verso) A.D. 243–244?

Transcription, commentary, and facsimile: *Final Rep.* v, no. 81 and plate 66, 1; *edidit* Gilliam.

Commentary:

1. R. O. Fink, "M. Aurelius Atho Marcellus," *AJP* 88 (1967) 84–85.
2. R. W. Davies, "M. Aurelius Atho Marcellus," *JRS* 57 (1967) 20–22.

If this is in fact a letter, the lack of a salutation indicates that at least one column preceded the present one; but it could be part of a monthly summary like **58**, **61**, and **62**, or of a morning report (cf. **47** ii 4–9), or, as Davies suggests, comparing **63** (evidently with ii 17–38 in mind), a pridianum. Because of these uncertainties, however, it has been kept under its original classification among the letters. If line 1 is to be restored *quorum nomina adplicui*, or the like (cf. **87** 7–9; **92** ii 14), the probability that it is a copy of a letter is enhanced.

Davies has presented the fullest interpretation of this text to date. His thesis is that Atho, as procurator of Syria Coele, cooperated with Philip the Arab in his overthrow of Gordian III and was rewarded with the procuratorship of Mauretania; and this may be basically right. We agree at least in identifying the present Atho Marcellus with the one named in *Ann. Ep.* 1908, no. 30, and *CIL* VIII 8809 (Dessau 5785) as both procurator Augusti of the two Philips and Otacilia Severa and also praeses. We also agree in ascribing the papyrus to the time of Gordian's campaign in Syria, though I should not exclude Philip's reign. This dating, however, should not be taken as proved; the case for it is no stronger than the assumption that the praetorian prefects (line 3) are present in Syria and that the emperor is accordingly also there. Actually, for all the papyrus shows, the reference to the officium of the praetorian prefects need not be more than a report of a directive received or a letter sent. Atho likewise may already have been in Mauretania at the time of the papyrus; there is no construction for the dative case of his name and so no evidence as to the reason why he was mentioned. The unread letters after his name even raise some doubt whether *praẹ*[at the end of line 4 is a title of his or of another person, or even a verb; and in any case the new reading eliminates his being a procurator.

With these reservations, however, Davies' reconstruction of the situation can be accepted as possible, perhaps even probable.

The recto is **31**.

]sentes quorụṃ ṇ[o]ṃiṇ[a
a]ḷẹxandr[i]ạ cuṃ ṇauiḅ[us .]s .[
o]ff̣ praeff praet e[. . .]ṭ.io[
]ị athonị ṃarcello .[. .]. . praẹ[
].uno uigụ.[. . .]. . .ẹṛ.[.]ẹ.[.]ṭạ.[
]ulares u c̣[. . .]. . . [
i]n his ord ị du[pl.] ṣ[e]ṣq[. . . . .]ị[
]. . . . . .[

1. *quorụṃ* .[.]. .[*:* D; app.: "*Prae*-] or *ab*]*sentes*?" Davies, on the grounds of the resemblance to **63**, prefers *absentes*; but the ablative of *alexandria* implies arrivals, "from Alexandria," and may justify *praesentes*.

2. *nauiḅ*[*u*]*s:* D. The Alexandria meant may be Alexandretta, the city *ad Issum* not far north of Antioch, but could very well be the city *ad Aegyptum*. In **63** ii 18–19 soldiers of the army of Moesia Inferior are as far away as Gaul on missions. Alexandria ad Tigrem is less likely because it was probably known at this time as Charax Spasinou.

3. *e*[. .]. .*ọ*[*:* D; app., "*O*]*f̣f̣*(*icio*)? *praef*(*ectorum*) *praet*(*orio*). At the end of the line perhaps *c* or *t*, *no* or .*io*."

4.].*athon*.; *pṛọc̣*[*:* D; app.: "Following -*athon* it appears that *o* was first written and then corrected to *i*. Possibly these letters are part of a name, perhaps the nomen of Marcellus. *Mathoni* would be possible, though surprising." At the end of the line, the letter before *p* is either *b*, *d*, or *h*; and either *prae*[*fect- or prae*[*posit-* could be restored. Perhaps *c*]*ọḥ*(*ortis*) *praẹ*[*posito* or *s*]*ụḅpraẹ*[*fecto*. Davies thinks also of *tr*]*ịḅ praẹ*[*tori-*; and a form of *praeses* or a verb such as *praeesse* also seem possible.

5. *vigin*[*ti*.].[.].*eṛ*[. .]. . .[*:* D. This reading may be right; but if so the *n* is unlike any other in the text. I have nothing to propose for *uigụ*.[; but at the beginning of the line just possibly *tri*]*ḅuno*?

6. *u*.[. .]. . .[*:* D; app.: "*Cons*]*ulares v*(*iri*) *c*(*larissimi*) is possible. The plural, however, would be unexpected." It would seem preferable to restore *sing*]*ulares u*(*iri*) *c*(*larissimi*) [*cos*(*ularis*) *n*(*ostri*)].

7. D in app.: "For this sequence of officers cf. [**47**], [**50**]. Another possible reading is *ordḍ du*[*o*."

97

Letter Mentioning Soldiers; Fragment with Date

PDur. 74 (inv. D. P. 21) A.D. 223–252

Transcription, commentary, and facsimile: *Final Rep*. v, no. 74 and plate 38, 2; *edidit* Gilliam.

"Two . . . fragments; some other smaller pieces containing a few scattered letters may belong to the same roll. . . . Large, careless hand, the character of which suggests that these letters are not from the provincial headquarters. There are illegible traces of ink along the fibers on the verso of Frag. *a*, possibly from the second line of the address. They seem to end with *t*. . . . to judge from Frag. *a*, 7, that letter may have been concerned with personnel. If the consul's cognomen in Frag. *b*, 4, ends *-ano*, the date may be any of eleven from 223 to 252" (*PDur*., p. 266).

Frag. a

.[
ṣ[a]ḷụṭ[e]m[
coh x̣x̣ p̣[alm(yrenorum)
anṭe c.[
decembr..[
rị[..]ụm ṣuor[um
n mil′ q[
]ṃ[

1. D in app.: "A long, slanting stroke, as e.g. in *a*, *i*, and *s*, which may mark the beginning of . . . the letter itself."
2. .[.]ọ..[: D. The letter read as *o* appears too large for that or for *b*; but cf. *u* in line 6.
3. The numerals are very uncertain.
4. *amiec*.[: D. The *t* is peculiarly formed; but the second letter is quite unlike the other *m*'s in this fragment.
5. The letter after *r* looks like *i*; but the next is hard to read as *b* for *decembrịḅ[us*.
6. D in app.: "Possibly *]ụm ṣuọṛ[um* or *ṭuọṛ[um*."
7. D in app.: "Perhaps *mil(ites) q[uos*, though the case and number of [both are uncertain]."

Frag. b

]..[
]ṛs s...[
i]dus iaṇ[
].no cos opt[o

1. D in app.: "Possibly *ḳạ[l*, in which case perhaps *c]os* should be restored in the next line."
2. *]osṣ..[*: D. See on line 1; read *c]ọs s(upra)-ṣcriptis*) or *coho]ṛs*?
4. *]ạṇo:* D; app.: "The consulship presumably completes the date begun in the preceding line. . . . *opto*, etc., was added in the author's own hand."

Letters About Finances and Matériel

98

Letter Regarding Entertainment of the Envoy Goces and Other Circular Letters

PDur. 60 (inv. D. P. 4) ca. 208

Transcription, commentary, and facsimile:

1. *Final Rep.* v, no. 60 and plate 41 (only nos. 1, 2, and 3 lines 6–10); *edidit* Gilliam.
2. M. I. Rostovtzeff, "Les Archives Militaires de Doura," *CRAI*, 1933, pp. 315–22. Facsimile only of no. 2, lines 1–10.

Transcription and facsimile:

1. *Prelim. Rep.* v (1934), pp. 297–98 and plate 30. Transcription of no. 2 only; facsimile as in *Final Rep.* v.
2. *EL*, no. 28, plate XIX. Facsimile of no. 2, lines 1–10.

Transcription and commentary: M. I. Rostovtzeff, "Das Militärarchiv von Dura," *Münchener Beiträge* 19 (1934) 373–78.

Commentary: U. Wilcken, *Archiv* 11 (1935) 315–16.

Text:

1. *L'Année Épigraphique*, 1933, no. 107.
2. *CPL*, no. 327.

The quoted matter in the descriptions and commentary which follow is taken from *Final Rep.* v.

"Five large and a number of small fragments from a roll of incoming letters. . . . The roll appears to have been a file of circulars sent out from the governor's office in Antioch. The opening formula in [nos. 2, 3] (probably), and Frag. f is addressed to all commanding officers in certain categories, not to the tribune of the Palmyrene cohort. The content of both [no. 2] and [no. 4] suggests a circular. In [no. 2] the concluding phrase *opto bene valeatis* is in the same hand as the rest of the letter, and not in that of Marius Maximus. There are no addresses on the verso, since it did not matter which copy reached any particular officer on the distribution list. All identifiable letters are from Marius Maximus, governor of Syria about 208 [**99**] . . . and the consular date in [no. 3] is restored to this year. In any event, in the light of *Augg nn* in line 2, [no. 2] cannot be later than 209 when Geta became a third Augustus" (p. 222).

1. Attached to the left edge of no. 2.

]ṃeorum

Perhaps to be divided]*ṃ eorum*.

2. "Copy of a letter to the provincial procurator commanding that the necessary preparations be made for the reception of a Parthian envoy. . . . The officers addressed commanded auxiliary units or in the case of the praepositi, possibly also legionary vexillations. Presumably they were stationed in the towns named at the bottom of the letter. These are listed in the order in which the courier would reach them going down the river. Though nothing is known about Goces or about this particular embassy . . . we may assume that a series of letters such as this preceded [him] all along the route of his journey to and from Imperial headquarters. He may have had to go all the way to Britain; Septimius and his sons crossed over to the island some time in 208. . . . It is natural to assume from *missus ad dd nn fortissimos impp* that Goces was on his way to them. But the possibility that he was returning from his mission does not seem to me to be ruled out; the order in which the towns are named may or may not be significant. . . . the expenses of entertaining him are likely to have been considerable. It is interesting to see what procedures were followed in meeting them. The governor authorized drafts on the quaesturae of units and required a detailed report of expenditures; *erogare* is of course a technical term meaning to disburse public funds. However, the procurator made the actual arrangements, sent the required orders to the individual units (which also received a copy of the governor's letter), and kept an account of what was spent. The quaesturae numerorum are obviously unit treasuries. . . . *Quaestura*, however, does not seem to appear elsewhere as a technical military term; but cf. *quaestorium* . . ." (p. 223).

It is worth noting that this letter and one other, **87**, are the only ones known to have survived reasonably complete from the hundreds of thousands that must have been written in the Roman army during the three centuries between Augustus and Diocletian.

ṃarius maximus tribb˙ et praeff˙ et praepositis n′ n′ salutẹṃ
quid scribserim minicio martiali proc˙ augg̣ n′ n′
et notum haberetis adplicuị opto bene ualeatis
ex(emplum)
curae tibi sit et quaesturas n′ n′ per quos transit goces
legatus parthọrum missus ad dd n′ n′ fortissimos impp
secundum morem xenia ei offere quid autem in
quoque numero erogaueris scribe mihi
gaẓịc̣a
appadana
dụ[r]a
eḍ[da]ṇa
bị[blada]

TRANSLATION

Marius Maximus to the tribunes, prefects, and praepositi of units. What I wrote to Minicius Martialis, procurator of our two Augusti, I have appended so that you may have the information. I hope that you are in good health.

Copy:

It is to be your care that the unit treasuries also of the posts through which Goces is passing, the Parthian envoy sent to our lords the most redoubtable emperors, offer him hospitality according to custom. What you spend, however, in each unit, write to me.

"However one emends the text, the clerk made errors, as Wilcken was the first to note. . . . *Et* for *ut* (lines 3 and 5) and *quaesturas* for *quaesturae* (line 5), Wilcken's suggestions, would be mistakes easily made by one glancing at a text in this hand without paying much attention to the content. But *offere* for *offerant*, again Wilcken's suggestion, is harder to understand. Other possibilities which have occurred to me in lines 5–7 are *et* or *ex quaesturis . . . offerre*, either of which is simpler than Wilcken's emendation. Perhaps the second of these is preferable" (p. 224).

"In [**98**, no. 2] Wilcken (op. cit. p. 315) suggested changing *et* to *ut* in two places, and changing an infinitive to a subjunctive. . . . This seems unnecessary . . . *notum haberetis* can mean 'you note' or 'are to note' . . . [and] the accusative *quaesturas* has the right case to be the subject of an infinitive, and *et* may be 'also' or 'even'" (Welles, p. 50).

1. Expand: *n*(*umerorum*), used here as a generic term for a military unit of any sort, not in the narrow sense of a body of irregulars under native leaders.

2. Expand: *proc*(*uratori*) *aug*(*ustorum*) *n*(*ostrorum*).

3. Read *ut* with Wilcken. *et* could be retained by making the mood of *haberetis* depend on *quid*; but the point of sending this letter is to acquaint the ranking officers of the various posts with these arrangements. One could still argue, of course, that even though the officers knew what was being done, the letter was necessary as written confirmation and authorization.

5. Rostovtzeff printed "*quaesturae* (or *-as*)" in CRAI; and *Prelim. Rep.* v has *quaesturae*; but there can be no doubt about *quaesturas*, as in both D and EL. The difficulty is in the interpretation. I take the word as the subject of *offerre*, line 7, and understand *et* as "also"—that is, that the military units were to participate officially with the civil authorities in entertaining the envoy. Wilcken emends to *ut quaesturae*.

6. Expand: *d*(*ominos*) *n*(*ostros*); *imp*(*eratores*).

7. Read *offer*⟨*r*⟩*e*. Wilcken emends to *offerant*.

8. "*secumdum* corrected by the clerk to *secundum*."

9. *Gasica:* CRAI and EL; but the third letter cannot be *s*.

3. "It is not certain that the two pieces here combined belong together. The appearance of the papyrus suggests that they do, and this is supported by the fact that the consular date of 208 would then begin on one piece and end on the other. . . . I have assumed that there is a space of only one or two letters lost between them in lines 5–6 at]*um* (line 5) and]*m* (line 6). The letter may direct that other documents and pridiana (line 3) be submitted for certain purposes or by a certain date, but obviously too little is left to reconstruct anything of its contents" (p. 224).

[marius m]aximus tri[bb
sạl[utem
[. . . . .]ṛ. . et pridian. [
[. . . . .]e. [.]. s item [
[. .]. . . [. . .]um iṃ[p] ant[onino aug iii et geta caesare] A.D. 208
ii cos qu[.]m. [. .]. ṃ. [
ptum[
sole. [
tiu. [
coṃ[

1. "Presumably the line was completed as in [no. 2] 1, but cf. Frag. *f* in which either the order was different or the praepositi are omitted."
3. "Possibly *dia*]*ṛịa et pridianạ*[".
4. "Possibly]*eạ*[*t*]*is*".
5. "The first letter preserved . . . probably is *c*, *p*, or *t*; *stip Kal*] [*Sep*]*ṭeṃ*[*bri*]*um* may be a remote possibility (cf. [**66**])."
6. "Probably *quem*, to judge from the trace of a connecting stroke joining *m*."
8. *soleṇ*[*t:* D.
10. "One of the many possibilities is *com*[*militon-*." But *con*[could also be read.

4. "The text . . . seems to have dealt with a prescribed method of paying soldiers. . . . Perhaps at the end, from line 6 or 7, it provides that up to a certain limit . . . amounts due soldiers are to be paid in full; beyond this . . . a fixed sum only was to be paid; and from any larger amount than the last stated, [? *ex maiore q*]*uantitate*, the soldier would receive only two aurei. The balance would be deposited in his account, one may assume. . . . Whether gold coins were actually issued is uncertain. None was found in the excavations. . . . It is conceivable that this is the second column of [no. 3]" (p. 225).

Gilliam's text.

].[.].[
]aug . . . [
].le.[*ca.* 15].ụṣ[.].[.]
]ṣẹç.ụṣ. . [*ca.* 10]ṣ dena
]ṣ praeci[s]e . .[.].[7] denarios
].ṇt primo qụ[i]ḍ[e]m [6 p]ariari
usqu]e ad denarios [. . .].[. . .].[. . . . a d]enaris
]ẹnt usqụẹ ad ḍẹṇạrios [.]. .[.]. . . .
q]ụantitạte solos binoṣ aureos
]ṣ

2. "*Augg* may be possible but not *Augg nn*. . . . The month is another possibility."
3. "Possibly *com*]*pleṭ*[."
4. "Possibly]*ṣẹçṭụṣ*; at the end of the line, *dena-* | [*rios*]?"
6. "An equally easy reading would be *p*]*ariati* = 'paid'?"
7. "Figures doubtless followed *denarios* in this line and the next."
8. "Possibly *deb*]*ẹnt* or, especially if there is any connection with [no. 3], *sol*]*ẹnt*."

Frags. e–f. "In addition to the following two fragments, there are half a dozen small pieces which may belong to this roll. None . . . contains any significant or intelligible sequence of letters. It is very possible that *e* is part of [no. 4]; Frag. f apparently comes from the first two lines of a letter" (p. 226).

Frag. e

]p. . .[
].ete. . .[
]a dena[ri-
]. . .[

Frag. f

praef]ectis n[n
]am prae[

e 3. *dena*[*riis:* D.

99

Letters Assigning Horses

PDur. 56 (inv. D. P. 8) ca. March 16–August 17, 208

Transcription, commentary, and facsimile: *Final Rep*. v, no. 56 and plates 33, 1–2 (addresses from the verso of nos. 1 and 2) and 34 (no. 1 and a fragment of the left edge of no. 2); *edidit* Gilliam.

Transcription and commentary: J. F. Gilliam, "Some Latin Military Papyri from Dura," *YCS* 11 (1950) 171–87.

Text: *CPL*, no. 330, reproduces the text of *YCS*.

The quoted matter in the following descriptions and commentary is from Gilliam in *Final Rep*. v, as are the texts of letters 1–3.

"One large and many small fragments from a roll. . . . Some of the detached fragments in the original edition [*YCS*, p. 186] have been placed in [nos. 2 and 3], and others are now rearranged.

"These letters concern the probatio and assignment of horses to cavalrymen of the Palmyrene cohort by the governor of Syria Coele, Marius Maximus. . . . Cf. [**97**], a copy of a similar letter, and especially [**83**], which in part was compiled from such letters as these. For the probation of horses see also [**89**, no. 42], [**1**] xxxviii 18; and [**27**] a, i, 1" (p. 217).

1. (*Frag. a*)
Recto:

].[.].i.[...]
marius ṃaxiṃ[us ua]ḷẹṇtiṇ[o] ṣ[uo]
(*Hand 2*) acc septimum decimum [k]ạḷ ạ[p]ṛịḷ[es dd nn imp a]ntonino aug ị[ii et ⟦geta caes ii⟧ cos]
ṣạḷ[ute]m
ecum quadrim[u]m rus persoṇ[a]ṭum
s·n· probatum a me iulio basso eq· coh· xx pal
c· p· 𐆖 ceṇtum ụiginti [q]uinq[ue] ịṇ ạc̣ṭ[a] ụ[t]
mos refer et ..[.....]ṇota ex die [qu]ạṛ[to ..]
iuṇịạṣ [dd nn imp antonino a]ụg iii′ [e]ṭ[⟦G]et[a]⟧
⟦caesare ịṭẹ[rum]⟧ cos]

Verso:

VLPIO VALENTINO TRIB COH
a
mario maximọ leg augg pr pr

TRANSLATION

Marius Maximus to Valentinus. (*Docket:* Received March 16, 208)

Enter in the records as usual and . . . a four-year-old horse, reddish, blazed face (?), no brand, approved by me, for Iulius Bassus, cavalryman of the coh. xx Palmyrenorum which you command, at 125 denarii . . . effective [May 29, June 2, or June 10], 208.

1. "It is uncertain what was . . . in this note at the top of the sheet and . . . whether it was on the letter when it was dispatched or was added later."

3. This line, in a second hand and much smaller letters, was run in between lines 2 and 4 to record the receipt of the letter at Dura. Cf. **88**, no. 2, line 4, and **91**, no. 1, line 2; no. 2, line 2. The letters in **89** were docketed at the bottom. For the cancellation of Geta's name, see on line 9.

5. Expand: *rus*(*seum*). "*Personatus*, 'masked,' is apparently a term for some marking on the horse's face."

6. Expand: *s*(*ine*) *n*(*ota*)*; eq*(*uiti*) *coh*(*ortis*)*; pal*(*myrenorum*).

7. "The same figure appears again in no. *3* and in [**83**]. [See also on **75**: ROF.] If the reading at the end of the line is correct, *acta* is apparently used for the cohort's records in general, as in Vegetius, ii, 19; cf. Gilliam, *Eos*, 48 (1957), pp. 207–216." Expand: *c*(*ui*) *p*(*raees*).

8. "The restoration *ạc̣*[*tis ad*]*nota*, though somewhat redundant, may be suggested. . . . It is not clear why the effective date should be later than that of the letter. It seems to be earlier in [no. *3*]." Perhaps, however, this is an order to brand the animal. In that case possibly read *iṇ lạ*[*tere*] *ṇota*.

9. "The letter may end with the date. A clerk crossed out Geta's name after his damnatio memoriae in 212. For a list of papyri in which his name is cancelled see *P. Mich.* VI, pp. 97 f., to which may be added *PSI* 1245, *P. Strasbourg* 192, *P. Mich. Inv.* 5763 (*TAPA* 82 [1951], p. 166; an altered seal)."

2. (*Frag. b*)

Recto:

[marius maximus ualentino suo]
[salutem]
[ecos quo]rum ịç[onismos subic]ị iussi
p̣[rob]at[os] ạ me equitibus ị[nf]ra [sc]riptis
coh xx˙ palmyr′ c˙ p singulos˙ ⚹ centenis˙
].[
[7 e]x vi˙ kal [. . . . apro et maxi]ṃo cos A.D. 207

Rest of letter lost

Notation in very small letters in left margin beside line 4:

dat(a)
iiii idus mai(as)
hieropo(li)

Verso:

[VLPIO] VALENTINO Ṭ[RIB COH]
[a mario maximo l]ẹg̣ [a]ụgg pr pr

TRANSLATION

[Marius Maximus to Valentinus]

[Enter in the records as usual . . .] horses approved by me, whose identifying marks I have ordered appended, for the cavalrymen named below, members of the coh. xx Palmyrenorum which you command, each horse at . . . denarii, effective [day, month], 207.

Given May 12 at Hierapolis.

2. "A docket noting date of receipt may have been entered at this point, as in [no. 1], but one was perhaps less necessary since the date of dispatch was given; so also in [no. 3]."

3. [*Ecos duos*? *quo*]*rum:* D. "For *iconismos* cf. [**87**] . . . . That letter deals with recruits, but the formulas and procedure were similar."

7. "Unless this letter is in fact earlier than [no. 1] and was written in 207, the effective date for the records is earlier than that of the letter by at least several months. I have assumed that the letters were filed in chronological order and were added to the right edge of the roll."

3. (Frag. c)

Recto:

[marius maximus ualentino suo]
[salutem]
eç[um ca]p̣pado[cem .]. . u . . [. .] . . [. . .]
ṇuṃ n f a s˙ pṛ[oba]tum a mẹ halathẹ
cxxv
ṃạrịṇ[i] eq′çoḥ [xx p]al c p [⳨]. . . . . [. .] . . . . . . [
iṇ [acta ut] ṃoṣ [refer ex k]ạl . [
Rest of letter lost
Notation in a second hand to the left of line 5:
dat(a)
xvi kal [s]ept(embres)
antiochia

Verso:

[VLPIO] VALENTIN[O TRIB COH]
[a mario maximo leg] augg pr pṛ

TRANSLATION

[Marius Maximus to Valentinus]

Enter in the records as usual a Cappadocian horse, approved by me, . . . branded on the left thigh and shoulder, for Halathes son of Marinus, cavalryman of the coh. xx Palmyrenorum which you command, at 125 denarii, effective [date].

Given August 17 at Antioch.

1. "The restoration of Marius Maximus' name in this letter is more uncertain than in [no. 2] since it is over three months later in date."

3. "The end of this line and the beginning of the next continued the description of the horse. Its age and color, possibly [*muri*] | *ṇuṃ*, were probably included."

4. Expand: *n*(*otatis*) *f*(*emore*) *a*(*rmo*) *s*(*inistris*); and cf. the abbreviations in **83**, especially line 2.

5. "The writing at the end of the line, over which *CXXV* is inserted, is small, irregular, and faded."

Frags d–g. "The following fragments belong to this roll and possibly to one or another of the letters . . . above" (p. 220).

Frag. d

m]ạrius [maximus

"From the first line of a letter, possibly [no. 2]."

Frag. e

]ị[.]ọ[

"Possibly *Valent*]*ị*[*n*]*ọ* or *ṣ*[*u*]*ọ* from the same line as [frag.] *d*."

Frag. f

]ẹta . . [

"Perhaps]*ẹt* *aç̣ṭ*[*is*; cf. [no. 1, line 8]."

Frag. g

] . d . [

100

Copy of a Letter Assigning Horses

PDur. 58 (inv. D. P. 63 verso) ca. 240–250

Transcription, commentary, and facsimile: *Final Rep.* v, no. 58 and plate 60, 1; *edidit* Gilliam.

Transcription and commentary: J. F. Gilliam, "Some Latin Military Papyri from Dura," *YCS* 11 (1950) 187–89.

Text: *CPL*, no. 343, reproduces the text of *YCS.*

"Written across the fibres. . . . The column was evidently quite wide, and much of the letter is lost in the lacuna to the right. The writer, Aurelius Aurelianus, is the governor or some other high official (cf. [**83**]). Aurelius Intenianus is almost certainly the tribune or praepositus commanding the Palmyrene cohort" (D, pp. 220–21).

The date is on the basis of the hand.

The recto is **41**.

[.]ec̣
One line blank
aurel [a]ụrẹl[i]anus aurel inteniano su[o
subici ịuṣ[si p]rob a me eqq˙ coh xx [palmyrenorum
iṇ [acta ut mo]ṣ refer ex˙ xvii kal ḍ[ec(embres)
[ ]data iiii idus ianụạ[r-

1. D in app.: "[*R*]*ec*(*ognitum*)? But I have found no parallel." Gilliam in *YCS*, p. 188: "*Ex*(*emplum*) cannot be read."

2. D in app.: "*Ingeniano* may have been intended but cannot be read. At the end of the line one may supply: *su*[*o salutem. equos* (number) *quorum iconismos*]. Cf. [**96**, no. 2]."

3. D in app.: "A second *s* is found below the *s* in *subici*, passing through part of *u*. Possibly the clerk after writing one letter decided to begin the line higher on the sheet. On Frag. *b* [the right-hand portion], the lacuna presumably contained after the name of the cohort: *c*(*ui*) *p*(*raees*) and a sum in denarii."

4. *Kal*[*:* D.

4–5. D in app.: "The descriptions of the horses may have been given in the lacunae in these lines."

5. *Ian*[*uarias:* D.

101

Letter Concerning Frumentationes

PDur. 61 (inv. D. P. 18) ca. 216

Transcription, commentary, and facsimile: *Final Rep*. v, no. 61 and plate 38, 1 (frag. a only); *edidit* Gilliam.

Quoted matter below is from Gilliam's introduction and apparatus.

"Two large and several small fragments incomplete on all sides. . . . No words have been read on six small scraps which are omitted here. . . . Col. ii and Frag. b are in a smaller, coarse hand, which is probably the same as that in [**89**, nos. 51–57]. It is possible that all these fragments come from one text. . . . Despite the striking difference in hands, the two columns in Frag. a seem to belong to the same text. There is no join of papyrus sheets between the columns, and what has been read in the second column supports the assumption that it continued the first" (p. 226). Note the similar situation in **90**, where the covering letter is Latin and the continuation Greek, and in **89**, no. 4, where the list of names is in a different hand from the covering letter. "Frag. *b* is very possibly part either of Frag. *a* ii or of a third column of the letter. . . . The hand in Frag. *a* i suggests that the letter was written in the office of the governor. . . . This column may have been a covering letter. It perhaps began with a statement that certain . . . instructions were appended . . . in accordance with which (*secundum quos*?) prescribed procedures were to be observed on the cohort's *frumentationes*. The column or columns that followed presumably contained the instructions in some detail. . . . It was among the duties of commanders of troops . . . *frumentationibus commilitonum interesse, frumentum probare: Digest*, xlix, 16, 12, 2 (Macer). For references concerning the provisioning of units see [**91**] and [*PDur*.] 129" (p. 226).

The dating rests on the resemblance of the second hand to **89**, nos. 51–57.

The verso is blank.

Frag. a

Col. i

]ṇ.[
]. . ẹgo.ẹ. . .[
.[.]. secunduṃ qu.[.]
]ṭam [fr]ụṃentaṭioni
]c̣oh˙ xx̣ p̣aḷṃyrenorum
]ịanae c˙ p ọbserụari
] *vacat*

1.]. . [*:* D. In place of *n*, *u* is possible.

2.]. . [.]*ẹgo.i.ẹ*. . . [*:* D; "The letter following]*ego* begins with a hook and may be *l*. The next to the last letter in the line has a hook at the bottom, as in *c*, *l*, *p*, and *t*."

3. "Possibly *qụ[i]ḍ*."

6. "If the reigning emperor was Caracalla, as is quite possible, or Elagabalus, [*Antoniṇ*]*ianae* should be restored. Nothing except part of a title of this type is lost in the lacuna." This means that the column was only 20–25 letters wide.

7. "A verb, such as *oportet* or *debent*, evidently ended this part of the text."

Col. ii

[. . .]. . . [
[.].s. . [.].[
[. .]ṇ.t. . . . [
[. .]. .ṛ.mc̣[
[. .]ṃạḍ[.].[.].[
.[. . .]ṛạ. . . . . [
.s.[.].dạ.ṣd. . . . [
suggẹ. .ṭ. . . [
inṣtr[u]mẹṇ[t-
ad qui. .os.[
teṣ frumẹ[nt-
sic̣i. .ṇ.[
[. . . . . .]. . [

1. [– *5* –].[*:* D.
2. [.]. . . [.].[*:* D.
3. [. . .]*n*[.]*t*. . . . [*:* D.
4. [. .]. . . . . [*:* D.
5. [. . .].*ạ*.[. .].[*:* D.
6. [. . . .]. . . . [.]. . [*:* D.
7. [.].*ṣ*.[.]. .*d*. .*ṣd*. . . [*:* D.
8. *ṣugge*. . . . . . . *:* D; "Presumably from *suggero*, but a fuller reading, *e.g. suggeṛạṇṭ*, is difficult." Still difficult, but much easier, is *ṣuggẹṛạt* or *ṣuggẹṛạtịṣ*.
10. *quiṇos:* D.
11. *teṛ:* D
12. *sic̣i*. . . . [*:* D.

Frag. b (Gilliam's text)

]. . . [
]. . f̣ṛụṃẹ[nt-
]sụggẹ[.]. . [
]. . . ịṇị[.]. . [
]. . . . . [
]. in[. .]a. . [.].[
]c̣.ịḅ. . . . [
].[. .]. . ịụ[
]. . . [
]. . [
]. . . . [
].[
]. . . . [
]me.[.]. . . [. .]. . [
]. . . [

3. "Cf. Frag. *a* ii 8. The lacuna may be followed by *in*[or *im*[, in which case an imperative would seem to be the only possible form of *suggero*."

7. "Possibly *c̣ṛịḅṛạ* or *c̣ṛịḅṛạṛịạ*."

102

Copies or Précis of Letters?

POxy. XII 1511; *vidi* First half of III p.
Bodleian Library, Ms. Gr. Class. c 83 (P) recto

Transcription and description: Bernard P. Grenfell and Arthur S. Hunt, in *POxy.* XII, no. 1511.

Transcription, commentary, and facsimile: *ChLA* IV, no. 265; cited as **M**.

Text: *CPL*, no. 140, reproduces the text of *POxy.*

This puzzling text was identified in the *Oxyrhynchus Papyri* as "fragments of a Latin military account"; but the new readings in lines 6 and 7 prove that we have here a file of copies or summaries of letters. Marichal in *ChLA* believes that the notation in lines 6–7, *data Emerito magistro*, proves that the text is a register of incoming letters received by tabularii, possibly those in "one of the bureaus of the *ἀρχιταβλάριος Αἰγύπτου* attested in 159 . . . or the *Fiscus Alexandrinus*." On this reasoning the prefects in lines 1, 7, and 12 become the senders of the letters; and the preposition *ab* is restored at the beginning of each of those lines.

It is not clear, however, how *data Emerito* proves that these are incoming letters. It could equally well mean that that letter had been given to him for delivery to the praefectus legionis. Nor is it clear why a register of incoming letters should be kept, since the letters themselves would be on file, as in e.g. **89**, **98**, and **99**. I should rather see in this text memoranda of outgoing letters addressed to the three prefects, for the names in lines 7 and 12 could be dative as well as ablative. Since the margin is complete above line 1, it follows that the pattern of each entry was first a line with the name and title of the addressee, then, much indented, several lines containing the substance of the letter, finally a line with the name of a tabularius, presumably in the ablative, "from," "sent by," "written by," "requested by," or the like. This suggests that the letters may come from the office of the Prefect of Egypt himself.

In favor of this interpretation is the variety of hands. Only three are distinguished in *POxy.*—frag. a, lines 1 and 4; frag. a, lines 5–12; and frag. b. Actually, although the samples are small and therefore undependable, and although some of the apparently different hands may have been written by the same clerk using different styles for heading, main text, and annotations, it still appears that we must distinguish at least five or six hands. Lines 1, 6, 7, 11, and 12 are in large letters which are basically epistolary cursive; but the letter *a*, for example, is formed quite differently in 1, 6, 7, and 11; 1 and 7 differ in the *e*, *f*, *m*, *o*, and *p*; 6 and 11 in the *b*; and 7 and 11 in the *n*. 7 and 12 are very similar but differ in the *f*. There are accordingly either four or five hands in these lines. The beginnings of three lines from the body of a letter preserved in lines 8–10 are in an ordinary epistolary hand; but the *b* of *iube* in line 9 is different from the *b*'s in lines 6 and 11. Line 13 is also from the body of a letter, but in a hand and pen quite different from lines 8–10. Finally, there is the hand of the notation in the margin at the left of line 8, and the possibly different hand of frag. b. This variety seems to indicate that different parts of the text were added at different times, as the letters were written, by different clerks as chance determined.

If previous editors are right in restoring forms of *tabularius* in lines 6 and 11, this, too, points to the office of an official ranking as high as the Prefect of Egypt, since Domaszewski (*Rang.*) records tabularii only for the praetorian prefect and the praefectus vigilum. But the word may instead be a form of *tabularium*. Cf. **87** 30: *in tabulario cohortis*.

The dating depends chiefly on the fact that the Greek text of the verso, *POxy*. 1418, a petition or appeal to the Boule of Oxyrhynchus, is dated A.D. 247. The recto might then be one to fifty years earlier.

Frag. a

pr]ạẹf coh apamẹ[norum
]   [
]   ọ[
]   .[
]   .[
].lano˙ tabu[lar-
].o marino praef legio[nis ii traianae fortis
]   littera . . [
8a data emerito magistro
]   tu iube ẹ[
]   ạḍc̣ur.ị age . . [
]ianọ proximo ṭabular[i-
].ecrino p[rae]f alae.[
] [   ]ṛỵba cui[

Frag. b

].ṃ.[
].[

Frag. a. M allows for only three lines between line 1 and my line 6.

6.]. *LARCO:* M; in app., "*Larco* for *largo*, cf. supra no. 234." But for the *n* cf. *marino*, line 7. *tabu[lario:* Oxy. and M.

7. The II Traiana was the only legion in Egypt after about 120. On the praefectus (castrorum) legionis, see now J. F. Gilliam, *AJP* 77 (1956) 365–72.

8. *Ḷ III ẹ. . . :* Oxy.; *Littera*.[*:* M. Emeritus is a cognomen; see Dessau's indices.

8a. *Mạx̣umó:* Oxy. M agrees with my reading; but Marichal interprets *magister* here as the chief of the bureau of tabellarii, the immediate superior of the proximus named in line 11. The word might, however, denote a magister campi of the legion.

9. *XVI* . . . .[*:* Oxy.; *iube* .[*:* M. At the end of the line perhaps *ẹ[um* or *ẹ[os*.

10. *apṭụṣ* . . . .[*:* Oxy.; *Actum Prem[i:* M, taking *Premi* as a place-name, the same as *Πρῆμνις*, *Πρῆμις*, or *Primis* (*i*-stem). M in app.: "The reading *Pre* is certain . . ."; but for *g* instead of *r*, cf. the *g*'s in *magistro*, line 8a, and *legionis*, line 7. Perhaps read *adcurẹs* for the first word?

11.]*irrió; tabular[io:* Oxy.;]*IRTIO; TABULAR[IORUM:* M. Marichal is right in taking *proximo* as "assistant to the tabularii." See Wilh. Ensslin, *RE* 23.1034, s.v. "proximus."

12.]*ferino:* Oxy. and M, which is possible. *H[ERCULIANAE:* M; but this is by no means certain. The als Apriana and ala Xoitana remain possible even if one eliminates the ala Augusta on the strength of Lesquier's statement, cited by Marichal, that it is not mentioned after 103.

13.]. .*ḅacus:* Oxy.;]*fẹbruạ[ri. . . :* M; but the letters after *b* cannot be *rua*. I assume that the line began with an oblique case of a personal name such as Rybas, Ar(r)ybas, or Atrybas.

Frag. b. Oxy. reports "traces of two lines in the 3rd hand."

1.]*ex*.[*:* M.
2.]*x*[*:* M.

103

Fragments of Letters

PDur. 57 (inv. D. P. 32) Perhaps ca. 208

Final Rep. v, p. 220 (Gilliam): "A series of seven fragments from a roll of letters. . . . Official epistolary hand resembling those in [**96**]. . . . No complete words can be read, but]*eli* may be *Aur*]*eli* or *A*]*eli*. Traces of the address on the verso."

No transcription.

104

Fragment of a Letter

PDur. 70 (inv. D. P. 68); plate 35, 2 A.D. 213

Final Rep. v, pp. 263–64 (Gilliam): "The interest of this fragment lies in the date and the large epistolary hand. . . . No other letter is dated in this year, which suggests that this scrap does not belong to any of the libri epistularum of which more substantial fragments are preserved. Verso blank."

The great rosters, **1** and **2**, also show that no soldiers were enrolled in this year, as likewise in 211 and 218. The speculations which these facts arouse make the loss of this letter all the more deplorable.

]. . .[
sa[lutem
antonino]ạụg ịị[ii] ẹt b[a]ḷbiṇ[o ii cos
].[

105

Fragment of a Letter

PDur. 71 (inv. D. P. 47) ca. 219

Final Rep. v, p. 265 (Gilliam): "Line 1, in another hand, probably contains the end of a name. If so,]*elius* may be receiving a copy of a letter written to Artemidorus, and is presumably the tribune of the Palmyrene cohort. Verso blank."

]elio
(*Hand 2*)]aṛ[te]midoro suo
[s]ạḷụṭ[em]

106

Fragments of Letters

PDur. 73 (inv. D. P. 42) ca. 210–220

Final Rep. v, p. 265 (Gilliam): "Eight scraps, incomplete on all sides. . . . Four other fragments, blank or with completely illegible traces of ink, have the same inventory number. Careful epistolary hand, probably that of a clerk at provincial headquarters, with some resemblances to the hands of [**96**] and Col. i of [**98**]. . . . Illegible remnants of letters on verso of Frags. *c* and *h*."

Frag. a	**Frag. b**	**Frag. c**	**Frag. d**
].......[	]ẹreḍ.[	].[	]..[
].assạ.[	]ẹred.[	]ịn[	].sc̣.[

Frag. e	**Frag. f**	**Frag. g**	**Frag. h**
]ụm[	]ṣc.[	]iụ[	].c̣[

Frag. b. If the remains on frag. b are one word, the letter may have concerned *heredes* or *hereditates* (cf. **77**); but of course each line may be two words, divided as]*e red*.[or]*ere d*.[.

107

Fragments of Letters

PDur. 75 (inv. D. P. 28) ca. 210–220

Final Rep. v, pp. 266–67 (Gilliam): "These small fragments . . . are from a block of fifteen layers which comes from the lower part of a roll. . . . Epistolary hands resembling those in [**89**]. On three fragments *mittas* can be read. Two preserve parts of signatures: *opto te*] *feliciss*[*imum* | *b*]*ene valere* and *opto te fel*]*ịcissiṃ*[*um* | *ben*]*e valere*, each perhaps in a fuller form. Others contain]*to haber*[*e* and]*xx*[, possibly part of the name of the Palmyrene cohort. A few Greek letters appear on another piece. Traces of writing on the verso of two fragments presumably belonged to addresses. To judge from the rather careless hands and the appearance of Greek, we may have here remnants of correspondence with other units and with lower ranking civilian officials, as in [**89**]."

No formal transcription.

108

Fragments of a Letter

PDur. 62 (inv. D. P. 33) ca. 216–220

Final Rep. v, p. 227 (Gilliam): "A series of four fragments containing parts of five lines of a letter and some of the margin on each side. . . . Coarse, irregular epistolary hand, resembling [**98**] *a* ii. Only scattered letters and parts of words are preserved, such as *die* and]*.nost*.[. The latter might be from the phrase *cos noster*. Verso blank."

No formal transcription.

109

Fragment of a Letter

PDur. 65 (inv. D. P. 23) A.D. 221

Final Rep. v, p. 234 (Gilliam): "The hand of lines 2 and 3 and the year are the same as those of the dockets in [**91**]. The writer of this letter, however, is not the Aurelius Rufinus of [**91**], and it is uncertain whether it belongs to the roll represented by those texts. A number of other fragments . . . have this inventory number, but they are too faded and tattered to provide any intelligible text or to permit one to determine whether they all in fact do belong together."

fl[aui-
(*Hand 2*) aç̣c[*day and month*
gṛ[a]ṭ[o et seleuco cos

1. *Fl[avius:* D.

110

Fragment of a Letter

PDur. 72 (inv. D. P. 43) A.D. 211–222

Final Rep. v, p. 265 (Gilliam): "If the epithet *Antoniniana* is correctly read and restored, the text was written under Caracalla or Elagabalus. Another small fragment . . . may come from the same letter. Verso blank."

].e[
coh x]x palmyr˙ ạṇ[toniniana
]..ẹ[

111

Fragment of a Letter

PDur. 78 (inv. D. P. 45) ca. 210–230

Final Rep. v, p. 268 (Gilliam): "Line 1, in a large epistolary hand, is from the last line of the letter proper. . . . Verso blank."

]. . . [
(*Hand 2*) [opto] ṭẹ f̣ṛạ[t]ẹṛ feḷicị[ssi-]
[mum] ṃụḷṭị[s] annis ḅ[ene]
ualere
vacat

112

Fragment of a Letter

PDur. 79 (inv. D. P. 52) ca. 210–230

Final Rep. v, p. 268 (Gilliam): "Of the letter itself on the recto only a few faded and illegible traces remain. The address on the verso follows the usual form. The name of the addressee in line 1 is in large letters approximately 1 cm. high. He was most probably the tribune of the Palmyrene cohort."

Verso:

]Ạ. . Ọ̣NIO[
]a. . . . . [.].[

1. D in app.: "The bottoms of three vertical strokes are preserved before -*ONIO*. *ANTONIO* and *AG*]-*ATHONIO* (cf. **88**) are possibilities."
2. D in app.: "If the letters in line 1 are from a nomen, we may have at this point *a* and the name of the writer. Otherwise, *leg*] *aụg pṛ pṛ* may be worth considering, though the second *p* is an unattractive reading."

113

Fragment of a Letter

PDur. 77 (inv. D. P. 51) ca. 220–230

Final Rep. v, p. 267 (Gilliam): "A small block of papyrus in layers, which the hand indicates is from a roll of letters. Nothing can be read to suggest the content. Verso blank."

Transcription of frag. a only.

]. [
]. . [. .]. . [
]. . nsc[. .]. [
]. . auctos . [

114

Fragment of a Letter

PDur. 59 (inv. D. P. 7) Probably 241

Transcription, commentary, and facsimile: *Final Rep.* v, no. 59 and plates 33, 6, and 40, 2; *edidit* Gilliam.

Facsimile: *Prelim. Rep.* v, plate 31, 1.

Mentioned in *CPL*, no. 329, but without text.

D, p. 221: "This fragment is from a liber epistularum. . . . The hand on the recto is [the chancery hand]. . . . There is no clue to the subject of this letter from Attius Rufinus, the governor of Syria, to Aurelius . . . r . . [. . .], praepositus of the Palmyrene cohort. It is possible . . . that it quotes some communication from a certain Aelius, and that it began *qui[d mihi scriberet] Aelius.* The date depends on that of [**29**], in which Attius appears as governor in either A.D. 239 or 241, and [**50**], in which another governor and another praepositus appear in A.D. 239; thus [**29**] should probably be dated to 241, and this letter to about the same time. The marginal docket can be restored in this sense."

The docket, in fact, seems to remove the need for hesitation.

Recto:

attiuṣ ṛ[u]f̣[inus
2 (*Hand 2*) ac̣c̣ẹp sextuṃ [*day and month* imp gordiano ii salutem]
2a et c̣l pomp̣[eiano cos
(*Hand 1*) qu . [
aeliuṣ . [
5 ad quiḍ[
rioriṣ . [
ḅillae . . [
coh xx p̣[almyrenorum

Verso:

AVRELIO . . . R . . [. .] PRAEP COH
attius ṛ[ufi]ṇus leg aug pr pr

Recto 1–2. Ṛ[*ufinus:* D, and below the *r*, . [; "marginal note opposite line 2": . . . ẹ. *sextum*[| . . .]*lpo* . . [But if the second line began this far to the left, the first line of the docket would have been written right through it. Therefore I take the stroke which runs down through *u* of *sextum* and curls to the left under the other letters as far as the *s* to be the tail of the *f* in *rufinus*, and assume that only *salutem* of the letter itself stood in line 2. This arrangement of the docket and *salutem* is exemplified in **88**, no. 2, line 4; **91**, no. 1, i, line 2, and no. 2, i, line 2; and **98**, no. 1, frag. a, line 3. The reading of the docket was suggested by Gilliam in his apparatus, though we differ in dotting letters.

7. D in app.: "The first letter in the line . . . has been read as *b*; . . . apparently one must take refuge in the explanation that this is part of a name, perhaps a place name in the locative."

Verso 1. D in app.: "The cognomen of the praepositus may include, beginnning with the second or third letter, *erm*. However, it does not appear to begin with either *g* or *h*."

115

Fragments of Letters

PDur. 80 (inv. D. P. 59) ca. 235–245

Final Rep. v, p. 268 (Gilliam): "Two small blocks of fragments, evidently from a roll of letters since there are partially preserved addresses on the verso. One block contained . . . Frags. *a–e* . . . two of which have writing on the recto and two on the verso. The other consists of . . . Frags. *f–r*. All are blank on the verso, but four have writing on the recto."

Recto:

Frag. b

]. .ḅ..[
vacat
]. z[

Frag. c

]ḷc̣ḥ[..]ṣ[.].ṃaṇị[
].a.nfa[
]....[

Frag. g

]h[
vacat
iụ[

Frag. h

]..[
].b.[
].g.[
]..b.[

Frag. i

]lc[
]c..[
].ṇ[
]..[

Frag. j

]hei[

c 1. D in app.: "*Ma*]*lc̣ḥ*[*us*] *s*[*a*]*lṃaṇị*?" More likely *ṣ*[*i*]*lụaṇị*.

g 2. *Iụ*[*l:* D; but many other possibilities exist, e.g. a form of *iubere*.

Verso:

Frag. a

] ÇỌḤ [

Frag. d

TRI]Ḅ ÇỌ[H

Tituli

116

Labels

PDur. 130 (inv. D. P. 60 A–D) ca. A.D. 215–245

Transcription: *Final Rep.* V, no. 130; *edidit* Gilliam.

These are four separate pieces of papyrus, each carefully cut for use. *A* was almost certainly meant for a roll of letters like those in **99**, or for a pigeon-hole where such rolls were kept. The names on the other three are probably those of clerks and would more likely be used on pigeon-holes than on rolls.

A has been published by J. F. Gilliam, *YCS* 11 (1950) 172, note 5, and in *CPL*, no. 342.

A

epistulae
equorum e.[
.[....].[.].[

B

zabdib maccaei

C

au]ṛel claudi[u]s

D

aurel ạ.[ ]..ạus

A 2. D in app.: "eṭ?"
D. D in app.: "Length of lacuna uncertain."

VI

Commentarii, Acta, Regulations, and Reference Materials

The materials covered in the preceding chapters have all, aside from a few of the letters, come from the archives of individual military units. But higher headquarters naturally kept military records, too. Letters like **87** and **99** prove that the provincial governor's office maintained files of individual personnel and matériel; and there must have been centralized pay-records and minutes of courts martial as well. In addition, every governor of a province and every field commander of expeditionary forces kept journals of his official activities in the form of commentarii and acta. Premerstein supposes that the distinction between the two consists in the acta's being limited to recording official decisions and directives, while commentarii might contain any sort of material, such as letters, which seemed pertinent.[1] This may be a valid observation, though lack of materials makes it difficult to test. At any rate, Caesar published under the title of *commentarii*, with the implication that he was merely offering his journals to the public as raw materials for historians; and, as might be expected, they include a very wide variety of subject-matter—personal observations, reports of subordinates, the conduct of individual soldiers and officers, tactical and strategic considerations, bons mots, casualty reports, and peace terms, as well as a great deal that is not military at all, particularly his description of the customs of the Gauls and Germans. A mixture of military and civilian affairs would inevitably characterize the journals of any provincial governor; the content of those kept for a field commander whose assignment was more specifically military may have had a narrower scope, though under the Roman system of organization even they probably contained some admixture of civilian matters. Some hint of the kind of thing found in a field commander's journals may be seen in the data cited for individual centurions during the military trials conducted by Germanicus after the mutiny of the legions along the Rhine—"citatus ab imperatore nomen, ordinem, patriam, numerum stipendiorum, quae strenue in proelio fecisset, et, cui erant, dona militaria, edebat." The record of dona militaria in particular, once entirely in the hands of the field general, must have been recorded in his journal, since the recommendation had to come from him, even after the awarding of such

[1] *RE*, s.v. "commentarii," cols. 734, 748–49, and 751.

distinctions had come to be reserved to the emperor.[2] Similarly all proceedings under military law and those in which the litigants were all military personnel (e.g. *PMich.* III 159) must have appeared in some detail in the journal of the presiding officer, and likewise as his report in the journal of his superior who appointed him to try the case.

Every field commander must also have had a file of reference works—itineraria,[3] regulations concerning discipline, promotion, and procedures of all sorts,[4] and perhaps treatises on tactics, strategy, and organization such as those now represented by the works of Frontinus, Aeneas Tacticus, and Vegetius. Imperial constitutiones of all sorts, such as Septimius Severus' permission to soldiers to marry, were no doubt sent to the governors of provinces, and the pertinent parts transmitted in turn by them to the commanders of the various units under their jurisdiction, while other regulations may have emanated from the governor himself.

Of all such general regulations and directives, the only representative to survive is the Feriale Duranum, **117**, a list of festivals and anniversaries designated for official observance by the army. Its presence among the archives of the coh. XX Palmyrenorum is evidence that some at least of the reference materials just mentioned were supplied not only to general officers but even to the headquarters of individual units.

[2] Tiberius' attitude is noteworthy (Suet. *Tib.* 32): "Corripuit consulares exercitibus praepositos . . . quod de tribuendis quibusdam militaribus donis ad se referrent quasi non omnium tribuendorum ipsi ius haberent."

[3] Vegetius 3.6: "itineraria omnium regionum in quibus bellum geritur plenissime debet habere perscripta ita ut locorum interualla non solum passuum numero sed etiam uiarum qualitate perdiscat, compendia, deuerticula, montes, flumina ad fidem descripta consideret usque eo ut sollertiores duces itineraria prouinciarum in quibus necessitas gerebatur non tantum adnotata sed etiam picta habuisse firmentur ut non solum consilio mentis uerum aspectu oculorum uiam profecturus eligeret."

[4] Pliny, *Epist.* 10.65, reports going through edicta and epistulae of Augustus, Vespasian, Titus, and Domitian without finding an applicable ruling. This was in Bithynia.

117

Feriae and Anniversaries for Official Military Observance

PDur. 54 (inv. D. P. 2) ca. A.D. 223–227

Transcription, commentary, and facsimile:

1. Robert O. Fink, Allan S. Hoey, and Walter F. Snyder, "The Feriale Duranum," *YCS* 7 (1940) 1–222 and plates I and II. Cited as **YCS**.
2. *Final Rep.* v, no. 54 and (col. ii only) plate 32; *edidi.*

Transcription and facsimile:

1. Col. ii, 14–19 only, *Prelim. Rep.* v, p. 296 (inaccurate and obsolete) and plate 31, no. 2.
2. Col. ii, 6–11, left half of lines only, Mallon, *Pal.*, plate 17, no. 4.

Commentary:

1. M. I. Rostovtzeff, "Les Archives militaires de Doura," *CRAI*, 1933, pp. 312–13.
2. Idem, "Das Militärarchiv von Dura," *Münchener Beiträge* 19 (1934) 364–67.
3. Allan S. Hoey, "Rosaliae Signorum," *HTR* 30 (1937) 15–35.
4. Idem, "The Feriale Duranum," *Actes du Ve Congrès International de Papyrologie* (Brussels 1938) 159–61.
5. Idem, "Official Policy toward Oriental Cults in the Roman Army," *TAPA* 70 (1939) 456–81.
6. James H. Oliver, "Notes on Documents of the Roman East," *AJA* 45 (1941) 540–41.
7. R. O. Fink, "*Victoria Parthica* and Kindred Victoriae," *YCS* 8 (1942) 81–101.
8. Robert O. Fink, "*Feriale Duranum* I, 1, and *Mater Castrorum*," *AJA* 48 (1944) 17–19.
9. J. Guey, "28 janvier 98 – 28 janvier 198 ou le siècle des Antonins. A propos du Feriale Duranum col. i, l. 14–16," *Revue des études anciennes* 50 (1948) 60–70.
10. James H. Oliver, "The Divi of the Hadrianic Period," *HTR* 42 (1949) 35–40.
11. Arthur Darby Nock, "The Roman Army and the Roman Religious Year," *HTR* 45 (1952) 187–252.
12. J. F. Gilliam, "The Roman Military Feriale," *HTR* 47 (1954) 183–96. Cited as **Gilliam.**
13. Herbert W. Benario, "The Date of the *Feriale Duranum*," *Historia* 11 (1962) 192–96.

Text: *CPL*, no. 324, reproduces the text of the editio princeps in *YCS* 7.

On the nature of this text, *Final Rep.* v, p. 192, may be quoted: "[Its] character as . . . a list of festivals is self-evident, and, as Hoey has demonstrated in detail, the use of the Latin language and capital script proves its official nature, its presence in the archives of the Cohors xx Palmyrenorum shows that it was intended for the army, the absence of any festivals of a strictly local nature is evidence that it was the standard feriale for all the armies of the empire, and the exclusion of all non-Roman gods and festivals is proof that this was the traditional calendar of observances which in its main outlines was as old as the time of Augustus."

Col. ii, 16–18 and 26, establish the time of this redaction of the Feriale within the reign of Severus Alexander; and if i 11–12 is in fact the natalis of Lucius Seius, Alexander's father-in-law, the latest possible date must be A.D. 227, when Alexander divorced Seia. On the other hand, Julia Maesa is already a diva in col. ii, 7. She died before Alexander's marriage, which occurred between August 225 and August 226; but the year of her death has not been determined with certainty. The number of divi in the Acta Fratrum Arvalium in A.D. 183, 218, and 224 indicates that neither Domna nor Maesa had been deified by November 7, 224; and because of the evidence of the Feriale itself this inference still seems valid despite the evidence of **5** that Commodus may have been deconsecrated by Macrinus.[1] Benario, however, argues that Maesa died in 223. He may be right; but his evidence, like that for placing her death in late 224 or in 225, is not entirely conclusive.

The verso is blank.

[1] *Final Rep.* v, i, p. 208; *YCS* 7.113–14 and 182–84. The sixteen divi in 183 were probably Augustus, Claudius, Vespasian, Titus, Nerva, Trajan, Hadrian, Antoninus Pius, Marcus Aurelius, Lucius Verus, Plotina, Sabina, Marciana, Matidia, and the two Faustinas. The twenty of 218 and 224 are presumably the same, with the addition of Commodus, Pertinax, Septimius Severus, and Caracalla. Of these, all are certainly present or readily accounted for in the Feriale Duranum except Plotina, Sabina, and one Faustina. One of these three was commemorated in i 10; and the other two may have been named in the lost portions of cols. iii or iv.

Col. i

[kal(endis) ianuaris *ca.* 42]
[iii nonas ianuarias quod soluantur ac nuncupentur u]ỌṬẠ ET OB SALVTEM
[domini nostri m aureli seueri alexandri aug et ob aetern]ỊṬẠTEM
[impe]RI P̣[r ioui o m b m iunoni reginae b f mineruae b f ioui uictori] B′ M′
[. . . .].S.[*ca.* 12 marti patri taurum marti uicotri ta]ṾRVM
[uict]ỌRIAE B [f
[vii idus] IANV[arias quod detur emeritis honesta missio cum usu priui]LEGIO-
[rum] ṾẸL NVMẸ[re]N[t]ṾṚ [militibus stipendia i o m b m iunoni b f mineruae] B′ F′
[salu]ṬI B F MARTI PẠṬṚỊ Ṭ[aurum
Ṿ[i idus i]ANVARIAS OB NATẠ[lem diuae . . . . diuae . . . . supp]ḶICAṬỊỌ
[. . idus i]ẠNVARIAS OB NẠṬALẸ[m luci 3–4 caesaris *ca.* 14]LVCI ⟦.Ṣ.[. . .] AṾG⟧
[3–4 c]AESARIS
VII[ii kal] FEBRAṚIAS OB ṆATẠ[lem diui hadriani diuo hadriano b m]
V Ḳ[a]Ḷ [feb]RARIAS OB V[i]C̣ṬORỊ[as *ca.* 20 et parthica]Ṃ MAXI-
Ṃ[a]M DIVI SEṾẸ[ri e]T OB [imperium diui traiani uictoriae part]ḤIC̣[a]Ẹ
B [f d]IVO TRAIAN[o b m

PRID Ṇ[onas f]EBRARIA[s o]B I[mperium diui antonini magni supplicat]ỊO ḌIVO
AṆṬỌNINO M[agno] B M
KAL Ṃ[a]RṬIS OB C̣[e]R[imo]NIẠ[s natalicias martis patris uictoris marti] P̣ẠTRI
VICṬOṚỊ TẠṾ[rum
P̣ṚỊḌ NỌN[is ma]Ṛ[tis ob] IM[perium diui marci antonini et diui luci ueri d]ỊVO MAR-
CO B [m diuo lucio] B M
III I[d]VS Ṃ[artias quod] IMP̣ [caesar m aurelius seuerus alexander im]PERATỌṚ
AP[pellat]Ṿ[s sit io]ṾỊ B Ṃ [iunoni b f mineruae b f *ca.* 16 ma]ṚṬI B M [quod]
[a mi]LITIB[us imp] ẠVG [marci aureli seueri alexandri alexande]R AVG Ṇ[
[primo] ỊMP̣[erator] ẠPEL[latus sit supplicatio
[pridie idu]Ṣ [martias q]VOD Ạ[lexander augustus no]Ṣ[ter augustus et pater]
[patriae et pontife]X̣ MAX̣[imus appellatus s]ỊṬ SVPP̣[licat]IO [genio do-]
[mini nostri alex]AND[ri augusti taurum

i 1. The existence of this line must be inferred from the fact that the line here numbered i 2 was exactly level with ii 2, and from the importance of January 1 for the imperial cult and for its military associations. See *YCS* 50–51 and notes 111 and 113–14. In the remainder of the line one could restore either *ob diem kalendarum* (cf. ii 1 and 22) or *ob kalendas* (cf. ii 8 and 14). The cult act was probably a supplicatio.

2. The letter before *ET* must be *M* or *A*; but the two preceding letters, restored as *OT*, are only unidentifiable traces.

2–6. The restorations in these lines are of course only an approximation of the original wording, exempli gratia.

4. Expand: *P(opuli) r(omani); o(ptimo) m(aximo) b(ouem) m(arem); b(ouem) f(eminam).*

5. The letter before *S* must be *H*, *I*, or *N*; the one after *S* cannot be *C*, *G*, *O*, *Q*, or *V*, but almost any other is possible. The beginning of the line might be restored as *[iunon]I̤ S̤[spiti b f saluti b f marti patri*, etc. The spelling *Seispes* or *Sispes* was still in use in the Severan period; cf. Dessau 9246.

7–9. The restoration of these lines has been questioned, most effectively by Gilliam, pp. 190–93; but see *Final Rep*. v, pp. 202–5 for a detailed discussion of January 7 as a day for the discharge of emeriti. On *vii idus* as a pay date see under **71**, above, p. 266.

8. The second letter of which traces are extant can only be *E* or *L*.

10. Because of severe abrasion, the remains of *TIO* at the end of the line resemble an *M*. The combination of a natalis with a supplicatio indicates an anniversary of a diva. The choice is limited to Plotina, wife of Trajan, Sabina, wife of Hadrian, or one of the Faustinas. See above, p. 423, note 1.

11. After *LVCI* at the right end of the line are traces of nine or ten letters which were erased. The last is certainly *G*; the second before it must be *A* or *M*; and the one between is pointed at the bottom. The first letter to the right of *LVCI* could be *A*, less likely *E*; the next is most like *S* but could possibly be *E*. All of the erased letters were overlined with a series of three horizontal strokes, one over the first three letters, a longer one over the central group, and one over the last three.

The ascription of this entry is far from certain. I am still inclined to give it to Lucius Seius Caesar, father-in-law of Severus Alexander; Hoey, *YCS* 183 note 870, and Gilliam, 189 note 19, prefer Lucius Aelius Caesar, Hadrian's original choice as his successor, who died shortly after his adoption. See *Final Rep*. v, pp. 205–6, for a detailed discussion of the evidence.

13. The two letters at the left of *F* in the *YCS* plate are on a separate scrap of papyrus whose position is not certain. If it belongs here, the letters are *AL*. For Hadrian's anniversaries see on ii 27.

14–16. *v[i]c̣ṭoṛị[as arabicam et adiabenicam et parthica]m maxiṃ[a]m divi seṿẹ[ri:* YCS and D. Guey proposes, in an article of which I was not aware when *Final Rep*. v was published, to restore *victori[am* (or *victori[as*) *Parthicam divi Traiani et Parthica]m Maximam*, etc. This is attractive, and barely possible; but the only evidence for it, apart from the Romans' fondness for coincidences, is that Trajan was voted the title Parthicus on February 20, 116. (Fasti Ostienses, published in *Notizie degli Scavi* 10 [1934] 254–56; *L'Année épigraphique* 1936, no. 97; and see especially the discussion in F. A. Lepper, *Trajan's Parthian War* [Oxford 1948] 39–41.) For the news of Trajan's capture of Seleucia–Ctesiphon, if it occurred on January 28, to have reached Rome by February 20 would require the messengers to travel at a speed phenomenal for the time of year. On the other hand, Guey has convinced me that *arabicam* and *adiabenicam* in my own restoration are not entirely consistent with the observance prescribed.

17–18. I have taken the restoration of this line proposed by Hoey (*YCS* 187 note 893) and accepted by Gilliam (194), though it is odd that Caracalla's dies imperii should be observed with more ceremony than his natalis.

21. There may have been an attempt to expunge the

first four letters; but in any case *PRID* was erroneous, for the dies imperii of Marcus Aurelius is attested as Nonis Martiis (*PIR*² I, p. 122, A 697).

23–26. Line 25: [*a mi*]*litib*[*us* . . .] *ạụg* [*imp caesar marcus aurelius severus alexande*]*r:* YCS; [*a mi*]*litib*[*us d n*] *Ạụg*[*Imp Marci Aureli Severi Alexandri Alexande*]*r:* D. In line 23 *IMP* and in lines 23–24 *PERATOR AP* show that the entry deals with the conferring of the title Imperator, while *B M* and *RTI B M* in line 24 mark the prescription of cult acts which usually concludes an entry; but *LITIB* in line 25 precludes restoring a new date and so requires the statement of a new occasion for observance under the same date. In the same line *AVG* and *AVG N*, and in line 26 *IMP* and *APEL*, show that this part of the entry deals again with the title Imperator, and that the recipient was the reigning emperor. His name has been restored in the genitive case in line 25 to modify *militibus*. In line 26 *primo* is somewhat too long for the space; but some such word is necessary.

27–29. As in lines 23–26, the remains of these lines are enough to establish their content and some notion of their wording. *VODA* in line 27 points to *quod* and hence to a new entry whose date, in view of the spacing, is best restored as the day immediately after the one in line 23. In line 28 *XMA*. leaves no alternative to *pontife*]*X̣ MAX̣*[*imus*; and in the next line *AND* is certainly part of Alexander's name. This, then, is the anniversary of the conferring of the usual titles of Augustus, Pater Patriae, and Pontifex Maximus on the new emperor; and it is interesting to see that this occasion, involving purely civil honors, is prescribed for celebration by the army.

Col. ii

XIIII KAḶ ẠPRILES OB DIEM QVINQ[u]A[trio]R[um] SVPPḶ[ic]ATIO IN X KA[l e]ẠSDEM SVPP̣ḶỊÇ[ationes]
PRIDIE ṆONAS APRILES OB NATALẸ[m] ḌỊ[u]I Ạ[n]TONIṆI ṂAGNI D[i]VO AṆ[t]ỌṆ[in]Ọ B M
V IDVS APRILES OB IMPERIVM DI[u]Ị PII SEVERI D[i]VO P̣[i]Ọ [s]ẸVER[o] ḄṂ
III IḌVS ẠP̣Ṛ[il]ES OB NATALEM DIVI PỊI SEVẸ[r]Ị Ḍ[iuo pio] Ṣ[euero] B [m]
X̣[i k]ẠḶ MAỊẠṢ OB NATALEM VRBIS [r]OMAẸ [a]ẸṬẸ[rnae u r a b f]
Ṿ[i k]AL MAIAS OB NATALEM DIVI MARCỊ ẠṆṬOṆ[ini diuo marco an]ṬỌ[nino b m]
NO[nas] MAIAS OB NATALEM DIVAE ỊVLỊẠE ṂẠ[esae diuae maes]ẠẸ [supplicatio]
VI.[d]ṾS MAIAS OB ROSALIAS SIGṆ[o]ṚVM ṢVPPL[icatio]
IIII ỊḌVS MAIAS OB CIRCENSES MẠ[rtiales] MARTI PẠ[tri ult]ORI ṬẠ[u]ṚVṂ
X̣II ḲẠḶ [i]VNIAS QVOD DIVS SEVERVS IMPERATOR Ạ[. . . . . . a]P̣P̣[ell]Ạ[tu]Ṣ Ṣ[it ḌIVO PỊ[o] SEVER[o]
ṾIỊỊI KAL IVNIAS OB NATALEM G[er]MANI[c]⟨i⟩ CAẸ[sa]RIS SVP̣[pli]CAT[i]O [me]ṂỌRI[ae ge]ṚM[anici] Ç[a]ESARIS
P̣Ṛ[i]Ḍ[ie] KAL IVNIAS OḄ ROSALIAS SIGNORVM SVPPḶ[i]CẠTIO
[v] ỊḌ[us i]VNIAS OB VẸSTALIA VESTE MATRỊ SVPPLICẠT[i]Ọ
[vi kal] IVLIAS QVOD DOMINVS NOSṬ[e]Ṛ [m]ARCVS AVRẸ[l]IVS SEVERVS AL[e]X̣Ạ[nder cae]ṢẠṚ ẠP̣P̣Ẹ[l-] [lat]ṾS SỊṬ ET TOGA VIRILI AMIÇ[tus] GEṆIO ẠḶEXANḌṚI AV[g]VSTI TAVRVM
[kal iuli]ỊṢ [qu]OD ALEXANDẸR AVG N P̣[r]IMO COṢ DESIG[n]ATVS SIT SVPPLỊÇẠṬ[io]
[n]ỌN(as) [i]ṾLIAS OḄ [n]ẠTALEM DIVAẸ ṂẠṬIDIAE DIVA[e] MATI[di]AE SVPPLỊ[cat]I[o]
[vi idus iulia]S OB IMPẸRIVM DIVI ANTONINI P̣II DIṾ[o] ANṬỌNINO B M
[iiii idus iul]ỊẠṢ ỌB NATALEM DIVI IVLI DỊVO IVLIO B M
[x kal augus]ṬAS OB DIEM NEPTVNALIORVM SVPPLICATIO; [i]MṂ[o]LATIO

[kal augustis ob n]ATALEM DIVI CLAVḌỊ ẸT DIVI PERṬ[in]ACIS [di]ṾỌ CL[audi]Ọ B M

[diuo pertinaci] B M

[nonis augustis] Ọ[b circenses sa]ḶVṬARES SẠLVT[i b f]

[.. kal septemb]ṚE[s ob na]TAḶ[em m]ẠMAEẠ[e aug matr]IṢ AVG N I[uno]N[i ma]ṂẠ[e]ẠE ẠVG [b f]

[. . . . .].VO[. . . .]ẠOḄ.[. . . . . .].IAM. .[. . . . .].[.]. .A. . .[

[.. kal septembr]ES Ọ[b nata]LẸ[m diu]ẠE MAṚ[cianae diuae marci]ẠṆ[ae supplicatio]

ii 2. It was noted under i 17 that Caracalla's dies imperii seems for some reason to have been celebrated more elaborately than his natalis.

3. This entry is the first evidence of the official date of Severus' proclamation by his troops at Carnuntum. The unusual order of name and titles, with Pius preceding Severus, appears also in ii 4 and ii 11.

5. Expand: *u(rbi) r(omae) a(eternae) b(ouem) f(eminam)*. Since the cult of Urbs Roma Aeterna was instituted by Hadrian, this anniversary cannot antedate his reign unless it appeared as the Parilia.

7. Most probably *nonas maias* is a blunder for *nonis maiis*, though a numeral may have been accidentally omitted.

8. *ṿị ị[du]s:* YCS; *V I.[– – u]s:* D. It is quite impossible to be sure of the numeral in the date, for it, with *idus*, occupied the same space as *v idus* in line 3 and *iiii idus* in line 9, and *IIII* in that line fills as much space as the first three characters in the present one. The numeral here could accordingly be *V*, *VI*, or *VII*.

On the possibility that this rosalia (the form *rosaliae* is otherwise unexampled) was a pay-day, see above on i 7–9, and Fink, *YCS* 70–71 and *Final Rep.* v, pp. 202–5. Against this view, Gilliam 191–93. The interpretation as a pay-day appears to me to be supported by the fact that another rosalia is scheduled in ii 14, only three weeks later, for it is difficult to understand why two completely identical holidays should be permitted to occur so close together. Col. iii 2 may be the occasion of the third stipendium.

9. The letters *ID* have been pulled together in patching the papyrus, so that the *I* appears to be the vertical stroke of the *D*. The phrase "Circenses Martiales," like *cerimonias natalicias* in i 19, does not refer to rites at Dura but is used as the name of the festival itself. The date is that of the dedication of the shrine of Mars Ultor, whose cult Augustus originated, built by Augustus to house Crassus' standards after their recovery from the Parthians.

10–11. In line 10, *DIVS* is probably a haplography for *DIVVS PIVS*, since the epithet *PIO* appears in line 11.

The occasion is either the anniversary of Severus' first acclamation in the First Parthian War by Niger's troops whom he had taken into his army (Hoey, *YCS* 131–34) or the anniversary of the "Ravenna incident" treated as the date of Severus' acknowledgment by the Senate (Hoey, *YCS* 130; Fink, *YCS* 134–36).

12–13. The first occurrence of the name in line 12 clearly ends in *ae*; but the date makes it certain that Germanicus is the person commemorated. Since he was not deified, he must be included because of his military reputation, deserved or not.

14. See above on ii 8.

18. The date is restored partly on considerations of space but chiefly because July 1 was by ancient republican tradition the earliest legal date for electing consuls. Since only the first consulship was commemorated for Augustus (*Feriale Cumanum*, *CIL* I, p. 229), the same is probably true here. This line consequently provides no evidence on the date of the present text. The prescription of the consulate in the military feriale is further evidence, like i 23–24, of Alexander's "constitutional" and civilian policy.

19. *[iiii n]ọṇ(as):* YCS; *[III N]ọn(as):* D. The reading *n]ỌN(as)* seems unavoidable, even though there is no other instance of this abbreviation in this text. The space available for the numeral would accommodate *IIII* best; but *VI* or *III* is not impossible. *PRID* is too long by one letter.

20. This date was previously attested only as that of Hadrian's death; but it is restored here because the Feriale regularly puts an emperor's dies imperii on the date of his predecessor's death. Cf. i 15–16, 17–18, and 21–22.

21. The space is a little narrow for the date restored; but this is the day usually celebrated rather than the actual date of Caesar's birth, *iii idus*.

22. The prescription of an immolatio as well as supplicatio on an occasion which was otherwise only a popular festival (*YCS* 148–49 and 167–70) may testify to an element of real worship of Neptune as a deity with some military significance. Perhaps immolatio rather than a *bos mas* or *taurus* because the choice of victim was left to the commanding officer of each garrison.

23–24. Claudius' presence here is strong evidence that no other divus had been dropped from the official list by the date of the Feriale, for he is absent from Decius' series of consecration coins and is survived by Pertinax in the *Fasti* of Philocalus (Snyder, *YCS* 147).

25. This is the festival of the Salus publica populi Romani, not of Salus Augusti.

26–28. The placing of the two fragments (9 and 10 in *YCS*, plate I) at the foot of this column has been challenged because they preclude restoring either the Volcanalia, *x kal septembres*, or Hadrian's dies imperii, *iii idus augustas*, in line 27. The spacing of the lines on the two fragments, however, is the same as in the last four lines on the main body of the papyrus, and in their present position they allow restoration of normal readings in lines 26 and 28. Line 27 remains a crux; it is not even certain whether it is a continuation of the entry begun in 26 or a new, separate entry. The first extant letter in line 27 is *B*, *D*, *O*, or *Q*; the third is *O* or *Q*. On the next fragment the letters are *A* or *M* followed by *O* and *B*, *P*, or *R* and an unidentifiable speck high in the line. On the first tab of the main papyrus is *A*, *L*, *M*, or *R* followed by *IAM*, a trace, and *A* or *M*. On the second tab the readings are much less clear: *E*, *F*, *G*, or *T*, followed by *A* or *N*, then *D*, *E*, or *L*. The next two letters might be *E*, *L*, or *T* followed by *D* or *E*. Nothing in the extant remains forbids reading and restoring *]Q̣VO[d uot]A OḄ Ṿ[icto]ṚIAM P̣Ạ[rthicam] ẠṾG̣ ẠḶẸX̣[andri*; but there are great difficulties in the way of beginning or ending such a line. For a more detailed discussion see *Final Rep.* v, pp. 210–211.

28. Since the letters *ẠEMAṚ* are on the first tab of the body of the papyrus, there can be little doubt that this line concerns the natalis of Diva Marciana.

Col. iii

[pr]ID [kal septembres ob nat]ẠLEṂ [diui commodi diuo] COṂ[modo b m]
[. .] IDṾ[s septembres *ca.* 6]. . [*ca.* 21]. [

Line 3 is entirely lost

[xiiii kal octo]ḄṚ[es] Ọ[b natalem diui traiani et ob imperium diui neruae diuo]
5 [traiano] [b m] [diuo neruae b m]
[xiii kal octobre]S O[b natalem diui an]T[onini pii diuo antonino b m]
[. . kal] OCṬ[obres o]Ḅ ṆAṬ[alem di]VAE F̣[austina]Ẹ DỊṾ[ae fau]STI[nae suppl]ỊCAT[io]
8 [viiii] ḲAḶ [octobres o]B N[atalem] DỊ[ui augusti] DỊ[uo aug]VṢ[to b m]

Lines 9 and 10 are entirely lost

11 [*ca.* 13]. [*ca.* 17]. . [.]. [*ca.* 15]. . [.]. . [
12 [*ca.* 7 no]ṾẸ[m]BṚ[e]S [*ca.* 14]ỊṬ[.]NVṢ. [*ca.* 13]. Ḅ[. .]. [.]Ẹ[
13 [*ca.* 15]Ị[*ca.* 11]. [*ca.* 6]Ṇ[
20? [ ]. [
21? [ ]. [*ca.* 19]. [
24? [k]AḶ[

iii 1. This is certainly Commodus' natalis; but his dies imperii, *xvi kal apriles* (the date of Marcus Aurelius' death; see on ii 20), appears not to have been celebrated. It should be found at the end of col. i or the beginning of col. ii.

2. Comparison with line 1 shows that the space before *idus* requires *viii* or *vii* for the numeral. No anniversaries are known for these dates; but if *vii idus ianuarias* (i 7–9) was in fact one date for paying the troops (cf. also ii 8), this line may record a holiday for the payment of the third and last stipendium of the year.

4–6. The restoration of these three lines appears sound despite the exiguity of the remains. The natales of Trajan and Antoninus Pius, only a day apart, could not have been omitted; and they must be placed here because lines 8 and 7 are occupied by the natales of Augustus and Faustina. Nerva's dies imperii has been added because the spacing of the lines on frag. B 2 (*YCS*, plate II) shows that the entry begun in line 4 was run over into another line. The condition of frag. B 2 is enough to account for its failure to reveal any traces of line 5.

7. The lack of any distinguishing epithet leaves unanswered the question of which Faustina is honored here, and whether the other was also commemorated. The younger Faustina was the first empress to bear the title of Mater Castrorum; but the elder anticipated her in some important respects (A. Alföldi, "Insignien und Tracht der römischen Kaiser," *Römische Mittheilungen* 50 [1935] 96; *YCS* 158 note 721). In all probability the cults of both were present at this time in both the civil and the military religious calendars.

11. On frag. G 4 (*YCS*, plate II) a segment of a curved stroke, concave above, with the serif of another letter below it on the right. On G 5 a stroke slanting upward to the right followed by the lower left quadrant of *C*, *G*, *O*, or *Q*. On G 6 two strokes somewhat like those on G 5 followed by a vertical stroke. On G 7 possibly *G* and the foot of a vertical hasta. On G 8 perhaps *E* or *L* followed by *A* or *M*.

12. After *nouembres*: [*ca.* 14] . . [.]*nuṣ.* [*ca.* 13]. . [. .]. [.]*ẹ*[: YCS and D. On G 5 probably *IT*, perhaps *NT*. On H 2 after *S* a vertical stroke. On G 7, *O* or *D* followed by *B* or, less likely, *R*. On G 8, *A* or *M*; on H 3, *E* or *F*.

13. The doubtful letter in the middle of the line is on frag. G 5. It is either *D*, *O*, or *Q*.

Col. iv

7? [xvi k]Ạ[l ianuar]Ị Ạ[s]ẠṬẠ[sup]PLỊ[c]ATỊ[o

8? [i]N X [kal eas]ḌEṂ

iv 7–8. These lines are so numbered because they are on the same level as lines 7–8 of col. iii. The remains in line 8 on frags. D 11 and 12 lead to the same phrase as that used in ii 1 to indicate an extended holiday. In this part of the year the only such holiday known is the Saturnalia; and the date in line 7 has been restored accordingly. The traces on frags. D 13, 14, and 15, however, do not accord with this restoration or with each other. The traces on D 13 are almost certainly *n*]*ẠṬẠ*[*lem*; but in an entry for a natalis, *supplicatio* (D 14 and 15) could not have followed so closely. Hoey's suggestion (*YCS* 162) that the papyrus had split into separate panels at this end, and that panels sliding up or down brought these words into line 7 from other lines above or below, is entirely reasonable and adequate.

TRANSLATION

Col. i

1 January 1 – –

2–6 January 3. Because vows are paid and undertaken both for the welfare of our Lord Marcus Aurelius Severus Alexander Augustus and for the eternity of the empire of the Roman nation, [to Jupiter Optimus Maximus an ox, to Juno Regina a cow, to Minerva a cow, to Jupiter Victor] an ox, [to Juno Sospes? a cow, – – – to Mars Pater a bull, to Mars Victor] a bull, to Victoria a cow [

7–9 January 7. [Because honorable discharge with the enjoyment of (customary)] privileges [is given to men who have served their time] or (because) stipendia are counted [for the soldiers, to Jupiter Optimus Maximus an ox, to Juno a cow, to Minerva] a cow, to Salus a cow, to Mars Pater a bull[

10 January 8. For the birthday of the deified (*empress*) [ ], to the deified (*empress*) [ ] a supplicatio.

11–12 January [9–23]. For the birthday of Lucius [. . . .] Caesar, [ ] of Lucius [. . . .] Caesar.

13 January 24. For the birthday [of the deified Hadrian, to the deified Hadrian an ox.]

14–16 January 28. For the [– – – and] very great Parthian victory of the deified Severus and for [the accession of the deified Trajan, to Victoria] Parthica a cow, to the deified Trajan [an ox].

17–18 February 4. For the accession [of the deified Antoninus Magnus] a supplicatio; to the deified Antoninus Magnus an ox.

19–20 March 1. For the [birthday] ceremonies [of Mars Pater Victor to Mars] Pater Victor a bull.

21–22 March 7. For the accession [of the deified Marcus Antoninus and the deified Lucius Verus], to the deified Marcus an ox, [to the deified Lucius] an ox.

23–26 March 13. [Because] the Emperor [Caesar Marcus Aurelius Severus Alexander] was named emperor, to Jupiter an ox, [to Juno a cow, to Minerva a cow – – –] to Mars an ox; [because] Alexander our Augustus was saluted as Imperator [for the first time] by the soldiers [of the Emperor Augustus Marcus Aurelius Severus Alexander, a supplicatio – – –].

27–28 [March 14.] Because Alexander our [Augustus] was named [Augustus and Pạter Patriae and] Pontifex Maximus, a supplicatio; [to the Genius of our Lord] Alexander [Augustus a bull – – –].

Col. ii

1 March 19. For the day of the Quinquatria, a supplicatio; until March 23, supplicationes.

2 April 4. For the birthday of the deified Antoninus Magnus, to the deified Antoninus an ox.

3 April 9. For the accession of the deified Pius Severus, to the deified Pius Severus an ox.
4 April 11. For the birthday of the deified Pius Severus, to the deified [Pius] Severus an ox.
5 April 21. For the birthday of the Eternal City Rome, [to the Eternal City Rome a cow].
6 April 26. For the birthday of the deified Marcus Antoninus, to [the deified Marcus] Antoninus [an ox].
7 May 7. For the birthday of the deified Julia Maesa, to [the deified] Maesa [a supplicatio].
8 May [9–11]. For the Rose-festival of the standards, a supplicatio.
9 May 12. For the circus-races in honor of Mars, to Mars Pater Ultor a bull.
10–11 May 21. Because the deified Severus was saluted as Imperator by [. . . . . . , – – –] to the deified Pius Severus.
12–13 May 24. For the birthday of Germanicus Caesar, a supplicatio to the memory of Germanicus Caesar.
14 May 31. For the Rose-festival of the standards, a supplicatio.
15 June [9]. For the Vestalia, to Vesta Mater a supplicatio.
16–17 June [26]. Because our Lord Marcus Aurelius Severus Alexander was named Caesar and clothed in the toga virilis, to the Genius of Alexander Augustus a bull.
18 July [1]. Because Alexander our Augustus was designated consul for the first time, a supplicatio.
19 July [2–5]. For the birthday of the deified Matidia, to the deified Matidia a supplicatio.
20 July [10]. For the accession of the deified Antoninus Pius, to the deified Antoninus an ox.
21 July [12]. For the birthday of the deified Julius, to the deified Julius an ox.
22 July [23]. For the day of the Neptunalia, a supplicatio (and) a sacrifice.
23–24 [August 1. For] the birthday of the deified Claudius and the deified Pertinax, to the deified Claudius an ox; [to the deified Pertinax] an ox.
25 [August 5.] For [the circus-races] in honor of Salus, to Salus [a cow].
26 August [14–29. For] the birthday of Mamaea [Augusta] mother of our Augustus, to the Juno of Mamaea Augusta [a cow].
27 *No coherent text.*
28 August [15–30]. For the birthday of the deified Marciana, [to the deified] Marciana [a supplicatio].

Col. iii

1 [August] 31. [For] the birthday [of the deified Commodus, to the deified] Commodus [an ox].
2 September [7 ?].
4–5 September [18]. For [the birthday of the deified Trajan and the accession of the deified Nerva, to the deified Trajan an ox, to the deified Nerva an ox.]
6 [September 19]. For [the birthday of the deified] Antoninus [Pius, to the deified Antoninus an ox.]
7 September [20–22]. For the birthday of the deified Faustina, to the deified Faustina a supplicatio.
8 September [23]. For the birthday of the deified [Augustus], to the deified Augustus [an ox].
12 October 16–November 12.

Col. iv

7 December [16] – – – birthday? – – – supplicatio
8 until December 23.

VII

Unclassifiable Fragments

The texts in this chapter are all from Dura, so that there is little hope that additional pieces of them will turn up. Some, however, such as **123**, possess a certain intrinsic interest; and all are published to remind papyrologists and other scholars of their existence. I have omitted a few whose military character seemed especially doubtful; but some of those included are not certainly military.

118

PDur. 134 (inv. D. P. 50) A.D. 220–222?

Transcription, commentary, and facsimile: *Final Rep.* v, no. 134 and plate 67, 2; *edidit* Gilliam, the source of quoted matter below.

"It could be a fragment of acta diurna, but it could equally well come from documents of many other kinds. If Elagabalus' name preceded that of Comazon in line 3, as seems probable, the papyrus almost certainly comes from his reign (218–222)."

The verso is blank.

com]ạzọ[nte
]comazoṇṭẹ .[
]et comazontẹ [ii cos? A.D. 220
coh xx p]almụrenor[um
]septim.[.] se[
an]toṇini ..[

"The space between lines 3 and 4 is greater than between the other lines." Line 4 may accordingly be a heading of some sort.

5.]*Septimi*.[.] *ṣẹ*[: D; "*Septimiọ Ṣẹ*[*vero?*" The rletter after *m*, however, seems to be an *n* or another *m* ather t han *i*.

6. (*centuria*), (*turma*), or a personal name are all equally possible restorations before *an*]*tonini*.

119

PDur. 135 (inv. D. P. 61) A.D. 210–230

Transcription and commentary: *Final Rep.* v, no. 135; *edidit* Gilliam, whose comment is quoted below.

"Line 2 is carefully written in large letters resembling those sometimes used in addresses. Verso blank."

].[...]..ọ[
coh] xx palmyr[e]ṇọ[rum

120

PDur. 142 (inv. D. P. 39 recto) A.D. 220–230

Transcription and commentary: *Final Rep*. v, no. 142; *edidit* Gilliam, whose comment is quoted below.

"Datable only by the script. Possibly the text contained monthly summaries of strength." Cf. **66** b ii 9–15, and perhaps **60** and **62**.

]. kal octọḅr[-
]. kaḷ no[uembr-

121

PDur. 143 (inv. D. P. 56) A.D. 221–242

Transcription and commentary: *Final Rep*. v, no. 143; *edidit* Gilliam, whose comment is quoted below.

"For the date in line 2, *Grato et Seleu*]*co cos* (A.D. 221) seems the most probable restoration. Perhaps *Atti*]*co* (A.D. 242), without his colleague, or *Fus*]*co* (A.D. 225), without either colleague or *II*, are also possible. In any event, the date need not have been the current year. . . . Verso blank."

]. . kal .[
]co cos[
]. . . .[. . . .].ị.o. . [
]. . .[.]. .[

122

PDur. 136 (inv. D. P. 78) ca. A.D. 230

Transcription and commentary: *Final Rep.* v, no. 136; *edidit* Gilliam, whose comments are quoted below.

"Place of finding unknown, but from season of 1932/33. Verso blank. If the Marianus of line 4 is the centurion, the date will be before *ca.* A.D. 233. The hand points to a date about A.D. 230."

].[..].[
].ụisorụṃ[
]e.ari.ṣ..[
]ṃariani[
]ṣ...[
].esar....[
]eoṣṛị[

3. "Possibly a word ending *-arios* or *-arius*. The second letter may be *r* or *t*. It appears . . . to be in ligature with the bottom of the following *a*."

4. "Possibly Y] *Ṃariani*."

5. "*C*]*ạesar* is a difficult reading, and the letter that follows is not *e* and probably not *i*."

123

PDur. 133 (inv. D. P. 66) A.D. 213–217 or 235–238

Transcription, commentary, and facsimile: *Final Rep.* v, no. 133 and plate 67, 1; *edidit* Gilliam, the source of quoted matter below.

"These [three] fragments are from the bottom of the same column, to judge from the amount of blank papyrus at the bottom . . . and the spacing of lines. Frag. a, 5, is in a larger and quite different hand. . . . Verso blank.

"It may be possible to determine the nature of this text when line 4 is read. . . . It is striking to find the titles of the emperor listed so fully, especially in the accusative. For his identity, *Germanicus Maximus* (line 2) is the chief clue. This title, within the limits of dated Latin papyri found at Dura (208–*ca.* 255), was borne only by Caracalla (from 213) and Maximinus. The hand is too irregular to be used with much confidence to decide between the two. *Aurel-* in line 3 perhaps suggests Caracalla if *et* links its bearer with the emperor.

"In detail, the text raises other questions. In line 3 *Caesaris filia* is difficult to identify, either as an emperor's daughter or as the daughter of an Imperial heir. It is also natural, despite the absence of a praenomen, to take *Aurel-* in the same line as another member of the Imperial family, though he might also be a governor or some other official. . . . One can hardly suppose that Elagabalus was Aurelius Antoninus in Caracalla's life-time . . . Maximinus at least had a son and Caesar."

If, however, frag. c (not mentioned in *PDur*. 133 but shown on the plate) is a part of this text, then *aurel* in frag. b 2, is probably one of a list of names, perhaps of soldiers. In frag. a 3, it is not certain that *caesaris* modifies *filiạ*[-; another possibility is *procuratore*]*m caesaris* or *libertu*]*m caesaris*, in the accusative perhaps as the subject of an infinitive of which *filia*[*m* or *filia*[*s* is the object. But of course *filia*[could be in any case, or could be *fili* in apposition with *caesaris* followed by *ạ*[*ug n* or *ṃ*[*arci* or *ạ*[*ureli* or *ṃ*[*aximini*. Frag. a 4 is still a mystery.

Frag. a

]ẹm x̣. . . . .[.].ṇ.[
g]eṛm ṃaximuṃ .[
]m cạesaṛịs filiạ[
].ọsṣopc̣i ịmm . . .ẓ.[
Space of three lines
]. .ḍm (*Hand 2*)

Frag. b

].[. .].[. .].[. . .].[.].[
a]ụgustum . . . .[
]et aụṛel . .[.]g̣[
]ṛ.ius .ụ. .ạeti

Frag. c

a]ụrẹḷ[
a]ụrel[

a 1.].*m*. . . . .[.]. . . .[*:* D; "Only a connecting stroke is preserved before *m*. The next letter might be *x*, but there is no trace of an *a* to make *max* possible." The *x* may be a numeral; and the line might very well read *x̣ịị ḳạḷ ạpriḷ*[*es*; but the traces are too few and slight for much confidence, especially in an unknown context.

2. "After *maximum*, *ạ* is possible, e.g., *Ạ*[*rabicum* or *Ạ*[*diabenicum*."

3. *filiạ*[*m:* D; "]*m* presumably is the end of a name."

4.]. . . .*ọṛc̣iimmii*.*z*[*:* D; "None of the first four letters is completely preserved. For the last two [of the four]—*ṣạ* is perhaps the most obvious reading. Then, after a space which may indicate a word division, *o* or *a* and *a* or *r*. Following *ci* or *pi*, *imm*(*unes*) *III Z*[would be a satisfactory reading in some contexts. The second *m* has a long trailing stroke which may indicate that it is the last letter in an abbreviated word." *imm*(*unes*) *iii* seems very probable. The preceding four letters might conceivably be read *opt*(*io*) *i* or *ort*(*inatus*) *i*; but the third letter is a very doubtful *t*, almost certainly *c*.

5.].*um:* D. The remains might also be read].*ụṃa*.

b 2. "*Augustum* was corrected from *Augusti*. *Augustus* usually precedes such titles as *Germ maximus*. Perhaps we have here *Augustum n*(*ostrum*), but the traces of ink are insufficient to test the possibility." *ṇọṣ*[*trum* seems barely possible; but the *n* would be very broad.

3. *Aurel*. .[.].[*:* D; "The *l* in *Aurel* is so long as to suggest an abbreviation. The letters following are blurred, but -*ịụṃ* may be possible."

4.]*ọ*. .*ṣ*[.].*ua*. . . . .*:* D; "possibly]*osis*,]*orius*,]*ores*, or other combinations of these letters. A complete letter may not be lost in the lacuna. The remaining letters might be read in ways as different as *auasasti* and *Marini*."

124

PDur. 145 (inv. D. P. 80 recto) A.D. 208–256

Transcription and commentary: *Final Rep.* v, no. 145; *edidit* Gilliam, whose description is quoted below.

"Place of finding unknown but from season of 1932/33. On verso faint traces of two lines of Greek or Latin. There is nothing to show the significance of the figure preserved, which appears to be complete. The denarius sign regularly precedes the number, and presumably a second figure is lost in the lacuna to the right."

] lxxxi ⳨[

125

PDur. 137 III p.

Description: *Final Rep.* v, no. 137; *edidit* Welles, who is quoted below.

"On the verso of [**55**], and written with the fibres, this text consists of nothing but scraps.... The lower margin of [**55**] is the left margin here. . . . One fragment shows a free interval between lines of 1 cm., suggesting that the document consisted of a number of separate items. The entries were dated. On four fragments, the month name *Εὐδυνέου* can be read, twice accompanied by numerals (*ιϛʹ, λʹ*), and on a fifth the numeral *πέμπτῃ* is visible. On one fragment, the turma sign (Ŧ) occurs, showing that the document had a military character."

In spite of the turma sign, the Greek language and the Macedonian name of the month cast doubt on the military nature of this text. At most it may have been half-military like *PDur.* 129; but more probably it was a contract to which a soldier was a party, and the turma was part of his identification, as the century was in *PDur.* 30, line 7, and *PDur.* 32, line 6.

126

PDur. 138 (inv. D. P. 116) III p.

Description: *Final Rep.* v, no. 138; *edidit* Welles, quoted below.

"This is a tiny scrap which was inventoried in the season of 1933/34, but which is so similar to [**55/125**] that it probably belongs to the season of 1931/32, if it is not, in fact, a part of that other document. The recto contains traces of three lines of Latin, only Ŧ (*turma*) *A – – III ·e -ri* being recognizable. The verso contains, at right angles in the same relation as the verso of [**55/125**], two lines of Greek in a fine and fluent hand, but beyond individual letters, nothing can be read (*ουαλ* for *Οὐαλης*?)."

127

PDur. 139 (inv. D. P. 113) III p.

Description: *Final Rep.* v, no. 139; *edidit* Welles, quoted below.

"Like [**126**], this . . . fragment may well have been part of [**55/125**], although it is listed in the inventory of the season of 1933/34. The recto contains little more than the turma sign:

]. . .ep[
]. Ŧ .[

The verso contains bits of four lines of Greek, with only what may be the beginning of the letters *τοῦ βο*[legible."

128

PDur. 146 (inv. D. Pg. 18) III p.?

Description: *Final Rep.* v, no. 146; *edidit* Welles, quoted below.

"This parchment sliver was found with the military documents of the season of 1931/32, and is similar to [**42**] in being a golden yellow in color. [**16**] and [**19**] show this coloring in a less pronounced way, and there are a number of similarly colored but smaller fragments which have not been given inventory numbers or included in this publication. [**128**] is the only one of these, with the possible exception of a small scrap where I seem to see the one word *ἵτεμ* (cf. [**35**]), which is written in Greek. Few letters are preserved in any line and fewer still are legible, and the fragment is worthy of mention only for its hand. The letters are small and neat, suggesting the hands of the early second century, but the *delta* is of the pure Latin type (d). For this reason, as well as from the circumstances of its finding, I am inclined to see in the script a late survival of this type of writing."

Addenda

129

Accounts in Denarii

Bodleian Library Ms. Lat. Class. g 3 P — II p.

Transcription, commentary, and facsimile: *ChLA* IV, no. 272; cited as **M**.

Marichal, the first to publish this text, has said nearly all that can be said of its contents: "It is certainly not concerned with wages, but may be a record of 'deposits' or 'expenses incurred on a mission'; from l. 4 it seems likely that legionary infantry are involved, perhaps exclusively commissioned officers, since the only other qualification mentioned is *custos armorum*, l. 6." The size of the sums in lines 3–5, however, would indicate that these are deposits or debits as in **73**. I know of no example of an account of expenses for an expedition.

The first two lines are taken by Marichal as remains of the date, which he restores as A.D. 87. This appears to be too early for the hand; and the name in cursive in line 6, along with the title *p(rimus) p(ilus)* in line 4, inclines me to believe that at least lines 1, 4, 5, and 6 contained the names and ranks of soldiers. My dating rests accordingly on paleographical grounds. I have worked from a photograph obtained through the courtesy of the Bodleian Library.

The verso contains the beginnings of three lines in Greek, of which only the first, *φαρμουθι* δ[, is intelligible.

] marti[
]xiii ịṇ ẹ[
]dc̣lxxxxvị[
]. p̄p̄ ⚹ dc [
].e ⚹ mlxxxxv [
] agrippa a˙ c˙
]ṭiui i ⚹ ccl
]..[.]xi ⚹ cclxxv

1.]*Marti*[*as:* M; but perhaps *marti*[*alis* or a similar personal name.
2. [*Imp Domitiano*] *XIII e*[*t Saturnino Cos:* M; but my photograph shows two or three partially effaced letters between the numeral and the *e*.
3.]*ṂLXXXXV* .[*:* M. For *dc* cf. line 4. In both occurrences the *d* has a bar through it.
4.]*.ṣ:* M. Expand *p*(*rimus*) *p*(*ilus*).
5.]*ṛe:* M.
6. Expand *a*(*rmorum*) *c*(*ustos*).
7.]*.c*[*.*]*XI:* M.

130

Account in Denarii

Bodleian Library Ms. Lat. Class. g. 4 (P.) End of II p.

Transcription, commentary, and facsimile: *ChLA* IV, no. 273; cited as **M**.

Marichal, who first published this text, rightly says that it is similar to but not identical with **70**. One may go further and say that the hands of both are also quite alike, as a photograph obtained through the courtesy of the Bodleian Library shows. A date at the very end of the second century is therefore reasonable, though the early years of the third cannot be excluded. Marichal says merely "Second/Third Century."

Since the papyrus is mounted on cardboard, the verso is presumably blank.

                                   .[
]ṂVS   ARTYSPARSIẠ .[
 ]. depositis ⚹ cix
   ]ḷ ix n˙ ⚹ viii ob iv

2.]*AUS ARTYSPARDIS K*(*astris*): M; but at the beginning]*MVS* seems a trifle more likely because the junction of the two strokes is lower than in the *A*'s which follow. In the second name the remains of Marichal's *D* are like a round Greek cursive delta and very similar to the preceding *S*, which is quite round above and below. Of the final letter only two flecks are left; but the lower one suffices to show that the letter was probably not *S*. The name is at any rate Iranian. On Iranians in the Roman army even in the first century, see now Hans Petersen, "New Evidence for the Relations between Romans and Parthians," *Berytus* 16 (1966) 61–69.

The character at the right edge of the papyrus resembles an *H* of double width. Marichal's *K*(*astris*) may be right but does not appear to me certain.

3. *i*]*n:* M. Probable, though almost nothing remains of the *n*.

4.]*lian:* M; in app., "Read *acceptos ab* or *datos Aure*]*liano* or *Iu*]*liano* etc. or *missos? ad Aure*]*lian*(*um*) etc.?" But in my photograph the third letter is a clear *x*, though I have no explanation of this combination of letters beyond pointing out the obvious, that *n* may be an abbreviation of *numerus* or *nummus*.

131

Accounts

PHawara 19 — Date uncertain. II p. ?
University College, London

Mentioned, without text, in *Hawara, Biahmu, and Arsinoe* (London 1889) no. 19; *CPL*, no. 319.

Transcription, commentary, and facsimile: *ChLA* IV, no. 239; cited as **M.**

As with the two preceding texts, Marichal was the first to publish the actual text of these fragments. I have worked from a photograph secured through the kindness of Professor E. G. Turner, who took the trouble to have the fragments detached from their cardboard backing and reports that the verso is blank.

In spite of Marichal's analysis and restorations, it does not appear possible to determine what sort of accounts these are. It is not certain that the numerals represent sums of money, or if they do, what unit of currency is involved, whether denarii, drachmae, or sesterces, for the character in frag. a 1 and 6 and frag. b 2, which Marichal read as the symbol for sesterces, is actually a simple *h* and may represent *h*(*abet*) to indicate a deposit, or *h*(*omines*) in a list of persons. Nor does the fact that the number *lxxx* in b 4 is the same as the amount deducted *in uictum* in **68** provide a sound basis for interpretation or restoration, since none of the other numbers corresponds with any of the sums named in **68** or **70**. Moreover, the standard deductions of **68** for *faenaria* and *caligas fascias* are missing here. In view of all this, it seems better to refrain from attempting to reconstruct the text. There is in fact no firm evidence that this account is even a military record.

Marichal's date of A.D. 6–83 rests on the assumption that the figure in b 2 is equivalent to the annual pay of a legionary, or one installment of a centurion's pay. But the interpretation of the figures in **68** and **70** on which he bases his calculations is highly uncertain; see above in the introductions to those texts. The date must therefore be judged on paleographical grounds, and numerals provide little evidence. A date in the second century might serve as a guess.

Frag. a

]ḥ dc̣c̣[
One or two lines blank
]ṿii [
]ius i [
] h .cxx̣..[

Frag. b

] viii ...[
]h dccị[
] iii [
] lxxx [
] xxxxv ṣ[
] x̣x̣v [

a 1.](*sestertios*) *DCC*[*:* M. Expand *h*(*abet*)?
4.].*II:* M.
5.]*ius t:* M. The *t* is explained in the apparatus as "tesserarius." But cf. the *i*'s in the line above and frag. b 1 and 3.
6. (*sestertios*) *CXXVI*[*:* M.

b 2.](*sestertios*) *DCCL*[*:* M. The numeral on the edge of the papyrus, however, is a very tall vertical stroke, quite unlike the *l* in line 4.
5. *XXXXXVI*[*:* M; but the last numeral has a long tail which extends back under the *v*. Expand *s*(*emis*).
6. No reading in M.

132

Account?

PAberd. Inv. 2h   II/III p.

Text, commentary, and facsimile: *ChLA* IV, no. 230; cited as **M**.

Marichal notes that this papyrus is "unpublished and nowhere referred to"; and at the time of this writing the Aberdeen University Library was unable to locate the papyrus or provide a photograph. My readings are therefore made from the plate in *ChLA* IV, which Marichal generously sent me.

Whether the text is military appears doubtful, as Marichal himself recognizes. If my readings are right, *accepit* disappears; if his *s*]*eruus* is the correct reading in line 3, the text must be civilian. The only indication that it may be an account is the possible reference to a depositum in line 2.

Marichal reports a Greek cursive text on the verso.

The date is Marichal's.

]. . . .ṭ. . [
] in dep sit. [
]ẹnus ṣe ạn. [
]ạnnịers. [
].   [
Two lines blank
]. ịo
]ịuṛạ   [
]. .   [

1.]*accepi*[*t stipendi* (*denarios*) . . . ?: M; app., "The first three letters seem certain, the *e* is doubtful, however cf. *se*, l. 3." The *a* nevertheless appears impossible because the left-hand stroke rises above the almost horizontal second stroke—possibly *e* or *f*, or with the next stroke, *h*. The doubtful *t* which I read might be *a*; and the other remains could be made to fit a variety of letters.

2.] *in deposito* [(*denarios*): M. I can not find the *o* after *p*; and the letter at the right edge is only a fleck.

3.]*eruus se an*. [: M; app., "*s*]*eruus?*" At the right end *ann*[is a possible reading;]*ẹnus* may be the end of a name, such as Serenus or Labienus, or an adjective like *terrenus*.

4.]. . *inters*. [: M; app., "*intersi*[*t?*". There is a horizontal line above my *i* which is evidently the basis for Marichal's reading *t*. It is not clear from the plate whether the line is an ink-stroke or merely the shadow of a raised fiber. If ink, one should read the *i* as a numeral: *ann*( ) *I*. I have no suggestion for *ers*.[The *r* may have been corrected from *l*.

8.]. . *o*: M; app., "*depoṣ*]*ịto?*"

9.]. *u*. . .: M; app., "*i*]*ṇ uịạ*[*tico*]*?*"

133

Legal Document?

PAberd. 150 (inv. 2 i) — Early II p.

Description: E. G. Turner, *PAberd.*, no. 150. Text of lines 1 and 3 only.

Text, commentary, and facsimile: *ChLA* IV, no. 229; cited as **M**.

Text: *CPL*, no. 127, and Daris, no. 18. Both reproduce Turner's readings, lines 1 and 3.

In spite of the words *coh vii*. . [in line 3, this is almost certainly not a military text; but it is included here because all other editors have accepted it as military. Marichal, the only one to offer a complete text, interprets it as possibly "a rough draft or note" and sees in L. Valerius a veteran of the legio II Traiana. A tentative identification with a L. Valerius discharged from that legion in A.D. 194 (*CIL* III 6580 = 12045, line 45) then leads him to date the papyrus ca. 194. But some of Marichal's readings are doubtful or impossible; and the very full statement of Valerius' name, with filiation and tribe, is not compatible with the usage of military texts in this century, especially toward the end. The latest instance of such formality is **64**, A.D. 156; and in it only the name of the prefect of the cohort is so treated. See Introduction, pp. 4–5. Few of the readings here are really secure; but on the basis of what appears to be read the text has the air of a legal document in which some person may be identified by his membership in a cohort, whether legionary or auxiliary.

The date is on the basis of the hand.

The writing is at right angles to the fibers; but since the other side is blank, one cannot say whether this text belongs to the recto or the verso.

l ualerius l f̣ ṣeṛ˙ crisp̣. . . [
auḍ . tṣẹmiṣ. . . est . t . ạ . c̣ . . [
ẹmẹcṭẹ coh vi̅i̅ . . [
] . ẹ. . . . . . [. .] . q̣[
] . orm . [. .] . . [
] . . . . [

1. *l˙ fil cru*. . . . [*:* Aberd.; *L FIL CRESC*[*E*]*NS:* M. But the *l* of *fil* is impossible; the character is entirely unlike the three *l*'s which precede it. The cognomen cannot be *crescens* because the third letter is not tall enough for *e* and the fifth is too tall for *c*. The remains are too scanty to encourage a choice between *crispus* and *crispinus*.

2. *acto˙ stip*(*endio*) *miss*[*us*] *est stati*. [*:* M. For *acto stipendio* Marichal compares *praetoriani actis stipendiis*, Tac. *Ann*. 6.3; but the singular would seem to limit Valerius' service to one year, and the expression is unparalleled in the military texts. In any case, *missus* can hardly stand. The first stroke of the *m* was ligatured with the preceding letter, and there is not room at the end for *sus*, considering the breadth of *u* in this hand. At the end of the line there is one stroke too many for the four letters *stat*, and the second *t* is more like *c*. Marichal's speculation that we have here a

veteran acting as a stationarius needs supporting parallels.

As I see it, the beginning of the line could be read in several ways, e.g. *auḍit ṣemisṣeṣ, auḍiṭi ẹmiss..*, none of which, admittedly, makes sense without a context.

3. *coh᾽ viii᾽* alone: Aberd.; *miles᾽ coh VII.*[: M. The reading *miles* is hard to reconcile with the idea that Valerius has been discharged; and is doubtful in itself. Another letter preceded *m*; there is too much space for *i*; the *l* is unlike the other *l*'s and most probably a *c*; and the *e* and *s* are also unlike the certain examples of those letters. If this text were military, an indication of rank or status should precede *coh*; but I can make nothing of the letters I find on my photograph.

The numeral was overlined; but the overlining breaks up at the right end so that one cannot say whether to read e.g. *vii iṭ[uraeorum* or *viiii[*. Marichal's deduction that this must be a legionary cohort because no auxiliary cohort in Egypt had a number as high as VII is based on Lesquier's emendation of *CIL* III 59 which is now invalidated by *PMich.* VII 441. (Daris, *Aegyptus* 36 [1956] 241, questions Sanders' restoration of III, V, and VII *Ituraeorum* but accepts them in *Documenti*, no. 87, app.)

4. No readings in M.

5. *].orm.*[: M, suggesting in app. *ad h]ormo[s* with a reference to **10** 12. But if the content of this text is legal, *] formu[la* would be preferable.

134

Names

BASP 3 (1965) p. 28   III p.

Bulletin of the American Society of Papyrologists 3 (1965) p. 28; *edidit* Welles.

Welles identifies these scraps, which belong to different layers in the same roll, as a roster.

a	**b**
seleuc[	]us
	]ianus

Index 1: Persons

This index, so far as the evidence permits, is prosopographical. It includes all persons named in the papyri except (a) emperors and members of the imperial family (see Index 2) and (b) the consuls named in dates (see Index 3).

The others are entered in one of two ways. Higher military officers and all civil officials are identified by rank or status and the place and date of the texts in which they appear. Military personnel of the rank of decurion, centurion, or lower are identified where possible by their unit, or at least the province or region, their century or turma, and their date of enlistment. A single date, e.g. 216, indicates that the exact year is known. An inclusive date such as 154–179 supplies a terminus ante quem; but because soldiers might be kept in service beyond the theoretical term, the earlier date is not a certain terminus post quem. A question mark indicates that both dates are approximate.

Nomenclature in these texts exhibits some variation. Non-Romans in all periods have a personal name and patronymic; but Roman citizens in the earliest papyrus (**36**) have only praenomen, gentilicium, and filiation, while somewhat later lists, e.g. **10** and **37**, show the familiar pattern of the tria nomina. This was soon approximated to the two-name system of the non-citizens by omission of the praenomen (**34**); and the two systems were further approximated, especially at Dura, by the breakdown of the old distinctions of nomen, praenomen, and cognomen, which resulted in all three being used indiscriminately in any position. In this index, accordingly, I have arbitrarily used *nomen* for any name which is the first of a pair, and *cognomen* for the second, in the names of both Romans and non-Romans.

All names are listed under the *nomen* in this sense if it is known, except those in **1** and **46**. In those two papyri it seems that everyone had the name "Aurelius," sometimes as a genuine *nomen* followed by one other name, more often prefixed to the pair of names which the soldier already had. For that reason no person found in **1** or **46** is listed under "Aurelius" unless there is confirmatory evidence that his name consisted of two elements only, with Aurelius as the first.

Naturally, where only one name survives it must be used even though this introduces distortions into the record.

Names in the Greek alphabet have been transliterated into the Roman except in a few instances where the reading was doubtful. These exceptions, however, are alphabetized as if in Roman, ϵ and η under e, ο and ω under o, rough breathing under h, and so on.

Men with identical names are listed in chronological order; and references to each person are likewise in chronological order. Where the precise date of a text is uncertain, the reference to it assumes the latest of the possible range of dates.

The following abbreviations are employed:

app: apparatus criticus
aux: auxiliary
c.: century
ca.: circa
cent: centurion
coh: cohort
cogn: cognomen
dec: decurion
drom: dromedarius
dupl: duplicarius
eq: eques *or* equitata
gen: genitive
marg: in the margin
nom: nomen
post: posterior
pr: prior
praef: praefectus
proc Aug: procurator Augusti
sesq: sesquiplicarius
sig: signifer
sing: singularis
t.: turma
trib: tribune
Vet Gall: ala Veterana Gallica
vex: vexillarius

I a.; III p.: first century B.C.; third century post Christum natum
I Aug Lus: coh. I Augusta Lusitanorum

I Hisp Vet: coh. I Hispanorum veterana
I Theb: coh. I Thebaeorum equitata
II Traian: leg. II Traiana fortis
III Cyr: leg. III Cyrenaica
III Itur: coh. III Ituraeorum
XVI FF: leg XVI Flavia Firma
xx Palm: coh. xx Palmyrenorum
XXII Deiot: leg. XXII Deiotariana

A[, *see also* ḅẹạṣṭ[. .]s, Iulius, Romanus
Ạ[. .]b.b[, xx Palm, 194–219: **1** xli 15 marg
Ạ[. . .].[.]s Ạṭ[, Egypt, I/II p.: **38** ii 8
A[. . . . .].o.[, xx Palm, t. Octaui, 199: **2** xxxix 1
A.[, *nom*, xx Palm, c. Malchi, 197–200: **2** i 3
Ạ.[, *nom*, xx Palm, c. Malchi, 198–201: **2** i 6
Ạ[-*ca.* 9- Z]ebida, xx Palm, 197–201: c. Castrici, **1**, Aurel, xvi 26; c. Antonini pr, **2** xxii 4
Aurel A.ea[, xx Palm, c. Danymi, 201–202?: **1** ii 9
Aurel Ạ[, xx Palm, c. Malchiana, 203: **1** xxvii 21
A.[ ]ṇus, xx Palm, c. Danymi, 209: **2** viii 16
A[. . . . .].[.]. .[, xx Palm, drom c. Malchi, 206 or 212: **2** xliii 25
Aurel Ạ[-*ca.* 8-].manus, xx Palm, c. Malchiana, 214: **1** xxix 16
Ạ[, xx Palm, c. Marci, 214: **2** xv 2
Ạ[, xx Palm, c. Seleuciana, 214: **6** xi 37
Ạ[, xx Palm, c. Antonini post, 202–215, *prob.* 214: **6** v 13
Ạ[ ]us c.[, xx Palm, c. Antonini pr, 214: **8** ix 3
Ạ. .[, xx Palm, c. Antonini pr, 215: **2** xxv 2 and 4
Ạ[, sing xx Palm, c. Marci, 216: **2** xv 5
Ạ[ ]. .ḥ[.].[, xx Palm, c. Marci, 216: **8** v 2
A. .[, writer of letter, status unknown, Dura, 216: **89** *15* verso 2
Ạ[, xx Palm, c. Malchi, 217?: **2** vi 2
Ạ[, xx Palm, c. Antonini post, 197–228: **8** x 5
Ạ[. .].e.[.]. . . .i, xx Palm, c. Antonini pr, 211–236: **33** ii 6
Ạ.[-*ca.* 7-], xx Palm, ca. 215–240: **15** i 7
A[, vex xx Palm, ca. 220–225: **25** a 3
Ạ[, xx Palm, 217–256: **17** a 11
Ạ[. .]. .e., xx Palm, 214–239: **50** a 3
Ạ[. . . .] Abumarius, eq xx Palm, 226–251: **83** 15
Ạ[. . . .] Malch[, xx Palm, c. Antonini pr, 215: **2** xxiv 22 and app
Ạ[. . . .] Mannus, xx Palm, c. Antonini pr, 215: **2** xxiv 19 and app
Ạ[. . . .] Sabinus, xx Palm, c. Antonini pr, 215: **2** xxiv 21 and app
A[. . . .]es Siuṣ[, xx Palm, c. Antonini pr, 215: **2** xxiv 24
A.ṛe.[.]ạṣ Terentianus, xx Palm, ca. 215–240: **15** ii 13
Ạ. .uinus, cent I Hisp Vet, ca. 75–105: **63** ii 32
Aạdeus, *see* Aurelius
Aathibelus, *see* Aethibelus
Ab.[, *see* Aurelius, Iulius
Ab.[, xx Palm, c. Antonini pr, 215: **2** xxv 3
]ạb[. .]. .[.]i, *cogn*, xx Palm, c. Antonini post, 208–225: **92** vi 15
Aḅ. .[, xx Palm, c. Germani, 217–256: **17** a 5
Aḅ[. .]bianu[s]: **15** ii 3 app
[A]ụṛ[el]Abb[, xx Palm, c. Mariani, 205–207: **1** xxii 25
Abb.[.]sarị, *cogn*, cent (?) xx Palm, 239: **50** i 14
Aurel Abbạ[, xx Palm, c. Marci, 214: **1** ix 16
Ạbḅ[a]l[. .].[, *see* Abdon
Aḅbalmaei, *cogn*, xx Palm, ca. 215–225: **92** ix 16 app; **15** i 23; ii 18
Abbas . .[.]ui. . .: **50** i 14 app
Abbas L. .[, xx Palm, c. Marci, 196: **6** ii 29; **2** xi 20
Abbas Zeb[ida, eq xx Palm, t. Antonini, 201: **1** xlii 9; **2** xlii 4
Abbedas Nicaei, xx Palm, c. Danymi, 204: **6** i 20
Abbis, *see* Habbis
Abbosas, *see also* Aurelius, Marinus, Priscus
]s Abbosa, xx Palm, c. Marci, 207: **2** xiii 15 and app
[A]bbo[sa-, *nom*, xx Palm, c. Antonini pr, 205: **2** xxiii 4
Abdạ[.].[.].sḅi: **15** ii 11 app
Ab[d]aeus Baraei, eq xx Palm, t. Antonini, 201: **1**, [Aur]el, xlii 12; **2** xlii 7, Barhaei
]abdaeus, *nom*, xx Palm, 224: **3** a 7
Abdaeus Zabb[, xx Palm, c. Seleuciana, 214: **6** xi 31; c. Antonini pr, **8** (ẓaḅḍ[) viii 20
Abdalathus, *cogn*, xx Palm, c. Castrici, 214: **1** xviii 18 app
'Αβδάλλαθος: **1** xxviii 19 app
Abdas, *see also* Aurelius
Aurel Abd[as T]hemarsa, xx Palm, c. Mariani, 192: **1** xxi 8
Abdas Zebida, xx Palm, c. Marci, 209: **1** viii 5; **2** xiii 17; **92** viii 12
Aurel Abdasthor Mocimi, eq xx Palm, t. Demetri, 193: **1** xxxvi 11
'Αβδελάθ: **1** xxviii 19 app
'Αβδεσαρος, 'Αβδισαρου: **50** i 14 app
Abdon Ạbḅ[a]l[. .].[, eq xx Palm, t. Zebida, 198–225: **92** ix 16 and app
Abdona, *see* Priscus

[*Αβ*]*δωνας̣*, status unknown, Dura in 216: **89** *41* 13 app
Abdus, *see* Aurelius
Abe[d-, *see also* Hiereus
Abed[, xx Palm, ca. 205–230?: **55** d 3
]. .en Aḅẹḍ.ẹ.[, xx Palm, ca. 200–235: **61** ii 14
Ạbẹḍ[. .] c̣ṛẹ[. . .]. . Malchi, xx Palm, ca. 210–240: **13** 12
Abed.[. .]mra, *see* Aurelius
Abedadadus, *see also* Mauelas
Abedadadus: **89** *2* 18 app
Abedalahas: **1** xxviii 19 app
Aurel Abedala[th-, xx Palm, c. Malchiana, 207: **1** xxviii 19
Abedalathus: **1** xliv 12 app
'Αβιδγινει, *cogn*, xx Palm, 213–256: **35** 11
Abedlahas, *see also* Aurelius, Ocbanes
Abedlahas: **1** xiii 1 app
Aurel Ạ[bed]ḷaha[s, xx Palm, c. Antonini post, 207: **1** xiii 1
Aurel Abedlahas Buccaei, xx Palm, c. Danymi, 195: **1** i 6
Abedlahas Maximi, xx Palm, c. Mariani, 204: **1** xxii 11; **2** xvii 18, Abid-; **8** v 13, Abid-
Abedlahin, *cogn*, eq xx Palm, t. Zebida, 204: **1** xxxii 37; **2** xxxiii 17
Abedmalchus, *see also* Aurelius
Abedmalchus Authaei, eq xx Palm, t. Octaui, 204: **1**, Aurel, xl 13; **2** xl 20
Abedmalchus Marosa, xx Palm, 204: c. Seleuciana, **6** xi 4; c. Castricii, **1** xvii 9; c. Antonini pr, **2** xxii 19
Abedṇ[, *see* Aurelius
Abednabus Themarsa, xx Palm, 203: c. Malchiana, **1**, Aurel, xxvii 14; c. Pudentis, **92** ix 8
Abednamares Marona, sing xx Palm, t. Demetri, 212: **1**, Aurel, xxxviii 8; **2** xxxviii 16
[.]ẹ.ị[. A]bedsalme, eq xx Palm, 226–251: **83** 8
Abedsalmas Iarhaei, xx Palm, c. Antonini post, 214: **1**, Aurel, xiv 4; **2**, drom, xlv 14
Aurel Abedsalmas Thema[rsa, eq xx Palm, t. Octaui, 201: **1** xxxix 10
Abedsalmạ[Them]arsa, eq xx Palm, t. Octaui, 214: **2** xl 31
Abedsemias, *see also* Iulius
Abedsemias Pupli, xx Palm, c. Danymi, 204: **6** i 7
Abertes: **73** a i 25 app
Abgari, *see also* Aurelius, Barathes, Belaacabus, Iarhaeus, Malchus, Themarsas
Aurel [-*ca.* 8?- Ab]gari, eq xx Palm, t. Demetri, 201: **1** xxxvi 35
[A]bgari, *cogn*, eq xx Palm, t. Demetri, 201: **1** xxxvi 39
Abgarus, *cogn*, xx Palm, c. Antonini post, 205: **2** xxviii 8
Abgarus Iarhaei, xx Palm, c. Marci, 201; **6** iii 2
Abgarus Iarhaei, eq xx Palm, t. Antonini, 205 or 208: **1** xliii 9; **2** xliii 7
Abgarus Iarhaei, xx Palm, 211–236: **33** iii 4
Abgarus Themarsa, xx Palm, c. Antonini post, 217: **6** v 29; **1**, Aurel, xvi 2; **2** xxxi 15; **92** iii 18, Themasa
Abgarus Themes, xx Palm, 199–201: c. Malchiana, **6** ix 5; **1**, Aurel, xxvii 2, Theme; c. Malchi, **2** i 7
Abgellus Bassi, xx Palm, c. Antonini post, 214: **2** xxix 30
Abianes, *see also* Aurelius
Abianes Macchana, eq xx Palm, t. Zebida, 201: **1**, Aurel, xxxii 6; **2** xxxii 19
Abid-, *see* Abed-
Abifur, Abidfur, *see* Barhadadus, Gaius; **33** iii 3 app
Absaena, *cogn*?: **15** i 7 app
Absaẹṛia, xx Palm, ca. 215–240: **15** i 7; cf. ii 13 app
Absas, *see* Aurelius
Aḅṣe.[.]as: **15** ii 13 app
]absеus (Abseus ?), xx Palm, ca. 205–240: **12** a–c 5
Aḅṣṣ.ạ.ịẹị.[, xx Palm, ca. 215–240: **15** f 2
Abumarius, *see* Ạ[*and* Aurelius
Acceptus: **91** *1* i 6 app
Achaeus, cent xx Palm, ca. 226–240: pp. 128, 132, 133; **15** i 6, 10, 14, 20, 23; ii 8, 18, 21; **16** verso 1; **32** 8; **66** (A.D. 250–251) a ii 13; b i 19 app
Achilles, *see also* Achilles, Antenor, Aurelius
Achilles Achillis, Vet Gall, t. Herodiani, 154–179: **76** iii 8, 17; v 8, 17; xi 18
Achilles Pibechas, Egypt, c. *or* t.].rliani, I/II p.: **38** i 13
Achilleus, Vet Gall, t. Donaciani, 105–130: **80** 36, Acilleus
[A]chilleus Malch[-, eq xx Palm, t. Antonini, 204: **1** xliii 3; **2** xliii 1
Acibas, *see also* Aurelius, Maesomas, Theotecnus
Acib[a- -*ca.* 9-]ṇi, xx Palm, c. Marci, 198: **2** xi 22
]uṣ Ạc̣ịbạs, xx Palm, 242? (226–243): **44** 2
Acibas Bora, xx Palm, c. Mariani, 204: **2** xvii 26; **8** v 18; **92** iii 6
Acibas Ginnaei, xx Palm, 199–201: c. Malchiana, **1**, Aurel, xxvii 5; c. Malchi, **2** i 10
Acrabanes Simon, eq xx Palm, t. Demetri, 195: **1** xxxvi 19
Actius, *name*?: **53** b 8
Ἄκυλας: **34** recto ii 2 app
Ἀκύλιος: **34** recto ii 2 app
Aculus, *see* Afrius
Aurel Aḍ[. . . . .]gṇ. .[. .]i, dupl xx Palm, t. Zebida, 202: **1** xxxi 26
Add[-*ca.* 6-]ṇdṛ[, xx Palm, c. Antonini post, 204: **1** xii 9
Addaaus?, xx Palm, 194–219: **1** xxxv 14 marg

Addaeus, *see also* Aurelius, Biaeus, Iarhaboles M.[, Nisamsus, Sọ.ṃọbiaeus, Themarsa
Addaei, *cogn*, xx Palm, ca. 215–240: **15** ii 20
Addaeus Iarhaei, eq xx Palm, t. Demetri, 205: **1**, Aurel, xxxviii 1; **2** xxxviii 9
Addaeus Maccaei, xx Palm, c. Mariani, 210: **1** xxiii 14; **2** xviii 21; **8** vi 2
Add[as Alexa]ṇdṛ[i: **1** xii 9 app
Aurel Addas Malch[, xx Palm, c. Malchiana, 203: **1** xxvii 15
Aurel Addas Ẓ[, xx Palm, c. Malchiana, 203: **1** xxvii 17
A[urel] Addas Z[e]bida, xx Palm, c. Malchiana, 214: **1** xxix 10
['*A*]δωναῖος]: **89** *41* 13 app
Ael[ ]sa..sius, eq xx Palm, t. Antonini, 201: **1** xli 35; **2** xli 23
Ael...l.aẹ.s, xx Palm, ca. 210–240: **13** 10
..[.].esurus [A]ẹlạṃi, eq xx Palm, t. Zebida, 196: **1** xxxi 35; **2** xxxii 8
Ael[ami]s A..sius, **2** xli 23 app
Aelamis Belsur, xx Palm, c. Mariani, 214: **1** xxiv 7; **2** xix 16; **8** vi 18
[A]elius? Dura, ca. 208: **103**
M Aur Elius, **46** 2 app
[A]elius [...]ụs, xx Palm, c. Mariani, 209: **1** xxiii 11
[A]eliụ[s *-ca.* 7-].n, xx Palm, c. Antonini pr, 214: **2** xxiv 5
Aelius .[.] genianus, status unknown, Dura in 216: **89** *6* 2; *7* 2; *8* 2
Ạeliu.[, status unknown, Dura in 216: **89** 22 app
[A]elius, status unknown, Dura ca. 219: **105** 1
Aeli[u]s, xx Palm, 213–223: **3** a 3 app
Aeliụṣ .[, status unknown, Dura ca. 241: p. 417; **114** 4
Aelius, xx Palm, 213–247: **3** b 8 and app
Aelius [.].[...].t..r[, Egypt, end of III p.: **11 bis** a 4
Aelius: **1** xvi 9 app; **23** iii 1 app; **24** 6 app
Ael[iu]s A..sius: **2** xli 23 app
Aelius Alexandrus, eq xx Palm, t. Zebida, 204: **1** xxxii 35; **2** xxxiii 15
Aelius Antoninus, xx Palm, t. Demetri, 205: **1**, notation lost, xxxvii 38; **2**, vex (centuriae), xxxviii 8
Aelius Antoninus, drom xx Palm, c. Marci, 201: **1** xliii 29; **2** xliv 14
[A]el(ius) Antoninus, eq xx Palm, t. Nifraotes, 207–232: **27** b i 14
Ael(ius) Auitus, legionary cent, praepositus xx Palm in 239: **50** i 7, 13; ii 7
Aelius Aurelius, xx Palm, c. Marci, 214: **8** vi 14
[Aurel?] Aelius B[, xx Palm, c. Antonini post, 204: **1** xii 12
Aelius Barnaeus, dupl xx Palm, t. Tiberini, 207: **1**, Aurel, xxxiii 28; **2** xxxiv 6
Aelius Bassus, xx Palm, c. Danymi, 196: **1**, Aurel, i 11; **2** vi 24
Aurel Aelius Bolan[-, xx Palm, c. Danymi, 202–206?: **1** iii–v, a–b–c 9
Aelius Bolanus, eq xx Palm, t. Zebida, 201: **1**, Aurel, xxxii 8; **2** xxxii 21
Aelius Capito, Vet Gall, t. Optatiani, 154–179: **76** iii 20
Aelius Fortunatus, eq xx Palm, t. Octaui, 205: **1**, Aurel, xl 16; **2** xl 23; **92** vii 11
Aurel Aelius Fronton, eq xx Palm, t. Demetri, 193: **1** xxxvi 12
Aurel Aelius Gaius, eq xx Palm, t. Demetri, 195: **1** xxxvi 24
[A]el[iu]s Ge.[ ]s, xx Palm, c. Antonini pr, 214: **8** ix 4
Aurel Aelius German[-, xx Palm, c. Marci, 201: **1** vi 25
Aelius Ger[ma]nus, xx Palm, c. Antonini pr, 215: **2** xxiv 26
Aelius Heliodorus, sig xx Palm, 202: **1**, Aurel, c. Malchiana, xxvii 7; xxviii marg; **2**, c. Malchi, i 12
Aelius Heliodorus, eq xx Palm, t. Zebida, 203: **1**, Aurel, xxxii 31; **2** xxxiii 11
Ael(ius) Heliodorus, xx Palm, c. Danymi, 209: **6** i 27
Aelius Heliodorus, xx Palm, c. Antonini post, 214: **1**, Aurel, xv 1; **2** xxx 11
Ael(ius) Heliod[orus], xx Palm, ca. 198–235: **47** i 18
Aelius Heracl.[, xx Palm, c. Mariani, 203: **1**, Aurel, xxii 6; **2** xvii 14; **8** v 10
Aelius Herennianus, xx Palm, c. Antonini post, 203: **2** xxvii 23
Aelius Herm[, Egypt, coh. equitata, ca. 132–217: **78** *47* 1
Aelius Hieronumus, Egypt, principalis?, 184: **39** 18
Aelius Licinnius, eq xx Palm, t. Zebida, 209: **1**, Aurel, xxxiii 17; prob. same as following two
Aelius Licinnius, dupl xx Palm, t. Demetri, 209: **2** xxxvi 18; prob. same as preceding and following
Aelius Licinnius, eq(?) xx Palm, t. Romulli, 209: **23** ii 10 and p. 144; prob. same as preceding two
Aelius Longinus, eq xx Palm, t. Antonini, 203: **1**, Aurel, xlii 23; **2** xlii 14
Aelius Marcellus, sing xx Palm, t. Demetri, 206: **1**, Aurel, sing cos, xxxviii 3; **2**, Ṃạrcẹḷlin[u]s, sing, xxxviii 11; **92**, [M]ạṛçẹḷlus, vii 9
Aurel Aelius Marcia[n-, xx Palm, c. Malchiana, 203: **1** xxvii 18
Aurel Aelius Marinus, xx Palm, c. Danymi, 195: **1** i 8

Aelius Marinus, Egypt, cent (?) numeri Emesenorum, II/III p. : **30** ii 9
Ael(ius) Menander, xx Palm, ca. 198–235: **47** i 18
Aelius Pudentillus: **64** i 10 app
Ael(ius) S.[.]on, Egypt, c. Theopropi, 194: **5** ii 13
Aelius Sarapion, Egypt, sesq t. Ammoniani post, 217: **24** 13
Aelius Serenus, dec Vet Gall, 154–179: **76** xv ⟦10⟧, 11; xviii 14; xx 25; xxi 1; GG 9
Aurel Aelius Th[, xx Palm, c. Malchiana, 207: **1** xxviii 20
Ael(ius) Theodorus, xx Palm, c. Danymi, 210: **6** i 29
Aeluri[, *cogn*, Egypt, late II p. : **71** a 8
Aurel Aem.[ ].i, eq xx Palm, t. Antonini, 193: **1** xli 13
M Aemilius: **51** i 24 app
C Aemilius [ ].[, III Cyr, 65–96: **9** 19 a
[A]ẹ[mi]ḷius [..]ẹocraṭes: **20** 21 app
C Aemilius C f Pol Proculus, Egypt, legionary, 65–90: **37** 2
C Aemilius Valens, III Cyr, 65–96: **9** 3 a
Aeson Mo[.]ịi[, xx Palm, c. Pudentis, 197–225: **92** vi 22
Aethibelus, *see* Azizus, Iaḍ[..]eus, Haeranes
Afarnes Bassi, eq xx Palm, t. Antonini, 203: **1**, Aurel, xlii 22; **2** xlii 13
Afranius: **85** 1 app
].ṣṣa arrọ Africanus: **63** i 25 app
Afrius, *see* Aufrius
Ạ[urel]ṛas Aḟrọ[, xx Palm, c. Marci, 204: **1** vii 15
Ag[, xx Palm, c. Antonini post, 209: **8** x 16. *See also* Agrippas Them[
Ag...s..ṃịạ.. Vai..., xx Palm, 193–244: **49** 3
Agathon, *see* Claudius
Agathonius, trib? xx Palm, ca. 186–211: p. 355; **88** *1* 1; *2* 1; *2* verso; **112** verso and app
Agathus Daemon, *see* Iulius
Agenor, *nom*, Vet Gall, 154–179: **76** i 10
Agilius Cosmianus: **83** 4 app
Agillius, *see* Lucius
Agrippas, *see* Claudius
Agrippas, dec Vet Gall, 154–179: **76** iii 11–12; iv 2; viii 14; ix 2–3; x 16; xiv 17; HH i 2
Agrippa, *cogn*, armorum custos, Egypt, II p.: **129** 6
Agrippas Male, xx Palm, c. Mariani, 198: **1** xxi 15; **2** xvi 21
Agrippas Male, eq xx Palm, t. Tiberini, 207: **1**, Aurel, xxxv 22; **2** xxxv 23
Agrippas Them[, xx Palm, c. Antonini post, 209: **1**, Aurel, xiii 11; **8** x 15–16 app
Agrippas Themarsa, xx Palm, c. Danymi, 199: **6** i 4; **1** i 17; **2** vi 29
Ạḷ..[, *see* Aurelius
Al.[, cent xx Palm, ca. 210–240: **13** 16
Alafes, Vet Gall, t. Donaciani, 105–130: **80** 9
Albinus: **37** 5 app
Albus: **37** 5 app
Ạlẹ.ẹ[..]dr..[, Egypt, end of III p.: **11 bis** a 6
Alexa, *see* Vlpius
Alexander, Alexandrus, *see also* Aelius, Aurelius, Iulius, Licinnius, Theophilus
].[....].[Al]exan[dr-, xx Palm, 225–247: **3** b 4
Aure[l A]lexand[r-, xx Palm, c. Castrici, 196–200: **1** xvi 21
Alexandri, Egypt, end of III p.: **11 bis** a 6
Alexandrus: **1** xvi 9 app
Alexandrus .[...].a, dupl xx Palm, t. Antonini, 194–219: **1** xli 4; **2** xli 4; **92** iv 12 app
Alexandrus [...].us, xx Palm, c. Mariani, 204: **2** xvii 22; **8** v 16
Alexandrus, xx Palm, ca. 210–240: **13** 6
Alexandrus, Egypt, eq aux, second half of II p.: **73** a iii 16
[.....].s Alexandrus, Egypt, coh eq, c. Longieni, 132–217: **78** *73* 1
Alexandrus, Egypt, coh eq, 154–179 or 186–211: **78** *2* 5
Alexandrus, Egypt, cibariator coh eq, 153–177 or 185–209: p. 311; **78** *34* 3; *36* 2; *37* 2; *38* 2; *41* 2; *42* 2; *43* 2; *67* 2; *71* 2
Alexandrus, Egypt, cent coh eq, 155–180 or 187–212: **78** *39* 2
Alexandrus Antonini, cornicularius xx Palm, t. Zebida, 203: **1**, Aurel, xxxii 29; **2** xxxiii 10
Alexandrus Antonini, eq xx Palm, t. Octaui, 199: **1**, Aurel, xxxix 1; **2** xxxix 7
Alexandrus Theofil[, sing xx Palm, t. Octaui, 202: **1**, Aurel, notation lost, xxxix 35; **2**, sing cos, xl 7
Alfeanus, *cogn*: **34** recto i 15 app
Allaeus, *see* Romanus
Allaeus: **2** viii 12 app
Q Allius Q f Col Pudentillus, praef I Aug Lus ending April 23, 154: **64** i 10
Alpinus, *see* Antonius
Am..[...]ịuṣ, *see* Aurelius
Amaeus, *nom*, xx Palm, 223?: **3** a 4
Aurel Amaeus Iadibeli, eq xx Palm, t. Octaui, 193: **1** xxxviii 17
Aurel Amaeus Zạ[bdibo]li, eq xx Palm, t. Antonini, 193: **1** xli 14
Amaeus Zebida, xx Palm, c. Marci, 212: **6** iii 32; **1** viii 16; **2** xiii 28
[-*ca.* 6-]ụs Amaḷ[, eq xx Palm, t. Octaui, 199: **1** xxxviii 36; **2** xxxix 3
Amerimnus Ammoni, Vet Gall, t. Lycarionis, 154–179: **76** xviii 11
Amerys, *see* Iulius
[Am]fidius: **20** 1 app
Aṃṃ.[, Egypt, eq coh quingenaria, first quarter of III p.: **52** b 16

Ammaeus (Amaeus *or* Hammaeus?), *see* Iadibelus
Ammon, *see* Anubas
Ammonianus, *see also* Antonius, Aprius, Aurelius, Iulius, Priscus
]... Ammoniani, Egypt, (cent or dec?), coh eq quingenaria, first quarter of III p.: **52** b 4 and app
Ammonianus posterior, Egypt, dec, 213–242: **24** 12
Ammonianus prior, Egypt, dec, 213–242: **24** 20
Ammonianus, dec Vet Gall, 154–179: **76** i 17; viii 7; xi 12; xiv 3
Ammonius, *see also* Amerimnus, Ammonius
Ammonius: **73** a iii 11 app
Ammonius, *nom*, I Aug Lus, c. Semproni, 156: **64** i 43
Ammonius, Egypt, eq aux, second quarter of II p.: **73** a ii 7
Ammonius Ammonius, Egypt, sig coh eq, 153–178 or 185–210: **78** *37* 1
Ammonius Casis, Vet Gall, t. Petroni, 154–179: **76** xv 2
Ammonius Marci, Egypt, c. or t.].rliani, I/II p.: **38** i 14
Ammonius Serenus, Vet Gall, t. Senti, 154–179: **76** ix 4
Ampliatus: **91** *1* i 6 app
Aurel Amṛ[-, *nom*, xx Palm, c. Marci, 214: **1** ix 24
Amṛ[us: **1** ix 24 app
Aurel Amrus Milens, eq xx Palm, t. Demetri, 204: **1** xxxvii 26
[...]salmus An[.].ọ[, xx Palm, c. Danymi, 203–216: **92** viii 9
Ananus, *see* Malchus
Andronicus, *see* Aurelius
Andrus Paer.[, Egypt, practor (military?), 136–161, 178–193, or 192–217: **78** *77* 4
Androsthenes, Vet Gall, t. Donaciani, 105–130: **80** 38
Anṃiochus, *see* Theodorus
Annaë.[..], *see* Orsenuphis
Annarius: **76** viii 19 app
Annellus Quodratus, p. 285
Annianus, praef. Aegypti, **20** 23 app
Anniochus, **76** xiii 2 app
Q Anniu[s].[, III Cyr 65-96: **9** 28 a
Annona, *see* Priscus
]. Ạṇṣirapọ.., Egypt, 217: **40** i 13
Ant[, *see* Iulius
Ant[, *nom*, xx Palm, c. Mariani, 214: **2** xix 22
Ant[, xx Palm, c. Mariani, 206: **8** v 24
Antenor Achillis, Vet Gall, 154–179: **76** xii 16, eq t. Clari; xv 8, custos armorum
Antigonus, *see* Aurelius
Antin(ous), *see* Aurelius
Antiochianus, *see* Aurelius
Antiochus, *see also* Aurelius
Antiochus: **76** xiii 2 app
Antiochus, Egypt, cent or dec, coh eq, 153–178 or 185–210: **78** *37* 6
Antiochus, dec xx Palm, 211–236: p. 144; **15** i 8; ii 2, 12, 17; **23** ii 5
].s Antiochus, xx Palm, c. Danymi, 215: **2** x 12
Antiochus, xx Palm, 194–219: **1** xxxvi 32 marg
Antiochus, *cogn*, xx Palm, ca. 215–240: **15** i 9
.[.]ẹ[.. Ant]iochus, xx Palm, ca. 215–240: **15** ii 20
[Ant]ị[o]cḥus, *cogn*, xx Palm, 217–242?: **44** 6
Antistius, XXII Deiot, c. Neri, early I p.: **51** ii 18
Anto[, Anton[, Antoni[, *see also* Aurelius, Claudius, Iulius, Mocimus
Anto[, *nom*, Egypt, aux, 183–188: **70** a iii 21
Anto[ ]siṇ[, xx Palm, c. Mariani, 205: **8** v 21
Aṇṭọ[, *nom*, xx Palm, c. Antonini post, 202–215: **6** v 8
A[urel An]toni[- ——, xx Palm, c. Marci, 216: **1** x 22
Anto[, status unknown, Dura in 216: **89** *10* 2
[A]nton[, status unknown, Dura in 216: **89** *43* 4
Antoṇ[, Egypt, middle of III p.: **67** 6
Antoni[, xx Palm, 194–219: **1** xvi 10 marg
Anton( ) Val( ), ci(rcitor?) xx Palm, 198–235: **47** i 17
Antoninianus: **67** 6 app
Antoninus, *see also* Aelius, Alexandrus, Aurelius, Azizus, Bassus, Claudius, Domitius, Flauius, Iulius, Mocimus, Seleucus, Vlpius
Antoninus: **67** 6 app
]ṛ.auius Antoninus, Egypt, early II p.: **77** b 7
Ạ[urel ——] Antoninus, sing xx Palm, t. Zebida, 194–195: **1** xxxi 33
]c̣ius Antonin[, xx Palm, c. Antonini post, 200: **2** xxvii 10
]Ạ[nto]ṇinus, *cogn*, xx Palm, c. Danymi, 203: **2** vii 15
Antoninus, *cogn*, xx Palm, c. Mariani, 205–207: **1** xxiii 2 app
[A]ṇṭọṇiṇ[, *cogn*, xx Palm, c. Danymi, 206–208: **2** viii 11
Antoninus, *cogn*, xx Palm, c. Danymi, 214: **2** x 8
Antoninus, *cogn*, xx Palm, c. Marci, 209–216: **92** viii 14. Cf. **2** xiii 26 and 29, for this and following entry.
]l Antoninus, *cogn*, xx Palm, c. Marci, 209–216: **92** viii 15
Antoninus, *cogn*, Egypt, 216: **40** i 5
['*Α*]ν̣τωνε̣ι̣[ν-, status unknown, Dura in 216: **89** *9* 5
['*Αντω*?]ν̣ειvος, Egypt, coh eq, 132–217: **78** *9* 1
Antoninus, *cogn*, xx Palm, c. Danymi, 202–219: **1** iii–v f 5
Antoninus, *cogn*, prior, cent xx Palm, 211–222: pp. 157, 183; **2** xlv 3; **118** 6?; **92** iii 9; **27** a i 7; **47** i 15; i 12?; **23** i 4; **33** ii 1

[An]tonini, xx Palm, 195–222: **118** 6
]. . Antoninus, xx Palm, c. Mariani?, 198–235: **47** i 12
[An]ṭọninus . . [, xx Palm, ca. 205–230: **55** b 3
]l Antoninus, eq xx Palm, t. Nifraotes 207–232: **27** b i 15
[A]ntoninus, *cogn*, xx Palm, 215–240: **15** ii 7
[Aurel Anto]ninus Hiạ[, xx Palm, c. Marci, 212: **1** viii 15
Aurel Antoninus Marinus, eq xx Palm, t. Tiberini, 195: **1** xxxiv 6
Antonius: **67** 6 app
[A]ntonius L f, Egypt, legionary, III Cyr or XXII Deiot, I a.: **36** 13
[An]tonius, Egypt, eq aux, second quarter of II p.: **73** a iii 13
Antonius, Egypt, eq aux, second quarter of II p.: **73** a iii 20
Aurel Antonius [——, xx Palm, c. Antonini post, 204: **1** xii 11
Antonius, Egypt, dec coh eq, 152–177 or 184–209: **78** *30* 4
Antonius[ ]ụs, xx Palm, c. Mariani, 214: **8** vi 21
Antonius?, trib? xx Palm, ca. 185–230: **112** verso 1 and app
Antonius Alexandri, xx Palm, c. Mariani, 207–232: **27** a i 6
M Antonius M f Pol Alpinus, Egypt, legionary, 65–90: **37** 5
Antonius Ammonianus, Egypt, dec alae, 234: **20** 7
Antonius Barlaha, xx Palm, c. Antonini post, 216: **2** xxx 28
Aurel Antonius Bassus, eq xx Palm, t. Antonini, 201: **1** xlii 13
Aurel Ạ[nto]ṇius [B]assus, xx Palm, c. Malchiana, 214: **1** xxix 15
Antonius Chaeremonianus, Vet Gall, t. Sereni Melanos, 154–179: **76** xx 7
Antonius Cleme[n-, xx Palm, c. Marci, 210: **1**, Aurel, notation lost, viii 10; **2**, sing cos, xiii 21
M Antonius Crispus, III Cyr, 65–96: **9** 15 a
Antonius Hierax, Egypt, drom coh, t. Longini, 132–217: p. 313; **78** *48* 1
Antonius Iu[stinus: **77** b 7 app; 9 app
Antonius Longinus, cent III Cyr, 91–116: **34** recto ii 6
Antonius Longo, cent III Cyr, 91–116: **34** recto ii 15
Antonius Ṃ[, xx Palm, ca. 205–240?: **42** 7
Antonius Marcianus, Vet Gall, sig t. Lucilli, 154–179: **76** xvi 7; xx 15
Antonius Maximus, III Cyr, c. Suburiana, 91–116: **34** recto i 14
Antonius Maximus, xx Palm, c. Danymi, 196: **6** i 1; **1**, Aurel, i 12
Antonius Maximus, drom? xx Palm, c. Marci, 197–225: **92** vii 16 and app
C Antonius Pri[, Egypt, early II p.: **11** ii 5
Antonius Romanus, Vet Gall, t. Herodiani, 154–179: **76** xv 18
Antonius Romanus, drom xx Palm, c. Malchi, 206 or 212: **2** xliii 26
Antonius Satuṇịl[us, III Cyr, c. Antoni Longini, 91–116: **34** recto ii 7
Antonius Seleucus, vir clarissimus, consularis Syriae, Dura in 221: p. 383; **91** *1* i 4; *2* i 3–4; 7–8
M Antonius Valens, tiro III Itur, 103: **87** 21
Antonius Valens, III Cyr?, c. Pompei Epane, 91–116: **34** recto ii 23; same as preceding?
Antonius Zabbaei, xx Palm, c. Antonini post, 214: **2** xxix 16
Anu[, Egypt, aux, 181–186: **70** a iii 8
Anubas, *see also* Mences
Anubas Amm[on], I Aug Lus, c. Marci, 156: **64** i 38
Anubion Harpocration, curator alae, Vet Gall, t. Agrippas, 154–179: **76** iv 1, 9, 17
Ap[. . .]. [, *see* Longinus
Api. . , Egypt, coh eq, 152–177 or 184–209: **78** *28* 5
Ἄπιδος, gen., **76** xi 2 app
Apitus, *see* Casis
απο. . . .[, *name*?, Egypt, coh eq, 156–181 or 188–213: **76** *14* 3
[A]pọḷ[l-, *cogn*, eq xx Palm, t. Tiberini, 212: **2** xxxvi 4
Apọḷ[l-, eq xx Palm, t. Antonini, 197–225: **92** iv 14 and app
Ạpọḷḷ[, *nom*, xx Palm, c. Marini, 217–256: **17** a 1
Apoll[.]n. [, *see* Aurelius
Apollinarius, *see also* Aurelius, Claudius, Eponuchus, Iulius
Apollinar(ius), Egypt, eq aux, second quarter of II p.: **73** a i 11; a ii 17; b 8. It is uncertain whether these are two men, or the same.
]. . ius Apolinaris, Egypt, classiarius, 146: **59** i 4
Apollinarius, dec Vet Gall, 154–179: **76** v 2; viii 28; xv 3; xvi 20; xix 13; BB 9
Apollinarius, status unknown, Egypt in 193–197: **39** verso, p. 170
Apollinarius, *cogn*, Egypt, 217: **40** i 12
[A]pọḷḷ[inarius?, xx Palm, 216?: **1** iii–v i 6 app; **2** x 16 and 24 app
[Apolli]ṇaris?, Egypt, early I p.: **51** i 20 app
Apolliṇarius G[ai]ani, sing xx Palm, c. Antonini post, 222: **2** xxi 25
Apollo[, *see also* G[, Longinus
Apollo[, status unknown, Egypt, Arsinoite nome, Heraclide meros, ca. 120–140: p. 271
Apollonas, *see* Vlpius

Apollonides, Egypt, coh eq, 151–176 or 183–208: **78** *24* 6
Apollonius, *see* Licinnius
Apollonius, *see also* Aurelius, Heliodorus, Isidorus, Iulius
Apollonius, dec xx Palm, 215–240; p. 128; **15** i 14; ii 22. Possibly same as Aurelius Apollonius Mesenus?
Apollonius Ḅạ[, xx Palm, c. Mariani, 199: **2** xvi 23
Apollonius Mesenus, *see* Aurelius Apollonius Mesenus
Apollos, Egypt, eq aux, second quarter of ɪɪ p.: **73** a ii 5
Apollos, Egypt, cibariator coh eq, 137–162 or 169–194: **78** *15* 2
Apollos Didymi, Egypt, eq? aux, t. (?) Longini, 114–139: **75** 6
Apollos Herminus, ɪ Aug Lus, c. Herculani, 156: **64** i 36
Apollos Serenus, Vet Gall, t. Aeli Sereni, 154–179: **76** xviii 12–13
]sia.iu..[.].us Aponianus, Egypt, faber Aug. n. classiarius, 127–164: **59** i 11
Gaius Aponius Vlp[, Egypt, eq? aux, 114–139: **75** 18
Apontinus: **59** i 11 app
Aponius Germanus, Vet Gall, t. Ammoniani, 154–179: **76** viii 7
Appianus, Egypt, cent coh eq, 156–181 or 188–213: **78** *5* 1
Aprianus, *see* Aurelius
Aprilis, *see* Petronius
Aprius Ammonianus, cent, Egypt, coh eq quingenaria, first quarter of ɪɪɪ p.: p. 201; **52** a 6 and app; b 4?; b 15
Apuleius: **46** 6 app
Apynchis, *see* Hermacis
Apynch[is]ẹchnutas, Egypt, aux, ɪ/ɪɪ p.: **38** i 2
Aquilus, *see* Aufrius
Areius Ci.[, Egypt, pedes coh eq, 132–217: **78** *54* 5
Argius, cent ɪ Aug Lus, 92–117: **74** iii 2
Argotes, Egypt, eq aux, second quarter of ɪɪ p.: **73** a iii 14
Argotius: **73** a iii 14 app
Ạṛi.[, *see* Aurelius
Arianus, *see* Longinus
Ariston, *see* Iulius
Ariston, *cogn*, xx Palm, c. Antonini post, 206: **2** xxviii 13
Aristus, *see* Iulius
Ạṛ.emụṣdorus, **15** ii 22 app
Armais, *see* Tosthenes
Arnei[..]i, *gen*, *see* Harmiusis
'*Αρνείτου*, *gen*, **76** xii 20 app
Arpocration, *see* Harpocration
Aṛṛ.[, *nom*, Egypt, c. Theopropi, 194: **5** ii 18
Arrianus, *see* Arrius, Auidius, Longinus
Arrius (?) Ammonianus: **52** a 6 app
Arrius Arrianus, Vet Gall, t. Lucili Bassi, 154–179: **76** xx 8
M. Arrius Niger, ɪɪɪ Cyr, 65–96: **9** 7 a
Arrius Vs[, Egypt, aux, ɪ/ɪɪ p.: **38** ii 11
].ụṣ Arruntianus, praef. ɪ Hisp vet, 75–105: **63** i 25
Arruntius: **36** 12 app
Arrybas: **102** a 13 app
Artemidorus, *see also* Aurelius, Cassius, Dionysius, Zenodorus
Artemidorus, dec ɪ Aug Lus, 131–156: **64** ii 7 and 33
[Arte]midorus, *cogn*, Egypt, 208: **5** i 14
Artemidorus, *cogn*, addressee, status unknown, Dura in ca. 219: **105** 2
Artemidorus, *cogn*, **24** 10 app
Artemon, *nom*, Egypt, ɪ/ɪɪ p.: **38** ii 16
Artorius, *see* Lucilius
]aus Artyspardis: **130** 1 app
]ṃus Artysparsia, Egypt, end of ɪɪ p.: **130** 1
Aurel Asadus Themarsa, eq xx Palm, t. Antonini, 195: **1** xli 20
Asclas Ascla[, Egypt, coh eq, 132–217: **78** *54* 1
Asclepiades, *see also* Aurelius, Gerelius
Asclepiades, *cogn*, xx Palm, ca. 215–240: **15** ii 8
Asclepiades *Δεμουρους*, Egypt, *κορνιξ*, coh eq, c. Olympi, 157–182 or 189–214: **78** *40* 2
Asclepiades *Ερ*[, Egypt, coh eq, t. Longini, 132–217: **78** *45* 1
M Aurelius Asclepiades Hermin.., Egypt, coh eq, c. Alexandri, 155–180 or 187–212: **78** *39* 1
Asianus: **15** ii 3 app
Asinius: **9** 12 e app
Asprius Maximus, legionary immunis ɪɪ Traian, 219: **21** 13
Assorius: **21** 13 app
Ạṭ[, *see* Ạ[...].[.]s
Atectus, Atestus: **80** 17 app
Atestas, Vet Gall, t. Donaciani, 105–130: **80** 17
Athmonis, *see* Isidorus
M Aurelius Atho Marcellus, proc Aug, praeses Maur Caes, Dura ca. 250: pp. 396–7; **96** 4
Atilius Cosminus, vir clarissimus, consularis Syriae, Dura in 250–251: **66** b i 5; **83** 4, 8, 14
Atreus, *see* Maximus
Atrybas, **102** a 13 app
Attius Rufinus, vir clarissimus, consularis Syriae, Dura in 241: pp. 154, 192, 417; **29** 3, 10; **114** 1; **114** verso 2
Aụ[, *nom*, Egypt, 192–217: **5** iii 11
Au.[.]ṣhus: **15** ii 12 app
Au.[, xx Palm, ca. 205–240: **12** a–c 14
Au...[.].[, *nom*, xx Palm, ca. 215–240: **15** i 9
Auadas, *see* Zabdas

Auctus: **91** *1* i 6 app
Audas Zebida, xx Palm, c. Antonini post, 203: **2** xxvii 25
Aufaeus, *see* Monimus
Aufelli Acculei: **34** recto ii 2 app
M Aur Aufelli[us, Egypt, 206: **46** 6 app
Auferi Accolei: **34** recto ii 2 app
[Au]fidius: **20** 1 app
Aufis: **80** 9 app
Aufrius Aculus, cent III Cyr, 91–116: **34** recto ii 2
Aufrius Aculus minor, cent III Cyr, 91–116: **34** recto ii 12
Auidalathus, *see also* Barhotarus, Simaones
[Aui]dalathus, *cogn*, xx Palm, c. Castrici, 214: **1** xviii 18 app
Auidalathi, *cogn*, xx Palm, c. Malchi, 197–222: **2** ii–iv h 3
Auidalathus: **1** xliv 12 app and **2** xliii 17 app. *See* Theoboli
Audalathus: **92** vii 2 app
Auidas, *see also* Aurelius, Mammaeus
Auidas, *cogn*, xx Palm, 191–216: **89** *4* ii 6
Auidas, *cogn*, xx Palm, ca. 190–230: **41** 11
Auidas: **66** a ii 17 app; **81** ii 16 app
Aurel Auidiṇ.[ ].[, xx Palm, c. Antonini post, 204: **1** xii 10
Auidius Arrian(us), cornicularius III Itur, 78–103: **87** 27
Auidius Heliodorus, Praef. Aeg. in 139: **75** 4
Auidus, *see* Gaddes
Auitus, *see also* Aelius: **81** ii 16 app
Aululanus, Vet Gall, t. Donaciani, 105–130: **80** 22
Aululanus, Vet Gall, t. Donaciani, 105–130: **80** 28
Auṛ[, *nom*, Egypt, 192–217: **5** iii 15
Aụre.[.]ạṣ: **15** ii 13 app
Αὐρη[λι-, *[Α]ὐ̣ρη̣λ̣ι̣.[*, status unknown, Dura in 216: **89** *33* 2; **89** *29* 2 and app
Aurelianus, *see also* Aurelius, Postumius
Aurelianus, dec xx Palm in 225: p. 387
Aurel[ianus ?], proc Aug, Dura in 216: **89** *15* 3 and app
Aurelius *as name*, pp. 311–12
Aurelius, *see also* Aelius, Lucius

In the names from **1** and **46**, because "Aurelius" (in **46** "M Aurelius") was apparently prefixed to all of them, it is impossible to decide whether an isolated "Aurelius" is such a prefix or an essential part of the man's name. The same usage appears sporadically elsewhere. Conversely, "Aurelius" was omitted in **1** xxxv 9, a name inserted after the roll was drawn up, and in **1** xliv 9.

Aurẹ[l(ius)]ḍ[...].[, sing dupl xx Palm, c. Malchiana, 194: **1** xxvi 14
Aur[el(ius), dupl xx Palm, c. Malchiana, 194–219: **1** xxvi 16
Aurel(ius)[, principalis, rank lost, xx Palm, c. Malchiana 195–199: **1** xxvi 24
Ạ[urel(ius)], principalis, rank lost, xx Palm, c. Antonini post, 201–203: **1** xii 23
Aurel(ius), xx Palm, c. Danymi, 201–205?: **1** ii 1, 6, 10; 202–206?: iii–v a 3, 4; 207–219?: e 2, 4–5; g 2, 4, 5; h 3–5
— c. Marci, 214: **1** ix 11, 15, 28–29, 32; 216: **1** x 13, 14, 17–20, 23, 25
— c. Antonini post, 196: **1** xi 13: aurel [-8?-].ces; xi 14: aurel [-9?-]aior; 201–203: **1** xii 2–5; 204: **1** xii 21: a[urel -?-]ẹị, 22; 205–207: **1** xii 25; 207: **1** xiii 2; 212?: **1** xiii 22–26; 214: **1** xiv 17–20; **1** xiv 21: a[urel -2?-]ma[; 216: **1** xv 8, 13–14
— c. Castrici, 195: **1** xvi 19; 197–201: **1** xvi 27: au[rel -12?-]ḷe, 29–30; 204: **1** xvii 19; 210: **1** xviii 6: ạ[urel -5?-]eus[; 212: **1** xviii 11: aurel [-8?-].haei; 214: **1** xviii 18: [aurel]-ḍalạṭhụ[s; 214–215: **1** xix 1, 3–5; 214–215: **1** xix 9: [a]ụrel .ar.[; 216: **1** xx 12: [aur]el [-5?-].[.].[.].ius; **1** xx 22–25
— c. Mariani, 199: **1** xxi 18–19; 200–201: **1** xxi 21–22; 24: auṛ[el] .siur.[; 204: **1** xxii 17–20; 210: **1** xxiii 18–20; 212–214: **1** xxiii 22; 214: **1** xxiv 16–20, 22–23; 215: **1** xxv 21, sing; 22; 23, sing cos; 24
— c. Malchiana, 193–197: **1** xxvi 18–19; 194–198: **1** xxvi 21–22; 195–199: **1** xxvi 25; 203: **1** xxvii 20; 207: **1** xxviii 23; 24, sing; 209: **1** xxviii 26–27; 214: **1** xxix 18: aurel [-10?-]ẹṃ[; **1** xxix 19: aur[el -9?-].us[; 20–22; 216: **1** xxx 20; aụṛ[el -7?-].ạs; **1** xxx 21; **1** xxx 22: aurel [-7?-]..[.]sci; 23–27; **1** xxx 30: [au]r[el -7?-]es
— t. Zebida, 193: **1** xxi 28
— t. Demetri, 201: **1** xxxvi 36; 1 xxxvi 37: aurel[-10?-]ṭẹ.[
— t. Octaui, 199: **1** xxxviii 36: [au]ṛẹḷ [-10?-]amaḷ[; 39; 203: **1** xl 5; 204: **1** xl 11: sing, aure[l -8?-].ḅịda[
— t. Antonini, 201: **1** xlii 6; 204: **1** xlii 32–33
— margin: **1** xxvi 1
M Aurelius[, Egypt, 205?: **46** 2
Ạuṛẹ[l, xx Palm, c. Marci, 191–216: **89** *12* ii 7

In all the names which follow there is good reason to believe that "Aurelius" plays the part of the "nomen" in a two-element name. See above, p. 445, on nomenclature and the terminology used here.

Aur[el(ius), principalis, rank lost, xx Palm, c. Mariani, 214: **2** xx 8
Aurel(ius), xx Palm, c. Malchi, 217?: **2** v 10–14; c. Danymi, 216: **2** x 20–21, 23, 27, 30; c. Marci, 216: **2** xv 20–24; 222: **2** xvi 6, sing; c. Mariani,

Aurel(ius), xx Palm—*contd.*
214: **2** xix 17; 217–219: **2** xxi 12, sing; 13, sing; 221: **2** xxi 16, sing; c. Antonini pr, 215: **2** xxiv 12; xxv 6, 10–11; 217–220: **2** xxvi 4–5; c. Antonini post, 216: **2** xxxi 3, sing?; 4, sing; drom c. Mariani, **2** xlv 2
Au[rel(ius), xx Palm, c. Aureli, 231: **4** b ii 9–10, sing; 11
Aure[l, xx Palm: **4** j 1; 2, sing
Aurel, xx Palm, c. Marci, 214?: **6** iv 1
Aurel .[.]ḷ[, xx Palm, c. Antonini post, 216: **6** v 23
Ạụṛ[el, xx Palm, c. Mariani: **6** vii 5
Aụṛẹ[l, xx Palm, c. Seleuciana, 214: **6** xi 36
[A]ụṛẹḷ, canceled, xx Palm, c. Danymi, 214: **8** ii 8
[A]ụṛ[el, xx Palm, c. Danymi, 215: **8** ii 24
[Aur]ẹḷ, xx Palm, c. Danymi, 216: **8** ii 30–31
Aụṛ[el, xx Palm, c. Mariani, 206: **8** v 26
Aurel, xx Palm, c. Mariani, 214: **8** vi 25, 28, 29
Aurel, xx Palm, c. Antonini pr, 214: **8** viii 27–31; ix 1
Aụṛ[el, xx Palm, c. Antonini pr, 215: **8** ix 11
Aurelius, Egypt, end of III p.: **11 bis** b ii 6 and 16
Ạụṛẹḷ [. . .]ḥ. . . . . . .[, xx Palm, ca. 210–240: **13** 3
Aur[e]l, xx Palm, ca. 210–240: **13** 11
Aurelius, xx Palm, c. Achaei, ca. 215–240: **15** i 20
Aurel, xx Palm, c. Germani, ca. 215–240: **15** ii 10
Auṛ[el *and* Aụ[rel, xx Palm, c. Heliodori, ca. 215–240: **15** ii 15 and c 5
Aurel, xx Palm, c. Nasonis, ca. 215–240: **15** i 15
Aurel, xx Palm, c. Prisci, ca. 215–240: **15** ii 19
Aurel, xx Palm, t. Antiochi, ca. 215–240: **15** i 8
Aurel, xx Palm, ca. 215–240: **15** i 9, 12–13, 18; ii 1, 5, 10–11, 18–19; b 3; c 6; i 4
Aurel, cent xx Palm, 217–256: **17** a 12. May be same as Aurelius Germanus, **50** i 1–2, 8–9 and elsewhere. Cf. also **4** b i 1–2
Aureliu[s -?-].ạ. .[, xx Palm, 211–236: **23** ii 4
Ạụṛẹ[l, eq xx Palm, ca. 199–224: **26** a
[Au]ṛẹl[, xx Palm, 211–236: **33** v 7
Ạ[ure]ḷ[, xx Palm, c. Antonini pr, 198–235: **47** i 15
Aurel[, xx Palm, 214–239: **50** b 8
Aure[l, xx Palm?, 191–216: **89** 1 5
Aurel[, writer of letter, status unknown, Dura in 216: **89** *6* 2; *7* 2; *7* verso 3; *8* 2
Aurelius, xx Palm?, 191–216: **89** *7* 4
[Au]re[l -*ca.* 10-], cent, xx Palm?, 191–216: **89** *10* verso 1
Aurel[. . . .], proc Aug, Dura in 216: **89** *15* 3 and app. Probably "Aurelianus"; see s.v.
[Au]ṛẹl[, addressee, status unknown, Dura in 216: **89** *15* verso 1
[Au]ṛeliu.[? *or*]Ạeliu.[, status unknown, Dura in 216: **89** *22* app
[Aure]ḷ, status unknown, Dura in 216: **89** *25* verso 3 app
Aurel[, Aure[l, status unknown, Dura in 216: **89** *34* 3 and *50* 3
Aurel(ius) .[. . .]s, xx Palm, c. Pudentis, 197–216: **92** iii 21
[Aur]eli *or* [A]eli?, status unknown, Dura, ca. 208: **103**
[Aur]elius *or* [A]elius? status unknown, trib xx Palm?, Dura, ca. 219: **105** 1
Aurel, Dura in 213–217 or 235–238: **123** b 3; c 1 and 2

In the names which follow, the "cognomen" is too damaged to be read with certainty. They are arranged in three groups: (1) soldiers whose rank is indicated, (2) names in which the *end* of the "cognomen" is preserved, arranged in a *reverse index*, and (3) names in which only the middle of the "cognomen" remains. These are listed, perforce, by the first extant letter of the "cognomen."

Aurelius . . .r. .[. . .], praepositus cohortis (xx Palm?), Dura in 241: p. 417; **114** verso 1 and app
Ạụṛ[el . . .]ụṣ[, cent xx Palm, 225–256?: **4** b i 2
Aurel[iu]s . .[. .]ḷ.r.ị, librarius *or* cieap?, III Cyr, 65–90: **58** ii 11 and 9 app
Aurel [-3?-]a[. .].io, sing xx Palm, c. Antonini post, 214: **2** xxx 9
Ạ[u]ṛ[el -7?-]ei, xx Palm, c. Antonini pr. 202: **2** xxii 10
[Au]ṛel [-3?-]nion, xx Palm, c. Danymi, 214: **2** ix 21
Au[rel . . .].ṛo, xx Palm, ca. 215–240: **15** ii 10
[Au]rel .[.].[. . .] prior, xx Palm, ca. 215–240: **15** ii 7
[A]urẹ[l 1?-]. .[. . . . .]ṣ, xx Palm, c. Marci, 216: **1** x 27
[Au]ṛel[?-]b[. .]s, xx Palm, c. Mariani, 214: **1** xxv 12. Probably Aurelius Absas: see s.v.
Aurel [5?-]as, xx Palm, c. Antonini pr, 215: **2** xxiv 11
Aurel .eaṛc̣hes, xx Palm, 211–236: **33** iv 5
Aurel [. . .].eịabus, xx Palm, ca. 215–240: **15** ii 9. [Bel]ịḥabus?
Ạụ[re]ḷ 2?-].ạẹ.heus, xx Palm, c. Antonini pr, 214: **8** ix 2
Aurel 4?-].eus, xx Palm, c. Antonini post, 216: **1** xv 6
[A]ụṛẹ[l 3?-].eus, xx Palm, c. Antonini pr, 215: **8** ix 9
Aurel [. . . .].ṛius, xx Palm, c. Pudentis, 197–216: **92** iii 20. Probably Aurelius Demetrius, 214, **1** xxx 15; **47** i 4
Aur[el 4?-]ḅelus, xx Palm, c. Malchiana, 216: **1** xxx 29

Aurel .[ ].imus, xx Palm, ca. 215–240: **15** ii 14
Aurel ....[.]anus, xx Palm, c. Achaei, 240: **66** a ii 14
Aurel 8?-]nus, xx Palm, c. Marci, 216: **1** x 26
Aurel[6?-]nus, xx Palm, c. Danymi, 216: **2** x 16
Ạ[urel 3?-].rus, xx Palm, c. Marci, 216: **1** x 21
[Au]ṛel ..ṇṛus: **92** v 11 app
[Aur]ẹḷ[ ]ụẹ.ṣụṛus, xx Palm, c. Danymi, 197–225: **92** v 10
Aurel .[....]ụs, xx Palm, c. Castrici, 216: **1** xx 7
[Aur]el [...]us, xx Palm, c. Mariani, 214: **1** xxv 9; **2** xx 6
[Aur]ẹl .[....].us, xx Palm, c. Mariani, 216: **1** xxvi 8
Au[rel] ...us, xx Palm, c. Aureli?, 227: **4** b i 15
A[u]ṛẹl ....aṣ.[, xx Palm, 234?: **4** d 2
[A]ụṛẹl .aṣiliạ[, xx Palm, c. Antonini post, 197–205: **92** vi 18. Basilianus?
Aur[eliu]s .[ ].eṃ.[ ].[, principalis? xx Palm, c. Rufiani, 215: **23** iv 9
A[ure]l [..]..eṛ.[, xx Palm, c. Nasonis, ca. 215–240: **15** ii 9
Aurel ....l[, xx Palm, c. Barga, 216–250: **16** recto 2
[A]ụṛẹḷ[6?-]ṃa[, xx Palm, c. Antonini post, 216: **2** xxxi 2
Au[rel] .nsio.[, xx Palm, c. Antonini post, 216: **2** xxxi 7
Aure[l .]ṇti..[.].[, xx Palm, c. Antonini post? 197–225: **92** ix 6 and app. Antiochianus?
Aurel .oraṛẹẹṛạḷị[, xx Palm, 217–256: **19** 8 and app. Perhaps Aurelius Gora followed by something corresponding to *sfetules* in **15**
[A]ụṛẹ[l] .....o.[, xx Palm, 235?: **4** k 2
[Aur]el ...ṛṃ[, Egypt, dupl?, t.].ṇị[, 230: **24** 10
Aurel A[-*ca.* 9-]., xx Palm, c. Antonini post, 216: **1** xv 9
Aurel A[-*ca.* 9-]., canceled, xx Palm, c. Antonini post, 216: **1** xv 10
Aurel A.........[, writer of letter, status unknown, Dura in 216: **89** *14* verso 2
Aurel Ạ.[ ]..aus, Dura, ca. 190–245: **116** D
Aurel Aạdaeus, drom xx Palm, c. Danymi, 216: **2** xliv 8
Aurel Ab.[, eq xx Palm, t. Antiochi, ca. 215–240: **15** ii 7
Aurel Abbosas, xx Palm, c. Mariani, 216: **1** xxvi 1; **2** xxi 4·
Aurel Abdas, eq xx Palm, t. Paulini, ca. 215–240: **15** ii 13
Aurel Abdus, xx Palm, c. Antonini post, 214: **1** xiv 7; **2** xxix 27
Aurel Ạḅẹḍ....[..]....[, writer of letter, status unknown, Dura in 216: **89** 25 verso 2 and app
Aurel Abed.[..]mra, xx Palm, c. Antonini post, 214: **1** xiv 11
Aurel Abidlahas, xx Palm, c. Mariani, 216: **2** xx 20; **8** vii 5; **92** v 21
Aurel Abedmalchus, xx Palm, c. Malchiana, 206: **1** xxviii 16
Au[rel A]bidmạ[lch]ụṣ, xx Palm, c. Antonini pr, 216: **2** xxv 23
Aurel Abiḍṃạḷçḥ[, xx Palm, c. Barga, 217–256: **17** a 9
Aurel Ạḅịḍṇ[, xx Palm, 208–233: **48** 9
Aurel Abgarus, xx Palm, c. Mocimi, ca. 216–242: **32** 7
Au[rel A]biane[s], xx Palm, ca. 215–240: **15** ii 3
Aurel Absas, xx Palm, c. Heliodori, 214? (cf. **1** xxv 12), sesq ca. 230: **47** i 17; **15** ii 13–14
Ạ[urel] Abumarius, eq xx Palm, 226–251: **83** 15 and app
Aurel Ạch.[, xx Palm, 193–244: **49** 2. Same as the following?
Aurel Achileus, xx Palm, c. Gaiani, 207–232: **27** a ii 11
Aurel Ạçi[bas: **17** a 8 app
Aurel Addaeus, xx Palm, c. Malchiana, 216: **6** x 20; **1** xxxi 3
Ạ[urel] Addaeus, drom xx Palm, c. Danymi, 216: **8** iii 5. Same as preceding?
M Aur Elius: **46** 2 app
Aurel Ạḷ..[, xx Palm, ca. 215–240: **15** i 7
Ạ[urel] Alexandrus, xx Palm, 191–216: **89** *4* ii 12
Aurel Alexandrus, xx Palm, c. Malchiana, 216: **6** x 14; **1** xxx 28
Aurel Alexandrus, canceled, xx Palm, c. Malchiana, 216: **1** xxxi 9
Aurel[iu]s Alexander, principalis? xx Palm, 219: **23** iv 4
Aurel Alexander, canceled, xx Palm, c. Pudentis, 207–232: **27** a ii 5
Aurel [A]lẹx̣ạṇ[drus, xx Palm, ca. 210–240: **14** 2
[Aur]ẹḷ Alex[a]nd[rus, eq xx Palm, 226–251: **83** 4
[A]u[r]ẹḷ Am..[...]ịụṣ, xx Palm, c. Germani, ca. 215–240: **15** ii 6
Aurel Ammonianus, Egypt, sesq? aux, t. Flamini, 224: **24** 15. Same as next?
Aurel Ammonianus, Egypt, cent coh eq quingenaria, first quarter of III p.: **52** b 4?; b 12
Aurel An[, cent, Egypt, middle of III p.: **67** 11
Aurel Andronicus, xx Palm, c. Malchiana, 214: **1** xxx 6
A[u]r[el A]ṇtigonus, xx Palm, c. Marci, 214: **1** ix 7; **2** xiv 18
M Aur Antin(ous), Egypt, 207: **46** 9
Aurel Antiochianus, xx Palm, c. Antonini post, 208: **1** xiii 7; **2** xxviii 24; **92** ix 6 app
Aurel Antiochus, xx Palm, 203: c. Malchiana, **6** ix 14; **1** xxvii 22; c. Malchi, **2** ii a 3

Aurel Anto[n-, sing xx Palm, c. Antonini pr, 209: **2** xxiii 17
Aurel Antọṇ[-, xx Palm, c. Antonini post, 216: **6** v 20
[Au]rel Ạntọ[n-, xx Palm, ca. 215–240: **15** ii 10
Aurel Antoninus, eq xx Palm, t. Tiberini, 204: **1** xxxv 11
Aurel Antoninus, sing cos xx Palm, c. Antonini post, 208: **2** xxviii 22
Aurel Antoninus, xx Palm, c. Malchiana, 214: **1** xxx 11
Aurel Antoninus, xx Palm, c. Marci, 214: p. 97; **8** iv 1; **92** v 15
Aurel Antoninus, xx Palm, c. Antonini post, 214: **2** xxix 31
Aurel Antoninus, xx Palm, c. Antonini (post?), 215: **31** i 5
Aurel Antoninus, xx Palm, c. Malchiana, 216: **6** x 18
Aurel An[toni]nus, xx Palm, 216: c. Castrici, **1** xx 8; c. Antonini pr, **2** xxv 17
[Au]rel Antoninus, xx Palm, c. Antonini post, 219: **2** xxxi 19
Aurel Antoninus, xx Palm, c. Aureli, 229: **4** b i 19
Aurel Antoninus, xx Palm, c. Marini post, 240: **66** a ii 11
Aurel Antoninus, xx Palm, c. Marini pr, 240: **66** b i 18
Aurel Antoninus post, xx Palm, c. Nasonis, ca. 215–240: **15** i 21
Aurel Antoninus, xx Palm, c. Mocimi, ca. 216–242: **32** 6
Aurel Apoll[.]n.[, xx Palm, c. Antonini post, 216: **2** xxi 10
Aurel Apollinarius, xx Palm, c. Danymi, 216: **6** ii 15; **2** x 25
Aurelius Apollinarius, immunis? II Traian, 216: **21** 20: Aplunaris
Aurel Apolinarius, xx Palm, c. Nigrini, 198–235: **47** i 12
Aurel Apollonius, xx Palm, c. Danymi, 214: **6** ii 3; principalis, rank lost, **2** x 4; **8** ii 17
Aurel Apollonius Mes(s)enus, xx Palm, c. Malchiana, 215: p. 144; **6** x 9; **1** xxx 17; dupl, **27** b i 7; principalis?, **23** ii 6
Aurel Apollonius, xx Palm, c. Antonini post, 216: **1** xv 7; **2** xxx 19
Aurel Apollonius, xx Palm, c. Marci, 216: **6** iv 12
Aurel Apollonius, xx Palm, 211–236: **33** v 4
Aurel Aprianus, xx Palm, c. Danymi, 216: **6** ii 16
Aurel Ari.[, xx Palm, c. Germani, 217–256: **17** a 8
Aurel Artemidorus, xx Palm, 212: c. Castrici, **1** xviii 8; c. Antonini pr, **2** xxiii 24
Aurel Artemidorus, xx Palm, ca. 215–240: **15** ii 22
Aurel Artemidorus, sing xx Palm, c. Antonini pr, 224: **23** i 5
M Aurelius Asclepiades, Egypt, optio coh eq, 146–173 or 180–205; p. 311; **78** *1* 2; *2* 2; *3* 3; *4* 1; *5* 1; *6* 3; *7* 2; *8* 2; *9* 2; *10* 2; *11* 1; *12* 2; *23* 2; *72* 4
Aurel Asclepiades, xx Palm, c. Aureli, 229: **4** b i 20
[Aurel] Auidas, xx Palm, c. Marci, 214: **1** ix 1; **2** xiv 12; **8** iv 4
Aurelius Aurelianus, gov. of Syria?, Dura, ca. 240–250: p. 406; **100** 2
Aurel Azizus, xx Palm, c. Mariani, 214: **1** xxv 6. Probably same as next
Aurel Azizus, eq xx Palm, t. Demetri, 214: **2** xxxviii 18
Aurel B...[, xx Palm, 214: c. Seleuciana, **6** xi 35; c. Antonini pr, **8** viii 26
Aurel Ḅ[.....] eias, xx Palm, c. Achaei, ca. 215–240: **15** ii 21
Aurel Ba[, xx Palm, c. Danymi, 214: **2** ix 32
Aurel Ba[, xx Palm, c. Marci, 216: **2** xv 19
Aurel Bạ[, xx Palm, c. Antonini post, 216: **6** v 24
Aurel Ḅạbạ, xx Palm, 211–236: **33** iv 7
Aurel Babuius, xx Palm, c. Mariani, 214: **1** xxiv 5; **2** xix 14
Aurel [B]ạbuius, xx Palm, c. Aureli, 230: **4** b i 23
Ạ[ur]ẹl Bạṛ...[, xx Palm, c. Antonini pr, 215: **2** xxiv 17
Aurel Baṛ.[, sing xx Palm, c. Aureli, 232: **4** b ii 14
Aurel Barathe, xx Palm, c. Danymi, 214: **2** ix 24 and app
Aurel Barbaesomen, xx Palm, c. Mariani, 216: **8** vii 10. Same as next?
Aurel Barbesomenius, xx Palm, 211–236: **33** iii 6
Aurel Ḅaṛc̣a.[, xx Palm, drom c. Danymi, 195–215: **2** xliv 4
Aurel Barcha[, canceled, xx Palm, c. Antonini pr, 216: **8** ix 20
Aurel Barchalbas, xx Palm, c. Marci, 201: **6** iii 5; **1** vi 22
Aurel Bargas, xx Palm, c. Danymi, 215: **6** ii 7
Aurel Bargas, xx Palm, ca. 210–240: **13** 7
Aurel Barhadadus, xx Palm, ca. 215–240: **15** ii 15
Aurel Barlahas, xx Palm, c. Marci, 216: **6** iv 10; **1** x 16
Aurel Barnaeus, xx Palm, 216: c. Malchiana, **1** xxxi 8; c. Pudentis, **92** iii 22
Aurel Barnaeus, xx Palm, ca. 215–240: **15** i 12
Aurel Ḅaṛṇisiaṇụṣ, xx Palm, c. Nasonis, ca. 215–240: **15** i 22
A[u]ṛẹḷ Bars[....]ṣ, eq xx Palm, 226–251: **83** 13
Aurel Barsemias, xx Palm, c. Malchiana, 216: **6** x 23; **1** xxxi 11, Barsemia
Aurel Ḅaṛ[s]ẹṃeas, xx Palm, ca. 215–240: **15** i 16
Aurel Barsimsus, xx Palm, 214: c. Seleuciana, **6** xi 32; c. Castrici, **1** xviii 23; c. Antonini pr, **8** viii 21; **92** vi 4

Aurel Barsumṃạṛẹ[s], xx Palm, c. Achaei, ca. 215–240: **15** ii 21
Aurel Ḅaṛsuthẹ[, xx Palm, 217–256: **19** 7
Aurelius Basileus, Praef. Aeg. in 242–256: **20** 6, 9, 3 app, 15 app
Aurelius Basileus, xx Palm, c. Malchiana, 216: **6** x 15 and app; **1** xxx 31
Aurel Bassạ.., xx Palm, 211–236: **33** iv 4
Aurel Bas[su]s, sing xx Palm, c. Antonini post, 206: **2** xxviii 15
Aurel Bassus, xx Palm, c. Danymi, 214: **2** ix 26; **8** ii 11
Aurel Bassus, xx Palm, c. Mariani, 214: **1** xxv 7; **2** xx 4
Aurel Bassus, xx Palm, c. Malchiana, 215: **6** x 10; **1** xxx 18
Aurel Bassus, xx Palm, c. Marci, 209–216: **92** viii 19
Aurel Bassus, xx Palm, c. Danymi, 216: **6** ii 19; **2** x 28
Aurel Bassus, xx Palm, c. Marci, 216: **6** iv 13
Aurel Bassus, xx Palm, c. Marci, 216: **92** v 17
Ạ[ure]ḷ Bassus, sing xx Palm, c. Mariani, 216?: **2** xx 21
Aurel Bassus, xx Palm, 216: c. Castrici, **1** xx 10; c. Antonini pr, **2** xxv 19; **8** ix 17
Aurel Bassus, xx Palm, 216; c. Castrici, **1** xx 13; c. Antonini pr, **2** xxv 21
Aurel Bassus, xx Palm, 198–235: **47** ii 13
Aurel Bassus, xx Palm, c. Felicis, ca. 215–240: **15** i 19
Aurel Bassus: **13** 7 app
Aurel Ḅ[e]lạçạ[b]ụs, xx Palm, c. Danymi, 214: **8** ii 4
Ạụṛẹl Ḅelahaḅẹaṛus, xx Palm, c. Nasonis, ca. 215–240: **15** ii 15
Aurel Bernicianus, xx Palm, c. Antonini pr, 207–232: **27** a i 9. Probably same as following
Aurel Bernici[a]n[us, xx Palm, c. Germani, ca. 216–242: **32** 2
Aurel Bolaeus, xx Palm, c. Pudentis, 207–232: **27** a ii 4
Aurel Bolianus, eq xx Palm, t. Tiberini, 204: **1** xxxv 8
Aurel Buccaeus, xx Palm, c. Mariani, 202: **1** xxii 3; **2** xvii 11
Aurel Ç[. . . .]ụs, xx Palm, c. Mariani, 216: **1** xxvi 7
Aurelius Caecilianus, immunis? II Traian, 217–242: **21** 4
Aurel Calpurnius, xx Palm, c. Danymi, 216: **6** ii 12; drom, **2** xliv 6; **8** iii 3
Aurel Capiton, librarius xx Palm, 198–235: **47** i 17
Aurel Cassianus, xx Palm, c. Malchi, 204: **2** ii a 5 and app
Aurel Castor, xx Palm, 216: p. 83; c. Antonini post, **2** xxxi 13; sing dupl, c. Aureli, **4** b i 4
Aurel Claudius, xx Palm, ca. 210–240: **13** 12; ca. 215–240: **15** i 3; ca. 190–245: **116** c. All the same man?
Aurel Cọ[, xx Palm, ca. 210–240: **13** 8
Aurel Cocceius, dupl xx Palm, c. Danymi, 214: **1** i 4; **2** vi 21. Same as dec Cocceius? See "Cocceius" below
Aurel Coceius, xx Palm, c. Prisci, ca. 215–240: **15** ii 19
Aurel Coddaeus, xx Palm, c. Malchiana, 199–201: **6** ix 4; **1** xxvii 1
Aurel Çrị[s]pị[nus, xx Palm, 235?: **4** k 3
Aurel Cronion, Egypt, dupl? aux, t. Nicola, 224: **24** 2
Aurel Cyrillus, xx Palm, c. Antonini post, 216: **6** v 21; **1** xv 11; **2** xxx 23, Curịḷḷ[u]s; **89** *16* 9 app
Aurel Ḍ[, xx Palm, c. Danymi, 215: **8** ii 22
Aurel D [, xx Palm, c. Aureli, 226: **4** b i 13
Aurel Ḍ[, xx Palm, ca. 215–240: **15** e 2
Aurel De.[, xx Palm, c. Marci, 216: **2** xv 17
Aurel Demetrius, xx Palm, c. Malchiana, 214: **1** xxx 15
Aurel Demetrius, xx Palm, c. Danymi, 214: **2** ix 25; **8** ii 10
Aurel Demetrius, xx Palm, c. Danymi, 215; **6** ii 8; **2** x 11
Aurel Demetrius, xx Palm, c. Antonini post, 215: **2** xxx 14
Aurel [Deme]ṭrius, xx Palm, c. Pudentis, 198–216: **92** iii 20 and app
Aurel Ḍẹṃ[et]ṛiụṣ, xx Palm, c. Antonini pr, 216: **2** xxv 25
Aurel Demetrius, xx Palm, c. Marci, 216: **6** iv 7; **1** x 7
Aurel Demetrius, xx Palm, 216: c. Castrici, **1** xx 4; c. Antonini pr, **2** xxv 14; **8** ix 14
Aurel Demetrius, eq xx Palm, t. Tiberini, 216: **2** xxxvi 8
Aurel Demetrius, xx Palm, c. Antonini pr, 216: **8** ix 18
Aurel Demetrius, xx Palm, c. Pudentis, 198–235: **47** i 4
Aurel Demostenes, immunis? II Traian, 221: **21** 14
Aurel Diodorus, xx Palm, c. Marci, 216: **2** xv 15; **92** v 16
Aurel Diodorus, principalis? xx Palm, 219: **23** iv 5
Aurel Diomedes, xx Palm, ca. 215–240: **15** ii 18
Aurel Dionusius, sing xx Palm, c. Antonini pr, 222: **2** xxvi 11
Aurel Domitianus, sing xx Palm, c. Aureli, 225: **4** b i 8
Aurel Domittius, xx Palm, c. Mariani, 214: **8** vi 13

Aurel Domitius, xx Palm, c. Antonini post, 215: **1** xv 3, Domettius; sing, **2** xxx 15, Domittius
Aurel Domitius, xx Palm, c. Marci, 216: **6** iv 9, Domittius; **1** x 10, Dometius
Aurel Domitius, xx Palm, c. Mariani, 216: **1** xxvi 6, Dometius; **2** xxi 9; **8** vii 14, Domittius
Aurel Domitius, xx Palm, c. Marci, 209–225: **92** viii 20. Same as second preceding?
Aurel Domitius, xx Palm, c. Antonini (post?), 217: **31** i 10
[Aure]l Domnus, xx Palm, 204: c. Castrici, **1** xvii 14; c. Antonini pr, **2** xxii 23
Aurelius Eudaemon, Egypt, coh eq c. Cassiani, 162–187?: **78** *69* 1
A[ure]ḷ Euxemon, xx Palm, c. Malchiana, 214: **1** xxix 8
Aurel Faustus, xx Palm, c. Danymi, 199: **6** i 3; **1** i 16; **2** vi 28
Aurel Filo.s, xx Palm, c. Danymi, 214: **2** ix 34
Aurel F̣ḷ.[, xx Palm, c. Danymi, 214: **8** ii 6
Aurel Flauius, xx Palm, c. Malchiana, 214: **6** x 2
Aurel Flauius, xx Palm, c. Marci, 216: **6** iv 14; **1** x 24
Aurelius Flauius, xx Palm, 191–216: **89** *5* 4
Aurel Fronton, xx Palm, c. Danymi, 203–216: **92** viii 8
Ạ[ure]ḷ G̣[.].[, xx Palm, c. Antonini post, 216: **6** v 26
Aurel G[, xx Palm, c. Antonini post, 216: **6** v 27
Aurel Gaianus, xx Palm, ca. 207–238: **94** c 2. Same as next?
Aurel Gaian[, xx Palm, c. Barga?, 217–256: **19** 4 and app. Same as next?
Aurel Gaianus, xx Palm, c. Barga, 225–251: **66** b ii 22
[Aurel] Gaius, xx Palm, c. Marci, 214: **1** ix 5; **2** xiv 16
Aurel Gaius, xx Palm, 214; c. Seleuciana, **6** xi 28, Gai; c. Castrici, **1** xviii 16, [G]aius
Aurel Germanus, eq xx Palm, t. Tiberini, 205: **1** xxxv 17; **2** xxxv 18
Aurel Germanus, xx Palm, c. Danymi, 214: **1** iii–v d 3; **2** ix 29; **8** ii 13
Aurel Germanus, xx Palm, c. Antonini post, 214: **1** xiv 10
Aurel Germ[anus, xx Palm, c. Antonini post, 202–215, probably 214 (*see* Aurel Hadrianus): **6** v 15
Aurel Germanus, xx Palm, c. Mariani, 216: **1** xxvi 4; **2** xxi 7
Aurel Germ[anus, xx Palm, c. Aureli, 232: **4** b ii 17
Aurel Germanus, cent xx Palm, 226–236: pp. 126, 128, 133; **23** i 8; **50** i 1, ord princeps; 2, 8, 9; ii [1]; a 1, 2; **13** 18; **14** 1; **15** i 10; ii 6, 10, 16; c 4; **29** 5; **32** 1; **66** a ii 5, 16; b i 19 app; **17** a 5, 7, 8, 12?; **19** 6
Aurel Germanus, xx Palm, 211–236: **33** v 2
Aurel Germanus, tiro, xx Palm, vi id maias, 239: **50** i 14
Aurelius Gora, xx Palm, 208–233: **48** 9
Aurel Gordius, xx Palm, c. Antonini post, 216: **1** xv 12; **2** xxx 24
Aurel Gr[, xx Palm, c. Antonini post, 216: **2** xxxi 6
Aurel G̣ṛaṭuṣ, xx Palm, ca. 197–222: **31** ii 4
Aurel H[, xx Palm, ca. 208–233: **56** 3
[A]ụṛẹḷ H[.].[....]s, Egypt, dupl? aux, t. Flamini, 230: **24** 8
Aurel H.[..]ofur, xx Palm, 211–236: **33** iii 3
Ạụ[r]ẹ[l] Ha.[...]s, xx Palm, c. Antonini pr, 216: **2** xxv 26
Aurel Hadrianus, xx Palm, c. Malchiana, 214: **1** xxx 13
Aurel Hadṛiạ[nus, xx Palm, c. Antonini post, 202–215: **6** v 18. Probably same as preceding
Aurelius Arpocration, cent III Itur, 230: **20** 21
Aurel Ḥẹ[, xx Palm, c. Danymi, 214: **8** ii 7
[Au]ṛẹ[l] Hel[, xx Palm, ca. 210–240: **14** 4
Aurel Heliodorus, xx Palm, 216: c. Castrici, **1** xx 9; c. Antonini pr, **2** xxv 18; **8** ix 16
Aurel Heliodorus, xx Palm, c. Malchiana, 216: **6** x 17; **1** xxx 32
Aurel Heliodorus, canceled, xx Palm, c. Antonini (pr?), 198–235: **47** i 12
Aurel Heliodorus, xx Palm, 198–235: **47** ii 13
Ạụṛẹḷ Ḥẹliọdọṛụ[s, xx Palm, ca. 215–240; **15** ii 3
Aurel Heliodorus, xx Palm, ca. 215–240: **15** ii 18
Aurel Ḥẹlla[ni]c̣ụ[s, xx Palm, c. Mocimi, ca. 216–242: **32** 5
Aurelius Eraclịḍ[, immunis? II Traian, 217–242: **21** 5
Aurel Heraclidas, xx Palm, c. Antonini post, 209: **1** xiii 13
Aurel Heras, Egypt, sesq, aux, t. Titi, 222: **24** 19
Aurel Erenn[ius *or* Erenn[ianus, xx Palm, c. Malchiana, 214: **1** xxx 1
Aurelius Herm[, Egypt, coh eq, 132–217: **78** *57* 8
Aurel Hermaiscus, Egypt, dupl?, aux, t. Quintiani, 220: **24** 4
Aurel Hermogenes, xx Palm, c. Antonini post, 219: **2** xxxi 18
Aurelius Heronia[nūs, **39** 16 app
Aurelius Hier[, Egypt, coh eq, 136–181 or 188–213: **78** *14* 1
Aurelius Hierax, Egypt, dec aux, 218–244: **20** 10
Aurel Ị[, xx Palm, 214–239: **50** i 10
Ạụṛẹḷ Ia..[, xx Palm, c. Aureli, 226: **4** b i 12 and app
Aurel Iaddạẹ[, xx Palm, c. Aureli, 226: **4** b i 11
Aurel Iadibelus, xx Palm, c. Danymi, 202–206?: **1** iii–v a–c 8
Aurel Iaqubus, xx Palm, c. Antonini post, 214: **2** xxix 14

Aurel Iaṛ.[.].ṣo, xx Palm, ca. 215–240: **15** i 13
Aurel Ieraboles, xx Palm, c. Malchiana, 214: **1** xxx 10
Aurel Iarhaboles, xx Palm, c. Mariani, 216: **1** xxvi 5, Ieraboles: **2** xxi 8; **8** vii 13
Aurel Iarhaboles, xx Palm, 214–239: **50** i 3; i 9 app, 10 app
Aurel Iarheus, xx Palm, c. Mariani, 216: **2** xx 18
Aurel Iarhaeus, xx Palm, c. Prisci, ca. 215–240: **15** i 1
Aurel Intenianus, tribune or praepositus? xx Palm, Dura ca. 240–250: p. 406; **100** 2
Aurelius Isidorianus, Egypt, coh eq, t. Saturnini, II/III p.: **30** ii 5; **78** *46* 4 app
M Aurelius Isidorus, Egypt, optio coh eq, 157–182 or 189–214: **78** *11* 1
Aurelius Isidor[, Egypt, coh eq, 132–217: **78** *46* 4
Aurel Isidorus, eq xx Palm, t. Tiberini, 207–232: **27** b i 5
Aurelius Iu.[, Egypt, end of III p.: **11 bis** a 21
Aurel Iulius, xx Palm, c. Antonini post?, 204?: **92** ix 5 and app
Aurel Iulius, sing xx Palm, c. Marci, 210: **2** xiii 22
Aurel Iulius pr, xx Palm, c. Castrici, 214–215: **1** xix 12
Aurel Iulius post, xx Palm, c. Castrici, 214–215: **1** xix 13
Aurel Iulius, xx Palm, c. Antonini post, 216: **1** xv 18; **2** xxx 27
Aurel Iulius, xx Palm, c. Antonini post, 220: **8** ix 25
Aurel Licinnius, xx Palm, c. Mariani, 216: **1** xxvi 3; **2** xxi 6; **47** i 4
Aurel Liuianus, xx Palm, c. Malchiana, 216: **6** x 9; **1** xxxi 2
Aurel Ḷọ[, xx Palm, c. Danymi, 216: **2** x 24
Aurel Lọ[..]oṇụṣ, xx Palm, c. Antonini pr, 211–236: **33** ii 5
Aurel Lon[: **1** iii–v i 5 app; **2** x 16 and 24 app
Aurel Long( ), xx Palm, 225–256: **4** 1 2 and app
Aurel Longi[n-, xx Palm, c. Antonini pr, 215: **2** xxiv 16
Aurel Longin[, xx Palm, c. Antonini post, 216: **1** xv 24: **2** xxxi 9
Aurel Longinus, xx Palm, c. Danymi, 216: **6** ii 11; **1** iii–v i 5 app; **2** x 16 and 24 app
Aurel Lucius, xx Palm, c. Mariani, 216: **2** xx 22; **8** vii 6
Aurel Lucius, xx Palm, c. Antonini pr, 217: **8** ix 23
Aurel Ṃ[, xx Palm, c. Mariani, 214: **2** xix 18
Aurel Ṃ[..].sus, xx Palm, c. Mariani, 214: **8** vi 22 and app
Aurel M.l[.]abiṃị, xx Palm, c. Antonini pr, 215: **8** ix 10
Aurel M....ṣ[, xx Palm, c. Danymi, 216: **2** x 22 and app
Aurel M[, xx Palm, c. Marci, 216: **2** xv 18
Aurel Ṃ[-*ca.* 8-]ṣ, xx Palm, c. Pudentis, 214–217: **92** ix 13
Aurel Ṃ[, xx Palm, 229: **95** b 9
Aurel Ṃ.[..].ịus, xx Palm, 211–236: **33** iii 2
Aurel Ma..[, xx Palm, c. Danymi, 214: **1** iii–v d 5; **2** ix 31
Aurel Ma.h[..]s, xx Palm, c. Marci, 214?: **6** iv 4
Aurel Ma[, xx Palm, c. Castrici, 214–215: **1** xix 10
Aurel Mạ[...]i[, xx Palm, c. Antonini post, 216: **6** v 22
Aurel Maal, xx Palm, ca. 210–238: **95** k 3
Aurel Macrinus, xx Palm, c. Heliodori, 225: p. 153; **29** 13
Aurel Magnus, xx Palm, c. Antonini pr, 214: **8** viii 17; **92** iii 14
Aurel Magnus, xx Palm, c. Danymi, 216: **6** ii 13; **2** x 22 app
Aurel Malchus, xx Palm, c. Malchiana, 214: **1** xxix 14
Aurel Malchus, xx Palm, c. Malchiana, 214: **1** xxx 3
Aurel Malchus, xx Palm, c. Danymi, 216: **6** ii 10; **2** x 15; **8** ii 29
Aurel Malchus, xx Palm, c. Danymi, 216: **6** ii 14
Aurel Malchus, xx Palm, c. Antonini post, 216: **2** xxxi 8
Aurel Malchus, xx Palm, c. Antonini post, 216: **2** xxxi 12
Aurel Malchus, sig xx Palm, 214–239: **50** i 3, 9; ii 4 app
Aurel Ṃạ[l]ḷc̣h[u]s, eq xx Palm, t. Cocceiana, ca. 215–240: **15** ii 2, 12
Aurel Malchus, xx Palm, ca. 215–240: **15** ii 11
Aurel Malchus, xx Palm, c. Marini pr, 240: **66** a ii 9
Aurel Man.ḍeus: **8** vi 12 app
Aurel Mannaeus, xx Palm, c. Mariani, 214: **8** vi 12
Aurel [M]ạṇṇus, xx Palm, c. Danymi, 197–225: **92** v 11
Aurel Mar.[, xx Palm, c. Mariani, 214: **1** xxv 4; **2** xx 3
Aurel Maṛ[, xx Palm, c. Antonini post, 214: **2** xxx 8
Aurel Marcellus, eq xx Palm, t. Octaui, 201: **1** xxxix 8
Aurel Marinus, xx Palm, c. Antonini post, 206: **2** xxviii 14
Aurel Marinus, sing xx Palm, c. Mariani, 208: **1** xxiii 8; **2** xviii 13, notation lost
Aurel Marinus, xx Palm, c. Malchiana, 214: **6** x 1
Aurel Marinus, xx Palm, c. Malchiana, 214: **6** x 6
Aurel Marinus, xx Palm, c. Antonini post, 214: **1** xiv 6; **2** xxix 26
[Aurel] Marinus, xx Palm, c. Mariani, 214: **1** xxiv 11

Aurel Marinus, xx Palm, c. Malchiana, 214: **1** xxix 11
Aurel Marinus, sesq xx Palm, t. Demetri, 214: **2** xxxvi 20
Aurel Marinus, drom xx Palm, c. Marci, 214: **2** xliv 17; **8** v 5
Aurel Marinus, xx Palm, c. Danymi, 215: **6** ii 6
Aurel Marinus, xx Palm, c. Antonini pr, 215: **8** ix 8
Aurel Marinus, xx Palm, c. Danymi, 216: **6** ii 20
Aurel Marinus, xx Palm, c. Malchiana, 216: **6** x 21; **1** xxxi 4
Aurel Marinus, xx Palm, c. Malchiana, 216: **6** x 22; **1** xxxi 10
Aurel Marinus, xx Palm, c. Antonini pr, 216: **2** xxv 24
Aurel Marinus, xx Palm, c. Mariani, 216: **8** vii 11
Aurel Marinus, xx Palm, c. Antonini pr, 216: **8** ix 21
Aurel Marinus, xx Palm, ca. 190–230: **41** 5
Aurel Marinus, xx Palm, ca. 215–240: **15** i 18
Aurel Marinus, xx Palm, c. Antonini (pr?), 198–235: **47** i 12
Aurel Marinus, xx Palm, c. Achaei, ca. 216–242: **32** 10
Aurel [M]aṛọṇ[as, xx Palm, c. Mariani, 225?: **8** vii 16
Aurel Maxim. . [, xx Palm, c. Germani, 225–251: **66** a ii 7
Aurel Maximus, Egypt, immunis? II Traian, 210–242: **21** 12
Aurel Maximus, xx Palm, c. Marci, 216: **6** iv 8; **1** x 8
Aurel Maximus, xx Palm, c. Mariani, 216: **8** vii 9
Aurel Maximus, xx Palm, c. Marci?, 207–232: **27** c 4
Aurel Maximus, xx Palm, c. Gaiani, 207–232: **27** a ii 9
[Aure]l Maximus, xx Palm, c. Achaei, ca. 216–242: **32** 9
Aurel Maximus, xx Palm, c. *or* t.]. iẹra, 238: **66** b i 20
Aurel Me. . d[, xx Palm, ca. 215–240: **15** i 4
Aurel Mo. [imu]s, xx Palm, c. Marci, 209–225: **92** viii 21 and app
Aurel Mocimus, xx Palm, c. Antonini post, 214: **1** xiv 5; **2** xxix 25
Aurel Mocimus, xx Palm, c. Mariani, 216: **8** vii 7
Aurel Mocimus, xx Palm, ca. 215–240: **15** i 11
Aurel Mocimus, sing xx Palm, c. Nigrini, 224: **23** i 7
Aurel Mocimus, eq xx Palm, t. Tiberini, 207–232: **27** b i 4
[Aure]l Mocimus, xx Palm, ca. 190–230: **41** 3
Aurel Mocimus, tesserarius xx Palm, 214–239: **50** i 3, 9
Aurel Mombogeus, xx Palm, c. Malchiana, 203: **1** xxvii 11
Aurel Mombogeus, xx Palm, c. Pudentis, 207–232: **27** a ii 3. Same as preceding?
Aurel Mambogeus, eq xx Palm, 226–251: **83** 17
Aurel Monimi, drom xx Palm, c. Malchiana, 204: **1** xliv 16 and app; **2** xliii 21 and app
Aurel Monimus, xx Palm, c. Malchiana, 214: **6** x 4
Aurel Monimus, eq xx Palm, t. Coccei, 207–232: **27** b i 12
[Aurel] Mu[, xx Palm, c. Castrici, 204: **1** xvii 24
Aurel Mucianus, stator? xx Palm, c. Mariani, 214: **1** xxiv 6; **2** xix 15; **89** *1* 5a and 5 app
Aurel Mucianus, xx Palm, c. Danymi, 216: **2** x 29
Aurel Mucianus, xx Palm, c. Malchiana, 216: **6** x 12
Aurel Mucianus, xx Palm, 205: c. Seleuciana, **6** xi 12; c. Antonini pr, **8** viii 4
Aurel Mucianus, xx Palm, c. Antonini pr, 214: **8** viii 19
Aurel Munnis, xx Palm, c. Antonini post, 215: **2** xxx 16
Aurel Ṇ. ị. [.]. s: **15** ii 11 app
Aurel Nebumarius, xx Palm, ca. 215–240: **15** i 11; ii 19
Aurel Nemas, Egypt, c. Theopropi, 194: **5** ii 16
Aurel Neon, xx Palm, c. Antonini post, 216: **1** xv 5; **2** xxx 18
[Aurel] Ni. [. .]eus, xx Palm, c. Mariani, 214: **1** xxiv 10
Aurel Nisraeus, xx Palm, c. Antonini post, 214: **1** xiv 9; **2** xxix 29
Aurel Ọạ. . l: **16** recto 2 app
Aurel Ọg[as], xx Palm, c. Achaei, ca. 215–240: **15** i 14
Aurel Ogelus: **4** b i 17 app
Aurel Ọḥrasus, xx Palm, c. Mariani, 216: **8** vii 8
Aurel Ṗạ[. .]ṃ. . . . [, eq xx Palm, t. Romulli, ca. 215–240: **15** ii 4
[Aur]ẹ[l] Ṗạụ. . . ạ[, xx Palm, c. Felicis, ca. 216–242: **32** 14
Aurel Paulus, xx Palm, 216: c. Malchiana, **6** x 13; drom, c. Malchi, **2** xliii 28
Aurel Philon, xx Palm, c. Marci, 216: **1** x 9; **2** xv 12
Aurel Priscus, sing xx Palm, c. Marci, 206: **2** xiii 11
Aurel Priscus, principalis, notation lost, xx Palm, c. Mariani, 214: **1** xxv 11; **2** xx 8 app
Aurel Priscus, bucinator, xx Palm, c. Marci, 214: **2** xiii 31; **50** i 2, 9; b 2
Aurel Ṗ[u]ṗḷ[, xx Palm, c. Antonini pr, 215: **2** xxv 12
Aurel Qu. [, xx Palm, c. Antonini pr, 215: **2** xxiv 13
Aurel Quinṭ[, xx Palm, 205–240: **22** 5

Aurelius R. . . ụṣ, principalis? xx Palm, 224?: **23** iv 7
Aurelius Regulus, p(rimi)p(ilus?), p(rae)-p(ositus?), Dura in 216: **89** *1* verso 1
Aurel Roṃ[, xx Palm, c. Danymi, 214: **6** i 36
Aurel Romanus, xx Palm, c. Antonini post, 214: **2** xxix 18
Aurel Romanus, xx Palm, c. Danymi, 214: **8** ii 5
Aurel Romanus, xx Palm, c. Danymi, 216: **6** ii 18
Aurel Romanus, xx Palm, c. Marci, 216: **1** x 12; **2** xv 14
Aurel Romanus, xx Palm, c. Mariani, 216: **2** xx 19; **8** vii 4
Aurel Romanus, xx Palm, c. Antonini post, 216: **2** xxx 20
Aurel Romanus, xx Palm, c. Antonini post, 216: **2** xxx 26
Aurel Romanus, drom xx Palm, c. Danymi, 216: p. 97; **2** xliv 7; **47** i 4 app; cf. **8** iii 4
Aurel Romanus, drom xx Palm, c. Danymi, 216: p. 97; **2** xliv 10; **47** i 4 app; cf. **8** iii 4
Aurel Romanus, drom xx Palm, c. Danymi, 216: p. 97; **8** iii 4; cf. **2** xliv 7 and 10; **47** i 4 app
Aurel Romanus, xx Palm, c. Antonini pr, 216: **8** ix 19
Aurẹ[l Ro]manus, xx Palm, c. Antonini post, 197–217: **92** iii 17
Aur]ẹl Romanus, xx Palm, c. Danymi, 197–225: **92** viii 10
Aurel Romanus, drom? xx Palm, c. Nigrini, 198–235: **47** i 4
Aurel Rubathus, curator xx Palm, 198–235: **47** i 7
Aurelius Rufinus, procurator Augustorum and praepositus praetenturae, Dura in 221: pp. 383, 414; **91** *1* i 1; *1* verso 2; *2* verso 2; *2* i 1 app; *2* i 12 app
Aurel Rufus, xx Palm, c. Nigrini, 198–235: **47** i 4. Cf. **23** iv 8 app
A[urel] Rumas, xx Palm, c. Mariani, 208: **1** xxiii 9; **2** xviii 14
Aurel Sa[, xx Palm, c. Antonini post, 216: **6** v 25
Aurel Sa.a.[, xx Palm, 211–236: **33** iv 3
Aurel Sabinus, xx Palm, c. Antonini post, 202: **2** xxvii 21
Aurel Sabinus, drom xx Palm, c. Danymi, 216: **2** xliv 9
Aurel Ṣạlṃ[, xx Palm, 215–240: **15** ii 4
Aurel Salma[n-, xx Palm, c. Felicis, ca. 215–240: **15** ii 20
Aurel Salmanes, xx Palm, c. Felicis, ca. 216–242: **32** 13
Aurel Seleuc[, xx Palm, c. Seleuciana, 214: **6** xi 30
Ạ[urel S]eleucus, xx Palm, 191–216: **89** *4* ii 11
Aurel Seleucus, xx Palm, c. Marci, 216: **1** x 11; **2** xv 13
Aurel Seleucus, xx Palm, c. Malchiana, 219: **1** xxxi 16
Aurel Seleucus, sing xx Palm, c. Antonini post, 222: **2** xxxi 24
Aurel Sempronius, Egypt, c. Theopropi, 194: **5** ii 12
Aurel Sentianus, xx Palm, c. Marci, 203: **8** iii 11
Aurel Serenus, Egypt, coh eq, t. Maximi, II/III p.: **30** ii 7
Aurel Si. . . .ṣẹs: **15** ii 14 app
Aurel Siluanus, drom xx Palm, c. Mariani, 210: **8** vii 18
Aurel Siluanus, xx Palm, c. Malchiana, 214: **1** xxx 4
Aurel Siluanus, xx Palm, c. Malchiana, 214: **1** xxx 7
Aurel Siluanus alter, xx Palm, c. Malchiana 214: **1** xxx 8
Aurel Siluanus, xx Palm, c. Antonini (post?), 215: **31** i 6
Aurel Siluanus alter, xx Palm, c. Antonini (post?), 215: **31** i 7
Aurel Siluanus, xx Palm, 216: c. Castrici, **1** xx 11; c. Antonini pr, **2** xxv 20
Aurel Siluanus, xx Palm, 216: c. Castrici, **1** xx 14; c. Antonini pr, **2** xxv 22
Aurel Siluanus, xx Palm, c. Mariani, 216: **1** xxvi 2; **2** xxi 5; **8** vii 12
Aurel Siluanus, xx Palm, c. Antonini post, 216: **2** xxx 29
Aurel Siluanus, drom xx Palm, c. Antonini pr, 216: **2** xlv 9
Aurel Siluanus, aedituus, xx Palm, 198–235: **47** i 7, 17; ii 12
Aurel Siluanus, xx Palm, c. Aureli, 230: **4** b i 24
Aurel Siluanus prior, xx Palm, ca. 215–240: **15** i 16: **16** recto 2 app
Aurel Siluanus, xx Palm, 216–250: **16** recto 2
Aurel Simaones, xx Palm, ca. 215–240: **15** ii 14
Aurel Ṣimọạṛus, xx Palm, 217–256: **19** 5
Aurel Siṭọṛṛ[, xx Palm, 211–236: **33** iv 1
Aurel Sopạ[, xx Palm, c. Danymi, 214: **2** ix 33 and app
Aurel Sossianus, xx Palm, c. Danymi, 214: **2** ix 27; **8** ii 12
Aurel Sp[, Egypt, c. Theopropi, 194: **5** ii 17
Aurel Summares, xx Palm, 216: c. Castrici, **1** xx 6; c. Antonini pr, **2** xxv 16; **8** ix 15
Aurel Th[, eq xx Palm, t. Antiochi, ca. 215–240: **15** ii 2; ii 12?
Aurel Them.[, xx Palm, c. Danymi, 214: **1** iii–v d 4; **2** ix 30
Aurel Them[, xx Palm, c. Aureli, 232: **4** b ii 13 and app
Aurel Themarsa, xx Palm, c. Malchiana, 214: **1** xxx 9

Aurelius Th[e]ṃạṛṣạ[, xx Palm, 205–240: **22** 3
Aurelius Themars[, xx Palm, 213–256: **35** 12
Aurel Theo[, xx Palm, c. Antonini pr, 221: **2** xxvi 8
Aurelius Theocles, Egypt, immunis? II Traian, 221: **21** 15
Aurelius Theodorus, procurator Augusti, Dura in 216: **89** *4* i 5
Aurel Theodorus, xx Palm, c. Achaei, ca. 215–240: **15** i 20
Aurel Theodorus, eq xx Palm, 226–251: **83** 20
Aurel Theodotus, xx Palm, 211–236: **33** v 5
Aurel Theopropus, Egypt, 192–217: **5** ii 2
Aurel Tiber[, xx Palm, c. Achaei, ca. 215–240: **15** ii 18
Aurel Titus, Egypt, immunis? II Traian, 221: **21** 16; **24** 5 and 18 app
Aurel Tra..[.]us, xx Palm, c. Malchiana, 214: **1** xxix 13. Traianus?
Aurel V[, xx Palm, c. Antonini post, 216: **2** xxxi 5
Aurel Valẹ[......]s, xx Palm, c. Marci, 214: **1** ix 13
Aurel Valens, eq xx Palm, t. Octaui, 214: **1** xl 24; **2** xl 30
Aurel Valens, drom xx Palm, c. Marci, 214: **2** xliv 16
Aurel Valens, xx Palm, c. Aureli, 229: **4** b i 21
Aurel Valerius, principalis? xx Palm, 224: **23** iii 4
Aurelius Victor, Egypt, principalis?, 177: **39** 10
Aurel Victorinus, xx Palm, c. Felicis, ca. 215–240: **15** i 19
[Aurel Vl]ṗius: **8** iii 1 app
Aurel Z.[.]..[.]s, eq xx Palm, t. Cocceiana, ca. 215–240: **15** ii 1
Aurel Zab[, xx Palm, c. Castrici, 214–215: **1** xix 11
Aurel Zabaeus, xx Palm, c. Antonini pr, 215: **2** xxiv 23
Aurel Ẓ[a]ḅḍ[, xx Palm, ca. 210–240: **14** 1
Aurel Zabdas, xx Palm, c. Marci, 216: **6** iv 11
Aurel Zabdas, xx Palm, 217: c. Malchiana, **6** x 25; **1** xxxi 13, Zabde; c. Pudentis, **92** ix 14
Aurel Zabdibolus, xx Palm, c. Antonini post, 214: **1** xiv 2; **2** xxix 24
Aurel Zabdibolus, xx Palm, 191–216: **89** *8* 4
Aurel Zabdib[ol-, drom xx Palm, c. Marci, 216: **8** v 7
Aurel Zabdib(olus), xx Palm, ca. 190–230: **41** 1
Aurel Zabdibolus, xx Palm, c. Achaei, ca. 216–242: **32** 11
Aurelius Zeḅ[...]m..[, principalis? xx Palm, 211–236: **23** iv 2
Aurel Zebinnus, xx Palm, c. Malchiana, 216: **1** xxxi 7
Aurel Zeṇ[, xx Palm, c. Aureli, 232: **4** b ii 15
Aurel Zeṇ.[.]o.r, xx Palm, 211–236: **33** v 6
Aurel Zenobius, xx Palm, c. Antonini post, 216: **2** xxxi 11
Aurelius Zenobius, xx Palm, ca. 215–240: **15** b 11
Aurel Zenodorus, xx Palm, c. Germani, ca. 215–240: **15** ii 16
Aurel Zinnẹ[..]s, xx Palm, c. Malchiana, 216: **6** x 16
Aurel Ẓo.[, xx Palm, c. Antonini pr, 215: **2** xxiv 14 and app
Authaei, *see* Abedmalchus
Aziz..[, *nom*, xx Palm, 225–256: **4** a i 4 and app
Azizus, *see also* Aurelius
Azizus Aethibeli, xx Palm, c. Marci, 214: **1** ix 3, Aathibeli; **2** xiv 14; **8** iv 6
Azizus Antonini, eq xx Palm, t. Zebida, 205: **1**, Aurel, xxxiii 10; **2** xxxiii 26
Azizus Salamalathi, drom xx Palm, c. Marci, 195: **1** xliii 27
Azizus Zaora, eq xx Palm, t. Tiberini, 209: **1** xxxv 24; **2** xxxv 26
Azizus Zebida, xx Palm, c. Antonini pr, 215: **2** xxiv 25

B[, *see also* Aelius, Aurelius, Iulius
B[, *nom*, xx Palm, c. Danymi, 204: **2** vii 32
].[.....]ḥus Ḅ[.]ḷ[, principalis, notation lost, xx Palm, t. Antonini, 204: **2** xlii 24
Aurel B..ḍs.[....]ae.[, xx Palm, c. Mariani, 205–207: **1** xxiii 3
Ḅ..ba.[..]d......[, xx Palm, c. Danymi, 214: **8** ii 14
B[, *nom*, xx Palm, c. Marci, 216: **2** xv 4
B.[...], Egypt, tesserarius, coh eq, 132–217: **78** *42* 5
Ḅ.[ ]bḅi.[, xx Palm, c. Pudentis, 197–225: **92** vi 23
Ḅ[, *nom*, xx Palm, c. Antonini post, 197–228: **8** x 10
Ḅ[.].ḅ[, xx Palm, ca. 205–240: **12** a–c 5
Ḅ[.....].eias, *see* Aurelius
Ba[, *see also* Apollonius, Aurelius
Ba..[.].[, Egypt, eq aux, second quarter of II p.: **73** a i 10
Ba[, xx Palm, c. Danymi, 202–206?: **1** iii–v a–c 10
Ba.[, *nom*, xx Palm, c. Antonini post, 210?: **8** x 19
Ba.[, *cogn*, xx Palm, c. Marci, 214: **2** xiv 23
Ḅạ[, *nom*, xx Palm, c. Antonini pr, 214: **2** xxiv 1
Bạ[, *nom*, xx Palm, c. Antonini post, 201–214: **6** v 6
Ba.[, xx Palm, ca. 210–240: **13** 2
Ḅạ[...]ẹ...a, xx Palm, ca. 210–240: **13** 11
Ḅạ[, *nom*, eq xx Palm, t. Romulli, ca. 215–240: **15** i 6
Ba.ạ[, eq xx Palm, 226–251: **83** 23
Baadadadus: **89** *2* 18 app

Ḅaḅa, *see* Aurelius
Babuius, *see also* Aurelius
Babuiu[s M]ọc̣im[, xx Palm, c. Danymi, 201: **2** vii 5
Bac̣[.]ḅ..ịụs Malch.[, xx Palm, 213–247: **3** b 9
Bachareụ[, *nom*, xx Palm, c. Antonini post, 212: **2** xxix 11
Baebius: **36** 8 app
Baebius Q. f., Egypt, III Cyr or XXII Deiot, I a.: **36** 3
Baebius Iu[..]us, cent hastatus primus, XXII Deiot?, early I p.: p. 198; **51** ii 5
Baibulas, Egypt, eq aux, second quarter of II p.: **73** a iii 3
Balini(us) Hecataeus, Egypt, III Cyr, c. Antoni Longini, 91–116: **34** recto ii 9, Ecateus
Ballaei, *see* Vabalathen
Βαλλησιανος, Egypt, coh eq, 158–183 or 190–215: **78** *7* 1
]baṇ.[, *cogn*, xx Palm, c. Mariani, 207: **2** xviii 5 and app
Baṇṇ[ae-: **2** xviii 5 app
Bannaei, *see also* Demetrius
Bannaei, *cogn*, xx Palm, c. Mariani, 197–204: **92** iii 5
Bannaeus: **92** iii 22 app
Baṛ...[, *see* Aurelius, Raamas
Baṛ.[.]..[: **2** xxxii 10 app
Aurel Bar.[.......]. Ierhaei, eq xx Palm, t. Octaui, 201: **1** xxxix 30
Bar[, *nom*, xx Palm, c. Marci, 214: **1** ix 14
Aurel Bar[, xx Palm, c. Marci, 214: **1** ix 17
Baṛ[, *cogn*, xx Palm, c. Marci, 214: **2** xiv 9
Ḅaṛ.[, *nom*, xx Palm, 214–239: **50** i 9 and app
baṛ[, *name?*, xx Palm, 225–251: **66** b ii 19
Ḅaṛ[.]ṇṇiaṇaṣ: **15** i 22 app
]ḅas Baraḅ[, xx Palm, c. Marci, 196: **6** ii 31
Barasthor: **19** 7 app
Barathe, *see also* Aurelius, Marinus, Seleucus, Zabdas
[Ba]ratḥ[es, *nom*, eq xx Palm, t. Antonini, 201: **2** xlii 2
Aure[l Ba]ṛath[es ....]..i, vex xx Palm, t. Zebida, 202: **1** xxxii 21
[B]ạraṭḥẹ, *cogn*, xx Palm, c. Malchiana, 209: **6** ix 25
Aurel Barathes Abgari, vex xx Palm, t. Demetri, 195: **1** xxxvi 18
Barathes Abgari, eq xx Palm, t. Antonini, 203: **1**, Aurel, xlii 24: **2** xlii 15
Barathes Buccaei, eq xx Palm, t. Demetri, 203: **1**, Aurel, xxxvii 13; **2** xxxvii 15
Barathes Hagus, eq xx Palm, t. Tiberini, 203: **1**, Aurel, xxxv 4; **2** xxxv 7
Barhathes Maesom, eq xx Palm, 226–251: **83** 19
Barathes Zebida, eq xx Palm, t. Tiberini, 198: **1**, Aurel, xxxiv 13; **2** xxxiv 11
Baṛḅ...[, xx Palm, ca. 207–238: **94** c 3
Barbaesomen, -ius, *see also* Aurelius, Domitius, Seleucus
Barbaesamen, *cogn*, eq xx Palm, t. Tiberini, 202: **1** xxxiv 30; **2** xxxiv 28
Barbaesamen, *nom*, xx Palm, c. Antonini post, 205: **2** xxviii 10
[Barba]essam[en], *cogn*, xx Palm, c. Danymi, 202–219: **1** iii–v f 3
Barbaesamen Male, eq xx Palm, t. Zebida, 203: **1**, Aurel, xxxii 32, Barbaessamen; **2** xxxiii 12
Barbaiatis: **64** ii 11 app
Barbasatis, *see* Cronius
Barca.[, *see* Aurelius
Barcha[, *see* Aurelius
Ḅ[ar]c̣ḥ[alb-, status unknown, Dura in 216: **89** *42* 3 and app
Barchalbas, *see also* Aurelius, Zabbaeus: **8** ix 20 app; **56** 2 app
Barchalba[, addressee, status unknown, Dura in 216: **89** *14* verso 1; *15* verso app
Bareus [-6?-]c̣hi, xx Palm, c. Antonini post, 202: **2** xxvii 19 and app
Bargas, *see also* Aurelius
Aurel Bargạ[, xx Palm, c. Malchiana, 214: **1** xxix 7
Bargas, cent xx Palm, 216–251: pp. 128, 132, 133, 136; **16** recto 2; **17** a 2, 3, 4, 6, 9; **19** 4 app; 5; **66** b ii 21; b i 19 app
Barginnaia, *see* Meheridates
Barhadadus, *see also* Aurelius, Gaius, Iulius
Barhadadus: **89** *2* 18 app
Aurel Barhadad[, xx Palm, c. Malchiana, 216: **1** xxxi 5
Barhadadus Abidfur, eq xx Palm, t. Octaui, 201: **1** xxxix 23, Abifur; **2** xxxix 26
Barhadadus Haeran[, eq xx Palm, t. Zebida, 199: **1** xxxi 37; **2** xxxii 10 and app
A[urel Barha]ḍadus Mombogei, eq xx Palm, t. Zebida, 194–195: **1** xxxi 30
Barhaei, *see* Abdaeus
Barhathes, *see* Barathes
Barhotarus, xx Palm: **1** xxxiii 10 marg
Barhotarus Auidalathi, eq xx Palm, t. Antonini, 199: **1**, Aurel, xli 27; **2** xli 15
Baricas Iarhaei, xx Palm, c. Antonini post, 214: **1**, Aurel, xiv 1; **2** xxix 23
Baricbelus Bassi, xx Palm, 204: c. Seleuciana, **6** xi 8; c. Castrici, **1** xvii 16; c. Antonini pr, **2** xxii 25
Barichius [, *nom*, Egypt, c. Belei, 180–205: **81** iii 2
Bariton: **34** recto ii 1 app
Barlahas, *see also* Antonius, Aurelius, Iulius, Mocimus

Barlahas [I]arḥ[-, xx Palm, c. Mariani, 200–201: **1**, Aurel, xxii 1; **2** xvii 9
Barn[, *see* Themarsa
Barnabus: **83** 10 app
Barne[, *see* Mocimus
Barne[, *nom*, xx Palm, c. Mariani, 214: **2** xix 20
Barnaeus, *see also* Aelius, Aurelius, Demetrius, Domitius, Iarhaeus, Mocimus, Zebida
Barnaeus, *cogn*, xx Palm, c. Marci, 204: **1** vii 23; **2** xiii 2
Barnae[us . . . .]ḷ, eq xx Palm, t. Octaui, 197–225; **92** x 3
Barneus Iaraḅ[ol-, xx Palm, c. Danymi, 214: **6** i 35; **50** i 9 app
Barnaeus Iarhaei, eq xx Palm, t. Antonini, 203: **1**, Aurel, xlii 20, Ierhaei; **2** xlii 12, Barneus
Barnaeus Themarsa, eq xx Palm, t. Demetri, 206: **1**, Aurel, xxxviii 4; **2** xxxviii 12, Barneus
Aurel Barnaeus Zabdil . [, xx Palm, c. Marci, 201: **1** vi 26
Aurel Barnaeus Zebida, eq xx Palm, t. Tiberini, 195: **1** xxxiv 5
[Aure]l Barneus Zebi(da), xx Palm, ca. 190–230: **41** 6. Same as preceding?
Barnebus, *see* Mombogaeus, Themarsas, Vlpius
Barnisianus, *see* Aurelius
Baṛṛil . [, *cogn*, xx Palm, c. Antonini post, 216: **1** xv 22. Aurelius B. ?
Bars[. . . .]ṣ, *see* Aurelius
Baṛs . [, *cogn*, xx Palm, c. Marci, 214: **2** xiv 6
Bars . [, *cogn ?*, xx Palm, c. Antonini post, 216: **1** xv 23. Aurelius B. ?
Barsemias, *see also* Aurelius, Domitius, Vlpius; **83** 13 app
Barsemias Bụḅ[, xx Palm, c. Marci, 195: **6** ii 27
Barṣẹ[mias, *cogn*, xx Palm, 191–216: **89** *4* ii 3
Barsimsus, *see also* Aurelius, Bassus, Hadadsabus, Romanus, Vareus, Vlpius
Aurel Barsim[, xx Palm, c. Malchiana, 216: **1** xxxi 1
[B]arsịnes Mannosin, xx Palm, ca. 215–240: **15** ii 12
Barsumius, *see* Vlpius Barsimsus
Barsummares, *see* Aurelius
Barzas Marea, xx Palm, c. Marci, 204: **1**, Aurel, vii 12: **2** xii 25
Aurel Bas . . [, xx Palm, c. Marci, 214: **1** ix 26
Basileus, *see* Aurelius
Ḅaṣiliạ[nus ?: **92** vi 18 app
Basṣạ . . [, *see* Aurelius
Aurel Ḅaṣṣ[-, xx Palm, c. Marci, 207: **1** viii 2
Bassus, *see also* Abgellus, Aelius, Afarnes, Antonius, Aurelius, Baricbelus, Iulius, Lucilius, Rabbulas, Valerius, Vlpius
Bassus, cent, xxii Deiot ?, early i p.: **51** ii 16
Bassus, *nom*, xx Palm, c. Danymi, 204: **2** vii 27
Aurel Bassus[, xx Palm, c. Danymi, 201–205: **1** ii 7
Bạ[ssu]s, *cogn*, xx Palm, c. Marci, 214: **2** xiv 25. Cf. 25–26 with **8** iv 11–12
Bassus [-3 ?-] . bọl[.]a, xx Palm, c. Danymi, 203–216: **92** viii 7
] . l Bassus, xx Palm, c. Marci, 209–216: **92** viii 16
Aurel Bassus[, xx Palm, c. Marci, 216: **1** x 6
Bassus, xx Palm: **1** xxx 14 marg
Bassus, xx Palm, ca. 205–240: **12** a–c 4
] . el Bassus, xx Palm, ca. 210–240: **13** 13
Bassus [. . . .] . ịṃi, xx Palm, c. Prisci, ca. 215–240: **15** ii 8
Bassus Antoni[n-, eq xx Palm, t. Antonini, 201: **1**, Aurel, xlii 3; **2** xli 27
Bassus Barsimsi, xx Palm, 205: c. Seleuciana, **6** xi 13; c. Antonini pr, **2** xxiii 5; **8** viii 6
Bassus Bibi, sing xx Palm, t. Octaui 204: **1** xl 11 app; **2** xl 18 and app
Bassus Diomedi: **1** viii 2 app; **2** xiii 14 app
Bassus Gora, xx Palm, c. Danymi, 216: **6** ii 17; **2** x 26
Bassus Maccei, xx Palm, c. Prisci, ca. 215–240: **15** i 17
Aurel Bassus Malchi, eq xx Palm, t. Antonini, 195: **1** xli 18
Bassus Montan[, eq xx Palm, t. Antonini, 199: **1**, Aurel, xli 29; **2** xli 17
Bassus Nassibeli, xx Palm, c. Mariani, 214: **1**, Aurel, xxiv 3; **2** xix 12; **8** vi 16
Aurel Bassus Salman, vex xx Palm, t. Octaui, 195: **1** xxxviii 23
Bassus Sịạ . . . ṇ, xx Palm, ca. 215–240: **15** ii 2
Bassus Tiberini, eq xx Palm, t. Zebida, 201: **1**, Aurel, xxxii 12; **2** xxxii 24
[B]aṣṣus Tiberini, xx Palm, c. Danymi, 210: **6** i 30
]ḅẹaṣṭ[. .]s A[, xx Palm, ca. 205–240: **42** 8
Βηκις Νεωτ, Egypt, coh eq, 157–182 or 189–214: **78** *11* 6
Bel[, *see* Malchus; **15** f 1 app
Belaacabus, *see also* Aurelius, Iarhaeus, Iulius, Mammaeus, Mazabanas
Bẹḷạç[abi: **1** xxxii 27 app
Belaacabus Abgari, eq xx Palm, t. Tiberini, 201: **1**, Aurel, xxxiv 24; **2** xxxiv 22
Belaacabus Hala, eq xx Palm, t. Zebida, 199: **1** xxxi 40 app; **2** xxxii 13
Belaacabus Iarhaei, xx Palm, c. Marci, 214: **2** xiv 10; **8** iv 2
Belacabus Z . [, eq xx Palm, t. Antonini, 201: **1**, Aurel, xlii 1; **2** xli 25
Belahaḅẹaṛus, *see* Aurelius
Beleni: **34** recto ii 9 app
Beleus (Bellaeus ?) Zabdeus, cent, Egypt, 180–205: **81** ii 12–13
Belihabi, *see* Garmelus

Bellaei, *see* Hanina- and cf. Beleus
Bellaeus: **2** viii 12 app
Bellaeus Oga, magister campi xx Palm, 208–233: **48** 8
Bellenius: **34** recto ii 9 app
Belsur, *see* Aelamis
Bernicianus, *see also* Aurelius
Bernicianus Silua[n-, xx Palm, c. Marci, 204: **1** vii 9; **2** xii 23
Berosas Valens, eq xx Palm, t. Octaui, 196: **1**, Aurel, xxxviii 31; **2** xxxviii 31
Besarion, *see* Leon
Besarion, *cogn*, Egypt, 217: **40** i 9
Besarion, Egypt, coh eq, 132–217: **78** *10* 6
Besarion Isidori, Vet Gall, t. Sereni Melanos, 154–179: **76** xii 19; 22, βησαρ; xiii 7
Biaeus Addaei, xx Palm, ca. 215–240: **15** i 4 app
Bibi, *see* Bassus
Bitecus, Vet Gall, t. Donaciani, 105–130: **80** 21, 27 app
Bitsius, Vet Gall, t. Donaciani, 105–130: **80** 27
Bius Longon, III Cyr, c. Subureana, 91–116: **34** recto i 17
Bland[, *see* Petronius
Bobe.[, *see* Mammaeus
Bode, *see* Malchus
Bolaeus, *see also* Aurelius
Bolaeus Mocimi, eq xx Palm, t. Tiberini, 200: **1**, Aurel, xxxiv 18; **2** xxxiv 16
Bolanus, *see also* Aelius, Bolanus, Mocimus
Bolanus Bolani, eq xx Palm, t. Octaui, 201: **1**, Aurel, xxxix 17; **2** xxxix 20
Boliadaeus Iarhaei, xx Palm, c. Marci, 214: **1** ix 2; **2** xiv 13; **8** iv 5
Aurel Boliadaeus Ẓ[a]ọṛa, eq xx Palm, t. Antonini, 193: **1** xli 15
Boliadaeus Zebida, eq xx Palm, t. Antonini, 204: **1** xliii 1; **2** xlii 25
Bolianus, *see* Aurelius
Bora, *see* Acibas, Iarhaeus
Bore, *see also* Gaddes
Bores Nisamsi, eq xx Palm, t. Zebida, 199: **1**, Aurel, xxxii 1; **2** xxxii 14
Boui[us?, Egypt, cent XXII Deiot?, early I p.: p. 198; **51** i 1
Bụḅ[, *see* Barsemias
Bu[.]ṛaṇ[.].us Maccei, xx Palm, c. Antonini post, 203: **2** xxvii 24. Bucranius?
Buccaeus, *see* Abedlahas, Aurelius, Barathes, Iarhaboles, Themarsas
Buzi, *see* Themarsas

Ç[, xx Palm, 225–256: **4** j 5
Çạ[, *see* Ofellius
Caecilianus, *see* Aurelius
Caecilius: **9** 24 b app
A Caecilius Faustinus, legatus, Moesia Inf.: pp. 219, 220, 221; **63** i 30, 31 app, 32 app; ii 4
Caeli(anus), *see* Domitius
Caerellius: **34** recto i 4 app
Cerelius Rufus, III Cyr, c. Ninni Rufi, 91–116: **34** recto i 4 and app
Καιμης: **79** 14 app
Caesarion: **40** i 9 app
Aurel Cal[, xx Palm, c. Marci, 214: **1** ix 27
L Cal..[ ].us, III Cyr, 65–96: **9** 27 a
Ç[al]efofes: **20** 18 app
Calligonus Cleonici, curator, Vet Gall, t. Aeli Sereni, 154–179: **76** xxi 5
Calpurnius, *see* Aurelius
Calpu[rn]ius Gaulianus, xx Palm, c. Marci, 214?: p. 394; **6** iv 2 and cf. **1** ix 27, **94** b ii 3
Camaṛiusis, Egypt, eq aux, second quarter of II p.: **73** a iii 2
Καμης (Καιμης) Ορσει (Ορσε), Vet. Gall, t. Gemelli, 154–179: **76** xiii 9 and 22
Candidus, *see* Sempronius
[C]anidius C.f., Egypt, III Cyr or XXII Deiot, I a.: **36** 2
Cantius, Egypt, cent aux, early II p.: **77** b 1
[Κ]ανωπου, *cogn*, Egypt, end of III p.: **11 bis** c 6
Capito Fana: **34** recto ii 10 app
Capiton, *see also* Aelius, Aurelius, Salius
Capiton, Egypt, eq aux, second quarter of II p.: **73** a ii 4
Capra, *see* Cuṛ..ịṭịụs
Çapṭ[, *see* Fabius
Car...: **9** 18 a app
Carus, dec I Hisp Vet, ca. 76–105: **63** ii 25
Κασιανος, *see* Cassianus
Casis, *see* Ammonius
Κασις Απιτος, Vet Gall, t. Lucilli, 154–179: **76** xi 2 and 11
Casius: **67** 7 app
Cassianus, *see also* Aurelius, Iulius, Lucius, Rufus
Cassianus, Egypt, cent coh eq, 162–187?: **78** *69* 2; *14* 3 app
Cassianus Ni...ṛ, xx Palm, 204: c. Malchiana, **1**, [Aurel], xxvii 25; c. Malchi, **2** ii a 5 and app; c. Pudentis, **92** ix 9
Cassi, *see* Seleucus
Cassius Artemidorus, Egypt, eq coh eq, 152–177 or 184–209: **78** *34* 8–9
Q Cassius Ḍọ[r]us, III Cyr, 65–96: **9** 10 a; 34–37 app
Cassius Habitus: **76** xi 2 app
Cassius Heronianus, Egypt, principalis aux, 183: **39** 16
Cassius Malchus, xx Palm, ca. 215–240: **15** ii 20
Cassius S...mi, Egypt, principalis aux, 177: **39** 9
Cassius Sacoṇ[a, xx Palm, c. Malchiana, 204: **6** ix 20; **1** xxviii 2

Castor, *see* Aurelius, Iulius
Ạ[urel -2?-].ius Castricius, cent xx Palm, 205: **1** xvi 8–9; 10 app
]πρριω Κελε̣[, xx Palm, ca. 213–247: **35** 5
Celer, *see also* Domitius, Flauius, Sossius: **10** 26 app
C[ele]r?, cent I Aug Lus, 92–117: **74** ii 2: κ[ελε?]ρος, *genitive*
Celerianus: **10** 26 app
Celerinus: **10** 26 app
Celerius: **34** recto i 4 app
Celsianus, praefectus III Itur in 103: **87** 2
]c̣ina Celsus, III Cyr, 65–90: **58** i 37
Κενες, Vet Gall, t. Aeli Sereni, 154–179: p. 285; **76** xxi 1
Lucius Cerel[: **34** recto i 4 app
Cerelius: **52** b 12 app
Cerelius Rufus, III Cyr, c. Ninni Rufi, 91–116: **34** recto i 4 and app
C. Cerficius Fuscus, III Cyr, 65–96: **9** 25 a
Cḥ[, Egypt, cent?, end of III p.: **11 bis** a 2
Chaeremon Maximi, Vet Gall, t. Aeli Sereni, 154–179: **76** xv 10 and 17
Ç[ha]ẹremon Se.[ ]., xx Palm, c. Marci, 216: **2** xv 16
Chaeremonianus, *see* Antonius, Iulius
Chares, Egypt, eq aux, second quarter of II p.: **73** a iii 9
Charifas Iuli, xx Palm, c. Danymi, 204: **6** i 22
Charinus: **32** 3 app
Chaseti, *see* Themarsas
Chierax: **20** 10 app
Çḥresp[, *see* Erasmius
...λεις (ι̣ο̣υ̣λεις?) Χρ̣η̣σ̣τ̣ο̣ρ̣α̣ν̣.[, Egypt, coh eq, 150–175 or 182–207: **78** *16* 1
Chu.[: **81** iii 12 app
Cl[, *nom*, Egypt, c. Theopropi, 194: **5** ii 19
[....]idaṣ Çḷ.b....[, xx Palm, c. Germani, 246: **66** a ii 17
Clarus, dec Vet Gall, 154–179: p. 285; **76** xii 17
Claudius, *see* Aurelius
Claudius, Egypt, eq aux, second quarter of II p.: **73** a iii 18
Aurelius Claudius[, xx Palm, c. Mariani, 214: **1** xxv 2
[C]laụḍị[us, *nom*, xx Palm, c. Danymi, 215: **8** ii 23
Claudius, Egypt, optio? coh eq, 132–217: **78** *9* 6–7
Claudius Agatho, III Cyr, c. Aufri Aculi minoris, 91–116: **34** recto ii 13
Cl Agrippas, curator xx Palm, 200–230: **47** i 7
Aurel Claudius Antoni.[, xx Palm, c. Malchiana, 209–212: **1** xxix 2
Claudius Antoninus, xx Palm, c. Antonini post, 207: **1**, Aurel, xiii 4; **2** xxviii 20
Claudius Antoninus, III Cyr, c. Ninni Rufi, 91–216: **34** recto i 7
Claudius Apollinarius, III Cyr, c. Pompei Epane, 91–116: **34** recto ii 22, Apulinar
Claudius Apollinarius, Egypt, principalis aux, 175: **39** 7
Claudius Clemens, III Cyr, c. Pompei Epane, 91–116: **34** recto ii 21, Clemes
Claudius Dadona, eq xx Palm, 205 or 208: **1** xliii 11; **2** xliii 9; **89** *41* 13 app
Cl Hairan, xx Palm, c. Malchiana, 214: **6** x 3
Cl Iul Maximus, sing xx Palm, c. Antonini post, 222: **2** xxxi 21; ii a 5 app
Çḷ Iul Secundus, sing xx Palm, c. Antonini post, 222: **2** xxxi 22; ii a 5 app
P Claudius Iustus, praefectus I Theb eq: **63** i 24 app
Cl Maximus, eq xx Palm, t. Coccei, 207–232: **27** b i 9
Claudius Milens, xx Palm, c. Mariani, 214: **8** vi 11
Aurel Claudius Mombogeus, dupl xx Palm, t. Demetri, 193: **1** xxxvi 4
Claudius Natalius, eq xx Palm, t. Demetri, 205: **1**, Aurel, xxxvii 29; principalis, notation lost, **2** xxxvii 29; sig, **47** i 17
Claudius Romanus, cent, Egypt, early II p.: **77** a i 2 and 7
Claudius Sabinus, Egypt, c. Belei, 180–205: **81** ii 14
Claudius Siluanus, sing xx Palm, t. Demetri, 205: **1** xxxvii 32
Claudius Sotericus, xx Palm, c. Mariani, 214: **1** xxiv 12; **2** xix 19
Claudius Terentianus, p. 245, note 1
Claudius Theanus, III Cyr, c. Subureana, 91–116: **34** recto i 12, Feanus
Claudius Tiberinus, xx Palm, c. Marci, 212: **6** iii 29; **1**, Aurel, viii 12; **2** xiii 24
Cl Zebida, xx Palm, c. Danymi, 203: **6** i 14; **92** viii 6
Cl Zebidas, xx Palm, 191–216: **89** *4* ii 5. Same as preceding?
Claudius Zenon, III Cyr, c. Subureana, 91–116: **34** recto i 11
Cleme[n-, *see* Antonius
Clemens, *see also* Claudius, Cocceius, Flauius, Marius, Suedius
]ṇụs Clemens, Egypt, 217: **40** i 7
Cleonici, *see* Calligonus
Cleides, *see* Iulius
P Clodius Secundus, III Cyr, 65–96: **9** 6 a
Cọ[, *see* Aurelius
Co..ṇụṣ, *see* Marrius
Co.[.....]s Theon, Vet Gall, t. Subatiani, 154–179: **76** ix 13

Cocas, Vet Gall, t. Donaciani, 105–130: **80** 16
Cocceianus: **6** v 16 app
Cocceius, *see also* Aurelius, Didas
Cocceius, dec xx Palm, 207–232: **27** b i 8. Same as Aurel Cocceius, dupl c. Danymi, 214?
Cocceius Clemens, III Cyr, c. Ninni Rufi, 91–116: **34** recto i 5
Cocceius S.[, xx Palm, c. Antonini post, 202–215: **6** v 16
Coddaeus, *see* Aurelius
Coenodis, *see* Positus
Colluthi, *see* Onnophris
Colluthes, Egypt, eq aux, second quarter of II p.: **73** a iii 17
Colluthi, *cogn*, Vet Gall, t. Iuli, 154–179: **76** iv 11
Coṃ[, *see* Gaius
Coṃạṛ[: **81** ii 3 app
Comari, *see* Comarus
Comarini: **81** ii 3 app
Comarinus, *see* Victor
Comarus Comari, Egypt, coh eq, c. Heracliani, 150–175 or 182–207: **78** *23* 1
Comazon, *see* Valerius
Conilus: **78** *21* 1 app
Conọṇ[, *nom*, xx Palm, c. Antonini pr, 214: **2** xxiv 4
Conon, Egypt, dec coh eq, 152–177 or 184–209: **78** *8* 2; *29* 1–2; *63* 1; *66* 1
Κονού[*φιος*: **78** *8* 2 app
Copres, Egypt, cibariator coh eq, 132–217: **78** *46* 1
Coranus: **81** ii 3 app
[C]ordius: **20** 4 app
Cornelian̩[, *cogn*, Egypt, 218: **40** i 18
Cornelianus, *see* Iulius
Cornelius: **34** verso i 2 app; **58** i 37 app
Cornelius Sex. f., III Cyr or XXII Deiot, I a.: **36** 4
Cornelius Egrilianus, cent III Cyr: **38** i 11 app
Cornelius Iulianus, cent, Egypt, middle of III p.: **67** 12
Cornelus, *cogn*, Egypt, c. Domiti Caeli(ani), 91–116: **34** verso i 2
Cosanus: **24** 12 app; **81** ii 3 app
Cosminus, *see* Atilius
Cottius: **67** 7 app
Crescens, *see also* Vibius; **133** 1 app
Crescens, cent I Aug Lus, 92–117: **74** i 9–10
Crisp.[, *see* Marin˙, Valerius
Crispinus, *see* Aurelius, Iulius; **72** 5 app; **133** 1 app
Crispus, *see also* Antonius; **72** 5 app; **133** 1 app
Crispus, *cogn*, III Cyr, 65–90: **58** i 38
Crispus, Egypt, eq aux, second quarter of II p.: **73** a i 16
Cronion, *see also* Aurelius
Cronion: **2** ix 21 app
Cronius Barbasatis, I Aug Lus, t. Saluiani, 156: **64** ii 11
Cronṇ[, *see* Flauius
Cru....[: **45** 1 app
Cumesiu[s]: **81** iii 10 app
Cuṛ..ịtịuṣ Capra, librarius? III Cyr, 65–90: **58** ii 10
Curiatius: **58** ii 10 app
Cutratus, *see* Quadratus
Cyrillus, *see* Aurelius
[Cy]rillus: **17** a 6 app

D[, *see* Aurelius, Dioscorus
D[, *nom*, Egypt, 192–217: **5** iii 2
Aurel D[, xx Palm, c. Marci, 214: **1** ix 12
].ṣas D.[, xx Palm, c. Marci, 214: **2** xiv 5
Aurel Ḍ..[, xx Palm, c. Marci, 214: **1** ix 20
]ẹl Ḍ[, *cogn*, xx Palm, ca. 215–240: **15** i 4
D...ụpor, Vet Gall, t. Donaciani, 105–130: **80** 31
Dadona, *see also* Claudius
[δα]δωνας[: **89** *41* 13 app
Dalathus: **2** xliii 17 app
Danymus, *see* Septimius
Ḍạocle[i]ḍẹṣ: **66** a ii 17 app
Ḍaṛṇachẹụ[s: **19** 7 app
Δχηουτος, *gen*, *see* Paësis
De.[, *see* Aurelius
De.[, *cogn*, xx Palm, c. Marci, 214: **2** xiv 22
D Decri(us?), cent III Cyr, 65–96: **9** 8 f–n; 20 f–k
[De]ḷfidius: **20** 1 app
]dem.[, xx Palm, c. Antonini post, 210?: **2** xxix 7
Demetrius, *see also* Aurelius, Flauius, Futtianius, Sempronius, Serapion, Vlpius; **73** d 4 app
[D]ẹṃetṛịụs, *cogn*, xx Palm, c. Malchiana, 214: **1** xxix 32
Demetrius, *cogn*, xx Palm, c. Marci, 214: **8** iv 13
[Dem]etrius, *cogn*, xx Palm, 191–216: **89** *4* ii 15
Demetrius, *cogn*, xx Palm, 208–233: **48** 8
Demetrius, xx Palm, ca. 215–240: **15** i 12
]ḍṛus Demetrius, xx Palm, ca. 215–240: **15** ii 13
Demetrius Bannaei, xx Palm, c. Antonini post, 199: **6** iv 26; **1** xi 19, Baṛ[n]ạẹi, and app
Demetrius Maccaei, eq xx Palm, t. Antonini, 200: **1**, Aurel, xli 32; **2** xli 20
Demetrius Z.[...]ṇ.[, eq xx Palm, t. Demetri, 205: **1** xxxvii 31; **2** xxxviii 2
[Deme]ṭrius Ẓạabal, xx Palm, ca. 190–230: **41** 2
Demnu.[, *name?*, xx Palm, ca. 207–238: **94** b ii 2
Δεμουρους, *genitive?*, *see* Asclepiades
Demosthenes, *see also* Aurelius
Demosthenes Eponuchus, Egypt, sesq, first half of III p.: **85** 2
Di.[, *see* Areius
Diadumeniacus, **30** i 3 app
δια*σ*....?, practor?, Egypt, coh eq, 156–182 or 189–214: **78** *6* 11 and app

Aurel Dicaeus Themarsa, drom xx Palm, c. Marci, 193: **1** xliii 25
Didas Coccei, eq xx Palm, t. Demetri, 201: **1**, Aurel, xxxvii 4; **2** xxxvii 6; **26** b 4
Didas Salman, xx Palm, 204; c. Castrici, **1** xvii 17; c. Antonini pr, **2** xxii 26
Didumachi, *see* Diosdorus
Didumanti: **52** b 13 app
Didymianus, Egypt, cent coh eq, 132–217: **78** *56* 1
Didymi, *see* Apollos
Didymus: **20** 4 app
Didumus Ẹ[, Egypt, end of III p.: **11 bis** a 14
Didymus Horigenes, Egypt, aux, I/II p.: **38** i 9
Didymus Pachom[, Egypt, coh eq, 153–178 or 185–210: **78** *67* 1
Διηουτος, genitive: **76** xv 11 app
Dinaei, *see* Maronas, Themarsa
Diodorus, *see* Aurelius
Diogenes, *see* Herennius, Malchus, Pompeius
Diomedes, *see also* Aurelius, Bassus
.[-8?- Di]ọmedi, xx Palm, 197–201: c. Castrici, **1**, Aurel, xvi 25; c. Antonini pr, **2** xxii 3
Diomedi, xx Palm, c. Marci, 207: **2** xiii 14 and app
Dionysianus, Egypt, cent? coh eq, 154–189 or 186–217: **78** *2* 7
Dionysius, *see also* Aurelius, Sopatrus
Dionysius, Egypt, eq aux, second quarter of II p.: **73** a i 19; ii 2 and 18
]s Dionysii, Vet Gall, t. Herodiani, 154–179: **76** iii 2
Dionysius, *cogn?*, xx Palm, c. Marini post, 240: **66** a i 10
Dionysius Artemidorus, Vet Gall, t. Herodiani, 154–179: **76** iii 1; BB 1
Dionysius Heraclei, Egypt, aux, I/II p.: **38** i 8
Dionysius Luçạ[, Egypt, early II p.: **11** ii 2
Dio[nysi]us P.[.]ọ[.]..ẹs, Vet Gall, t. Lycarionis, 154–179: **76** xix 1
Dionysius Sarapionis, sig Vet Gall, t. Apollinari, 154–179: **76** viii 28; xvi 19; BB 8
Diophanius: **77** a i 1 app
Dioscori, *see* Pasion, Polion
Dioscorus, Egypt, eq aux, second quarter of II p.: **73** a i 13; e 7 app
Dioscorus, Vet Gall, 154–179: **76** HH ii 3
Dioscoros, Egypt, practor, 136–161, 168–193, or 192–217: **78** *77* 3
Dioscorus D[, Egypt, coh eq, 152–178 or 184–210: **78** *68* 1
Dioscorus Didumanti: **52** b 13 app
Dioscorus Paḷ[, Egypt, coh eq, 132–217: **78** *70* 6
Diosdorus Didumachi, Egypt, coh eq quingenaria?, first quarter of III p.: **52** b 13
Dịr..[..]ạmuṣ .[, III Cyr, 65–96: **9** 18 a
Dius: **1** xvi 9 app
Dius, *nom*, xx Palm, c. Castrici, 204: **1** xvii 20
Ḍị[u]ṣ G.[.].us, xx Palm, c. Danymi, 214: **1** iii–v d 2; **2** ix 28
Aurel Ḍ[i]ụs Iarhaei, eq xx Palm, t. Tiberini, 195: **1** xxxiv 4
Dọ.ọ..ṣ[, III Cyr, 65–90: **58** ii 13
Doctus: **91** *1* i 6 app
Dolens: **80** 23 app
Domitius, *see* Aurelius, Iulius
Domitius, XXII Deiot?, early I p.: **51** ii 20
M Domitius [ ]..ạṭo, III Cyr, 65–96: **9** 31 a
Domitius, III Cyr or XXII Deiot, c. Domiti Caeli(ani?), 91–116: **34** verso i 4
Domittius, Vet Gall, t. Donaciani, 105–130: **80** 9
Domittius, Vet Gall, t. Donaciani, 105–130: **80** 24
Domitti, xx Palm, c. Antonini pr, 197–201: **2** xxii 5
Aurel Domẹ[ti-, xx Palm, c. Marci, 214: **1** ix 23
Domitius Antoninus, cent xx Palm, 200: pp. 157, 183; **6** iv 16–17, Antonini, Domittius Antoninus; **1** xi 1–2; xliii 30, Antonini; **2** xlv 10, Antonini post; **27** a i 13, Anton post; **92** iii 15, Anton post; **89** *12* ii 8 app; **118** 6?; **31** i 4?; **47** i 12?
Aurel Dometius Antoninus, eq xx Palm, t. Zebida, 207: **1** xxxiii 13. Same as following?
Domittius Antoninus, eq xx Palm, t. Tiberini 207: **2** xxxv 24
Dometius Barbaessamen, sesq drom xx Palm, c. Marci, 196: **1** xlii 23 and app; **2** xliv 12 and app, Dometius Barsemea
Domitius Barnaei, eq xx Palm, t. Tiberini, 202: **1** xxxiv 28; **2** xxxiv 26
Dometius Barsemea, *see* Dometius Barbaessamen
Domitius Caeli(anus?), cent III Cyr or XXII Deiot, 91–116: **34** verso i 1
C Domitius Ce[le]r, III Cyr, 65–96: **9** 2 a and app
Domitius F..[..]., III Cyr, 65–90: **58** ii 15
Domitius Germạ[n-, III Cyr, c. Antoni Longini, 91–116: **34** recto ii 8
Aurel Dometius Marcianus, xx Palm, c. Malchiana, 216: **1** xxxi 6
Dometius Nicolaus, xx Palm, c. Marci, 216: p. 97; **6** iv 6; **1** x 4; drom, **2** xliv 19; *not* drom, **8** v 3; *not* drom, **92** v 18
Domitius Philippus, praefectus Aegypti: **20** 3 app
[Do]metius P[ro]çlus, xx Palm, t. Octaui, 204: eq, **1**, Aurel, xl 12; vex, **2** xl 19, Domittius Proç[ul]us
C Domitius Rufus, sig I Aug Lus, c. Ta...., 92–117: **74** ii 9
Domittius Salman, xx Palm, c. Marci, 201: **6** iii 1
[Do]mitius Ṿ[ ].[, Egypt, classiarius, 144: **28** 8
Domẹ[tti]us Zeṇ[, xx Palm, c. Marci, 216–221: **2** xvi 3
Domnus, *see* Aurelius, Siluanus

Donacianus, dec Vet Gall, 105–130: **80** 1–2
Donatus, *cogn*, Egypt, 215?: **40** i 3
Dorus, *see* Cassius
Dositheus: **70** a i 18 app
Dulens, Vet Gall, t. Donaciani, 105–130: **80** 23
Dumans: **52** b 13 app
Ḍụṃanus Na.[, xx Palm, 211–236: **33** iv 2

E[, *see* Didymus, Eros, Herminus, Malchus
ϵ̣...γι, *genitive*, Egypt, cent coh eq, 132–217: **78** *53* 2. Herennius?
]eḅsuṛṃius: **15** ii 11 app
Ebucaei, *see* Iarhabus
Ecatus, Vet Gall, t. Donaciani, 105–130: **80** 26 and app
Egla, *see* Zebidas
Egnati(anus), *see* Paconius
L Egnatius, Egypt, optio c. Iuli[, early II p.: **77** a i 7
Egrilianus: **38** i 11 app
L Egrilius Optus: **77** a i 7 app
Emeritus: **91** *1* i 6 app
Emeritus, magister campi II Traian, first half of III p.: **102** a 8
Ẹṇ[, Egypt, cent coh eq, 148–174 or 185–206: **78** *19* 1; cf. *53* 2
T Ennius: **68** ii 32 app
Epane, *see* Pompeius
epị[.]..c.., *name?*, Egypt, second quarter of III p.: **53** a i 6
Eponuchus, *see also* Demosthenes
Eponuchus, Egypt, eq aux, second quarter of II p.: **73** a ii 15; b 5
Eponuchus, Egypt, c. Belei, 180–205: **81** iii 12
Eponuchus Apollinarius, Egypt, principalis, 174: **39** 5
Eponuchus Heraclidae, Egypt, coh aux, c. ϵ̣...γ̣ι, 149–174 or 181–206: p. 313; **78** *20* 1; *53* 1
Eppani, *genitive*: **34** recto ii 20 app
ἐρ[(*or* ἑρ[ ), *see* Asclepiades, Longinus
Ẹr.scia: **15** i 20 app
Eraclid, *see* Heraclid[
Erasmius Chresp[, Egypt, coh eq, 132–217: **78** *44* 1
Erasmus: **2** xx 23 app
Erennius, *see* Herennius
ἐρμ[(or ἑρμ[ ), *see* Aelius
Ermogenes, *see* Hermogenes
Eros Ẹ[, I Aug Lus, c. Semproniani, 136 or 154: **64** ii 31
Eṣsuṛṃius, xx Palm, ca. 215–240: **15** ii 11
Eṭiopịus Chu.[: **81** iii 12 app
Ẹụ[, *cogn?*, xx Palm, ca. 200–235: **61** ii 1
Euclides, *see* Flauius
Eudaemon, *see* Aurelius, Sossius
[Eu]daemon (Patermuthi?), Egypt, coh eq, 132–217: **78** *13* 1 and app
Eudaemon, *cogn*, Egypt, 217: **40** i 14
Eudaemon Sar[apa]m[monis], Egypt, coh eq, c. ωρη⟨γϵ⟩νους 148–173 or 180–205: **78** *72* 1
Eugenianus: p. 361
Eup⟨h⟩ranor, *see* Iulius
Euxemon, *see* Aurelius

F[, *see* Domitius, Iulius
Faber: **9** 22 a app
Fabianus, Egypt, coh eq, second quarter of II p.: **73** a ii 16; b 6 app
Q Fabius Ċapṭ[, III Cyr, 65–96: **9** 22 a
L Fabius Iustus, legatus, Moes. Inf.? in 101? 105?: pp. 219–21; **63** i 31 app; ii 4 app, 5, 25
Fanius Rulius (Fannius Rullus?), III Cyr, c. Ninni Rufi, 91–116: **34** recto i 9
Faustinus, *see* Caecilius, Vibius
Faustius Vib.[, Egypt, coh eq quingenaria, first quarter of III p.: **52** a 9
Faustus, *see* Aurelius
Feanus, *see* Claudius Theanus
Felix, *see also* Iulius, Valerius
Felix, Vet Gall, t. Donaciani, 105–130: **80** 29
Felix, *cogn*, eq xx Palm, t. Octaui, 203–224: **26** c 6
Felix, cent xx Palm, ca. 215–240: pp. 133, 158; **15** i 8, 19; ii 14, 20; d 2; b 10 app; **32** 12
Felici (*dative? genitive?*), xx Palm, ca. 215–240: **15** b 10
Filo.s, *see* Aurelius
Filotas?: **2** ix 34 app
].l[.]ẹsa[...]. Firmicus, Egypt, gubernator, 127–164: **59** i 6
Firminus, *see* Neratius
Firmus, *see also* Valerius: **59** i 6 app
Firmus, cent, XXII Deiot?, early I p.: **51** ii 22
[F]iṛṃus, *cogn*, xx Palm, c. Mariani, 210: **2** xviii 26
Ḟḷ.[, *see* Aurelius
Fl.[.....].sus, sing xx Palm, c. Danymi, 206–208: **2** viii 13
Ḟḷ[, *nom*, xx Palm, c. Germani, ca. 215–240: **15** c 4
Flamininus: **24** 7 and 14 app
Flaminus (Flaminius?), dec, Egypt, 213–242: p. 146; **24** 7 and 14
Fla[ui-, *nom*, xx Palm, c. Antonini post, 208?: **8** x 15. Flauius Flauianus? *see* 15–16 app
Fl[aui-, xx Palm, status unknown, Dura in 221: **109** 1
Flau[i-, xx Palm, ca. 215–240: **15** i 3
Flauianus, *see* Flauius; Flauia(nus), **58** ii 8 app
Flauius, *see also* Aurelius, Iulius; **8** viii 25 app; **85** 1 app

Flauius, III Cyr, 65–96: **9** 21 a
Flauius, *nom*, xx Palm, c. Antonini pr, 214: **8** viii 25 and app
Flaui[us -4?-]erni[a]ṇus, xx Palm, c. Antonini pr, 214: **2** xxiii 29 and app
Flauius, *nom*, xx Palm, c. Antonini pr, 221: **2** xxvi 7
Flauius, xx Palm, ca. 215–240: **15** i 15
Flauius? Antoninus: **77** b 7 app
Flauius Antoninus, Egypt, coh eq, 132–157: **78** *73* 2
T Flauius Celer, Egypt, 62–80: pp. 116, 117; **10** 26
Flauius Clemens, III Cyr, c. Subureana, 91–116: **34** recto i 18, Flaus Clemes
Fḷ(auius) Cronụ[, Egypt, I/II p.: **38** ii 13
Ạ[urel] Flauius Demetri[, sesq xx Palm, t. Tiberini, 206; **1** xxxiii 30
Aurel Flauius Demetrius, eq xx Palm, t. Zebida, 209: **1** xxxiii 16
Fl(auius) Demetrius, xx Palm, c. Seleuciana, 214: **6** xi 34; **8** viii 25 app
Fl(auius) Demetrius, principalis xx Palm, 229: **95** b 8
Flauius Demetrius alt(er), sig xx Palm, 214–239: **50** i 3 and 9
Flauius Demetrius, xx Palm, c. Prisci, ca. 215–240: **15** i 23
Flauius Demetrius, dupl, Egypt, first half of III p.: **85** 1
Fl(auius) Demetrius, xx Palm, ca. 205–240: **12** e 3
Aurel Flauius Euclides, sig xx Palm, t. Zebida, 201: **1** xxxii 16
Flauius Flauianus, xx Palm, c. Antonini post, 208: **1**, Aurel, xiii 8: **2** xxviii 25; **8** x 15–16 app
T Flauius Frontinus Heraclius, vir perfectissimus, Praef Aegypti?: **11** ii 3 app
Flauius Gerthianus, III Cyr, c. Subureana, 91–116: **34** recto i 13, Flaus Gerfeanus
Fl(auius) Heliodorus, eq xx Palm, t. Coccei, 207–232: **27** b i 10
Flauius Marinus, eq xx Palm, t. Octaui, 196: **1**, Aurel, xxxviii 30; **2** xxxviii 30
Flauius Marinus, eq xx Palm, t. Tiberini, 205: **1**, Aurel, xxxv 18; **2** xxxv 19
Flauius Monimus, eq xx Palm, t. Tiberini, 201: **1**, Aurel, xxxiv 26; **2** xxxiv 24
Flauius Ṇẹ..[, xx Palm, ca. 215–240: **15** i 5
Flauius Nicomachus, sig xx Palm, c. Danymi, 196: notation lost, **1**, Aurel, i 10; sig, **2** vi 23
T Flauius Niger, III Cyr, 65–96: **9** 14 a; 34–37 app
Ḟḷạ[ui]us Numerị[, sing xx Palm, c. Antonini pr, 222: **2** xxvi 12
T Flauius Priscus, III Cyr, 65–96: **9** 13 a; 34–37 app
Flauius Ṛọṃạṇ[u]s, sing xx Palm, c. Antonini post, 222: **2** xxxi 23
T Flauius Satur[, Egypt, 62–90: **10** 11; 16 app
Flauius Serenus, curator Vet Gall, t. Sereni, 154–179: **76** xvii 8
Flauius Seuerianus, immunis? II Traian, 216: **21** 19
Flauius Seuerus: **85** 1 app
Flauius Siluanus, eq xx Palm, t. Octaui, 205: **1**, Aurel, xl 15; **2** xl 22
T Flauius Vale.[, Egypt, 62–81: p. 117; **10** 17
T Flauius Vale..., III Cyr, 65–96: **9** 34 a
A Flauius Vespasianus, dec I Aug Lus, 134: **64** i 39
Flauius Vlpianus, immunis? II Traian, 210–242: **21** 7
Flauus, III Cyr, 65–90: **58** ii 8
Fortius Fortius, Egypt, principalis?, 178: **39** 12; **38** i 7 app
Fortunatus, *see* Aelius
Fra..., xx Palm, 194–219: **1** xxxiv 19 marg; xl 15 marg
Franius Seuerus, cent, Egypt, first half of III p.: **85** 1 and app
Ḟront[, *see* Iulius
Fronton, *see also* Aelius, Aurelius
Fronton Marea, eq xx Palm, t. Zebida, 204: **1**, Aurel, xxxii 34; **2** xxxiii 14
C Fu.g......ṛc̣.., III Cyr, 65–96: **9** 26 a
[Fu]fidius: **20** 1 app
Fuluius: **76** xx 1 app
Furianus, *see also* Messius
Furianus, dec Vet Gall, 154–179: **76** vi 1; xii 20; GG 2; vi 1 app
Furius: **9** 26 a app
Fuṣc̣ianius Demọ[: **21** 9 app
Fuscus, *see* Cerficius
Fuṭṭianius Demẹ[trius?, immunis? II Traian, 217–242: **21** 9

G̣[, *see* Aurelius, Iulius
G.[.].us, *see* Dius
G̣[.]l[, Egypt, eq, 180–205: **81** ii 1
G̣[....]eụ.[, droṃ xx Palm, c. Malchiana, 219: **1** xliv 19
G̣[-7?- Apo]ḷḷọ[, eq xx Palm, t. Tiberini, 203: **2** xxxv 3
G̣[..]sces Maxim[, xx Palm, c. Antonini post, 212: **2** xxix 9 and app
Gạ[, *cogn*, xx Palm, c. Mariani, 204–206: **2** xviii 3
[-7?-] es G̣abrion, drom xx Palm, 196; c. Malchiana, **1**, Aurel, xliv 14; c. Malchi, **2** xliii 19
Gabrion Obean, eq xx Palm, t. Zebida, 205: **1**, Aurel, xxxiii 9; **2** xxxiii 25
Gadde, *see* Maronas, Theobol(us)

Gaddes Auidus, Egypt, c. Belei, 180–205: **81** ii 16
Gaddes Bore, xx Palm, c. Antonini post, 217: **6** v 30; **1**, Aurel, xvi 3, Gadde; **2** xxxi 16
Γαδδειβωλιοι: **1** xli 34 app
Ga[ddi]bolus, eq xx Palm, t. Antonini, 201: **1** xli 34 app
Gaddius: **81** ii 16 app
L Gae.[, Egypt, 187–230: **46** 1
Gai[, *see* Licinnius
Aurel Gai..[, xx Palm, c. Marci, 214: **1** ix 21
Gaianus, *see also* Aurelius, Apollinarius, Iulius, Vlpius; **55** b 4 app
Gaianus, Vet Gall, t. Donaciani, 105–130: **80** 18
Gaianus, cent I Aug Lus, 131–156: **64** i 40; ii 1 app
Aurel [.].[..]s Gaia[n]us, eq xx Palm, t. Octaui, 214: **1** xl 23. Perhaps same as sesq, **2** xxxviii 28, and cent, **27** a ii 6
[G]aianus, *cogn*, drom xx Palm, c. Mariani, 215?: **8** vii 24
Gaianus, *cogn*, xx Palm, ca. 190–230: **41** 9
Gaianus, cent xx Palm, 207–232: **27** a ii 6. Perhaps same as **1** xl 23; sesq **2** xxxviii 28
Gaianus Iarhabole: **47** i 3 app
Gaianus Themarsa, eq xx Palm, t. Tiberini, 200: **1**, Aurel, xxxiv 17; **2** xxxiv 15
Gainus: **80** 25 app
Gaius, *see also* Aelius, Aurelius, Iulius, Priscus, Sammas
]d[.]a[nus] Gai, xx Palm, 204: c. Castrici, **1** xvii 8 and app; c. Antonini pr, **2** xxii 18
Gaius Abidfur, eq xx Palm, t. Octaui, 201: **1**, Aurel, xxxix 19; **2** xxxix 22
Gaius Barhadadus, drom xx Palm, c. Antonini pr, 195: **2** xlv 4
Gaius Com[, Egypt, aux, I/II p.: **38** ii 12
Aurel Gaius Germanus, xx Palm, c. Malchiana, 219: **1** xxxi 17
Gaius Sal[, xx Palm, 193–244: **49** 2
Gaius Serenus, Vet Gall, t. Gemelli, 154–179: **76** vii 2 and 13
Galates, Egypt, eq aux, second quarter of II p.: **73** a iii 12
Galeris, *see* Gerelius
Gall...: **9** 27 a app
Gan[, cent I Aug Lus, 131–156: **64** ii 1
gar..[, *name?*, xx Palm, ca. 205–230: **55** b 4
Garmelus Belihabi, eq xx Palm, t. Antonini, 204: **1**, Aurel, xlii 30; **2** xlii 21
Gaulian[, xx Palm, 207–238: **94** b ii 3. Cf. **6** iv 2
Gaulianus, *see* Calpurnius
Ge.[-2?-]s, *see* Aelius
Gemellus, *see also* Veturius
Gemellus, Egypt, eq aux, second quarter of II p.: **73** a ii 12; b 2
Gemellus, dec Vet Gall, 154–179: **76** vii 2 and 14; xiii 9 and 16
Gemellus Themarsa, eq xx Palm, t. Tiberini, 203: **1**, Aurel, xxxv 3; **2** xxxv 6
Gemellus, Egypt, dec coh eq, 151–177 or 184–209: **78** *27* 1–2; *33* 1; *34* 3; *66* 5; *3* 2 app; *27* 1 app
[Geme]llus?: **2** vii 10 app
Genucius: **36** 1 app
Aurel Ger[, xx Palm, c. Antonini post, 204: **1** xii 8
Gerelius Asclepiades, xx Palm, c. Marci, 204: p. 97; **2** xii 27; **8** iii 16; **92** v 13, Galeris
Gerfeanus, *see* Flauius Gerthianus
Gerfennus: **34** recto i 13 app
Germa[n-, *see also* Domitius
Germa[n-, xx Palm, ca. 215–240: **15** i 9
].reip..inasianus G[er]ma[n-, xx Palm, ca. 215–240: **15** ii 3
Germanicus: **34** recto ii 8 app
Germanus, *see also* Aelius, Aponius, Aurelius, Gaius, Iulius, Sarapion, Sextilis, Valerius, Vlpius
Germanus, Vet Gall, t. Donaciani, 105–130: **80** 13
Germanus, *cogn*, sing xx Palm, c. Antonini post, 216: **2** xxx 21
Germanus, *nom*, xx Palm, 223?: **3** a 5
Germanus, *cogn*, xx Palm, ca. 190–230: **41** 12
Germanus, *cogn*, xx Palm, 255?: **44** 17
Germanus: **34** recto ii 8 app
Γερθιᾶνις: **34** recto i 13 app
Gerthianus, *see* Flauius
Ginnaei, *see* Acibas
Glauci[, *see* Marrinus
Glycon, Egypt, cent coh eq, 144–175 or 176–207: **78** *18* 1–2; *23* 6; *40* 1?; *48* 6; *55* 1; *65* 1
Glycon, Egypt, coh eq, 157–214: **78** *40* 1. Same as preceding?
Gnoster: **78** *12* 1 app
Goces, legatus Parthorum, Dura ca. 208: p. 400; **98** *2* a 5
Gora, *see* Aurelius, Bassus, Malchus, Themarsa, Zabdibolus
Gordius, *see* Aurelius
Goremis Iadaei, eq xx Palm, 201: **1**, Aurel, xxxvii 5; **2** xxxvii 7; **26** b 5
Gorippus, *see also* Iulius
Gorippus Valenti(ni), eq xx Palm, t. Octaui, 204: **1** xl 9, Valenti; **2** xl 16, Valentini
Gr[, *see* Aurelius
Gra.ius ...eanus, III Cyr, c. Subureana, 91–116: **34** recto i 15
Gradius: **81** ii 16 app
Granius, Grattius: **34** recto i 15 app
Gratus, *see* Aurelius
Guris Nisamsi, eq xx Palm, t. Antonini, 199: **1**, Aurel, xli 28; **2** xli 16

H[, *see* Aurelius, Iulius, Tryphon
H.[..]ofur, *see* Aurelius
H[..]ụ[.]liṛi, *see* Lycophron
].ius Ḥ[, Egypt, classiarius, 136: **28** 2
H[-8?-].[..]ẓạ[, xx Palm, c. Marci, 199: **2** xi 24
H[, *nom*, xx Palm, c. Antonini post, 208?: **8** x 14 and 15–16 app
Ḥ...[ ]ṣ.[..]ṣ[, drom xx Palm, c. Mariani, 212: **8** vii 20
H[.]aruạl.[.]., xx Palm, 194–219: **1** xii 3 marg
H[, *nom*, xx Palm, 225–256: **4** j 4
Ḥ[.]ḍṛẹ.[, xx Palm, 225–256: **4** m 4
Ḥ...ṇ[.]nus Phlei, Egypt, aux, 180: **70** a ii 37
Ha.[...]s, *see* Aurelius
Ha[, *cogn*, xx Palm, c. Mariani, 212–214: **1** xxiii 26
Aurel Hab[, xx Palm, c. Mariani, 205–207: **1** xxii 24
Habbis Marona, xx Palm, 207: c. Seleuciana, **6** xi 18, Abbis; c. Antonini pr, **8** viii 9
Habbis Ogeli, xx Palm, c. Mariani, 212: **8** vi 9
Habiḅạ[s -3?-].m.[, xx Palm, c. Antonini post, 214: **2** xxx 10
Habiba[s N]ebudaei, xx Palm, c. Antonini post, 201: **1** xi 27; **2** xxvii 15
Habibi, *see* Zebidas
Habibis Zebida, eq xx Palm, t. Antonini, 205 or 208: **2** xliii 5
Habitus, *see* Cassius
Haḍ.[, *see* Iulius
Aurel Hadadsabus Barsimsi, eq xx Palm, t. Antonini, 195: **1** xli 19
Hadrianus, *see* Aurelius
[Ha]d[ri]anus: **1** xvii 8 app; **2** xxii 18 app
Hadymus: **20** 4 app
Haeran, Heran, *see* Barhadadus, Claudius, Maccaeus, Malchus, Themarsas, Victor
[H]ạẹran, *cogn*, xx Palm, c. Antonini pr, 197–201: **2** xxii 6
].s Haerạ[n-, xx Palm, c. Antonini pr, 210: **2** xxiii 21
[Ha]ẹran, *cogn*, xx Palm, c. Malchiana, 214: **1** xxix 28
]hus H[ae]ṛan, xx Palm, c. Malchiana, 214: **1** xxix 31
Hạ[e]ṛan, *cogn*, xx Palm, c. Marci, 214: **2** xiv 27
Haeranạ.ḷ, xx Palm, 194–219: **1** vii 6 marg
Aurel Heranes Aithibeli, eq xx Palm, t. Demetri, 195: **1** xxxvi 21
Aurel Heranes Ierabole, eq xx Palm, t. Antonini, 203: **1** xlii 18; **47** i 13 app
Aurel Heranes Malchi, drom xx Palm, c. Danymi, 195: **1** xliii 20
Hagus, *see also* Barathes
Hagus Ierhaei, eq xx Palm, 203: t. Antonini, **1**, Aurel, xlii 19; t. Tiberini, **2** xxxv 8
Hagus Malchi, eq xx Palm, t. Zebida, 201: **1**, Aurel, xxxii 5; **2** xxxii 18
Aurel Hagus Salme, eq xx Palm, t. Demetri, 195: **1** xxxvi 23
Hairanes, *see* Haeranes
Hala, *see also* Belaacabus
A[urel]ạs Hala, eq xx Palm, t. Zebida, 194–195: **1** xxxi 32
Halas, *nom*, xx Palm, 204: c. Castrici, **1** xvii 6; c. Antonini pr, **2** xxii 16, imaginifer?
Halas, eq xx Palm, t. Paulini, ca. 207–238: **94** b ii 6
]...us Halas, xx Palm, 217–256: **17** a 12
Halathẹ Ṃaṛiṇ[i], eq xx Palm, 183–208: **99** *3* 4–5
Hammae[, *see* Zabdibolus
Hammaeus, xx Palm, 194–219: **1** xxxvii 15 marg
Hammaeus Ogeli, xx Palm, c. Malchiana, 205: **6** ix 23; **1**, Aurel, xxviii 12
Hanina, *see* Ogas, Vabalathus
Haninas: **1** xi 28 app
Haninas, status unknown, Dura in 221: **91** *2* i 7 and app; *2* ii 6
Haṇị[na-] Bellaei, xx Palm, c. Antonini post, 201: **1** xi 28; **2** xxvii 16, [B]elei; **91** *2* i 7 app
Hareschis Nechtherotis, Vet Gall, t. Iuli, 154–179: **76** v 2–3
Harmiusis Arnei[..]i (αρνει[..]ọụ), Vet Gall, t. Furiani, 154–179: **76** xii 20
Harpocration, *see* Anubion, Aurelius
[ἁρ]ποκρατου ερμου: **11 bis** c 5 app
Hascia, *see* Zebinnus
Ḥẹ[, *see* Aurelius
He.[, Egypt, aux, 184–189: **70** c 1
].esuṛ.ṃius He[, xx Palm, c. Antonini post, 212: **2** xxix 10 and app
Heberi, *see* Hermias
Hecataeus, *see* Balini(us)
Hecatus: **80** 26 app
Hel[, *see* Aurelius
Heliodorus, *see also* Aelius, Auidius, Aurelius, Flauius, Iulius, Marinus, Nisamsus, Septimius, Themes
Heliodorus [......]ịus, Vet Gall, t. Agrippae, 154–179: **76** iii 11
Helioḍ[or-, *cogn*, xx Palm, c. Danymi, 202–219: **1** iii–v f 6
[Aurel].ḍ[.]s Ḥẹḷio[dor-, xx Palm, c. Antonini post, 210: **1** xiii 15
[He]l[i]ọdori, *cogn*, xx Palm, c. Marci, 214: **8** iv 14
Aure[l ——] Heliodorus, drom xx Palm, c. Castrici, 194–219: **1** xliv 2
Heliodorus, sig xx Palm, 194–219: **1** xxviii 14 marg
].us Heliodori, xx Palm, ca. 215–240: **15** ii 1

Heliodorus, cent xx Palm, 214–241: pp. 126, 133; **13** 8; **14** 4 app; **15** i 9; ii 6, 12, 13 (twice), 15; **15** c 5; **29** 12
Heliodorus, xx Palm, 193–244: **49** 3
Heliodorus: **1** xiii 15 app
[He]l[i]oḍọrụṣ, *cogn:* **23** iii 1 app
Heliodorus Apolloni, xx Palm, c. Antonini post, 208: **1**, Aurel, xiii 6; **2** xxviii 23; **8** x 15–16 app; **92** vi 11
Helio(dorus) Max(imi), xx Palm, 194–219: **1** xxii 15 marg
Heliodorus Patroclus, Vet Gall, t. Agrippae, 154–179: **76** x 15
Aurel Heliodorus Seleuci, eq xx Palm, t. Zebida, 202: **1** xxxii 19
Heliodorus Sereni, Vet Gall, t. Ammoniani, 154–179: **76** xi 12, 20, 21
Heliodorus Zebida, xx Palm, c. Marci, 201: **6** iii 8; **1**, Aurel, vi 28; **2** xii 7
Heli(us?), cent III Cyr, 65–96: **9** 3 d and app; 6 m; 11 g
Helius, Egypt, eq aux, second quarter of II p.: **73** a iii 5
Ḥẹlla[ni]çụ[s], *see* Aurelius
Hẹḷụịus P̣[e]ṛ[tin]ạx, immunis? II Traian, 217–242: **21** 6
Her[, *see* Aelius, Asclepiades, Longinus
Heracl.[, *see* Aelius
Heracla[, *see* Iulius
Heraclammon Q[, I Aug Lus, c. Gan[, 156: **64** ii 5
Heraclas, drom xx Palm, c. Mariani, 214: **2** xliv 28 and app; **8** vii 22
Heraclid, Heraclida[, *see* Aurelius
Heraclidae, *see* Eponuchus
Heraclidas: **1** xiii 13 app
Heracleus, *see* Dionysius
Heracleus, Praefectus Aegypti: **11** ii 3 app
Heraclianus, *see also* Iulius
Heraclian(us), cent?, Egypt, early II p.: **11** ii 3 and app
Heraclianus, cent, Egypt, coh eq, 150–175 or 182–207: **78** *21* 2; *23* 2
Heraclius, *see* Flauius
Heranes, *see* Haeranes
Heras, *see* Aurelius
Herculanus, cent I Aug Lus, 131–156: **64** i 34; ii 1 app
Herennianus, *see* Aelius, Horatius; **1** xxx 1 app
Herennius, *see also* Aurelius; cent, **78** *53* 2 app
Quintus Herennius, sig I Aug Lus, c. Longiani, 92–117: **74** iii 8
Herennius Diogenes, Egypt, status unknown, 114–139: **75** 2, 12, 19
Aurel Erennius Marinus, xx Palm, c. Malchiana, 214: **1** xxx 5
Herennius Melas, sesq Vet Gall, 154–179: **76** vii 20–21
L Herennius Saturninus, legatus Moesiae Sup.: pp. 219–21; **63** ii 7
Herm[, *see also* Aurelius
Herm[, Egypt, coh eq, 146–171 or 178–203: **78** *18* 8
Herma[, Egypt, pedes coh eq, 152–178 or 184–210: **78** *35* 1
Hermacis Apynç[his, eq I Aug Lus, t. Artemidori, 156: **64** ii 8
Hermacisapyni: **64** ii 8 app
Hermaiscus, *see also* Aurelius
Hermaiṣg[, Egypt, eq aux, second quarter of II p.: **73** a ii 9. *Probably* Hermaiscus
Hermas, Egypt, coh eq, 132–217: **78** *44* 2
ερμεν[, (Herminus?), Egypt, coh eq, 150–175 or 182–207: **78** *22* 2
ερμου, *see* ἁρποκρατου
Hermiae, *see* Hermias
Hermias Heberi, Vet Gall, t. Lucili Bassi, 154–179: **76** xvi 1
Hermias Hermiae, optio campi Vet Gall, t. Iuli, 154–179: **76** ii 8; xix 9
Hermin[, Egypt, coh eq, c. or t. Antiochi, 153–178 or 185–210: **78** *37* 6
[.....]θιν ερμειν[, Egypt, coh eq, 156–181 or 188–213: **78** *4* 8
Herminus, *see also* Apollas, Asclepiades; **78** *18* 8 app
Herminus, Egypt, dec coh eq, 137–162 or 169–194: **78** *15* 2; *51* 7 app
Herminus E[, Egypt, coh eq, c. Trunni, 132–217: **78** *70* 1
Herminus Tyrannus, Egypt, curator coh eq, 152–181 or 184–213: **78** *4* 15; *34* 1 and app; *60* 3
Hermion, Egypt, coh eq, 150–175 or 182–207: **78** *22* 5
Hermogenes, *see also* Aurelius, Maximus
Hermogenes Maçċio.[.]s, xx Palm, c. Achaei, ca. 215–240: **15** ii 8
Hermofil(us), Egypt, eq aux, second quarter of II p.: **73** a i 22
Herodianus, dec Vet Gall, 154–179: **76** i 7, 9; iii 2, 9, 18; iv, 3, 19, 25; v 9, 17; vi 17; viii 25; xi 19; xiii 3; xv 19; xx 1; BB 1–2; FF 1; i 7 app
Heron Isidorus, Vet Gall, t. Lucili, 154–179: **76** ix 18; x 22; xi 9; FF 8
Heronianus, *see* Aurelius, Cassius, Iulius
Herontianus: **39** 16 app
Ἡρῶντις Ψεναμο(ύνιος) Ἀβῶτ(ος): **39** 16 app
Hiạ[, *see* Antoninus
Aurel Hia.[..]..[..]ṇ, eq xx Palm, t. Octaui, 195: **1** xxxviii 27
]s Hiçṃạ, Egypt, 218: **40** i 17

Hier[, *see* Aurelius
Hierax, *see also* Antonius, Aurelius, Isidorus, Petenefotes
Hierax, Egypt, eq aux, second quarter of II p.: **73** a i 20
Hierax, *cogn*, Vet Gall, 154–179: **76** ii 2
Hierax, Egypt, coh eq, 132–217: **78** *57* 7
Hiereus Abẹ[d-, status unknown, Dura in 211: p. 355; **88** *2* 6
Hieronymus, *see* Aelius
Hila[r-, *see* Iulius
Hila[ri-: **46** 7 app
Hispanus, *see* Valerius
Honoratianus, Praefectus Aegypti: **20** 15 app; 23 app
Hoṛ[, *nom*, Egypt, c. Ammoniani?, first quarter of III p.: **52** b 4
]ạẹ Hor[, Egypt, late II p.: **71** b 3
(H)orạpo[ll]oni[: **52** a 3 app
Horatius Herennianus, I Aug Lus, c. Candidi, 148: **64** ii 20
Ὡρη⟨γέ⟩νοụṣ (*genitive*), Egypt, cent coh eq, 148–173 or 180–205: **78** *72* 2
Horigenes, *see also* Didymus
]ḷius Horigenes, Egypt, dupl? t. Titi, 228: **24** 6
Origenes, *cogn*, dec, Egypt, 229: **20** 13; 15 app
Horion, *see also* Iulius
Horion, Egypt, coh eq, cent or dec?, 156–182 or 188–214: **78** *6* 2 and 12; cf. *22* 2
Horion Isidori, Egypt, aux, I/II p.: **38** i 5
Marc̣[us] Aurelius Horion Sarapion, Egypt, armorum custos coh eq, 155–180 or 187–212: **78** *39* 4–5
Horus, Egypt, eq aux, second quarter of II p.: **73** a iii 7
Horus Piat[.].., Vet Gall, t. Iuli, 154–179: **76** xv 3
Hos[: **52** b 4 app
Hotaraei, *see* Marinus, Maximus

I.[, *see* Aurelius, Iosephus
I.[, *nom*, xx Palm, c. Mariani, 206: **8** v 29
Aurel I.[..].[, xx Palm, c. Castrici, 214–215: **1** xx 1
Ị[, *nom*, xx Palm, c. Mariani, 193–218: **6** vii 8
Ị..[, Egypt, end of III p.: **11 bis** b ii 4
I.[..]ṃammus: **27** b ii 12 app
I[.]ṇu[...]ṣ, *see* Iulius
Ia..[, *see also* Aurelius
Ịạ[, *nom*, xx Palm, c. Antonini post, 197–228: **8** x 7
Ịạḍ.[.]..[, xx Palm, ca. 215–240: **15** i 2
Aurel Iaḍ[..]eus Aithibeli, xx Palm, c. Malchiana, 209–212: **1** xxix 4. *Possibly* Iaddaeus?
Iabaei, *see also* Goremis, Zebidas
Iadaeus [Ier]haei, xx Palm, c. Mariani, 193: **1** xxi 10
Iadaeus Themarsa, xx Palm, 204: c. Seleuciana, **6** xi 9; c. Castrici, **1** xvii 18; c. Antonini pr, **2** xxii 27; **8** viii 1
Iaddae[, *see* Aurelius
Iaddaeus: **4** b i 11 app
Iadibelus, *see also* Aurelius, Amaeus
Iadib[el-, xx Palm, c. Malchi, 197–222: **2** ii–iv f 6
Iadibelus Ammaei, xx Palm, c. Danymi, 214: **6** i 34
Iadibelus Iarhaei, eq xx Palm, t. Demetri, 198: **1**, Aurel, xxxvi 26; **2** xxxvi 22
Aurel [Iadi]ḅẹḷuṣ Malchi, eq xx Palm, t. Tiberini, 195: **1** xxxiv 1
Iadibelus Zebida, xx Palm, c. Danymi, 201: **6** i 6; **1** i 2; **2** vii 2
Iamlichi, *see also* Salmanes
Ạ[ure]ḷ [3?].a...[I]amlichi, eq xx Palm, t. Zebida, 203: **1** xxxii 30
Iamlichus Mocimi, eq xx Palm, t. Demetri, 203: **1**, Aurel, xxxvii 15; **2** xxxvii 16
Ịaṇ[-5?-], eq xx Palm, 226–251: **83** 22
Ianuarius, Praefectus Aegypti: **20** 20; 23 app
Ianuarius: **1** xxviii 3 app
Iaqubus, *see also* Aurelius
[Ia]qubus, xx Palm, c. Malchi, 197–222: **2** ii–iv f 3
[Iaq]ubus, *cogn*, xx Palm, 255?: **44** 18
Aurel Iaqubus Themarsa, xx Palm, c. Malchiana, 203: **1** xxvii 12
Iaqubus Zebida, eq xx Palm, t. Tiberini, 205: **1**, Aurel, xxxv 14; **2** xxxv 15
Iar.[, *see also* Aurelius, Ṃ.[..]ṃụs
Aur[el I]er.[, xx Palm, c. Mariani, 200–201: **1** xxi 23
Aure[l I]er.[, xx Palm, c. Mariani, 205–207: **1** xxii 22
Iar.[, xx Palm, 194–219: **1** xlii 2 marg
Iaraboles, *see* Iarhaboles
Iarḥ[, *see also* Barlahas, Zebidas
Iarḥ[, *nom*, xx Palm, c. Antonini pr, 215: **2** xxv 5
Iarhaboles, *see also* Aurelius, Barnaeus, Gaianus, Haeranes
...ianes Iarhabole, xx Palm, 198–235: **47** i 13
[I]ạṛḥạḅ[o]l[.], xx Palm, ca. 210–240: **13** 5
[Iar]ḥạḅọleṣ, *cogn*, xx Palm, ca. 215–240: **15** i 7
Iaraboles, *nom*, xx Palm, c. Achaei, ca. 215–240: **15** i 14
Iarhaboles: **1** xvi 27 app; **4** b i 12 app
Iaraboles, *nom*, xx Palm, ca. 220–255: **25** b 3
[Iar]haboles, *cogn*, xx Palm, 255?: **44** 16
[Iarha]ḅọlẹṣ, *cogn*, xx Palm, 217–256: **17** a 2
Iarhaboles Addaei, eq xx Palm, t. Zebida, 201: **1**, Aurel, xxxii 10; **2** xxxii 23 and app
Aurel Ierabol[es Bu]ccaei, xx Palm, c. Mariani, 205–207: **1** xxiii 1

Iarhaboles Iarhaei, xx Palm, c. Gaiani, 198–235: **47** i 12
Iarhaboles Luci, eq xx Palm, t. Demetri, 205: **1**, Aurel, xxxvii 30, Ierabole; **2** xxxviii 1; **26** b 8
Iarhaboles Obean, xx Palm, 214: c. Seleuciana, **6** xi 27; c. Castrici, **1**, Aurel, xviii 15, [Ierab]ole
Iarhaboles Odeati, eq xx Palm, t. Anton(ini), 198–235: **47** i 4
Iarhaboles Themarsa, xx Palm, c. Marci, 202: **6** iii 11; **1**, Aurel, Ierabole, vi 31; **2** xii 10
Iarhaboles Themarsa, eq xx Palm, t. Zebida, 199: **1** xxxi 38; **2** xxxii 11
[Iarh]ạboles Theme, eq xx Palm, t. Antonini, 201: **2** xli 29
Iarhaboles Vdathi, xx Palm, c. Marci, 212: **6** iii 30; **1**, Aurel, viii 13; **2** xiii 25
Iarhaboles Zebida, drom xx Palm, 196: c. Malchiana, **1**, Aurel, xliv 13 and app; c. Malchi, **2** xliii 18
Iarhabus Ebucaei, eq xx Palm, t. Antonini, 196: **1**, Aurel, xli 23, Ierabus; **2** xli 11
Ie.[: **4** b ii 13 app
Ieraboles, Ierhaboles, *see* Iarhaboles
Ierabus, *see* Iarhabus
Iarhaei, Iarhaeus. *Regularly* Ierhaeus *in* **1**, Iarheus *in* **2**, Iaraeus *in* **6**, Iarhaeus *in* **8**. *See also* Abedsalmas, Abgarus, Addaeus, Aurelius, Bar.[.......]., Baricas, Barnaeus, Belaacabus, Boliadaeus, Dius, Hagus, Iadaeus, Iadibelus, Iarhaboles, Malchus, Maris, Mocimus, Seleucus, Themarsas, Zebidas
Iarhaei: **1** xxii 1 app; **2** xvii 9 app
Aurel [——] Ị[e]ṛaẹi, *cogn*, xx Palm, c. Antonini post, 195: **1** xi 11
]es Iarhẹ[, xx Palm, c. Mariani, 200–201: **2** xvii 6
[Ia]ṛhei, eq xx Palm, t. Tiberini, 203: **2** xxxv 1
Iarhaei, eq xx Palm, t. Demetri, 197–206: **92** vii 6
Ierhaei, xx Palm, c. Castrici, 214–215: **1** xix 18
Ị[ar]ḥe[us -8?-].i, dupl xx Palm, c. Marci, 197–222: **2** xi 18
]ṇ.ṣ Iarhaei, xx Palm, c. Danymi, 197–225: **92** v 7
Iarhaeus Abgari, xx Palm, c. Malchiana, 214: **6** x 5; **1** xxx 12
[I]erḥ[aeu]ṣ Barnaei, xx Palm, c. Mariani, 195: **1** xxi 13
Iarhaeus Barnaei, eq xx Palm, t. Demetri, 204: **1**, Aurel, xxxvii 23; **2** xxxvii 24; **26** b 7
Iarhaeus Barnaei, xx Palm, 207: c. Seleuciana, **6** xi 19; c. Antonini pr, **8** viii 10
Iarhaeus Barnaei, xx Palm, c. Antonini post, 214: **2** xxix 22
Iarhaeus Belaacabi, eq xx Palm, t. Zebida, 203: **1**, Aurel, xxxii 27; **2** xxxiii 8
Iarhaeus Bora, eq xx Palm, t. Tiberini, 205: **1**, Aurel, xxxv 13; **2** xxxv 14
Ierraeus Macchana, Egypt, c. Belei, 180–205: **81** ii 15
Iarhaeus Malchi, eq xx Palm, t. Tiberini, 212: **1**, Aurel, xxxv 27; **2** xxxv 30
Iarhaeus Malchi, xx Palm, 198–235: **47** i 7. Same as preceding?
Iarhaeus Marea, eq xx Palm, t. Zebida, 205: **1**, Aurel, xxxiii 7; **2** xxxiii 23
Iarhaeus Nisams[, xx Palm, 214: c. Seleuciana, **6** xi 33 and app; **1** xviii 24 and app
Iarhaeus Ṇisṃọṣa, xx Palm, ca. 215–240: **15** i 2
Iarhaeus Salman, xx Palm, c. Mariani, 212: **8** vi 7
Iarhaeus Th[, xx Palm, c. Antonini pr, 214: **8** viii 24; **1** xviii 24 app
Iarhaeus Themarsa, eq xx Palm, t. Tiberini, 200: **1**, Aurel, xxxiv 19; **2** xxxiv 17
Iarhaeus Themarsa, eq xx Palm, t. Demetri, 201: **1**, Aurel, xxxvii 6; **2** xxxvii 8
Iarhaeus Themarsa, eq xx Palm, t. Zebida, 201: **1**, Aurel, xxxii 17; **2** xxxii 27 and app
Iarhaeus Themarsa, xx Palm, c. Danymi, 214: **2** ix 22
Iarhaeus Themarsa, xx Palm, c. Antonini post, 214: **2** xxix 17
Ịạṛḥ[a]eus? Ṭ[he]ṃạṛṣạ[, xx Palm, c. Antonini pr, 214: **8** ix 6 and app
Iarhaeus Themarsa, xx Palm, c. Gaiani, 207–232: **27** a ii 10
Ịạ[rha]eus Themarsa, xx Palm, 211–236: **33** v 1
Iarhaeus Theoboli, xx Palm, c. Malchiana, 214: **6** x 7; **1**, Aurel, xxx 14
Aurel Ierhaeus Zab[.]ua, eq xx Palm, t. Octaui, 201: **1** xxxix 27
Iarhaeus Zebida, xx Palm, c. Marci, 201: **6** iii 6; **1**, Aurel, vi 23
Iarhaeus Zebida, xx Palm, 210: c. Seleuciana, **6** xi 21; c. Castrici, **1** xviii 5; c. Antonini pr, **2** xxiii 20
Iarhaeus Zebida, xx Palm, c. Marci, 214: **1** ix 4; **2** xiv 15; **8** iv 7
Aurel Ierhaeus Zebi[da-, xx Palm, c. Antonini post, 214: **1** xiv 3
Aurel Iar[haeus Zebi]da, xx Palm, c. Marci, 191–216: **89** *12* ii 5
Iarhaeus Zebida, xx Palm, c. Antonini pr, 211–236: **33** ii 2
Idus ..[, *name?*, Egypt, 160–185: **72** 11
Aurel Ie..[..].ene.nis, eq xx Palm, t. Octaui, 195: **1** xxxviii 25
Ịẹạṣtel[, xx Palm, c. Germani, 217–256: **19** 6
Iebbael[: **81** iii 1 app
Ịẹḍḍael[, Egypt, c. Belei, 180–205: **81** iii 1
Ierhaeus, *see* Iarhaeus
Illi....[...]s, xx Palm, 225–256: **4** a i 5
Im[uthes ?, Egypt, dec coh eq, 154–189 or 186–217: **78** *3* 2 and app

Ingenianus: p. 361 and **100** 2 app
Innocens, *see* Rennius
Intenianus, *see* Aurelius
Inuentus: **91** *1* i 6 app
Iosepus, Egypt, aux, I/II p.: 38 ii 14
Iperan..: **73** a i 20 app
Isas Sarapionis, Vet Gall, t. Agrippae, 154–179: **76** HH i 1, ii 1
Isiḍ..[, *nom*, xx Palm, 225–256: **4** m 5
Isidorianus, *see* Aurelius
Isidori, Isidorus, *see also* Aurelius, Besarion, Heron, Horion, Iulius, Sarapion, Valerius
Isidorus ..sidon, eq xx Palm, t. Tiberini, 203: **1**, Aurel, xxxv 1; **2** xxxv 4
Isidorus, Egypt, coh eq, t. Cononis, 152–177 or 184–209: **78** *29* 1
Isidori, *cogn*, Egypt, pedes coh eq, 132–217: **78** *51* 1
Isidorus, *cogn*, Egypt, 217: **40** i 10
Isidori, *cogn*, Egypt, coh eq quingenaria, first quarter of III p.: **52** b 6
Isidorus Apolloni, Vet Gall, t. Apollinari, 154–179: **76** v 2
Isidorus Athmonis, Egypt, coh eq, t. Gemelli, 152–177 or 184–209: **78** *34* 2
Isidorus Hierax, Egypt, coh eq, 157–182 or 189–214: **78** *40* 3
Isiogenes: **64** i 35 app
Isiognis, *see* Philon
Ision Petsireos, eq I Aug Lus, t. Artemidori, 141 or 155: **64** ii 35
Iu.[, *see* Aurelius
Iu[..]us, *see* Baebius
]na Iu[, Egypt, classiarius, liburna Mercurius, 127: **28** 14
Iu[, *nom*, Egypt, aux, 180: **70** a iii 1
Iu[, *nom*, Egypt, aux, 167–192: **70** g 3
Iụ[, *nom*, Egypt, c. Theopropi, 195?: **5** ii 22
Ịụ[, *nom*, Egypt, 196–216: **5** iii 12
Ịu[, *nom*, Egypt, 197–217: **5** iii 14
Iu[, *nom*, Egypt, 197–217: **5** iii 18
Iudus, *see* Nepheros
Iuḷ[, *nom*, Egypt, c. Theopropi, 195?: **5** ii 21
Iul...[, *nom*, xx Palm, c. Germani, 217–256: **17** a 7
Iul[, *nom*, Egypt, end of III p.: **11 bis** b ii 11
Iuliͅ[, xx Palm, c. Antonini post, 209?: **8** x 17 and 15–16 app
Iuli[, *nom*, xx Palm, c. Germani, 217–256: **17** a 7
Iuli[, *nom*, xx Palm, 213–256: **35** 3
Iulianus, *see also* Cornelius, Iulius, Quintus
]us Iulianus, sing xx Palm, c. Marci, 204: **2** xii 22
[Iu]ḷianus, *cogn*, xx Palm, 191–216: **89** *4* iii 3 app
Iulianus, *cogn*, xx Palm, ca. 201–230: **41** 13
Iulianus Themarsa, sesq xx Palm, t. Antonini, 202: **1**, Aurel, xli 8; **2** xli 8
Iuli, Iulius, *see also* Aurelius, Charifas, Claudius; **36** 6 app; **63** i 22 app; **78** *16* 1 app
Iulius, Vet Gall, t. Donaciani, 105–130: **80** 11
C Iulius[, I Aug Lus, c. Gan[, 155: **64** ii 2
Iulius, *nom*, Egypt, aux, 192: **70** b ii 18
Aurel Iulius[, xx Palm, c. Castrici, 195: **1** xvi 17
Aurel Iulius [-5?-]s, eq xx Palm, t. Octaui, 201: **1** xxxix 29
Iulius [-4?-]entianus, xx Palm, c. Antonini post, 202: **2** xxvii 20 and app
Aurel Iulius [-2?-].anus, xx Palm, c. Mariani, 203: **1** xxii 8
Aurel Iulius [, xx Palm, c. Antonini post, 204: **1** xii 7; **92** ix 5 app
Iulius, *nom*, xx Palm, c. Castrici, 204: **1** xvii 25
Iulius, *nom*, xx Palm, c. Castrici, 204: **1** xvii 26
Iulius, *nom*, Egypt, c. Belei, 180–205: **81** iii 11
Ịul[ius ..]..[, eq xx Palm, t. Demetri, 205: **1** xxxvii 35
Aurel Iuliu[s, xx Palm, c. Danymi, 201–205: **1** ii 2
Iulius[ ].ṇ[.]ẹus, xx Palm, c. Antonini pr, 205: **8** viii 5
Iuli[us, *nom*, Egypt, eq t. Eạ[.]..c[, I/II p.: **30** ii 2
M Aur Iulius .[, Egypt, 206: **46** 5
Iuli[us]ụs, xx Palm, c. Antonini pr, 207: **2** xxiii 12
Iulius [ ]b[-7?-]ṣ, drom xx Palm, c. Antonini post, 205 or 208: **2** xlv 11
Iulius .[.......]ụs, xx Palm, c. Antonini post, 212: **2** xxix 12
Iulius ...log[, Egypt, coh eq, 154–179 or 186–211: **78** *2* 1
Iul .[.....]ius, xx Palm, c. Antonini pr, 197–214: **92** iii 11
Aurel Iulius[, xx Palm, c. Mariani, 212–214: **1** xxiii 25
Aurel Iulius .[, xx Palm, c. Marci, 214: **1** ix 18
Iulius, *nom*, xx Palm, c. Mariani, 214: **2** xix 21
Iulius [.]..[ ]ius, drom xx Palm, c. Antonini post, 214: **2** xlv 13
Iulius, Egypt, coh eq, 157–182 or 189–214: **78** *40* 10
Aurel Iuliu[s, xx Palm, c. Castrici, 214–215: **1** xix 7
Iulius [.....], Egypt, coh eq, 132–217: **78** *57* 4–5
I[u]l[ius -5?-]us, xx Palm, c. Antonini pr, 215: **2** xxiv 10
Ị[ul ....]asraeus: **89** *4* ii 8 app
Iụḷ[-3?-]nus, xx Palm, 191–216: **89** *4* ii 10
M Aurelius Iulius [......], Egypt, t. Cononis, 132–217: **78** *8* 1
Iul[ius, sing xx Palm, c. Marci, 222: **2** xvi 8
Iul(ius) ...[..]ục̣.ṣ, xx Palm, c. Antonini pr, 211–236: **33** ii 4
Iul(ius) ..[.]sus, xx Palm, 211–236: **33** iv 6

Iulius, *cogn*, xx Palm, ca. 210–240: **13** 15
Iulius, *nom*, xx Palm, c. Felicis, ca. 215–240: **15** i 19
Iulius: **1** xvi 9 app; **4** b i 25 app; **24** 6 app
Aurel Iulius Ạ[. . .]ṇi.[, xx Palm, c. Mariani, 205–207: **1** xxiii 2
Iul(ius) Ạb[. . . . .]s, xx Palm, c. Seleuciana, 204: **6** xi 7
Iulius Abidsemias, xx Palm, c. Mariani, 204: **1** xxii 12, Abedsemia; **2** xvii 19; **8** v 14
C Iulius Aelurio, cent III Aug: **71** a 8 app
Iulius Agathus Daemon stator, Vet Gall, t. Ammoniani, 154–179: **76** xiv 2
Iulius Alexander, immunis? II Traian, 217–242: **21** 10
Iulius Alexandrus, xx Palm, 205: c. Malchiana, **1**, Aurel, xxviii 9; c. Pudentis, **92** ix 11
Iulius Alexandrus, eq xx Palm, t. Zebida, 212: **1**, Aurel, xxxiii 19; **2** xxxiii 31
Iul Alexandrus, Egypt, second quarter of III p.: **53** a i 9
Iulius Amerys, Vet Gall, t. Furiani, 154–179: **76** GG 6
Iulius Ammonianus, principalis?, Egypt, 174: **39** 4
Iul Aṇṭ[, xx Palm, c. Germani, 216–241: **29** 6
Iulius Antoni[, eq xx Palm, t. Octaui, 202: **1**, Aurel, xxxix 34; **2** xl 6
Aurel Iuḷ[ius] Ạn[t]ọṇ[i]nus, eq xx Palm, t. Octaui, 199: **1** xxxviii 33
Iulius Antoninus, eq xx Palm, t. Octaui, 200: **1**, Aurel, xxxix 4; **2** xxxix 10
Iulius Antoninus alter, eq xx Palm, t. Octaui, 200: **1**, Aurel, xxxix 5; **2** xxxix 11
Iul(ius) Antoninus, xx Palm, c. Danymi, 203: **6** i 12
Iulius Antoninus, dupl xx Palm, t. Tiberini, 203: **1**, Aurel, xxxiii 26; **2** xxxiv 4
Iulius Antoninus, eq xx Palm, t. Demetri, 205: **1** xxxvii 33; **2** xxxviii 5
Iulius Ạṇṭọṇịṇ[u]ṣ, xx Palm, c. Marci, 212: **2** xiii 29
Iul(ius) Anṭọ[n]ị[u]s, xx Palm, c. Marci, 209–225: **92** viii 18
Iulius Antonius Seleucus, leg. Moes. Inf.: **91** *1* i 4 app
Iulius Apollinarius, Vet Gall, t. Sereni Melanos, 154–179: **76** x 2
Iulius Apollinarius, Vet Gall, t. Apollinarii, 154–179: **76** xix 12
Iulius Apollinarius, sing dupl xx Palm, c. Mariani, 203: **1**, Aurel, xxi 4; **2** xvi 19
Iul(ius) Apolinarius, xx Palm, c. Aureli, 225: **4** b i 9
Iulius Apollonius, xx Palm, c. Antonini post, 199: **6** iv 27; **1** xi 20; **2** xxvii 8
Iulius Ariston, xx Palm, 203: c. Malchiana, **1**, Aurel, xxvii 10; c. Malchi, **2** i 15
Iulius Aristus, eq xx Palm, t. Tiberini, 204: **1** xxxv 9
Iul(ius) Ḅ[, xx Palm, c. Antonini post, 202–215, *probably* 214, *see* Aurelius Hadrianus: **6** v 14
Iulius Barhadadus, xx Palm, c. Antonini post, 195: **6** iv 21; **1**, Aurel, xi 10
Iulius Barlaha, eq xx Palm, t. Octaui, 201: **1**, Aurel, xxxix 26; **2** xxxix 28
Iulius Bassus, drom xx Palm, c. Antonini post, 199: **1** xliii 33
Iulius Bassus, xx Palm, 205: c. Seleuciana, **6** xi 11; c. Antonini pr, **8** viii 3
Iulius Bassus, eq xx Palm, t. Zebida, 205: **1**, Aurel, xxxiii 3; **2** xxxiii 20
Iulius Bassus, xx Palm, c. Mariani, 205: **8** v 20
Iulius Bassus, eq xx Palm, 183–208: **99** *1* 6
Aurel Iulius Bassus, xx Palm, c. Malchiana, 214: **1** xxix 6
Iul(ius) Bassus, xx Palm, c. Danymi, 215: **6** ii 5
Iulius Bassus, xx Palm, c. Antonini pr, 215: **2** xxiv 15
Iulius Belaacabus, eq xx Palm, t. Demetri, 207: **1**, Aurel, xxxviii 6; **2** xxxviii 14
Iulius Cassianus, eq xx Palm, t. Zebida, 204: **1** xxxii 36; **2** xxxiii 16
Iulius Castor, Vet Gall, t. Pactumei Sereni, 154–179: **76** xii 11
Iulius Chaeremonianus, Vet Gall, t. Agrippae, 154–179: **76** ix 2 and 10
Iulius Cleides, Egypt, eq coh eq, 154–179 or 186–211: **78** *1* 5
Iulius Cornelianus, Egypt, middle of III p.: **67** 11
Iulius Crispinus, xx Palm, c. Marci, 204: **2** xii 21; **8** iii 15
Iulius Domitius, xx Palm, c. Marci, 202: **6** iii 10; **1**, Aurel, vi 30; **2** xii 9
Iul(ius) Eupranor, Egypt, c. Theopropi, 192: **5** ii 8
Iulius Ḟ[, sing xx Palm, c. Antonini pr, 208: **2** xxiii 14
M Aur Iulius F[, Egypt, ca. 187–230: **46** 5
M Iulius Felix, III Cyr, 65–96: **9** 33 a; 34–37 app
Iulius Flauius, xx Palm, 214: c. Malchiana, **1**, Aurel, xxix 9; c. Pudentis, **92** ix 12
C Iulius Front[, Egypt, early II p.: **11** ii 8
Iulius Ġ. .[, xx Palm, ca. 205–240: **42** 5
Iulius Gaianus, xx Palm, c. Mariani, 214: **8** vi 20
Iulius Gaius, sing xx Palm, c. Antonini pr, 221: **2** xxvi 9
Iulius Germanus, eq xx Palm, t. Demetri, 202: **1**, Aurel, xxxvii 9; **2** xxxvii 11
Iulius Germanus, eq xx Palm, t. Demetri, 203: **1**, Aurel, xxxvii 16; **2** xxxvii 17
Iulius Germanus, same as one of two preceding: **26** b 6

Iulius Germanus, eq xx Palm, t. Antonini, 205 or 208: **1** xliii 10; **2** xliii 8; **92** vii 13
Iulius Germanus, Egypt, pedes coh eq, c. Sabini, 152–177 or 184–209: **78** *32* 1
Iulius Gorippus, eq xx Palm, t. Demetri, 203: **1**, Aurel, xxxvii 11; **2** xxxvii 12
Aurel Iulius H[. . . .].[, xx Palm, c. Malchiana, 206: **1** xxviii 17
Iul(ius) Haḍ.[, xx Palm, c. Antonini post, 205–215, *probably* 214, *see* Aurelius Hadrianus: **6** v 17
Iul(ius) Hel[, xx Palm, ca. 220–255: **25** b 2
Iulius Heliodorus, xx Palm, 204: c. Seleuciana, **6** xi 6; c. Castrici, **1** xvii 11; c. Antonini pr, **2** xxii 21
Iulius Heliodorus, xx Palm, ca. 215–240: **15** ii 5
Iulius [He]ṛacla[, xx Palm, c. Mariani, 214: **1** xxiv 9
Marc(us) Aurelius Iulius Heracleianus, Egypt, pedes coh eq, c. Tithoeus, 154–179 or 186–211: **78** *1* 1
Iulius Heronianus: **39** 16 app; **76** i 7 app
M Aur Iul(ius) Hila[r-, Egypt, 206: **46** 7
Iulius Horion, Egypt, optio coh eq, 132–217: **78** *41* 1
Aurel Iulius I[.]ṇu[. . .]ṣ, xx Palm, c. Malchiana, 204: **1** xxviii 3
Iul(ius) Isid[or-, Egypt, pedes coh eq, c. Vippị[, 132–217: **78** *76* 1
Aurel Iulius Iulianus, eq xx Palm, t. Octaui, 194: **1** xxxviii 21
Iulius Iulianus, eq xx Palm, t. Zebida, 207: **1**, Aurel, xxxiii 14; **2** xxxiii 29
Iulius Iulianus, xx Palm, ca. 215–240: **15** ii 22
C Iulius Ḷo[. .].[, III Cyr, 65–96: **9** 9 a
Iulius Lọ[. .]. .[, eq xx Palm, t. Demetri, 205: **1** xxxvii 37; **2** xxxviii 7
C Iulius Longus (Sidon), III Cyr, 65–96: **9** 11 a
C Iulius Longus (Amisus), III Cyr, 65–96: **9** 12 a; 34–37 app
M Iulius Longus, III Cyr, 65–96: **9** 37 a
Iulius Ṃ[. .]nus, xx Palm, c. Mariani, 204: **2** xvii 24 and app
Iụ[liu]s Ṃa. .[, xx Palm, c. Antonini pr, 214: **8** viii 23 and app
Iulius Magn[, eq xx Palm, t. Antonini, 201: **1** xlii 10; **2** xlii 5 and app
Iul(ius) Malchus, xx Palm, c. Danymi, 201: **6** i 7
Iụ[l(ius)] Mammes, xx Palm, c. Gaiani, 207–232: **27** a ii 12
Iulius Marc.[, xx Palm, c. Mariani, 214: **1** xxv 3; **2** xx 2
Iulius Marcianus, sing xx Palm, c. Antonini post, 208: **1**, Aurel, xiii 9; **2** xxviii 26
Iulius Marcus, sig Vet Gall, 154–179: **76** xviii 31
Iulius Marcus, cent xx Palm, 201: **89** *12* ii 4; **6** ii 22–23; **1** xliii 22; **2** xi 14–15; xliv 11; **8** iii 7; **92** v 12; vii 15; viii 11; **94** a 2 app
Iulius Mạṛị[, xx Palm, ca. 200–235: **61** ii 4
Iulius Marianus, cent xx Palm, 205: **89** *1* 5a (canceled); **1**, Aurel, xxi 1–2; **2** xvi 16–17; **8** v 9; **92** iii [4]; v 19; **47** i 4; ii 5 and 19; **27** a i 2; **122** 4?
Iulius Marinus, eq xx Palm, t. Zebida, 201: **1**, Aurel, xxxii 13; **2** xxxii 25
Iulius Marinus alter, eq xx Palm, t. Zebida, 201: **1**, Aurel, xxxii 14; **2** xxxii 26
Iulius Marinus, eq xx Palm, t. Antonini, 201: **1** xlii 11; **2** xlii 6
Aurel Iulius Marinus, eq xx Palm, t. Octaui, 201: **1** xxxix 24
Iulius Marinus, xx Palm, 204: c. Castrici, **1** xvii 7; c. Antonini pr, **2** xxii 17
Iulius Marinus, eq xx Palm, t. Demetri, 205: **1** xxxvii 35 app; **2** xxxviii 6
Iulius Marinus, eq xx Palm, t. Octaui, 205: **1**, Aurel, xl 17; **2** xl 24
Aurel Iulius [M]ạrinus, xx Palm, c. Malchiana, 206: **1** xxviii 14
Iulius Marinus, eq xx Palm, t. Antonini, 205 or 208: **2** xliii 4
Iulius Marinus, xx Palm, c. Mariani, 214: **1**, Aurel, xxiv 1; **8** vi 15
Iụ[lius] Mari[nu]ṣ, sing xx Palm, c. Antonini post, 216: **2** xxx 22
C Iulius Maximus, III Itur, 103: **87** 15
Iulius Maximus, III Cyr, c. Nini Rufi, 91–116: **34** recto i 6
Iulius Maximus, cent, Egypt, early II p.: **77** a i 7?, 9, 15
Iulius Maximus, Egypt, faber classiarius, 127–164: **59** i 10
Iul(ius) Maximus, Egypt, c. Theopropi, 190: **5** ii 6
Ịụ[lius] Ṃạ[xi]mus, eq xx Palm, t. Zebida, 203: **1**, Aurel, xxxii 28; **2** xxxiii 9
Aurel Iulius Maximus, xx Palm, c. Malchiana 204: **1** xxviii 6
Iulius Maximus, eq xx Palm, t. Demetri, 204: **1**, Aurel, xxxvii 22; **2** xxxvii 23
Iulius Maximus, eq xx Palm, t. Tiberini, 205: **1**, Aurel, xxxv 15: **2** xxxv 16
Iulius Maximus, xx Palm, c. Mariani, 208: **1**, Aurel, xxiii 7; **2** xviii 12
Iul(ius) Maximus, Egypt, dupl or sesq, c. Theopropi, 212: **5** ii 4
Iulius Menandrus, xx Palm, c. Marci, 210: **6** iii 27; **1** viii 8; **2** xiii 20
Iulius Nepotianus, Vet Gall, t. Herodiani, 154–179: **76** iv 19–20; FF 1–2
Iulius Niger, III Cyr, c. Antoni Longo, 91–116: **34** recto ii 17

Iulius Nilus, Egypt, eq coh eq, t. Longini, 132–217: **78** *42* 1
L Iulius Oc ụianus, III Cyr, 65–96: **9** 5 a
Iulius Paniscus, Egypt, principalis?, 187: **39** 20
Iul(ius) Pomponianus, status unknown, Dura in 211: p. 355; **88** *2* 3; *2* verso; *1* 2 app
Q Iulius Q f Col Ponticus, Egypt, legionary, 65–90: **37** 3
Q Iulius Proculus, Egypt, legionary, 56–81: **68** ii 2
Iulius Proculus, XX Palm, 205–240: **22** 2
Iulius Protarchus, dec Vet Gall, 154–179: **76** ii 9; iv 11; v 3; xii 2; xv 4; xx 19; GG 12
Iulius Quadratus?, III Cyr, c. Nini Rufi, 91–116: **34** recto i 8, Cutratus
Aurel Ị[u]ḷ[i]us Romanus, eq XX Palm, t. Octaui, 195: **1** xxxviii 24
Iulius Romanus, XX Palm, 207: c. Seleuciana, **6** xi 17; c. Antonini pr, **8** viii 8
Iulius Romanus, XX Palm, c. Antonini pr, 209: **2** xxiii 16; **8** viii 12
Iul(ius) Romanus, XX Palm, c. Antonini pr, 197–214: **92** iii 13. Same as preceding?
Iulius Romanus: **1** xiii 12 app; **8** x 15–16 app
Iulius Rufianus, tribune XX Palm, ca. 230: p. 183; **47** i 3, 11; ii 3, 16
Iulius Rusticus, III Cyr, c. Aufri Aculi, 91–116: 34 recto ii 3, Ruticus
Iulius Sabinus, XX Palm, c. Mariani, 214: **8** vi 23
Iulius Salman, XX Palm, c. Marci, 201: **6** iii 7; **1**, Aurel, vi 27; **2** xii 6
Iulius Salman, eq XX Palm, t. Octaui, 201: **1**, Aurel, xxxix 12: **2** xxxix 16
Iulius Salman, XX Palm, 203: c. Seleuciana, **6** xi 2; c. Castrici, **1** xvii 4; c. Antonini pr, **2** xxii 14
Aurel Iulius Salman, eq XX Palm, t. Antonini, 203: **1** xlii 21
Iulius Sarapion, Egypt, sesq t. Sarapionis, 221: **24** 17
Iulius Saturnilus, eq XX Palm, t. Zebida, 203: **1**, Aurel, xxxii 26; **2** xxxiii 7
C Iulius Saturninus, III Itur, 103: **87** 19
Iulius Scaurianus, eq XX Palm, t. Tiberini, 201: **1**, Aurel, xxxiv 25; **2** xxxiv 23
Iulius Secundus, III Itur, 103: **87** 17
L? Iulius Serenus, summus curator Vet Gall, 154–179: **76** i 2, 11, 18, 22; ii 3, 12; iii 3, 12, 21; iv 3, 12, 21; v 4, 12; vi 2, 10, 17; vii 3, 9, 17; viii 3, 8, 14, 19, 25; ix 4, 14; x 9, 16; xi 3, 14; xii 2–3, 12, 20; xiii 3, 10, 17; xiv 3, 11; xv 4, 12, 19; xvi 2, 11, 20; xvii 2, 10, 15; xviii 2, 14, 25–26; xix 4, 13, 19; xx 2, 10, 20; xxi 1; xxiv 2; BB 2; FF 3; GG 2, 10; HH i 2; ii 1
Iulius Serenus (1), Vet Gall, t. Herodiani, 154–179: **76** iv 19; FF 1
Iulius Serenus (2), curator Vet Gall, t. Lycarionis. 154–179: **76** vi 14, 21; x 9
Iulius Serenus (3), Vet Gall, t. Lycarionis, 154–179: **76** viii 2, 11
Iulius Serenus (4), Vet Gall, t. Ammoniani, 154–179: **76** xi 13
Iulius Serenus (5), Vet Gall, t. Herodiani, 154–179: **76** xx 1. Literate; hence not same as 1 above
Iulius Serenus (6), Vet Gall, 154–179: **76** xxiv 1
Iul(ius) Serenus, Egypt, c. Theopropi, 193: **5** ii 10
Iulius Seuerus, secutor tribuni III Cyr, ca. 65–90: **58** ii 7
M Iulius M f Siluanus, praef. I Aug Lus in 154: **64** i 6–7
Iulius Soemus, XX Palm, c. Marci, 204: **6** iii 18; **1** vii 10, sing; **2** xii 24
Iulius Terentius, trib XX Palm: **50** i 11 app
Iulius Th[, sing XX Palm, c. Mariani, 221: **2** xxi 15
Aurel Iulius Themarsa, eq XX Palm, t. Zebida, 201: **1** xxxii 11
Iulius Themarsas, XX Palm, c. Mariani, 210: **1** xxiii 16; **2** xviii 23; **8** vi 3 (**1** and **8**, Themarsa)
[I]ụḷịus Va[b]ạḷạ[t]ḥụṣ, XX Palm, c. Antonini pr, 214: **8** ix 5
C Iulius Valens, III Cyr, 65–96: **9** 4 a
Iulius Valens, Egypt, t. Rufi, II–III p.: **30** ii 15
Iul(ius) Valentinus, XX Palm, ca. 190–230: **41** 8
Iulius Valerianus, Egypt, t.? Saturnili, 114–139: **75** 11
Aurel Iulius [Za]bde, XX Palm, c. Malchiana, 205: **1** xxviii 10
Iul(ius) Zabdibolus, XX Palm, c. Nigrini, 198–235: **47** ii 6
M Iun Crispu[s]: **72** introd
Iunius Martiaḷ[is], immunis? II Traian, 210–242: **21** 3
Ius.[, cent?, Egypt, second quarter of III p.: **53** d
Iustillus, trib XX Palm in 221: p. 383; **91** *1* 1; *1* verso 1; *2* verso 1; *2* i 1 app
Iustus, *see also* Fabius Minicius
]cịṣ.s Iustus, XXII Deiot, early I p.: **51** i 8

L[, *see also* Abbas, Melas
C Ḷ. . .ụs[, Egypt, early II p.: **77** a ii 2
]Ḷa. .us Themarsa, XX Palm, c. Danymi, 201: **1** i 19 and app; **2** vii 1
Laetianus, *see* Pomponius
Lappus, cent I Aug Lus, 131–156: **64** ii 16, 26; ii 1 app
Largus: **102** a 6 app
Laronius Secundianus, trib XX Palm: p. 183
Latinianus, proc Aug, ca. 101–105: **63** ii 26
Λχηους: **76** xv 11 app
Leon, trib, Dura in 216: p. 367; **89** *18* verso; *28* verso 2 app

Leon Besarion, Egypt, coh eq t. Antoni, 152–177 or 184–209: **78** *30* 3
Leonid[, *see* Ṣ.[..]ṃius
Lepidianus, cent, XXII Deiot?, early I p.: **51** i 5; ii 3
Letianus, *see* Pomponius Laetianus
Liberalis, *see also* Sempronius
Liberalis: **10** 16 app
Licinnius, *see also* Aelius, Aurelius
Licinnius Alexan[d-, XX Palm, c. Nasonis, ca. 215–240: **15** ii 17
Licinnius Apolloninus, eq XX Palm, t. Antonini, 205 or 208: **1** xliii 12; **2** xliii 10; **92** iv 14 app
Liciṇ[niu]ṣ Gaị[, *canceled*, XX Palm, c. Marci, 216–221: **2** xvi 4
Licin(nius) Loce (Locceius?), III Cyr, c. Capitoniana, 91–116: **34** recto ii 11 and app
Licinnius Pacatianus, dux, Dura in 245: **83** 21 and 23
Liuianus, *see* Aurelius
Litorinus, *see* Oppius
Lo[, *see* Aurelius, Iulius
Lo[..]oṇụṣ, *see* Aurelius
Lọ.[.]us Salmẹ[, XX Palm, 226: **95** b 4
Locceius, *see* Licinnius Loce
Loce, *see* Licinnius
M Aur Loḷḷiụ[s, Egypt, 205?: **46** 3
Lon[, *see* Au[
Loṇ[, *cogn*, eq XX Palm, t. Octaui, 201: **2** xl 2
Aurel Lon[, XX Palm, c. Danymi 202–206?: **1** iii–v i 5
M Aur Ḷon[: **46** 1 app
Long( ), *see* Aurelius
Longianus, cent I Aug Lus, 92–117: **74** iii 9
Longie[nus, Egypt, cent coh eq, 132–157: **78** *73* 1 and app
Longin[: **1** xv 24 app
Longinus, *see also* Aelius, Antonius, Aurelius; **9** 30 a app, **76** vii 16 app; **78** *73* app
Longinus, XXII Deiot?, early I p.: **51** ii 2
M Longinu[s]sus, III Cyr, 65–96: **9** 30 a
Longinus, dec, Egypt, 114–139: **75** 7 and 15
Longinus, Egypt, eq aux, second quarter of II p.: **73** a i 12
M Longinus .[, dec? sig?, Egypt, aux, second quarter of II p.: **73** a iii 1
Longinus (1), Egypt, eq aux, second quarter of II p.: **73** a iii 22
Longinus (2), Egypt, eq aux, second quarter of II p.: **73** a iii 25
Longinus, Egypt, dec coh eq, 132–217: **78** *42* 2; *45* 2; *48* 2; *49* 1
Lọṇgi[nu]ṣ, status unknown, Dura in 216: **89** *49* 3
Longinus: **46** 1 app; **4** 1 2 app
M Longinus Ap[...].[, III Cyr, 65–96: **9** 32 a
C Lọngius Apollọ[, I Aug Lus, c. Lappi, 141 or 155: **64** ii 27
Longinus Arianus, Vet Gall, t. Lucilli Bassi, 154–179: **76** vii 16
Longinus Er[(or Her[ ), Egypt, coh eq, t. Gemelli, 151–177 or 183–209: **78** *27* 1
Longinus Longus, sig I Aug Lus, c. Titulei, 92–117: **74** i 1
Longinus Nerius, Vet Gall, t. Sereni Melanos, 154–179: **76** xx 19
Aurel Longinus Numei, sing XX Palm, t. Demetri, 203: **1** xxxvii 14
C Longinus Priscus, III Itur, 103: **87** 13
Longinus Ru[....].[, Egypt, c. Theopropi, 194: **5** ii 15
Longinus Rufus: **9** 30 a app
Longinus Tituleius, cent I Aug Lus, 92–117: **74** i 2–3, 10; ii 2, 10; iii 2, 9–10
Longius: **87** 13 app
Longon, *see* Antonius, Bius; **34** recto ii 15 app
Longus, *see also* Iulius, Longinus; **46** 1 app
Luçạ[, *see* Dionysius
Lucianus: **34** recto ii 11 app
Aurel Lucianus Themarsa, eq XX Palm, t. Demetri, 193: **1** xxxvi 9
Lucilius Artorius, dupl XX Palm, t. Tiberini, 207–232: **27** b i 2
Lucilius Bassus, dec Vet Gall, 154–179: **76** vii 16–17, ix 18; x 23; xi 3; xv 12; xvi 2 and 8; xx 9 and 16; FF 9
Lucilius Luci, sing XX Palm, c. Antonini post, 208: **2** xxviii 27
Lucillus: **34** recto ii 11 app
Lucius, Luci, *see also* Aurelius, Iarhaboles, Lucilius, Marinus
Lucius, trierarchus liburnae, Egypt, II p.: **82** 3, 4, 9
Lucius Agillius, Egypt, aux, 177: **70** a ii 1
Aurel Lucius Aurelius, eq XX Palm, t. Demetri, 194: **1** xxxvi 14
Lucius Cassianus, eq XX Palm, t. Antonini, 204: **1**, Aurel, xlii 31; **2** xlii 22
Luçị[us] Ịuḷiạṇ[u]s, sesq XX Palm, c. Aureli, 226: **4** b i 6 and app
Lucius Octauius, dec XX Palm, 201: pp. 149, 387; **1**, Aurel, xxxviii 11–12; **2** xxxviii 24–25; **92** vii 10; x 2
Aurel Lucius Salme, eq XX Palm, t. Demetri, 214: **1** xxxvi 15
Aurel Lucius Thema[rsa-, sesq XX Palm, c. Mariani, 204: **1** xxi 6
Lucius Valerianus, sig XX Palm, t. Octaui, 207: **1**, Aurel, xl 19; **2** xl 26
Lucretius, XXII Deiot, c. Firmi, early I p.: **51** ii 22
Lupus, pr[, status uncertain, Dura in 216: **89** *7* 10; *14* 3–5 app
Lycarion, dec Vet Gall, 154–179: **76** vi 15 and 21; viii 2 and 12; ix 3; x 9; xviii 2, 12, 21; xix 2

Lycarion Pasaus, Vet Gall, t. Apollinarii, 154–179: **76** xv 3
Lucofron H[..]ụ[.]liri, Egypt, principalis?, 173: **39** 2

M[, *see also* Antonius, Aurelius, Marinus, Marius, Paasechus, Seleucus, Vlpius
Ṃ.[..].ịus, M.l[.]abimi, *see* Aurelius
Ṃ[..]nus, *see* Iulius
M....ṣ[, *see* Aurelius
Ṃ[, Egypt, aux, 184–189: **70** c 8
M.[ ] Addei, xx Palm, c. Marci, 199: **2** xi 25
]as Ṃ[, eq xx Palm, t. Octaui, 201: **2** xl 3
Ṃ.[..]ṃụs Iaṛ[, eq xx Palm, t. Octaui, 202: **1**, Aurel, xxxix 33; **2** xl 5
Aurel M.[..]iṃ[, xx Palm, c. Antonini post, 204: **1** xii 14
M.[ ]ei, xx Palm, c. Danymi, 209: **2** viii 15
]thus M[, sing xx Palm, c. Antonini pr, 210: **2** xxiii 22
Ṃ[, *nom*, xx Palm, c. Antonini post, 210?: **8** x 20
Aurel M[, xx Palm, c. Marci, 214: **1** ix 30
Aurel M[, xx Palm, c. Mariani, 214: **1** xxiv 21
Aurel M[, sing xx Palm, c. Castrici, 214–215: **1** xx 2
Aurel Ṃ[......].ma[, dupl xx Palm, t. Zebida, 194–219: **1** xxxi 24
M.[ ]ḥ..[, xx Palm, ca. 200–235: **61** ii 6
M[, xx Palm, ca. 215–240: **15** b 10
Ṃ..ḷ[, xx Palm, ca. 215–240: **15** b 12
Ṃ[, *nom*, xx Palm, ca. 220–255: **25** b 4
Ṃ[.]ternus: **30** ii 10 app
M[..]*ναν*[*ο*]*υ*: **81** ii 5 app
Ma[, *see also* Aurelius, Iulius, Mocimus, Themarsa
Ma.h[..]s, *see* Aurelius
Aurel Ma.[, xx Palm, c. Danymi, 202–206: **1** iii–v i 2
Ma[, *nom*, xx Palm, c. Danymi, 204: **2** vii 31
Mạ[, xx Palm, c. Antonini post, 210?: **8** x 18
Aurel Ma[, xx Palm, c. Marci, 214: **1** ix 31
Aurel Ma.[...]ụs .[, xx Palm, c. Mariani, 214: **1** xxiv 2
]ma.[...]ṣ, *cogn*, xx Palm, c. Marci, 214: **2** xiv 21. Probable, but not certain, that this name begins with *m*.
Aurel Ma[, xx Palm, c. Antonini post, 216: **1** xv 19
Aurel Ma[, xx Palm, c. Antonini post, 216: **1** xv 21
Ma.[, *nom*, sing xx Palm, c. Marci, 222: **2** xvi 7
Ṃạ..[, *nom*, xx Palm, ca. 200–235: **61** ii 5
Maal, *see* Aurelius
Mabogaeus, -eus, *see* Mombogeus
Mac[, *see* Salmes
Maccaei, *see also* Addaeus, Bassus. Bu[.]ṛaṇ[.].us, Demetrius, Malchus, Salmanes, Zabdibolus, Zebidas
Aurel .[......] Maccaei, eq xx Palm, t. Tiberini, 195: **1** xxxiv 3
Macceus H[ae]ran, xx Palm, c. Antonini post, 207: **2** xxviii 17
Maccaeus Themarsa, eq xx Palm, t. Demetri, 200: **1**, Aurel, xxxvi 32; **2** xxxvi 28; **26** b 2
Macchana, *see* Abianes, Iarhaeus, Males
Maçcio.[.]s, *see* Hermogenes
Macrinius Maximi, xx Palm, 212: c. Seleuciana, **6** xi 24; c. Castrici, **1**, Aurel, xviii 12; drom, c. Antonini pr, **2** xlv 7, Macrinus, and **8** ix 17
Macrinus, *see* Aurelius
Macrinus Maximi, *see* Macrinius
Ṃạẹg ..[, *name?*, Egypt, II p.: **72** 10
Maesom(as), *see also* Barathes
Maesomas Aciba, eq xx Palm, t. Tiberini, 199: **1**, Aurel, xxxiv 15: **2** xxxiv 13, Maesamas
Maeuius Margellus (Marcellus?), I Aug Lus, c. Candidi, 136: **64** ii 24
Magdaei, *see* Saedus
Magn-, Magnus, *see also* Aurelius, Iulius
Aurel Magnus[, xx Palm, c. Antonini post, 204: **1** xii 13
Magnus Vabalathi, xx Palm, c. Danymi, 203: **6** i 13; **92** viii 5
Maimins (Maeminius?) Puteolanus, dupl Vet Gall, t. Agrippae, 154–179: **76** xiv 16
Maior, *see* Marcus and **1** xi 14 app
Mal[, *see* Zabdibolus
Malacheli, *see* Zabdibolus
Malch[, *see also* Addas, Achilleus
Aurel Malc[h-, xx Palm, c. Mariani, 200–201: **1** xxi 25
Aurel Malc[h-, xx Palm, c. Malchiana, 203: **1** xxvii 23
Malch[, xx Palm, ca. 205–240: **12** a–c 8
[M]ạḷç[h-, xx Palm, ca. 210–240: **13** 19
Malchi, *see also* Abed[..].cre[...].., Bac[.]b..ius, Bassus, Haeranes, Hagus, Iadibelus, Iarhaeus, Marinus, Mombogeus, Nisamsus, Ogelus, Salmes, Seleucus, Seleus, Themarsa, Themes, Valerius, Zabathes, Zabbaeus, Zabdaathes, Zabdes, Zabdibolus, Zebidas
].th[ ] Malchi, xx Palm, c. Mariani, 193: **1** xxi 11
A[urel -10?-] Malchi, xx Palm, c. Castrici, 196–200: **1** xvi 22
[Ma]ḷcḥi, xx Palm, c. Malchiana, 203: **6** ix 11
]..[.] Malchi, xx Palm, c. Danymi, 203: **2** vii 13
[-7?-ḷus Mal]çhi, xx Palm, c. Marci, 205: **1** vii 27; **2** xiii 6
]hes Malchi, xx Palm, c. Marci, 205: **1** vii 29; **2** xiii 8
].aeus Malchi, xx Palm, c. Danymi, 210: **6** i 31

]. . . .as Malchi, xx Palm, ca. 215–240; **15** ii 4
Malchi: **1** xxvii 15 app
Malchus, *see also* Aurelius, Cassius, Iulius, Ṛ[; **55** b 5 app
Malchus, *nom*, xx Palm, c. Antonini post, 202: **2** xxvii 18
Malchus, *nom*, xx Palm, c. Mariani, 209?: **6** vi 1
Aurel Malchus[, xx Palm, c. Marci, 214: **1** ix 22
Malchus, *cogn*, xx Palm, c. Mariani, 214: **1** xxv 13
Malchus, cent xx Palm, 197–222: pp. 183, 387; **2** i 1 app; xliii 15
Malchus, *nom*, xx Palm, 225: **3** a 9
Malchus: **2** xiii 6 app
Aurel Malchus Abgari, eq xx Palm, t. Octaui, 195: **1** xxxviii 26
Malchus Anani, xx Palm, c. Antonini post, 193: **6** iv 19; **1**, Aurel, xi 8
Aurel Malchus Bel[, xx Palm, c. Marci, 210: **1** viii 9
Malchus Bode, eq xx Palm, t. Tiberini, 204: **1**, Aurel, xxxv 7; **2** xxxv 11
Malchus Diogeni, xx Palm, c. Antonini post, 196: **6** iv 23; **1**, Aurel, xi 15; **2** xxvii 4
Malchus Ẹ[, xx Palm, c. Marci, 193: **6** ii 25
Malchus Goras, eq xx Palm, 226–251: **83** 3
Malchus Haeran, eq xx Palm, t. Octaui, 199: **2** xxxix 6
Malchus Haeran, eq xx Palm, t. Octaui, 201: **1**, Aurel, xxxix 11; **2** xxxix 15
Malchus Iarhaei, eq xx Palm, t. Octaui, 201: **1**, Aurel, xxxix 15; **2** xxxix 18
Malchus Maccaei, eq xx Palm, t. Octaui, 201: **1**, Aurel, xxxix 7; **2** xxxix 13; **26** c 2
Malchus Mombogei, eq xx Palm, t. Zebida, 202: **1**, Aurel, xxxii 20; **2** xxxiii 2, Mambogei
Malchus Mombogei, xx Palm, 211–236: **33** iii 5
Malchus Muciani, eq xx Palm, t. Demetri, 204: **1**, Aurel, xxxvii 19; **2** xxxvii 20
Aurel Malchus Nisamsi, eq xx Palm, t. Octaui, 193: **1** xxxviii 19
Malchus Salman, drom xx Palm, c. Antonini pr, 195: **2** xlv 5
[Ma]ḷc̣ḥ[us] Ṣ[a]ḷṃaṇị: **115** c 1 app
Malchus Salme, xx Palm, c. Heliodori, ca. 215–240: **15** ii 14
Mal(chus?) Siluan[.], xx Palm, 194–219: **1** xli 28 marg
[Ma]ḷc̣ḥ[us] Ṣ[i]ḷụaṇị: **115** c 1 app
Malchus Themarsa, eq xx Palm, t. Tiberini, 201: **1**, Aurel, xxxiv 22; **2** xxxiv 20
Aurel Malchus Ṭ[hemar]ṣạ, xx Palm, c. Malchiana, 214: **1** xxx 2
Malchus Themarsa, xx Palm, c. Antonini post, 207–232: **27** a i 14
Aurel Malchus Theme, eq xx Palm, t. Demetri, 195: **1** xxxvi 17
Malchus Vabalathi, xx Palm, c. Antonini post, 207: **2** xxviii 19
Malchus Vabalathi, xx Palm, c. Mariani, 210: **2** xviii 24; **8** vi 4; **92** v 20
Aurel Malchus Zebida, xx Palm, c. Malchiana, 214: **1** xxix 12
Malchus Zebida, xx Palm, 198–235: **47** i 18. Same as next two?
Malchus Zebida, sig xx Palm, 208–233: **48** 8
Malchus Zebida, xx Palm, c. Antonini pr, 211–236: **33** ii 3
Male, *see also* Agrippas, Barbaesamen, Nisraeus
Male, *cogn:* **1** xvi 27 app
A[urel M]ạḷẹ Mannaei, drom xx Palm, c. Antonini post, 195: **1** xliii 31
Aurel Male Macchana, eq xx Palm, t. Zebida, 201: **1** xxxii 15
Males Macchana, eq xx Palm, t. Tiberini, 201: **2** xxxiv 21. Same as preceding?
Males Themarsa, eq xx Palm, t. Tiberini, 207–232: **27** b i 3. Canceled
Malichi, *see* Themes
Malichus Sạ[, Egypt, c. Belei, 180–205: **81** iii 7
Ṃạḷḷịọ[, *cogn:* **21** 5 app.
Malochus (*Μαλωχως*) .[. .]mii, Egypt, optio, 180–205: **81** ii 5
Mambogaeus, -eus, *see* Mombogeus
Aurel Mammaeus Auida, xx Palm, c. Danymi, 195: **1** i 7
Mammaeus Belaacabi, xx Palm, c. Antonini post, 201: **6** iv 31; **1** xi 25; **2** xxvii 13
Mammaeus Bọbe.[, xx Palm, c. Marci, 214?: **6** iv 3
Mammes, *see* Iulius
Man.deus: **8** vi 12 app
Mandatus: **91** *1* i 6 app
Mannaeus, *see* Aurelius
[M]annas, *cogn:* **89** *4* ii 14 app
Aurel Mannas Themarsa, eq xx Palm, t. Octaui, 201: **1** xxxix 28
Mannosin, *see* Barsines
Mannaei, *see* Male
Mannus *see* Ạ[, Aurelius
Mar[, *see also* Aurelius
Ṃạṛ.[, *nom*, xx Palm, c. Antonini pr, 214: **2** xxiv 2
]s Mar[. .]us, xx Palm, c. Mariani, 214: **1** xxiv 14
Aurel Mar[ ] Salman, xx Palm, c. Malchiana, 205: **1** xxviii 11
Maras Themarsa, eq xx Palm, t. Demetri, 204: **1**, Aurel, xxxvii 20; **2** xxxvii 21
Marc.[, *see* Iulius
Μαρκ̣[, status unknown, Dura in 216: **89** *9* 2 app
Marcellinus, *cogn*, Egypt, 217: **40** i 15
Marcellus, *see* Aelius, Atho, Aurelius, Vlpius; **64** ii 24 app

Marcianus, *see also* Aelius, Antonius, Domitius, Iulius; **1** xxvii 18 app; **50** i 9 app
Marcianus, Egypt, actuarius equitum promotorum?, 268–293: **86** 6
Marcius, *nom:* **9** 23 a app; **38** ii 7 app
Marcus, *see also* Ammonius, Iulius, Menodorus
Marcus, *cogn*, cent I Aug Lus, 131–156: **64** i 37; ii 1 app
Marcus, *cogn*, xx Palm, 216–250; **16** recto 3
Marcus Fuscus: p. 285
Marcus Maior, eq xx Palm, t. Tiberini, 201: **1** xi 14 app; xxxiv 21; **2** xxxiv 19
Marcus Titus *or* Titi, Vet Gall, t. Agrippae, 154–179: p. 285; **76** viii 14 and 23
Marcus Valerius, stator Vet Gall, t. Petroniana, 154–179: **76** xvii 1
Marcus Victor, xx Palm, c. Mariani, 204: **1** xxii 10; **2** xvii 17
Marcus Victor, principalis? xx Palm, t. Antiochi, 222: **23** ii 8
Mardontes: **78** *18* 1 app
Marea, *see* Barzas, Fronton, Iarhaeus, Vlpius
Margellus, *see* Maeuius
Mari..[.]..[, *nom?*, xx Palm, ca. 215–240: **15** i 15
].mari.[, xx Palm, ca. 215–240: **15** e 3. *Possibly*]. Mari.[
Mariani, xx Palm, ca. 205–230: **122** 4 and app
Marianus, *see* Iulius, Vlpius
Aurel Marimelus Reibeli, eq xx Palm, t. Demetri, 201: **1** xxxvii 2
Marin˙ Crisp.[, Egypt, II p.: **72** 5
Aurel Marin[, xx Palm, c. Danymi, 202–206: **1** iii–v i 3
Marini, xx Palm, c. Mariani, 200–201: **2** xvii 5
]mus Marini, eq xx Palm, t. Tiberini, 202: **1** xxxiv 29
]s Marini, xx Palm, c. Marci, 214: **1** ix 6; **2** xiv 17; **8** iv 8
Marini, Marinus, *see also* Aelius, Antoninus, Aurelius, Claudius, Flauius, Halathes, Herennius, Iulius, Salme, Timon, Vlpius; **8** viii 23 app
[Aur]el [-7?- M]arinus, eq xx Palm, t. Octaui, 199: **1** xxxviii 34
]ius Marinus, eq xx Palm, t. Zebida, 202: **1**, Aurel, xxxii 23: **2** xxxii 4
[Ma]rinus, *cogn*, xx Palm, c. Danymi, 203: **2** vii 19
Marinus, *cogn*, xx Palm, c. Marci, 204: **1** vii 24; **2** xiii 3
Marinus .[.].ron, xx Palm, c. Mariani, 204: **2** xvii 23; **8** v 17
Marinus, *cogn*, sing xx Palm, c. Mariani, 208: **2** xviii 15
]ius M[a]rinus, vexillarius xx Palm, c. Mariani, 209: **1** xxiii 12; **2** xviii 19
]..[..].ius Marinus, xx Palm, c. Danymi, 214: **2** x 5; **8** ii 18
Marinus, xx Palm, 194–219: **1** xxxii 9 marg
Marinus, *nom*, xx Palm, c. Heliodori, ca. 215–240: **15** ii 13
Marinus, *cogn*, praefectus II Traian, first half of III p.: **102** a 7
Marinus post, cent xx Palm, 225–251: pp. 128, 133; **66** a i 9; a ii 10; b i 19 app; **17** a 1?
Marinus pr, cent xx Palm, 225–251: pp. 128, 133; **66** a ii 8; b i 17; b ii 23; b i 19 app; **17** a 1?
Marinus, cent xx Palm, 217–256: pp. 128, 133; **17** a 1. Probably same as one of the two preceding
Marinus Abbos[a, xx Palm, c. Germani, ca. 216–242?: **32** 3
Marinus Barathe, xx Palm, c. Marci, 203: **6** iii 13; **1**, Aurel, vii 1
Marinus Bobe.[: **6** iv 3 app
Marinus Glauci[, *see* *Μαρρινος*
M[a]rinus Heli[od]ori, xx Palm, c. Mariani, 216: **2** xx 23
Marinus Hotaraei, eq xx Palm, t. Demetri, 204: **1**, Aurel, xxxvii 18; **2** xxxvii 19
Marinus Luci, xx Palm, 204: c. Malchiana, **6** ix 21; **1**, Aurel, xxviii 4; c. Pudentis, **92** ix 10
Marinus M[, xx Palm, c. Aur[eli, 232: **4** b ii 16
Marinus M[.]l[, xx Palm, 217–256: **17** a 10. Probably same as next
Marinus Malchi, xx Palm, ca. 215–240: **15** ii 10–11
Marinus Maximi, xx Palm, c. Malchiana, 204: **6** ix 19; **1**, Aurel, xxviii 1
Marinus Seleuci, xx Palm, c. Marci, 201: **6** iii 3
Mari[nus] Themarsa[, xx Palm, c. Malchiana, 196: **6** viii 17
Maris Iarhaei, xx Palm, c. Marci, 203: **6** iii 15; **1** vii 2; **8** iii 10
A Marius Clemens, III Cyr, 65–96: **9** 23 a; 34–37 app
Marius M[, Egypt, I/II p.: **38** ii 15
Marius Maximus, governor of Syria, Dura ca. 208: pp. 399, 403; **98** *2* 1; *3* 1; **99** *1* 2; *1* verso 3; *2* [1]; *2* verso [2]; *3* verso [2]; *3* 1 app; *d*
Marona, *see also* Abednamares, Aurelius, Habbis
Maronas Dinaei, eq xx Palm, t. Octaui, 204: **1**, Aurel, xl 8; **2** xl 15
Maronas Gadde, eq xx Palm, t. Tiberini, 196: **1**, Aurel, xxxiv 10; **2** xxxiv 9
Marosa, *see* Abedmalchus
[Au]re[l] Marr..[, *canceled*, xx Palm, c. Marci, 201: **1** vi 19
Μαρρινος Γλαυκι[, xx Palm, 213–256: **35** 7
Aurel Marrius .[..]man[, xx Palm, c. Castrici, 194: **1** xvi 14
Marrius Com..us, Egypt, eq, 180–205: **81** ii 3

Marti[, Egypt, II p.: **129** 1
Martialis, *see* Iunius, Minicius; **129** 1 app
Martinus: **38** i 15 app
Martius, *see* S. . tius
[Mat]ernianus: **2** xxiii 19 app
Matharaei, Matrhaei, *see* Signas
Matthana: **1** xxxii 6 app; 15 app; **2** xxxii 19 app; xxxiv 21 app. The name in **81** ii 15 is clearly Macchana; and re-examination of the Dura papyri shows that the same reading is preferable in them.
Matinus, *see* Vettienus
Mauelas Abedadadi, xx Palm, c. Marci, 204: **6** iii 19; **1**, Aurel, vii 14; **2** xii 28
max[, *nom* if a name: xx Palm, ca. 207–238: **94** g 3
Maxiṃ[-, *see also* Ç[. .]sces
[Ma]xịṃ[-, *cogn*, xx Palm, c. Marci, 200: **2** xi 28
Maxim[-, *cogn*, xx Palm, c. Marci, 204: **1** vii 11 and app
[Ma]xi[m-, *cogn*, xx Palm, c. Danymi, 205: **2** viii 4
Maximi, *see also* Abedlahas, Chaeremon, Heliodorus, Macrinius, Marinus
Maximi, *cogn*, xx Palm, c. Danymi, 197–225: **92** v 8
Maximinus: **66** a ii 7 app
Maximus, *see also* Antonius, Asprius, Aurelius, Claudius, Iulius, Marius, Valerius; **8** viii 23 app; **66** a ii 7 app; **102** a 8a app
[. . . .]ius Maximus, sig I Aug Lus, c. Celeri?, 92–117: **74** ii 1
Maximus, Vet Gall, t. Donaciani, 105–130: **80** 35
Maximus, Egypt, eq aux, second quarter of II p.: **73** a i 24
]s Maximus, Egypt, aux, 178: **70** a ii 23
Aurel Maxim[us]ạḷ[. .]i, xx Palm, c. Malchiana, 204: **1** xxviii 5; app, [m]ạḷ[ch]i?
Maximus, *cogn*, principalis xx Palm, title lost, c. Antonini post, 205: **2** xxviii 11
Maximus, *cogn*, eq xx Palm, t. Demetri, 197–206: **92** vii 7
Maximus . . .y. .[, Egypt, coh eq, c. Glyconis, 150–175 or 182–207: **78** *23* 5
Maximus, *cogn*, Egypt, 212?: **5** i 17
Maximus, *cogn?*, tesserarius?, Egypt, coh eq, 132–217: **78** *55* 5
Maximus, Egypt, libertus: **10** 16
Maximus Atrei, Egypt, I/II p.: **38** i 10
Maximus Ermogeni, xx Palm, c. Danymi, 204: **6** i 18
Maximus Hotaraei, xx Palm, 204: c. Seleuciana, **6** xi 5; c. Castrici, **1** xvii 10; c. Antonini pr, **2** xxii 20
Maximus Malchi: **1** xxviii 5 app
Maximus N[. . . . .]ianus, Egypt, aux, 177: **70** a i 26
Maximus Salman, xx Palm, c. Mariani, 214: **1**, Aurel, xxv 10; **2** xx 7
Aurel Maximus Seleuci, eq xx Palm, t. Tiberini, 212: **1** xxxv 26
Maximus Zaora, xx Palm, c. Mariani, 204: **1** xxii 15; **2** xvii 21; **8** v 15
]maẓ[, *cogn*, xx Palm, c. Marci, 216–221: **2** xvi 2
Ạ[urel M]azaba[na-, imaginifer?, xx Palm, c. Malchiana, 207: **1** xxviii 21
Mazab[anas, *nom*, xx Palm, c. Mariani, 214: **8** vi 24
Mazabanas Belaacabi, eq xx Palm, t. Octaui, 201: **1**, Aurel, xxxix 21; **2** xxxix 24, Mazabbanas
Mazd. [, *see* Zabdibolus
Ṃe. . d[, *see* Aurelius
Me. aṣius, *nom:* **21** 11 app
Aurel Me[. . . . . The]marsa, xx Palm, c. Seleuci, 191–216: **89** *12* ii 3
Meheridates Barginnaia, xx Palm, c. Danymi, 201: **2** vii 4
Melas, *see also* Herennius, Serenus, Taurinus
Melas L[, Egypt, aux, 181–186: **70** a iii 13
Memnon Psenpres, sig Vet Gall, t. Petronii, 154–179: **76** vi 6; xvii 6
Menander, Menandrus, *see also* Aelius, Iulius, Vlpius
Menander, *cogn*, xx Palm, ca. 215–240: **15** ii 11
Mences Anubas, Vet Gall, t. Herodiani, 154–179: **76** vi 17
Menodorus Marci, Vet Gall, t. Sereni Melanos, 154–179: **76** xviii 24
Mesenus, Messenus, *see* Aurelius Apollonius
Messianus, *cogn*, xx Palm, 248?: **44** 13
Messius Furianus, dec Vet Gall in 199: **76** vi 1 app (Dessau 2543)
Milens, *see also* Amrus, Claudius
]us Milens, xx Palm, ca. 215–240: **15** ii 14
Milo, *see* Naaroüs
[C] Minicius Italus, Praefectus Aegypti, 101–103: **87** 2
Minicius Iustus, princeps xx Deiot?, early I p.: p. 198; **51** ii 6
Minicius Martialis, proc Aug, Dura, ca. 208: **98** *2* a 2
Miso: **9** 12 a app
Aurel Mo[, xx Palm, c. Antonini post, 216: **1** xv 20
Mo. . . . [, xx Palm, ca. 205–240: **12** a–c 10
Mo. [imu]s, *see* Aurelius
[M]ocim[, *see also* Babuius
Mocị[m-, *cogn*, eq xx Palm, t. Octaui, 201–203: **26** c 3
Ạ[urel M]oçiṃ[, xx Palm, c. Malchiana, 207: **1** xxviii 22
Aurel Moci[m-, xx Palm, c. Mariani, 212–214: **1** xxiii 24

Mocimi, *see* Abdasthor, Bolaeus, Iamlichus, Mocimus, Siluanus, Themarsas, Zabdaathes
Mocimus, *see also* Aurelius
Mocimus, *nom*, eq xx Palm, t. Antonini, 201: **1** xlii 8
]ius Mocimus, eq xx Palm, t. Tiberini, 212: **1** xxxv 29; **2** xxxvi 2
Moci[mus, *nom*, xx Palm, c. Danymi, 214: **6** i 37
Mocimus, *cogn*, xx Palm, c. Marci, 214: **8** iv 15
Mocimus, cent xx Palm, 216–250: pp. 132, 133, 157; **32** 4; **16** recto 3
Mocimus: **4** a i 2 app
Mocimus Antoni[, xx Palm, 214: c. Seleuciana, **6** xi 29; c. Castrici, **1** xviii 17
Mocimus Antonini, xx Palm, 212: c. Seleuciana, **6** xi 25; **1**, Aurel, xviii 13
Mocimus Antonini, eq xx Palm, 226–251: **83** 7
Mocimus Barlaha, eq xx Palm, t. Octaui, 199: **1**, Aurel, xxxix 2; **2** xxxix 8
[Mo]ç[i]mus Barnei, eq xx Palm, t. Tiberini, 202: **2** xxxiv 27; **1** xxxiv 29 app
Mocimus Bạṛṇẹ[, xx Palm, c. Danymi, 214: **2** ix 23; **8** ii 9
Mocimus Bolani, xx Palm, c. Danymi, 203: **6** i 11
Aurel Mocimus Ierhaei, eq xx Palm, t. Demetri, 201: **1** xxxvii 1
Mocimus Ṃ[, xx Palm, c. Antonini post, 207: **2** xxviii 18
Mocimus Ma.[, xx Palm, c. Antonini pr, 214: **8** viii 22
Mocimus Marini: **1** xxxiv 29 app
Mocimus Mocimi, sing xx Palm, t. Zebida, 205: **1**, Aurel, xxxiii 11; **2** xxxiii 27
[Mo]cimus Ṣ...[, xx Palm, c. Mariani, 210: **6** vi 3
Mocimus Salman, eq xx Palm, t. Tiberini, 210: **2** xxxv 28
M[o]ç̣ịṃụṣ Salme, xx Palm, c. Heliodori, ca. 215–240: **15** ii 12
Mocimus Simon, eq xx Palm, t. Tiberini, 205: **1**, Aurel, xxxv 16; **2** xxxv 17, Simaoni
Mocimus Themar[sa-, dupl *or* sesq xx Palm, c. Castrici, 204: **1** xvi 12
Mocimus Themarsa, xx Palm, c. Antonini pr, 207–232: **27** a i 11
Mocimus Themarsas, xx Palm, ca. 215–240: **15** ii 9
Mocimus Theme[, xx Palm, 203: c. Castrici, **1** xvii 1; c. Antonini pr, **2** xxii 12
Mocimus Theme, eq xx Palm, t. Tiberini, 205: **1**, Aurel, xxxv 19; **2** xxxv 20
Aurel Mocimus Zabd[, xx Palm, c. Malchiana, 209–212: **1** xxix 1
Mocimus Zaora, eq xx Palm, t. Antonini, 204: **1** xliii 2; **2** xlii 26
Mocimus Zebida, eq xx Palm, t. Zebida, 205: **1**, Aurel, xxxiii 6; **2** xxxiii 22
Mocimus Zebida, xx Palm, c. Danymi, 214: **6** i 33
[Moc]ọpor: **89** *5* 15 app
Mombogei, Mombogeus, *see also* Aurelius, Claudius, Malchus, Ṿ[.....]
A[urel ....a]ḍadus Mombogei, eq xx Palm, t. Zebida, 194–195: **1** xxxi 30 and app
Mombogeus Barnebus, xx Palm, c. Marci, 204: p. 97; **92** v 14; **8** iii 18 and app
[Mom]bogeus M[a]lch[, xx Palm, ca. 205–240: **12** e 2. These may be the names of two men
Mombogeus Themarsa, xx Palm, c. Mariani, 198–235: **47** ii 19
Mombogeus Zaora, xx Palm, c. Antonini post, 201: **6** iv 32, Mabogeus; **1** xi 26; **2** xxvii 14, Maṃ[bogeus
Monimi, Monimus, *see also* Aurelius, Flauius, Monimus, Valerius
Aurel Mon[im-, xx Palm, c. Danymi, 201-205: **1** ii 8
Aurel [ ] Monimi, drom xx Palm, c. Malchiana, 204: **1** xliv 16 and app; **2** xliii 21
Monimus [..]..a, xx Palm, c. Marci, 212: **2** xiii 27
Monimus, *cogn*, Egypt, 217: **40** i 11
Monimus Aufei, xx Palm, c. Danymi, 204: **6** i 16
Monimus Monimi, xx Palm, c. Danymi, 204: **6** i 19
Monimus (*cogn?*) prior, xx Palm, ca. 215–240: **15** i 17
Monimus Salluma, xx Palm, c. Danymi, 204: **6** i 21
Montan[, *see* Bassus
Montanus, Egypt, eq aux, second quarter II p.: **73** a ii 10, Muntanus
Mu[, *see* Aurelius
Muciani, Mucianus, *see also* Aurelius, Malchus, Valerius; **50** i 9 app
Mucianus Zabbei, xx Palm, c. Danymi, 214: **2** x 3; **8** ii 16
Aurel Mucianus Zabdibolus, eq xx Palm, t. Demetri, 193: **1** xxxvi 10
Munnis, *see* Aurelius
Muntanus, *see* Montanus
Murenus Taeni: **30** ii 12 app

Ṇ.ị.[.].ṣ, *see* Aurelius
N[.....]ianus, *see* Maximus
Na[, *see* Dumanus
Naamaei, *see* Salmanes
Ναaραους: **76** xvii 15 app
Naaroüs Milonis, Vet Gall, 154–179: **76** xvii 15
Ναaρωσις: **76** xvii 15 app
Naḥaṛọṭis, *genitive:* **27** b i 13 app
Nahestabus Themarsa, eq xx Palm, t. Zebida, 200: **1**, Aurel, xxxii 3; **2** xxxii 16

Aurel Ṇaọ.[, xx Palm, c. Mariani, 212–214: **1** xxiii 23
]...ạṛies Ṇaṛ.[..]ḥ.[, xx Palm, ca. 215–240: **15** b 5
Ναρωους: **76** xvii 15 app
Narsi, *genitive:* **53** b 5 app
Naso, cent xx Palm, ca. 205–240: pp. 125, 132, 133; **12** a–c 10; **15** i 11, 15, 21, 22; ii 5, 7, 9, 15, 17; g; **16** verso 2
Nassibeli, *see* Bassus
Ṇ[a]ṭal( ), xx Palm, 194–219: **1** xxxvii 6 marg
Natalis?, xx Palm, 194–219: **1** xxxvi 23 marg
Natalius, *see* Claudius
Natali(us?), xx Palm, 194–219: **1** xxxv 3 marg
Ṇẹ..[, *see* Flauius
Nebudaei, *see also* Habibas
Nebudaes Themarsa, eq xx Palm, t. Antonini, 204: **1**, Aurel, xlii 27; **2** xlii 18; **92** x 5
Nebumarius, *see* Aurelius
Nechtherotis, *genitive*, *see* Hareschis
Nechutus: **59** i 16 app; 19 app
Nedimus (Nedymus); **20** 4 app
Nefotianus, *see* Nephotianus
Nemaesianus: **70** a i 26 app
Nemas, *see* Aurelius
]h.s˙ Neoh..[..]dus, Egypt, classiarius, 127–164: **59** i 19
Neon, *see* Aurelius
Neot( ), *see* Becis
Neoterius, *cogn*, sing xx Palm, c. Mariani, 216: **2** xx 16
Nepherotis, *genitive*, *see* Nepheros
[*Νε*]*φερῶ*: **76** GG 1 app
Nepheros, Egypt, eq aux, second quarter II p.: **73** a iii 15
Nepheros, *alias* Nephos, Vet Gall, t. Soterichi, 154–179: p. 285; **76** xix 18
Nepheros Iudi, Egypt, I/II p.: **38** i 4
Nepheros Nepherotis, Egypt, optio coh eq, 153–178 or 185–210: **78** *36* 1
Nephos, *alias of* Nepheros, Vet Gall
Nefotianus, Egypt, eq aux, second quarter of II p.: **73** a ii 14; b 4
]...s. Nephyas, Egypt, classiarius: 127–164: **59** i 16
Nepotianus, *see* Iulius, Valerius
Neptunianus: **70** a i 26 app
Neratius Firminus, principalis, II Traian, rank unknown, 217–242: **21** 11
Nerius, *see also* Longinus
Nerius, cent, XXII Deiot?, early I p.: **51** ii 18
Neruaas, Vet Gall, t. Donaciani, 105–130: **80** 15
Aurel Ni[, xx Palm, c. Antonini post, 201–203: **1** xii 1
Aurel [ ]ẹus Ni.[, xx Palm, c. Malchiana, 203: **1** xxvii 19
Ni...r, *see* Cassianus
Nicaei, *see* Abbedas
Nicolas, dec, Egypt, 213–242: **24** 1
Nicolaus, *see* Domitius
Nicomachus, *see* Flauius
Nifṛạọṭes, dec xx Palm, 207–232: **27** b i 13
Niger, *see also* Arrius, Flauius, Iulius, Vlpius
Niger, Egypt, early II p.: **77** a ii 8 and app
Nigrinianus: **70** a i 26 app
Nigrinus, cent xx Palm, 211–236: p. 183; **47** i 4, 12; ii 6, 9: **23** i 6
Nilas, Vet Gall, t. Donaciani, 105–130: **80** 20
Nilus, *see* Iulius; **78** *21* 1 app
Ninius (Ninnius) Rufus, cent III Cyr, 91–116: **34** recto i 3
Ṇịṣạṃṣ[, *see also* Iarhaeus
]...eus Nisams[-, xx Palm, c. Malchiana, 195: **6** viii 14
Nisams[-, *cogn*, xx Palm, c. Mariani, 200–201: **2** xvii 7
Nisamsi, *see also* Bores, Guris, Malchus, Themarsas
Nisamsi, *cogn*, xx Palm, c. Malchiana, 203: **6** ix 12
Nisamsi, *cogn*, xx Palm, ca. 215–240: **15** i 15
Nisamsus, *nom*, xx Palm, c. Mariani, 206: **8** v 23
Nisamsus, xx Palm, 194–219: **1** xxxvii 13 marg
Ṇ[isa]ṃsus: **8** vi 22 app
Nisamsus Addaei, xx Palm, c. Marci, 201: **6** ii 4; **1**, Aurel, vi 21
Aur[el Nis]amsus Heliodori, eq xx Palm, t. Antonini, 212: **1** xliii 15
Nisamsus Malchi, xx Palm, c. Mariani, 207–232: **27** a i 4
Nisamsus Zabdiboli, eq xx Palm, t. Demetri, 199: p. 149; **1**, Aurel, xxxvi 29; **2** xxxvi 25; **26** b 1
Nismosa, *see* Iarhaeus
Nisraei: **6** xi 33 app; **1** xviii 24 app
Nisraeus, *see also* Aurelius
Nisraeus Male, xx Palm, c. Marci, 203: **8** iii 13
Nisraeus Vaḅ[, xx Palm, c. Antonini post, 214: **2** xxx 7
Nonius: **34** recto i 3 app
Ṃ Num[..].uius..[, III Cyr, 65–96: **9** 16 a
Numei, *see* Longinus
Numeri[, *see* Flauius
Numerianus: **89** *1* verso 1 app
Numissianus: **70** a i 26 app; **89** *1* verso 1 app
Nuocrinis: **64** ii 11 app
[Nym]fidius: **20** 1 app

Aurel Ọ[, xx Palm, c. Danymi, 202–219: **1** iii–v e 3
Obean, *see also* Gabrion, Iarhaboles
Obeanes Themarsa, xx Palm, c. Gaiani, 207–232: **27** a ii 8

Oc.ụianus, *see* Iulius
[Oc]baṇẹ[: **2** xviii 5 app
Ocbanes Ạ[..].ạẹị: **1** xxvii 3 app
Ocbanes Abidlaha, xx Palm, 198–201: c. Malchiana, **6** ix 6; **1**, Aurel, xxvii 3 and app; c. Malchi, **2** i 8
A[urel ..]ṣ Ọcç[...]ṃsa, xx Palm, c. Marci, 215: **1** x 2
Ocçḅạnas .[....], xx Palm, c. Nasonis, ca. 215–240: **15** i 21
Aurel Occḥạ[, xx Palm, c. Marci, 201: **1** vi 20
Octauianus: p. 285; **9** 5 a app; **76** iii 20 app
Octauius, *see also* Lucius
Octauius A f, Egypt, legionary, I a.: **36** 9
Octauus, *see* Peducaeus
Odeati, *see* Iarhaboles
Oenilus: **78** *21* 1 app
Ofilius (Ofellius) Ç̣a[, Egypt, I/II p.: **38** ii 5
Ogas, *see also* Aurelius, Bellaeus
...ụṃ[..]s Oga, xx Palm, c. Antonini post, 200: **6** iv 29; **2** xxvii 11
Aurel Ọgạṣ .[, xx Palm, c. Antonini post, 207: **1** xiii 3
[....]ṛnabus [O]gạ, eq xx Palm, 226–251: **83** 10
Ogas Hanina, eq xx Palm, t. Octaui, 212: **1**, Aurel, xl 21; **2** xl 28
Ogeli, *see* Habbis, Hammaeus
Ogelus, *see also* Aurelius
Ogelus ..[..]boli, eq xx Palm, t. Antonini, 201: **1**, Aurel, xli 34 and app; **2** xli 22. *Possibly* Gaddiboli
Ogelus .[, eq xx Palm, t. Paulini, 207–232: **27** b i 17 and app
Ogelus Malchi, optio xx Palm, 205–232: **27** b i 17 app; **47** i 17
Ogelus Malchi, xx Palm, ca. 215–240: **15** i 9
Ogelus Malchi, xx Palm, 226–251: **83** 2
Ogelus Themarsas, xx Palm, c. Achaei, ca. 215–240: **15** i 23; ii 21
Ogelus Vabalathi, eq xx Palm, t. Octaui, 203: **1**, Aurel, xl 3; **2** xl 11; **26** c 4
Ογτατιανι, *genitive:* p. 285; **76** iii 20 app
Ohrasus, *see* Aurelius
Olympus, Egypt, cent coh eq, 157–182 or 189–214; **78** *40* 3
Onnophris Colluthi, Vet Gall, t. Sentii, 154–179: **76** xix 2
Oppius Litorinus, Vet Gall, t. Sentii, 154–179: **76** xvi 10
Optatianus, dec Vet Gall, 154–179: p. 285; **76** iii 20
]..ẹus Optatus, I Hisp Vet, 79: p. 219; **63** i 22
Or[....], Egypt, practor, coh eq? in 161, 193, or 217: **78** *77* 2. Not certainly military
Ordinatus, libertus Augustorum, Dura in 221: **91** *1* i 5
Orees, Egypt, cent coh eq, 148–173 or 180–205; **78** *72* 2
Origenes, *see* Horigenes
Orsenuphis, *see also* Pathermuthis
Orsenuphis Annaë.[..], Vet Gall, t. Soterichi, 154–179: **76** viii 19
Orsei, *see* Cames

P[, *cogn*, xx Palm, c. Antonini post, 214: **1** xiv 23
P.[, *nom*, Egypt, 195–215?: **5** iii 3
P[, *nom*, Egypt, 196–216?: **5** iii 9
].ạẹtagụs P̣.[, xx Palm, ca. 205–240: **42** 6
P.[.]ọ[.]..ẹs, *see* Dionysius
Pa[, *cogn*, xx Palm, c. Antonini post, 214: **2** xxx 6
P̣ạ[, xx Palm, 194–219: **1** xxvi 5 marg
Pạ[.]ẹ[.]ọṛ[.]ụs, *cogn:* **76** xix 1 app
P̣ạ[..]ṃ....[, *see* Aurelius
Paasechus Ṃ[, Egypt, I/II p.: **38** ii 6
Paç..m( ), xx Palm, 194–219: **1** xxviii 28 marg
Pacatianus, *see* Licinnius
Pacebis, *nom*, Egypt, c. Belei, 180–205: **81** iii 13
Pacebius P[: **81** iii 13 app
Pache..: **59** i 17 app
Pachnoutis: **38** i 2 app
]ṇ Pachny..., Egypt, classiarius, 127–164: **59** i 17
Pachom[, *see* Didymus
Pachomius: **78** *67* 1 app
Pachompetenephotes: **20** 18 app
Pacoebis, *see* Paminis
Pacon(ius) Egnati(anus), III Cyr, c. Antoni Longo, 91–116: **34** recto ii 16
Pactumeius Serenus, dec Vet Gall, 154–179: p. 285; **76** iv 21; v 1–2; vi 9–10; xii 12; xiv 11; BB 2?; BB 5; FF 3
P̣ạẹṛ.[.....], Egypt, practor?, coh eq? in 161, 193, or 217: **78** *77* 4. Not certainly military
P̣aë[sis?, Egypt, coh eq? in 161, 193, or 217: **78** *77* 6. Not certainly military
Paësis Dcheutis, Vet Gall, t. Lucilli Bassi, 154–179: **76** xv 11
Pal̤[, *see* Dioscorus
Παλαματης: **76** vii 8 app
Palamotes, *see* Pathermuthis
Pambecis, Egypt, coh eq, 157–182 or 189–214: **78** *11* 2
Paminis Pacoebis, citator campi, Vet Gall, t. Aelii Sereni, 154–179: **76** xx 24
Παμμ...: **78** *26* 3 app
Pammones, Egypt, eq aux, second quarter of II p.: **73** a iii 11
Paṇa[.....], Egypt, practor, coh eq? in 161, 193, or 217: **78** *77* 3. Not certainly military
Panechates, *see* Puonsis
Panilus: **78** *21* 1 app
Paninutas, Egypt, eq aux, second quarter of II p.: **73** a iii 8

Paniscus, *see* Iulius
Pantarchus, *cogn*, Egypt, aux, 178: **70** a ii 14
M Papirius Rufus, Egypt, 62–80: **10** 1
Papontos Ṣ.[, Egypt, I/II p.: **38** ii 3
Papontos S[, Egypt, I/II p.: **38** ii 4
Pasaus, *see* Lycarion
Pasenis Ptole[maei, Egypt, practor?, coh eq? in 161, 193, or 217: **78** *77* 1. Not certainly military
Pasion, Egypt, eq aux, second quarter of II p.: **73** a i 15, 23; a ii 6
Pasion, Egypt, coh eq, 152–177 or 184–209: **78** *32* 6
Pasion Dioscori, Vet Gall, t. Gemelli, 154–179: **76** xiii 16
[Pat]ernianus: **2** xxiii 29 app
Pathermuthis, *see also* Eudaemon, Sarapion; **78** *51* 7 app
Patermouthis, Egypt, coh eq, 154–179 or 186–211: **78** *1* 7; *13* 1?
Pathermuthis Orsenuphis, Vet Gall, t. Pactumeii Sereni, 154–179: **76** iv 20; FF 2, *Πατερμουθις*
Pathermuthis Palamotes, Vet Gall, t. Sereni Melanos, 154–179: **76** vii 8
Pathermuthis Ptolemei, Egypt, aux, 180: **70** a ii 31
Patroclus, *see* Heliodorus
P̣aụ...ạ[, *see* Aurelius
Paulianus: 63 ii 32 app
Paulinus, *see* Timinius
Paullinus: **63** ii 32 app
Paulus, *see also* Aurelius, Priscus
Paulus, Vet Gall, t. Donaciani, 105–130: **80** 19
Pautina: **32** 14 app
Pẹ[.]yr.ịs, *see* Pechysis
Πεβερος: **76** xvi 1 app
Pechnutas: **38** i 2 app
Pechysis Pẹ[.]yr.ịs, Vet Gall, t. Herodiani, 154–179: **76** iv 2 and 9
Peducaeus: **63** i 22 app
Peducaeus Octauus, III Cyr, c. Aufri Aculi, 91–116: **34** recto ii 4, Petucaeus Otaus
Pei: **34** recto i 20 app
Pertinax, *see* Heluius
Petalis, Egypt, coh eq, 148–173 or 180–205: **78** *72* marg
[Pe]teesis, Egypt, eq coh eq, 132–217: **78** *59* 1
Peteesius, Egypt, coh eq, 157–182 or 189–214: **78** *11* 3
Peteminis Psenosiris, Vet Gall, t. Petronii Sereni, 154–179: **76** v 11
[Pet]ẹṇefotes Hierax, cent III Itur, 230: **20** 18
Petepsa[etis?], *see* Ṭẹṛ.chon
Petesius Papa, Egypt, coh eq, 157–181 or 188–213: **78** *14* 4
]ḍịmus Petosiris, dec, Egypt, 221: **20** 4
Petsiris, *see* Ision
Ṃ Petronius, III Cyr, 65–96: **9** 17 a
Petronius, dec Vet Gall, 154–179: p. 285; **76** v 11–12; vi 7; xv 2–3
Petronius, Egypt, cibariator, coh eq, 155–171 or 187–203: pp. 311, 312; **78** *18* 2; *21* 2; *24* 2; *25* 1; *27* 2; *30* 5; *32* 2; *39* 2; *47* 2; *48* 2; *49* 2; *50* 2–3; *51* 3; *52* 2; *53* 2; *54* 2; *68* 2; *69* 3; *74* 1
Petronius, Egypt, *χιριστης* (curator?) coh eq, 132–217: **78** *64* 1
Petronius Aprilis, cent?, Egypt, early II p.: **77** a i 13
Petronius Bland[, Egypt, early II p.: **77** a i 15
Philo-, *see also* Filo-
Philon, *see also* Aurelius
Philon Isiognis, I Aug Lus, c. Herculani, 156: **64** i 35
Philotas: **2** ix 34 app
Philotas, *cogn*, sing XX Palm, c. Mariani, 208: **2** xviii 16
Phlei, *see* Ḥ...ṇ[.]nus
Piat[.].., *see* Horus
Pibechas, *see* Achilles
Pibechis: **38** i 13 app
Pisas, Egypt, coh eq, 132–217: **78** *62* 3
Pitheeus, Pitheous: **70** a i 18 app
Platon, Vet Gall, t. Donaciani, 105–130: **80** 12
Plotinus, carrarius III Cyr, ca. 65–90: **58** ii 6
Plotius, trib III Cyr in ca. 90: **58** ii 8
P̣luti[..]cis, *see* Plution
Plutilus, *cogn:* **39** 14 app
Plution, *see also* Tithoes
Plution, *cogn*, Egypt, 206: **5** i 8
Plution P̣luti[..]cis, principalis?, Egypt, 180: **39** 14
Polion Dioscori, Egypt, aux, 178: **70** a ii 8
]us Poly.[, Egypt, classiarius, 141: **28** 4
Polydas, Egypt, coh eq, 148–173 or 180–205: **78** *72* marg
Pompeius Diogenes, Vet Gall, t. Iulii, 154–179: **76** GG 12
Pompeius Epane, cent, III Cyr?, 91–116: **34** recto ii 20
Pompeius Sarapionis, principalis?, Egypt, 188: **39** 23
Pomponianus, *see* Iulius
Pomponius Letianus (Laetianus), uir egregius, proc Aug, Dura in 251: **83** 15 and 17
C Pon[, Egypt, II p.: **46** 3
Ponticus, *see* Iulius
Poppaeus: **63** i 22 app
Porcius, conductor, III Cyr, ca. 65–90: **58** ii 5
Pos[, cent, Egypt, coh eq, 132–217: **78** *50* 2
Posidonius: **79** 1 app
Posidonius, Egypt, eq aux, second quarter of II p.: **73** a iii 4
Positus Coenodis, Egypt, coh eq, 132–217: **78** *62* 1

Posius: **78** *50* 2 app
Postumius Aurelianus, trib xx Palm in 216: pp. 362, 363, 366, 367, 377; **89** *1* verso 4; *2* 2; *6* 1; *7* 1; *8* 1; *10* verso 2; *17* 11; *25* verso 1; *28* verso 1; *29* 2 and app; *36* verso 1; *37* 1; *47* verso 1
pr.[, *name?*, Egypt, early II p.: **77** b 1
Pri[, *see* Antonius
Primus: **11** ii 5 app
Princeps: **9** 5 h app
Aurel P[ri]scian[, xx Palm, c. Marci, 216: **1** x 15
Prisci: **55** c 3 app
Priscus, *see also* Aurelius, Flauius, Longinus
Priscus, sing, Egypt, 103: **87** 26
Aurel Priscus .[, xx Palm, c. Marci, 207: **1** viii 3
Priscus, cent xx Palm, ca. 215–240: p. 133; **15** i 1, 17, 23; ii 8, 19; **95** a 2 app
Priscus: **11** ii 5 app
Priscus Abbosa, xx Palm, 216: c. Castrici, **1**, Aurel, xx 5; c. Antonini pr, **2** xxv 15
Priscus A[bbosa]: **1** viii 3 app; **2** xiii 15 app
Priscus Abdona, xx Palm, c. Marci, 204: **1**, Aurel, vii 13; **2** xii 26; **89** *41* 13 app
Priscus Ammonianus, Egypt, coh eq, 152–177 or 184–209: **78** *30* 9–10
Priscus Annona, xx Palm, 204: c. Castrici, **1** xvii 15; c. Antonini pr, **2** xxii 24
Aurel Priscus Gai, sesq xx Palm, t. Demetri, 204: **1** xxxvi 6
Priscus Paulus, Egypt, eq coh eq, t. Hermini, 137–162 or 169–194: **78** *15* 1
Proculus, Proclus, *see* Aemilius, Domitius, Iulius
Protarchus, *see* Iulius
Protas, Egypt, eq aux, second quarter of II p.: **73** a ii 8
Ps[e]nam[.].[, *nom*, Egypt, I/II p.: **38** ii 2
Psenosiris, *see* Peteminis
Psenosirius, *nom*, Egypt, c. Belei, 180–205: **81** iii 8
Psenpres, *see* Memnon
Pseutheous: **70** a i 18 app
Psois, Egypt, eq aux, second quarter of II p.: **73** a i 21
Ptolemaei, *see also* Pasenis, Pathermuthis
Ptolemaeus, Egypt, eq aux, second quarter of II p.: **73** a iii 19; j 4
Ptolemaeus M[, xx Palm, c. Pudentis, 208–233: **48** 2
Publius, Egypt, eq aux, second quarter of II p.: **73** a iii 10
Pudens, cent xx Palm, 207–232: pp. 183, 387; **27** a ii 1; **47** i 4; **48** 2
Pudentillus, *see* Allius
Pulius Mafinus: **77** a i 9 app
Puonsis Panechates, Vet Gall, t. Iulii, 154–179: **76** xx 1
Pupl[, *see* Aurelius
Pupi, *see* Abedsemias
Puplianus, *see* Vlpius
Puteolanus, *see* Maimins

Q[u- *and* Qu.[, *see* Aurelius, Heraclammon
Qu.[...]us Va[, eq xx Palm, t. Demetri, 205: **1** xxxvii 36
Quadratus, *see* Iulius
[Qu]adratu[s, Egypt, legionary?, ca. 59–84: **69** 1
Quint[, *see* Aurelius
Aurel Quint[, xx Palm, c. Marci, 216: **1** x 5
Quintianus, dec Egypt, 213–242: **24** 3
Quintus Iulianus, xx Palm, c. Marci, 210: **6** iii 26; **1**, Aurel, viii 7; **2** xiii 19
Quirini, Quirinus, *see* Valeras, Vlpius

R.n....[.].r., Egypt, coh eq, 156–182 or 188–214: **78** *6* 9
R...us, *see* Aurelius
R[-4?-] Malchus, xx Palm, c. Antonini pr, 215: **2** xxiv 20
Raammas Bar[.]..[, sing xx Palm, c. Antonini post, 215: **2** xxx 13
Rabbelus, *nom*, xx Palm, 225: **3** a 10
Rabbulas Bassi, eq xx Palm, t. Octaui, 204: **1**, Aurel, xl 10; **2** xl 17
Raibelus, *see* Reibelus
Regulus, *see* Aurelius
Reibeli, *see* Marimelus
Reibelus, xx Palm, 194–219: **1** xxiv 23 marg; 26 marg, Raibelus
Rennius Innocens, Egypt, legionarius, 56–81: **68** ii 32
Rom[-9?-]ni, dupl? xx Palm, t. Zebida, 197–222: **2** xxxii 4
Romanus, *see also* Antonius, Aurelius, Claudius, Flauius, Iulius; **66** a i 4 app
Aurel [ ]us Romanus, xx Palm, c. Antonini post, 209: **1** xiii 12. *Perhaps* [Iuli]us Romanus; *see* **8** x 15–16 app
Roman(us) A[, Egypt, c. Belei, 180–205: **81** iii 9
Aurel Romanus Allaei, sesq xx Palm, t. Octaui, 192: **1** xxxviii 15. Canceled
Romanus Barsimsi, xx Palm, c. Antonini pr, 215: **8** ix 12
Romullus, dec xx Palm, 225–236: **23** ii 9; **15** i 6; ii 4; **66** a i 4; **4** a i 7
Rossi: **52** b 13 app
Ru[....].[, *see also* Longinus
[.].rcius Ru[, Egypt, I/II p.: **38** ii 7
Rubathus, *see also* Aurelius
Rubathus S..[, xx Palm, c. Malchiana, 199: **6** viii 12 and app
Rufianus, *see also* Iulius
Rufianus, cent xx Palm, 211–236: **23** iv 8
Rufin[ianu]s: **4** a i 5 app
Rufinus, *see also* Attius, Aurelius

Rufinus, Egypt, eq aux, second quarter of II p.: **73** a iii 21
Rufus, *see also* Aurelius, Caerellius, Domitius, Longinus, Ninnius, Papirius, Valerius
Aurel Rufus [, xx Palm, c. Mariani, 214: **1** xxv 5
Rufus: **9** 10 a app
Rufus Cassiani, principalis?, Egypt, 188: **39** 22
Rulius, Rullus, *see* Fannius
Rumas, *see* Aurelius
]ḍạṣ Runnaei, drom xx Palm, c. Castrici, 194–219: **1** xliv 3
Rusticus, *see* Iulius
Ruticus, *see* Iulius Rusticus
Rybas?, *cogn?*, Egypt, first half of III p.: **102** a 13 and app

S.[, *see also* Cocceius, Mocimus, Rubathus
Ṣ[ ]i, eq xx Palm, t. Demetri, 198–206: **92** vii 8
S. . . ., *name?*, practor, Egypt, coh eq, 156–182 or 188–214: **78** *6* 11 app
Ṣ[, *nom*, Egypt, 192–217: **5** iii 10
].us S[. .]g̣ill[, xx Palm, 211–236: **33** iii 7
S. . .mi, *see* Cassius
Aurel Ṣ.[. .]ṃius Leonid.[, xx Palm, c. Malchiana, 209–212: **1** xxix 3
S.[.]ọn, *see* Aelius
S. .tius Martius, Egypt, eq aux, 114–139: **75** 1
Sạ[, *see* Aurelius, Malichus
Sa.a.[, *see* Aurelius
Aurel Ṣab.[, xx Palm, c. Mariani, 214: **1** xxv 1
Sabinus, *see also* Ạ[, Aurelius, Claudius, Iulius
Sabinus, Egypt, cent coh eq, 152–177 or 184–209: **78** *31* 1; *32* 2
Sacona, *see* Cassius; **33** iv 1 app
Ṣaçọt[.]ix: **30** ii 8 app
Sạḍ[. .].i, *see* Zaidibolus
Sadach: **6** x 29 app
Sadalathi, *see also* Siluanus
. . .[.]e.s Ṣạḍạḷạthi, eq xx Palm, 226–251: **83** 21
Aur[el S]adalathu[s . . . . . .].i, eq xx Palm, t. Antonini, 192: **1** xli 11. Canceled
Sadalathus, *cogn:* **1** xviii 18 app
Sadalathus: **1** xliv 12 app; **2** xliii 17 app
Sadallathus: **44** 15 app
Ṣạdus . . .[.].[, Egypt, eq, 180–205: **81** ii 2
Sadus, *nom*, Egypt, c. Belei, 180–205: **81** iii 3
Aurel Saedus Magdaei, eq xx Palm, t. Octaui, 193: **1** xxxviii 18
Sal[, *see* Gaius
Salamalathi, *see* Azizus
Salius Capiton, III Cyr, c. Subureana, 91–116: **34** recto i 16
Salluma, *see* Monimus
Sallusti: **58** ii 8 app
[Sal]lustius C f, Egypt, legionary, I a.: **36** 11
Salm[, *see* Aurelius
Ṣaḷṃ[, *cogn*, xx Palm, c. Danymi, 212?: **2** viii 21
Ạ[urel . . . .].es Salṃ[, dupl xx Palm, c. Antonini, 194–219: **1** xi 6
Salmạ[n-, *see* Aurelius
Salman, *see also* Bassus, Didas, Domitius, Iarhaeus, Iulius, Malchus, Mar[, Maximus, Mocimus, Themarsas, Themes, Zabdibolus, Zebidas
Salman, *cogn*, xx Palm, c. Marci, 214: **2** xiv 11; **8** iv 3
Salmanes, *see also* Aurelius
Salmanes Iamlichi, xx Palm, c. Marci, 203: **6** iii 14; **8** iii 9
Salmanes Maccaei, eq xx Palm, t. Demetri, 199: **1**, Aurel, xxxvi 28; **2** xxxvi 24
Aurel Salmanes Naamaei, eq xx Palm, t. Demetri, 195: **1** xxxvi 20
Salmanes Signa-, xx Palm, c. Marci, 204: **1** vii 17; **2** xii 30; **8** iii 17
[Sal]manes Theme, xx Palm, c. Malchiana, 195: **6** viii 15
Aurel Salmanes Za[, eq xx Palm, t. Antonini, 192: **1** xli 10. Canceled
Salmanes Zabdiboli, xx Palm, c. Antonini pr, 207–232: **27** a i 8
Salmanes Zebida, dupl xx Palm, t. Octaui, 201: **1**, Aurel, xxxviii 13; **2** xxxviii 26
Salme, *see also* Hagus, Lucius, Lọ.[.]us, Malchus, Mocimus
Salmes, *see also* Bassus
Salmes, *nom*, xx Palm, c. Malchiana, 199–201: **6** ix 3
Salmes, *cogn*, xx Palm, c. Danymi, 203: **2** vii 17
Salmes, *nom*, Egypt, c. Belei, 180–205: **81** iii 5
Salmes, *cogn*, xx Palm, ca. 215–240: **15** i 4
Salmes Maç[, xx Palm, 213–247: **3** b 2
Salmes Malchi, eq xx Palm, t. Antonini, 205 or 208: **1** xliii 13; **2** xliii 11; **92** vii 14
Aurel Salme Marini, eq xx Palm, t. Demetri, 193: **1** xxxvi 8 and app
Ṣạ[l]mẹṣ Thẹṃ[, xx Palm, ca. 200–235: **61** ii 3
Salmes Zebida, eq xx Palm, t. Antonini, 201: **1**, Aurel, xlii 2; **2** xli 26
Salmeus: **81** iii 5 app
Saluianus, dec I Aug Lus, 131–156: **64** ii 10, 36 app
Saluius, Egypt, eq aux, second quarter of II p.: **73** a iii 23
Sammas Gai, eq xx Palm, t. Tiberini, 207: **1**, Aurel, xxxv 21; **2** xxxv 22
Sarapammon, *see* Eudaemon, Valerius
Sarapion, Sarapionis, *see also* Serapion *and* Aelius, Dionysius, Horion, Isas, Iulius, Pompeius, Valerius
Sarapion, Vet Gall, t. Donaciani, 105–130: **80** 37
]ẹi.ịtus Sarapion, Egypt, eq, second half of II p.: **79** 8

Sarapion, *cogn*, dec, Egypt, 213–242: **24** 16
Sarapion, *cogn?*, Egypt, coh eq quingenaria?, early III p.: **52** a 3
Sarapion Germanus, sig, Egypt, first half of III p.: **85** 3
Sarapion Isidori, Vet Gall, t. Lycarionis, 154–179: **76** ix 3
Sarapion Isidori, principalis?, Egypt, 189: **39** 25
Sarapion Pathermuthis, Vet Gall, t. Herodiani, 154–179: **76** viii 25
Sarapion Tauris, Vet Gall, t. Sereni, 154–179: **76** xvii 9
Sattius: **75** 1 app
Satur[, *see* Flauius
Satur[nianus: **10** 11 app
Saturnilus, *see also* Antonius, Iulius, Vlpius
Saturnilus, dec?, Egypt, aux, 114–139: **75** 12
Saturnilus, *cogn*, Egypt, coh eq, 151–176 or 183–208: **78** *24* 1
[Satu]ṛnịli, xx Palm, 197–225: **92** iv 4
Saturninus, *see also* Herennius, Iulius
Saturninus, Egypt, eq aux, second quarter of II p.: **73** a iii 24
Saturninus, status unknown, Dura in 211: p. 355; **88** *1* 2; *2* 3
Satur[ninus], *cogn:* **10** 11 app
Scaurianus, *see* Iulius
Se.[ ]., *see* Chaeremon
Secundinus Verus: p. 285
Secundus, *see* Claudius Iulius, Clodius, Iulius
Seleuc[, *see also* Aurelius
Seleuc[, xx Palm, III p.: **134** a
Seleuci, *see* Heliodorus, Marinus, Maximus
Seleucus, *see also* Antonius, Aurelius
Seleucus, cent xx Palm, 191–211: p. 355; **88** *1* 5; **89** *12* ii 2
[S]ẹlẹụcụ[s, xx Palm, c. Malchi, 197–222: **2** ii–iv f 2
Seleucus Antonin-, eq xx Palm, t. Antonini, 201: **1** xliii 4; **2** xli 28 and app
Seleucus Barathe, eq xx Palm, t. Antonini, 202: **1**, Aurel, xlii 15; **2** xlii 9
Seleucus Barbaessamen, xx Palm, c. Marci, 203: **1**, Aurel, vi 33; **8** iii 8
Seleucus Cassi, xx Palm, c. Antonini post, 214: **2** xxix 20
Seleucus Iarhaei, eq xx Palm, t. Octaui, 201: **1**, Aurel, xxxix 20; **2** xxxix 23
Seleucus Ṃ[, xx Palm, c. Marci, 204: **1**, Aurel, vii 16; **2** xii 29
Seleucus Malchi, xx Palm, 211–236: **33** iii 1
Seleucus Theme, xx Palm, c. Antonini post, 214: **2** xxix 15
Seleus Malchi, xx Palm, 199–201: c. Malchiana, **6** ix 7; **1**, Aurel, xxvii 4; c. Malchi, **2** i 9
Sempronianus, cent I Aug Lus, 131–156: **64** i 42; ii 29; ii 1 app
Sempronius, *see also* Aurelius; Sem[pronius, *see* **51** ii 18 app
Sextus Sempronius Candidus, cent I Aug Lus, 156: **64** i 23; ii 19, 23; ii 1 app
Sempronius Ḍ[e]metrius, Egypt, II/III p.: **30** ii 10
Sempronius Liberalis, Praefectus Aegypti: **11** ii 3 app: **64** i 20–21, 32
Sen[, *nom*, XXII Deiot?, c. Seruili, early I p.: **51** ii 18
Seneca, *see* Volusius
Senecio, *see* Q Sosius
Senephotes: **20** 18 app
Sentianus, *see* Aurelius
Sentius, dec Vet Gall, 154–179: **76** ix 4; xvi 11; xix 3
Septim.[.]se[, Dura in ca. 220–222: **118** 5 and app
Septimius Danymus, cent xx Palm, 201: p. 183; **1**, Aurel, i 1–2; xliii 19; **2** vi 18–19; xliv 1; **92** v 6; viii 4
Septimius Heliodor-, xx Palm, 206: c. Seleuciana, **6** xi 15; c. Antonini pr, **2** xxiii 7
].rus Serap[ion, xx Palm, c. Marci, 205: **1** vii 30; **2** xiii 9
Serapion Demetri, Egypt, c. or t.].rliani, I/II p.: **38** i 12
Serẹ[, *see* Theon
]us Seren[, Egypt, classiarius, 142: **28** 6
Seren[, *nom*, cent?, Egypt, II p.: **45** 4
Sere[ni filius: **24** 21 app
Sereni, Serenus, *see also* Aelius, Ammonius, Apollos, Aurelius, Flauius, Gaius, Heliodorus, Iulius, Valerius, Vincleius
Serenus, cent III Cyr, 65–96: **9** 9 f–n; 13 f app; 19 c app
Serenus, procurator Vet Gall, t. Donaciani, 105–130: **80** 2 and 25
Serenus, Egypt, eq aux, second quarter of II p.: **73** a ii 11
Serenus, Egypt, eq aux, second quarter of II p.: **73** a ii 13; b 3
Serenus: **73** b 1 app
Serenus, dec Vet Gall, 154–179: **76** xvii 9, Aelius? Melas? Pactumeius?; BB 2, Pactumeius?, cf. line 5.
Serenus Melas, dec Vet Gall, 154–179: p. 285; **76** i 10; vii 9; x 3; xii 19; xiii 7; xviii 25; xx 8 and 20
Serenus, dec, Egypt, end of III p.: **11 bis** a 17
[Se]ṛenus: **11 bis** b i 18 app
Serraeus: **81** ii 15 app
Seruilius, cent XXII Deiot?, early I p.: **51** ii 18
M Seruilius Silanus: **39** 21 app
Q Seruilius Silanus: **39** 21 app
Seuerianus, *see also* Flauius
[S]euerianus, Egypt, coh eq quingenaria, early III p.: **52** c 7. Cf. **21** 19

Seuerus, *see also* Franius, Iulius, Vlpius
Seuerus Antonini, xx Palm, c. Danymi, 207: **6** i 25
L Sextilius Germanus, III Cyr, 65–96: **9** 8 a
Sextius: **75** 1 app
Aurel Si.ba.[..]us Vabalathi, eq xx Palm, t. Octaui, 195: **1** xxxviii 28
Sia...n, *see* Bassus
Sidonius: **79** 1 app
S[i]gill[: **33** iii 7 app
C Sigillius Valens, I Aug Lus, c. Gaiani, 156: **64** i 41
Signa-, *see also* Salmanes
Sign(as?), xx Palm, 194–219: **1** xxxiv 30 marg
Signas Matharaei, eq xx Palm, t. Demetri, 204: **1**, Aurel, xxxvii 21, Matrhaei; **2** xxxvii 22
Siluan[, Siluani, Siluanus, *see also* Aurelius, Bernicianus, Claudius, Flauius, Iulius, Malchus, Vlpius
]al.[.]bius [Si]luani, eq xx Palm, t. Zebida, 202: **1**, Aurel, xxxii 22; **2** xxxiii 3
Siluani: **1** vii 9 app
Siluanus, *cogn*, xx Palm, ca. 215–240: **15** i 5
[Si]luanus, *cogn*, xx Palm, 244: **66** b i 26
Sil[uanus?, xx Palm, 217–256: **18** 1
S[il]uanus [Do]mni, **2** xvii 25 app
Siluanus Mocimi, eq xx Palm, t. Octaui, 204: sing, **1**, Aurel, xl 7; *not* sing, **2** xl 14
Siluanus Sadalathi, xx Palm, c. Mariani, 210: **2** xviii 25; **8** vi 5
Simaones, *see also* Aurelius, Mocimus
Simaones Auidalathi, eq xx Palm, t. Tiberini, 196: **1**, Aurel, xxxiv 9; **2** xxxiv 8; **92** vii 2 app
Simoarus, *see* Aurelius
Simon, *see* Acrabanes, Mocimus
Sipo: **9** 11 a app
Sisois: **73** a i 21 app
Sitorr[, *see* Aurelius
Sittius: **75** 1 app
Sius, *see* A[-4?-]es
So.mobiaeus Addei, xx Palm, ca. 215–240: **15** i 4
So(h)aemus, *see also* Iulius
So(h)aemus Taesii, Egypt, eq coh equitata, t. Rufi, II/III p.: **30** ii 12, Suaemus
Solas, Vet, Gall, t. Donaciani, 105–130: **80** 10
Sopa[, *see* Aurelius
Sopatrus: **2** ix 33 app
Sopatrus Dionysius, Vet Gall, t. Aelii Sereni, 154–179: **76** GG 9
Sorechus, xx Palm, 194–219: **1** xxxvi 15 marg
Sosius, *see also* Sossius
Q Sosius Senecio: p. 220
Sossianus, *see* Aurelius
Sossius, *see also* Sosius
C Sossius, optio III Cyr, c. Celsi: p. 198
C Sossius C f, III Cyr, c. Aquilae, I a./I p.: p. 198
Sossius, cent, XXII Deiot?, early I p.: p. 198; **51** i 14
C Sossius Celer, III Cyr, 65–96: **9** 35 a
Sossius Eudaemon, sig Vet Gall, t. Herodiani, 154–179: **76** iv 25
Sosthenes: **38** i 6 app
Sotericus, *see also* Claudius; **53** b 25 app
Soterichus, dec Vet Gall, 154–179: **76** viii 19; xix 19
Sozon, librarius XVI F F, Dura, 196–221: **91** *2* i 6; *2* i 12 and app
Sozymus: **39** 9 app
Sp[, *see* Aurelius
Staius: **58** ii 8 app
Stilbo(n), *see* Theon
Suaemus, *see* Sohaemus
Subatianus, dec Vet Gall, 154–179: p. 000; **76** ix 13
Subur Fanii: **34** recto i 10 app
T Suedius Clemens, praef castrorum, Egypt in 80: **10** 2–3
Sulpicius L f, Egypt, legionary, I a.: **36** 5
Summares, *see* Aurelius
Summareus: **1** xx 6 app
]mbrius Suri..us, xx Palm, ca. 215–240: **15** i 10
]nus Syrion, Egypt, 217: **40** i 8
Sy[ri]on?, *cogn:* **5** ii 13 app

T.b..s, Vet Gall, t. Donaciani, 105–130: **80** 32
Ta...., cent I Aug Lus, 92–117: **74** ii 9
Taeni, *see* Murenus
Taesis, Thaesis, *feminine:* **30** ii 12 app
Taesius, *see* Sohaemus
Taurinus: **76** xvii 9 app; **80** 30 app
[.]..imes Taurini Melanos, Egypt, eq, second half of II p.: **79** 14
Tauris, *see* Sarapion
Te[, *nom*, drom xx Palm, c. Malchi, 204: **2** xliii 23
Τειμης: **79** 14 app
Ter.chon Petepsa[etis?, Egypt, coh eq, 154–189 or 186–217: **78** *3* 1
Terentianus, *see* A.re.[.]as, Claudius; **2** xxvii 20 app
Terentius, Vet Gall, t. Donaciani, 105–130: **80** 33
Tertius, *see* Valerius, Vlpius
Th[, *see also* Aurelius, Iarhaeus, Iulius
Th[, *cogn*, eq xx Palm, t. Tiberini, 203: **1** xxxiv 33 and app
Th[, *cogn*, eq xx Palm, t. Antonini, 204: **2** xlii 23
Th..[, xx Palm, ca. 205–240: **12** a–c 9
The[, Egypt, aux, second half of II p.: **70** g 9
The[, *cogn*, eq xx Palm, t. Tiberini, 202: **1** xxxiv 31
Aurel The[, xx Palm, c. Danymi, 201–205?: **1** ii 5
The[, *nom*, xx Palm, c. Mariani, 214: **8** vi 26
Theacabus Themarsa, xx Palm, c. Gaiani, 207–232: **27** a ii 7
Theanus, *see* Claudius

Them[, *see also* Agrippas, Aurelius
]es Them[, xx Palm, c. Mariani, 200–201: **2** xvii 8
Themarsa, *see also* Abdas, Abednabus, Abedsalmas, Abgarus, Agrippas, Asadus, Aurelius, Barnaeus, Dicaeus, Gaianus, Gemellus, Iadaeus, Iarhaeus, Iaqubus, Iarhaboles, Iulianus, Iulius, La.[.]us, Lucianus, Lucius, Maccaeus, Malchus, Males, Mannas, Maras, Marinus, Mocimus, Mombogeus, Me[.....], Nahestabus, Nebudaes, Obeanes, Ogelus, Theacabus, Zabdibolus
A[urel -5?-]ẹ. Thema[rsa-, eq xx Palm, t. Tiberini, 193: **1** xxxiii 32
Themarsa.[-6?-]..[, *nom*, xx Palm, c. Malchiana, 198: **6** viii 19
Themars[a-, *cogn*, xx Palm, c. Mariani, 200–201: **2** xvii 4
Themarsa[, cent? xx Palm, ca. 205–240: p. 125; **12** e 4
Themars[a-, xx Palm, ca. 215–240: **15** d 3
A[urel -6?-].us Themarsa, eq xx Palm, t. Zebida, 194–195: **1** xxxi 31
Themarsa, *cogn*, xx Palm, c. Castrici, 196–200: **1** xvi 23
A[urel -10?- Th]emarsa, xx Palm, c. Castrici, 197–201: **1** xvi 28
Themarsa, *cogn*, xx Palm, c. Malchiana, 203: **6** ix 13
]b[..].as Themarsa, xx Palm, c. Danymi, 203; **2** vii 14
Themarsa, *cogn*, xx Palm, c. Mariani, 214: **6** vi 12
Aurel [-8?–].as Themarsa, xx Palm, c. Malchiana, 214: **1** xxix 17
....[.]eus Themarsa, xx Palm, c. Antonini pr, 214: **8** ix 6 and app
Themarsa *cogn*, xx Palm, c. Mariani, 216: **2** xx 17
Themasa (*sic*), *cogn*, xx Palm, c. Antonini post, 197–225: **92** vi 16
Themarsa, *cogn*, xx Palm, ca. 195–230: **43** 6
Themarsa, *cogn*, xx Palm, 242?: **44** 8
Themarsa: **1** xvi 2 app
Themarsas, *see also* Mocimus
Themarsas, xx Palm, 191–216: **89** *2* 16, Θ[εμαρσ]α̣[ς]
Themarsas, *nom*, xx Palm, c. Mariani, 214–218: **6** vii 3
Themarsas, *nom*, xx Palm, 227: **95** b 6
Ṭḥ[ema]ṛṣ[a]s, *cogn*, xx Palm, ca. 215–240: **15** ii 16
Themarsas: **13** 9 app
Themarsas Abgari, eq xx Palm, t. Zebida, 201: **1**, Aurel, xxxii 19, Themarsa; **2** xxxii 22
Aurel Tḥ[e]ṃ[ar]ṣa Addaei, eq xx Palm, t. Tiberini, 195: **1** xxxiv 7
Themarsas Addaei, eq xx Palm, t. Coccei, 207–232: **27** b i 11
Aurel Themarsa Barn.[, xx Palm, c. Marci, 201: **1** vi 24
Themarsas Barnebus, xx Palm, c. Danymi, 214: **2** x 6; **8** ii 19
Themarsas Buccaei, drom xx Palm, c. Malchiana and Malchi, 196; **1** xliv 11; **2** xliii 16
Themarsas Buzi, eq xx Palm, t. Tiberini, 212: **1** xxxv 28, Themarsa; **2** xxxvi 1
Themarsas Chaseti, eq xx Palm, t. Octaui, 201: **1**, Aurel, xxxix 14, Themarsa; **2** xxxix 17
Aurel Tḥ[emars]ạ Dinaei, eq xx Palm, t. Antonini post, 200: **1** xli 19; **2** xli 19, Themes Dinaei
Themarsa Gora, xx Palm, c. Mariani, 207–232: **27** a i 3
Themarsas Haeran, eq xx Palm, t. Zebida, 201: **1**, Aurel, xxxii 7, Themarsa; **2** xxxii 20
Themarsas Iarhaei, eq xx Palm, t. Octaui, 203: **1**, Aurel, xl 2, Themarsa; **2** xl 10
Themarsas Iarhaei, xx Palm, c. Danymi, 214: **6** ii 1; **2** x 1; **8** ii 15
Aurel Themarsa Ma[, xx Palm, c. Malchiana, 203: **1** xxvii 16
Themarsas Malchi, xx Palm, ca. 215–240: **15** i 22
Themarsas Mocimi, eq xx Palm, t. Tiberini, 214: **1** xxxv 32; **2** xxxvi 6
Themarsa Nisamsi, eq xx Palm, t. Antonini, 204: **1**, Aurel, xlii 29, Themarsa; **2** xlii 20, Themarsa[
Themarsas Nisamsi, xx Palm, 212: c. Seleuciana, **6** xi 23; c. Castrici, **1**, Aurel, xviii 10, Themarsa; c. Antonini pr, **2** xxiii 26, Themarsa[; **8** viii 15, Themarsa[s]
Themarsas Salman, xx Palm, c. Mariani, 214: **1**, Aurel, xxv 8; **2** xx 5
Themarsas Salman, *see* Themes Salman
Themarsas Ṭḥ[e]ṃẹ, xx Palm, c. Antonini pr, 214: **8** viii 18
Aurel Themarsas Themuami, drom xx Palm, c. Danymi, 195: **1** xliii 21
Themarṣ[a] Tiberini, dec xx Palm, 207: p. 387; **1**, Aurel, xxxiii 23–24 and app; **2** xxxiv 1–2 and app; **92** ix 17; **47** i 5; **27** b i 1
Aurel Themaṛṣạ Ṿ.[, vex, xx Palm, t. Octaui, 201: **1** xxxix 13
Themarsa Ve[, status unknown, Dura in 216: p. 363; **89** *9* verso 1
Themarsas Zebida, xx Palm, 198: eq t. Antonini, **1**, Aurel, xli 25; sig, **2** xli 13
Themar[sas Zebi?]da, status unknown, Dura in 211: p. 355; **88** *2* 5–6. Same as preceding?
Theme, Themes, *see also* Abgarus, Iarhaboles, Malchus, Mocimus, Salmanes, Seleucus, Themarsas, Zabdibolus
Themes, *nom*, Egypt, c. Belei, 180–205: **81** iii 4
Ṭ[h]ẹṃẹs, xx Palm, 225–247: **3** b 7
Themes: **1** xvi 2 app
Theme: **1** xxxiv 31 and 33 app

Themes: **89** *2* 16 app
Themes Dinaei, *see* Themarsa Dinaei
Themes Heliodor-, xx Palm, c. Mariani, 214: **1** xxiv 4; **2** xix 13; **8** vi 17
Themes Malchi, xx Palm, c. Mariani, 203: **1**, Aurel, xxii 7; **2** xvii 15; **8** v 11
Themes Malchi, xx Palm, c. Castrici, 204: **1** xvii 12
Themes Malichi, Egypt, c. Belei, 180–205: **81** ii 17
Themes Mocimi, sacerdos xx Palm, 214–239: **50** i 2, 9; b 2
Aurel Themes Salman, eq xx Palm, t. Octaui, 201: **1** xxxix 18 and app. *See also* Themarsas Salman
Aurel Themes Zeb[, xx Palm, c. Danymi, 202–206?: **1** iii–v a–b–c 7
Themes Zebida, xx Palm, 212: c. Castrici, **1**, Aurel, xviii 9; c. Antonini pr, **2** xxiii 25; **8** viii 14
Themuamas: **1** xliii 21 app
Themuamus, *see* Themarsas: **89** *2* 16 app
Theo[, *see* Aurelius
Aurel Theo[, xx Palm, c. Danymi, 202–206?: **1** iii–v i 4
Theoboli, *see also* Iarhaeus, Zabdibolus
]dalathus Theoboli, drom xx Palm, 196: c. Malchiana, **1**, Aurel, xliv 12 and app, Teoboli
Theobolus Gadde, xx Palm, c. Danymi, 201: **6** i 8; **2** vii 3
Theobol(us) Gadde, xx Palm, 195–230: **41** 7. Same as preceding?
Theocles, *see* Aurelius
Theodorus, *see also* Aelius, Aurelius
[....]llus Ṭḥẹọḍ[o]ṛ[i], sing xx Palm, c. Danymi, 202: **2** vii 10
Theodorus Anṃiochi, Vet Gall, t. Herodiani, 154–179: **76** xiii 2 and app
Theodorus Zebida, eq xx Palm, t. Antonini, 201: **1** xli 36; **2** xli 24
Theodotus, *see* Aurelius
Theon, *see also* Co.[.....]s
Theon Serẹ[, Egypt, sesq? t. Ammoniani pr, 217: **24** 21
Theon Stilbonis, Vet Gall, t. Pactumei Sereni, 154–179: **76** v 1; BB 2
Theofil[, *see* Alexandrus
Theofili: **1** xxxix 35 app
Theophilus Alexandri, Vet Gall, t. Lycarionis, 154–179: **76** xviii 1
Theopropus, *see* Aurelius
Theotecnus Aciba, xx Palm, c. Pudentis, 207–232: **27** a ii 2
Thestor: **78** *12* 1 app.
Tiber[, *see* Aurelius
Tiberini, Tiberinus, *see also* Bassus, Claudius, Themarsa
[Ti]berinus: **11** ii 6 app
Tiberis, *cogn*, Egypt, aux, 190: **70** b i 7
Tiberius, *see* Titius
Timetus, trierarchus liburnae, Egypt, II p.: **82** 10 and 13–14
Timinius, cent, Egypt, 65–90: **10** 14
Timinius Paulinus, dec xx Palm, 198–232: pp. 189, 394; **47** i 6, 16, 17; ii 11, 12; **27** b i 16; **15** ii 12
Timon Marini, sing xx Palm, t. Antonini, 202: **1**, Aurel, xlii 16; **2** xlii 10
Tineius Val[, Egypt, aux, 192: **70** b ii 9, TINHIVS; a i 18 app
Tithoes, cent, Egypt, 154–173 or 186–205: **78** *1* 2; *72* 4
Tithoes Plutionis, Vet Gall, t. Pactumei Sereni, 154–179: **76** xiv 10
Aurel Titius Tiberius, xx Palm, c. Malchiana, 206: **1** xxviii 15
Tituleius, *see* Longinus
Titus, *see also* Aurelius, Marcus
Titus, dec, Egypt, 213–242: p. 146; **24** 5 and 18. Same as Aurelius Titus, 221, in **21** 16?
Torquatus: **91** *1* i 6 app
Tosthenes Armais, Egypt, I/II p.: **38** i 6
Ṭrạ..[.]us, *see* Aurelius
Ṭrạịạ[n]us?: **1** xxix 13 app
Trebius: **36** 8 app
Trethonius, oeconomus Caesaris, second half of II p.: **79** 9
Trunnius, Egypt, cent coh eq, 132–217: **78** *70* 2 and 7
Tryphon H[, Egypt, c. Belei, 180–205: **81** iii 10, ⟦Tru⟧fon
Ṭụbạṣ: **80** 32 app
Turbon, Egypt, aux, second quarter of II p.: **73** a iii 26
Turranius, xx Deiot?, c. Vari, early I p.: **51** ii 19
Tyon: **63** i 34 app; ii 13 app
Tyrannus, *see* Herminus

Ṿ.[, *see* Aurelius, Domitius, Themarsa
C V.ḷ.ṛ.x̣[..]..[.]ṣ.ṣ, III Cyr, 65–96: **9** 20 a
V.[, cent, Egypt, early II p.: **77** b 7 and 9
Ṿ[, Egypt, aux, 184–189: **70** a iii 28
Ṿ[, *nom*, xx Palm, c. Mariani, 206: **8** v 28
Ṿ[..]ṇina, xx Palm, 194–219: **1** xli 14 marg
Ṿ.[...].[, xx Palm, ca. 210–240: **13** 18
Ṿ[, xx Palm, ca. 215–240: **15** b 12
Aurel Ṿ[..... Mo]mbogeus, eq xx Palm, t. Tiberini, 195: **1** xxxiv 2
Va[, *see* Qu.[...]us
Vạ[, *nom*, xx Palm, c. Mariani, 214: **8** vi 30
Vaḅ[, *see* Nisraeus
Aurel Vabala[th...]z[..]i, eq xx Palm, t. Zebida, 205: **1** xxxiii 4 and app

Vabala[th-, *cogn*, xx Palm, c. Antonini post, 205: **2** xxviii 9
Ṿạbal[ath-, *cogn*, xx Palm, c. Danymi, 212?: **2** viii 22
Vabalathen Ballaei, xx Palm, c. Mariani, 207–232: **27** a i 5
Vabalathi, Vabalathus, *see also* Iulius, Magnus, Malchus, Ogelus, Si.ba...us
Vabballathi, xx Palm, 191–216: **89** *4* ii 9
Vabalathi, xx Palm, 198–235: **47** i 7
.[.]..us Vhabalathi, eq xx Palm, 226–251: **83** 12
Vabalathi: **92** v 9 app
Vaballathus: **44** 15 app
Vabalathus Hanina, eq xx Palm, t. Tiberini, 212: **1** xxxv 30; **2** xxxvi 3
Val[, Val..., *see also* Ag...s..mia.., Tineius
]ụal..[, *nom*, xx Palm, 225–256: **4** m 2
Vale..., *see* Flauius
Valẹ[......]ṣ, *see* Aurelius
Valeṇ[: 15 ii 11 app
Valens, *see also* Aemilius, Antonius, Aurelius, Berosas, Flauius, Iulius, Sigillius
Vale⟨n⟩s, *cogn*, Egypt, c. Domitii Caeliani, 91–116: **34** verso i 3
Valens, *cogn*, xx Palm, c. Antonini post, 203–204: **2** xxviii 6
Aur[el -6?-]ịus Valens, xx Palm, c. Marci, 214: **1** ix 8
Valens: **10** 17 app
Valenti, Valentini, *see* Gorippus
Valentinus, *see* Antonius, Iulius, Valerius, Vlpius; **10** 17 app
Valeṛ[: **15** ii 11 and app
Aurel Valeras Quirini, eq xx Palm, t. Tiberini, 196: **1** xxxiv 11
M Aur Ṿạleṛị.[, Egypt, ca. 187–230: **46** 6
Valerianus, *see* Iulius, Lucius; **9** 34 a app; **10** 17 app
Valerius, *see also* Aurelius, Marcus
Valerius, Egypt, aux, second quarter of II p.: **73** a iii 6
Aurel Valerius [, xx Palm, c. Marci, 214: **1** ix 25
M Aur Valeriu[s: **46** 6 app
Valerius: **9** 20 a app; **28** 12 app
C Valerius C f Bassus, Egypt, legionary, 65–90: **37** 4
L Valerius L f Ser(gia) Crisp...[, Egypt, early II p.: **133** 1
L Valerius Felix, III Cyr, 65–96: **9** 24 a
Aurel Valerius Firmus, xx Palm, c. Malchiana, 205: **1** xxviii 8
Valerius Firmus, eq xx Palm, t. Zebida, 205: **1**, Aurel, xxxiii 2; **2** xxxiii 19
C Valerius Germanus, Egypt, legionary, 56–81: **68** iii 1
Valerius Hispanus, principalis II Traian, 217–242: **21** 2
Valerius Isidori, Egypt, 180–205: **81** ii 4
Valer(ius) Malchi, xx Palm, c. Marci, 203: **6** iii 16; **2** xii 19
Valerius Maximus, eq xx Palm, t. Demetri, 204: **1**, Aurel, xxxvii 25; **2** xxxvii 26
Valerius Monimus, eq xx Palm, t. Zebida, 203: **1**, Aurel, xxxii 25; **2** xxxiii 6
Valerius Mucia[n-, xx Palm, c. Mariani, 208: **1**, Aurel, xxiii 5; **2** xviii 10
Valerius Nepotianus, Vet Gall, t. Lycarionis, 154–179: **76** xviii 7–8 and 20
Valerius Rufus, sig I Aug Lus, c. Crescentis, 92–117: **74** i 9
Valerius Rufus, Egypt, classiarius, 127–164: **59** i 8
Valerius Sarapammon, Vet Gall, t. Iulii Protarchi, 154–179: **76** xii 1 and 9
Valerius Serapion, Vet Gall, t. Pactumei Sereni, 154–179: **76** vi 9
Valerius Serenus, Egypt, middle of III p.: **67** 10
Valerius Tertius, I Aug Lus, c. Lappi, 151: **64** ii 17
Valerius Valentinus, sing xx Palm, t. Antonini, 196; **1**, Aurel, xli 22; **2** xli 10
Vareus Barsimsi, xx Palm, c. Mariani, 204: **1** xxii 14; **2** xvii 20
Varini: **34** recto ii 9 app
Varius, cent XXII Deiot?, early I p.: p. 198; **51** ii 11, 19, 21
Ṿaṛṣụtheu[s: **19** 7 app
Vdathi, *see* Iarhaboles
Ve[, Verus?, *see* Themarsa
Verecun[dus: **63** ii 4 app
Vespasianus, *see* Flauius
Vettienus Matinus, Egypt, dupl, c. or t.].rliani, I/II p.: **38** i 15
C Veturius Gemellus, III Itur, 103: **87** 11
Ṿị[, xx Palm, c. Danymi, 202–215?: **1** iii–v d 1
Vib.[, *see* Faustius
Vibiani[, *nom*, xx Palm, 207-238: **94** b ii 4
Vibianus: **78** *76* 2 app
Vibius, *see also* Vippi[
Vibius Crescens, principalis II Traian, 217–242: **21** 8
Vibius Faustinus, principalis II Traian, 217: **21** 18
Victor, *see also* Aurelius, Marcus
Victor, Egypt, eq aux, second quarter of II p.: **73** a i 18
Victor Comarinus, vicarius of oeconomus, Egypt in 205: **81** ii 5–6
Victor Haeran, eq xx Palm, t. Demetri, 199: **1**, Aurel, xxxvi 30; **2** xxxvi 26
Victorinus, *see also* Aurelius
]ḟidius Victorinus, dec, Egypt, 217: **20** 1

L Vincleius Serenus, III Cyr, 65–96: **9** 36 a
Vinius: **34** recto i 3 app
C Ṿịṿ[, Egypt, II p.: **45** 5
Vippị[, cent, Egypt, coh eq, 132–217: **78** *76* 2
Vlp[, *see also* Aponius
Vlp[, Egypt, early II p.: **77** a ii 8
Vlpianus, *see* Flauius; **75** 18 app
Vlpius, *see also* Aurelius; p. 161
Vlpius .[..]ịnus, xx Palm, c. Mariani, 203: **1**, Aurel, xxii 5; **2** xvii 13
Vlpius, xx Palm, ca. 215–240: **15** ii 16; **57** 2
Vlpius Alexa, III Cyr, c. Pompei Epane, 91–116: **34** recto ii 25, Vpis
Vlpius Antoninus, dec xx Palm, 206: pp. 144, 387; **1**, Aurel, xli 1–2; **2** xli 1–2; **92** iv 11; vii 12; x 4; **47** i 4; **27** b i 6; **118** 6?
Vlpius Antoninus, xx Palm, c. Marci, 212: **6** iii 31; **1**, Aurel, viii 14; **2** xiii 26
Vlpius Apollona[-: p. 149; **1**, Aurel, xxxviii 38; **2** xxxix 5; **26** c 1
Vlpius Barneb[, eq xx Palm, t. Octaui, 199: **1**, Aurel, xxxviii 37
Vlpius Barsimsus, eq xx Palm, t. Tiberini, 204: **1**, Aurel, xxxv 6; **2** xxxv 10, Barsumius
Ṿ[lp(ius)] Barsẹ[mias], xx Palm, c. Marci, 191–216: **89** *12* ii 6
Vlpius Bassus, eq xx Palm, t. Octaui, 203: **2** xl 12
Vlpius Demetrius, dec xx Palm, 200: pp. 144, 149, 387; **1**, Aurel, xxxvi 1–2; **2** xxxvi 15–16
Vlpius Demetrius, eq xx Palm, t. Tiberini, 201: **1** xxxiv 23
Ṿḷp[i]ụs Gaiaṇ[us], sesq xx Palm, t. Octaui, 214: **2** xxxviii 28. Perhaps same as **1** xl 23 and cent, **27** a ii 6
Vlpius Germanus, xx Palm, t. Apolloni, ca. 215–240: **15** ii 22
Vlpius Ṃ......, Egypt, c. Theopropi, 194: **5** ii 14
Vlpius Marcellus, eq xx Palm, t. Tiberini, 204: **1**, Aurel, xxxv 10; **2** xxxv 12
Aurel Vlpius Marea, eq xx Palm, t. Demetri, 195: **1** xxxvi 22
Vlpius Marianus, sig xx Palm, 214–239: **50** i 2 and 9
Vlpius Marinus, eq xx Palm, t. Demetri, 201: **1**, Aurel, xxxvii 3; **2** xxxvii 5; **26** b 3
Vlpius Marinus, xx Palm, c. Marci, 203: **8** iii 12
Vlpius Marinus, eq xx Palm, t. Demetri, 204: **1**, Aurel, xxxvii 27; **2** xxxvii 27
Vlpius Marinus, xx Palm, c. Mariani, 208: **1**, Aurel, xxiii 6; **2** xviii 11
Vlpius Marin[, xx Palm, c. Antonini post, 216: **2** xxx 25
Vlpius Menandrus, eq xx Palm, t. Zebida, 199: **1** xxxi 39; **2** xxxii 12
Ṿ[lpius Mo]mbogeus: **1** xxxiv 2 app
Vlp[ius] Niger: **77** a ii 8 app
Vlpius Puplianus, xx Palm, 204: c. Castrici, **1** xvii 13; c. Antonini pr, **2** xxii 22
Vlpius Quirinus, principalis II Traian, 216: **21** 21
Vlpius Saturnilus, III Cyr, c. Pompei Epane, 91–116: **34** recto ii 24, Vpis Satunilus
Vlpius Seuerus, xx Palm, 203: c. Seleuciana, **6** xi 1; actuarius, c. Castrici, **1** xvii 3; actuarius, c. Antonini pr, **2** xxii 13
Vlpius Siluanus, xx Palm, c. Danymi, 197: **1**, Aurel, i 14; **2** vi 26
Vlpius Siluanus, eq xx Palm, t. Octaui, 203: **1**, Aurel, xl 1; vexillarius centuriae, **2** xl 9
Vlp(ius) [Sil]ụanus, xx Palm, 191–216: **89** *4* ii 4
Vlpius Siluanus, xx Palm, 214–239: **50** i 3 and 9
Vlpius Siluanus, xx Palm, 216–250: **16** recto 3
Vlpius Tertius, dux, Dura in 248: **83** 24
Vlpius Valentinus, trib xx Palm in 208: **99** *1* 2; *1* verso 1; *2* 1; *2* verso 1; *3* 1; *3* verso 1; frag. e app
Vpis, *see also* Vlpius Alexa and Vlpius Saturnilus
Vpis Pei: **34** recto i 20 app
Volusius Seneca, Egypt, ascita, classiarius, 127–170: **59** i 13
Vs[, *see* Arrius
Ṿṣẹtus: **63** ii 25 app
P Vxị.nụ[ ].o, III Cyr, 65–96: **9** 29 a

Xanthippus: **73** c 9 app
[Xi]fidius: **20** 1 app

Z.[, Z.[...]ṇ.[, Z.[.]..[.]s, *see also* Aurelius, Belaacabus, Demetrius
Ẓ[, *cogn*, eq xx Palm, t. Octaui, 201: **2** xl 1
Z.[, *nom*, xx Palm, c. Marci, 214: **1** ix 9
Aurel Z[, xx Palm, c. Castrici, 214–215: **1** xix 8
Z.....[.].ạieṛ[, xx Palm, c. Pudentis, 197–225: **92** vi 20
]ctụ[....]n Ẓ.[, xx Palm, ca. 205–240: **42** 4
]....ạṇụṣ Ẓ.ḅ...[, xx Palm, 225–247: **3** b 3
Za[, *see also* Salmanes
Ẓạ[, *cogn*, xx Palm, 225–247: **3** b 5
Zaabal, *see* Demetrius
Zab[.]ua, *see* Iarhaeus
Zab...ṣ.....[.].ẹ..[, xx Palm, ca. 215–240: **15** i 16
Zabaeus, *see* Aurelius
Zabathes Malchi, *see* Zabdaathes
Zabḅ[, *see* Abdaeus
Zabbaei, *see also* Antonius, Mucianus
Zabbei, *cogn*, xx Palm, c. Antonini pr, 197–201: **2** xxii 7
Zabbeus, *cogn*, xx Palm, c. Antonini pr, 215: **2** xxiv 18
Zabbaeus Barchalba, eq xx Palm, t. Demetri, 201: **1**, Aurel, xxxvii 7; **2** xxxvii 9

Zabbaeus Malchi, eq xx Palm, t. Demetri, 203: **1**, Aurel, xxxvii 12; **2** xxxvii 14, Zabaeeus
Zabd[, *see also* Abdaeus, Aurelius, Mocimus
Zaḅḍ.[, *cogn*, xx Palm, c. Malchi, 205–216: **2** ii–iv h 4
Zabdaathes Malchi, eq xx, t. Octaui, 201; **1**, Aurel, xxxix 16 and app, vexillarius, Zabathes; **2** xxxix 19 and app
Zabdaathes Mocimi, xx Palm, c. Antonini post, 196: **6** iv 24; **1**, Aurel, xi 16; **2** xxvii 5
Zabdas, *see also* Aurelius
Zabdas Auada, xx Palm, c. Antonini post, 214: **1**, Aurel, xiv 8; **2** xxix 28
Zabdas Barathe[, xx Palm, c. Marini pr, 233?: **66** b ii 24
Zabde, *see* Aurelius, Iulius
Zabdes Malchi, xx Palm, c. Marci, 205: **6** iii 21; **1** vii 26; **2** xiii 5
Zabdeus, *see* Beleus
Zabdibol[, *see also* Aurelius
Zabdib[ol-, xx Palm, ca. 205–240: **12** a–c 7
Zabdiboli, *see also* Amaeus, Nisamsus, Salmanes
Zabdiboli, *cogn*, xx Palm, c. Antonini post, 199: **1** xi 18; **2** xxvii 7
Aurel[-12?- Za]ḅḍịboli, eq xx Palm, t. Octaui, 203: **1** xl 4
Zabdiboli, *cogn*, xx Palm, c. Danymi, 203: **2** vii 16
Zabdibolus, *see also* Aurelius, Iulius, Mucianus, Zaidibolus
Zabdibolus, *cogn*, xx Palm, c. Danymi, 214: **2** x 7
Zaḅḍịḅo[lus, *nom*, xx Palm, c. Mariani, 193–218: **6** vii 7
Zabdibolus Gora, eq xx Palm, t. Antonini, 204: **1**, Aurel, xlii 28; **2** xlii 19
Zabdibolus Gora, xx Palm, c. Antonini post, 207–232: **27** a i 15
Zabdibolus Hammae[, xx Palm, c. Marci, 205: **6** iii 22; **1** vii 28 app; **2** xiii 7
Zabdib(olus) Maccaei, xx Palm?, 190–245: **116** B
Zabdibolus˙ Mal[, xx Palm, c. Antonini pr, 210: **2** xxiii 19 and app
Zabdibolus Malacheli, xx Palm, 195: c. Seleuciana, **6** x 28 and app; c. Castrici, **1**, Aurel xvi 16 and app, Zaidibolus
Zabdibol(us) Malchi, xx Palm, ca. 190–230: **41** 4
Zabdibolus Malchi, xx Palm, c. Antonini pr, 207–232: **27** a i 12
Zabdibolus Ṃaẓḍ.[, xx Palm, c. Antonini post, 214: **2** xxix 21
[Zabdi]bolus Saḍ[..].i, xx Palm, 195: c. Seleuciana, **6** x 29 and app; **1**, Aurel, xvi 18 and app, Zaidibolus
Zabdibolus Salman, eq xx Palm, t. Zebida, 205: **1**, Aurel, xxxiii 5; **2** xxxiii 21, canceled
Zabdibolus Themarsa, eq xx Palm, t. Zebida, 203: **1**, Aurel, xxxv 2; **2** xxxv 5; **92** ix 18, Themasa
Zabdibolus Theme, xx Palm, c. Danymi, 214: **6** ii 2; **2** x 2
Zabdibolus Theoboli, xx Palm, 202: c. Malchiana, **1**, Aurel, xxvii 8; c. Malchi, **2** i 13
Zabdil.[, *see* Barnaeus
[Ζα]βειδ[, status unknown; Dura in 216: **89** *16* 8
Zaidibolus, *see* Zabdibolus
Zaora, *see* Azizus, Boliadaeus, Maximus, Mocimus, Mombogeus
Aurel Ze[, xx Palm, c. Marci, 214: **1** ix 19
]es Ẓe[, xx Palm, c. Marci, 214: **2** xiv 19
Aurel Ze.[, xx Palm, c. Castrici, 214–215: **1** xix 6
Zeb[, Zeḅ[...]ṃ..[, *see also* Aurelius, Themes
Zeb[, *nom*, xx Palm, c. Mariani, 200–201: **1** xxi 26
Aurel Zeb[-7-]ại, eq xx Palm, t. Octaui, 201: **1** xxxix 31
Zeb[, *cogn*, xx Palm, c. Danymi, 202–206?: **1** iii–v a–b–c 6
Zebid[, xx Palm, ca. 205–240: **12** a–c 12
Zebida, *see also* Ạ[, Abbas, Abdas, Addas, Amaeus, Audas, Aurelius, Azizus, Barathes, Barnaeus, Boliadaeus, Claudius, Habibis, Heliodorus, Iadibelus, Iaqubus, Iarhaboles, Iarhaeus, Malchus, Mocimus, Salmanes, Salmes, Themarsas, Themes, Theodorus, Zebidas
Aurel .[-7?- Z]ebida, eq xx Palm, t. Demetri, 201: **1** xxxvi 34
Aure[l -8?- Ze]bida, eq xx Palm, t. Demetri, 201: **1** xxxvi 38
Zebida, *cogn*, xx Palm, c. Malchiana, 203: **6** ix 15 and app
Zebidas, *nom*, Egypt, c. Belei, 180–205: **81** iii 6
Aure[l Z]ebida[, xx Palm, c. Mariani, 205–207: **1** xxii 23
[Ze]b[i]ḍạs ..[.]ạlac[, vexillarius xx Palm, t. Antonini, 205 or 208: **2** xliii 3
Zebida, *cogn*, xx Palm, c. Mariani, 212: **6** vi 5
Zebida, *cogn?*, xx Palm, 193–212: **7** a 1
Zebida, *cogn*, xx Palm, c. Antonini pr, 197–214: **92** iii 12
A[urel Z]ebida[, xx Palm, c. Antonini post, 214: **1** xiv 22
Zebida, *cogn*, xx Palm, c. Mariani, 214: **1** xxiv 13
Zebida, *cogn*, xx Palm, c. Malchi, 197–222: **2** ii–iv h 2
Zebida, *cogn*, xx Palm, 197–225: **92** iv 3
Zebida, *cogn*, xx Palm, ca. 190–230: **41** 10
Zebida, *cogn*, xx Palm, ca. 195–230?: **43** 3
Zebida, xx Palm, ca. 210–240: **13** 10
[Ze]ḅida: **1** vi 1 app
Zebidas: **66** a ii 17 app
Zebidas Barnaei, xx Palm, c. Danymi, 207: **6** i 24. Same as next?

Zebidas Barnei, xx Palm, c. Nigrini, 207: **47** ii 9
Zebidas Egla, xx Palm, t. Octaui, 201: vex, **1**, Aurel, xxxix 9; *not* vex, **2** xxxix 19
Zebidas Habibi, eq xx Palm, t. Antonini, 205 or 208: **2** xliii 6
Zebidas Iadaei, eq xx Palm, t. Octaui, 201: **1**, Aurel, xxxix 22; **2** xxxix 25
Zebidas Iarḥ[, xx Palm, 226: **95** b 3
Zebidas Iarhaei, dec xx Palm, 199: p. 387; **1**, Aurel, xxxi 21–22; **2** xxxii 1; **92** ix 15
Zebidas Iarhaei, eq xx Palm, t. Octaui, 201: **1**, Aurel, xxxix 25; **2** xxxix 27
Zebidas Iarhaei, eq xx Palm, t. Zebida, 205: **1**, Aurel, xxxiii 8; **2** xxxiii 24
Zebidas Iarhaei, xx Palm, c. Mariani, 212; **8** vi 8
[Ze]bida Iarhaei, xx Palm, c. Antonini post, 197–217: **92** iii 16
Zebidas Iarhaei, xx Palm, c. Antonini pr, 207–232: **27** a i 10
Zebidas Maccaei, eq xx Palm, t. Demetri, 204: **1**, Aurel, xxxvii 24; **2** xxxvii 25
Zebidas Malchi, eq xx Palm, t. Antonini, 203: **1**, Aurel, xlii 25; **2** xlii 16
Aurel Zebidas Salman, eq xx Palm, t. Antonini, 195: **1** xli 17
Aurel Zebidas Salman, xx Palm, c. Malchiana, 203: **1** xxvii 13
Zebidas Salman, xx Palm, c. Antonini post, 214: **2** xxix 19
Zebidas Zebida, xx Palm, c. Danymi, 201: **6** i 9; **2** vii 6
Zebidius: **81** iii 6 app
Zebịṇṇụṣ Hạsçịa, xx Palm, c. Achaei, ca. 215–240: **15** i 20
Zen[, Zeṇ.[.]o.ṛ, *see also* Aurelius, Domitius
Ẓẹṇ[, *cogn*, xx Palm, c. Marci, 214: **2** xiv 1
Zenobi, *cogn*, xx Palm, c. Marci, 214: **2** xiv 26 and app
Zenobius, *see also* Aurelius
[Zen]ọbiụṣ, *cogn*, xx Palm, c. Marci, 214: **2** xiv 26 app; **8** iv 12 and app
Zenodorus, *see also* Aurelius
].l[ ] Ẓ[e]ṇodọṛụṣ, principalis? xx Palm, 211–236: **23** iii 1
Zenodorus Artemidori, xx Palm, c. Marci, 207: **6** iii 24; **1**, Aurel, viii 1; **2** xiii 13
Zenon, *see also* Claudius, Zenon
Zenon Ẓẹ(non), Egypt, I/II p.: **38** i 7
Zinnẹ[..]ṣ, *see* Aurelius
Ẓo.[, *see* Aurelius
Zoilus, sig Vet Gall, 154–179: **76** xii 7
Zoster: **78** *12* 1 app

The following are broken names of which enough remains to provide some clue for restoration. The list is divided into two parts. The first consists of names of which only the end is preserved. These are alphabetized as a reverse index. The second is made up of names of which only some part of the middle is extant. These are alphabetized by the first extant letter.

]se.[-9?-].ẹḷḍṣ.ạ, xx Palm, c. Marci, 203: **1** vii 6
].ẹa, xx Palm, c. Malchiana, 197–222: **2** ii–iv g 2
]ḷifa, xx Palm, c. Marci, 199: **2** xi 26
]gạ, xx Palm, 197–222: **31** i 8
]aḅ..ga, *cogn*, xx Palm, 191–216: **89** *4* ii 13
].umịạ, Eygpt, legionary cent?, ca. 59–84: **69** 2
]ba.na, xx Palm, c. Malchi, 197–222: **2** ii–iv g 3
]..ṣạṛạ, xx Palm, 210–240?: **13** 10
].ịẹra, dec or cent? xx Palm, 225–251: **66** b i 19 and app
].ṇṇọsa, *cogn*, xx Palm, c. Antonini pr, 197–201: **2** xxii 8
]me, *cogn*, eq xx Palm, t. Tiberini, 203: **2** xxxv 2 and app
]me, *cogn*, xx Palm, ca. 215–240: **15** i 6
.ạ.[.]çịạ.ị, xx Palm, ca. 215–240: **15** i 7
]bbaei, *cogn*, xx Palm, c. Danymi, 197–212?: **8** i 2
].balaẹi, *cogn:* **92** v 9 app
]ḅẹi, *cogn*, xx Palm, c. Mariani, 193–218: **6** viii 6
]...ọụpẹị, *cogn*, xx Palm, ca. 210–240: **13** 7
].çhi, *cogn*, xx Palm, 217–256: **17** a 4
]..ọ.us ..ṣi..açhi, xx Palm, 217–256: **17** a 10
].balaçḥi, xx Palm, c. Danymi, 197–225: **92** v 9 and app
[...]thi, *dative*, Egypt, cibariator coh eq, 132–217: **78** *55* 2
]ẹli, *cogn*, xx Palm, 208–233: **48** 2
].iụ.[.].gaani, xx Palm, c. Danymi, 201: **2** vii 7
.[..].uani, xx Palm, 194–219: **1** xxxix 14 marg
].ṇịni, xx Palm, c. Antonini post, 203–204: **2** xxviii 5
].rini, xx Palm, c. Danymi, 202: **2** vii 9
]ṭṭịṇị, *name?*, xx Palm, 225–251: **66** b i 15
.[..].anus [..]mni, Siluanus Domni?, xx Palm, c. Mariani, 204: **2** xvii 25 and app
[....]ωνι̣, *dative*, Egypt, cibariator coh eq, 150–175 or 182–207: **78** *22* 2
]..ịoni, *dative*, Egypt, optio, early II p.: **77** a i 13
]ṇri, xx Palm, ca. 205–230: **55** b 4
]ạ[........]mṣi, xx Palm, c. Marci, 203: **1** vii 3 and app
]...ran, *cogn*, Haeran?, xx Palm, c. Danymi, 202–219: **1** iii–v f 2
]ṇdon, *cogn*, xx Palm, c. Danymi, 215: **2** x 13; **8** ii 27?
[...]ạριων, Egypt, coh eq, c. Glyconis, 132–217: **78** *55* 1
]sọṇ, xx Palm, c. Marci, 193–201: **1** vi 5
]φερω, Vet Gall, t. Furiani, 154–179: **76** GG 1

]. κωστ . ρ, Egypt, tesserarius coh eq, 132–217: **78** *12* 1
.ạṣṣẹṛ( ), xx Palm, 193–219: **1** xlii 1 marg
]. . ṭoṛ, *cogn*, xx Palm, 225–256: **4** 1 3
]bdạṣ, *cogn*, xx Palm, 214–239: **50** b 8
]dṛo . ọṛṭịḍạṣ, Egypt, early II p.: **77** a i 1
]mḷas, *cogn*, Egypt, 208: **5** i 15
]annas, *cogn*, xx Palm, 191–216: **89** *4* ii 14
]. . sas, *nom*, Absas?, xx Palm, 225–256: **4** a i 3
]ẹchnutas, *see* Apynchis
]. [. .]. ụas, *cogn*, Egypt, 205?: **5** i 4
]ḍọcẹs, Egypt, II/III p.: **30** i 2
]νιδης, Egypt, coh eq, c. Glyconis, 132–217: **78** *48* 6
]ạthes, xx Palm, ca. 210–240: **13** 19
. . . ules, Vet Gall, t. Donaciani, 105–130: **80** 34
]. ṃẹṣ, xx Palm, c. Malchi, 216?: **2** v 1
]ạṃes, *cogn*, xx Palm, 242?: **44** 7
]. ọgenes, xx Palm, ca. 210–240: **13** 11
[. . .]δοντης, Mardontes?, Egypt, coh eq, c. Glyconis, 146–171 or 178–203: **78** *18* 1
. . . artes, Egypt, eq aux, second quarter of II p.: **73** a i 25
]. . . ṇacis, XXII Deiot?, early I p.: **51** i 11
]μονις, Egypt, pedes coh eq, 132–217: **78** *61* 1
. [. .]geṇ . ḷ. ụs, Iul(ius) Gemellus?, xx Palm, c. Aureli, 230: **4** b i 25
]. raṭṣ[.]us, Egypt, eq aux, second quarter of II p.: **73** b 7
]ḅus, xx Palm, ca. 215–240: **15** e 4
]ḷ[.]cus, xx Palm, c. Malchiana, 216: **1** xxx 33
. . . [. . . .]ḥ. lcuṣ, eq xx Palm, 226–251: **83** 14
[. . . . . . .]δαδος, xx Palm, 191–216: **89** *2* 18 and app
]llaẹ[u]ṣ, xx Palm, c. Danymi, 206–208: **2** viii 12
]narieus, *cogn*, xx Palm, c. Malchiana, 204: **6** ix 17
]. ειν ευς, Egypt, optio coh eq, 152–177 or 184–209: **78** *31* 5
]. . . . . ηρευς, Egypt, coh eq, 132–217: **78** *17* 3
. [. . . .]arreus, xx Palm, 191–216: **89** *4* ii 8
]ẹni . . gus, Egypt, II/III p.: **30** i 3
]. ṭhehus, Egypt, aux, 176: **70** a i 18
]. pḥus, *cogn*, Egypt, 206: **5** i 10
]. . . . ṣ. thus, *cogn*, Egypt, 205: **5** i 5
]ạḍallathus, *cogn*, xx Palm, 255?: **44** 15
[. . . . . .]καιος, xx Palm, 191–216: **89** *2* 17
]bius, Egypt, legionary, I a.: **36** 8
]enucius, Genucius?, Egypt, legionary, I a.: **36** 1
]. lius M' filius, Egypt, legionary, I a.: **36** 6
. elius . . o . . ṛ. [, Aelius?, xx Palm, 225–247: **3** b 8 and app
]. ịṃ[.]us, *cogn*, xx Palm, c. Danymi, 214: **8** ii 2
]ẹssuṛṃius, xx Palm, ca. 215–240: **15** ii 11
]nius, Egypt, second half of II p.: **70** e 8
]nius, governor of Syria in 239: **50** i 14
]nius, xx Palm, ca. 215–240: **15** b 6
]. ranịus Q filius, Granius?, Egypt, legionary, I a.: **36** 7
]ọnius, Egypt, classiarius, 144: **28** 9
]ṗius, *cogn*, Vlpius?, drom xx Palm, c. Danymi, 197–216: **8** iii 1
]. . ṛịus, *cogn*, xx Palm, 214: **17** a 6
]. rius, *cogn*, xx Palm, 214: **8** ii 1
]ṃbrius Suṛi . . us, xx Palm, ca. 215–240: **15** i 10
]ṭerius, *nom*, Egypt, classiarius liburnae Mercuri, 125: **28** 12
]ṭọrius, Egypt, legionary, I a.: **36** 14
]untius L filius, Egypt, legionary, I a.: **36** 12
. [.]lo[.]. [.]ḷus, xx Palm, c. Aureli, 228: **4** b i 17 and app
]ẹlus, *nom*, eq xx Palm, t. Demetri, 201: **2** xxxvii 1
]νιλου, Egypt, coh eq, 150–175 or 182–207: **78** *21* 1
]llus, *cogn*, xx Palm, 243?: **44** 10
]. ellus, *nom*, sesq xx Palm, t. Romulli, 225–256: **4** a i 13
]. ụammillus, *name*?, XXII Deiot?, early I p.: **51** i 21
]ṛiḷlus, Cyrillus?, xx Palm, c. Barga, 217–256: **17** a 6
]imus, III Cyr, 65–90: **58** i 32
[. . .]ṣalṃus An[.]. ọ[, xx Palm, c. Danymi, 203–216: **92** viii 9
]ṇiṇ[.]rṃus, Egypt, eq aux, second quarter of II p.: **73** b 8
]. . ṇ. . [. .]. . ạṇ[u]s, Egypt, c. or t.]. rliani, I/II p.: **38** i 16
]. ạnus, Egypt, eq aux, second quarter of II p.: **73** b 6
]ạnus, *cogn*, Egypt, 206: **5** i 9
]. [.]ạnus, xx Palm, c. Danymi, 205–207: **2** viii 8
]ạṇus, xx Palm, c. Antonini pos', 214: **1** xiv 13
]. . anus, *cogn*, xx Palm, 242?: **44** 3
]ianus, *cogn*, proximus tabular., Egypt, first half of III p.: **102** a 11
]. . ianus, *cogn*, xx Palm, 195–230?: **43** 4
]διανος, Egypt, coh eq, c. Sabini, 152–177 or 184–209: **78** *31* 1
]lian(us): **130** 4 app
]ḷianus, *cogn*, xx Palm, 191–216: **89** *4* iii 3
]. lianos, Egypt, coh eq, t. Gemelli, 152–177 or 184–209: **78** *66* 5
]. rlianus, dec or cent, Egypt, I/II p.: **38** i 11
]ριανος, sig I Aug Lus, c. Argii, 92–117: **74** iii 1
]. lanus, *cogn*, tabularius, Egypt, first half of III p.: **102** a 6
]ẹnus: **132** 3
]. . çiṇus, xx Palm, ca. 200–235: **61** i 14
]. eịṇus, *cogn*, Egypt, end of III p.: **11 bis** b i 18

].ecrinus, *cogn*, praefectus alae, Egypt, first half of III p.: **102** a 12
]ferinus: **102** a 12 app
]orinus, *cogn*, xx Palm, c. Danymi, 215: **2** x 10
[..]urinus, Vet Gall, t. Donaciani, 105–130: **80** 30
]ṃ..ọus, *cogn*, Egypt, 212?: **5** i 18
]pus, Egypt, aux, 172: **70** a i 5
].ṛus, xx Palm, 217–256: **19** 6
]ṛus, xx Palm, ca. 215–240: **15** f 3
].aṛus, xx Palm, ca. 215–240: **15** ii 10
]ωρος, Egypt, eq coh eq, 144–169 or 176–201: **78** *65* 5
]dorus, xx Palm, c. Marci?, 207–232: **27** c 1
].sus, *cogn*, xx Palm, 242?: **44** 4
]dṣus, xx Palm, c. Danymi, 197–222: **2** xi 8
]bedṣus, Abedsus?, xx Palm, c. Castrici, 214–215: **1** xix 15
]ntus, *cogn*, Quintus?, xx Palm, ca. 215–240: **15** i 11

]..abbu[, xx Palm, ca. 215–240: **15** ii 11
[.].ạetẹnuṣ[, Egypt, I/II p.: **38** ii 17
].ạṇera[, Egypt, I/II p.: **38** ii 10
].[..]ạṛẹạ...., xx Palm, ca. 210–240: **13** 10
]aro..[, *cogn*, Barotarus?, xx Palm, c. Antonini pr, 203–204: **8** vii 28
]arṣi..grạ....., xx Palm, ca. 210–240: **13** 9
]b.elba[.]..[, xx Palm, ca. 205–240: **12** d 3
].ḅ..ụalạh.ị[, xx Palm, ca. 215–240: **15** ii 5
]ḅẹ.ẹdiọ.m[, xx Palm, 217–256: **17** b 1
].bel[, xx Palm, ca. 215–240: **15** f 1
]bia.[, *cogn*, xx Palm, c. Antonini post, 201: **1** xi 30
]bus[, eq xx Palm, t. Tiberini, 203: **1** xxxiv 35
].[.]ccei...., xx Palm, 236: **4** k 5
]e..ṛiasa.[, xx Palm, 217–256: **17** a 4
].ebụ[, xx Palm, c. Danymi, 205: **2** viii 2
]elạ...ọṃ[, xx Palm, ca. 215–240: **15** i 8
]elp.[, xx Palm, ca. 215–240: **15** ii 17
].[.]l .ẹnṭạ[, xx Palm, ca. 200–235: **61** ii 13
[....]επτ̣ια[, Egypt, pedes coh eq, c. Pos[, 132–217: **78** *50* 1
]erṃ[, xx Palm, ca. 215–240: **15** ii 9
]eṣam[, Barbaesamen?, xx Palm, c. Castrici, 214: **1** xviii 25
.[...]ḥ[...]ẹleạ..[, xx Palm, 211–236: **33** v 3
]....ḥariod.[, xx Palm, 217–256: **17** a 8
].[ ]ḷaṭḥ[, eq xx Palm, t. Antonini, 201: **2** xlii 1
].lqụ[, xx Palm, ca. 205–240: **12** a–c 11
].ṃ.ogyn.[, *cogn*, xx Palm, 191–216: **89** *4* iii 2
].ṃaṛị.[, xx Palm, ca. 215–240: **15** e 3
]...ṃuṭị[, xx Palm, ca. 215–240: **15** ii 4
].n.s[.].ạaṭh[, xx Palm, c. Antonini pr, 212: **2** xxiii 27
]...[..]ṇas...sti[, xx Palm, ca. 210–240: **13** 4
]ṇdri.[, xx Palm, 217–256: **17** b 3
]ṇiṃị[ ].ṛiṃ[, xx Palm, ca. 200–235: **61** ii 15
].nisa[, eq xx Palm, t. Octaui, 199: **1** xxxviii 35: **2** xxxix 2
]ṛeịọqu..ariṣ[, xx Palm, 217–256: **17** a 3
].ṛoṃ..[, xx Palm, ca. 215–240: **15** i 3
].....ṛọni[, Egypt, coh eq, first quarter of III p.: **52** a 3
]........ṣ.p..pạẹṣ.[, xx Palm, ca. 210–240: **13** 11
].ṣaḅ[, eq xx Palm, t. Tiberini or Zebida, 197–225: **92** vii 3
]..sam.[, xx Palm, ca. 205–240: **12** a–c 13
].ste..ẹss.[, xx Palm, 217–256: **17** a 5
]ueṣ[, xx Palm, c. Danymi, 202–207?: **1** iii–v j 3
]ugṇ[, *cogn*, xx Palm, c. Antonini post, 216: **2** xxxi 1
.ụṛạeṇiạ[, *nom*, xx Palm, 225–256; **4** m 3

Index 2: Emperors and the Imperial Family

For Augusti and Caesars as consuls see also Index 3.

Aelius Caesar, *see* Lucius

Alexander, *see* Severus

Antoninus Pius, pp. 311, 423 note; **75** 10: Imp Antonin[; 16: *Αἴλιος*; 22–23: *Αἴλ[ιος Ἁδριανὸς] Ἀντωνεῖνος*; **78** *73* 6–7: *Αὐτοκράτωρ Καῖσαρ Τίτος Αἴλιος Ἁδριανὸς Ἀντωνῖνος Σεβαστὸς Εὐσεβής*; **117** ii 20 and iii 6: diuus Antoninus Pius, diuus Antoninus; iii 4–6 app

Augustus, pp. 1, 4, 6, 8, 141 note, 242, 421 note 4, 423 note; **117** iii 8: diuus Augustus; ii 9 app, 18 app; iii 4–6 app

Aurelius Antoninus, *see* Caracalla *and* Elagabal

Balbinus, p. 395

Caesar, C Iulius, *dictator*, pp. 8, 349, 420; **117** ii 21: diuus Iulius; ii 21 app

Caracalla, pp. 88, 90 note 1, 311, 312, 336, 349, 357, 414, 423 note; **5** i 13 app; **89** *3* 7 app; *39* 5 app; **101** a i 6 app; **117** i 17–18: diuus Antoninus Magnus; ii 2: diuus Antoninus Magnus, diuus Antoninus

Claudius, p. 423 note; **117** ii 23: diuus Claudius

Commodus, pp. 88, 170, 255, 311, 312, 423 note; **39** 13 app; **70** a ii 7 app, 30 app; **76** i 5–6; ii 7, 16–17; iv 24; v 14–15; vi 5–6, 13–14, 20–21; vii 5–6, 11–12, 19–20; viii 5, 10–11, 22; ix 7–8, 9, 16–17; x 7–8, 13, 20–21; xi 7–8; xii 6–7, 15, 24; xiii 5–6, 14–15, 20–21; xiv 6–7, 8–9; xv 7–8, 16; xvi 22; xvii 4–5, 13–14, 17–18; xviii 5–6, 17–19; xix 8–9, 16–17, 22–23; xx 4–5; xxiv 3–4; FF 6–7; HH i 5–6: *Αὐρήλιος Κόμμοδος ὁ κύριος Σεβαστός*

—— **76** i 14–15, 20–21, 25; iii 13–14, 16–17, 25–26; v 5–6; xi 16–17: *Αὐρήλιος Κόμμοδος Καῖσαρ ὁ κύριος*

—— **76** iii 6–7; v 7–8, 16; xiii 12–13, 19; xiv 15; xv 14–15, 21; GG 5, 11: *Κόμμοδος ὁ κύριος Σεβαστός*

—— **76** iii 23–24; iv 7–8, 15–16; viii 17, 27; xvi 5–6; xx 12–13, 22–23; xxi 3–4; BB 7: *Αὐρήλιος Κόμμοδος ὁ κύριος αὐτοκράτωρ*

—— **76** x 5–6: *Κόμμοδος ὁ κύριος*

—— **76** xvi 15–17: *Λούκιος Αὐρήλιος Κόμμοδος ὁ κύριος αὐτοκράτωρ*

—— **76** xviii 29–30: *Αὐρήλιοι Ἀντωνῖνοι οἱ κύριοι καὶ Κόμμοδος Σεβαστοί*

—— **76** FF 5: *Αὐτοκράτωρ Κόμμοδος*

—— **117** iii 1: [diuus] Com[modus]

Constantius Caesar, **86** 2: Constantius nobilissimus Caesar

Decius, p. 235; **117** ii 23–24 app

Diocletian, pp. 1–2, 3, 122, 242, 400; **86** 1: d(ominus) n(oster) Diocletianus Aug(ustus)

Domitian, pp. 4, 107, 118, 210, 220, 251, 256, 421 note; **10** 3 app; **63** i 17 app; **68** ii 3 app; **69** 27 app; **10** 5, 20, 22, 31; **37** 1: Imp Domitianus

—— **10** 7, [8], [12], 16, [23], 25, 32, 33: Domitianus

Elagabal, pp. 13, 14, 52, 88, 90 note 1, 141, 144, 172, 177, 380, 414, 431, 434; **49** 1 app; **55** g 2 app; **89** *3* 7 app; **90** *1* a 1–2: d(ominus) n(oster) sanctissimus [Imp(erator)] Marcus Aurel(ius) Inuictus; **91** *1* i 4 app, 6 app; *2* i 6 app; **101** a i 6 app

Faustina, p. 423 note; **117** iii 7: diua Faustina; i 10 app; iii 4–6 app, 7 app

Galerius, *see* Maximian Caesar

Gallienus, p. 175

Gallus, p. 175; **83** 15 app

Germanicus Caesar, p. 420; **117** ii 12: Germanicus Caesar

Geta Caesar, pp. 349, 399; **5** i 13 app

Gordian III, pp. 82, 133, 137, 154, 191, 192, 396; **20** 15 app; **49** 1 app; **50** i 1–2 and 8: d(ominus) n(oster) M Antonius Gordianus Pius Felix Inuictus Aug

Hadrian, pp. 271, 423 note; **64** i 28 app; **117** i 13: [diuus Hadrianus]; i 10 app, 11 app; ii 5 app, 20 app, 26–28 app

Iụ.ḷ . . . . . . [, emperor, **49** 1

Iulia Domna, pp. 349, 423

Iulia Maesa, p. 423; **117** ii 7: diua Iulia Ma[esa]

Iulia Mamaea, **117** ii 26: Mamaea Augusta

Lucius Aelius Caesar, **117** i 11 app

Lucius Seius Caesar, p. 423; **117** i 11 app

Lucius Verus, p. 423; **11** ii 1 app; **117** i 21: diuus Lucius Verus, diuus Lucius
Macrinus, pp. 88, 90 note 1, 380, 423
Marciana, p. 423 note; **117** ii 28: diua Marciana
Marcus Aurelius, pp. 156, 312, 350, 423 note; **76** i 5–6; ii 7, 16–17; iv 24; v 14–15; vi 5–6, 13–14, 20–21; vii 5–6, 11–12, 19–20; viii 5, 10–11, 22; ix 7–8, 9, 16–17; x 7–8, 13, 20–21; xi 7–8; xii 6–7, 15, 24; xiii 5–6, 14–15, 20–21; xiv 6–7, 8–9; xv 7–8, 16; xvi 22; xvii 4–5, 13–14, 17–18; xviii 5–6, 17–19; xix 8–9, 16–17, 22–23; xx 4–5; xxiv 3–4; FF 6–7; HH i 5–6: *Αὐρήλιος Ἀντωνῖνος ὁ κύριος Σεβαστός*
—— **76** i 14–15, 20–21, 25; iii 13–14, 16–17, 25–26; v 5–6; xi 16–17: *Αὐρήλιος Ἀντωνῖνος Καῖσαρ ὁ κύριος*
—— **76** iii 6–7; v 7–8, 16; xiii 12–13, 19; xiv 15; xv 14–15, 21–22; xvii 29–30; GG 5, 11: *Ἀντωνῖνος ὁ κύριος Σεβαστός*
—— **76** iii 22–23; iv 7–8, 15–16; viii 17, 27; xvi 5–6, 15–17; xx 12–13, 22–23; xxi 3–4; BB 7: *Αὐρήλιος Ἀντωνῖνος ὁ κύριος αὐτοκράτωρ*
—— **76** x 5–6; *Ἀντωνῖνος ὁ κύριος*
—— **117** i 21: [diuus Marcus Antoninus], diuus Marcus; ii 6: diuus Marcus Antoninus; iii 1 app
Matidia, p. 423 note; **117** ii 19: diua Matidia
Maximian, **86** 1: d(ominus) n(oster) Ma[x]imian[Aug]
Maximian Caesar (Galerius), **86** 2: [Maximianus] nobilissimus Caesar
Maximinus Thrax, pp. 82, 146, 157, 159, 395, 433; **4** k 4 app
Nerva, pp. 161, 423 note; **117** iii 4–5: [diuus Nerua]
Otacilia Severa, p. 397
Pertinax, pp. 255, 423 note; **117** ii 23: diuus Pertinax
Pescennius Niger, p. 350; **117** ii 10–11 app
Philip, pp. 82, 175, 396–97; **66** b i 14 app
Plotina, p. 423 note; **117** i 10 app
Pupienus, p. 395
Sabina, p. 423 note; **117** i 10 app
Seia, p. 423
Seius, *see* Lucius
Septimius Severus, pp. 88, 156, 255, 312, 336, 400, 421, 423 note; **91** *1* verso 2–3 app; **117** i 15: diuus Seuerus; ii 3, 4, 10–11: diuus Pius Seuerus; **118** 5 app
Severus Alexander, pp. 14, 52, 82, 144, 146, 183, 395, 423; **4** b ii 12 app; **47** i 6 and 17: d(ominus) n(oster) Alexander Aug(ustus); **55** g 2 app; **91** *1* i 6 app; **117** i 3: [dominus noster M Aurelius Seuerus Alexander Aug]; 23: Imp(erator) [Caesar M Aurelius Seuerus Alexander 25: [Imperator] Augustus [Marcus Aurelius Seuerus Alexander], [Alexande]r Aug(ustus) n(oster); 27: A[lexander Augustus no]s[ter]; ii 16: dominus noster Marcus Aurelius Seuerus Alexander; 17: Alexander Augustus; **117** i 11 app, 27–29 app; ii 18 app, 26–28 app
Tiberius, pp. 4, 199
Titus, pp. 116, 246, 421 note, 423 note; **10** 3, 18, 27, 29: [Imp Titus]
Trajan, pp. 161, 219, 220, 221, 278, 348, 423 note; **63** i 14 app; **74** i 7, 14; ii 7, 13; iii 7, 15: *Τραιανὸς Ἄριστος Καῖσαρ ὁ κύριος* (iii 15: ⟨*τρα*⟩*ιανου*); **87** 25: Imp Traianus n(oster); **117** i 15 and 16: diuus Traianus; iii 4–5: [diuus Traianus]; i 10 app
Trebonianus, *see* Gallus
Vespasian, pp. 168, 421 note, 423 note
Volusian, **83** 15 app

Index 3: Notable Persons, Including Consuls

The consuls, because their large number would seriously interrupt the remainder of the list, have been placed at the end. Tribunes and other high ranking military officers will be found in Index 4: Military Affairs.

adiutor Praefecti Aegypti
Sex Attius L f Volt Suburanus Aemilianus, **34** recto i 10 app
Ardashir, **4** b ii 12 app
Crassus, "triumvir," **117** ii 9 app
dux
Egypt, name lost, **20** 3
Dura, Licinnius Pacatianus, **83** 23
Vlpius Tertius, **83** 24
eutheniarch of Oxyrhynchus
T Flauius Valerianus, p. 242
legatus Parthorum
Goces, p. 400; **98** *2* a 5
legatus Augusti
Germaniae Superioris
Hordeonius, p. 350
Moesiae Inferioris
A Caecilius Faustinus, pp. 219, 220, 221; **63** i 30, 31 app, 32 app; ii 4
L Fabius Iustus, pp. 219, 220, 221; **63** i 31 app; ii 4 app, 5, 25
Iulius Antonius Seleucus, **91** *1* i 4 app
Moesiae Superioris
L Herennius Saturninus, pp. 219, 220, 221; **63** ii 7
Syriae
Antonius Seleucus, p. 383; **91** *1* i 4 and app; *2* i 3–4, 7–8
Atilius Cosminus, **66** b i 5; **83** 4, 8, 14
Attius Rufinus, pp. 154, 192, 417; **29** 3, 10; **114** 1; **114** verso 2
Aurelius Aurelianus, p. 406; **100** 2
Caese(nnius?) Vinius, **50** i 14 app
L Iulius Apronius Maenius Pius Salamallianus, **50** i 14 app
Marius Maximus, pp. 399, 403; **98** *2* 1; *3* 1; **99** *1* 2; *1* verso 3; *2* 1; *2* verso 2; *3* 1 app; *3* verso 2; d
]nius, **50** i 14 and app
C. Marius, pp. 7, 8
Pliny the Younger, p. 348
Pompey, p. 348
Praefectus Aegypti, pp. 242, 409, 410; **9** 2 m app; **11** ii 3 app; **20** 3 app; **87** 2 app; **91** *1* i 5 app
(Alphabetically by cognomina)
Annianus, between A.D. 236 and 240, **20** 23 app
Aurelius Basileus, A.D. 242–245, **20** 3 app, 6, 9, 15 app
L Peducaeus Colonus, A.D. 69/70, **34** recto ii 4 app
Tineius Demetrius, A.D. 189/90–190, **70** b ii 9 app
L Munatius Felix, A.D. 150–152/3, **11** ii 3 app
C Auidius Heliodorus, A.D. 138–141, **75** 4
Heracleus, date uncertain, **11** ii 3 app
T Flauius Frontinus Heraclius, date uncertain, **11** ii 3 app
Meuius Honoratianus, A.D. 232–236, **20** 15 app, 23 app
M Aurelius Zeno Ianuarius, A.D. 229/30–231, **20** 20, 23 app
C Minicius Italus, A.D. 101–103, **87** 2
M Sempronius Liberalis, A.D. 154–158/9, **11** ii 3 app; **64** i 20–21, 32; ii 14–15
L Volusius Maecianus, A.D. 160–161, **59** i 13 app
C Domitius Philippus, A.D. 241–242, **20** 3 app
L Valerius Proculus, A.D. 144–147, **11** ii 3 app
M Annius Syriacus, A.D. 162–163, **11** ii 3 app
Iulius Vrsus, A.D. 84, **34** recto i 10 app
].an[, between A.D. 230 and 244, **20** 23
praefectus praetorio, pp. 397, 410
P Valerius Comazon, p. 380; **90** *1* b 1; c 1
praepositus praetenturae
Aurelius Rufinus, pp. 383, 414; **91** *1* i 1; *1* verso 2; *2* i 1 app, 12 app; *2* verso 2
praeses Mauretaniae Caesariensis
M Aurelius Atho Marcellus, p. 397; **96** 4

procurator Augusti
Aurel[ianus ?], Dura in A.D. 216, **89** *15* 3 and app
M Aurelius Atho Marcellus, Mauretania, p. 397; **96** 4
Aurelius Rufinus, pp. 383, 414; **91** *1* i 1; *1* verso; *2* i 1 app, 12 app; *2* verso 2
Aurelius Theodorus, Dura in A.D. 216, **89** *4* i 5
Latinianus, Moesia Inferior, A.D. 101–105, **63** ii 26
Minicius Martialis, Dura ca. A.D. 208, **98** *2* a 2
Pomponius L⟨a⟩etianus, Dura in A.D. 251, **83** 15, 17
Servius Tullius, p. 6
Shapor, p. 83; **20** 15 app

Consuls. All dates are A.D.

ạ...ċto, ca. 140–165: **59** i 15
Aduento, 218: p. 172; **40** i 16
Aeliano, *see* Marullo, 184; Crispino, 187; Maximo II, 223
Aemiliano, *see also* Albino, 206
Aemiliano II et Aquilino, 249: **66** a ii 12 and 15; **83** 12 and 19
Africano, *see also* Maximino, 236: **4** k 4
Afro, *see* Catulino, 130
Agricola et Clementino, 230: **20** 19, 20, 22
Agricola, 230: **4** b i 22; **24** 7 and 9
Agricola et Maximo II, 233, 234?, **20** 20 app
Albino et Aemiliano, 206: **1** xxviii 13; xxxviii 2; xli 1; **2** xxiii 6; xli 1; **5** i 6; **46** 4
Albino, 206: **1** xxxiii 29; **2** xiii 10; xxviii 12; xxxviii 10; xliii 22 app; **6** xi 14; **8** v 22
Albino et Maximo, 227: **95** b 5
Albino, 227: **4** b i 14
Albino, 246, *see* Praesente
Alexandro Aug, 222: p. 82; **2** xvi 5; xxvi 10; xxxi 20; **31** i 12; ii 6
diuo Alexandro, 222: **24** 18
diuo Alexandro II, 226: **4** b i 5 and 10
diuo Alexandro et Dione, 229: **24** 14; *see also* Cassio Dione
diuo Alexandro III, 229: **4** b i 18
Ambibulo, 126, *see* Vero III
Antonino, **59** i 18 app
Antonino II, 205: **1** vii 25; xvi 8; **2** xlv 10?; **6** iii 20; ix 22
diuo Antonino II, 205: **1** xxi 1; xxviii 7; xxxiii 1; xxxv 12; xxxvii 28; xl 14; **2** viii 1; xiii 4; xvi 16; xviii 7; xxxiii 18; xxxv 13; xxxvii 28; xl 21; xliii 2?; xlv 10?; **5** i 1 and app; **6** xi 10; **8** v 19; viii 2
Antonino Aug III et Geta Caesare II, 208: **98** *3* 5–6; **99** *1* 3, 9–10
diuo Antonino III, 208: **1** xiii 5; xxiii 4; xliii 4?; **2** xviii 9; xxiii 13; xxviii 21; xliii 2?; xlv 10?; **5** i 13 and app
Antonino Aug IIII et Balbino, 213: **104** 3
Antonino IIII, **40** i 2 app
Antonino Aug II et Sacerdote II, 219: **1** xxxi 14–15; xliv 17–18; p. 141
Anullino II, 199: **1** i 15; xi 17; xxi 16; xxxi 21, 36; xxxiv 14; xxxvi 27; xxxviii 32; xli 26; xliii 32; **2** vi 27; xi 23; xvi 22; xvii 6; xxxii 1, 9; xxxiv 12; xxxvi 23; xli 14; **6** i 2; iv 25; viii 11
Anullino, 216, *see* Sabino II
Apollinari et Mamertino, suffecti, 150: **72** 10 app
Apro II, 176, *see also* Pollione II; **70** a i 17 app
Apro et Maximo, 207: **1** vii 31; xi 3; xxviii 18; xxxiii 12, 23, 27; xxxv 20; xxxviii 5; xl 18; **2** xxiii 8; xxxiv 1, 5; xxxv 21; **5** i 11 app; **6** iii 23; xi 16; **46** 8; **99** *2* 7
Apro, 207: **1** iii–v j 4?; **2** xiii 12; xviii 4; xxviii 16; xxxiii 28; xxxviii 13; xl 25; **6** i 23; **8** viii 7
Aquilino, *see* Asiatico, 125; Rustico II, 162; Aemiliano II, 249
Arriano et Papo, 243: **20** 15; **44** 9
Asiatico II et Aquilino, 125: **28** 11
Aspero, **59** i 15 app
duobus Aspris, 212: **1** viii 11; xviii 7; xxxiii 18; xxxv 25; xxxviii 7; xl 20; xliii 14; **2** viii 17?; xiii 23; xxiii 23; xxix 8; xxxiii 30; xxxv 29; xxxviii 15; xl 27; xliii 22 app; xlv 6; **5** i 16 app; ii 3; **6** iii 28; vi 4; xi 22; **8** vi 6; vii 19; viii 13; ix 26; x 21?
Atiliano, 135, *see* Pontiano
Attico, 143, *see* Torquato II
Attico et Praetextato, 242: **20** 3, 6, 9, 12
[Atti]co?, 242, p. 432
Augurino, 156, *see* Siluano
Auito et Maximo, 144: **28** 7
Auito, 144: **59** i 5
Auito, 209, *see* Pompeiano
Balbino II, 213, *see* Antonino IIII
Barbaro et Faustino, suffecti 99: **63** i 30 app
Basso, 211, *see* Gentiano
Catulino et Afro, 130: **80** 7–8
Celso II et Marcello II, 129: p. 120; **11** ii 7 app
Cereale, 215, *see* Laeto II
Cilone II, 204: **1** vii 8; xii 6; xvi 11; xvii 5; xxi 5; xxii 9; xxvii 24; xxxii 33; xxxv 5; xxxvi 5; xxxvii 17; xl 6; xlii 26; xliv 15; **2** ii a 4; vii 22; xii 20; xvii 16; xxii 15; xxxiii 13; xxxv 19; xxxvii 18; xl 13; xlii 17; xliii 20; **6** i 15; iii 7; ix 16; xi 3; **8** iii 14; v 12
Claro it(erum), 146: **59** i 3
Claro, 193, *see* Erucio Claro
Clementino, 230, *see* Agricola
Comazonte II, 220: pp. 380, 431; **8** ix 24; **20** 14 app; **24** 3; **118** 1, 2, 3
Commodo et Laterano, 154: **64** i 9; ii 30?
Commodo et Pompeiano, 136: **28** 1; **64** ii 23; 30?
Commodo Aug et Quintillo, 177: **70** a i 24–25

Commodo Aug II et Vero II, 179: **76** FF 5
Commodo Aug IIII et Victorino II, 183: **40** i 4 app
Commodo Aug V et Glabrione II, 186: **70** a iii 26–28 app
Commodo Aug VII et Pertinace II, 192: **70** b ii 7–8
Commodo Aug VII, 192: p. 88; **1** xxi 7; xxxviii 14; xli 9
Condiano et Maximo, 151: **64** ii 16
Condiano II, 180: **39** 13 app; **70** a ii 30 app; *see also* Praesente II
Crispino et Aeliano, 187: **39** 19
Crispino, 224: p. 82; **3** a 6; *see also* Iuliano II
Decio Aug et [, 244–249?: **66** b i 14 app
Decio Aug et Grato, 250: **66** a i 11–12; b i 1–2, 7–8, 21–22, 27–28; ii 25–26
Dextro, 225, *see* Fusco II
Dextro II, 196: **1** i 9; xi 12; xxxi 12 app, 34; xxxiv 8; xxxviii 29; xli 21; xliii 22; xliv 10; **2** vi 22; xi 19; xxvii 2; xxxii 7; xxxiv 7; xxxviii 29; xli 9; xliii 15; xliv 11; **5** iii 2 app; **6** ii 28; iv 22; viii 16; x 27 and app
Diocletiano Aug v et Maximiano Aug III, 293: **86** 6
Cassio Dione II, 229: **95** b 7; *see also* Alexandro Aug
Domitiano Aug XIII et Saturnino, 87: **129** 2 app
Domitiano Aug XV, 90: **37** 1
Erucio Claro, 193: pp. 88, 90 note; **1** xi 7; xxi 9; xxxi 27; xxxiii 31; xxxvi 3, 7; xxxviii 16; xli 12; xliii 24; **6** ii 24; iv 18; *see also* Falcone
Extricato II, 217: pp. 90 note, 147; **1** xvi 1; xxxi 12; **2** v 3?; xxxi 14; **6** v 28; x 24; **8** ix 22; **31** i 9; *see also* Praesente
Fabiano, 201: p. 90 note; *see also* Muciano
Falcone, 193: pp. 88, 90 note; **5** ii 9
Faustino, 99, *see* Barbaro
Faustino, 210: **1** viii 6; xiii 14; xviii 4; xxiii 13; **2** xiii 18; xviii 20; xxiii 18; xxxv 27; **6** i 28; iii 25; vi 2; xi 20; **8** vi 1; vii 7
Flacco, 174, *see* Gallo
Fusciano, 188: **39** 21
Fusco II et Dextro, 225: **20** 14 app
Fusco II, 225: p. 432; **3** a 8; **4** b i 7; **29** 12
Gallicano et Titiano, 127: **28** 13
Gallieno Aug II, 255: p. 175
Gallo et Flacco, 174: **39** 3; **70** a i 11 app
Gentiano et Basso, 211: **88** *2* 4
Geta Seniore II, 203: **1** vi 32; xxi 3; xxii 4; xxvii 9; xxxii 24; xxxiii 25; xxxiv 32; xxxvii 10; xxxix 36; xlii 17; **2** i 14; vii 11; xii 11; xvi 18; xvii 12; xxii 11; xxvii 22; xxxiii 5; xxxiv 3, 29; xxxvii 12; xl 8; xlii 11; **6** i 10; iii 12; ix 10; **8** iii 7; v 9
Geta Caesare II, *see* Antonino Aug III
Glabrione et Homullo, 152: **59** i 7 app; **64** ii 37
Glabrione II, 186, *see* Commodo V
Gordiano Aug, 239: **50** i 14
Gordiano Aug, 239? 241?: **29** 1, 8, 15
Gordiano Aug II et Pompeiano, 241: p. 133; **114** 2–2a
Grato et Seleuco, 221: p. 432; **20** 5; **91** *1* i 2 a; *2* i 2a; **109** 3
Grato, 221: **2** xxi 14; xxvi 6; **6** vii 6 app; **21** 14; **24** 16
Grato, 250, *see* Decio Aug II
Homullo, 152: **59** i 7; *see also* Glabrione
Iuliano, 148, *see* Torquato
Iuliano, 175, *see* Pisone
Iuliano II et Crispino, 224: p. 82; **23** i 4, 6; iii 3; iv 6
Iuliano II, 224: **24** 1, 14
Laeto II et Cereale, 215: **23** ii 5; iv 8
Laeto II, 215: **1** x 1; xv 2; xxv 14; xxx 16; **2** x 9; xxiv 6; xxx 12; **6** ii 4; vii 6 app; x 8; **8** ii 21; vii 15, 23; ix 7; **31** i 4; **40** i 2?
Laterano, 154, *see* Commodo
Laterano, 197: **1** i 13; **2** vi 25
Libone, 128, *see* Torquato II
Lupo et Maximo, 232: **27** a ii 15, 16
Lupo, 232: **4** b ii 12 and app; **27** a ii 14
Mamertino, 150, *see* Apollinari
Aufidio Marcello II, 226: **95** b 2
Marcello II, **11** ii 7: *see also* Celso II
Marullo et Aeliano, 184: **39** 17
Maxim[, **22** 4
Maximiano Aug IIII, 293, *see* Diocletiano Aug v
Maximino Aug et Africano, 236: **33** i 1–2
Maximo, 144, *see* Auito
Maximo, 151, *see* Condiano
Maximo, 172, *see* Orfito
Maximo, 207, *see* Apro
Maximo II et Aeliano, 223: **23** i 2 app
Maximo, 227, *see* Albino
Maximo, 232, *see* Lupo
Maximo et Paterno, 233: **48** 5, 6; **66** b ii 23 app
Maximo et Vrbano, 234: **20** 8
Messalla et Sabino, 214: **1** i 3; **2** xxxviii 27
Messalla, 214: **1** viii 17 *or* 27; xviii 14; xxix 5; xxxv 31; xl 22; **2** vi 20; viii 26; xiii 30; xxiii 28; xxix 13; xxxvi 5, 19; xxxviii 17; xl 29; xliv 15, 27; xlv 12; **6** i 32; vi 9; vii 6 app; xi 26; **7** a 2; **8** v 4; vi 10; vii 21; viii 16; **40** i 2 app
Modesto II, 228: **4** b i 16, *modes*(*to ii*) *cos*; **24** 5, *modesto cos*
Muciano et Fabiano, 201: **1** i 1; **2** vi 18; xi 14
Muciano, 201: p. 90 note; **1** i 18; xi 21 app; xxxii 4; xxxiv 20; xxxvi 33; xxxviii 11; xxxix 6; xli 33; xliii 28; **2** vi 30; xi 29; xxvii 12; xxxii 17; xxxiv 18; xxxvi 29; xxxviii 24; xxxix 12; xli 21; xliv 13; **6** i 5; ii 22; iv 30
Nerua II, 90: **37** 1 app

Orfito et Maximo, 172: **70** a i 4
Orfito et Rufo, 178: **39** 11; **70** a ii 7; **76** BB 4
Papo, 243: **66** b ii 23 app; *see also* Arriano
Paterno, 233: **66** b ii 23; *see also* Maximo
Peregrino, 244: **66** b i 25; ii 23 app
Pertinace, 192: **5** ii 7 and app; *see also* Commodo VII
Pio, 238: **66** b i 19 app
Pisone et Iuliano, 175: **39** 6
Po.[, **46** 2
Asinio (Pollione), 81: **68** ii 1
Pollione II et Apro II, 176: **46** 2 app; **70** a i 17 app
Pollione II, 176: **70** a i 17
Pollione, ca. 218/19: **89** *3* 7 app
Pompeiano, *see* Commodo, 136; Seuero, 173
Pompeiano et Auito, 209: **23** ii 9
Pompeiano, 209: **1** viii 4; xiii 10; xviii 2 app; xxiii 10; xxviii 25; xxxiii 15; xxxv 23; **2** viii 14; xiii 16; xviii 17; xxiii 15; xxviii 28; xxxv 25; xxxvi 17; xli 5; **6** i 26; ix 24; **8** viii 11
Pompeiano, 241, *see* Gordiano Aug II
Pontiano, 238: **46** 2 app; **66** b i 19; ii 23 app
Pontiano et Atiliano, 135: **46** 2 app
Pontiano et Rufino, 131: **46** 2 app; **64** i 5
Praesente, **66** b ii 23 app
Praesente et Albino, 246: p. 147; **66** a ii 16; **83** 2
Praesente II et Condiano II, 180: **40** i 16 app; **70** a ii 30
Praesente II, 180: **39** 13
Praesente et Extricato, 217: **20** 2
Praesente, 217: pp. 90 note, 146, 147, 172; **21** 18; **24** 12 and 20; **40** i 6
Praetextato, 242, *see* Attico
Pupp(ieno)?, 234: **4** d 1 and app
Quadrato, 142, *see* Rufino
Quintiano, *see* Seuero, 235
Quintillo, 177: **39** 8; *see also* Commodo
Rufino, 131, *see* Pontiano
Rufino et Quadrato, 142: **28** 5
Rufo, 178, *see* Orfito
Rustico et Aquilino, 162: **77** b 6 app
Sabiniano, *see* Seuero, 155
Sabino, 214, *see* Messalla
Sabino II et Anullino, 216: **89** *1* 7; *4* iii 5–6; *17* 13–14; *19* 10–11; *20* 4–5?, 7–8; *21* 3; *23* 19; *25* 7, 9; *26* 7; *28* 9–10; *29* 15–16; *31* 9–10; *32* 8; *34* 6 and app; *38* 3, 7 app; *39* 6; *45* 4–5 and app; *48* 2–3; *50* 5 and app
Sabino II, 216: **1** x 3; xv 4; xx 3; xxx 19; **2** x 14; xx 15?; xxv 13; xxx 17; xxxvi 7; xliii 27; xliv 5, 18; xlv 8; **4** b i 3; **6** ii 9; iv 5; v 19; x 11; **8** ii 28; iii 2; v 6; ix 13, 28; **21** 19, 20, 21; **40** i 4; **89** *42* 5
Sabino II, 240: **66** a i 9; ii 8, 10, 13; b i 17
Sacerdote II, 219; *see also* Antonino Aug II; **2** xxxi 17; **21** 13; **23** iv 3
Saturnino, 87, *see* Domitiano Aug XIII
Saturnino, 198: **1** xxi 14; xxxiv 12; xxxvi 25; xli 24; **2** xi 21; xvi 20; xxxiv 10; xxxvi 21; xli 12; **6** ii 30 and app; viii 18
Seleuco, 221, *see* Grato
Septimiano II, 190: **5** ii 5; **70** b i 6
Seruiano, 134: **64** i 28 app
Seuero, 141, *see* Stloga
diuo Seuero, 194: **1** xvi 13; **5** ii 11 and app
diuo Seuero II, 194; **1** xxvi 13; xxxviii 20
Seuero II, 194; **1** xxxi 13
(Ti Claudio) Seuero (Proculo), 200: p. 90 note
diuo Seuero III, 202: **1** xxxi 25; xxxii 18; **2** xvii 10; xxii 9; xxvii 17; xxxiv 25; xxxvii 10; xl 4; xli 7; xlii 8
Seuero III, 202: **1** vi 29; xxii 2; xxvii 6; xxxvii 8; xxxix 32; xlii 14; **2** i 11; vii 8; xii 8; xxxii 28; **6** iii 9
Seuero et Pompeiano, 173: **39** 1; **70** a i 11 app
Seuero et Quintiano, 235: **20** 15 app
Seuero et Sabiniano, 155: **64** ii 1; 26?, 34?
Silanis duobus, 189: **39** 24
Siluano et Augurino, 156: **64** i 2, 22, 34; ii 4
Stloga et Seuero, 141: **28** 3; **64** ii 26? 34?
Suburano, 101 and 104: **34** recto i 10 app
III et I, 251: p. 144; **83** 4, 9, 14, 16, 17, 22
III et II, 248: p. 144; **44** 12; **83** 24
Tertullo, 195: **1** i 5; xi 9; xvi 15; xxi 12; xxxiii 35; xxxvi 16; xxxviii 22; xli 16; xliii 19, 26, 30; **2** xlv 3; **6** ii 26; iv 20; viii 13; x 27 and app
Titiano, 127, *see* Gallicano
Titiano, 245: **83** 5, 10, 21, 23
Tito Aug VIII, 80: **63** i 17 app
Torquato et Iuliano, 148: **64** ii 19
Torquato II et A[, **11** ii 4
Torquato (II?) et Attico, 143: p. 120; **11** ii 4 app
Torquato II et Libone, 128: p. 120; **11** ii 4 app
Varo, 134: **64** i 28
Vero II, 179, *see* Commodo Aug II
Vero III et Ambibulo, 126: p. 120
Vero III et D.[, **11** ii 1
Vespasiano Aug VI et Tito Caesare IIII, 75: p. 220; **63** i 15
Vespasiano Aug VIIII, 79: **63** i 21
Victorino, 200: p. 90 note; **1** xi 1, 21 app; xxxii 2; xxxiv 16; xxxvi 1, 31; xxxix 3; xli 30; **2** xi 27; xxvii 9; xxxii 15; xxxiv 14; xxxvi 15, 27; xxxix 9; xli 18; **6** iv 16, 28
Victorino II, 183: **39** 15; *see also* Commodo Aug IIII
Vipstano, 115: **63** i 30 app
Vi[, after 225, before 247: **3** a 11
Volusiano, p. 175
Vrbano, *see* Maximo, 234
]ino, *ca.* 194–219: **1** xi 5

Index 4: Military Affairs

This index is concerned primarily with military ranks and organizational units. Any terms not found here should be sought in Index 8, Greek Words, or Index 9, Latin Words.

actuarius
  Marcianus, **86** 6
  Vlpius Seuerus, **1** xvii 3; **2** xxii 13
ad hostias, pp. 12, 14, 17; **1** xxxvi 22 and 26; xlii 23
  Aurel Aelius Longinus, **1** xlii 23
  Aurel Iadibelus Iarhaei, **1** xxxvi 26
  Aurel Vlpius Marea, **1** xxxvi 22
adiutor? corniculariorum
  Aurelius Apollinarius, **21** 20
  Flauius Seuerianus, **21** 19
  Vibius Faustinus, **21** 18
  Vlpius Quirinus, **21** 21
aedituus, p. 192
  Aurelius Siluanus, **48** i 7, 17; ii 12
ala
  Apriana, **73** a iii 25; **102** a 12 app
  III Asturum ciuium Romanorum pia fidelis, **53** b 22 app
  Augusta, **102** a 12 app
  I Flauia Gallorum Tauriana, **63** i 21 app
  I Flauia singularium ciuium Romanorum pia fidelis, **53** b 22 app
  Herculiana, **102** a 12 app
  prima, **73** a iii 25 app
  quinta, **38** i 10 app
  II Thracum, **64** i 25 app
  Thracum Herculiana, **89** *39* 5 and app
  Thracum Mauretana, **64** i 25–26; p. 285
  ueterana Gallica, **20** 11; **39** 16 app; **53** b 27; **76** i 1, 9; ii 1, 8, 11, 18; iii, 1, 2, 8, 11, 20; iv 1, 11, 17, 19; v 1, 3, 11; vi 9, 18; vii 2, 8, 13, 16, 21; viii 2, 7, 11, 14, 19, 25; ix 2, 13, 18; x 2, 10, 15, 22; xi 2, 9, 12, 13, 18; xii 1, 11, 16, 19; xiii 2, 9, 16, 22; xiv 2, 10, 16; xv 2, 10, 18; xvi 1, 7, 10, 19; xvii 1, 8; xviii 1, 8, 11, 13, 20, 24; xix 1, 3, 12, 18; xx 1, 7, 9, 15, 18, 19, 25; xxi 1, 5; xxiv 1; BB 1, 8; FF 1, 8; GG 1, 6, 9, 12; HH i 1; **80** 1; pp. 202, 204, 270, 283, 285, 333
  Xoitana, **102** a 12 app
aquila, **51** ii 11, 17; **53** b 15
arma, **58** ii 4; **71** a 3, 12; **73** a ii 18; iii 10 app; **76** xv 8; **78** *39* 5
armorum custos
  Agrippa, **129** 6
  Antenor Achillis, **76** xv 8
  M Aurelius Horion Sarapion, **78** *39* 4–6
  ].ei, **78** *71* 1
ascita
  Volusius Seneca, **59** 13 and 12 app
bucinator
  Aurelius Priscus, **2** xiii 31; **50** i 2, 9; b 2
carrarius
  Plotinus, **58** ii 6
centuria
  Achaei, **15** i 6, 10, 14, 20, 23; ii 8, 18, 21; **16** verso 1; **32** 8; **66** a ii 13
  Afri Aquili, **34** recto ii 2
  Afri Aquili minoris, **34** recto ii 12
  Alexandri, **78** *39* 2
  Antonini, **31** i 4; **47** i 12
  Antonini posterioris, (Domitius), **1** xi 1; xliii 30; **2** xlv 10; **6** iv 16; **8** x; **27** a i 13; **31** i 4?; **89** *12* ii 8 app; **92** iii 15; vi; ix 6 app; **118** 6 and app; p. 16
  Antonini prioris, **2** xxii; xlv 3; **8** vii 26 and app; **27** a i 7; **33** ii 1; **47** i 12?, 15; **92** iii 9; vi
  Antonii Longini, **34** recto ii 6
  Antonii Longonis, **34** recto ii 15
  Appiani, **78** *5* 1
  Aquilae, p. 198
  Argii, **74** iii 2
  Aurelii [. . .]i, **4** b i 1–2
  Aurel Aṇ[ton-, **67** 11
  Aurelii Germani, *see* Germani
  Barga, **16** recto 2; **17** a 2, 3, 4, 6, 9; **19** 4 app, 5; **66** b ii 21
  Belei Zabdei, **81** ii 12
  Bouii, **51** i 1
  Caec(ilii)?, **9** 24 b app
  Candidi, **64** ii 19, 23
  Cantii, **77** b 1
  Capitoniana, **34** recto ii 10
  Cassiani, **78** *14* 3 app; *69* 2
  Castricii, **1** xvi 8; xliv 1; **2** xxii 1 app; **8** vii 26 app; p. 90
  Celeris?, **74** ii 2
  Claudii Romani, **77** a i 2, 7
  Cornelii Iuliani, **67** 12
  Crescentis, **74** i 9–10

centuria—*cont.*
Danymi (Septimius), **1** i 1; xliii 19; **2** vi 18; xliv 1; **47** i 4 app; **92** v 6; viii 4; pp. 16, 90, 91, 97, 173
Decrii, **9** 8 f–n; 4 m app; 20 f, k and app, m app
Didymiani, **78** *56* 1
Domitii Caeliani, **34** verso i 1
Domitii Antonini, *see* Antonini posterioris
ε̣. . . γι, **78** *53* 2
Ẹṇ[, **78** *19* 1
Felicis, **15** i 8, 19; ii 14, 20; b 10 app; d 2; **32** 12
Firmi, **51** ii 22
Gaiani, A.D. 131–156, **64** i 40; ii 1 app
Gaiani, ca. 207–232, **27** a ii 6; **47** i 12, 14
Gaṇ[, **64** ii 1
Germani (Aurelius), **13** 18; **14** 1; **15** i 10; ii 6, 10, 16; c 4; **17** a 5, 7, 8, 12?; **19** 6; **23** i 8; **29** 5; **32** 1; **66** a ii 5, 16
Glyconis, **78** *18* 2; *23* 6; *40* 1?; *48* 6; *55* 1; *65* 1
Heliodori, **15** i 9; ii 6, 12, 13 (twice), 15; **29** 12
Heraclian-, **11** ii 3
Heracliani, **78** *21* 2; *23* 2
Herculani, **64** i 34; ii 1 app
Iuli[-, **77** a i 7
Iulii, *see* Marci *and* Mariani
Lappi, **64** ii 16, 26
Lepidiani, **51** i 5
Longiani, **74** iii 9
Longieni, **78** *73* 1
Malchi, **2** i; xliii 15
Malchiana, **6** viii 11; **1** xxvi 13; xliv 10; **2** i 1 app; p. 17
Marci, A.D. 131–156, **64** i 37
Marci (Iulius), **1** vi 1; xlviii 22; **2** xi 14; xliv 11; **6** ii 22; **8** iii 7; **89** *12* ii 4; **92** v 12; vii 15; viii 11; pp. 16, 97, 150
Mariani (Iulius), **1** xxi 1; **2** xvi 16; **6** vi; **8** v 9; **27** a i 2; **47** i 4; ii 5, 19; **89** *1* 5a; **92** iii 4; v 19; p. 16
Marini, **17** a 1
Marini posterioris, **66** a i 9; ii 10
Marini prioris, **66** a ii 8; b i 17; 24 app; ii 23
Maximi, **77** a i 44 app
Mocimi, **16** recto 3; **32** 4
Nasonis, **12** a–c 10; **15** i 11, 15, 21, 22; ii 5, 7, 9, 15, 17; g; **16** verso 2
Neri, **51** ii 8
Nigrini, **23** i 6; **47** i 4, 12; ii 6, 9
Nin⟨n⟩i Rufi, **34** recto i 3
O[.]ạnti, **77** b 1 app
Olympi, **78** *40* 3
Oreis, **78** *72* 2
Pompei Epane, **34** recto ii 20
Pos[, **78** *50* 2
Prisci, **15** i 1, 17, 23; ii 8, 19
Pudentis, **27** a ii 1; **47** i 4; **48** 2; **92** iii 19; vi 19; ix 6 app, 7; p. 387
Quarti, **77** b 1 app
Rufiani, **23** iv 8
Sabini, **78** *31* 1
Seleuci, **88** *1* 5 and app; **89** *12* ii 2; p. 355
Seleuciana, **2** xxii 1 app; **6** x 27; **8** vii 26 app; p. 90
Semproniani, **64** i 42; ii 29
Septimii Danymi, *see* Danymi
Sereni, **9** 4 m app; 9 f–n
Seruilii, **51** ii 18
Sossii, **51** i 14
Suburiana, **34** recto i 10
Ta. . . ., **74** ii 9
Ter[entii, **77** a i 9 app
Themarsa?, **12** e 4
Theopropi, **5** ii 2
Tithoeis, **78** *1* 2
Titulei, **74** i 2
V.[, **77** b 7, 9
Varii, **51** ii 19
Vippị[(Vibi[?), **78** *76* 2
Vlpiana (Vpiana), **34** recto i 20
centurio *or* decurio
Ammonianus, **52** b 4 and app
Antiochus, **78** *37* 6
Horion, **78** *6* 1–2, 12; *22* 27
Saturnilus, **75** 12
].rlianus, **38** i 11
centurio
Ạ. . uinus, **63** ii 32
Abb.[.]sarus?, **50** i 4
Achaeus, **15** i 6, 10, 14, 20, 23; ii 8, 18, 21; **16** verso 1; **32** 8; **66** a ii 13; b i 19 app; pp. 128, 132, 133
Aelius Auitus, **50** i 7, 13; ii 7
Aelius Marinus, **30** ii 9
Aelurio, *see* Iulius
Afrius Aquilus, **34** recto ii 2
Afrius Aquilus minor, **34** recto ii 12
Al.[, **13** 16; p. 126
Alexandrus, **78** *39* 2
Ammonianus, *see* Aprius *and* Aurelius
Antoninus, **31** i 4; **47** i 12; pp. 52, 156–57, 183; *see also* Domitius Antoninus
Antoninus posterior, *see* Domitius Antoninus
Antoninus prior, **2** xlv 3; **23** i 4; **27** a i 7; **33** ii 1; **47** i 12?, 15; **92** iii 9; pp. 157, 183
Antonius Longinus, **34** recto ii 6
Antonius Longo, **34** recto ii 15
Appianus, **78** *5* 1
Aprilis, *see* Petronius
Aprius Ammonianus, **52** a 6; b 4?, 15
Aquila, p. 198
Aquilus, *see* Afrius
Argius, **74** iii 2

Auitus, *see* Aelius
Aurel[, **17** a 12
Aurel [. . .]us, **4** b i 1–2
Aurelius Ammonianus, **52** b 4?, 12
Aurelius An[ton-, **67** 11
Aurelius Germanus, **13** 18; **14** 1; **15** i 10; ii 6, 10, 16; c 4; **17** a 5, 7, 8, 12?; **19** 6; **23** i 8; **29** 5; **32** 1; **50** i 1, 2, 8, 9; ii 1; a 1, 2; **66** a ii 5, 16; b i 19 app; pp. 126, 128, 133
Aurelius Harpocration, **20** 21
Aurelius Theopropus, **5** ii 2
Baebius Iu[. .]us, **51** ii 5; p. 198
Bargas, **16** recto 1; **17** a 2, 3, 4, 6, 9; **19** 4 app, 5; **66** b i 19 app; ii 21; pp. 128, 132, 133, 136
Bassus, **51** ii 16
Beleus Zabdeus, **81** ii 12, 13
Boui[us, **51** i 1; p. 198
Caeli(anus), *see* Domitius
Candidus, *see* Sempronius
Cantius, **77** b 1
Cassianus, **78** *14* 3 app; *69* 2
Ạ[urel].ius Castricius, **1** xvi 8–9; xliv 4
C[ele]r?, **74** ii 2
Cḥ[, **11 bis** a 2
Claudius Romanus, **77** a i 2, 7
Cornelius Egrilianus, **38** i 11 app
Cornelius Iulianus, **67** 12
Crepereius, **51** i 13 app
Crescens, **74** i 9–10
Danymus, *see* Septimius
D Decri(us?), **9** 8 f–n; 20 f–k
Didymianus, **78** *56* 1
Dionysianus, **78** *2* 7
Domitius Antoninus (A. posterior), **1** xi 1–2; xliii 30; **2** xlv 10; **6** iv 16; **27** a i 13; **31** i 4?; **47** i 12; **89** *12* ii 8 app; **92** iii 15; **118** 6?; pp. 157, 183
Domitius Caeli(anus?), **34** verso i 1
ϵ̣. . .νι, *gen*, **78** *53* 2: Herennius?
Egrilianus, *see* Cornelius
Ẹṇ[, **78** *19* 1; cf. *53* 2
Epane, *see* Pompeius
Felix, **15** i 8, 19; ii 14, 20; b 10 app; d 2; **32** 12; pp. 133, 158
Firmus, **51** ii 22
Franius Seuerus, **85** 1
Gaianus, **64** i 40; ii 1 app
(Vlpius?) Gaianus, **27** a ii 6; **47** i 12, 14; p. 183
Gaṇ[, **64** ii 1
Germanus, *see* Aurelius
Glycon, **78** *18* 2; *23* 6; *40* 1?; *48* 6; *55* 1; *65* 1
Harpocration, *see* Aurelius
Heliodorus, **13** 8; **14** 4 app; **15** i 9; ii 6, 12, 13 (twice), 15; c 5; pp. 126, 128
Helius, **9** 3 d; 6 k app; 6 m; 11 g
Heraclianus, early II p., **11** ii 3
Heraclianus, A.D. 175 or 207, **78** *21* 2; *23* 2
Herculanus, **64** i 34; ii 1 app
Herennius, **78** *53* 2 app
Hierax, *see* Petenefotes
Iu[. .]us, *see* Baebius
C Iulius Aelurio, **71** a 8 app
Iulius Marcus, **1** xliii 22; **2** xi 14–15; xliv 11; **6** ii 22–23; **8** iii 7; **89** *12* ii 4; **92** v 12; vii 15; viii 11; **94** a 2 app; p. 183
Iulius Marianus, **1** xxi 1–2; **2** xvi 16–17; **8** v 9; **27** a i 2; **47** i 4; ii 5, 19; **89** *1* 5a; **92** iii 4; v 19; **122** 4?; pp. 183, 433
Iulius Maximus, **77** a i 7?, 9, 15
Ius.[, **53** d
Lappus, **64** ii 1 app; ii 16, 26
Lepidianus, **51** i 5; ii 3
Longianus, **74** iii 9
Longienus, **78** *73* 1
Longinus, *see also* Aurelius
Longinus Tituleius, **74** i 2–3, 10; ii 2, 10; iii 2, 9–10
Longo, *see* Antonius
Malchus, **2** xliii 15; pp. 183, 387
Marcus, *see also* Iulius
Marcus, **64** i 37; ii 1 app
Marianus, *see* Iulius
Marinus, *see also* Aelius; **17** a 1; p. 133
Marinus posterior, **17** a 1?; **66** a i 9; ii 10; b i 19 app; pp. 128, 133
Marinus prior, **17** a 1?; **66** a ii 8; b i 17, 19 app; ii 23; pp. 128, 133
Maximus, *see* Iulius
Minicius, **51** ii 6; p. 198
Mocimus, **16** recto 3; **32** 4; pp. 132, 133, 158
Naso, **12** a–c 10; **15** i 11, 15, 21, 22; ii 5, 7, 9, 15, 17; g; **16** verso 2; pp. 125, 132, 133
Nerius, **51** ii 18
Nigrinus, **23** i 6; **47** i 4, 12; ii 6, 9; p. 183
Ninnius Rufus, **34** recto i 3
Olympus, **78** *40* 3
Orees, **78** *72* 2
Paulianus, **63** ii 32 app
Paullinus, **63** ii 32 app
Petenefotes Hierax, **20** 18
Petronius Aprilis, **77** a i 13
Pompeius Epane, **34** recto ii 20
Pos[, **78** *50* 2
Priscus, **15** i 1, 17, 23; ii 8, 19; **95** a 2 app; p. 133
Pudens, **27** a ii 1; **47** i 4; **48** 2; **92** iii 19; vi 19; ix 7; pp. 183, 387
Romanus, *see* Claudius
Rufianus, **23** iv 8
Rufus, *see* Ninnius
Sabinus, **78** *31* 1; *32* 2

centurio—*cont.*
Seleucus, **88** *1* 5; **89** *12* ii 2; p. 355
Sempronianus, **64** i 42; ii 1 app, 29
Sex Sempronius Candidus, **64** i 23; ii 1 app, 19, 23
Aurelius Septimius Danymus, **1** i 1–2; xliii 19; **2** vi 18–19; xliv 1; **92** v 6; viii 4; p. 183
Serenus, **9** 9 f–n; 13 f app; 19 c app
Seruilius, **51** ii 18
Seuerus, *see* Franius
Sossius, **51** i 4; p. 198
Ta. . . ., **74** ii 9
Themarsas, **12** e 4; p. 125
Theopropus, *see* Aurelius
Tiberinus, **11** ii 6 app
Timinius, **10** 14
Tithoes, **78** *1* 2; *72* 4
Tituleius, *see* Longinus
Trunnius, **78** *70* 2, 7
V.[, **77** b 7, 9
Varius, **51** ii 11, 19, 21; p. 198
Vippị[, (Vibi[?), **78** *76* 2
Vlpius?, *see* Gaianus
Zabdeus, *see* Beleus
].ịẹra, **66** b i 19 and app
]nus, **11 bis** b i 17
]nto (*case*?), **77** a i 15
cibariator, p. 311
Alexandrus, **78** *34* 3; *36* 2; *37* 2; *38* 2; *41* 2; *42* 2; *43* 2; *67* 2; *71* 2
Apollos, **78** *15* 2
Copres, **78** *46* 1
Hermas, **78** *44* 2
Hermen[, (Herminus?), **78** *22* 2–3; *45* 2
Isidorus Hierax, **78** *40* 3
Petronius, **78** *18* 2; *21* 2; *24* 2; *25* 1; *27* 2; *30* 5; *32* 2; *39* 2; *47* 2; *48* 2; *49* 2; *50* 2–3; *51* 3; *52* 2; *53* 2; *54* 2; *68* 2; *69* 3; *74* 1; pp. 311, 312
[. . .]this, **78** *55* 2
circitor
Anton( ) Val( ), **47** i 7
Aurelius Ach.[, **49** 2
Gaius Sal[, **49** 2
Iarhaeus Malchi, **47** i 7
citator campi
Paminis Pacoebis, **76** xx 24
classis Flauia Moesica, **63** ii 4
cohors
Apamenorum, **73** a iii 10 app; **102** a 1
I Ascalonitanorum, **1** xiii 9
II Brittonum miliaria ciuium Romanorum pia fidelis, **53** b 22 app
I Cilicum equitata, **77** a i 13 app
I Flauia Cilicum equitata, **53** b 16 app; **64** ii 22
I Corsorum ciuium Romanorum, **77** a i 7 app
Cyrenaica equitata, **77** a i 7 app
III Delmatorum equitata ciuium Romanorum pia fidelis, **53** b 22 app
Ị. .[, **1** xii 28
II eq[, **47** ii 8 and app
Gallorum, **63** i 21 app
I Hispanorum, **63** i 15 app, 24 app
I Hispanorum equitata, p. 311
I Hispanorum ueterana quingenaria, **63** i 21 app, 24; 32 app; ii 7 app, 13 app
II Ituraeorum equitata, **63** i 24 app; **77** a i 7 app; **87** 28 app; p. 311
III Ituraeorum, **20** 16; **87** 2 app; 28 and app; **133** 3 app
V Ituraeorum, **133** 3 app
VII Ituraeorum, **45** 3 app; **133** 3 app
Lepidiana, **51** i 5 app
I Augusta praetoria Lusitanorum equitata, **64** i 1; ii 16–17 app; **74** i 1, 9; ii 1, 3, 9; iii 1, 3, 8, 10; pp. 202, 277
I Nomidarum, **52** c 6; p. 202
I Flauia Numidarum, p. 202
XX Palmyrenorum, **47** i 1 app, 2, 10; ii 2, 15; **48** 4; **50** i 5, 6, 11, 12, 13, 14 app, 15; ii 5, 6; **89** *1* 2; *1* verso 4; *4* i 3–4; *7* 10; *8* 5; *14* 4; *18* app; *20* 1–2; *25* 2–3; *28* 2; **90** *1* a 6; **91** *1* i 8 app; *2* i 1 app, 7 app; **97** a 3; **99** *1* 6, 7 app; *1* verso 1; *2* 5; *2* verso 1; *3* 5; *3* verso 1; **100** 3; **101** a i 5; **110** 2; **114** 8; verso 1; **118** 4; **119** 2; pp. 14, 16, 128, 138, 146, 153, 180, 182, 198, 202, 216, 233, 255, 340, 350, 355, 357, 358, 362, 363, 364, 367, 380, 383, 399, 403, 406, 412, 413, 415, 417, 421, 423
VI Praetoriana?, **20** 15
I Thebaeorum equitata, **63** i 24 app; p. 311
II Thebaeorum, **77** a i 21
Traiana, **63** i 21 app
VII. .[, **133** 3 and app; p. 442
conductor
].ṣ.[. . .] Pantarchus?, **70** a ii 18 and app
Porcius, **58** ii 5
cornicen?
Asclepiades Demonres, **78** *40* 2
cornicularius
Aurelius Alexandrus Antonini, **1** xxxii 29; **2** xxxiii 10
? Asclepiades Demonres, **78** *40* 2
Auidius Arrianus, **87** 27
curator
Aurelius Rubathus, **47** i 7
Claudius Agrippas, **47** i 7
Herminus Tyrannus, **78** *4* 5 and app; *34* 1
curator alae
Anubion Harpocration, **76** iv 1, 9, 17
Calligonus Cleonici, **76** xxi 5
Flauius Serenus, **76** xvii 8
curator turmae
Iulius Serenus, **76** vi 14–15, 21; x 9

summus curator
L? Iulius Serenus, **76** passim; *see* Index 1, Persons
custos, *see also* armorum
custos domi
Flauius, **58** ii 8
decurio *or* centurio
Ammonianus, **52** b 4 and app
Antiochus, **78** *37* 6
Horion, **78** *6* 1–2, 12; *22* 2?
Saturnilus **75** 12
].rlianus, **38** i 11
decurio *or* signifer
M Longinus .[, **73** a iii 1
decurio
Ạ.[, **55** g 1 app
Aelius Serenus, **76** xv 10, 11; xviii 14; xx 25; xxi 1; GG 9; p. 285
Agrippa, **76** iii 12; iv 2; viii 14; ix 3; x 16; xiv 17; HH i 2
Ammonianus, *see also* Antonius
Ammonianus, **76** i 17; viii 7; xi 12; xiv 3; p. 285
Ammonianus posterior, **24** 12; *cf.* Antonius Ammonianus
Ammonianus prior, **24** 20
Annellus Quodratus, p. 285
Antiochus, **15** i 8; ii 2, 12, 17; **23** ii 5; p. 144
Antoninus, *see* Vlpius
Antoni(us?), **78** *30* 4
Antonius Ammonianus, **20** 7
Apollinarius, **76** v 2; viii 28; xv 3; xvi 20; xix 13; BB 9
Apollonius, **15** i 14; ii 22; p. 128
Artemidorus, **64** ii 7, 33
Aurelianus, p. 387
Aurelius Hierax, **20** 10
Bassus, *see* Lucilius
Carus, **63** ii 25
Clarus, **76** xii 17; p. 285
Cocceius, **27** b i 8; *cf.* duplicarius, Aurelius Cocceius
Conon, **78** *8* 2; *29* 2; *63* 1; *66* 1
Ç̣ṛ[, **30** ii 1 app
Donacianus, **80** 1–2
Demetrius, *see* Vlpius
Eạ[.]..ç[, **30** ii 1
Flaminus, **24** 7, 14; p. 146
A Flauius Vespasianus, **64** i 29
Furianus, **76** vi 1; xii 20; GG 2; *see also* Messius
Fuscus, *see* Marcus
Gemellus, **76** vii 2, 14
Gemellus, **78** *3* 2 app; *27* 1–2; *33* 1; *34* 3; *66* 5
Herminus, **78** *15* 2; *51* 7 app
Herodianus, **76** i 7 and app; 9; iii 2, 9, 18; iv 3, 19, 25; v 9, 17; vi 17; viii 25; xi 19; xiii 3; xv 19; XX 1; BB 1; FF 1
Hierax, *see* Aurelius
Horigenes, **20** 13
Iarhaei, *see* Zebidas
Imuthes, **78** *3* 2 and app
Iulius Protarchus, **76** ii 9; iv 11; v 3; xii 2; xv 4; xx 19; GG 12
Longinus, **75** 7, 15
Longinus, **78** *42* 2; *45* 2; *48* 2; *49* 1
Lucilius Bassus, **76** vii 16–17; ix 18; x 23; xi 3; xv 12; xvi 2, 8; xx 9, 16; FF 9
Lucius Octauius, **1** xxxviii 11–12; **2** xxxviii 24–25; **92** vii 10; x 2; pp. 149, 387
Lycarion, **76** vi 15, 21; viii 2, 12; ix 3; x 9; xviii 2, 12, 21; xix 2
Marcus Fuscus, p. 285
Maximus, **30** ii 6
Messius Furianus, **76** vi 1 app
Melas, *see* Serenus
Nicolas, **24** 1
Nifṛạọṭes, **27** b i 13
Octauius, *see* Lucius
Optatianus, **76** iii 20; p. 285
Pactumeius Serenus, **76** iv 21; v 1–2; vi 9–10; xii 12; xiv 11; BB 2?; BB 5; FF 3; p. 285
Paulinus, *see* Timinius
]ḍịmus Petosiris, **20** 4
Petronius, **76** v 11–12; vi 7; xv 2–3; p. 285
Protarchus, *see* Iulius
Quintianus, **24** 3
Quodratus (*sic*), *see* Annellus
Ṛ.[, **55** g 1 app
Romullus, **4** a i 7; **15** i 6; ii 4; **23** ii 9; **66** a i 4; p. 144
Rufus, **30** ii 11, 14
Saluianus, **64** ii 10, 36?
Sarapion, **24** 16
Saturninus, **30** ii 4
Secundinus Verus, p. 285
Sentius, **76** ix 4; xvi 11; xix 3
Serenus (*see also* Aelius *and* Pactumeius) **76** xvii 9; BB 2; p. 285
Serenus, **11 bis** a 17
Serenus Melas, **76** i 10; vii 9; x 3; xii 19; xiii 7; xviii 25; xx 8, 20; p. 285
Soterichus, **76** viii 19; xix 19
Subatianus, **76** ix 13; p. 285
Themarsas Tiberini, **1** xxxiii 23–24; **2** xxxiv 1–2; **27** b i 1; **47** i 5; **92** ix 17; p. 387
Timinius Paulinus, **15** ii 12; **27** b i 16; **47** i 6, 7, 16, 17; ii 11, 12; **94** b ii 5; pp. 189, 394
Titus, **24** 5, 18; p. 146
Verus, *see* Secundinus
Vespasianus, *see* Flauius
]fidius Victorinus, **20** 1
Aurelius Vlpius Antoninus, **1** xli 1–2; **2** xli 1–2; **27** b i 6; **47** i 4; **92** iv 11; vii 12; x 4; pp. 144, 387

decurio—*cont.*
Aurelius Vlpius Demetrius, **1** xxxvi 1–2; **2** xxxvi 15–16; pp. 144, 149, 387
Aurelius Zebidas Iarhaei, **1** xxxi 21–22; **2** xxxii 1; **92** ix 15; p. 387
].ịẹra, **66** b i 19
].ṇị[.]..[, **24** 9
]ni, **11 bis** b i 17
discens fabrum?
Aurelius Gr[, **2** xxxi 6
discens mensorem
Aurelius Iarhaboles, **50** i 3
Bar.[, **50** i 9 and app
discens signiferum?
Flauius Seuerianus, **21** 19
domus, *see* origo
dromadarius
Ạ[.....].[.]..[, **2** xliii 25
Abidsalmas Iarhaei, **2** xlv 14
Aurel Aelius Antoninus, **1** xliii 29; **2** xliv 14
Antonius Hierax, **78** *48* 1; *49* 1
Antonius Maximus?, **92** vii 16
Antonius Romanus, **2** xliii 26
Aur[el]s, **2** xlv 2
Aurelius Aadaeus *or* Addaeus, **2** xliv 8; **8** iii 5
Aurelius Barca.[, **2** xliv 4
Aurelius Calpurnius, **2** xliv 6; **8** iii 3
Aurelius Marinus, **2** xliv 17; **8** v 5
Aurelius Paulus, **2** xliii 28
Aurelius Romanus, **2** xliv 7; **8** iii 3?
Aurelius Romanus, **2** xliv 10; **8** iii 3?
Aurelius Sabinus, **2** xliv 9
Aurelius Siluanus (216), **2** xlv 9
Aurelius Siluanus (210), **8** vii 18
Aurelius Valens, **2** xliv 16
Aurelius Zabdib[ol-, **8** v 7
Aurel Azizus Salamalathi, **1** xliii 27
Cronius Barbasatis, **64** ii 11
Aurel Dicaeus Themarsa, **1** xliii 25
Domitius Nicolaus, **2** xliv 19
G[....]eụ.[, **1** xliv 19
Aure[l ....].ẹs Gabrion, **1** xliv 14; **2** xliii 19
[G]aianus, *cogn*, **8** vii 24
Gaius Barhadadus, **2** xlv 4
Ḥ...[ ]ṣ.[, **8** vii 20
Aure[l —] Heliodorus, **1** xliv 2
Heraclas, *cogn*, **2** xliv 28; **8** vii 22; *cf.* **1** xxiv 9
Aurel Heranes Malchi, **1** xliii 20
Aurel Iarhabole Zebida, **1** xliv 13; **2** xliii 18
Iulius [ ]b[ ]ṣ, **2** xlv 11
Iulius ..[......]ius, **2** xlv 13
Iulius Bassus, **1** xliii 33
Macrinius Maximi, **2** xlv 7; **8** ix 27
Malchus Salman, **2** xlv 5
Aurel Male Mannaei, **1** xliii 31
Aurel [— M]onimi, **1** xliv 16; **2** xliii 21
]das Runnaei, **1** xliv 3
Tẹ[, **2** xliii 23
Aurel Themarsas Buccaei, **1** xliv 11; **2** xliii 16
Aurel Themarsas Themuami, **1** xliii 21
A[urel ?dalathu]ṣ Theoboli, **1** xliv 12; **2** xliii 17
]aṣ[, **2** xliv 20
]m[, **2** xliv 2
dromadarius sesquiplicarius
Aurel Domitius Barbaessamen, **1** xliii 23; **2** xliv 12
duplicarius *or* sesquiplicarius
Iulius Maximus, **5** ii 4
Mocimus Themarsa, **1** xvi 12
duplicarius
Aur[el, **1** xxvi 16
Aurẹ[l]ḍ[...].[, **1** xxvi 14
? Aurel ...ṛṃ[, **24** 10
Aurelius Aḍ[.....]gṇ..[..]i, **1** xxxi 26
Aurelius Aelius Barnaeus, **1** xxxiii 28; **2** xxxiv 6
Aelius Licinnius, **2** xxxvi 18; **23** ii 10; *cf.* **1** xxxiii 17
Aurelius Alexandrus .[...].a, **1** xli 4; **2** xli 4; **92** iv 12 app
Aurelius Apollonius Mesenus, **23** ii 6; **27** b i 7; *cf.* **6** x 9; **1** xxx 17
Aurelius Castor, **4** b i 4; *cf.* **2** xxxi 13
Aurelius Cocceius, **1** i 4; **2** vi 21; *cf.* decurio, Cocceius
? Aurelius Cronion, **24** 2
? Aurelius H[.].[....]s, **24** 8
? Aurelius Hermaiscus, **24** 4
Aurelius Claudius Mombogeus, **1** xxxvi 4
Flauius Demetrius, **85** 1
?]ḷius Horigenes, **24** 6
Ị[ar]ḥe[us -8?-].i, **2** xi 18
Aurelius Iulius Antoninus, **1** xxxiii 26; **2** xxxiv 4
Aurelius Iulius Apollinarius, **1** xxi 4; **2** xvi 19
Lucilius Artorius, **27** b i 2
Aurelius Ṃ[......].ma[, **1** xxxi 24
Maimins Puteolanus, **76** xiv 16
? Rom[-9?-]ni, **2** xxxii 4
Ạ[urel].es Salṃ[, **1** xi 6
Aurelius Salmanes Zebida, **1** xxxviii 13; **2** xxxviii 26
Vettienus Matinus, **38** i 15
dux, **20** 3
Licinnius Pacatianus, **83** 23
Vlpius Tertius, **83** 24
emeritus
sesq Aurel Romanus Allaei, **1** xxxviii 15
Aurel Sadalathu[s ......]i, **1** xli 11
Aurel Salmanes Za[, **1** xli 10
excubatio, excubitor, *see* Index 5, Religion
faber, *see also* discens
].us Aponianus, **59** 11
Iulius Maximus, **59** 10

gubernator
  ].l[.]ẹsa[...]. Firmicus, **59** 6
hiberna, **50** i 5, 11, 13; ii 5; **89** *10* 10
hibernatur, **64** i 3
imaginifer
  Ạ[urelius M]azabạ[na-, **1** xxviii 21
  ? Halas [, **2** xxii 16
immunis?
  Iul[ ]nus, **89** *4* ii 10
legio
  II Traiana Fortis, **9** 2 m app; **20** 2 and app; **34** verso ii 12 app; **53** a ii 2 app; **64** ii 13; **77** a i 7 app, 21 app; **102** a 7; pp. 141, 161, 165 note 2, 442
  III Cyrenaica, **34** recto i 1; ii 5, 14; verso ii 9?; **38** i 11 app; **58** i 1; **77** a i 7 app; pp. 107, 161, 165, 166, 198 note, 244
  IIII Scythica, **1** xxvi 21 and app; **66** f 2; p. 16
  XVI Flauia Firma, **89** *1* verso 1 app; **91** *2* i 6 and app; p. 383
  XXII Deiotariana, **34** recto i 19; verso ii 11; pp. 165, 166, 198 and note
librarius
  Aurelius ..[..]ḷ.r.ị?, **58** ii 11
  Aurelius Capiton, **47** i 17
  Cuṛ..ịtius Capra?, **58** ii 10
  Sozon, **91** *2* i 6
liburna, trierarch
  Lucius, **82** 3, 4, 9
  Timetus, **82** 10, 14
magister campi
  Bellaeus Oga, **48** 8
  Emeritus, **102** a 8–8a
mater castrorum, p. 349
medicus centurio?
  Longinus Tituleius, **74** i 2–3 and 3 app
mensor, *see* discens
mulio, **91** *1* i 7
natio, *see* origo
numerus
  Emesenorum, **30** ii 8
  I equitum, **81** ii 8 app
  Orientalium, **30** ii 13
  I peditum, **81** ii 8 app
optio
  M Aurelius Asclepiades, **78** *1* 2; *2* 2; *3* 3; *4* 1; *5* 1; *6* 3; *7* 2; *8* 2; *9* 2; *10* 2; *11* 1; *12* 2; *23* 2; *72* 4; p. 311
  M Aurelius Isidorus, **78** *11* 1
  Claudius [....?]tion, **78** *9* 6–7
  L Egnatius, **77** a i 7
  Iulius Horion, **78** *41* 1
  Malochus, **81** ii 5
  Nepheros Nepherotis, **78** *36* 1–2
  Ogelus Malchi, **47** i 17
  ].eineus, **78** *31* 5
optio campi
  Hermias Hermiae, **76** ii 8; xix 9
origo
  Altinum, **36** 14
  Amisus, **9** 12 a
  Ancyra, **36** 2, 3, 4
  Antaeopolites, **70** a ii 37
  Antinoites, **39** 25; **46** 9 app
  Apamea, **36** 8
  c.[, **10** 1 and app (*castris*? *castrensis*?)
  castris, castrensis, **37** 2 app, 3, 4; **39** 4, 5, 16, 18, 22, 23; **70** a i 2, 5, 18, 26; ii 8, 14, 23; b i 20 app; d 11
  Chrysopolis, **36** 15
  ciuis Romanus, **70** b i 14
  Coptites, **39** 20
  Cremona, **36** 6
  Damascus, **68** ii 2
  Gadara, **37** 3 app
  Hadrumetum, **36** 9
  Heliopolitanus, **70** a ii 31; iii 13; Aberd. 2
  Laodicea, **36** 7 app, 12, 13
  Lycopolites, **39** 2, 7, 10, 14
  Oxyrhynchites, **70** e 1
  Pessinus, **36** 1, 5
  Philomedia, **36** 10
  Prosopites, **39** 12
  Sidon, **9** 11 a
  Syenites, **39** 9
  Thinites, **70** b i 7
  Tyrus, **68** iii 1
  Vtica, **36** 11
  ]it(es), **70** d 5
pạṛ[, paṣ( ) centuriae, **2** viii 24
  Iulius Maximus, **2** xxxiii 9
practor, *military*? *See* **78** *6* 11 and app; *77* 1–4 and app
praefectus, *see also* Index 9, Latin Words
praefectus alae
  ].ecrinus, **102** a 12
praefectus castrorum
  T Suedius Clemens, **10** 2–3
praefectus cohortis
  Q Allius Q f Pudentillus, **64** i 10
  ].ụṣ Arruntianus, **63** i 25
  Celsianus, **87** 2
  P Claudius Iustus, **63** i 24 app
  M Iulius M f Quir Siluanus, **64** i 6–7
praefectus legionis
  ].us Marinus, **102** a 7
  ..[..]...ianus, **89** *1* verso 1
praepositus, *see also* Index 9, Latin Words
  ? Aurelius Regulus, **89** *1* verso 1
praepositus cohortis
  Aelius Auitus, **50** i 7, 13; ii 7
  Aurelius ...r..[...], **114** verso 1; p. 417
  Aurelius Intenianus, **100** 2; p. 406

praepositus praetenturae
Aurelius Rufinus, **91** *1* i 1; *1* verso 2; *2* i 1 app, 9 app, 12 app; *2* verso 2
praesidium, **63** ii 21, 27; **70** b ii 13 a app
praetorium, **1** xxi 8; xxxvi 7; **2** xxxiii 11; **17** a 8 app; **34** recto i 8 app; **47** ii 8; **63** ii 34; **66** a i 2, 8 app; **82** 7; **96** 3; p. 14
pridianum, **63** i 24; **64** i 1; ii 1 app; **98** *3* 3; pp. 2, 4, 177, 180–82, 201, 214, 217, 233, 235, 401
primipilaris, **89** *1* verso 1 app
primipilus, **9** 20 b app
? Aurelius Regulus, **89** *1* verso 1
princeps, **9** 5 h, 27 h; **13** 18 app; **51** ii 6; **55** b 2; **62** 6 app; p. 198
Minicius Iustus, **51** ii 6
princeps posterior, **21** 5, 6, 9, 10, 11, 13; **45** 3 app
princeps prior, **21** 4, 8, 14, 16, 21
ordinatus princeps
Aurelius Germanus, **50** i 1 and app, 2, 8; ii 1; a 1; *cf. under* centurio *above*
principalis, *exact rank unknown*, **1** viii 17; **2** viii 24
Aelius Hieronymus, **39** 18
Asprius Maximus, **21** 13
Ạ[urelius, **1** xii 23
Aurelius[, **1** xxvi 24
Aurelius .[, **2** xx 8
Aurelius Alexander, **23** iv 4
Aurelius Apollonius, **2** x 4; *cf.* **6** ii 3 and **8** ii 7
Aurelius Caecilianus, **21** 4
Aurelius Demosthenes, **21** 14
Aurelius Diodorus, **23** iv 5
Aurelius Heraclid[, **21** 5
Aurelius Maximus, **21** 12
Aurelius Priscus, **1** xxv 11; **2** xx 8
Aurelius Quint[, **22** 5
Aurelius R. . .ụṣ, **23** iv 7
Aurelius Themarsa, **22** 3
Aurelius Theocles, **21** 15
Aurelius Titus, **21** 16
Aurelius Valerius, **23** iii 4
Aurelius Victor, **39** 10
Aurelius Zeḅ[. . .]ṃ. . [, **23** iv 2
Aureliu[s].ạ. . [, **23** ii 4
Aurelius .[.].eṃ.[ ].[, **23** iv 9
].[. . . . .]ḥus Ḅ[.]ḷ[, **2** xlii 24
Cassius Heronianus, **39** 16
Cassius S. . .mi, **39** 9
Claudius Apollinarius, **39** 7
Eponuchus Apollinarius, **39** 5
Flauius Demetrius, **95** b 8
Flauius Vlpianus, **21** 7
Fortius Fortius, **39** 12
Futtianius Demẹ[trius?, **21** 9
Heluius Pertinax, **21** 6
Iulius Alexander, **21** 10
Iulius Ammonianus, **39** 4
Iulius Paniscus, **39** 20
Iulius Proculus, **22** 2
Iunius Martialis, **21** 3
Lycophron H[. .]ụ[.]liri, **39** 2
Marcus Victor, **23** ii 8
Maximus, **2** xxviii 11
Mocimus Themarsa, **1** xvi 12
Neratius Firminus, **21** 11
Plution Pluti[. .]cis, **39** 14
Pompeius Sarapionis, **39** 23
Rom[ ]ni, **2** xxxii 4
Rufus Cassiani, **39** 22
Sarapion Isidori, **39** 25
Valerius Hispanus, **21** 2
Vibius Crescens, **21** 8
].l[ ] Zenodorus, **23** iii 1
]eụṣ .[, **1** xxxviii 34
principia, **51** ii 5 app; **54** a–c 5; **55** a 4; **62** 6 app; p. 207
sacerdos, p. 192
Themes Mocimi, **50** i 2, 9; b 2
secutor tribuni
Iulius Seuerus, **58** ii 7
sesquiplicarius *or* duplicarius
Iulius Maximus, **5** ii 4
Mocimus Themarsa, **1** xvi 12
sesquiplicarius
? Aelius Sarapion, **24** 13
Aurelius Absas, **47** i 17; *cf.* **15** ii 13–14
? Aurelius Ammonianus, **24** 15
? Aurelius Heras, **24** 19
Aurelius Marinus, **2** xxxvi 20
Demosthenes Eponuchus, **85** 2
Aurelius Domitius Barbaessamen, **1** xliii 23; **2** xliv 12
Aurelius Flauius Demetri, **1** xxxiii 30
Herennius Melas, **76** vii 20–21
Aurelius Iulianus Themarsa, **1** xli 8; **2** xli 8
? Iulius Sarapion, **24** 17
Lucius Iulianus, **4** b i 6
Aurelius Lucius Themarsa, **1** xxi 6
Aurelius Priscus Gai, **1** xxxvi 6
Aurelius Romanus Allaei, **1** xxxviii 15
? Theon Serẹ[, **24** 21
Vlpius Gaianus, **2** xxxviii 28
].ellus, **4** a i 13
signifer *or* decurio
M Longinus .[, **73** a iii 1
signifer
Aurelius Aelius Heliodorus, **1** xxvii 7; xxviii 14–15 marg; **2** i 12
Ammonius Ammonius, **78** *37* 1–2
Antonius Marcianus, **76** xvi 7; xx 15
Aurelius Malchus, **50** i 3, 9; ii 4 app
Aurelius Claudius Natalius, **2** xxxvii 29?; **47** i 17; *cf.* **1** xxxvii 29
Dionysius Sarapionis, **76** viii 28; xvi 19; BB 8

C Domitius Rufus, **74** ii 9
Flauius Demetrius alter, **50** i 3, 9
Aurelius Flauius Euclides, **1** xxxii 16
Flauius Nicomachus, **1** i 10; **2** vi 23
Iulius Marcus, **76** xviii 31
Longinus Longus, **74** i 1
Aurelius Lucius Valerianus, **1** xl 19; **2** xl 26
Malchus Zebida, **48** 8
[....]ius Maximus, **74** ii 1
? Maxim[, **1** vii 11 and app
Memnon Psenpres, **76** vi 6; xvii 6
Quintus Herennius, **74** iii 8
Sarapion Germanus, **85** 3
Sossius Eudaemon, **76** iv 25
Aurelius Themarsas Zebida, **2** xli 13; *cf.* **1** xli 25
Valerius Rufus, **74** i 9
Vlpius Marianus, **50** i 2, 9
Zoilus, **76** xii 7
]ṛianus, **74** iii 1

singularis
A̡[, **2** xv 5
Abenamares Marona, **1** xxxviii 8; **2** xxxviii 16
A̡[urelius —] Antoninus, **1** xxxi 33
Apollinarius Gaiani, **2** xxxi 25
Aurel[ius, **1** xxv 21
Aure[lius, **2** xvi 6; xxi 12, 13, 16; xxxi 3, 4
Au[relius, **4** b ii 9, 10; j 2
Aurelius [-3?-]a[..].io, **2** xxx 9
Aurelius [ ]b.[, **1** xxviii 24
Aure[lius].ḅịda[, **1** xl 11
Aurelius Anto[n-, **2** xxiii 17
Aurelius Artemidorus, **23** i 5
Aurelius Baṛ.[, **4** b ii 14
Aurelius Bassus, **2** xx 21
Aurelius Bassus, **2** xxviii 15
Aurelius Dionysius, **2** xxvi 11
Aurelius Domitianus, **4** b i 8
Aurelius Domitius, **2** xxx 15; *cf.* **1** xv 3
Aurelius Iulius, **2** xiii 22
Aurelius Marinus, **1** xxiii 8; *cf.* **2** xviii 13
Aurelius Mocimus, **23** i 7
Aurelius Priscus, **2** xiii 11
Aurelius Seleucus, **2** xxxi 24
Bassus Bibi (Zebida?), **1** xl 11; **2** xl 18
Claudius Iulius Marinus, **2** xxxi 21; ii a 5 app
Claudius Iulius Secundus, **2** xxxi 22; ii a 5 app
Claudius Siluanus, **1** xxxvii 32
Fl.[.....].sus, **2** viii 13
Flauius Numeri[, **2** xxvi 12
Flauius Romanus, **2** xxxvi 23
[....]. Germanus, **2** xxx 21
[-3?-]us Iulianus, **2** xii 22
Iul[ius, **2** xvi 8
Iulius Ḟ[, **2** xxiii 14
Iulius Gaiụ[s, **2** xxvi 9
Iulius Marinus, **2** xxx 22
Iulius Soemus, **1** vii 10; *cf.* **2** xii 24; **6** iii 18
Iulius Th[, **2** xxi 15
Longinus Numei, **1** xxxvii 14
Lucilius Luci, **2** xxviii 27
]thus M[, **2** xxiii 22
Aurelius M[, **1** xx 2
Ma.[, **2** xvi 7
Marinus, **2** xviii 15
Neoterius, **2** xx 16
Philotas, **2** xviii 16
Priscus, **87** 26
Ṛạạṃmas Ḅạṛ[.]..[, **2** xxx 13
Aurel Siluanus Mocimi, **1** xl 7; *cf.* **2** xl 14
]llus Theodori, **2** vii 10
Aurelius Timon Marini, **1** xlii 16; **2** xlii 10

singularis consularis
Aelius Marcellus, **1** xxxviii 3; *cf.* **2** xxxviii 11: singul, *and* **92** vii 9
Aurelius[, **1** xxv 23
Aurelius Alexandrus Theofil[, **2** xl 7; *cf.* **1** xxxix 35
Aurelius Antoninus, **2** xxviii 22
Aurelius Antonius Clemẹ[n-, **2** xiii 21; *cf.* **1** viii 10
Aurelius Iulius Marcianus, **2** xxviii 26; *cf.* **1** xiii 9
Aurelius Mocimus Mocimi, **1** xxxiii 11; *cf.* **2** xxxiii 27
Aurelius Valerius Valentinus, **1** xli 22; *cf.* **2** xli 20

singularis decurio
Romullus, **4** a i 7

singularis duplicarius, p. 11
Aurẹ[lius]ḍ[...].[, **1** xxvi 14
Aurelius Castor, **4** b i 4
Aurelius Iulius Apollinarius, **1** xxi 4

speculator
C Iulius Lo[..].[, **9** 9 d
L Sextilius Germanus, **9** 8 c

stator
? Aurelius Mucianus, **89** *1* 5 a and 5 app
Iulius Agathos Daemon, **76** xiv 2
Marcus Valerius, **76** xvii 1

tabularius
?]ianus, **102** a 11
].lanus, **102** a 6

tesserarius
Aurelius Mocimus, **50** i 3, 9
B.[...], **78** *42* 5–6
? Maximus, **78** *55* 5–6
].κωστ.ρ, **78** *12* 1

tribunus
? Agathonius, **88** *1* 1; *2* 1; *2* verso 1; **112** verso 1 and app; p. 355
? Aurelius Intenianus, **100** 2; p. 406
Iulius Rufianus, **47** i 3, 11; ii 3, 16
Iulius Terentius, **50** i 11 app
].[.]..ịus Iustillus, **91** *1* verso 1; *2* verso 1

tribunus—*cont.*
Laronius Secundianus, p. 183
Leon, **89** *18* verso; *28* verso 2 app; p. 367
Plotius, **58** ii 8
Postumius Aurelianus, **89** *1* verso 4; *2* 2; *6* 1; *7* 1; *8* 1; *10* verso 2; *17* 11; *25* verso 1; *28* verso 1; *29* 2 and app; *36* verso 1; *37* 1; *47* verso 1
Vlpius Valentinus, **99** *1* 2; *1* verso 1; *2* 1; *2* verso 1; *3* 1; *3* verso 1
trierarchus liburnae, **82** 3 app
Lucius, **82** 3, 4, 9
Timetus, **82** 10, 14
turma
Aelii Sereni, **76** xv 11; xviii 14; xx 25; xxi 1, 5–6; GG 9
Agrippae, **76** iii 11–12; iv 2; viii 14; ix 2–3; x 16; xiv 17; HH i 2
Ammoniani, **76** i 17; viii 7; xi 12, 13; xiv 3
Ammoniani posterioris, **24** 12
Ammoniani prioris, **24** 20
Antiochi, **15** i 8; ii 2, 12, 17; **23** ii 5
Antonini (Vlpius), **1** xli 1; **2** xli 1; **27** b i 6; **47** i 4; **88** *2* 5–6 app; **92** iv 11; vii 12; x 4; pp. 17, 387
Antonii, **78** *30* 4
Apollinarii, **76** v 2; viii 28; xv 3; xvi 20; xix 13; BB 9
Apollonii, **15** ii 22
Artemidori, **64** ii 7, 33
Attae, **53** b 26 app
Clari, **76** xii 17
Cocceiana, **15** i 11; ii 1, 2, 12
Coccei, **27** b i 8
Cononis, **78** *8* 2; *29* 2; *63* 1; *66* 1
Ç̣ṛ[, **30** ii 1 app
Demetri (Vlpius), **1** xxxvi 1; **2** xxxvi 15; **92** vii 5; p. 17
Donaciani, **80** 1–2
Eạ[.]..ç[, **30** ii 1
Flamini, **24** 7, 14
Furiani, **76** vi 1; xii 20; GG 2, 7
Gemelli, **76** vii 2, 14; xiii 16, 22–23
Gemelli, **78** *27* 1–2; *33* 1; *3* 2 app
Hermini, **78** *15* 2; *51* 7 app
Herodiani, **76** i 7, 9; iii 1–2, 3, 8–9, 17–18; iv 3, 19, 20, 25; v 9, 17; vi 17; viii 25; xi 19; xiii 3; xv 19; xx 1; BB 1; FF 1, 2
Imuthae, **78** *3* 2 app
Iulii Protarchi, **76** ii 9; iv 11; v 3; xii 2; xv 4; xx 19; GG 12
Longini, **75** 6–7, 15
Longini, **78** *42* 2; *45* 2; *48* 2; *49* 1
Lucilii Bassi, **76** vii 16–17; ix 18; x 23; xi 3, 9–10; xv 12; xvi 2, 8; xx 9, 16; FF 9
Lycarionis, **76** vi 15, 21; viii 2, 12; ix 3; x 9; xviii 2, 8–9, 12, 21; xix 2
Maximi, **30** ii 6
Narsi, **53** b 5 app
Nifṛạọṭis, **27** b i 13
Octauii (Lucius), **1** xxxviii 11; **2** xxxviii 24; **92** vii 10; x 2; p. 17
Optatiani, **76** iii 20
Pactumei Sereni, **76** iv 21; v 1–2; vi 9–10; xii 12; xiv 11; BB 2?; FF 3
Paulini (Timinius), **15** ii 12; **27** b i 16; **94** b ii 5; p. 394
Petronii, **76** v 11–12; vi 7; xv 2–3
Petroniana, **76** xvii 2
Romulli, **15** i 6; ii 4; **23** ii 9; **66** a i 4
Rufi, **30** ii 11, 14
S[, **64** ii 36
Saluiani, **64** ii 10, 36?
Sarapionis, **24** 16
Saturnini, **30** ii 4
Sentii, **76** ix 4; xvi 11; xix 3
Sereni, **76** xvii 9, 10; BB 2
Sereni, **11 bis** a 17
Sereni Melanis, **76** i 10; vii 9; x 3; xii 19; xiii 7; xviii 25; xx 8, 20
Soterichi, **76** viii 19; xix 19
Subatiani, **76** ix 13
Tiberini (Themarsas), **1** xxxiii 23; **2** xxxiv 1; **27** b i 1; **47** i 5; **92** vii 2 app; ix 17
Titi, **24** 5, 18
Zebida Iarhaei, **1** xxxi 21; **2** xxxii 1; **92** vii 2 app; ix 15
uexillarius
A[, **25** a 3
Aure[lius Ba]rath[es ....]..i, **1** xxxvii 21
Aurelius Barathes Abgari, **1** xxxvi 18
Aurelius Bassus Salman, **1** xxxviii 23
Aurelius Domitius Proculus, **2** xl 19; *cf.* **1** xl 12
]ius Marinus, **1** xxiii 12; **2** xviii 19
Aurelius Themarsa Ṿ.[, **1** xxxix 13
Aurelius Zabathes Malchi, **1** xxxix 16; *cf.* **2** xxxix 19
Aurelius Zebidas Egla, **1** xxxix 9; *cf.* **2** xxxix 14
Zebidas ..[.]ạlac[, **2** xliii 3
uexillarius centuriae
Aelius Antoninus, **2** xxxviii 8; *cf.* **1** xxxvii 38
Aurelius Vlpius Siluanus, **2** xl 9; *cf.* **1** xl 1

Index 5: Religion: Gods, Divi, Temples, Festivals

adytum, **53** b 14
aedes, **53** b 15
aeterna, *see* Roma
aquila, **51** ii 11, 17; **53** b 15
Azzanathkona, p. 233
bos, *as victim*
—— femina, **117** i 4 (twice), 6, 8 (twice), 9, 16, 24 (twice); ii 5, 25, 26
—— mas, **117** i 4 (twice), 8, 13, 16, 18, 22 (twice), 24 (twice); ii 2, 3, 4, 6, 20, 21, 22 app, 23, 24; iii 1, 5 (twice), 6, 8
caerimonia, **117** i 19
circenses
—— Martiales, **117** ii 9
—— Salutares, **117** ii 25
cult, imperial, **117** i 1 app; iii 7 app
diuus, diua, pp. 82, 146, 255, 423 and note; **63** i 21 app; **117** i 10 and app
—— Alexander, **4** b i 5, 10, 18; **20** 14; **24** 18
—— Antoninus Pius, **117** ii 20; iii 6
—— M Antoninus (M Aurelius), **117** i 21; ii 6
—— Antoninus (Caracalla), **1** xiii 5; xxi 1; xxiii 4; xxviii 7; xxxiii 1; xxxv 12; xxxvii 28; xl 14; xliii 4; **2** xiii 4; xvi 16; xviii 9; xxiii 13; xxviii 7, 21; xxxiii 18; xxxv 13; xxxvii 28; xl 21; xliii 2; **5** i 13; **6** xi 10; **8** v 19; viii 2; **117** i 17, 18; ii 2
—— Augustus, **117** iii 8
—— Claudius, **117** ii 23 and app
—— Commodus, **117** iii 1
—— Faustina, **117** iii 7
—— Hadrianus, **117** i 13
—— Iulia Maesa, **117** ii 7
—— Iulius, **117** ii 21
—— Marciana, **117** ii 28
—— Matidia, **117** ii 19
—— Nerua, **117** iii 4, 5
—— Pertinax, **117** ii 23, 24 and app
—— Seuerus, **1** xvi 13; xxvi 13; xxxi 25; xxxii 18; xxxiv 27; xxxviii 20; **2** xvii 10; xxii 9; xxvii 17; xxxiv 25; xxxvii 10; xl 4; xli 7; xlii 8; **5** ii 11; **117** i 15; ii 3, 4, 10, 11
—— Traianus, **117** i 15, 16; iii 4, 5
—— L Verus, **117** i 21, 22
Dolicheneum, **47** ii 8 app
Dolichenus, *see* Iuppiter
excubare (ad signa), **15** ii 7 app; **47** i 6, 17; **49** 1; **50** i 1, 8; **51** ii 17; **52** b 3?; **67** 10 app?
excubatio (ad aquilam), p. 198
excubatio (ad signa), pp. 180, 189, 191, 201
excubitor, pp. 192, 197, 209; **50** ii 4 app
Feriale Duranum, pp. 421, 422–23; **47** i 16 app; **117**; **117** ii 18 app, 20 app, 23–24 app
feriatus, **53** b 10
festival, **117** 9 app, 22 app, 25 app; pp. 421, 422
Genius, **117** i 28; ii 17
hostia, pp. 12, 14, 17; **1** xxxvi 22, 26; xlii 23
imago, p. 14; *cf.* **1** i 4; ii 12; xii 2; xiii 7; xxi 11; xxxii 12
immolatio, **47** i 16; **117** ii 22 and app
Iuno, **117** i 8, 24
—— Mammaeae Augustae, **117** ii 26
—— Regina, **117** i 4
—— Sị[spes], **117** i 4
Iuppiter, **48** 14; **117** i 24
—— Dolichenus, **50** i 13
—— Optimus Maximus, **117** i 4, 8
—— Victor, **117** i 4
Mars, **117** i 24
—— Pater, **117** i 5, 9
—— —— Victor, **117** i 19 (twice)
—— —— Vltor, **117** ii 19 app
Martialis, *see* Circenses
mater, *see also* Vesta
—— castrorum, **117** iii 7 app; p. 349
Mercurius, **47** i 3
Minerva, **117** i 4, 8, 24
Neptunalia, **117** ii 22
Neptune, **117** ii 22 app
Parilia, **117** ii 5 app
pontifex maximus, **117** i 28
Quinquatria, **117** ii 1
Regina, *see* Iuno
Roma aeterna, **117** ii 5
Rosaliae signorum, **117** ii 8 and app, 14
sacer, p. 14; **90** *1* b 2
sacerdos, **47** i 7 app; p. 192
—— Themes Mocimi, **50** i 2, 9; b 2
sacramentum, **50** i 4 app; **63** i 21 app

salus, **54** d 1 app; **117** i 9; ii 25 app
salutaris, *see* circenses
s(anctus)?, **47** i 3 app; **50** i 13 app
sanctissimus, **90** *1* a 1, 7–8 app
Saturnalia, **117** iv 7–8 app
saturnalicium, **68** ii 8 and app; iii 7; **69** 5 app; **76** FF 4 app
Securitas, **50** i 7
Seispes, Sispes, Sospes, *see* Iuno
septizonium, **47** i 3, 11
signa, *military standards*; *see also* Rosaliae; pp. 128, 180; **9** 8 c app; **15** ii 7 app; **17** a 12; **47** i 6, 17; **49** 1; **50** i 1, 8; **51** ii 11, 17; **52** b 9; c 4; **68** ii 19 and app; iii 18; **69** 15 app; **90** *1* a 7–8 app; **117** ii 8, 14
signum, *pass-word*, **51** ii 14; **52** a 6
—— Iouis, **50** i 13
—— Mercuri, **47** i 3
—— Securitatis, **50** i 7
supplicatio, **47** i 16; **117** i 1 app, 10, 17, 26, 28; ii 1, 7, 8, 12, 14, 15, 18, 19, 22 and app, 28; iii 7; iv 7
taurus, *as victim*, **117** i 5, 9, 20, 29; ii 9, 17, 22 app
templum, p. 218; **15** ii 22
Venus, **47** i 11 app
Vesta mater, **117** ii 15
Vestalia, **117** ii 15
Victor, *see* Iuppiter *and* Mars
Victoria, **117** i 6, 14; ii 26–28 app
—— Parthica, **117** i 15
Vltor, *see* Mars
Volcanalia, **117** ii 26–28 app
uota, **50** i 4 app; **117** i 2; ii 26–28 app
Vrbs Roma Aeterna, **117** ii 5

Index 6: Calendar

A[, **10** 22: *A[prilibus* or *A[ugustis*
April, pp. 88, 137, 183, 255, 285; **10** 22 app
Aprilis, **20** 3, 6 app, 15; **47** i 1, 9, 19; ii 1, 14; **64** ii 9, 18; **82** 4, 8, 15; **99** *1* 3; **117** ii 1, 2, 3, 4
Ἀθύρ, *see* Hathyr
Audynaios (Αὐδυναῖος), p. 435: Εὐδυνέου
August, pp. 97, 118, 122, 181, 218, 219, 255, 277, 341; **10** 22 app; **64** ii 1 app
Augustus, p. 122; **5** ii 1; **11 bis** b i 1, 15; a 1 app; **31** i 11; **53** a ii 1; b 2, 3; **64** i 2; **66** a i 1, 11; ii 15; b i 3; **83** 21, 23; **89** *6* 10; *12* i 5 app; *20* 7; *21* 2; *23* 18; **98** *4* 2 app; **117** ii 22, 23, 25
]bṛẹṣ, **20** 6; **54** a–c 6
Choiak (Χοίακ), **78** *1* 5; *2* 5; *4* 3; *5* 4; *6* 6; *7* 5; *8* 6; *14* 2; *25* 3; *34* 8; *65* 4
December (English), pp. 157, 181, 255, 266, 357; **20** 15 app; **64** ii 1 app
December (Latin), **10** 8, 15; **20** 6 app, 12; **27** a ii 13; **38** i 10 app; **89** *42* 13; *45* 4 and app; **91** *2* i 2 app; **97** a 5; **100** 4
Domitianus (*October*), pp. 107, 116 and note; **9** 1 b, c, d, e, f, g, h, k, m, n
epagomenai, **78** *32* 6; *69* 6
Epiph (Ἐπίφ), **78** *18* 7; *54* 5; *57* 4; *72* 8; *77* 5
Eudyneos, *see* Audynaios
Februarius, **10** 4, 13, 16 marg, 19, 21, 28; **64** ii 28; **66** a ii 18; **83** 14; **117** i 13, 14, 17
February, pp. 118, 285, 353; **10** 27 app; **117** 14–16 app
Hathyr, **78** *1* 6; *2* 6; *4* 4; *6* 6; *12* 4
I[, **66** a ii 11: *kal i[*
Ianuarius, **60** b 3; **63** i 26, 29; **64** i 15, 19; ii 3; **72** 2, 7, 13 app; **73** h 2; **83** 5, 10; **86** 3; **97** b 3; **100** 5; **117** i 1, 2, 7, 10, 11; iii 2 app; iv 7
Idus, pp. 118, 122; **5** ii 1 app; **9** 1 k, m, n; **10** 6, 22, 24, 28; **11 bis** a 1, c 1; **18** 2; **20** 15; **50** i 14; **53** a ii 1; b 2, 3; **64** i 5, 36; ii 20, 28; **66** a i 10; b i 3; **72** 11 app; **75** 8; **82** 1, 6, 15; **83** 12, 15, 17, 21, 23; **89** *4* iii 4 and app; *23* 18; *28* 8; *29* 15; *31* 8; *32* 7; *34* 6 app; **97** b 3; **99** *2* marg; **100** 5; **117** i 7, 10, 11, 23, 27; ii 3, 4, 8, 9, 15, 20, 21, 26–28 app; iii 2
Iu[, **29** 7: *Iunias* or *Iulias*
Iulius, **10** 6, 9, 24, 33; **64** i 5; **77** a i 12, 20; b 6; **83** 24 app; **88** *2* 4; **89** *1* 6; *4* iii 4; **117** ii 16, 18, 19, 20, 21
Iunius, p. 128; **10** 30; **15** ii 7; **50** i 5, 11; ii 5; **80** 5; **83** 24 app; **99** *1* 9; **117** ii 10, 12, 14, 15
January, pp. 117, 180, 181, 246, 251, 266, 277, 283, 285, 341; **64** ii 1 app; **66** b i 5–10 app; **76** vii 1 app; **117** i 1 app; 7–9 app; 14–16 app; iii 2 app
July, pp. 88, 116, 235, 357; **117** ii 18 app
June, pp. 88, 154, 219, 235, 380; **75** 8 app
Kalendae, pp. 118, 128, 159, 181; **5** ii 1 and app; **8** iii 4, 18, 23; **9** 1 b; **10** 4, 7, 13, 15, 19, 21, 25, 30, 32, 33; **15** ii 7; **20** 6 app, 9, 20; **27** b ii 4; a ii 13; **29** 7; **31** i 8, 11; ii 5; **47** i 1, 9, 16; ii 1, 14; **50** i 5, 11; ii 5; **54** a–c 6 app; **60** b 3; **62** 1; **63** i 23, 26, 29; **64** i 8, 12, 14, 19, 23; ii 2, 12, 17; **66** a i 1; ii 11, 14, 18; b i 9, 20, 30; ii 3, 4 app, 7 app, 9, 10, 11, 12, 13, 14, 15; **71** a 1, 10; b 5; **72** 2, 7, 13; **73** h 2; **76** BB 3; **83** 2, 4, 5, 9, 10, 14, 19, 22, 24; **86** 3; **87** 7, 24; **88** 2, 4; **89** *6* 10; *12* i 5; *20* 7; *25* 8; *26* 6; **92** ii 16; **97** b 1 app; **98** *3* 5 app; **99** *1* 3; *2* 7; *3* 6; *3* marg; **100** 4; **117** i 1, 13, 14, 19; ii 1, 5, 6, 10, 12, 14, 16, 18, 22, 23, 26, 28, 26–28 app; iii 1, 4, 6, 7, 8, 24; iv 7, 8; **120** 1, 2; **121** 1; **123** a 1 app
Kalends, pp. 180, 216, 235, 255, 266
M[(*Maias* or *Martias*), **64** ii 6; **75** i; **92** ii 16
Maius, **5** ii 1 app; **10** 7, 8 app; **50** i 14; **64** i 8, 24, 35; ii 12; **66** b i 1, 30; **71** a 1, 10; b 5; **82** 1, 6, 15; **83** 17, 24; **99** 2 marg; **117** ii 5, 6, 7, 8, 9
March, pp. 137, 172; **66** b i 5–10 app
Martius, **10** 8 app, 32; **64** i 30; **87** 7, 24; **117** i 19, 21 and app, 23, 27; **129** 1 app
May, pp. 128, 154, 219, 220, 246, 255, 256, 266, 341; **10** 27 app
Mechir (Μεχίρ), **76** xv 16, 22; xvi 6, 18, 24; xvii 6, 14, 18; xviii 7, 19, 30; **78** *3* 7; *6* 6; *9* 6; *20* 6; *29* 5; *30* 8; *61* 5; *66* 4
Mesore (Μεσορή), **78** *39* 7
Nonae, pp. 118, 235; **8** ix 20; **9** 1 c, d, e, f, g, h; **10** 9, 31; **20** 3, 6 app, 23; **48** 6; **64** i 29, 35, 38; ii 6; **66** b i 26; **77** a i 11, 20; b 6; **89** *1* 6; **117** i 2, 17, 21 and app; ii 2, 7, 19, 25
November (English), pp. 97, 157, 219
Nouember (Latin), **8** ix 20; **20** 6 app, 9, 15 app; **31** i 8; **54** a–c 6 app; **64** ii 21; **83** 2; **91** *2* i 2 app; **117** iii 12; **120** 2
October (English), pp. 107, 115, 116 and note, 118, 180, 210; **9** 34–37 app; **10** 4 app; **91** *2* i 2 app
October (Latin), p. 235; **8** iii 18, 23; **10** 4, 25, 31; **20** 12 app; **27** b ii 4; **31** ii 5; **48** 5 app; **54** a–c 6 app; **62** 1; **63** i 23; **66** b ii 9, 10, 11, 12, 13, 14, 15, 25; **83** 19; **117** iii 4, 6, 7, 8; **120** 1

Pachon (*Παχών*), **76** xx 24; xxi 4; **78** *6* 7
Pauni (*Παῦνι*), **75** 17; **78** *2* 6 app; *22* 8; *37* 7; *76* 3
Phamenoth (*Φαμενώθ*), **76** xix 9, 17, 24; xx 6, 14; xxiv 5; GG 6, 12; **78** *6* 6; *9* 5; *11* 5; *31* 4; *36* 6
Phaophi (*Φαῶφι*), **78** *33* 5
Pharmuthi (*Φαρμοῦθι*), **76** HH i 6; **78** *6* 7; *16* 4; *21* 6; *24* 8; *40* 9; *53* 8; *56* 4; *58* 5; *73* 9
pridie, p. 181; **8** ix 20; **9** 1 g; **10** 24; **11 bis** c 1; **27** a ii 13; **48** 6; **63** i 26; **64** i 12, 14 app; **75** 8; **83** 1, 17, 22; **89** *23* 18; **117** i 17, 21, 27; ii 2, 14; iii 1
September (English), pp. 107, 115, 116, 117, 118, 181, 210, 219, 234–35, 246, 251, 256, 266, 283; **69** 27 app; **76** BB 3 app, 4 app; **91** *2* i 2 app
September (Latin), p. 181; **8** iii 4; **20** 6 app, 20; **48** 5 app, 6; **54** a–c 6 app; **64** i 12; **66** b i 5–10 app, 21, 27; ii 3, 4 app; **71** b 5 app; **76** BB 4; **83** 12, 22; **89** *25* 8; *26* 6; *28* 8; *29* 15; *31* 8; *32* 7; *34* 6 and app; **98** *3* 5 app; **99** 3 marg; **117** ii 26, 28; iii 1, 2
]s, **20** 22;]ṛẹs, **48** 5
Thoth (*Θώθ*), p. 283; **74** i 8, 14; ii 8, 14; iii 7, 16; **81** ii 9, 11
Tybi (*Τῦβι*), **76** i 6, 15, 21, 26; ii 8, 17; iii 7, 17, 26; iv 8, 16, 25; v 8, 17; vi 6, 14, 21; vii 6, 12, 20; viii 6, 11, 18, 23, 28; ix 10, 17; x 8, 14, 21; xi 8, 18; xii 7, 16, 25; xiii 6, 15, 21; xiv 9, 15; xv 8; BB 8; FF 8; **78** *3* 6; *6* 6; *7* 6; *15* 7; *26* 2; *67* 4
Φ[, **78** *28* 4
Φα[, **78** *35* 5
Φαμενώθ, see Phamenoth
Φαρμοῦθι, see Pharmouthi
Φαῶφι, see Phaophi
Χοίακ, see Choiak

Index 7: Geography and Ethnics

Achaea, **63** ii 7 app
ad leones, *place-name*? *See* Index 9, Latin Words
Adatha, **47** ii 6 and app
Adiabene, p. 357
Adiabenicus, *imperial title*, **117** i 14–16 app; **123** a 2 app
Africa, pp. 82, 291 note 2
. . . . ạgr . [.]e, *place-name*?, **11 bis** a 3
Alexandretta, **96** 2 app
[a]lexandr[i]a, **96** 2
Alexandria ad Aegyptum, pp. 107, 165; **9** 5 k app; **96** 2 app
Alexandria ad Issum, **96** 2 app
Alexandria ad Tigrem, **96** 2 app
Alexandrinus, **9** 16 c app; 32 g app
Altinum, p. 165; **36** 14
Amisus, **9** 12 a
Ancyra, **36** 2, 3, 4
Antaeopolis, **70** a ii 37
Antin(oites), **39** 25; **46** 9 app
Antioch, pp. 15, 16, 399; **96** 2 app; **99** *3* marg
Apamea, pp. 15, 165; **36** 8
Aphrodito, p. 122; **11 bis** b i 16; **76** i 4; xii 5; xvi 23; vii 6–7 app
Αφρ/λινωι, **76** vii 6–7
Appadana, pp. 13, 14–15, 17, 383; **1** i 6; iii a 1, 5, 6, 7; g 4; vii 9, 15; viii 5, 9, 20, 21, 28, 29, 31; ix 22, 24; xi 13 app; xiii 1, 19, 23; xiv 3 (?), 7, 10; xv 3, 10; xvii 8; xviii 8, 9; xxii 20; xxiii 11, 15, 23; xxiv 1, 3, 6, 8; xxviii 26; xxix 7, 9, 13, 14, 15; xxx 11, 15; xxxi 26; xxxiii 6; xxxiv 11, 17, 25; xxxv 1, 10, 22; xxxvi 20; xxxvii 1, 9, 21; xxxix 8, 15, 21, 24; xlii 9, 15, 20; **2** vii 7; ix 5, 6 app, 8, 9, 10, 11, 19, 20, 26; x 5, 12, 23; xii 21, 26, 29, 30; xiii 17; xv 23; xvii 5; xviii 18; xix 3, 15, 17, 21, 22, 23; xxiii 24, 25; xxiv 12; xxvii 3, 16; xxviii 19; xxix 10, 14, 27; xxx 8, 10; xxxi 7; xxxiv 15, 23; xxxv 12; xxxvi 2; xxxvii 11; xxxix 18, 24; xl 5; xli 28; xlii 4, 12; xliii 7; **3** c 7; **8** iii 17; vi 7, 15, 16, 19, 20; viii 14, 22, 23; ix 11; **23** ii 6; **47** i 5; **88** 2, 9; **91** *1* i 8 app; ii 2 app; *2* i 7 app; **98** *2* a 10
Appadanensis, **91** *1* i 8
Arabia, p. 161
Arabicus, *imperial title*, **117** i 14–16 app; **123** a 2 app
Arsinoite nome, p. 270; **76** x 12; xiv 5; xvii 5; xviii 28; HH ii 6
Asia Minor, p. 165 note 2
Asianus, **74** i 5, 13; ii 5, 12; iii 5, 13
Atha, **47** ii 6 and app
Ausonius, **9** 12 a app
Babylon, in Egypt, **11 bis** ii 14; **70** b ii 9, 13a; **70** a iii 8 app; 13 app
Barbalissus, p. 15; **2** vi 3; ix 34; xii 13; xv 1; xx 19; xxviii 14; **47** ii 6 app
Bartha, *see* Birtha
Becchufrayn, p. 15; **1** i 2, 7; iii a 3, 4; g 5; vi 25; vii 14; viii 26; ix 1, 25, 26, 29; x 5, 6, 9, 18, 19; xi 11, 15; xii 9, 12; xiii 15, 20; xiv 22; xv 1, 6, 7, 8, 9, 13, 16; xvii 14; xviii 6; xix 2, 24; xx 5, 6, 17, 19, 23, 24; xxi 6, 13; xxii 5, 23; xxiii 5 and app, 6; xxiv 2, 11; xxv 17, 18, 22; xxvi 2, 4, 7; xxvii 11, 20; xxviii 10; xxix 2, 4, 10, 11, 22; xxx 10, 21, 22, 23, 26, 27; xxxi 1, 5, 6; xxxii 1, 5, 10, 13, 27; xxxiii 13, 28; xxxiv 7, 28; xxxv 2, 15; xxxvii 3; xxxviii 5, 21; xxxix 1, 26; xl 2, 10, 17; xli 18, 31; **2** vii 23; ix 3, 14, 21, 30; x 17, 22; xii 5, 25; xiii 2, 13; xv 4, 14, 17, 20, 22; xvii 13; xx 18; xxi 4; xxii 19, 22, 23; xxiii 21; xxv 22; xxvii 1; xxviii 18; xxx 11, 19, 26, 28, 29; xxxi 8, 9, 11; xxxii 14; xxxvi 26; xli 19; **47** i 14
Berenice, **11** ii 6
Bi[blada], **98** 3 a 13
Billae. . [(*place*?), **114** 7 app
Birtha (Bartha), p. 15; *bartha*: **1** xv 9; xxiv 12; *birtha*: **1** xiii 2, 6; xviii 10; xxv 19; xxvi 8; xxviii 5; **2** i 13, 15; xii 3, 7; xxii 5, 26; xxiii 26; xxvii 11
Bithynia, pp. 165, 421 note 4
Βωμος, **78** *59* 2 app
Boridava, **63** ii 28: *buridauae*
Britain, p. 400
Bucolia, **76** ii 15; vi 4, 19; viii 16; xi 15; xv 6; xvi 4, 14
Cae[s(area), **37** 3 app
Caper, *see* Chafer
Cappadox, **30** i 2 app; **99** *3* 3
Capua, p. 7 note 3
Carnuntum, **117** ii 3 app
Castellum Arabum, p. 15; **1** vii 6; xxii 13; xxiv 13, 17; xxv 4; xxviii 11; xxx 14; **2** xix 20; xxii 10, 12; **65** 3 app
Castra, **63** ii 21
Castra Augustoflauianensia, **63** ii 21 app

Cercasora, Cercasorum, **70** a iii 8 app
Cercasorus, **11 bis** a 16 app; **70** a iii 8: [*ce*]*rkas·*
Cercesaite, Cercesthe, **11 bis** a 16 app
Cercesdite, **11 bis** a 16
Chabur River, p. 14
Chafer (Caper) Auira, pp. 15, 17; *caper*: **2** xix 16; xxxiii 31; *chafer*: **1** xxxiv 26; xxxv 17; xxxviii 19; xxxix 16, 29; xl 8; xliii 1; **2** xxxiii 23; xxxix 14; **65** 2
Charax Spasinou, **96** 2 app
[Chr]ysọpolis pạ[.].m[, **36** 15
Circesium, **66** b ii 28 app
Clysma, **76** xviii 4 and 16
Cọmṃa[genus], **83** 8
Contrapollonospolis maior, **64** i 34
Coptites, **39** 20
Corcois, **66** b ii 28 app
Corcosio (locative?), **66** b ii 28; b i 23 app
Cremona, p. 165; **36** 6
Ctesiphon, **117** i 14–16 app
Cyme, **52** b 15 app
Cyrrhus, p. 16
Dacia Inferior, 63 i 24 app
Dakkeh, p. 310
Dalmatia, **63** ii 21 app
Damascus, **68** ii 2
Danube River, **63** ii 29: *trans danuuium*; **77** a i 7 app
Dardania, **63** ii 22
Delta, Egypt, **70** a iii 1 app; 8 app
Dura-Europos, pp. 1, 5, 14, 15, 52, 83, 175, 233, 235, 242, 336, 380, 382, 430, 433; **47** ii 8 app; **50** i 11 app; **66** a ii 7 app; **89** *2* 18 app; *11* 11; *23* 1 app; *41* 13 app; **91** *2* i 6 app; **98** *2* a 11; **99** *1* 3 app; **117** ii 9 app
E....[, **11 bis** b ii 9
Ed[da]na, **98** *2* a 12
Egypt, pp. 2, 87, 116, 137, 161, 165, 166, 170, 181, 182, 202, 242, 244, 278; **9** 3 h app; **20** 2 app; **52** c 6 app; **53** a ii 2 app; b 22 app; **63** i 24 app; **64** ii 25 app; **70** a ii 19 app; **77** a i 7 app; **89** *39* 5 app; **102** a 5 app
Epirus, **63** i 14 app
Erạṛ[.]m, **63** ii 20: *trans erạṛ*[.]*m*
].ẹrro (locative?) **70** g 4
Euphrates River, p. 15
Gadara, **37** 3 app
Galatia, p. 165; **50** i 14 app
Gallia, **63** ii 18
Gazica, **98** *2* a 9
Germanicus, *imperial title*, **123** a 2
Germany, **77** a i 7 app; **89** *3* 7 app
Graecia, **63** ii 18 app
Hadrumetum, p. 165; **36** 9
Haemus, **63** ii 35
Heliopolis, Egypt, **70** a ii 31; a iii 13; Aberdeen 133, 2
Heracleia Lyncestis, **63** ii 21 app
Heracleouspolis Parva, **70** a iii 1
Heraclide meros, Arsinoite nome, p. 271
Heroonpolis, **70** g app
Hieropolis (Bambyce), **99** *2* marg
Italy, pp. 6, 165 note 2
Kastello, p. 15
Laodicea, p. 165; **36** 7 app, 12, 13
Laura, **76** xii 5; xv 20–21; xix 6, 22; xx 12
ad leones, *place-name*? *See* Index 9, Latin Words
Lycaonia. p. 165
Lycia Pamphylia, p. 202
Lycopolites, **39** 2, 7, 10, 14
Macedonia, **63** ii 21 app
Magdala, pp. 11, 12, 14, 15; **1** ix 28; xiv 1; xv 15; xx 1, 4; xxv 10, 16; xxviii 6; xxx 24; xxxi 7, 11; **2** ix 23?, 24?, 29; x 6, 30?; xviii 21; xx 17; xxi 8? 9; xxiv 14, 15 app, 21 app; xxv 14?; xxix 17, 21, 23; xxxi 10; xxxviii 14
Mareotis, **76** iii 5; viii 26 a; BB 5; BB 4 app
Marus River, **63** ii 20 app
Mauretania, pp. 396–97; **64** i 25–26; **77** a i 7 app; **91** *1* verso 2–3 app
με[.]λα̣ (*place*?), **90** *2* a 6 and app
Mendes, **70** d 6–7 app
Mercurium, quarter of Alexandria, **10** 5, 8, 23
Mesopotamia, p. 357; **4** b ii 12 app; **20** 15 app; **89** *3* 7 app
Moesia Inferior, pp. 219–220; **50** i 14 app; **63** i 24 app; ii 7 app, 21 app; **91** *1* i 4 app
Moesia Superior, pp. 219–220; **63** ii 7 app, 21 app
Mons Claudianus, p. 242
Neapolis, suburb of Alexandria, **9** 31 g; **10** 2, 27, 8 app; **51** ii 23
Nicopolis, suburb of Alexandria, **9** 5 k and app; 16 k, 27 k
Nicopolis in Epirus, **63** i 14
Nicopolis ad Haemum (ad Istrum), **63** i 14 app
Nicopolis ad Nestum, **63** i 14 app
Numidia, **50** i 14 app
Ogḅo[, Ogḍo[, **70** d 6 and app
Ogdoekontarouros, **70** d 6–7 app
Ombos, **70** d 6–7 app
Ostracina, **70** a ii 37; d 18 app
Oxyrhynchus, pp. 242, 410; **70** e 1
Palmyra, **66** b ii 28 app
Pamphylia, p. 202; **52** c 6 app
Pannonia, **63** i 24 app; ii 8 app
Pannonia Inferior, **63** ii 21 app
Paphlagonia, p. 165
Paraetonium, p. 165
Parapotamia, **90** *1* a 9; **92** ii 7 app
Parsa Dagh, p. 16
Parthen, Parthes, p. 16
Parthia, p. 16; **1** xix 3; xxii 3; xxx 9, 17; xl 1
Parthorum, **98** *2* a 6
Pessinus, **36** 1 and 5

Pharos, **9** 10 b app
Philadelphia, **67** 8
Philae, **78** *45* 5
Philomede, p. 166
Philomedia, p. 165; **36** 10
Philomelium, p. 165
Phrygia, p. 165
Piroboridava, **63** ii 27
Pontus, p. 165
Πρῆμις, *Πρῆμνις*, Primis, **102** a 10 app
Prosopites, **39** 12
Pselcis, pp. 310, 311; **78** *73* app
Ravenna, **117** ii 10–11 app
Rhine River, p. 420
Rhinocorura, **70** a ii 31
Rome, **117** ii 5; i 14–16 app
ad sacrahim, *place-name? See* p. 14
Salonae, **63** ii 21 app
Samos, p. 202
Scenae, **76** iv 5 and 14; v 13
Scenae Mandrae, **52** b 5 app; **76** iii 15; v 13 (?); vi 12; vii 19; x 19; xii 14 and 23; xiii 5 (?)
Scenae Megalae, **76** iii 24; v 13 (?); ix 16; xi 5–6; xx 3–4
Scenae Micrae, **76** viii 4–5, 10, 21; x 6; xiv 13–14
Scenae Naartrae, **76** xiii 5
Scenae Veteranorum, **52** b 5 app
Seleucia-Ctesiphon, **117** i 14–16 app
Servitium, **63** ii 21 app
Sidon, **9** 11 a
Silva, **89** *1* 3
Stobi, **63** i 13, 16, 18, 19, 24
Syenites, **39** 9
Syria, pp. 150, 154, 165 and note 2, 192, 202, 348, 382, 383, 396–97, 399, 403, 417; **20** 15 app; **89** *39* 5 app; **90** *2* a 5; **91** *1* i 4 app
Taposiris, **76** ii 6
Tell Edfou, p. 242
Thaubasti, **70** c 8
Thebaid, **64** i 4
Theogenous, **70** d 6–7 app
This, **70** b i 7: *thinit(es)*
Thubursica, **64** i 7–8
Tripoli (Syria), **66** b ii 28 app
Tyras, **63** ii 21 app
Tyrus, **68** iii 1
ụạ. . . . [(*place-name*?), **11 bis** b ii 2
Ulcisia Castra, **63** ii 21 app
Utica, p. 165; **36** 11
Veii, p. 6
Zenobia (*city*), p. 15
Zeugma, p. 15

Index 8: Greek Words

agon: agonas, **67** 8
ἀδελφός, *see also Index 9*, frater; pp. 170, 349 and note 9
ἀδελφοῦ, **39** verso; p. 170
ἀδελφῷ, **76** HH ii 4
ἄδελφε, **89** *16* 2; *17* 11; *29* 12
adytum, **53** b 14
ἀεί, **76** HH ii 8
αἰτέω?: αιτε[, **89** *2* 10
ἀλλά?, **89** *41* 9
ἄλλος: ἄλλα, **76** BB 3; **89** *41* 9
ἅλς: ἁλός, **78** *15* 5
amphora, **82** 2: amp(hora)
αν( ), **79** 12
ἀνά, **76** iii 5; v 6; xi 16; xx 23
Ἀνατολικῶν, *see also Index 4, Military Affairs*, numerus Orientalium; **30** ii 13 app
ἀνήρ: ἀνδρῶν, **74** i 6; ii 6, iii 6
ἄνιππος, **73** c 9 app
αντ[, **89** *33* 4
ἀντί, **78** *11* 6
ἄνω: ἀνομένου, **79** 12 app
ἀπό, **39** verso, p. 170; **78** *14* 3?; *15* 4; *44* 3 app; *65* 3; *66* 3; *67* 3; *68* 3; *69* 4; *71* 4; **89** *9* verso 2; *26* 3
ἀπογράφω: ἀπογρ(άφομαι?), **78** *5* 5
ἀποδίδωμι: ἀπόδος, **39** verso, p. 170
]απολυσ[, **89** *26* 2; *27* 2 app
ἀπολύσιμος, *see also Index 9*, libertus; **89** *26* 2 app; p. 242
ἀπολύω, **89** *26* 2 app
ἀποχή: ἀποχήν, **76** HH ii 7
ἀργυροῦς: ἀργυρᾶ, 74 i 11
ἀριθμός, *see also Index 4, Military Affairs*, numerus
ἀριθμοῦ, **30** ii 13 app
ἀριθμῷ, **74** i 13; ii 12; **81** ii 8 app; **89** *41* 11 and app
ἀριθμῶν, **81** ii 8
ἄριστος, *see also Index 9*, optimus; ἀρίστου, **74** i 8, 14; ii 7, 13; iii 7, 15
ἀρμόρου, ἀρμοκούστωρ, ἀρμωρωκούστωρ, *see Index 4, Military Affairs*, armorum custos; **76** xv 8; **78** *12* 1 app; *39* 5–6; *71* 1
ἀρτάβη, p. 313
ἀρτάβαι, **79** 13
ἀρτάβην, **78** *1* 5; *2* 4; *7* 4; *12* 3
ἀρτάβας, **78** *3* 5; *4* 4; *6* 8; **81** ii 9
(ἀρτάβας), *symbol* ∸, **78** *11* 4 (twice), 7; *14* 4; **85** 4
ἄρχων, p. 8
authenticam, **87** 29
αὐτοκράτωρ, *see also Index 9*, imperator
αὐτοκράτορος, **74** iii 15; **76** FF 5; **78** *73* 6
αὐτοκρατόρων, **76** iii 23; iv 8, 16; viii 17, 27; xvi 6, 17; xx 13, 23; xxi 4; BB 7
αὐτόκρατορ, **11 bis** c 2–3 app
αὐτός, **78** *12* 5 app; *18* 6; *33* 6 app
αὐτοῦ, **76** i 7, 27; iii 18; iv 18; v 18; vi 7, 15, 22; vii 14, 21; viii 12, 23, 28; ix 19; x 23; xi 10; xii 8 (twice), 17; xiii 8, 23; xiv 17; xvi 8; xvii 7; xviii 9, 32; xxi 6; GG 7, 13 (twice); HH ii 5; **78** *4* 7; *6* 9; *9* 7; *10* 7; *22* 6 (twice); *23* 7; *39* 6; *42* 6; *56* 6; *58* 7; *79* 15
αὐτῆς, **74** ii 3; iii 3, 10; **76** i 27; ii 2, 3, 9, 20; iii 2, 3, 8 (twice); iv 17, 20; v 3, 9; vii 13, 21; viii 7, 12; ix 18; x 10, 22; xi 9, 10, 13 (twice), 18; xiii 22 (twice); xiv 12, 16; xv 11; xvi 7; xvii 10; xviii 8, 9, 13, 21; xix 3; xx 9, 16, 25; xxi 5, 6; BB 8; FF 2, 8; GG 6, 7, 12; **89** *23* 2
αὐτῷ, **78** *77* 2
αὐτόν, **76** i 8, 27; ii 9; iii 18; iv 10, 18; v 18; vi 8, 15, 22; vii 15, 22; viii 13, 24; x 24; xii 18; xiii 8, 24; xiv 18; xvi 9; xvii 7; xviii 10, 32; xix 10; xxi 6; GG 8, 13
αὐτῶν, **76** iii 9; iv 26; ix 11; xi 19; xv 8; xviii 22; xx 16, 25; BB 9; FF 9; **89** *23* 5
αὐτοῖς, **78** *62* 2 app
αὐτούς, **76** i 16; ii 10; iii 10; iv 26; v 10; ix 12; xv 9; xviii 22; xix 11; xx 17, 26; FF 10; **90** *2* a 1–2 app
αφσσηταων (= absentium?), **35** 2, 4, 8
ἄχρι, **78** *11* 5; *23* 5; *31* 3
βαλλ[, **89** *23* 8
βαρίδων, **34** recto ii 1 app
βιβλίον ἐφήμερον, p. 179
bouleutes, p. 242
βραδέως, **76** xi 20
γάρ, **90** *2* a 4
γε̣[. . . .]α, **89** *2* 9
geometres, p. 242
γίγνομαι
γίγνεται, **78** *32* 5
γίγνονται, **78** *6* 7; *79* 13
γενομ[εν-, **90** *2* a 5
gossipion, **9** 3 h app

γράμμα
γράμμασιν, **89** *16* 4 and app, 10
γράμματα, **76** i 8, 16, 27; ii 10; iii 10, 19; iv 10, 18, 27; v 10, 18; vi 8, 16, 22; vii 15, 22; viii 13, 24, 29; ix 12; x 24; xii 18; xiii 8, 24; xiv 18; xv 9; xvi 9; xvii 7; xviii 10, 23, 32; xix 11; xx 17, 26; xxi 6; BB 10; FF 10; GG 8, 13; **78** *9* 8; *22* 7; *23* 7; *26* 3; *39* 7; *56* 7
γραμματεύς, **78** *26* 3 app
γράστις, *see* κράστις
γράφω
ἔγραψα, **76** i 7, 15, 27; ii 9; iii 9, 18; iv 9, 17, 26; v 9, 17; vi 7, 15, 21; vii 14, 21; viii 12, 23, 28; ix 11, 19, 23; xi 10, 19; xii 8, 17; xiii 23; xiv 7; xv 8, 17; xvi 8; xvii 7; xviii 9, 21, 31; xix 10, 16, 25; xxi 6; BB 9; FF 9; GG 7, 13; **78** *1* 6; *2* 6; *4* 6; *6* 9; *9* 7; *10* 7; *12* 5 app; *15* 8; *18* 6; *22* 6; *23* 6; *24* 7; *25* 3; *26* 3; *30* 10; *31* 5; *33* 6; *34* 10; *37* 7; *39* 6; *40* 10; *42* 6; *48* 6; *54* 6; *55* 7 app; *56* 5; *57* 5, 6; *58* 6; *60* 2; *65* 5; *66* 6; *67* 4; *75*; **79** 15
ἔγραψον, **76** xiii 7
γράφοντος, **76** xi 20
gubernator, **59** i 5
δέκα, **76** FF 6; **78** *54* 4
δεκάδαρχος: δεκαδάρχου, **76** BB 5; *see also Index 4, Military Affairs*, decurio
δεκαέν, **74** ii 11
δεκαέξ, **74** iii 4
δεκαέπτα, **74** i 13
δέκατος, **76** x 11
δέομαι, **90** *2* a 3 and app; *cf.* p. 380
δεομε.[, **89** *41* 15
δεύτερος
δευτέρου, **75** 16, 22
δευτέρᾳ, **76** x 14
δηλόω: δηλουμένοις, **89** *23* 3
διά, **76** i 8, 16, 27; ii 10; iii 9, 18; iv 10, 18, 26; v 10, 18; vi 8, 15, 22; vii 14, 22; viii 12, 23; ix 11; x 23; xi 20; xii 17; xiii 8, 23; xiv 17; xv 9; xvi 8; xvii 7; xviii 10, 22, 32; xix 10; xx 17, 26; xxi 6; FF 9; GG 7, 13; **78** *6* 12; *17* 2; *18* 8; *20* 8; *25* 3–4 app; *28* 5; *34* 1; *59* 2; *60* 3; *62* 3; *70* 7; *71* 3; *72* 5
διακόσιοι: διακόσια, **74** i 11; ii 11; iii 4 app
δίμοιρον, **78** *11* 4
δίδωμι
δέδομεν, **11 bis** c 3
δώσειν, **89** *29* 4
δούς, **76** HH ii 3
δοθέντες, **89** *2* 5; *41* 2
δίπλευρος, **70** a ii 19 app
δίπλινθος, **70** a ii 19 app
diota, **53** b 24
δοχη[, **89** *41* 16 and app
δραχμή, pp. 122, 243–44, 251, 255, 306–307, 440; **68** i 17–18 app; **69** 3 app; 9 app; 17–18 app; 26 app
δραχμῆς, **78** *34* 7
dr, **77** a i 4; b 4
drachma[, **77** a ii 7
drachmae, **77** a i 18, 19
drachmarum, **77** a i 8 app
drachmas, **68** ii 3, 5, 6, 7, 8, 9, 10, 11, 12, 13, 14, 16, 17, 18, 19, 20, 21, 22, 23, 24, 26, 27, 28, 29, 30, 31; iii 2, 4, 5, 6, 7, 8, 9, 10, 11, 12, 13, 15, 16, 17, 18, 19, 20, 21, 22, 23, 25, 26, 27, 28, 29; **69** 2, 3, 4, 5, 6, 7, 9, 10, 11, 12, 13, 14, 15, 17, 18, 19, 21, 22, 23, 24, 25; **77** a i 3, 9, 10, 16, 17 app
δρασα. . . .ε, **78** *30* 2
dromas, **8** iii 5 app
dromon, **8** iii 5 app
dromone, **8** iii 5; vii 22
δύο, **74** ii 5; **78** *3* 6; *27* 3; *32* 4; *34* 7; *39* 4; *68* 5; *69* 5; *70* 5; **79** 13 (twice)
ἑβδομήκοντα, **75** 21
ἐγώ
ἐμοῦ, **76** HH i 4; **78** *11* 3; *59* 2
μου, **76** i 3, 19, 23; ii 14; iii 13, 22; iv 13; v 13; vi 3, 11, 18; vii 4, 10, 18; viii 9, 15, 20, 26; ix 15; x 5, 11, 18; xi 5; xii 4, 13; xiii 4, 11, 18; xiv 5, 13; xv 20; xvi 3 (twice), 12, 13, 21; xvii 3, 17; xviii 4, 27; xix 15, 21; xxi 2; xxiv 3; GG 3, 10; HH i 4; ii 8; **78** *1* 4; *4* 3; *5* 3; *7* 4; *8* 5; *9* 4; *10* 4; **79** 11
μοι, **89** *2* 6; *41* 2
με, **89** *2* 8?; *31* 4
ἡμῶν, **76** i 12; ii 5; iii 4; iv 4, 22, 23; v 5; ix 6, 8; xi 15; xii 22; xv 5, 6, 13, 15; xviii 16; xix 5, 11; xx 14, 21, 23; BB 6; FF 4; **90** *2* a 6
ἡμεῖν, **90** *2* a 4
iconismus, **87** 14, 16, 18, 20, 22
iconismo, **87** 12
iconismos, **50** i 15; **87** 8; **99** *2* 3; **100** 2 app
εἴκοσι, **74** iii 12; **76** i 5, 13, 19, 24; ii 6, 15; iii 5, 15, 25; iv 6, 13, 23; v 6, 15; vi 5, 13, 20; vii 5, 12, 18; viii 4, 9, 16, 21; ix 8; x 7, 11, 20; xi 7, 16; xii 5, 14, 23; xiii 5, 13, 20; xv 7, 15, 22; xvi 6, 17, 23; xvii 6, 12; xviii 7, 19, 30; xix 6, 17, 24; xx 14, 23; xxi 4; xxiv 5; BB 6; HH i 4; ii 6; **78** *36* 5; *72* 7; *73* 6
εἰκοσιδύω, **74** ii 13
εἰκοσιέξ, **74** ii 11
εἰκοσιπέντε, **76** xx 6
εἰκοσιτεσσάρων, **74** iii 6
εἰκοσιτρείων (*gen*), **74** iii 13
εἰκοσιτρία, **74** i 4
εἰκοστός
εἰκοστοῦ, **74** i 7, 13
εἰκοστῇ, **76** x 14
εἴλη, *see* ἴλη

εἰμί (*sum*) **76** xx 17?
εἰς, **74** i 12; **76** i 4, 13, 19; ii 6, 15; iii 5, 15, 24; iv 5, 14; v 13; vi 4, 12, 19; vii 7, 19; viii 4, 10, 16, 21, 26a; ix 6, 16; x 6, 11, 19; xi 5, 15; xii 5, 14, 22, 23; xiii 5; xiv 5, 13; xv 6, 20; xvi 4, 14, 23; xvii 5; xviii 4, 16, 28; xix 6, 22; xx 3, 12; **78** *73* 5; **89** *2* 9; **90** *2* a 2; k 3
εἷς, μία, ἕν
ἑνός, **74** i 7?; **78** *53* 6
μίαν, **78** *1* 5; *2* 4; *4* 4; *6* 8?; *7* 4; *11* 4; *12* 4
ἕν, **74** i 7?; **78** *18* 5; *19* 4; *21* 5; *23* 4; *24* 4; *25* 2; *26* 1; *28* 3; *30* 7; *31* 3; *33* 4; *34* 6; *36* 5; *38* 4; *39* 4; *40* 6, 7; *45* 4; *46* 2; *49* 4; *51* 5; *53* 5; *54* 3; *55* 4; *56* 3; *57* 3; *58* 3; *59* 3
ἐκ, ἐξ, **76** ii 6; xvii 12; xix 6; xxiv 4; BB 3; FF 6; **78** *16* 2; *17* 2; *18* 4; *20* 4; *21* 4; *22* 4; *28* 2; *30* 6; *33* 3; *34* 5; *35* 3; *37* 3; *47* 3; *48* 3; *49* 3; *50* 5; *54* 2; *55* 3; *56* 2–3 app; *58* 3; *61* 2; *63* 3
ἕκαστος, **76** iv 23; ix 8; xii 23; xv 6, 15; xx 14, 23; BB 6
ἑκατόν, **74** iii 11
ἕκτος
ἕκτῃ, **74** ii 8, 14; iii 7
ἕκτην, **74** iii 16
ἐν, **74** i 6; ii 6, 12; iii 6, 14; **76** i 3, 12, 19; ii 5, 14; iii 4, 14, 23; iv 5, 14; v 4, 15; vi 3, 12; vii 18; viii 4, 9, 16, 20, 26; ix 6, 15; x 4, 18; xi 5, 15; xii 13, 21; xiii 4, 11, 18; xiv 5, 13; xv 5, 13, 20; xvi 4, 13, 21; xvii 3; xviii 4, 16, 27; xix 5, 15, 21; xx 3, 11; BB 5; HH ii 6; **78** *9* 4; *13* 2; *45* 5; *55* 7 and app
ἐνενηκονταδύο, **74** iii 12
ἐννεακαιδέκατος: ἐννεακαιδεκάτου, **76** i 4, 24; ii 5, 14; iii 6, 13, 22; xiii 11, 18; xv 5, 14; xviii 5, 17; xix 7; xx 12; GG 4
ἐξ, **78** *6* 8; *24* 6 app; *27* 4
ἐξέρχομαι
ἐξερχομενομεν, **76** xii 22
ἐξερχόμενος, **76** i 4, 19; ii 15; iii 15, 24; iv 14; v 13; vi 4, 12, 19; vii 6, 19; viii 4, 9, 16, 21, 26a; ix 15; x 6, 11, 18; xi 5; xii 4, 14; xiii 4; xiv 5, 13; xv 20; xvi 4, 14, 23; xvii 5; xviii 4, 28; xix 6, 21; xx 3
ἐξερχόμενοι, **76** i 13; ii 6; iii 5; iv 5; v 7; ix 6; xi 15; xv 6, 13; xviii 16; xx 11
ἐξουσία, **89** *29* 4
ἐπεί, **76** HH ii 5
ἐπί, **78** *2* 3; **90** *2* 5, 6
ἐπιδέδομεν, **11 bis** c 2–3 app
epimeletes, p. 242
epistratego, **11** ii 9; **81** iii 10 app
ἑπτά, **78** *6* 8; *72* 6
ἔρχομαι: ἦλθαν, **90** *2* a 7
ἐρωτάω: ἐρωτηθείς, **76** ii 9; iii 9, 18, 26; v 9, 18; vii 14, 21, 23; ix 11, 19; xi 10, 19; xiii 8, 23; xiv 17; xviii 9, 32; xix 10; xx 16; FF 9; GG 13
ἐρωτηθέντων, **76** xx 25
ἔτος, **74** iii 14; **76** iii 22
ἔτους, **74** i 7, 13; ii 13; **75** 16, 22; **76** i 4, 24; ii 5, 14; iii 6, 13; vi 3, 11, 19; ix 16; x 11, 20; xi 7; xiii 12, 13, 20; xv 6, 14; xviii 5, 17; xix 7; xx 12; FF 6; GG 4 (twice), 11; **79** 12; **89** *2* 14?
(ἔτους), *symbol* ∟, **74** ii 7; iii 7, 14; **76** i 5, 14, 20, 25; ii 7, 16; iii 16, 25; iv 7, 15, 24; v 7, 16; vi 5, 13, 20; vii 4, 5, 11, 19; viii 5, 10, 16, 17, 21, 22, 27; ix 7, 9; x 5, 7, 13, 19; xi 6; xii 6, 15, 24; xiii 5; xiv 8, 14; xv 7, 16, 21; xvi 4, 5, 15; xvii 13, 17, 18; xix 15; xx 4, 22; xxi 3; xxiv 3; BB 7; HH i 5; **78** *1* 6; *2* 6; *3* 7; *4* 4; *5* 4; *6* 8, 10; *7* 6; *9* 6; *11* 5; *14* 2; *15* 7; *16* 4; *18* 7; *19* 5; *20* 6; *21* 6; *22* 8; *23* 8; *24* 7; *25* 3; *26* 2; *27* 5; *28* 4; *29* 5; *30* 8; *31* 4; *32* 6; *33* 5; *34* 8; *35* 5; *36* 6; *37* 7; *38* 4; *39* 7; *40* 8; *45* 5; *53* 8; *54* 4; *57* 4; *61* 5; *65* 4; *66* 4; *67* 4; *68* 5; *69* 6; *70* 5; *72* 8; *73* 6; *77* 5; **81** ii 10
(ἔτους), *symbol* ʃ′ or ʃ, **76** iv 5, 13, 23; v 5, 13; xi 16; xvi 21; HH i 4, 5; ii 4
ευν[, **89** *24* 2
εὐσεβής (=pius, *title*): εὐσεβοῦς, **78** *73* 8
εὔχομαι, p. 349, note 9; **76** HH ii 8; **89** *17* 12; *29* 11; *41* 15 app
ἔχω
ἔχειν, **89** *41* 15
ἔσχον, **78** *68* 3
ἕως, **78** *33* 4; *38* 5; *40* 7; *42* 4; *63* 4
ζ.β..σ^υ, **11 bis** c 4
ηλ[.].[, **75** 11
ἡμεῖς, *see* ἐγώ
ἐφήμερος, p. 179
ιζ′ (*numeral*?), **11 bis** c 7
ι [....]ṭανας, **78** *73* 5–6
ἰατρός: ἰατρῷ, **74** i 3
ἴδιος
ἰδίᾳ, **78** *25* 3–4; *60* 2; *67* 4?
ἴδιον, **78** *5* 5; *12* 5 app
ἴλη: ἴλης, *see also Index 4, Military Affairs*, ala; **76** i 1, 9; ii 1, 2, 8, 11; iii 1, 2, 8, 11, 20; iv 1, 11, 19; v 1, 3, 11; vi 9, 18; vii 2, 8, 13, 16, 21; viii 2, 7, 11, 14, 19, 25; ix 2, 13, 18; x 2, 10, 15, 22; xi 2, 9, 12, 13, 18; xii 1, 11, 16, 19; xiii 2, 9, 16, 22; xiv 2, 10, 12, 16; xv 2, 10, 11, 18; xvi 1, 7, 10, 19; xvii 1, 8; xviii 1, 8, 11, 13, 20, 24; xix 1, 3, 12, 18; xx 1, 7, 9, 15, 18, 19, 25; xxi 1, 5; xxiv 1; BB 1, 8; FF 1, 8; GG 1, 6, 9, 12; HH i 1
ἱππεύς, *see also Index 9*, eques; **76** i 1, 9; ii 2, 8; iii 1, 2, 8, 11, 17, 20; iv 11, 19; v 1, 3, 9, 11, 17; vi 9; vii 1, 8, 13, 16; viii 2, 7, 14, 19, 25; ix 2, 13, 18; x 2, 15, 22; xi 2, 9, 12, 13, 18; xii 1, 11, 16, 19; xiii 2, 9, 16, 22; xiv 2, 10; xv 2, 10, 11, 18; xvi 1, 7, 10; xvii 1, 15; xviii 1, 8, 11, 13, 20, 24; xix 1, 3, 12, 18; xx 1, 7, 9, 15, 18, 19; xxi 1; xxiv 1; BB 1; FF 1,

8; GG 1, 6, 9, 12; HH i 1; **78** *1* 6; *3* 2; *8* 2; *15* 1; *27* 1; *30* 4; *33* 1; *34* 3, 9; *42* 1; *45* 1; *63* 1; *65* 5; *66* 1, 5; **79** 8, 14
ἱππεῖς, **81** ii 8
ιτε[, **89** *2* 14
καθοράω: *καθορῶμεν*, **90** *2* a 1
καί, **74** i 7; **76** i 5, 10 (twice), 14, 20, 25; ii 7, 16, 19; iii 2, 7, 14, 16, 23, 26; iv 2, 7, 15, 19, 20, 24; v 2, 6, 7, 14, 16; vi 5, 13, 20; vii 5, 11, 19; viii 5, 10, 17, 22, 27; ix 3, 4, 7, 9, 17; x 5, 8, 11, 13, 14, 20, 21; xi 8, 13, 17, 20; xii 6, 15, 20, 24; xiii 6, 12, 14, 19, 21; xiv 6, 8, 15; xv 3 (twice), 7, 11, 14, 16, 21; xvi 5, 15, 22; xvii 4, 9, 13, 17; xviii 6, 12, 18, 29; xix 2, 8, 16, 18, 23; xx 5, 8, 13, 19, 22; xxi 3; xxiv 4; BB 2, 4, 7; FF 1, 2, 5, 7; GG 4, 5, 11; HH i 5; ii 7, 8; **78** *3* 6; *6* 6 (twice); *11* 2; *14* 2; *15* 5 (twice); *40* 6; *44* 4?; *49* 4; *57* 5, 6; *72* 3, 6; *77* 2; **85** 1, 2, 3; **89** *2* 7; *23* 9; **90** *2* a 5
καινός, **78** *44* 4 app
καλῶς, **76** HH ii 3; **89** *41* 15 app
κατέχω: *κατέχειν*, **90** *2* m 3 and app
κεντουρία, *κεντυρία*, *see Index 9, Latin Words, and Index 4, Military Affairs*, centuria
κεράμιον, **78** *23* 4; *27* 3 app; *44* 4 app; p. 312, note 4
κίκι, **78** *57* 3–4 app, 7–8
κλίβανος: *κλιβάνου*, **78** *16* 2–3; *17* 2
κολοφώνιον, pp. 312 note 4, 313; **78** *18* 5; *19* 4; *21* 4; *24* 4; *25* 2; *26* 1; *27* 3 app; *28* 3; *29* 4; *30* 7; *33* 4; *34* 6; *39* 3; *40* 6; *42* 4; *44* 3 app; *54* 3; *56* 3; *57* 3; *58* 2 app, 3; *59* 3; *64* 2, 6
  κολοφωνίου, **78** *69* 4–5
  κολοφώνια, **78** *27* 3; *32* 4; *57* 3
  [*κολ*], [*κολ*]*ο̣φ*[, *κο*[*λ*, **78** *35* 4; *41* 4; *55* 4
κοπτιτικός: *κοπτιτικόν*, **78** *23* 4
κορνιξ (=cornicem? cornicularius?), **78** *40* 2
κουστωρ (=custos), *see ἁρμόρου, and Index 4, Military Affairs*, armorum custos
κράστις (*γράστις*): *κράστιν*, **76** i 3, 12, 18, 23; ii 4, 13; iii 4, 13, 22; iv 4, 13, 22; v 5, 12; vi 3, 11, 18; vii 4, 10, 18; viii 3, 9, 15, 20, 26; ix 6, 15; x 4, 11, 18; xi 4, 15; xii 4, 13, 21; xiii 4, 11, 18; xiv 4, 13; xv 5, 13, 20; xvi 3, 13, 21; xvii 3, 12, 17; xviii 3, 15, 27; xix 5, 15, 21; xx 3, 11, 21; xxi 2; xxiv 3; BB 3 app; GG 3, 10; HH i 3; ii 4
κριθή: *κριθῆς*, **78** *11* 6; **85** 4
κύριος
  κυρι[, **89** *16* 9 and app
  κυρίου, **74** i 8, 14; ii 8, 14; iii 7
  κύριε, **89** *16* 2 app
  κυρίων, **76** i 6, 15, 21, 25; ii 7, 17; iii 7, 14, 17, 23, 26; iv 7, 15, 24; v 6, 8, 14, 16; vi 6, 14, 20; vii 6, 12, 20; viii 5, 11, 17, 22, 27; ix 7, 9, 17; x 6, 8, 13, 21; xi 8, 17; xii 6, 15, 24; xiii 6, 12, 14, 19, 21; xiv 7, 9, 14, 15; xv 8, 14, 16, 21; xvi 5, 16, 22; xvii 4, 14, 18; xviii 6, 18, 29; xix 8, 16, 23; xx 5, 13, 22; xxi 3; xxiv 4; BB 7; FF 7; GG 5, 11; HH i 6; **81** ii 10
κωπητῆρ, **82** 5 app
λδ[e] (*numeral*?), **11 bis** c 5
λαμβάνω
  λήμψη, **76** HH ii 7
  ἔλαβα, **75** 20; **76** xi 21; xvii 16; **78** *17* 1
  ἔλαβαν, **76** xvi 3
  ἔλαβον, **74** i 3, 11; ii 3, 10; iii 3, 11, **75** 13; **76** i 3, 18, 23; ii 13; iii 12, 21; iv 12; v 12; vi 2, 11, 18; vii 3, 10, 17; viii 3, 8, 15, 20, 26; ix 14; x 4, 10, 17; xi 4, 11; xii 4, 13; xiii 4, 10, 17; xiv 4, 12; xv 13, 19; xvi 12, 21; xvii 3; xviii 3, 26; xix 14, 20; xx 2; xxi 2; xxiv 2; GG 3, 10; HH i 3; **78** *7* 3; *8* 4; *9* 3; *10* 3; *12* 3; *15* 3; *16* 2; *18* 3; *19* 3; *20* 3; *21* 3; *22* 3; *23* 3; *24* 3; *25* 1; *26* 3 app; *27* 3; *28* 1; *29* 3; *30* 6; *31* 2; *32* 3; *33* 3; *34* 4; *35* 3; *36* 3; *37* 3; *38* 3; *39* 3; *40* 5; *41* 3; *42* 3; *43* 3; *44* 3; *45* 3; *46* 2; *47* 3; *49* 2; *51* 4; *52* 4; *53* 3; *54* 2; *55* 3; *56* 2; *57* 2; *58* 2; *61* 2; *63* 3; *65* 3; *66* 3; *67* 2; *69* 4; *70* 3; *71* 3; *72* 5; *73* 4?; *74* 3
  ἐλάβαμεν, **76** i 12; ii 4; iii 4; iv 4, 22; v 4; ix 5; xi 14; xii 21; xv 5; xvii 11; xviii 15; xix 4; xx 10, 21; BB 3; FF 4
  εἰληφήναι, **78** *50* 4–5
λαμπτῆρ, **82** 5 app
λόγος
  λόγου, **11 bis** c 4 app; **78** *11* 5
  λόγον, **78** *73* 5
μ̣αρ[, **89** *33* 1
μαρα[, **89** *9* 2
μέγιστε, **11 bis** c 2
μεσίτης, p. 242
μετά, **76** BB 5
μετιστε, **11 bis** c 2–3 app
μετρέω, p. 332
  ἐμετρήθην, **79** 11
  ἐμετρήθησαν, **81** ii 7
μετρητής, p. 312 note 4
μή, **76** i 8, 16, 27; ii 10; iii 9, 18; iv 10, 18, 26; v 10, 18; vi 8, 15, 22; vii 14, 22; viii 12, 23, 28; ix 12; x 23; xii 17; xiii 8, 23; xiv 17; xv 9; xvi 8; xvii 7; xviii 10, 22, 32; xix 10; xx 17, 26; xxi 6; BB 9; FF 9; GG 7, 13; **78** *9* 8; *22* 7; *23* 7; *39* 6; *56* 6
μήν
  μηνός, **78** *1* 4; *2* 4; *4* 3; *6* 5; *7* 5; *8* 5; *9* 5; *10* 4; *12* 4; **81** ii 9
  μηνῶν, **78** *3* 6; *6* 5, 8; **79** 12
μισθοδότης, p. 7
νεκροτάφος, **78** *73* 3
xenia, **98** *2* 7
ὁ, ἡ, τό
  ὁ, **76** i 15; iv 9; ix 10; xii 9; xix 18

τοῦ, **74** i 8, 14; ii 7, 13; iii 7, 16; **76** i 4, 20, 24; ii 5, 14; iii 6, 14, 22; iv 5, 13, 23; v 5, 13; vi 3, 14, 19; vii 4, 11, 18; viii 4, 9, 15, 21, 27; x 5, 11, 19; xi 6, 16; xiii 11, 18; xiv 6, 14; xv 5, 14, 21; xvi 4, 16, 21; xvii 4; xviii 5, 17, 28; xix 7, 15, 22; xx 4, 12, 22; xxi 3; xxiv 3; GG 3, 4, 11; HH i 4; ii 4; **78** *16* 2; *17* 2; *18* 4; *20* 4; *21* 4; *22* 4; *23* 5; *28* 2; *30* 6; *33* 3; *34* 5; *35* 5; *37* 3; *47* 3; *48* 3; *49* 3; *50* 5; *54* 2; *55* 3; *56* 2–3 app; *58* 3; *61* 2; *63* 3; **79** 12

τῆς, **74** ii 3; iii 3, 10; **76** i 26; ii 2, 3, 8; iii 2, 3, 8; iv 17, 20; v 3; vii 13, 21; viii 7, 11; ix 18; x 10, 22; xi 9 (twice), 13 (twice) 18; xiii 22 (twice); xiv 12, 16; xv 11; xvi 7; xvii 10; xviii 8, 9, 13, 20; xix 3; xx 9, 15, 25; xxi 5; BB 8; FF 2, 8; GG 6, 7, 12; **89** *2* 8?; *26* 3; *41* 2; **90** *2* a 4

τῷ, **76** HH ii 1, 3; **78** *18* 2

τῇ, **74** i 6; ii 6, 12; iii 6, 14

τόν, **78** *1* 4; *4* 3; *5* 3; *7* 4; *8* 5; *9* 4; **89** *23* 15?

τήν, **75** 20; **76** i 3, 12, 18, 23; ii 4, 13; iii 13, 21; iv 13, 22; v 5, 12; vi 3, 11, 18; vii 4, 10, 17; viii 3, 8, 15, 20, 26; ix 5, 15; x 4, 11, 18; xi 4, 14; xii 4, 13, 21; xiii 4, 11, 17; xiv 4, 13; xv 5, 13, 20; xvi 3, 13, 21; xvii 3, 12, 17; xviii 3, 15, 27; xix 5, 15, 21; xx 3, 11, 21; xxi 2; xxiv 3; GG 3, 10; HH i 3; ii 4, 7; **90** *2* a 4

τό, **75** 14?; **76** i 16, 27; ii 10; iii 9, 18; iv 10, 18, 26; v 10, 18; vi 8, 15, 22; vii 14, 22; viii 12, 23; ix 12; x 23; xi 20; xii 8 (twice), 17; xiii 8, 23; xiv 17; xv 9; xvi 8; xvii 7; xviii 10, 22, 32; xix 10; xx 17, 26; xxi 6; FF 4, 5 (twice), 9; GG 7, 13; **78** *5* 5

οἱ, **78** *77* 2; **81** ii 8

τῶν, **76** i 3, 6, 14, 21, 25; ii 7, 16; iii 4, 7, 17, 23, 26; iv 7, 15, 24; v 6, 8, 14, 16; vi 6, 20; vii 6, 11, 20; viii 5, 11, 17, 22, 27; ix 7, 9, 17; x 6, 8, 13, 21; xi 8, 17; xii 6, 15, 24; xiii 6, 12, 14, 19, 21; xiv 7, 9, 14, 15; xv 7, 14, 16, 21; xvi 5, 16, 22; xvii 4, 14, 18; xviii 6, 18, 29; xix 8, 16, 23; xx 5, 13, 22; xxi 3; xxiv 4; BB 7; FF 7; GG 5, 11; HH i 6; **81** ii 10

τοῖς, **78** *62* 2; *67* 5

τούς, **89** *2* 5; *31* 2; *41* 2

τά, **74** i 12; **76** ii 15; vi 4, 19; viii 16; ix 6; xi 15, 22; xv 6; xvi 4, 14; BB 3

οβ[. . .], **11 bis** c 4 app

ὀβολός

obolus, obol, abbreviated in **69** as *a*, in **70** as *ob*, in **73** as *b*. Pp. 122, 244, 254; **68** i 17–18 app; **69** 6a app; **78** *45* 6 app; *55* 4 app; *72* 5–6 app

a = a(s) = obol-, **69** 6a, 7, 8, 9, 10, 21, 24, 25, 25a, 26

ob( ), **70** a i 3; ii 20; f 1

ob(oli), **70** a i 8, 14, 21, 29; ii 4, 11, 17, 26, 34, 40; b i 3, 10, 17, 23; d 1, 8, 14, 20; e 4

ob(olos), **70** a i 7, 9, 13, 15, 20, 22, 28, 30, 32; ii 3, 5, 10, 12, 15, 16, 21, 22, 25, 27, 29, 33, 35, 39, 41; b i 2, 4, 9, 11, 13, 16, 18, 22, 24; d 2, 7, 9, 13, 15, 21; e 3, 5; f 2

(o)b(ol-), **73** a i 1, 5, 11, 14, 15, 17, 18, 19, 20, 21, 22, 23, 24, 26; ii 3, 4, 5, 6, 7, 8, 9, 10, 11, 12, 13, 14, 15, 16, 17; c 3, 6; f 4, 6

(o)b(oli), **73** a iii 27, 28, 29, 30

(o)b(olos), **73** a iii 17, 22, 23, 26

ὀβολ( ), **78** *37* 5 (twice); *51* 6

ὀβολοῦ, **78** *53* 6

ὀβολῶν, **76** FF 6; **78** *18* 6; *21* 5; *24* 5; *32* 5; *36* 5; *45* 4?; *46* 3; *48* 5; *49* 5; *54* 4; *55* 4; *66* 4

ὀβολοί, **78** *15* 6; *24* 10; *32* 5; *69* 5

ὀβολούς, **74** i 4, 12; ii 4, 11; iii 4, 12; **78** *72* 7; *70* 5 app

οἶδα

εἰδέναι, **76** i 8, 16, 27; ii 10; iii 9, 18; iv 10, 18, 26; v 10, 18; vi 8, 15, 22; vii 15, 22; viii 12, 23; ix 12; x 23; xii 17; xiii 8, 23; xiv 17; xv 9; xvi 8; xvii 7; xviii 10, 22, 32; xix 10; xx 17, 26; xxi 6; BB 10; FF 9; GG 7, 13

εἰδότος, **76** viii 28; **78** *9* 8; *22* 7; *23* 7–8; *39* 6; *56* 6

οἰκονόμος, pp. 332, 335

οἰκονόμου, **81** ii 6

οἰκονόμῳ, **79** 10

οἶνος: οἴνου, **78** *18* 4; *20* 4; *21* 4; *22* 5; *23* 4; *24* 4; *25* 2; *27* 3; *28* 2; *29* 4; *30* 7; *31* 3; *32* 3; *33* 4; *34* 6; *36* 4; *37* 4; *38* 3; *40* 5; *41* 4; *42* 4; *43* 3; *44* 4; *46* 2; *47* 4; *48* 4; *50* 6; *51* 5; *52* 5; *53* 4; *54* 3; *56* 2–3 app; *57* 3; *58* 3; *61* 3; *65* 3; *66* 3; *67* 3; *68* 4; *69* 4; *70* 4; *71* 4

ὀκτώ, **76** FF 6; **78** *15* 7; *37* 5 (twice); *49* 5; *69* 5

ὀκτωκαιδέκατος: ὀκτωκαιδεκάτου, **76** GG 3

ὁμοίως, **76** GG 4

ὁμολογέω, **76** xii 3; **78** *50* 4

ὁμοῦ, p. 313; **78** *57* 9 app

ὄνομα

ὀνομ[, **78** *12* 5

ὄνομα, **76** xii 8; **78** *5* 5

ὀνόμασι, **78** *62* 2?

ὀξίς: ὀξίδιν, **78** *64* 2

ὄξος: ὄξεος, **78** *15* 5

horm[, hormos, **9** 23 b–d app; **10** 12; **133** 5 app

ὅς, ἥ, ὅ: οὗ, **76** HH ii 7

ὅτι, **90** *2* a 1

οὐκ, **90** *2* a 1–2 app

ὀψώνιον: ὀψωνίου, **78** *23* 5

παρά, **74** i 3, 11; ii 3, 10; iii 3, 11; **75** 13, 20; **76** i 3, 12, 18, 23; ii 4, 13; iii 4, 12, 21; iv 4, 13, 22; v 4, 12; vi 3, 11, 18; vii 4, 10, 17; viii 3, 8, 15, 20, 26; ix 5, 14; x 4, 10, 17; xi 4, 14; xii 4, 13, 21; xiii 4, 10, 17; xiv 4, 12; xv 5, 13, 20; xvi 3, 13, 21; xvii 3, 11, 16; xviii 3, 15, 27; xix 5, 14, 20; xx 3, 11, 21; xxi 2; xxiv 3; BB 3; GG 3, 10; HH i 3; ii 5, 7; **78** *1* 4; *3* 4;

4 2; *5* 3; *6* 4; *7* 3; *8* 4; *9* 4; *10* 3; *12* 3; *15* 4; *17* 1; *18* 4; *19* 3; *20* 3; *22* 3; *23* 3; *24* 3; *25* 2; *27* 3; *28* 1; *29* 3; *30* 6; *31* 3; *32* 3; *33* 3; *34* 5; *36* 4; *38* 3; *39* 3; *40* 5; *41* 3; *42* 4; *43* 3; *44* 3; *46* 2; *47* 3; *48* 3; *49* 3; *50* 5; *51* 4; *52* 5; *53* 3; *56* 3; *57* 2; *58* 2; *61* 2; *63* 3; *65* 3; *66* 3; *67* 3; *68* 3; *69* 4; *70* 3; *71* 3; *72* 5; *73* 5; *74* 3; **79** 11; **90** *2* a 4

παραδέχομαι

παράδεξον, **78** *11* 3

παραδείξατε, **78** *11* 3 app

παραλήμπτης: παραλήμπτῃ, **78** *1* 3; *3* 3–4; *5* 2; *6* 3; *7* 2–3; *8* 3; *10* 2

παραλήμταις, **78** *11* 2

πάρειμι: παρόντος, **76** GG 13

πᾶς: πάντα, **90** *2* a 2

πέμπω: ἔπεμψα, **89** *41* 10 and app

πέντε, **76** i 5, 13, 20, 24; ii 6, 15; iii 5, 16, 25; iv 6, 14, 23; v 6, 15; vi 5, 13, 20; vii 5, 12, 18; viii 4, 9, 16, 21; ix 8; x 7, 11, 20; xi 7, 16; xii 5, 14, 23; xiii 5, 13, 20; xv 7, 15, 22; xvi 6, 17, 23; xvii 6, 13; xviii 7, 19, 30; xix 7, 17, 24; xx 14, 23; xxi 4; xxiv 5; BB 6; HH i 4; ii 7; **78** *48* 5; **89** *41* 11 and app

πεντήκοντα, **74** ii 4; **81** ii 10

πεντηκονταδύω, **74** i 12

πιττουργεῖον, **82** 2 app

πλήρης: πλήρες, **76** i 13, 24; ii 16; iii 5, 25; xvi 23; xvii 6; BB 6

πλεῖστα, **89** *2* 4 and app

ποιέω: ποιήσεις, **76** HH ii 3

πόλις: πόλιν, **90** *2* k 3

πολύς, p. 349 note 9

πολλοῖς, **89** *17* 11; *29* 12

potamofulacide (*abl.*), **10** 29

πραιτος?: πραιτων, **81** ii 8

πράκτωρ, **78** *6* 11

πράκτορες, **78** *77* 2

πρό, **89** *23* 1; **90** *2* i 2?

προγράφω: προγεγραμμένος, **76** i 15; iv 9; ix 10; xii 9; **78** *26* 3 app; **79** 9

προεῖπον: προείπομεν, **89** *41* 8 and app

πρόκειμαι

πρόκειται, **76** xi 21; xii 9

προκείμενοι, **81** ii 8

προκόπτω: προκοπέσθαι, **76** HH ii 8

πρός, **89** *31* 4?

προσφέρω: προσφερομένων, **76** BB 9

πρότερος: προτέρου, **79** 12

πρόχειρος?: προχείρωι, **76** xii 22

προχράω: προεχρησάμεν, **76** HH ii 5

προχρεία

ἐν προχρείας, **76** iii 23; iv 5, 14; vi 4; xii 4 (ἐν *om.*), 13; xiii 4, 11, 18; xv 5; xvi 4, 13; xvii 3; xx 11

ἐν προχρείᾳ, **76** i 3, 12, 19; ii 5, 14; iii 4, 14, 23; v 5, 15; vi 12; vii 18; viii 4, 9, 16, 20, 26; ix 6, 15; x 4, 18; xi 5, 15; xiv 5, 13; xv 13, 20; xvi 21; xviii 4, 16, 27; xix 5, 15, 21; xx 3; **78** *9* 4; *13* 2

ἐπὶ προχρείᾳ, **78** *2* 3

ἐν προχείρωι, **76** xii 22

πρῶτος

]πρωτ[, **89** *23* 11

πρώτου, **74** i 13

πρώτων, **81** ii 8 app

πυρός: πυροῦ, **78** *2* 4; *6* 8; **81** ii 9

(πυροῦ), *symbol* +, **78** *11* 4 (twice)

ργε (*numeral*?), **11 bis** c 6

ῥώννυμι, p. 349 and note 9

ἔρρωσο, **89** *2* 15; *9* 7; *26* 5 app; *29* 11

ἐρρῶσθαι, **76** HH ii 8

Σεβαστός; *see also Index 9*, Augustus

Σεβαστοῦ, **75** i 6; ii 7, 17; iii 7; iv 24; v 8, 15, 16; vi 6, 14, 21; vii 6, 12, 20; viii 5, 11, 22; ix 8, 9, 17; x 8, 13, 21; xi 8; xii 7, 15, 24; xiii 6, 13, 15, 19, 21; xiv 7, 9, 14, 15; xv 8, 15, 16, 22; xvi 22; xvii 5, 14, 18; xviii 6, 19, 30; xix 9, 17, 23; xx 5; xxiv 4; FF 7; GG 5, 11; HH i 6; **81** ii 10

σημειοφόρος, *see also Index 9*, signifer; **74** i 4, 9; ii 1, 9; iii 1, 8; **76** iv 25; vi 7; viii 28; xii 7; xvi 7, 19; xvii 6; xviii 31; xx 15; **78** *37* 1

σημειοφόρῳ, **85** 4

σημειόω

ἐσημιοσόμην, **78** *68* 7

σεσημείωμαι, **78** *2* 8; *4* 9; *11* 8; *22* 10

σῖτος

σιτο (*nom*?), **79** 11

σίτου, **78** *1* 3; *3* 4, 5; *5* 2; *6* 4, 5?; *7* 3; *8* 4; *10* 3; *11* 3, 6; *12* 3

σῖτον, **78** *1* 4; *4* 3; *5* 3; *6* 5?; *7* 4; *8* 5; *9* 4; *10* 4

σπεῖρα, *see also Index 4, Military Affairs*, cohort

σπείρης, **74** i 1, 9; ii 1, 3, 9; iii 1, 3, 8, 10; **89** *41* 2; **90** *2* a 4

στήγη, **82** 2, 8, 11, 12

στρατηγός, p. 271

στρατιώτης, *see also Index 9*, miles

στρατιωτη[, **89** *27* 3

στρατιωτα[, **90** *2* q 2

στρατιώτης, **78** *1* 1; *7* 1; *10* 1; *18* 1; *21* 1; *23* 1; *32* 1; *35* 1–2; *48* 6; *50* 1–2; *51* 2; *53* 1; *54* 6; *61* 1; *69* 2; *70* 1; *72* 2

στρατιώτῃ, **78** *11* 3

στρατιῶται, **90** *2* a 1–2 app

στρατιωτῶν, **90** *2* k 4

στρατιώτας, **89** *2* 6; *31* 2; *41* 2

σύ

σου, **74** i 3, 11; ii 3, 10; iii 3, 11; **75** 13, 20; **76** i 3, 12, 18, 23; ii 4, 13; iii 4, 13, 21; iv 4, 13, 22; v 4, 12; vi 3, 11, 18; vii 4, 7, 10; viii 3, 8, 15, 20, 26; ix 5, 15; x 4, 10, 17; xi 4, 14; xii 4, 13, 21; xiii 4, 10, 17; xiv 4, 12; xv 5, 13, 20; xvi 3, 13, 21; xvii 3, 12, 16; xviii 3,

σύ—cont.

σου—cont.

15, 27; xix 5, 14, 20; xx 3, 11, 21; xxi 2; xxiv 3; BB 3; GG 3, 10; HH i 3; **78** *1* 4; *3* 5; *4* 2; *5* 3; *6* 4; *7* 4; *8* 4; *9* 4; *10* 4; *12* 3; *15* 4; *17* 2; *18* 4; *19* 3; *20* 4; *22* 3; *23* 3; *24* 3; *25* 2; *27* 3; *28* 1; *29* 4; *30* 6; *31* 3; *32* 3; *33* 3; *34* 5; *36* 4; *38* 3; *39* 3; *40* 5; *41* 3; *42* 4; *43* 3; *44* 3; *45* 3; *46* 2; *47* 3; *48* 3; *49* 3; *50* 5; *51* 5; *52* 5; *53* 4; *56* 3; *57* 2; *58* 2; *61* 2; *63* 3; *65* 3; *66* 3; *67* 3; *68* 3; *69* 4; *70* 4; *71* 3; *72* 5; *74* 3; **79** 11; **90** *2* a 3

σοι, **89** *41* 15

σε, **76** HH ii 8; **89** *29* 11

ὑμῶν, **78** *73* 5

σύν, **78** *77* 2; **89** *23* 9?

συνευδοκέω: συνευδωκῶ, **78** *57* 5, 6

σύναρσις: συνάρσεως, **78** *11* 5

συντιμάω: συντιμήθη, **78** *31* 3; *33* 4; *38* 5; *40* 7; *42* 5; *63* 4

συστρατιώτης, **78** *2* 5; *23* 6

sphaeromachiam, **67** 8

σῶμα, **76** xii 8

τάσσω: τεταγμένοις, **90** *2* a 1–2 app

τεσ̣[, **89** *2* 13

τέσσαρες, **74** i 12

τέσσαρα, **78** *15* 6

τεσσάρων, **78** *32* 4; *46* 3; *57* 3–4 app

τετρακόσιοι: τετρακόσια, **74** i 4; ii 4

τιμή

τιμῆς, **78** *15* 4; *44* 3 app; *65* 3; *66* 3; *67* 3; *68* 4; *69* 4; *70* 4; *71* 4

τιμήν, **75** 20 app

τίμιος

τιμιωτάτῳ, **76** HH ii 1

το..σα.χ̣ρ̣της.[, **75** 13

τρεῖς, τρία

τριῶν, **78** *18* 6; *21* 5; *24* 5; *25* 3; *36* 5; *45* 4?; *46* 3; *51* 6; *53* 5; *54* 4; *56* 3?; *58* 4; *61* 4

τρεῖς, **74** iii 4

τρία, **74** i 4, 12; **89** *2* 10?

τριάκοντα, **74** i 11

τριακόσιοι: τριακόσια, **74** iii 4 app

τρικέραμον, p. 312 note 4

τρικέρ[αμ-, **61** 3

τρικεράμιον, **78** *31* 3; *62* 2

τρικέραμον, **78** *36* 4; *38* 4; *40* 6; *43* 3; *45* 3; 3–4; *46* 2; *49* 4; *51* 5; *53* 4; *60* 4, 5

τρικέραμα, **78** *48* 4

triceramon, **78** *44* 3 app; *45* 6 app; *49* 4 app; *58* 2 app

tricerama, **78** *27* 3 app

τροπωτήρ, **82** 5 app

ὑγιαίνω, p. 349 note 9

ὑγιαίνειν, **89** *17* 12

υἱός, **78** *22* 6

ὑμεῖς, *see σύ*

ὑπατεία: ὑπατείας, **76** BB 4; FF 5

ὑπείκω: ὑπείκουσι, **90** *2* a 2

ὑπέρ, **74** i 5; ii 5, 11; iii 4, 12; **76** i 4, 7, 15, 20, 24, 27; ii 5, 9, 14; iii 6, 9, 18; iv 9, 17, 23, 26; v 9, 17; vi 3, 7, 11, 15, 22; vii 4, 11, 14, 18, 21; viii 4, 9, 12, 15, 21, 23, 26, 28; ix 11, 19; x 5, 11, 19, 23; xi 6, 10, 16, 19; xii 17; xiii 7, 11, 18, 23; xiv 6, 14, 17; xv 5, 8, 14, 21; xvi 4, 8, 14; xvii 4, 7; xviii 5, 9, 17, 21, 28, 31; xix 7, 10, 15, 22; xx 4, 12, 16, 22, 25; xxi 6; xxiv 3; BB 9; FF 9; GG 3, 7, 11, 13; **78** *1* 4; *2* 4; *3* 6; *4* 3, 6; *6* 9; *7* 5; *8* 5; *9* 5, 7; *10* 4, 7; *11* 3; *12* 4; *16* 3; *22* 6; *23* 7; *39* 6; *42* 6; *56* 6; *58* 7; *70* 4; **79** 12, 15; **81** ii 9; **90** *2* a 1–2 app

ὑπογράφω

ὑπογράφομαι, **78** *5* 5 app

ὑπογράφοντος, **76** xii 8

φακός: φακοῦ, **78** *15* 4

χαίρω

χαῖρε?, **78** *34* 4

χαίρειν, **74** i 3, 10; ii 3, 10; iii 3, 10; **75** 13; **76** i 3, 12, 18, 23; ii 4, 13; iii 4, 12, 21; iv 4, 12, 22; v 4, 12; vi 2, 10, 18; vii 3, 10, 17; viii 3, 8, 15, 20, 26; ix 5, 14; x 4, 10, 17; xi 4, 14; xii 3, 13, 21; xiii 3, 10, 17; xiv 4, 12; xv 4, 12, 19; xvi 3, 12, 20; xvii 3, 11, 16; xviii 3, 15, 26; xix 4, 14, 20; xx 2, 10, 21; xxi 2; xxiv 2; BB 3; FF 4; GG 2, 10; HH i 3; ii 12; **78** *1* 3; *2* 3; *3* 4; *4* 2; *5* 2; *6* 4; *7* 3; *8* 4; *9* 3; *10* 3; *11* 2; *12* 2; *15* 3; *16* 2; *18* 3; *19* 3; *20* 3; *21* 3; *22* 3; *24* 3; *25* 1; *27* 2; *28* 1; *29* 3; *30* 6; *31* 2; *32* 3; *33* 2; *35* 3; *36* 3; *37* 3; *38* 2; *39* 3; *40* 4; *41* 3; *42* 3; *43* 2; *44* 2; *45* 3; *46* 2; *47* 2; *48* 3; *49* 2; *50* 4; *51* 4; *52* 4; *53* 3; *54* 2; *55* 2; *56* 2; *57* 2; *58* 2; *61* 2; *63* 2; *65* 2; *66* 2; *67* 2; *68* 2; *69* 3; *70* 3; *71* 3; *72* 5; *73* 4; *74* 2; **79** 10; **81** 7; **89** *2* 4; *37* 2; *40* 2

chartam, **10** 18

χείρ: χειρί, **78** *25* 4; *60* 2; *67* 4?

χειριστής (=*curator*?), **78** *25* 3–4 app; *64* 1

cheirographum, p. 242

chora, **10** 25

[cho]ran, **11** ii 3

χορηγέω: χορηγηθέντα, **74** i 12 app

χοῦς, p. 312 note 4

χρόνος, p. 349 note 9

χρόνοις, **89** *17* 12; *29* 13

χωρηγέντα, **74** i 12

ὡς, **76** xi 21; xii 9; **90** *2* a 5, 6

Broken words listed in a reverse index

]τρια, **89** *2* 10

].ακοσιοι, **74** iii 4

..φιων..σ̣αν, **35** 1

]ε̣σπου̣α̣ι̣γευθημεν, **76** BB 4–5

]ογου, **11 bis** c 4

. . . μου, **11 bis** c 5
]ενβωμου, **78** *59* 2
]. κρατου, **11 bis** c 5
]ọστου, **89** *2* 13

Broken words listed by the first extant letter
]μαλεθ. [*or*]μαληα. [, **89** *37* 3
]. πịφ. [.]., **76** vi 1
]φοροụ[, **90** *2* a 7

Index 9: Latin Words

a, ab, **5** iii 6; **14** 4 app; **20** 6, 9, 20, 15 app; **34** verso ii 12 app; **47** ii 3 app; **50** i 14; **51** ii 23; **63** i 30 app, 32 app; ii 10; **64** i 20, 25, 32; ii 14; **66** a ii 2?; **67** 6 app; **75** 3; **77** a i 9; **83** 2, 4, 5, 8, 10, 11, 12, 14, 15, 17, 19, 21, 23, 24; **87** 4; **88** *2* verso; **89** *1* verso 3; *7* 10; *7* verso; *10* 1? (twice); *10* verso 2; *14* verso 2; *15* verso 2; *25* verso 2; *47* verso 2; **98** *4* 7; *e* 3; **99** *1* 6; *1* verso 2; *2* 4; *2* verso 2; *3* 4; *3* verso 2; **100** 3; **112** verso 2; **117** i 25; ii 10

a = a(s) = obolus, *see Index 8*, ὀβολός

a[, ạ. . . , *notation*, **1** viii 22; ix 6; xxix 21; **2** vii 29; **9** 27 m; 31 h; **37** 4; **40** ii 14

ạ.ạrio, **63** ii 33

a.c·, *rank*, *duty*?, **49** 3

ạ.l[, *notation*, **38** ii 9

ạḅ.[, **89** *10* 1

]ạbep.[, *ab epị[stul-* ?, **89** *10* 1 and app

absens (abs, apsentes), **61** ii 8; **62** 3; **63** ii 17, 23, 38; **91** *2* ii 6 and app; **96** 1 app; pp. 180, 181, 201, 202, 215, 216, 233

ac, **117** i 2

ạċ[, *actuarius*?, **50** i 3

accedere

- [accedun]ṭ, **63** i 29 app
- [access]ẹ[r(unt)], **63** i 29
- accesserunt, **63** i 35; **64** i 19

accipere, *see also Index 8*, λαμβάνω

- accepi[, **132** 1
- accepi, **75** 2–3; **80** 4
- accep(it), **72** 7 and 13
- accepi[t, **132** 1 app
- accepit, **68** ii 3, 14, 24; iii 2, 13, 23; **69** 3, 11, 19; **70** a i 7, 13, 20; ii 3, 10, 16, 33, 39; iii 3, 10, 23; c 3; e 3; g 5 and 11; b i 2 and 17; ii 13 and 20; **71** a 1 and 10; b 5
- acceper(unt), **27** a i 1
- accepisse **77** a i 2, 8, 14; b 2 and 8; accepi[sse, **132** 1 app
- accepta **87** 24
- acc(epta) **88** *2* 4; **89** *4* iii 4; *6* 10; *8* 8; *12* i 5 app; *19* 10; *20* 7; *21* 2; *23* 18; *25* 8; *26* 6; *28* 8; *29* 14; *31* 8; *32* 7; *34* 10; **91** *1* i 2; *2* i 2; **92** ii 16 and app; **99** 1, 3; **109** 2
- accep(ta) **27** b ii 4; **114** 2
- accepti, **63** i 34 app; ii 13

acta, actum, *see* agere

actuarius (actarius), *see also Index 4, Military Affairs*; **1** xvii 3 app; **2** xxii 13 app; **86** 6; pp. 11, 12

actuitum, **53** b 20 and 28

ad, **1** i 4; ii 6, 7, 12, 13?; iii a 2; h 2, 3, 4, 5; vii 7; viii 25; ix 2, 3, 4, 5, 7, 18, 19, 20, 21; xii 2, 3, 4, 5, 11; xiii 3, 7, 22; xiv 11, 12, 16, 17, 18, 19, 20, 21; xvi 12; xvii 7 and 12; xviii 3; xix 5, 6, 7, 8, 9, 10, 11; xx 20; xxi 2, 8, 11; xxii 1, 7; xxiv 10; xxv 1 and 9; xxvi 5 and 6; xxvii 14; xxviii 3, 16, 17; xxix 3 and 6; xxx 1, 2, 3, 4, 5, 6, 7, 8; xxxi 3 and 8; xxxii 12; xxxiii 2 and 19; xxxiv 4, 10, 24, 30; xxxv 3; xxxvi 7, 9, 19, 22, 26; xxxvii 26; xxxviii 18; xxxix 28 and 30; xli 17 and 25; xlii 8 and 23; xliii 29; **2** i 1; vi 29; ix 6 and app, 16; x 19 and app; 21 app; xi 28 and 31; xii 10; xiii 6; xiv 16; xv 19; xvi 17; xix 4; xxix 24; xxx 24; xxxi 6; xxxii 20 and 26; xxxiii 8, 11, 12, 14, 15; xxxiv 17 and 28; xxxv 17, 19, 24; xxxvi 3; xxxvii 7, 8, 9, 16, 17, 21, 24; xxxviii 31; xxxix 10, 15, 19; xl 17 and 28; xli 17; xliii 16, 18, 19, 26; xliv 20 and 26; xlv 2 and 14; **4** m 5 app; **9** 4 d; 12 f app; 13 f; 23 b–d app; 31 e; 32 g app; **10** 2, 5, 8, 12, 18, 20, 23, 27; **13** 13; **15** ii 7; **17** a 12 (*at*); **47** i 6 (twice), 13, 16, 17; ii 2, 6?, 7, 8, 21?; ii 3 app; **48** 5, 7, 9; **49** *1*; **50** i 1 (twice), 4, 8 (twice), 10; **51** i 23; ii 2?, 8, 11, 13 (twice), 15, 17, 20; **52** b 9, c 4; **53** b 2; **63** i 24 app, 26 app; ii 4 app, 7, 22, 31, 33, 34, 35 (twice); **64** i 26; **65** 5, 6, 4 app; **66** a i 2; ii 1; b i 23 and 29; ii 1, 3, 4, 6, 8; **67** 5, 6, 7; **68** ii 19; iii 18; **69** 10 app; **70** b ii 13 a; **71** a 11; b 6; **81** ii 14; **88** *1* 14; **89** *1* 5; *42* 13; **90** *1* a 4; *1* c 2; **91** *2* i 14; **92** ii 10, 11?; **93** a 1; **98** *2* 6; *4* 7 and 8; **101** a ii 10; **114** 5; p. 225

ad dom(inum) n(ostrum), pp. 13, 14; *see also* dominus

ad frum(entum), *see also* frumentum; **2** xvi 17; p. 11

ad hordeum, *see also* hordeum; **2** xvi 17 app; pp. 11, 15

ad hostias, pp. 12, 14, 17; *see also* hostias

ad leones, pp. 13, 14, 15; *see also* leones

ad mamm(aeam?), pp. 14, 17; *see also* mamm

ad man ambul, pp. 13, 15; *see also* ambul

ad opinionem peten(dam), p. 14; *see also* opinio

ad opinionem quaerendam, p. 14
ad opinionem stipendii, p. 14; *see also* stipendium
ad praetori(um), p. 14; *see also* praetorium
ad sacrahimag, pp. 14, 15; *see also* sacrahimag
ad[. . .]mọpiṇị, **65** 4
ad.[.].[. .]ṭiọnẹm, **92** ii 8
ad bonas, **67** 7
ạḍc̣ur.ị, **102** a 10
adcurare, **102** a 10 app
adducere, **63** ii 35
Adiabenicus, **117** i 14–16 app; **123** a 2 app
adiutor, **34** recto i 10 app; verso ii 16 app; p. 141; *see also Index 4, Military Affairs*
adl.[, **51** ii 2
adlectus, **47** ii 21 app
admittere
  admissa, **47** i 6 and 16; ii 11; **50** i 1 and 8; **51** ii 6?; pp. 189, 191, 201
  admiss[us], **63** ii 4 app
  admittenda, **52** b 2 and 14; p. 201
adnare: adnavit, **53** b 11 app
adnotare, **99** *1* 8 app
adplicare
  adplicari, **92** ii 14
  adplicui, **98** *2* a 3
adytum, **53** b 14
aedes, **53** b 15
aedit(uus), **47** i 7 and 17; ii 12; p. 192; *see also Index 4, Military Affairs*
aeg, *aeg(ypti)*?, *aeg(er)*?, **9** 23 **d**
aeger, **8** viii 4 app; x 11 app; **63** ii 44; **66** b ii 6; **89** *4* i 7 app; p. 181
aequatum, -am, **83** 4, 19, 23, 24; p. 341
aerarium, **69** 10 app
aestimare
  aestima, **91** *2* ii 8; *in app*, aestimarem
  aestimatum, **83** 15; p. 340
aeternus, **117** ii 5
aeternitas, **117** i 3
ạeti, **67** 17
ạge. .[, **102** a 10
agere
  agant, **90** *1* b 5
  act(um), **77** a i 11; **102** a 10 app
  acta, **99** *1* 7 and app; 8 app; *3* 6; f app; **100** 4; pp. 2, 179, 180, 420, 431
  acto, **133** 2 app
  ag(ens), agens, **53** a ii 2 and app; **58** ii 14; p. 14
ạgẹsc̣. .a[, **86** 2
aggerem, **9** 13 f app
agita. . . . .e.ṭọṣ, agitare, agitatae, **50** i 15 and app
ala, *see also Index 8*, ἴλη *and Index 4, Military Affairs*; **11** ii 2 app; **20** 5, 8, 11; **38** i 10 app; **39** 16 app; **53** b 27; b 10 app, 22 app, 29 app; **63** i 21 app; **64** i 25–26; **73** a iii 25 and app; **75** 6 app; **76**, *see* ἴλη; **80** 1; **89** *39* 5 and app; **102** a 12; pp. 84, 138, 146, 155, 168, 171, 179, 202, 204, 270, 283, 285, 333, 346
alarium, **63** ii 33 app
album, *noun*, **2** xl 19 and app
albus, -a, -um, **83** 2, 8, 14
Al(exandrino)?, **9** 32 g app
alexạ[, **2** xxiv 18
Alexandriana, **47** i 2, 10; ii 2, 15; **48** 4; p. 183
Alecsandrini, **9** 16 c app
alimentatum, *supine*, **63** ii 19 app
a[l]ị[o]ṣ, **89** *4* i 6
alter, **1** xxx 8; xxxii 14; xxxix 5; **2** xxxii 26; xxxix 11; **31** i 7; **50** i 3; p. 5
ambul( ), ambulare, ambulatio, *see also* ad man; **2** xli 25, 29; xlii 18; xliii 4; **23** ii 8; pp. 13–14
amicire: amic̣[tus], **117** ii 17
amittere
  amisi, **89** *5* 14
  amisit, **8** iii 5 app; **83** 1, 3, 6, 7, 13, 22
amphora, **82** 2
an[, **77** a i 19; **132** 3
annona, **63** ii 31; pp. 245, 350
annus, *see also Index 8*, ἔτος
  anni, **68** ii 3, 14, 24; iii 2, 13, 23; **69** 3, 11, 19; **132** 4?
  anno, **10** 3, 4, 5, 6, 7, 8, 9, 12, 13, 15, 18, 19, 20 (twice), 21, 22, 23, 24, 25, 27, 28, 29, 30, 31 (twice), 32, 33; **63** i 22; p. 118
  ann(o), **87** 24
  ann(orum), **87** 15 and 22; annor(um), **87** 12, 14, 18, 20
  annis, **89** *1* 10; *5* 12; **91** *2* i 10; **111** 3; p. 349 note 8
ante, **5** ii 16; **66** b ii 8; **97** a 4
Antoniniana, **89** *1* 3; *1* verso 2; *18* 2 and app; *20* 2; *39* 5; **91** *2* i 6; **101** a i 6 app; **110** 2
[αντ]ω̣νειν̣[ιανης], **89** *41* 3
apolusimos, p. 242
Appadanensis, **91** *1* i 8
appellatus, **117** i 24, 26, 28; ii 10 and 16
Apriana, **73** a iii 25
aqua, **63** ii 9
aquaria (porta), **13** 13 app; **15** i 7 app; ii 10, b 4 app; **17** a 6 and app; p. 128
aquila, **51** ii 11, 17; **53** b 15
ar. . . . .s, **50** i 15 and app
Arabicus, **117** i 14–16 app; **123** a 2 app
Arabs, **53** a i 2
  Arabum, **15** ii 13; p. 128
arca, **69** 2 app
ạṛṃ, **9** 17 c app
arma: armorum, **58** ii 4; **71** a 3 and 12: *arm(orum)*; **73** a ii 18; a iii 10 app: *c(ustos?) a(rmorum?)*; **76** xv 8: αρμορου; **78** *39* 5–6: αρμωρω; **129** 6: *a(rmorum) c(ustos)*; p. 438

armamenta(rium), armamentar(ium), **9** 3 k and app; 4 f–g, k app; 26 h
armentum, **63** ii 35
armus: a(rmo), **83** 2, 5, 10, 15; **99** *3* 4
aṛṣ, **62** 5
arx: arcis, **20** 6 app
a(s) = obolus, **69** 6a and app; 7, 8, 9, 10, 21, 24, 25, 25a, 26
ascita, **59** i 12 and app; p. 382
Asianus: ασιανων, **74** i 5, 13; ii 5, 12; iii 5, 13
asin, **9** 12 e and app
asinarius: asinaṛịs, **9** 12 e–f app
asserere: asserente, **86** 6
auctoritas: auctoritate, **90** *1* b 2
aud.ṭi, **133** 2
audire, **133** 2 app
augere: auctos, **113** 4
augustus, -a, -um
  coh I Augusta Lusitanorum, **64** i 1
Augustus, *title*; *see also* Σεβαστός
  aug, **98** *4* 2 and app
  Aug(ustus), **117** i 27; ii 18; i 27–29 app
  Augustum, **123** b 2
  castra Aug(usti), **77** a i 11 and 19; b 6
  equites promoti Aug(ustorum), **86** 1 and 6
  fab(er) Aug(usti), **59** i 9
  Genius Aug(usti), **117** i 29; ii 17
  Iuno Aug(ustae), **117** ii 26
  leg(atus) Aug(usti), **53** a ii 2 app; **112** verso 2 app; **114** verso 2
  leg(atus) Aug(ustorum), **99** *1* verso 3; *2* verso 2; *3* verso 2
  lib(ertus) Aug(ustorum), **91** *1* i 6; p. 383
  mater Aug(usti), **117** ii 26
  milites Aug(usti), **117** i 25
  natalis Aug(ustae), **117** ii 26
  proc(urator) Aug(usti), **63** ii 26; ii 5 app; **89** *4* i 5; *5* 3; *8* 9; *14* 5; *15* 3; *18* 3; pp. 350, 361
  proc(urator) Aug(ustorum), **83** 15 and 17; **91** 1 verso 2; *1* i 6 app; *2* verso 2; **98** *2* 2; pp. 383, 397; *see also* procurator
  salus Aug(usti), **117** i 3
  signa Aug(usti), **47** i 6 and 17; **50** i 2 and 8
  socer? Aug(usti), **117** i 11
  Aug(usto) cos, **2** xvi 5; xxvi 10; xxxi 20; **10** 16 app; **20** 15 app; **31** i 12; ii 6; **33** i 1; **50** i 14; **66** a i 12; b i 2, 8, 14, 21, 27; b ii 26; **86** 6; **98** *3* 5; **99** i 3 and 9
aureus: aureos, **98** *4* 9; p. 402
autem, **98** *2* a 7
authenticus: authenticam, **87** 29

b, **9** 2 m and app
b = obolus, *see under* ὀβολός
b[.]..[, **9** 21 e
baḍịo..nus, -a, -um: baḍ[i]ọ[ca]nam, **83** 21 and app
ballio, *see* balneum
ballista
  ad balistas, **13** 13; p. 128
  bal(listarum), **52** b 8 app
balneum
  bal, **52** b 8; c 3
  balnei, **9** 3 m app; **47** ii 9
  ballio, **9** 3 m and app; 4 e app, h, k app, n; 5 g; 8 d; 15 b, d app; 17 e, f; 18 e app; 21 e app, f, g; 22 b, e–m
bareton, **34** recto ii 1; verso ii 13
bene, **89** *1* 10; *12* i 9; *38* 10; *39* 10; *46* 2; *48* 8; **91** *2* i 10; **98** *2* a 3; **107**; **111** 3; p. 349
beneficiarius, **9** 2 m app; **51** ii 18a app
beneficium: beneficio, **9** 2 m app; **9** 14 b and app
bes, **73** i 17 app, 18 app
bilateris, **70** a ii 19 app
bimum, **83** 5; p. 341
binos, **98** *4* 9
bonisessus, bonosessus, **50** i 4 app
bonus
  bonos?, **48** 9
  bonis?, **50** i 4 and 10
  bona, **88** *1* 8
  bonas?, **67** 7
bos: b(ouem), **117** i 4 (four times), 6, 8 (three times), 9, 13, 16 (twice), 18, 22 (twice), 24 (four times); ii 2, 3, 4, 5, 6, 20, 21, 23, 24, 25, 26; iii 1, 5 (twice), 6, 8; ii 22 app
bouleutes, p. 242
breviculus, p. 2
brevis, pp. 2, 3, 4
bucinator, p. 11; **58** i 35 app
  buc̣[, **2** xiii 31 and app
  buc, **50** i 2 and 9; b 2
  bucina[, **51** i 4

c̣, *meaning unknown*, **4** a i 9
c, *see* ciuis, clarissimus, coepit, commeatus
c̣.c̣ḥ, **9** 24 b
cdot, p. 146; **24** 4 app, 6 app, 8 app, 10 app
c̣ ẹ, **53** b 16
c̣ạ[, **9** 10 n; **40** ii 23
ca.[, **51** ii 13 and app: *car*[*cerem*?
C̣Ạ[, **52** f 2
cacula, caculatus, **9** 4 k app
c̣ạec̣, **9** 24 6 app
caerimonia: cerimonias, **117** i 19
Caesar, *name*, **117** ii 12 and 13
Caesar, Καῖσαρ, *title*
  Caesar, **117** i 23; ii 16; **91** *1* i 6 app; **122** 5 app
  Caesaris, **79** 4; **117** i 11 and 12; **123** a 3; pp. 332, 434
  Καίσαρος, **74** i 8 and 14; ii 7 and 13; iii 7, 15, 16; **78** *73* 7; **79** 10
  Caesare, **98** *3* 5; **99** *1* 3 and 10
  Caesarum, **86** 2

Καισάρων, **76** i 14, 20, 25; iii 14, 17, 26; xi 17; **81** ii 6
cal, *see also* cunicul(os); **9** 10 n app; 12 d–g app
cal(ceamenta), **9** 6 m; 4 e app; 6 k app
calcem, **9** 6 k; cal(cem), **9** 4 e app; 12 f app
calị.[, **73** c 12
calidam, *adj.*, **83** 19 app
caliga
caligae, **73** c 12 app
caligas, **68** ii 7, 18, 28; iii 6, 17, 27; **69** 6, 14, 23
caligatus, **73** c 12 app
caligati, **59** i 14; **61** ii 10 app; p. 212
cal(igatorum), **47** i 1 and 9; ii 1 and 14; **54** a–c 3; [caliga]t[o]ṛ(um), **50** i 5
calo, **9** 4 k app
camelus
camelorum, **52** b 5 app
camelos, **89** *5* 6 app
campus
campi, **48** 8; **102** a 8a app
καμπι, **76** ii 8; xx 24
καμπου, **76** xix 9
Cappadox
Cappadocem, **99** *3* 3
[Cappa]doces?, **30** i 2 app
carcer
ḳarc·, **52** b 15
caṛ[cerem?, **51** ii 13
ç̣ari.i, **55** c 3
carrarius, **58** ii 6; p. 180
karissiṃ[e], **87** 10; p. 349
casṭ[, **40** ii 18
castellum, **5** ii 6 app
castello, **65** 3; **19** 6 app
cas(trensis) *or* cas(tris), **37** 4
castr(ensis) *or* castr(is), **39** 4, 5, 16, 18, 22, 23
castrensis, p. 165 and note 2
castrum, castra
castri, **5** ii 14; ii 6 app
kas⟨t⟩rae, **63** ii 21 and app
castrorum, **10** 3
castra, **48** 5; **89** *44* 2; *45* 1 and app; **90** *1* b 3
castris, **51** ii 9; **90** *1* a 8; [castr(is)], **77** a i 11
[cedun]t, **63** i 29 app
celeber: celebres, **54** a–c 6 app
centenis, **99** *2* 5
centum, **75** 5; **77** a i 3; **99** *1* 7
(centuria) *or* (centurio), *symbol* ϒ, **92** ii 6; **94** a 2
centuria: *for individual centuries see Index 4, Military Affairs*; **2** xxxviii 8 app; xl 9 app; **38** i 11 app; **58** i 35 app; **69** 2 app; p. 12
κεντυρια, *dat*, **74** i 6; ii 6 and 12; iii 6 and 14
κεντυριας, *gen*, **78** *65* 1
(centuria-), *symbol* ϒ, **1** i 1; xi 1; xxi 1; xxvi 13; xliii 19, 22, 30; xliv 1, 10; **2** vi 18; xi 14; xvi 16; xxxiii 9; xxxviii 8; xliii 15; xliv 1, 11; xlv 3, 10; **4** b i 1; **6** ii 22; iv 16; x 28; **8** iii 7; v 9; vii 26; x 1; **9** 4 b app, d app, m; 5 f, m; 7 d; 8 f–n; 9 f–n; 11 g; 15 d app; 15 f; 16 f, g, m; 17 d; 20 f–k; 24 b app; 25 k app; 26 f app, g; 29 b; 32 g app; **11** ii 3; 6 app; **11 bis** a 2; **12** a–c 10; e 4; **13** 8, 15, 16, 18; **14** 1, 4 app; **15** i 1, 6, 8, 9, 10 (twice), 11, 14, 15, 17, 19, 20, 21 (twice), 22, 23 (twice); ii 3, 5, 6 (twice), 7, 8 (twice), 9, 10, 12, 13 (twice), 14, 15 (twice), 16, 17, 18, 19, 20, 21; b 2, 10 app; c 4, 5; d 2; g; **16** recto 2, 3; verso 1, 2; **17** a 1, 2, 3, 4, 5, 6, 7, 8, 9; **18** 3, 4; **19** 3, 5, 6; **21** 2–16 and 18–21; **23** i 4, 6, 8; iv 8; **27** a i 2, 7, 13; ii 1, 6; **29** 5, 12; **31** i 4; **32** 1, 4, 8, 12; **33** ii 1; **34** recto i 3, 10, 20; ii 2, 6, 10, 12, 15, 20; verso i 1; **46** 3; **47** i 4 (three times), 12 (twice), 14, 15; ii 5, 6, 9, 18, 19; **48** 2; **49** 3 app; **51** i 1, 5, 14; ii 18 (twice), 19; **53** b 26; d; e 4, 5 app; **55** b 5; **64** i 34, 37, 40, 42; ii 1, 16, 19, 23, 26, 29; **66** a i 9; a ii 5, 8, 10, 13, 16; b i 17; b ii 21, 23 and app; **67** 7, 11, 12; **69** 2; **77** a i 2, 6, 13, 14; b 1, 7, 9; **81** ii 12; **88** 1, 5; **89** *1* 5 a; *12* ii 2, 4, 8 app; **92** iii 4, 9, 15, 19; v 6, 12, 19; vi 19; vii 15; viii 4, 11; ix 3, 7
(centuria-), *symbol* ⳩, **74** i 2, 9; ii 2, 9; iii 2, 9; **78** *1* 2; *2* 7; *5* 1; *10* 1; *14* 3; *18* 1; *19* 1; *21* 2; *23* 2, 6; *31* 1; *32* 2; *35* 2; *39* 2; *40* 3; *48* 6; *50* 2; *51* 2; *53* 2; *55* 1; *56* 1; *61* 1; *69* 2; *70* 2; *72* 2, 3; *73* 1; *76* 2
centurio, *for individual centurions see Index 4, Military Affairs*
centurio, **74** i 3 app; pp. 12, 277
centurionis, **13** 18 app; p. 128
(centurion-), *symbol* ϒ, **10** 14; **11** ii 3; **13** 18; **15** i 22; **50** i 7, 13, 14; ii 7; **51** ii 3, 11, 16, 21; **52** a 6; b 10, 12; c 5; **53** b 26; c 5 app; d; e 4, 5 app; **54** a–c 3; **58** i 2, 35; **63** i 27, 28; ii 1, 15, 32, 39, 42; **64** i 15, 20; **69** 2; **77** a i 9, 15 (twice); **89** *10* verso 1
cerae, *gen*, **82** 8
ceraius, cerarius, **58** ii 9 app
cerinus, *adj.*, ceruinus, *adj.*, **83** 2 app and 24 app
cetero[, **90** *1* b 4
chartam, **10** 18
cheirographum, p. 242
chora, **10** 25; [cho]ran?, **11** ii 3
cibariator, pp. 311, 312; *for individual* cibariatores *see Index 4, Military Affairs*
κιβαριατορι, **78** *15* 2; *16* 2; *18* 2; *19* 2; *20* 3; *21* 3; *22* 2; *24* 2; *25* 1; *27* 2; *29* 2; *30* 5; *31* 2; *32* 2; *33* 2; *34* 4; *35* 3; *36* 2; *37* 2; *38* 2; *39* 2; *40* 4; *41* 2; *42* 3; *43* 2; *44* 2; *45* 2; *46* 1; *47* 2; *48* 2; *49* 2; *50* 3; *51* 3; *52* 3; *53* 2; *54* 2; *55* 2; *56* 2; *57* 2; *58* 2; *61* 1; *63* 2; *65* 2; *66* 2; *67* 2; *69* 3; *70* 3; *71* 2; *74* 2; *22* 2 app; *33* 1–2 app; *56* 2–3 app

cibarium, p. 311
κιβαρίου, **78** *18* 4; *20* 4; *21* 4; *22* 4; *28* 2; *30* 7; *33* 3; *34* 5; *35* 4; *37* 4; *47* 3; *48* 4; *49* 3; *50* 6; *54* 3; *55* 3; *58* 3; *61* 2; *62* 3; *56* 2–3 app
cịẹạpi, *nom pl*, **58** ii 9
Cil(icum), **64** ii 22
cincturas, **70** b ii 14
circenses, **117** ii 9 and 25
ci(rcitor)?, **47** i 7 and 17
circitores, **49** 2
circumiu.[, **67** 9; in app, *circumiue[runt*
cirratum, *adj.*, **83** 8 app
citator, **76** xx 24
ciuis, **70** b i 14; **73** a iii 10 app
c(iuium), **53** b 22
ciuitas
ciuita[t-, **67** 2; p. 239
ciuitatis, **52** a 1
ciuitatem, **53** b 11
ciuitatibus, **52** a 2
ciuitas sine suffragio, p. 7 note 3
clarissimus, **29** 3 and 10; **50** i 14; **66** b i 5; **91** *1* i 4; *2* i 4 and 8
classem, **63** ii 4
classiarius, pp. 4, 152, 212, 242
clauus
clauum, **82** 10
claui, **82** 5 app, 7, 9, 11
clericus, **58** ii 9 app
clinici, **9** 4 d app
ċo....[, **71** a 13
Cocceiana, **15** i 11; ii 1 and 2
c(oepit), **63** i 21; coepit, **64** i 8; c(oeperunt), **63** i 21 app
cogendum, **70** a iii 9 app
cogn(itionem), **81** ii 14 app
cognlega?, **81** ii 14 marg
cognomen, **5** i 16 app; **9** 9 a app; **24** 7 app, 14 app; **34** recto ii 11 app; verso i 1 app, 2 app; **52** b 15 app; **53** b 26 app; **70** a i 26 app; **74** iii 8 app; **89** *1* 5 app, *1* verso 1 app, *25* verso 2 app, 3 app; **114** verso 1 app; pp. 4, 5, 165, 198, 284, 285, 334, 361, 398
cogn(oscendum), **81** ii 14 app
cohors, *see also* σπεῖρα, *and for individual cohorts Index 4, Military Affairs*
coh, **20** 16; **52** d 3; **66** b ii 4 app; **73** j 4 app; **77** a i 7; **89** *10* 11; *14* 4; **93** c 2; **97** a 3; **101** a i 5; **110** 2; **114** 8; **115** a verso, d verso; **118** 4; **119** 2; **133** 3
cohors, **52** c 6; **97** b 2 app; p. 349
cohortis, **89** *25* 2
chortis, **64** i 26
χορτης, **75** 14 app
cohor(tis), **20** 6 app
coh(ortis), **20** 15; **47** i 2 and 10; ii 2 and 15; **48** 4; **50** i 5, 6, 11, 12, 13; ii 5, 6, 7; **63** i 24; **64** i 1; **87** 28 and 30; **89** *1* 2 and 6; verso 4; *1* 5 app; *3* 7 app; *4* i 3 and verso; *7* 10; *8* 5; *10* verso 2; *18* 1–2; *20* 1; *25* 2 and verso 1; *28* verso 1; *36* verso 1 app; *47* verso 1; *56* 3; **90** 1 a 6; **91** *1* verso 1; **96** 4 app; **99** *1* 6; verso 1; *2* 5; verso 1; *3* 5; verso 1; **100** 3; **102** a 1; **114** verso 1
coh(ortem), **1** viii 30; **50** i 15; **53** b 11 app; **87** 5
coh(orte), **1** xii 28; xiii 9; **40** ii 17; **47** ii 8; **51** ii 12; **64** ii 22
cohortes, **53** b 28 app; 29 app
cohors equitata, **75** 6 app; pp. 155, 168, 202, 270, 311
cohors equitata miliaria, pp. 138, 146
cohors equitata quingenaria, **64** ii 1 app; p. 202
cohors miliaria, p. 202
cohors quingenaria, p. 202
collatio, **70** a i 8, 14, 21, 29; ii 4, 11, 17, 26, 34, 40; iii 16, 24; e 4; b i 3, 10, 17, 23; ii 12, 21?, 2 app; **71** a 2 app; **76** FF 4 app; pp. 255, 256
collega, **81** ii 14 app
collegam, **91** *2* ii 5
coṃ[, **98** *3* 10
comes, **9** 15 g–k app; 18 b–c app; 19 c app; 20 b app
comess, **9** 33 b–c
comitatus, p. 242
comitia centuriata, p. 6
cọṃṃa[genum?], **83** 8
commeatus, **9** 2 m and app; n app; 24 b app; 34–37 app
commentarii, pp. 8, 420
com[militon-, **98** *3* 10 app
commilit[ones], **90** *1* b 3
comparandum, **2** xxxiii 15 and app; **47** i 13; ii 4
comparet, **47** ii 20
compellas, **91** *1* i 6; *2* i 5
[com]pleṭ[, **98** *4* 3 app
conductione, **70** a ii 18 app; 30 app
conductor, **58** ii 5; **70** a ii 18 app; pp. 180, 333, 335
conductoribus, **80** 3
conficiendam, **10** 18
confodiendos, **10** 12
congiarium, **69** 27 app
constitutio Antoniniana, pp. 87, 177, 311
consul, co(n)s(ul), **117** ii 18
co(n)s(ule), co(n)s(ulibus), **1** i 1, 3, 5, 9, 13, 15, 18; iii–v j 4?; vi 2, 29, 32; vii 8, 25, 31; viii 4, 6, 11, 17, 27; x 1, 3; xi 1, 3, 5, 7, 9, 12, 17, 21; xii 6, 24; xiii 5, 10, 14; xv 2, 4; xvi 1, 8, 11, 13, 15, 20; xvii 5; xviii 2, 4, 7, 14; xx 3; xxi 1, 3, 5, 7, 9, 12, 14, 16; xxii 2, 4, 9; xxiii 4, 10, 13; xxv 14; xxvi 13; xxvii 6, 9, 24; xxviii 7, 13, 18, 25; xxix 5; xxx 16, 19; xxxi 12, 15, 21, 23, 25, 27, 34, 36; xxxii 2, 4, 18, 24, 33; xxxiii 1, 12, 15, 18, 23, 25, 27, 29, 31,

35; xxxiv 8, 12, 14, 16, 20, 27, 32; xxxv 5, 12, 20, 23, 25, 31; xxxvi 1, 3, 5, 7, 13, 16, 25, 27, 31, 33; xxxvii 8, 10, 17, 28; xxxviii 2, 5, 7, 11, 14, 16, 20, 22, 29, 32; xxxix 3, 6, 32, 36; xl 6, 14, 18, 20, 22; xli 1, 3, 7, 9, 12, 16, 21, 24, 26, 30, 33; xlii 14, 17, 26; xliii 4, 14, 19, 22, 24, 26, 28, 30, 32; xliv 1, 10, 15, 18
2 i 11, 14; ii–iv a 4; v 3; vi 18, 20, 22, 25, 27, 30; vii 8, 11, 22; viii 1, 14, 17, 26; x 9, 14; xi 14, 17, 19, 21, 23, 27, 29; xii 8, 11, 20; xiii 4, 10, 12, 16, 18, 23, 30; xvi 5, 16, 18, 20, 22; xvii 10, 12, 16; xviii 4, 9, 17, 20; xx 15; xxi 14; xxii 9, 11, 15; xxiii 6, 8, 13, 15, 18, 23, 28; xxiv 6; xxv 13; xxvi 6, 10; xxvii 2, 6, 9, 12, 17, 22; xxviii 7, 12, 16, 21, 28; xxix 8, 13; xxx 12, 17; xxxi 14, 17, 20; xxxii 1, 5, 7, 9, 15, 17, 28; xxxiii 5, 13, 18, 28, 30; xxxiv 1, 3, 5, 7, 10, 12, 14, 18, 25, 29; xxxv 9, 13, 21, 25, 27, 29; xxxvi 5, 7, 15, 17, 19, 21, 23, 27, 29; xxxvii 10, 12, 18, 28; xxxviii 10, 13, 15, 17, 24, 27, 29; xxxix 9, 12; xl 4, 8, 13, 21, 25, 27, 29; xli 1, 5, 7, 9, 12, 14, 18, 21; xlii 8, 11, 17; xliii 2, 15, 20, 27; xliv 5, 11, 13, 15, 18, 21, 27; xlv 3, 6, 8, 10, 12
3 a 6, 8; **4** b i 3, 5, 7, 10, 14, 16, 18, 22; ii 12; d 1 app; k 4; **5** i 1, 6, 11, 13, 16 app; ii 3, 5, 7, 9, 11; iii 2 app; **6** i 2, 5, 10, 15, 23, 26, 28, 32; ii 4, 9, 22, 24, 26, 28, 30; iii 9, 12, 17, 20, 23, 25, 28; iv 5, 16, 18, 20, 22, 25, 28, 30; v 19, 28; vi 2, 4, 9; vii 4, 6 app; viii 7, 11, 13, 16, 18; ix 1, 10, 16, 22, 24; x 8, 11, 24, 27, 28; xi 3, 10, 14, 16, 20, 22, 26
7 a 2; **8** ii 21, 28; iii 2, 7, 14; v 4, 6, 9, 12, 19, 22; vi 1, 6, 10; vii 15, 17, 19, 21, 23; viii 2, 7, 11, 13, 16; ix 7, 13, 22, 24, 26, 28; **11** i 1, 6, 9; ii 1 app
20 2, 3, 5, 6, 8, 9, 11, 12, 14, 15, 19, 20, 22; **21** 13, 14, 15, 16, 18, 19, 20, 21; **23** i 4, 6, 8; ii 5, 7, 9; iii 3; iv 1, 3, 6, 8; **24** 1, 3, 5, 7, 9, 12, 14, 16, 18, 20; **27** a ii 15, 16; **28** 1, 3, 5, 7, 11, 13; **29** 1, 8, 15; **31** i 9; **32** 1, 4, 8, 12; **33** i 2; **37** 1; **39** 1, 3, 6, 8, 11, 13, 15, 17, 19, 21, 24; **40** i 2, 4, 6, 16; **44** 9, 12, 14; **46** 4, 8; **48** 5, 6; **50** i 14; **63** i 12, 15, 17, 21, 30 app, 32 app; **64** i 2, 5, 9, 22, 34, 37, 40, 42; ii 1, 4, 7, 10, 16, 19, 23, 26, 30, 34, 37; **66** a i 9, 12; ii 8, 10, 12, 13, 15, 16; b i 2, 8, 19, 22, 25, 28; ii 23, 26; e; a i 2 app; b i 23 app; **70** a i 1, 4, 17, 25; a ii 7, 30; e 7; Aberd. 1; b i 6; ii 8; **71** a 7; **80** 8
83 1, 2, 4, 5, 9, 10, 11, 13, 14, 16, 17, 19, 21, 22, 23, 24; **86** 6; **88** *2* 4; **89** *1* 7; *4* iii 6; *17* 14; *19* 11; *20* 8; *21* 3; *23* 19; *25* 7 and 10; *26* 7; *28* 10; *29* 16; *31* 10; *32* 8; *34* 6 app; *38* 3 and 7; *42* 13; *45* 5; *48* 3; **91** *1* i 2 a; *2* i 2a; **95** b 5, 7; **97** b 2 app, 4; **98** *3* 6; **99** *1* 3, 10; *2* 7; **104** 3; **109** 3; **114** 2a; **121** 2

consularis (=legatus Augusti pro praetore), *see also Index 3, Notable Persons*
[co]ṣ, **108**
co(n)s(ularis), *nom*, **91** *1* i 4; *2* i 4 and 8
co(n)s(ularis), *gen*, **1** xxv 23; xxxiii 11; xxxviii 3; xli 22; **2** xiii 21; xxviii 25 and 26; xl 7; **29** 3 and 10; **53** b 4; **66** ii 28 app; **96** 6 app
co(n)s(ulari), *abl*, **50** i 14; **66** b i 5–10 app; b ii 28 app; **83** 4, 8, 14
contectio?: contuctione, **70** a ii 18
contemsit, **53** b 23
contubernium, **68** ii 4 app
contuctione, **70** a ii 18
conturmalibus, **80** 4
[con]ualescen[tes], **51** ii 2 app
corcọsio?, **66** b ii 28 and app
cornicen, *see κορνιξ*
cornicularius, *see also κορνιξ, and for individual cornicularii Index 4, Military Affairs*; **1** xxxii 29; **2** xxxiii 10; **87** 27; **66** b ii 28 app; pp. 10, 11, 12, 17, 141, 352
corniculariorum, **21** 17
c̣ṛẹ[, **53** b 13 app
cribra, cribraria, **101** b 7 app
cultus, **9** 15 e
cum, **1** ix 31 app; xii 26; xiii 8; xix 25; xxviii 1; xxix 24; xxxiv 31; xliv 2; **2** vii 19 app; xii 28; xiv 20; xxi 3 app; xxv 18; xl 19; **9** 12 d–e; 20 b, 23 b–d app; **10** 14, 16, 29, 32; **11** ii 9; **47** i 5; ii 7, 8; **51** ii 21 app; **63** ii 32 and 34; **67** 3; **77** a i 5 app; **81** iii 10 app; **89** *14* 4; *43* 10; **96** 2; **117** i 7
cumẹṣịnus? **81** iii 10
].cumque, **93** a 1
cuneos, **51** ii 8
cuniculos, **9** 4 d–e and app
cura
curae, *dat*, **98** *2* 5
curam, **91** *2* ii 8
curare, **90** *1* b 4
curator, *for individual* curatores *see Index 4, Military Affairs*; **47** i 7 (twice); **63** i 24 app; **75** 2 app and 19 app; p. 283
κουρατ( ), **78** *60* 4
κουράτωρ, **76** iv 1 and 17; vi 14; xvii 8; xxi 5; **78** *58* 6
κουράτορος, **78** *34* 1
κουράτορι, **76** i 2, 11, 18, 23; ii 3; iii 3, 12, 21; iv 3, 12, 22; v 4, 12; vi 2, 10, 17; vii 3, 9, 17; viii 3, 8, 15, 20, 26; ix 5, 14; x 3, 17; xi 4, 14; xii 3, 12, 21; xiii 3, 10, 17; xiv 4, 12; xv 4, 12, 19; xvi 2, 12, 20; xvii 2, 11, 16; xviii 3, 14, 26; xix 4, 14, 20; xx 2, 10, 21; xxi 2; xxiv 2; BB 3; FF 4; GG 2, 10; HH i 2
κουράτορσι, **78** *60* 5
cuṣ[, **10** 6

custodia
cuṣṭọḍ[, **2** xxi 3
custodiam, **10** 6 app
custodia, *abl*, **63** ii 36, 37
custodiarum, **56** b 8; c 3
custodias, **67** 5
custos, **10** 6 app
custos armorum, **58** ii 4; **73** a iii 10 app; **129** 6; p. 180
custos domi, **58** ii 8
αρμορου (=armorum custos), **76** xv 8
αρμωρου κουστωρ, **78** *39* 5–6
αρμουκουστωρ, **78** *71* 1
[custo]ḍes, **52** b 8 app
Cyrenaica (legio III), **34** recto i 1; ii 5; **58** i 1

d: d(educitur)?, d(educentur)?, **77** b 3
d: quingenaria?, **63** i 24
ḍ ḅ . Y, **9** 17 d
d c c, **33** ii 2, 3, 4, 6; iii 1, 3, 4, 5; iv 1, 3, 4, 6; v 4, 5, 7; p. 159
d f: d(iscens) f(abrum)?, **2** xxxi 6
]d s, d(e)s(ideratus)? d(e)s(eruit)? d(iscens) s(igniferum)? **21** 19
Dacicus, **63** ii 8 app
damnatio memoriae, pp. 88, 90 note 1, 144, 170, 220, 225 note 1, 341, 349; **5** i 13 app; **59** i 7 app; **66** b i 19 app; **70** a i 17 app; **99** *1* 9 app
dare, **91** *1* i 9
dari, **79** 5; **91** *1* ii 3
dantur, **77** a i 19 app
detur, **117** i 7
dedi, **89** *4* i 6
dedit?, **51** ii 14
dedimus, **89** *8* 6; *34* 6 app
datus, **63** ii 4; dati, **64** ii 14
data, **99** *2* marg; *3* marg; **100** 5; **102** a 8; datae?, **86** 4
de, **88** *2* 7; **90** *1* b 4; **9** 14 b?; **90** *1* b 2?
de.se.se, **9** 14 b–c and app
ḍẹ[..]..[.]os, **27** b ii 2
debere
debet, **70** a i 28, 30, 32; ii 25, 29; iii 15, 17, 19; f 2; b i 9, 11, 13, 22, 24; ii 11, 15, 17; **69** 2 app, 16 app; **70** a iii 10a app; f app; g app; **72** 3 app; **73** k 4 app; p. 256
debent, **98** *4* 8 app; **101** a i 7 app
debuit, **68** i 17–18 app
debita, p. 256
debitores, **73** a i 17; ii 3; k 4 app; p. 269
decedere, **63** ii 3 app
decedunt, **63** ii 3
decesserunt, **63** ii 12; i 29 app, 35 app
decem, **27** b marg 3 app; **86** 5; **89** *25* 5; **90** *1* a 1 app
decernere, **91** *2* ii 7 and app
decernente, **86** 6 app
decimum, **89** *12* i 5; *26* 6; **99** *1* 3
decuma[nam]?, **51** i 23 and app
decurio, *see also δεκάδαρχος, and for individual decurions Index 4, Military Affairs*; **1** xxxi 22; xxxiii 24; xxxvi 2; xxxviii 12; xli 2; **2** xxxvi 16; xxxviii 25; xli 2; **4** a i 7; **15** i 14; **20** 2, 5, 8, 11, 14, 19, 15 app, 17 app; **47** i 1, 6, 7, 9, 16, 17; ii 11, 12; **48** 11; **50** i 5, 11; **52** b 10; c 5; **55** f; **63** i 27; ii 1, 15, 25 app, 33, 39, 42; **64** i 15, 25; **66** b ii 5 app
decursores, **62** 7
ḍeḍ[.]ẹc̣tuṣ, **52** b 6
deducere
deducuntur, **77** a i 9 and 16; b 3 app
deduxit, **51** ii 11
defection[, **53** b 24 app
defendendam, **63** ii 31
defunctus
defuncti, *gen*, **77** a i 15; defuncto, **77** a i 9
degere
degunt, **89** *4* 9 app; **91** *1* i 8
d(egentis), *gen*, **63** i 24 app
degentes, **89** *1* 3
Deiotariana, **53** b 24 app
demissu[, **52** b 6 app
demnu.[, **95** b ii 2
dena, dena[rios]? **98** *4* 4 and app
denarius
dena[ri-, **98** e 3
δηναρι-, **78** *44* 5
denarios, **75** 5; **98** *4* 5, 7, 8; *4* 4 app; **132** 1 app, 2 app
denariis, **98** *4* 7
δηναρίων, **76** ii 6; xvii 12; xix 6; xxiv 5; FF 6; **78** *18* 5; *19* 4; *20* 5; *21* 5; *24* 4–5: *δηνάρια τριῶν*; *25* 2; *26* 1; *27* 4; *28* 3; *32* 4; *34* 7; *37* 4: *δηνάρια*; *39* 4; *45* 4; *46* 3; *48* 4; *49* 4; *51* 6; *53* 5; *54* 3; *56* 3; *57* 3; *58* 4: *δηναρίου τρ̣ι̣[ιῶν]*; *45* 6 app; *49* 4 app
δηνάρια, **74** i 4, 11; ii 4, 10; iii 4, 11; **75** 21; 15 app; **76** i 5, 13, 19, 24; ii 15; iii 5, 15, 24 (twice); iv 5, 13, 23; v 6, 15; vi 4, 12, 19; vii 4, 12, 18; viii 4, 9, 16, 21; ix 8; x 7, 11, 19; xi 6, 16; xii 5, 14, 23; xiii 5, 13, 20; xiv 7; xv 7, 15, 22; xvi 6, 17, 23; xvii 5; xviii 7, 19, 30; xix 17, 24; xx 5: *δηνάριον*, 14, 23; xxi 4; BB 6; HH i 4; ii 6; **78** *15* 5; *67* 3?; *68* 4; *69* 5; *70* 4–5: *[δηνα]ρίων δύο*; *72* 6; pp. 122, 244, 254–55, 256, 266, 270, 277, 284, 311, 313, 345, 435, 440; **65** 10 app; **69** 27 app; **73** a ii 3 app, 5 app, 19 app; iii 14 app, 25 app; **75** 5 app; **78** *55* 4 app; *57* 3–4 app; *72* 5–6; **83** 13 app, 16 app; **100** 3 app
(denari-), *symbol* ⋇, **65** 10; **70** a i 3, 6 (twice), 7, 8, 9, 10 (twice), 12 (twice), 13, 14, 15, 16 (twice), 19 (twice), 20, 21, 22, 23 (twice), 27 (twice), 28, 29, 30, 31 (twice), 32; ii 2

(twice), 3, 4, 5, 6, 9 (twice), 10, 11, 12, 13 (twice), 15, 16, 17, 19, 20, 21, 22 (twice), 24 (twice), 25, 26, 27, 28, 29, 32, 33, 34, 35, 36 (twice), 38 (twice), 39, 40, 41, 42 (twice); d 10, 12, 16, 18, 22; e 2, 3, 4, 5, 6; f 2, 3; Aberd. 3; b i 1, 2, 3, 4, 5 (twice), 8 (twice), 9, 10, 12 (twice), 13, 15, 16, 17, 18, 19, 21, 22, 23, 24, 25; ii 10, 16, 17; h 3, 4, 7, 8, 9; **71** a 2, 4, 5, 6, 9, 11, 12, 13; b 4, 6, 7, 8, 9, 10; **72** 1, 4, 6, 12, 15; **73** a i 12, 13, 14, 15, 16, 17, 18, 19, 20, 21, 22, 23, 24, 25, 26; ii 2, 3, 4, 5, 6, 7, 8, 9, 10, 11, 12, 13, 14, 15, 16, 17, 18, 19; iii 15, 16, 17, 18, 19, 20, 21, 22, 23, 24, 25, 26, 27, 28, 29, 30, 35; b 4, 5, 6, 7, 8; c 2, 3, 4, 5, 6; d 1; e 5, 6, 7, 8; f 4; g 6; h 1; **78** *22* 5, 9; *30* 7; *32* 5; *36* 5; *37* 5; *55* 4; *61* 4; **83** 2, 4, 5, 9, 10, 11, 13, 14, 16, 17; **84** 1, 2, 3, 4, 5, 6, 7; **99** *1* 7; *2* 5; *3* 5; **124**

(denari-), *symbol* H, **78** *24* 10; *25* 5; *45* 6; *57* 9; *65* 6, 7; *66* 7; *67* 6; *70* 8

denum, **29** 11, *de num(ero)*?

deponere

[d]ẹp, *dep(osuit)*?, **69** 9

deposuit, **68** ii 11, 21; iii 10, 20; **69** 18 app

depositos, **73** a iii 13, 14, 16, 17, 18, 19, 20, 21, 22, 23, 24, 25, 26

deposco, **90** *1* b 2 app

depositum, *noun*, pp. 243, 244, 269, 270, 307

depositi, **71** a 9

δηποσίτου, **74** i 5; ii 5, 11; iii 5

δηπόσιτον, **74** i 12

deposito, **68** ii 31, iii 29; **70** a i 6, 10, 12, 16, 19, 23, 27, 31; ii 2, 6, 9, 13, 15, 22, 24, 28, 32, 36, 38, 42; iii 14, 18, 22; e 2, 6; b i 1, 5, 8, 12, 15, 19, 21, 25; ii 5, 6, 10, 16; d 18 app; **132** 2?, 8 app

depositorum, **73** a ii 1; iii 27

δηπωσέτων, **74** iii 12

depositis, **130** 2

ḍeputatus, **47** i 5 app

derelictis, **90** *1* a 7

deseruit, **21** 19 app

deses, **9** 14 b app

desiderare

desidera[-, **89** *42* 11

desideratus, **21** 19 app

designatus, **117** ii 18

dexter, **83** 2, 5, 10, 15; **87** 23

dḟ.ạṣa[, **71** a 5

diaria, **98** *3* 3 app

dicere, **91** *2* i 9 app

dicit, **77** b 2

dictis, **50** i 4 app

dies, **50** i 4 app

diem, **117** ii 1, 22

die, **53** b 9; **63** i 20; **83** 11; **86** 3; **99** *1* 8; **108**

dies imperii, **117** i 17–18 app; 21 app; ii 2 app, 20 app, 26–28 app; iii 1 app, 4–6 app

dignatus, **91** *1* i 3; *2* i 9

dignitas, p. 3

dim[, **89** *1* 6 and app; *39* 4 and app

ḍiṃ...us, **9** 23 c

dimittere, **89** *26* 2 app

dim[, **89** *1* 6; *39* 4

dimis[, **89** *6* 9; *7* 11

dimisi, **89** *42* 13

d(imissi), **63** i 21 app

diota, **53** b 24

discens, **25** a 5; **50** i 3, 9; **2** xxxi 6 app; **21** 19 app; **58** ii 9 app

disciplina, **90** *1* a 8; b 5

dispensator, *see also* οἰκονόμος; p. 232 and note 1

dispensatore, **79** 4

dispositus, **1** xxxii 9, 23; xxxiv 9, 23, 36; xxxv 14, 28, 32; xxxvi 4, 28, 29; xxxvii 7, 13, 15; xxxviii 1; **2** xxxii 22, 25; xxxiv 22; xxxv 6, 15; xxxvi 4, 25; xxxvii 27; xxxviii 9, 18; xxxix 4; xl 24, 30; xlii 3; xliii 6; **8** v 16; **2** x 18 app; xvi 4 app; **47** i 5 app; pp. 13, 15

διστριβούτων, **74** i 5; ii 6, 12; iii 5, 14

diuus, **117** ii 10; 23–24 app; **63** i 21 app; pp. 82, 146, 255, 423 and note 1

diui, *gen*, **117** i 13, 15, 17, 21; ii 2, 3, 4, 6, 20, 21, 23 (twice); iii 1, 4 (twice), 6, 8

diuo, *dat*, **117** i 13, 16, 17, 21; ii 2, 3, 4, 6, 11, 20, 21, 23, 24; iii 1, 4, 5, 6, 8

diuo, *abl*, **1** xiii 5; xvi 13; xxi 1; xxiii 4; xxvi 13; xxviii 7; xxxi 25; xxxii 18; xxxiii 1; xxxiv 27; xxxv 12; xxxvii 28; xxxviii 20; xl 14; xli 7; xliii 4?; **2** xiii 4; xvi 16; xvii 10; xviii 9; xxii 9; xxiii 13; xxvii 17; xxviii 7, 21; xxxiii 18; xxxiv 25; xxxv 13; xxxvii 10, 28; xl 4, 21; xli 7; xlii 8; xliii 2; **4** b i 5, 10, 18; **5** i 13 and app; ii 11; **6** xi 10; **8** v 19; viii 20; **20** 14; **24** 18

diuae, *gen* and *dat*, **117** i 10 (twice); ii 7 (twice), 19 (twice), 28 (twice); iii 7 (twice); i 10 app

doctor, **59** i 9 app

dodrans, *see* 'e' *and* 'f'

Dolicheni, **50** i 13

dominus, **88** *2* 8 and app; **117** ii 16; pp. 13, 52, 349

domini, *gen*, **47** i 6, 17; **49** 1; **50** i 1, 8; **68** ii 3; iii 2; **117** i 3, 28

dominorum, **86** 1

dominum, **1** ii 6, 7, 13?; iii a 2; h 3, 4, 5; vii 7; ix 2, 3, 4, 5, 7, 18, 19, 20, 21; xii 4, 5, 11; xiii 3, 22; xiv 11, 12, 16, 17, 18, 19, 20, 21; xvii 7, 12; xviii 3; xix 5, 6, 7, 8, 9, 10, 11; xxii 1; xxv 1; xxviii 3; xxix 6; xxx 1, 2, 3, 4, 5, 6, 7, 8; xxxvi 19; xxxvii 26; xxxix 30

dominos, **98** *2* a 6

domino, *abl*, **2** xvi 5; xxvi 10; xxxi 20; **31** i 12; ii 6; **33** i 1, 17; **50** i 14; **66** a i 11; b i 1, 7, 21, 27; ii 25; **90** *1* a 1

dominus—*cont.*
dominis, *abl*, **99** *1* 3, 9
domine, **88** *1* 4 app; *2* 5; **89** *4* i 3; *5* 11–13 app; *6* 8; *12* 7; *38* 8; *39* 9; *48* 7; **91** *1* i 5; *2* i 4, 9
domini, *voc*, **89** *1* 2, 8
domus, *see also Index 4, Military Affairs*, origo
"house," **53** b 9; **58** ii 8
"origo," **64** i 7
dona militaria, p. 420
ḍṛ[, **37** 5
drachma, *see Index 8, Greek Words*
dromadarius, **1** xliii 18; **2** i 1 app; xliii 14; **8** iii 2 app; v 4; vii 17; ix 26; **47** i 1, 4 and app, 9 and app; **49** 4; **50** i 5 and app, 11 and app; **52** b 9; **61** ii 9, 10 app; **64** i 16, 33; ii 11; **65** 4; **92** vii 15–16 app
δρομαδάριος, **78** *48* 1; *49* 1
dromas, **8** iii 5 app
dromon, **8** iii 5 app
dromone, **8** iii 5; vii 22
duxit, **51** ii 3; **89** *25* 4?
duo, **96** 7 app
duos, **50** i 15; **51** ii 13
duas, **51** ii 4, 12
duobus, **1** viii 11; xviii 7; xxxiii 18; xxxv 25; xxxviii 7; xl 20; xliii 14; **2** viii 17?; xiii 23; xxiii 23; xxix 8; xxxiii 30; xxxv 29; xxxviii 15; xl 27; xliii 22 app; xlv 6; **5** i 16 app; ii 3; **6** iii 28; vi 4; xi 22; **8** vi 6; vii 19; viii 13; ix 26; x 21?; **39** 24
duplicarius, **1** i 4; x 28; xi 4, 6; xvi 4, 10 app, 12 app; xxi 4; xxvi 9, 14, 16; xxxi 18, 24, 26; xxxiii 20, 26, 28; xxxv 33; xxxvi 4, 22 app, 26 app; xxxviii 9, 13; xl 25; xli 4, 6 app; xlii 16; **2** vi 21; xi 16, 18; xvi 19; xvii 1; xxxii 4 app; xxxiv 4, 6; xxxvi 18; xxxviii 26; xli 4, 6; **4** a i 9 app; 11; b i 4; **5** ii 3–4 app; **22** 6; **27** b i 2, 7; **38** i 15; **47** i 1 (twice); 9 (twice); 17 app; ii 17; **50** i 5 (twice), 11 (twice); **63** i 27, 28; ii 1, 2, 15, 16, 42, 43; **76** xiv 16; **85** 2; **92** iv 12 app; **96** 7 and app; pp. 11, 12, 14, 15, 16, 17, 84, 143, 146, 181, 201
dupl(icario), *abl*, **20** 11
δουπλικαρίῳ, *dat.*, **85** 2
dupla, **88** *1* 8; p. 355
dux, **89** *23* 1 app; **91** *2* i 6 app
ducis, **17** a 8 app
duce, **20** 3; **83** 21, 23, 24

e, *see under* quadrans
e e, e(xemplum) e(pistulae)?, **50** i 15; **53** b 8
e, ex, **1** xii 28; xxii 8; **2** xx 22?; **10** 2; **20** 2, 5, 8, 11, 14, 19, 22; **29** 2, 9; **30** ii 8, 13; **38** i 10 app; **47** i 3, 11; ii 8 (twice), 17, 21, 22; ii 3 app; **50** i 14; **51** ii 8, 12, 16, 22; **52** b 17?; **58** ii 2; **62** 2, 5; **63** i 34 app; ii 3, 13 app, 17, 44; **64** i 4, 8, 20, 23, 29, 35, 36, 38; ii 2, 5, 8, 11, 13, 17, 20, 22, 24, 25, 27, 29; **66** b i 29, 33; ii 4, 6, 8, 27, 28, 29; ii 3 app; **68** ii 4, 12, 15, 22, 25; iii 3, 14, 21, 24; **69** 3a, 11a, 20; 10 app; **70** a i 8, 14, 21, 28; ii 4, 11, 17, 25, 34, 40; iii 15, 24; c 4; e 4; g 6; b i 3, 9, 17, 22; ii 5, 5a, 11, 21?; **72** 3 app, 8 app; **77** a i 3, 9, 16; **83** 1, 13, 16; **86** 3; **87** 5; **89** *4* i 4, 6a, 8, 9 app; *8* 9; *25* 2 app; **90** *1* b 5; **91** *1* i 9; **92** v 16; vi 8; ix 14; **99** *1* 8; *2* 7; *3* 6; **100** 4
e.[, **53** b 7
ẹ...[, **71** b 5
eaṃ[, **53** b 24
edicere, **50** i 4 app
ego, **101** a i 2
mihi, **79** 5; **91** *1* i 3; *2* i 3; *2* i 9 app; **98** 2 a 8; p. 417
me, *acc*, **77** a i 2, 8, 14; b 2, 8; **80** 6; **88** *1* 4; **91** *2* i 14?
me, *abl*, **87** 4; **99** *1* 6; *2* 4; *3* 4; **100** 3
egregius: egregio, **83** 15, 17
ei.[, **88** *1* 9; **90** *1* e
emansit, **1** xxii 8; xxiii 15 app; **53** b 7 app
emansioṇ[, **53** b 6
emere
ẹmiṣṭi, **45** 2
empti, **82** 3 app
emeritus, **1** xxxviii 15; xli 10, 11; **47** ii 18; **65** 8; **70** b ii 4 app; **117** i 7
Emesenorum, **30** ii 8
emiss.., **133** 2 app
emṇạ, *liquid measure*?, **82** 3
enim, **51** ii 9
epimeletes, p. 242
epistratego: **11** ii 9; **81** iii 10 app
epistula, pp. 150, 348, 349, 421 note 4
epistul( ), **89** *5* 13; *10* 1 and app; epis[tul-], **27** b ii 5; **89** *5* 14 and app
epistulae, *nom*, **116** *A* 1
epistulae, *gen*, **50** i 15; **52** b 8
epistulae, *dat*, **87** 9
epistulam, **87** 30; **89** *1* 7–8 app
epistula, *abl*, **10** 2; **29** 2, 9; **47** ii 7
epistulis, *abl*, **1** xliv 2; **4** b i 9 app; **89** *25* 2 app
epulụ.[, **89** *35* 3
epulum, **76** FF 4; p. 284
epulis, **4** b i 9
equatum, *supine*, **63** ii 20
eques, *see also* ἱππεύς; pp. 17, 90, 96, 122, 150, 179, 181, 201, 208, 216, 245, 270, 336, 340, 341, 350
eq[, eq( ), **53** b 1; 28 app; **58** i 30; **89** *42* 11
eq(ues), **11 bis** a 16; b i 16; **40** ii 17; **47** i 4, 7, 17, 18; ii 4, 20; **52** b 16; **63** ii 5, 6, 9 app, 10; **64** i 33; ii 8; **66** b ii 5; b i 31 app; **68** ii 4 app; **75** 6?; **88** *2* 5–6 app; **92** ii 9
eq(uites), equites, **47** i 1, 9, 18; ii 20; **48** 11; **49** 4; **50** i 4, 5, 11; **55** e 2; i 1; **58** i 36; **61** ii

10 app; **63** i 27; ii 1, 15, 20, 21, 23, 25 app, 30, 32, 39, 42; **64** i 16; ii 32; **65** 7; **80** 7; **81** ii 8 app; **92** vii 15–16 app
eq(uitum), **62** 1; **81** ii 8 app
eq(uiti), **99** *1* 6; *3* 5
equitibus, **86** 1; **91** *1* i 7; **99** *2* 4; eqq, **100** 3
eq(uite), **20** 2, 14, 22, 15 app
equites promoti, **86** 1; p. 347
equites singulares, **20** 15 app
eq[uester?, **47** ii 8 and app
eq[u]i[, **23** iii 2
equitata (cohors), **53** b 16 app, 22 app; **63** i 24 app; **64** i 1; pp. 90, 138, 155, 168, 202
equus, pp. 349, 350
equi, *gen*, **75** 3
equorum, **116** *A* 2
equum, **1** xxxviii 18; **8** iii 5 app; **89** *42* 12; **99** *1* 5; *3* 3; eq(uum), **83** 1, 2, 3, 4, 6, 7, 8, 10, 11, 12, 13, 14, 17, 22, 23, 24; eq(uam), **83** 19, 21
equos, **27** a i 1; **99** *2* 3; **100** 2 app; equas, **86** 5 app
era.[, **1** xxii 8
erogaueris, **98** *2* a 8
esse, **87** 31; **89** *11* 3?
est, **69** 8, 17; **91** *2* i 9
sit, **91** *1* i 3; **98** *2* a 5; **117** i 24, 26, 28; ii 10, 16, 18
sunt, **50** i 4, 5, 10, 11; ii 5; b 3; **51** ii 9; **67** 6; **73** a ii 19
erat, **29** 4
erimus, **47** i 6, 16; **49** 1; **50** i 1, 8
fuit, **53** b 17
fuerit, **47** i 6, 16; **48** 7; **50** i 1, 8; b 7; **53** b 30
]...erunt, **89** *4* 7
et, **1** i 1, 3; vii 31; xi 3; xxviii 13, 18; xxxi 15; xxxiii 12, 23, 27; xxxv 20; xxxviii 2, 5; xl 18; xli 1; xliv 18; **2** vi 18; xi 14; xxiii 6, 8; xxxiv 1, 5; xxxv 21; xxxviii 27; xli 1; **5** i 6, 11 app; **6** iii 23; xi 16; **11** ii 1, 4; **20** 2, 3, 5, 6, 8, 9, 12, 14, 15, 19, 20, 22; **23** 1, 3, 5, 7, 11, 13; **33** i 2; **38** ii 1?; **39** 1, 3, 6, 11, 17, 19; **44** 9, 12?; **46** 4, 8; **47** i 6, 16; ii 21; **48** 5, 6, 7; **50** i 1 (twice), 4, 8 (twice), 10, 15; **51** ii 3, 7, 10, 11, 17, 19; **53** b 1, 13 app, 27, 29; **58** ii 9; **64** i 2, 5, 9, 19, 22, 34; ii 1, 4, 16, 19, 23, 26, 30, 34, 37; **66** a i 12; ii 12, 15, 16; b i 2, 8, 14, 22, 23?, 28; ii 26; **67** 3, 4, 9; **68** ii 12, 22; iii 11, 21; **69** 10 app; **70** a i 4, 24; ii 7, 30; b i 7; **71** b 5 app; **77** a i 10; **80** 5, 6, 8; **81** iii 10 app; **82** 2, 4, 9, 10, 11, 14, 16 (twice?), 17, 19, 22, 24; **86** 1 (twice), 2, 5, 6; **87** 8; **88** *2* 4, 6; **89** *1* 7; *4* i 7; iii 5; *6* 2; *7* 2, 4; *8* 2; *17* 14; *19* 10; *20* 8; *21* 3; *23* 19; *25* 9; *26* 7; *28* 9; *29* 16; *31* 9; *32* 8; *34* 6 app; *38* 3; *39* 6; *48* 2; *53* 2; **90** *1* b 4; **91** *1* i 2a, 6; *2* i 2a, 5; **93** d 2; **95** b 5; **98** *2* 1 (twice), 3, 5; *3* 3, 5; **99** *1* 3, 8, 9; *2* 7; f app; **104** 3; **109** 3; **114** 2a; **116** *A* 2 app; **117** i 2, 3, 14, 15, 21, 27, 28; ii 17, 23; iii 4
ẹto, **72** 4
etọṛ, **9** 21 h
euocatus, **47** ii 18 app
ex.[.].., **2** xx 22
ex...ụ..ẹroe..[, **52** b 17
exceptor, **10** 2 app; **75** 19 app
excubare, **52** b 3
excubant, **47** i 6, 17; **49** 1; **50** i 1, 8, 4 app
excubuerunt, **51** ii 17; **15** ii 7 app
[ex]cubit(um), **67** 10 app
excubatio ad signa, pp. 180, 189, 191, 198, 201
excubitor, **50** ii 4 app; pp. 192, 197, 209
exeṃ[, **54** d 2
exemplum, **50** i 15 app; **53** b 8; **54** d 2 app; **87** 1; **88** *2* 2 app; **89** *54* 5; **90** *1* c 1 app; **91** *2* i 11 app; **98** *2* a 4; **100** 1 app
exercitum, **63** ii 8
eximere, **54** d 2 app
exit, **9** 10 b app; 12 d; 23 b; 31 d; 34–37 app; **10** 2, 5, 6, 8, 12, 14, 16, 18, 20, 21, 23, 24, 27, 29, 30, 32; **38** i 10 app?; p. 115
exit ad frumentum Mercuri, **10** 5, 8
exit ad frumentum Neapoli, **9** 31 d–g; **10** 2
exit cum asin, **9** 12 d–e and app
exit cum frumentariis, **10** 32; **9** 12 d–g app
exit in ḍiṃ...us Aeg, **9** 23 b–d and app
expeditio, pp. 350, 387
expeditionem, **63** ii 29; **92** ii 8
expeditione, **92** ii 12
expensas, **68** ii 10, 20, 30; iii 9, 19
expertos, **50** i 15 app
explorator, **1** xiii 11; xv 14; xx 21; xxiii 19; xxvi 18; xxxii 3, 38; xxxiii 3; xxxv 21, 24; xxxvii 4, 20; xxxix 12, 25; xliii 12; **2** ix 15, 31; xxvii 25; xxix 26; xxxv 22; xxxvii 6; xxxviii 12; xliii 10; xx 22 app; p. 15
exploratum, *supine*, **63** ii 32; **1** xxxii 38 app
expungentur, **47** i 16
exruḥụḍec, **38** i 10
extra, **63** ii 23

f, *see under* quadrans
f.ri (porta), ḟọṛi?, **15** ii 15; p. 128
f..sia (porta), **13** 12; p. 126
faber, **59** i 9; **2** xxxi 6 app; p. 212
fabricae, fabriciensis, **59** i 9 app
facere
faciet, **67** 6
faciemus, **47** i 6; **48** 7; **50** i 1, 8; **53** b 30
fact[, **65** 11
factus, **20** 2, 5, 8, 11, 14, 19, 22; **40** ii 17; **64** i 20; p. 157
facti, **64** ii 32; **65** 7
faenaria, *acc*, **68** ii 5, 16, 26; iii 4, 15, 25; **69** 4, 12, 21 app

faenarius, *adj.*, **80** 3
faenum, **73** c 10, 8 app; **80** 4
fascias, **68** ii 7, 18, 28; iii 6, 17, 27; **69** 6, 14, 23
fateor, **77** a i 2, 8, 14; b 2, 8
fatotro, **15** ii 21 app
felix
  felicis, **50** i 2, 8
  felicissim-, **89** *50* 6–7 app
  felicissimum, **89** *12* i 8; *38* 9; *39* 10; *46* 1; *48* 7; **91** *2* i 9; **107** (twice); **111** 2; p. 349
  felicissimos, **89** *1* 9; *5* 11
femina (bos), **117** i 4 (twice), 6, 8 (twice), 9, 16, 24 (twice); ii 5, 25, 26
femore, **83** 2, 5, 10, 24; **99** *3* 4
fercla, **9** 15 c; 4 k app
feriatae, **53** b 10
ferre
  tulit, **70** a i 9, 15, 22; ii 5, 12, 21, 35, 41; iii 25; c 5; e 5; b i 4, 18; **71** a 9 app; **72** 4 and app, 9?; **47** ii 21? 22?
ferream, **82** 13
ferri, **82** 7, 9, 10, 11, 14
fidelis, **53** b 22
fidei, **86** 4
fieri
  fit, **68** ii 13, 23; iii 12, 22; **69** 10a app; **73** a iii 30
  fiunt, **58** ii 17 app; **70** a i 30; ii 27; iii 17; f 2; b i 11, 24; ii 15; **80** 6
  fient **53** b 30 app
filiạ[, **123** a 3
filius, **24** 21 app; **36** 1, 2, 3, 4, 5, 6, 7, 8, 9, 10, 11, 12, 13, 14; **37** 2, 3, 4, 5; **45** 1 app; **64** i 6; **133** 1
  fili, *voc*, **91** *1* i 5; *2* i 4, 9
firma, **91** *2* i 6
fiscalibus, **91** *1* i 9
Flauia, *title of unit*, **63** ii 4; **64** ii 22; **91** *2* i 6
formula, **133** 5 app; pp. 6, 7
fortis, *gen*, **20** 2; *abl*, **64** ii 13
  fortissimos, **98** *2* a 6
fra. . .[, **89** *1* 2 app
frater, pp. 170, 349; *see also* ἀδελφός
  voc, **87** 10; **88** *2* 5; *1* 4 app; **89** *6* 8; *38* 3; *39* 9; *43* 7; *48* 7; **111** 2
  fratres, *voc*, **89** *5* 11
frontis, **87** 22
fru[, **89** *56* 3
frui, p. 378
fru[m, **2** ix 6 app; fru[ment-, **89** *56* 3 app; frume[nt-, **101** a ii 11; b 2
frum, **47** ii 21
frumentatum, *supine*, **63** ii 19 app
frumentarius
  frum[entariis, **10** 32
  frumentarias, **63** ii 33
frumentatio, pp. 350, 407
  frumentationi, **101** a i 4
frumentum, pp. 126, 378; **2** xvi 17; **9** 31 e–f; **10** 2, 5, 8, 23, 27; **47** i 13; **79** 5
  frumenti, **13** 17; **14** 3
  frumento, **51** ii 23
frumentum menstruum, p. 255
fumị. . ṭat[u]m, **63** ii 19
fumigatum, **63** ii 19 app

g[.], **51** ii 21
galeariato, **9** 4 k and app
galearii, **9** 4 k app
Gallica (ala), **20** 11; **53** b 27; **80** 1
  Γαλλικῆς, *gen*, **76** i 2, 9; ii 1, 11; iii 1, 11, 20; iv 1, 11, 19; v 1, 11; vi 9, 18; vii 2, 8, 16; viii 2, 14, 19, 25; ix 2, 13; x 2, 15; xi 2, 12; xii 2, 11, 16, 19; xiii 2, 9, 16; xiv 2, 10; xv 2, 10, 11, 18; xvi 1, 11, 19; xvii 1, 8; xviii 1, 12, 25; xix 1, 13, 18; xx 1, 8, 18, 20; xxi 1; xxiv 1; BB 1; FF 1; GG 1, 9; HH i 1
gel, **9** 24 b app
gentilicium, **46** 2 app; pp. 177, 284
geometres, p. 242
Germanicus, *title*, **123** a 2
gla[, *adj.*, **83** 24
glaucus, **83** 24 app
go. .[.]s, **9** 3 h and app
go/gendum, **70** a iii 8–9
Gordiana, *title of unit*, **20** 11, 16 app; **50** i 5, 6, 11, 12, 15; ii 6; p. 137
gossipion, **9** 3 h app
gregalis, pp. 198, 284
groma, **15** ii 9; **19** 6; pp. 128, 136
gubernator, **59** i 5; p. 212

ḥ/. ., **9** 32 d
eas ḥ qụạli, **53** b 29
h.ṣ.[, **89** *5* 7
ḥạ., **72** 12
habere, **107**
  h(abet?), **131** a 1 and 6; b 2; p. 440
  habet, **68** ii 31; iii 28; **69** 16 app; **70** a i 10, 16, 23, 31; ii 6, 13, 22, 28, 36, 42; iii 6, 11, 18, 26; c 6; e 6; g 8; b i 5, 12, 19, 25; ii 6, 16; **72** 1 app, 6 app, 12 app; **73** a iii 10, 13, 14, 15, 16, 17, 18, 19, 20, 21, 22, 23, 24, 25, 26
  habeatur, **51** ii 5 app
  haberetis, **98** *2* a 3
  habuit, **68** ii 12, 22; iii 11, 21; **69** 10 app
  habuistis, **51** ii 7
harena, **9** 4 b
hastatus, **21** 12, 18, 19, 20; **51** ii 5; pp. 7, 198
ḥe[, **88** *1* 7
ḥẹḷ, **9** 3 n app
hemi-, **82** 3 app
hereditas, **77** a i 8 app, 17 app; **106** app
herede, **73** k 4 app; **106** app

hiberna
hib[ern-, **89** *10* 10
hibernis, **50** i 5, 11, 13; ii 5
hibernatur, **64** i 3
hic
huic, **87** 9
hos, **89** *54* 6
his, *abl*, **47** i 1 (three times), 4, 9 (three times); ii 4, 17; **48** 11; **49** 4; **50** i 5 (three times), 11 (three times); **52** a 11; b 10; c 5; **62** 4, 12; **66** b i 31; **89** *4* i 6a, 8; **92** ii 9, 13; v 4; **96** 7
Hispana (cohors), **63** i 24
hodie, **51** ii 7
h(omines?), p. 440
honestus
honesta (missio), **37** 1 app; **63** i 21 app; **117** i 7
honeste (emeritus), **47** ii 18; **65** 8; **70** b ii 4 app
hor..ṣ, **66** b i 23
hora, **53** b 18, 21
horcos, **66** b ii 28 app
hord[, **1** xxxvi 10
hordearius, **1** xix 4 app
hordeum, *see also* κριθή; **1** xxxiii 26; xli 2 and app; **47** ii 4; **66** b i 23 app; **91** *1* i 8; ii 1; p. 311
hordiator, **1** xxx 18; **47** ii 5
hordinacus, **30** ii 9 app
horm, **9** 23 b–d app
hormos, **10** 12
horreum, **1** xli 2 and app; **13** 17; **14** 3; p. 126
hospitio, **15** i 9, 14, 22; ii 16; p. 128
hostias, **1** xxxvi 22, 26; xlii 23; pp. 12, 14, 17

i, *letter*?, *numeral*?, **51** i 13 marg; **66** b ii 3
i.[, **40** ii 19; **50** ii 7
ị., **34** verso ii 17
ạd iat[, **2** x 19 and app
ịạṭo.., **15** ii 4; ịạṭọẹṣso, **15** ii 21
iconismus, **87** 14, 16, 18, 20, 22
iconismo, **87** 12
iconismos, **50** i 15; **87** 8; **99** *2* 3; **100** 2 app
iḍ.[..]., **9** 26 f
idem
eiusdem, **68** ii 14, 24?; iii 13?, 23?; **69** 19 app; **89** *1* 6
eodem, **10** 4, 6, 7 app, 9, 15, 21, 24, 28, 30, 31; p. 118; **32** 1, 4, 8, 12; **64** i 37, 40, 42; ii 7, 10, 14
easdem, **53** b 2?; **117** ii 1; iv 8?
iḷ[, **53** e 1
ille, **53** b 25, 27
illa, **53** b 9, 18
ịṃ[, **53** b 3
imaginifer, **1** xxviii 21 app; **2** xxii 16 app; pp. 11, 12, 17
imago, p. 14
immobilis, **89** *4* i 7 app
immolatio, **47** i 16; **117** ii 22
immunis, **89** *4* i 7 app; ii 10 app; **123** a 4 app; pp. 192, 210, 212
immunes, **30** ii 3
imperatum, **47** i 6; **48** 7; **50** i 1, 8; b 7; **53** b 30; **67** 6 app
imperator, *see also* αὐτοκράτωρ
ịṃ[, **53** b 3 app
imp, **63** i 21; **75** 10
imperator, **117** i 23 (twice), 26, 23–26 app; ii 10
imp(eratoris), **10** 3, 5, 12, 18, 20, 22, 27, 29, 31; **20** 15 app; **49** 1 app; **50** i 1, 8; **87** 25; **117** i 25
imp(eratore), **33** i 1; **37** 1; **70** a i 24; b ii 7; **90** *1* a 2; **98** *3* 5; **99** *1* 3, 9; **114** 2; p. 255
imp(eratores), *acc*, **98** *2* 6
imperium, **117** i 15, 17, 21; ii 3, 20; iii 4
imperi, **117** i 4
in, **1** viii 30; x 28; xv 18; xxvi 9, 21 app; xxx 18; xxxi 18; xxxiii 20; xxxv 33; xxxviii 9; xl 25; xliii 16; **2** xxxiii 21; xxxiv 24; **9** 4 m; 5 f, m; 7 d; 11 g; 15 d app, f; 16 f, g, m; 23 b; 25 k app; 26 f app, g; 29 b; 32 g app; **10** 6 app; **29** 2, 9; **40** ii 17; **47** i 1 (three times), 4, 9 (three times), 14; ii 4, 5, 17; **48** 11; **49** 4; **50** i 5 (four times), 11 (four times), 15 (twice); ii 5; **51** ii 9, 12, 15, 21; **52** a 11; b 10, 16; c 5; **53** b 11, 14, 15, 26? 28?; **54** a–c 5; **55** a 4; **62** 4, 12; **63** i 27 (twice), 35; ii 1 (twice), 4, 5, 6, 8, 9, 12, 15 (twice), 18, 20, 21 (twice), 22, 23, 27, 28, 29 (twice), 33 (twice), 36 (twice), 37, 39 (twice), 42 (twice); **64** i 15, 33, 34, 37, 40, 42; ii 1, 7, 16, 19, 23, 26, 29, 33, 36; **66** b i 23, 31; ii 3 app, 5; **68** ii 6, 17, 27, 29, 31; iii 5, 8, 16, 26, 28, 29; **69** 5, 7, 13, 22; **70** a i 6 (twice), 10 (twice), 12 (twice), 16 (twice), 19 (twice), 23 (twice), 27 (twice), 31 (twice); ii 2 (twice), 6 (twice), 9 (twice), 13 (twice), 42 (twice); iii 14, 18, 22; d 10, 12, 16, 18; e 2 (twice), 6; Aberd. 3; b i 1, 5 (twice), 8 (twice), 12, 15, 19, 21, 25; ii 5, 6, 10, 16; **73** a iii 25; **77** a i 11; **82** 2, 3, 4, 7, 8, 9, 10, 11, 12, 13; **87** 4, 5, 30; **89** *4* i 6; **90** *1* b 3; **91** *1* i 8; **92** ii 9, 13; v 4; **96** 7; **98** *2* a 7; **99** *1* 7; *3* 6; **100** 4; **117** ii 1; iv 8?; **129** 2; **130** 2 app; **132** 2, 9 app
in[, **1** xv 18; **9** 11 n
iṇ..[, **71** b 9
inalbis, *adj.*, **83** 21
ịṇḍ[, **47** ii 21
inducere, **90** *1* b 4
infiti[, **53** b 17
infra, **63** i 21 app; **99** *2* 4
inscription.[, **70** b ii 5a
inseruit, **53** b 11 app
instar, **77** a i 8
instrumen[t-, **101** a ii 9
insula, **9** 10 b; 34–37 app
inṭ[, **51** ii 5

interesse
interfuit, **53** b 13
intersit, **53** b 14 app; **132** 4 app
intra, **63** ii 24
inuictus
inuicti, **50** i 2
inuicto, **90** *1* a 2
ire
eunt, **67** 10 app
]eạ[t]ịs ?, **98** *3* 4 app
is
ei[?, **90** *1* e
eius, **53** c 5; **68** ii 24?; iii 13? 23? **93** b 2
ei, *dat*, **93** *2* a 7
ẹ[um, **102** a 7 app
eo, **70** a i 8, 14, 21; ii 4, 11, 17, 34, 40; iii 24; c 4; e 4; g 6; b i 3, 17; **77** a i 5; **91** *2* ii 6
ea, **89** *5* 16
eorum, **30** ii 3; **87** 8; **89** *4* 7 app; **98** 1 app
eos, **89** *56* 3; **102** a 7 app
eas, **53** b 29? and app
eis, **47** ii 8; **51** ii 8, 16, 21 app; **58** ii 2; **62** 2; **63** i 20?, 27 (twice), 35; ii 1 (twice), 3, 5, 6, 12, 15 (twice), 17, 20, 21, 23, 29, 33, 36, 39 (twice), 42 (twice), 44 (twice); **64** i 15, 33; **66** b i 23, 33; ii 3?, 4, 5, 6, 8, 27, 28, 29; d 1, 2; **68** ii 4, 15, 25; iii 3, 14, 24; **69** 3a, 11a, 20; **70** b ii 5, 21?
it[, **40** ii 20
item, **11 bis** a 7, 16; b ii 9, 14; **27** b marg 3 app; **30** ii 3, 8, 13; **34** verso ii 17; **40** ii, app to 18, 19, 20; **50** i 8 app, 15; **63** ii 19, 31, 32, 33 app, 37; **64** ii 25, 32; **66** a ii 3; **70** a i 29; ii 26; iii 16; b i 10, 23; ii 4 app, 12; **73** a ii 3, 18; **81** ii 12; **83** 18; **89** *1* 5 app; *4* i 10 app; *43* 2; **98** *3* 4
ἴτεμ, **35** 2; **128**
iterum, **53** b 13; **59** i 3; **99** *1* 10
ito..o, **15** i 10
iubere, **115** g 2 app
iube, **87** 6; **102** a 9
iussi, **49** app to 2, 5, 6, 7, 9; **89** *20* 3; **99** *2* 3; **100** 3
iumentum, p. 376
iumentorum, **63** ii 36
iumenta, **89** *11* 5 app
iunxi, **89** *53* 3
iurauerunt, **53** b 28
iussu, **63** ii 4, 5

ḳạ[.]., **5** iii 7
kar...[, **89** *1* 2 app
karcer, karus, kastellum, etc., *see under* 'c'.

laịsọ, **51** i 16
lam⟨i⟩nas, **82** 13
laterit, **70** a ii 19 app
latronibus, **63** ii 10
laureatae (litterae), p. 348
leaenu?, **9** 13 f app
leg, **15** i 20; **53** a ii 2; **63** i 32;
legatum, *legacy* **77** a i 8 app
legati, *gen*, **77** a i 8
legato, 77 a i 5, 14
lega(tur), **81** ii 14 app
legatus (Augusti), **63** i 31 app, 32 app; **91** *1* verso 2–3 app; **114** verso 2; pp. 220, 221
leg(ati), *gen*, **53** a ii 2 app; **63** ii 4, 5, 25; **81** ii l4a pp
leg(ato), **63** i 30 and app; 32 app; **99** *1* verso 3; *2* verso 2; *3* verso 2; **112** verso 2 app
legatum, **67** 6
legatus (legionis), **81** ii 14 app
legatus Parthorum, **98** *2* a 6
legio, *see also Index 4, Military Affairs, under the names of individual legions*; **34** recto i 1, 19; ii 5, 14; verso ii 9, 11; **58** i 1; **66** f 2; **77** a i 7 app, 21 app
leg(ionis), **20** 2, 15 app; **21** 19 app; **51** ii 4; **89** *1* verso 1 app; **91** *2* i 6; **102** a 7
legionem, **1** xxvi 21 app
leg(ione), **34** verso ii 12 app; **53** a ii 2 app; **63** ii 25 app; **64** ii 13
legionarius, **50** i 7, 13
legionariorum, **53** b 24
ad leones, **1** xx 20; xxii 7; xxvi 5, 6; xxxi 3; xxxiv 30; xxxvi 9; **2** xiii 6; xiv 16; xv 19; xxxiv 28; **4** m 5 app
liber (epistularum), pp. 355, 356, 411, 417
liberalitas, **47** i 16 app
libertus, *see also* ἀπολύσιμος; **28** 10 app; pp. 383, 434
lib(ertum), **91** *1* i 7
liberto, **10** 16
librarius, **47** i 17; pp. 180, 383
librarium, **91** *2* i 6
librarii, *pl*, **58** ii 9
librariorum, **28** 10 app
librariis, **63** ii 34
λιβραρίοις, **78** *67* 5
liburna, **28** 10; pp. 4, 152, 338
lib(urnam), **82** 3, 4, 9, 10, 13, 16
lignare, **47** ii 9 app
lignator, **9** 3 m app;.**47** ii 9
limitis, **91** *1* verso 2–3 app
liq(uidae), **82** 2
littera, p. 348
littera..[, **102** a 8
litterarum, **90** *1* c 1
litteras, **90** *1* a 3
litteris, **89** *8* 9
li[tora], **51** ii 2 app
lixa, **9** 4 k app
locus, **70** a ii 19 app
loco, **11 bis** a 5–6 app, 13, 20; **64** i 10; **89** *4* i 6; p. 122
loricem, **70** a i 6 and app; iii 22; b ii 10

lorictitis, **70** a i 27; ii 2, 9, 15, 24, 32, 38; iii 2, 14; b i 8; d 18 app
loric-, **70** a i 6, 12, 19; iii 9; c 2, 9; e 2; g 4, 10; b i 1, 15, 21; ii 19
Lus(itanorum), **64** i 1
Λουσιτανῶν, **74** i 2, 9; ii 2, 9; iii 2, 9

ṃ, **9** 32 c
m[, **29** 11
m.[..].[, **37** 1
ad ṃ[.]..ṃạ., **1** xii 3 and app
m[...]ụs, **89** *10* 1 and app
mạ...., **52** a 5
macelli, **51** ii 13
magister (campi), **48** 8; **102** a 8a app
magistro, **102** a 8a
magni.[, **70** b ii 4
Magnus, *title*, **117** i 17, 18; ii 2
m′ ambul, ad m ambul, ad man′ ambul; p. 14; *see also under* mamm; **1** xii 3 app; xxxiii 2, 19; xxxiv 4, 10, 24; xxxv 3; xxxvi 12; xxxvii 24, 29, 30, 34; xxxviii 26, 27; xxxix 2, 11; xli 17, 19, 32 app; xlii 8, 25; xliv 13
ad mamm, **2** xxxii 20; xxxiii 8, 12, 14; xxxvii 7, 8, 9, 16, 17, 21, 24; xxxviii 31; xxxix 10, 15, 19; xl 17, 28
mandra, **2** x 21 and app
manere
m[anent], **89** *4* i 7 app
manserunt, **15** ii 7 app; **47** ii 8
manus, **87** 20
m(arem) (*bouem*), **117** i 4, 8, 13, 16, 18, 22 (twice), 24 (twice); ii 2, 3, 4, 6, 20, 21, 23, 24; iii 1, 5 (twice), 6, 8
Martialis, *adj.*, **117** ii 9
mater
matris, **117** ii 26
matri, **117** ii 15
mater castrorum, **117** iii 7 app; p. 349
ṃạṭị, **73** a iii 33
matricula, **37** 1 app; pp. 2, 3, 167
matrix, pp. 2, 3
maximus, **117** i 4, 8, 14, 28; **123** a 2
ṃe..., **11 bis** a 8; **89** *8* 10
medicus, medicus centurio, medicus ordinarius, **74** i 3 app
memoriae, **117** ii 12; pp. 88, 90 note 1, 144, 170, 220, 255 note 1, 341, 349
mensis, *see also μήν*; *gen*, **64** i 2; **80** 5
mensor, **25** a 4
mensorem, **50** i 3, 9
Mercuṛ[, *liburna*, **28** 10
Mercuri, *quarter of Alexandria*, **10** 5, 8, 23
ad metella (*sic*), **63** ii 22
meus, **88** *2* 8 and app
meorum, **98** *1* and app
meis, **80** 5; **89** *8* 9 app
mị[, **89** *10* 8
miles, *see also στρατιώτης*
mil( ), **47** ii 17; **52** a 5; **89** *14* 3 app; *18* 1; *20* 1; *25* 2; *54* 4; **97** a 7
mil(es), **9** 3 m app; **47** i 14; ii 9
miles, **133** 3 app
mil(item), **34** verso ii 17 app
mil(ite), **53** b 12
mil(ites), *nom.* **47** i 1, 4, 9, 13; ii 1, 4, 5, 6, 14, 18; **50** i 5; **52** b 11; **53** b 26; **61** ii 8; **63** i 21 app; **65** 2, 3, 5, 7, 8, 9; **66** a i 6 (twice), 8; ii 1, 4; b i 6, 24, 31; ii 1, 2, 3, 4, 7, 27, 28; **90** *1* a 6; **92** ii 9, 13
mil(itum), **54** a–c 3 app; **63** i 26, 36 app
mil(itibus), *dat*, **117** i 8, 25
mil(ites), *acc*, **89** *1* 2 app; *4* i 3
miliaria (cohors), p. 90
militare, **63** i 21; **64** i 8
militia, **63** i 21 app
m(ille), **63** i 21
m(ilia), **27** b marg (four times)
ad ministerium, **63** ii 4 app
ex ministerio, **89** *4* i 4
minor(is), **34** recto ii 12
missicius, **89** *26* 2 app
missio, **117** i 7; **37** 1 app; **63** i 21 app; pp. 158, 218
missio causaria, **63** i 11 app; p. 220
mittere
mittas, **88** *1* 4 app; **107** (three times)
mitte, **93** b 1
misi, **89** *1* 4; *3* 5?
misit, **47** i 3, 11; **50** i 7, 13
m(issus), **1** xxxviii 15; xli 10, 11
mis(sus), **2** xii 28 and app; **9** 3 m app; 12 f; **37** 1 app; **47** ii 9; **70** b ii 13 a; **89** *10* 1 app; **92** ii 11?; **98** *2* a 6
missus, **98** *2* 6; **133** 2 app; p. 400
missi, **47** i 4, 13; ii 4, 5; **53** a i 4?; **65** 8; p. 192
Moesicam (classem), **63** ii 4
moneta, **10** 20
mora, **89** *1* 2 app; **90** *1* b 3
mos, **99** *1* 8; *3* 6; **100** 4
morem, **91** *1* 9–10 app; **98** *2* 7
mulionibus, *dat*, **91** *1* i 7
multatus, multati, **47** ii 21 app
multis (annis), **89** *1* 9; *5* 12; **91** *2* i 10; **111** 3; p. 349 note 8
murinum (equum), **83** 10; **99** *3* 3 app
mutare
mutant, **89** *43* 9 and app
mutantes?, **51** ii 21 app
mutatus, mutati, **47** ii 21, 22

ṇ, **50** i 4
n(auales?), **59** i 9 app
n s (*non sanus*?), **8** iv 1?; v 3; vii 3, 7; x 8, 12, 13?, 14; pp. 13, 16

ṇạoci.[, **15** ii 1
natalicias, **117** i 19
natalem, **117** i 10, 11, 13; ii 2, 4, 5, 6, 7, 12, 19, 21, 23, 26, 28; iii 1, 4, 6, 7, 8; iv 7?; i 10 app; 17–18 app; ii 2 app; 28 app; iii 1 app; 4–6 app; iv 7–8 app; p. 423
natio, *see Index 4, Military Affairs*, origo
nauarium, **63** ii 33 app
nauis
  nauis, **82** 11 app
  nauem, **1** xix 4, 25; xxix 24
  naues, *acc*, **2** xxxi 6; **63** ii 33
  nauibus, **96** 2
naulum, **80** 5
Ṇemọṣenoi, **30** ii 8 app
Nico(politana?), **9** 5 k, 16 k, 27 k
nigrum, **83** 5
nobilissimorum, **86** 2
nomen, **2** ii a 5 app; **11** ii 2 app; **52** a 6 app; b 15 app; **63** i 25 app; **74** iii 8 app; **89** *15* verso app; **91** *1* verso 2–3 app; **96** 4 app; **112** verso 2 app; pp. 4, 5, 161, 165, 245, 284, 285, 312
  nomen, *acc*, **51** ii 15
  nomina, **50** i 15; **55** c 1; **87** 7; **89** *4* i 10; **92** ii 14; **96** 1
nominatio, **50** i 14 app
non (*see also* n s), **1** xlii 18; **2** xii 18; **47** ii 20; **51** ii 9 (twice); **63** i 34; ii 13; **66** b ii 2
nonaginta, **77** a i 4, 11, 18; b 5
nonus: nona, **53** b 18
noscere
  notum, **92** ii 15; **98** *2* 3
noster, **91** *1* i 4; *2* i 4, 8; **108**; **117** i 25, 27; ii 16, 18
  nostri, *gen*, **29** 3, 10; **47** i 6, 17; **49** 1; **50** i 1, 8; **59** i 9; **87** 25; **96** 6 app; **117** i 3, 29; ii 26
  nostrorum, **83** 15; **86** 1; **91** *1* i 7, verso 2; *2* verso 2; **98** *2* 2
  nostrum, **67** 6; **88** *1* 6 app; **123** b 2 app
  nostros, **98** *2* 6
  nostro, **2** xvi 5; xxvi 10; xxxi 20; **31** i 12; ii 6; **33** i 1; **50** i 14 (twice); **66** a i 11; b i 1, 7, 21; ii 25; **90** *1* a 1
  nostris, **99** *1* 3, 9
  nn, **98** *4* 2 app
nota, **83** 8, 14, 19, 21; **99** *1* 6, 8 and app
notare
  n(otat-), **83** 2, 5, 10, 15, 23, 24; **99** *1* 8?; *3* 4
nouis, **82** 11
num, **89** *1* 7–8 app
numerare, **65** 10
  numerentur, **117** i 8
numerus, *see also* ἀριθμός *and Index 4, Military Affairs*; **47** i 1, 9; ii 1, 14; **50** i 5, 11; **62** 1; **66** b ii 9, 10, 11, 12, 13, 14, 15; **81** ii 8 app; p. 192
  numeri, *gen*, **89** *1* verso 1 app
  numero, **29** 11?; **30** ii 8, 13; **50** i 14; **51** ii 16; **52** b 11; **62** 3; **63** ii 14; **82** 5
  numerorum, **98** *2* 1, 5, 8; f 1; p. 400
  numeros, **29** 2, 9; **50** i 15; **87** 5; **89** *4* i 3; *25* 2 and 5 app
Numidae, **52** c 6: nom[idarum
nummorum, **73** a iii 30; **86** 4
nuncupentur, **117** i 3

o., **34** recto i 6 marg
ob, **54** a–c 6 app; **89** *1* 7–8 app; **117** i 2, 3, 10, 11, 13, 14, 15, 17, 19, 21; ii 1, 2, 3, 4, 5, 6, 7, 8, 9, 12, 14, 15, 19, 20, 21, 22, 23, 25, 26, 28; iii 1, 4, 6, 7, 8; ii 26–28 app
obiit, **34** recto i 6 app; **77** a i 7 app
obolus, *see* ὀβολός
obseruari, **101** a i 6
occidere: occisus, **63** ii 10
octingenti: octogentum, **86** 4
octo, **84** 4; **89** *4* i 3
of[, **70** d 18
offerre, **98** *2* a 7
officina, **58** i 37 app
officium
  off, **4** b ii 11; f 3; j 1 and app; **66** a i 8 app; b ii 27; **96** 3
  offi.[, **48** 5
  offici, *loc*, **5** iii 8; **63** ii 26
  officio, **1** i 12, 16; ii 8, 9; vii 16; viii 2; x 8 app; xiii 21; xv 12; xvii 9; xviii 11; xix 1; xxii 18; xxiii 7; xxv 3; xxviii 4; xxix 1, 5, 12; xxxi 10; xxxii 28; xxxv 6, 13; xxxvi 17, 24; xxxvii 2, 31; xl 12, 24; xli 20; xlii 21; **2** i 8; vi 1, 8; xii 24; xiv 21; xix 18; xxi 10; xxii 27; xxviii 3, 13; xxx 6; xxxi 18, 19; xxxv 4, 10, 16; xxxix 11; xlii 7; **34** recto i 6 app; **70** b 18 app; **92** v 16; vi 8; ix 14
olei, **82** 3
omnis, **68** ii 23; iii 12, 22
  omnes, **50** i 12; **65** 9 app
  omnem, **47** i 6, 16; **48** 7; **50** i 1 (*omniam*)
ọṇ..., **34** verso ii 8
onero, **34** recto i 2 app
onro, **34** recto i 19 app; verso ii app
opera, *abl*, **58** ii 3
opinio, pp. 14, 235
  opinionem, **1** viii 25; xxi 2; xxvii 14; xxviii 16, 17; xxix 3; xxxi 8; xxxix 28; xli 25; xliii 29; **2** i 1; ix 16; xi 28, 31; xii 10; xix 4; xxix 24; xxx 24; xxxii 26; xxxiv 17; xxxv 24; xxxvi 3; xliii 16, 18, 19; xliv 20, 26; xlv 2, 14; **65** 5, 6; **66** b i 29; ii 1; ii 2? (*opinione*)
oportet, **101** a i 7 app
optimo, **117** i 4, 8
optio, *see also Index 4, Military Affairs*; **47** i 17 (*option*); **75** 19 app; **77** a i 1?; a i 7; pp. 198, 311
  ὀπτίων, **76** ii 8; xix 9; **78** *31* 5; *36* 2; **81** ii 5; **89** *3* 4; **123** a 4 app

optioni, **77** a i 13; ὀπτίωνι, **78** *1* 2; *2* 2; *4* 2; *5* 2; *7* 2; *8* 3; *9* 3, 7 app; *11* 1; *12* 2 (ὀπτίων); *23* 3; *72* 4
opto, **89** *1* 8; *12* i 7; *38* 7; *39* 9; *48* 6; **91** *2* i 9; **97** b 4; **98** *2* a 3; **107** (twice); **111** 2; p. 349
ordinare, **91** *1* i 6 app
ordinarius, *see* ordinatus
medicus ordinarius, **74** i 3 app
ordinatus, pp. 10, 11, 12, 137; **1** i 2; xi 2; xvi 9; xxi 2; **2** xvi 17; **4** a i 9 app; **6** ii 23; iv 17; **17** a 12; **20** 19 app, 22; **25** a 1; **30** ii 9 (*hordinatus*); **47** i 1; **50** i 1, 2, 8, 9; ii 1; a 1, 2; **52** b 4?; **66** b i 31; ii 5 app; **96** 7 and app; **123** a 4 app
ordinati, **20** 17; **50** i 5, 11
ordinatus decurio, **20** 22 app
ordinatus princeps, **50** i 1, 8, 14 app; ii 1; a 1
ordo decurionum, **20** 17 app
origo, *see also Index 4, Military Affairs*; *Index 7, Geography, Ethnics*; *and this index s.v.* domus; pp. 4, 5, 7, 165, 169, 181; **9** 11 a app; **69** 1 app; **70** a i 11 app; ii 31 app; d 17 app
ornatus, *noun*, **9** 3 c–d; 4 k app
Orontalium, *gen*, **30** ii 13 app
ọṣṭṛ, **9** 15 h–k

p d cc, **33** ii 5; iii 2; iv 2, 5; v 1, 2, 3, 6; vi 1, 7; p. 159
pp, **89** *1* verso 1 and app
pạ.[, **9** 5 n
pạ[.].ṃ[, **36** 15
pagane, paganic( ), **9** 15 e app
paganus: pagano, **9** 15 e; **64** i 20
pallidus, **83** 19 app
Palmyrenus
Palmyreni, **90** *1* c 3
Palmyrenorum, **47** i 2, 10; ii 2, 15; **48** 4; **50** i 5, 6, 11, 12, 13, 15; ii 5, 6; **81** ii 8 app; **89** *1* 2; *4* i 4; *7* 10; *8* 5; *14* 4; *18* 1–2 app; *20* 1; *25* 3; *28* 2; *57* 2; **90** *1* a 6; **91** *2* i 1 and app; **97** a 3; **99** *1* 6; *2* 5; *3* 5; **100** 3; **101** a i 5; **110** 2; **114** 8; **118** 4; **119** 2
Παλμυρηνων, **89** *31* 2 and app; *41* 2
palos, **9** 6 b–f app
Pannoni[cum, **63** ii 8 app
papili, **9** 21 h app
paṛ, paṣ, **2** viii 24; xxxiii 9
parati, **47** i 6, 16; **50** i 4, 8, 10; b 3; **52** b 3; **67** 7 app
parcus?, **53** b 5
pariare
pariari, **98** *4* 6
pariati, **98** *4* 6 app
pars: parte, **87** 23
Parthicus
Parthicae, *dat*, **117** i 15
Parthicam, **117** i 14; ii 26–28 app
Parthorum, **98** *2* a 6
patriae, **117** i 27–28 and app
pater, **117** i 27–28
patris, **117** i 19
patri, **117** i 5, 9, 19; ii 9
patres, *voc*, **89** *1* 7–8 app
pe[, **89** *10* 7
peç.[, **9** 3 n and app
pecua(rius)?, **9** 27 d and app; 3 n app
pecus: pecoribus, **89** *43* 10; p. 350
ped (*pedes* or *pedester*), **63** i 28; ii 2, 16, 30, 43
pedes, pedites, **64** i 17; **81** ii 12; ii 8 app; **92** vii 15–16 app; pp. 16, 17, 90, 97, 150, 181, 336
pedester, *see* ped
penum, **2** xxxiii 15 and app; xxxv 19; **89** *35* 4 app
per, **80** 6; **87** 25; **89** *1* 5; **98** *2* a 5
perfe.[, **53** a ii 4
perferre: perlatam, **89** *1* 7–8 app
perfectus
perfecti, **53** a ii 4 app
perfecta, **63** i 36 app; **64** i 14 app
perfectissimo, **20** 3, 9, 15 app
perfo.[, **53** a ii 3
perfoṛ[tes, **53** a ii 3 app
perfunctione, **2** xxxiii 21 and app
perire: peri<i>t, **63** ii 9
permanserunt, **50** i 6
personatus, **99** *1* 5
pertinet, **90** *1* c 2 app
pes: pedibus, **83** 8, 14, 21
petere
peto, **88** *1* 4 app; *2* 5; **89** *1* 2 app; 7–8 app; **91** *1* i 6; *2* i 5
petat, **93** b 1
petendam, **65** 6 app; **66** b ii 1
phal (*phalaricis*? *phalaris*? *phalis*?), **9** 4 c and app; 8 e; 9 c, 27 d app
pili (i.e. *primipili*), **9** 20 b app
pilọ[, **9** 20 b
pilus, *see also* primipilus
pil(us) pos(terior), **21** 3 and 7
pin.[, **70** b ii 22
pius
pii, *gen*, **50** i 2, 8; **117** ii 3, 4, 20
pio, **117** ii 3, 4, 11
pia, **53** b 22
pix: picis, **82** 2
pḷ.ụ.tụ...ṭ, **66** a ii 4
pollio: pollione, **89** *3* 7
pondo, *adv.*, **82** 4, 7, 8, 9, 10, 11, 14
pondus: pondera, **51** ii 13
pontifex, **117** i 28
populus Romanus, p. 6
populi Romani, **117** i 4
por (*portae*? *portorii*? *portus*?), **9** 6 h; 8 b; 21 h; 22 c; 25 e app; 25 f; 29 h app; 33 g

porta, **13** 6, 12, 13; **15** i 17, 18; ii 8, 10, 11, 15; b 4 app; **17** a 6, 7; pp. 126, 128, 133
portae, *gen*, **9** 6 h app
portam, **51** i 23 app
portare: portetur, **89** *5* 10; *5* 15?
portorii, **9** 6 h app
portus, **9** 6 h app
poscere: poscit *or* poscimus, **90** *1* d and app
poscu.[, **70** b ii 4a
poss[, **53** b 24; **70** b ii 23
posse: poterit, **91** *2* ii 7
post, **63** i 29; **64** i 19
posterior, **15** i 21; **34** recto ii 12 app; **66** b i 19 app; **92** vi; pp. 5, 157, 320
posterioris, **2** xlv 10; **21** 3, 5, 6, 7, 9, 10, 11, 12; **24** 12; **27** a i 13; **66** a i 9; **92** iii 15
posterioribus, **83** 8, 14
potamofulacide, **10** 29
p̣ọụḷilfuṣo, **75** 7
pr, **34** recto i 8
]pr, **66** b i 24
pr[, **9** 5 n app; **66** a ii 2; **89** *7* 10
pr[..]ụṣ/ạṃ.ọc̣ụla, **9** 17 c and app
pṛ[.].us, **53** a i 8
pra[e-, prae[, **53** b 25; **91** *1* ii 3; **96** 4; **98** f 2
praecipere: praecepi, **48** 5; **50** i 15; **89** *4* i 10 app; *5* 9 app; **91** *1* ii 3 app
praecise, *adv.*, **98** *4* 5
praedium: praediis, **91** *1* i 9; ii 3 app; p. 383
praees, **87** 5; **89** *4* i 4; **99** *1* 7; *2* 5; *3* 5; **100** 3 app; **101** a i 6
praefect-, **5** ii 6 and app; **52** a 4; **55** d 2?; **96** 4 app
praefectus, *see also Index 4, Military Affairs*; p. 362
praefecti, *gen*, **9** 2 m
praefecto, *dat*, **89** *1* verso 1?
praefectis, *dat*, **98** *2* 1; f 1
—— Aegypti, *see also Index 3, Notable Persons*; **20** 6, 9, 20, 23; 15 app; **64** i 21, 33; ii 14–15; **75** 4
—— alae, *see also Index 4, Military Affairs*; **102** a 12
—— annonae, **20** 3 app
—— arcis, **20** 6 app
—— castrorum, *see also Index 3, Notable Persons, and Index 4, Military Affairs*; **5** ii 6 app; **9** 2 m app; **10** 3; p. 241
—— cohortis, *see also Index 4, Military Affairs*; **63** i 24 app, 25; **64** i 6; **102** a 1
—— fabrum, p. 241
—— legionis, *see also Index 4, Military Affairs*; **89** *1* verso 1?; **102** a 7; pp. 4, 241, 409
—— praetorio, **83** 2, 5, 10, 11, 12, 19; **96** 3
—— urbi, p. 82
—— uigilum, p. 409
praenomen, pp. 4, 5, 137, 176, 177, 284, 311, 434; **11** ii 2 app; **20** 1 app; **74** ii 9 app; iii 8 app; **75** 1 app; **76** viii 14 app
Aulus, **9** 23 a; **36** 9; **64** i 29
Gaius, **9** 2 a, 3 a, 4 a, 9 a, 11 a, 12 a, 19 a, 20 a, 25 a, 26 a, 28 a app, 35 a; **11** ii 5, 8; **36** 1, 2, 10, 11; **37** 2, 4; **46** 3, 5; **64** i 41; ii 2, 27; **68** iii 1; **77** a ii 2?; **87** 2, 11, 13, 15, 19
γ(άιος), **74** ii 9; γάιος, **75** 18
Decimus, **9** 8 f–n, 20 f–k
Lucius, **9** 5 a, 8 a, 24 a, 27 a, 36 a; **36** 5, 12, 13; **45** 1; **46** 1; **58** ii 15 app; **117** i 11 (twice), 21, 22; **133** 1 (twice)
λ(ουκίω), **76** viii 14 app; λουκίου, **76** xvi 15
Manius, **36** 6
Marcus, *see also* Marcus Aurelius; **9** 7 a, 15 a, 16 a, 17 a, 30 a, 32 a, 33 a, 37 a; **10** 1; **20** 15 app; **46** 1 app, 2?; **50** i 2, 8; **51** i 24 app; **64** i 6 (twice); **87** 21; **117** i 3, 23; ii 6 (twice)
μ(ᾶρκος), **78** *9* 2; *11* 1; *39* 1?; *39* 4–5?
Marcus Aurelius, p. 311; **46** 1 app, 2?, 3, 5, 6, 7
μᾶρκ(ος) αὐρῆλις, **78** *1* 1; μ(ᾶρκος) αὐρῆλις, **78** *8* 1; *39* 1?; *39* 4–5?
Publius, **9** 6 a, 29 a
Quintus, **9** 10 a, 17 a app, 22 a, 28 a; **36** 3, 7; **37** 3; **68** ii 2
κούιντος, **74** iii 8
Sextus, **36** 4; **64** i 23
Titus, pp. 116, 117; **9** 13 a, 14 a, 21 a app, 26 a app, 34 a; **10** 2, 11, 17, 26; **68** ii 32 app
τίτου, **78** *73* 7
p̣ṛep̣, **5** ii 6 app
praepositus, *see also Index 4, Military Affairs*; pp. 128, 361, 377, 383, 400, 406, 417
prae[posit-, **96** 4 app; praeposi[, **89** *5* 3
praepositus, **20** 6 app; **50** i 7, 13, 11 app; ii 7
praepositi, **15** i 22; ii 16
praeposito, *dat*, **89** 1 verso 1?; **114** verso 1
praepositus praetenturae, **89** *47* verso 2 and app; **91** *1* verso 3 and app; *2* verso 3
praeses, p. 397
praesidis, **47** ii 8; **66** a i 8; **89** *42* 9 and app
praesidem, **70** b ii 13a app
praesentes, pp. 180, 181, 201, 215, 216, 233; **52** b 7; c 2; a 4 app; **62** 4; **63** ii 41; **89** *5* 8 app; **96** 1 app
]sente, **91** *2* ii and app
praesidium, **70** b ii 13a app
praesidio, **63** ii 21, 27
praetentura, pp. 377, 383
praetenturae, **89** *47* verso 2 and app; **91** *1* verso 3; *2* verso 3
praetenturam, **91** *1* verso 3 app
praetore, **63** i 30 app; **89** *5* 3 app; **99** *1* verso 3; *2* verso 2; *3* verso 2; **112** verso 2 app; **114** verso 2
praetoriana (porta), pp. 126, 128; **13** 6; **15** i 18; ii 11; **17** a 7

praetorium, p. 14
pr, **34** recto i 8 app
praetorio, **17** a 8 app; **96** 3
praetorium, **1** xxi 8; xxxvi 7; **2** xxxiii 11; xl 11?; **4** a i 9 and app; **47** ii 8; **63** ii 34; **66** a i 2 and app; i 8 app; **82** 7
praetoria (cohors), **20** 15; **64** i 1
p̣ṛẹḅ[, **53** b 5
premere:]p̣ṛẹṣṣ, **53** a i 5
pretium, **75** 3; p. 3
p[r]ẹtora, **2** xl 11
pridianum, pp. 2, 4, 177, 180–82, 201, 214, 217, 218, 233, 235, 401; **63** i 24; **64** i 1; ii 1 app
pridian.[, **98** *3* 3
primipilus, primus pilus, *see also Index 4, Military Affairs*; **9** 20 b app; **89** *1* verso 1 app; **129** 4
primipilari, **89** *1* verso 1 app
primo, *adv.*, **117** i 26; ii 18
primus, **51** ii 5; **53** a 1, 8 app
primo, *adj. or adv.?*, **47** ii 16; **52** a 5; **98** *4* 6
princeps, *see also Index 4, Military Affairs*; pp. 7, 198, 277; **50** i 1, 2, 8; ii 1; **51** ii 6; **55** b 2; **62** 6 app; **67** 4
principis, **9** 5 h; 27 h; **13** 18 app
princeps prior, **21** 4, 8, 14, 16, 21
princeps posterior, **21** 5, 6, 9, 10, 11, 13; **45** 3 app
ordinatus princeps, **50** i 1, 2, 8; ii 1
principalis, *see also Index 4, Military Affairs*; pp. 2, 4, 10, 12, 143, 144, 146, 169, 192, 212; **62** 6 app
principia: principiis, **51** ii 5 app; **54** a–c 5; **55** a 4; **62** 6 app; p. 207
prior, **92** vi; pp. 5, 157, 183
prioris, **2** xlv 3; **15** i 16, 17; ii 7; **21** 4, 8, 14, 16; **23** i 4; **24** 20; **27** a i 7; **33** ii 1; **34** recto ii 12 app; **47** i 15; **66** a ii 8; b i 17, 19 app, 23; **92** iii 9
priore, **68** ii 12, 22; iii 21; **69** 10; **70** a i 28; ii 25; iii 15; b i 9, 22; ii 11; **72** 3 app, 8 app
priorem, **72** 6 app
prioribus, **83** 21
priuilegiorum, **117** i 7
pro, pp. 12–13; **1** vii 6; xii 3; xiii 6, 30; xvi 10; xviii 10; xxii 15; xxvi 1, 5, 6; xxviii 14, 28; xxx 14; xxxii 9; xxxiii 10; xxxiv 19, 23, 26, 30; xxxv 3, 14; xxxvi 15, 23, 32; xxxvii 6, 7, 13, 15; xxxviii 27, 28; xxxix 11, 14; xl 15; xli 14, 15, 28; xlii 1, 3; xliii 21; **2** xvi 4; **9** 6 b–f; 11 b–f; 17 g–m; 19 g–m; **63** i 30 app; **70** a ii 18; **89** *5* 3 app; **99** *1* verso 3; *2* verso 2; *3* verso 2; **112** verso 2 app; **114** verso 2
probare, p. 340
probandum, **1** xxxviii 18; **89** *42* 2
probatus, **66** b i 5–10 app
probati, **50** i 14; **63** i 30 app; **64** i 31; **75** 3
probatum, **83** 2, 4, 5, 8, 10, 11, 12, 14, 19, 24; **99** *1* 6; *3* 4
probatos, **50** i 15; **87** 4; **99** *2* 4; **100** 3
probatio, p. 403; **50** i 14 app
procurator, *see also Index 3, Notable Persons*; pp. 14, 16, 333, 350 and note 16, 357, 358, 359, 361, 362, 363, 366, 367, 383, 397, 400, 434
proc, **88** *1* 8; **89** *5* 3; *8* 8; *14* 5; *15* 3; *18* 3
procurator, **80** 2; **91** *1* i 5 app, 6 app; verso 2 and 2–3 app; ii 1 app; *2* i 9 app; verso 2
procuratoris, **4** b ii 11; f 3; j 1 app; **63** ii 26; **66** b ii 27; **89** *4* i 5
procuratori, **98** *2* a 2
procuratore, **83** 15, 17
proferre:]profers.[, **73** h 3
proficisci, **48** 5
promotus, **34** recto i 8 app
promotis (equitibus), **86** 1
pronuntiare: pronuntiauit, **47** i 6, 16; ii 11; **50** i 1, 8; **51** ii 6?; **52** b 2, 14; **53** b 29
proreṣaratum, **83** 8
proroṣṭratum, **83** 8 app
prosecutionem, **1** xxx 18; **2** xxxiv 24; **47** ii 5
prosedit, **53** b 25
prouinciam, **63** ii 23, 24
proxime, **67** 5 app
proximus, **102** a 11 and app
Ptolemaicus, **77** a i 8 app
punc, **4** b i 9
purus, **47** i 1, 9; ii 1, 14; **50** i 5, 11; **66** b ii 9, 10, 11, 12, 13, 14, 15
puro, **63** ii 14
putare: puta, putat, putate, **53** b 16 app
p̣utateṣa, **53** b 16

q d p, pp. 192, 234, 235; **47** i 5 and app; ii 6, 7, 8, 21; **66** b i 23, 29, 33; ii 3, 4, 6, 8, 18, 27, 28; d 1, 2; f 1; **89** *20* 2 app
q[(porta), **13** 13
qụ[, **77** b 3; **89** *10* 6 and 9; **93** b 1
qụ[.]m.[, **98** *3* 6; in app, *qu[e]m*
qu..ṇt, **52** a 2
quadrans, *see* **70** a i 9 app *and* **73** a i 17 app; *transcribed in* **70** *as* 'e'; *in* **73** *as* 'f'; **70** a i 7, 9, 13, 15, 20, 22; ii 3, 5, 10, 12, 16, 21, 33, 35, 39, 41; d 2, 7, 9, 13, 15, 19, 21; e 3, 5; b i 2, 4, 16, 18; **73** a i 9, 17, 18, 26; iii 22, 23, 29, 30; f 4, 6?; a iii 30 app
quadrimum (equum), **83** 2, 14, 17, 21; **99** *1* 5
quadringenti, **86** 5
quaerendum, **2** xii 28 and app; **65** 6 app
quaestionario, *abl*, **20** 2 app
quaestura, pp. 341, 400, 401; **78** *55* 7 app
[quae]ṣṭur....[, **89** *55* 3 and app
quaesturam, **70** a ii 18
quaesturas, **98** *2* a 5
quaes⟨t⟩ura, *abl*, **83** 16
qualis: quali, **53** b 29

quantitate, **98** *4* 9
quarto, **99** *1* 8
quater, **50** i 4 app
quattuor, **50** i 4 app; **84** 5
querendum?, **2** xii 28 and app; xxxv 17; xli 17
qui, *relative-indefinite*, q[u, **53** b 19; qu.[, **77** b 10; quị[, **89** *4* i 8; quae, **89** *4* i 8; quod, **90** *1* c 2
qui, *sing*, **88** *1* 6; **89** *42* 11; **93** b 1
qui, *pl*, **51** ii 8; **63** i 21; **89** *4* i 7 app; *14* 3–5 app; *36* 3; **91** *1* i 7
quorum, **50** i 15; **89** *4* i 6 and 9; **92** ii 14; **96** 1; **99** *2* 3; **100** 2 app
cui, *masc*, **89** *4* i 5; *36* 3; **102** a 13
quibus, *dat*, **51** ii 14
quem, **89** *1* 6; *42* 13; **98** *3* 6 app
quos, **70** a i 30; ii 27; iii 17; f 2; b i 11, 24; ii 15; **97** a 7 app; **98** *2* 5
quibus, *abl*, **77** a i 3, 9, 16; **88** *2* 7
quae, *sing*, **63** ii 38 app; **64** i 3
quarum, **52** a 2 app; **89** *54* 5
cui, *fem*, **87** 5; **89** *4* i 4; **99** *1* 7; *2* 5; *3* 5; **100** 3 app; **101** a i 6
quam, **51** ii 7
quas, **77** b 4?; **90** *1* a 3
quod, *nom*, **47** i 6; **48** 7; **50** i 1, 8; b 7
quodam, **90** *1* c 2 and app
quidem, **98** *4* 6
quingenaria?, *abbreviated* 'd', **63** i 24
quinos, **101** a ii 10 and app
quinque, **77** a i 4, 11, 17, 18; b 3?, 5; **84** 1; **99** *1* 7
quintanesio, **9** 6 b–f; 11 b–f; 17 g–m; 19 g–m
quintus, **38** i 10 app
quintum, **89** *1* 6; *29* 14 app
quis: quid, **91** *1* i 3; *2* i 3; **98** *2* a 2 and 7; **101** a i 3 app; **114** 3 and p. 417; quid[, **114** 5
quisque: quoque, **98** *2* a 8
quo Arabum, p. 128; **15** ii 13
quọạḍ.[, **13** 9
quod, *conj.*, **117** i 2, 7, 23, 24, 27; ii 10, 16, 18, 26–28 app
quondam, **47** i 5 app; **89** *1* 3

r, *meaning unknown*, **4** a i 5; **53** b 24
r (*rediit* or *reuersus*), **10** 4 and app, 6, 7, 9, 13, 19, 20, 22, 24, 28, 30, 31, 33; **38** i 10 app
ṛ[, **9** 2 b, 13 d; **52** a ii 2
ṛ...ṭa, **70** a ii 20
ṛ[..]utor, **34** verso ii 16 and app
ratio, pp. 3, 6, 235, 350
rat( ), **72** 6
rationem, **66** b ii 3, 4, 6, 8 app
ratione, **70** a i 28; ii 25; b i 9, 22; **72** 3 app, 8 app
recedere
recessit?, **69** 25 a app
recesserunt, **63** i 20; p. 218
recessa, **69** 25 a app; **73** a ii 1, 19; a i 26 app; p. 269
recognoscere
recogn[, **51** ii 10
recognitum?, **100** 1 app
recognitam, **51** ii 7
recognitos, **51** ii 15
reddere: reddita, **53** b 24 app
redimere: redemit, **63** i 21 app
refectio, **71** a 3, 12; b 7
referre
referri, **87** 6
refer, **99** *1* 8; *3* 6; **100** 4
relatus, **29** 2, 9
regina, **117** i 4; *see Index 5, Religion*, Iuno
reicere: reiectus, **63** ii 7 app; **64** i 25
relinquere: relicta **70** a ii 20 app
relictos, **72** 6 app
reliquus
reliqui, **52** b 7, 9; c 2, 4; **58** ii 1, 17; **62** 4; **63** i 36 app; ii 14, 41; **65** 10
reliquae, **77** a i 18; b 4 app
reliquos, **70** a i 9, 15, 22; ii 5, 12, 21, 35, 41; iii 25; c 5; e 5; g 7; b i 4, 18
reliquas, **68** ii 11, 21; iii 10, 20; **69** 18 app
remanere: remansit, **1** xxiii 15 app; **8** viii 4 and app; **66** b ii 6
remittere
remittatis, **89** *1* 2 app
remisi, **89** *3* 5?; *4* i 6; *25* 5 app
remisimus, **89** *7* 8 app
remissus, **63** ii 7
res, **54** a–c 6 app
resinae (*gen*), **82** 12
responderunt, **51** ii 7–8
restituere: restitutus, **63** ii 13
reuersus, pp. 115, 192; **1** xlii 18; **47** ii 8, 10; **53** b 23
reuersi, **47** i 5; ii 6, 7; **66** b i 29 app; ii 3, 4, 8, 27, 28, 29; d 1, 2
ṛịex, **81** iii 2 marg
rogare: roge.[, **90** *1* g
Roma, *as deity*, **117** ii 5; *see also Index 5, Religion*
roma.[, **5** iii 5 and app
Romanus, **70** b i 14
Romani (populi), **117** i 4
Romanorum, **53** b 22
rosaliae, *see also Index 5, Religion*
rosalias, **117** ii 8 and app; 14
ṛsp, **72** 6
rumpere: rumpantes, **53** b 19
russeobadium, **83** 15
russeosordidam, **83** 23
russeus: russeum, **99** *1* 5

s, p. 146; **24** 4, 6, 8; **47** i 3; **50** i 13
s...[, **71** b 7
ṣ.[.]a, **9** 30 d
s.ċaro[, **52** d 2
s[..]ṛ, **9** 2 f

ṣ[ ]ṛ. . ., **34** verso ii 7
sacer: sacra, **90** *1* b 2
sacerdos, **47** i 7 app; **50** i 2, 9; b 2; p. 192; *see also Index 5, Religion*
sacrahimag, **1** i 4; ii 12; xii 2; xiii 7; xxi 11; xxxii 12; p. 14
sacramentum, **50** i 4 app; **63** i 21 app
saepius, **51** ii 10
sagittarii, **30** ii 8 and app; p. 156
sal[, **83** 18
ṣalu. .[, **54** d 1
salubris: salubres, **54** a–c 6 app
Salus, *deity, see also Index 5, Religion*; **117** i 9; ii 25 and app
salus, p. 348
  salutis, **54** d 1 app
  salutem, **67** 1; **75** 2; **77** a i 2, 8, 14; b 2; **80** 3; **87** 3; **88** *1* 3; *2* 4; **89** *4* i 2; *6* 3; *7* 3; *8* 3; **91** *1* i 2; *2* i 2; **97** a 2; **98** *2* 1; *3* 2; **99** *1* 4; *2* 2; *3* 2; **100** 2 app; **104** 2; **105** 3; **114** 2; **117** i 2
salutauit, **53** b 11; b 20
salutares, **117** ii 25
saluus, **83** 18 app; p. 341
s(anctus?), **47** i 3; **50** i 13
  sanctis, **90** *1* a 7–8 app
  sanctissimo, **90** *1* a 1
saṇt. . . .[, **90** *1* a 7
sanus, p. 16
satisfacere, **91** *2* i 7
saturnalicium, **68** ii 8; iii 7; **69** 5 app; **76** FF 4 app
sc̣enopọ[, **52** b 5
sci.[, **89** *55* 1
scire: scires, **91** *1* i 5; *2* i 5
scoparius, **9** 28 b–c; 29 b and app; 4 m app
ṣc̣ṛ[, **30** ii 10
scriba, **30** ii 10 app; **79** 3
scribere, *see also* suprascriptus
  scr[, **89** *6* 6; scrib[, **88** *2* 7; scribe. .[, **93** a 2
  scribere, **91** *1* i 3; *2* i 9 app; **93** a 2 app
  scribatis, **89** *1* 7
  scribe, **98** *2* a 8; **93** a 2 app?
  scriberet, **114**, p. 417
  scripsi, **75** 9; **87** 29; **89** *5* 9 app
  scripserim, **98** *2* a 2
  scripserit, **91** *2* i 3
  s(cripti), **63** i 21 app
Scythicam, **1** xxvi 21 and app; **66** f 2
sebum; sebi, **82** 4
secundum, *prep.*, **63** i 24 app; **72** 6 app; **91** *1* i 9; **98** *2* a 7; **101** a i 3
secundo, *abbreviated* iio, **70** a i 29; ii 26; iii 16; b i 10, 23
securitas: securitatis, **50** i 7
secutor, **58** ii 7; *see also Index 4, Military Affairs*
seetules, *see* sfetules
Seispes, Sispes (=Sospes), *epithet of Juno*, **117** i 5 app
semis, **68** i 8, 9, 17, 23; ii 3, 11, 13, 14, 21, 22, 24, 29, 30; iii 2, 10, 12, 13, 20, 21, 23, 28; **69** 6a, 7, 8, 9, 25a, 26; **70** a i 3, 7, 8, 13, 14, 20, 21, 28, 29; ii 3, 4, 10, 11, 15, 16, 17, 20, 22, 25, 26, 33, 34, 39, 40; d 1, 7, 8, 13, 14, 19, 20; e 2, 3, 4, 6; b i 2, 3, 9, 10, 16, 17, 22, 23; **73** a i 1, 5, 6, 9, 11, 14, 15, 17, 18, 20, 21; ii 4, 9, 10, 11, 12, 13, 14, 15, 16, 17; iii 27, 28; f 6?; **82** 3, 4, 10?, 14; **131** b 5 app
  semisses, **133** 2 app
]sep.[, **54** f 1
sepositum, *noun*, p. 269; **69** 27 app
  sepositorum, **73** a iii 28
septem, **89** *29* 14
septimum, **86** 3; **99** *1* 3
septizonium: septizonis, **47** i 3, 11
sequi: secuti, **66** b ii 2
  secutis, **63** i 34; ii 13
[s]eruus, **132** 3 app
sesquiplicarius, *see also Index 4, Military Affairs*; pp. 11, 12, 14, 15, 16, 17, 84, 181, 201; **1** xvi 12 app; xxi 6; xxxiii 30; xxxvi 6, 7 app; xxxviii 15; xli 6 app, 8; xliii 23; **2** xxxii 6; xxxvi 20; xxxviii 28; xli 8; xliv 12; **4** a i 13; b i 6; **5** ii 3–4 app; **20** 5, 8, 14 app; **24** 11; **30** ii 10 app; **40** ii 17 app; **45** 3 app; **47** i 1 (three times), 9 (three times), 17 and app; **50** i 5 (twice), 11 (twice); **55** frag. i 2 app; **63** i 27, 28; ii 1, 15, 16, 25 app, 29, 30, 36, 40, 43; **73** b 10; **96** 7 and app
  σησκουπλικάρις, **76** vii 21; *σησκουβλιταρίω*, *dat*, **85** 3
sessor, **50** i 4 app
sestertius, **63** i 21: *IIS*; **86** 4: *HS*; **131** a 1 app, 6 app; b 2 app
Seueriana, p. 183; **47** i 2, 10; ii 2, 15; **48** 4
sex, **84** 3; **87** 4
sextans, **73** i 17 app, 26 app; f 4 app
sextum, **89** *29* 14 app; **114** 2
sfetules, p. 128; **15** i 5, 19; ii 12, 14; c 3; **17** a 3
si, **51** ii 10; **53** b 19, 22?
si.[, **53** b 22; **89** *54* 6
sias·, **13** 14
siċi. .ṇ.[, **101** a ii 12
sido.[, **79** 1
signare: signata, **83** 21, 23; p. 340
signifer, *see also σημειοφόρος, and Index 4, Military Affairs*; pp. 11, 12, 13, 16, 17, 146, 269, 277, 350, 366; **1** i 10 app; vii 11 app; xxvii 7, 27; xxviii 15 marg; xxxii 16; xl 19; **2** i 12; vi 23; xxxvii 29 app; xl 26; **4** a ii 1 app; **21** 19 app; **25** a 2 app; **47** i 17; ii 12; **48** 8; **50** i 2, 3 (twice), 9 (twice); **51** ii 19a; **67** 3; **68** ii 32 app; **89** *15* 4
signum, pp. 128, 180; **47** i 3, 7 app, 11; **48** 14; **50** i 7, 13; **51** ii 14; **52** a 6
  signorum, **117** ii 8, 14

signum—*cont.*
signa, **15** ii 7 app; **17** a 12; **47** i 6, 17; **49** 1; **50** i 1, 8; **51** ii 11, 17; **52** b 9; c 4; **68** ii 19 and app; iii 18; **69** 15 app
signis, **9** 8 c app; **90** *1* a 7–8 app
silua: siluae, **89** *1* 3: *place-name*?
sine, p. 97; **8** iii 5; vii 22; **83** 8, 14, 19, 21; **87** 12, 16, 18; **89** *1* 2 app; **90** *1* b 3; **99** *1* 6
singularis, pp. 16, 144, 146, 220; *see also Index 4, Military Affairs*;
1 vii 10, 11 app; ix 23; xiii 9; xix 26; xx 2; xxiii 8; xxv 21; xxviii 24; xxxi 33; xxxvii 14, 32; xxxviii 8; xl 7, 11; xlii 16;
2 vi 6; vii 10; viii 12, 13; x 13; xii 22; xiii 3, 11, 22; xv 5; xvi 6, 7, 8; xviii 15, 16; xx 13, 16, 21, 23; xxi 1, 2, 12, 13, 15, 16; xxii 8; xxiii 11, 14, 17, 22; xxvi 9, 11, 12; xxviii 15, 27; xxix 2; xxx 9, 13, 15, 21, 22; xxxi 4, 21, 22, 23, 24, 25, 27; xxxviii 11, 16; xl 7, 18; xli 10; xlii 10; **4** a ii 1 app; b i 8; ii 8, 9, 10, 14; j 2; **20** 15 app; **23** i 5, 7; **51** ii 12 and app; **53** b 7
singularis consularis, **1** xxv 23; xxxiii 11; xxxviii 3; xli 22; **2** xiii 21; xxviii 22, 26; xl 7; **53** b 4
singularis decurio, **4** a i 7
singularis duplicarius, **1** xi 4; xxi 4; xxvi 14; **2** xvi 19; **4** b i 4
singularem, **87** 26
singulares, **63** ii 25; **96** 6 app
equites singulares, **20** 15 app
singuli: singulos, **51** ii 12?; **99** *2* 5
sinister, **83** 10, 23, 24; **87** 14; **99** *3* 4
sit.[, **132** 2
siue, **20** 15 app; **91** *1* i 7
sole.[, **98** *3* 8
solere: solent, **98** *3* 8 app; *4* 8 app
soluere
soluantur, **117** i 2
solui, **80** 6
solus: solos, **98** *4* 9
Sospes (*Iuno*), **117** i 5 app
speculator, **9** 8 c, 9 d
spectare; spectatum (*supine*), **51** ii 3
ssṇ.[, **50** b 6
statio
statione, **9** 5 h, 6 h, 8 b, 13 f, 16 c app, 21 h, 22 c, 25 e app, f, 27 h, 29 b app, h, 33 g, 34–37 app
stationem, **58** ii 14; **67** 2
stationarii, **9** 6 h app; **133** 2 app
stator, *see also Index 4, Military Affairs*
statorem, **89** *1* 5 and app
στάτωρ, **76** xiv 2; στατορ[, **76** xvii 1
statura: staturas, **50** i 15
stega (στέγη): stegis, **82** 2, 8, 11, 12
stenocoriasis, **52** b 5 app
stercus, **9** 32 g
stipendium, *see also* opinionem; pp. 3, 6 and note 2, 7, 144, 182, 235, 242, 243, 244, 245, 246, 251, 254, 255, 256, 266, 270
stip, **73** h 2, j 3?, k 3; **98** *3* 5 app
stipendi, **66** b i 30; ii 3, 4, 7; **70** a i 7, 13, 20, 29; ii 3, 10, 16, 20 app, 26, 33, 39; e 3; b i 2, 10, 16, 23; **132** 1 app
stipendium, *acc*, **68** ii 3, 14, 24; iii 2, 13, 23; **69** 3, 11, 19, 26 app, 27 app; **71** a 1, 10; b 5; **72** 7, 13
stip(endio), **133** 2 app
stipendia, **23** i 8; ii 7; **117** i 8; ii 8 app; iii 2 app
striga: strigis, **9** 4 k app, 7 f–n
[s]ụbḍa[, **92** ii 7
subicere
subici, **50** i 15; **99** *2* 3; **100** 3
subieci, **87** 9; **89** *4* i 10 app; **91** *1* i 5; *2* i 5
subpraefectus: subpraefecto, **96** 4 app
suggerere, **101** a ii 8: sugge..ṭ..[; b 3: suggẹ[
sui
sibi, **89** *42* 12
se, **132** 3
sum[, **71** a 2; b 6
sumifṣṇọ[, **71** a 11
summa, *noun*, **34** verso ii 14 and app; **50** i 6, 12; **58** ii 16; **63** i 26, 35, 36 app; ii 12, 23, 38; **64** i 14; **65** 9 app; **68** ii 13, 23; iii 12, 22; **69** 8, 10a app, 17, 25; **70** b ii 13; **73** a iii 27, 30; f 1 app
summittere: summisi, **89** *4* i 8
summus, *adj.*: σούμμῳ, **76** i 2, 11, 18, 23; ii 3, 12; iii 3, 12, 21; iv 3, 12, 21; v 4, 12; vi 2, 10, 17; vii 3, 9, 17; viii 3, 8, 15, 20, 26; ix 5, 14; x 3, 10, 16; xi 3, 14; xii 3, 21; xiii 3, 10, 17; xiv 3, 11; xv 4, 12, 19; xvi 2, 12, 20; xvii 2, 10, 16; xviii 2, 14, 26; xix 4, 14, 19; xx 2, 10, 20; xxi 2; xxiv 2; BB 2; FF 3; GG 2, 10; HH i 2
supercilium: supercil(ii?), **87** 14
supplicatio, **47** i 16; **117** i 1 app, 10, 17, 26, 28; ii 1 (twice), 7, 8, 12, 14, 15, 18, 19, 22 and app, 28; iii 7; iv 7
supranumẹṛaṛ.[, **58** ii 12
s(upra)s(cript-), **21** 2, 15, 16; **38** i 3; **50** i 4 app; **53** b 22; **63** i 22 app, 32 app; **64** i 36, 38; **66** a i 2 app; **69** 8, 17, 25; **83** 11; **89** *1* 5 app; **93** c 2; **97** b 2 app
suscipere, **50** i 4 app
suus, p. 348
suo, **87** 2; **88** *1* 2; *2* 3; **91** *1* i 1; *2* i 1 app; **99** *1* 2; *2* 1; *3* 1; e app?; **100** 2; **105** 2
suum, **51** ii 14
sua, *n. pl.*, **90** *1* b 4
suorum, **97** a 6
suas, **90** *1* a 3

tabularium, p. 410; **89** *55* 2?; **102** a 6?, a 11?
tabulario, **87** 30

tabularius, p. 410; *see also Index 4, Military Affairs*; 102 a 6? a 11?
taurus: taurum, **117** i 5 (twice), 9, 20, 29; ii 9, 17, 22 app
templum: templo, p. 218; **15** ii 22
temptare, tentare, **92** ii 12 and app
tendere, **63** i 24 app
ter, **101** a ii 11 app
teres, **82** 5
teṛigụṣ, **53** b 25
terrenum, **9** 13 f app
ṭẹrtcị.[, **45** 2
tes.[, **53** b 23
tessera, p. 7
  tesseram, **47** i 6, 16; **48** 7; **50** i 1, 8; **53** b 23 app, 28 app
tesserarius, *see also Index 4, Military Affairs*; **50** i 3, 9; **51** ii 19; **53** b 23 app; 28 app; **78** *12* 1; **131** a 5 app
  τεσσεράριος, **78** *12* 1; *42* 6; *55* 6; *56* 5 app; *75*
testari, **92** ii 12 and app
  testatus, **53** b 23 app
therạpẹ[, **53** b 4
thetatus, pp. 13, 97; **8** iii 4 app; **34** recto i 6 app, 14 app; **47** i 4 app
  te(tatus), **34** recto i 12, 13, 17
  tetati, **34** verso ii 14
  tetates, **34** recto ii 19
  θetati, **63** ii 11
  (thetatus), *symbol* θ, **8** iii 4; vi 13, 22; vii 6; x 22; **73** a iii 26
Thrax: Thracum (*ala*), **64** i 25
tiro, pp. 3, 5, 153, 158, 277; **50** i 14 and app, 15; f; **51** ii 3; **63** i 30 app; **64** i 31; ii 1 app; **87** 4
  τιρώνων, **74** i 5, 12; ii 5, 11; iii 5, 13
toga, **117** ii 17
tollere
  sustuli, **80** 6 app
  sublatis, **90** *1* a 7
totus
  totum, **51** ii 10
  toti, **65** 9
Traiana (*legio*), **20** 2; **64** ii 13
trans, **63** ii 20, 29, 31
transferre: translatus, p. 16; **1** viii 30; xii 28; xiii 9; xxvi 21 app; xxxi 9; **34** recto i 8 app, 14 app; verso ii 12 app; **63** ii 8; **64** ii 22, 25; **73** a iii 24
ṭṛ.[, **72** 3
triarii, p. 7
trạṇ.[, **70** b ii 3
transire
  transit, **98** *2* a 5
  transeuntes, **53** b 26
tres, **77** a i 5
  tribus, **54** a–c 6?; **84** 2
tribụ[, **54** a–c 6
tribunus, *see also Index 4, Military Affairs*; p. 349
  trib(un-), **23** iii 2; **89** *25* 2
  tribunus, **45** 3 app; **47** i 3, 11; ii 3, 16; **54** a–c 5; a–c 6?
  tribuni, *gen*, **9** 14 c?; 15 g–k app; **58** ii 7, 8
  tribuno, *dat*, **89** *4* i verso; *25* verso 1; *28* verso 1; *36* verso 1; *47* verso 1; **91** *1* verso 1; *2* i 1 app; *2* verso 1; **99** *1* verso 1; *2* verso 1; *3* verso 1; **115** d verso?
  tribuno, *abl*, **20** 15 app; **89** *10* verso 2; *28* verso 2 app
  tribuno, *dat or abl*?, **89** *56* 3; **96** 5 app
  τριβύνω, **89** *2* 2
tribus: tribu, **64** i 6
  Aemilia, **36** 1, 5
  Claudia, **36** 6
  Clustumina, **133** 1 app
  Collina, **37** 3
  Cornelia, **36** 11 app, 12, 13
  Fabia, **36** 14
  Lemonia, **36** 5 app, 6 app
  Pollia, p. 165; **37** 2, 4, 5
  Pomptina, **36** 2, 3, 4
  Quirina, **64** i 6
  Romilia, **36** 7, 8, 9
  Sabatina, **36** 11
trierarchus (*liburnae*), *see also Index 4, Military Affairs*; **82** 3 app
triginta: triginti, **80** 7
tu, **102** a 9
  tibi, **80** 6; **88** *2* 7; **89** *4* i 4; *5* 9 app; **98** *2* a 5
  te, *acc*, **89** *12* i 7; *38* 8; *39* 9; *48* 6; **90** *1* b 3; **91** *2* i 9; **93** a 1; **107** (twice); **111** 2
  vos, **89** *1* 5, 8; *42* 13
  te, *abl*, **75** 3
tul, **47** ii 21, 22; **72** 4, 9?
tunc, p. 220 and note 2; **20** 3, 20; **66** a ii 2; **83** 3, 4, 5, 8, 10, 11, 12, 14, 19, 21, 23, 24
turma, *see also Index 4, Military Affairs*; pp. 2, 4, 5, 12, 18, 52, 83, 122, 126, 128, 143, 144, 146, 149, 155, 181, 269, 270, 283, 285, 311, 333–34, 340, 341, 350, 387, 435; **2** xxxviii 8 app; **38** i 1 app, 11 app; **53** b 26 app; **64** ii 7, 10, 32 app, 33, 36; **67** 16?; **75** 6; **80** 1
  (turm-), *symbol* Ͳ, **1** xxxi 21; xxxiii 23; xxxvi 1; xxxviii 11; xli 1; **2** xxxvi 15; xxxviii 24; xli 1; **11 bis** a 17; b ii 3, 5, 15; **24** 1, 3, 5, 7, 12, 14, 16, 18, 20; **27** b i 1, 6, 8, 13, 16; a i 1; **30** ii 1, 4, 6, 11, 14; **53** b 26 app; **55** g 1; **73** a i 26; ii 19; c 10 app; **76** viii 28; xx 1; GG 9, 12; **78** *15* 2; *27* 1; *29* 1; *30* 4; *33* 1; *34* 3; *42* 2; *45* 2; *48* 2; *49* 1; *63* 1; *66* 1, 5; **89** *5* 16; **92** iv 11; vii 10, 12; ix 15, 17; x 2, 4; **125**; **126**; **127**
  (turm-), *symbol* T^{u}, **15** i 6, 8, 11; ii 1, 2, 4, 12 (three times), 17, 22; **23** ii 2, 5, 9
  τουρμα, **75** 15

turma—*cont.*
τουρμης, **76** i 2, 6, 9, 10, 17, 26; ii 1, 3, 9, 12; iii 1, 3, 8, 11, 17, 20; iv 2 (twice), 11, 19, 20, 21, 25; v 1, 2, 3, 9, 11, 17; vi 1, 7, 9, 15, 17, 21; vii 2, 8, 13, 16; viii 2, 7, 12, 14, 19, 25; ix 2, 3, 4, 13, 18; x 2, 9, 16, 22; xi 2, 9, 12, 13, 19; xii 2, 12, 17, 19; xiii 2, 7, 9, 16, 22; xiv 3, 11, 16; xv 3, 4, 10, 11, 12, 18; xvi 2, 8, 11, 19; xvii 2, 9, 10; xviii 2, 8, 12, 13, 21, 25; xix 2, 3, 13, 19; xx 8, 9, 16, 19, 20, 24; xxi 1, 5; xxiv 1; BB 1, 2, 9; FF 1, 2, 3, 8; GG 2, 7; HH i 2; **78** *3* 2; *8* 2; **79** 14 app
tuus: tuorum, **97** a 6 app

uacare: uacantes, **58** ii 3
ualere, p. 349; **89** *1* 11; *12* i 9; *38* 10; *46* 2; *48* 9; *52* and 2; **91** *2* i 10; **107** (twice); **111** 4
uale, **87** 10
ualeatis, **98** *2* a 3
ualescen.[, **51** ii 2
ualetudinarium, **51** ii 20
uallum: uallo, **51** ii 12
uas: uasa, **82** 12
ubi, **70** a ii 19 app
uehementer, **90** *1* a 5
uel, **53** b 10, 17; **117** i 8
uelites, p. 7
uenalis, p. 3
uendere: uendidisse, **88** *1* 7
uerbum, **50** i 4 app
uerus: uera, **63** ii 38 app
uester, uoster, **88** *1* 6 app
uestimentum: uestimentis, **68** ii 29; iii 8, 28; **69** 7?
uestire: uestitum, **63** ii 18
uestitorium, **68** ii 9 app; **69** 2 app, 16 app, 24 app
ueteranus: ueterana (*ala*, *coh*), **53** b 27; **63** i 24; **80** 1
οὐετρανῆς, **76** i 1; ii 1, 11, 18; viii 2; xii 1, 11, 16; xiv 10; xv 2, 10, 18; xvi 1, 10; xvii 1; xviii 11, 24; xix 12; xx 7, 18, 19; GG 1, 9; HH 1
uetus
ueterem, **82** 14
ueteres, **82** 5 app
ueteribus, **82** 8
uex?, **51** ii 21
οὐεξι[*λλα-*, **90** *2* k 2 and app
uexillarius, *see also Index 4, Military Affairs*; pp. 11, 12, 15, 17; **1** xxiii 12; xxxii 21; xxxvi 18; xxxviii 23; xxxix 9, 13, 16; **2** xviii 19; xxxviii 8; xl 9, 19; xliii 3; **25** a 3; **89** *4* i 9 app
uexillatio
οὐεξι[*λλατιων-*, **90** *2* k 2 app
uexillationis, **91** *1* verso 2–3 app
uexillatione, **47** i 14; **63** ii 28; **89** *4* i 9 app; **91** *1* i 8

ụị, **38** i 1
uia, **9** 4 m app; 5 k, 16 k, 27 k; **63** ii 21 app
uiaticum, pp. 269–70, 277
uiatico, **70** a i 6, 10, 12, 16, 19, 23, 27, 31; ii 2, 6, 9, 13, 15, 22, 24, 28, 32, 36, 38, 42; d 10, 12, 16, 18; e 2, 6; Aberd. 3; b i 1, 5, 8, 12, 15, 19, 21, 25; d 18 app; **132** 9 app
uiaticorum, **73** a i 14; iii 29
uical?, **9** 32 g
uicarius, p. 335
οὐικαρίου, **81** ii 7
uices agens, **53** a ii 2 app
uicesima (hereditatium), p. 306; **77** a i 10, 17; b 3
uictor, *see also Index 5, Religion*, Iuppiter *and* Mars; **117** i 4, 19, 20
uictoria: uictorias, **117** i 14; ii 26–28 app
uictus, *noun*, **68** ii 6, 17, 27; iii 5, 16, 26; **69** 5, 13, 22
uicus: uico, **9** 32 g app
uigil: uigiles, **51** ii 15
uigilia: uigiliam, **67** 9; uigilias, **51** ii 11, 21; **52** a 10?
uiginti, **84** 1; **86** 3, 4; **89** *4* i 3; **99** *1* 7
uigu.[, **96** 5
ụịḷ..ṛ., **9** 15 d and app
ụin [...], **63** ii 4
uino, **9** 23 b–c app
uir
clarissim-, **96** 6
clarissimus, **91** *1* i 4; *2* i 4, 8
clarissimi, *gen*, **29** 3, 10
clarissimo, *abl*, **50** i 14; **66** b i 5
egregio, *abl*, **83** 15, 17
perfectissimo, *abl*, **20** 3, 9
uirga, **64** i 26
uirilis: uirili (toga), **117** ii 17
uis: ui, **88** *1* 6?
uitis, **64** i 25 app
ultor (*Mars*), **117** ii 9
unus, **58** i 35 app
unam, **51** ii 14
uno, **84** 6, 7
uoluntarius: uoluntari, **64** i 31
uotum: uota, **117** i 2; ii 26–28 app; 50 i 4 app
urbs: urbis (*Roma*), **117** ii 5
us?: **50** i 4
usque, **53** b 22; **98** *4* 7, 8
usus: usu, **117** i 7
ut, **89** *5* 9; **90** i b 5; **91** *1* i 5; *2* i 4; **99** *1* 7; *3* 6; **100** 4
uterque: utraque, **63** ii 38

xenia, **98** *2* a 7

yscription.[, **70** b ii 5a

The following section consists of broken words of which enough remains to give some hope of restoration. Possible restorations are sometimes suggested in the apparatus. The list is divided into two parts, the first containing words of which only the end is preserved. These are alphabetized as a reverse index. The second part consists of words which have lost both the beginning and the end. These are alphabetized by the first extant letter.

].ruṭịc̣ia, **5** ii 19
]ṭẹṣia, **15** i 21
]ndra, **2** x 21, *in app*, [ad ma]ndra
..[..]ṇ..AG̣G̣, **33** iii 6
].ạnạṭị.i, **15** ii 1
...mprinci, **9** 16 c app
].orḍi, **73** e 6
]ṣ.u..ẹperei, **51** i 13
].rụṃṭii, **13** 17
].ạbḷị, **34** verso ii 12
...csạndriṇi, **9** 16 c
]xịti, **73** g 10
]ṣtui, **53** c 3
.c̣eriṇ[..]m, **83** 24
]...ạlidam, **83** 19
]..idem, **84** 4
]ṃịṣem, **84** 1
].niṣem, **84** 2
]ẹṭem, **27** b
.[.]..ṣṣc̣uṃ, **9** 15 g–h
....r..torium, **68** ii 9
]gelorum, **52** b 5
].uisorụṃ, **122** 2
]ọstrum, **88** *1* 6
].eṇtum, **86** 3
]ṇtuc̣ọ, **53** c 1
].upp, **4** d 1
]ạṭer, **84** 3
].oscor, **73** e 7
........ḍior, **53** a i 4
]ni.aḷoṛ, **27** c 6
]ḍes, **52** b 8
]ḅ[.]ị[.]beḷeṣ, **27** b marg
]ulares, **96** 6
]rentes, **51** i 22
]ṇaris, **51** i 20
]nans, **1** xxiii 15 marg
]ṣec̣.ụṣ, **98** *4* 4
]nibus, **53** c 2
]ṣ...ubus, **53** c 5
[.]lạ.ṭiọ.ạc̣us, **13** 13
]ebrusạdus, **53** a i 3
]..ạṛius, **53** a i 6
]ẹnus, **132** 3
].nịsus, **63** i 32
].ụ.ṛatus, **53** a i 8
]nic̣iṭ, **50** i 13
]..brịt, **55** a 5
].ssit, **52** a 9
]....ṇiụit, **50** i 7
].eṛ[.]nṭ, **15** ii 7
].[.]eruṇṭ, **55** c 2
.eṛẹnu, **9** 13 f

]ạg.aṭ., **58** i 31
]ạnalib.[, **89** *11* 4
]ạṛạ..., **9** 19 c
]eredebe.[, **73** k 4
].esar....[, **122** 6
]ịpposcor..[, **73** d 3
]iume.[, **89** *11* 5
].ixṭi.[, **70** b ii 2
..laitin[.].[, **11 bis** a 12
].lano·, **102** a 6
]mesḷḷạ[, **89** *5* 6
].n..ssum[, **66** f 3
]odis..ṣ[, **11 bis** b i 24
]orm.[, **45**
-ptum[, **98** *3* 7
]ṛemitṛ..[, **73** d 4
]..rie.., **59** i 7
]seraṭị[, **89** *11* 3
].tẹar.[, **59** i 2
-tiu.[, **98** *3* 9

Index 10: Abbreviations and Conventional Symbols

See also pp. 11–16 for abbreviations in the notations in **1** and **2**. It is obvous that, aside from standard abbreviations like *Kal*(*endae*) and *leg*(*atus*), most of the following were devised by the clerk on the spur of the moment to suit his own convenience.

Latin

a: aeternus, Alexandrinus ?, armus, as (= obolus), Aulus
abs: absens, absentes
a c: armorum custos
acc, accep: accepta
accep: accepit
acceper: acceperunt
accesser: accesserunt
act: actum
actuar: actuarius
aedit: aedituus
aeg: aeger ?, Aegypti
aegupt: Aegypti
aem: Aemilia (*tribus*)
ag: agens
al: Alexandrinus ?
amb, ambul: ambulare ?, ambulatio ?
amp: amphora
ann: annus
annor: annorum
antaeopol: Antaeopoli, Antaeopolitanus
anti: Antinoites
april: Apriles
arm: armorum
armamenta, armamentar: armamentarium
asc⟨a⟩l: Ascalonitanorum (*cohors*)
asin: asinus ?, asinarius ?
aug: Augustus, Augusta (*emperor and empress*), Augustus (*month*)
aurel: Aurelius
b: beneficium, bos, obolus
bal: ballista, balneum
bene: beneficium
buc: bucinator
c: ciuis, clarissimus, coepit, Gaius
c a: custos armorum, ciuis Alexandrinus
caes: Caesar
cal: calcarius, calceamentum, caligatus, calx
caligator: caligatorum
cas, castr: castrensis, castris
c d o t: c(iuitate) do(natus) t(estatur) *or* t(estatus) ?
ç ẹ: ?
cen: centurio
ci: circitor ?
cil: Cilicum (*cohors*)
cl: Claudius
cla: Claudia (*tribus*)
cogn: cognitio ?, cognoscendum ?
coh: cohors
col: Collina (*tribus*)
com: comes, commeatus
comp: comparandum
cor: Cornelia (*tribus*)
cor, corniclar: cornicularius
cos: consul, consularis
c p: cui praees
c r: ciuis Romanus
cru: Clustumina (*tribus*)
cunic, cunicul: cuniculi
cyr: Cyrenaica (*legio III*)
d: Decimus, deducitur ?, deducuntur ?, degens ?, depositus, dexter, discens ?, diuus, dominus, quingenaria ?
dam: Damasco, Damascenus
dat: data
ḍ ḅ.: ?
d c c: ?, *also* p d c c
dec: decurio
dec, decembr: Decembres
decur: decursores ?
deg: degunt
dep: depositum (*noun*), deposuit ?
depo: deposuit
dextr: dexter
d f: discens fabrum ?
disc: discens
dispos, disposi, disposit: dispositus

do, dom, domin: dominus
d p: d(e)p(utatus)?, d(is)p(ositus)?
dr: drachma
dro, drom: dromadarius
dromo, dromon: dromone, *abl*
]d s: d(e)s(ideratus)?, d(e)s(eruit)?, discens signiferum?
duc: duce
dup, dupl, duplic?: duplicarius
e: egregius, emeritus, epistula, exemplum, quadrans
e e: exemplum epistulae
eius, eiusd: eiusdem
emans: emansit
emer: emeritus
emesenor: Emesenorum (*numerus*)
eor: eorum
epistrat: epistrategus
epis⟨t⟩ul: epistula
eq: eques, equitatus, equus
era.: ?
ẹs: ?
excubit: excubitum (*supine*)
ex: exemplum
expl, explor, explora, explorat, explorato: explorator
f: factus, femur, fidelis, filius, firma, fiunt, Flauia, quadrans
fab: faber, Fabia (*tribus*)
febr: Februarius
fel: felix
fer: ferrum
f f: Flauia firma (*legio XVI*)
fil: filius
fl: Flauia (*classis, cohors, legio XVI*), Flauius
frum: frumentatio?, frumentum
gall: Gallica (*ala*)
germ: Germanicus (*title*)
gub: gubernator
h: habet, hastatus, his, honeste, homines
hab: habet
heliopol: Heliopoli, Heliopolitanus
hisp: Hispanorum (*cohors*)
hor: hordeum?, horreum?
hord, hordiator: hordiatorum
i: iconismus, in?, Ioui
id, idib: Idus, Idibus
iio: secundo
imag: imaginifer
imp: imperator, imperatum
isteg: stegis (στεγή), *abl*
it: iterum
iul: Iulius
k: castrensis, castris, Kalendae
kal: Kalendae
karc: carcer?
l: Lucius
leg: legatus, legio, legionarius
lega: legatur?, legatus?
lem: Lemonia (*tribus*)
leon: leones
lib: libertus, librarius, liburna
lig: lignator
liq: liquidus
lus: Lusitanorum (*cohors*)
lycop: Lycopoli, Lycopolites
m, ḿ: man( ), Marcus, mas, maximus, mille, milia, militare, missus
ḿ: Manius
mag: magister
mai: Maius
maiar: Maiarum
mamm: ?
man: ?
m e: missus emeritus
mens: mensor
mil: miles
minor: minoris
mis: missus
n: naualis?, Nonae, noster, nota, notatus, numerus, nummus
nico: Nicopolitana?, Nicopolis (*gen*)?
no: Nonae
nouembr: Nouembres
n s: non sanus?
nu: numeros
num, numo: nummus, nummorum
o: optimus
ob: obiit, obolus
oct, octobr: Octobres
of, off, offi, offic: officium
op, opin, opinio, opinion: opinionem
ord: ordinarius, ordinatus
p: perfectissimus, pius, pondo, praees, pro?, Publius, purus
palm, palmur, palmyr, palmureno, palmyrenor: Palmyrenorum (*cohors*)
par, pas (centuriae): ?, *title of rank*
p d c c: ?, *also* d c c
pecua: pecuarius?
ped: pedes?, pedester?
pen: penus
perf: perfectus
perfunc: perfunctio?
peten: petendam
pf: praefectus
phal: phala?, phalarica?, phalerae?
pil: pilus
p n t: promotus nominante tribuno?
pol: Pollia (*tribus*)
pom: Pomptina (*tribus*)
por: porta?, portorium?, portus?
pos, post: posterior
pp: p(rae)p(ositus)?, primipilus

p r: populus Romanus
pr: praetor, praetorius, praetorium?, princeps, prior, pro, promotus?
pr pr: princeps prior, pro praetore
praef: praefectus
praep, praepos: praepositus
praes: praeses
praesi: praesidem?, praesidium?
praet, praetent: praetentura
praet, praetor, praetori: praetorium
pr, prid: pridie
princ: princeps?, principalis?
prio: priore
prob: probatus, probandus
proc: procurator
prosec, proseq: prosecutio
ptol: Ptolemaicus
punc: ?
q: qui, Quintus, quondam?
q d p: quondam deputati?, quondam dispositi?
q m c: qui militare coepit (coeperunt)
quaes⟨t⟩ur: quaestura
quere, queren, querend: qu⟨a⟩erendum?, querendum?
quir: Quirina (*tribus*)
r: ?, redditus?, rediit, relictus, reuersus, Romanus
rat, ration: rationem, ratione
[r]ec: recognitus?
recesser: recesserunt
ref: refectio?
refec: refectio
rel: relatus
rel, reliq: reliquus
remans: remansit *or* remansor
reuer: reuersus
rom: Roma, Romilia (*tribus*)
rus: russeus
s: ?, sanctus?, semis, sine, sinister, summa
sab: Sabatina (*tribus*)
sacer: sacerdos
sagit[.]: sagittarius
scopa: scoparius
scy: Scythica (*legio IIII*)
sep, sept, septem, septembr: Septembres
ser: Sergia (*tribus*)
sesq, sesqui⟨p⟩liciar: sesquiplicarius
sex: Sextus
sias: ?
sido: Sidone, Sidonius
s?, sig, sign, signif: signifer
sing, singul: singularis
  cos: singularis consularis
  dec: singularis decurio
  dupl: singularis duplicarius
sinistr: sinister
specula, speclat: speculator
ss: suprascriptus
sta, station: statione
stip, stipendi?: stipendium
supercil: supercilium
t: Titus
Ŧ: turma
tess: tesserarius
test: ?
thinit: Thinites
thrac: Thracum (*ala*)
tr: Traiana (*legio II*), translatus
trans, tra⟨n⟩sl: translatus
tr, tri, trib: tribunus
T^{u}: turma
tul: tulit?
tyr: Tyro, Tyrius
u: ueterana, urbs
uaca: ?
u c: uir clarissimus
u e: uir egregius
ueter: ueterana
ueterib: ueteribus
uex: uexillum?, uexillatio?, uexillarius
uexil, uexill: uexillarius, uexillatio
uexillation: uexillationis
uic: uicus?
u p: uir perfectissimus
u r a: urbs Roma aeterna
us: ?
z: *ζήτει*? *See* **1** xxv 17 app

Greek

αν: *ἀνομένου*? (*ἔτους*)
απογρ: *ἀπογράφομαι*
αρτ: *ἀρτάβη*
αυ: *αὐτῷ*
γ: *γίνεται*, *γίνονται*
γρα: *ἔγραψα*
γραμμς, *γραμας*: *γράμματα*
δρομαδαρ: dromadarius
εγρα: *ἔγραψα*
εἰδ: *εἰδότος*
ερρω⟨σ⟩θ: *ἐρρῶ⟨σ⟩θαι*
ετ: *ἔτους*
⟨ε⟩υχο: *εὔχομαι*
ζ: *ζήτει*? *See* **1** xxxv 17 app
ιπ: *ἱππεύς*
κ: *καί*
κικ: *κίκεως* (*gen*)
κολ, *κολοφ*: *κολοφώνιον*
κριθ: *κριθῆς*
μαρκ: Marcus
ο: *ὁμοῦ*
οβ, *οβολ*: *ὀβολός*
οιν: *οἴνου*
ον, *ονομ*: *ὄνομα*

παραλημπτα: παραλήμπταις (*dat*)
πρακ: πράκτωρ, πράκτορες
προκοπ: προκόπεσθαι
προτερ: προτέρου
πυρ: πυροῦ
σ: σου
σεσμ, σεσημ: σεσημείωμαι
σιτ: σίτου
στρ, στρα, στρατιω, στρατιωτ: στρατιώτης
συ: σύν
συνστ, συστρατιωτ: συστρατιώτης
τρικ: τρικέραμον
υ, υπ: ὑπέρ
υπογρ: ὑπογράφομαι
υπογφ: ὑπογράφοντος
φαρμ: Φαρμοῦθι
χ, χα, χαι: χαίρειν

The following are conventional symbols, alphabetically arranged in so far as they are composed of letters or resemble letters.

αβʹ: 1⅔
Ɣ: centuria *or* centurio; cohors?: **21** 2 app
ƆNERO: ? **34** recto i 2, 19; ii 1 app
HS *or* IIS: sestertius
H: denarius, **78** *24* 10; *25* 5; *45* 6; *57* 9; *65* 6, 7; *66* 7; *67* 6; *70* 8
θ: "thetatus," deceased (killed in combat?)
L: ἔτους; αὐτοῖς?, **78** *62* 2 and app
m̈: ?, **50** i 3, 9
⳩: centuria *or* centurio (ἑκατονταρχία, ἑκατοντάρχης)
⚹: denarius
——›: *See pp.* 11–12
——: *See pp.* 11–12
—∸—: artaba, ἀρτάβη
●, ●●, ●●: *See p.* 12
+: πυροῦ
ʃ, ʃʹ: *ἔτους or mark of abbreviation*: **76** iv 5, 13, 23; v 5; vii 18; xi 16; xvi 21; HH i 4, 5; ii 4; **78** *1* 6; *45* 6; *66* 7, 8
//: *follows the number of the regnal year in e.g.* **78**, *4* 4; *5* 4; *6* 10; *etc.*; *and in* **81** ii 10

Index 11: Inscriptions, Ostraca, and Papyri

Inscriptions

Acta Fratrum Arualium, p. 423
Année Epigraphique 97: **117** i 14–16 app
207: p. 166
CIL I p. 229: Feriale Cumanum: **117** ii 18 app
I 206: p. 11
CIL III 14; Supp. 6581 (*ILS* 2543): **39** 16 app; **76** i 7 app; vi 1 app
59: **133** 3 app
103 (*IGRR* III 1328): **38** i 11 app
333: p. 332 note 1
3412 (*ILS* 2409): **52** b 15 app
3490: **89** *1* 3 app
3543 (*ILS* 2391): p. 141
5949 (*ILS* 2430): **89** *3* 7 app
6580 (=12045): **133** int
6591: p. 198
6592 (*ILS* 2345): p. 141
6607 (*ILS* 2247): **9** 30 a app
6627 (*ILS* 2483): **9** 30 a app; **63** ii 21 app; pp. 165, 198
12045 = 6580
14147[2] (*ILS* 8907): **63** i 24 app
14356, 3a (*ILS* 9103): p. 334
20996: **81** ii 8 app
CIL III pp. 801–41, Edictum de pretiis rerum venalium (*ILS* 642) ii 10: p. 3
CIL VI 209 (*ILS* 2097): **63** i 11 app
220: p. 2
228 (*ILS* 2187): **20** 15 app
1056–59: p. 2
1057: **34** recto i 4 app
1585: p. 3 note 7
1984 (*ILS* 5025): p. 147
2009 (*ILS* 466): p. 147
2977 (*ILS* 2173): **20** 15 app
3289: **63** ii 21 app
6627 (*ILS* 2483): p. 165; **9** 30 a app
31151: **20** 15 app
32415 (*ILS* 4932): **21** 16 app; **24** 5 app, 18 app
CIL VIII 2494 (*ILS* 2636): **71** a 8 app
2877 (*ILS* 2653): p. 84
8809 (*ILS* 5785): p. 397
9725 = 21531: **63** ii 21 app
9786: p. 361
9790 (*ILS* 3251): **91** *1* verso 2–3 app
21567: **20** 15 app
CIL IX 795: **63** ii 21 app
CIL X 7845 (*ILS* 6107): **21** 13 app
7953 (*ILS* 6766): **64** i 10 app
CIL XI 630: **59** i 9 app
CIL XIII 583 (*ILS* 3732) and 5677 (*ILS* 4609): **77** b 1 app
CIL XVI dipl. 4 (p. 219) and 29: **63** i 24 app
23, 36, 55, 94, 117, 118, 121: **53** b 22 app
35: p. 202
44: **63** i 24 app
46 and 110: **53** b 22 app
50 and 54: p. 219
56: **77** a i 7 app
73: **53** b 22 app
75: **63** i 24 app
79, 92, 100: p. 152
128: p. 202
CIL XVI pp. 157–58: **63** i 11 app
Dessau, *ILS* 466 (*CIL* VI 2009): p. 147
1327: **91** *1* verso 2–3 app
2097 (*CIL* VI 209): **63** i 11 app
2102: **64** ii 26 app
2156–57 (*CIL* VI 1056–59): p. 2
2163 (*CIL* VI 220): p. 2
2173 (*CIL* VI 2977) and 2187 (*CIL* VI 228): **20** 15 app
2200: **34** recto ii 11 app
2210: **24** 5 app, 18 app
2247 (*CIL* III 6607): **9** 30 a app
2303: **64** ii 26 app
2345 (*CIL* III 6592): p. 141
2390 and 2391 (*CIL* III 3543): p. 141
2409 (*CIL* III 3412): **52** b 15 app
2430 (*CIL* III 5949): **89** *3* 7 app
2483 (*CIL* III 6627): **9** 30 a app; **63** ii 21 app; pp. 165, 198 and note
2529: p. 84
2543 (*CIL* III 14, 6581): **39** 16 app; **76** i 7 app; vi 1 app; p. 285
2636 (*CIL* VIII 2494): **71** a 8 app
2653 (*CIL* VIII 2877): pp. 84, 141

2654 and 2655 (*CIL* III 1480 and VIII 14698): p. 141
2891: **24** 5 app, 18 app
3035 (*CIL* III 894): p. 141
3251 (*CIL* VIII 9790): **91** *1* verso 2–3 app
3732 (*CIL* XIII 583): **77** b 1 app
4609 (*CIL* XIII 5677): **77** b *1* app
4932 (*CIL* VI 32415): **21** 16 app; **24** 5 app, 18 app
5025 (*CIL* VI 1984): p. 147
5785 (*CIL* VIII 8809): p. 397
6085 (*CIL* I 206): p. 6
6107 (*CIL* X 7845): **21** 13 app
6766 (*CIL* X 7953): **64** i 10 app
7226: **32** 14 app
8865: p. 202
8907 (*CIL* III 14147^2): **63** i 24 app
8977: **91** *1* verso 2–3 app
9103 (*CIL* III 14356, 3a): p. 334
9493: **89** *3* 7 app
9246: **117** i 5 app
Fasti Ostienses: **117** i 14–16 app
Fasti of Philocalus: **117** ii 23–24 app
Feriale Cumanum (*CIL* I, p. 229): **117** ii 18 app
IGRR III 1328 (*CIL* III 103): **38** i 11 app
1333 and 1337: **51** i 13 app

Ostraca and Papyri

P. Aberdeen 133: p. 263
P. Aberdeen 150 (**133**): p. 11
P. Berlin 6866 (**70**): **39** 13 app; **64** i 36 app
BGU 8: **34** recto ii 11 app
67: **34** recto ii 15 app
372: **11** ii 3 app
568: **74** i 2 app
610: p. 9
1046: **34** recto ii 11 app
Chester Beatty papyri: **64** i 36 app
P. Clermont-Ganneau 1 b: **64** i 10 app
P. Dur. 17 A 3: **1** xxviii 19 app
26: **1** xxviii 19 app
30 and 32: p. 435
46: p. 15, s.v. "becchufrayn"
48: p. 233
49: **6** x 29 app
59: **53** b 8 app; p. 154
82: **64** i 14 app
83: **47** i 6 app
88: **47** i 6 app, 7 app
89: **47** i 6 app; **48** 9 app
94: **64** ii 32 app
97: **8** iii 5 app
125 and 126: p. 183
129: pp. 242, 347, 387, 407, 435
133: p. 434
140: p. 386
141: p. 143
P. Flor. II 278: **30** ii 13 app
P. Gen. 52: **89** *1* 7–8 app
P. Giess. 54: **38** i 15 app
P. Hamb. 40–53: p. 283, note 1
P. Lond. inv. 229 (British Museum): p. 1 note 2
2723: **46** 2 app
P. Mich. inv. 5763: **99** *1* 9 app
III 159: p. 421
161: p. 242
VII 435: p. 13
441: **133** 3 app
447: p. 9; **11** ii 3 app; **46** 2 app
448: p. 9
Wilcken, *Ostraca* 1487: **39** 16 app
P. Oxy. 39: p. 1
43 recto: p. 242
489: p. 278
1047: p. 241
1115 and 1194: p. 242
1204: **47** i 16 app
1313: **11** ii 3 app
1418: p. 410
1446: **34** recto i 13 app
1511: p. 242
2349: **34** recto ii 4 app
Corp. Pap. Raineri 28, 14: **70** d 6–7 app
PSI 1245: **99** *1* 9 app
1307: **47** i 6 app
P. Strasbourg 192: **99** *1* 9 app
SB 1319: **34** recto ii 11 app
2067: **39** 16 app
4117: p. 278
4595: **34** recto ii 11 app
7181: p. 242

Index 12: Classical Authors Cited

Accius, *trag.* 16: **63** ii 21 app
Appian, *Bell. Civ.* 5.46: pp. 2 note 5, 179 note 1
Arrian, *Epicteti Diss.* 4.13.5: **9** 15 e app
Augustine, *Confessiones* 4.14.21: **88** *2* 6 app
Caesar, *Bell. Gall.* 1.29.1: p. 8
Cicero, *Ad Atticum* 8.12 A–D: p. 348 note 3
Ad fam. 5.2, 7, 10a; 15.1, 2: p. 349 note 10
Cod. Just. 8.55.1: **83** 4 app
Digest 49.16.3–4 and 14: **47** ii 18 app
49.16.3–6: **47** ii 21 app
49.16.12.2: p. 407
Dio Cassius 69.14.3: p. 349 note 10
77.18.2: p. 349 note 11
Herodian, *Hist.* 3.8.4: p. 312 note 3
Hyginus, *De mun. castr.* 16: p. 138
27: **64** ii 1 app
Isidore, *Etym.* 12.1.52: **83** 19 app
Orig. 1.24.1: p. 3
Livy 1.44.2: p. 6
2.12.6–7: p. 7
4.59.11: p. 7
5.7.12–13: p. 7
28.29.13: **51** ii 15 app
29.15: p. 7
29.37.7: p. 7
45.1: p. 348 note 2
Pliny, *Epist.* 7.25.5: **9** 15 e app
10.27–28: p. 350 note 16; **47** ii 4–5 app; **63** ii 4 app; **89** *4* i 3–6 app
10.65: p. 421 note 4
Pliny, *Hist. Nat.* 15.133: p. 348 note 2
Polybius 2.23.9: p. 7
6.19: p. 7 note 2
6.19–20: p. 7
6.21.4–5: p. 7 and note 3
6.34.7–6.36.9: p. 7
6.39.12–14: p. 8 and note 4
Procopius, *Anecd.* 18.42: p. 165
Rufinus, *Adv. Hieron.* 2.36: p. 3
Scholia on Persius 2.13: **47** i 16 app
SHA *Alex.* 21: p. 3
Commodus 4.10: **70** a ii 7 app
Niger 4.1–2: p. 350
Suetonius, *Domitian* 7.3: p. 256
Iulius 56.6: pp. 348 note 1, 349 note 12
Iulius 61: **50** i 4 app
Tiberius 32: p. 421 note 2
Tacitus, *Agric.* 18: p. 348 note 2
Ann. 1.16–18; 26.2; 35.2; 36.4: **63** i 11 app
6.3: **129** 2 app
15.8.9: p. 348 note 1
Hist.: p. 348
1.85: **9** 15 e app
4.25: p. 349
Tertullian, *De corona mil.* 1.1: **47** i 16 app
Vegetius 1.10: **9** 4 k app
1.11 and 14–15: **9** 6 b–f app
1.26: p. 3
1.27: p. 14
2.2: p. 2
2.5: p. 2
2.7: pp. 2, 349 note 14
2.9–10: p. 241 note 1
2.11: **9** 4 k app; p. 241 note 2
2.19: pp. 2 note 6, 106; **99** *1* 7 app
2.20: p. 245; **68** ii 19 app
2.25: p. 241 note 3
3.2, 3, 7: p. 241 note 3
3.6: p. 421 note 3; **9** 4 k app
3.8: **49** 2 app
4.6–9, 11, 34: p. 241 note 3

Concordance of Papyri and Ostraca

(Numbers in bold-face type are those of the present corpus)

Papyri

P. Aberdeen
- 132: **45**
- 133: **70**
- 150: **133**

P. Antinoopolis 41 recto: **46**
P. Berlin 6866: **70**
BGU
- 696: **64**
- 1083: **36**

British Museum Papyrus 2851: **63**
ChLA IV
- 230: **132**
- 239: **131**
- 270: **67**
- 272: **129**

P. Clermont-Ganneau 4a: **79**
P. Dura
- 54: **117**
- 55: **90**
- 56: **99**
- 57: **103**
- 58: **100**
- 59: **114**
- 60: **98**
- 61: **101**
- 62: **108**
- 63: **88**
- 64: **91**
- 65: **109**
- 66: **89**
- 67: **92**
- 68: **94**
- 69: **95**
- 70: **104**
- 71: **105**
- 72: **110**
- 73: **106**
- 74: **97**
- 75: **107**
- 76: **93**
- 77: **113**
- 78: **111**
- 79: **112**
- 80: **115**
- 81: **96**
- 82: **47**
- 83: **48**
- 84: **56**
- 85: **54**
- 86: **57**
- 87: **55**
- 88: **49**
- 89: **50**
- 90: **60**
- 91: **61**
- 92: **62**
- 93: **22**
- 94: **65**
- 95: **66**
- 96: **25**
- 97: **83**
- 98: **6**
- 99: **7**
- 100: **1**
- 101: **2**
- 102: **8**
- 103: **26**
- 104: **3**
- 105: **4**
- 106: **13**
- 107: **15**
- 108: **14**
- 109: **19**
- 110: **17**
- 111: **18**
- 112: **16**
- 113: **12**
- 114: **41**
- 115: **27**
- 116: **23**
- 117: **33**
- 118: **44**
- 119: **42**
- 120: **31**
- 121: **29**
- 122: **32**
- 123: **35**
- 124: **43**
- 130: **116**
- 133: **123**
- 134: **118**
- 135: **119**
- 136: **122**
- 137: **125**
- 138: **126**
- 139: **127**
- 142: **120**
- 143: **121**
- 145: **124**
- 146: **128**

P. Fayum 105: **73**
P. Gen. lat. 1 recto,
- part I: **68**
- part II: **10**
- part III: **37**
- part IV: **58**
- part V: **9**

P. Gen. lat. 4: **69**
P. Giess. Bibl. Inv. 282: **85**
P. Grenfell II 110: **86**
P. Hamburg 39: **76**
P. Hawara 19: **131**
P. London 482: **80**
P. Mich.
- III 162: **39**
  - 163: **40**
  - 164: **20**
- VII 435 and 440: **77**
  - 450 recto and 455 recto: **52**
  - 450 verso and 455 verso: **53**
  - 454: **30**

P. Oslo III 122: **24**
P. Oxy.
- IV 735: **81**
- VII 1022: **87**
- XII 1511: **102**

Princeton Garrett Deposit 7532 recto: **21**
P. Rylands
- 79: **28**
- 223: **82**
- 273a: **72**

PSI
- 1063: **74**

PSI—cont.
1307: **51**
1308: **59**
P. Vienna
L 2: **34**
L 4: **11 bis**
L 72 and L 82: **71**
L 99 recto: **38**
L 100 recto: **5**
L 111: **84**
L 112: **11**
P. Yale 249: **75**

Ostraca

Greek Ostraca in the Bodleian Library, Tait and Préaux
2003: **78** *73*
2004: **78** *65*
2005: **78** *20*
2006: **78** *19*
2007: **78** *16*
2008: **78** *21*
2009: **78** *24*
2010: **78** *25*
2011: **78** *26*
2012: **78** *27*
2013: **78** *29*
2014: **78** *66*
2015: **78** *28*
2016: **78** *34*
2017 (*SB* 6971): **78** *67*
2018: **78** *35*
2019 (*SB* 6975): **78** *38*
2020: **78** *40*
2021 (*SB* 6973): **78** *70*
2022: **78** *71*
2023: **78** *46*
2024: **78** *47*
2025: **78** *61*
2026: **78** *45*
2027: **78** *53*
2028: **78** *59*
2029: **78** *51*
2030: **78** *56*
2031: **78** *17*
2032: **78** *55*
2033: **78** *63*
2034: **78** *41*
2035: **78** *54*
2036: **78** *76*
2037: **78** *74*
2038: **78** *58*
2039: **78** *43*
2040: **78** *52*
2041 (*SB* 6969): **78** *64*

Griechische Ostraka aus Aegypten und Nubien II, Wilcken
1128: **78** *72*
1129: **78** *23*
1130: **78** *1*
1131: **78** *2*
1132: **78** *4*
1133: **78** *14*
1134: **78** *5*
1135: **78** *11*
1136: **78** *6*
1137: **78** *7*
1138: **78** *77*
1139: **78** *9*
1140: **78** *3*
1141: **78** *10*
1142: **78** *44*
1143: **78** *12*
1144: **78** *8*
1145: **78** *13*
1146: **78** *75*
1265: **78** *69*

Sammelbuch griechischer Urkunden aus Ägypten III, Preisigke, Bilabel, Kiessling
6955: **78** *50*
6956: **78** *68*
6957: **78** *32*
6958: **78** *42*
6959: **78** *33*
6960: **78** *30*
6961: **78** *39*
6962: **78** *37*
6963: **78** *36*
6964: **78** *31*
6965: **78** *49*
6966: **78** *48*
6967: **78** *15*
6968: **78** *60*
6969 (*GOB* 2041): **78** *64*
6970: **78** *18*
6971 (*GOB* 2017): **78** *67*
6972: **78** *62*
6973 (*GOB* 2021): **78** *70*
6974: **78** *22*
6975 (*GOB* 2019): **78** *38*
6976: **78** *57*